NUMBERING in AMERICAN SIGN LANGUAGE

Number Signs for Everyone

NUMBERING IN AMERICAN SIGN LANGUAGE: Number Signs for Everyone

Manufactured in the United States of America
Published by DawnSignPress

SIGN MODELS

Library of Congress Cataloging-in-Publication Data
Numbering in American Sign Language: number signs for everyone.
p. cm.
ISBN 0-915035-72-3 (alk. paper)
1. American Sign Language—Handbooks, manuals, etc. 2. Counting.
3. Grammar, comparative and general—Quantifiers.
HV2474.N86 1998
419—dc21 98-25013
CIP

10 9 8 7 6 5 4 3 2 1

ABOUT THIS BOOK

Several years ago Joe Dannis and Ben Bahan committed DawnSignPress to the development of a book about the number sign system in American Sign Language. A lot of effort has gone into this book and there are many people to be recognized for their contribution toward making this book a reality.

Cinnie MacDougall, with Ben's guidance, spent a great deal of time and effort researching and developing vocabulary lists of numbers signs. Cinnie worked closely with Joe on the materials used for Paul Setzer's detailed sign illustrations that bring ASL to life on the printed page. Don Newkirk's consultation and advice about the vocabulary and text were an important contribution to the manuscript stage. DawnSignPress' production team, Rebecca Ryan, Robin Taylor, Tina Jo Breindel, Robb Pawlak, Andy Granda, and Ryan Stern, put in many hours refining the manuscript and turning vocabulary lists, illustrations, and text into a finished book.

DawnSignPress offers sincere appreciation for the collaborative efforts of the people who made this book possible. We know you will benefit from their efforts to make *Numbering in American Sign Language* the best book possible.

Table of Contents

INTRODUCTION

HOW TO USE THIS BOOK

NUMBER SIGNS FOR EVERYONE **gives basic information about how numbers are used in American Sign Language (ASL). In twelve chapters you will be introduced to basic number signs such as counting from 1 to 10, and complex number signs, such as how to describe the placement of a team in a volleyball tournament.**

Over one thousand illustrations of number signs constitute the majority of the book. Illustrations can never take the place of learning signs from a live instructor or from interacting with signers, but the sign illustrations do have detailed content that will help you learn to form the sign correctly.

HOW TO READ THE ILLUSTRATIONS

The basic four parameters of every sign are *handshape*, *palm orientation*, *location*, and *movement*. When evaluating a sign illustration, first identify how each of these elements contributes to the sign.

HANDSHAPE

There are approximately forty commonly used handshapes in ASL and many others that are seen only occasionally. Many of the handshapes appear similar, but are in fact very specific.

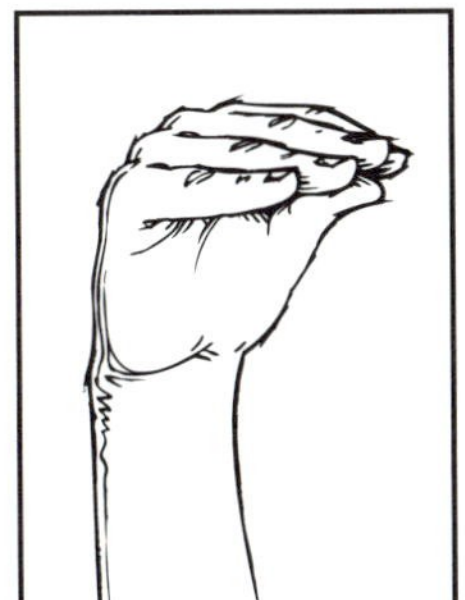

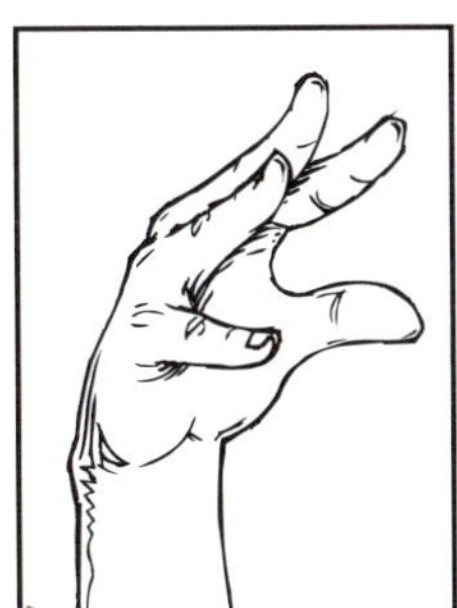

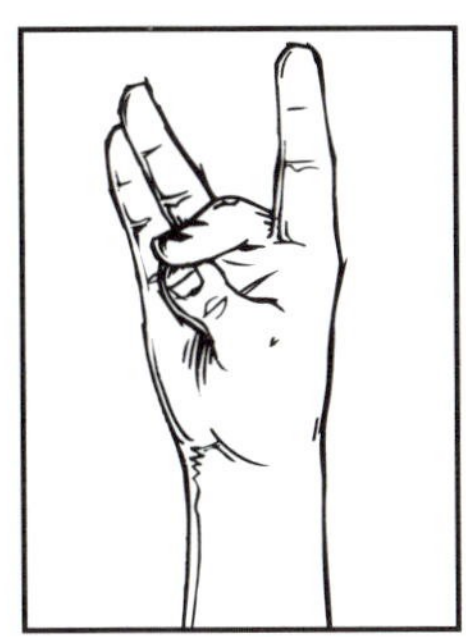

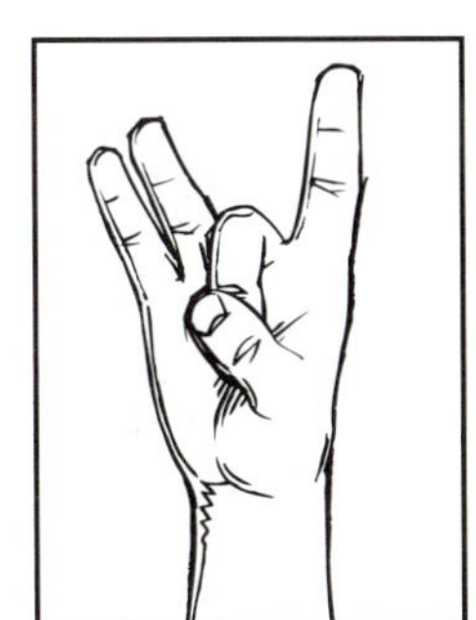

The following chart shows the common handshapes for ASL.

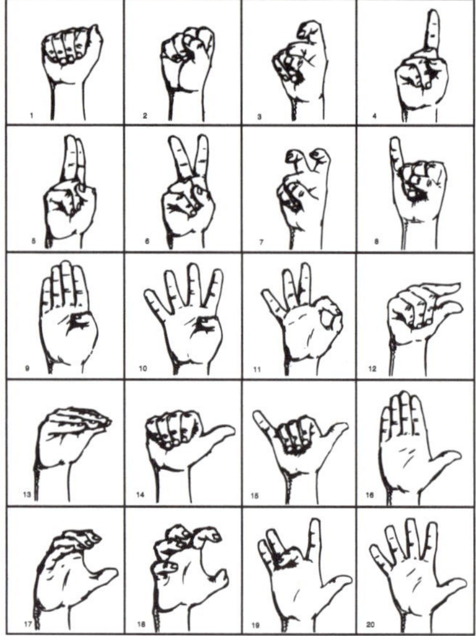

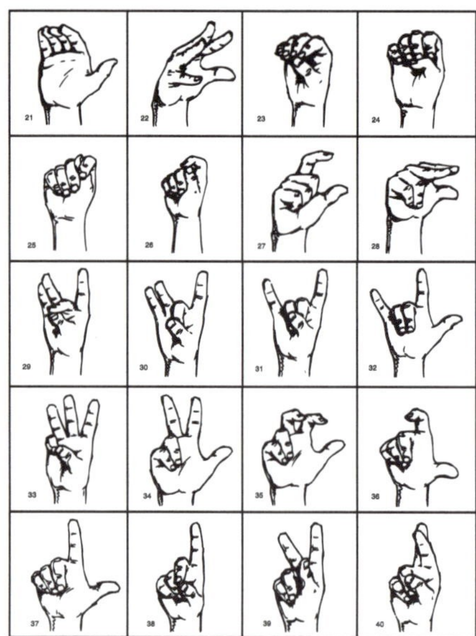

Palm Orientation

Orientation of the hands, such as palm facing outward, palm facing inward, and thumb side of the hand pointing up or down, is an important part of expressing a sign. With number signs you will notice that palm orientation sometimes changes depending on the context.

1

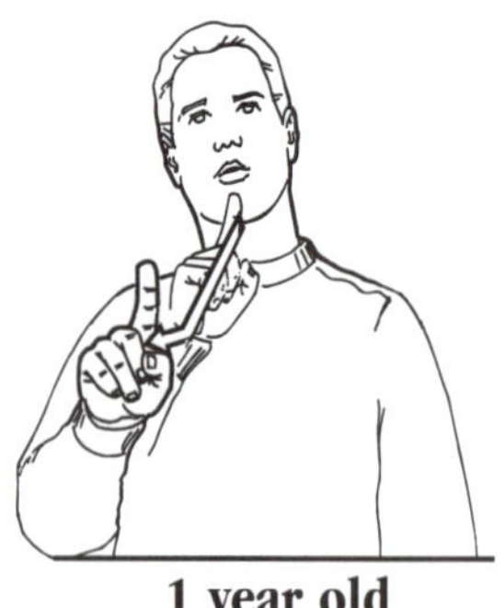

1 year old

Location

Understanding the location of a sign means that you know where to express the sign in relation to your body. Some signs are made near the chest, while others are made near the forehead or shoulder. Changing the location of a sign can change the meaning.

MOVEMENTS

Because ASL is a visually active language, the most difficult requirement of a sign illustration is to show movement. To fascilitate the three-dimensional nature of signs, illustrations incorporate a number of helpful features.

Arrows show the direction, path, and repetition of the movement. Here are the arrows you will see.

Directional arrows point in the direction the sign is to be made. See sign examples below.

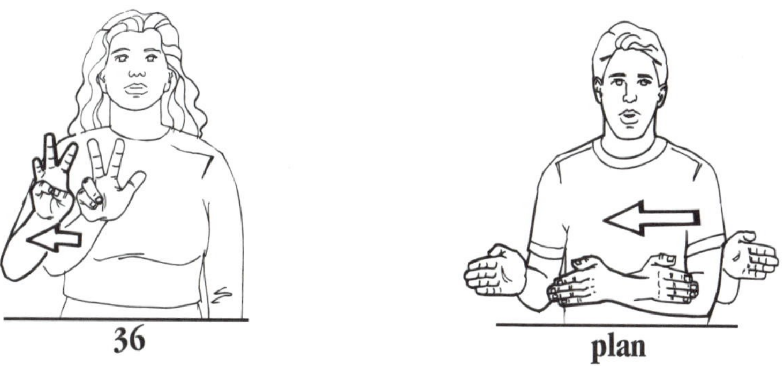

36 plan

Bi-directional arrows indicate a back and forth motion. See sign examples below.

2 of them baby

Path arrows show you the path of movement of the sign. See sign examples below.

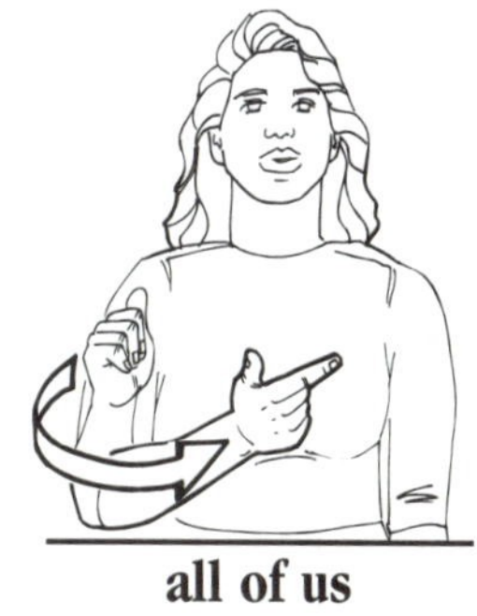

all of us

next week

Repetive arrows show you the sign's movement is repeated twice or more. See sign examples below.

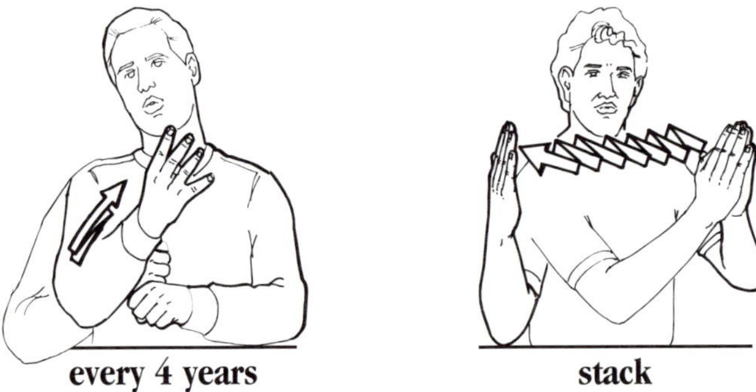

every 4 years stack

A touch is when part of the handshape touches the chest, shoulder or other part of the body. Touches are shown this way.

Examples of touch marks:

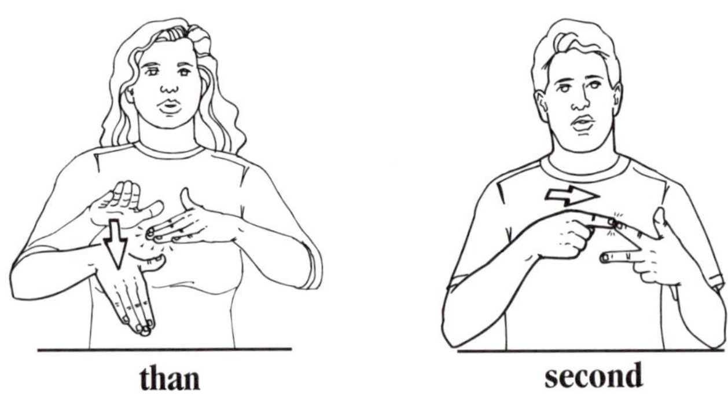

than second

When a handshape is supposed to be "wiggled" or moved back and forth slightly, there will be wiggle marks indicating this.

Examples of wiggle marks:

2:00 30-something

To illustrate how motion can affect the meaning of a sign, and how the detail of a sign illustration can help you evaluate that motion, look at the following three signs.

As you can see, the handshapes, movements, and locations of these signs are all similar, but the meanings are different.

Some signs begin and end in the same location, while other change location from beginning to end and the sign illustration indicates this. In this book, line thickness is used to distinguish the position of the arms and hands at the beginning of the sign's motion from that at the end of the sign's motion. If the lines of the arms and hands are thin, they indicate the placement of the arms and hands at the beginning of the sign. If, at a different place in the drawing, the lines of the arms and hands are thick, they indicate the placement of the arms and hands at the end of the movement. Here are some examples of signs with movement indicated by line thickness.

If you are able to indentify and evaluate the four parameters of a sign, your ability to use sign illustrations as a learning tool will be increased.

ASL Illustration Conventions

All sign illustrations depict a right-handed signer. Imagine that the person in the illustration is facing you. For a right-handed reader to copy a sign illustration, remember that the hand in the illustration will appear opposite of the way you will need to make the sign. For a left-handed signer, the illustration can be used as a mirror image.

The order in which you read sign illustrations and phrases that have multiple illustrations is very important. Words or phrases that contain multiple illustrations need to be read illustration by illustration from left to right. Individual illustrations then need to be read according to the direction or movement of the sign shown.

The following examples show vocabulary with multiple illustrations.

1 yard **3,535**

The Videotape *Number Signs for Everyone*

The chapters and sections of this book are set up to coincide with the topics and order of the videotape *Number Signs for Everyone*. Although the signs included here and in the video are not identical, the content is similar. This book and the video have been designed to reinforce each other and both have special features and capabilities that are unique and valuable to the learning process.

A final note to the reader. ASL is a dynamic, ever growing and changing language. The signs you see in this book are intended to give a person learning ASL basic information about the number sign system. In the signing community you will see other variations of number signs, but, after studying the illustrations here you will be well on your way to mastering numbers and their use in context in ASL.

CHAPTER 1
HOW MANY

CARDINAL numbers are used to describe quantities: 1 shoe, 2 trees, 3 lbs of flour. ASL uses cardinal numbers for counting and expressing quantities. The ASL number system is based on whole numbers in units of 10.

NUMBERS 0–10 1.1

Zero, and the basic signs for counting from 1 to 10 are shown here (note that numbers 1 through 5 have the palm facing inward toward the signer; 0, and 6 through 9 have the palm facing outward).

1.2 NUMBERS 11–30

The following signs are for numbers 11 through 30. Note the variations in palm orientation here. The signs for 16 through 19 begin with the 10 handshape, and end with the hand twisting outward to form the sign for 6, 7, 8, or 9. The signs for 20 through 29, except 22, use a different handshape, an L-handshape to represent 2.

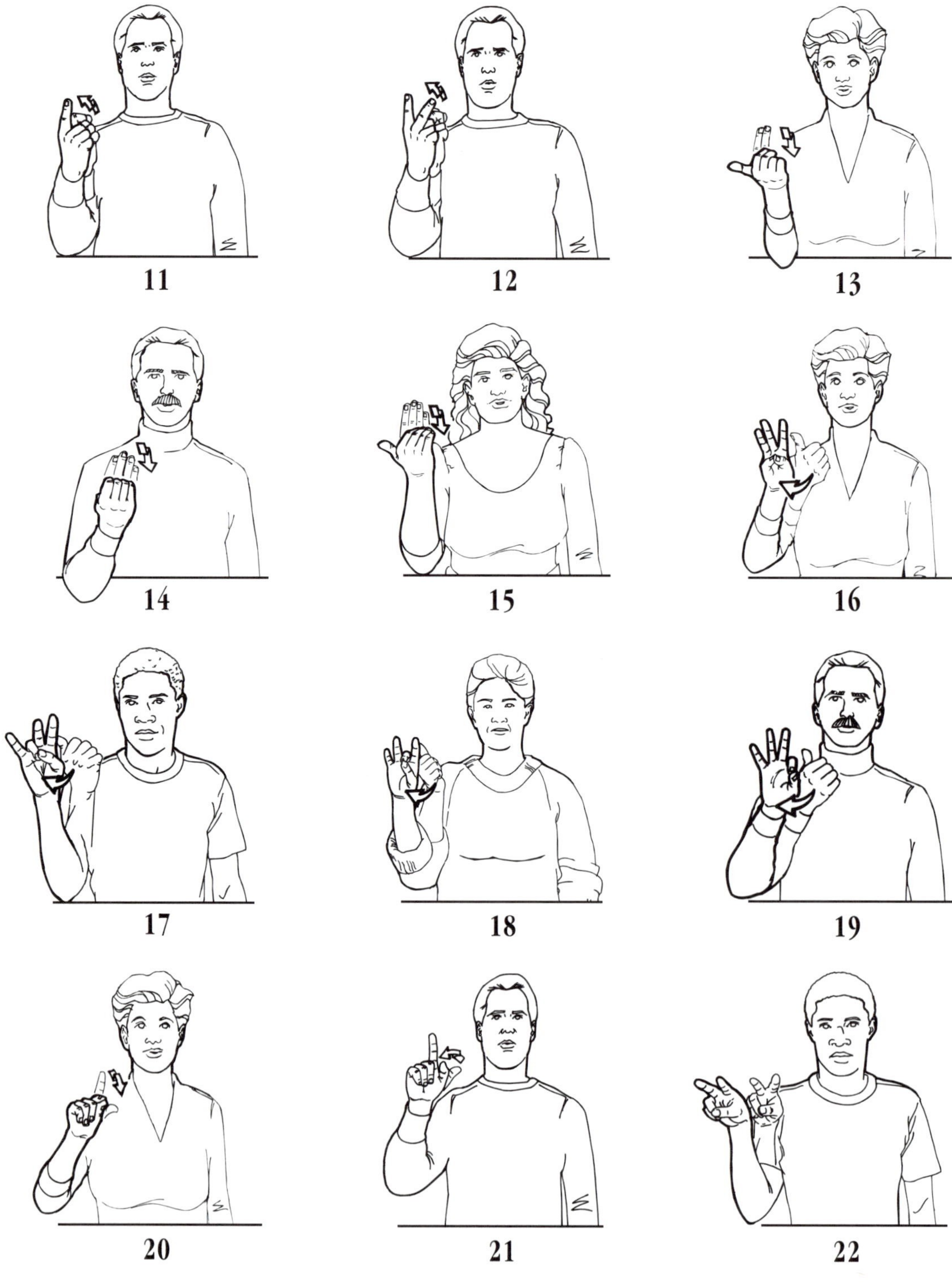

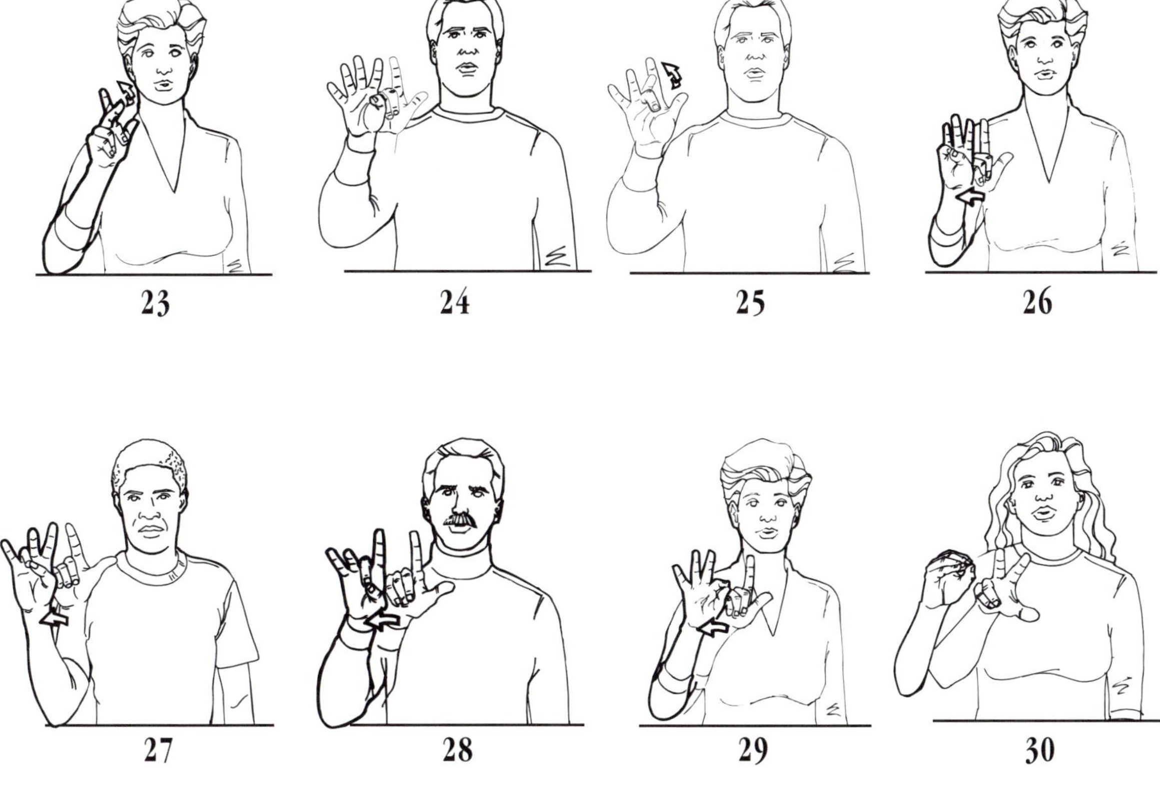

1.3

NUMBERS 31–109, AND MULTIPLES OF 100

This section presents sign illustrations for numbers 31 through 109. Special attention should be paid to multiples of 11 (22, 33, 44, etc.). When these numbers are signed, the same number is repeated, with the handshape bouncing twice. Another unique group of signs comprises two-digit combinations using the numbers 6, 7, 8, and 9 (such as 68, 76, or 97). The signs have a twisting movement to emphasize and clarify the position of the thumb as it shifts from one fingertip to the other, creating the number combination required. Notice the numbers 101-109 are handled so the 0 is clearly shown. Additionally, illustrations for 200, 300, and 400 through 900 are shown.

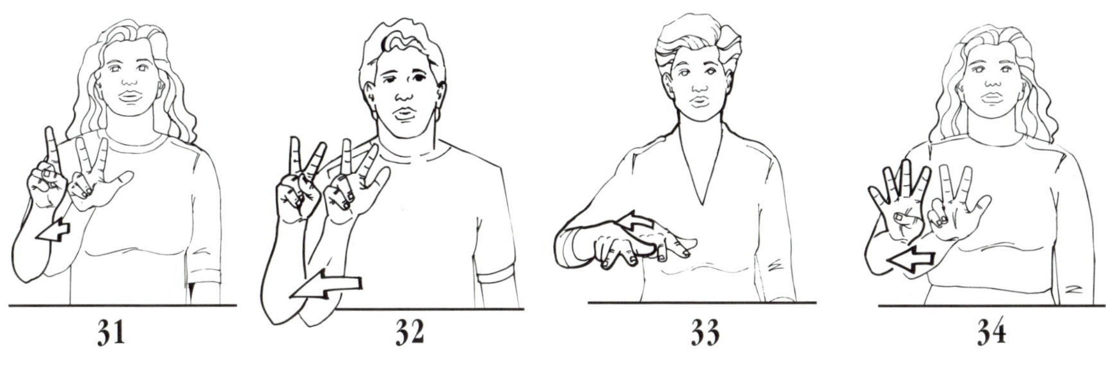

35
36
37
38
39
40
41
42
43
44
45
46
47
48
49
50

51
52
53
54
55
56
57
58
59
60
61
62
63
64
65
66

67
68
69
70
71
72
73
74
75
76
77
78
79
80
81
82

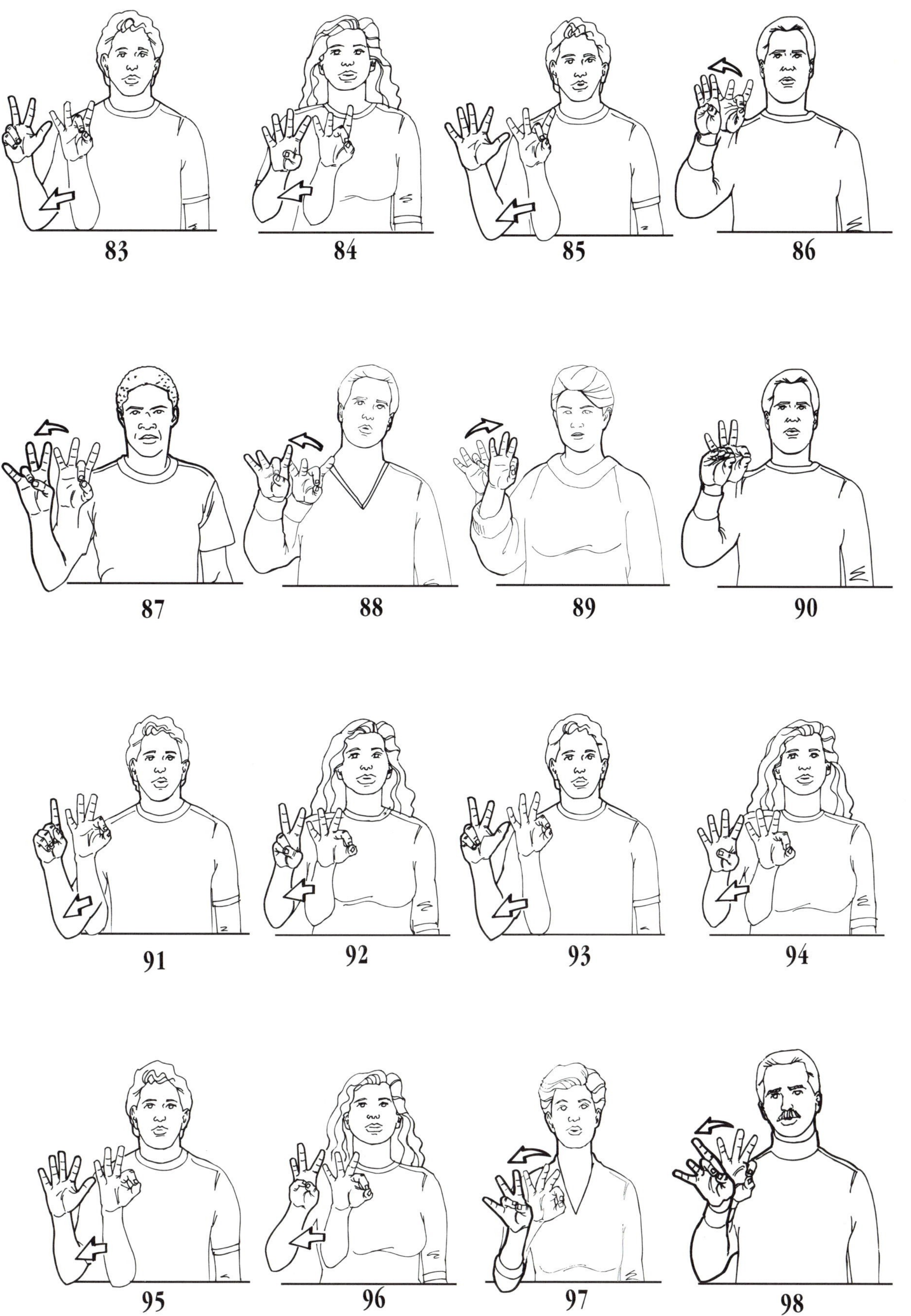
83
84
85
86
87
88
89
90
91
92
93
94
95
96
97
98

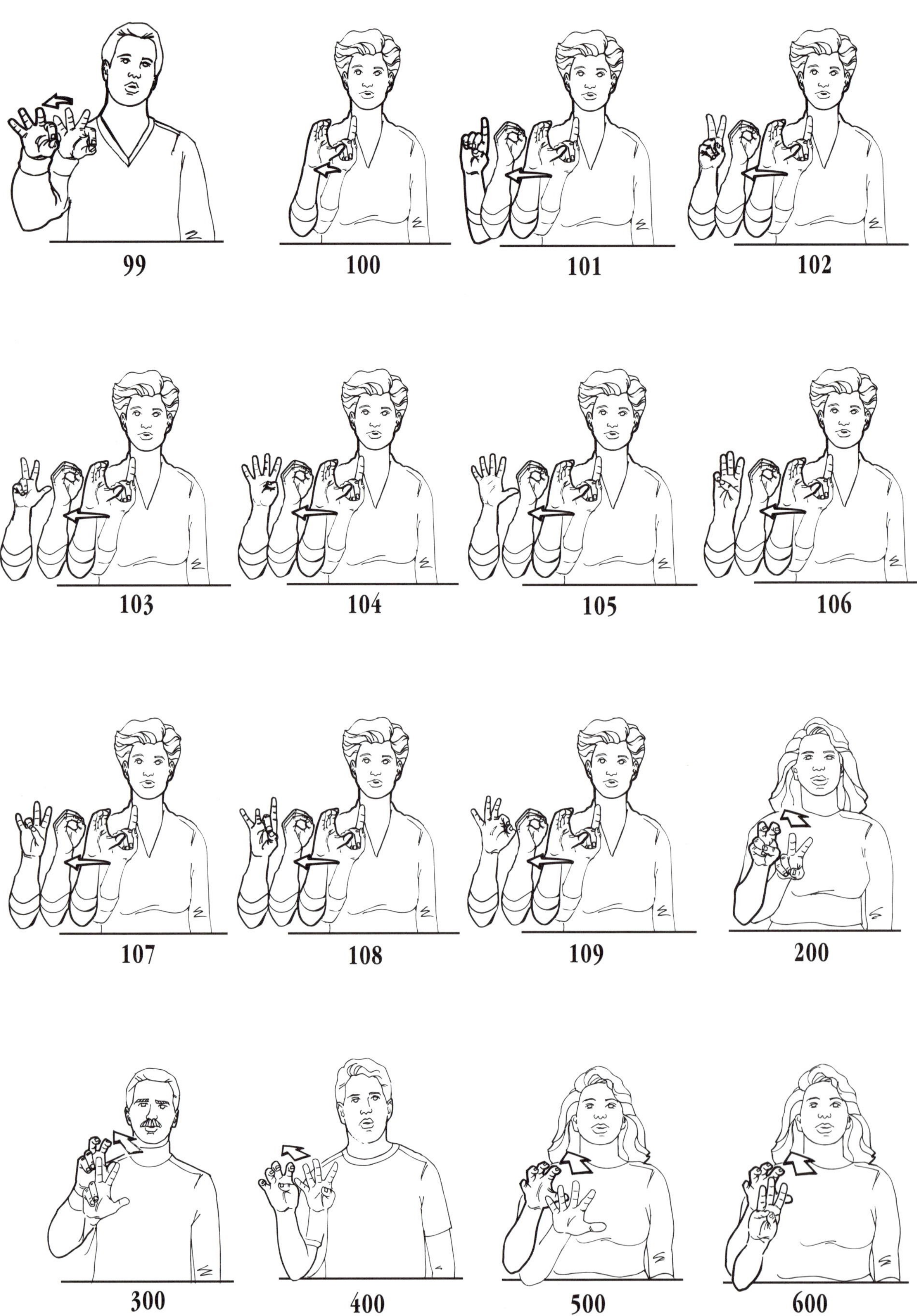
99
100
101
102
103
104
105
106
107
108
109
200
300
400
500
600

700

800

900

EMPHASIS

1.4

Number signs include emphasis, which adds context to ASL sentences by showing whether the person signing feels the quantity they are discussing is normal or exceptional. The following illustrations use a sharp singular motion and facial expressions to show emphasis. In ASL, sign formations often lose repetition of movement when they are emphasized.

200

300

400

500

LARGE NUMBERS AND MIXED NUMBERS

1.5

Here illustrations of larger numbers, such as 1,000 to 1 billion, and mixed numbers are shown. Mixed numbers are signed in parts as in three hundred, sixty-five, not three, six, five.

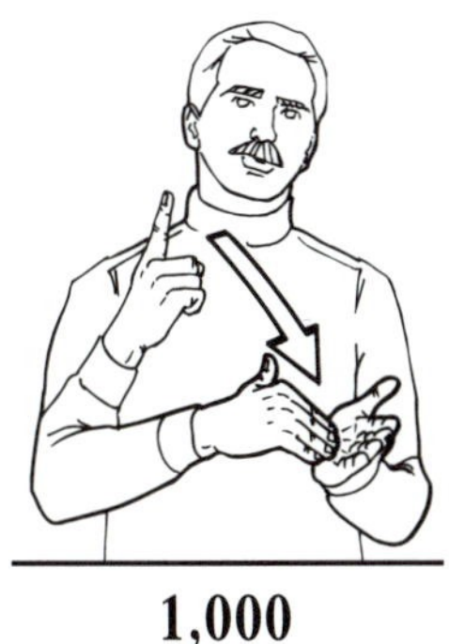
1,000

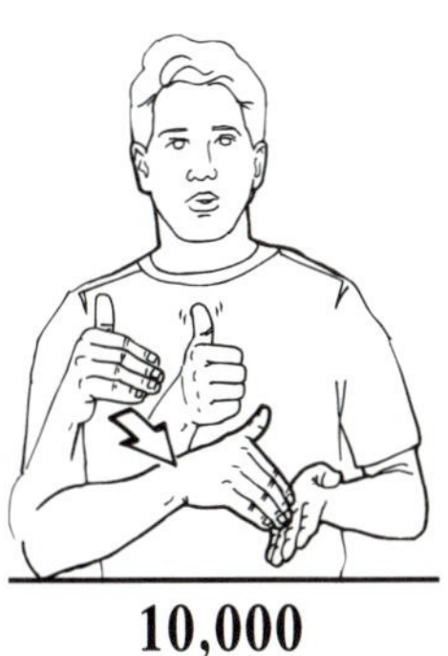
10,000

50,000

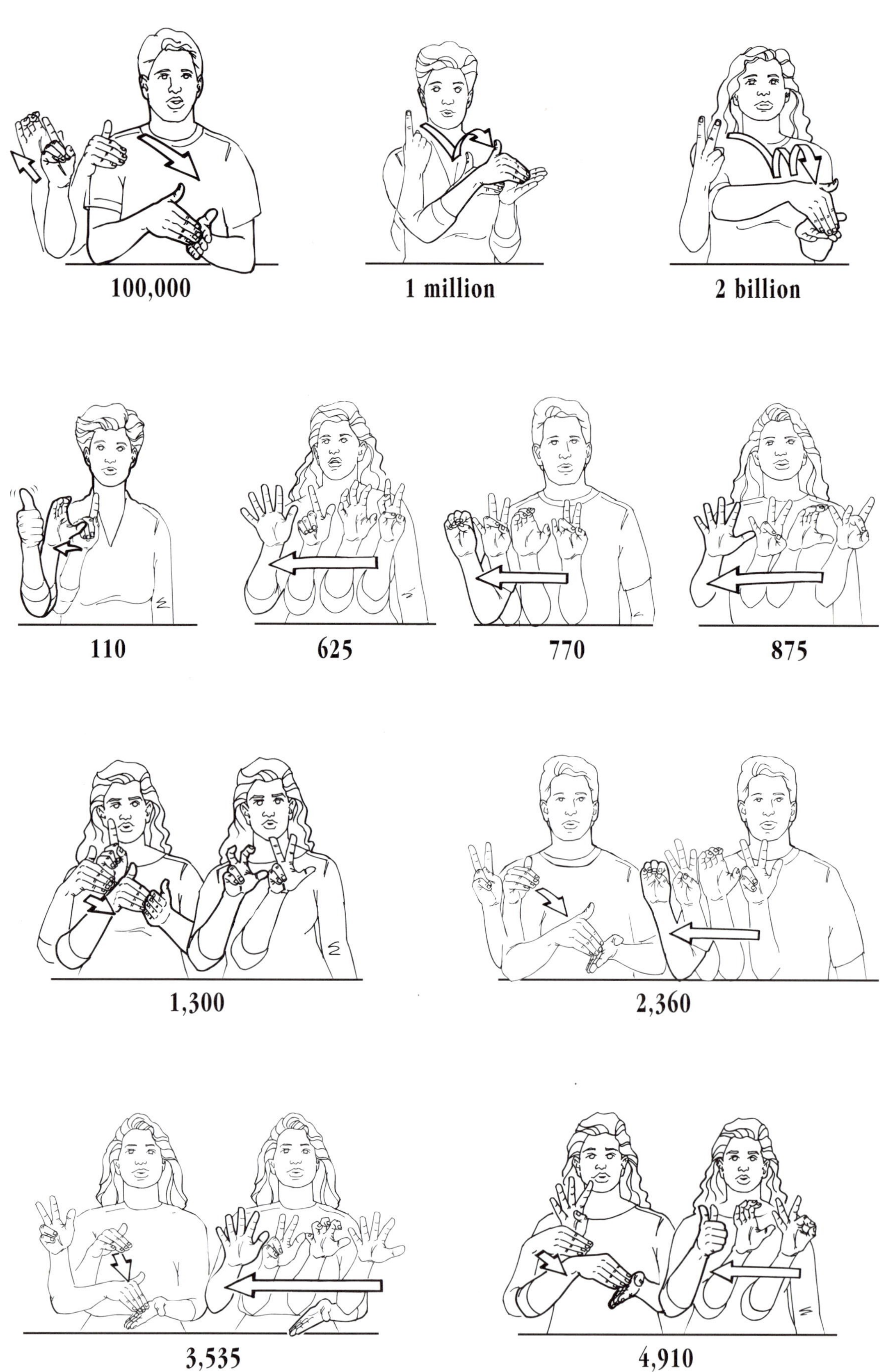
100,000
1 million
2 billion
110
625
770
875
1,300
2,360
3,535
4,910

APPROXIMATIONS

Sometimes it is useful or necessary to express an approximate number. There are several ways of doing this in ASL. One is to sign the number, but add a facial expression indicating that you are not sure of the exact amount. Another is to add a sign indicating that you are estimating, or add a wiggling motion.

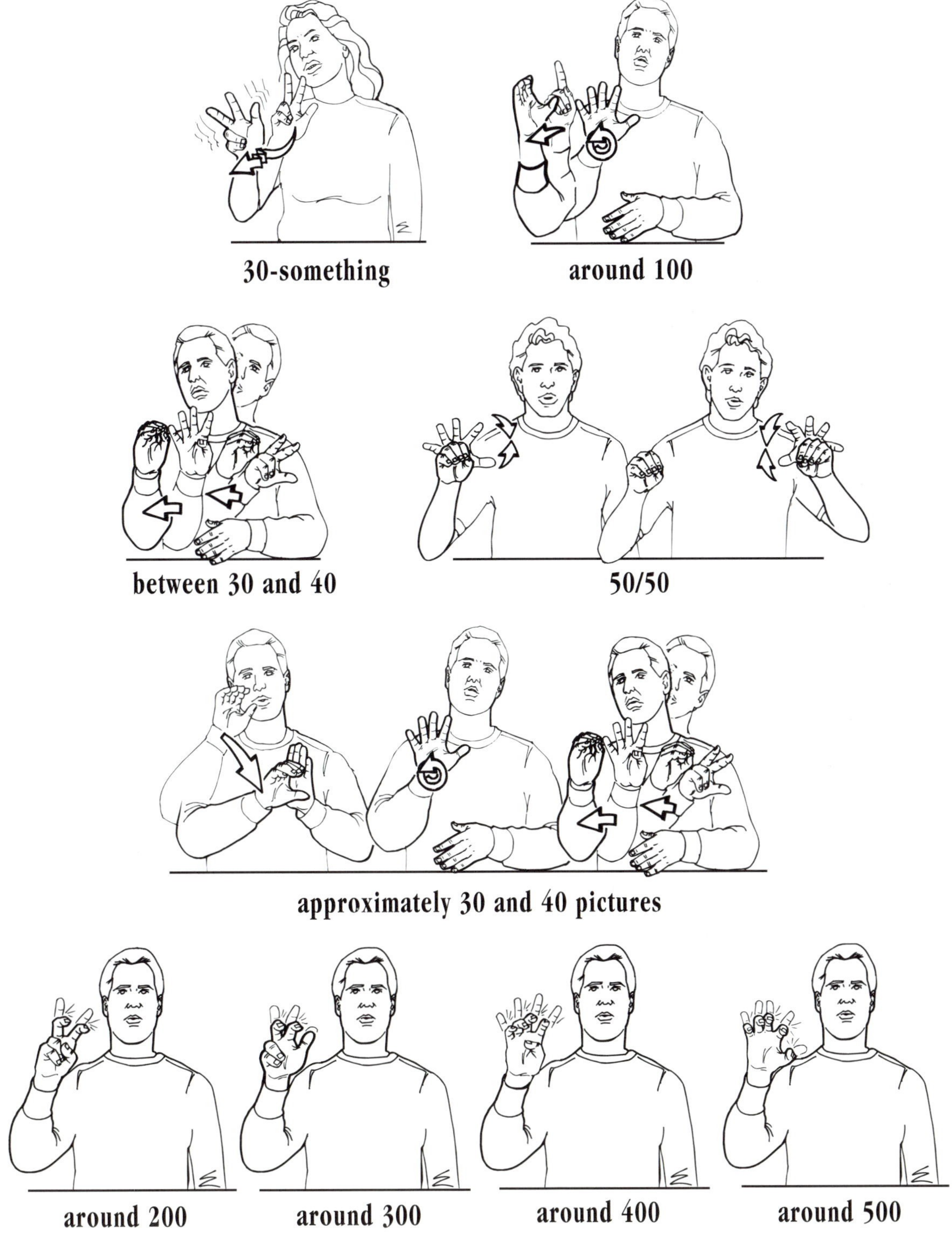

30-something **around 100**

between 30 and 40 **50/50**

approximately 30 and 40 pictures

around 200 **around 300** **around 400** **around 500**

1.7 NUMBER REPRESENTATION

Number representation is an important part of ASL structure. These signs use a number handshape with modified motion or location, or a noun to express a meaning.

number of baby teeth | **double date** | **4 couples together**

1 person moving | **1 person approaching 2 people** | **5 people approaching**

2 of us | **2 of them** | **3 of us**

4 of us | **5 of you** | **6 of us** | **all of us**

QUANTIFIERS

So far, we have been using numbers to express absolute quantities, that is, amounts that can be understood correctly out of context. In addition to absolute numbers, ASL has another kind of sign for showing quantity using quantifiers. Quantifiers represent attributes of things in a relative sense, rather than discussing exact amounts with whole numbers. Words like many, more, and few are examples of generic quantifiers.

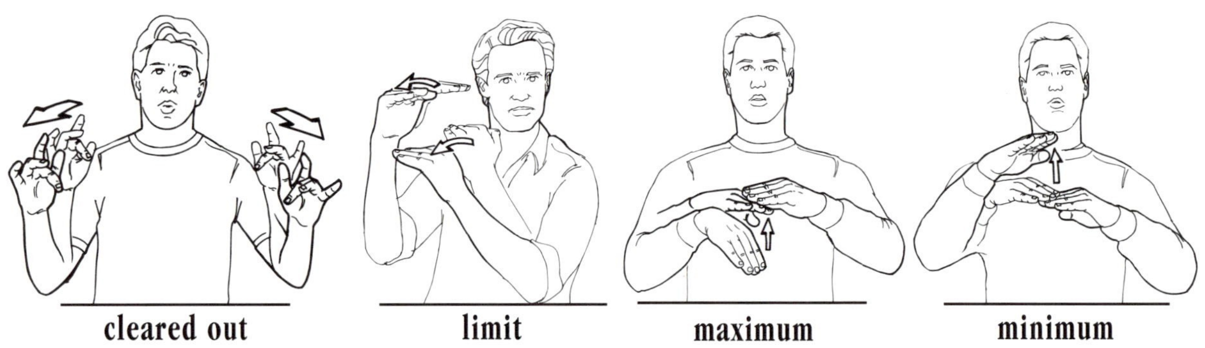

cleared out | limit | maximum | minimum

Phrases using Quantifiers

How many?

Thirty people came.

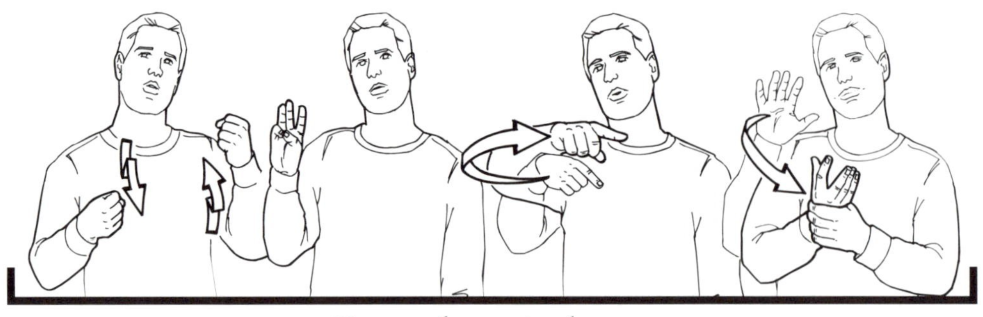

Six people are in the car.

I have rows of shoes.

I gave a book to both of you.

I assume 2 cars left, one following the other.

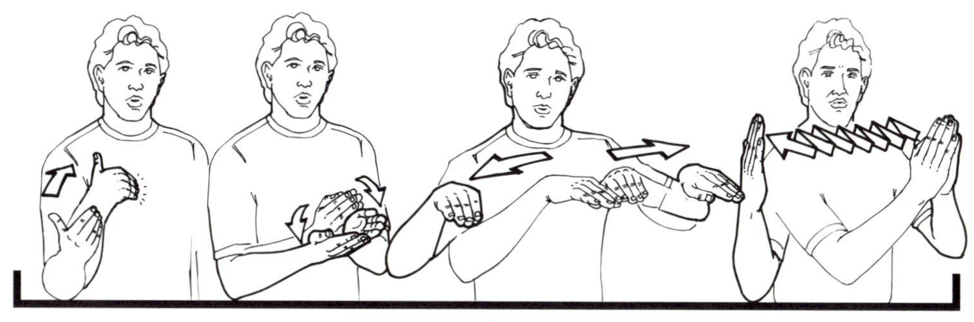

I have a whole shelf of books.

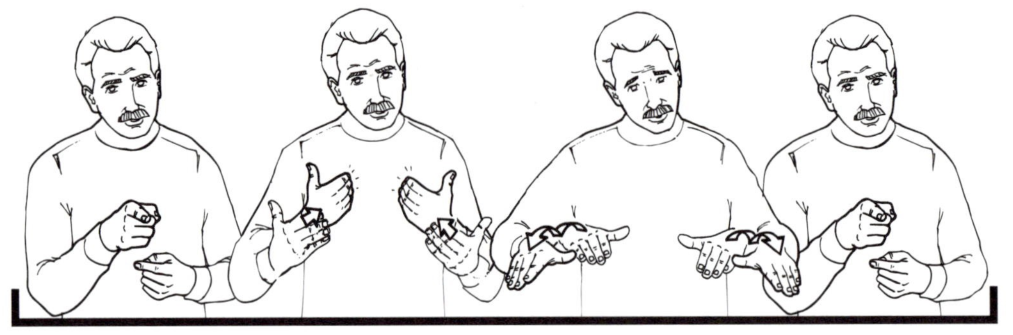

Do you have children?

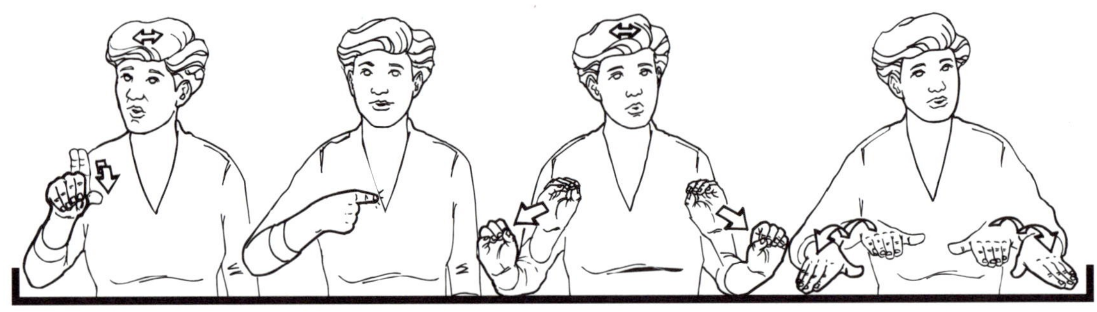

No, I don't have any children.

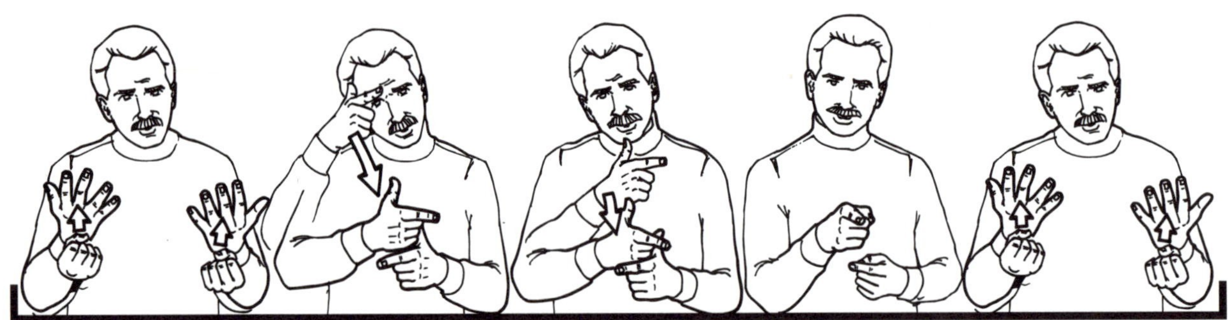

How many brothers and sisters do you have?

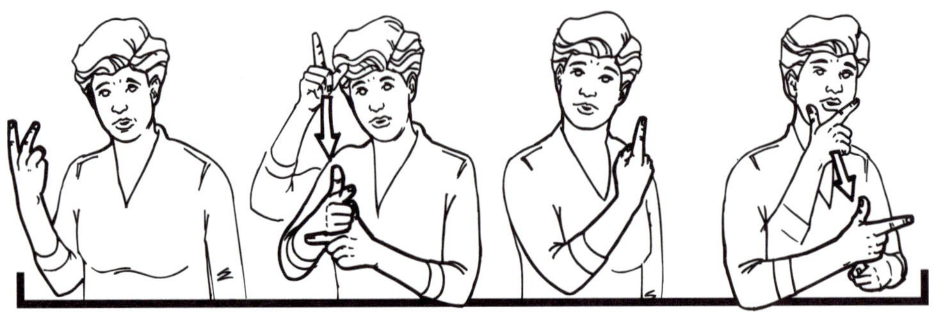

I have 2 brothers and 1 sister.

CHAPTER 2
MONEY

MONEY is a part of everyday life. The following examples of number signs for monetary values show the basic signs for dollars and cents and show phrases using money signs.

CENTS

2.1

Cents are the smallest monetary value in ASL. The following are various quantities of cents. Notice that 25 cents uses a common variation of the number 25.

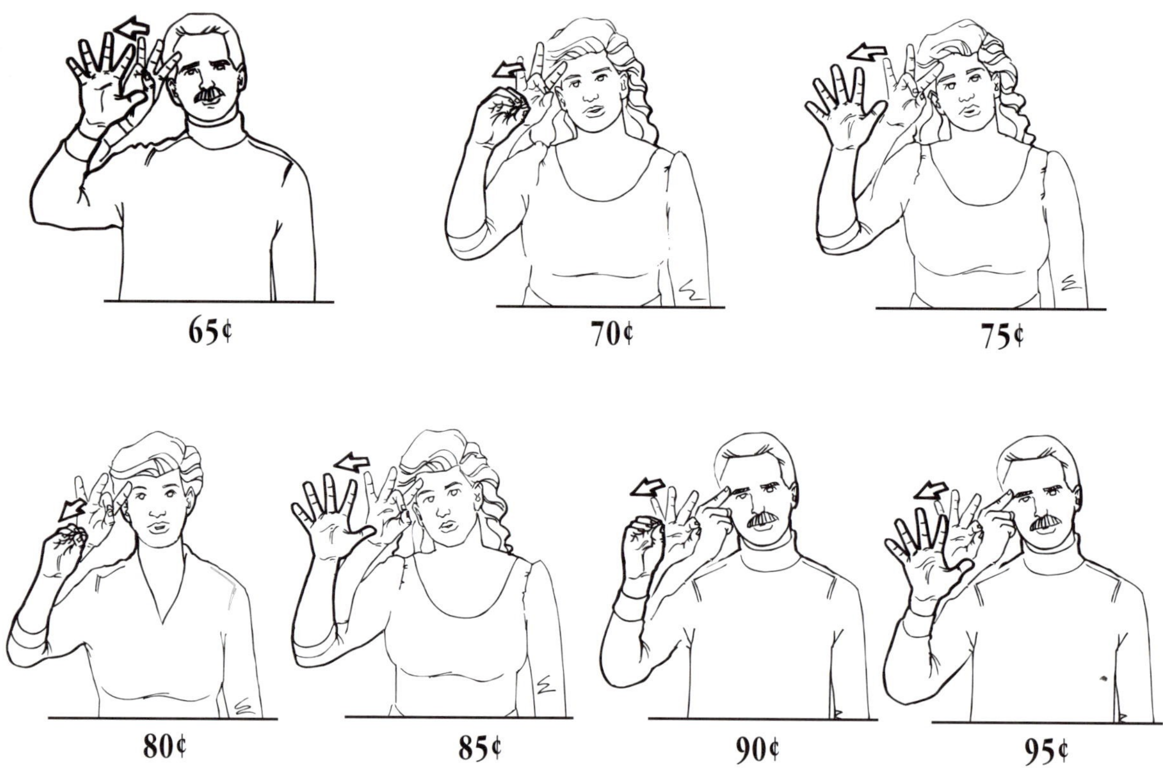

65¢ 70¢ 75¢

80¢ 85¢ 90¢ 95¢

2.2 FINGERSPELLING CENTS

You can also sign a number and fingerspell the word *"C-E-N-T-S"* to show the amount. Remember, if the amount is a number from 1 to 5, you sign the number with your palm facing toward your body, and then turn your hand palm-outward to fingerspell *cents*.

5 c-e-n-t-s 46 c-e-n-t-s

DOLLARS

Following are various signs for dollar values. With dollar numbers 1 through 9 you do not separate the number and dollar sign; you use the number handshape with a twisting motion to indicate dollars. For numbers 10 or greater the signs change. The signs for numbers and dollars are separated.

2.4 MIXED MONEY SIGNS

The previous rules for signing dollars and cents apply to mixed monetary values such as $10.25. In English, people may say "ten twenty-five" when discussing cost. For mixed money signs in ASL with 10 dollars or greater, the signs for dollars and sign for cents are sometimes lost when incorporated in a sentence. The samples below show mixed money signs.

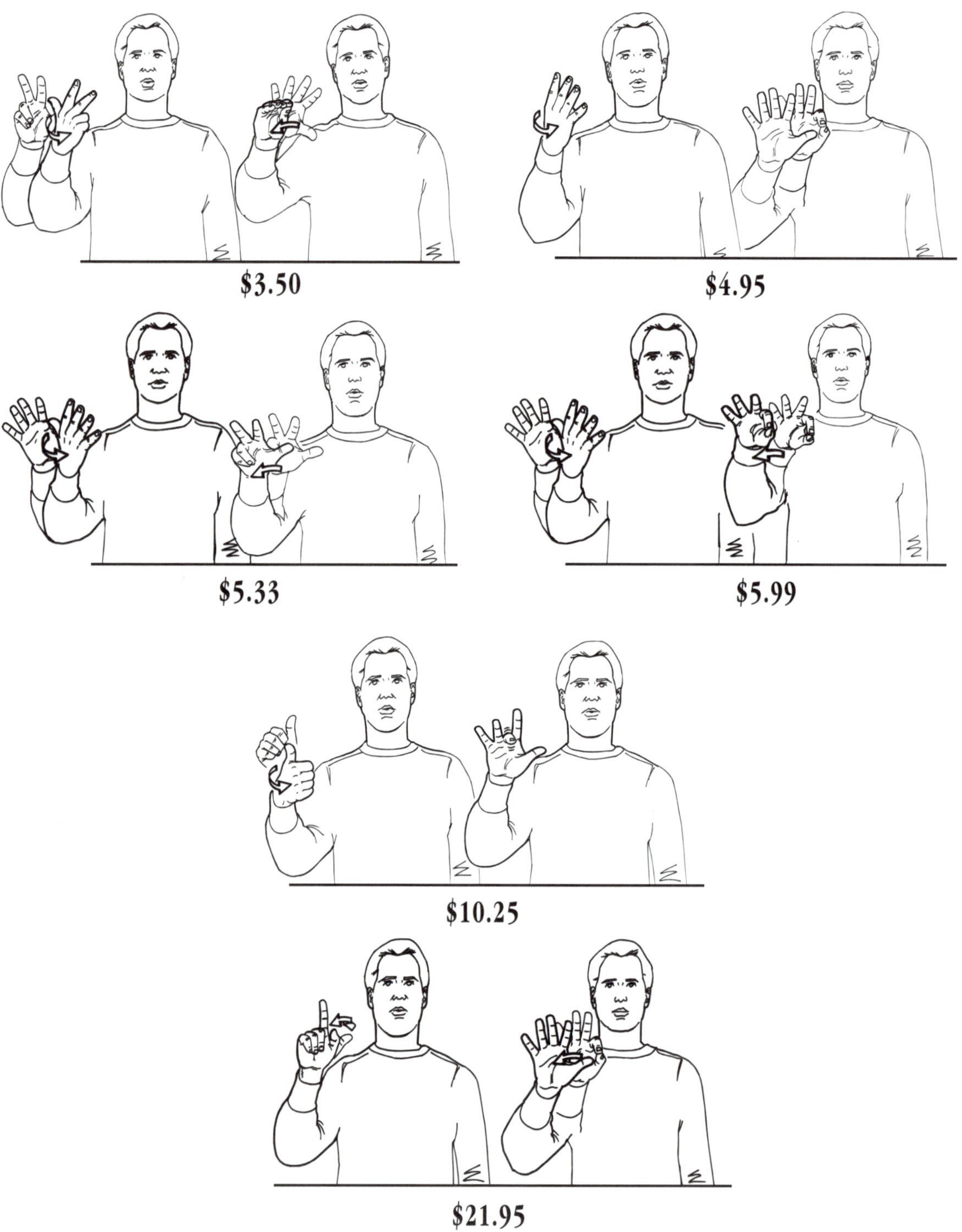

Approximate Money Signs

Sometimes, we do not know, or it is not important, exactly how many cents are involved. The next sign shows how to approximate a monetary value.

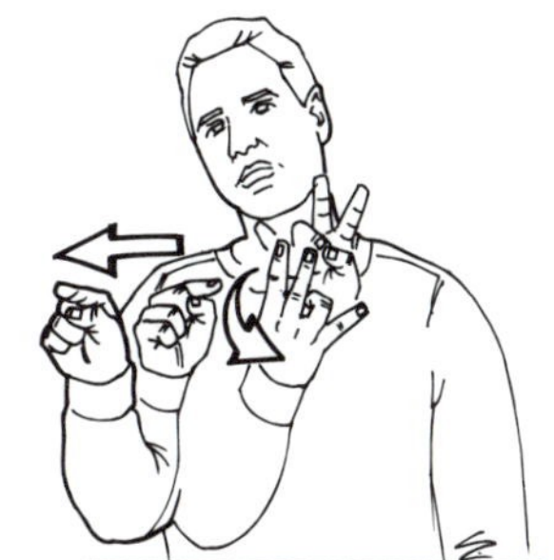

7 dollars and some odd cents

Phrases Using Money Signs

How much?

How much?

How much is the admission fee?

It's $3.00.

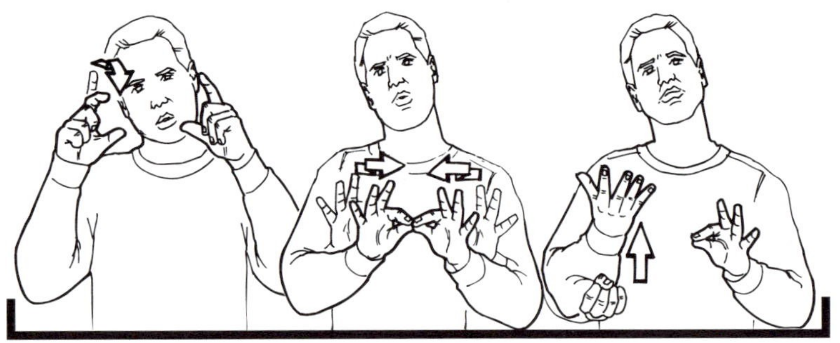

How much is the camera worth?

It's nice . . . it's worth 80 dollars and 46 c-e-n-t-s.

It's cheap! It costs $9.05 plus tax.

CHAPTER 3
FINANCES

THIS chapter focuses on vocabulary related to money. Examples of phrases using the vocabulary in the proper context are given.

PAYMENT AND SPENDING

3.1

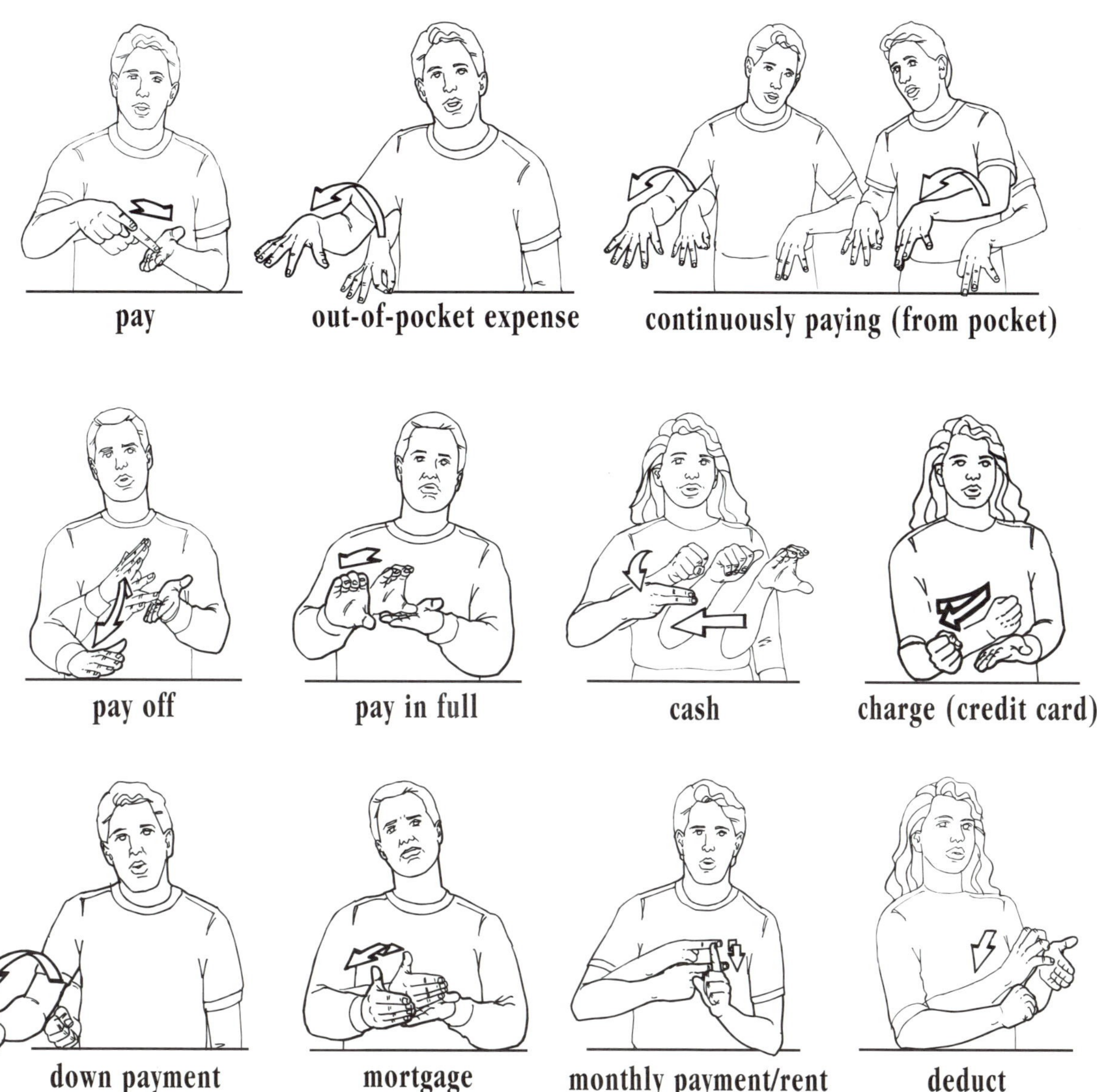

pay

out-of-pocket expense

continuously paying (from pocket)

pay off

pay in full

cash

charge (credit card)

down payment

mortgage

monthly payment/rent

deduct

Phrases Using Payment Signs

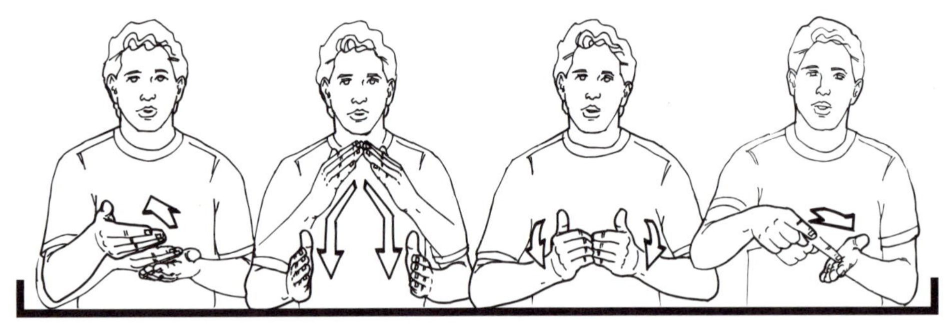

How did you pay for the house you bought?

I paid in full!

INCOME

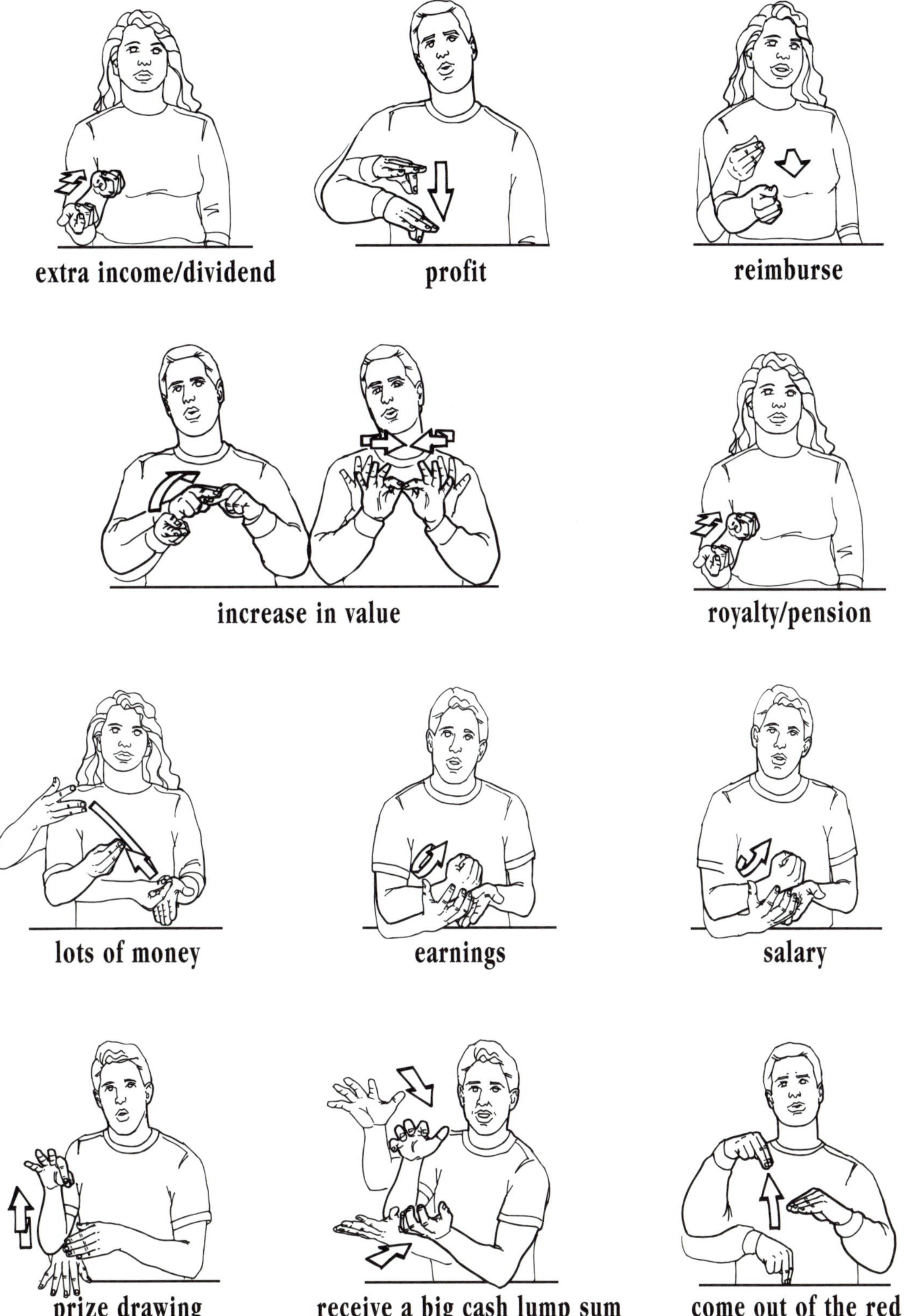

extra income/dividend

profit

reimburse

increase in value

royalty/pension

lots of money

earnings

salary

prize drawing

receive a big cash lump sum

come out of the red

Phrases Using Income Signs

Does your job pay well?

I make good money!

3.3 LOSSES

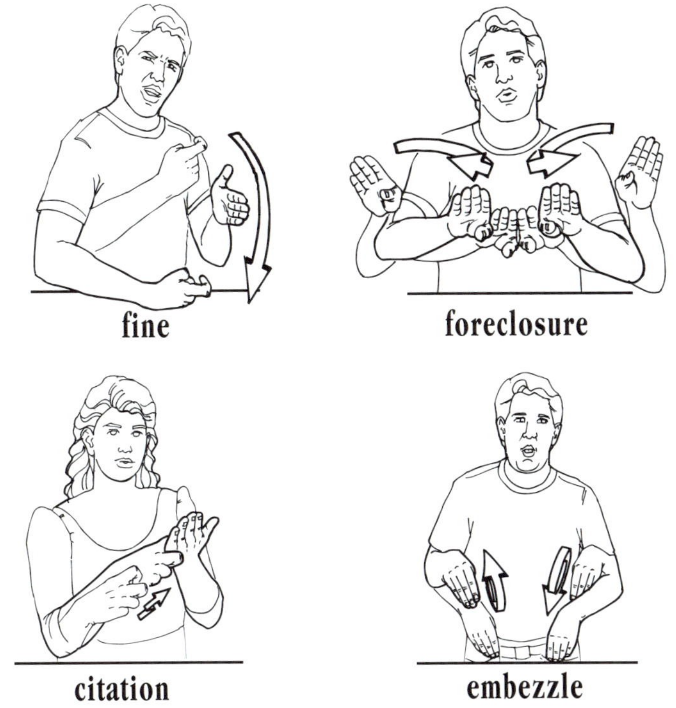

FINANCE-RELATED SIGNS

3.4

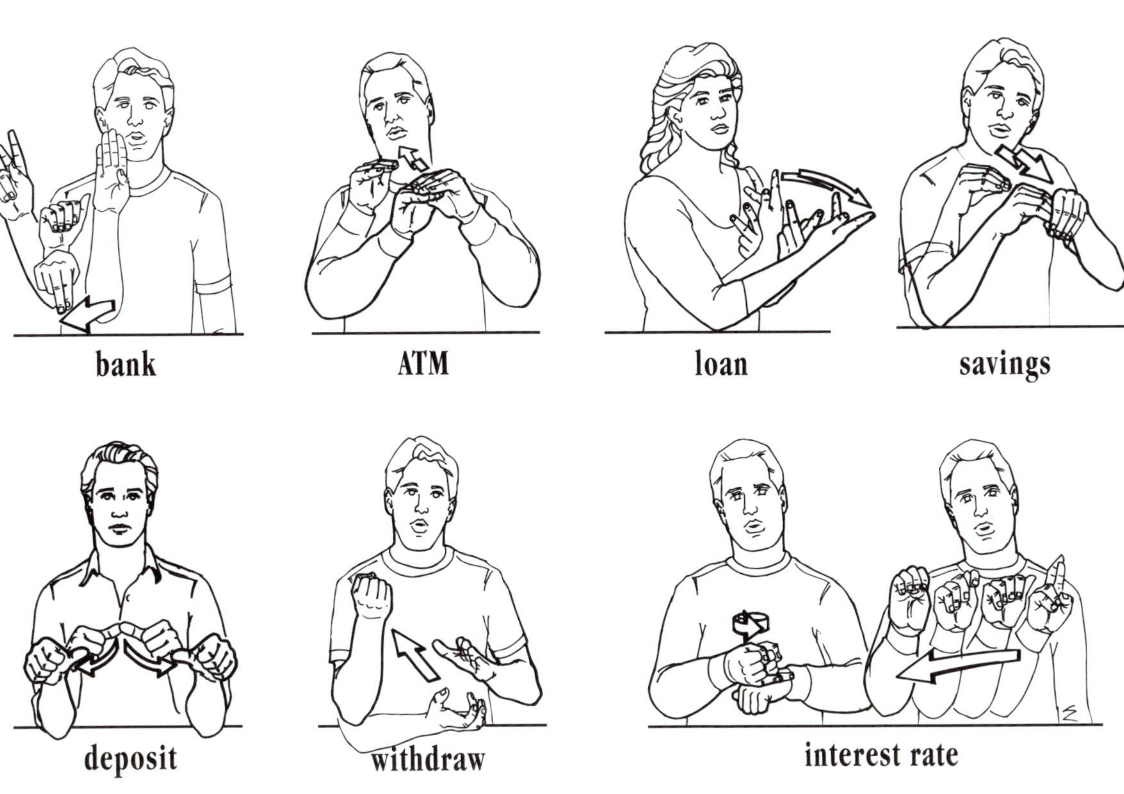

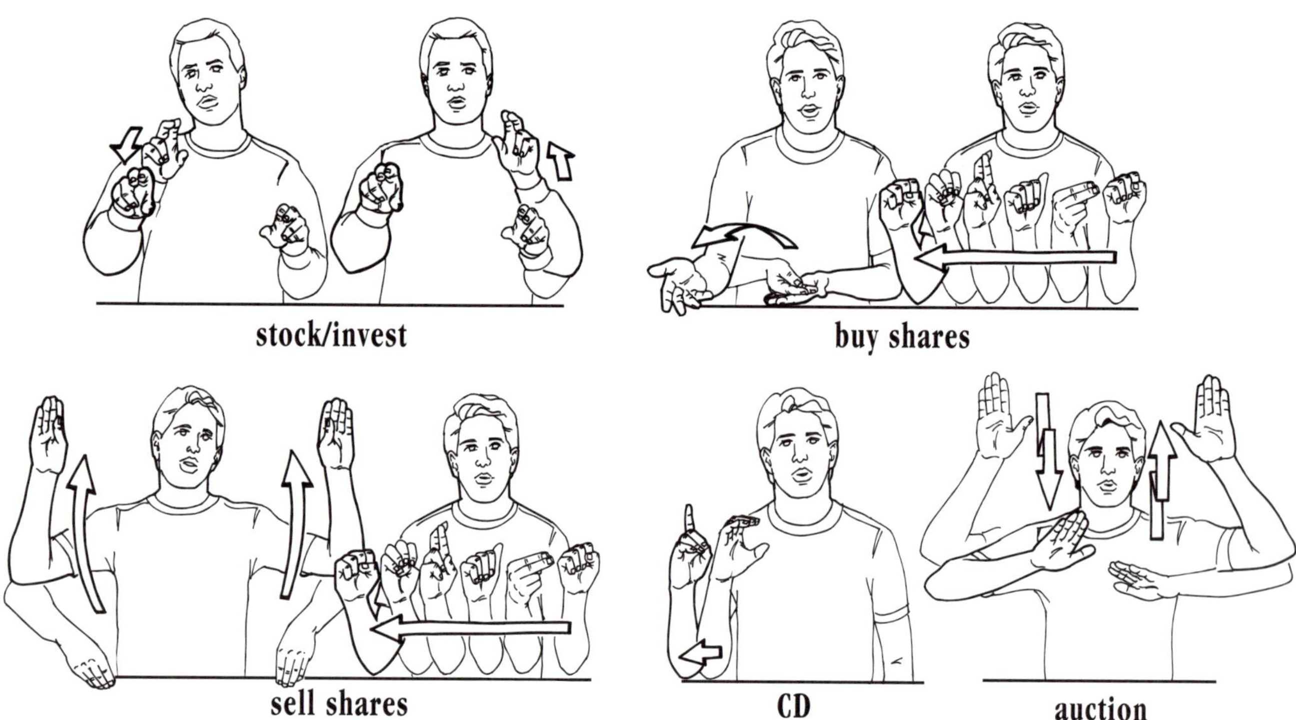

Phrases Using Finance-Related Signs

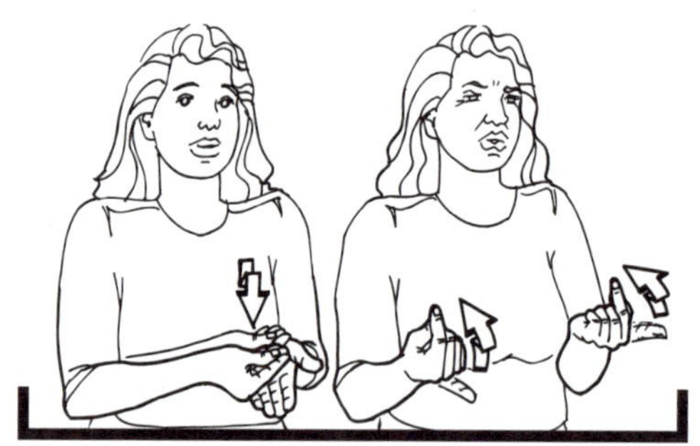

What do you do with your money?

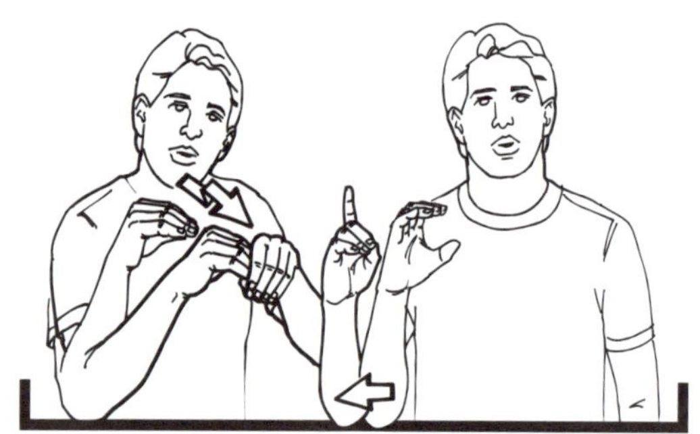

Put it in my savings or CD's.

FINANCE-RELATED OCCUPATIONS

Most of the signs in this next group are compounds of a verb sign for the activity plus a sign that is often translated as "-er" to indicate that an occupation is being discussed.

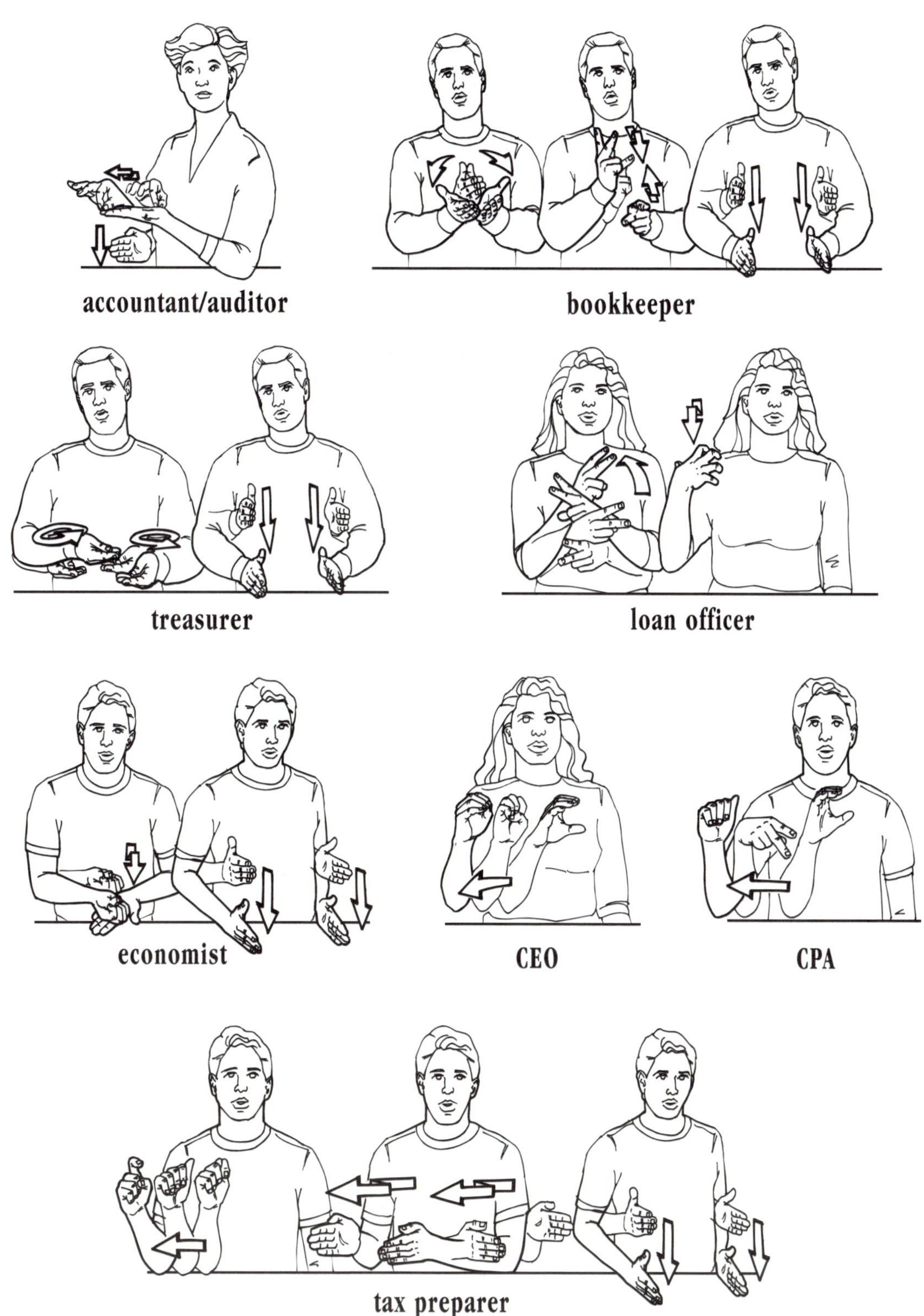

accountant/auditor

bookkeeper

treasurer

loan officer

economist

CEO

CPA

tax preparer

financial planner

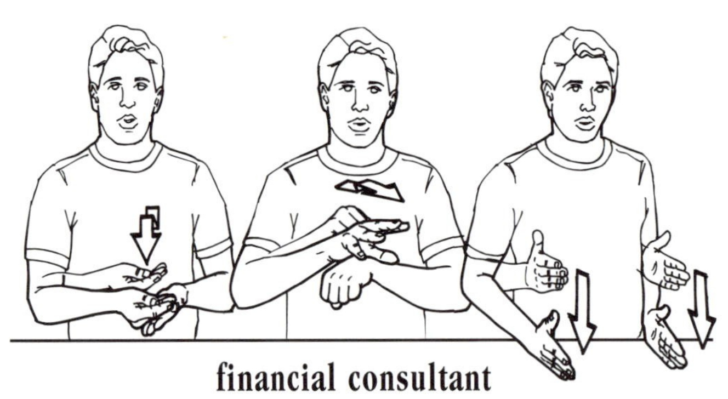

financial consultant

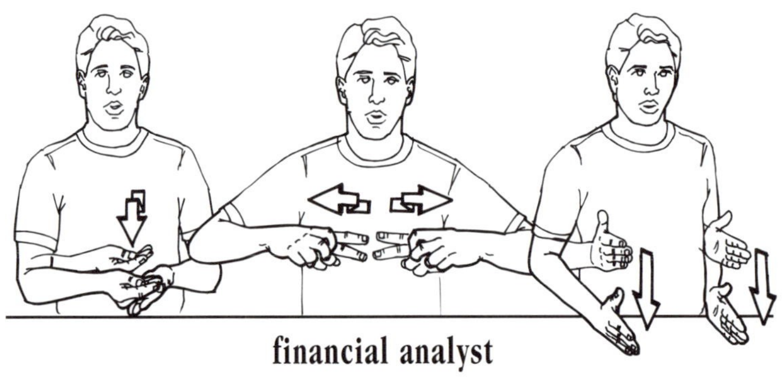

financial analyst

CHAPTER 4
MEASUREMENTS

NUMBERS are not only used for counting, but also for measuring, comparing, and otherwise commenting on quantity. This chapter shows number signs that give information about "how much" and "how many."

NUMERICAL SIGNS SHOWING QUANTITY AND FREQUENCY 4.1

ASL has a common pattern from once all the way up to five times, using the corresponding handshape for the numbers 1 to 5. Notice in the following sign illustrations how the different numeric handshapes use different fingertips in contact with the base hand to begin the sign.

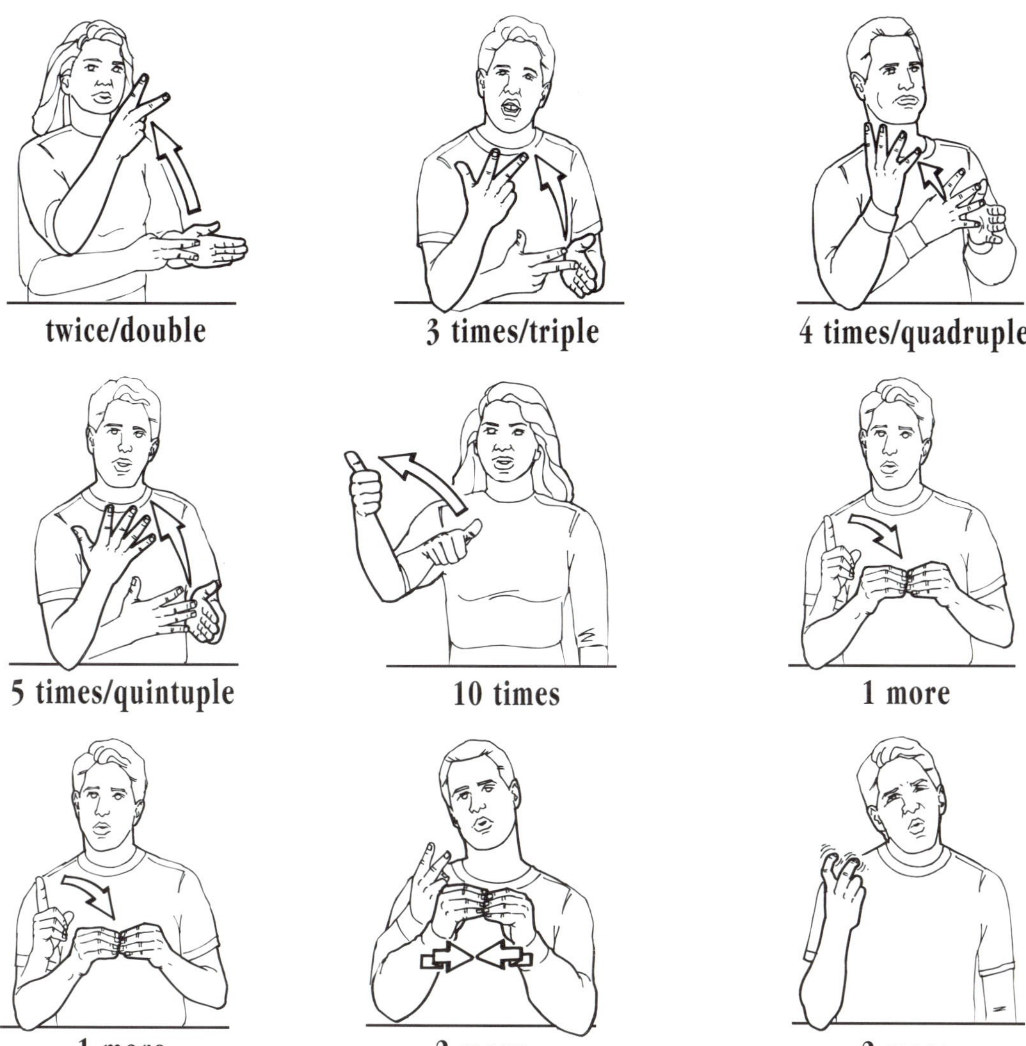

twice/double **3 times/triple** **4 times/quadruple**

5 times/quintuple **10 times** **1 more**

1 more **2 more** **2 more**

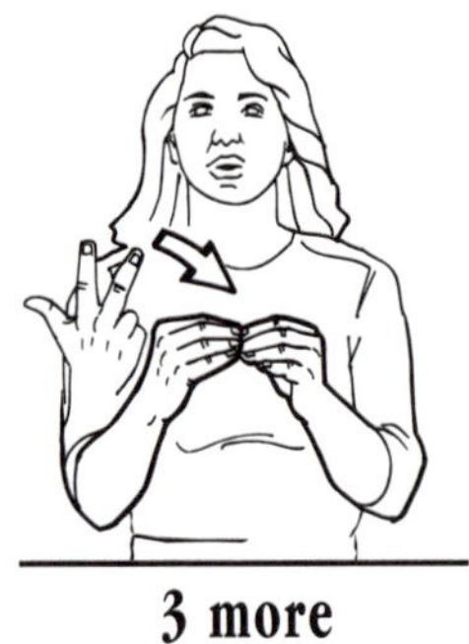

3 more

3 more

Phrase Using Quantity and Frequency Signs

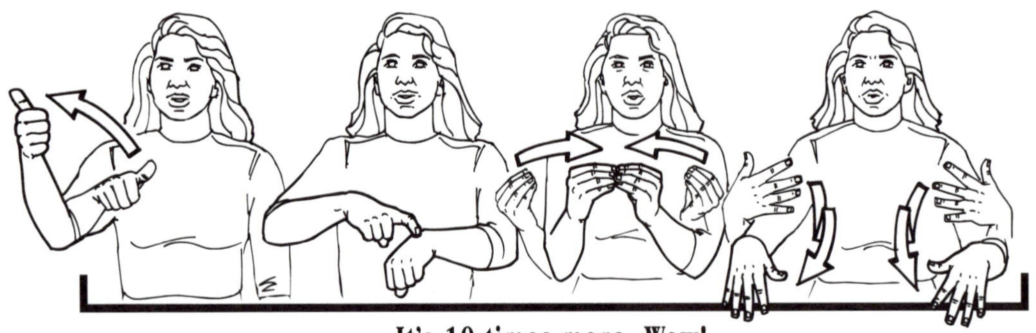

It's 10 times more, Wow!

4.2 QUANTIFIERS

As seen in Chapter 1, Section 8, a quantifier is a word like "all" or "some" that indicates the quantity of something without using an absolute number. The following signs are quantifiers that specifically discuss measurement.

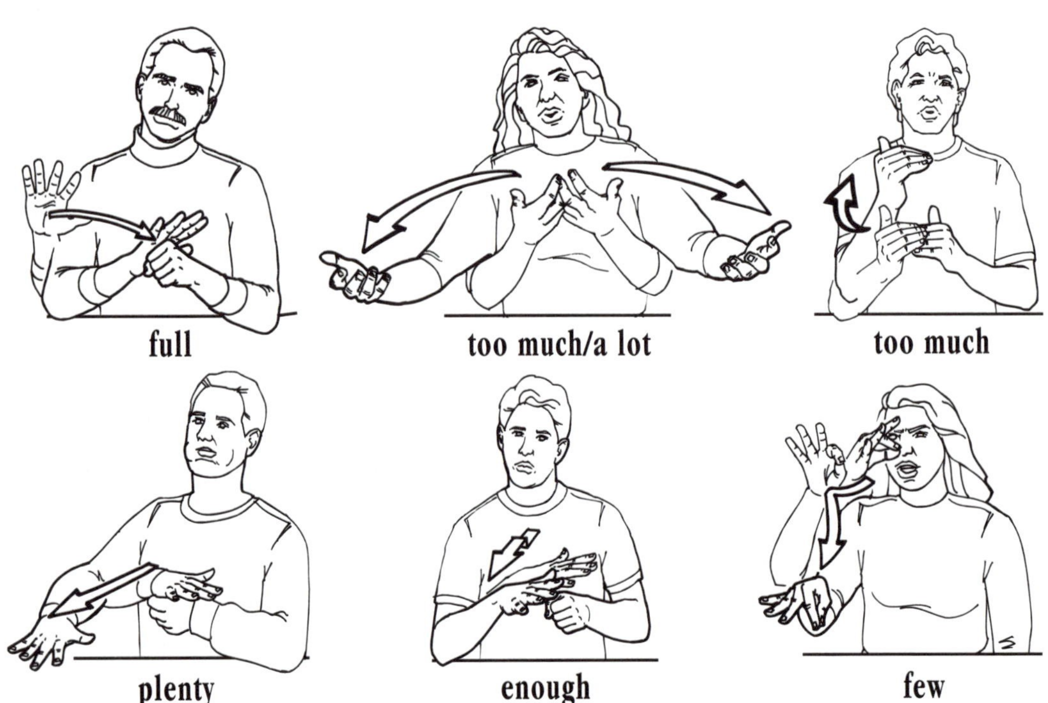

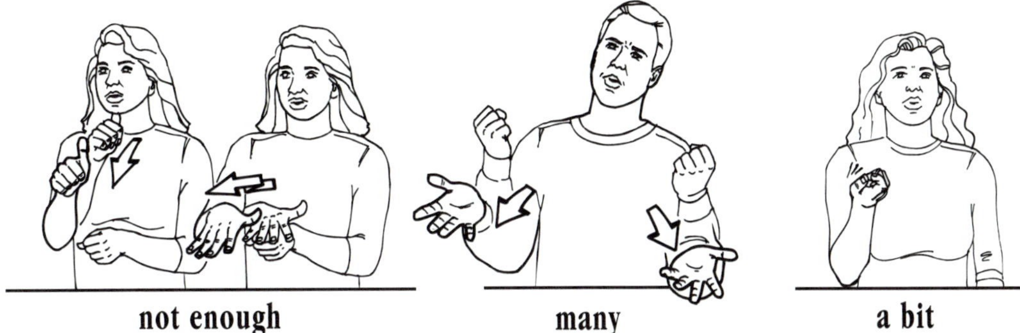
not enough | many | a bit

Phrases Using Quantifier Signs

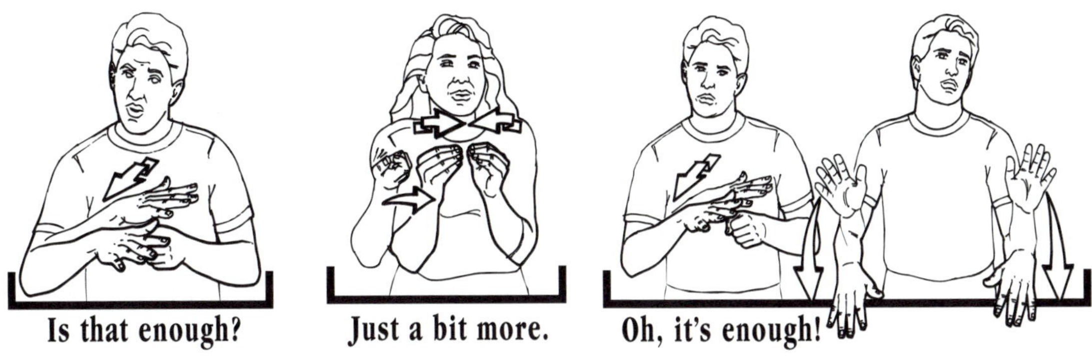
Is that enough? | Just a bit more. | Oh, it's enough!

4.3

FRACTIONS

ASL uses space to indicate a fraction, signing the upper number (the numerator), and then dropping the hand slightly and signing the lower number (the denominator). Fractions where both the numerator and the denominator are single digits, for example, *1/2, 1/3, 1/4,* and up to *3/9, 4/9,* and *5/9* are made with the palm facing in toward the signer for both digits. Here are some common fractions.

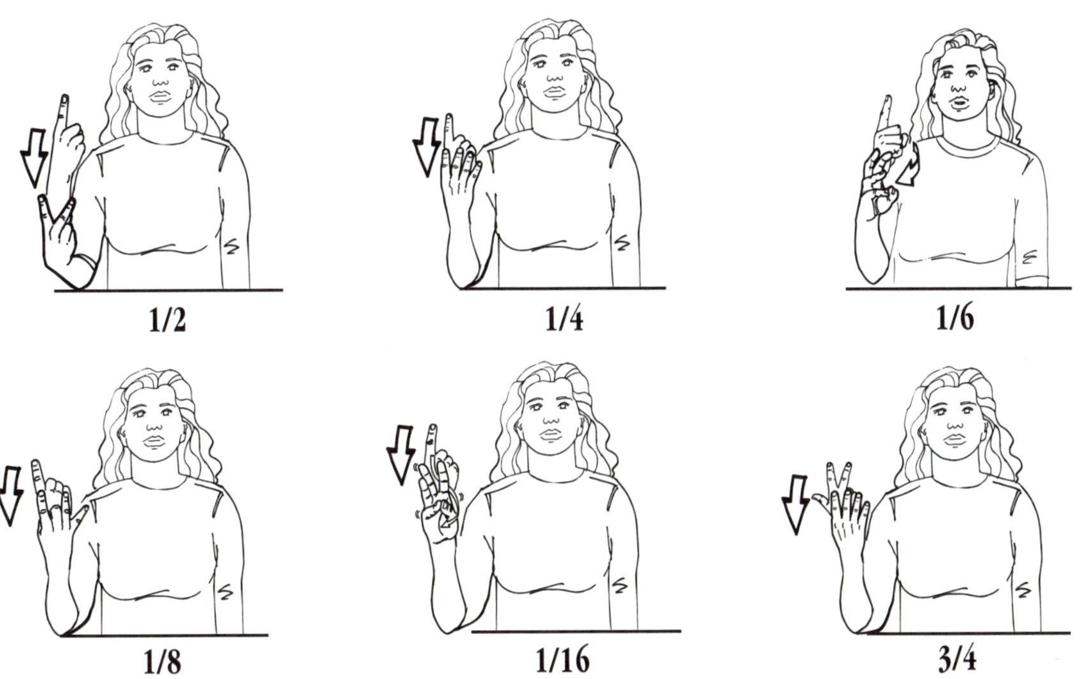
1/2 | 1/4 | 1/6
1/8 | 1/16 | 3/4

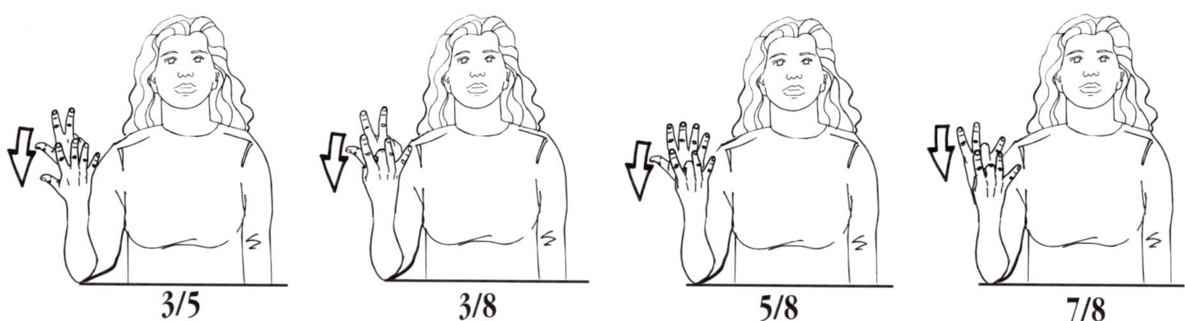

3/5 3/8 5/8 7/8

Half

Following are signs for *half*. One follows the simple pattern described previously to make the fraction 1/2. The second shows a two-handed sign, translated as "1/2 for you, and 1/2 for me." The third is a special sign based on the verb *cut in half* and does not incorporate any numbers.

1/2

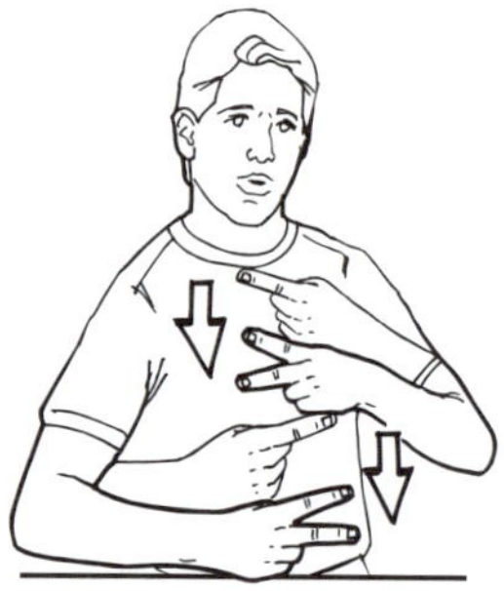

1/2 for you, 1/2 for me

half/split

half and half

50/50

half French, half Italian

Body Measurements

Height and other body measurements such as dress size are shown here. One important note in expressing a person's height in ASL is that the numbers are signed with the palm facing toward the signer. As the handshape changes from expressing number of feet to number of inches, the hand moves sharply in the direction of the thumb-side of the hand (that is, to the right if you are right-handed and to the left if you are left-handed).

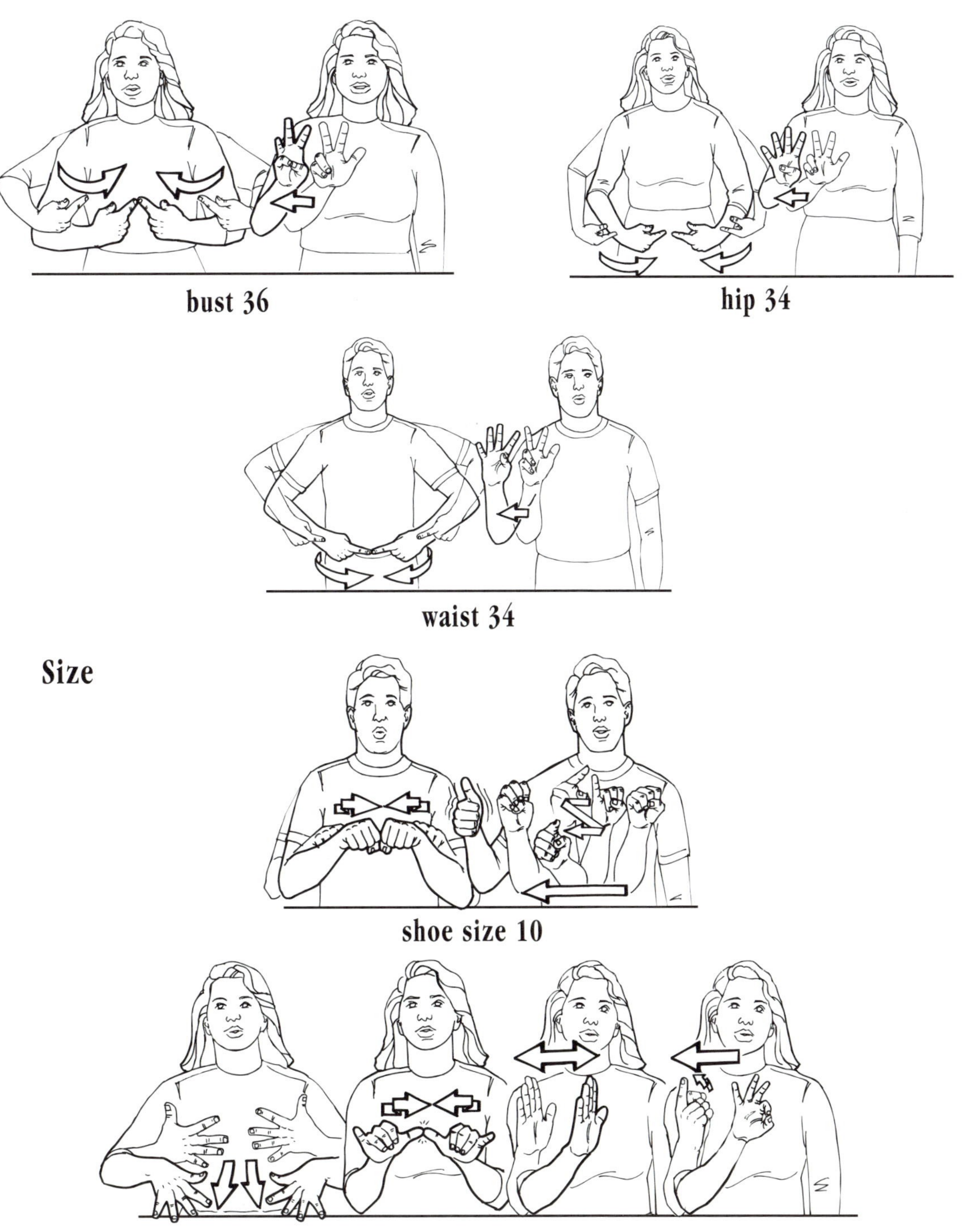

bust 36

hip 34

waist 34

Size

shoe size 10

dress size between 9 and 11

Height

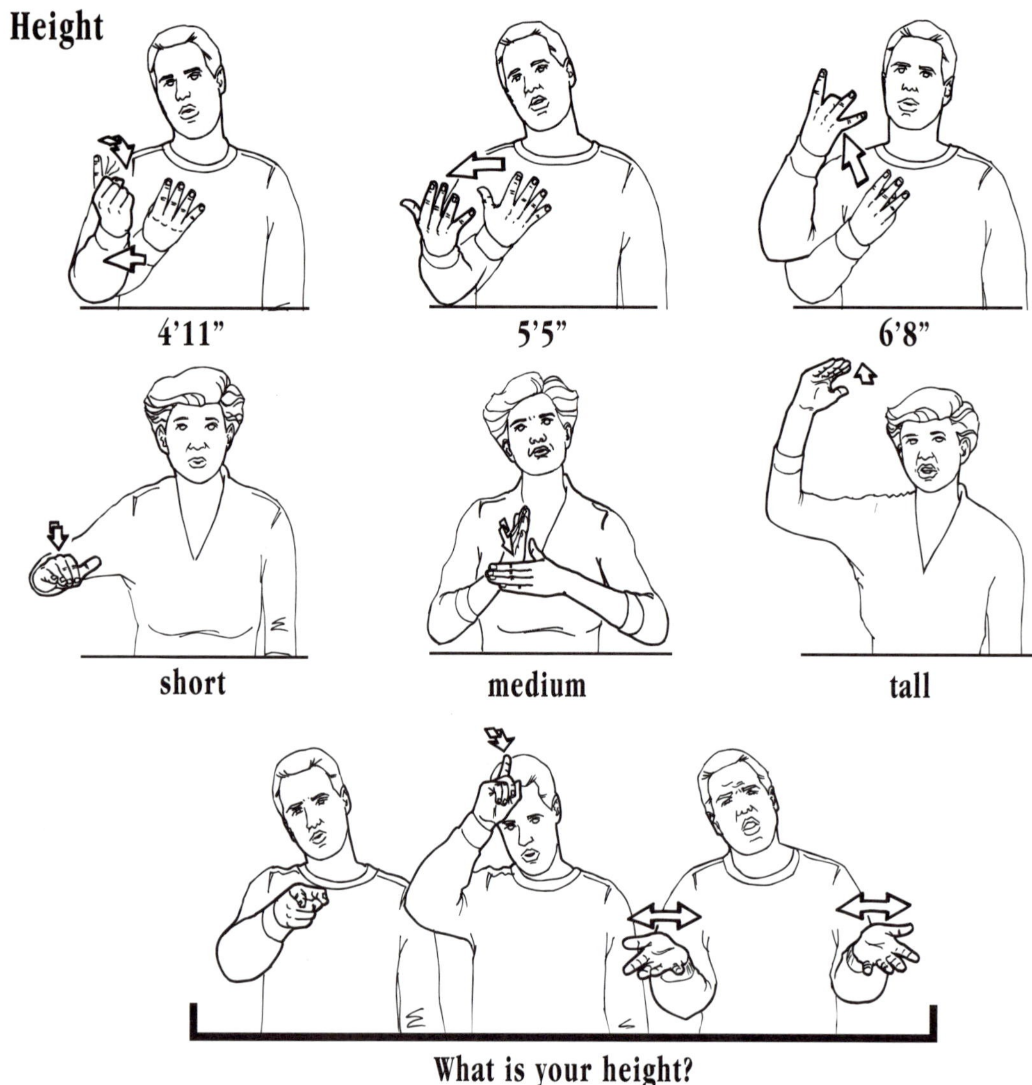

4'11" 5'5" 6'8"

short medium tall

What is your height?

Other Measurements

Length, volume, weight, and temperature are expressed as a counting number or a fraction, followed by the unit of measurement. The units of measurement are most often fingerspelled abbreviations of the English equivalents, rather than sign translations. For example, "one foot" is signed *1 ft*, rather than *1 foot.*

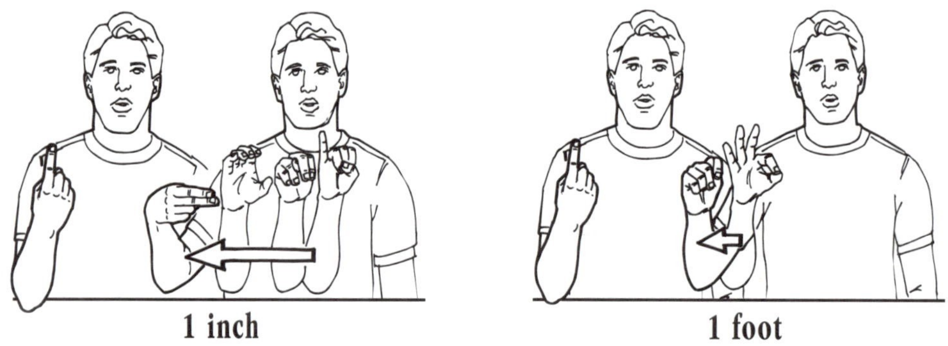

1 inch 1 foot

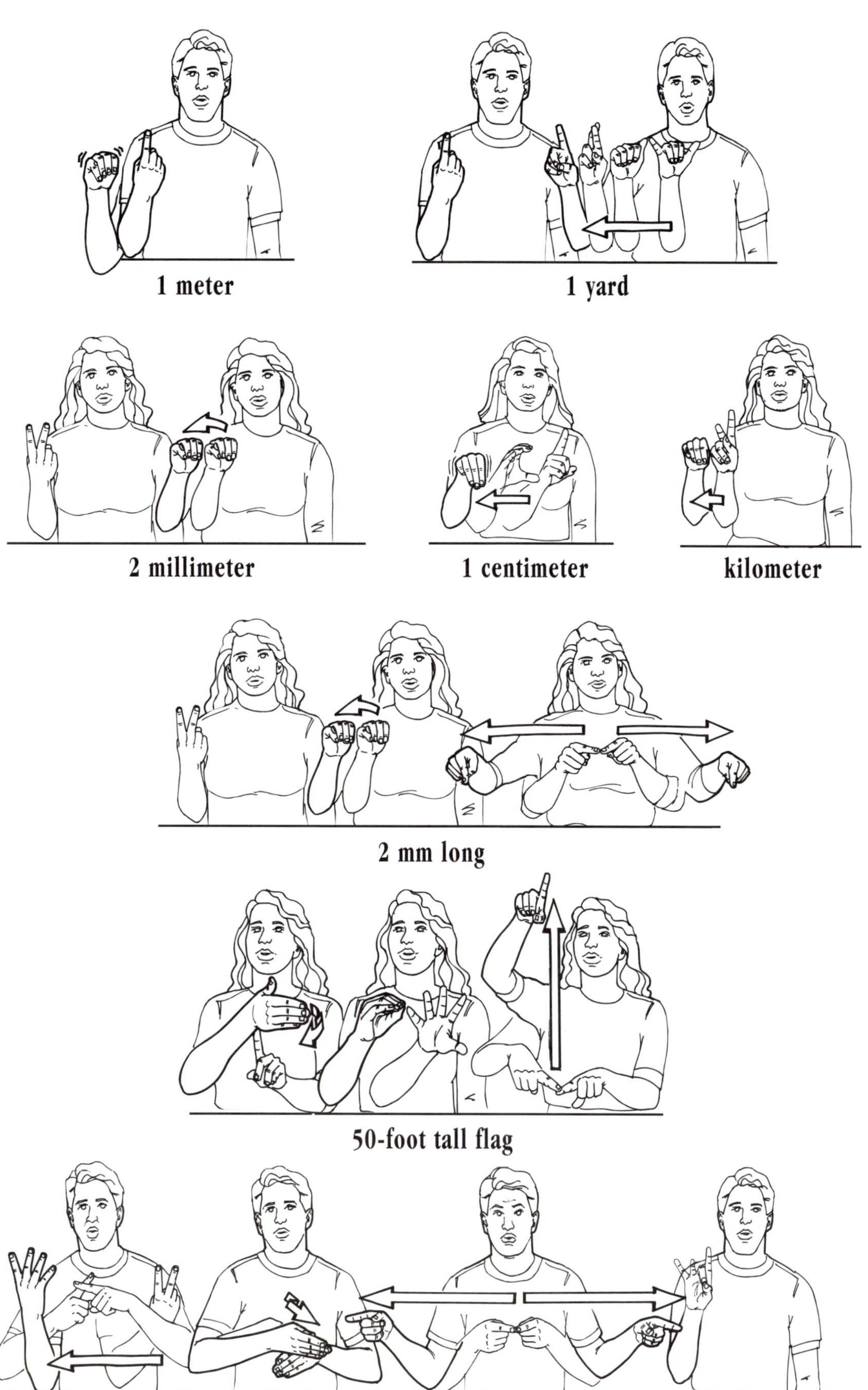

1 meter

1 yard

2 millimeter

1 centimeter

kilometer

2 mm long

50-foot tall flag

8-foot 2 x 4 board

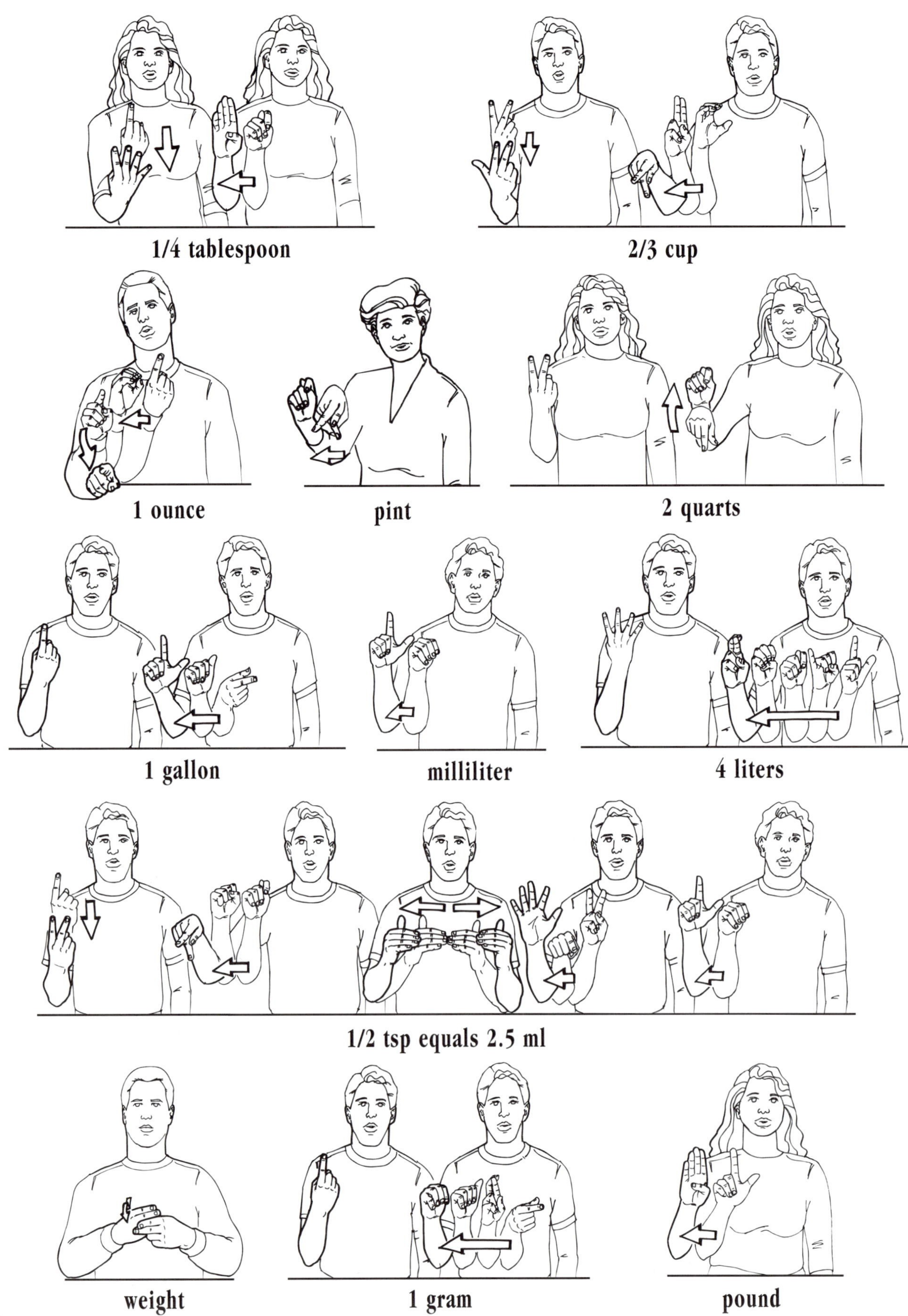

1/4 tablespoon

2/3 cup

1 ounce

pint

2 quarts

1 gallon

milliliter

4 liters

1/2 tsp equals 2.5 ml

weight

1 gram

pound

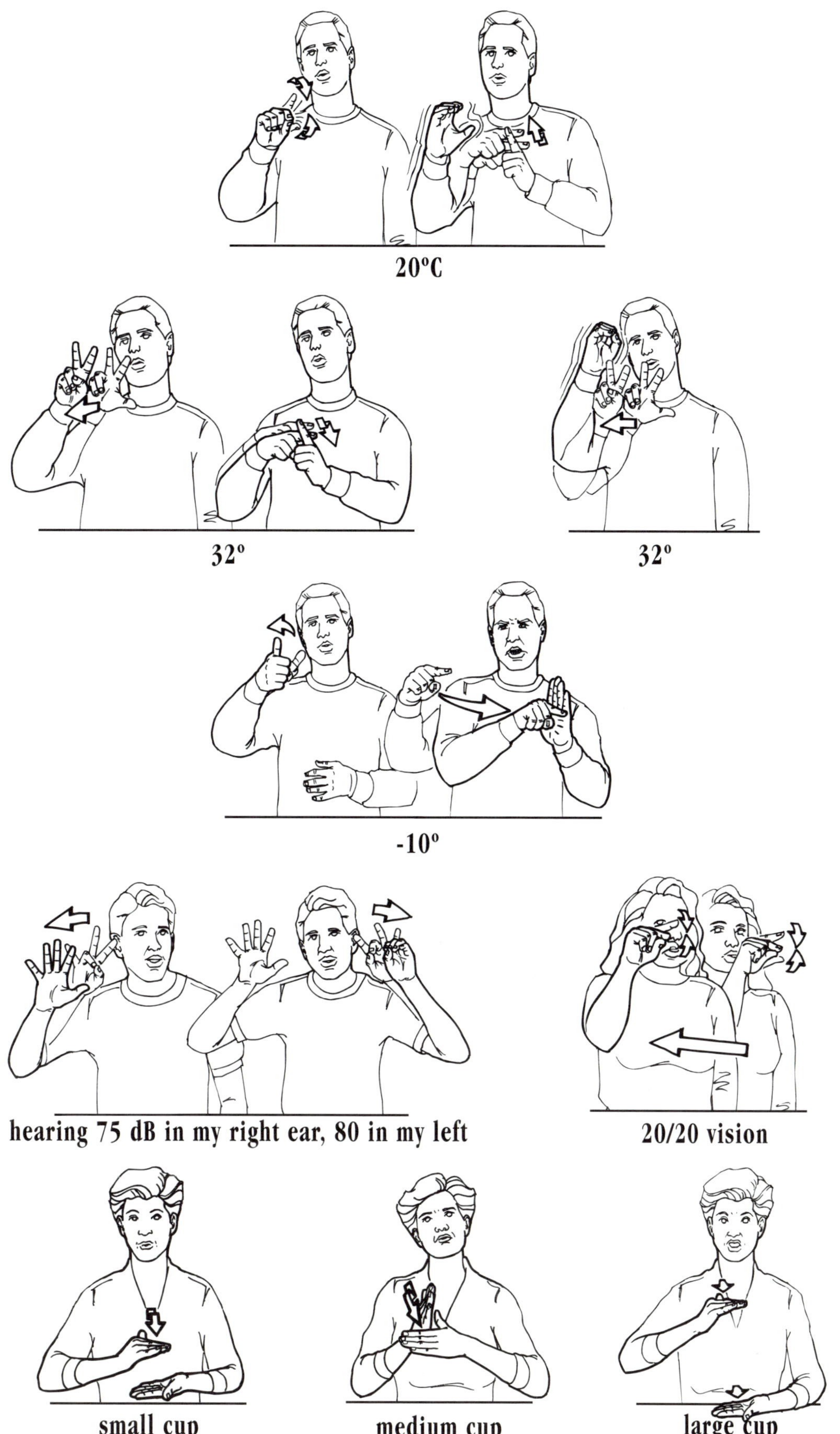

20°C

32°

32°

-10°

hearing 75 dB in my right ear, 80 in my left

20/20 vision

small cup

medium cup

large cup

4.5 VEHICLE-RELATED AND COMPUTER-RELATED SIGNS

Fingerspelled abbreviations such as *m-p-h* and *r-p-m* are commonly used in conjunction with numbers to convey vehicle-related information.

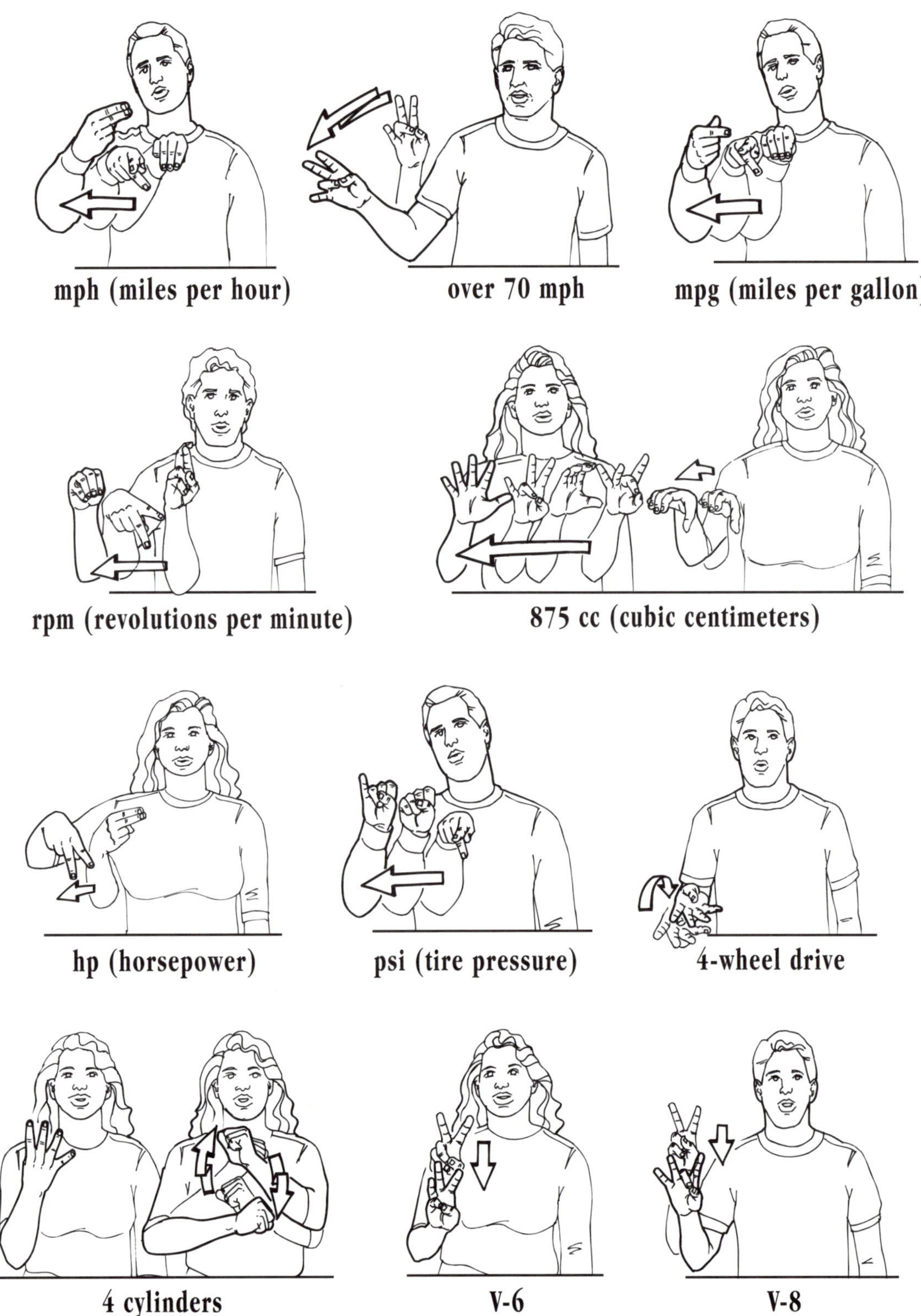

mph (miles per hour) · over 70 mph · mpg (miles per gallon)

rpm (revolutions per minute) · 875 cc (cubic centimeters)

hp (horsepower) · psi (tire pressure) · 4-wheel drive

4 cylinders · V-6 · V-8

Phrases Using Vehicle Signs

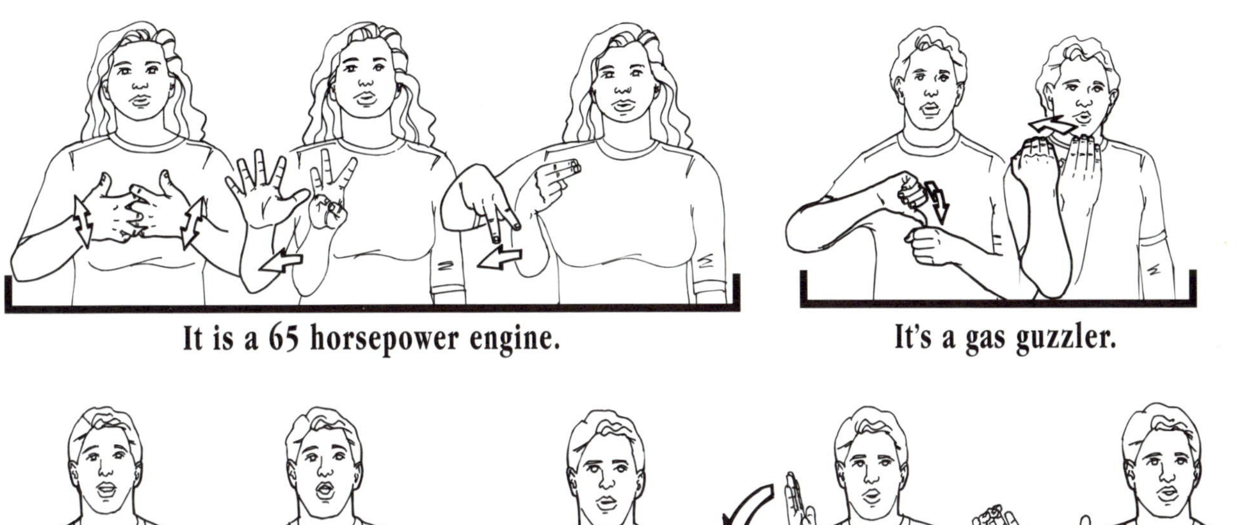

It is a 65 horsepower engine.

It's a gas guzzler.

My car's mileage is now over 100,000.

The next signs show numbers with abbreviations for high-tech computer concepts, such as *mb* for "megabytes."

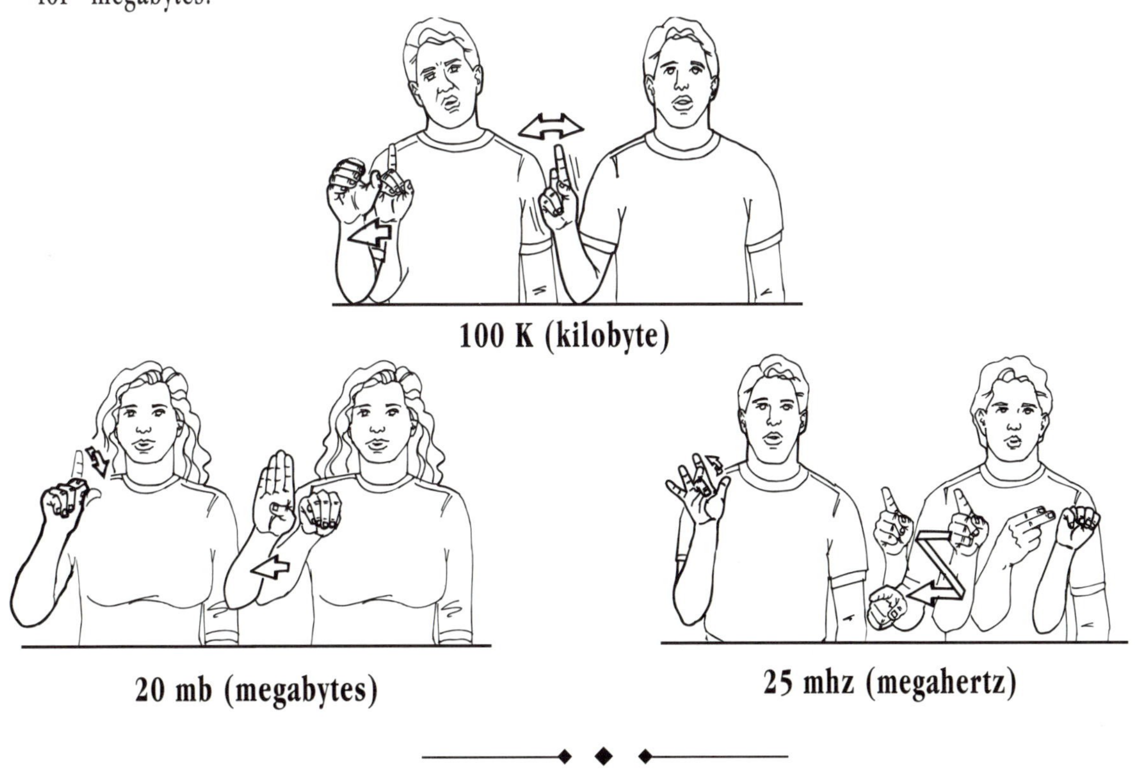

100 K (kilobyte)

20 mb (megabytes)

25 mhz (megahertz)

CHAPTER 5
HOW LONG

THIS chapter discusses the ways to sign time units. For most units of time in ASL there is a Rule of Nine, where any number from 1 to 9 is incorporated into the sign for the time unit. For example, *two minutes* incorporates the handshape for *two* into the sign for *minute*. For numbers 10 and greater, the number is signed and then the singular sign for the time unit is signed separately.

SECONDS 5.1

Second is most often fingerspelled as *S-E-C*.

3 s-e-c

MINUTES, HOURS, DAYS, WEEKS, AND MONTHS 5.2

The sign for *minutes* follows the Rule of Nine, but signers may optionally fingerspell it as *M-I-N*. Following are several examples of signing *minutes*.

1 minute

3 minutes

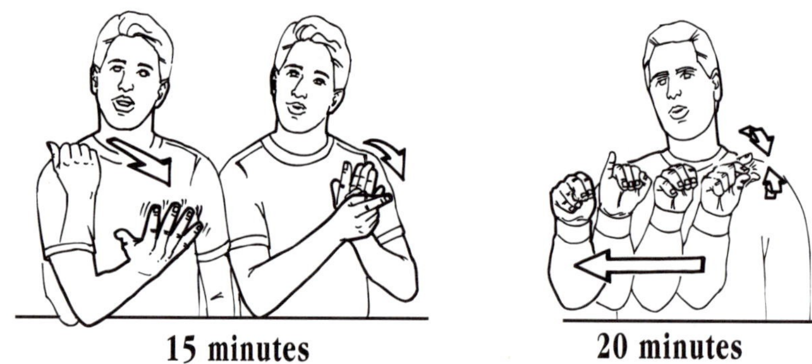

15 minutes 20 minutes

The sign for *hour* follows the Rule of Nine. Following are examples of ways to sign *hour*.

1/2 hour

1 hour

2 hours

4 hours

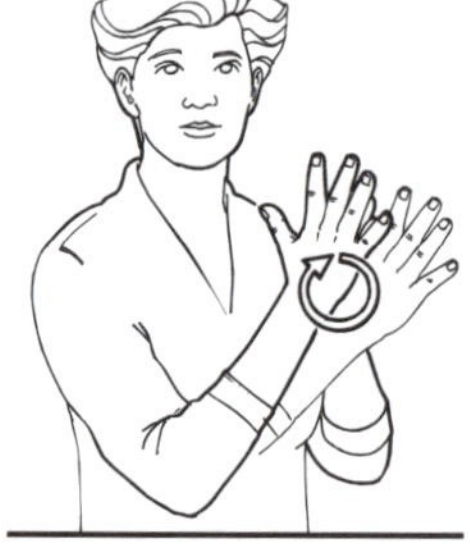

5 hours

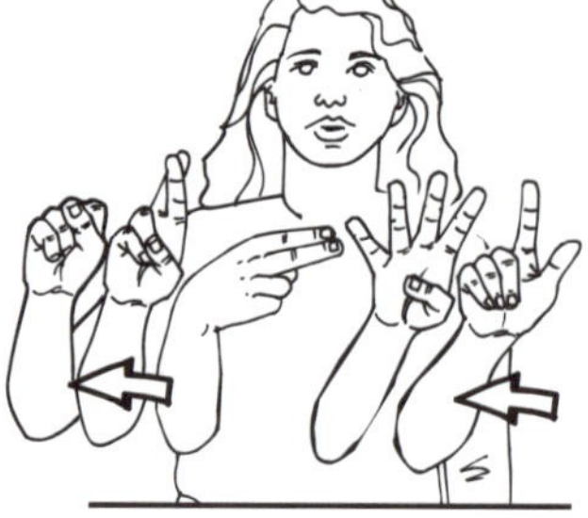

24 hours

Here are examples of *day*.

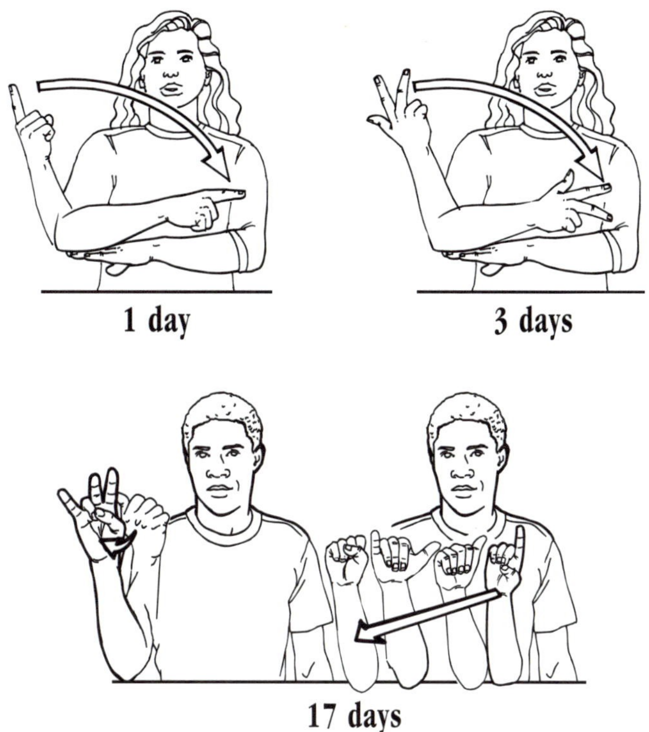

1 day **3 days**

17 days

Week follows the Rule of Nine. Here are sign examples using *week*.

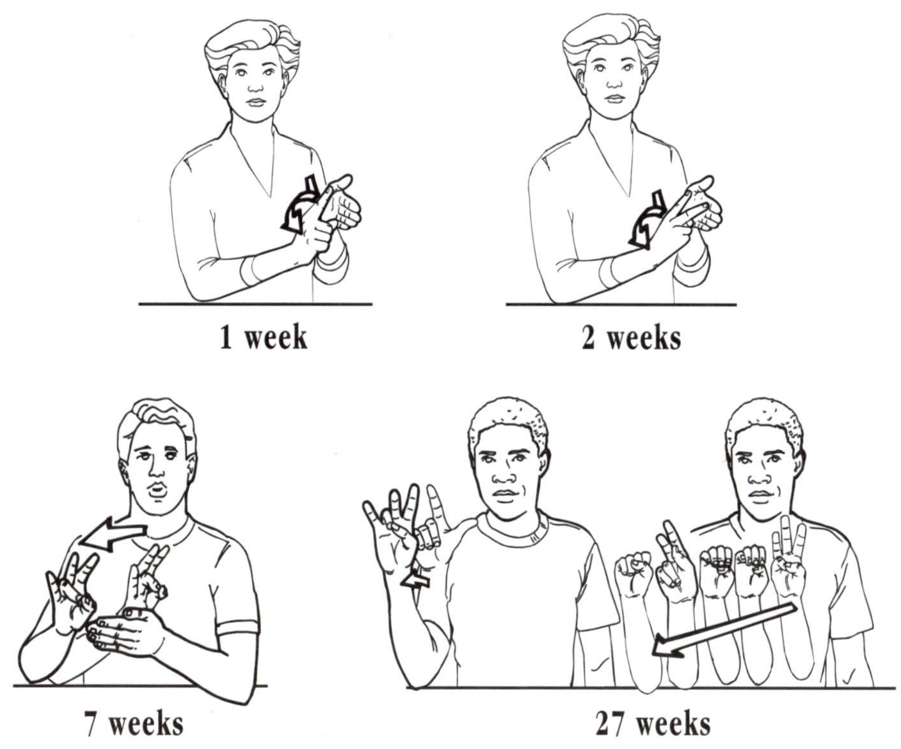

1 week **2 weeks**

7 weeks **27 weeks**

The sign for *month* also follows the Rule of Nine. Here are examples of *month*.

1 month

4 months

18 months

36 months

5.3 YEARS

Year does not use the Rule of Nine. Here are examples of *year*.

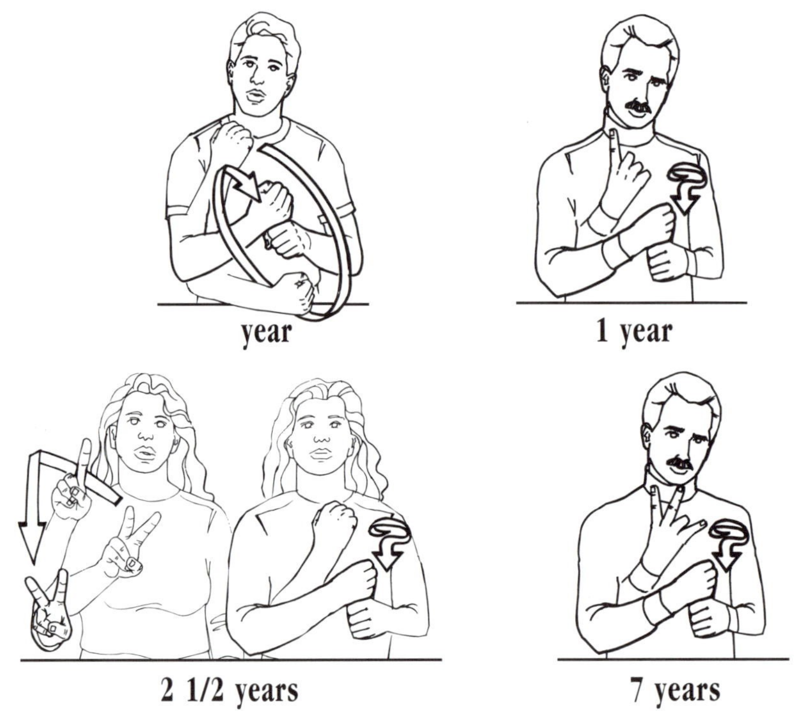

year

1 year

2 1/2 years

7 years

DURATION

Signing time units in terms of duration shows how long something lasts. In English, it is possible to convey a feeling of normal length, "it lasted an hour," or express that an event felt as if it took a long time, "it lasted an *hour*." Emphatic forms of signs using motion and expression convey this same meaning. Following are examples of signs for time that show duration.

1 whole hour

7 long hours

3 whole days

3 long weeks

7 weeks!

1 whole month

4 long months

20 years!

Phrases Using Time Duration Signs

How long?

I drove and drove for 3 days.

I waited and waited for 15 minutes!

I was sick for 3 weeks!

How long have you worked for that company?

Four months!

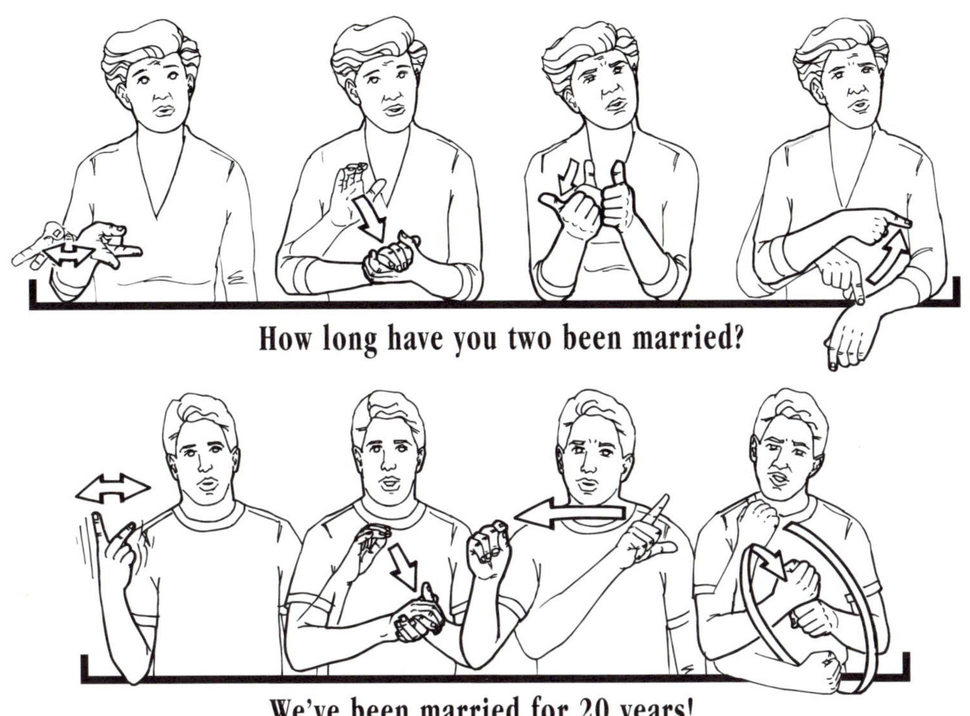

How long have you two been married?

We've been married for 20 years!

Other Time Vocabulary

quarter
semester
infinity
continuous

Chapter 6
How Often

When something happens at regular intervals, it can be described as occurring, for example, "every hour" or "every two hours." ASL expresses these meanings with special signs, based on a number handshape, a time unit, and repeated movement.

Numerical Time Frequency Signs

6.1

One week is a period of time, and the repetition of the sign *1 week* shows that something happens "weekly" or "every week." The signs that follow show how to combine the elements of a number handshape, time unit, and movement when talking about frequency.

every 2 minutes

every 1/2 hour

every 4 hours

everyday

every Monday

every 5 days

once a week
every week
every 2 weeks
once a month
monthly
every 2 months
once a year
every year
twice a year
4 times a year
every 5 years
every 8 years

Phrases Using Time Frequency Signs

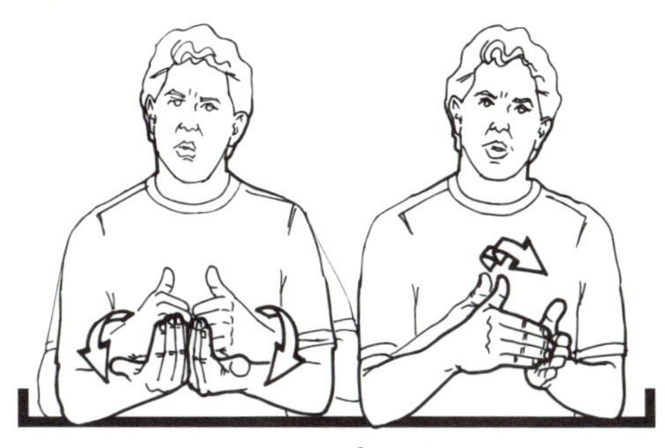

How often?

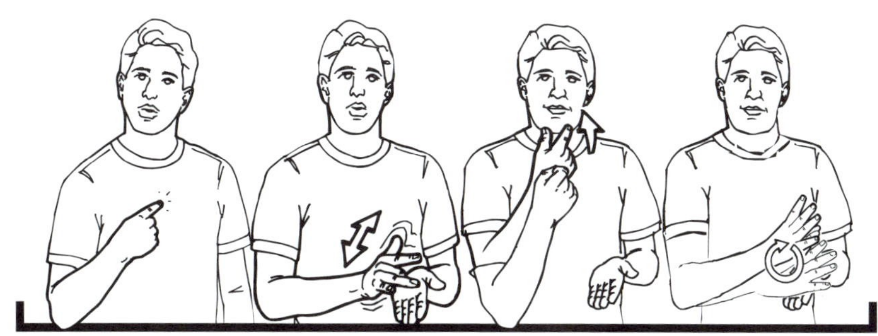

I take medication every 4 hours.

I tend to go out to eat every other week.

I call my mother once a month.

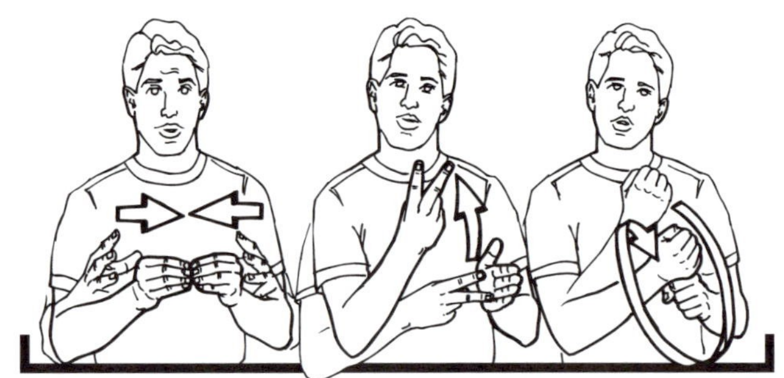

The meeting occurs twice a year.

Presidential elections are held every 4 years.

6.2 OTHER FREQUENCY SIGNS

Some signs that discuss frequency do not use a combination of number handshape, time sign, and repeated movements. These signs describe frequency in more general terms like "always."

always **often** **daily**

sometimes **once in a while** **never**

first time

many times

regularly

every other weekend

Other Phrases Using Time Frequency Signs

I work 9 to 5 daily.

I've seen that many times.

Chapter 7
When

If you ask someone when an event occurred, the answer could contain a time, a date, or both. The information in this chapter deals with times and dates and explains ASL's physical timeline.

Signs for Telling Time

7.1

Signs for telling time ("1 o'clock," "2 o'clock") are made up of a version of the sign *time* plus a number sign from 1 to 12.

When signing *1 o'clock* through *5 o'clock*, remember that this is an instance in which the first five numbers appear palm-outward.

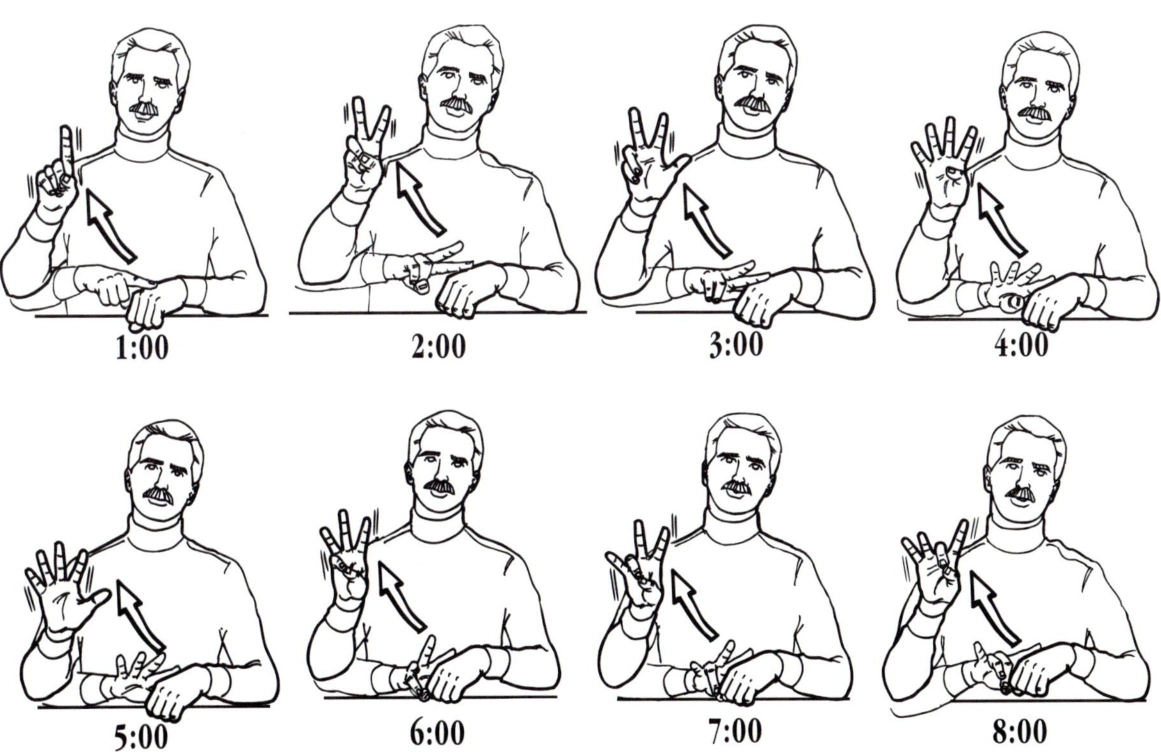

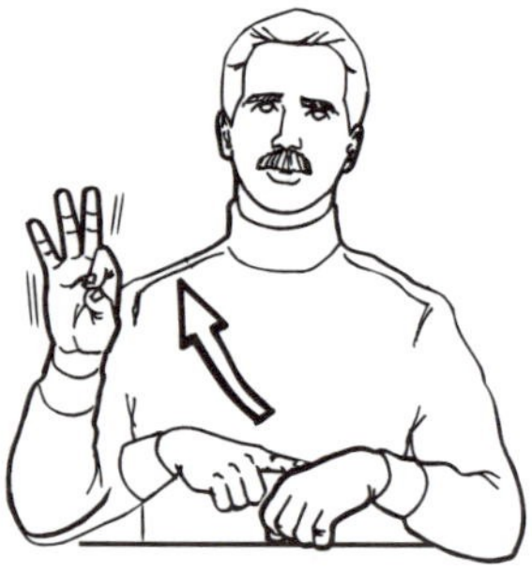

9:00

10:00

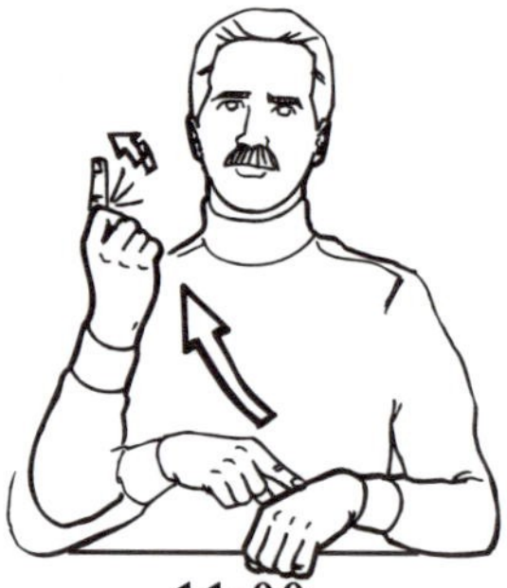

11:00

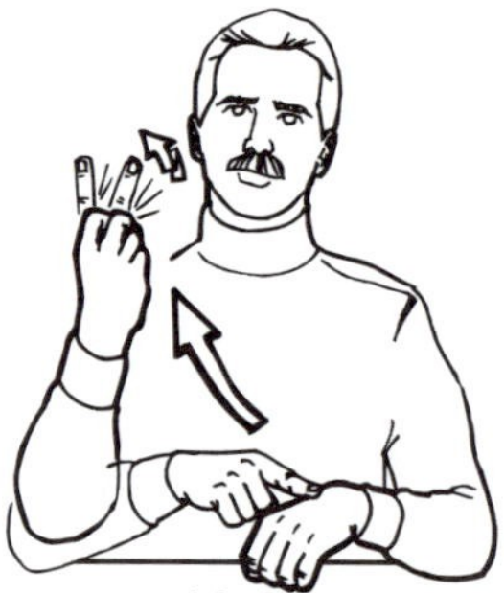

12:00

11:30

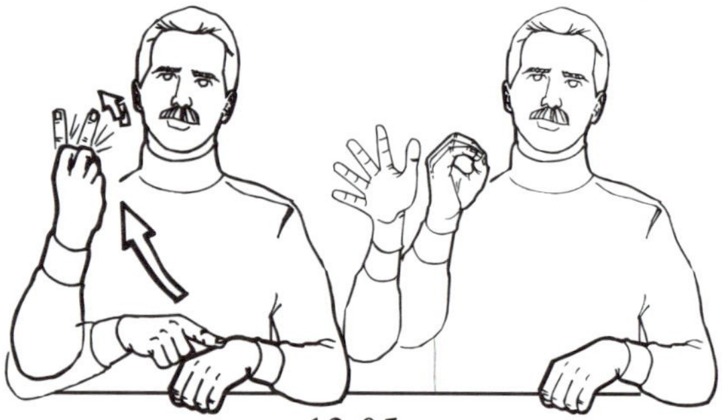

12:05

1:15

7.2 Time Estimates

When it is necessary to express an approximate time, facial expression or a sign that suggests something will happen "around" 2 o'clock is used.

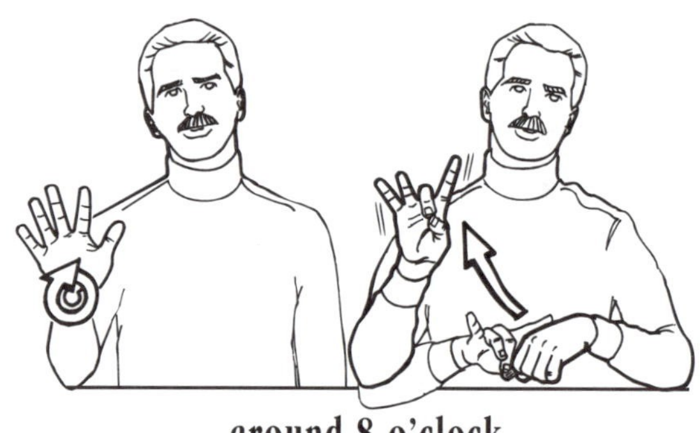

around 8 o'clock

Phrases Using Time Signs

What is the best time to go?

At 2:00.

On Friday afternoon at 2:00.

Between 10:00 and 11:00.

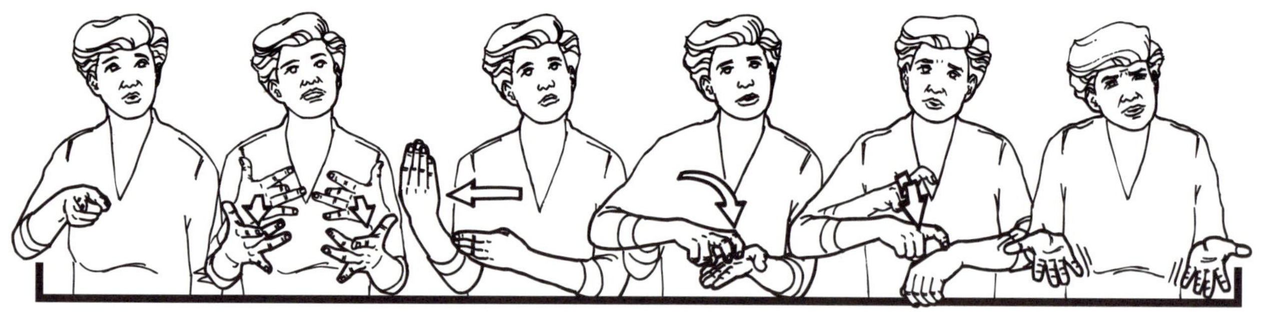

What time in the morning do you usually get up?

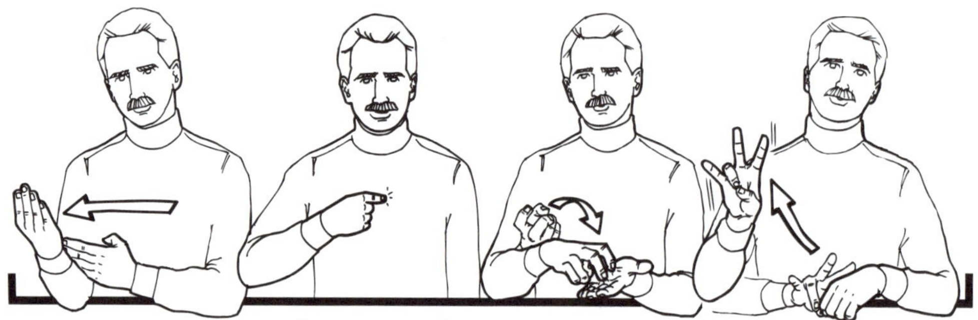

I get up at 7 am every morning.

What time do you work?

I work from 10 am to 3 pm.

THE TIMELINE IN ASL

One of the most important uses of space in ASL can be found in the relation of physical space to time. The physical timeline created in ASL has standard locations for the past, the present, and the future. The past is the area behind the signer. Signs such as *yesterday* and *last week* reflect that the area behind the signer represents the past. The future is the area moving out away from the signer. Forward movement in signs such as *will*, *future*, *tomorrow*, and *next week* reflect that the area in front of the signer represents the future. The space directly in front and close to the signer represents the present, as seen in the sign *now*.

Past

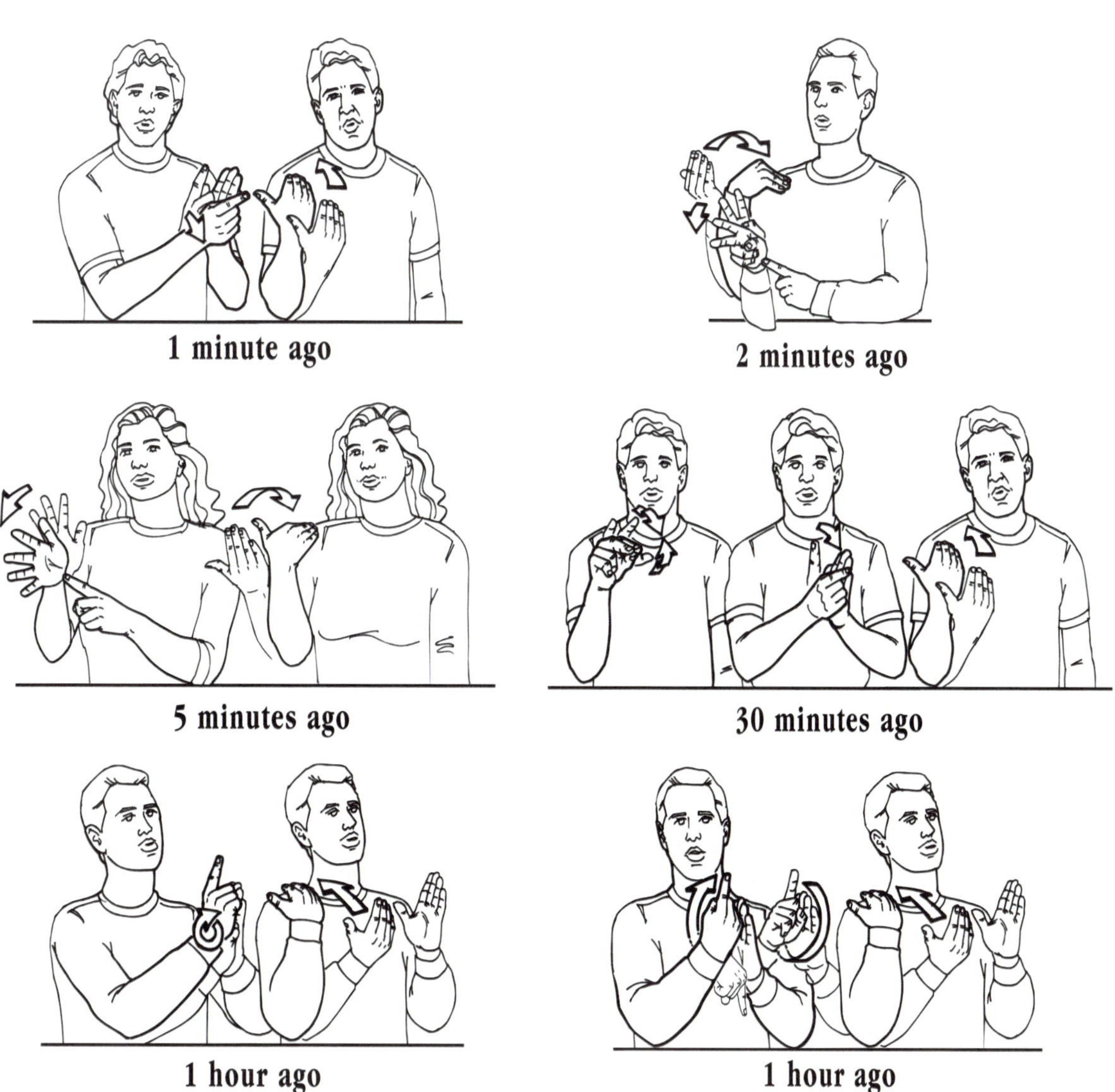

1 minute ago

2 minutes ago

5 minutes ago

30 minutes ago

1 hour ago

1 hour ago

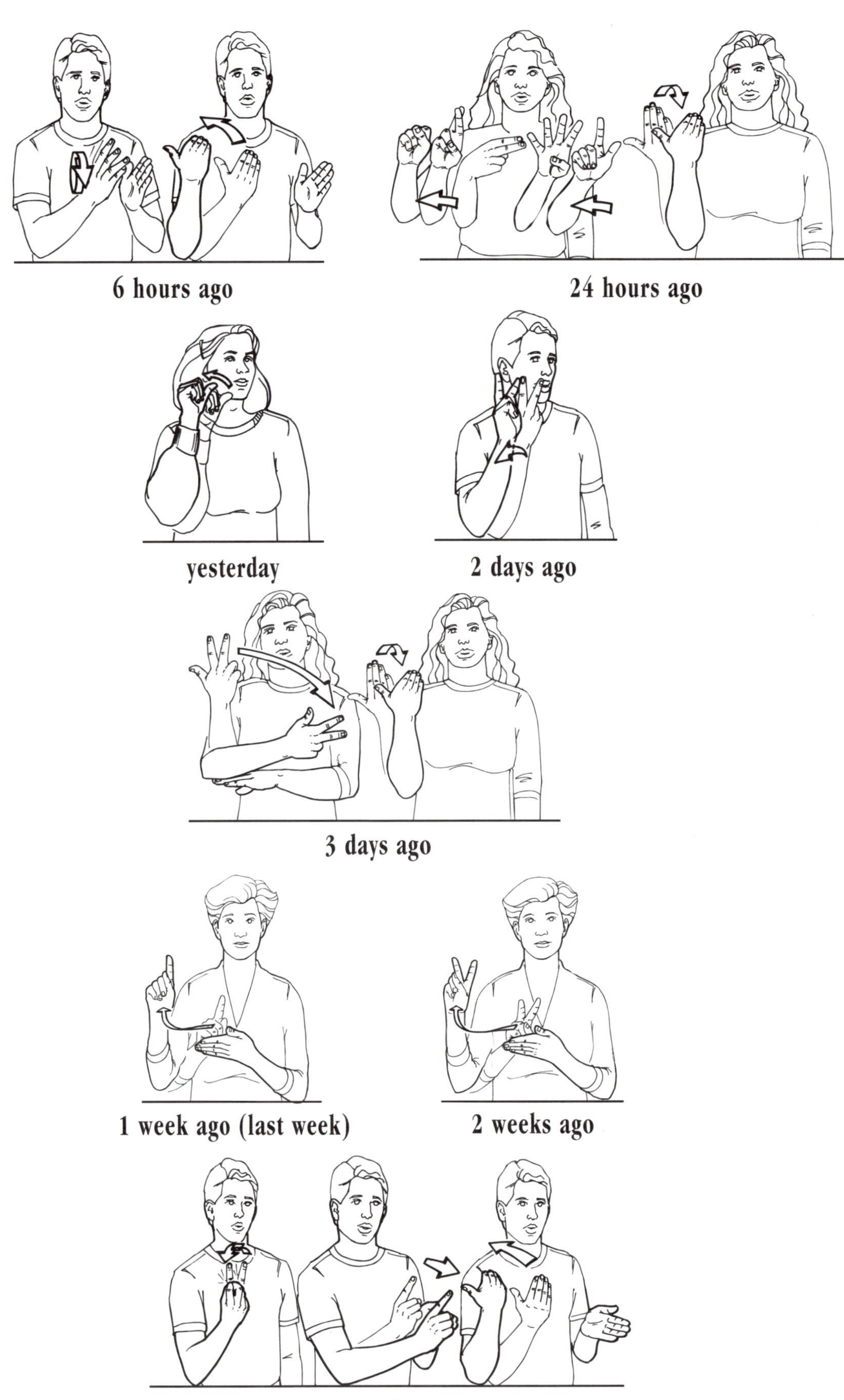

6 hours ago

24 hours ago

yesterday

2 days ago

3 days ago

1 week ago (last week)

2 weeks ago

12 weeks ago

1 month ago

8 months ago

last year

last year

2 years ago

3 years ago

4 years ago

4 years ago

6 years ago

Future

future

in few days

next week

in 2 weeks

4 weeks from now

in 7 weeks

next month

next 3 months

next 8 months

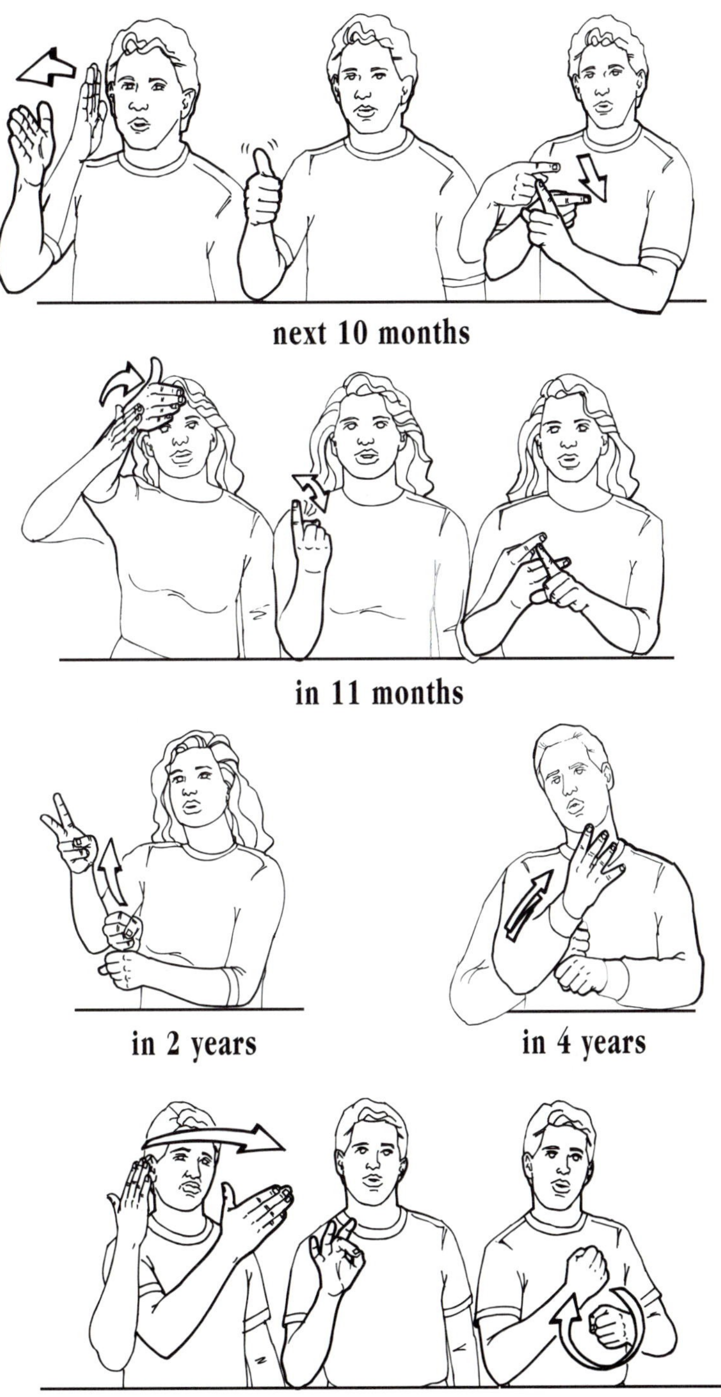

next 10 months

in 11 months

in 2 years

in 4 years

8 years from now

Phrases Using Signs and the Physical Space Timeline

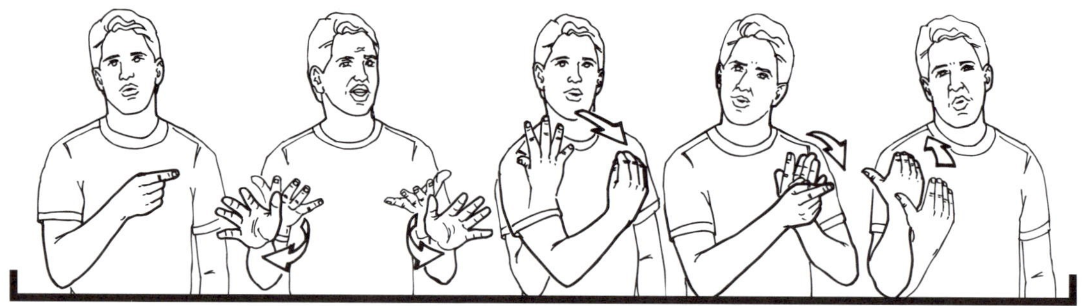

She already left a minute ago.

I just arrived 5 minutes ago.

It will start in 15 minutes.

We'll get it in 2 weeks.

Year and Date Signs

Years are most often signed as two digit numbers. Nineteen seventy-six is signed 19 for the first two digits, 76 for the second two digits. In years where the second two digits are within the range of 01—09 the zero is emphasized for clarity. Signs for even century years vary depending on context. If speaking generally, the sign for the double zero is the sign for *hundred*. If speaking specifically, the double zero is emphasized.

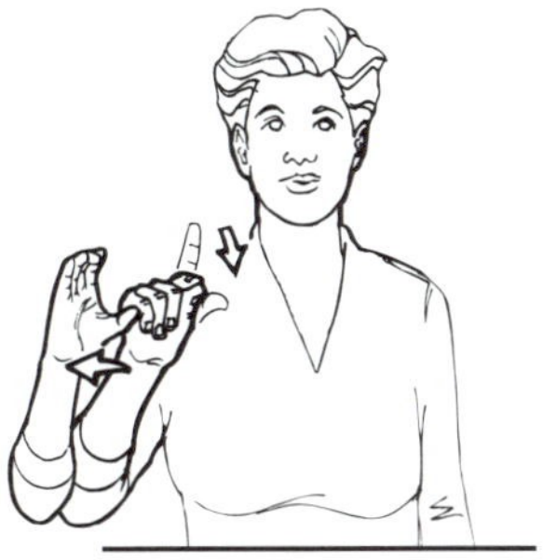

2000

2000

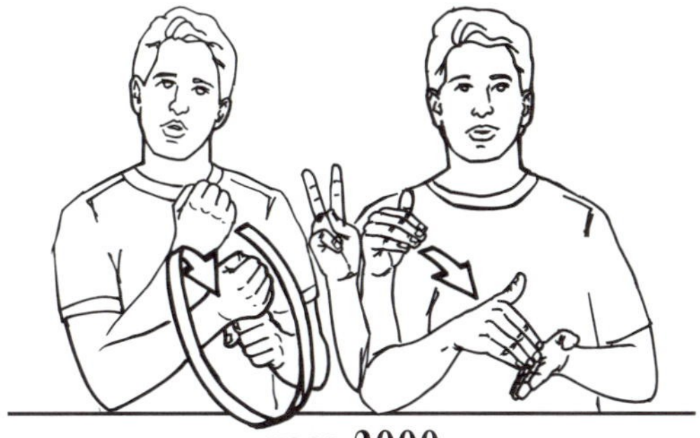

year 2000

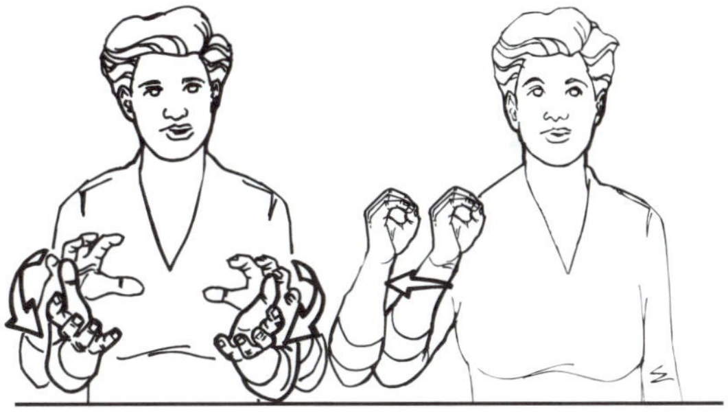

class of '00

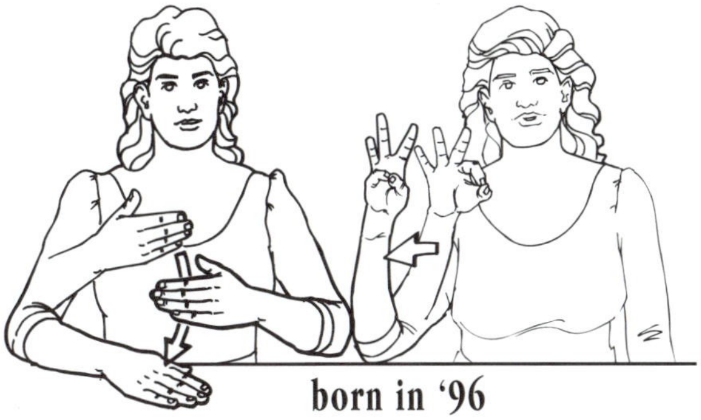

born in '96

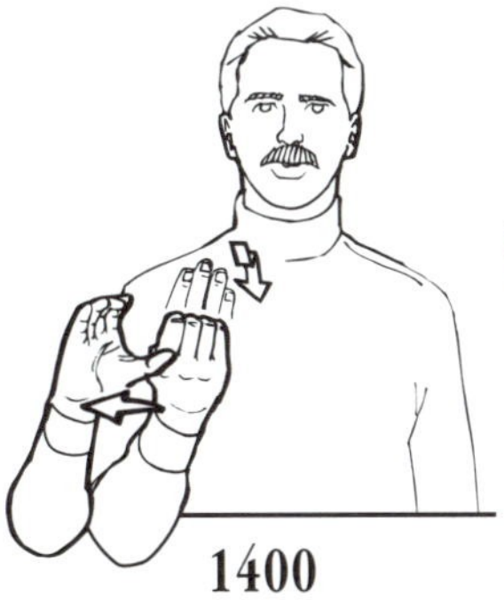

1400

1776

1805

2002

Approximate Signs for Years

thereabout 1921

1950s

Specific dates with month, day, and year in ASL are easy to sign. First, fingerspell the month (some months are commonly signed as abbreviations):

J-A-N	*F-E-B*	*M-A-R-C-H*	*A-P-R-I-L*	*M-A-Y*	*J-U-N-E*
J-U-L-Y	*A-U-G*	*S-E-P-T*	*O-C-T*	*N-O-V*	*D-E-C*

The day of the month is expressed as an ordinal number if it is the first through the ninth day of the month, for instance *J-A-N second* or *N-O-V ninth*. For dates of the tenth through the thirty-first day of the month, a cardinal or counting number is used; for example, *J-u-l-y fourteen* is proper in ASL, and the English equivalent is "July fourteenth."

December 3, 1955

November 8, 2000

1865-1877

1910 to 1983

CHAPTER 8
AGE

WHEN someone is asked how old they are, they will answer by telling their age. In ASL age is expressed by combining the movement and location of the sign "old" with the number of years. When talking about age, the numbers 1 through 5 face palm-outward, unlike when counting. Pay careful attention to how the various handshapes touch the chin in the following age signs.

AGE

8.1

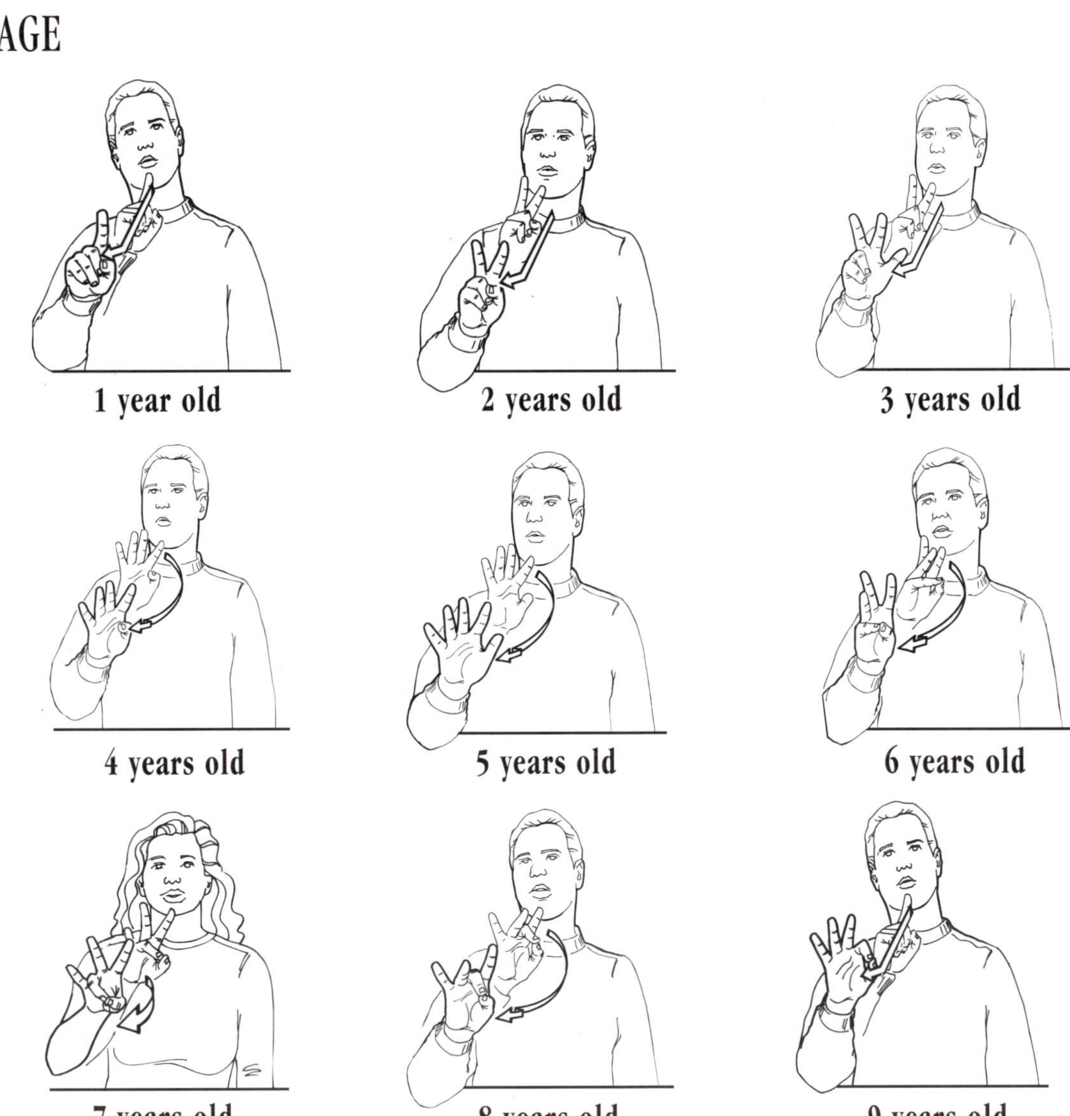

1 year old

2 years old

3 years old

4 years old

5 years old

6 years old

7 years old

8 years old

9 years old

10 years old

11 years old

15 years old

18 years old

19 years old

20 years old

25 years old

34 years old

40 years old

65 years old

5 days old

8 months old

Ages Signed with Emphasis

40 years old!

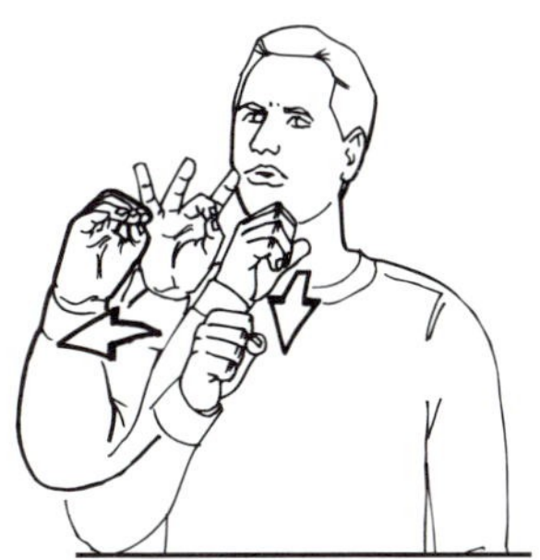
80 years old!

Approximate Signs for Ages

around 30 years old

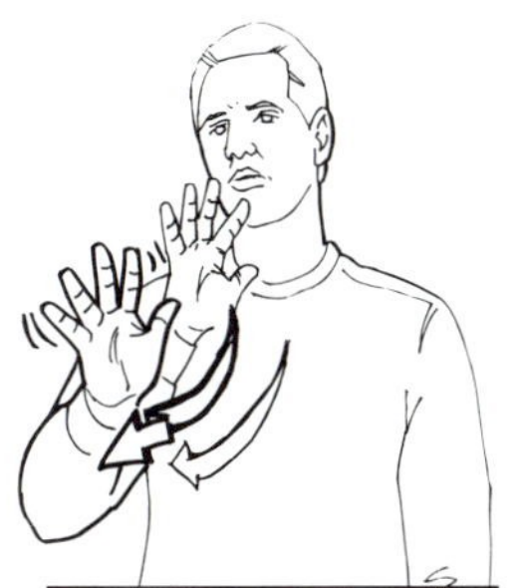
in his/her 50s

Phrases Using Age Signs

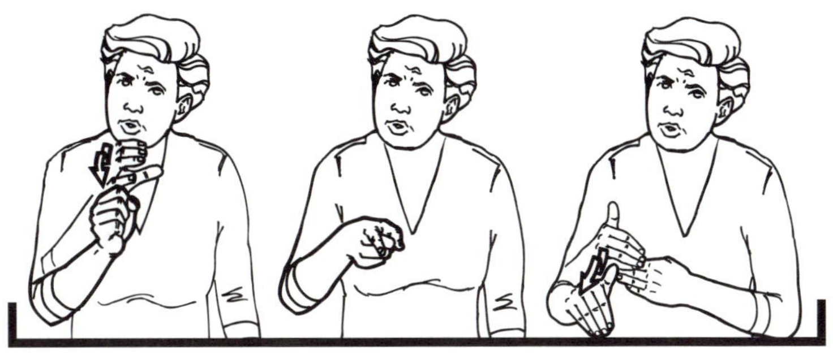
How old is that bread?

5 days old.

The baby is 8 months old.

My oldest child is now 15 years old.

How old were you when you first flew?

I was 40 years old.

How old were you when you started reading?

I was 3 years old.

CHAPTER 9
SPORTS

WHEN discussing sports, numbers are used to give information about scores, placement, and players' jersey numbers. Following are both number signs and signs for additional vocabulary related to sports.

SPORTS-RELATED VOCABULARY

9.1

Baseball

baseball

1st base

2nd base

3rd base

single

double

triple

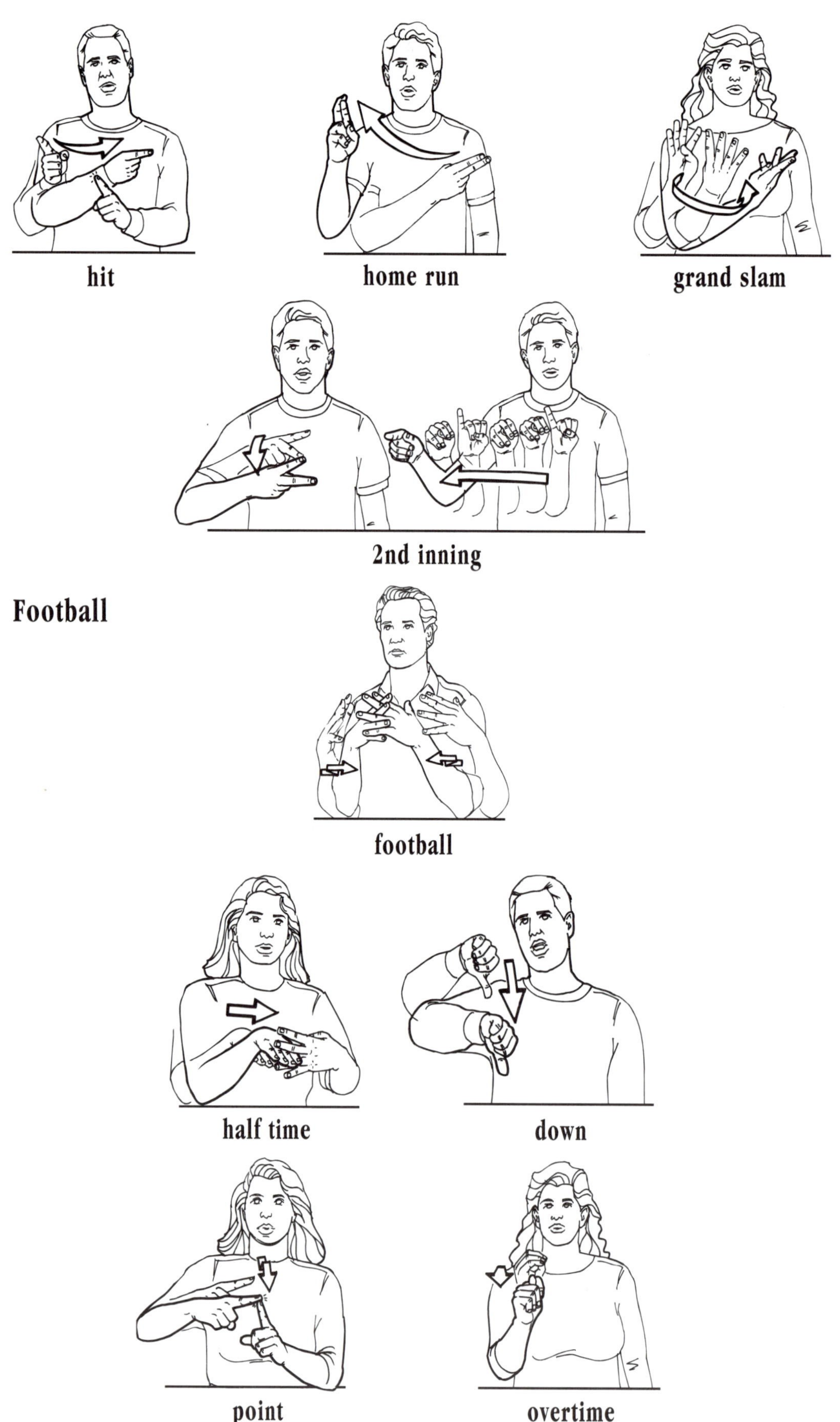
hit
home run
grand slam
2nd inning
Football
football
half time
down
point
overtime

Track

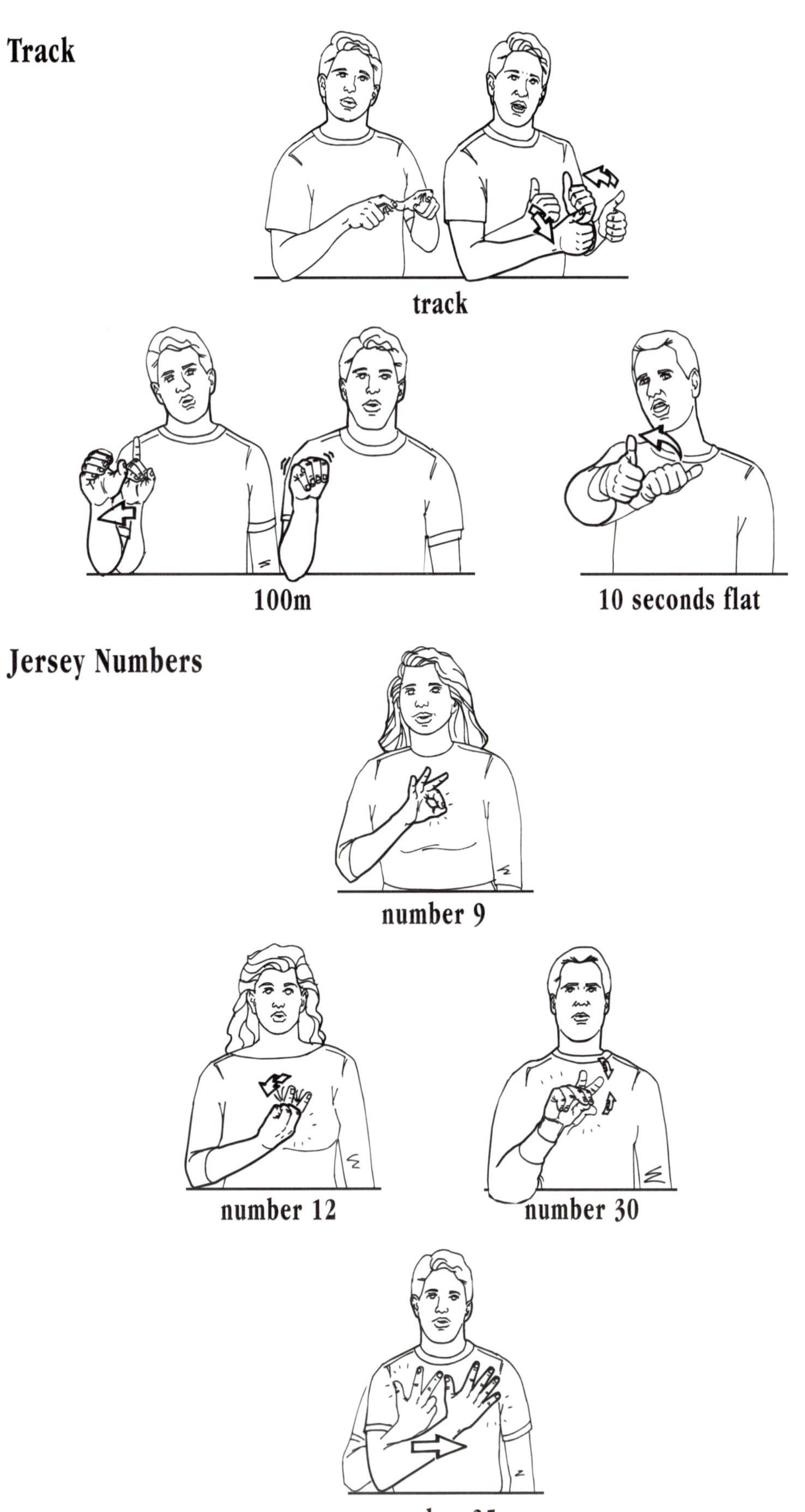

track

100m

10 seconds flat

Jersey Numbers

number 9

number 12

number 30

number 35

9.2 PLACEMENT AND SCORES

In ASL, ordinal numbers with a horizontal movement to indicate place are used to express who wins a competition or a how a person or team has finished.

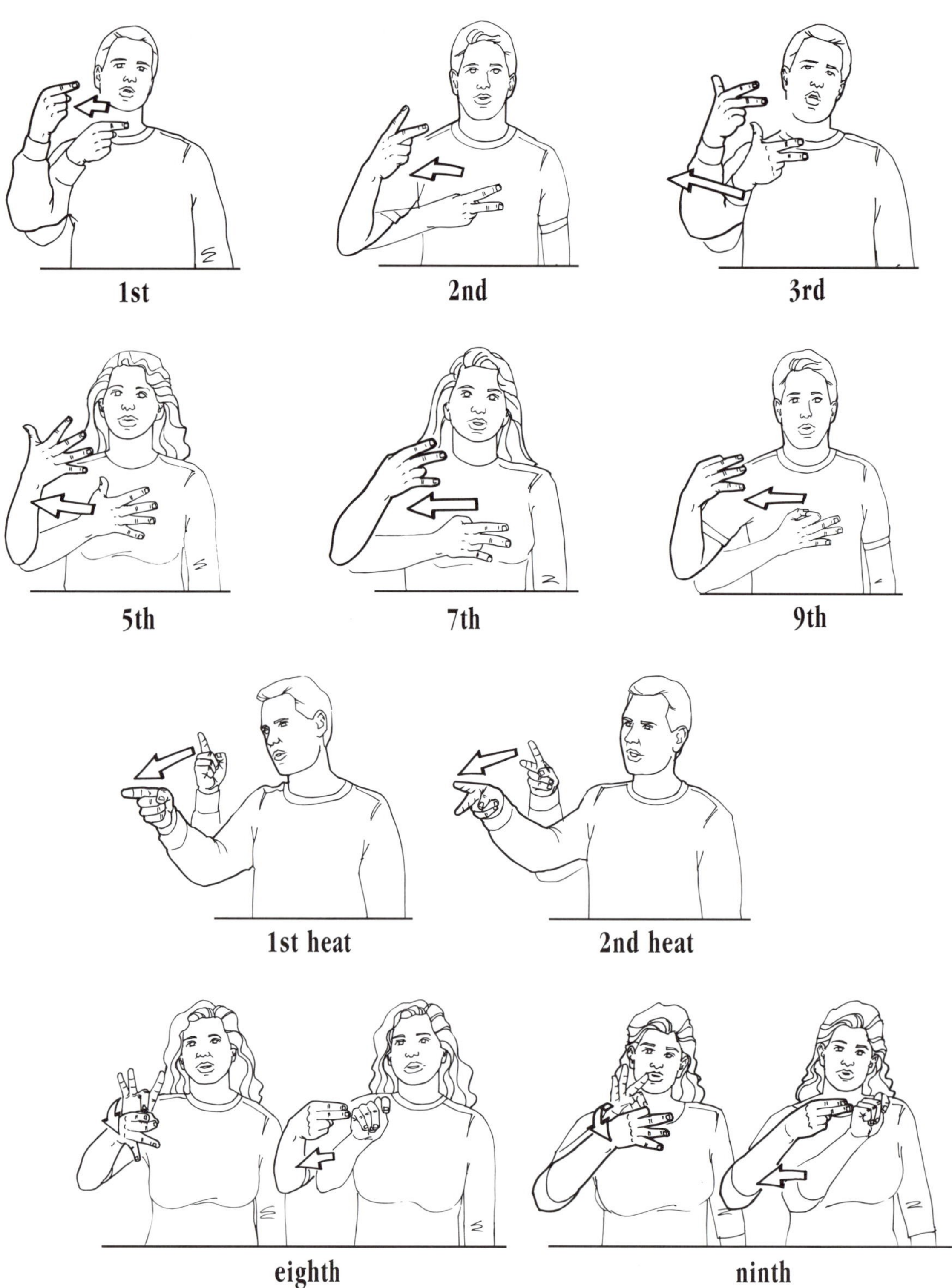

1st 2nd 3rd

5th 7th 9th

1st heat 2nd heat

eighth ninth

Phrases About Placement and Scores

What is the score?

The second team won 5 to 2.

Did you win?

I finished third.

Signs about teams and their scores use space to represent one team against another.

my team 3, their team 5

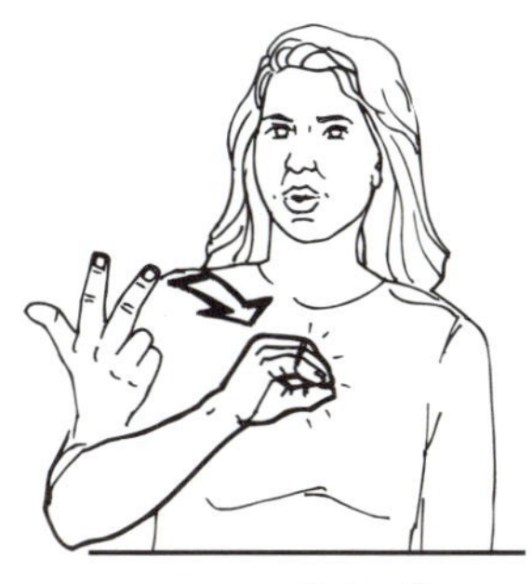
score 3 to 0

tie game

tied 2 to 2

tied 4 to 4

11 to 9

my team 5, their team 0

win–loss record 15-0

blowout

shutout

CHAPTER 10
WHERE, WHICH

THIS chapter includes vocabulary for describing specifics, such as where to find a particular book, which hat you prefer, and the address of your favorite restaurant.

LOCATION

10.1

Numbers used to locate an object, such as a book on a particular shelf of a bookcase, or a specific car in a parking lot combine ASL's use of physical space with ordinal number signs. Spatial patterns are used to describe locations. Two patterns that occur frequently are (1) a straight-downward pattern, in which each item is on a different line, like shelves in a bookcase that are stacked one below the other, and (2) a straight-sideways pattern, similar to a row of books on a shelf or to cars in one aisle of a parking lot. The following signed locations give the physical location that tells you where and the ordinal number that describes which.

first shelf

fourth drawer down below

eighth hat up there

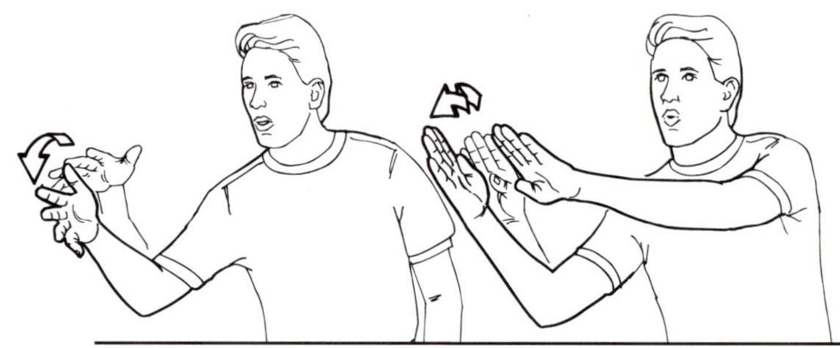

fifth door to the right

third car

downstairs on the second floor

upstairs on the tenth floor

PLACES

10.2

The following signs show how to describe locations by street names. In numbered street names, there is an important difference between English and ASL. English uses ordinal numbers, such as "22nd Street" or "35th Avenue" for numbered streets. ASL more often uses a cardinal (counting) number sign for numbered streets above "Ninth," for example, *Twenty-two Street* or *Thirty-five A-V-E*. Note that these are names nonetheless and the "nd" or "th" part of the street name that English speakers pronounce is understood in ASL without adding the ordinal information.

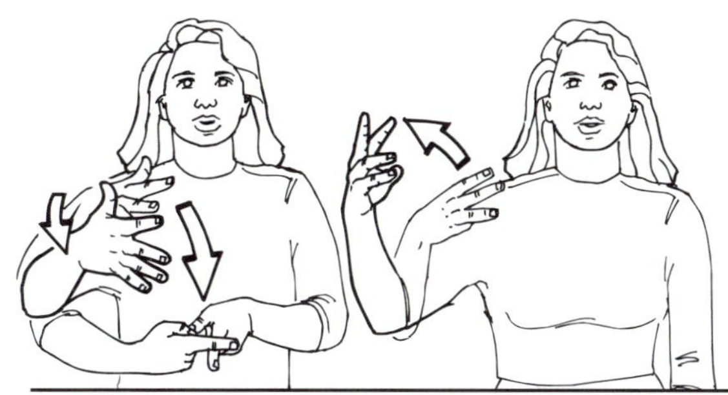

the intersection of 5th and Washington

22nd Street and 35th Avenue

RANK OR ORDER IN FAMILY

10.3

When discussing family, it is common to talk about siblings and yourself in terms of birth order, who was born first, second, third, and so on. A signer represents the number of people being discussed on one hand, showing by number how many people are involved, and then explains their order from the thumb (first in order) on down. This method of describing order is not limited to the family, however, the following signs are examples of rank or order in the family. Also shown are signs for *twin* and *only child*.

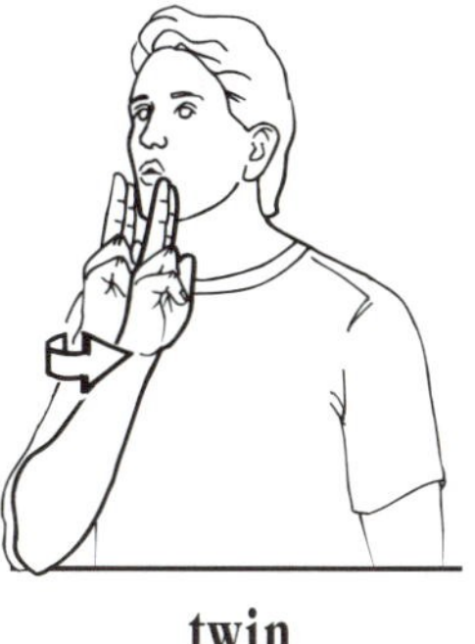

twin

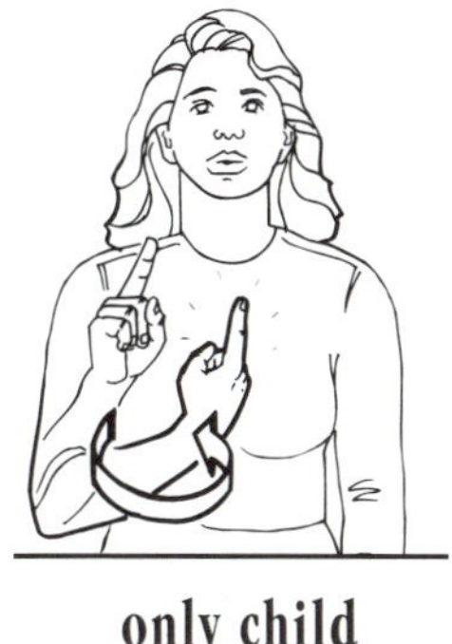

only child

Phrases Showing Order in Family

She is an only child.

I am the second of 3 children.

I am the sixth child of 7 children.

Out of 8 brothers and sisters, I am the last child born.

My son is the third of my 5 children.

ORDINAL NUMBERS

10.4

As shown in previous chapters, ordinal numbers explain the position of something in an ordered set or group. Following are ASL's basic signs for ordinal numbers that show placement, rank, or order.

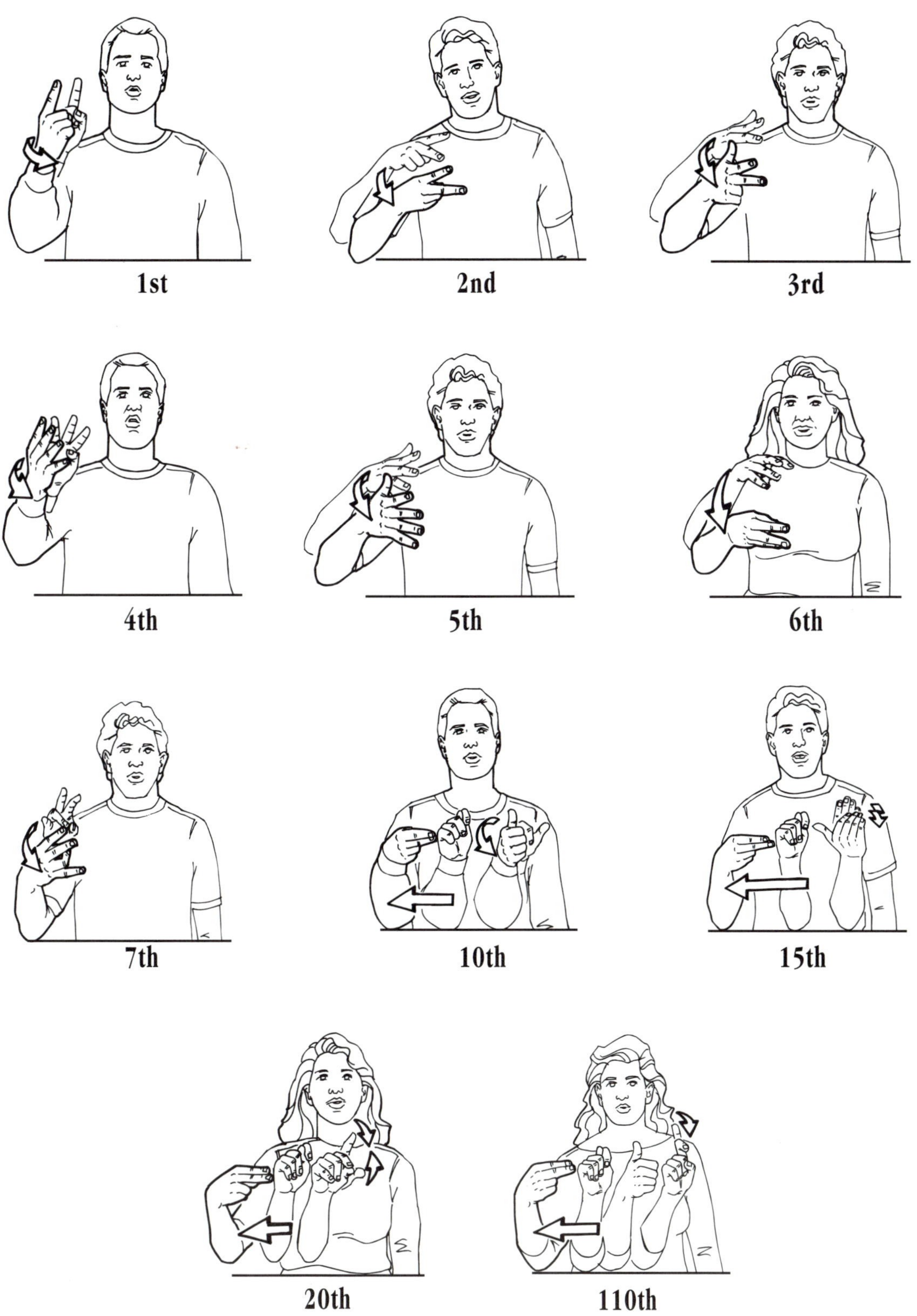

1st 2nd 3rd

4th 5th 6th

7th 10th 15th

20th 110th

Phrases for Sequence of Events

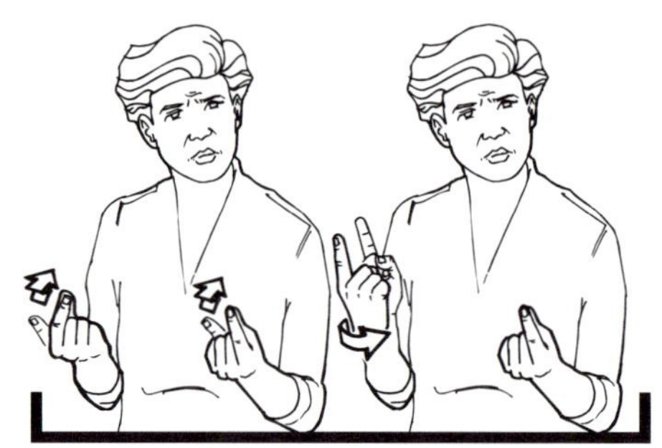

What did you do first?

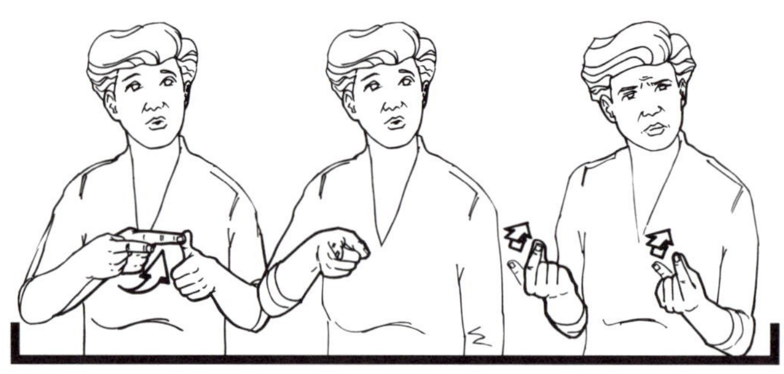

What did you do first?

first

second

third

Chapter 11
Personal Numbers

NUMBERS are often used to give information; addresses, phone numbers, and social security numbers are all numbers that people use in their personal lives.

Identification Numbers

11.1

Personal identification numbers do not represent quantities and are therefore signed differently than quantitative numbers. For example, a TTY number or a street address is signed more like a fingerspelled word. The street number "1524" would be signed as *1-5-2-4* , rather than as *one thousand five hundred twenty-four*. In this case, the numbers 1 through 5 are signed palm-out, not palm-inward as in counting. In ASL, it is also possible to combine two-digit groups, so "1524" can be signed *fifteen twenty-four.* The two signs appear as regular ASL number signs, as shown in Chapter 1.

Phone Numbers

716-3929

(TTY number) 482-3006

Social Security Numbers

163-10-9119

309-77-0825

Addresses

address

34518 Taos Road

2341 Pine Street

SIGNS FOR SPECIFIC THINGS

11.2

Ordinal numbers with a wiggling movement are used in ASL when discussing one-digit room numbers, TV channels, or highway numbers.

Which channel is it?

It's channel 7.

It's Room 5.

Highway 1

I-5

CHAPTER 12
SCIENTIFIC NUMBERS

THE following are examples of vocabulary used in math and science. Mathematical and chemical formulas, which are often written with superscript and subscript numbers, are usually signed in ASL so their spatial layout is reflected.

SCIENTIFIC NUMBERS

12.1

scientific number

math

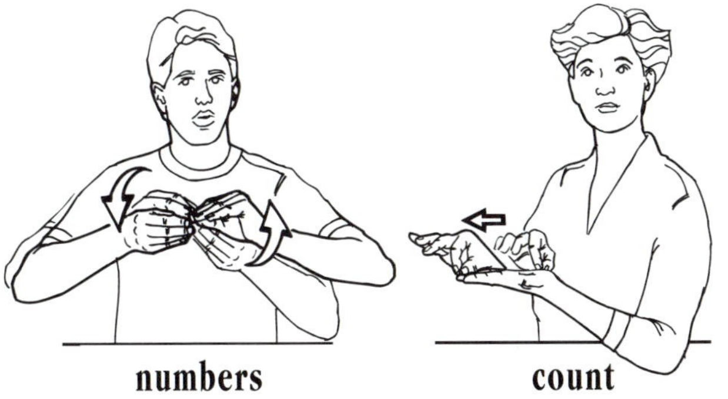
numbers count

equal

left

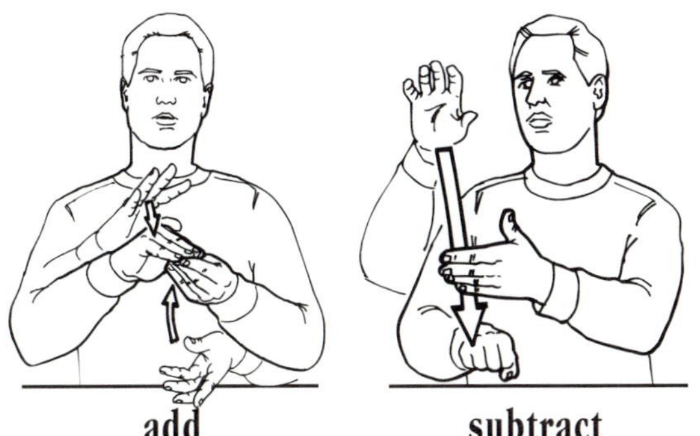
add subtract

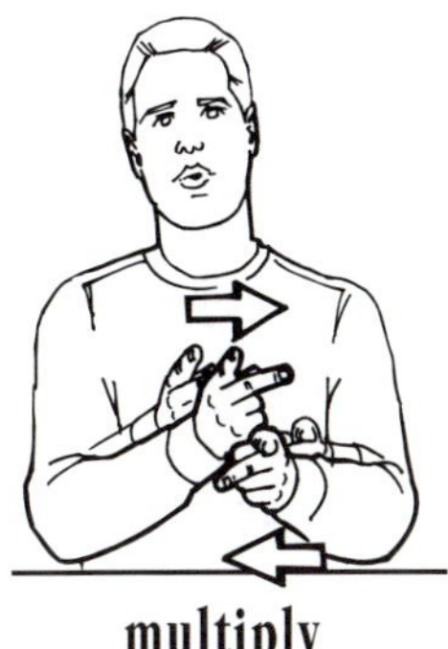
multiply

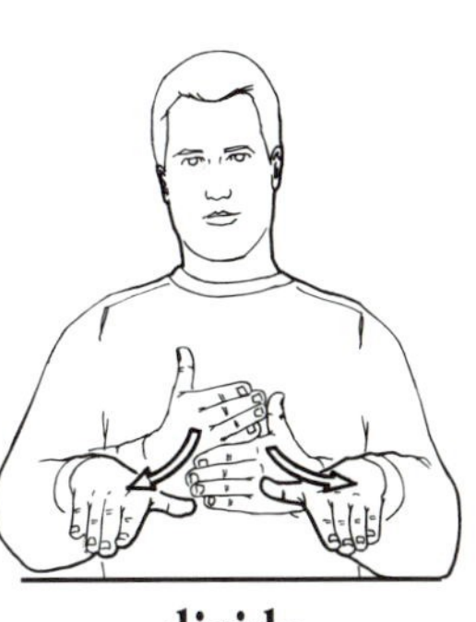
divide

estimate/guess
figure
average
percentage
greater than
less than
even number
odd number
algebra
geometry
trigonometry
calculus
angle
perpendicular
parallel
formula

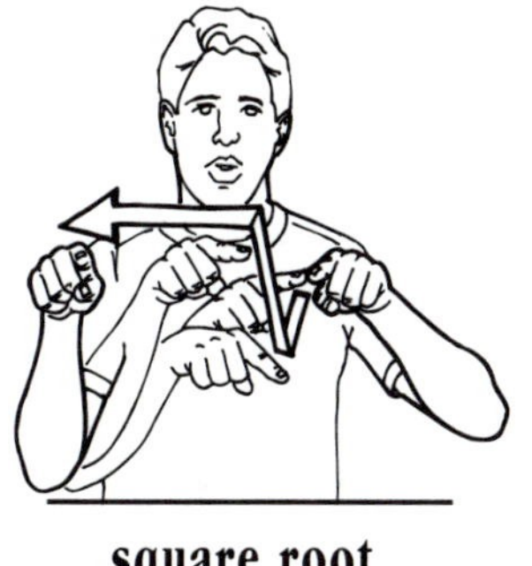
square root

square root

Phrases Using Scientific Number Signs

Do you like math?

Three and 9 is 12.

Four times 8 equals 32.

Eleven and 9, adds up to 20.

Two times 2 is how many?

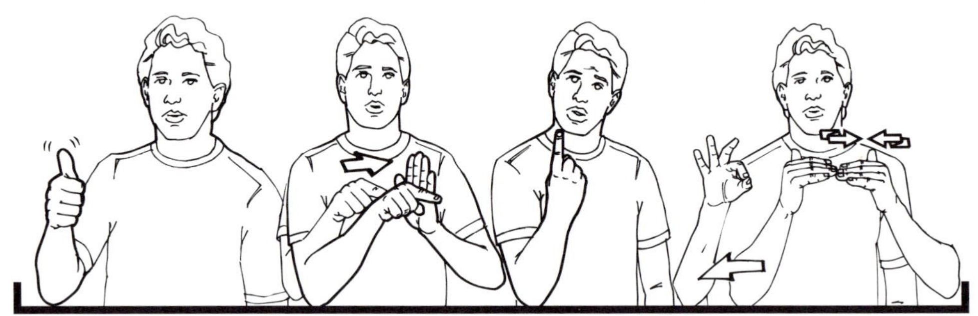

Ten minus 1 equals 9.

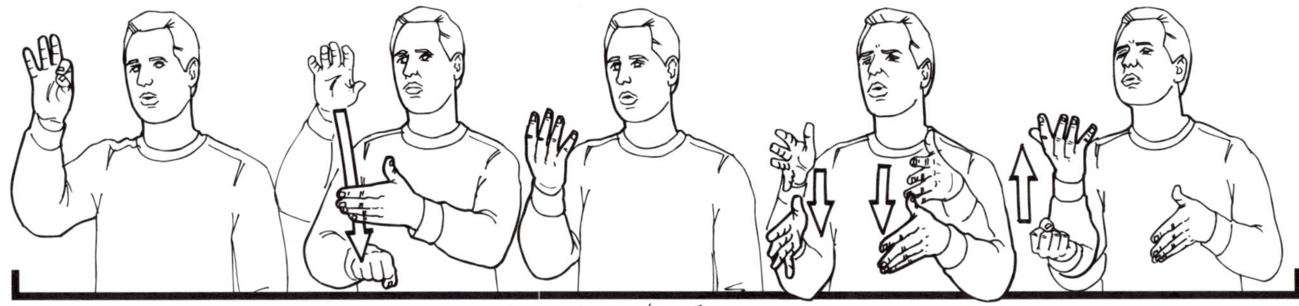

Nine minus 4 is how many?

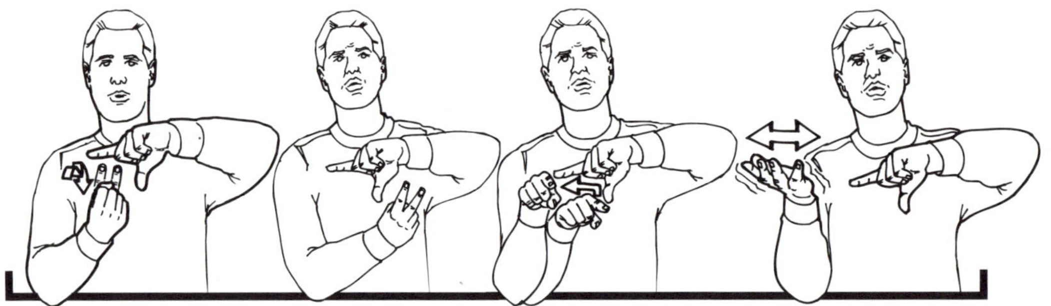

Twelve divided by 2 equals what?

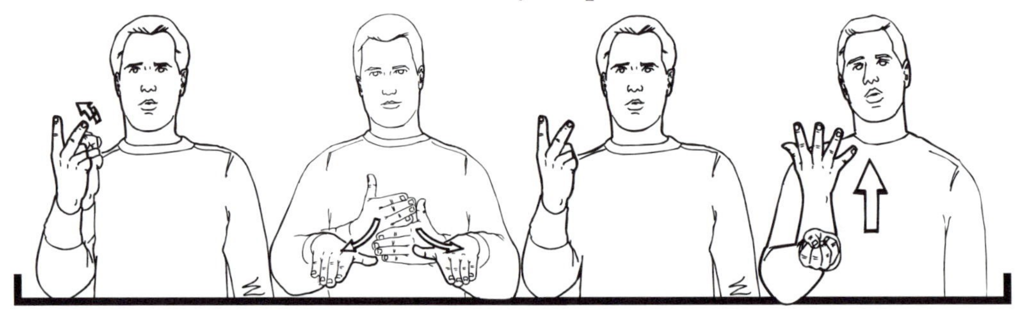

Twelve divided by 2 is how many?

X^2 plus Y^2 equals Z^2

chemistry

CO_2

CO_2

H_2O

NOTES

NOTES

Quality Educational Videos from DawnSignPress

NUMBER SIGNS *for* EVERYONE

Watch the *Numbering in American Sign Language* book in action! Now you can receptively enhance your newly acquired skills.

Numbers play an important role in everyday life. We constantly communicate numbers relating to time, age money—everything. Here's the first video where Deaf trainer Cinnie MacDougall shows all the different rules and handshapes for clearly, accurately communicating number within sentences and in proper context.

NUMBER SIGNS FOR EVERYONE:
Numbering in American Sign Language
by Cinnie MacDougall
One 90-minute video
Closed-Captioned
Voice-Over

Fingerspelled Names & Introductions

A powerful learning tool to improve recognition of fingerspelled words, *Fingerspelled Names & Introductions* allows any signer to increase comprehension and build self-confidence. Deaf people introduce themselves in unrehearsed settings with fingerspelled words presented in a four-step template building approach.

FINGERSPELLED NAMES & INTRODUCTIONS:
A Template Building Approach
by Carol Patrie, Ph.D.
One 90-minute Video

DAWNSIGNPRESS
6130 Nancy Ridge Drive, San Diego, CA 92121-3223
Voice/TTY: (619) 625-0600 Fax: (619) 625-2336
Toll Free: 1-800-549-5350 www.dawnsign.com

291. **(B)** False. Normally the hCG doubles every 2 days. However, the hCG titers in ectopic pregnancy are usually lower than in a normal intrauterine pregnancy (IUP). *(1:293–294)*

292. **(C)** Gravida is a woman who is pregnant. *(8)*

293. **(A)** Multipara is a woman who has given birth two or more times. *(8)*

294. **(D)** Nullipara (P0) is a woman who has never given birth to a viable infant. *(8)*

295. **(H)** Primipara (PI) is a woman who has given birth one time to a viable infant, regardless of whether the child was living at birth and regardless of whether the birth was single or multiple. *(8)*

296. **(B)** Nulligravida (G0) is a woman who has never been pregnant. *(8)*

297. **(E)** Primigravida (GI) is a woman who is pregnant for the first time. *(8)*

298. **(F)** Multigravida is a woman who has been pregnant several times. *(8)*

299. **(G)** Para is the number of pregnancies that have continued to viability. *(8)*

300. **(I)** Trimester is a 3-month period during gestation. *(8)*

301. **(C)** Adnexa is any accessory part, structure, or mass lateral to the uterus. *(8)*

302. **(B)** Eclampsia is toxemia of late pregnancy characterized by convulsion and coma. *(8)*

303. **(A)** Meconium is a dark green substance in the intestines of a full-term fetus. *(8)*

304. **(F)** Postpartum means after birth. *(8)*

305. **(E)** Hydramnios is also called polyhydramnios, both of which refer to an amount of amniotic fluid above 2000 cc at term. *(8)*

306. **(G)** Oxytocin is a hormone that stimulates uterine contraction. *(8)*

307. **(D)** Oligohydramnios is an amount of amniotic fluid below 300 cc at term. *(8)*

308. **(H)** Preeclampsia is toxemia of late pregnancy characterized by hypertension, albuminuria, and edema. *(8)*

309. **(C)** Lightening is when the fetal head engaged into the pelvis. *(8)*

310. **(F)** Chadwick's sign is the bluish purple color of the vagina. *(8)*

311. **(B)** Hegar's sign is the softening of the lower uterine segment. *(8)*

312. **(D)** Goodell's sign is the softening of the cervix. *(8)*

313. **(A)** Braxton Hicks' sign is painless uterine contraction. *(8)*

314. **(E)** Quickening is the mother's first perception of the movements of the fetus felt in utero. *(4)*

315. **Class A diabetes (A)** Chemical diabetes before pregnancy. *(28:865)*

316. **Class B diabetes (D)** Onset of clinical diabetes after age 20, duration less than 10 years, no evidence of vascular disease. *(28:865)*

317. **Class C diabetes (C)** Onset between ages 10 and 19, duration of 10–19 years, no evidence of vascular disease. *(28:865)*

318. **Class D diabetes (B)** Onset before age 10, duration over 20 years, vascular lesions of benign retinopathy. *(28:865)*

319. **(C)** The start of the first menstrual cycle is called menarche. *(7:4)*

320. **(D)** Implantation of the blastocyst occurs approximately 7 days (3 weeks menstrual age) after fertilization. *(29:61)*

321. **(C)** A benign invasion of endometrial tissue into the myometrium is called adenomyosis. *(27:443)*

322. **(G)** All of the above. Pelvic inflammatory disease (PID) can be caused by a variety of organisms. Gonorrhea can be the most frequent and the most destructive depending upon the area involved. *(27:462; 29:583)*

323. **(I)** All of the above. The signs and symptoms of pelvic inflammatory disease (PID) are severe pelvic pain, high fever, leukocytosis, rapid pulse rate, vaginal discharge, and rebound tenderness due to peritoneal involvement. *(27:467)*

324. **(F)** The incidence of endometriosis is less among women with frequent pregnancies. It is suggested that frequent pregnancies have a guarding effect

against endometriosis. The incidence is also less in black women and women in their thirties. *(27:625; 29:593)*

325. **(D)** All of the above. Endometriosis is associated with metromennorhagia, dysmenorrhea, and dyspareunia. *(29:592)*

326. **(A)** Endometriosis is ectopic location of endometrial tissue. *(29:593)*

327. **(G)** All of the above. Endometriosis has a variety of sonographic appearances. *(29:593)*

328. **(C)** Pelvic inflammatory disease in IUCD users is most often associated with actinomycosis. *(29:583)*

329. **(F)** All of the above. Marked hypertrophic change in the endometrium occurs in an ectopic pregnancy. The uterine mucosa responds with a decidua as a result of hormonal stimuli. Other conditions associated with prominent endometrial echo are PID, endometritis, and the secretory phase of menstruation. *(29:583–596; 39:123)*

330. **(E)** All of the above. Most adnexal complex masses can mimic PID, which include endometriosis, ectopic pregnancy, hemorrhagic cyst, and multicystic ovarian cancer. *(29:583–596)*

331. **(B)** An aerobe is an organism that requires oxygen for life. *(8)*

332. **(C)** An anaerobe is an organism that does not require oxygen for life. *(8)*

333. **(D)** Pyocolpos is pus in the vagina. *(8)*

334. **(A)** Pyosalpinx is pus in the oviduct. *(8)*

335. **(D)** Dermoid cysts have a variety of sonographic appearances. The most common sonographic appearance is a complex mass with internal echoes and distal acoustic shadow. *(39:54)*

336. **(D)** Dermoid cysts are most commonly located superior to the uterine fundus. *(39:54)*

337. **(A)** Krukenberg's tumor is a secondary carcinoma of the ovaries with the primary carcinoma in the gastrointestinal tract (stomach and pancreas). *(40:1293)*

338. **(D)** All of the above. The causes for ectopic pregnancy are usually factors that prevent the transit of the zygote into the uterine cavity, which include tubal obstruction due to chronic salpingitis, tubal adhesions from pelvic inflammatory disease (PID), and tubal malfunction. *(27:636–637)*

339. **(D)** The best time to perform amniocentesis is 16–19 weeks of gestational age. *(39:52)*

340. **(D)** The femur length is most accurate between 14 and 20 weeks of gestational age. *(29:144)*

341. **(C)** For safe amniocentesis, the needle should avoid the fetus, umbilical cord, and placenta. *(29:376)*

342. **(D)** All of the above. Amniocentesis is usually performed for genetic disorders, fetal maturity, hemolytic disease, bilirubin, α-fetoprotein, chromosome studies, and sex identification. *(2:335–343)*

343. **(A)** The serum β chorionic gonadotropin (β-hCG) is very reliable in the diagnosis of ectopic pregnancy and intrauterine pregnancy. Therefore, a sonogram may not be warranted with a negative result. *(29:404; 42:951)*

344. **(C)** The fetal iliac crests can be depicted at about 12 weeks. *(29:133)*

345. **(C)** Corpus luteum cysts are associated with normal intrauterine pregnancies and usually regress by 12–15 weeks. *(29:438)*

346. **(E)** Both subserous and submucous can become pedunculated. *(29:541)*

347. **(D)** Normally, breathing does not start before birth. This is due to blood in the intervillous spaces that gives oxygen to the fetus. The baby begins to breathe after the umbilical cord is cut. Breathing is the expansion of the lungs with air. This is not to be confused with airless thoracic movement or in utero mechanical respiratory activity detected by ultrasound. The fetal lungs in utero are echogenic and homogeneous in texture. Their echogenicity is similar to the liver. *(2:198; 29:219)*

348. **(A)** Real-time sonography can depict the fetal thoracic movements at 12–60 times per minute. This is not to be confused with normal breathing—the exchange of gases after birth. *(29:221)*

349. **(E)** All of the above. The fetal lungs are seen on sonography and so are congenital abnormalities of the lungs. *(29:221–223)*

350. **(D)** Ectopic pregnancy in the ampullary portion of the fallopian tube is not as critical as in the isthmus or the interstitial portion of the tubes in which rupture occurs early in the course of the ectopic pregnancy owing to the tube maximum expansion tolerance. *(29:400–401)*

351. **(A)** The β chorionic gonadotropin (β-hCG) can be detected at 10 days. *(29:401)*

352. **(C)** Follicular cysts are usually small, about 10–20 mm in size. *(29:487)*

353. **(A)** Normal-sized adult ovaries measure 3 × 2 × 2 cm. *(29:475)*

354. **(D)** Multiple follicles grow when stimulated by the medications Clomid (clomiphene citrate) and Perganol (menotropins). *(29:517)*

355. **(B)** The approximate uterine measurement of a nulligravida is 6 × 3 × 3 cm. *(39:123)*

356. **(E)** First identify the ovaries, which are located anterior to the internal iliac vessels, then measure the length and thickness in the longitudinal scan, and the width in the transverse scan. *(3:86–87)*

357. **(B)** False. The ovaries in postmenopausal patients are usually atrophic. *(3:86–87)*

358. **(G)** The innominate bone comprises three bones: the ilium, ischium, and pubic bones. Do not confuse ilium with ileum. See Fig. 8–116. *(29:99)*

359. **(A)** Suction curettage is the method used for terminating a pregnancy up to 12 weeks' menstrual age. *(28:526)*

360. **(A)** After 12 weeks, the fetal head and the body is too large for the suction tube. When the last menstrual period (LMP) is uncertain, sonography can be used to predict gestational age in order to help the obstetrician in selecting the best technique for pregnancy termination for that particular gestational age. *(28:524–530)*

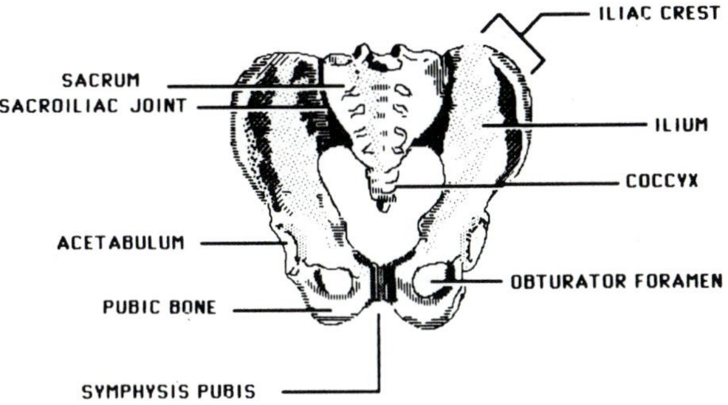

Figure 8–116. Diagram of the pelvic bones. *Note:* It is important to be able to distinguish between ileum and ilium. A good memory key is to associate the letter e in ileum with intestine and the i in ilium with pelvis.

361. **(B)** Masses can be confirmed by water enema. *(29:531)*

362. **(J)** All of the above. Normally, 90% of the adult uterus occupies an anteverted position and forms a 90° angle with the long axis of the vagina. The other 10% are retroverted, antiflexed, retroflexed, midposition, right lateral deviation, and left lateral deviation, all of which are normal variations of the positions of the uterus. *(11:158; 27:365–369)*

363. **(A)** T-shaped uterus is seen in the daughter of a woman who took diethylstilbestrol (DES). *(29:536)*

364. **(A)** Hydrometrocolpos is watery fluid in the uterus and vagina. *(29:539)*

365. **(C)** Hematometrocolpos is blood in the uterus and vagina. *(29:539)*

366. **(B)** Pyometrium is pus in the uterus. *(29:539)*

367. **(D)** Pseudopolyp is a tab of mucous membrane resembling a tumor with a pedicle. *(29:539)*

368. **(I)** All of the above. The sonographic appearance of leiomyoma is an enlargement of the uterus with nodular or irregular contours that may produce an abnormal indentation on the bladder or rectum. The uterus may also be heterogeneous in texture with high-level echoes with distal acoustic shadowing due to calcification. A solid mass that cannot be separated from the uterus also is another sonographic appearance. *(26:30–47; 29:541–542)*

369. **(G)** The sonographic criteria for a cystic mass are anechoic (echo-free), well-defined wall, and distal acoustic enhancement. *(14:40)*

370. **(H)** The sonographic criteria for a solid mass are irregular and poorly defined margins; distal acoustic shadow; and internal echoes. *Note:* A homogeneous solid mass can appear anechoic; however, no distal acoustic enhancement will be seen. *(14:40)*

371. **(D)** Septations are less frequent in serous cystadenomas and are more frequent in mucinous cystadenomas. *(14:138–139; 29:492–494)*

372. **(A)** See explanation for question 371. *(14:138–139; 29:492–494)*

373. **(F)** All of the above. If a malignant tumor is depicted, the sonographer should scan the entire abdomen and pelvis and look for any other mass or fluid collection. Scans should also be taken of the lower chest for pleural effusions. *(29:475)*

374. **(C)** If the peritoneal cavity becomes filled with a mucinous material from a ruptured ovarian cyst or cystadenocarcinoma, it is called pseudomyxoma peritonei. *(29:494)*

375. **(F)** Stage IVB is distant metastases.

376. **(E)** Stage 0 is carcinoma in situ.

377. **(C)** Stage IA is microinvasive.

378. **(D)** Stage II is carcinoma extending beyond the cervix.

379. **(A)** Stage IB is carcinoma confined to the cervix.

380. **(B)** Stage IIB is lateral parametrial involvement. *(29:547–548)*

381. **(G)** All of the above. Stein-Leventhal syndrome is characterized by obesity, infertility, hirsuitism, menstrual dysfunction, and polycystic ovaries. *(27:744; 29:489)*

382. **(D)** The cyst would be most likely a parovarian cyst. *(27:501–503; 29:486)*

383. **(A)** Postpartum refers to after childbirth or delivery. *(29:449)*

384. **(D)** Puerperium refers to 6–8 weeks after delivery. *(29:449)*

385. **(D)** The ovaries are least likely to be seen on a postpartum pelvic sonogram. This may be due to extrapelvic position of the ovaries caused by the large uterus. *(29:451)*

386. **(A)** Immediately following delivery, the fundal height is at the level of the umbilicus. The uterus will continue to contract and involute for several weeks. *(29:449)*

387. **(E)** Hemorrhage, thromboembolism, and infection are the most common complications during the postpartum period. Placenta previa is an antipartum complication. *(29:449)*

388. **(C)** The volume of amniotic fluid increases with gestational age until about the 38th week of gestation when the volume decreases. *(29:310)*

389. **(B)** Numerous measuring techniques have been applied to biparietial diameter (BPD) measurements. However, the most accepted method is outer to inner edge (leading echo to leading echo). *(29:148)*

390. **(C)** A change in head shape, such as brachycephaly or dolichocephaly, affects accurate measurement in predicting gestational age. The degree to which fetal head shape affects BPD can be estimated with this formula:

$$CI = \frac{BPD}{OFD} \times 100.$$

(29:150)

391. **(F)** All of the above. Head circumference (HC) can be obtained with real-time electronic calipers, a light pen, a map measurer, and with the following formula:

$$HC = \frac{BPD + OFD}{2} \pi.$$

(29:151)

392. **(D)** Doppler measurement. Studies demonstrate that linear-array and sector scanners give measurements that are in agreement to the true value. *(29:153; 40:525–530)*

393. **(G)** The fetal head should be ovoid (egg-shaped) and the cavum septum pellucidum, thalamus, and the anterior horns of the lateral ventricles should be seen. *(1:29; 29:1147)*

394. **(A)** In the fetus, the kidneys develop in the pelvis and gradually migrate upward into the retroperitoneal space of the abdomen. *(22:260)*

395. **(A)** The urinary bladder of the fetus is completely developed by 12 weeks. *(29:137)*

396. **(D)** Fetal gender can be determined as early as 16 weeks. *(29:195)*

397. **(E)** Evidence of a male fetus is obtained by the depiction of the penis, scrotum, and testicles. *(29:195)*

398. **(C)** There is no pathologic significance of isolated hydrocele in utero. *(29:195)*

399. **(C)** Evidence of a female fetus is confirmed by depiction of the labia. *(29:195)*

400. **(D)** Accuracy of gender prediction in the second and third trimesters is 95–99.9%. *(29:197)*

401. **(C)** The umbilical vein provides oxygenated blood to the fetus and the umbilical arteries and provides deoxygenated blood from the fetus to the placenta. *(29:369)*

402. **(A)** See explanation for question 401. *(29:369)*

403. **(D)** Placenta previa is the implantation of the placenta in the lower uterine segment. *(7:500–516; 11:220–223; 29:357–363)*

404. **(A)** Placenta accreta is the abnormal adherence of part or all of the placenta to the uterine wall. *(7:500–516; 11:220–223; 29:357–363)*

405. **(C)** Placenta succenturiata is an accessory lobe of placenta. *(7:500–516; 11:220–223; 29:357–363)*

406. **(B)** Abruptio placentae is the premature separation of the placenta after 20 weeks of gestation. *(7:500–516; 11:220–223; 29:357–363)*

407. **(E)** Placenta increta is the abnormal adherence of part or all of the placenta in which the chorionic villi invade the myometrium. *(7:500–516; 11:220–223; 29:357–363)*

408. **(F)** Placenta percreta is the abnormal adherence of part or all of the placenta in which the chorionic villi invade the uterine wall. *(7:500–516; 11:220–223; 29:357–363)*

409. **(E)** The McDonald and Shirodkar procedures are the treatments for an incompetent cervix. *(2:600–601; 29:365)*

410. **(B)** Twins have the largest percentage of single umbilical arteries when compared to singleton births, abortuses, and fetuses with trisomy D. *(29:371)*

411. **(D)** All of the above. The causes of an incompetent cervix are several dilation and curettage procedures (D&Cs) and exposure to diethylstilbestrol in utero. Hormonal influences on the sphincteric ring also are noted. *(29:363)*

412. **(C)** Incompetent cervix should be treated at 14–18 weeks of gestation. *(29:363)*

413. **(B)** The erect position is used as an aid to diagnose incompetent cervix. *(20:601–602; 29:363)*

414. **(F)** Twins resulting from one sperm and one ovum are monozygotic (identical) twins. *(7:63; 29:321)*

415. **(E)** Twins resulting from two sperm and two ova are dizygotic (fraternal) twins. *(7:63; 29:321)*

416. **(A)** A neonate is considered growth retarded when the mean weight for gestational age falls below the 10th percentile. *(18:99)*

417. **(A)** Total intrauterine volume (TIUV) is least reliable for the diagnosis of intrauterine growth retardation (IUGR). This method was used primarily with the static B-scanner. The new concept involves measurement of the head and abdominal circumference. *(29:162)*

418. **(C)** The formula for head circumference is:

$$HC = \frac{BPD + OFD}{2}\pi$$

(32:268)

419. **(D)** Abdominal circumference measurement primarily reflects liver size. *(29:164)*

420. **(A)** The formula for abdominal circumference is

$$AC = (D_1 + D_2) \times 1.57$$ *(32:268)*

421. **(C)** The kidneys are responsible for amniotic fluid production. *(29:197)*

422. **(B)** Hydramnios is not associated with renal agenesis. *(29:198)*

423. **(A)** The most common fetal renal anomaly is hydronephrosis. *(29:199)*

424. **(D)** Most unilateral hydronephrosis is due to ureteropelvic junction obstruction. *(29:199)*

425. **(G)** All of the above. Hydronephrosis is the most common fetal anomaly and is associated with "prune belly" syndrome, also known as Eagle-Barrett syndrome, ureteropelvic junction obstruction, oligohydramnios, and dilated urinary bladder. *(29:201)*

426. **(D)** "Prune belly" syndrome is an abdominal muscle deficiency that produces dilatation of the ureters, bladder, and posterior urethra, it is associated with cryptorchidism and urachal cyst, and it is predominantly a male disorder. *(29:201)*

427. **(E)** Both polycystic and multicystic disease can be diagnosed before birth. *(29:204)*

428. **(E)** See explanation for question 427. *(29:204)*

429. **(D)** Absence of hair from the skin (alopecia) cannot be depicted with sonography. *(29:229)*

430. **(B)** Hydramnios, also called polyhydramnios, is an excessive amount of amniotic fluid over 2,000 mL at term. *(8)*

431. **(C)** Oligohydramnios denotes reduction in the amount of amniotic fluid below 300 mL at term. *(8)*

432. **(G)** Formation of the umbilical cord results from the fusion of the body stalk and yolk stalk. *(29:369)*

433. **(C)** Wharton's jelly protects the blood vessels inside the umbilical cord. *(29:369)*

434. **(A)** Both femur length and biparietal diameter (BPD) are most accurate between 14 and 20 weeks. *(29:142)*

435. **(C)** Monozygotic twins are produced by a single ovum and are known as identical twins. Dizygotic twins are produced from separate ovum and are known as fraternal twins. Approximately 75% of dizygotic twins are of the same sex. *(28:755; 29:325–326)*

436. **(B)** The most common anomaly affecting the central nervous system (CNS) is anencephaly. *(29:301)*

437. **(D)** Fetal ascites seen in a mother with an elevated Rh titer indicates heart failure. *(29:283)*

438. **(B)** Pseudoascites can be differentiated from true ascites by changing the patient's position and observing the fluid movement. Pseudoascites will not be altered by a change in the patient's position. Ascites is an abnormal accumulation of intraperitoneal serous fluid. *(8; 29:237–238, 282)*

439. **(F)** All of the above. The anomalies associated with erythroblastosis are hydramnios, hepatosplenomegaly, hydrops, and increased umbilical vein diameter. *(29:279)*

440. **(D)** Cleft palate is associated with hypotelorism and alobar holyprosencephaly. *(29:262–263)*

441. **(A)** Sacrococcygeal teratoma is the most common in utero tumor. The tumor is located in the region of the coccyx and comprises both solid and cystic elements (complex) with some areas of calcification that produce distal acoustic shadow. *(29:207)*

442. **(A)** The maxillary bone is partially or completely absent below the nose on sonography. *(29:262–263)*

443. **(D)** The internal iliac artery can be depicted posteromedial to the ovary. The external iliac artery is anterolateral to the ovaries. *(29:475)*

444. **(D)** Hypertension in pregnancy results from preeclampsia (toxemia). This condition occurs in the last months of gestation and is characterized by blood pressure of 140/90 mm Hg or more with proteinuria and edema. Hypertension also results from eclampsia (toxemia). This condition is characterized by the same symptoms as preeclampsia but with convulsions. *(12:80–81)*

445. **(C)** See explanation for question 444. *(12:80–81)*

446. **(B)** The hemolytic disease of newborns described is erythroblastosis fetalis. *(12:85)*

447. **(F)** A patient who contracts German measles in the first 12 weeks of gestation may give birth to an infant with microcephaly, heart lesions, and auditory defects. *(12:85)*

448. **(B)** The three stages of labor are dilation of the cervix, delivery of the baby, and expulsion of the placenta. *(12:103–104)*

449. **(E)** The external os of the cervix is completely dilated at 10 cm (100 mm). *(12:103)*

450. **(B)** The fetal kidneys can be depicted at 14 weeks. *(29:195)*

451. **(A)** The fetal head grows 5 mm per week at 16 weeks of gestation. *(18:38)*

452. **(B)** The scanning plane is too high. When performing a biparietal diameter measurement (BPD), the fetal head should be ovoid and the measurement obtained at the level of the thalami and cavum septum pellucidum. *(3:134; 29:148)*

453. **(D)** The fetal head grows 3.6 mm per week at 20 weeks gestation. *(18:38)*

454. **(C)** The fetal head grows 2.3 mm per week at 32 weeks gestation. *(18:38)*

455. **(B)** The fetal head grows 1.4 mm per week at 40 weeks of gestation. Fetal head growth reduces with the advancement of gestational age. *(18:38)*

456. **(D)** Corpus luteum cyst is usually enlarged, but regresses after the 14th week of gestation. Fibroid enlargement is due to high levels of hormones. Ovarian cystadenoma also enlarges. *(39:53)*

457. **(B)** Leiomyomas are the most common solid masses associated with pregnancy. *(39:53)*

458. **(H)** The most common cause for a uterus too large or too small for dates is incorrect or mistaken dates from the patient's last menstrual period (LMP). Other causes for the uterus too large for dates are multiple gestation, hydramnios, hydatidiform mole, and myoma. *(10:78–79; 41:184)*

459. **(G)** Causes for a uterus too small for dates are fetal death, oligohydramnios, and intrauterine growth retardation (IUGR). See also question 458. *(10:78–79; 41:184)*

460. **(D)** 90%. Remaining 10% have retroverted, right lateral deviation, or left lateral deviation. *(11:158)*

461. **(E)** 90% of women have an anteverted uterus with a 90° angle with the long axis of the vagina. *(10:84)*

462. **(F)** Anterior cul-de-sac or vesicouterine pouch. *(11:89)*

463. **(F)** Posterior cul-de-sac, retrouterine pouch, or pouch of Douglas. *(11:89)*

464. **(D)** Retropubic space or space of Retzius. *(11:89)*

465. **(H)** The three major pelvic side wall muscles are iliopsoas, pubococcygeus, and obturator internus muscles. *(11:89)*

466. **(B)** Mittelschmerz is intermenstrual pain. *(11:88)*

467. **(A)** The placenta is almost never removed in abdominal pregnancy due to high risk of hemorrhage. *(2:546; 13:353)*

468. **(A)** An acardius anencephalic twin occurs in monozygotic-twin pregnancy. *(33:109)*

469. **(B)** An acardius fetus may move around with absence of cardiac motion. This is most likely due to vascular placental anastomosis between the twins. *(38:108)*

470. **(B)** Ancephaly results from failure of the neural tube to close at its cephalic end. *(33:109)*

471. **(C)** The standard range of error for biparietal diameter measurements (BPD) is 2 mm. *(18:36)*

472. **(A)** The range of error for biparietal diameter (BPD) can be tested by a repeat scan in 24-hours on the same patient. *(18:38)*

473. **(A)** The multiple echogenic interfaces probably arising from a Lippes loop IUCD. *(39:157)*

474. **(C)** An intrauterine contraceptive device (IUCD) should be within the upper portion of the uterine lumen to be effective. *(39:132)*

475. **(B)** The sonographic findings include a mature follicle and two immature follicles. A mature follicle measures approximately 2 cm in average dimension. *(39:156)*

476. **(A)** The maturity of the oocyte can be inferred by the size of the follicle. Most mature follicles measure approximately 2 cm in average dimension. *(39:131)*

477. **(B)** A loculated, predominately cystic adnexal mass is shown. *(39:120)*

478. **(D)** The mass was found to represent an endometrioma. It also could represent a cystic ovarian tumor such as cystadenoma. It is unlikely that a physiologic ovarian cyst would have this appearance. *(39:141)*

479. **(B)** This sonogram demonstrates matted bowel loops surrounded by echogenic fluid. This appearance is unusual for bowel loops and is strongly suggestive of malignancy. *(63:271)*

480. **(A)** This condition results from ovarian malignancy secondary to pseudomyxoma peritonei. The presence of ascites usually indicates that the ovarian tumor has extended beyond its capsule. *(63:271)*

481. **(A)** The presence of multiple tumor implants on the surface of bowel loops producing matting and abnormal bowel thickening with surrounding echogenic fluid are characteristic of pseudomyxoma peritonei. *(63:271, 29:494)*

482. **(A)** The incidence of ovarian carcinoma in women in the United States over 50 years of age is 33 per 100,000. *(64:557)*

483. **(D)** This sonogram shows normal fetal lips and nose without evidence of cleft lip or palate. *(63:163)*

484. **(A)** Cleft lip is a common congenital facial deformity that is associated with chromosomal disorders (trisomy 13) and can occur with or without cleft palate. *(63:163)*

485. **(D)** Evaluation of the hand is helpful in some congenital anomalies associated with polydactyly or syndactyly. This sonogram demonstrates all five digits in normal position. A fixed lateral position of the thumb, called "hitchhiker thumb," is not demonstrated in this sonogram. *(63:136)*

486. **(D)** Either Rh isoimmunization or masses that obstruct venous return to the heart have been associated with hydrops fetalis. Hydrops fetalis refers to a fetus that has massive edema and usually fluid within the peritoneal, pleural, and/or pericardial spaces. *(39:62)*

487. **(B)** The chorion and the amnion typically fuse between 10 and 14 weeks. Prior to this, the amnion can be identified as a linear echogenic structure within the gestational sac. *(39:53)*

488. **(A)** The chorion has been elevated and immediately beneath it are venous lakes. *(39:75)*

489. **(C)** The term *limb reduction abnormalities* refers to the absence of a limb or segment of a limb to include (1) acheiria (absence of a hand) or (2) acheiropodia (absence of a hand and foot). *(60:373)*

490. **(D)** Since mothers are asked to drink fluid prior to obstetric studies, the fetus may have brisk diuresis and show mild separation of the renal collecting system. *(39:204)*

491. **(A)** This is a normal four-chamber view of the fetal heart. The large arrows point to the atria. *(63:133)*

492. **(B)** The short arrows point to the ventricles. *(63:133)*

493. **(C)** Maternal conditions that are associated with increased incidence of fetal heart malformations include diabetes mellitus, alcoholism, and infection. Certain medications such as lithium can also increase the incidence of fetal heart malformations. *(65:390)*

494. **(B)** Only the shaft of the femur should be measured in femur length, excluding the femoral neck and other epiphyseal calcification centers. *(39:88)*

495. **(B)** The uterus should return to normal size approximately 4 weeks after delivery. *(39:65)*

496. **(D)** All of the above are associated with an increased incidence of placenta previa. *(39:59)*

497. **(D)** M-mode echocardiogram is important in assessing fetal cardiac arrhythmias. This M-mode demonstrates normal rate and rhythm. *(63:133)*

498. **(B)** The presence of retrochorionic hemorrhage does not exclude the possibility of carrying to term, although it lessens somewhat the likelihood of completion of pregnancy. It can be associated with first- and second-trimester bleeding. *(39:59)*

499. **(D)** All of the above may be associated with arrhythmias. *(63:133)*

500. **(B)** A cervix that measures less than 3 cm in length should be considered suspect for cervical incompetence. *(39:54)*

501. **(D)** The normal heart rate and rhythm of a second-trimester fetus is between 120 and 160 beats/minute. Certain arrhythmias, such as premature atrial or ventricular contractions are benign, whereas arrhythmias under 60 beats/minute or over 200 beats/minute are potentially life threatening. The normal heart rate and rhythm of a second-trimester fetus can vary with the fetal state, breathing, and activities and also demonstrate periodic premature ventricular contractions. *(63:133)*

502. **(C)** The adrenal can be approximately 30% the size of the kidney in the term fetus. *(39:104)*

503. **(A)** This sonogram is diagnostic of a hydatidiform mole. Sonographically, the characteristic of hydropic villi present within molar tissue give rise to multiple small anechoic structures within the echogenic tissue resulting in this recognizable pattern. *(63:92–95)*

504. **(A)** The most common place for implantation of an ectopic pregnancy is in the ampullary portion of the fallopian tube. *(39:48)*

505. **(B)** The hydropic villi cannot be recognized until after 14 weeks. *(63:92–95).*

506. **(A)** Even though one can diagnose the completeness of a miscarriage, one cannot exclude the possibility of an ectopic pregnancy because in at least 20% of ectopic pregnancies, no abnormal sonographic findings will be encountered. *(39:40)*

507. **(E)** This fetus has two abnormal findings involving the fetal head. A "lemon head" and "banana sign" both associated with meningomyelocele. *(63:131)*

508. **(A)** See question 507 for explanation. *(63:131)*

509. **(A)** Besides meningomyelocele, elevation of serum α-fetoprotein can be encountered with several other conditions, including anencephaly, cystic hygroma, and omphalocele. *(63:131)*

510. **(A)** The yolk sac is largest between 5 and 9 weeks. *(39:70)*

511. **(A)** This fetus has herniation of the meninges and a portion of the brain through a defect in the posterior cranial fossa. *(39:111)*

512. **(C)** Cystic hygromas are due to a malfusion of lymphatic channels behind the neck and can be associated with Turner's syndrome. *(39:57)*

513. **(B)** The most common nontrophoblastic primary tumor of the placenta is chorioangioma. Teratoma is a rare tumor of the placenta. *(64:151)*

514. **(A)** This sonogram demonstrates retained products of conception. The normal involuting uterus should have a thin linear central interface representing the coapted uterine surfaces. *(63:208)*

515. **(B)** The arrow points to fetal ascites, which is usually seen in association with fetal hydrops. However, this image does not demonstrate any marked skin and subcutaneous thickening or skin edema (anasarca). There is no sonographic evidence of pericardial effusion. If fetal ascites occurs alone, it is called isolated ascites. *(63:134,65:563–570)*

516. **(B)** Immune hydrops is caused by incompatibility of maternal antibodies with antigens in the fetal red blood cells, resulting in Rh isoimmunization. *(63:134,65:563–570)*

517. **(B)** This sonogram demonstrates an amniotic band or sheet crossing the lower uterine segment. Amniotic band syndrome may result in amputated fetal parts. *(63:202)*

518. **(B)** The amniocytes have the highest likelihood for a better culture if obtained between 16 and 18 weeks. *(39:56)*

519. **(E)** All of the above. Amniotic band syndrome is associated with gastroschisis, omphalocele, anencephaly, clubfeet, and amputated fingers, toes, and extremities. *(63:202)*

520. **(A)** Usually normal because anencephaly does not involve an open neural tube defect. The α-fetoprotein may be normal. *(39:97)*

521. **(B)** Bowel should return to the abdomen by 12 weeks. When there is an amniotic band, this return of bowel into the abdomen may be hindered. *(63:202)*

522. **(C)** There is a high association of renal malformation with uterine malformations. *(39:91)*

523. **(B)** This mature fetus has a meconium-filled large bowel. *(63:133)*

524. **(E)** None of the above. Normal structures that should be seen at the appropriate level for an abdominal circumference in a third trimester fetus are demonstrated. *(63:133)*

525. **(A)** Fig. 8–43 shows the typical appearance of a Copper-7 (Cu-7) intrauterine contraceptive device (IUCD). *(48:797)*

526. **(D)** There is a higher incidence of ovarian abscesses and ectopic pregnancies in users of intrauterine contraceptive devices (IUCDs). *(48:797)*

527. **(B)** Blighted ovum implies lack of development of the fertilized ovum past the blastocyst phase. *(46:336)*

528. **(D)** Fig. 8–44 demonstrates the normal anatomy that should be present for measuring the biparietal diameter. *(63:45)*

529. **(A)** Fig. 8–45 demonstrates the normal anatomy that should be present for measuring the abdominal circumference. *(63:45)*

530. **(C)** An overly distended bladder may compress the placenta, resulting in a false impression of anterior or posterior placenta previa. *(45:169)*

531. **(C)** Situs inversus is reversal (transposition) of the abdominal and thoracic viscera forming a mirror image of the organs' positions. *(65:350)*

532. **(A)** True. There is a 30% incidence of spinal dysraphism in anencephalic fetuses. *(49:319)*

533. **(B)** This transvaginal sonogram demonstrates a developing gestational sac within the decidualized endometrium. The pseudogestational sac that occurs with ectopic pregnancy lacks the localized thickening of the chorion frondosum seen in a viable intrauterine pregnancy. *(63:91)*

534. **(A)** The Chiari malformation is associated with meningomyelocele. This disorder involves low placement of the cerebellar tonsils, enlargement of the precerebellar cistern, pointing of the frontal horns, and enlargement of the massa intermedia. *(49:319)*

535. **(A)** This sonogram shows herniation of the liver outside of the abdomen. *(51:14)*

536. **(A)** Both omphalocele and gastroschisis are herniations of the bowel; however, gastroschisis presents a normal umbilical cord, whereas omphalocele is herniated at the umbilical cord insertion. *(1:71–72; 51:13)*

537. **(D)** The amount of β subunit of human chorionic gonadotropin (hCG) can be quantitated and correlated with the week of gestation. The level of serum β-hCG in which the normal intrauterine gestation sac can be seen on transabdominal sonography differs from transvaginal sonography. The level for transvaginal sonography is about 500 mIU/mL (2nd International Standard). *(63:40;66:169)*

538. **(C)** Cumulus oophorus consists of the oocyte and surrounding granulosa cells. *(52)*

539. **(A)** The cystic structure shown in Fig. 8–48 most likely represents a follicular cyst. *(53)*

540. **(A)** Physiologic cysts may have hemorrhage within them, thus giving them internal echoes. *(53)*

541. **(B)** This sonogram demonstrates an early intrauterine pregnancy in addition to an intramural leiomyoma. A uterine contraction would have less defined borders. *(63:125)*

542. **(D)** All of the above. *(54)*

543. **(D)** When the gestation sac reaches a size of 8–10 mm, a yolk sac should be seen within the gestation sac. *(63:40)*

544. **(A)** This well-circumscribed cystic mass of the umbilical cord results from cystic dilation of an allantoid remnant, and it is commonly referred to as allantoic cyst. *(60:392)*

545. **(D)** The uterus is retroverted in position with a small cystic mass in the cervix. The cervical mucosa has numerous glands that form a retention cyst known as nabothian cyst when occluded. *(59:397)*

546. **(D)** Although there is some decreased probability of completion to term, the presence of retrochorionic hemorrhage does not always indicate that the pregnancy will not be brought to full term. *(55:975)*

547. **(D)** The placenta is anterior and is bulging into the amniotic fluid. A well-defined hematoma is seen between the placenta and uterine wall (retroplacental hematoma). The primary area of detachment results in hemorrhage predominantly beneath the placenta. This premature separation of the normally implanted placenta with its associated hemorrhage is called abruptio placentae. *(59:309)*

548. **(A)** As opposed to the decidual cast in an ectopic pregnancy that has only one layer of decidua, an intrauterine pregnancy typically has two. *(44:755)*

549. **(C)** The open arrows point to a structure called the cerebral peduncle. *(61:39)*

550. **(D)** The open arrow points to the third ventricle, located between the thalami. *(61:36)*

551. **(A)** The open arrow points to the cavum septum pellucidum. *(61:30)*

552. **(B)** The solid arrow points to the thalamus. *(61:38)*

553. **(D)** The presence of intrauterine contraceptive devices (IUCDs) is associated with only 50% of pregnancies brought to term and are also associated with excessive vaginal bleeding and spontaneous abortion. *(48:797)*

554. **(D)** The open arrow points to the choroid plexus in the lateral ventricle. *(61:32)*

555. **(C)** Clinically, hydatidiform mole frequently presents with early preeclampsia and/or hyperemesis gravidarum. The sonographic appearance in Fig. 8–57 has a typical vesicular texture. *(29:387–394)*

556. **(B)** Leiomyoma, a missed abortion, hematoma, and a multiloculated papillary serous cystadenoma can all mimic a hydatidiform mole. Pseudocyesis is false pregnancy and is not associated. *(29:387–394)*

557. **(D)** Fig. 8–58 shows the uterus as enlarged without any sonographic evidence of an intrauterine gestation sac. A right adnexal ring is seen, which is highly suggestive of an unruptured ectopic pregnancy. The clinical history of a negative urinary chorionic gonadotropin (UCG) has very little significance in sonographic correlation owing to high false-positive and false-negative results. Quantitative serum β-hCG is the recommended test for sonographic correlation. *(1:291–294)*

558. **(E)** All of the above. A hemorrhagic cyst and an infection in the fallopian tube could mimic an ectopic pregnancy. *(29:412–414)*

559. **(C)** The uterus as shown in Fig. 8–59 is enlarged. The uterus may enlarge in the presence of an ectopic pregnancy. *(1:291–303; 29:206–412)*

560. **(A)** This sonogram shows the typical appearance of a calcified fibroid. Note the acoustic shadowing below the calcified ring. *(1:239; 29:541–542)*

561. **(A)** A Zipper ring intrauterine contraceptive device (IUCD) could mimic a ringlike intrauterine mass. All the others are less likely to be differential. Dermoid and hemorrhagic cysts are adnexal in location. A gestation sac does not normally demonstrate an acoustic shadow. *(1:239; 29:541—542)*

562. **(A)** The distal acoustic shadow is due to deposition of calcium salts within the hard ball of solid tissue. *(1:239; 27:434; 29:541–542)*

563. **(E)** This mass is solid and calcified. Its calcification is characterized by distal shadowing. *(1:239; 29:541–542)*

564. **(D)** Failure to demonstrate any heart motion on real-time is highly suggestive of fetal demise. After death, liquefaction of the brain occurs resulting in overlapping of the fetal cranial sutures (sonographic Spalding's sign). *(29:432–434)*

565. **(C)** If the fetal heart motion was demonstrated on real-time and a double-ring sign (Druel's sign) of the fetal head is seen, this finding could represent fat deposition of the scalp or scalp edema in sickle-cell anemia. However, in view of this patient's history of Rh^- blood type, this study would highly suggest erythroblastosis fetalis with edema of the scalp. *(3:308; 39:46)*

566. **(C)** Scalp edema. Diabetes mellitus and sickle-cell anemia can present with a similar double-ring sign. *(3:308)*

567. **(B)** This sonogram shows the endometrial lumen, which indicates that the uterus is empty. An adnexal ring is seen with internal echoes, which would be suggestive of ectopic pregnancy. *(1:299)*

568. **(C)** Hemorrhagic corpus luteum cyst or an inflammation process in the pelvis can produce a ringlike structure that mimics an ectopic pregnancy. *(1:299)*

569. **(B)** A sonographer in a private ultrasound clinic should *not* give any patients Polaroid pictures, VHS tapes, or x-ray films without permission from the physician to whom he or she is responsible. The fee the patient pays is for service rendered and *not* for purchase of medical records. *(36:222; 37:305)*

570. **(B)** See explanation for question 569. *(36:222; 37:305)*

571. **(B)** The rule regarding patient records in a hospital ultrasound department is the same as in a private ultrasound clinic. See explanation for question 569. *(36:222; 37:305)*

572. **(B)** The patient's medical chart is hospital property. Neither a patient nor his or her authorized representative has a legal right to physical ownership. However, a patient has a legal right to the information in the medical record and can have legal access to its contents through an attorney. *(36:222; 37:305)*

573. **(C)** The physician is ultimately responsible for any diagnosis made by the sonographer. *(26:619)*

574. **(C)** The umbilical cord should be cut between the two clamps. *(2:421)*

575. **(C)** The description is of the broad ligaments. *(2:25)*

576. **(D)** Anything the sonographer does in the role of employment is ultimately the physician's responsibility. *(29:619)*

577. **(B)** This unethical behavior would be outside the normal duties and responsibilities of a sonographer and therefore the sonographer would be responsible. *(29:619)*

578. **(D)** The physician is responsible. *(29:619)*

579. **(B)** The resulting infant will be a boy. The mature ovum has 23 X chromosomes (female factor) and the mature sperm has 23 Y chromosomes (male factor). *(12:28–29)*

580. **(C)** Fertilization usually takes place in the ampullary portion of the fallopian tube. Implantation occurs in the uterus. *(29:619)*

581. **(D)** Frank breech is described as the buttocks descending first with the thighs and legs extending upward along the anterior fetal trunk. *(28:925)*

582. **(C)** Complete breech is described as the buttocks descending first, with the knees flexed, and the baby sitting cross-legged. *(28:925)*

583. **(A)** A footling breech is when one or both feet are prolapsed into the lower uterine segment. *(28:925)*

584. **(C)** Cephalic is a general term for head first. Vertex is when the region between the anterior and posterior fontanelles and the sagittal suture are the presenting part. *(13:574; 28:925)*

585. **(H)** PROM is premature rupture of membranes.

586. **(E)** CPD is cephalopelvic disproportion.

587. **(D)** FUO is fever of unknown origin.

588. **(C)** NPO is nothing by mouth.

589. **(J)** D&C is dilation and curettage.

590. **(F)** TAH is total abdominal hysterectomy. *(8)*

591. **(D)** Fetal kidneys can be depicted 14 weeks after the last menstrual period. *(29:195)*

592. **(D)** The seal is called the mucous plug. *(2:224)*

593. **(A)** The normal circumference of the fetal kidneys in relationship to fetal abdominal circumference is 27–30%. *(41:746)*

594. **(C)** Piriformis muscle. *(2:21–35)*

595. **(D)** Iliopsoas muscle. *(2:21–35)*

596. **(B)** Uterus. *(2:21–35)*

597. **(A)** Ovary. *(2:21–35)*

598. **(A)** False pelvis and pelvic major. *(1:199)*

599. **(B)** True pelvis and pelvic minor. *(1:199)*

600. **(E)** Linea terminalis *(1:199)*

601. **(B)** The line the solid arrow points to is the falx cerebri (interhemispheric fissure). *(3:30)*

602. **(B)** The line the open arrow points to is sylvian fissure/insula. *(61:23)*

603. **(B)** The open arrow points to the ambient cistern. *(61:41)*

604. **(B)** The line the solid arrow points to is the basilar artery; pulsating echo can be appreciated on real-time. *(61:41)*

605. **(D)** The two open arrows point to umbilical arteries. *(61:121)*

606. **(A)** The open arrow points to the lens. *(61:44–45)*

607. **(A)** The open arrow points to the fetal bladder. *(61:111)*

608. **(B)** The solid arrow points to the fetal stomach. *(61:88)*

609. **(C)** The open arrow points to the fetal aorta seen anterior to the spine. *(61:119)*

610. **(A)** The arrow points to the umbilical cord. *(61:120)*

611. **(D)** The arrow points to the subcutaneous tissue/skin of the thigh. *(61:153)*

612. **(A)** The solid arrow points to the femur. *(61:153)*

613. **(C)** The hypoechoic line the closed arrow points to is the fetal diaphragm, which separates the thoracic from the abdominal cavity. *(61:102)*

614. **(D)** The open arrow points to the fetal aorta seen anterior to the spine. *(61:115)*

615. **(C)** The open arrow points to the hypoechoic subcutaneous muscle layer commonly referred to as pseudoascites. *(61:97)*

616. **(A)** The two open arrows point to the cerebellar hemispheres. *(61:36)*

617. **(D)** The anechoic structure the closed arrow points to is the cisterna magna. *(61:38)*

618. **(A)** The structures the black arrows point to are the kidneys. *(61:111)*

619. **(B)** The structures the black arrows point to are the adrenal glands. The shape and echo texture of the fetal adrenal glands is similar to the kidneys; however, the adrenal glands are recognized by their position and triangular shape. *(61:113)*

620. **(A)** The structure the closed arrow points to is the umbilical cord. A common pitfall is the misinterpretation of the umbilical cord as a penis. The penis appears as a solid structure, whereas the umbilical cord could appear as interrupted linear echoes or fluid-filled round areas depending on the plane in which the cord is imaged. *(61:127–129)*

621. **(B)** This transverse sonogram shows three typical ossification centers in the spine. The anterior center is the developing vertebral body and the two posterior centers are the lamina. *(61:64)*

622. **(A)** The structure the open arrow points to is the cervical spine. *(61:67)*

623. **(A)** The structure the "0" arrow points to is the uterine fundus. *(59:287, 376)*

624. **(B)** The structure the "1" arrow points to is the vagina. *(59:287, 376)*

625. **(D)** The structure the "2" arrow points to is the cervix. *(59:287, 376)*

626. **(D)** The structure the arrow points to is the right ovary. *(59:287, 376)*

627. **(D)** The arrows point to the male genitalia demonstrating the scrotum and the penis. *(61:127–130)*

628. **(C)** The structure the open arrow points to is the portal vein/portal sinus. *(61:96)*

629. **(D)** The arrows point to both clavicles. *(61:78)*

630. **(D)** The location of the ovaries is variable, especially in women who have had previous children. *(59:386)*

631. **(A)** The brief evaluation of the kidneys post void is essential to identify any degree of obstructive uropathy (hydronephrosis) resulting from a pelvic mass or pregnancy. *(59:389)*

632. **(A)** The broad ligaments are identified sonographically when surrounded by ascites or when the uterus is retroverted. *(59:389)*

633. **(C)** The most common cause for enlargement of the uterus is pregnancy and a myoma. *(59:394)*

634. **(C)** The uterine texture is normally homogeneous. Myomas usually cause a change in the texture of the myometrium. Focal hypo- and hyperechoic areas or calcifications are suggestive of a myoma. *(59:396)*

635. **(A)** The thickness of the endometrium in the proliferative phase is approximately 2–4 mm. *(59:397)*

636. **(B)** The thickness of the endometrium in the secretory phase is approximately 5–6 mm. *(59:397)*

637. **(A)** In the postmenopausal patient in the absence of estrogen replacement therapy, the thickness of the endometrium is approximately 1–3 mm. *(59:397)*

638. **(D)** The endometrial cavity is central in location. Leiomyomas sometimes cause displacement of its cavity in an eccentric position. *(59:403)*

639. **(D)** All of the above. The muscle groups forming the boundaries of the true pelvis that can be depicted sonographically are iliopsoas, piriform, and obturator. *(59:426)*

640. **(A)** Follicular cysts may be first identified when they approach the size of 4–5 mm. *(59:427)*

641. **(C)** The presence of the proximal tibial epiphyseal ossification center indicates a menstrual age of 35 weeks. *(59:328)*

642. **(C)** The presence of the distal tibial epiphyseal ossification center indicates a menstrual age of 33 weeks. *(59:328)*

643. **(D)** The cisterna magna appears sonographically as an echo-free space inferior to the cerebellum and is best demonstrated sonographically between weeks 16 and 28. *(59:99–100)*

644. **(D)** Cranial bone defect resulting in herniation of the brain and meninges is referred to as encephalocele. *(59:125)*

645. **(C)** Incompetent cervix denotes premature dilation of the endocervical canal in pregnancy before the onset of labor. *(59:408)*

646. **(C)** Focal myometrial contraction (FMC) is a physiologic mass that is produced by uterine contractions. The features that distinguish this mass from myomas are (1) FMC disappears with time, (2) FMC is always homogeneous and myomas are heterogeneous in texture, (3) FMC does *not* attentuate but myomas do, (4) FMC distorts only the endometrial surface and myomas tend to distort both the serosal and endometrial contour. *(59:43)*

647. **(C)** The two arrows point to the right and left iliac crests. The sacral spine is seen in the center. *(3:92)*

648. **(B)** This sagittal sonogram demonstrates both the tibia and fibula. *(59:148)*

649. **(A)** This image is a cross-section through the leg demonstrating the tibia and fibula. The tibia is centrally located, whereas the fibula is eccentric in position. *(61:146)*

650. **(A)** This image is a four-chamber view of the fetal heart. The solid arrow points to foramen ovale. In the fetus, blood is shunted from the right atrium to the left atrium through this opening. *(61:81)*

651. **(B)** The open arrow points to the interventricular septum that separates the ventricles. *(61:81)*

652. **(D)** A fold of peritoneum extending from the posterior surface of the uterus to the anterior rectum forms a deep pouch known as the pouch of Douglas, or posterior cul-de-sac. This image demonstrates fluid accumulation in this region. *(59:394)*

653. **(A)** The arrows point to the broad ligaments, a double fold of peritoneum that extends from the lateral margins of the uterus to the pelvic side walls, forming a partition across the pelvic cavity dividing it into anterior and posterior compartments. The uterus and proximal tube are suspended by the broad ligament but not the fimbriated end of the fallopian tube. *(59:386–391)*

654. **(D)** The open arrow points to focal myometrial contraction (FMC) that can easily be distinguished from the placenta or a myoma by its physiologic and sonographic characteristics. *(59:42–43)*

655. **(B)** The open arrow points to the distal femoral epiphysis ossification center. *(61:153)*

656. **(A)** The open arrow points to the internal os of the cervix. *(61:305)*

657. **(C)** The solid arrow points to the endocervical canal. *(59:305)*

658. **(B)** The open arrow points to the inferior vena cava (IVC). Next to and parallel with the IVC is the aorta. *(61:86)*

659. **(D)** The open arrow points to a reverberation artifact (echoes that are not real). *(61:375–384)*

660. **(A)** The fetal component of the placenta. *(59:22)*

661. **(B)** The maternal component of the placenta. *(59:22)*

662. **(D)** The two general types of intrauterine growth retardation (IUGR) are symmetrical and asymmetrical. Measurements of the fetal body parts can depict the ratio changes in the fetal body organ size. Asymmetrical IUGR results from uteroplacental insufficiency. This results in an abnormal fetal growth in which weight gain stops but the head growth is maintained. Both the head to abdominal circumference (H/AC) and the femur length to ab-

dominal circumference (FL/AC) ratios are helpful in predicting abnormal growth symmetry. *(29:161–171)*

663. **(D)** This transverse sonogram demonstrates jet echoes discharged at a slight angle to the left. The spontaneous intervals of urine spurting into the urinary bladder from the ureteral orifice are seen during bladder filling on real-time sonography. The shear force of fluid entering fluid produces a disturbance (turbulence) within the urine-filled bladder call "ureteral jet." *(59:389–390)*

664. **(C)** The open arrows in this sagittal sonogram point to the iliac bones. *(61:71)*

665. **(B)** The cistern magna appears as a fluid-filled space located between the dorsum of the cerebellar hemisphere and the inner calvarium and is best identified from 15 to 28 weeks of gestation, after which the ability to image this region declines sharply. *(65:90;67;52)*

666. **(A)** This sonogram demonstrates the labia majora. *(61:31)*

667. **(D)** The solid arrow points to fluid in the vagina, hematocolpos and Gartner's duct cyst has similar sonographic appearance. Urine in the vagina also can give similar sonographic appearance. Hematometra is blood in the uterus. *(41:56)*

668. **(A)** The open arrow points to fluid in the posterior cul-de-sac. *(63:610)*

669. **(A)** The arrow points to hydrocephalus. *(59:112)*

670. **(B)** The arrow points to the falx cerebri. *(61:29)*

671. **(D)** The arrow points to the lateral ventricle. *(61:29)*

672. **(A)** The arrow points to the inferior vena cava. *(61:119)*

673. **(B)** The arrow points to the umbilical cord. *(59:221)*

674. **(A)** The arrowhead points to the umbilical vein. *(59:221)*

675. **(C)** The arrow points to the umbilical artery. *(59:221)*

676. **(D)** The arrow points to the dividing membrane in a twin pregnancy. *(59:304)*

677. **(A)** The arrow points to fetal ascites. *(59:218)*

678. **(D)** The arrow points to pleural effusion. *(59:216)*

679. **(C)** The arrowhead points to the fetal lung *(59:216)*

680. **(B)** The arrowhead points to the fetal liver *(59:213)*

681. **(B)** The arrow points to a relatively large mass extending from the fetal anterior abdominal wall. Note the intrahepatic portion of the umbilical vein coursing directly through the mass and the echotexture of the mass similar to liver echotexture. These findings are characteristic of an omphalocele. *(59:245)*

682. **(C)** In the four-chamber view, the foramen ovale, which normally moves in and out of the left atrium, and the moderator band within the apex of the right ventricle shows left/right orientation in the fetal heart. *(72:344)*

683. **(B)** Flow through the foramen ovale is right to left. The blood flow is directed from the inferior vena cava through the right atrium by the eustachian valve and crista dividens. Blood flow then traverses the foramen ovale to the left atrium. *(84:335)*

684. **(C)** The eustachian valve acts as a steering device, along the crista dividens, to direct blood flow to the foramen ovale. *(87:813)*

685. **(C)** When performing M-mode on a fetal heart, both atria and ventricles must be evaluated. Arrhythmias may originate either from the atrium or ventricles and may or may not conduct to each other. *(77:793)*

686. **(B)** Without question, the four-chamber view is the most important view in fetal echocardiography. Most fetal cardiac abnormalities will be initially seen in the four-chamber view, which should be performed on all obstetric sonograms. *(68:529, 72:343)*

687. **(D)** 60% of the right atrial blood volume will traverse the foramen ovale, whereas the remaining 40% will traverse the tricuspid valve for right-hearted circulation. *(73:345)*

688. **(A)** 90% of the right ventricular outflow tract/main pulmonary artery blood volume continues through the ductus arteriosus. *(73:345;85:565)*

689. **(B)** Because 90% of the main pulmonary artery volume continues through the ductus arteriosus, the remaining 10% of this volume circulates through the pulmonary arteries/veins. *(85:565;73:345)*

690. **(D)** 96% of all fetal cardiac malformations can be identified from the fetal four-chamber view. *(71:648)*

691. **(C)** If a sonographer is looking for narrowing of the aortic arch, one would have to image this structure; therefore, the aortic arch (suprasternal) view would be the ideal one to visualize this area. *(73:343;76:249)*

692. **(A)** To easily visualize the great vessels, the five-chamber view with anterior angulation of the transducer will allow the sonographer to see the aorta and main pulmonary artery. *(73:345;76:249;74:300)*

693. **(A)** Generally, the left heart perfuses the fetal cranium. *(73:345;77:982;86:43;83:12010;88:813)*

694. **(B)** The fetal right heart generally perfuses the systemic circulation of the fetus. *(73:345;77:982;86:43;83:12010;88:813)*

695. **(A)** The crista dividens is a part of the eustachian valve that connects to the foramen ovale for right to left shunting of fetal atrial blood flow. *(73:345;85:565)*

696. **(C)** Because the umbilical vein carries highly oxygenated blood, the right atrium, via the inferior vena cava, has the highest oxygenated blood in the fetal heart. *(73:345;88:811;85:565)*

697. **(B)** The ductus arteriosus becomes the ligamentum arteriosus after birth. *(85:565;88:811)*

698. **(C)** The moderator band is the other portion of anatomy one should strive for for left/right fetal cardiac orientation. The moderator band lies within the right ventricular apex. *(73:343)*

699. **(B)** Because the fetal right heart would not be perfusing the systemic circulation, the fetal left heart would continue to perfuse the cranial aspects of the fetus. *(73:343;85:565;88:811;22:590)*

700. **(D)** Doppler in fetal echocardiography is helpful in diagnosing dysplastic valves, septal defects, and great vessel abnormalities. It is not useful in diagnosing fetal arrhythmias because contractions over time, both atrial and ventricular, are needed for fetal arrhythmia diagnosis. *(77:982;78:792;81:250)*

701. **(B)** In the fetus, the apex of the fetal heart lies perpendicular to the fetal spine because the lungs are not aerated and the fetal diaphragm remains in a high position. *(73:343)*

702. **(B)** Because the fetal heart lies perpendicular to the fetal spine, when imaging the fetal heart in its short/transverse axis, the sonographic plane will be imaging the fetus in a sagittal plane. *(73:343;74:299)*

703. **(D)** The right atrium primarily receives blood from the inferior vena cava and superior vena cava. This fetal cardiac anatomy is not different from adult cardiac anatomy. *(73:343;76:249)*

704. **(A)** The decline of the S/D ratio during pregnancy is a reflection of the decreasing resistance to flow offered by the placenta as the fetus matures. As pregnancy progresses, the fetal vessels occupy a greater portion of the chorionic villus and there is a progressive increase in umbilical blood flow. *(89:988)*

705. **(D)** The pulsatility index = (A-B)/mean. This index is capable of reflecting changes in the waveform shape that do not affect peak systolic or end-diastolic shift. It does require the digitizing of the entire time-velocity waveform. See Fig. 8–117. *(90:291)*

706. **(E)** The flow velocity waveform of term pregnancies in early labor did not change despite uterine contractions, amniotomy infusion of dilute concentrations of oxytocin, and the usual doses of analgesics given intravenously. *(92:35)*

707. **(C)** The wall filter may be necessary to remove low-frequency, high-intensity Doppler signals produced by pulsatile movements of the vessel wall. When the wall filter is set too high, usable information in systole and diastole may be removed. *(91:570)*

708. **(A)** The umbilical artery has a typical triangular appearance derived from the relatively slow upstroke of systolic velocity, itself a consequence of the elasticity of the long arterial segment between the heart and the point of sampling. See Fig. 8–118. *(90:267)*

709. **(D)** The A/B ratio of the umbilical artery in the third trimester is less than 3.0. Studies are interpreted to mean that the impedance to blood flow in the umbilical arterial circulation decreases with advancing maturity with increased forward flow throughout the cardiac cycle. *(92:34)*

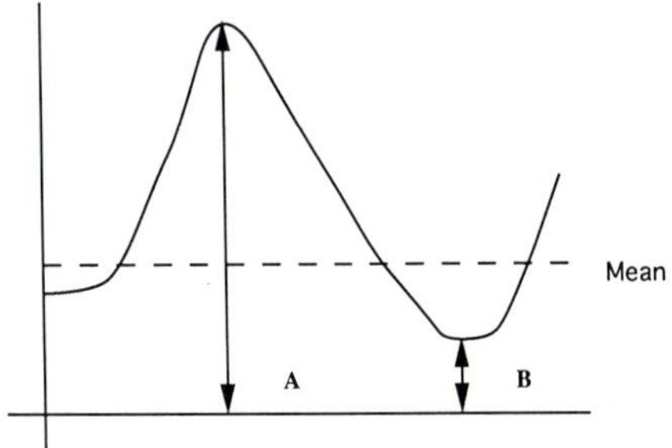

Figure 8–117. Waveform demonstrating peak-systolic (**A**) and end-diastolic (**B**) pressures.

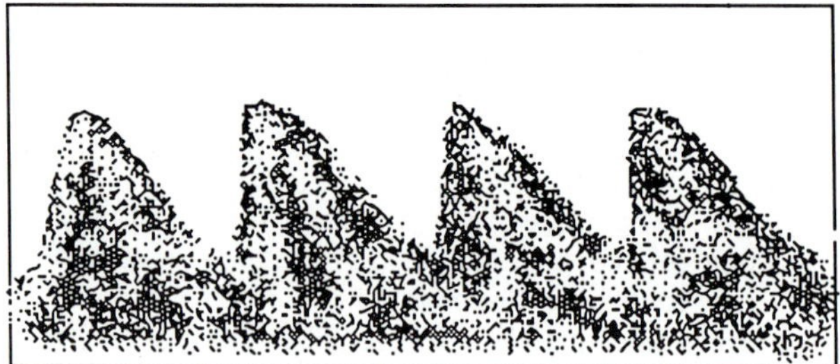

Figure 8–118. Waveform demonstrating an umbilical artery.

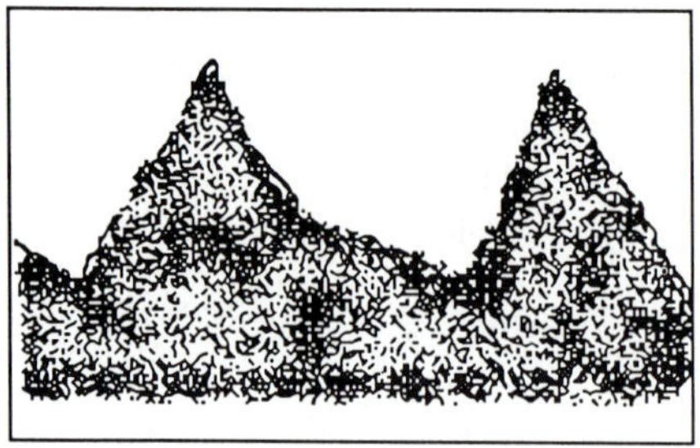

Figure 8–120. Waveform demonstrating a uteroplacental artery.

710. **(B)** The pourcelot or resistance index = (A-B)/A. As diastolic flow approaches zero, the pourcelot index approaches unity. *(90:290)*

711. **(D)** All of the above. Fetuses of diabetic women in whom blood glucose is poorly controlled may have higher A/B ratios of the umbilical arteries. Pregnancies complicated by hypertension, proteinuria, and suspected fetal growth retardation often had abnormal uterine artery flow velocity waveforms (FVWs). *(92:35.38)*

712. **(E)** All of the above. Sector scanners have the advantages of being suitable for both the uterine and fetal circulations but have the disadvantage that conventional systems are limited in their ability to measure volumetric flow rates. Electronically steered sector scanners offer real-time imaging at a reduced frame rate at the same time pulsed Doppler signal is being acquired. Linear arrays have a well-established place in obstetric imaging. See Fig. 8–119. *(90:266)*

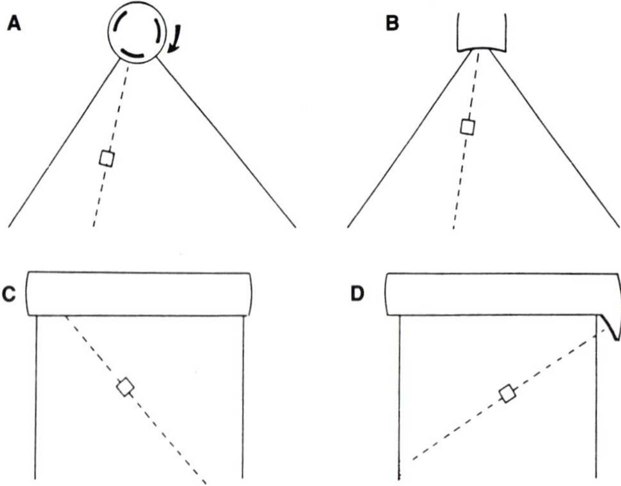

Figure 8–119. Four common configurations of the duplex scanner: (**A**) the mechanical sector scanner; (**B**) the electronically steered sector scanner; (**C**) the electronically steered linear array; (**D**) the linear array with offset Doppler transducer. (*Reprinted with permission from Burns PN, J Clin Ultrasound 15:575, 1987.*)

713. **(A)** The fetal descending aorta offers an alternative method of studying fetal cardiac dysrhythmias. Information on timing and relative aortic stroke volume over a cardiac cycle can be obtained by inspection of the sonogram. *(91:590)*

714. **(B)** Umbilical artery A/B ratios near the placenta are lower than those near the fetal abdomen. The fall in ratio from the fetal to the placental end of the cord may be the result of dampening and attenuation of the propagated wave. *(93:174)*

715. **(C)** The uteroplacental arteries have a pattern of low pulsatility and high end diastolic frequencies. See Fig. 8–120. *(94:365)*

716. **(B)** The A/B ratio of the uterine or arcuate artery is less than 2.6. Persistence or development of a dicrotic notch in the third trimester is correlated with intrauterine growth retardation and preeclampsia. *(90:292)*

717. **(A)** The waveform of the umbilical artery has a relatively slow rise time in systole, followed by a decelerating flow that persists throughout diastole. The umbilical vein may be seen as a continuous flow vessel beneath the baseline. *(90:292)*

REFERENCES

1. Callen PW. *Ultrasonography in OB/GYN,* 2nd ed. Philadelphia: WB Saunders, 1983.
2. Pritchard JA, MacDonald PC. *Williams Obstetrics,* 16th ed. New York: Appleton-Century-Crofts, 1980.
3. Sanders RC, James AE. *The Principles and Practices of Ultrasonography in Obstetrics and Gynecology,* 2nd ed. New York: Appleton-Century-Crofts, 1980.
4. Miller BS, Keane CB. *Encyclopedia and Dictionary of Medicine and Nursing.* Philadelphia: WB Saunders, 1972.
5. Van Bergen WS. *Obstetric Ultrasound Application and Principles.* Menlo Park, CA: Addison-Wesley, 1980.

6. Burrow PE, Lyons EA, Phillips JH, et al. Intrauterine membranes: sonographic findings and clinical significance. *J Clin Ultrasound* **10:**1–8, January 1982.
7. Taber BZ. *Manual of Gynecologic and Obstetric Emergencies.* Philadelphia: WB Saunders, 1979.
8. Agnew LRC, Aviado DM, Brody JI, et al. *Dorland's Illustrated Medical Dictionary,* 24th ed. Philadelphia: WB Saunders, 1965.
9. Morris W. *The American Heritage Dictionary of the English Language.* New York: Houghton Mifflin, 1971.
10. Taylor KJW, Jacobson P, Talmont CA, et al. *Manual of Ultrasonography.* New York: Churchill Livingstone, 1980.
11. Netter FH, Oppenheimer E, Rock J. *The Ciba Collection of Medical Illustrations: Reproductive System,* Vol. 2, 4th ed. Summit, NJ: Ciba Pharmaceutical, 1965.
12. Anderson BG, Shapiro PJ. *Obstetrics for the Nurse,* 3rd ed. New York: Delmar, 1979.
13. Danforth DN, Dignam WJ, Hendricks CH, et al. *Obstetrics and Gynecology,* 3rd ed. New York: Harper & Row, 1977.
14. Fleischer AC, James AE. *Introduction to Diagnostic Sonography.* New York: John Wiley & Sons, 1980.
15. Mayden KL. Orbital distance measurements: techniques for prenatal diagnosis and dating. *Med Ultrasound* **8:**117, August 1984.
16. Mayden KL, Tortora M, Berkowitz RL, et al. Orbital diameters: a new parameter for prenatal diagnosis and dating. *Am J Obstet Gynecol* **144:**289, 1982.
17. Robbins SL, Angell M. *Basic Pathology,* 2nd ed. Philadelphia: WB Saunders, 1971.
18. Hobbins J, Winsberg F. *Ultrasonography in Obstetrics and Gynecology.* Baltimore: Williams & Wilkins, 1977.
19. Sanders R. *Ultrasound Annual 1982.* New York: Raven Press, 1982.
20. Sarti DA, Sample WF. *Diagnostic Ultrasound Text and Cases.* Boston: GK Hall, 1980.
21. Hole WH Jr. *Human Anatomy and Physiology,* 2nd ed. Dubuque, Iowa: Wm C Brown, 1978.
22. Moore KL, Read G. *The Developing Human,* 3rd ed. Philadelphia: WB Saunders, 1982.
23. King DL. *Diagnostic Ultrasound.* St. Louis: CV Mosby, 1974.
24. Burrows PE, Lyons EA, Phillips JH, et al. Intrauterine membranes: sonographic findings and clinical significance. *J Clin Ultrasound* **10:**1–8, January, 1982.
25. Athey PA, Hadlock FP. *Ultrasound in Obstetrics and Gynecology.* St. Louis: CV Mosby, 1981.
26. Kobayashi M. *Illustrated Manual of Ultrasound in Obstetrics and Gynecology,* 2nd ed. Tokyo: Igaku-Shoin, 1980.
27. Jones HW Jr, Jones SG. *Novak's Textbook of Gynecology,* 10th ed. Baltimore: Williams & Wilkins, 1981.
28. Benson RC, Schaubert LV. *Current Obstetric and Gynecologic Diagnosis and Treatment,* 4th ed. Los Altos, CA: Lange Medical Publications, 1982.
29. Sanders RC, James AE. *The Principles and Practices of Ultrasonography in Obstetrics and Gynecology,* 3rd ed. Norwalk, CT: Appleton-Century-Crofts, 1985.
30. Nicholas K, Taylor KJ, Rosenfield AT, et al. Combined use of serum hCG and sonography in the diagnosis of ectopic pregnancy. *Am J Roentgenol* **141:**609–615, 1983.
31. Hagen-Ansert SL. *Textbook of Diagnostic Ultrasonography,* 2nd ed. St. Louis: CV Mosby, 1983.
32. Raymond HW, Zwiebel JW, Gottesfeld KR, et al. *Seminars in Ultrasound: Obstetrical Ultrasound Update,* Vol. 1, No. 4. New York: Grune & Stratton, 1980.
33. Billah KL, Shah K, Odwin C. Ultrasonic diagnosis and management of acardius anencephalic twin pregnancy. *Med Ultrasound* **8:**108–109, August 1984.
34. Hobbins JC, Winsberg F, Berkowitz RL. *Ultrasonography in Obstetrics and Gynecology,* 2nd ed. Baltimore: Williams & Wilkins, 1983.
35. Chinn DH, Bolding DB, Callen PW, et al. Ultrasonographic identification of fetal lower extremity epiphyseal ossification centers. *Radiology* **147:**815–818, June 1983.
36. Hayt E. *Medico-legal Aspects of Hospital Records,* 2nd ed. Berwyn, IL: Physicians Record, 1977.
37. Southwick AF, Siedel GJ III. The Law of Hospital and Health Care Administration. University of Michigan, Health Care Administration Press, 1978.
38. Odwin C. Sonographic appearance of a vaginal contraceptive sponge. J DMS, **1**(2):65–67, March 1985.
39. Fleischer AC, James AE Jr. *Real-Time Sonography: Textbook and Videotape.* Norwalk, CT: Appleton-Century-Crofts, 1984.
40. Robbins SL, Cotran RS. *Pathologic Basis of Disease,* 2nd ed. Philadelphia: WB Saunders, 1979.
41. Kenneth T. *Atlas of Ultrasonography,* Vols 1 and 2, 2nd ed. New York: Churchill Livingstone, 1985.
42. Nyberg DA, Filly RA, Mahony BS, et al. Early gestation: correlation of hCG levels and sonographic identification. *Am J Radiol* **144:**951–954, 1985.
43. Jeanty P, Beck G, Chervenak F, et al. A comparison of sector and linear array scanners for the measurement of the fetal femur. *J Ultrasound Med* **4:**525, 1985.
44. Nyberg D, Laing F, Filly R, et al. Ultrasonographic differentiation of the gestational sac of early intrauterine pregnancy from the pseudogestational sac of ectopic pregnancy. *Radiology* **146:**775, 1983.
45. Jeffery R, Laing F. Sonography of the low-lying placenta: value of Trendelenburg and traction scans. *Am J Roentgenol* **137:**547, 1981.
46. Bernard K, Cooperberg P. Sonographic differentiation between blighted ovum and early viable pregnancy. *Am J Radiol* **144:**597, 1985.

47. Mahony B, Filly R, Nyberg D, et al. Sonographic evaluation of ectopic pregnancy. *J Ultrasound Med* **4**:221, 1985.
48. Callen P, Filly R, Munyes T. Intrauterine contraceptive device. *Am J Roentgenol* **135**:797, 1980.
49. Slotnick N, Filly R, Callen P, et al. Sonography as a procedure complementary to α-fetoprotein testing for neural tube defects. *J Ultrasound Med* **1**:319, 1982.
50. Graham D, Johnson T, Winn K, et al. The role of sonography in the prenatal diagnosis and management of encephalocele. *J Ultrasound Med* **1**:111, 1982.
51. Klein M, Kosloske A, Hertzier, J: Congenital defect of the abdominal wall: a review of the experience in New Mexico. *JAMA* **245**(16), 1981.
52. Fleischer A, Pittaway D. Uses of sonography for moneritering ovarian follicular development. In *Ultrasound Annual.* New York: Raven Press, 1983.
53. Fleischer A, Wentz A, Jones H. Ultrasound evaluation of the ovary. In Callen P (ed): *Ultrasonography in Obstetrics and Gynecology,* 2nd ed. Philadelphia: WB Saunders, 1983.
54. Callen P. *Ultrasonography in Obstetrics and Gynecology: Ultrasound of the Uterus,* 2nd ed. Philadelphia: WB Saunders, 1983.
55. Goldstein S, Subramanyam B, Raghavendra B, et al. Subchorionic bleeding in threatened abortion: sonographic findings and significance. *Am J Roentgenol* **141**:975, 1983.
56. Goldberg BB, Kotler MN, Ziskin MC, et al. *Diagnostic Uses of Ultrasound.* New York: Grune & Stratton, 1975.
57. Sanders RC, Campbell J, Guidi S, et al. *Clinical Sonography: A Practical Guide.* Boston: Little Brown, 1984.
58. Jeanty P, Romero R. *Obstetrical Ultrasound.* New York: McGraw-Hill, 1984.
59. Callen PW. *Ultrasonography in Obstetrics and Gynecology,* 2nd ed. Philadelphia: WB Saunders, 1983.
60. Romero R, Pilu G, Jeanty P, et al. *Prenatal Diagnosis of Congenital Anomalies.* Norwalk, CT: Appleton & Lange, 1988.
61. Bowerman RA. *Atlas of Normal Fetal Ultrasonographic Anatomy.* Chicago: Year Book Medical Publications, 1986.
62. Sabbagha R. *Diagnostic Ultrasound: Application to OB/GYN,* 2nd ed. Philadelphia: JB Lippincott, 1987.
63. Fleischer A, James E. *Diagnostic Sonography: Principles and Clinical Applications.* Philadelphia: WB Saunders, 1989.
64. Fleischer A, Romero R, Manning F. *The Principles and Practice of Ultrasonography in Obstetrics and Gynecology,* 4th ed. Norwalk, CT: Appleton & Lange, 1991.
65. Nyberg D, Mahony B, Pretorius DH: *Diagnostic Ultrasound of Fetal Anomalies: Test and Atlas.* St. Louis: Mosby-Year Book, 1990.
66. Fleischer A, Kepple D. *Transvaginal Sonography: A Clinical Atlas.* Philadelphia: JB Lippincott, 1992.
67. Kurtz A, Goldberg B. *Obstetrical Measurements in Ultrasound: A Reference Manual.* Chicago: Year Book Medical Publications, 1988.
68. Allan LD, Chita SK, Al-Ghazali, et al. Doppler echocardiographic evaluation of the normal human fetal heart. *Br Heart J* **57**:528–533, 1987.
69. Allan LD, Joseph MC, Boyd EGCA, et al. M-mode echocardiography in the developing human fetus. *Br Heart J* **47**:573–583, 1982.
70. Benacerraf BR, Pober BR, Sanders SP. Accuracy of fetal echocardiography. *Radiology* **165**:847–849, 1987.
71. Copel JA, Pilu G, Green J, et al. Fetal echocardiographic screening for congenital heart disease: the importance of the four-chamber view. *Am J Obstet Gynecol* **157**:648–655, 1987.
72. Cyr DR, Guntheroth WG, Mack LA, et al. A systematic approach to fetal echocardiography using real-time/two-dimensional sonography. *J Ultrasound Med* **5**:343–350, 1986.
73. Cyr DR, Komarniski CA, Guntheroth WG, Mack LA. The prevalence of imaging fetal cardiac anatomy. *J Diagn Med Sonography* **6**:299–304, 1988.
74. DeVore GR. Fetal echocardiography: a new frontier. *Clin Obstet Gynecol* **27**:359–377, 1984.
75. DeVore GR, Donnerstein RL, Kleinman CS, et al. Fetal echocardiography. I. normal anatomy as determined by real-time–directed M-mode ultrasound. *Am J Obstet Gynecol* **144**:249, 1982.
76. DeVore GR, Siassi B, Platt LD. Fetal echocardiography. IV. M-mode assessment of ventricular size and contractility during the second and third trimesters of pregnancy in the normal fetus. *Am J Obstet Gynecol* **150**:981–988, 1984.
77. DeVore GR, Siassi B, Platt L. Fetal echocardiography. III. the diagnosis of cardiac arrhythmias using real-time–directed M-mode ultrasound. *Am J Obstet Gynecol* **146**:792, 1983.
78. DeVore GR, Horenstein J, Siassi B, Platt LD. Fetal echocardiography. VII. Doppler color flow mapping: a new technique for the diagnosis of congenital heart disease. *Am J Obstet Gynecol* **156**:1054–1064, 1987.
79. Hertzberg BS, Mahoney BS, Bowie JD. First trimester fetal cardiac activity: sonographic documentation of a progressive early rise in heart rate. *J Ultrasound Med* **7**:573–575, 1988.
80. Huhta JC, Strasburger JF, Carpenter RJ, et al. Pulsed Doppler fetal echocardiography. *J Clin Ultrasound* **13**:247–254, 1985.
81. Jeanty P, Romero R, Hobbins JC. Fetal pericardial fluid: a normal finding of the second half of gestation. *Am J Obstet Gynecol* **149**:529–532, 1984.
82. Kenny JF, Plappert T, Doubilet P. Changes in intracardiac blood flow velocities and right and left ventricular stroke volumes with gestational age in the

normal human fetus: a prospective Doppler echocardiographic study. *Circulation* **74:**1208–1216, 1986.

83. Kleinman CS, Copel JA, Weinstein EM, et al. Treatment of fetal supraventricular tachyarrhythmias. *J Clin Ultrasound* **13:**265–273, 1985.
84. Moore KL. *The Developing Human: Clinically Oriented Embryology,* 3rd ed. Philadelphia: WB Saunders, 1982.
85. Reed KL, Meijboom EJ, Sahn DJ, et al. Cardiac Doppler flow velocities in human fetuses. *Circulation* **73:**41–46, 1986.
86. Reed KL, Sahn DJ, Scagnelli S, et al. Doppler echocardiographic studies of diastolic function in the human fetal heart: changes during gestation. *J Am Coll Cardiol* **8:**391–395, 1986.
87. Rudolph AM. Distribution and regulation of blood flow in the fetal and neonatal lamb. *Circulation Res* **57:**811–821, 1985.
88. Sahn DJ, Lange LW, Allen HD, et al. Quantitative real-time cross-sectional echocardiography in the developing normal human fetus and newborn. *Circulation* **62:**588–597, 1980.
89. Schulman H, Fleischer A, Stern W et al. Umbilical velocity wave ratios in human pregnancy. *Am J Obstet Gynecol* **148:**985–990, 1984.
90. Taylor KJ, Burns PN, Wells P. *Clinical Applications of Doppler Ultrasound.* New York: Raven Press, 1988.
91. Griffin D, Cohen-Overbeek T, Campbell S. Fetal and utero-placental blood flow. *Clin Obstet Gynecol* **10**(3):565–602, 1983.
92. Rightmire D. Clinical doppler ultrasonography: Uterine and umbilical blood flow. *Clin Obstet Gynecol* **31**(1):27–43, 1988.
93. Mehalek KE, Rosenberg J, Berkowithz, GS et al. Umbilical and uterine artery flow velocity waveforms: effect of the sampling site on Doppler ratios. *J Ultrasound Med* **8**(4):171–176, 1989.
94. Campbell S, Bewley S, Cohen-Overbeek T. Investigation of the uteroplacental circulation by Doppler ultrasound. *Semin Perinatol* **11:**362–368, 1987.
95. Willams JD, Zuspan FP. *Manual of Obstetrics and Gynecology OB/GYN.* St. Louis: CV Mosby, 1990.

CHAPTER 9

SONOGRAPHIC AND DOPPLER INVESTIGATION OF THE PERIPHERAL VEINS AND ARTERIES AND THE CEREBROVASCULAR SYSTEM

PART I
Peripheral Veins and Arteries

Sandra Katanick and Thomas G. Hoffman

Study Guide

VENOUS ANATOMY

The three distinct tissue layers of a vein are the tunica intima, tunica media, and tunica adventitia.

Tunica intima. The innermost lining of the vein consisting of endothelial tissue. Semilunar valves are formed by folds of endothelial tissue.

Tunica media. The middle layer of the vein and varies in thickness in different veins. The superficial veins have a thicker layer than many deep veins. It consists of varying degrees of connective and smooth muscle tissue.

Tunica adventitia. The outer layer of the vein consisting of collagen and smooth muscle.

Venous Valves

Venous valves are found in the tunica intima. They are thin, paired structures consisting of endothelial and connective tissue. A normal valve allows blood to flow only in a forward direction. The valve is found in a broadened area of the vein called a valve sinus. Valves open in the deep system when venous blood is forced upward by muscular contractions of the calf (Fig. 9–1).

Valves close when pressure on the venous blood is released. Blood pools in the valve sinus when the valve is closed. A functioning valve is said to be competent when it will not allow reversal of blood flow (Fig. 9–2).

Formation of deep vein thrombosis in the valve sinus may cause injury to the valve. Valve leaflets may become frozen in the open position and venous blood will flow retrograde when pressure on the venous system is released. This is referred to as an incompetent valve.

Valves in the deep veins prevent reversal of flow in the deep system. Valves in the communicating veins prevent flow from the deep to superficial veins. Those in the superficial veins prevent flow from the deep to superficial system as well as retrograde flow in the superficial system. Valves are more numerous in the deep calf veins and decrease in number in the popliteal and femoral veins. They are located throughout the greater and lesser saphenous veins. For a comparison of veins and arteries, see Table 9–1.

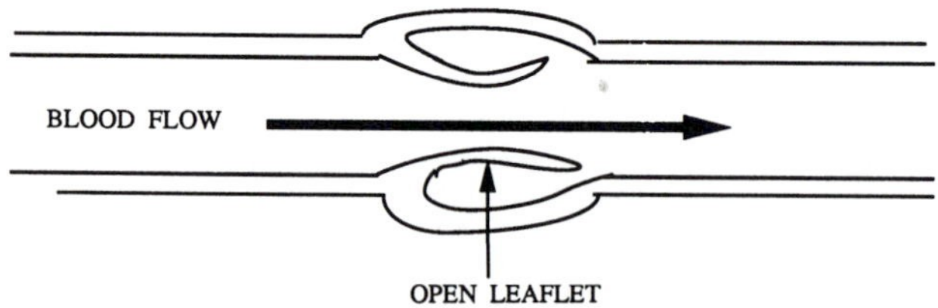

Figure 9–1. Venous valves open.

TABLE 9–1. COMPARISON OF VEINS AND ARTERIES

Veins	Arteries
Thin walls	Thick walls
Walls collapse easily	Rigid walls
Valves	No valves
Nonpulsatile	Pulsatile

Types of Veins

- Deep veins
- Superficial veins
- Communicating veins
- Soleal sinuses

Deep Veins. These veins run in close association with corresponding arteries. There are frequent communications with the superficial veins. The deep veins are comprised of the calf veins (anterior and posterior tibial and peroneal veins); popliteal vein; superficial, deep, and common femoral veins; and external iliac veins (see Figs. 9–13 and 9–14).

Calf Veins. These veins are paired structures and correspond to a single artery. Ten to 12 valves are found in each calf vein. The calf veins join to form the popliteal vein. There are three sets of calf veins.

Anterior Tibial Veins. These veins are found on the anterior surface of the leg between the tibia and fibula.

Posterior Tibial Veins. These veins begin posterior to the medial malleolus and course in the posteromedial calf to become the tibioperoneal trunk.

Peroneal Veins. These veins begin posterior to the lateral malleolus and course in the lateral calf to become the tibioperoneal trunk.

Popliteal Vein. This vein is formed by the confluence of the tibial and peroneal veins. It is found posterior to the popliteal artery and continues to the level of the adductor canal to become the superficial femoral vein. The lesser saphenous vein (superficial vein) joins it posteriorly. The popliteal vein is found behind the knee.

Superficial Femoral Vein. This vein extends from the adductor canal medially to the upper thigh where it joins with the deep femoral vein to form the common femoral vein.

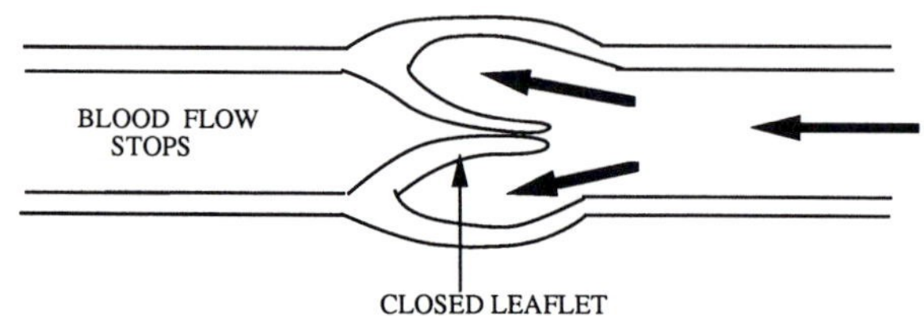

Figure 9–2. Valve leaflet closed.

Deep Femoral Vein (Deep Profunda Vein). This vein brings venous blood flow from the thigh muscle to the common femoral vein.

Common Femoral Vein. This vein lies medial to the artery in the groin. The greater saphenous vein (superficial vein) joins the common femoral vein at its medial aspect. A valve is found at the saphenofemoral junction.

External Iliac Vein. This vein brings venous return from the common femoral vein to the common iliac vein into the inferior vena cava.

Superficial Veins. These veins have no associated arteries. They are located just below the skin surface and communicate with the deep system by communicating veins. The superficial veins are comprised of the greater and lesser saphenous veins (see Figs. 9–13, 9–14, and 9–20).

Greater Saphenous Vein. This vein arises anterior to the medial malleolus in the ankle and travels superiorly along medial aspect of leg until joining with the common femoral vein. It is the longest vein in the body (see Fig. 9–22).

Lesser Saphenous Vein. This vein arises posteriorly from the lateral malleolus and courses posteriorly up the calf to enter the popliteal vein behind the knee. It is often referred to as the stocking-seam vein (see Fig. 9–22).

Communicating Veins. These veins provide a connection of the superficial veins with the deep veins. They contain valves that allow blood flow from the superficial to the deep system.

Soleal Sinuses. These venous sinuses are located in the calf muscle. They carry venous return from the muscle into the posterior tibial and peroneal veins.

Upper Extremity Venous Anatomy

Fig. 9–15 illustrates deep and superficial veins of the upper extremity.

VENOUS HEMODYNAMICS

Respiratory Effect on Venous Flow in the Lower Extremities

Respiration causes phasic changes in venous flow. In the supine position, inspiration causes increased abdominal

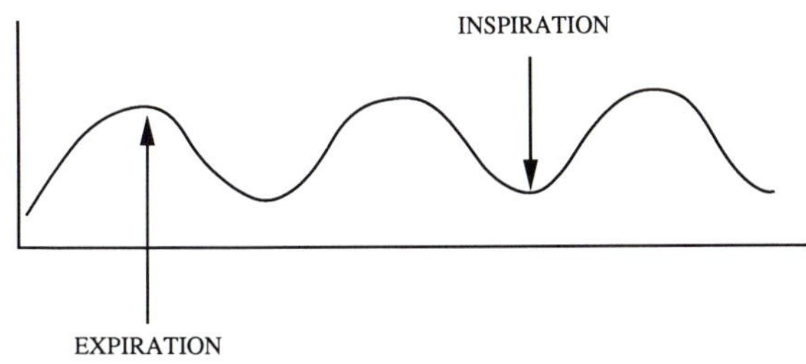

Figure 9–3. Phasic flow pattern.

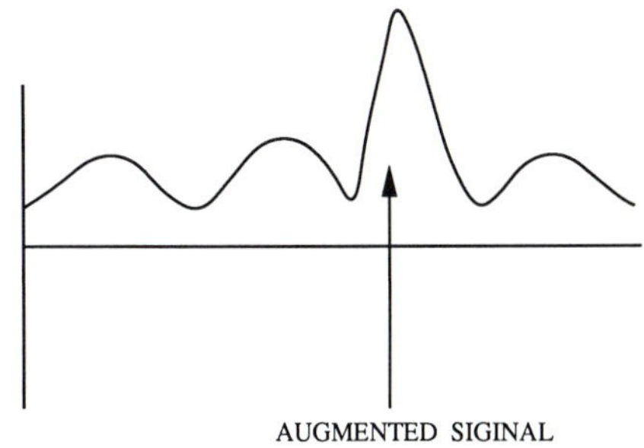

Figure 9–5. Augmentation.

pressure and a decrease of venous flow. On expiration, abdominal pressure decreases and venous flow increases (Fig. 9–3).

The Calf Muscle Pump

Calf muscle contractions cause compression of the venous sinuses and deep veins (posterior and anterior tibial veins, and peroneal veins). This forces blood upward into the more proximal deep venous system. Venous valves prevent reversal of blood flow (Fig. 9–4).

NORMAL DOPPLER SIGNALS

Spontaneity of Flow

A phasic signal should be evident in the femoral and popliteal veins when the Doppler sample volume is placed within the lumen.

Phasic Flow

The flow signal of the normal femoral and popliteal veins should correspond to the respiratory pattern of the patient. In the supine position, the greatest flow is during expiration. A decrease or cessation in flow will be noted during inspiration (Fig. 9–3).

Augmentation

Compression of a venous segment inferior to the site being investigated will enhance flow on the spectral display. This indicates patency of the venous channels from the site of compression to the site of investigation, although it does not exclude partial obstruction of the veins (Fig. 9–5).

Competency of Valves

When examining the common or superficial femoral veins, a Valsalva maneuver (forcibly exhaling against a closed glottis), can be performed by the patient. The venous flow should stop until the maneuver is discontinued. There should be no reversal of venous flow. Release of the maneuver will show a brief compensatory increase in the venous flow velocity (Fig. 9–6)

Valve competency in the lower segment of the femoral vein, popliteal vein, and calf veins can be determined by using a compression maneuver on veins superior to the site being examined. A change in the phasic pattern may be noted but no reversal of venous flow should be demonstrated.

ABNORMAL DOPPLER SIGNALS

Loss of Spontaneous Signal

Placement of the sample volume into the vein results in little or no flow. This may indicate obstruction at the site by thrombus.

Loss of Phasic Signal

A level spectral display may indicate obstruction superior to the site being examined (Fig. 9–7).

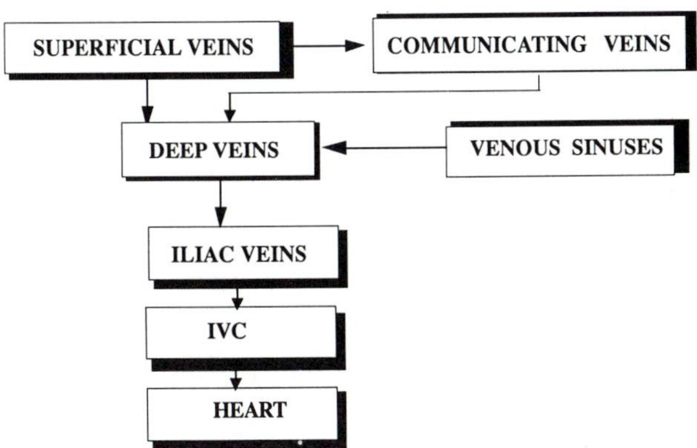

Figure 9–4. Pattern of venous flow in lower extremity.

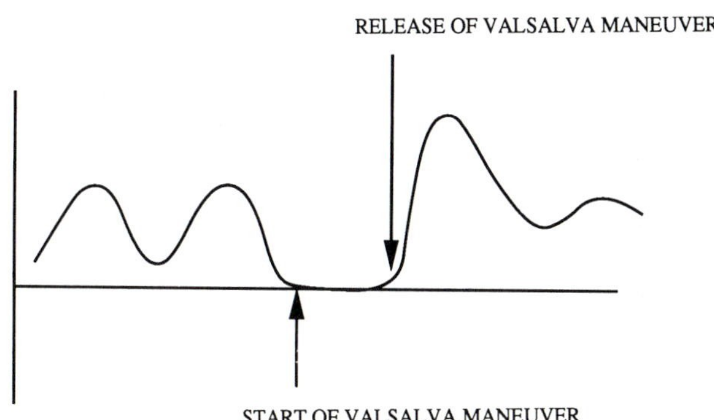

Figure 9–6. Normal venous response to a Valsalva maneuver.

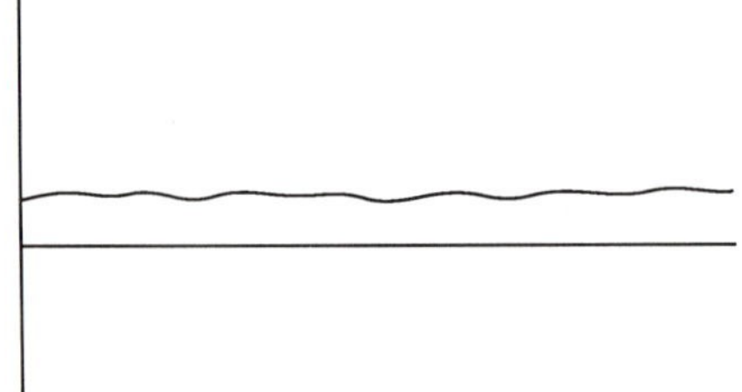

Figure 9–7. Loss of phasic flow pattern.

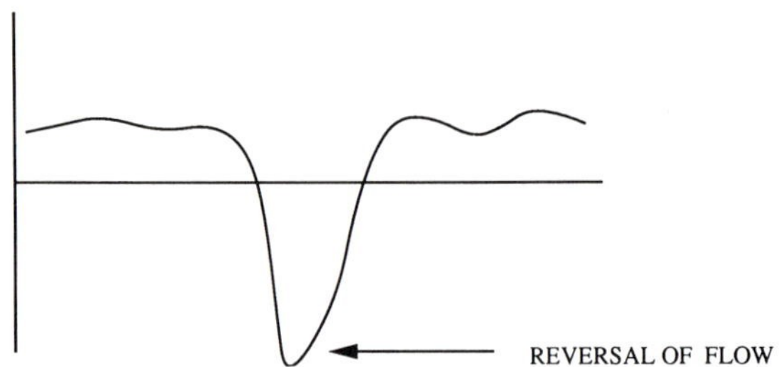

Figure 9–9. Reversal of flow with proximal compression.

Loss of Augmented Blood Flow

When manually compressed, an inferior venous segment will not force venous blood flow through superior channels. This may indicate obstruction of the venous channels from the site of compression to the site being examined (Fig. 9–8).

Reversal of Flow on Spectral Display

When venous flow is reversed, it indicates that venous valves are incompetent. It may be noted during a Valsalva maneuver, with proximal vein compression or in severe cases, with normal respiratory patterns (Fig. 9–9).

Pulsatile Venous Flow

A vein may have pulsatile flow rather than a smooth phasic flow pattern. This may occur with an arteriovenous fistula or with heart failure (Fig. 9–10).

IMAGING CHARACTERISTICS OF LOWER EXTREMITY VEINS (Figs. 9–11 through 9–14)

Compression of Veins

By far the most important imaging characteristic of a vein is its compressibility. When external compression is applied with a transducer, a normal vein will collapse until opposing walls touch. A partially occluded vein will compress only partially and a totally occluded vein will not compress at all (Fig. 9-11).

Respiratory Changes in Vein Diameter

Vein dimensions may change when a patient takes a deep inspiration or performs a Valsalva maneuver. A vein that is totally occluded with thrombus will not change at all (Fig. 9–12).

Sonographic Characteristics of Deep Vein Thrombosis

Acute Deep Vein Thrombosis. In acute deep vein thrombosis, the thrombus may be anechoic (not visible on ultrasound), isoechoic (echogenic filling of vein but less echogenic than vein walls), or hyperechoic (vein filled with bright echoes). The diameter of the vein increases, the obstruction may be partial or complete, and the vein may partially compress but the vein walls do *not* touch completely.

Chronic Deep Vein Thrombosis. In chronic deep vein thrombosis, the thrombus may be hyperechoic (usually brighter than vein walls), is adherent to the vein wall (nonmobile), and becomes rigid (difficult to compress at all). The diameter of the vein decreases, recanalization of the obstructed vein can occur, the vein wall becomes thickened, and collateral veins may begin to appear.

PATHOLOGY OF LOWER EXTREMITY VEINS

Deep Vein Thrombosis (DVT). Deep vein thrombosis of the lower extremity is a major cause for pulmonary embolus. A combination of major contributing factors for DVT formation is known as Virchow's triad: (1) blood stasis, (2) hypercoagulability, and (3) damage to the endothelial layer of the vein.

Influencing Factors. Factors that influence DVT are patient immobility; major abdominal, pelvic, or orthopedic surgery; malignancy; pregnancy and postpartum state; trauma to lower limbs; heart failure; use of oral contraceptives; obesity; and previous DVT.

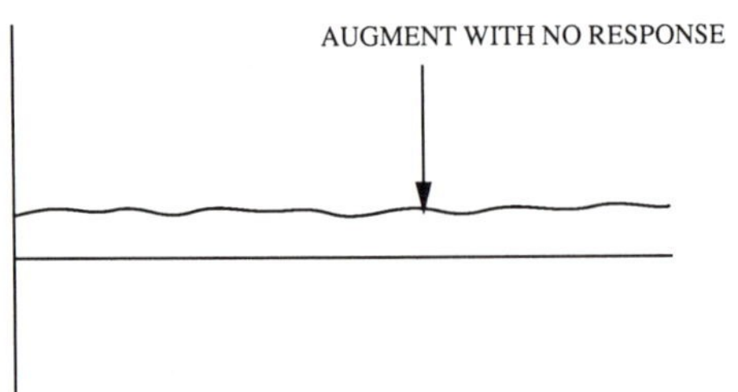

Figure 9–8. Loss of augmented blood flow.

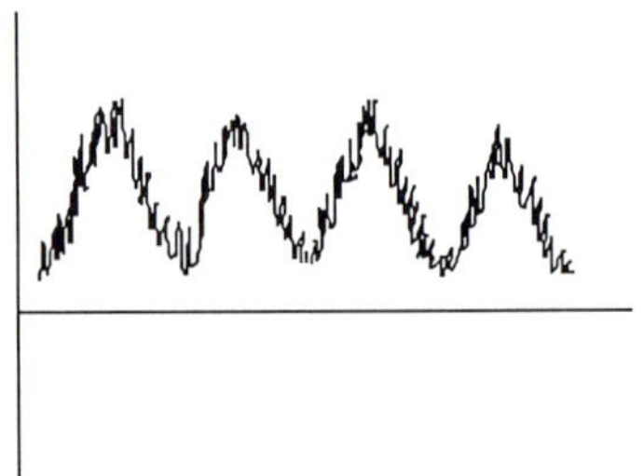

Figure 9–10. Pulsatile venous flow.

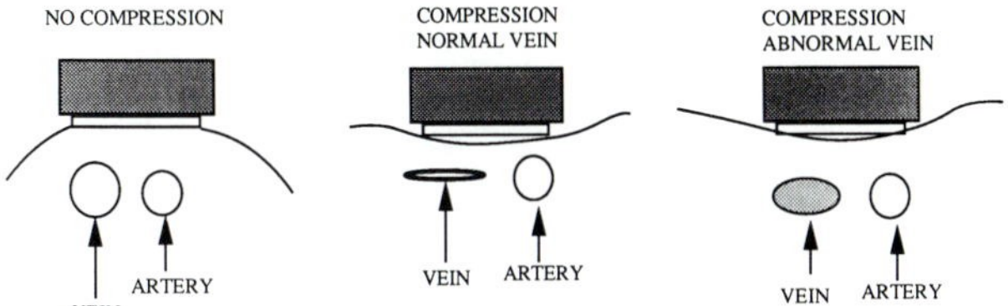

Figure 9–11. Compression of veins.

Symptoms. Clinically, DVT may be difficult to diagnose because patients with DVT may be asymptomatic. However, there may be pain in the lower extremity, swelling and edema, redness, warmth of the thrombosed segment, and fever.

Varicose Veins

Primary Varicose Veins. The valves of the superficial veins are incompetent, which allows venous flow to reverse itself. The greater and lesser saphenous veins are the veins that are affected. The valves of the deep and communicating veins remain competent. Primary varicose veins are usually hereditary.

Secondary Varicose Veins. This occurs when either the valves of the communicating and/or deep systems are incompetent or in the presence of long-standing DVT. Venous blood pools in the lower leg with the eventual formation of collateral venous pathways.

Postthrombotic Syndrome

Venous insufficiency often occurs due to previous DVT. Incompetency of the communicating and deep valves occurs. Retrograde blood flow can be demonstrated by Doppler with proximal compression of the vein. Blood pools in the lower leg. Physical symptoms include ankle edema followed by skin discoloration, skin thickening, and ankle ulceration.

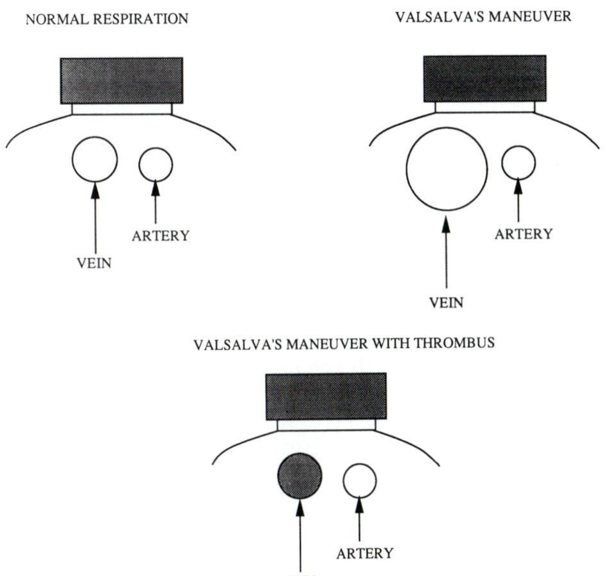

Figure 9–12. Respiratory changes in vein diameter.

Superficial Thrombophlebitis

Thrombus formation occurs in the greater or lesser saphenous veins with an inflammatory reaction. Painful cords (thrombosed veins) may be palpated below the skin surface. Thrombus in the saphenofemoral confluence should be treated as DVT.

Other Lower Extremity Pathology

- cellulitis of the calf with painful swelling
- Baker's cyst causing swelling and pain in the popliteal fossa and calf
- lymphedema causing swelling of the lower extremity
- swelling caused by external compression of pelvic or thigh veins
- muscle pain
- plantaris tear

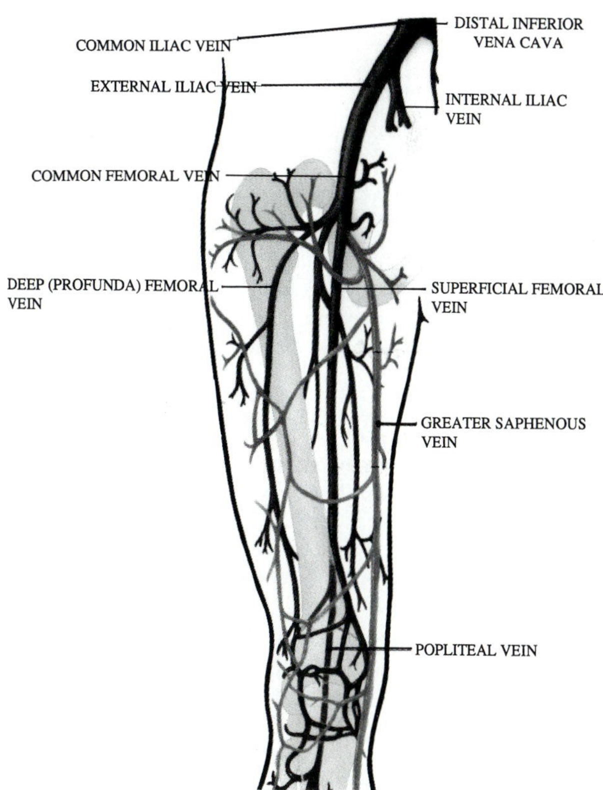

Figure 9–13. Veins of the thigh. *(Reprinted with permission from Abbott Laboratories, North Chicago, IL. Medical illustration by Scott Thorn Barrows, AMI.)*

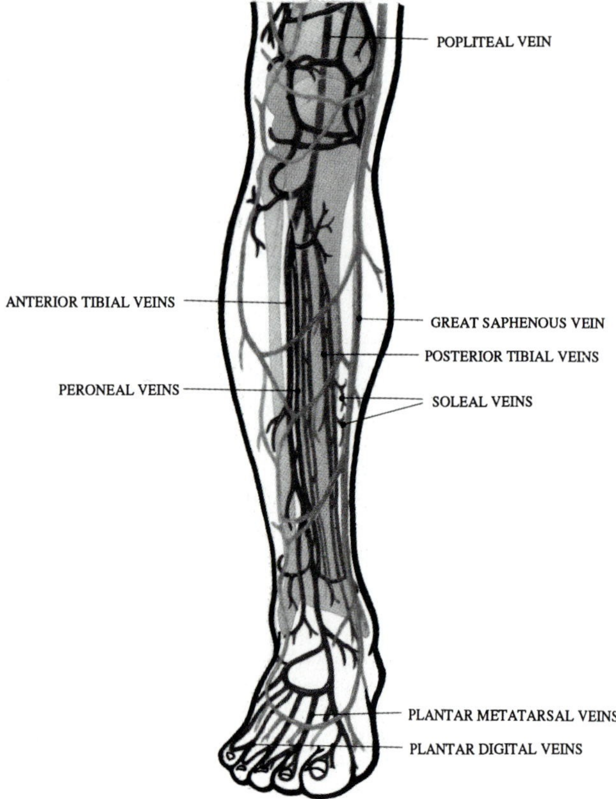

Figure 9–14. Veins of the leg. (*Reprinted with permission from Abbott Laboratories, North Chicago, IL. Medical illustration by Scott Thorn Barrows, AMI.*)

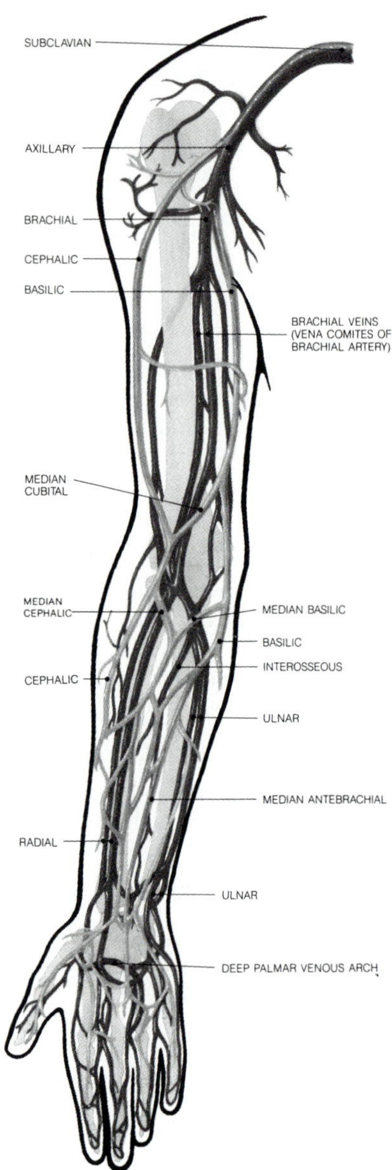

Figure 9–15. Veins of the arm. (*Reprinted with permission from Abbott Laboratories, North Chicago, IL. Medical illustration by Scott Thorn Barrows, AMI.*)

LOWER EXTREMITY ARTERIAL ANATOMY (Figs. 9–16, 9–17, and 9–19 through 9–22)

The arteries of the lower extremity are the external iliac artery; common, superficial, and deep femoral arteries; popliteal artery; anterior and posterior tibial arteries; and peroneal artery.

External Iliac Artery

The external iliac artery courses through the lower abdomen from the common iliac artery to the common femoral artery.

The Common Femoral Artery

The common femoral artery begins as the external iliac artery and passes under the inguinal ligament. It is found lateral to the common femoral vein. It bifurcates into the superficial femoral artery and the deep femoral artery.

Superficial Femoral Artery

The superficial femoral artery is found anterior to the superficial femoral vein. It courses distal in the thigh to the level of the adductor canal.

Deep Femoral Profunda Artery

The deep femoral artery courses deep into the thigh muscles and is paired with the deep femoral vein.

Popliteal Artery

The popliteal artery is a continuation of the superficial femoral artery. It courses inferiorly from the level of the adductor canal to the proximal portion of the calf. It divides into the anterior tibial artery and the tibioperoneal trunk.

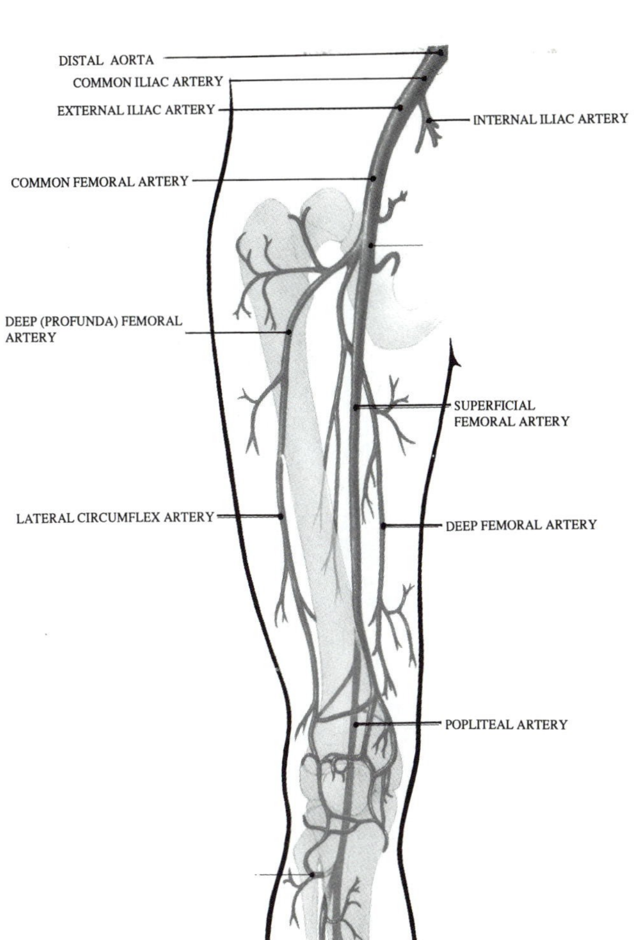

Figure 9–16. Arteries of the thigh. (*Reprinted with permission from Abbott Laboratories, North Chicago, IL. Medical illustration by Scott Thorn Barrows, AMI.*)

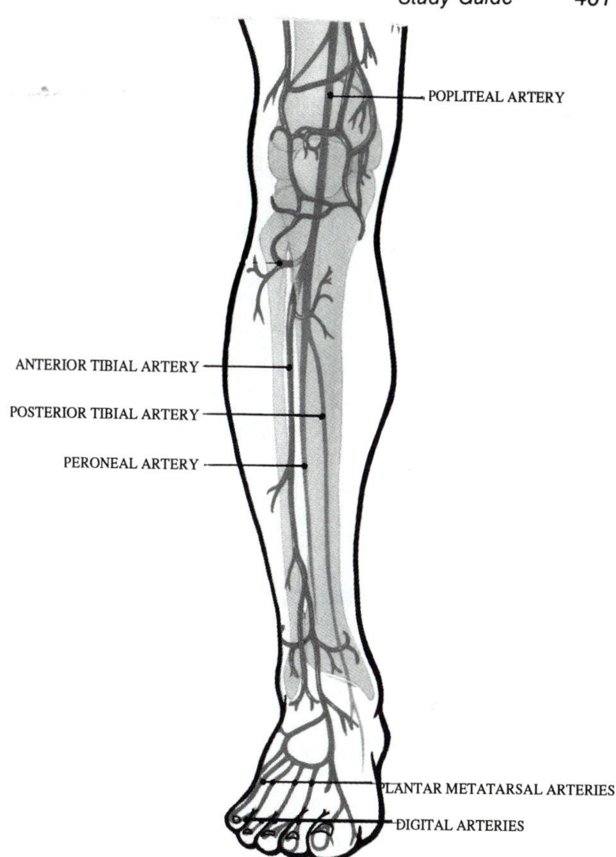

Figure 9–17. Arteries of the leg. (*Reprinted with permission from Abbott Laboratories, North Chicago, IL. Medical illustration by Scott Thorn Barrows, AMI.*)

Anterior Tibial Artery

The anterior tibial artery courses anteriorly through the interosseous membrane and travels inferiorly to form the dorsalis pedis artery in the foot.

Posterior Tibial Artery

The posterior tibial artery courses medially and posteriorly from the tibioperoneal trunk and ends at the medial aspect of the ankle.

Peroneal Artery

The peroneal artery courses posteriorly and laterally from the tibioperoneal trunk and ends at the lateral aspect of the ankle.

Upper Extremity Arterial Anatomy

Fig. 9–23 illustrates the arterial anatomy of the upper extremity.

NORMAL SONOGRAPHIC ARTERIAL ANATOMY

The normal sonographic characteristics of the anatomy are smoothness of the internal walls of the vessel lumen, pulsatility of the vessel, gradual narrowing of the artery, firmness of the artery (with compression, it remains pulsatile).

ABNORMAL SONOGRAPHIC FINDINGS

Plaque Formation

Plaque may be fatty, fibrotic, or calcified; the borders may be smooth or irregular; and may exhibit homogeneous or heterogeneous echogenicity.

Identification of Totally Occluded Artery

To identify a totally occluded artery, look for echoes throughout the lumen, loss of pulsatility, and a decrease in the size of the lumen of the artery.

Aneurysmal Dilatation of the Artery

True aneurysmal dilatation of an artery can be fusiform or saccular. A pseudoaneurysm can occur after arterial cannulation or at graft anastomotic sites.

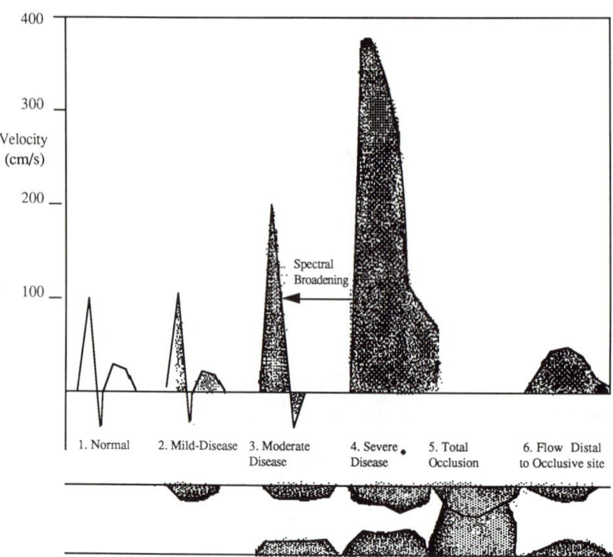

Figure 9–18. Spectral Doppler waveform in progressive disease states.

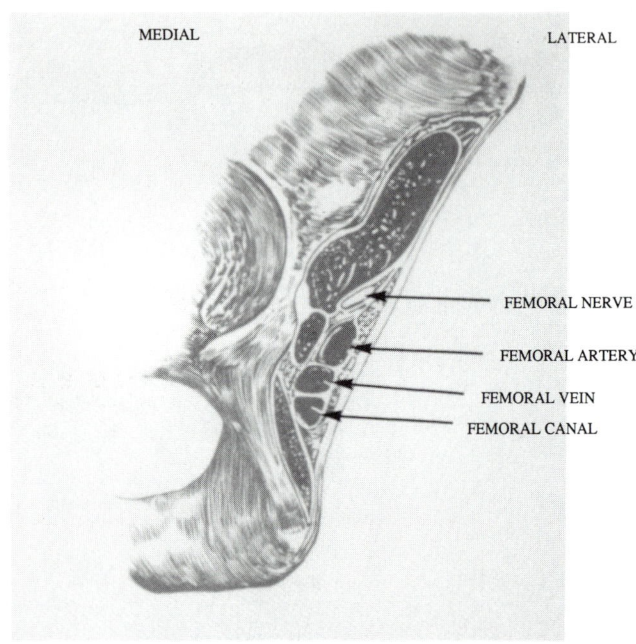

Figure 9–19. Lateral surface of the right pelvic girdle. (*Reprinted with permission from Gray H, Clemente CD: Anatomy of the Human Body. Philadelphia: Lea & Febiger, 1985.*)

CLINICAL SYMPTOMS

The clinical symptoms of lower extremity arterial disease are intermittent claudication, cold feet, leg pain at night, pain at rest, absent peripheral pulses, dependent rubor, dry and scaly skin, thickened toenails, loss of hair on toes and feet, gangrene, and lesions on the plantar surface of the foot.

PULSED WAVE DOPPLER SPECTRAL DISPLAY[9] (Fig. 9–18)

1. *Normal*
   - triphasic waveform
   - clear, crisp spectral window
   - quick upstroke to systolic peak
2. *Mild disease* (less than 20% diameter reduction)
   - triphasic waveform
   - minimal spectral broadening
   - quick upstroke to systolic peak
3. *Moderate disease* (less than 50% diameter reduction)
   - peak systolic velocity at least 30% greater than the proximal segment waveform
   - biphasic waveform
   - spectral window filling, spectral broadening
4. *Severe disease* (diameter reduction greater than 50%)
   - peak systolic velocity increases by 100% or greater over the proximal segment waveform
   - severe disease may have monophasic pattern with increased diastolic flow
   - severe spectral broadening
5. *Occluded artery*
   - Absence of spectral information
6. *Flow distal to an occluded site* (due to collateral channels)
   - decreased systolic flow
   - sluggish upstroke to peak systole
   - spectral broadening
   - monophasic

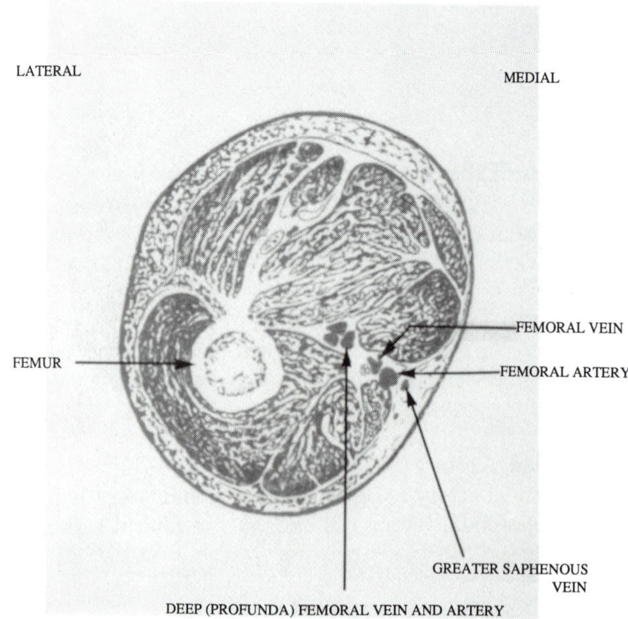

Figure 9–20. Cross section proximal thigh. (*Reprinted with permission from Gray H, Clemente CD: Anatomy of the Human Body. Philadelphia: Lea & Febiger, 1985.*)

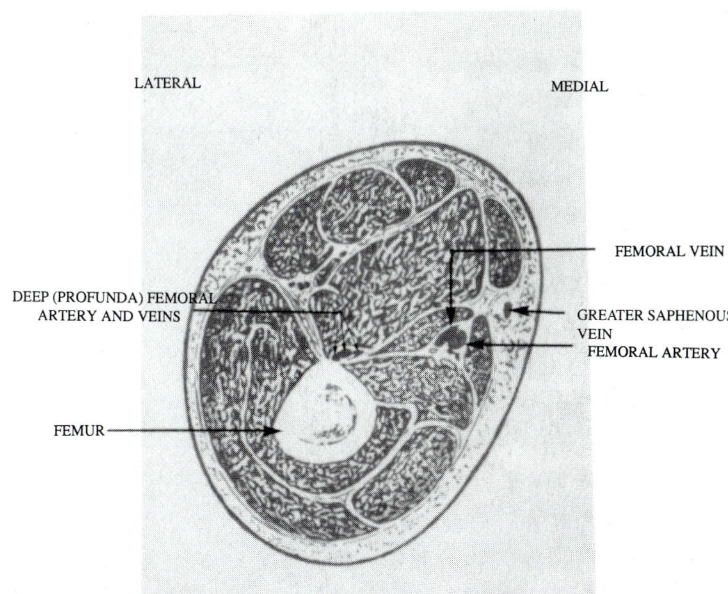

Figure 9–21. Cross section midthigh. *(Reprinted with permission from Gray H, Clemente CD: Anatomy of the Human Body. Philadelphia: Lea & Febiger, 1985.)*

CEREBROVASCULAR ANATOMY

Aortic Arch

The aortic arch has three arteries coursing cephalad (Fig. 9–24):

1. The brachiocephalic trunk, also known as the innominate artery, courses to the right and branches into the right common carotid artery superiorly and the right subclavian artery laterally.
2. The left common carotid artery.
3. The left subclavian artery.

Extracerebral Circulation (Fig. 9–25)

Common Carotid Artery. This artery is the main branch of the carotid system. Located in the cervical section of the neck, it has no arterial branches. It bifurcates into the internal carotid artery and the external carotid artery. The location of the bifurcation is variable but is usually at the level of the thyroid cartilage.

Internal Carotid Artery. This artery carries blood to the cerebral hemispheres of the brain. It is divided into four sections. There are no branches of the internal carotid

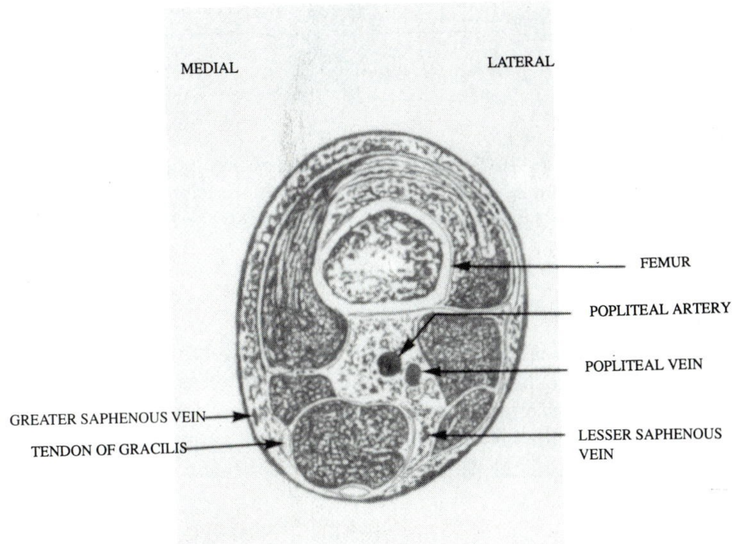

Figure 9–22. Cross section at the popliteal space. *(Reprinted with permission from Gray H, Clemente CD: Anatomy of the Human Body. Philadelphia: Lea & Febiger, 1985.)*

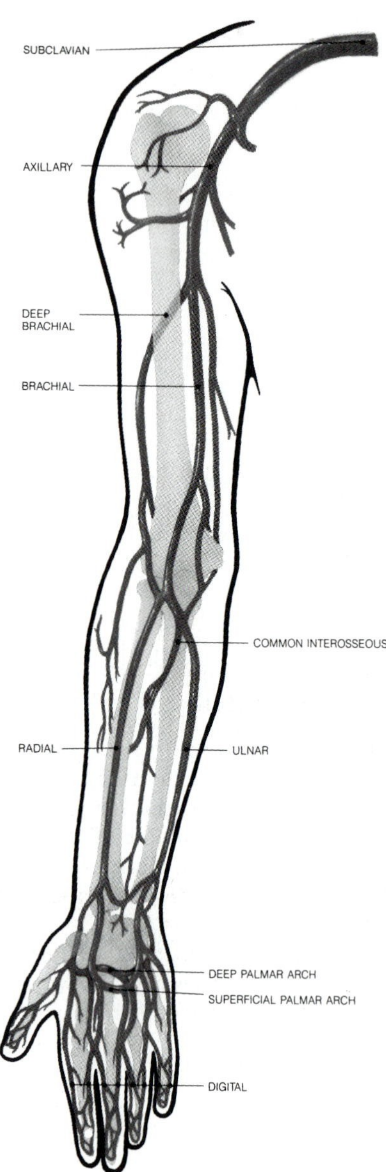

Figure 9–23. Arteries of the arm. (*Reproduced with permission from Abbott Laboratories, North Chicago, IL. Medical illustration by Scott Thorn Barrows, AMI.*)

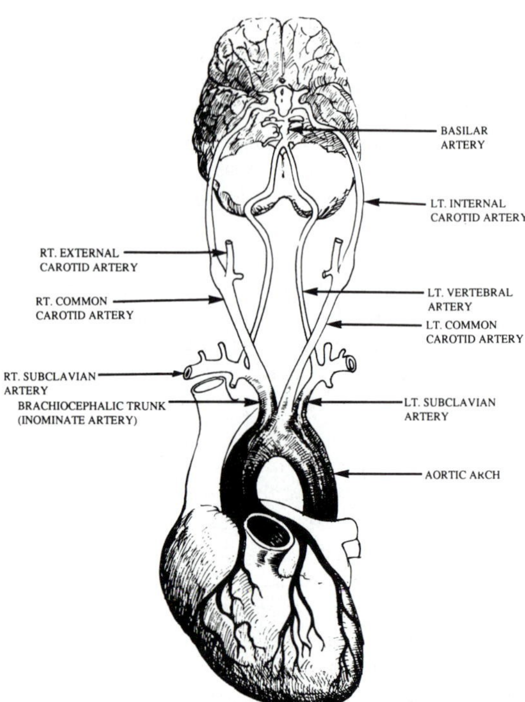

Figure 9–24. Blood supply to the brain.

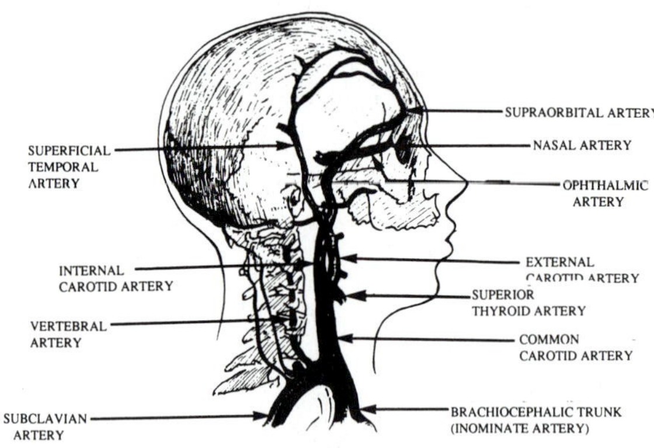

Figure 9–25. Cerebrovascular anatomy. (*Reproduced with permission from Zwiebel, W. J.: Introduction to Vascular Ultrasonography, 2nd ed. Philadelphia: WB Saunders, 1986.*)

artery in the cervical section. Small branches arise from the petrous and cavernous portions. The ophthalmic artery is the first major branch coursing from the cavernous portion. The intracranial portion feeds the middle cerebral artery, the anterior cerebral artery, and the posterior communicating artery.

Ophthalmic Artery. This artery courses anteriorly from the cavernous portion of the internal carotid artery. It supplies blood to the eye. The three distal branches are the supraorbital, frontal, and nasal arteries. These arteries can become sources of collateral circulation with the distal branches of the external carotid artery in the event of internal carotid artery occlusive disease.

External Carotid Artery. This artery carries blood to the face and scalp. Unlike the internal carotid artery, it can be identified by its numerous branches in the cervical region. The superior thyroid artery is the first branch noted. The location of the superficial temporal artery is important for performing a tapping maneuver for positive identification of the external carotid artery during Doppler examination.

Vertebral Artery. This artery courses superiorly and enters the foramina of the transverse processes of the sixth cervical vertebra. It enters the skull at the foramen magnum. The two vertebral arteries unite to form a single basilar artery (Fig. 9–24).

Circle of Willis (Fig. 9–26)

The circle of Willis is an anastomosis found at the base of the brain formed by a network of arteries that arise from the internal carotid arteries and the basilar artery.[5] The internal carotid artery, which courses superiorly into the base of the brain, branches into the anterior cerebral artery, middle cerebral artery, and the anterior and posterior communicating arteries.

The vertebral arteries converge to form a single basilar artery, which bifurcates to form the posterior cerebral arteries.

Communicating arteries form an important network

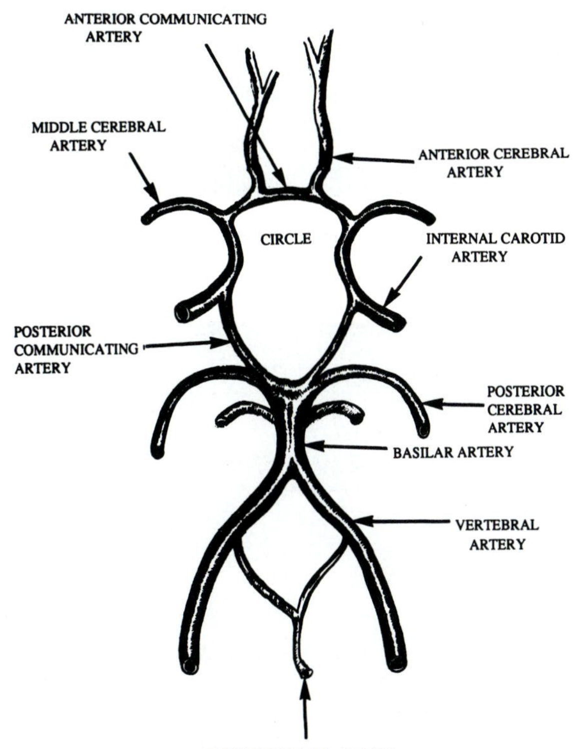

Figure 9–26. Arteries forming the circle of Willis. Circle of Willis is a network of arteries that arise from the internal carotid arteries and the vertebral arteries.

of collateral circulation in the circle of Willis. The anterior communicating artery connects the two anterior cerebral arteries. The posterior communicating arteries connect the posterior cerebral arteries with the anterior circulation (middle cerebral and anterior cerebral arteries).

Important: The circle of Willis is an important collateral pathway for circulation. However, it is not intact in a large percentage of the population.

Arterial Anatomy

Like veins, arteries have three distinct tissue layers (Table 9–1):

1. The tunica intima is the innermost layer of endothelial tissue.
2. The tunica media is the smooth muscle layer of the artery. It is elastic in nature allowing for constriction and dilation of the artery.
3. The tunica adventitia is the outer layer of tissue which gives the artery its rigidity.

ATHEROMA FORMATION AND CLASSIFICATION OF PLAQUE

Atheroma Formation

Atheroma formation is a complicated process whereby plaque is initially formed in the intimal layer of tissue and evolves into an accumulation of fibrotic materials, hemorrhagic products, and calcifications.

Atheroma formation begins with the infiltration of lipid materials into the endothelial layer of the intima of the artery. On two-dimensional (2D) images, the intimal echo is bright with a uniform, narrow width. Lipid infiltration is depicted as an irregular thickening that varies throughout the length of the lumen (Fig. 9–27).

The simple lipid (fatty) plaque can evolve into a more complex structure. Hemorrhage may occur within the plaque. The endothelial layer may become eroded and the surface of the intima can become irregular. Ulceration of the plaque can lead to the release of platelet aggregates into the circulation. These become microemboli, and neurologic symptoms may occur as small vessels become occluded.

Irregular plaque surfaces can lead to thrombus formation. Thrombus can narrow the arterial lumen and eventually cause a total occlusion. It can also break free from the plaque site and become a large embolus, causing neurologic symptoms.

Arterial bifurcations are common sites for plaque formation. The most common site in the extracerebral vascular circulation is the bifurcation of the common carotid artery into the internal and external carotid arteries.

Two-Dimensional Characteristics of Plaque

Types of Plaque

Soft Plaque. It may be technically difficult to visualize a soft plaque because of the low-level echoes it contains.

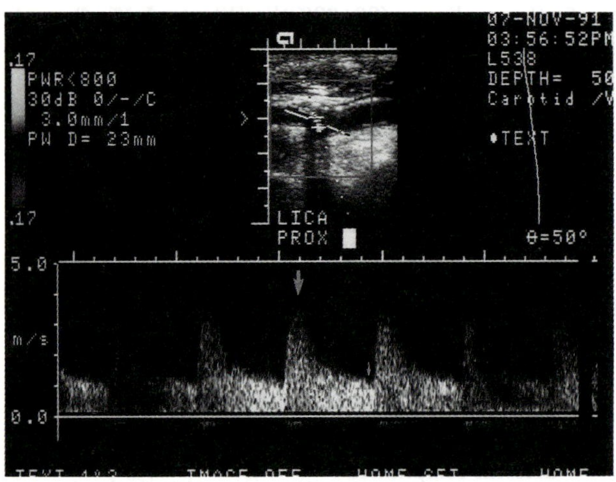

Figure 9–43. Sample site at the stenotic area. There is a dramatic increase in the peak systolic velocity (large arrow) and the end-diastolic velocity (small arrow). Note the spectral window filling.

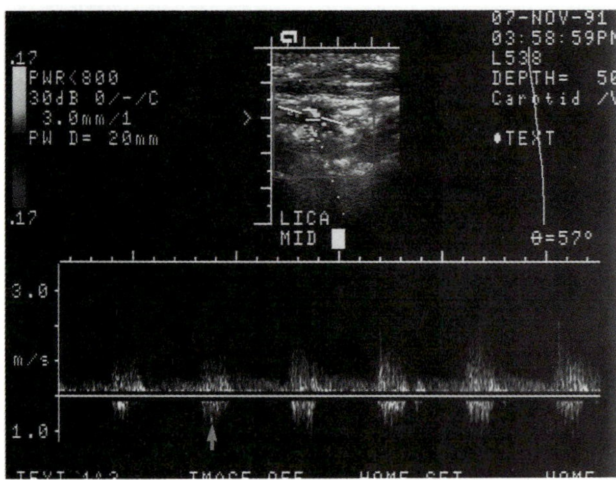

Figure 9–44. Sample site located distal to the stenosis. The post-stenotic peak systolic velocities and end diastolic velocities are decreased. Turbulent flow is noted as flow reversal (arrow).

2. *Stenotic site* (Fig. 9–43)
   - peak systolic velocities increase
   - end-diastolic velocities increase
   - spectral broadening is noted
3. *Poststenotic site* (Fig. 9–44)
   - peak systolic velocities decrease
   - end-diastolic velocities decrease
   - turbulent flow is noted (flow reversal as well as forward flow)

REFERENCES

1. Anthony CP, Kolthoff NJ. *Textbook of Anatomy and Physiology.* St Louis: CV Mosby, 1971.
2. Rutherford RB. *Vascular Surgery,* 2nd ed. Philadelphia: WB Saunders, 1984.
3. Barnes R. Ultrasound techniques for evaluation of lower extremity venous disease. *Semin Ultrasound* **2**(4):276–282, 1981.
4. Zweibel W. *Introduction to Vascular Ultrasonography,* 2nd ed. Philadelphia: WB Saunders, 1986.
5. Dodd H, Cocket F. The *Pathology and Surgery of the Veins of the Lower Limbs.* New York: Churchill Livingstone, 1976.
6. Gerlock, A, Giyanani V, Krebs C. *Applications of Noninvasive Vascular Techniques.* Philadelphia: WB Saunders, 1988.
7. Rollins D, Lloyd W, Buchbinder D. Venous thrombosis: The clinical picture. *Semin Ultrasound CT MR* **9**(4): 277–283, 1988.
8. Zweibel W. Anatomy and duplex characteristics of the normal veins. *Semin Ultrasound CT MR* **9**(4):269–275, 1988.
9. Jager KA, Phillips DJ, Martin RL, et al. Noninvasive mapping of lower limb arterial lesions, *Ultrasound Med Biol* **11**(3):515–521, 1985.
10. Belanger A: *Vascular Anatomy and Physiology: An Introductory Text.* Pasadena, CA: Appleton Davies, 1986.
11. Bernstein E. *Noninvasive Diagnostic Techniques in Vascular Disease.* 3rd ed. St. Louis: CV Mosby, 1985.
12. Fields W. Aortocranial occlusive vascular disease (stroke). *CIBA Clin Symp* **26**(4):1–31, 1974.
13. Kremkau F. *Doppler Ultrasound: Principles and Instruments.* Philadelphia: WB Saunders, 1990.
14. Rutherford R. *Vascular Surgery,* 3rd ed. Vols I and II. Philadelphia: WB Saunders, 1989.
15. Taylor K, Burns P, Wells P. *Clinical Applications of Doppler Ultrasound.* New York: Raven Press, 1988.
16. Roederer GO, Strandess DE Jr. A simple spectral parameter for the classification of severe carotid disease. *Bruit* **8**:174–178, 1984.

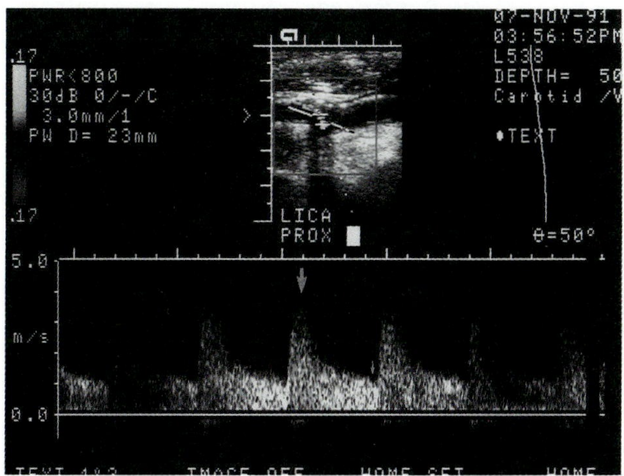

Figure 9–43. Sample site at the stenotic area. There is a dramatic increase in the peak systolic velocity (large arrow) and the end-diastolic velocity (small arrow). Note the spectral window filling.

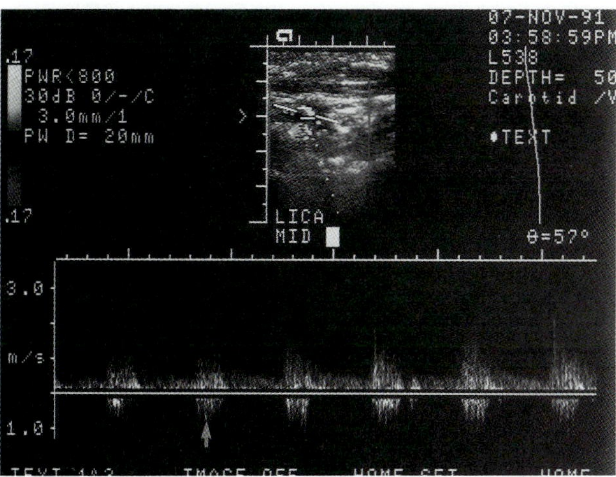

Figure 9–44. Sample site located distal to the stenosis. The poststenotic peak systolic velocities and end diastolic velocities are decreased. Turbulent flow is noted as flow reversal (arrow).

2. *Stenotic site* (Fig. 9–43)
   - peak systolic velocities increase
   - end-diastolic velocities increase
   - spectral broadening is noted
3. *Poststenotic site* (Fig. 9–44)
   - peak systolic velocities decrease
   - end-diastolic velocities decrease
   - turbulent flow is noted (flow reversal as well as forward flow)

REFERENCES

1. Anthony CP, Kolthoff NJ. *Textbook of Anatomy and Physiology.* St Louis: CV Mosby, 1971.
2. Rutherford RB. *Vascular Surgery,* 2nd ed. Philadelphia: WB Saunders, 1984.
3. Barnes R. Ultrasound techniques for evaluation of lower extremity venous disease. *Semin Ultrasound* **2**(4):276–282, 1981.
4. Zweibel W. *Introduction to Vascular Ultrasonography,* 2nd ed. Philadelphia: WB Saunders, 1986.
5. Dodd H, Cocket F. The *Pathology and Surgery of the Veins of the Lower Limbs.* New York: Churchill Livingstone, 1976.
6. Gerlock, A, Giyanani V, Krebs C. *Applications of Noninvasive Vascular Techniques.* Philadelphia: WB Saunders, 1988.
7. Rollins D, Lloyd W, Buchbinder D. Venous thrombosis: The clinical picture. *Semin Ultrasound CT MR* **9**(4): 277–283, 1988.
8. Zweibel W. Anatomy and duplex characteristics of the normal veins. *Semin Ultrasound CT MR* **9**(4):269–275, 1988.
9. Jager KA, Phillips DJ, Martin RL, et al. Noninvasive mapping of lower limb arterial lesions, *Ultrasound Med Biol* **11**(3):515–521, 1985.
10. Belanger A: *Vascular Anatomy and Physiology: An Introductory Text.* Pasadena, CA: Appleton Davies, 1986.
11. Bernstein E. *Noninvasive Diagnostic Techniques in Vascular Disease.* 3rd ed. St. Louis: CV Mosby, 1985.
12. Fields W. Aortocranial occlusive vascular disease (stroke). *CIBA Clin Symp* **26**(4):1–31, 1974.
13. Kremkau F. *Doppler Ultrasound: Principles and Instruments.* Philadelphia: WB Saunders, 1990.
14. Rutherford R. *Vascular Surgery,* 3rd ed. Vols I and II. Philadelphia: WB Saunders, 1989.
15. Taylor K, Burns P, Wells P. *Clinical Applications of Doppler Ultrasound.* New York: Raven Press, 1988.
16. Roederer GO, Strandess DE Jr. A simple spectral parameter for the classification of severe carotid disease. *Bruit* **8**:174–178, 1984.

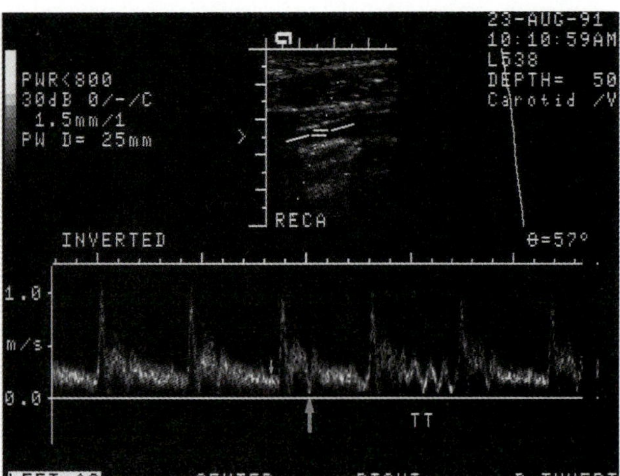

Figure 9–40. Resistive flow pattern in the external carotid artery. Note the return of flow to the baseline (large arrow) in early diastole and the close proximity to the baseline in end diastole (small arrow). Positive identification of the external is made by tapping the superficial temporal artery and noting the transmitted pulsations along the diastolic portion of the waveform (TT).

2. *Mild disease* (0–15% diameter reduction)
   - range of velocities in diastole mildly increases
   - spectral window may still remain clear
   - peak systolic velocities do not exceed 125 cm/s
3. *Moderate disease* (16–49% diameter reduction)
   - spectral broadening (range of velocities increases)
   - spectral window filling
   - peak systolic velocities do not exceed 125 cm/s
4. *Severe disease* (50–79% diameter reduction)
   - marked spectral broadening with spectral window filling
   - peak systolic velocities exceed 125 cm/s
   - end diastolic velocity increases but does not exceed 100 cm/s

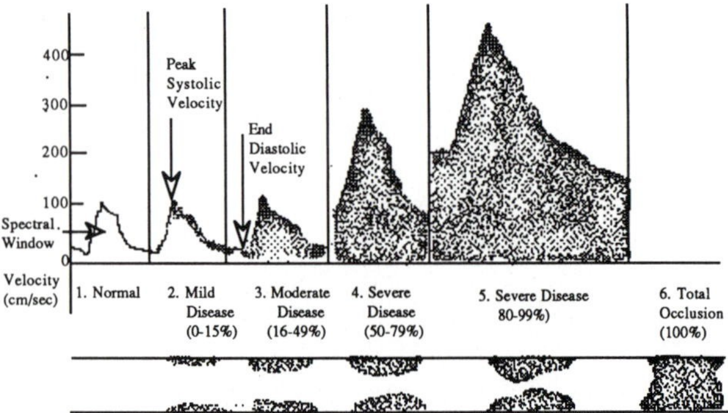

Figure 9–41. Spectral Doppler waveform in progressive disease states in the internal carotid artery.

5. *Severe disease* (80–99% diameter reduction)
   - marked spectral broadening with spectral window filling
   - peak systolic velocities exceed 125 cm/sec and may be in the 300–400 cm/sec range
   - end-diastolic velocity exceeds 140 cm/s
6. Total occlusion
   - absence of spectral information because of no flow

Factors Affecting Flow Velocities

- cardiac output
- blood pressure
- peripheral resistance
- obstruction of contralateral carotid artery
- arterial compliance

Hemodynamically Significant Stenosis

A hemodynamically significant stenosis is one that exceeds 50–60% diameter reduction (75% area reduction). It is at this point when flow velocities begin to increase (both systolic and end diastolic) and flow volume begins to decrease. Therefore, stenotic lesions in the fourth and fifth category in Fig. 9–41 are considered hemodynamically significant.

When a hemodynamically significant lesion is present, certain flow characteristics are evident at the prestenotic, stenotic, and poststenotic sample sites. The location of these sample sites is noted in Fig. 9–42, 9–43, and 9–44.

1. *Prestenotic site* (Fig. 9–42)
   - located proximal to a hemodynamically significant stenosis
   - peak systolic velocities are within normal limits
   - a resistive flow pattern may be noted in diastole

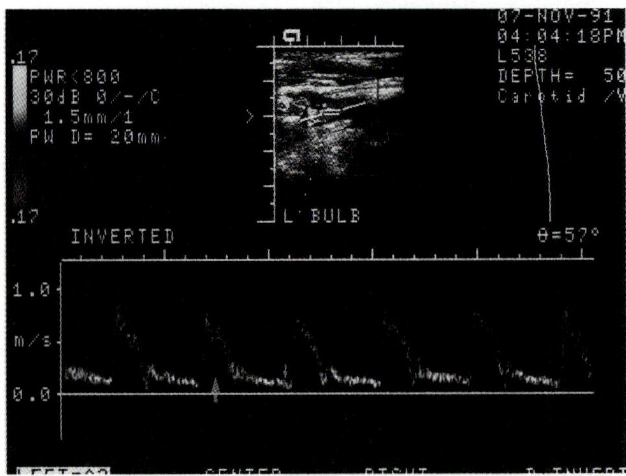

Figure 9–42. Sample site located proximal to a stenosis. Note the decreased diastolic portion of the spectral waveform due to distal resistance (arrow). Note the laminar flow pattern with a clear spectral window (large arrow).

Sample Volume (Fig. 9–37)

Sample volume placement in an artery is controlled by the operator. The sample volume can be moved up and down an electronic cursor that can be steered on the 2D image to obtain the appropriate angle for Doppler. (The angle must not exceed 60° to the flow stream.)

The length of the sample volume, ie, the axial dimension, is controlled by the operator. Information from only the sample area is displayed on the velocity spectrum. The ability to range gate allows the operator to select the depth from which the Doppler information will be obtained. In reality, a time delay is being utilized to decipher information only from the sample volume area.

The lateral dimension of the sample volume is determined by its placement within the ultrasound beam.

Spectral Display (Fig. 9–38)

Information obtained from the spectral display includes direction of blood flow, peak-systolic velocity, end-diastolic velocity, range of velocities (narrow range vs spectral broadening), time, and amplitude of the velocities.

The spectral analysis waveform displays flow characteristics in the carotid arteries. Plaque buildup within the artery can cause flow disturbances depending upon the reduction in the diameter of the artery.

Types of Flow in the Extracerebral Circulation

Nonresistive Flow. This type of flow demonstrates continuous flow in the diastolic portion of the spectral display. Flow is unimpeded as it flows through the artery. The internal carotid artery displays nonresistive diastolic flow (Fig. 9–39) because it is flowing to the circle of Willis.

Resistive Flow. This type of flow has diastolic flow that returns to the baseline of the spectral display. After the peak systolic phase, blood flow returns to a very low velocity because of the resistance to flow. The external carotid artery demonstrates a resistive flow pattern because it is feeding the face and scalp. In very resistive arterial beds, such as distally occluded internal carotid arteries, diastolic flow can actually be reversed (Fig. 9–40).

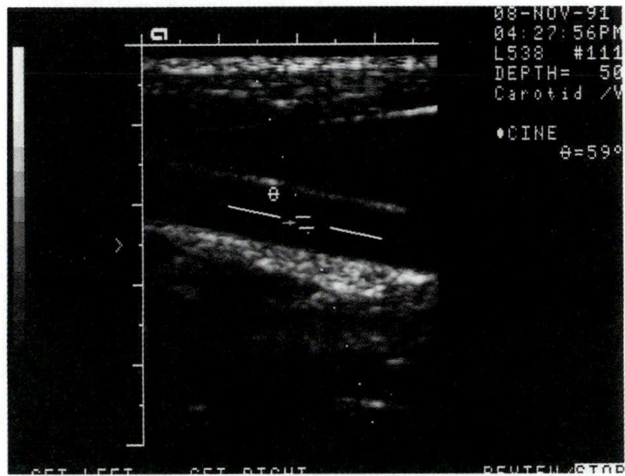

Figure 9–37. The sample volume (arrowhead) is noted here as two parallel lines. The axial dimension (how wide the gate is open) is determined by the operator.

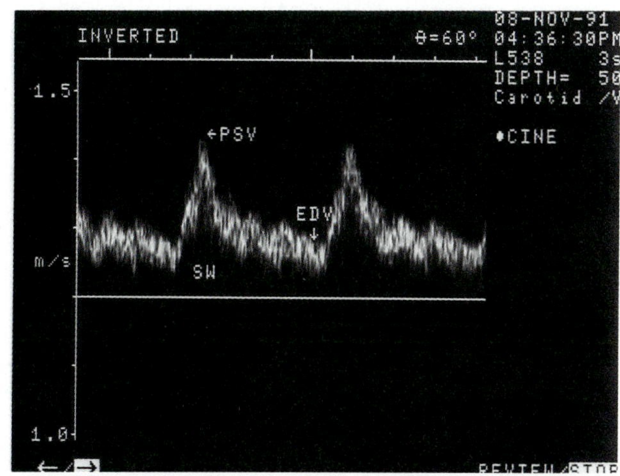

Figure 9–38. The spectral display demonstrates peak systolic velocity (PSV), end-diastolic velocity (EDV), and the spectral window (SW). In this example, a narrow range of velocities is demonstrated. The spectral window is clear. Time (in seconds [s]) is the horizontal scale. Velocity (in meters/second [m/s]) is the vertical line.

Spectral Doppler Waveform in Progressive Disease States of the Internal Carotid Artery (Fig. 9–41)

The following gradations[16] are for short-segment stenosis:

1. *Normal*
   - narrow range of velocities in systole and diastole
   - clear spectral window
   - peak systolic velocities do not exceed 125 cm/s

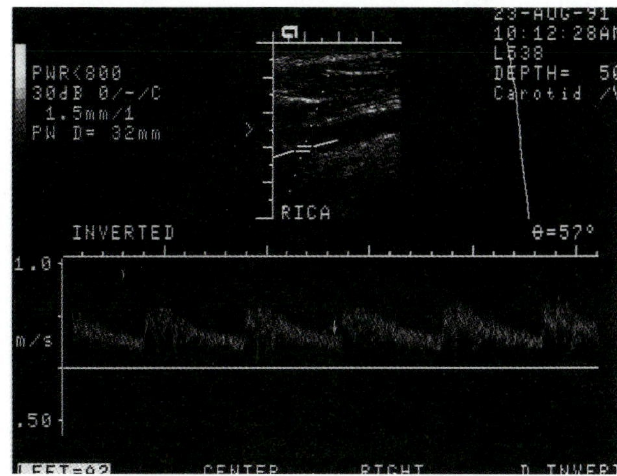

Figure 9–39. Nonresistive flow pattern in the internal carotid artery. The arrow points to the characteristic continuous flow in diastole.

pulses (incident frequency) and waits for the returning frequency (reflected frequency). The use of a small sample volume (range gating) eliminates Doppler information from any sites other than where the sample volume is located. When the Nyquist limit (one half the pulse repetition frequency) is exceeded, aliasing occurs. Aliasing is a Doppler artifact resulting in erroneous distribution of the Doppler information. This usually occurs with very high-frequency shifts.

TESTING METHODS

Indirect Cerebrovascular Testing

Ocular Pneumoplethysmography (OPG). This is based on pressure measurements of the opthalmic artery to detect hemodynamically significant lesions (greater than 50%). A significant stenosis will cause an arterial pressure decrease. When there are opthalmic artery pressure differences of 5 mm Hg or more between the right and left sides, a hemodynamically significant lesion can be considered present.

The examination is performed by anesthesizing the eye, placing eye cups on the sclera, and applying a vacuum (300–500 mm Hg). When the vacuum is released, tracings are made of the returning pulsations of both eyes. This examination can be used in the assessment of collateral circulation.

Periorbital Doppler. This examines the direction of blood flow in the opthalmic artery branches (supraorbital, frontal, and nasal arteries). These arteries serve as collateral pathways with internal carotid artery disease.

The direction of flow in the periorbital arteries requires a directional Doppler velocity detector. The frontal and supraorbital arteries are examined separately. Flow in each artery is assessed in its normal state and with compression of the superficial temporal, facial, and infraorbital arteries. In the normal state, the periorbital arterial flow is toward the face. Compression of the external carotid artery branches can cause no change or can increase the periorbital arterial flow. With internal carotid artery stenosis or occlusion, flow in the periorbital arteries can be reversed; that is, flowing back into the orbit. Compression of the external carotid artery branches will decrease or obliterate the Doppler signal.

Direct Cerebrovascular Testing

Continuous Wave Doppler. With a directional velocity detector, this allows for direct examination of the extracerebral circulation. Audio and spectral display are used. Identification of the characteristic Doppler patterns is crucial for each artery examined (common, internal and external carotid arteries). Careful examination is essential because of anatomic variations. No two-dimensional imaging is used with this technique.

Pulsed Doppler. Imaging with pulsed Doppler is used to display the course of the superficial vessels of the extracerebral circulation. This consists of a pulsed Doppler probe, a position-sensing arm, and an oscilloscope. A 2D image is created by moving across the vessel. Abnormalities, other than occlusion, are usually made from the Doppler signal. The advantage of pulsed Doppler imaging is the use of range gating that includes only the desired information.

Pitfalls with the use of pulsed Doppler imaging include atheromatous plaque, overlying vessels, and tortuous anatomy.

Pulsed Doppler imaging depicts only flowing blood and the images obtained are not equivalent to B-mode images.

Duplex Imaging. In duplex imaging of the extracerebral arteries, both B-mode imaging and pulsed-wave Doppler are used for spectral analysis. Detailed images of the arteries are obtained and precise placement of the Doppler sample volume can be determined. Duplex imaging is discussed further below.

Transcranial Doppler. This is the examination of the intracerebral arteries. A 2- or 3-MHZ transducer with range gating features is used. The anterior cerebral, middle cerebral, and posterior cerebral arteries can be examined through the temporal region of the skull. The basilar artery can be examined through the foramen magnum. The transcranial Doppler examination also can assess vasospasm and the collateral circulation of the circle of Willis.

Arteriography. This is an invasive examination of the extracerebral and intracerebral circulations. A catheter is inserted into an artery through a percutaneous puncture. Radiopaque contrast medium is injected through the catheter for visualization of the arteries of interest. Atheromatous plaque, tortuous vessels, and collateral pathways are outlined.

Duplex Investigation of the Extracerebral Vascular System

Two-dimensional B-mode imaging and pulsed-wave Doppler are both used to examine the extracerebral vascular system.

B-Mode Imaging

B-mode imaging allows for identification of the particular artery being investigated, morphologic description of atheromatous plaque, and placement of the sample volume (area sensitive to pulsed-wave Doppler) into a specific site for Doppler investigation.

Pulsed-Wave Doppler

Pulsed-wave Doppler of a particular artery supplies spectral information about direction of flow, velocity of blood flow, amplitude of blood flow, and pulsatility features of the artery being examined.

Stroke in Evolution. In stroke in evolution, the neurologic defects become progressively worse over time. The duration can be up to 2 weeks.

Neurologic Symptoms. In an abbreviated text, it is difficult to discuss precise neurologic symptoms. One must consider the area of the brain being affected as well as the portion of the cerebral circulation affected. The following gives the general symptoms that are associated with the area of interest.

Symptoms of Internal Carotid Artery Disease. Internal carotid artery disease affects the cerebral hemispheres and can cause hemiparesis or hemiplegia on the contralateral side of the affected hemisphere; speech deficit with involvement of the dominant hemisphere; hemianopsia (blindness in one half the field of vision, can be bilateral or unilateral) from occlusion of the middle cerebral artery; decreased level of consciousness; and amaurosis fugax (fleeting blindness) on the side of the diseased artery, which is caused by an embolus in the opthalmic artery or one of its branches.

Symptoms of Vertebrobasilar Artery Disease. Vertebrobasilar artery disease affects the posterior areas of the brain, including the occipital lobes, brain stem, and cerebellum, and can cause vertigo (loss of equilibrium); ataxia (muscular uncoordination); cranial nerve symptoms that include dysphagia, dysphonia, and abnormal eye movements; visual field disturbances, including diplopia; vomiting; headache; and occipital hemianopsia.

Subclavian Steal Syndrome. Obstructed flow in the subclavian artery or innominate artery proximal to the origin of the vertebral artery can result in retrograde flow in the vertebral artery on the affected side. A steal syndrome occurs as blood reverses direction to the occluded artery from the ipsilateral vertebral artery. Vertebrobasilar neurologic symptoms may occur as circulation to the posterior portion of the brain is compromised.

HEMODYNAMIC CONSIDERATIONS

Laminar Flow

Blood flows through an artery in concentric layers with the fastest flow in the central portion of the lumen. Blood flow becomes slower as each layer becomes closer to the arterial wall. In theory, the layer next to the arterial wall will display little or no flow. This is typical of flow in a normal artery (Fig. 9–35).

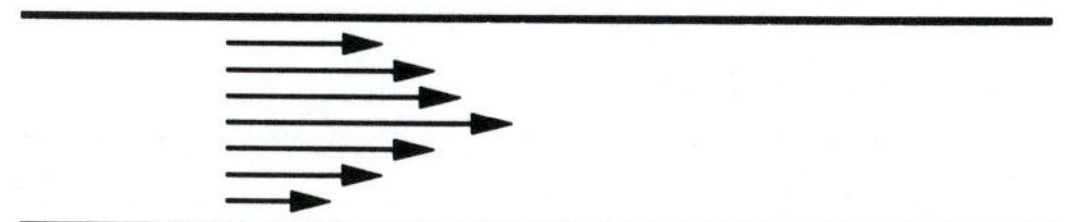

Figure 9–35. Artery with a laminar flow profile. The fastest flow is in the central portion of the artery.

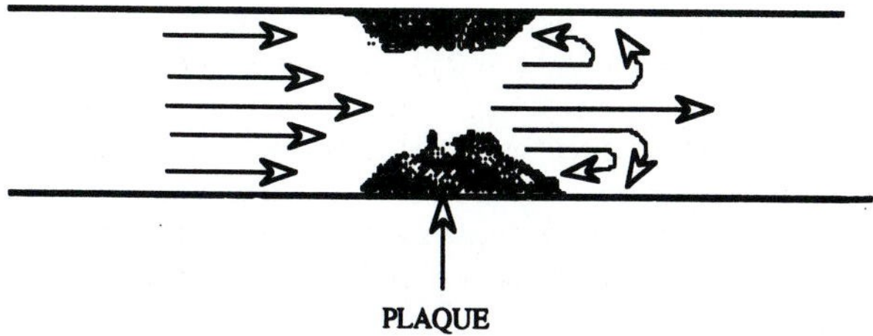

Figure 9–36. Turbulent flow in a narrowed arterial segment. Forward and reverse flow components are noted after blood flow has passed the plaque.

Turbulent Flow

Blood flow loses its laminar characteristics as it travels past areas of atheromatous deposits. The degree of turbulent flow depends upon the degree of disease; as the stenotic area becomes increasingly narrow, the degree of turbulence increases.

Turbulent flow consists of both forward and reverse components as blood flow changes direction after passing through a stenotic area. The flow reversal occurs because of boundary layer separation. The boundary layer is the slowest flow that is found along the wall of the artery (Fig. 9–36).

DOPPLER

Doppler Effect

The Doppler effect occurs when a wave is reflected by a moving target. The frequency of the reflected wave is different from the transmitted wave.

Doppler Shift

The Doppler shift is the difference between the incident (transmitted) frequency and the reflected (received) frequency. The difference depends upon the speed at which the target moves and its direction of movement. Doppler shift frequencies are found in the audible range of human hearing (20–20,000 Hz). Red blood cells are the source of the Doppler signal.

Types of Doppler

Continuous Wave Doppler. This uses a transmitting crystal and a receiving crystal that continuously transmit and receive Doppler information along the path of insonation. Continuous-wave Doppler is not able to differentiate where the Doppler shift originates, and it cannot separate the signal from overlying vessels. It is inexpensive, and it does allow for the determinations of very high frequencies without aliasing. In conjunction with a directional velocity detector, flow direction can be determined.

Pulsed-Wave Doppler. This uses a single crystal to emit and receive the Doppler information. Rather than continuous transmission and reception of the signal, the pulsed-wave Doppler crystal emits a short burst of ultrasound

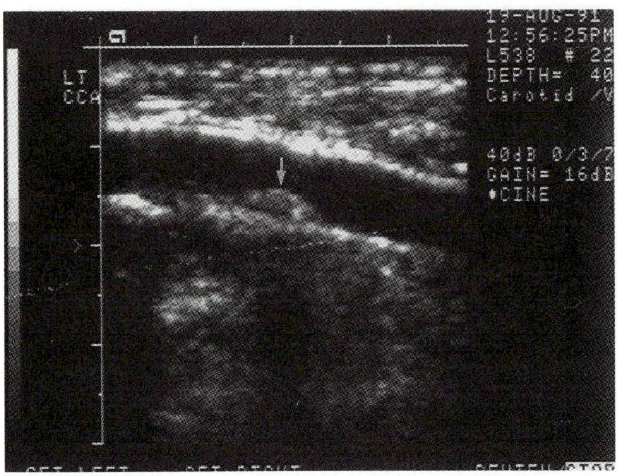

Figure 9–31. Smooth-bordered plaque (arrow).

Internal Echo Characteristics

Homogeneous Echo Content. In a homogeneous plaque, all the echoes within the plaque are uniform. The borders are usually smooth. On the two-dimensional images, the plaque may range from mildly echogenic to very echogenic (Fig. 9–33).

Heterogeneous Plaque. In a heterogeneous plaque, a complex echo pattern is noted. Echo-poor areas may be caused by intraplaque hemorrhage. Calcifications may be noted. Irregular surfaces, ulcer formation, and thrombus formation may occur (Fig. 9–34).

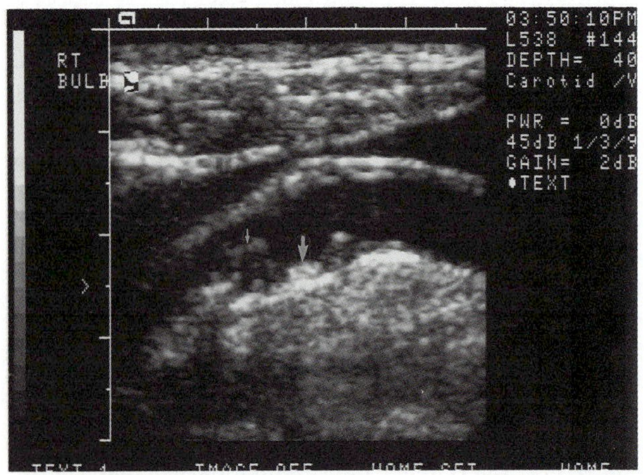

Figure 9–32. Irregular-bordered plaque with echogenic (large arrow) and echo-poor (small arrow) regions noted.

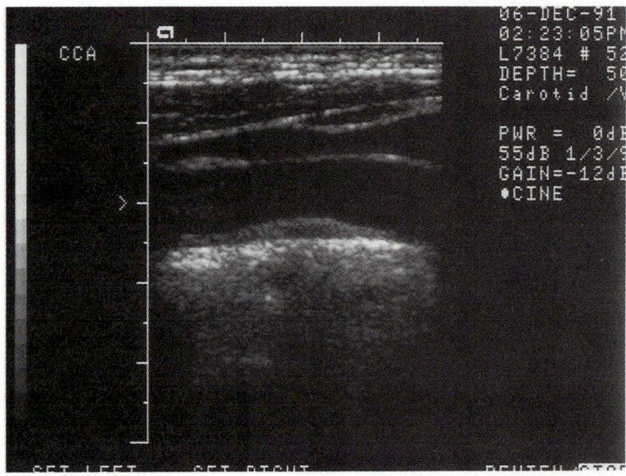

Figure 9–33. Homogeneous echo content in smooth-bordered plaque.

Neurologic Events

Transient Ischemic Attack (TIA). A TIA is a neurologic event in which there are neurologic deficits but the symptoms resolve in less than 24 hours.

Reversible Ischemic Neurologic Deficit (RIND). A RIND lasts longer than 24 hours but resolves within a week.

Completed Stroke. In completed stroke, neurologic defects last longer than 24 hours and do not resolve; symptoms may be severe and cell death occurs in the brain tissue.

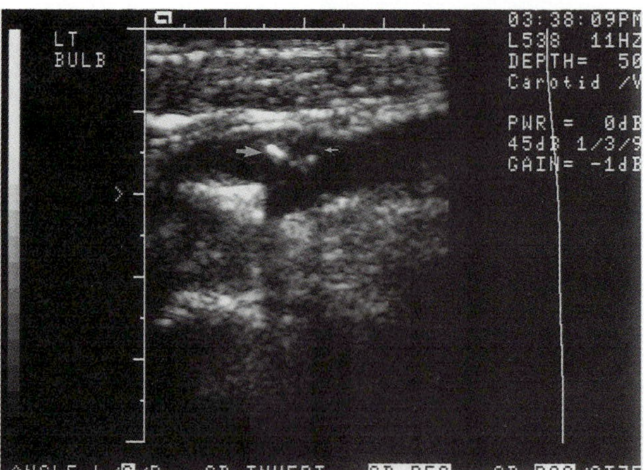

Figure 9–34. Heterogeneous plaque with echo-poor (small arrow) and echogenic areas (large arrow). The echo-poor area may be hemorrhage within the plaque.

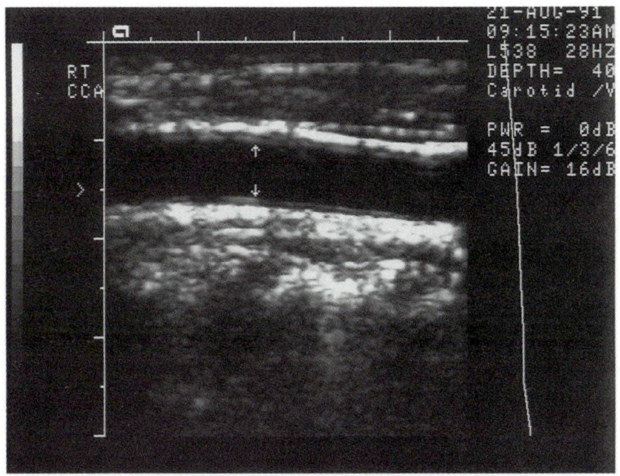

A

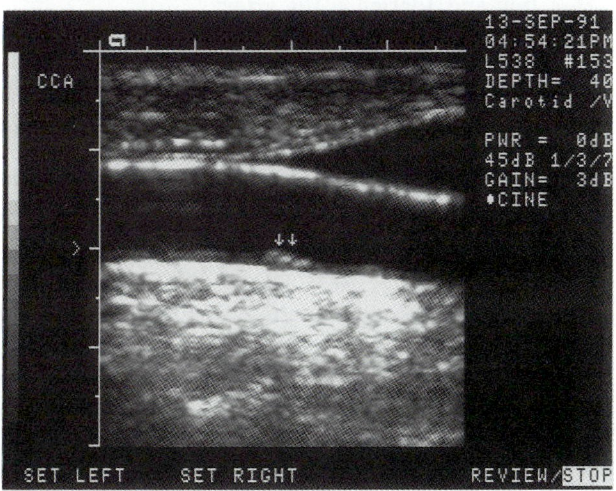

B

Figure 9–27. (**A**) Normal intimal echo in the carotid artery (arrows). (**B**) Abnormally thickened intimal echo consistent with lipid (fatty) infiltration (arrows).

Careful scanning techniques must be utilized to optimize visualization (Fig. 9–28).

Dense Plaque. It is easy to identify a dense plaque because it is echogenic on the 2D images. It is usually fibrotic in nature and may be associated with calcifications (Fig. 9–29).

Calcified Plaque. A calcified plaque is noted by its bright appearance and its posterior acoustic shadowing on the 2D image (Fig. 9–30).

Surface Characteristics of Plaque

Smooth Borders. Plaque may have a smooth surface with no irregularities (Fig. 9–31).

Irregular Borders. Plaque may have irregularities and pitted surfaces and the presence of ulcers (Fig. 9–32).

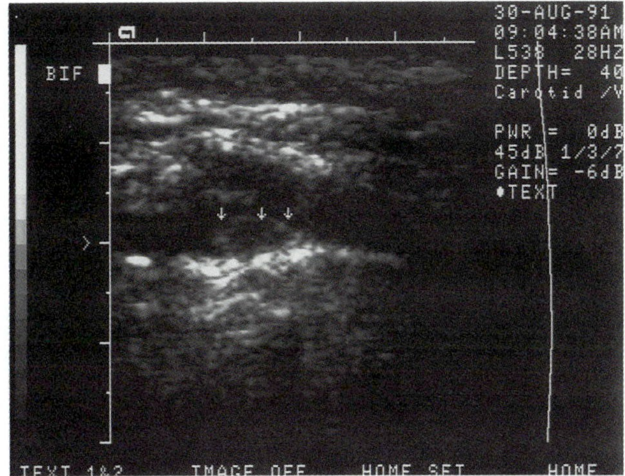

Figure 9–28. Soft plaque in the carotid artery (arrows).

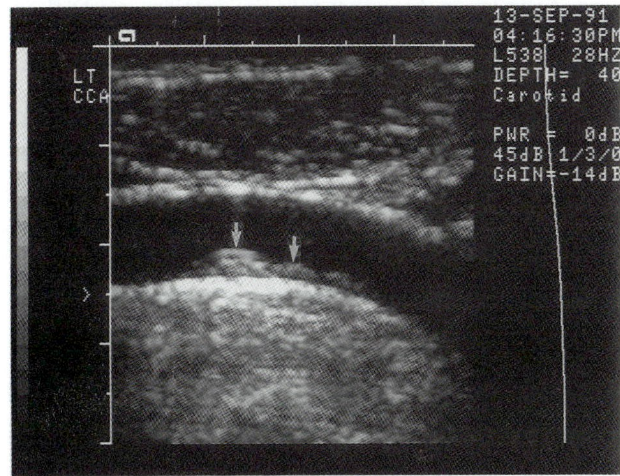

Figure 9–29. Dense plaque in the carotid artery (arrows).

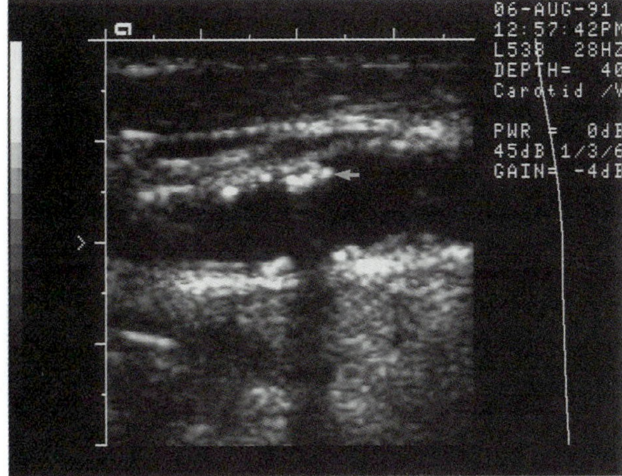

Figure 9–30. Calcified plaque in the carotid artery (arrow). Note the posterior acoustic shadowing.

External Carotid Artery. This artery carries blood to the face and scalp. Unlike the internal carotid artery, it can be identified by its numerous branches in the cervical region. The superior thyroid artery is the first branch noted. The location of the superficial temporal artery is important for performing a tapping maneuver for positive identification of the external carotid artery during Doppler examination.

Vertebral Artery. This artery courses superiorly and enters the foramina of the transverse processes of the sixth cervical vertebra. It enters the skull at the foramen magnum. The two vertebral arteries unite to form a single basilar artery (Fig. 9–24).

Circle of Willis (Fig. 9–26)

The circle of Willis is an anastomosis found at the base of the brain formed by a network of arteries that arise from the internal carotid arteries and the basilar artery.[5] The internal carotid artery, which courses superiorly into the base of the brain, branches into the anterior cerebral artery, middle cerebral artery, and the anterior and posterior communicating arteries.

The vertebral arteries converge to form a single basilar artery, which bifurcates to form the posterior cerebral arteries.

Communicating arteries form an important network of collateral circulation in the circle of Willis. The anterior communicating artery connects the two anterior cerebral arteries. The posterior communicating arteries connect the posterior cerebral arteries with the anterior circulation (middle cerebral and anterior cerebral arteries).

Important: The circle of Willis is an important collateral pathway for circulation. However, it is not intact in a large percentage of the population.

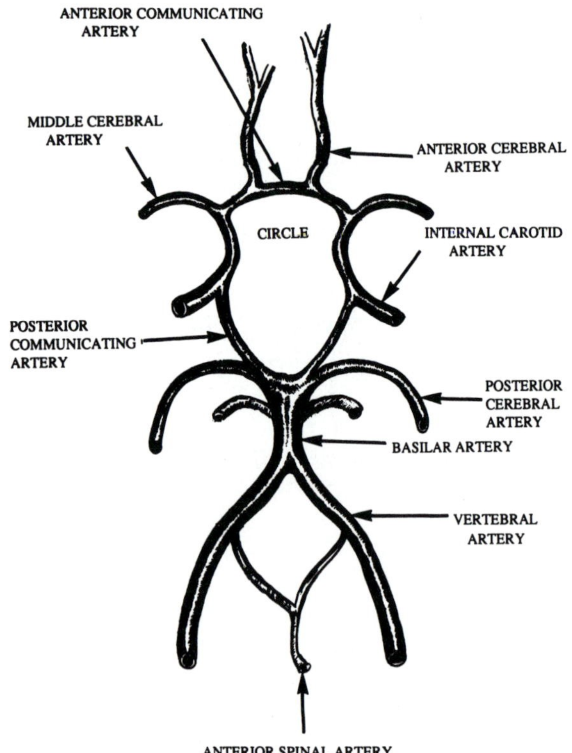

Figure 9–26. Arteries forming the circle of Willis. Circle of Willis is a network of arteries that arise from the internal carotid arteries and the vertebral arteries.

Arterial Anatomy

Like veins, arteries have three distinct tissue layers (Table 9–1):

1. The tunica intima is the innermost layer of endothelial tissue.
2. The tunica media is the smooth muscle layer of the artery. It is elastic in nature allowing for constriction and dilation of the artery.
3. The tunica adventitia is the outer layer of tissue which gives the artery its rigidity.

ATHEROMA FORMATION AND CLASSIFICATION OF PLAQUE

Atheroma Formation

Atheroma formation is a complicated process whereby plaque is initially formed in the intimal layer of tissue and evolves into an accumulation of fibrotic materials, hemorrhagic products, and calcifications.

Atheroma formation begins with the infiltration of lipid materials into the endothelial layer of the intima of the artery. On two-dimensional (2D) images, the intimal echo is bright with a uniform, narrow width. Lipid infiltration is depicted as an irregular thickening that varies throughout the length of the lumen (Fig. 9–27).

The simple lipid (fatty) plaque can evolve into a more complex structure. Hemorrhage may occur within the plaque. The endothelial layer may become eroded and the surface of the intima can become irregular. Ulceration of the plaque can lead to the release of platelet aggregates into the circulation. These become microemboli, and neurologic symptoms may occur as small vessels become occluded.

Irregular plaque surfaces can lead to thrombus formation. Thrombus can narrow the arterial lumen and eventually cause a total occlusion. It can also break free from the plaque site and become a large embolus, causing neurologic symptoms.

Arterial bifurcations are common sites for plaque formation. The most common site in the extracerebral vascular circulation is the bifurcation of the common carotid artery into the internal and external carotid arteries.

Two-Dimensional Characteristics of Plaque

Types of Plaque

Soft Plaque. It may be technically difficult to visualize a soft plaque because of the low-level echoes it contains.

QUESTIONS

GENERAL INSTRUCTIONS: For each question, select the best answer. You are to select only one answer for each question unless otherwise indicated.

Questions 1 through 8: Match the structures in Fig. 9–45 with the terms in Column B.

COLUMN A	COLUMN B
1. _____	(A) popliteal vein
2. _____	(B) greater saphenous vein
3. _____	(C) superficial femoral vein
4. _____	(D) distal inferior vena cava
5. _____	(E) internal iliac vein
6. _____	(F) deep femoral vein (profunda femoral vein)
7. _____	(G) external iliac vein
8. _____	(H) common femoral vein

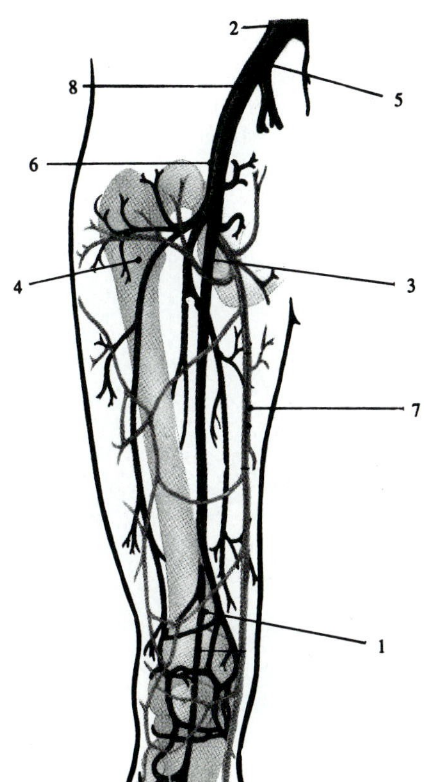

Figure 9–45. Veins of the thigh. (*Reprinted with permission from Abbott Laboratories, North Chicago, IL. Medical illustration by Scott Thorn Barrows, AMI.*)

Questions 9 through 16: Match the structures in Fig. 9–46 with the terms in Column B.

COLUMN A	COLUMN B
9. _____	(A) anterior tibial veins
10. _____	(B) plantar digital veins
11. _____	(C) soleal veins
12. _____	(D) posterior tibial veins
13. _____	(E) plantar metatarsal veins
14. _____	(F) peroneal veins
15. _____	(G) popliteal vein
16. _____	(H) greater saphenous vein

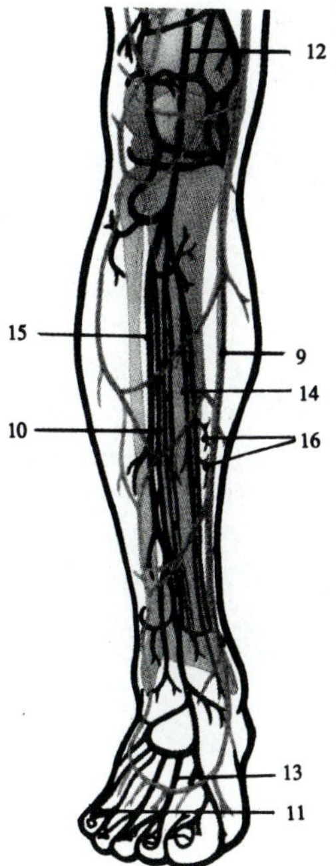

Figure 9–46. Veins of the leg. (*Reprinted with permission from Abbott Laboratories, North Chicago, IL. Medical illustration by Scott Thorn Barrows, AMI.*)

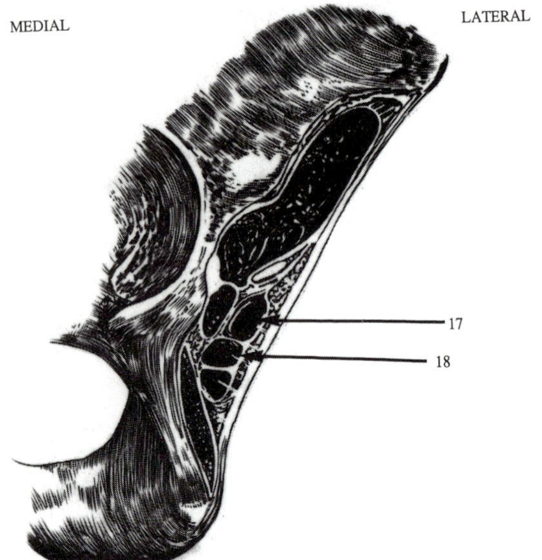

Figure 9–47. Lateral surface of the right pelvic girdle. (*Reprinted with permission from Gray H, Clemente CD: Anatomy of the Human Body. Philadelphia: Lea & Febiger, 1985.*)

Questions 17 through 18: Match the structures in Fig. 9–47 with terms in Column B.

COLUMN A	COLUMN B
17. _____	(A) femoral artery
18. _____	(B) femoral vein

Questions 19 through 22: Match the structures in Fig. 9–48 with the terms in Column B.

COLUMN A	COLUMN B
19. _____	(A) profunda (deep) femoral vein and artery
20. _____	(B) femoral artery
21. _____	(C) greater saphenous vein
22. _____	(D) femoral vein

Questions 23 through 26: Match the structures in Fig. 9–49 with the terms in Column B.

COLUMN A	COLUMN B
23. _____	(A) greater saphenous
24. _____	(B) femoral arteries
25. _____	(C) profunda (deep) femoral artery and vein
26. _____	(D) femoral vein

Questions 27 through 30: Match the structures in Fig. 9–50 with the terms in Column B.

COLUMN A	COLUMN B
27. _____	(A) lesser (small) saphenous
28. _____	(B) popliteal vein
29. _____	(C) greater saphenous
30. _____	(D) popliteal artery

31. The diagnosis of deep vein thrombosis (DVT) can be clinically accurate in about 50% of cases based on presenting signs and symptoms. The clinical signs and symptoms of acute DVT include(s)

(A) pain and swelling
(B) increased temperature
(C) cyanosis of the limb

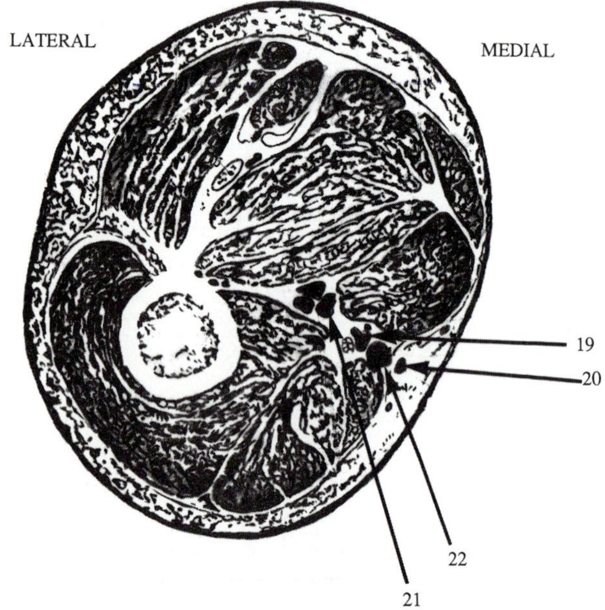

Figure 9–48. Cross section proximal thigh. (*Reprinted with permission from Gray H, Clemente CD: Anatomy of the Human Body. Philadelphia: Lea & Febiger, 1985.*)

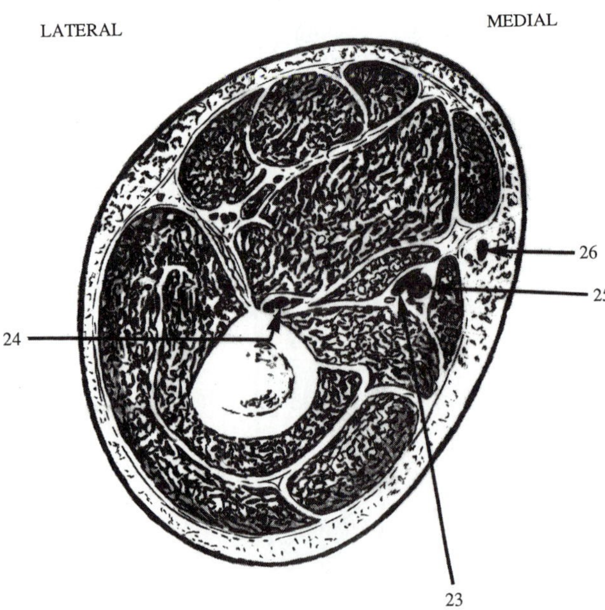

Figure 9–49. Cross section midthigh. (*Reprinted with permission from Gray H, Clemente CD: Anatomy of the Human Body. Philadelphia: Lea & Febiger, 1985.*)

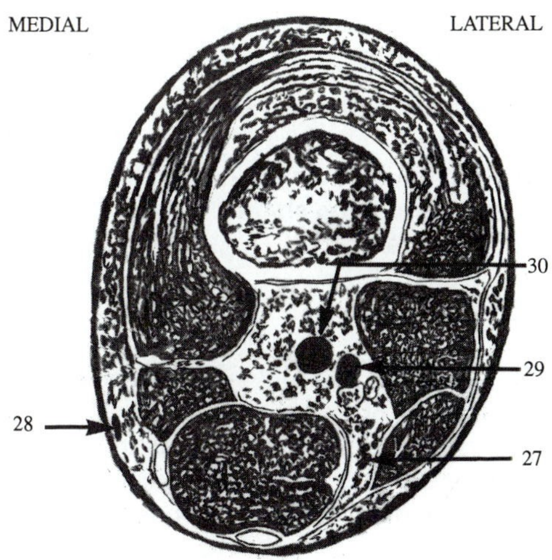

Figure 9–50. Cross section at the popliteal space. (*Reprinted with permission from Gray H, Clemente CD: Anatomy of the Human Body. Philadelphia: Lea & Febiger, 1985.*)

(D) A and B only
(E) all of the above

32. Patients who are at high risk for developing deep vein thrombosis are

(A) those who have had recent major surgical procedures
(B) those with metastatic disease
(C) those who have taken oral contraceptives
(D) A only
(E) all of the above

33. What are the multiple factors affecting venous circulation

(A) veins are collapsible
(B) veins contain valves
(C) collateral pathways rarely develop
(D) venous system is low pressure system
(E) effect of gravity affect volume and function
(F) all of the above except C
(G) all of the above

34. Treatment of acute deep vein thrombosis may consist of

(A) 7–10 days of intravenous heparin
(B) aspirin every 6 hours
(C) thrombolytic agents such as streptokinase or urokinase
(D) elevation of the limb
(E) bed rest
(F) coumadin (warfarin sodium)
(G) all of the above
(H) B, D, and E
(I) all of the above except B

35. Virchow's triad contains the key elements of the etiology of deep vein thrombosis. The triad consists of

(A) stasis
(B) lysis
(C) hypercoagulability
(D) endothelial damage
(E) recanalization
(F) B, C, and E
(G) A, C, and D

36. The most common site for thrombi to appear is

(A) soleal sinuses
(B) right common femoral vein
(C) venous valve sinus
(D) left iliofemoral venous segment
(E) A, C, and D
(F) A, B, and C
(G) all of the above

37. Varicose veins are generally divided into two categories, primary and secondary. Primary varicose veins

(A) involve perforating veins
(B) are confined to the superficial venous system
(C) occur in the presence of deep vein thrombosis
(D) involve the deep veins of the calf

38. Secondary varicose veins occur when

(A) the deep venous system is obstructed
(B) the valves are destroyed or rendered incompetent
(C) flow in communicating veins is reversed and the direction of flow changes from deep to superficial
(D) venous blood is forced to follow alternate pathways to reach the heart
(E) A, B, and D
(F) all of the above

39. Superficial thrombophlebitis is a distinctly separate entity from deep venous thrombosis in signs, symptoms, and treatment. The signs and symptoms for superficial thrombophlebitis include

(A) local tenderness
(B) redness
(C) palpable cord
(D) A and B
(E) A, B, and C

40. The treatment of superficial thrombophlebitis consists of

(A) 7–10 days of intravenous heparin
(B) oral anti-inflammatory drug (aspirin)
(C) heat to the affected area
(D) all of the above
(E) B and C

41. Venous Doppler flow patterns in the legs are normally dominated by the pressure changes that occur with respiration. During inspiration, there is an increase in intraabdominal pressure. What would you expect to happen to the venous Doppler signal in the common femoral vein during inspiration

(A) decrease or stop
(B) increase
(C) have no appreciable change
(D) none of the above

42. With expiration, the intraabdominal pressure decreases, therefore the venous Doppler signal from the common femoral vein during expiration should

(A) decrease
(B) increase
(C) have no appreciable change
(D) stop

43. In acute deep vein thrombosis (DVT), the venous Doppler signal at the level of obstruction will be

(A) increased
(B) decreased
(C) absent
(D) continuous and unaffected by respiration

44. In acute deep vein thrombosis (DVT), proximal to the level of obstruction, the Doppler flow will be

(A) increased
(B) decreased
(C) absent
(D) continuous and unaffected by respiration

45. Diagnosis of deep vein thrombosis by ultrasound alone relies mostly on compressibility of the vein walls, size of the vein, and visible thrombus. What veins are always difficult or unable to be compressed normally?

(A) common femoral veins
(B) superficial femoral veins
(C) iliac veins
(D) inferior vena cava
(E) C and D

46. Duplex scanning aids in the diagnosis of deep vein thrombosis by the addition of Doppler analysis to B-mode imaging. The regions that benefit most from Doppler are

(A) pelvic
(B) hiatus canal
(C) mid thigh
(D) adductor canal
(E) A and D
(F) A and C

47. The proper patient position for a lower extremity duplex scan is

(A) supine with head elevated 10° to 20°
(B) prone
(C) supine with head elevated 50° to 60°
(D) knee and hip slightly externally rotated
(E) leg straight
(F) A and D
(G) A and E

48. Because the signs and symptoms of acute deep vein thrombosis often are similar to those of postphlebitic syndrome, it is important to be able to differentiate chronic from acute deep vein thrombosis. The sign(s) of chronic deep vein thrombosis is

(A) increased diameter of vein
(B) thickened vein walls
(C) difficult compression of vein walls
(D) presence of venous flow
(E) incompetence of valves
(F) all of the above
(G) B, C, D, and E

49. Claudication is a discomfort or disability associated with exercise. Depending on the level and extent of disease, the patient may present with buttock, thigh, calf, or foot claudication. Which of the following are consistent with true arterial claudication?

(A) cramping pain above the level of arterial stenosis
(B) cramping pain below the level of arterial stenosis
(C) nocturnal muscle cramps
(D) pain completely relieved after a minute or so of rest
(E) pain completely relieved after 30–40 minutes of rest
(F) C and D
(G) B and D

50. Signs and symptoms of arterial disease of the lower extremity include

(A) intermittent claudication
(B) dependent rubor
(C) pallor on elevation
(D) impotence in males
(E) trophic skin changes
(F) all of the above
(G) A, B, D, and E

51. There are many known risk factors that play a part in the development of atherosclerosis of the extremities. These include

(A) family history
(B) cigarette smoking
(C) hypertension
(D) malignancies
(E) diabetes
(F) all of the above
(G) A, B, C, and E

52. Duplex scanning, especially with color, is an effective and accurate means of following patients who have undergone endovascular procedures (balloon angioplasty, laser atherectomy). The generally accepted criteria for a high-grade hemodynamically significant stenosis include

(A) velocities greater than 150 cm/s
(B) absent reverse flow velocity
(C) velocities greater than 400 cm/s
(D) marked spectral broadening
(E) A and B
(F) B, C, and D

53. Fig. 9–51 shows the orientation of the superficial femoral artery to the superficial femoral vein in the mid thigh. The superficial femoral vein in this sonogram is

(A) posterior to the superficial femoral artery
(B) anterior to the superficial femoral artery
(C) filled with thrombus
(D) normal in appearance
(E) A and D
(F) B and C

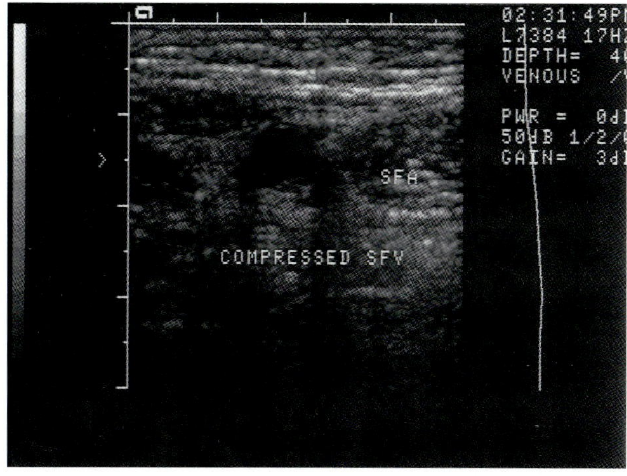

Figure 9–52. Sonogram demonstrating a compressed superficial femoral vein.

54. Fig. 9–52 demonstrates a compressed superficial femoral vein. The sonographic finding(s) is

(A) acute deep vein thrombosis
(B) normal appearance during compression maneuver
(C) chronic deep vein thrombosis
(D) none of the above

55. The Doppler signal in Fig. 9–53 represents

(A) abnormal continuous venous flow
(B) normal phasic venous flow pattern
(C) abnormal arterial flow
(D) normal arterial waveform

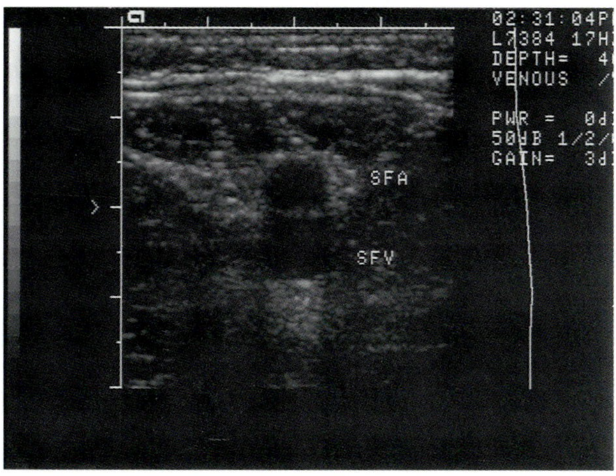

Figure 9–51. Sonogram of a superficial vein.

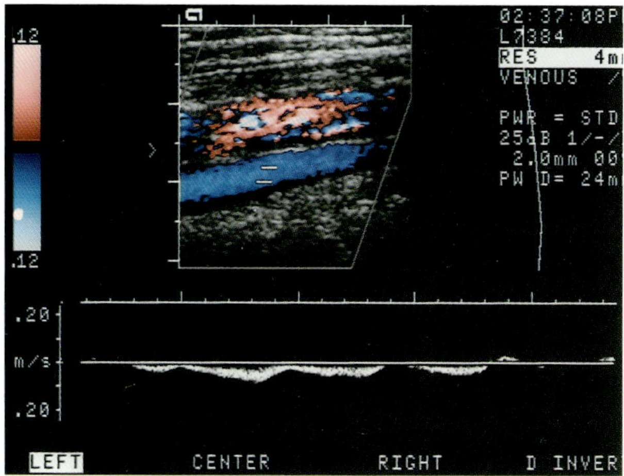

Figure 9–53. Sonogram of a Doppler signal.

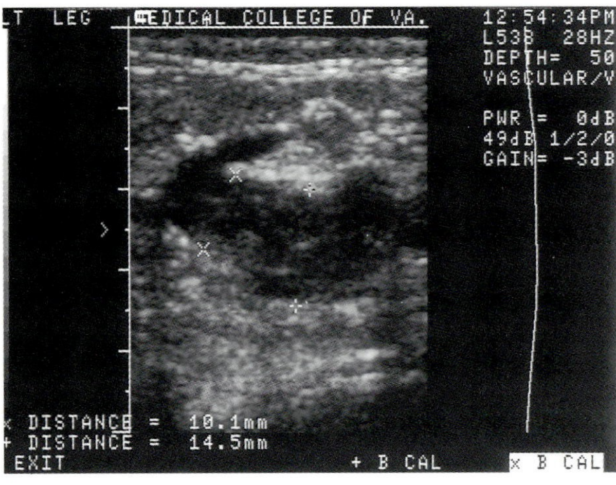

A

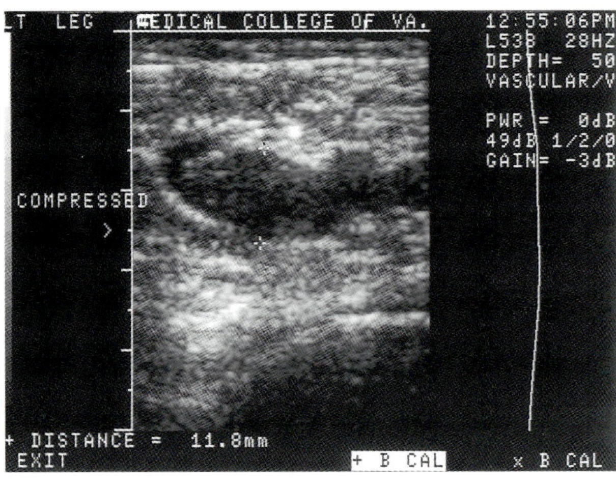

B

Figure 9–54. (**A and B**) Sonogram of the leg.

56. This patient was evaluated for slight bilateral leg edema without pain, with a history of lung resection 3 weeks previously for metastatic cancer of the lung. The most likely sonographic finding(s) in Fig. 9–54 is

(A) thrombosis of the left common femoral vein
(B) thrombosis of the saphenous vein
(C) thrombosis of the left iliac vein
(D) normal sonographic appearance
(E) A and B
(F) all of the above

57. The sonographic finding in Fig. 9–55 is

(A) normal arterial wall
(B) isolated irregular plaque on the vessel wall
(C) thrombus within the vessel lumen
(D) high-grade stenosis of the common femoral artery

58. The Doppler signal in Fig. 9–56 demonstrates

(A) triphasic flow
(B) marked spectral broadening
(C) normal velocity profile at 83 cm/s
(D) abnormal velocity profile at 83 cm/s
(E) A and C
(F) B and D

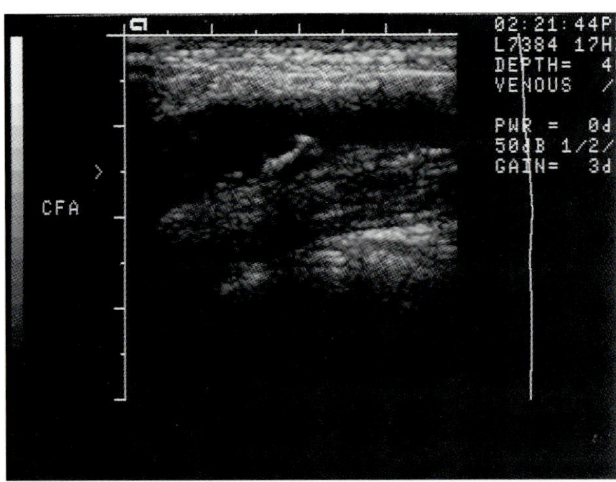

Figure 9–55. Sonogram of an artery.

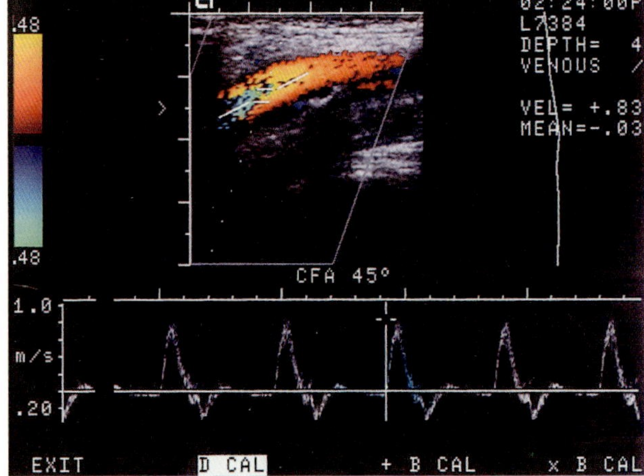

Figure 9–56. Doppler signal.

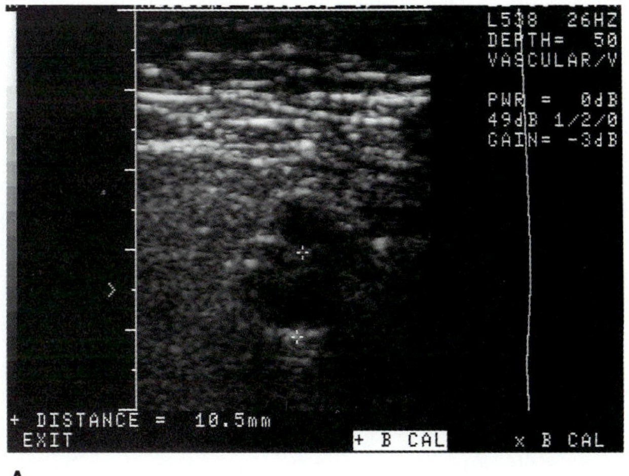

A

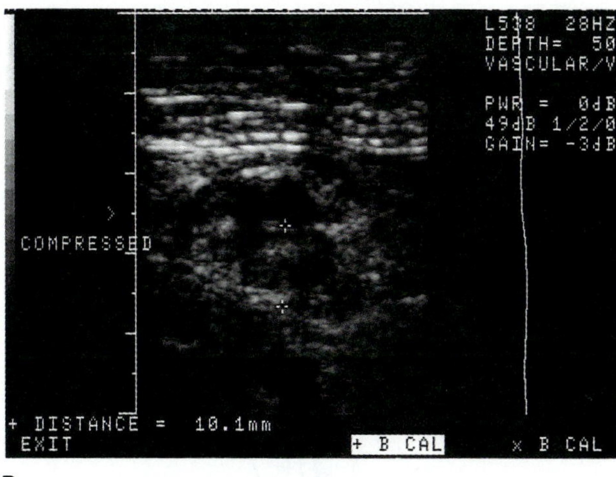

B

Figure 9–57. (A and B) Sonogram of the leg.

59. The sonographic finding(s) in Fig. 9–57 is

(A) slightly dilated superficial femoral vein
(B) increased echogenicity within the lumen of the superficial femoral vein
(C) noncompressibility of the superficial femoral vein
(D) absence of Doppler flow
(E) A, B, and C
(F) all of the above

Questions 60 through 66: Match the structures in Fig. 9–58 with terms in Column B.

COLUMN A	COLUMN B
60. _____	(A) internal iliac artery
61. _____	(B) popliteal artery
62. _____	(C) superficial femoral artery
63. _____	(D) profunda (deep) femoral artery
64. _____	(E) common femoral artery
65. _____	(F) distal aorta
66. _____	(G) external iliac artery

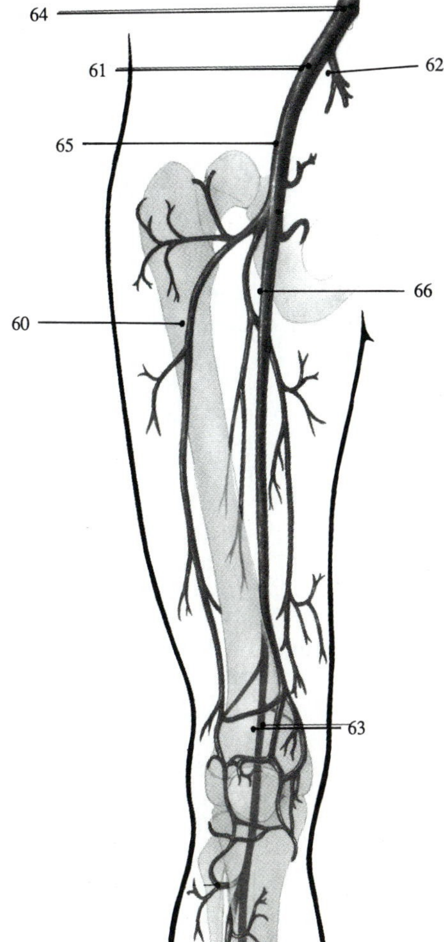

Figure 9–58. Arteries of the thigh. (*Reprinted with permission from Abbott Laboratories, North Chicago, IL. Medical illustration by Scott Thorn Barrows, AMI.*)

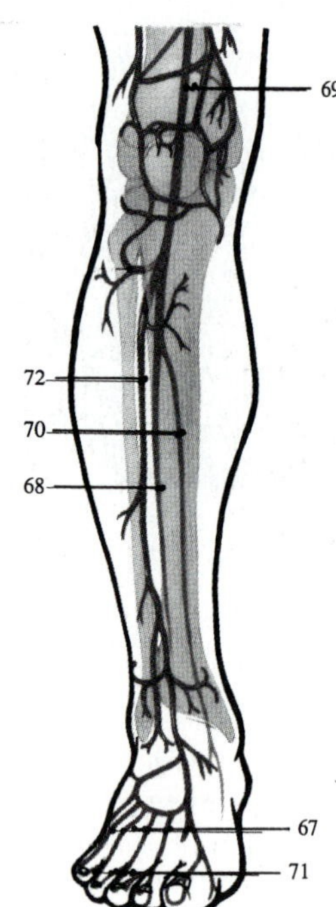

Figure 9–59. Arteries of the leg. (*Reprinted with permission from Abbott Laboratories, North Chicago, IL. Medical Illustration by Scott Thorn Barrows, AMI.*)

Questions 67 through 72: Match the structures in Fig. 9–59 with the terms in Column B.

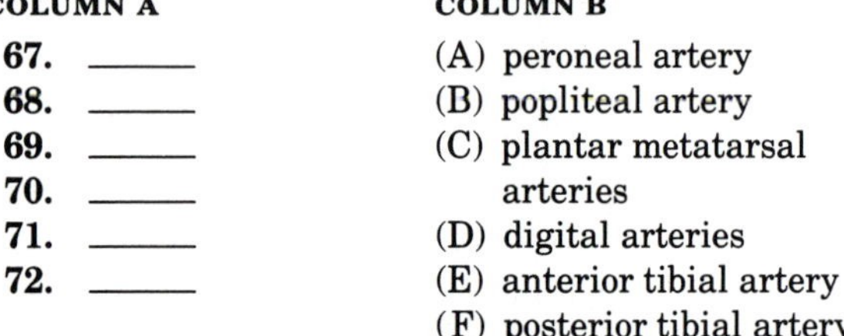

COLUMN A	COLUMN B
67. ______	(A) peroneal artery
68. ______	(B) popliteal artery
69. ______	(C) plantar metatarsal arteries
70. ______	(D) digital arteries
71. ______	(E) anterior tibial artery
72. ______	(F) posterior tibial artery

Questions 73 through 76: Match the velocity waveforms in Fig. 9–60 with the terms in Column B.

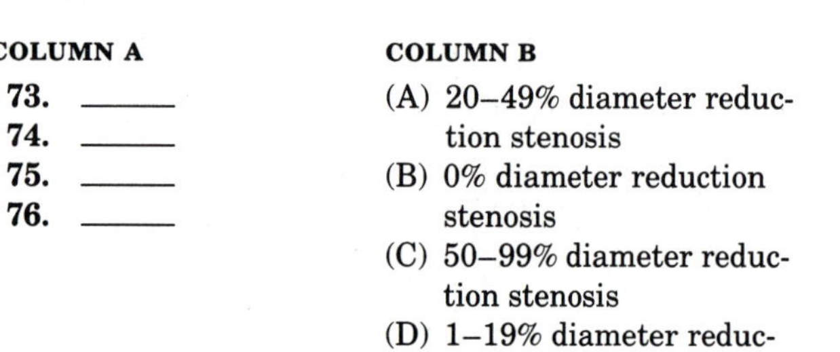

COLUMN A	COLUMN B
73. ______	(A) 20–49% diameter reduction stenosis
74. ______	(B) 0% diameter reduction stenosis
75. ______	(C) 50–99% diameter reduction stenosis
76. ______	(D) 1–19% diameter reduction stenosis

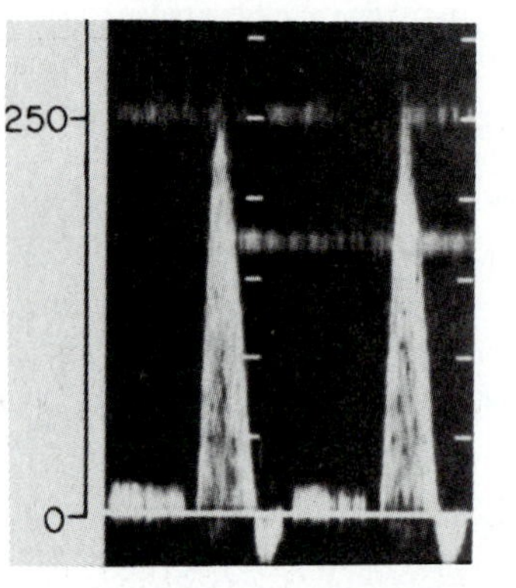

Question 73

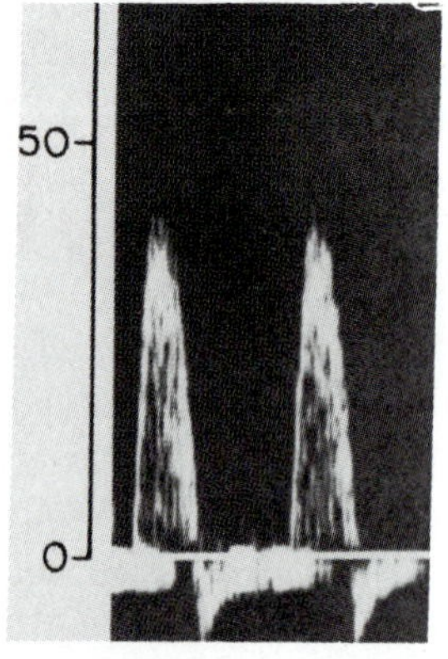

Question 74

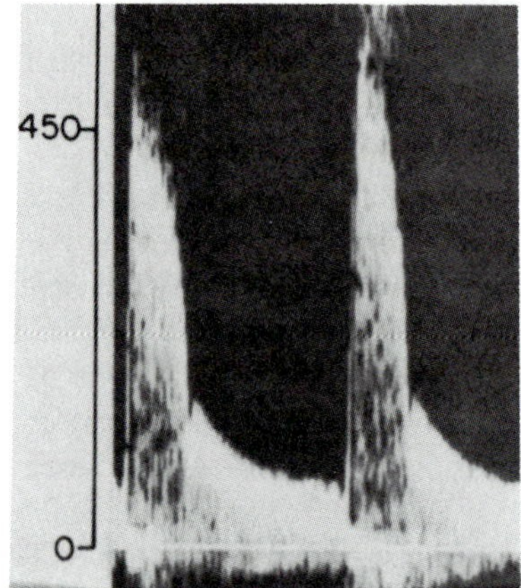

Question 75

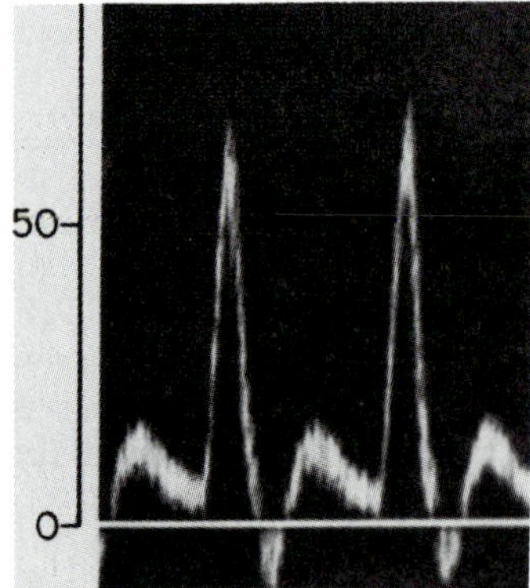

Question 76

Figure 9–60. Velocity waveforms (cm/sc.) (*Reprinted from Bergan JJ, Yao JST: Arterial Surgery: New Diagnostic and Operative Techniques. Philadelphia: Grune & Stratton, 1988, p 441.*)

77. The most likely cause of a transient ischemic attack (TIA) is
    (A) a decrease in blood flow caused by a narrowed segment of an arterial lumen
    (B) release of embolic debris from atheromatous plaque that occludes distal arteries
    (C) orthostatic hypotension
    (D) turbulent arterial flow distal to a severe stenosis in the internal carotid artery

78. An ischemic deficit that lasts greater than 24 hours but clears completely within 1 week is

(A) transient ischemic attack
(B) reversible ischemic neurologic deficit (RIND)
(C) stroke in evolution
(D) completed stroke

79. A neurologic symptom related to atherosclerotic disease in the posterior circulation (vertebrobasilar artery disease) is

(A) amaurosis fugax
(B) contralateral extremity weakness
(C) orthostatic hypotension
(D) vertigo

80. A symptom that is *not* related to internal carotid artery disease is

(A) hemiplegia
(B) supraorbital or temporal headache on the occluded side
(C) dysphagia
(D) speech deficit with the involvement of the dominant hemisphere

81. All statements regarding a subclavian steal are true *except*

(A) it is caused by a severe stenosis or occlusion of the subclavian artery distal to the origin of the ipsilateral vertebral artery
(B) blood flow from the ipsilateral vertebral artery is reversed to compensate for the reduction in flow in the subclavian artery
(C) the patient may complain of basilar artery symptoms (vertigo, visual disturbances, headache)
(D) the patient may have a decreased pulse in the affected limb

82. An embolic episode involving the opthalmic artery (amaurosis fugax) or its branches can result in

(A) transient blindness of the ipsilateral eye
(B) transient blindness of the contralateral eye
(C) abnormal eye movements
(D) hemianopsia

83. The first major branch of the internal carotid artery with clinical significance is the

(A) middle cerebral artery
(B) anterior cerebral artery
(C) ophthalmic artery
(D) posterior communicating artery

84. There are three layers of tissue within the arterial wall. The structure that is *not* one of the three layers is

(A) media
(B) adventitia
(C) intima
(D) striated muscle

85. Of the statements below, the one that is true is

(A) veins have valves that protrude into the lumen from the medial layer
(B) the adventitial layer of the artery is stronger and thicker than that of the vein
(C) the tunica media of the artery is thinner than the tunica media of the vein
(D) the wall of the arterial capillaries consist of the tunica media and the tunica intima

86. With a hemodynamically significant, short-segment stenosis, one would expect

(A) an increased peak-systolic velocity and an increased end-diastolic velocity
(B) a decreased peak-systolic velocity and a decreased end-diastolic velocity
(C) an increased peak-systolic velocity and a decreased end-diastolic velocity
(D) a decreased peak-systolic velocity and an increased end-diastolic velocity

87. Information obtained from the pulsed-wave Doppler spectral display includes all the following *except*

(A) the source of origin of the Doppler signal
(B) pulsatility features of the waveform
(C) velocity or frequency shift of the blood flow
(D) direction of flow

88. Turbulent flow (loss of the laminar pattern) occurs in all instances *except*

(A) in the carotid bulb as blood flow changes occur
(B) after a severe stenosis
(C) at a site 2 cm proximal to a severe stenosis of 50% or greater
(D) placement of the sample volume near the arterial wall

89. Differentiation of the internal carotid artery waveform from the external carotid artery waveform is important. Characteristic flow in the normal internal carotid artery is

(A) decreased peripheral resistance with an increase in the diastolic flow component
(B) increased peripheral resistance with a decrease in the diastolic component
(C) increased peripheral resistance with an increase in the diastolic flow component
(D) decreased peripheral resistance with a decrease in the diastolic component

90. Positive identification of the external carotid artery from the internal carotid artery can be made by

(A) continuous diastolic flow noted on the spectral display
(B) a more lateral anatomic orientation in relation to the internal carotid artery
(C) identification of branching arteries of the external carotid artery
(D) diameter of the arterial lumen equal to or larger than the internal carotid artery

91. Spectral broadening results in the loss of the clear spectral window below the peak-systolic velocity spectral waveform in systole. Which of the following statements is *true?*

(A) a small sample volume placed centrally in the artery should decrease the size of the spectral window
(B) the spectral window filling occurs as flow disturbances produce vortices (swirling eddies) with varying flow direction
(C) vortices (rotating flow) will show only forward flow and produce a narrow band of velocities demonstrating a clear spectral window
(D) loss of the spectral window occur only with stenotic lesions of 75% or greater

92. A transient ischemic attack is

(A) a temporary neurologic loss that lasts longer than 24 hours but is less than 3 weeks in duration
(B) a neurologic deficit that progresses over time
(C) a neurologic deficit that clears after a 1-week duration
(D) a temporary motor or sensory disturbance lasting less than 24 hours in duration

93. A carotid bruit is heard because of

(A) arteriovenous malformation
(B) disease of the great vessels
(C) audible turbulence localized at the carotid bifurcation
(D) valvular stenosis

94. Appreciable changes in pressure and flow do not occur until the diameter of an artery is reduced by 50% or greater. This degree of narrowing is called

(A) critical stenosis
(B) Reynolds' number
(C) Bernoulli's principle
(D) Poiseuille's law

95. The principal control mechanisms affecting blood volume changes are

(A) viscosity and blood vessel diameter
(B) cardiac output and peripheral resistance
(C) blood pressure gradients and inertial losses
(D) energy losses and flow-reducing lesions

96. Ocular pneumoplethysmography performed with carotid compression

(A) provides information about collateral circulation
(B) can distinguish between a high-grade stenosis and total occlusion
(C) can determine the exact site of stenosis
(D) is important for determining flow volume in the carotid artery

97. Care should be taken in the performance of carotid compression because of

(A) discomfort to the patient
(B) stimulation of baroreceptors that can decrease heart rate
(C) stimulation of baroreceptors that can increase heart rate
(D) the possibility of totally occluding a severely stenosed internal carotid artery segment

98. One advantage of using continuous wave Doppler is

(A) the ability to differentiate overlying blood vessels
(B) minimal spectral broadening
(C) high velocities can be displayed without aliasing
(D) control of the depth selection of the sample site

99. When the external carotid artery supplies collateral circulation for an occluded internal carotid artery, the most noticeable change in the external waveform is

(A) flow reversal in the diastolic component
(B) a decrease in the peak-systolic velocity
(C) an increase in the end-diastolic velocity
(D) a decrease in the end-diastolic velocity

100. Factors affecting the Doppler shift frequency include

(A) Doppler angle
(B) transducer
(C) velocity of the red blood cells
(D) B and C
(E) A, B, and C

101. Nonatheromatous causes of turbulent flow in the carotid arteries may include

(A) sudden increase in the diameter of the blood vessel
(B) tortuosity of the internal carotid artery
(C) kinking of the internal carotid artery
(D) all of the above
(E) none of the above

102. An example of indirect cerebrovascular testing is

(A) Doppler imaging of the carotid bifurcation
(B) duplex Doppler of the carotid bifurcation
(C) continuous-wave Doppler investigation of the carotid arteries
(D) periorbital Doppler

103. An increased resistivity index in the common carotid artery may indicate

(A) stenotic disease proximal to the sample site
(B) stenotic disease distal to the sample site
(C) disease at the sample site
(D) sample volume placement too close to the arterial wall

104. As an arterial stenosis becomes hemodynamically significant, which statement is *true* about the hemodynamics of the stenosis?

(A) flow volume increases, peak-systolic velocity decreases
(B) flow volume decreases, peak-systolic velocity decreases
(C) flow volume decreases, peak-systolic velocity increases
(D) flow volume increases, peak-systolic velocity increases

105. Atheroma formation within the intimal layer of the artery is the primary cause of extracranial cerebrovascular disease.

(A) true
(B) false

106. The most common site for atherosclerotic plaque formation in the extracranial circulation is the carotid bifurcation.

(A) true
(B) false

107. Arterial plaque ulceration can ultimately lead to the formation of thrombus. This can increase the risk of arterial embolus.

(A) true
(B) false

108. In the event of occlusive disease in the internal carotid artery proximal to the carotid siphon, the external carotid artery provides collateral circulation through the ophthalmic artery via the distal branches off the superficial temporal artery.

(A) true
(B) false

109. Complete formation of the circle of Willis occurs in 60% of all individuals.

(A) true
(B) false

110. Digital compression of the ipsilateral superficial temporal artery during periorbital examination will result in an increase in periorbital artery flow.

(A) true
(B) false

111. The normal ophthalmic artery blood flow is directed out of the orbit toward the face.

(A) true
(B) false

112. Digital compression of the superficial temporal artery during the periorbital examination with a concurrent ipsilateral internal carotid stenosis inferior to the ophthalmic artery may result in an increase in ophthalmic artery flow.

(A) true
(B) false

113. Middle cerebral spectral analysis can be obtained through the thinnest portion of the temporal bone.

(A) true
(B) false

114. The basilar artery can be examined by cephalic angulation through the foramen magnum.

(A) true
(B) false

115. A transducer frequency of 2–3 MHz is required for transcranial Doppler.

(A) true
(B) false

116. A 50% diameter reduction of an arterial lumen is equal to an area reduction of 75%.

(A) true
(B) false

117. Blood flow volume remains stable until a diameter reduction of about 50–60%; at this point, the volume of blood flow begins to increase to compensate for the stenosis.

(A) true
(B) false

118. As the diameter reduction of the arterial lumen exceeds 50%, the peak systolic velocities begin to increase. This type of lesion is considered hemodynamically significant.

(A) true
(B) false

119. A narrow range of velocities with minimal spectral window filling will appear on Doppler examination of an irregular stenotic plaque of 50% or greater.

(A) true
(B) false

120. A sample site in the ipsilateral common carotid artery proximal to a short-segment stenotic lesion in the internal carotid artery should have an increase in the resistance to flow.

(A) true
(B) false

121. Highest peak systolic velocity is found at the narrowest portion of the stenotic lesion.

(A) true
(B) false

122. As flow passes through a stenotic lesion, it returns to a laminar flow pattern almost immediately.

(A) true
(B) false

123. Spectral broadening can be described as an increased range of velocities on the spectral display with spectral window filling.

(A) true
(B) false

124. The flow pattern throughout the stenotic lesion will remain laminar in nature.

(A) true
(B) false

Questions 125 through 154: Answer *true* or *false* for each of the statements.

Factors that can affect the peak-systolic and end-diastolic velocities in a stenotic lesion during the pulsed-wave Doppler examination are

125. blood pressure _____

126. cardiac output _____

127. peripheral resistance _____

128. arterial compliance _____

129. contralateral carotid obstruction _____

130. The carotid triangle is a depression in the neck formed by the sternomastiod, omohyoid, and digastric muscles

(A) true
(B) false

131. The carotid triangle is the usual location of the carotid bifurcation

(A) true
(B) false

132. Differences in pressures between one end of a tube and the other end is called a pressure gradient.

(A) true
(B) false

133. Flow of a liquid occurs even when a pressure gradient does not exist

(A) true
(B) false

134. The greater the difference in pressure between two points, the faster the fluid will flow.

(A) true
(B) false

135. All other factors being constant, the artery with the smallest radius will have a higher resistance to flow.

(A) true
(B) false

136. Ocular pneumoplethysmography (OPG) can measure the ophthalmic artery pressure, which can reflect the pressure in the distal internal carotid artery.

(A) true
(B) false

137. Ocular pneumoplethysmography will detect carotid artery obstruction only when there is a decrease in arterial pressure

(A) true
(B) false

Arteries that demonstrate high-volume, low-resistance flow include

138. the common carotid artery _____

139. the internal carotid artery _____

140. the external carotid artery _____

141. the vertebral artery _____

Certain patients are at greater risk for completed stroke. Which symptoms or conditions predispose a patient to stroke?

142. prior transient ischemic attack (TIA) _____

143. hypertension _____

144. cholesterol emboli in the retinal artery _____

145. neck bruit _____

The advantage(s) of pulsed-wave Doppler include

146. depth information _____

147. no limit on maximum velocities displayed _____

148. separation of overlying flow signals _____

149. continuous transmission and reception of Doppler information _____

Symptoms related to vertebrobasilar artery disease include

150. ataxia _____

151. dysphonia _____

152. hemiplegia _____

153. diplopia _____

154. numbness of an arm _____

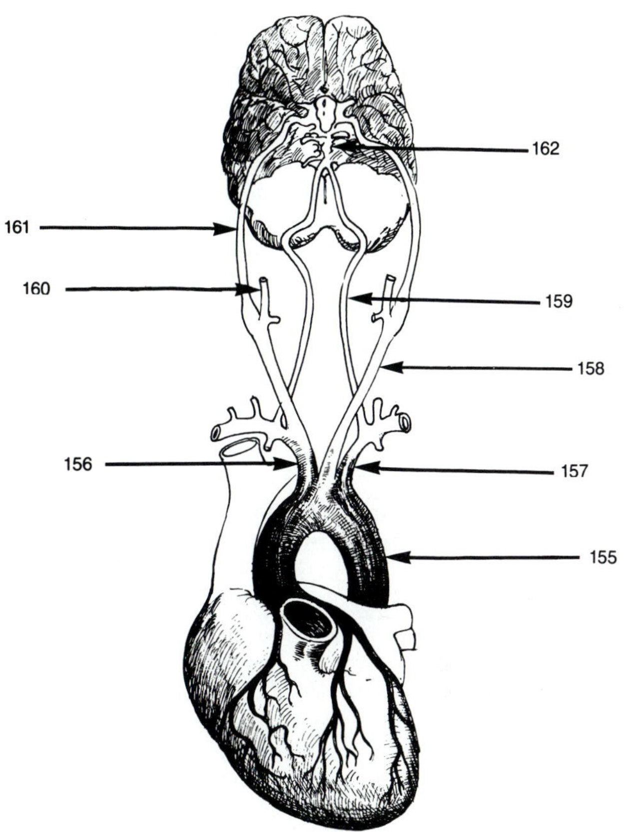

Figure 9–61. Blood supply to the brain.

Questions 155 through 162: Match the structures in Fig. 9–61 with the terms in Column B.

COLUMN A	COLUMN B
155. _____	(A) right internal carotid artery
156. _____	(B) right external carotid artery
157. _____	(C) left subclavian artery
158. _____	(D) basilar artery
159. _____	(E) brachiocephalic trunk
160. _____	(F) aortic arch
161. _____	(G) left common carotid artery
162. _____	(H) left vertebral artery

Questions 163 through 172: Match the structures in Fig. 9–62 with the terms in Column B.

COLUMN A	COLUMN B
163. ______	(A) subclavian artery
164. ______	(B) common carotid artery
165. ______	(C) brachiocephalic trunk
166. ______	(D) external carotid artery
167. ______	(E) vertebral artery
168. ______	(F) superficial temporal artery
169. ______	(G) supraorbital artery
170. ______	(H) superior thyroid artery
171. ______	(I) internal carotid artery
172. ______	(J) ophthalmic artery

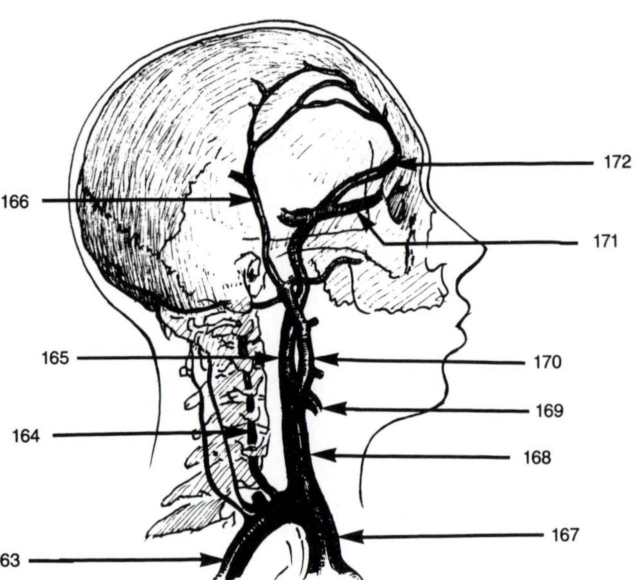

Figure 9–62. Cerebrovascular anatomy (*Reproduced with permission from Zwiebel, WJ: Introduction to Vascular Ultrasonography, 2nd ed. Philadelphia: WB Saunders, 1986.*)

Questions 173 through 180: Match the structures in Fig. 9–63 with the terms in Column B.

COLUMN A	COLUMN B
173. ______	(A) posterior communicating artery
174. ______	(B) anterior cerebral artery
175. ______	(C) anterior communicating artery
176. ______	(D) vertebral artery
177. ______	(E) middle cerebral artery
178. ______	(F) internal carotid artery
179. ______	(G) basilar artery
180. ______	(H) posterior cerebral artery

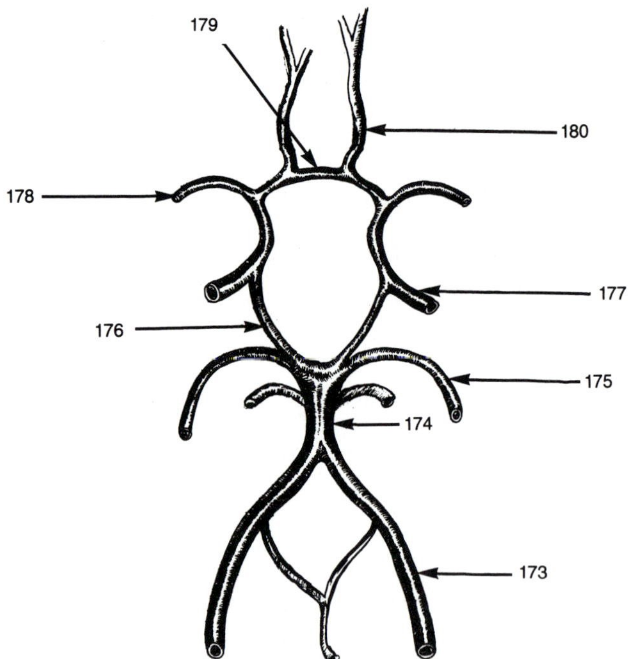

Figure 9–63. Circle of Willis.

Answers and Explanations

1. **(A)** Popliteal vein. *(Fig. 9–13, Study Guide)*

2. **(D)** Distal inferior vena cava. *(Fig. 9–13, Study Guide)*

3. **(C)** Superficial femoral vein. *(Fig. 9–13, Study Guide)*

4. **(F)** Profunda (deep) femoral vein. *(Fig. 9–13, Study Guide)*

5. **(E)** Internal iliac vein. *(Fig. 9–13, Study Guide)*

6. **(H)** Common femoral vein. *(Fig. 9–13, Study Guide)*

7. **(B)** Greater saphenous vein. *(Fig. 9–13, Study Guide)*

8. **(G)** External iliac vein. *(Fig. 9–13, Study Guide)*

9. **(H)** Greater saphenous vein. *(Fig. 9–13, Study Guide)*

10. **(F)** Peroneal veins. *(Fig. 9–14, Study Guide)*

11. **(B)** Plantar digital veins. *(Fig. 9–14, Study Guide)*

12. **(G)** Popliteal vein. *(Fig. 9–14, Study Guide)*

13. **(E)** Plantar metatarsal veins. *(Fig. 9–14, Study Guide)*

14. **(D)** Posterior tibial veins. *(Fig. 9–14, Study Guide)*

15. **(A)** Anterior tibial veins. *(Fig. 9–14, Study Guide)*

16. **(C)** Soleal veins. *(Fig. 9–14, Study Guide)*

17. **(A)** Femoral artery. *(Fig. 9–19, Study Guide)*

18. **(B)** Femoral vein. *(Fig. 9–19, Study Guide)*

19. **(D)** Femoral vein (also known as superficial femoral vein). *(Fig. 9–20, Study Guide)*

20. **(C)** Greater saphenous vein. *(Fig. 9–20, Study Guide)*

21. **(A)** Profunda (deep) femoral vein and artery. *(Figs. 9–20 and 9–22, Study Guide)*

22. **(B)** Femoral artery (also known as superficial femoral artery). *(Fig. 9–20, Study Guide)*

23. **(D)** Femoral vein (also known as superficial femoral vein). *(Fig. 9–22, Study Guide)*

24. **(C)** Profunda (deep) femoral artery and vein. *(Fig. 9–22, Study Guide)*

25. **(B)** Femoral artery (also known as superficial femoral artery). *(Fig. 9–22, Study Guide)*

26. **(A)** Greater saphenous. *(Figs. 9–20 and 9–22, Study Guide)*

27. **(A)** Lesser (small) saphenous. *(Figs. 9–21 and 9–16, Study Guide)*

28. **(C)** Greater saphenous. *(Figs. 9–21 and 9–22, Study Guide)*

29. **(B)** Popliteal vein. *(Fig. 9–21, Study Guide)*

30. **(D)** Popliteal artery. *(Figs. 9–21 and 9–16, Study Guide)*

31. **(E)** All of the above. The primary signs and symptoms of deep vein thrombosis (DVT) are pain and swelling. In cases of acute obstruction of the iliac or pelvic veins, a condition known as phlegmasia cerulea dolans, the limb turns a bluish to ashen color owing to total obstruction. In most other cases, the leg may be slightly reddened owing to incomplete venous return and venous engorgement, often with a slight increase in temperature of the extremity. Pulses will always remain intact except in severe cases of phlegmasia cerulea dolans. *(1:31–32)*

32. **(E)** All of the above. Lengthy surgeries and prolonged bed rest may cause stasis leading to the development of deep vein thrombosis. Malignancies and oral contraceptives may affect the blood coagulation factors, which also will lead to thrombus formation. *(6:90)*

33. **(F)** All of the statements are true about venous hemodynamics *except* the statement that venous collaterals rarely develop. Collateral pathways often develop in response to thrombosis and will decrease the severity of symptoms, especially swelling. The venous valves, gravity, and the muscle pumps of the calf are all responsible for proper venous return. *(1:40)*

34. **(I)** All of the statements are accepted treatments *except* aspirin therapy. This is usually reserved for the treatment of superficial thrombophlebitis and *not* deep. In extreme cases, surgical thrombectomy may also be employed. Placement of an inferior vena cava filter may be used to prevent pulmonary embolism. *(2:305)*

35. **(G)** Virchow's triad has been hypothesized as the cause of deep vein thrombosis. Stasis or blood pooling, hypercoagulability, or the increased tendency of blood to clot because of interruption of one or more of the clotting factors and endothelial damage to the vein wall are all, alone or in combination, considered causes in the development of deep vein thrombosis. *(1:32)*

36. **(E)** It is thought that thrombi most frequently develop in the soleal sinus of the calf around the area of valve cusps or in the left iliofemoral segment owing to the left iliac vein crossing the femoral artery. *(1:33)*

37. **(B)** Primary varicose veins are confined only to the superficial system without any involvement of the deep system. The causes are varied and often influenced by family history. Multiple pregnancies and previous episodes of superficial phlebitis are contributing factors. *(1:176)*

38. **(F)** All of the above. Secondary varicose veins occur in response to a deep venous obstruction that has resulted in valvular incompetence and subsequent poor venous return and stasis. Deep venous flow is then forced to seek alternate pathways of return to the heart. The most frequent pathway is reversal of flow in the communicating veins changing the venous pattern to deep draining into superficial to return to the heart. The normal pattern of return is superficial to deep veins to heart. *(1:176)*

39. **(E)** Superficial thrombophlebitis is an irritation or thrombus limited to the superficial system (ie, saphenous vein). The predominate symptoms are localized pain, redness along the involved vein, and often a palpable cord. It also can present with increased skin temperature. *(1:33)*

40. **(E)** The treatment of superficial thrombophlebitis consists of treating the symptoms. Generally, an anti-inflammatory drug such as aspirin is prescribed as well as bed rest and elevation of the limb and application of heat to the area. *(2:305–308)*

41. **(A)** During inspiration, the increase in intraabdominal pressure causes the inferior vena cava (IVC) to partially compress. Therefore, you would expect the venous flow signal to decrease or stop. *(1:60–63)*

42. **(B)** With the decrease in intraabdominal pressure, the inferior vena cava (IVC) expands and the venous flow signal should increase. *(1:60–63)*

43. **(C)** In acute deep vein thrombosis with obstruction, the venous flow signal will be absent owing to lack of flow at the area. *(1:60–63)*

44. **(D)** Proximal to the level of venous obstruction, owing to the increased velocity as the blood tries to return, the flow signal becomes continuous and is unaffected by respiration because the thrombus is obstructing the respiratory waves. *(1:60–67)*

45. **(E)** The iliac veins and the inferior vena cava are difficult to compress because of their location. The inguinal ligament makes compressing the iliac segments very difficult. The depth of the inferior vena cava along with surrounding organs makes compression nearly impossible in most patients. Another anatomic region where compression is difficult is the adductor canal in the distal thigh where the superficial femoral vein passes through before becoming the popliteal vein. *(1:83–86)*

46. **(E)** Even when compressibility is difficult, the Doppler will yield diagnostic information based on the flow characteristics in the iliac veins and the distal superficial femoral vein as it travels through the adductor canal. *(1:172–175)*

47. **(F)** Patient positioning plays an extremely important part in obtaining a complete and accurate examination. It is important to have the head elevated slightly to promote maximum venous filling by gravity. However, too much elevation can impede venous return in the groin region and yield inaccurate results. The external rotation of the hip and

knee also promote maximum venous return and make compression maneuvers easier to perform by relaxing the thigh muscles. *(4:352)*

48. **(G)** Chronic venous disease has some very distinct characteristics from the acute form. The vein diameter is generally smaller than normal in chronic disease. It usually increases in diameter when acute thrombus is present. As the thrombus ages and becomes chronic, the vein walls generally have a thickened appearance and are difficult to compress completely. Venous flow by Doppler will be present but may be diminished in velocity at rest and with augmentation. Often the valves are destroyed and the flow will be incompetent as well. *(8:739–742)*

49. **(G)** The pain of intermittent claudication occurs as a response to a lack of blood flow to the muscles below the level of stenosis during exercise (usually walking). At rest, the muscles do not demand as much blood supply; therefore there is no pain. However, when exercising, the blood and oxygen demands to the muscle are increased and the stenosis or occlusion prevents enough supply. As soon as exercise ceases, the pain is relieved because the demands for increased blood flow have stopped. *(2:4)*

50. **(F)** All of the above. Intermittent claudication is usually the first symptom of arterial disease. As the disease progresses to the point of rest pain, the trophic skin changes, dependent rubor, and pallor on elevation occur. If the level of disease is aortoiliac, it often renders the male impotent because the penile circulation branches from the internal iliac. *(2:5)*

51. **(G)** The most significant risk factor is the unavoidable family history. Cigarette smoking, diabetes, and hypertension all lead to the development of atherosclerosis. *(2:5)*

52. **(F)** As the arterial stenosis in an extremity reaches a critical (>75%) level, the peak systolic velocities usually rise in excess of 400 cm/s. The amount of spectral broadening increases as the stenosis increases. The reverse flow component of the normal arterial signal disappears first at a low percentage of stenosis. *(9:522–529)*

53. **(E)** The normal orientation in mid thigh is the superficial femoral vein, displayed posterior (or inferior) to the artery. *(4:352–356)*

54. **(B)** The opposing walls of the vein should completely collapse and touch with light probe pressure. *(4:352)*

55. **(B)** The Doppler signal in Fig. 9–53 represents a normal phasic flow signal that increases with expiration and decreases or stops with inspiration. *(4:338–340)*

56. **(E)** Fig. 9–54 represents both the common femoral and saphenous veins that are filled with thrombus and demonstrate dilation with *no* compressibility. These are all signs of acute deep vein thrombosis. The iliac veins are not shown. *(4:367–372)*

57. **(B)** Fig. 9–55 shows an approximately 1-cm length of irregular plaque on the inferior arterial wall. *(9:522–529)*

58. **(E)** The Doppler signal shows normal triphasic flow with a peak systolic velocity of 83 cm/s, which is within the normal range of velocities. *(9:522–529)*

59. **(E)** Fig. 9–57 demonstrates the presence of thrombus in the superficial femoral vein that is slightly dilated and filled with thrombus. There is no evidence of compressibility. The Doppler signal is not shown. *(4:367–372)*

60. **(D)** Deep femoral artery (profunda femoral). *(Fig. 9–16, Study Guide)*

61. **(G)** External iliac artery. *(Fig. 9–16, Study Guide)*

62. **(A)** Internal iliac artery. *(Fig. 9–16, Study Guide)*

63. **(B)** Popliteal artery. *(Fig. 9–16, Study Guide)*

64. **(F)** Distal aorta. *(Fig. 9–16, Study Guide)*

65. **(E)** Common femoral artery. *(Fig. 9–16, Study Guide)*

66. **(C)** Superficial femoral artery. *(Fig. 9–16, Study Guide)*

67. **(C)** Plantar metatarsal arteries. *(Fig. 9–17, Study Guide)*

68. **(A)** Peroneal artery. *(Fig. 9–17, Study Guide)*

69. **(B)** Popliteal artery. *(Fig. 9–17, Study Guide)*

70. **(F)** Posterior tibial artery. *(Fig. 9–17, Study Guide)*

71. **(D)** Digital arteries. *(Fig. 9–17, Study Guide)*

72. **(E)** Anterior tibial artery. *(Fig. 9–17, Study Guide)*

73. **(A)** 20–49%. When the diameter of stenosis increases in an artery, the velocity and spectral broadening increase in the Doppler waveform. *(Study Guide, p. 471)*

74. **(D)** 1–19%. *(Study Guide, p. 471)*

75. **(C)** 50–99%. *(Study Guide, p. 471)*

76. **(B)** 0–%. *(Study Guide, p. 471)*

77. **(B)** The primary cause for TIA is an embolic event caused by atheromatous debris from plaque or platelet aggregates dislodged from ulcerated plaque. *(15:1300–1302)*

78. **(B)** A reversible ischemic neurologic deficit (RIND) clears completely within 1 week. A transient ischemic attack (TIA) has symptoms that resolve within 24 hours. A patient with complete stroke has symptoms that do not clear. A stroke in evolution displays neurologic defects that become progressively worse over time, with maximum loss over a period of a week or more. *(15:1309)*

79. **(D)** Vertigo is one of the symptoms of vertebrobasilar insufficiency. *(15:1303–1304)*

80. **(C)** Dysphagia (difficulty in swallowing) is due to impairment of cranial nerve circulation that is supplied by the vertebrobasilar circulation and is *not* related to internal carotid artery disease. *(12:23)*

81. **(A)** A subclavian steal is caused by severe stenosis or occlusion of the subclavian artery proximal to the origin of the ipsilateral vertebral artery. Blood flow is reversed in the ipsilateral vertebral artery. The patient may complain of vertebrobasilar artery symptoms with a increase in flow to the affected limb. *(15:1310)*

82. **(A)** Transient blindness (amaurosis fugax) occurs in the eye on the side of the affected artery (ipsilateral). *(12:20)*

83. **(C)** The ophthalmic artery is the first major branch of the internal carotid artery with any clinical significance. *(10:81–83)*

84. **(D)** Striated muscle is not found in the wall of an artery. Smooth muscle can be found in the medial layer. *(10:27)*

85. **(B)** The adventitial layer of the artery is stronger and thicker than the vein. It gives the artery its rigidity. Venous valves are extensions of the tunica intima of the vein. The tunica media of the artery, and its muscular coat, is thicker in the vein. The wall of the arterial capillaries consists only of the tunica intima. *(10:27)*

86. **(A)** A hemodynamically significant lesion is a 50% diameter reduction or greater. As the stenotic segment exceeds 50%, the peak-systolic velocities begin to increase. The end-diastolic velocities also increase. The ratio of systolic to diastolic velocities begins to fall. *(4:181)*

87. **(A)** The source of origin of the Doppler signal is derived from the sample volume location on the 2D image *not* from the spectral display. Amplitude of the Doppler signal, pulsatility features of the waveform, velocity or frequency shift of the blood flow, and the direction of flow are all obtained from the spectral display. *(4:63–64)*

88. **(C)** A more resistive flow pattern may be noted proximal to a severe stenosis. However, flow velocity ranges should remain narrow. *(4:177)*

89. **(A)** Lower peripheral resistance in the internal carotid artery is depicted on the spectral display as higher end-diastolic velocities than those found in the external carotid artery. The cerebral circulation is a low-resistance system of which the internal carotid artery is a major source of blood supply. *(4:66–67)*

90. **(C)** Positive identification of the external carotid artery can be made by noting branching arteries distal to the carotid bulb. Other important features include a resistive pulsatility feature (decreased flow in diastole in comparison with the internal carotid artery), a more medial position in relation to the internal carotid artery, and usually a smaller luminal diameter than the internal carotid artery. *(4:151)*

91. **(B)** A clear spectral window indicates laminar flow with little flow disturbance. A small sample volume placed in the central portion of the normal flow stream will produce a crisp, clear window. Flow disturbances, such as vortices and swirling eddies, will decrease the size of the spectral window and should demonstrate flow reversal as well. Spectral broadening can occur with moderate stenotic lesions as well as severe lesions. *(16:103–104)*

92. **(D)** A transient ischemic attack is a temporary stroke lasting less than 24 hours. The event occurs on the contralateral side of the hemisphere that is affected. *(16:122)*

93. **(C)** A true carotid bruit is localized over the carotid bifurcation and is due to audible turbulence of the blood flow. A neck bruit occurs for a number of rea-

sons that include valvular stenosis, valvular disease in the great vessels, and arteriovenous malformations. *(16:126)*

94. **(A)** The critical stenosis occurs with a diameter reduction of 50% (area reduction of 75%) or greater. This is also called a hemodynamically significant lesion. *(15:23)*

95. **(B)** The two principal mechanisms that control blood volume are the cardiac output and the peripheral resistance. Cardiac output (mL/s) is the rate of blood flow per minute. Two factors that affect cardiac output are heart rate and stroke volume. Peripheral resistance is controlled by the arterioles and arterial capillaries. These tiny vessels control the volume of blood flow. *(10:157–159,163–165)*

96. **(A)** Ocular pneumoplethysmography with compression of the carotid artery low in the neck gives important information about collateral circulation from the vertebrobasilar and contralateral carotid arteries. *(4:250)*

97. **(B)** Compression of the carotid artery should always be performed low in the neck. Massage of the carotid bulb can cause a decrease of the heart rate by stimulation of baroreceptors. *(10:75)*

98. **(C)** The major advantage of continuous-wave Doppler is that it can display high velocities without the phenomena of aliasing occurring. Unfortunately, it has no range resolution and its sample size cannot be controlled. *(14:108)*

99. **(C)** When the external carotid acts as a collateral channel for a highly stenotic or occluded internal carotid artery, the diastolic portion of the external waveform will increase. The arterioles dilate in the distal branches of the external carotid artery, allowing for an increase in flow volume. The external carotid artery assumes a low resistance waveform. *(13:25)*

100. **(E)** Doppler shift frequencies are affected by Doppler angle, transducer frequency, and the velocity of the red blood cells. As the Doppler angle decreases between the Doppler beam and the flow stream, there will be an increase in the frequency shift. If the transducer frequency decreases, the frequency shift will decrease. The velocity of the red blood cells will affect the Doppler shift. As the red blood cells move faster, the frequency shift will increase. *(13:5–7)*

101. **(D)** Turbulent flow does not necessarily have to be caused by atheromatous plaque. Sudden increase in the diameter of the blood vessel can cause turbulence. This can be seen in the carotid bulb region where the boundary layer separates from the arterial wall with an inherent reversal of flow. Tortuous arteries also can cause turbulence as blood flow is forced to change direction. Carotid kinks can cause turbulence as the arterial lumen is narrowed. *(13:18–19)*

102. **(D)** Doppler imaging, duplex Doppler, and continuous-wave Doppler of the carotid arteries are all direct methods of assessing carotid artery hemodynamics. Periorbital Doppler assesses the condition of the internal carotid artery indirectly. Investigation of flow direction of arteries distal to the internal carotid artery and their hemodynamic response to compression maneuvers helps to evaluate the patency of the internal carotid artery. *(15:1338–1346)*

103. **(B)** An increased resistivity index in the common carotid artery can indicate stenotic or occlusive disease distal to the sample site. Total occlusion of the internal carotid artery can cause a decrease in diastolic flow in the common carotid artery because of increased resistance to flow. *(13:88)*

104. **(C)** As an arterial stenosis exceeds 60%, the peak-systolic velocity will increase and the volume of flow will decrease. *(16:62)*

105. **(True)** The primary cause of extracranial cerebrovascular disease is atheroma formation in the arterial intima. *(15:1295)*

106. **(True)** Arterial bifurcations are common sites of atheroma formation. In the extracranial circulation, the carotid bifurcation into the internal and external carotid arteries is the most common site. *(15:1295)*

107. **(True)** Ulcerations in arterial plaque increase the risk of arterial emboli. Formation of blood platelet aggregates within the ulcer as well as the potential for thrombus formation at the site increase the risk of embolic events. *(15:1296)*

108. **(True)** The supraorbital and nasal arteries are branches of the ophthalmic artery that terminate in the forehead. The superficial temporal artery, a branch of the external carotid artery, also terminates in the forehead. Compensatory circulation can occur between these branches in the event of internal carotid artery occlusion with a resultant reversal of flow through the ophthalmic artery. *(10:83)*

109. **(False)** Approximately 20% of all patients have a completed circle of Willis. Hypoplasia of one or more components occurs in a large percentage of the population. *(15:1321)*

110. **(True)** Compression of the superficial temporal artery should result in an increase in periorbital artery flow in the normal situation. *(15:1335–1337)*

111. **(True)** The normal ophthalmic artery blood flow is directed out of the orbit toward the face. *(15:1335–1337)*

112. **(False)** Compression of the ipsilateral superficial temporal artery during periorbital Doppler will result in a decrease or obliteration of ophthalmic artery flow if the internal carotid artery is occluded. *(15:1335–1337)*

113. **(True)** Transcranial Doppler of the middle cerebral artery, anterior cerebral artery, and the posterior cerebral artery can be obtained through the thinnest portion of the temporal bone. *(15:1345)*

114. **(True)** The basilar artery can be examined by cephalic angulation through the foramen magnum. *(15:1345)*

115. **(True)** A transducer frequency of 2–3 MHz is required for transcranial Doppler. *(15:1345)*

116. **(True)** A 50% diameter reduction of an arterial lumen is equal to an area reduction of 75%. *(4:179)*

117. **(False)** Blood flow volume decreases as the diameter reduction exceeds 60% or greater. *(4:180)*

118. **(True)** At 50% diameter reduction, a stenosis becomes hemodynamically significant. It is this point where the peak-systolic velocities begin to increase. Flow volume decreases as the degree of stenosis increases. *(4:179–180)*

119. **(False)** Although the spectral waveform may be laminar in appearance, spectral broadening will occur if the stenotic zone is irregular in its borders. *(4:177)*

120. **(True)** An increased resistivity index in the ipsilateral common carotid artery may indicate a hemodynamically significant lesion in the internal carotid artery. *(13:26)*

121. **(True)** Careful search through a stenotic lesion should lead to the demonstration of the highest peak systolic velocities. *(4:177)*

122. **(False)** As flow passes through a stenotic lesion, the flow stream separates from the wall of the artery. As a result, there is reversal of flow with a turbulent spectral waveform. The degree of post-stenotic turbulent flow depends on the severity of the stenotic lesion. *(4:177)*

123. **(True)** As blood flow becomes more disturbed by arterial plaque formations, the degree of spectral broadening increases. The actual range of velocities increase, which results in a loss of the clear spectral window. *(4:177)*

124. **(True)** The flow pattern throughout the stenotic lesion will remain laminar in nature. *(4:177)*

125. **(True)** See explanation in Answer 129.

126. **(True)** See explanation in Answer 129.

127. **(True)** See explanation in Answer 129.

128. **(True)** See explanation in Answer 129.

129. **(True)** Stenotic lesions can be overestimated or underestimated because of a number of influencing factors. These include blood pressure, cardiac output, peripheral resistance, arterial compliance, and obstruction of the contralateral carotid artery. *(4:180)*

130. **(True)** The carotid triangle is a depression in the neck formed by a sternomastoid, omohyoid, and digastric muscles. *(16:130)*

131. **(True)** The carotid triangle is the usual location of the carotid bifurcation. *(16:130)*

132. **(True)** Differences in pressure allow for fluid flow. Fluids flow from a high-pressure area to a lower-pressure area. *(10:139)*

133. **(False)** When a pressure gradient does not exist, there is no flow of fluid. Flow only occurs when there is a pressure gradient. *(10:139)*

134. **(True)** Blood flow rate increases as the pressure differences between two points increase. The greater the differences between two points, the faster the flow rate between them. *(10:141)*

135. **(True)** As the radius of an artery decreases, the resistance to flow will increase. *(10:147–149)*

136. **(True)** Ocular pneumoplethysmography (OPG) can measure the ophthalmic artery pressure that can reflect the pressure in the distal internal carotid artery. *(11:29)*

137. **(True)** Ocular pneumoplethysmography will detect carotid artery obstruction only when there is a decrease in arterial pressure. *(11:92)*

138. **(True)** See explanation in answer 141.

139. **(True)** See explanation in answer 141.

140. **(False)** See explanation in answer 141.

141. **(True)** The common carotid artery, the internal carotid artery, and the vertebral artery display, in their normal flow state, high-volume and low-resistance flow. This is because they handle a large amount of flow circulation to the brain. The internal carotid artery handles between 70 and 80% of the blood flow from the common carotid artery. *(13:16)*

142. **(True)** Patients who have experienced a transient ischemic attack (TIA) are at greater risk for a completed stroke within 5 years. *(16:122)*

143. **(True)** Hypertension contributes to stroke by increasing the risk of cerebral hemorrhage and possible dislodgement of atheromatous plaque. *(4:88)*

144. **(True)** Cholesterol emboli in the retinal artery indicates the occurrence of embolic events from vessels proximal to the site. These patients are at greater risk for stroke. *(16:128)*

145. **(False)** A neck bruit does not specifically indicate vascular disease because it can be caused by a number of entities, including valvular stenosis, great vessel disease, and arteriovenous malformations. A carotid bruit is localized over the carotid bifurcation. Patients with a carotid bruit may be at risk for stroke. *(16:126)*

146. **(True)** See explanation in answer 149.

147. **(False)** See explanation in answer 149.

148. **(True)** See explanation in answer 149.

149. **(False)** Pulsed-wave Doppler allows for the selection of depth information and the separation of overlying flow signals. Maximum velocities displayed are limited to one half the pulse repetition frequency (Nyquist limit). One crystal transmits the pulses and receives the Doppler information in pulsed-wave Doppler; therefore, continuous transmission and reception is impossible. *(11:25–26)*

150. **(True)** See explanation in answer 154.

151. **(True)** See explanation in answer 154.

152. **(False)** See explanation in answer 154.

153. **(True)** See explanation in answer 154.

154. **(False)** Symptoms of vertebrobasilar artery disease include ataxia, cranial nerve involvement (dysphagia, dysphonia, dysarthia, diplopia), bilateral extremity weakness, vertigo, and drop attacks. *(11:303)*

155. **(F)** Aortic arch. *(Fig. 9–24, Study Guide)*

156. **(E)** Brachiocephalic trunk. *(Fig. 9–24, Study Guide)*

157. **(C)** Left subclavian artery. *(Fig. 9–24, Study Guide)*

158. **(G)** Left common carotid artery. *(Fig. 9–24, Study Guide)*

159. **(H)** Left vertebral artery. *(Fig. 9–24, Study Guide)*

160. **(B)** Right external carotid artery. *(Fig. 9–24, Study Guide)*

161. **(A)** Right internal carotid artery. *(Fig. 9–24, Study Guide)*

162. **(D)** Basilar artery. *(Fig. 9–24, Study Guide)*

163. **(A)** Subclavian artery. *(Fig. 9–25, Study Guide)*

164. **(E)** Vertebral artery. *(Fig. 9–25, Study Guide)*

165. **(I)** Internal carotid artery. *(Fig. 9–25, Study Guide)*

166. **(F)** Superficial temporal artery. *(Fig. 9–25, Study Guide)*

167. **(C)** Brachiocephalic trunk. *(Fig. 9–25, Study Guide)*

168. **(B)** Common carotid artery. *(Fig. 9–25, Study Guide)*

169. **(H)** Superior thyroid artery. *(Fig. 9–25, Study Guide)*

170. **(D)** External carotid artery. *(Fig. 9–25, Study Guide)*

171. **(J)** Ophthalmic artery. *(Fig. 9–25, Study Guide)*

172. **(G)** Supraorbital artery. *(Fig. 9–25, Study Guide)*

173. **(D)** Vertebral artery. *(Fig. 9–26, Study Guide)*

174. **(G)** Basilar artery. *(Fig. 9–26, Study Guide)*

175. **(H)** Posterior cerebral artery. *(Fig. 9–26, Study Guide)*

176. **(A)** Posterior communicating artery. *(Fig. 9–26, Study Guide)*

177. **(F)** Internal carotid artery. *(Fig. 9–26, Study Guide)*

178. **(E)** Middle cerebral artery. *(Fig. 9–26, Study Guide)*

179. (C) Anterior communicating artery.
(Fig. 9–26, Study Guide)

180. (B) Anterior cerebral artery.
(Fig. 9–26, Study Guide)

REFERENCES

1. Strandness DE. *Duplex Scanning in Vascular Disorders.* New York: Raven Press, 1990.
2. Rutherford, RB. *Vascular Surgery,* 2nd ed. Philadelphia: WB Saunders, 1984.
3. Bergen J, Yao J. *Arterial Surgery New Diagnostic and Operative Techniques.* Philadelphia: Grune & Stratton, 1988.
4. Zweibel W. *Introduction to Vascular Ultrasonography,* 2nd ed. Philadelphia: WB Saunders, 1986.
5. Hershey F, Barnes R, Summer D. *Noninvasive Diagnosis of Vascular Disease.* Pasadena, CA: Appleton Davies, 1984.
6. White J, Katz M. Pathogenesis of deep vein thrombi. *J Vasc Technol.* **XII**:90, 1988.
7. Cronan J, Dorfman G, et al. Deep venous thrombosis: ultrasound assessment using vein compression. *Radiology* **10**(5):522–529, 1989.
8. Cronan J, Leen V. Recurrent deep vein thrombosis: limitations of ultrasound. *Radiology* **170**(3):739–742, 1989.
9. Cossman D, Ellison J, et al. Comparison of contrast arterogram to arterial mapping with color-flow duplex imaging in the lower extremities. *J Vasc Surg* **10**(5): 522–529, 1989.
10. Belanger A. *Vascular Anatomy and Physiology: An Introductory Text.* Pasadena, CA: Appleton Davies, 1986.
11. Bernstein E: *Noninvasive Diagnostic Techniques in Vascular Disease.* 3rd ed, St. Louis, CV Mosby, 1985.
12. Fields W. Aortocranial occlusive vascular disease (stroke). *CIBA Clin Symp,* **26**(4):1–31, 1974.
13. Gerlock A, Giyanani V, Krebs C: *Applications of Noninvasive Vascular Techniques.* Philadelphia: WB Saunders, 1988.
14. Kremkau F: *Doppler Ultrasound: Principles and Instruments.* Philadelphia: WB Saunders, 1990.
15. Rutherford R. *Vascular Surgery,* Vols I and II, 3rd ed. Philadelphia: WB Saunders, 1989.
16. Taylor K, Burns P, Wells P. *Clinical Applications of Doppler Ultrasound.* New York: Raven Press, 1988.

PART II
Diagnosis of Venous Disease

Carolyn M. Semrow and David L. Rollins

Study Guide

INTRODUCTION

The true incidence of acute deep vein thrombosis is difficult to determine. Randomized clinical trials on different prophylactic regimens in which serial testing of patients was performed from the time of hospital admission probably provides the most accurate prevalence data. These studies reported a 20% incidence of deep vein thrombosis (DVT) in general medical and surgical patients over 40 years old and a 60–80% incidence in patients with long bone fracture or undergoing total joint replacements.[1–5] An even more significant finding was that 50% of these patients were asymptomatic. Acute DVT that remains confined to the extremity is relatively benign in the short term. However, the primary clinical concern in DVT is the complication of pulmonary embolism, which is fatal in 1% of patients with diagnosed DVT. Although the clinical course of the majority of patients with acute DVT is uneventful, the thrombotic process causes permanent damage to the deep venous system. Scarring of the vein wall and residual thrombus leads to a later, postphlebitic syndrome. Symptoms of this condition appear between 18 months and 10 years after the thrombotic event. Eighty percent of patients who develop acute DVT will have some symptoms of postphlebitic syndrome within 10 years.

In the mid 19th century, Virchow postulated three factors that influence the development of acute DVT: stasis of the blood, trauma to the vessels, and a hypercoagulable state. Researchers in the 20th century have determined that some mechanical and medical conditions placed individual patients at a higher risk of developing acute DVT during their course of hospitalization. These risk factors include age, obesity, surgical procedures lasting longer than 2 hours, previous history of venous thrombosis, malignancy, heart disease, prolonged bed rest, and trauma. The risk factor with the highest predictive value is a previous history of venous disease. It has been associated with an 80–100% incidence of recurrent thrombosis.[1,6]

Varicose veins are the most common form of venous disease and, contrary to popular belief, are equally prevalent in men and women. Epidemiologic data indicate that the greatest risk factor for the development of varicose veins is genetic predisposition. This pattern is familial and sex linked to the male. Primary varicose veins are dilated tortuous superficial veins, often related to the saphenous system and its branches. The exact etiology of primary varicose veins remains controversial. However, they are most likely caused by mechanical factors such as pregnancy and prolonged standing. Secondary varicose veins occur following acute deep vein thrombosis. Chronic deep vein obstruction and reflux lead to ambulatory venous hypertension and incompetence of normal valves. Commonly, the saphenous veins and their branches become dilated as venous outflow channels are created through destruction of perforating vein valves and reflux into the saphenous system. In the past, the presence of incompetent perforating veins was thought to be indicative of previous deep vein thrombosis. However, with modern technology, a multitude of investigators have reported that incompetent perforating veins occur without any evidence of a previous thrombotic process.

Over the last few years, a resurgence of interest in the venous system has occurred and new technologies have been applied to increase our knowledge of the venous system. Advances in diagnostic techniques have far outpaced our knowledge of the disease itself. Clinical diagnosis of acute venous disease, even in the most skilled hands, is only about 50% accurate. Therefore, the diagnosis and differentiation of disease must be confirmed by objective testing. Until recently, ascending contrast venography was the standard method used. Today, noninvasive laboratory techniques have all but replaced venography to confirm the diagnosis of acute deep vein thrombosis.

Owing to the complex nature of the venous system and its diseases, the vascular laboratory staff must have a thorough knowledge of anatomy, physiology, and pathophysiology. Additionally, the technical aspects of diagnostic procedures must be well known in order to provide the clinician with an accurate appraisal of the pathology. The intent of this chapter is to provide an overview of venous anatomy and physiology as well as ultrasonic diagnostic procedures. This chapter focuses on the anatomy and physiology of this region because epidemiologic studies have found that 95% of venous disease originates in the lower extremities.

BASIC VENOUS ANATOMY

The tripartite structure of the vein wall is composed of an inner *intima* that consists of a thin layer of endothelial cells, a *media* containing smooth muscle cells with a loose network of collagen and elastin fibrils, and an outer *adventitia* that is primarily made up of nondistensible collagen. Vein wall structure is similar to that of an artery. In veins, the main differences are that the media is very thin with the elastin concentration substantially reduced and the muscle fibers predominantly oriented longitudinally. The adventitia is the thickest and strongest part of the vein wall (Fig. 9–64). To assure flow in a prograde direction back to the heart, veins contain one-way valves that are generally bicuspid and consist of smooth muscle cells and loose connective tissue covered by endothelial cells (Fig. 9–65). The valves are attached to the vein wall by a circular ring of collagen and elastin fibers.

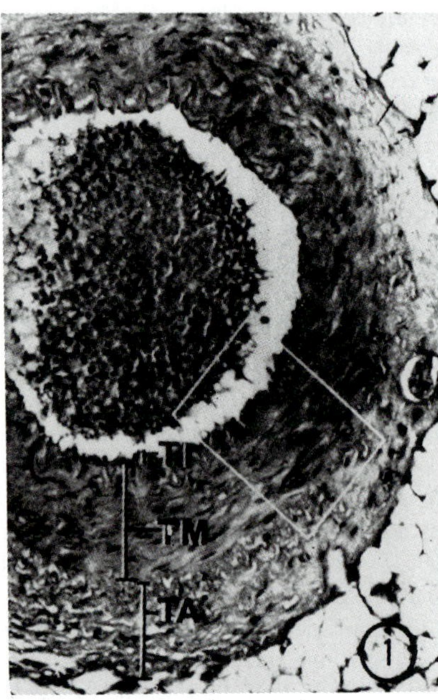

Figure 9–64. The microscopic vein structure. TA = adventitia, TM = media; TI = intima.

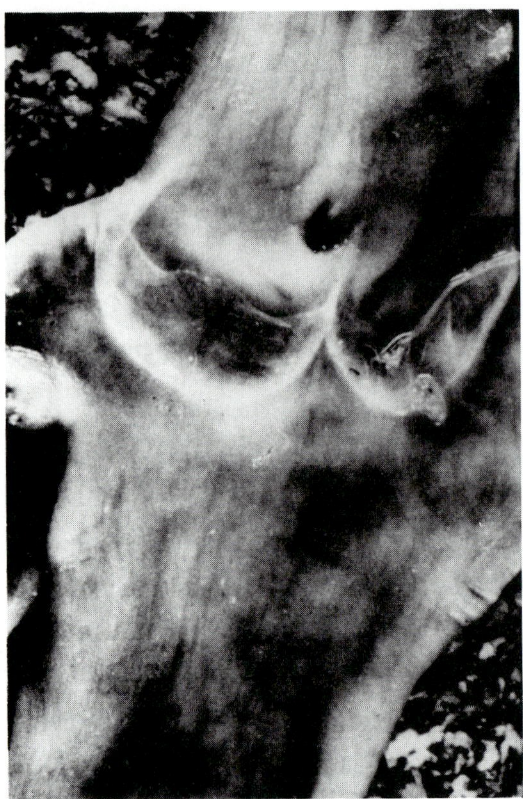

Figure 9–65. A vein with valve leaflets. *(Reprinted with permission from Gottlob R, May R: Venous Valves. New York: Springer-Verlag, 1986, p. 27.)*

This connection is associated with a localized area of vein wall dilatation or "sinus" immediately above the valve ring. The number of valves in the venous system varies depending on the distance from the heart. In the calf, valves can be found every 1.5 to 2 cm apart. As many as 10–15 valves may be present in each vein. In the thigh, there are three to five valves present, whereas valves are rarely found in the iliac veins and vena cava. The location of venous valves are inconstant within each vein, but they are most commonly found at the orifices of branches or just beyond the joining or confluence of two or more veins.

In the lower extremity, there are four components to the venous system. These are the deep, superficial, intramuscular, and perforating, or communicating, veins. The deep veins are the primary channels that transport the blood from the extremity to the heart. They are located beneath the muscle close to the bones from which their names are derived. These veins include the common femoral (CFV), superficial femoral (SFV), profunda femoral (PFV), popliteal (POP), posterior tibial (PTV), peroneal, and anterior tibial (ATV). The three deep veins of the calf (PTV, peroneal, and ATV) are classified as venae comitantes because they are intimately attached to the artery of the same name and are duplicated throughout their course. The superficial venous system consists of the greater and lesser saphenous veins along with their multitude of branches. These veins drain the skin, subcutane-

ous tissue, and foot and run beneath the superficial fascia but above the muscle fascia (Fig. 9–66). Perforating, or communicating veins as they are often called, connect the superficial to the deep veins and transport blood into the deep systems where more efficient flow is present. Intramuscular veins drain the muscles of the lower extremity into the deep venous system. These are often paired.

Precise knowledge of exact venous anatomy is necessary to assess the venous system adequately and accurately with ultrasonic techniques because there are often significant anatomic variations present that can be confusing.

ADVANCED VENOUS ANATOMY

The anatomy of the venous system is presented in the same order that venous imaging is performed so that it can easily be used as a reference.

Deep Veins

As noted above, the deep veins of the calf consist of three sets of paired vessels that are the venea comitantes accompanying the arteries. Each set of veins runs within a specific musculofascial compartment of the leg. The posterior tibial veins are formed by the union of the superficial and

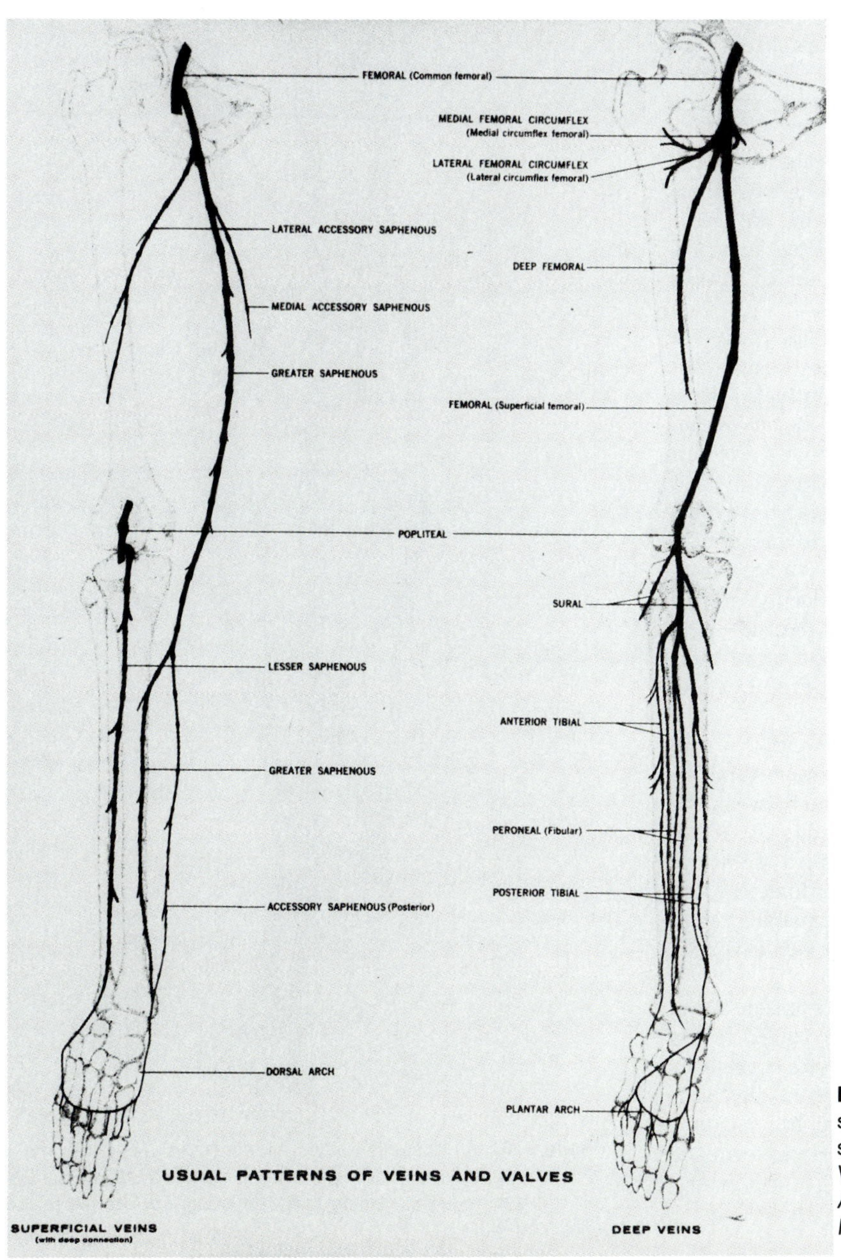

Figure 9–66. An illustration of the location of the superficial and deep veins relative to the bony structures. (*Reprinted with permission from DeWeese JA, Rogoff SM, Tobin CE: Radiographic Anatomy of Major Veins of Lower Limb (chart). Rochester, NY: Eastman Kodak Company.*)

deep plantar veins behind the medial malleolus. These veins course proximally lying on the tibialis posterior muscle, which separates them from the interosseous membrane. The posterior tibial veins lie in the posterior crural compartment and are covered superficially by the soleus and gastrocnemius muscles. They drain the flexors of the calf and soleus muscle and tributaries of the greater saphenous system and enter these veins through a series of perforating veins. In the upper third of the calf, posterior tibial veins unite to form a single vessel that ascends for 1–3 cm before anastomosing with the peroneal trunk to form the tibioperoneal confluence (Fig. 9–66). This ascends another few centimeters, where it is joined by the anterior tibial vein and forms the popliteal vein.

The popliteal vein lies deep in the popliteal fossa and is medial to the popliteal artery. It crosses from the medial to the lateral aspect of the artery as it courses upward into the adductor (Hunter's) canal. It is joined by the termination of the lesser saphenous vein (saphenopopliteal confluence) 1–5 cm above the popliteal fossa. The gastrocnemius veins usually enter the popliteal veins at the same level as the lesser saphenous.

The medial gastrocnemius vein anastomoses to the popliteal vein just inferior to the lesser saphenous. However, it may quite commonly anastomose with the lesser saphenous more directly and enter the popliteal as a single trunk. The lateral gastrocnemius vein almost always joins to the popliteal vein separately.

The peroneal veins lie directly beneath and medial to the fibula. In the distal third of the lower leg, the peroneal veins are small and run deep to the flexor hallucis longus (tendons) in close proximity to the interosseous membrane. Near the top of the lower third of the leg, the peroneal vein is joined by a lateral perforating vein that drains the soleus muscle. At this point, the peroneal veins dramatically increase and double in size. In the middle third of the lower leg, the peroneal veins emerge from under the flexor hallucis muscle in the deep posterior compartment. The peroneal veins unite to form a single trunk in the upper third of the leg and continue their ascension to join the posterior tibial vein at the tibioperoneal confluence.

The anterior tibial veins are a continuation of the dorsalis pedis veins coursing with the anterior tibial artery. They lie on the interosseous membrane between the tibia and fibula in the anterior compartment and are beneath the extensor muscles. In the upper third of the leg, these veins unite to form a single trunk. At this point, the anterior tibial vein travels posteriorly and medially close to the fibular head to join with the tibioperoneal to constitute the popliteal vein.

The superficial femoral vein is a continuation of the popliteal vein and begins at the adductor canal. It lies lateral to the artery. As it ascends into Scarpa's triangle, it crosses behind the artery to assume a more medial position. Five to 10 cm below the inguinal ligament, the profunda femoral vein unites with it posteriorly to form the common femoral vein that ascends medial to the artery. The common femoral vein passes underneath the inguinal ligament to become the external iliac vein.

Superficial Veins

The lesser saphenous vein is formed by the union of the lateral marginal vein and numerous small veins draining the outer side of the foot. It arises from behind the lateral malleolus and continues upward on the lateral aspect of the Achilles tendon in its lower third. From there it ascends superficially to the gastrocnemius muscle up the center of the calf to the popliteal fossa (Fig. 9–67). There is a large constant perforating vein draining into the per-

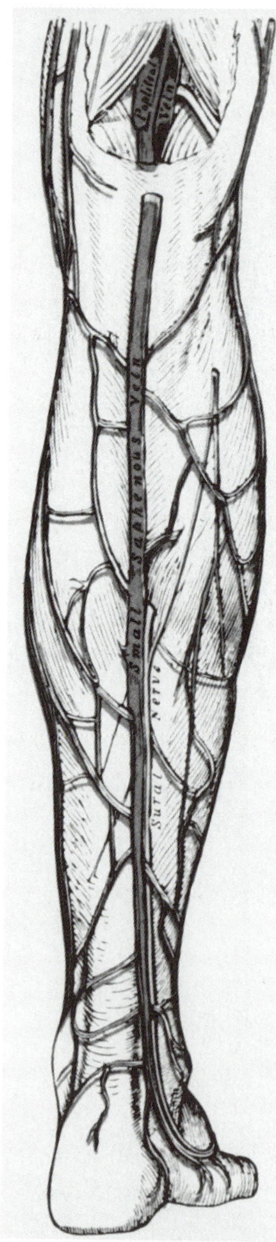

Figure 9–67. An illustration of lesser saphenous vein with some of its tributaries. (*Reprinted with permission from Gray H. In Goss CM (ed.): Anatomy of the Human Body. Philadelphia: Lea & Febiger, 1973, p. 718.*)

oneal vein at the point where the saphenous crosses the lateral edge of the gastrocnemius fascia. In the middle of the calf at the junction of the tendinous and muscular part of the gastrocnemius muscle, the lesser saphenous enters the intrafascial compartment of the gastrocnemius muscle. The point of the lesser saphenous entry into the popliteal space is variable, usually occurring 1.5 cm above the skin crease behind the knee.

The greater saphenous vein is formed by the union of veins from the inner part of the foot and the medial marginal vein. At the ankle, it lies in the groove between the anterior border of the medial malleolus and the tendon of the tibialis anterior. It ascends obliquely posteriorly over the subcutaneous medial surface of the lower fourth of the tibia and along the medial border of the tibia to the medial condyle at the knee. Around the knee the greater saphenous receives three large tributaries: a calf branch, which drains the posterior calf and connects with the lesser saphenous; an anterior branch, which arises from the dorsum of the foot and ascends on the anterior surface of the leg; and a posterior arch branch, which is formed by a series of small venous arches connecting the medial calf perforators that ascend the medial aspect of the leg. The greater saphenous vein then courses over the posteromedial aspect of the knee joint and behind the medial condyle of the femur. Above the knee, it ascends the anteromedial aspect of the thigh into the fossa ovalis, where it joins the common femoral vein. Just distal to its termination, it receives the posteromedial branch that runs up the posterior aspect of the thigh under the deep fascia, which later in its ascension pierces the deep-fascia to become subcutaneous and medial. The greater saphenous vein at this level also unites with an anterolateral branch that courses diagonally upward from the lateral side of the leg, knee, and thigh. The branches of the saphenous vein near its termination are highly variable in number and location (Fig. 9–68).

Muscular Veins of the Calf

The soleus muscle contains a series of large venous sinuses that are reported to be devoid of valves. They are drained by a series of short but compliant veins into the posterior tibial and peroneal veins, as previously described. During rest, they assume a tortuous appearance that may be mistaken for deep varicosities; however, this is necessary in order to accommodate the wide range of movement when the soleus muscle contracts.

The gastrocnemius muscles contain several parallel veins in each head that contain many valves and are accompanied by an artery and nerve. The paired gastrocnemius veins emerge from the inner (ventral) surface of the heads to form a singular trunk in each head. These veins join the popliteal vein at or above the level of the knee joint. Distally, the gastrocnemius veins are united in the posterior midline of the mid-calf, where they are joined by a mid-calf perforator that communicates with the lesser saphenous vein. This perforator is often referred to as the gastrocnemius point (Fig. 9–69).

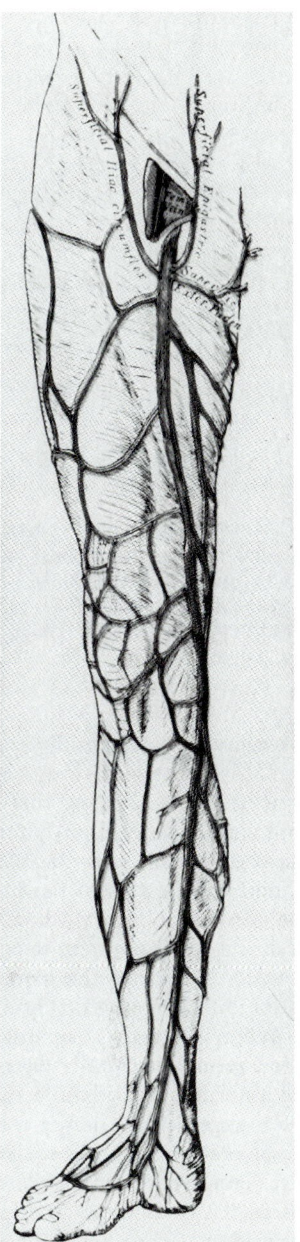

Figure 9–68. An illustration of the greater saphenous vein with its multitude of branches. *(Reprinted with permission from Gray H. In Goss CM (ed.): Anatomy of the Human Body. Philadelphia: Lea & Febiger, 1973, p. 717.)*

PHYSIOLOGY OF THE VENOUS SYSTEM

Veins are thin-walled vessels that collapse when empty. This feature of the venous system allows it to contain large volumes of blood with little change in venous pressure. As the vein begins to fill with blood, it changes from a collapsed state to an elliptical shape. The pressure within the vein is directly proportional to the force that is exerted on the vein wall by the volume of blood within it. The vein during this shape transition is very compliant;

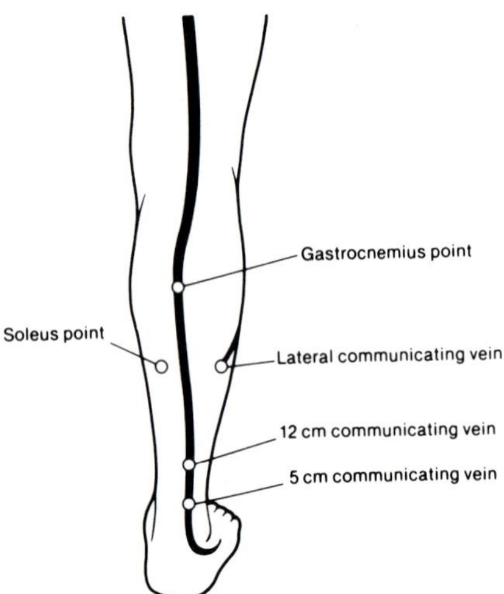

Figure 9–69. An illustration of the common posterior perforators associated with the lesser saphenous, including the gastrocnemius point. (*Reprinted with permission from Browse NL, Burnand KG, Thomas ML: Disease of the Veins: Pathology, Diagnosis and Treatment. Kent, England: Edward Arnold Division of Hodder & Stoughton, 1988, p 46.*)

therefore, the pressure change is minimal. As the volume of blood increases, the shape of the vein becomes oval and finally circular (Fig. 9–70). During this transition, the venous pressure increases only slightly until the circular state is reached. At this point, increased blood volume will result in large increases in pressure until the maximum expansion of the vessel has been reached.

The ability of the venous system to adjust shape and size makes it ideally suited for the storage of blood. In fact, 75–80% of the blood volume is contained within the venous system. When a person is resting in the supine position, the blood volume is equally distributed. The venous pressure of a normal individual at the ankle is ~7–10 mm Hg. When an erect position is assumed, approximately 500 ml of blood volume is redistributed to the lower extremities. This redistribution causes an increased venous pressure in the extremities and is referred to as the hydrostatic gradient. The change in pressure due to positional change can be calculated by multiplying the density of blood by the distance from the right atrium (Fig. 9–71) to a specific location in the extremity (eg, the ankle). The pressure (eg, in the ankle) is to be determined times gravity. Pressure increases due to gravity effect both the venous and arterial systems. However, owing to a lower initial pressure within the venous system, the effect of this change is more dramatic.

In the supine person, the venous pressure at the ankle is approximately 10 mm Hg, whereas the pressure in the right atrium is ±2 mm Hg. This pressure differential encourages flow toward the heart. Venous flow also is aided by the pressure differential created by movement of the diaphragm during respiration. During inspiration, the intra-abdominal venous pressure increases, preventing flow from the lower extremities but allowing inflow from the upper portions of the body. During exhalation, the building volume of blood in the lower extremities rushes into empty intrathoracic vessels. The phasic flow pattern created by the activity of respiration is characterized by sharp increases in flow followed by complete cessation. Flow patterns in the venous system can be altered by changing the breathing pattern. For instance, if you take a deep breath and hold it, venous flow will stop. Blood flow

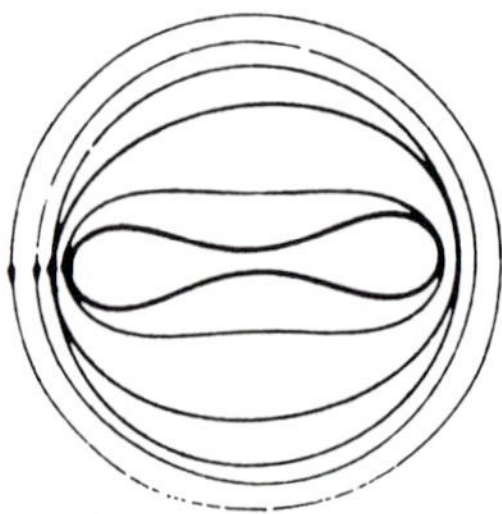

Figure 9–70. An illustration of the changes in shapes and sizes of veins as the volume is increased. (*Reprinted with permission from Strandness DE, Sumner DS: Hemodynamics for Surgeons. New York: Grune & Stratton, 1975, p. 128.*)

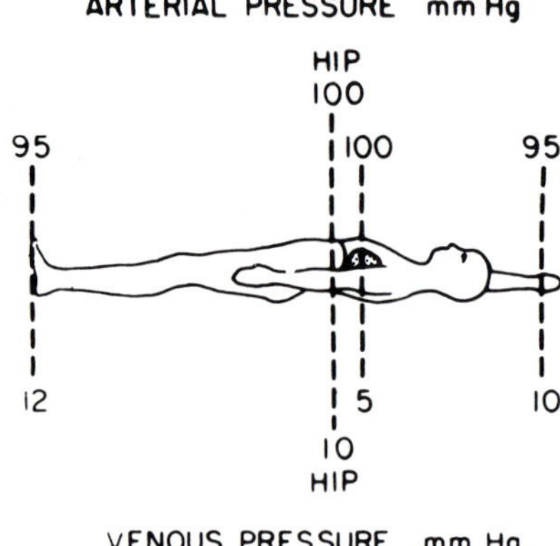

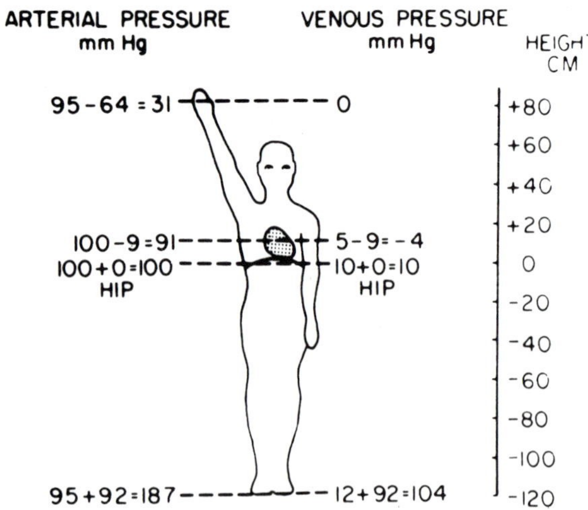

Figure 9–71. A graph showing the changes in venous pressure due to changes in body position. (*Reprinted with permission from Strandness DE, Sumner DS: Hemodynamics for Surgeons. New York: Grune & Stratton, 1975, p. 123.*)

also can be augmented by manual compression of an area. When a person stands upright, the venous return in not adequate. To augment, venous blood flow from the periphery muscular contractions helps propel blood toward the heart.

In the lower extremity, the predominant peripheral pumps are the muscles of the calf and to a lesser extent contraction of the foot and thigh muscles. Venous return also is enhanced by the network of valves. The venous valves open and close in response to a pressure differential. When the venous pressure is higher than the valve, it closes to prevent reverse flow (venous reflux). When the muscles of the leg contract, the venous pressure is higher and blood from the deep veins of the calf is expelled into the thigh and the calf veins collapse. Because some blood in the calf is forced downward by the collapse of the vein, the pressure increases distally and closes the inferior valves. During muscle relaxation, blood from the superficial system and the foot rushes into empty veins. Venous pressure in the thigh is now higher than in the calf, which closes the valves above the knee. The combination of competent valves and muscle pumps provides an efficient mechanism that propels blood from the lower extremities. If either the valves or the muscle pump do not function, then the efficiency of the venous return is compromised and ambulatory venous hypertension in the leg occurs.

DIAGNOSIS OF VENOUS DISEASE

From the clinical standpoint, venous disease is divided into two specific problems. Acute deep venous thrombosis may cause life-threatening pulmonary embolism, and the postthrombotic syndrome may result in chronic suffering due to leg swelling and ulceration. Early diagnosis of acute DVT is desirable because timely treatment will limit the extent of the thrombosis and decrease the sequelae of these problems. However, our current knowledge of the natural history of DVT is confusing because previous studies were based upon conclusions that were drawn solely from clinical features of the problem. These sometimes erroneous conclusions persist in medical practice even though our current knowledge of venous disease is based upon more accurate information derived from newer diagnostic techniques. Furthermore, the newer technologies detect venous disease much earlier in the thrombotic process than previous studies, which has created two conflicting bodies of information. In spite of these problems, reasonable diagnostic and therapeutic schemata have evolved and provide an acceptable basis for patient management.

Acute Venous Disease

The initial clinical evaluation of the venous system involves a careful medical history with emphasis on the risk factors noted above. Clinical findings in acute deep venous thrombosis are highly variable and extremely unreliable. It is estimated that more than half of the patients with calf vein thrombi are asymptomatic, and it has been demonstrated that an equal number of patients with signs and symptoms suggestive of acute deep venous thrombosis have normal deep venous systems.[7,8] However, clinical diagnosis is of significant value. Manifestations of thrombosis vary with the location of the venous segment involved and rapidity of clot formation.

Because DVT most commonly occurs in the calf veins, most symptoms begin at that level. Pain, consisting of a dull posterior calf ache that increases over several hours or days and is exacerbated by ambulation, is most common. This may be localized over the area of thrombosis. The physical findings include tenderness over the affected area, unilateral leg swelling and edema, and, if the proximal veins are involved, the calf may become erythematous and hot, mimicking a bacterial cellulitis. When major obstruction of the iliofemoral system occurs, massive swelling of the entire lower extremity associated with a white or deeply cyanotic limb may occur. The signs of iliofemoral thrombosis represent the few clinical features that reliably identify acute DVT.

Unfortunately, the overall diagnostic accuracy of physical examination is only about 50% and thus the diagnosis must be confirmed with objective testing. Historically, ascending contrast venography has been the standard test used. It is highly accurate compared with autopsy findings, but it is invasive and results in both patient discomfort and a low but defined morbidity. With the advent of Doppler and ultrasound technology over the last 20 years, noninvasive testing has replaced contrast venography for the diagnosis of deep venous thrombosis in most instances.[9–11] Duplex imaging allows us to visualize the entire deep venous system reliably and to diagnose acute and chronic thrombosis with an accuracy similar to contrast venography.[10–12]

Chronic Venous Disease

Diagnosis of chronic venous disease is more straightforward because varicose veins, leg swelling, and distal leg skin changes resulting from chronic venous obstruction and valvular reflux are often obvious. These clinical manifestations result from chronic venous hypertension due to anatomic derangements in the superficial, perforating, and deep veins.

Varicose Veins. These are the most common manifestation of chronic venous disease and appear as dilated tortuous superficial branches that often involve the greater and lesser saphenous systems. Primary varicose veins are often hereditary, as noted above. Perforating veins carry blood from the superficial venous system to the deep venous system. Reflux is prevented by subfascial valves. Occasionally, primary incompetence of perforating veins occurs; particularly in patients whose occupations require prolonged standing. Additionally, chronic superficial venous reflux in the saphenous vein may cause secondary dilatation and damage to the perforating veins with resulting valvular incompetence.

Etiology. The primary cause of chronic deep vein abnormalities is acute thrombosis. Following the initial event, thrombi variably lyse but persistent obstruction and valvular damage occur. The chronic venous hypertension that ensues causes a "blowout" of the perforating veins and results in "secondary" varices. Over a period of time, the chronic venous disease causes chronic leg pain and swelling, edema, hyperpigmentation, stasis dermatitis, and ankle ulceration. This is the well-known postthrombotic syndrome.

Diagnostic Imaging Techniques

Clinical diagnosis of chronic venous disease is quite reliable but the physical findings do not localize or quantitate the anatomic and physiologic abnormalities. In recent years, several noninvasive diagnostic techniques have been used to evaluate the physiologic alterations associated with chronic venous disease.[13] Doppler ultrasound and plethysmographic techniques assess valvular incompetence and obstruction, and venous photoplethysmography qualitatively assesses reflux and can grossly differentiate between superficial and deep incompetence. Although these techniques are reasonably accurate in confirming chronic disease and differentiating superficial from deep reflux, they only provide indirect information about the location and extent of venous insufficiency. B-mode and duplex ultrasonography provide anatomic and physiologic information that reliably assesses venous flow patterns, determine the extent of vascular incompetence, and identify sites of venous obstruction.

Thus, the diagnosis of acute and chronic venous thromboses initially rests with the clinician's suspicion of disease. The exact nature of acute and chronic venous thromboses must be confirmed by objective testing. Today, duplex ultrasonography is the noninvasive gold standard for detection of disease.

Venous Doppler Ultrasound. Doppler ultrasound has been used for the past two decades to assess the venous system for evidence of obstruction and abnormal flow due venous valvular dysfunction. In this technique, the ultrasound beam that is reflected back to the transducer at a frequency that is proportional to the speed or velocity of blood flow within the vessel being insonated is within the audible range. The mean velocity can be calculated by using the following formula:

$$V = \frac{C\,\Delta f}{2fe \cos \theta}$$

where Δf = frequency shift; fe = frequency of transmitted ultrasound; V = mean velocity of blood; Θ = angle of the incident sound beam with the vessel; and C = velocity of sound in the medium.

Venous Doppler evaluation can be performed with any commercially available continuous-wave Doppler velocity detector and a 5- or 8-MHz transducer. In our clinical experience, we have found that a 5 MHz hand-held Doppler velocity detector with a wide flat transducer surface provides the best results. The higher-frequency Doppler transducers often do not penetrate deep enough to assess accurately the superficial femoral vein or an extremely edematous or obese extremity. Pencil-probe transducers are adequate for assessment but have a narrow beam, and inadvertent vein compression by this small probe can lead to erroneous results.

Doppler ultrasound examination is a subjective test where the examiner compares the audible Doppler velocity signals in each extremity using limb compression maneuvers. It is performed with the patient in the supine position with the legs exposed and externally rotated. In a normal venous Doppler examination, the venous signal is heard when the transducer is placed over the vein located next to the accompanying artery. This characteristic is referred to as *spontaneity*. The only location where a spontaneous venous signal may normally not be heard is the posterior tibial vein at the ankle. In this location, the blood flow rate may be below the sensitivity of the Doppler velocity detector. Most commercially available Doppler velocity detectors cannot detect movement below 6 cm/s. The audible signal is evaluated to determine if it is *phasic* (waxes and wanes with respiration), continuous, or pulsatile. A normal venous signal is phasic.

A continuous venous signal indicates either internal obstruction of flow or external compression of the vein proximal to the position of the transducer. Compression of the vein by the transducer also can cause a continuous venous signal.

A pulsatile venous signal indicates increased venous blood volume (hypervolemic state). The extremity is manually compressed below the location of the transducer to augment blood flow past the transducer and the audible Doppler velocity signal is assessed for its response to this maneuver.

The normal response to distal *augmentation* is a rapid increase in the pitch (frequency) of the signal followed by a slow decay and then a return to the normal phasicity. If the Doppler velocity signal increases rapidly and then abruptly stops or no response is heard with augmentation, the vein is considered to be obstructed proximal to or at the location of the transducer.

Valvular *competence* of the vein is evaluated by manually compressing the extremity above the transducer. If the valves are competent between the transducer and the location of the manual compression, there will be no audible venous signal during the compression. On release of compression, the signal will resume in a manner similar to the response of the distal augmentation. If a signal is heard during proximal compression, the valves between the area of compression and the transducer are incompetent.

Venous Doppler examination is started at the posterior tibial vein and proceeds to the popliteal, superficial, and common femoral veins, respectively. The contralateral extremity should always be evaluated at each level before the examination continues to the more proximally located veins because deep vein thrombosis is rarely bilat-

eral. A bilateral abnormal evaluation may indicate technical error.

The venous Doppler evaluation is highly accurate in the detection of hemodynamically significant obstruction of the popliteal, superficial femoral, and common femoral veins. However, owing to the extreme compliance and redundancy of the venous system, it cannot reliably detect partial obstructions that do not cause changes in the venous flow pattern. This procedure also cannot accurately detect thrombosis confined to the calf veins. Additionally, owing to the physiologic nature of this examination, it cannot differentiate acute from chronic or intrinsic from extrinsic causes of obstruction.

Venous Imaging. For over two decades, noninvasive testing has been used to diagnose venous thrombosis and chronic deep venous insufficiency. As noted above, venous Doppler ultrasound combined with a form of outflow plethysmography are the tests most frequently used to diagnose venous disease. Although these techniques are highly accurate in skilled hands, they are unable to provide precise anatomic information or assess venous flow patterns. A continuing evolution of more sophisticated real-time ultrasound technology and computer software has enhanced our ability to investigate the venous system noninvasively.

Over the last 5 years, ultrasonic venography has been shown to image accurately the entire venous system and detect venous thrombosis with an accuracy similar to contrast venography.[10–12,14,15] More recently, it has been used to assess valve function, locate and map the sites of venous reflux, and differentiate between acute and chronic venous obstruction.[16–19] This makes ultrasonic venography an ideal noninvasive method to evaluate patients with both acute and chronic venous insufficiency.

Ultrasonic venography can be performed using any of the commercially available high-resolution B-mode imagers that have "small parts" capabilities. The ideal transducer frequency is 7.5 MHz, with an imaging field depth of 6–7 cm. Most 7.5-MHz mechanical sector transducers have a probe artifact created by the fluid standoff that limits the field depth to 4–5 cm. Therefore, a 5-MHz transducer must be used to visualize the venous system. Linear-array transducers with their rectangular shape and wide footprint are ideally suited for extremity imaging. The sequence and the extent of the venous evaluation is influenced by the patient population and the clinical indications for the examination.

Ultrasonic Venography in the Ambulatory Patient. The patient is seated on an examination table or high chair with the foot of the leg to be examined resting on the sonographer's knee. To locate venous pathology and correlate the examination results with contrast venography, a tape measure can be attached to the anterior aspect of the extremity from the ankle to the inguinal ligament. The study is videotaped in its entirety for off-line interpretation.

The examination is begun just above the medial malleolus where the posterior tibial vein is insonated behind the tibia. The evaluation proceeds superiorly to the tibioperoneal confluence where the scan path continues in a posteromedial direction into the popliteal fossa. The popliteal vein is evaluated from the popliteal fossa to above the abductor canal and then retraced inferiorly to the tibioperoneal confluence. As the popliteal space is traversed, the saphenopopliteal confluence and the termination of the gastrocnemius veins are visualized. The peroneal veins are evaluated next by moving the transducer laterally to a position next to the medial border of the fibula and then tracing the vessels inferiorly to the ankle. The anterior tibial veins are imaged with the transducer just lateral to the anterior border of the tibia, starting at the level of the fibular head and proceeding inferiorly to the lateral malleolus.

The superficial femoral vein is assessed by placing the transducer medial to the femur above the abductor canal and then tracing it superiorly to the common femoral vein. The confluence of the superficial femoral, profunda femoral, and greater saphenous with the common femoral are routinely evaluated.

The veins are continually evaluated for the presence of obstruction using frequent compressions of the vein with the transducer. Confirmation of finding can be obtained by using a different imaging plane or the pulsed or color Doppler on duplexed imaging systems. However, it should be remembered that a normal Doppler signal does not rule out a partially obstructing thrombus that does not fill more than 50% of the maximally expanded vessel.

Ultrasonic Venography in the Bedridden Patient. In the acutely ill bedridden patient, the ultrasonic evaluation is most easily performed with the patient supine and, if possible, the leg externally rotated. The bed can be placed in reverse Trendelenburg position to distend the veins and facilitate the examination; however, this is not necessary because the common and superficial femoral and the popliteal veins are large enough to be visualized without additional distension. In this patient population, the evaluation is begun at the common femoral and proceeds inferiorly to the tibioperoneal confluence, where the examination may be terminated. If it is necessary to evaluate the calf veins, the patient's foot is placed flat on the bed with the knee bent. After the patient has been repositioned, the evaluation should start at the popliteal vein above the skin crease. The vein is imaged moving down over the posteromedial aspect of the knee to the medial border of the tibia. The tibial peroneal confluence should be visualized at this level. As the evaluation continues to the ankle along the medial border of the tibia, the posterior tibial vein should be seen at a depth of 2–3 cm and the peroneal vein visualized in the far field at 4–6 cm in the calf and 1–3 cm in the lower leg. The transducer should next be placed on the anterior border of the tibia about 5 cm below the patella in the sagittal imaging plane, where the anterior tibia can be visualized resting above the interosseous membrane in the near field and the peroneal below the interosseous membrane in the far field. Once

these vessels are identified, the evaluation is continued by following the anterior border of the tibia to the ankle. If the patient is cooperative and easily repositioned, the popliteal and peroneal veins can be examined by placing the patient on his or her side with the knees slightly bent. The examination is again started with the popliteal vein above the skin crease and proceeds downward on the midline of the calf to the tibioperoneal confluence. The scan path should then descend obliquely lateral to the medial border of the fibula in the calf where the separation of the peroneal vein into paired venae comitantes should occur. The peroneal veins are evaluated using the medial border of the fibula as a guide to the ankle. The posterior tibial veins can be visualized in the far field from this position by angling the transducer beam toward the medial border of the tibia. By angling the transducer beam toward the anterior borders of the tibia and fibula, the anterior tibial vein can be seen in the far field. During the evaluation, frequent vein compression with the transducer is performed to determine the presence of obstruction. It is important during the compression maneuver that the vein walls are seen to come together. On release of the venous compression, the vein should be visualized on the screen as it appeared prior to the compression maneuver. If these criteria are not met, the maneuver must be repeated and making sure that the transducer is stabilized by using both hands to prevent slipping. The calf veins seen in the far field can be evaluated for obstruction by applying external digital compression to the location of the vein at the same level as the position of the transducer.

The methods of imaging described above can be performed with the transducer in either a cross-sectional (transverse) or long-axis (longitudinal) view. Both views are highly accurate in detecting obstruction in the thigh and knee. The longitudinal view of limb anatomy is preferred for identification and evaluation of the vast number of clinically important veins in the calf. This imaging view allows the examiner to discriminate between disease processes and to locate and assess venous valves. Valve competence can be determined by placing the pulsed Doppler sample volume into the vein near the valve. A manual distal compression augments flow from the leg. Release of compression will result in an absence of a venous signal in the presence of a competent valve. This procedure is performed with the Doppler sample volume placed above and below the valve leaflets. When assessing the competence of valves at the saphenofemoral and saphenopopliteal junction, it is recommended that the patient stand with the knee of the leg being examined slightly flexed and the body weight supported by the contralateral extremity. All veins at each confluence are evaluated both at the junction and distal to the valve. Distal

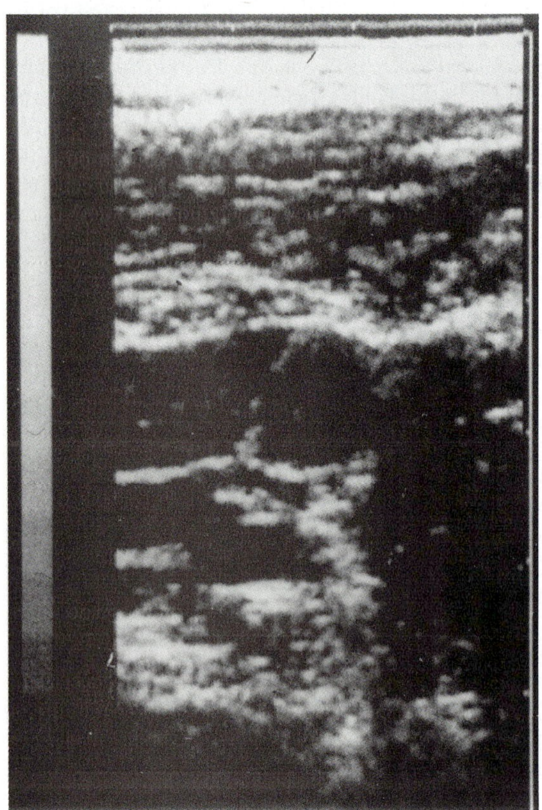

Figure 9–72. A normal vein with thin valve leaflets projecting into the vessel lumen.

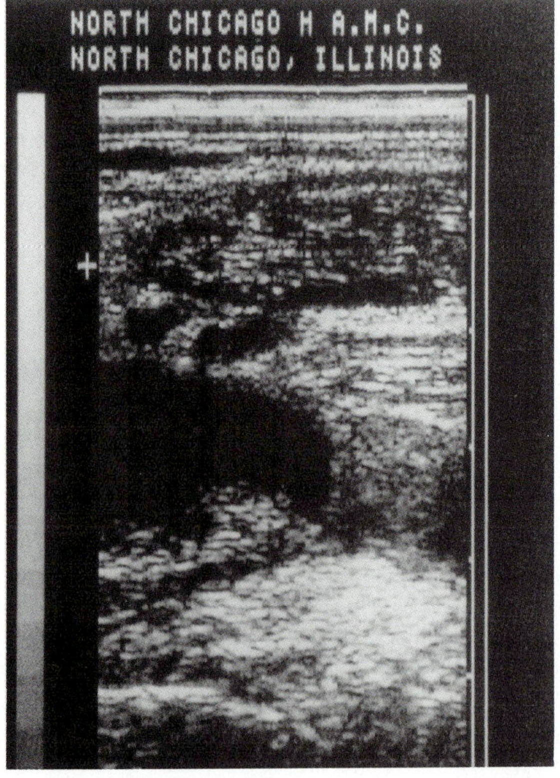

Figure 9–73. The anechoic area of this popliteal vein contains acute thrombus collateral channels that can be seen above and below the vessel.

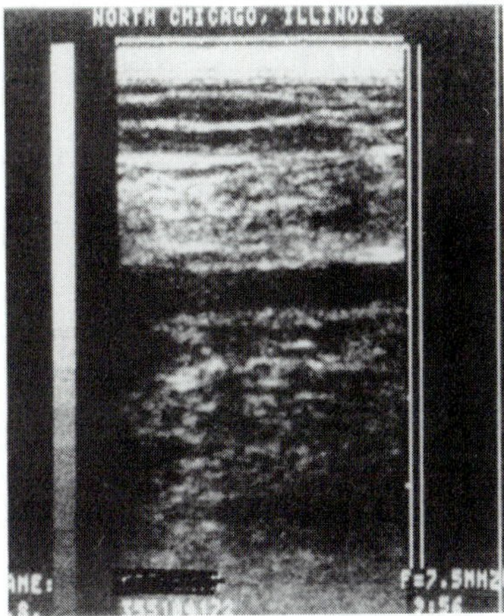

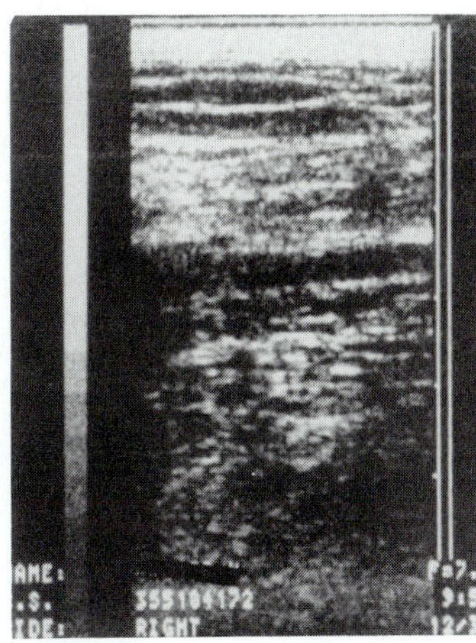

Figure 9–74. On the left the tibial artery (top) and vein (bottom) are visualized. The vein contains hypoechoic luminal echoes. The image on the right demonstrates the noncompressibility of the vein (bottom) and increased echogenicity.

augmentation and release is used to determine valve competence.

One criticism of longitudinal imaging is that during transducer compression the vein may be displaced to the side by the transducer. Although it is true that the superficial veins above the fascia in the subcutaneous tissue are not well anchored and may be displaced by transducer compression, the deep and muscular veins are encased within the fascial compartments next to bones and are tethered in place by their tributaries, preventing movement of the vessel. Therefore, this problem indicates operator error due to transducer slippage. It is easily overcome with practice.

Characterization of Images. The value of ultrasonic venography is not only its ability to locate disease within the vein but also its capability to differentiate acute from chronic disease processes. This is based on image characteristics that have been correlated with contrast venograms and clinical and pathologic findings.[20]

Normal veins have thin, echogenically homogeneous walls with elliptical valve sinuses that contain long thin valve leaflets (Fig. 9–72). Perforating and small tributary veins are rarely visualized in the normal venous system. Venous flow characteristic may be assessed by direct observation of moving luminal echoes created by the ultrasonic reflection of red blood cell aggregates.[20] The pulsed or color Doppler also may be used. However, its use extends the examination time and may not identify a partial acute obstruction, leading to a high false-negative rate. In veins containing acute thrombus, a hypoechoic or anechoic mass is seen with luminal echoes flowing around it (Fig. 9–73). The visualization of an anechoic mass usually indicates a very recent thrombotic process. When the vein is externally compressed with the transducer, the vein walls will not coapt and the echogenicity of the luminal mass will increase owing to the density change caused by the compression maneuver (Fig. 9–74). If the mass does not change in echogenicity, it is an older stable thrombus and is not considered to be part of the acute disease process. It is not unusual, however, to visualize acute thrombus on either side of an older obstruction. A careful inspection of the entire vessel is necessary to discriminate the different disease states.

Chronic venous disease is characterized by hyperechoic heterogeneous protrusions from the vein wall that may partially or totally occlude the vein (Fig. 9–75). Any vein not visualized in its normal anatomic position is clas-

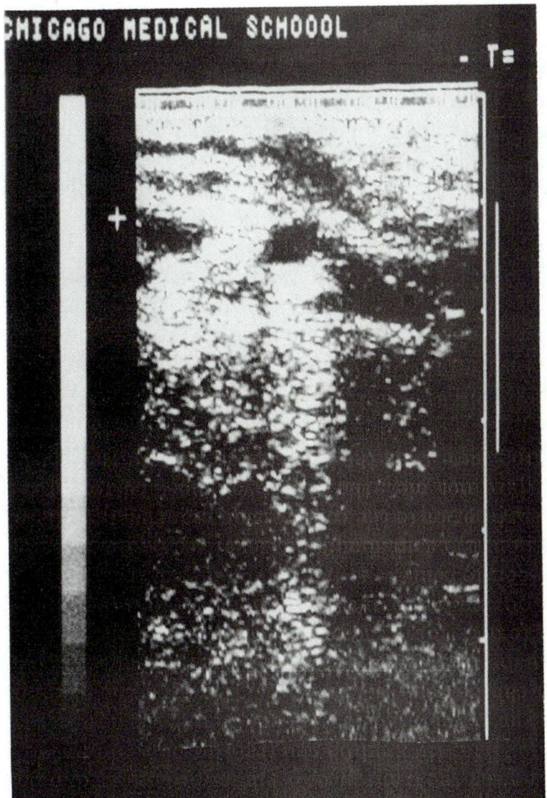

Figure 9–75. This image demonstrates a chronic total segmental obstruction of a distal tibial vein. A perforating vein to the greater saphenous can be seen to the right or distal to the occlusion.

sified as chronically obstructed. However, it is rare to find the entire length of the vein totally obstructed.[21] Veins that at one time contained thrombus that has resolved by the normal lytic process have hyperechoic thick walls and are classified as recanalized. Incompetent collateral and perforating veins leading to intramuscular or superficial varicosities are frequently observed. Valve sinuses are rarely distinguishable but, when present, have absent or short thickened nonfunctional valve leaflets that are frequently misaligned (Fig. 9–76).

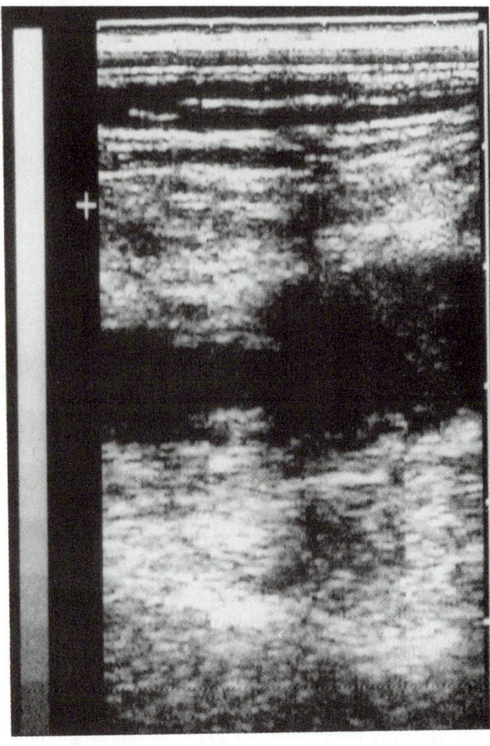

Figure 9–76. Within this proximal tibial vein can be seen short thickened valve leaflets protruding into the vessel lumen.

CONCLUSION

Diseases of the venous system are not new. One of the oldest depictions of varicose veins can be seen in the leg of an Athenian warrior in an ancient frieze in Greece. Epidemiologic studies suggest that approximately 50% of the adult population in the United States has some form of chronic venous disorder. Acute venous problems are often asymptomatic but carry with them sequelae that can either be fatal or cause chronic debilitation. Although we are very familiar with the risk factors for acute and chronic venous diseases, there is still very little scientific knowledge about the pathophysiology of these entities. Until recently, the diagnosis of all venous problems was made primarily by clinical assessment and contrast venography. With the arrival of noninvasive diagnostic methods in the early 1970s came an increased accuracy in the detection of hemodynamically significant venous obstruction of the popliteal and femoral veins. Today, real-time B-mode ultrasonic imaging has all but replaced other diagnostic testing for the diagnosis of venous problems. The accuracy of this modality is equivalent to the invasive gold standard, ie, ascending contrast venography without the risks or discomfort associated with it.

Ultrasonic venography is beginning to give us important new information on venous disease. This modality can be used at any stage in the thrombotic process. Serial scans are already providing insights into the natural history of venous disease. Additionally, ultrasonic venography is a valuable tool in the assessment of acute and chronic venous problems and mapping of the venous system prior to surgical intervention.[16,19] It is routinely employed in many clinical situations and provides important information to the physician that enables him or her to diagnose and treat venous disease more accurately.

REFERENCES

1. Borow M, Goldson H. Postoperative venous thrombosis—Evaluation of five methods of treatment. *Am J Surg* **141:**245–251, 1981.
2. Caprini JA, Chucker JL, Zuckerman L, et al. Thrombosis prophylaxis using external compression. *SG&O* **156:**599–604, 1983.
3. Hartman JT, Pugh JL, Smith RD, et al. Cyclic sequential compression of the lower limb in prevention of deep venous thrombosis. *J Bone Joint Surg* **64**A:1059–1062, 1982.
4. Hills NH, Pflug JJ, Jeyasingh K, et al. Prevention of deep vein thrombosis by intermittent pneumatic compression of calf. *Br Med J* **1:**131–135, 1972.
5. Oster G, Tuden RL, Colditz GA. Prevention of venous thromboembolism after general surgery; cost-effectiveness analysis of alternative approaches to prophylaxis. *Am J Med* **82:**889–899, 1987.
6. Janssen HF, Schachner J, Hubbard J, et al. The risk of deep venous thrombosis: A computerized epidemiologic approach. *Surgery* **101:**205–212, 1987.
7. Filip DJ, Eckstein JD, Veltkemp JJ. Heredity antithrombin three deficiency and the thrombo embolic diseases. *Med J Hematol* **1:**343–349, 1978.
8. Haeger K. Problems of acute deep vein thrombosis. *Angiology* **20:**219–223, 1969.

9. Yao JST, Horres JP, Rubo N, et al. Diagnosis of deep venous thrombosis by Doppler ultrasound and impedance plethysmography. In Kwaan HL, Bowie EJW (eds): *Thrombosis*. Philadelphia: WB Saunders, 1982, pp 224–235.

10. Raghavendra BN, Rosen R. Deep venous thrombosis: Detection by high resolution real time ultrasonography. *Radiology* **152:**789–793, 1984.

11. Hannan LJ, Stedke KJ, Cranley JJ, et al. Venous imaging of the lower extremities: Our first 2,500 cases. *Bruit* **10:**29–31, 1986.

12. Semrow CM, Friedell ML, Buchbinder D, et al. The efficacy of ultrasonic venography in the detection of calf vein thrombosis. *J Vasc Technol* **12:**240–244, 1988.

13. Barnes RW. Non-invasive techniques in chronic venous insufficiency. In Bernstein ER (ed): *Non-Invasive Diagnostic Techniques in Vascular Disease*. St Louis: CV Mosby, 1985, pp 724–729.

14. Flanagan LD, Sullivan ED, Cranley JJ. 1984 Venous imaging of the extremities using real-time B-mode ultrasound. In Bergan JJ, Yao JST (eds): *Surgery of the Veins*. Orlando, FL: Grune & Stratton, 1984, pp 89–98.

15. Langsfeld M, Hershey FB, Thorpe L, et al. 1987 Duplex B-mode imaging for the diagnosis of deep venous thrombosis. *Arch Surg* **122:**587–591, 1987.

16. Rollins DL, Semrow CM, Friedell ML, et al. The use of ultrasonic venography in the evaluation of venous valve function. *Am J Surg* **154:**189–191, 1987.

17. Rollins DL, Semrow CM, Buchbinder D, et al. Diagnosis of recurrent deep venous thrombosis using B-mode ultrasonic imaging. *Phlebology* **1:**181–188, 1986.

18. Szendro G, Nicolaides AN, Zukowski AJ, et al. 1986 Duplex scanning in the assessment of deep venous incompetence. *J Vasc Surg* **4:**237–242, 1986.

19. Semrow CM, Laborde A, Buchbinder D, et al. Preoperative mapping of varicosities and perforating veins: A preliminary report. *J Vasc Technol* **14**(2):72–74, 1990.

20. Semrow CM, Friedell ML, Buchbinder D, et al. Characterization of lower extreme venous disease using real-time B-mode ultrasonic imaging. *J Vasc Technol* **11:**187–191, 1987.

21. Rollins DL, Semrow CM, Friedell ML, et al. Origin of deep vein thrombi in an ambulatory population. *Am J Surg* **156:**122–125, 1988.

Questions

For each question, select the best answer. You are to select only one answer for each question unless otherwise indicated.

1. The function of perforating veins is to
   (A) transport blood from the deep to superficial system
   (B) transport blood to the heart
   (C) transport blood from the muscles
   (D) transport blood from the superficial to deep system

2. How many deep veins are there below the knee?
   (A) two
   (B) three
   (C) six
   (D) none

3. The lesser and greater saphenous veins are
   (A) deep veins
   (B) intermuscular veins
   (C) superficial veins
   (D) perforators

4. Deep veins are located
   (A) above the fascia
   (B) within the muscle
   (C) within the musclofascial compartment
   (D) none of the above

5. Veins are
   (A) thick-walled rigid vessels
   (B) thin-walled rigid vessels
   (C) thick-walled collapsible vessels
   (D) thin-walled collapsible vessels

6. The main differences between the vein wall and the arterial wall structure are
   (A) media is thick with a high concentration of elastin
   (B) media is very thin with reduced elastin concentration
   (C) intima contains a thick layer of endothelial cells and the adventitia is the thinnest part of the vein wall

7. The function of the venous valves is to
   (A) increase venous capacitance
   (B) regulate the amount of venous blood returned to the heart
   (C) assure prograde flow
   (D) all of the above
   (E) none of the above

8. As the volume of blood in a vein increases, the shape of the collapsed vein changes to
   (A) circular
   (B) elliptical
   (C) oval
   (D) no change

9. When the vein changes from the collapsed state to an elliptical shape, the venous pressure
   (A) increases dramatically
   (B) remains the same
   (C) increases minimally
   (D) decreases

10. When a person assumes the erect position, the venous pressure in the lower extremities
    (A) increases
    (B) decreases
    (C) is unchanged

11. The hydrostatic gradient effects
    (A) venous system
    (B) arterial system
    (C) capillaries
    (D) none of the above
    (E) all of the above

12. The pressure within the vein is
    (A) directly proportional to the cardiac output
    (B) equal to the arterial pressure

(C) directly proportional to force that is exerted on the vein wall by the blood volume within it
(D) directly proportional to the rate of respiration and the pulmonary status

13. In the supine position, venous return from the leg is related to

(A) pressure differential between the leg and the heart and the pressure differential created by the diaphragm during respiration
(B) cardiac output and arterial inflow to the leg
(C) volume of blood contained with the veins of the leg
(D) pressure differential between the arterioles and venuoles

14. In the erect position, blood is expelled from the lower extremities in response to

(A) pressure differential between leg and heart
(B) contraction of the muscles of the leg
(C) pressure differential created by the movement of the diaphragm
(D) none of the above
(E) all of the above

15. Venous valves close in response to

(A) change in position
(B) high blood volume in the vein above the valve
(C) high blood volume below the valve
(D) total blood volume in the leg
(E) cardiac cycle

16. The posterior tibial, peroneal, and anterior tibial veins are

(A) superficial veins of the leg
(B) muscular veins
(C) paired deep veins of the calf
(D) deep veins of the thigh

17. How many valves are there in the veins of the lower extremities?

(A) three
(B) 10
(C) varies from person to person
(D) none

18. Venous valves are located in

(A) the deep and superficial veins of the legs
(B) all veins except the vena cava
(C) only in the deep veins of the leg

19. Where are the majority of venous valves found?

(A) proximal veins
(B) distal veins
(C) deep veins
(D) varies depending on individual

20. Localized dilation of the vein wall is associated with

(A) aneurysm
(B) valve sinus
(C) thrombus

21. The function of the deep venous system is

(A) storage of blood
(B) conduit for transport of blood to heart
(C) drainage of skin

22. The posterior tibial vein is located in

(A) posterior lateral calf
(B) posterior medial calf
(C) anterior lateral calf

23. The superficial femoral vein is

(A) a superficial vein
(B) a deep vein
(C) a muscular vein

24. The peroneal vein is located

(A) anterior to the interosseous membrane
(B) directly behind and medial to the tibia
(C) directly behind and medial to the fibula

25. The gastrocnemious vein is a

(A) superficial vein
(B) deep vein
(C) muscular vein

26. The gastrocnemious vein terminates at

(A) posterior tibial vein
(B) popliteal vein
(C) superficial femoral vein

27. The lesser saphenous vein is located

(A) in the center of the posterior calf
(B) medial aspect of the leg
(C) lateral aspect of the leg

28. The lesser saphenous vein terminates with the

(A) superficial femoral vein
(B) common femoral vein
(C) popliteal vein

29. The greater saphenous vein is located in

(A) medial aspect of the leg
(B) posterior aspect of the leg
(C) abdomen

30. The greater saphenous vein terminates at

(A) external iliac vein
(B) popliteal vein
(C) common femoral vein

31. Distal to its termination, the greater saphenous vein

(A) unites into a posteromedial and antereolateral branches
(B) unites with the superficial femoral vein
(C) unites with the lesser saphenous vein

32. The volume of blood contained within the venous system is

(A) 10%
(B) 50%
(C) 80%

33. In the resting supine position, the venous blood distribution is

(A) located mostly in the abdomen
(B) equally distributed through the system
(C) stored in the lower extremities

34. When a person assumes the erect position, the venous blood distribution

(A) remains unchanged
(B) is redistributed to the lower and upper extremities
(C) is redistributed to the lower extremities

35. When a person assumes an erect position, the venous pressure at the ankle

(A) decreases
(B) increases
(C) is unchanged

36. Perforating veins are

(A) muscular veins
(B) connecting veins between superficial and deep veins
(C) veins of the arm

37. The function of perforating veins is to

(A) transport blood to the heart
(B) drain to subcutaneous tissue
(C) transport blood between the deep and superficial veins

38. The direction of flow through perforating veins is

(A) from superficial to deep veins
(B) from deep to superficial veins
(C) to the heart

39. Perforating veins

(A) are located in the subcutaneous tissue
(B) course from the subcutaneous tissue through the fascia
(C) are located within the muscle

40. Contraction of the calf muscle

(A) prevents blood flow out of the leg
(B) causes the venous valves to become incompetent
(C) expels blood from the calf into the thigh

41. Relaxation of the calf muscle

(A) allows blood flow to continue
(B) allows flow from the superficial and foot veins to enter the deep veins of the calf
(C) causes venous valves to become competent

42. Contraction of the calf muscle

(A) closes venous valves below the calf muscle
(B) causes valves to become incompetent
(C) opens valves below the calf muscle

43. Venous hypertension can occur when

(A) venous valves are nonfunctional
(B) calf muscle pump is nonfunctional
(C) systemic hypervolemia is present
(D) all of the above
(E) none of the above

44. Doppler ultrasound detects

(A) the velocity of blood
(B) volume flow rate
(C) resistance

45. In the Doppler equation, the angle Θ relates to

(A) angle of the transducer to the skin
(B) angle of the beam to the vessel
(C) a constant

46. The venous Doppler examination is conducted with the patient

(A) sitting
(B) supine
(C) in Trendelenburg position

47. The venous Doppler examination is

(A) an objective test
(B) compares the responses of one side of the body with the responses of the other side
(C) highly accurate in the detection of calf vein obstruction

48. The diagnostic parameters for venous Doppler study are

(A) presence of turbulence and high flows
(B) spontaneity, phasicity, and augmentation
(C) peak frequency and end-diastolic frequency

49. Distal augmentation is used to

(A) determine the presence of obstruction
(B) determine the competence of venous valves
(C) locate the vein

50. In normal veins, the venous Doppler signal is always

(A) high pitched
(B) continuous
(C) phasic

51. A spontaneous venous signal may be normally absent in

(A) all veins
(B) posterior tibial vein
(C) popliteal vein

52. The normal response to a distal augmentation maneuver is

(A) rapid increase in frequency followed by an abrupt cessation of the signal
(B) slow increase in frequency
(C) rapid increase in frequency followed by a slow return to precompression signal

53. The Doppler signal over a totally occluded common femoral vein is

(A) absent
(B) continuous
(C) pulsatile

54. The Doppler signals in a patient with severe bilateral lower extremity edema and severe congestive heart failure would be

(A) absent
(B) phasic
(C) pulsatile
(D) continuous

55. The Doppler signals in the mid superficial femoral vein in a patient with a large upper thigh medial hematoma would be

(A) absent
(B) phasic
(C) continuous
(D) pulsatile

56. The venous Doppler evaluation is highly accurate in

(A) detecting partially occluding thrombus in proximal veins
(B) determining acute or chronic obstruction
(C) detecting totally occluding thrombus in proximal veins

57. Proximal augmentation is used to

(A) detect venous obstruction
(B) assess perforators
(C) assess valve competence

58. In B-mode ultrasonic evaluation of the venous system, the posterior tibial vein is evaluated by placing the transducer

(A) medial to the femur
(B) slightly medial to the posterior border of the tibia
(C) posterolateral leg

59. To visualize the peroneal vein, the transducer is placed on

(A) posterior lateral aspect of leg
(B) medial aspect of leg
(C) anterior lateral aspect of leg

60. The ultrasonic characteristic(s) of a normal vein is

(A) thin echogenically homogeneous vessel wall
(B) thick rough-appearing vessel walls
(C) thick-walled pulsating vessel

61. The ultrasonic appearance of normal venous valve leaflets is

(A) thick, short, and stationary
(B) thin, long, and moving
(C) not usually visible

62. An acute thrombus is ultrasonically characterized as

(A) hypoechoic mass that does not change in intensity with external compression of the vein
(B) hyperechoic luminal mass
(C) hypoechoic luminal mass that increases in echogenicity with external compression of the vein

63. A chronic venous obstruction is ultrasonically characterized as

(A) hypoechoic luminal mass that increases with echogenicity with external compression of the vein
(B) anechoic luminal mass
(C) hyperechoic mass attached to the vein wall protruding into the lumen

64. In the mid 19th century, Bernoulli postulated three factors that influenced thrombus formation: stasis, trauma, and hypercoagulability.

(A) true
(B) false

65. The risk factor with the highest predictive value for the development of acute DVT is heart disease.

(A) true
(B) false

66. The thrombotic process can cause permanent damage to the venous system.

(A) true
(B) false

67. Pulmonary emboli and postphlebitic syndrome are sequelae of acute superficial vein thrombosis.

(A) true
(B) false

68. The incidence of DVT in the general medical and surgical patient population over 40 years old is 50%

(A) true
(B) false

69. Varicose veins are more prevalent in women than men.

(A) true
(B) false

70. The greatest risk factor for the development of primary varicose veins is genetic predisposition.

(A) true
(B) false

71. Acute DVT is the major contributing factor in secondary varicose veins.

(A) true
(B) false

72. Clinical diagnosis of acute venous disease is about 50% accurate.

(A) true
(B) false

73. Ninety-five percent of venous disease originates in the lower extremities.

(A) true
(B) false

74. The clinical manifestations of chronic venous disease result from venous hypertension.

(A) true
(B) false

75. Varicose veins appear as dilated tortuous muscular veins.

(A) true
(B) false

Answers and Explanations

The relevant information for questions 1 through 75 can be found in the Study Guide.

1. **(D)** The function of the perforating veins is to transport blood from the superficial to deep system. *(496, Study Guide)*

2. **(C)** Six. *(497, Study Guide)*

3. **(C)** The lesser and greater saphenous veins are superficial veins. *(496–497, Study Guide)*

4. **(C)** The deep veins are located within the musculofascial compartment. *(496–497, Study Guide)*

5. **(D)** Veins are thin-walled collapsible vessels. *(496, Study Guide)*

6. **(B)** The main differences between the vein wall and the arterial wall structures is the reduced elastin concentration and its very thin media. *(496, Study Guide)*

7. **(C)** The function of the venous valves is to assure prograde flow. *(496, Study Guide)*

8. **(B)** As the volume of blood in a vein increases, the shape of the collapsed vein changes to elliptical. *(496, Study Guide)*

9. **(C)** When the vein changes from the collapsed state to an elliptical shape, the venous pressure increases minimally. *(499–500, Study Guide)*

10. **(A)** When a person assumes the erect position, the venous pressure in the lower extremities increases. *(499–500, Study Guide)*

11. **(E)** All of the above. *(499–500, Study Guide)*

12. **(C)** The pressure within the vein is directly proportional to the force that is exerted on the vein wall by the blood volume within it. *(499–500, Study Guide)*

13. **(A)** In the supine position, venous return from the leg is related to the pressure differential between the leg and the heart and the pressure differential created by the diaphragm during respiration. *(499–501, Study Guide)*

14. **(E)** All of the above. *(499–501, Study Guide)*

15. **(B)** Venous valves close in response to high blood volume in the vein above the valve. *(499–501, Study Guide)*

16. **(C)** The posterior tibial, peroneal, and anterior tibial veins are paired deep veins of the calf. *(497–498, Study Guide)*

17. **(C)** The number of valves in the veins of the lower extremities varies from person to person. *(496, Study Guide)*

18. **(B)** Venous valves are located in all veins except the vena cava. *(496, Study Guide)*

19. **(B)** The majority of venous valves are found in distal veins. *(496–497, Study Guide)*

20. **(B)** Localized dilation of the vein wall is associated with valve sinus. *(496–497, Study Guide)*

21. **(B)** The primary function of the deep venous system is to transport blood from the extremity to the heart. *(496, Study Guide)*

22. **(B)** The posterior tibial vein is located in the posterior medial calf. *(498, Study Guide)*

23. **(B)** The superficial femoral vein is a deep vein. *(498, Study Guide)*

24. **(C)** The peroneal vein is located directly behind and medial to the fibula. *(498, Study Guide)*

25. **(A)** The gastrocnemius vein is a muscular vein. *(498, Study Guide)*

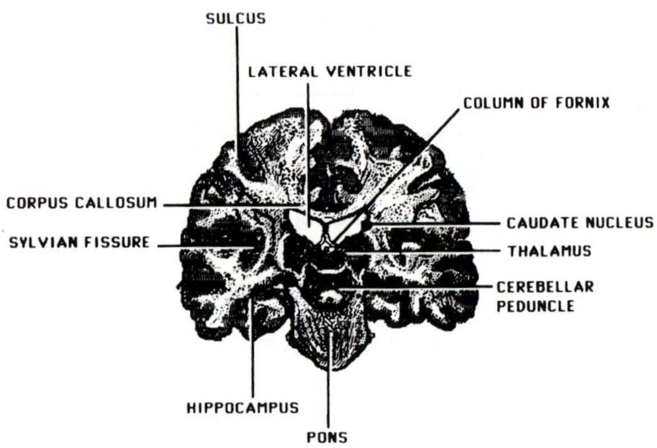

Figure 10–15. A diagram of a coronal section of the brain.

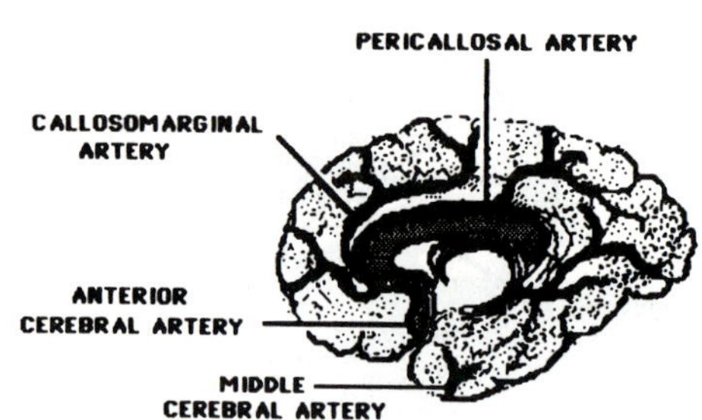

Figure 10–18. A diagram of lateral aspect of the internal carotid artery divisions.

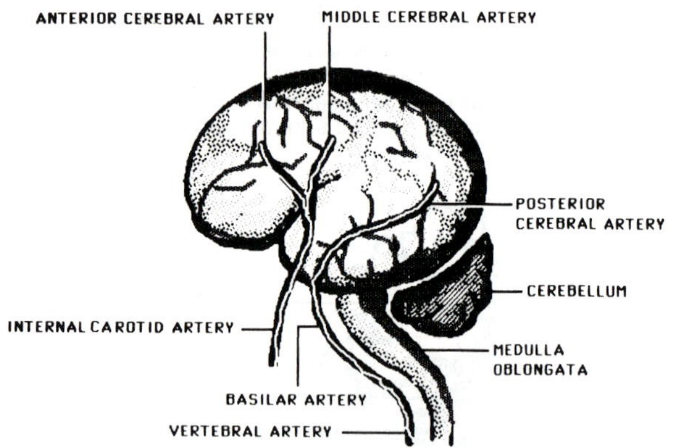

Figure 10–16. A diagram of the brain and arteries, sagittal section.

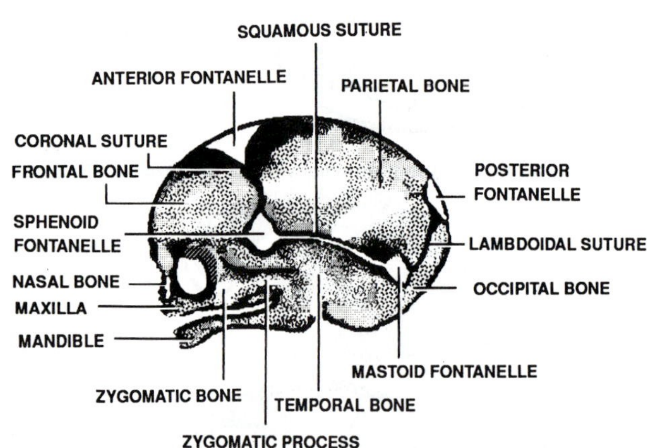

Figure 10–19. A diagram of a lateral view of the infantile skull.

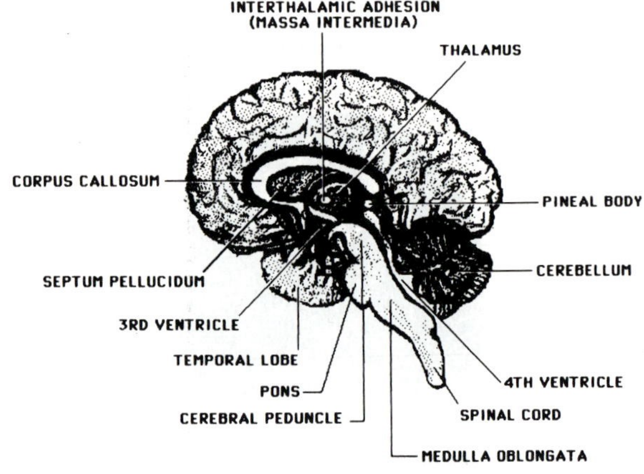

Figure 10–17. A diagram of the brain sagittal section.

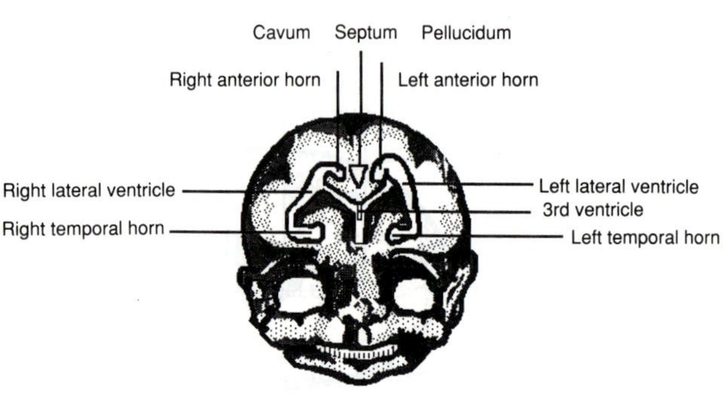

Figure 10–20. A diagram of an anterior view of the infantile skull with ventricular system.

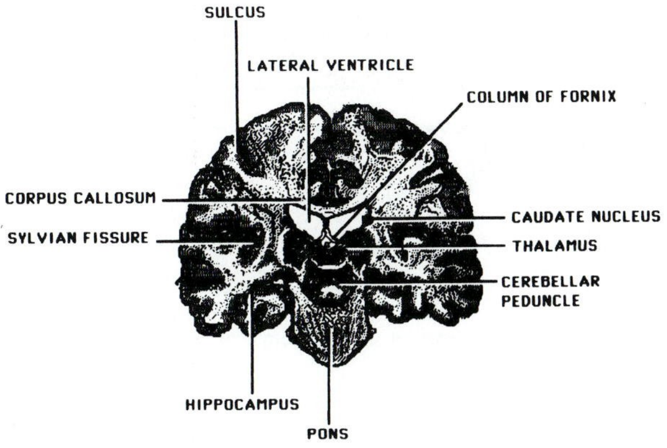

Figure 10–15. A diagram of a coronal section of the brain.

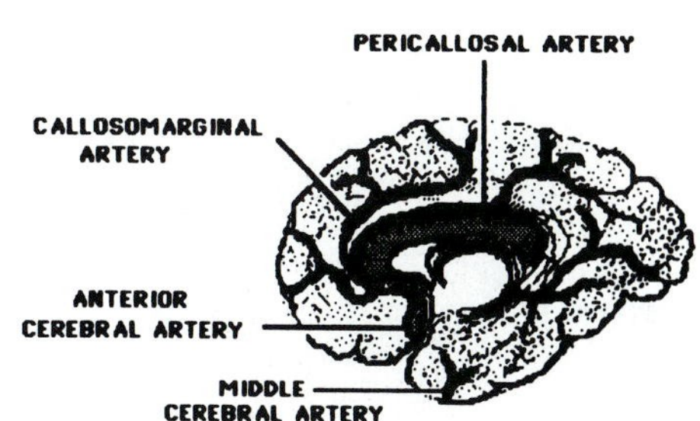

Figure 10–18. A diagram of lateral aspect of the internal carotid artery divisions.

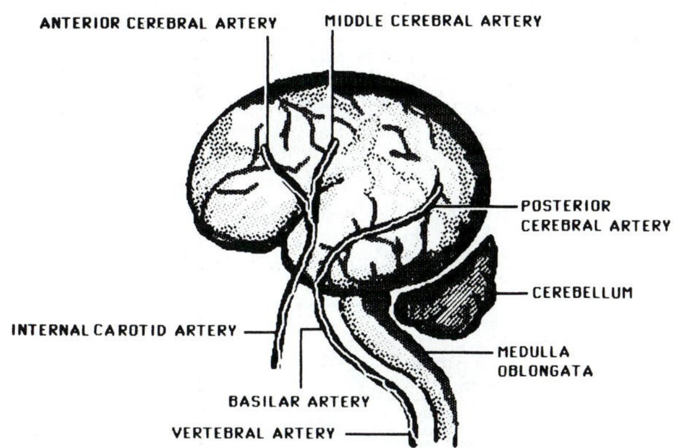

Figure 10–16. A diagram of the brain and arteries, sagittal section.

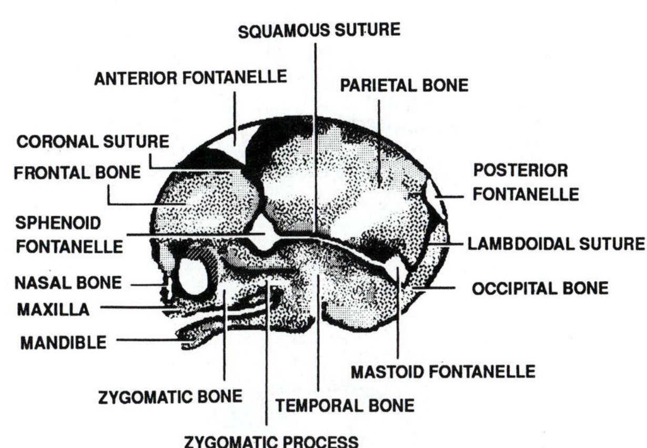

Figure 10–19. A diagram of a lateral view of the infantile skull.

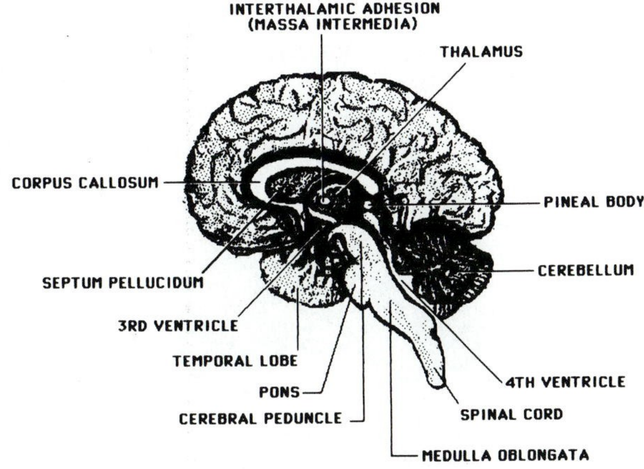

Figure 10–17. A diagram of the brain sagittal section.

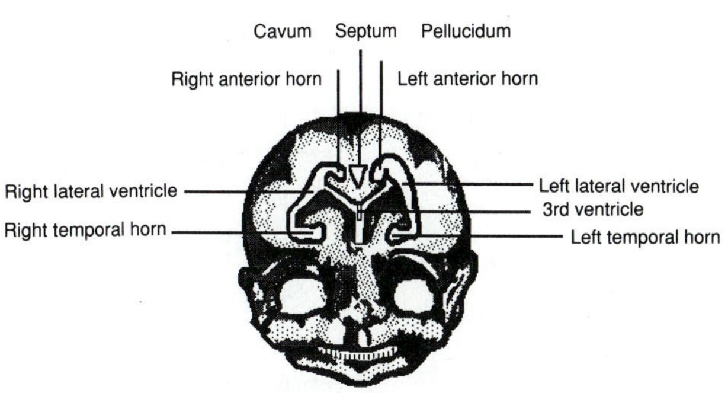

Figure 10–20. A diagram of an anterior view of the infantile skull with ventricular system.

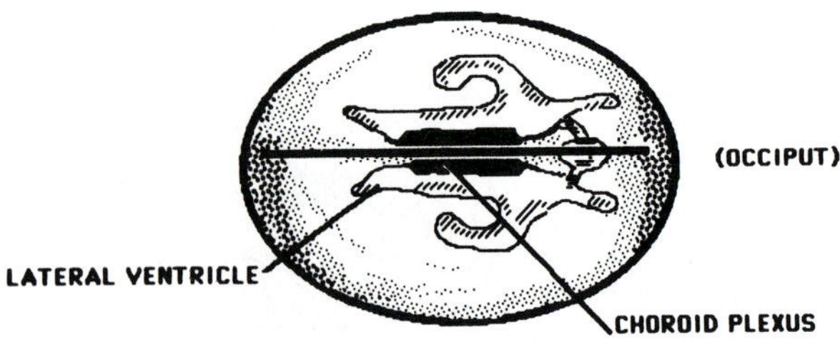

Figure 10–7. A diagram of an axial view at the level of the lateral ventricle.

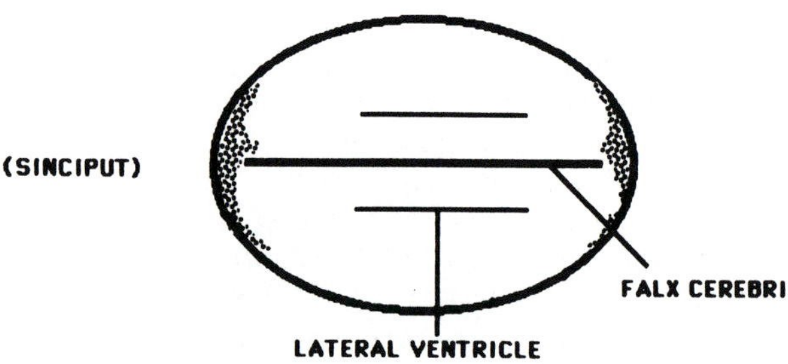

Figure 10–11. A diagram of an axial view at the level of the lateral ventricle.

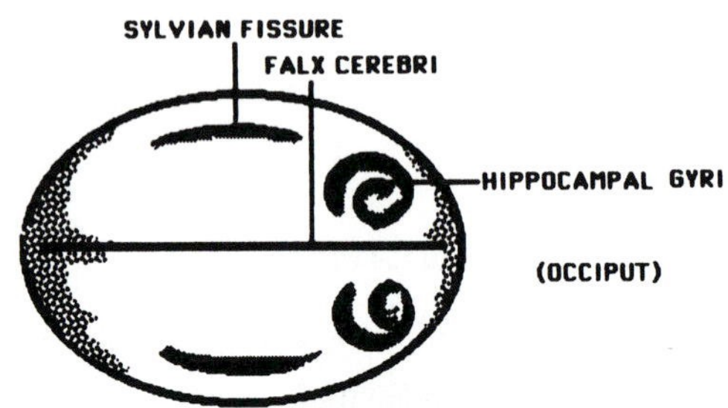

Figure 10–8. A diagram of an axial view at the level of the sylvian fissure.

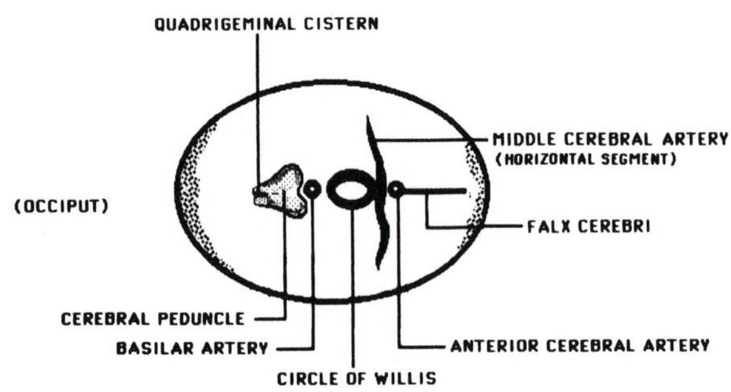

Figure 10–12. A diagram of an axial view at the level of the base of the skull.

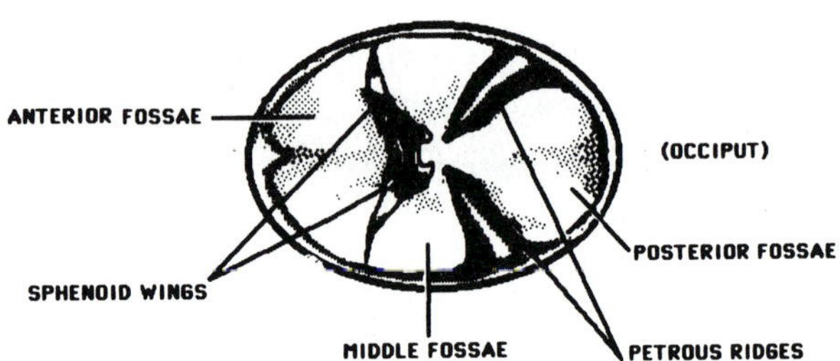

Figure 10–9. A diagram of an axial view at the base of the skull.

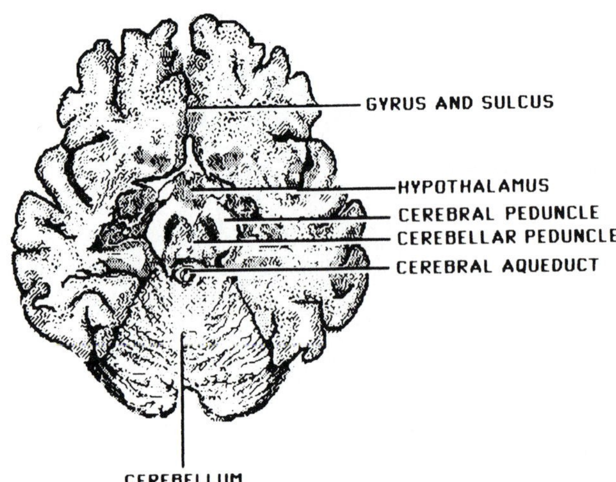

Figure 10–13. A diagram of a coronal section of the brain.

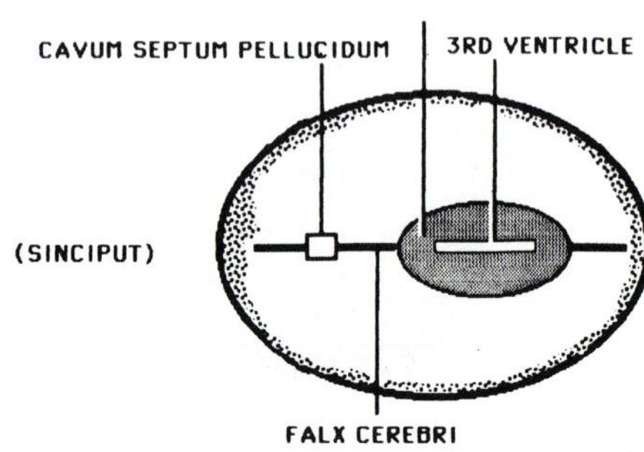

Figure 10–10. A diagram of an axial view at the level of the thalami.

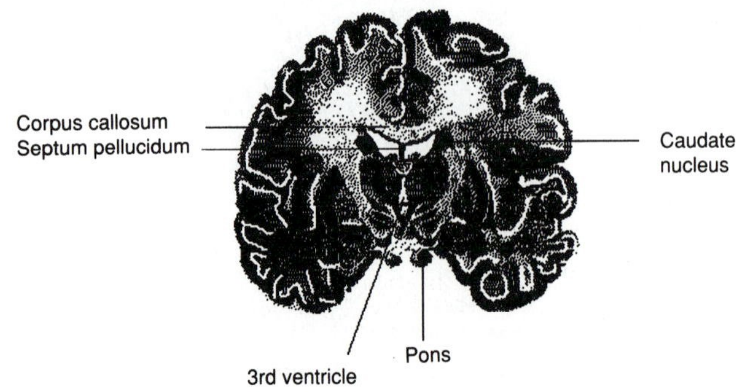

Figure 10–14. A diagram of a coronal section of the brain.

tration carefully, then close your examination book and try to form a photographic image of the illustration in your mind. Then draw and label the illustration on a separate sheet of paper without referring to the illustration.

Although this process may sound difficult at first, it is a simple method of developing a photographic memory. As sonographers, we see hundreds of sonographic images each day and have probably used photographic memory without even realizing it. Go ahead and try this with the following illustrations.

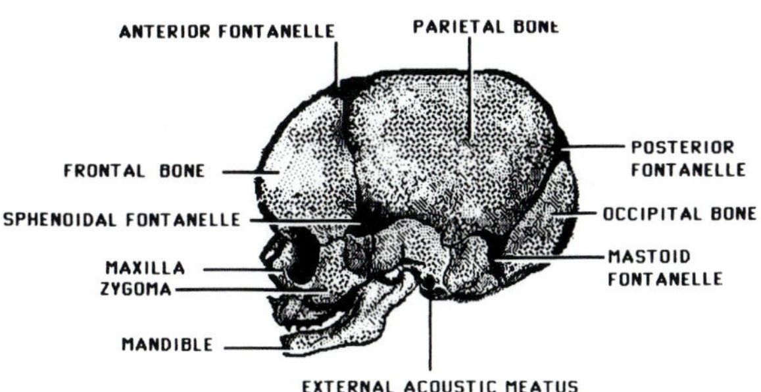

Figure 10–1. A diagram of a lateral view of the infantile skull.

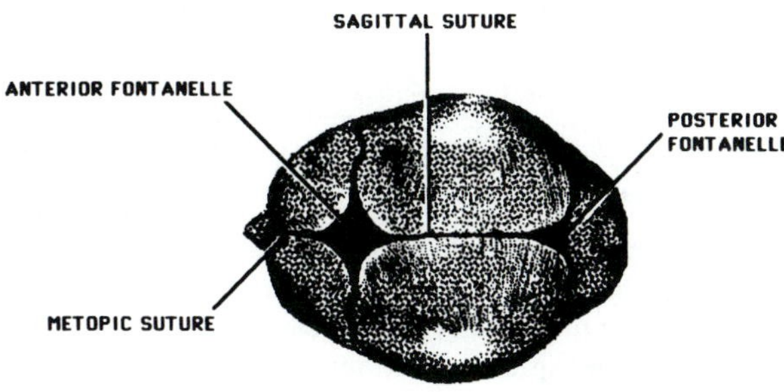

Figure 10–2. A diagram of a superior view of the infantile skull.

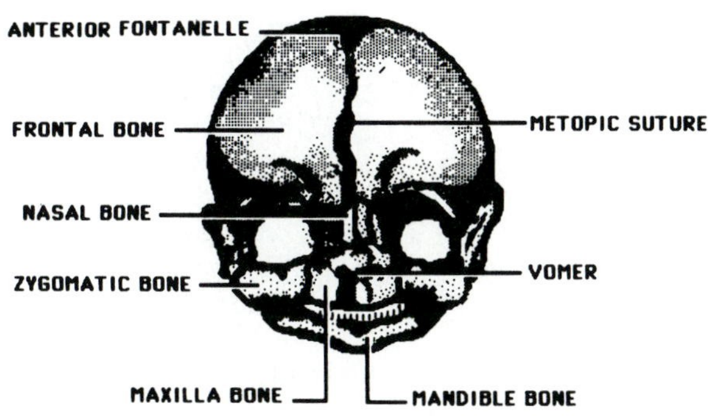

Figure 10–3. An anterior view of an infantile skull.

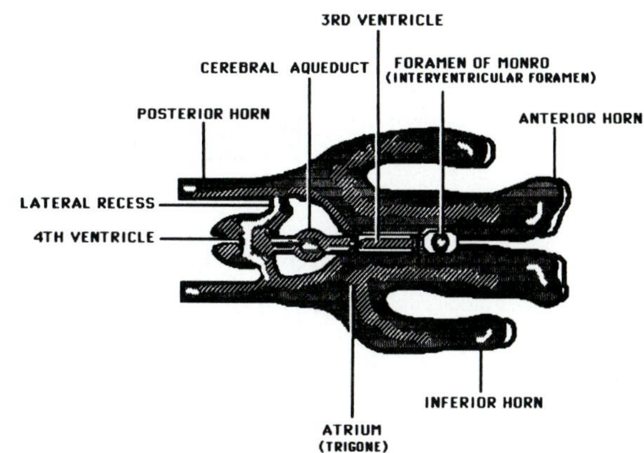

Figure 10–4. A diagram of the ventricular system; superior view.

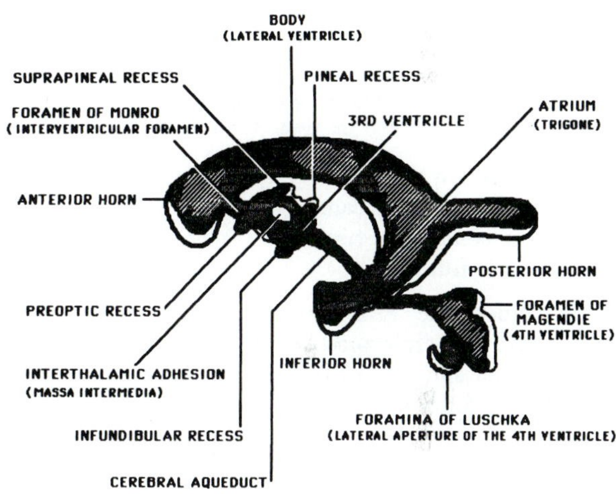

Figure 10–5. A diagram of the ventricular system; lateral view.

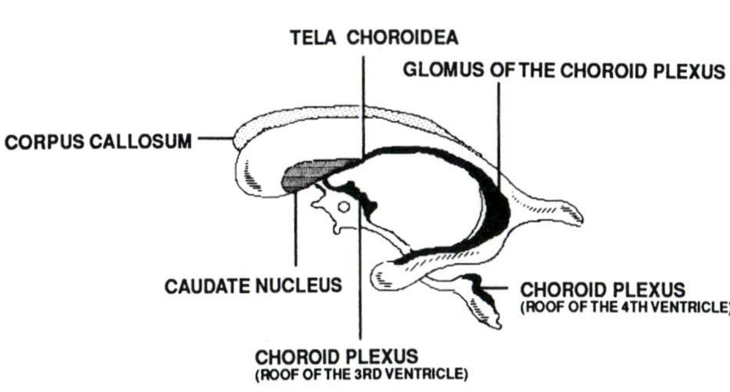

Figure 10–6. A diagram of the ventricular system and choroid plexus; lateral view.

CHAPTER 10

NEUROSONOLOGY

Charles S. Odwin, Chandrowti Devi Persaud, Arthur C. Fleischer, and Pamela M. Foy

Study Guide

The material in this guide will assist you. The mnemonics and illustrations in this Study Guide should help you to increase your knowledge and, as a result, improve your skills in taking examinations.

The mnemonic "SCALP" serves as a memory key for the five layers of the scalp listed below:

S skin
C connective tissue
A aponeurosis epicranalis
L loose connective tissue
P pericranium

The mnemonic "PAD" serves as a memory key for the three layers of membranes called meninges, which cover the brain and spinal cord from inner to outer. The three layers are as follows:

P pia
A arachnoid
D dura

A mnemonic for the 12 cranial nerves is "O, O, O TELL TED AND FRANCES ABOUT GOING VACATIONING AFTER HALLOWEEN":

O olfactory
O optic
O oculomotor
T trochlear
T trigeminal
A abducens
F facial
A acoustic
G glossopharyngeal
V vagus
A accessory
H hypoglossal

There are six fontanelles: one anterior, one posterior, two mastoidal, and two sphenoidal. The mnemonic "MAPS" serves as a memory key for these fontanelles:

M mastoidal
A anterior
P posterior
S sphenoidal

There are four ventricles. The first and second are called the right and left lateral ventricles. The third and fourth are below the first and second. Between the frontal horns of the lateral ventricle is the cavum septum pellucidum; between the bodies of the two lateral ventricles is the cavum vergae. The mnemonic SAC serves as a memory key for the three scanning planes used in neonatal cranial sonography.

S sagittal
A axial
C coronal

Mnemonics is just one of many useful ways to formulate words that will help you remember. How fast you learn, and how much you retain after you learn, may be a big factor in taking examinations.

The following are study groups. Formulate your own mnemonic device to help you remember them.

LOBES OF THE BRAIN

Occipital lobe
Parietal lobe
Temporal lobe
Frontal lobe

TYPES OF INTRACRANIAL HEMORRHAGE

SEH subependymal hemorrhage
GMH germinal matrix hemorrhage
CPH choroid plexus hemorrhage
SAH subarachnoid hemorrhage
IPH intraparenchymal hemorrhage

The following pages contain illustrations of anatomical structures (see Figs. 10–1 to 10–28). Study each illus-

58. **(B)** In B-mode ultrasonic evaluation of the venous system, the posterior tibial vein is evaluated by placing the transducer slightly medial to the posterior border of the tibia. *(504, Study Guide)*

59. **(A)** To visualize the peroneal vein, the transducer is placed on the posterior lateral aspect of the leg. *(504, Study Guide)*

60. **(A)** The characteristic of a normal vein is a thin echogenically homogeneous vessel wall. *(496, Study Guide)*

61. **(B)** The ultrasonic appearance of normal venous valve leaflets is thin, long, and moving. *(496, Study Guide)*

62. **(C)** An acute thrombus is ultrasonically characterized as a hypoechoic luminal mass that increases in echogenicity with external compression of the vein. *(504–505, Study Guide)*

63. **(C)** A chronic venous obstruction is ultrasonically characterized as a hyperechoic mass attached to the vein wall protruding into the lumen. *(504–505, Study Guide)*

64. **(B)** False. Virchow postulated this triad. *(504–505, Study Guide)*

65. **(B)** False. The risk factor with the highest predictive value is a previous history of venous disease. *(504–505, Study Guide)*

66. **(A)** True. *(504–505, Study Guide)*

67. **(B)** False. They are sequelae of acute deep vein thrombosis. *(505, Study Guide)*

68. **(B)** False. The incident in the patient population over age 40 is 20%. *(505, Study Guide)*

69. **(B)** False. Epidemiologic data indicates an equal distribution between sexes. *(505, Study Guide)*

70. **(A)** True. *(505, Study Guide)*

71. **(A)** True. *(505, Study Guide)*

72. **(A)** True. *(505, Study Guide)*

73. **(A)** True. *(505, Study Guide)*

74. **(A)** True. *(505, Study Guide)*

75. **(B)** False. Varicose veins are dilated tortuous superficial veins. *(505, Study Guide)*

26. **(C)** The gastrocnemius vein terminates at the popliteal vein. *(498, Study Guide)*

27. **(A)** The lesser saphenous vein is located in the center of the posterior calf. *(498, Study Guide)*

28. **(C)** The lesser saphenous vein terminates with the popliteal vein. *(498, Study Guide)*

29. **(A)** The greater saphenous vein is located in the medial aspect of the leg. *(499, Study Guide)*

30. **(C)** The greater saphenous vein terminates at the common femoral vein. *(499, Study Guide)*

31. **(A)** The greater saphenous vein distal to its termination unites into posteromedial and antereolateral branches. *(499, Study Guide)*

32. **(C)** The volume of blood contained within the venous system is 80%. *(500, Study Guide)*

33. **(B)** In the resting supine position, the venous blood distribution is equally distributed through the system. *(500, Study Guide)*

34. **(C)** When a person assumes the erect position, venous blood is redistributed to the lower extremities. *(500–501, Study Guide)*

35. **(B)** When a person assumes an erect position, the venous pressure at the ankle increases. *(500–501, Study Guide)*

36. **(B)** Perforating veins are connecting veins between superficial and deep veins. *(498–499, Study Guide)*

37. **(C)** The function of perforating veins is to transport blood between the deep and superficial vein. *(498–499, Study Guide)*

38. **(A)** The direction of flow through perforating veins is from superficial to deep veins. *(498–499, Study Guide)*

39. **(B)** Perforating veins course from the subcutaneous tissue through the fascia. *(498, Study Guide)*

40. **(C)** Contraction of the calf muscle expels blood from the calf into the thigh. *(499–500, Study Guide)*

41. **(B)** Relaxation of the calf muscle allows blood flow from the superficial and foot veins to enter the deep veins of the calf. *(499–500, Study Guide)*

42. **(A)** Contraction of the calf muscle closes venous valves below the calf muscle. *(499–500, Study Guide)*

43. **(D)** All of the above. *(500–501, Study Guide)*

44. **(A)** Doppler ultrasound detects the velocity of blood. *(502, Study Guide)*

45. **(B)** In the Doppler equation, the angle Θ relates to the angle of the beam to the vessel. *(502, Study Guide)*

46. **(B)** The venous Doppler examination is conducted with the patient in the supine position. *(503, Study Guide)*

47. **(B)** The venous Doppler examination compares the responses of one side of the body with the responses of the other side. *(503–504, Study Guide)*

48. **(B)** The diagnostic parameters for venous Doppler study are spontaneity, phasicity, and augmentation. *(502, Study Guide)*

49. **(A)** Distal augmentation is used to determine the presence of obstruction. *(502, Study Guide)*

50. **(C)** In normal veins, the venous Doppler signal is always phasic. *(502, Study Guide)*

51. **(B)** A spontaneous venous signal may be normally absent in the posterior tibial vein while the velocity of the blood within the vessel is moving too slowly to be detected by Doppler. *(502, Study Guide)*

52. **(C)** The normal response to a distal augmentation maneuver is a rapid increase in frequency followed by a slow return to precompression signal. *(502, Study Guide)*

53. **(A)** The Doppler signal over a totally occluded common femoral vein is absent. *(504–505, Study Guide)*

54. **(C)** The Doppler signal in a patient with severe bilateral lower extremity edema and severe congestive heart failure would be pulsatile. This history suggests systemic hypervolemia, where the arterial wave is transmitted through the venous system. *(504–505, Study Guide)*

55. **(C)** The Doppler signals in the mid superficial femoral in a patient with a large upper thigh medial hematoma would be continuous. Either intrinsic or extrinsic compression of the vein creates continuous flow. *(504–505, Study Guide)*

56. **(C)** The venous Doppler evaluation is highly accurate in detecting totally occluding thrombus in proximal veins. *(504–505, Study Guide)*

57. **(C)** Proximal augmentation is used to assess valve competence. *(502, Study Guide)*

Answers and Explanations

The relevant information for questions 1 through 75 can be found in the Study Guide.

1. **(D)** The function of the perforating veins is to transport blood from the superficial to deep system. *(496, Study Guide)*

2. **(C)** Six. *(497, Study Guide)*

3. **(C)** The lesser and greater saphenous veins are superficial veins. *(496–497, Study Guide)*

4. **(C)** The deep veins are located within the musculofascial compartment. *(496–497, Study Guide)*

5. **(D)** Veins are thin-walled collapsible vessels. *(496, Study Guide)*

6. **(B)** The main differences between the vein wall and the arterial wall structures is the reduced elastin concentration and its very thin media. *(496, Study Guide)*

7. **(C)** The function of the venous valves is to assure prograde flow. *(496, Study Guide)*

8. **(B)** As the volume of blood in a vein increases, the shape of the collapsed vein changes to elliptical. *(496, Study Guide)*

9. **(C)** When the vein changes from the collapsed state to an elliptical shape, the venous pressure increases minimally. *(499–500, Study Guide)*

10. **(A)** When a person assumes the erect position, the venous pressure in the lower extremities increases. *(499–500, Study Guide)*

11. **(E)** All of the above. *(499–500, Study Guide)*

12. **(C)** The pressure within the vein is directly proportional to the force that is exerted on the vein wall by the blood volume within it. *(499–500, Study Guide)*

13. **(A)** In the supine position, venous return from the leg is related to the pressure differential between the leg and the heart and the pressure differential created by the diaphragm during respiration. *(499–501, Study Guide)*

14. **(E)** All of the above. *(499–501, Study Guide)*

15. **(B)** Venous valves close in response to high blood volume in the vein above the valve. *(499–501, Study Guide)*

16. **(C)** The posterior tibial, peroneal, and anterior tibial veins are paired deep veins of the calf. *(497–498, Study Guide)*

17. **(C)** The number of valves in the veins of the lower extremities varies from person to person. *(496, Study Guide)*

18. **(B)** Venous valves are located in all veins except the vena cava. *(496, Study Guide)*

19. **(B)** The majority of venous valves are found in distal veins. *(496–497, Study Guide)*

20. **(B)** Localized dilation of the vein wall is associated with valve sinus. *(496–497, Study Guide)*

21. **(B)** The primary function of the deep venous system is to transport blood from the extremity to the heart. *(496, Study Guide)*

22. **(B)** The posterior tibial vein is located in the posterior medial calf. *(498, Study Guide)*

23. **(B)** The superficial femoral vein is a deep vein. *(498, Study Guide)*

24. **(C)** The peroneal vein is located directly behind and medial to the fibula. *(498, Study Guide)*

25. **(A)** The gastrocnemius vein is a muscular vein. *(498, Study Guide)*

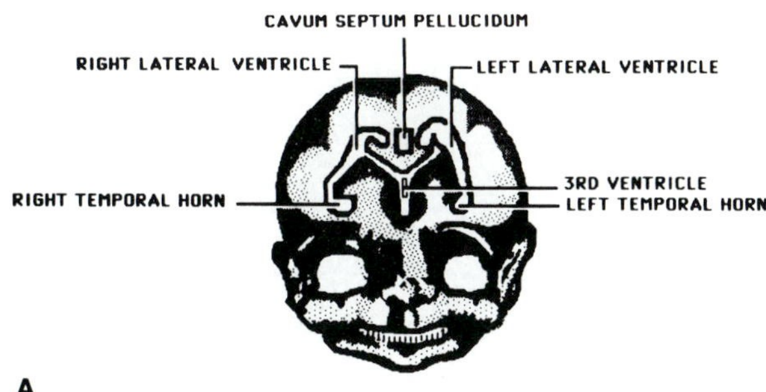

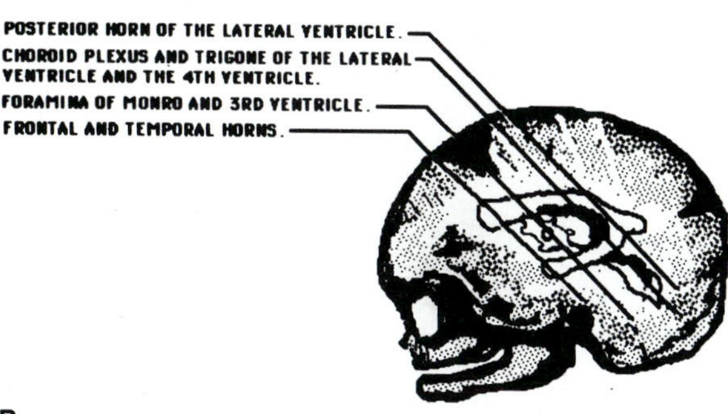

Figure 10–21. A diagram of **(A)** an anterior view and **(B)** a lateral view of the infantile skull with ventricular system.

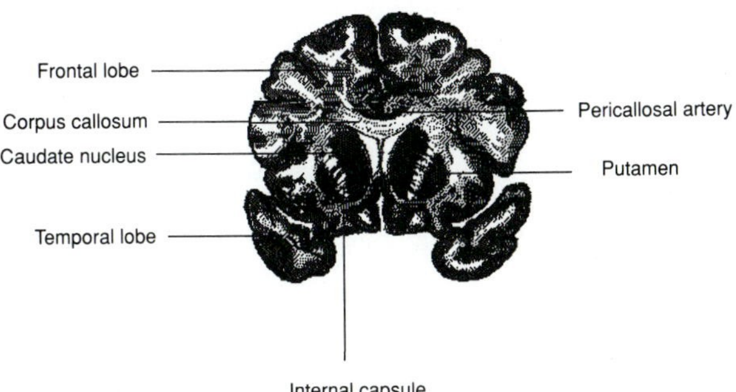

Figure 10–22. A diagram of a coronal section of the brain.

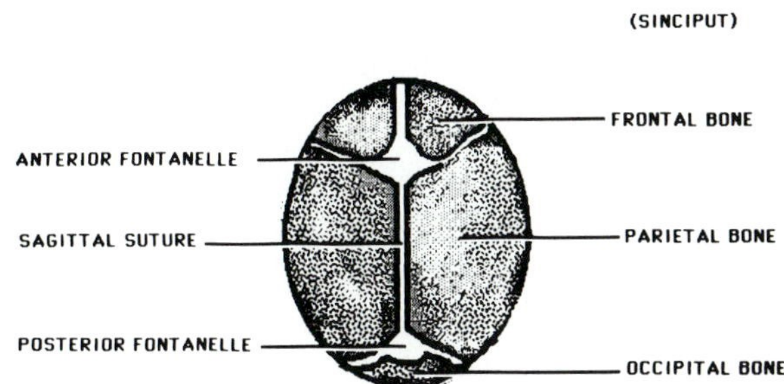

Figure 10–23. A superior view of an infantile skull.

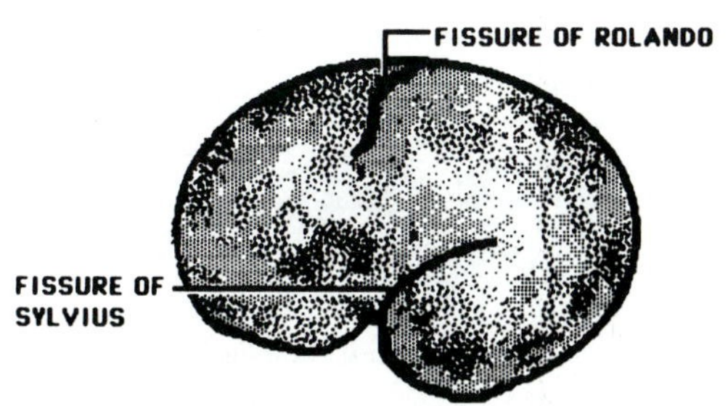

Figure 10–24. A lateral view of the brain.

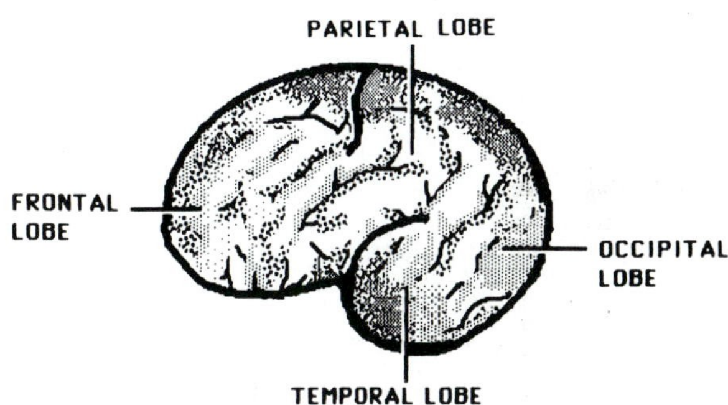

Figure 10–25. A lateral view of the brain.

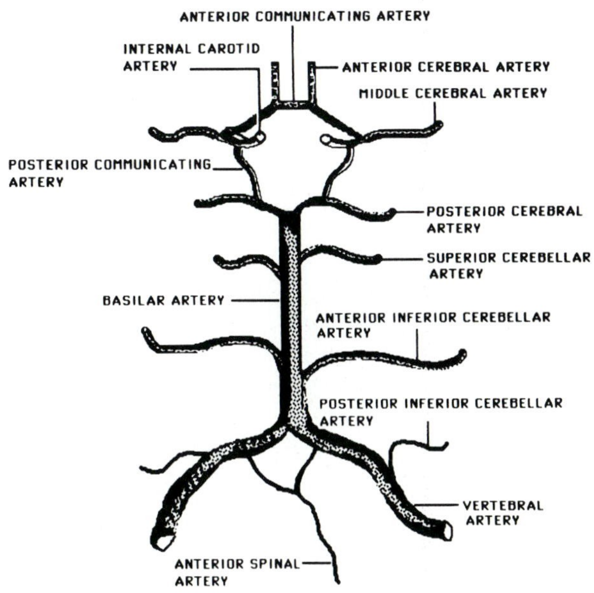

Figure 10–26. The circle of Willis.

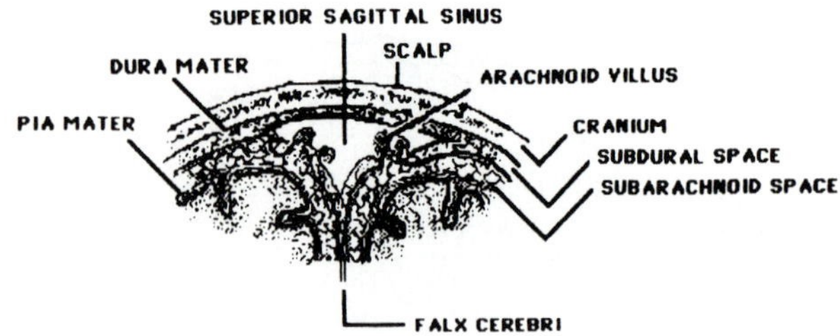

Figure 10–27. A diagram of a coronal section of the meninges and cortex.

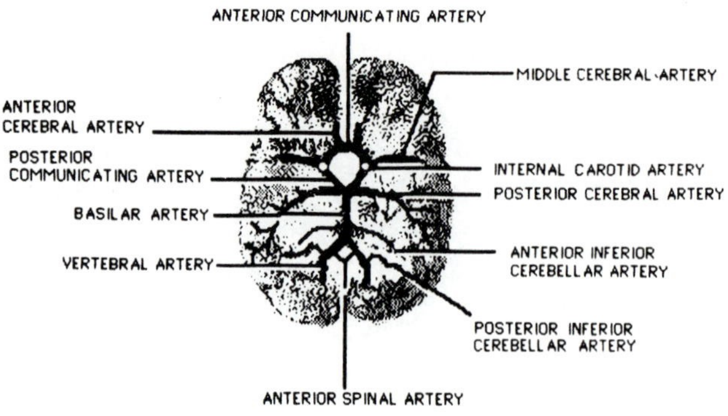

Figure 10–28. A diagram of the arteries at the base of the brain.

Questions

GENERAL INSTRUCTIONS: For each question, select the best answer. Select only one answer for each question unless otherwise instructed.

1. The acoustic windows used most often in neonatal cranial sonography are the (1) anterior fontanelle, (2) posterior fontanelle, (3) mastoidal fontanelle, (4) sphenoidal fontanelle.

   (A) 1 and 2
   (B) 1 and 3
   (C) 3 and 4
   (D) all of the above

2. On sonography, cytomegalovirus in the neonate is associated with

   (A) periventricular calcifications
   (B) small cystic lesions
   (C) encephalocele
   (D) anencephaly

3. The first sonographic images of the brain with the use of the A-mode were formerly called

   (A) echoencephalography
   (B) neurosonology
   (C) neonatal ultrasound
   (D) cranial ultrasound

4. Another name for the sphenoid fontanelle is

   (A) lambda
   (B) the anterolateral fontanelle
   (C) the posterolateral fontanelle
   (D) bregma

5. The mastoid fontanelle becomes progressively smaller and closes completely by age

   (A) 2 years
   (B) 2–3 months
   (C) 18 months
   (D) 12 months

6. The posterior fontanelle becomes progressively smaller and closes completely by age

   (A) 18 months
   (B) 2 years
   (C) 1 year
   (D) 2–3 months

7. The anterior fontanelle becomes progressively smaller and closes completely by age

   (A) 6 months
   (B) 2–3 months
   (C) 1 year
   (D) 18 months

8. The term *craniosynostosis* denotes

   (A) premature fusion of the cranial sutures
   (B) premature separation of the cranial sutures
   (C) a bluish discoloration of the cranium
   (D) a bluish discoloration of the scalp

9. Hypothermia denotes

   (A) high memory
   (B) low memory
   (C) high temperature
   (D) low temperature

10. Identify the causes of hydrocephalus in utero: (1) aqueductal stenosis, (2) a Dandy-Walker malformation, (3) an intrauterine infection, (4) isolated chromosomal abnormalities.

    (A) 1 and 3
    (B) 2 and 4
    (C) 3 only
    (D) all of the above

11. Another name for the mastoidal fontanelle is

    (A) anterior fontanelle
    (B) posterior fontanelle
    (C) lambda
    (D) posterolateral fontanelle

12. When the parietal bones are relatively thin, lateral ventricular measurements can be obtained up to

(A) 5 years
(B) 6 months
(C) 2–3 years
(D) 6–12 months

13. What percentage of premature infants with a birthweight of less than 1500 g develop intracranial hemorrhage?

(A) 40–60%
(B) 5–10%
(C) 80–90%
(D) 10–30%

14. The advantage(s) of real-time sonography for evaluating the neonatal brain is

(A) ionization
(B) depiction of vascular pulsation
(C) portability
(D) noninvasiveness
(E) B, C, and D
(F) all of the above

15. In cranial sonography, a real-time linear-array transducer is limited by (1) a limited field of view, (2) the inability to visualize the inner lateral table of both sides of the calvarium simultaneously, (3) being able to examine only the central portion of the brain, (4) producing only a 90° pie-shaped image, (5) low signal-to-noise ratio and artifact.

(A) 1 and 2
(B) 4 and 2
(C) 1, 2, and 4
(D) 1, 2, 3, and 5

16. To eliminate loss of information caused by a videotape, the sonographer should (1) obtain the image directly from the monitor with a multi-image camera, (2) freeze the videotape and make the image from the freeze frame, (3) put the tape on slow motion, (4) use a slow exposure time in high-speed fast forward.

(A) 1 only
(B) 2 and 3
(C) 1 and 4
(D) 1, 2, and 3

17. The original A-mode techniques were used to evaluate

(A) hydrocephalus
(B) mass lesions
(C) midline shift
(D) all of the above

18. Which of the following sonographic planes are most comparable with cranial computed tomography (CT)

(A) axial
(B) coronal
(C) sagittal
(D) B and C only

19. The sphenoid fontanelle becomes progressively smaller and closes by age

(A) 12 months
(B) 2–3 months
(C) 18 months
(D) 6 months

20. Axial cranial sonograms are taken at what interval?

(A) 2 cm
(B) 5 mm
(C) 5 cm
(D) 2 mm

21. Which of the following statements about temporal and occipital horns are true?

(A) they both diverge laterally as they project from the body of the lateral ventricles
(B) they both diverge medially as they project from the body of the lateral ventricles
(C) the occipital horn is lateral and the temporal horns are medial to the body of the lateral ventricles
(D) the right temporal horn and the occipital horn are medial and the left temporal horn is lateral

Figure 10–29 illustrates the sagittal projections through the anterior fontanelle taken from planes 1 to 4 for coronal-sectional images. For each numbered line, match the anatomic structures to be visualized in Column B with the correct numbered planes in Column A.

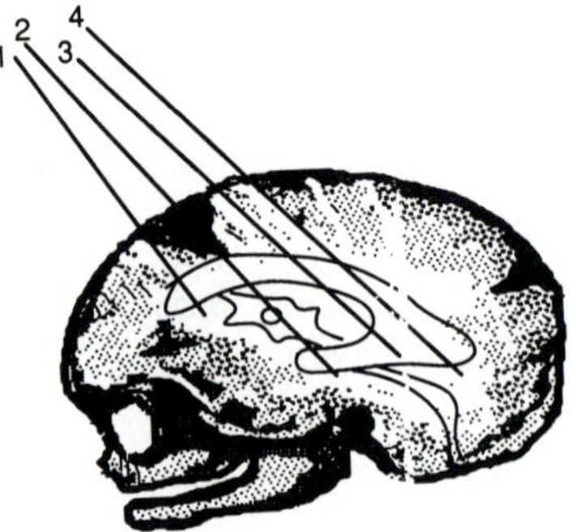

Figure 10–29. Sagittal projections through the anterior fontanelle taken from planes 1 to 4 for coronal-sectional images.

COLUMN A	COLUMN B
22. plane 4 ______	(A) foramina of Monro and the third ventricle
23. plane 3 ______	(B) choroid plexus and trigone of the lateral ventricle and the fourth ventricle
24. plane 2 ______	(C) posterior horn of the lateral ventricle
25. plane 1 ______	(D) frontal horn of the lateral ventricle

Figure 10–30 illustrates anatomic structures in a coronal image. For each numbered line, match the anatomic structures to be visualized in Column B with the correct number in Column A.

COLUMN A	COLUMN B
26. 3 ______	(A) third ventricle
27. 1 ______	(B) temporal horn
28. 2 ______	(C) cavum septum pellucidum
	(D) frontal horn

29. The lateral ventricular ratio can be obtained by measuring the distance from the

(A) anterior wall to the posterior wall of the lateral ventricle
(B) midline to medial wall of the lateral ventricle and from the inner wall of the table of the skull
(C) medial wall to the lateral wall of the lateral ventricle
(D) midline to the lateral wall of the lateral ventricle and dividing this by the distance from the midline echo to the inner table of the skull

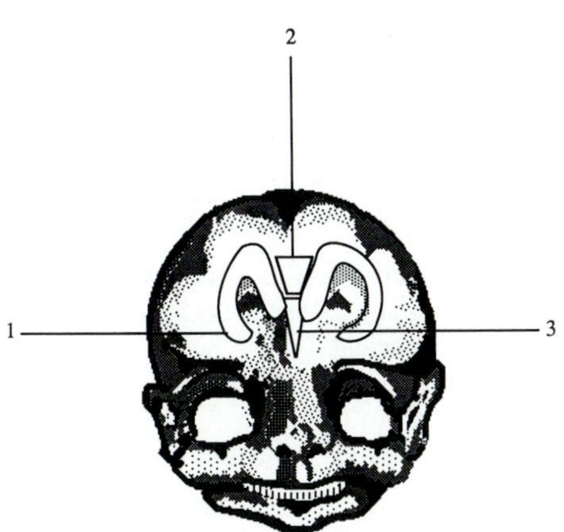

Figure 10–30. An anterior view of a newborn's skull demonstrating anatomic structures.

30. What percentage should the lateral ventricle width–hemispheric width ratio not exceed in the neonate?

(A) 100%
(B) 40%
(C) 35%
(D) 5–10%

31. The axial scan can be obtained by placing the transducer on the parietal bone just above the

(A) styloid process
(B) coronal suture
(C) glabella
(D) external auditory meatus

32. The axial technique is used primarily for (1) the lateral ventricle width hemispheric width (LVW/HW), (2) cerebrospinal fluid-blood level in the ventricle, (3) hypercarbia, (4) hypoxia.

(A) 1 and 4
(B) 1 and 2
(C) 3 and 4
(D) all of the above

33. Which of the following statements about the lateral ventricle in the axial scan are true: (1) the lateral wall is never seen, (2) the medial wall may not be visualized, thus the actual width of the lateral ventricle is not measured, (3) the medial and lateral ventricle are not measured, (4) the medial wall of the lateral ventricle is not perpendicular to the ultrasound beam?

(A) 1 and 2
(B) 1 and 4
(C) 3 and 4
(D) 2 and 4

34. In what position is the caudate nucleus in relation to the lateral ventricle: (1) superolateral border, (2) inferomedial border, (3) inferolateral border, (4) superomedial border?

(A) 1 only
(B) 2 and 3
(C) 1 and 3
(D) 3 only

35. Which of the following statements regarding the germinal matrix are true: (1) it cannot be visualized as a distinct structure, (2) it lies just above the caudate nucleus, (3) it disappears between 32 weeks to term, (4) it is a fetal structure?

(A) 3 and 2
(B) 3 and 4
(C) 1 and 3
(D) all of the above

36. Which one of the following statements about the choroid plexus is not true?

(A) the choroid plexus will fall to the dependent side when the head changes position
(B) there is no choroid in the occipital horn
(C) there is no choroid in the frontal horn
(D) the choroid is largest in the frontal horn and trigone region of the lateral ventricle

37. The most common site for subependymal germinal matrix hemorrhage is

(A) anterior to the telea choroidea
(B) body of the choroid plexus
(C) head of the choroid plexus
(D) head of the caudate nucleus

38. The normal location for the germinal matrix after 24 weeks of gestation is

(A) above the caudate nucleus in the subependymal layer of the lateral ventricle
(B) within the choroid plexus
(C) inferior to the caudate nucleus
(D) within the choroid plexus in the trigone

39. Which of the following is the true relationship of the thalami to the ventricles: (1) the thalami lies inferior to the body of the later ventricles, (2) oval symmetric, echogenic structures that form the lateral wall of the third ventricle, (3) the inferior margin of the thalami is closely applied to the roof of the temporal horns, (4) the thalami lies medial to the body of the later ventricles?

(A) 1, 2, and 3
(B) 1, 3, and 4
(C) 2, 3, and 4
(D) all of the above

40. The cisterna magna appears sonographically as

(A) echogenic space superior to the cerebellum
(B) echogenic space inferior to the cerebellum
(C) echo-free space superior to the cerebellum
(D) echo-free space inferior to the cerebellum

41. With the use of real-time sonography, vascular pulsation is sometimes seen in the sylvian fissure. This is most likely caused by the

(A) anterior cerebral arteries
(B) posterior cerebral arteries
(C) middle vertebral arteries
(D) middle cerebral arteries

42. Which of the following statements about the fissure and sulci is *true?*

(A) fissure and sulci both appear echogenic
(B) fissure is echo-free and the sulci is echogenic
(C) sulci is echo-free and the fissure is echogenic
(D) fissure and sulci are both echo-free

43. The choroid plexus is attached to the floor of the lateral ventricle. Its point of attachment is called

(A) telea choroidea
(B) interhemisphere fissure
(C) pineal body
(D) caudate nucleus

44. The germinal matrix normally regresses at what period of time?

(A) after 40 weeks
(B) between 32 and 40 weeks
(C) between 20 and 30 weeks
(D) the germinal matrix does not regress

45. A structure often confused with the third ventricle in the fetus and neonate is the

(A) cavum septum pellucidum
(B) choroid plexus
(C) thalamus
(D) telea choroidea

46. Which of the following statements are *true:* (1) the choroid plexus enlarges posterior to the caudate nucleus, (2) the choroid plexus does not taper, whereas the caudate nucleus does taper, (3) the tail of the caudate nucleus extends into the occipital horn, (4) the choroid plexus tapers anterior and the caudate nucleus tapers posterior?

(A) 2 and 3
(B) 1 and 3
(C) 4 only
(D) none of the above

47. The cavum septum pellucidum is located between (1) the corpus callosum, (2) the third ventricle, (3) the thalami, (4) the frontal horns of the lateral ventricles

(A) 1 and 4
(B) 2 and 3
(C) 3 and 4
(D) 4 only

48. The cavum vergae is located between the

(A) frontal horns of the lateral ventricles
(B) bodies of the lateral ventricles
(C) third ventricle
(D) thalami

49. The third ventricle is located between the

(A) cavum septum pellucidum
(B) frontal horns of the lateral ventricle
(C) thalami
(D) corpus callosum

50. A subependymal hemorrhage will usually appear sonographically as

(A) increased echogenicity inferior and lateral to the frontal horn and body of the lateral ventricle
(B) sonolucency in the choroid plexus
(C) increased echogenicity in the choroid plexus
(D) sonolucency in the brain parenchyma

51. The germinal matrix consists of which of the following structures: (1) rapidly developing neural tissue, (2) a loosely organized sheet of primitive cells, (3) connective tissues, (4) thin-walled veins?

(A) 1 and 2
(B) 1 and 4
(C) none of the above
(D) all of the above

52. Between 32 and 40 weeks, the incidence of germinal matrix hemorrhage drops. Approximately what percentage of germinal matrix hemorrhage occurs at 28 weeks of gestation?

(A) 25%
(B) 35%
(C) 40%
(D) 67%

53. What is the approximate incidence of germinal matrix hemorrhage at 40 weeks (term)?

(A) 67%
(B) 5%
(C) 50%
(D) 40%

54. The choroid plexus is enlarged after tapering anteriorly with a bulging density. This finding most likely represents

(A) subependymal hemorrhage
(B) intraventricular hemorrhage
(C) subdural hemorrhage
(D) intraparenchymal hemorrhage

55. Which of the following is the most common cause of a false-positive diagnosis of subependymal hemorrhage?

(A) too much far gain
(B) too much near gain
(C) a slightly oblique coronal view
(D) use of a 5-MHz 6-mm short-focused transducer

56. Increased echogenicity in the brain parenchyma is called

(A) subependymal hemorrhage
(B) intraventricular hemorrhage
(C) intraparenchymal hemorrhage
(D) choroid plexus hemorrhage

57. If dense echogenic material is seen in the ventricle, it is called

(A) intraventricular hemorrhage
(B) intraparenchymal hemorrhage
(C) subarachnoid hemorrhage
(D) subependymal hemorrhage

58. Sonographically, how early can an intraparenchymal hemorrhage show a central area of decreased density that may become hypoechoic in the center?

(A) 40–60 days
(B) 3–4 days
(C) 7–14 days
(D) 3–4 weeks

59. How long after an intraparenchymal hemorrhage does a rind of sonolucency develop at the edge, with the clot retracting at the edges and thus separating the edge of the clot from the brain parenchyma?

(A) 3–4 days
(B) 5–10 days
(C) 10–14 days
(D) 2–4 weeks

60. After an intraparenchymal hemorrhage, the clot retracts and may result in a cystic area communicating with the ventricle. This is now termed

(A) holoprosencephaly
(B) hydranencephaly
(C) hydrocephalus
(D) porencephaly

61. Which of the following is not a sonographic criterion for isolated choroid plexus hemorrhage: (1) echogenic clot is attached to the choroid plexus and extends into the subependymal area, (2) echogenic clot extends from the choroid plexus and into the ventricles, (3) choroid plexus is bulky and irregular in contour, (4) echogenic clot is attached only to the choroid plexus?

(A) 1 and 3
(B) 3 and 4
(C) 1 and 2
(D) all of the above

62. Which type of hemorrhage demonstrates the most echogenic gyri and sulci?

(A) intraventricular hemorrhage
(B) subependymal hemorrhage
(C) subdural hemorrhage
(D) all of the above

63. The distinction between a subdural and a subarachnoid hemorrhage can be made best with which of the following imaging modalities?

(A) sonography (real-time)
(B) electroencephalogram
(C) computed tomography
(D) sonography (static)

64. What percentage of sensitivity and specificity does sonography have in the detection of intracranial hemorrhage when compared to computed tomography?

(A) 40–60%
(B) 50–70%
(C) 90–100%
(D) 10–30%

65. Hemorrhage on computed tomography scans becomes isodense after

(A) 20–30 days
(B) 24 hours
(C) 2–4 days
(D) 5–10 days

66. The term isodense denotes the following:

(A) same density
(B) same as sonolucent
(C) same as echogenic
(D) same as anechoic

67. Which of the following is not a possible contributing factor to intracranial hemorrhage: (1) maternal ingestion of aspirin during the final weeks of pregnancy, (2) extrauterine stress, (3) intrapartum hypoxia, (4) pleural effusion?

(A) 1 only
(B) 1, 2, and 3
(C) 4 only
(D) all of the above

68. Which of the following is a possible cause of intracranial hemorrhage: (1) acidosis, (2) ischemia, (3) hypercapnia, (4) hypertension?

(A) 4 only
(B) 1, 2, and 3
(C) none of the above
(D) all of the above

69. Intraoperative spinal sonography is useful because it can localize lesions and differentiate between solid and cystic masses.

(A) true
(B) false

70. A neonate is defined as

(A) a child during the first 28 days after birth
(B) a child from 29 days after birth to 1 year
(C) a fetus at 20 weeks of gestation to a child 28 days after birth
(D) conception to birth

71. Which of the following is associated with an intracranial hemorrhage: (1) hyaline membrane disease, (2) sudden change in blood flow to the region of the germinal matrix, (3) increase in venous and arterial pressure, (4) an expanded volume of plasma?

(A) 1 and 2
(B) 3 and 4
(C) all of the above
(D) none of the above

72. The most common site for periventricular leukomalacia is

(A) white matter surrounding the ventricles
(B) gray matter surrounding the ventricles
(C) white matter inside the ventricles
(D) all of the above

73. Disruption of organogenesis in brain development causes specific, related brain defects. Such defects do *not* include

(A) diverticulation
(B) neural tube closure
(C) neuronal proliferation
(D) tuberous sclerosis

74. An infant is defined as a child

(A) from 29 days after birth to 1 year
(B) during the first 28 days after birth
(C) from 1–2 years after birth
(D) from 2–6 years after birth

75. Which of the following stages is *not* a congenital defect in the development of the brain?

(A) myelination
(B) organization
(C) sulcation
(D) neuronal migration

76. Which authors describe the classification of the grading systems for cerebroventricular hemorrhage as follows: Grade I. isolated subependymal hemorrhage; Grade II. rupture into the ventricle with no dilatation; Grade III. rupture into the ventricle with dilatation; Grade IV. intraventricular hemorrhage with parenchymal hemorrhage?

(A) Lazzara et al, 1980
(B) Papille et al, 1978
(C) Levene et al, 1982
(D) Shankaran et al, 1982

77. Because neonates are extremely sensitive to hypothermia, sonographers should

(A) use an air conditioner in the ultrasound room
(B) scan in the isolette with real-time equipment
(C) set the room temperature at 75–85° F
(D) set the room temperature at 75–78° C
(E) B and C
(F) A, B, and D

78. When scanning a neonate, the transducers should be cleaned between examinations with

(A) alcohol
(B) diluted bleach
(C) an autoclave
(D) hot-air sterilization

79. Which equipment was not designed for portable imaging of infant brains?

(A) computed tomography
(B) magnetic resonance scanners
(C) real-time sonography
(D) static scanners
(E) A, B, and D
(F) all of the above

80. What are the advantages of neonatal cranial sonography over computed tomography: (1) it can be done portably, (2) it has no partial volume effect, (3) it has no transducer artifact, (4) there is no bone interference?

(A) 1 and 2
(B) 1, 3, and 4
(C) none of the above
(D) all of the above

81. Which of the following allows a technically adequate ultrasound examination to be done in children older than 2 years: (1) craniotomy defects, (2) split sutures, (3) burr hole, (4) open fracture?

(A) 1 and 2
(B) 1 and 4
(C) none of the above
(D) all of the above

82. Technically adequate neonatal cranial sonograms are best obtained in which children: Those (1) with open sutures, (2) with open fontanelles, (3) with open orbits, (4) who are under the age of 18 months?

(A) 1 and 2
(B) 3 only
(C) 1, 2, and 4
(D) all of the above

83. Maintaining an infant's normal body temperature is extremely important, particularly for premature infants. Which of the following helps to do this: (1) servo-control radiant heaters, (2) infrared heaters, (3) heat lamp, (4) radiation?

(A) 1 and 2
(B) 1 and 3
(C) 1, 2, and 3
(D) all of the above

84. The term used to describe any hemorrhage within the cranial vault is

(A) subependymal hemorrhage
(B) germinal matrix hemorrhage
(C) intraventricular hemorrhage
(D) intracranial hemorrhage

Questions 85 through 88: Match the term in Column B with the types of hemorrhage in Column A.

COLUMN A	COLUMN B
85. Cerebrospinal fluid-blood level in the ventricles _____	(A) intraparenchymal hemorrhage (IPH)
86. Echogenic foci in the region of the caudate nucleus _____	(B) subependymal hemorrhage (SEH)
87. Echogenic area in the brain parenchyma _____	(C) intraventricular hemorrhage (IVH)
88. Enlarged and highly echogenic choroid plexus _____	(D) choroid plexus hemorrhage (CPH)

89. An imaginary line from the outer canthus to the external auditory meatus is called (1) orbitomeatal line, (2) canthomeatal line, (3) radiographic baseline, (4) Reid's baseline.

(A) 1, 2, and 3
(B) 2 only
(C) 2 and 4
(D) all of the above

90. Some infants are too strong for simple immobilization, and sedation may be required. Which of the following is the suggested medication?

(A) morphine sulfate
(B) chloral hydrate
(C) phenobarbital
(D) Valium

91. Cranial sonography of children under the age of 8 weeks postpartum rarely requires sedation. However, to ensure a quieter infant, which of the following is recommended: (1) darkened room, (2) quiet environment, (3) pacifier in the infant's mouth during examination?

(A) 1 and 2
(B) 3 only
(C) all of the above
(D) none of the above

92. The techniques most recommended for immobilizing an infant for cranial sonography are (1) wrapping the infant with sheets, (2) using an ace bandage to wrap the knees and feet, (3) placing sandbags around the legs, (4) wrapping the entire infant in a plastic bag and leaving only the fontanelle exposed.

(A) 1 and 2
(B) 1, 2, and 3
(C) 4 only
(D) all of the above

93. Intracranial hemorrhage is most common among which group of infants: (1) those weighing more than 1500 g, (2) those weighing less than 1500 g, (3) those born at less than 32 weeks' gestation, (4) those born at more than 32 weeks' gestation?

(A) 1 and 4
(B) 2 and 3
(C) none of the above
(D) all of the above

94. When scanning an infant's head, the axial scan should be performed at which plane?

(A) one perpendicular to a line 15° from the canthomeatal line
(B) one parallel to a line 10° from the radiographic baseline
(C) one perpendicular to a line 10° from the Reid's baseline
(D) parallel to a line 90° from the orbitomeatal line

95. What type of intracranial hemorrhage is most common among full-term infants?

(A) a subdural hemorrhage
(B) an intraventricular hemorrhage
(C) an intraparenchymal hemorrhage
(D) a subependymal hemorrhage

96. True coronal scans are performed at what angle with the orbitomeatal line?

(A) 60°
(B) 90°
(C) 150°
(D) they do not have an angle with the orbitomeatal line

97. Modified coronal scans are performed at what angle with the orbitomeatal line?

(A) 90°
(B) 60°
(C) 150°
(D) they do not have an angle with the orbitomeatal line

98. Posterior fossa scans are performed at what angle with the orbitomeatal line?

(A) 150° from the orbitomeatal line and perpendicular to the clivus
(B) 150° from the canthomeatal line and parallel to the clivus
(C) 90° perpendicular to the orbitomeatal line and parallel to the clivus
(D) none of the above

99. Which of the following designates the term "acoustic window" in cranial sonography: (1) a procedure to bypass bone interface, (2) an opening to which ultrasound can travel with little or no obstruction, (3) an area in which ultrasound is obstructed?

(A) 2 only
(B) 1 and 2
(C) 1 and 3

100. Which of the following disease(s) is *not* a common cause of congenital infections of the nervous system: (1) rubella, (2) toxoplasmosis, (3) gonorrhea, (4) syphilis, (5) cytomegalovirus?

(A) 1 and 2
(B) 3 only
(C) 4 only
(D) 5 only

101. Which of the following are the sonographic findings of congenital infection of the nervous system: (1) microcephaly with enlargement of the ventricles, (2) a prominent interhemispheric fissure and brain atrophy, (3) macrocephaly with enlargement of the ventricles, (4) calcification in the periventricular regions?

(A) 1 and 2
(B) 2 and 4
(C) 1, 2, and 4
(D) all of the above

102. According to the computed tomography grading system for intracranial hemorrhage, which of the following is a Grade I hemorrhage?

(A) subependymal hemorrhage with intraventricular hemorrhage and ventricular dilatation
(B) subependymal hemorrhage with intraventricular hemorrhage and no ventricular dilatation
(C) subependymal hemorrhage with intraventricular hemorrhage and intraparenchymal hemorrhage
(D) isolated subependymal hemorrhage

103. The trigone of the ventricular system is formed by the junction of which two structures?

(A) the temporal and occipital horns
(B) the frontal and temporal horns
(C) the third and fourth ventricles
(D) the foramen of Monro and cerebral aqueduct

104. Another name for the trigone of the ventricle is the

(A) antrum
(B) atrium
(C) arachnoid
(D) aqueduct of Sylvius

105. The foramen between the third and fourth ventricle is the

(A) cerebral aqueduct
(B) foramen of Monro
(C) foramen of Magendie
(D) foramen of Luschka

106. Which of the following are true regarding hydranencephaly: (1) usually only the brainstem and portion of the occipital lobe remain, (2) the falx is usually intact, (3) the falx is usually not intact because the head is largely filled with fluid, (4) there is a severe loss of cerebral tissue?

(A) 1, 2, and 4
(B) 1, 3, and 4
(C) 4 only
(D) all of the above

107. A Dandy-Walker cyst is usually associated with

(A) toxoplasmosis
(B) dysgenesis of the vermis of the cerebellum
(C) syphilis
(D) cytomegalovirus

108. Which of the following is the purpose of a ventriculoperitoneal (V-P) shunt: (1) shunt cerebrospinal fluid from the ventricle to another body compartment such as the peritoneum, (2) shunt peritoneal fluid from the abdomen to the ventricles, (3) decrease the intraventricular pressure, (4) shunt cerebrospinal fluid from the lateral ventricles to the brain parenchyma?

(A) 1 and 3
(B) 1 and 2
(C) 3 only
(D) all of the above

109. The treatment for hydrocephalus with increased intraventricular pressure is

(A) Javid's internal shunt
(B) ventriculoperitoneal (V-P) shunt
(C) radiation treatment
(D) ventriculoectomy

110. Which of the following are not clinical signs of hydrocephalus: (1) a skull bones halo sign on x-ray, (2) anterior fontanelle sinks, (3) bulging of the frontal bone of the skull, (4) rapid head growth?

(A) 1 only
(B) 2, 3, and 4
(C) 1, 2, and 3
(D) none of the above

111. The most common cause of congenital hydrocephalus is

(A) aqueductal stenosis
(B) subarachnoid hemorrhage
(C) interventricular hemorrhage
(D) intracranial infection

112. Which of the following is the most common etiology for acquired infantile ventricular enlargement: (1) cerebral atrophy, (2) subarachnoid hemorrhage, (3) intraventricular hemorrhage, (4) aqueductal stenosis?

(A) 2 and 3
(B) 2, 3, and 4
(C) none of the above
(D) all of the above

113. Subperiosteal hematomas are also called

(A) cephalohematomas
(B) subependymal hemorrhages
(C) intraventricular hemorrhages
(D) choroid plexus hemorrhages

114. A subperiosteal hematoma occurs more frequently in newborns as a result of

(A) hypoxia
(B) excess $NaHCO_3$
(C) maternal ingestion of aspirin
(D) a traumatic delivery

115. A subperiosteal hematoma is seen on the sonogram as

(A) a mildly echogenic mass separating the scalp from the bony skull
(B) an echogenic mass between the bony calvarium and the brain
(C) echogenic material in the brain parenchyma
(D) increased echoes in the region of the caudate nucleus

116. The cavum pellucidum begins to close at which week of gestation?

(A) 40 weeks
(B) 36 weeks
(C) 12 weeks
(D) 24 weeks

117. Which of the following ventricles is the largest: (1) first ventricle, (2) second ventricle, (3) third ventricle, (4) fourth ventricle?

(A) 1 and 2
(B) 3 and 4
(C) 4 only
(D) all ventricles are the same size

118. The frontal horn extends laterally from the foramen of Monro and divides it from the body of the ventricle posteriorly.

(A) true
(B) false

119. Which of the following best describes the position of the choroid plexus with the ventricles?

(A) the choroid plexus extends into the roof of the lateral, third, and fourth ventricles
(B) the choroid plexus extends to the floor of the lateral ventricle, the roof of the third ventricle and medial wall, and the floor of the fourth ventricle
(C) the choroid plexus extends from the floor of the lateral ventricle and medial aspects of the temporal horn, the roof of the third ventricle, and the roof of the fourth ventricle
(D) the choroid plexus normally extends into the roof of the lateral ventricle and temporal horn, and extends into the roof of the third and fourth ventricle

120. How many days after the birth of an infant at less than 32 weeks' gestation should sonography be used as a screening test for intracranial hemorrhage?

(A) 1–3 days
(B) 5–7 days
(C) 15–20 days
(D) 10–14 days

121. If the sonogram is negative for intracranial hemorrhage on day 1, this excludes the possibility for later intracranial hemorrhage.

(A) true
(B) false

122. Which of the following best defines the Dandy-Walker syndrome: (1) a cyst in the posterior fossa that does not communicate with the fourth ventricle, (2) a congenital cystic dilatation of the third ventricle, (3) a congenital cystic dilatation of the fourth ventricle, (4) a posterior fossa cyst that is continuous with the fourth ventricle?

(A) 1 and 2
(B) 2 and 4
(C) 3 and 4
(D) all of the above

123. Transillumination of the head of a newborn can readily demonstrate

(A) hydrocephalus
(B) hemorrhage
(C) intracranial tumor
(D) intracranial infection

124. If one sees echogenic material within the occipital horn, it would most likely be correct to assume that there is

(A) a choroid plexus in the occipital horn
(B) a choroid plexus in the lateral horn
(C) an intracranial hemorrhage because no choroid extends into this area
(D) an intracranial hemorrhage because the tail of the choroid extends into the occipital horn

125. Which of the following is the cause of hydranencephaly?

(A) aqueductal stenosis
(B) congenital toxoplasmosis
(C) atresia of the foramen of Magendie
(D) bilateral intrauterine occlusion of the supraclinoid internal carotid artery

126. Which of the following describes hydranencephaly: (1) the head is largely filled with fluid, (2) the falx is usually intact, (3) the loss of cerebral tissue is severe, (4) the brainstem and a portion of the occipital lobe remain?

(A) 1 and 3 only
(B) 1, 3, and 4
(C) 1 only
(D) all of the above

127. A differential diagnosis for hydranencephaly is

(A) severe hydrocephalus
(B) Dandy-Walker cyst
(C) arachnoid cyst

128. The roof of the lateral ventricle is formed by which structure?

(A) corpus callosum
(B) basilar artery
(C) caudate nucleus
(D) choroid plexus

129. The medial wall of the lateral ventricle is formed by which structure?

(A) corpus callosum
(B) germinal matrix
(C) caudate nucleus
(D) septum pellucidum

130. The lateral wall of the lateral ventricle is formed by which structure?

(A) septum pellucidum
(B) head of the caudate nucleus
(C) choroid plexus
(D) cavum vergae

131. The body of the ventricle extends from which anatomical point?

(A) posterior from the foramen of Monro to the collateral trigone
(B) anterior from the foramen of Monro to the collateral trigone
(C) posterior from the collateral trigone
(D) inferior from the foramen to the cerebral aqueduct

132. The pericallosal artery is normally seen

(A) above the corpus callosum
(B) below the corpus callosum
(C) in the sylvian fissure
(D) between the hippocampal sulcus

133. On cranial sonography, the middle cerebral artery is found in the

(A) region of the sylvian fissure and above the corpus callosum
(B) region of the sylvian fissure and in the circle of Willis
(C) genu of the corpus callosum and sylvian fissure
(D) genu of the corpus callosum and hippocampal sulcus

134. From which of the following are measurements of the cortical mantle obtained: (1) frontal horn to the inner surface of the skull, (2) frontal horn to the posterior horn, (3) occipital horn to the anterior horn, (4) occipital horn to the inner surface of the skull?

(A) 1 and 3
(B) 2 and 4
(C) 1 and 4
(D) all of the above

135. Which of the following statements is *not* true?

(A) blood within the ventricles is recognized as heterogeneous echogenic material
(B) ventricular hemorrhage is recognized as echogenic floating material with a halo effect
(C) it is easy to distinguish the choroid because it is attached medially and is homogeneous in texture
(D) it is impossible to distinguish between an intracranial hemorrhage and a choroid plexus hemorrhage because both blood and the choroid are echogenic and both are homogeneous in texture

136. The *most* severe form of hemorrhage is

(A) germinal matrix hemorrhage
(B) intraventricular hemorrhage
(C) subependymal hemorrhage
(D) intraparenchymal hemorrhage

137. Approximately how long after ventricular dilatation does the head circumference start to increase?

(A) 5–7 days
(B) 3–4 days
(C) 8 weeks
(D) 2 weeks

138. If hemorrhage is detected in a newborn on the first examination, studies should be performed

(A) every 3 days until 2 weeks of age
(B) every 3 days until 2 months of age
(C) every 5 days until 3 weeks of age
(D) every 7 days until 3 weeks of age

139. The neural plate begins to develop approximately how many days into embryonic life?

(A) 1 week
(B) 18 days
(C) 8 months
(D) 26 days

140. The forebrain is also called

(A) prosencephalon
(B) mesencephalon
(C) rhombencephalon
(D) myelencephalon

141. Axial scans can be performed by using a water bath system. Which of the following will make the examination more comfortable and successful: (1) a bath warmed to body temperature, (2) ordinary liquid soap in the bath water, (3) gel on top of and beneath the water bag, (4) depth of water greater than the structure examined?

(A) 1 and 3
(B) 1, 2, and 3
(C) 1, 3, and 4
(D) all of the above

142. The bones that separate the squamous suture are called

(A) frontal and parietal bones
(B) parietal and occipital bones
(C) sphenoidal and occipital bones
(D) temporal and parietal bones

143. The circle of Willis is formed by which of the following: (1) posterior cerebral arteries, (2) anterior cerebral arteries, (3) internal carotid arteries, (4) posterior and anterior communicating arteries?

(A) 2 and 3
(B) 1, 2, and 3
(C) 3 only
(D) all of the above

144. At which week of gestation is the choroid plexus prominent and may completely fill the lateral ventricle?

(A) 40 weeks
(B) 36 weeks
(C) 12–16 weeks
(D) 30–36 weeks

145. On neonatal sonography, two vertical linear echoes are seen extending from the posterior wall to the anterior wall of the cavum septum pellucidum. This finding is most likely to represent

(A) column of fornix
(B) cavum septi pellucidi kink
(C) normal septal veins
(D) multilocular cyst of the cavum septum pellucidum
(E) pathological septations of the septum pellucidum

146. Which of the following scans produce a rectangular shaped image?

(A) linear-array real-time
(B) sector real-time
(C) water-delay scanner
(D) static scanner

147. The bones that separate the coronal suture are the

(A) sphenoidal and parietal bones
(B) frontal and parietal bones
(C) parietal and occipital bones
(D) temporal and parietal bones

148. The bones that separate the lambdoidal suture are the

(A) temporal and parietal bones
(B) frontal bone and the two parietal bones
(C) the two parietal bones and the occipital bone
(D) sphenoidal and occipital bones

149. The ventricle occupies more than 50% of the hemisphere of the brain before which week of gestation?

(A) 36 weeks
(B) 40 weeks
(C) 8 weeks
(D) 20 weeks

150. Which of the following is true regarding noncommunicating hydrocephalus?

(A) it is also called nonobstructive hydrocephalus
(B) the cerebrospinal fluid pathways within the brain are blocked
(C) cerebrospinal fluid is blocked within the ventricular system
(D) none of the above

151. Which of the following best describes communicating hydrocephalus?

(A) it is also called obstructive hydrocephalus
(B) the cerebrospinal fluid pathways within the brain are blocked
(C) cerebrospinal fluid is blocked within the ventricular system
(D) none of the above

152. Hydranencephaly is defined as

(A) holospheric cerebrum
(B) posterior fossa cyst
(C) congenital cystic dilatation of the fourth ventricle
(D) a head that is largely filled with fluid and a severe loss of cerebral tissue

153. The etiology of Dandy-Walker syndrome is believed to be

(A) massive disruption of the cerebral hemisphere
(B) atresia of the foramen of Magendie and foramen of Luschka secondary to the failure of the vermis cerebellum to develop
(C) diverticulation of the fetal brain
(D) cystic dilatation of the third ventricle with patency of the foramen of Magendie

154. Microcephaly is associated with which of the following: (1) Meckel-Gruber's syndrome, (2) chromosomal abnormalities, (3) Soto's syndrome, (4) cerebral gigantism?

(A) 1 and 2
(B) 3 and 4
(C) 1 and 3
(D) all of the above

155. A Chiari II malformation is defined as

(A) a congenital abnormality of the brain with elongation of the pons and fourth ventricle and downward displacement of the medulla into the cervical canal
(B) congenital cystic dilatation of the fourth ventricle caused by atresia of the foramen of Magendie
(C) congenital formation of a holospheric cerebrum caused by a disorder of the diverticulation of the fetal brain
(D) none of the above

156. Dandy-Walker syndrome is defined as (1) congenital cystic dilatation of the fourth ventricle, (2) posterior fossa cyst that does not communicate with the fourth ventricle, (3) formation of a holospheric cerebrum, (4) severe loss of cerebral tissue and the head is largely filled with fluid

(A) 1 and 2
(B) 1 only
(C) none of the above
(D) all of the above

157. Which of the following are frequently associated with congenital hydrocephalus: (1) encephalocele, (2) meningomyelocele, (3) spina bifida, (4) Chiari II malformation?

(A) 1 and 2
(B) 1 and 3
(C) 2 and 3 only
(D) all of the above

158. Which of the following regions can be used for placement of the distal tip of the ventriculoperitoneal (V-P) shunt tube: (1) within the peritoneal cavity, (2) within the roof of the third ventricle, (3) in the right atrium, (4) in the gallbladder?

(A) 1, 3, and 4
(B) 2 only
(C) 1 only
(D) all of the above

159. Holoprosencephaly is described as which of the following: (1) formation of a holospheric cerebrum, (2) a disorder of diverticulation of the fetal brain, (3) cerebral hemispheres and lateral ventricles that develop as one vesicle, (4) a large, single, midline ventricular cavity?

(A) 3 and 4
(B) 1 and 2
(C) 1, 2, and 3
(D) all of the above

160. The ventriculoperitoneal (V-P) shunt used to remove excessive cerebrospinal fluid from the ventricular system is connected by a

(A) one-way valve at the distal portion of the tube
(B) one-way valve at the proximal portion of the tube
(C) two-way valve at the distal portion of the tube
(D) two-way valve with one valve at each end

161. Which of the following are complications secondary to placement of the shunt: (1) obstruction within the tubing or valve caused by pieces of choroid plexus or a hemorrhage, (2) loculation of cerebrospinal fluid at the distal tip of the peritoneal end of the shunt tubing, (3) cerebrospinal fluid pseudocyst, (4) poor absorption of cerebrospinal fluid by the peritoneal lining?

(A) 1 and 3
(B) 2 and 4
(C) 1 only
(D) all of the above

162. Which of the following statements about spinal and cranial nerves is true?

(A) there are 12 pairs of cranial nerves and 12 pairs of spinal nerves
(B) there are 12 pairs of cranial nerves and 30 pairs of spinal nerves
(C) there are 31 pairs of cranial nerves and 12 pairs of spinal nerves
(D) there are 12 pairs of cranial nerves and 31 pairs of spinal nerves

163. The spinal cord ends at about what vertebral level?

(A) L2
(B) L5
(C) S2
(D) S5

164. The arteries supplying the brain are

(A) one vertebral and one carotid artery
(B) one carotid and one vertebral artery
(C) two external carotid and two vertebral arteries
(D) two internal carotid and two vertebral arteries

165. The vertebral artery, at the level of the pons, is called the

(A) internal carotid artery
(B) basilar artery
(C) external carotid artery
(D) posterior cerebral artery

166. The basilar artery, at the level of the cerebrum, is called the

(A) basilar artery
(B) posterior cerebral artery
(C) anterior cerebral artery
(D) carotid artery

167. Obstruction of the right common or internal carotid artery causes

(A) loss of sensation on the left side of the body
(B) loss of sensation on the right side of the body
(C) total blindness
(D) total loss of muscle sensation

168. The central nervous system includes which of the following (1) spinal cord, (2) brain stem, (3) cerebellum, (4) cerebrum.

(A) 2 only
(B) 1 and 2
(C) 1, 2, and 3
(D) all of the above

169. The greatest proportion of the cerebrospinal fluid is elaborated by

(A) choroid plexus
(B) caudate nucleus
(C) lateral ventricles
(D) movement of extracellular fluid from blood

170. The germinal matrix is best depicted by

(A) computed tomography
(B) sonography
(C) cerebral angiography
(D) none of the above

171. The cerebral peduncles appear as a heart-shaped structure. The notch of the heart has a pulsation that represents the

(A) basilar artery
(B) middle cerebral arteries
(C) vertebral artery
(D) posterior cerebral artery

172. The occipital horn extends from what anatomical region?

(A) the trigone anteriorly
(B) the trigone posteriorly
(C) the foramen of Monro to the trigone
(D) the trigone inferiorly

173. Which of the following statements is not true regarding the cavum septum pellucidum?

(A) it normally connects with the subarachnoid or ventricular fluid
(B) the cavum vergae begins to close at 6 months
(C) the cavum septum pellucidum begins to close at 40 weeks
(D) the cavum septum pellucidum is anterior and the cavum vergae is posterior

174. The third ventricle is connected to the lateral ventricle by the

(A) aqueduct of Sylvius
(B) foramen of Monro
(C) thalamus
(D) caudate nucleus

175. Polymicrogyria is associated with

(A) toxoplasmosis
(B) cytomegalovirus
(C) Dandy-Walker syndrome
(D) abnormal thickening of the cortex
(E) B and C
(F) A, B, and D

176. The normal anatomical sequela of intracranial hemorrhage is

(A) subependymal cyst
(B) porencephaly
(C) hydrocephalus
(D) holoprosencephaly
(E) A, B, and C
(F) A and B

177. A pulsation is sometimes seen above the superior margin of the corpus collosum. This is most likely to represent the

(A) basilar artery
(B) internal carotid artery
(C) middle cerebral artery
(D) pericallosal arteries

178. Which foramen connects the third ventricle to the fourth ventricle?

(A) foramen of Monro
(B) foramen of Luschka
(C) foramen of Magendie
(D) cerebral aqueduct

179. The two anterior recesses on the third ventricle are the (1) supraoptic recess, (2) pineal recess, (3) infundibular recess, (4) suprapineal recess.

(A) 1 and 2
(B) 3 and 4
(C) 1 and 3
(D) 2 and 4

180. The two posterior recesses on the third ventricle are (1) preoptic recesses, (2) pineal recesses, (3) infundibular recesses, (4) suprapineal recesses

(A) 1 and 2
(B) 1 and 3
(C) 3 and 4
(D) 2 and 4

181. Another name for massa intermedia is

(A) interthalamic adhesion
(B) pineal recess
(C) preoptic recess
(D) infundibular recess

182. The modified system of grading the extent of intracranial and ventricular dilatation suggested separately by Levene and de Crespigny ranges from

(A) grade I–IV
(B) grade I–III
(C) grade O–IV
(D) grade O–V

183. The sonographic findings of ventriculitis do *not* include

(A) echogenic ventricular walls
(B) septated ventricles
(C) normal-sized ventricles with no debris within them
(D) debris within the ventricles

184. Which of the following is *not* a cranial bone?

(A) sphenoid
(B) ethmoid
(C) palatine
(D) frontal

185. How many cranial bones are there?

(A) 12
(B) 10
(C) 8
(D) 5

186. Which structure is *not* a partition of the dura mater?

(A) falx cerebelli
(B) falx cerebri
(C) tentorium
(D) cerebellum

187. Periventricular leukomalacia is *most* commonly observed in which of the following: (1) at the level of the white matter around the foramen of Monro, (2) near the occipital horns and trigone of the lateral ventricles, (3) in the inferior horn of the lateral ventricles, (4) between the bordering zones of the penetrating branches of the middle cerebral artery and the posterior cerebral artery?

(A) 1
(B) 2
(C) 3
(D) 1 and 4

188. Blood between the arachnoid membrane and the pia mater is called

(A) subarachnoid hematoma
(B) subdural hematoma
(C) epidural membrane
(D) intraparenchymal hematoma

189. Another name for the orbitomeatal line is which of the following: (1) radiographic baseline, (2) Reid's baseline, (3) canthomeatal line, (4) intraorbitomeatal line?

(A) 2 only
(B) 1 and 3
(C) 1, 2, and 4
(D) all of the above

190. Which of the following are the first and second ventricle?

(A) the cavum septum pellicidum and vergae
(B) the right and left lateral ventricles
(C) the caudate nucleus and choroid plexus
(D) there are no first and second ventricles

191. Approximately what percentage of cerebrospinal fluid is produced by the choroid plexus?

(A) 40%
(B) 60%
(C) 90%
(D) 10%

192. The amount of cerebrospinal fluid production in children is

(A) 140 mL/week
(B) 140 mL/day
(C) 532–576 mL/day
(D) 552–576 mL/week

193. Bleeding within the cerebral parenchyma is called

(A) subdural hematoma
(B) intraparenchymal hemorrhage
(C) cerebellar hemorrhage
(D) subarachnoid hematoma

194. Which of the following is not the cause of a subdural hematoma or effusion?

(A) meningitis
(B) hypervitaminosis
(C) trauma
(D) germinal matrix hemorrhage

195. The accumulation of blood between the dura mater and the inner table of the skull is called

(A) subarachnoid hemorrhage
(B) subdural hematoma
(C) epidural hematoma
(D) intraparenchymal hemorrhage

196. The accumulation of blood between the arachnoid membrane and dura mater is called

(A) subarachnoid hematoma
(B) subdural hematoma
(C) epidural hematoma
(D) intraparenchymal hematoma

197. Which of the following is not part of the lateral ventricle?

(A) occipital horn
(B) atrium
(C) infundibular horn
(D) temporal horn

198. Another name for the temporal horn is the

(A) anterior horn
(B) posterior horn
(C) inferior horn
(D) lateral horn

199. Another name for the occipital horn is the

(A) anterior horn
(B) posterior horn
(C) inferior horn
(D) lateral horn

200. The largest of all the horns is the

(A) temporal horn
(B) occipital horn
(C) frontal horn
(D) lateral horn

201. Another name for the foramen of Monro is the

(A) interventricular foramen
(B) cerebral aqueduct
(C) foramen of Luschka
(D) foramen of Magendie

202. Vascular pulsations are easily seen with real-time sonography. Which of the following *cannot* be visualized?

(A) ophthalmic artery
(B) middle cerebral artery
(C) basilar artery
(D) anterior cerebral artery

203. Which of the following are not midline structures?

(A) third ventricle and fourth ventricle
(B) cerebral hemispheres
(C) cavum septum pellucidum
(D) falx cerebri

204. The vein of Galen aneurysm is most likely to be located

(A) anterior to the third ventricle
(B) posterior to the foramen of Monro and superior to the third ventricle
(C) posterior to the foramen of Monro and inferior to the third ventricle
(D) posterior to the fourth ventricle

205. Which of the following is *not* part of the brain stem?

(A) spinal cord
(B) diencephalon
(C) midbrain
(D) pons

206. Chiari II malformation is associated with which of the following: (1) hydrocephalus, (2) meningomyelocele, (3) enlarged massa intermedia, (4) enlarged cavum septum pellucidum?

(A) 1, 2, and 3
(B) 2 and 3
(C) 2 only
(D) all of the above

207. Which two of the following abnormalities are characterized by severe loss of cerebral tissue when the head is largely filled with fluid: (1) hydranencephaly, (2) severe hydrocephalus, (3) arachnoid cyst, (4) porencephaly?

(A) 1 and 3
(B) 3 and 4
(C) 1 and 2
(D) 1 and 4

208. What are some bacterial causes of intracranial infection: (1) *haemophilus influenzae,* (2) herpes simplex, (3) *Diplococcus pneumoniae,* (4) toxoplasmosis?

(A) 1 and 3
(B) 2 and 4
(C) 4 only
(D) all of the above

209. Which of the following intracranial hemorrhages (ICHs) is *least* likely to occur in premature infants:

(1) subdural hemorrhage, (2) intraparenchymal hemorrhage, (3) epidural hemorrhage, (4) subependymal hemorrhage.

(A) 1 and 3
(B) 2 and 3
(C) 1 and 4
(D) 2 only

210. Midline facial anomalies are often associated with holoprosencephaly. These malformations can include which of the following: (1) cerebrocephaly, (2) cleft palate, (3) hypoplasia of the ethmoid bone, (4) cyclopia?

(A) 2 only
(B) 2 and 3
(C) 3 only
(D) all of the above

211. The incidence of intracranial infection is which of the following: (1) 2 in every 10,000 full term births, (2) 20 in every 10,000 premature births, (3) 50 in every 10,000 premature births, (4) 30 in every 10,000 full term births?

(A) 1 and 3
(B) 2 and 4
(C) 1 and 2
(D) all of the above

212. Which of the following are the functions of the hypothalamus: (1) it regulates the functioning of the autonomic nervous system, (2) it regulates body temperature, (3) it regulates water and electrolyte balance, (4) it controls hunger?

(A) 1 and 3
(B) 2 and 4
(C) 1 only
(D) all of the above

213. The meninges covers the brain and spinal cord. Which of the following is *not* one of its layers?

(A) dura mater
(B) white matter
(C) arachnoid membrane
(D) pia mater

214. The term *leukomalacia* denotes

(A) morbid softening of the white matter
(B) necrosis of the white blood cells
(C) an increase in the number of leukocytes in the blood
(D) a fatal disease of the blood-forming organs characterized by a marked increase in leukocytes

215. Neuropathic complications of periventricular leukomalacia include

(A) cavitation within cerebral white matter
(B) hemorrhage within the areas of leukomalacia
(C) both A and B

216. Which of the following is *not* one of the cranial nerves?

(A) trigeminal
(B) facial
(C) vagus
(D) thalamus

217. A deep groove in the brain is called

(A) fissure
(B) gyri
(C) sulcus
(D) lobes

218. The central fissure is also called

(A) sylvian fissure
(B) fissure of Rolando
(C) lateral fissure
(D) longitudinal fissure

219. The place of fusion between the third ventricle and the medial surface of the thalami is termed

(A) infundibular recess
(B) globus pallidus
(C) hypothalamus
(D) massa intermedia

220. Which of the following is *not* one of the cranial nerves?

(A) olfactory
(B) oculomotor
(C) trochlear
(D) pineal

221. Which of the following is a cranial nerve?

(A) glossopharyngeal
(B) optic
(C) accessory
(D) all of the above

222. Which of the following are not a part of the dura mater?

(A) falx cerebelli
(B) falx cerebri
(C) tentorium cerebelli
(D) septum pellucidum

223. The etiology of a porencephalic cyst is which of the following: (1) intracranial infection, (2) infarction, (3) intracranial hemorrhage, (4) trauma?

(A) 1 only
(B) 1 and 3
(C) 1, 2, and 3
(D) all of the above

224. Holoprosencephaly can be associated with other abnormalities, including (1) maternal diabetes mellitus, (2) toxoplasmosis, (3) intrauterine rubella, (4) endocrine dysgenesis.

(A) 1 only
(B) 1 and 2
(C) 2 and 3
(D) all of the above

225. Which of the following is best demonstrated by computed tomography: (1) subependymal hemorrhage, (2) subarachnoid hemorrhage, (3) intraparenchymal hemorrhage, (4) subdural hemorrhage?

(A) 1 and 2
(B) 2 and 4
(C) 1 and 3
(D) all of the above

226. Which of the following is demonstrated best by sonography: (1) subependymal hemorrhage, (2) subarachnoid hemorrhage, (3) intraparenchymal hemorrhage, (4) subdural hemorrhage?

(A) 1 and 2
(B) 2 and 4
(C) 1 and 3
(D) all of the above

227. Numerous sulci can normally be identified on the premature brain, particularly in the sagittal scan. Identify the condition or conditions that would *least* be likely to obscure the normal sulcal pattern.

(A) *Salmonella meningoencephalitis*
(B) subdural hematoma
(C) intracranial infection
(D) infarction

228. The germinal matrix is largest at which week of gestation?

(A) 40 weeks (term)
(B) 24–32 weeks
(C) 32–40 weeks
(D) 12–15 weeks

229. Which of the following is *not* an intracranial tumor?

(A) dermoid tumor
(B) choroid plexus papilloma
(C) medulloblastoma
(D) cyclopia

230. Brain tumors encountered in infants and children (1) constitute only 12–15% of tumors, (2) are less frequent in infants older than 2 years, (3) are less frequent in infants younger than 2 years, (4) constitute only 20–30% of tumors.

(A) 1 and 3
(B) 1 and 2
(C) 3 and 4
(D) all of the above

231. Periventricular leukomalacia is best described as

(A) ischemic lesions of the neonatal brain characterized by necrosis of periventricular white matter
(B) a disorder of premature newborns characterized by large white blood cells around the ventricle
(C) an increase in the number of leukocytes around the ventricles
(D) a marked decrease in leukocytes

232. Which of the following are associated with Dandy-Walker syndrome: (1) dysgenesis of the vermis of the cerebellum, (2) a large cerebrum, (3) agenesis of the corpus callosum, (4) holoprosencephaly?

(A) 1 and 2
(B) 1, 3, and 4
(C) 1 and 3
(D) none of the above

233. Which of the following is the etiology of an arachnoid cyst: (1) abnormal mechanism of leptomeningeal formation, (2) entrapment of subarachnoid space by adhesions, (3) entrapment of cisternal space by adhesions, (4) failure of development of the cerebral mantle?

(A) 1, 2, and 3
(B) 1 and 2
(C) all of the above
(D) none of the above

234. Which of the following is a possible explanation for periventricular leukomalacia?

(A) failure of arterial perfusion of the region
(B) ischemic injury
(C) hypoxic injury
(D) all of the above

235. The lateral cerebral fissure is also called

(A) sylvian fissure
(B) fissure of Rolando
(C) longitudinal fissure
(D) transverse fissure

236. A shallow groove in the cerebrum of the brain is called

(A) lobe
(B) gyrus
(C) fissure
(D) sulcus

237. What is the *most* common infection(s) acquired in utero?

(A) herpes simplex
(B) Dandy-Walker
(C) toxoplasmosis
(D) cytomegalovirus
(E) A and D
(F) A, C, and D

238. Toxoplasmosis in the newborn is clinically associated with

(A) skin rash
(B) seizures
(C) microcephaly
(D) macrocephaly
(E) A, B, and C
(F) all of the above

239. What is the major reason for placing a newborn in an isolette?

(A) to replace some of the newborn's fluid loss
(B) to lower the newborn's metabolic rate
(C) to provide an environment similar to the uterus
(D) to increase the viscosity of the newborn's respiratory secretions

240. The cerebrospinal fluid consists of (1) protein, (2) sodium chloride, (3) glucose, (4) potassium

(A) 1 only
(B) 3 and 4
(C) 2, 3, and 4
(D) all of the above

241. Which of the following is *not* true of anencephaly?

(A) it usually is not viable in utero
(B) it is associated with oligohydramnios
(C) it is associated with hydramnios
(D) it is usually viable in utero

Questions 242 through 244: Identify the structures to which the arrows point in Fig. 10–31, then place in Column A the letter corresponding to the appropriate item in Column B.

COLUMN A	COLUMN B
242. _____	(A) mastoidal fontanelle
243. _____	(B) coronal suture
244. _____	(C) sagittal suture
	(D) anterior fontanelle
	(E) parietal bone
	(F) posterior fontanelle

Questions 245 through 259: Identify the structures to which the arrows point in Fig. 10–32, then place in Column A the letter corresponding to the appropriate item in Column B.

COLUMN A	COLUMN B
245. _____	(A) mastoidal fontanelle
246. _____	(B) sphenoid fontanelle
247. _____	(C) parietal bone
248. _____	(D) maxilla bone
249. _____	(E) sphenoid bone
250. _____	(F) occipital bone
251. _____	(G) coronal suture
252. _____	(H) frontal suture
253. _____	(I) zygomatic bone
254. _____	(J) nasal bone
255. _____	(K) temporal bone
256. _____	(L) mandible bone
257. _____	(M) anterior fontanelle
258. _____	(N) squamous suture
259. _____	(O) lambdoidal suture
	(P) zygomatic process

(SINCIPUT)
242
243
244

Figure 10–31. A superior view of an infantile skull.

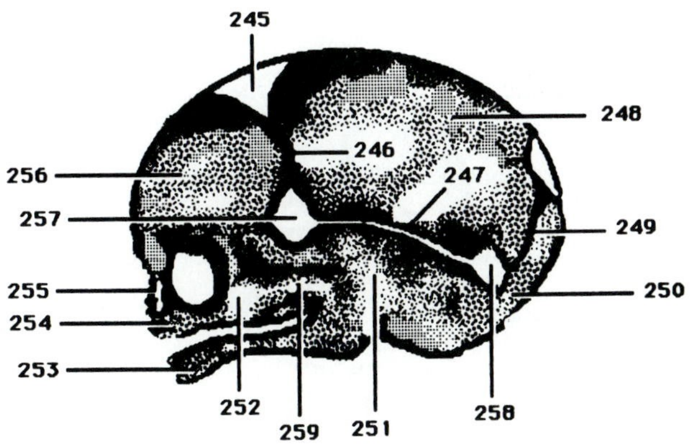

Figure 10–32. A lateral view of an infantile skull.

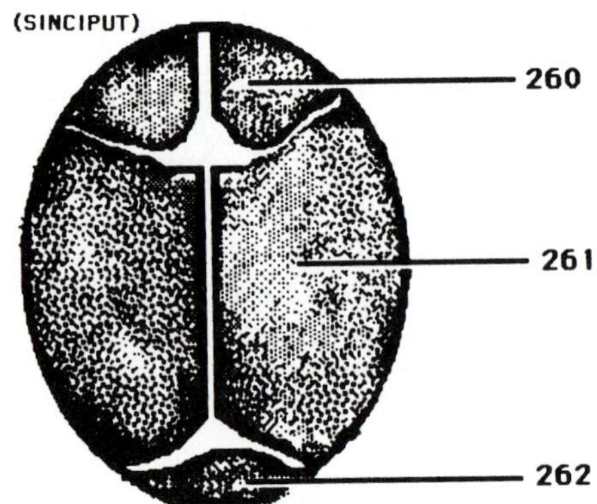

Figure 10–33. A superior view of an infantile skull.

Questions 260 through 262: Identify the structures to which the arrows point in Fig. 10–33, then place in Column A the letter corresponding to the appropriate item in Column B.

COLUMN A	COLUMN B
260. _____	(A) occipital bone
261. _____	(B) parietal bone
262. _____	(C) anterior fontanelle
	(D) temporal bone
	(E) frontal bone

Questions 263 through 270: Identify the structures to which the arrows point in Fig. 10–34, then place in Column A the letter corresponding to the appropriate item in Column B.

COLUMN A	COLUMN B
263. _____	(A) zygomatic bone
264. _____	(B) metopic suture
265. _____	(C) frontal bone
266. _____	(D) nasal bone
267. _____	(E) mandible bone
268. _____	(F) maxilla bone
269. _____	(G) vomer
270. _____	(H) anterior fontanelle

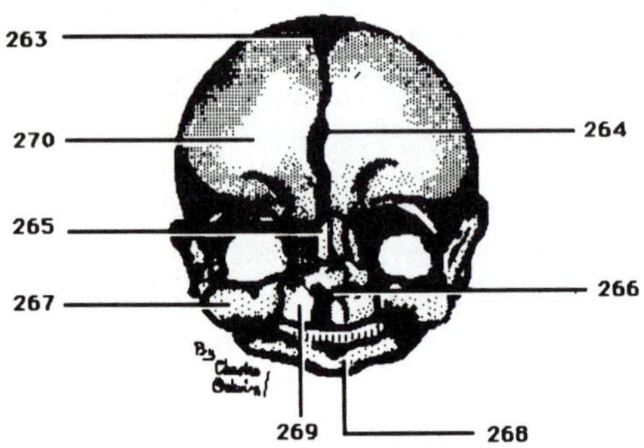

Figure 10–34. An anterior view of an infantile skull.

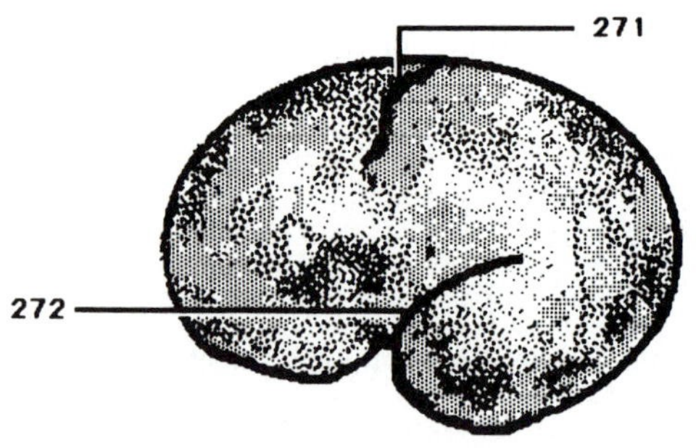

Figure 10–35. A lateral view of the brain.

Questions 271 through 272: Identify the structures to which the arrows point in Fig. 10–35, then place in Column A the letter corresponding to the appropriate item in Column B.

COLUMN A	COLUMN B
271. _____	(A) longitudinal cerebral fissure
272. _____	(B) sylvian fissure
	(C) fissure of Rolando

Questions 273 through 276: Identify the structures to which the arrows point in Fig. 10–36, then place in Column A the letter corresponding to the appropriate item in Column B.

COLUMN A	COLUMN B
273. _____	(A) occipital lobe
274. _____	(B) parietal lobe
275. _____	(C) temporal lobe
276. _____	(D) frontal lobe

Questions 277 through 284: Identify the structures to which the arrows point in Fig. 10–37, then place in Column A the letter corresponding to the appropriate item in Column B.

COLUMN A	COLUMN B
277. _____	(A) internal carotid artery
278. _____	(B) posterior cerebral artery

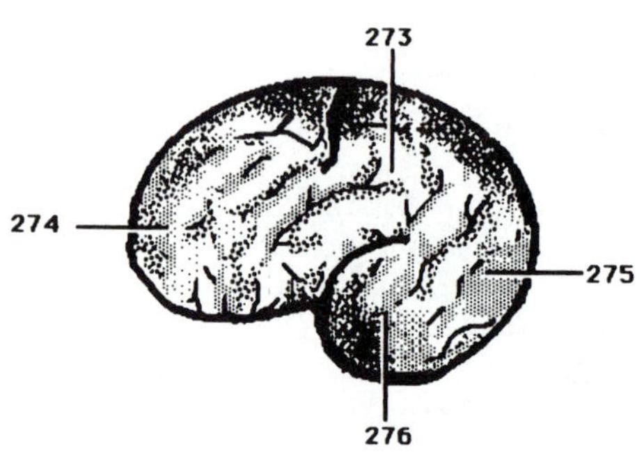

Figure 10–36. A lateral view of the brain

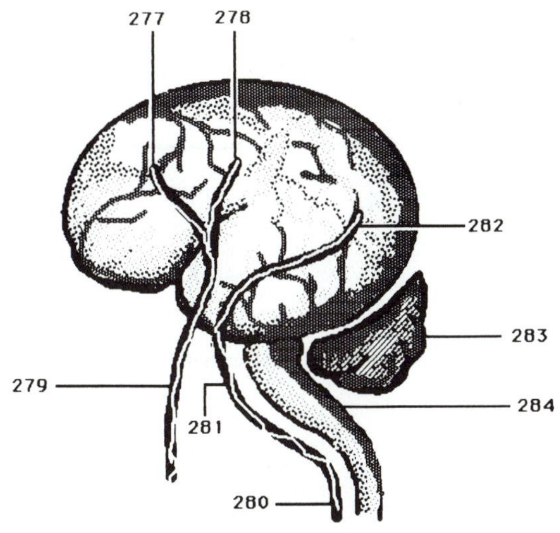

Figure 10–37. A diagram of the brain in the sagittal view.

279. ______	(C) vertebral artery
280. ______	(D) basilar artery
281. ______	(E) anterior cerebral artery
282. ______	(F) middle cerebral artery
283. ______	(G) cerebrum
284. ______	(H) cerebellum
	(I) medulla oblongata

Questions 285 through 296: Identify the structures to which the arrows point in Fig. 10–38, then place in Column A the letter corresponding to the appropriate item in Column B.

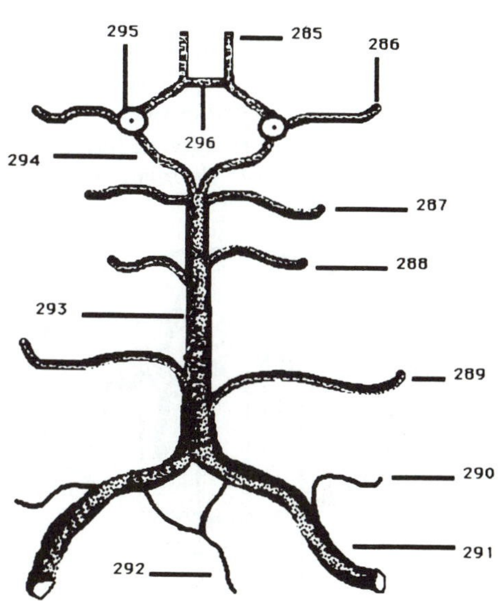

Figure 10–38. A diagram of the circle of Willis.

COLUMN A	COLUMN B
285. ______	(A) basilar artery
286. ______	(B) posterior cerebral artery
287. ______	(C) middle cerebral artery
288. ______	(D) internal carotid artery
289. ______	(E) anterior cerebral artery
290. ______	(F) anterior inferior cerebellar artery
291. ______	(G) vertebral artery
292. ______	(H) anterior communicating artery
293. ______	(I) posterior communicating artery
294. ______	(J) anterior spinal artery
295. ______	(K) posterior inferior cerebellar artery
296. ______	(L) superior cerebellar artery

Questions 297 through 311: Identify the structures to which the arrows point in Fig. 10–39, then place in Column A the letter corresponding to the appropriate item in Column B.

COLUMN A	COLUMN B
297. ______	(A) pineal recess
298. ______	(B) body of lateral ventricle
299. ______	(C) interventricular foramen
300. ______	(D) posterior horn
301. ______	(E) infundibular recess
302. ______	(F) third ventricle
303. ______	(G) preoptic recess
304. ______	(H) frontal horn
305. ______	(I) inferior horn
306. ______	(J) collateral trigone
307. ______	(K) suprapineal recess
308. ______	(L) foramen of Magendie (fourth ventricle)
309. ______	(M) cerebral aqueduct
310. ______	(N) foramina of Luschka
311. ______	(O) interthalamic adhesion

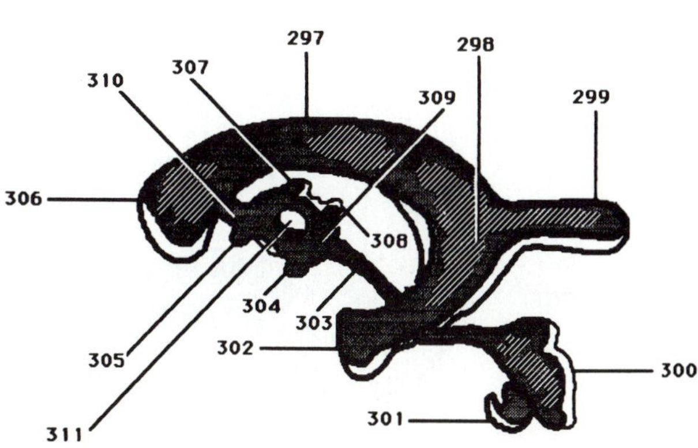

Figure 10–39. A diagram of the ventricular system in the lateral view.

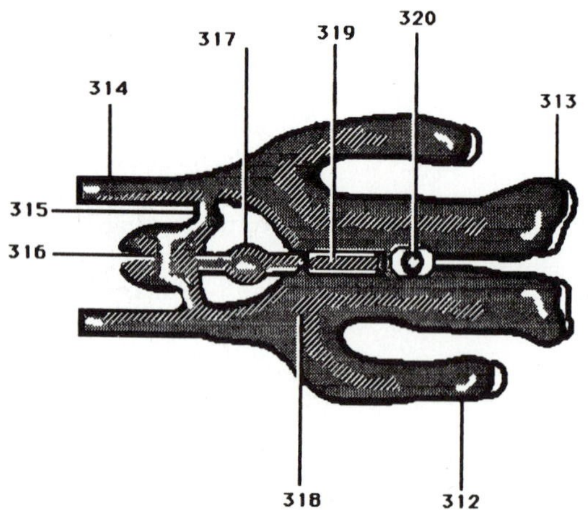

Figure 10–40. A diagram of the ventricular system in the superior view.

Questions 312 through 320: Identify the structures to which the arrows point in Fig. 10–40, then place in Column A the letter corresponding to the appropriate item in Column B.

COLUMN A	COLUMN B
312. _____	(A) third ventricle
313. _____	(B) anterior horn
314. _____	(C) inferior horn
315. _____	(D) foramen of Monro
316. _____	(E) lateral access
317. _____	(F) cerebral aqueduct
318. _____	(G) fourth ventricle
319. _____	(H) atrium
320. _____	(I) posterior horn

Questions 321 through 332: Identify the structures to which the arrows point in Fig. 10-41, 10-42, and 10-43; then place in Column A the letter corresponding to the appropriate item in Column B. Note that one of the answers will be used three times.

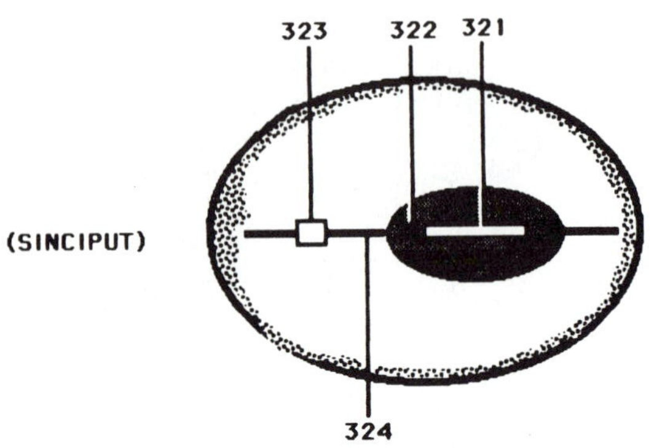

Figure 10–41. A diagram of an axial scan at the level of the thalami.

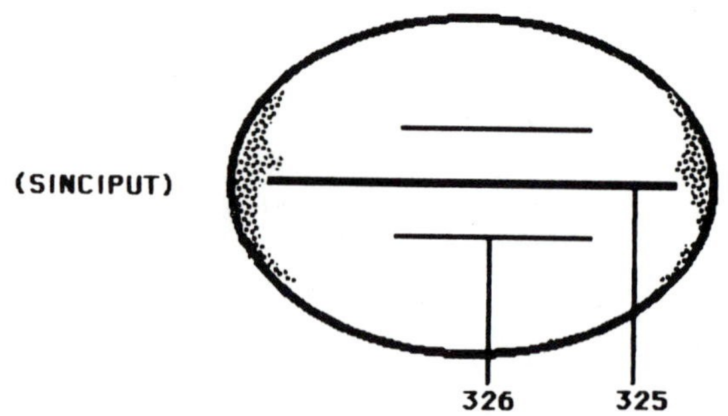

Figure 10–42. A diagram of an axial scan at the level of the lateral ventricle.

COLUMN A	COLUMN B
321. _____	(A) third ventricle
322. _____	(B) basilar artery
323. _____	(C) thalami
324. _____	(D) cerebral penduncles
325. _____	(E) lateral ventricle
326. _____	(F) circle of Willis
327. _____	(G) arterior cerebral artery
328. _____	(H) falx cerebri
329. _____	(I) middle cerebral artery
330. _____	(J) cavum septum pellucidum
331. _____	
332. _____	

Questions 333 through 342: Identify the structures to which the arrows point in Fig. 10–44, 10–45, and 10–46; then place in Column A the letter corresponding to the appropriate item in Column B.

COLUMN A	COLUMN B
333. _____	(A) falx cerebri
334. _____	(B) hippocampal gyri
335. _____	(C) posterior fossae
336. _____	(D) petrous ridges
337. _____	(E) middle fossae
338. _____	(F) anterior fossae
339. _____	(G) sphenoid wings
340. _____	(H) lateral ventricle
341. _____	(I) sylvian fissure
342. _____	(J) choroid plexus

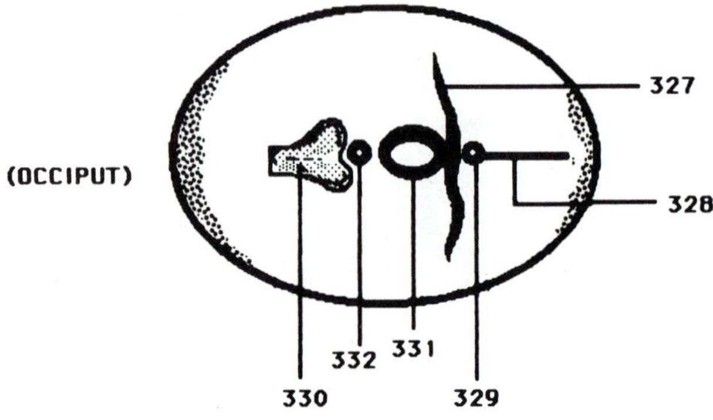

Figure 10–43. A diagram of an axial scan at the base of the skull.

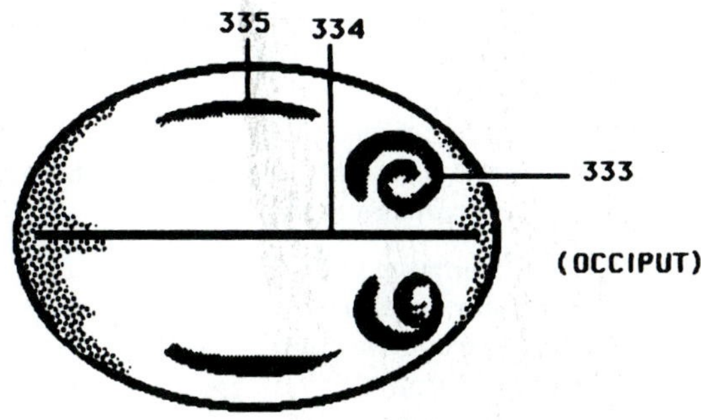

Figure 10–44. A diagram of an axial scan at the level of the sylvian fissure.

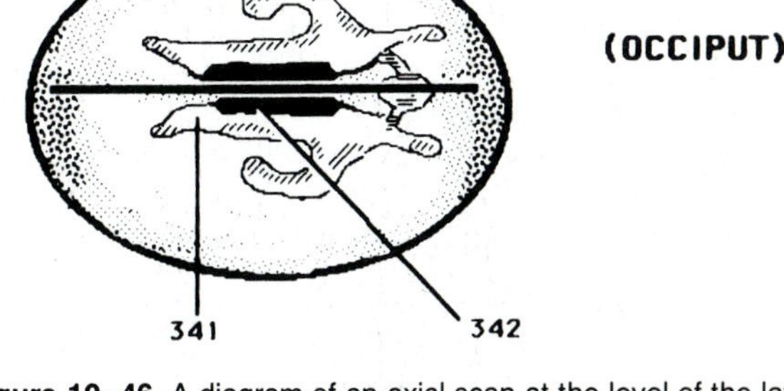

Figure 10–46. A diagram of an axial scan at the level of the lateral ventricles.

Questions 343 through 348: Identify the structures to which the arrows point in Fig. 10–47, then place in Column A the letter corresponding to the appropriate item in Column B.

COLUMN A	COLUMN B
343. ____	(A) caudate nucleus
344. ____	(B) choroid plexus of the third ventricle
345. ____	(C) telea chorida
346. ____	(D) corpus colosum
347. ____	(E) choroid plexus of the fourth ventricle
348. ____	(F) glomus of the choroid plexus

349. Which of the following results in the greatest number of neonatal deaths?

(A) hypoxia
(B) erythroblastosis
(C) trauma at birth
(D) premature placental separation

350. Which of the following is not a characteristic of lissencephaly?

(A) a decrease in the size of the sylvian fissure as the neonatal brain matures
(B) large ventricles
(C) less sonographic characteristics because of the inability to differentiate white from gray matter
(D) all of the above

Questions 351 through 360: Match the terms in Column A with the correct definition given in Column B.

COLUMN A	COLUMN B
351. Asphyxia ____	(A) cessation of breathing
352. Necrosis ____	(B) accumulation of body acid
353. Ischemia ____	(C) lack of oxygen
354. Hypoglycemia ____	(D) suffocation
355. Hypoxia ____	(E) low oxygen content
356. Acidosis ____	(F) death of tissue
357. Anoxia ____	(G) diminished content of glucose in the blood
358. Hypercarbia ____	(H) excess carbon dioxide in the blood
359. Apnea ____	(I) incomplete closure of the neural tube
360. Dysrhaphia ____	(J) deficiency of blood in a body part

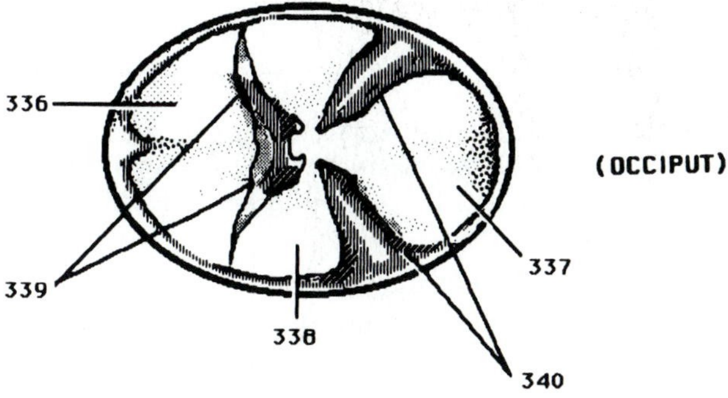

Figure 10–45. A diagram of an axial scan at the base of the skull.

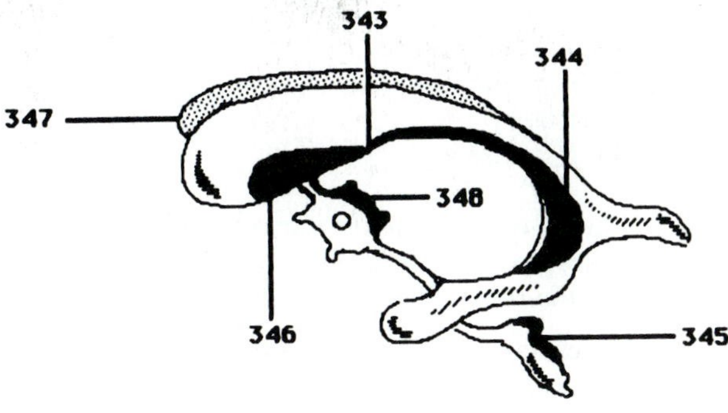

Figure 10–47. A diagram of the ventricular system in a neonate.

361. The fluid-filled cavity of the septum pellucidum seen on neonatal sonography is called

(A) the cavum septi pellucidi
(B) the third ventricle
(C) lateral ventricles
(D) massa intermedia

362. The anomalies associated with anencephaly are

(A) spina bifida
(B) hydrocephalus
(C) holoprosencephaly
(D) hydranencephaly

Question 363: Select the letter indicating the appropriate numbered choice or choices.

363. The most common intracranial infection(s) in the neonate is (1) *Hemophilus influenzae,* (2) β-streptococci, (3) meningitis, (4) *Escherichia coli.*

(A) 3 only
(B) 3 and 1
(C) 1, 2, and 3
(D) 2 and 4

364. Accidents are a major cause of death among infants. Sonographers should know what to do and what *not* to do to reduce unnecessary accidents. Which of the following should *not* be done?

(A) identify the patient properly before scanning
(B) keep crib sides up at all times when the infant is unattended
(C) wash your hands before and after scanning
(D) remove all dressings and fracture weights carefully before scanning

Question 365: Select the letter indicating the appropriate numbered choice or choices.

365. Premature babies are usually placed in incubators. The reasons for this are to (1) provide proper heat for the baby, (2) provide a cool and dry environment for the baby, (3) maintain environmental conditions similar to the uterus, (4) provide proper humidity and oxygen for the baby, (5) provide proper isolation and protection for the baby.

(A) all of the above
(B) 1, 2, and 4
(C) 1 and 5
(D) 1, 3, 4, and 5

366. When a sonographer or nurse turns an infant with severe hydrocephalus, he or she should always support the head. The reason for this is to

(A) prevent a strain on the neck
(B) prevent fluid from leaking out
(C) prevent the closure of the anterior fontanelle
(D) prevent the anterior fontanelle from opening

367. If an infant has a ventriculoperitoneal (V-P) shunt and the fontanelles are bulging, the usual position to assist in drainage is the

(A) Trendelenburg position
(B) lithotomy position
(C) semi-Fowler's position
(D) Sim's position

368. If an infant has a ventriculoperitoneal (V-P) shunt and the fontanelles are sunken, the usual position to assist in drainage is the

(A) Trendelenburg's position
(B) lithotomy position
(C) Fowler's position
(D) supine position

369. Because premature infants are highly susceptible to infection, sonographers who scan the newborn in the intensive care unit should know the fundamentals of asepsis. Which of the following is *not* the proper handwashing procedure in medical asepsis?

(A) turn on the water with your foot or knee
(B) open the faucets with your hands and close them with a paper towel
(C) do not allow your uniform to touch the sink, and use warm water
(D) use bar soap in preference to liquid soap.

370. The patient's medical chart is an important legal document and may be used in a court of law. Sonographers are sometimes required to enter the date, time, and type of sonogram performed, along with their signature. Which of the following should *not* be done: (1) enter information with a pen, (2) enter information with a pencil, (3) if you make an error, erase it and continue recording the correct information, (4) if you make an error, draw a single line through the mistake, write the word "error" and continue recording the correct information, (5) rewrite the entire chart?

(A) 1, 4, and 5
(B) 2, 3, and 5
(C) 2 and 3
(D) 2 and 5

371. When performing a neonatal sonogram, sonographers should be observant and be familiar with intravenous (IV) lines in children. The sonographer should

(A) handle the IV with care
(B) check to make sure the IV fluid does not run out

(C) report to the physician if blood returns up the line
(D) observe for any swelling around the site and report it
(E) all of the above
(F) do none of the above; sonographers need not be observant or familiarized with IV; this is the job of a nurse

372. Convulsions are *most* common in what year of life?

(A) first 2 years of life
(B) in children older than 6 years
(C) 18 years
(D) convulsions are more common in adults than in children

373. The sagittal real-time cranial sonogram in Fig. 10–48 shows

(A) an intraparenchymal hemorrhage
(B) an "old" germinal matrix hemorrhage that has undergone fibrinolysis
(C) ventricular dilatation only
(D) none of the above

374. The sonographic appearance of the abnormality in Fig. 10–48 indicates

(A) that there has been acute germinal matrix hemorrhage
(B) that the clot has undergone fibrinolysis and therefore has been present for at least 3 days
(C) that there has been extensive intraventricular extension of the hemorrhage
(D) none of the above

375. The cranial sonograms in Figs. 10–49A and B demonstrate

(A) no abnormality
(B) bilateral germinal matrix hemorrhage with mild ventricular dilatation involving the left lateral ventricle only
(C) germinal matrix hemorrhage with ventricular dilatation of the right lateral ventricle

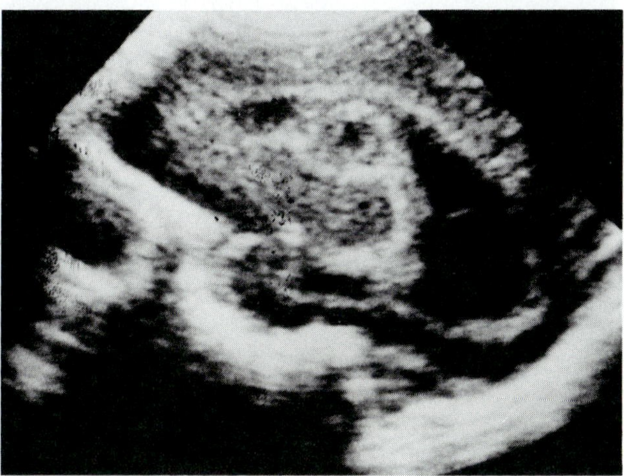

Figure 10–48. A parasagittal sonogram.

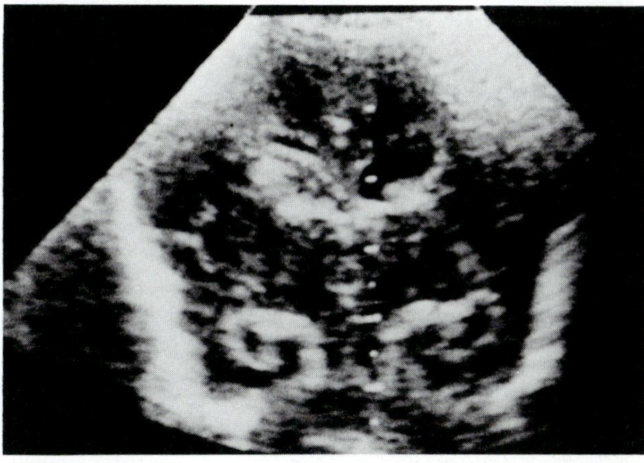

A

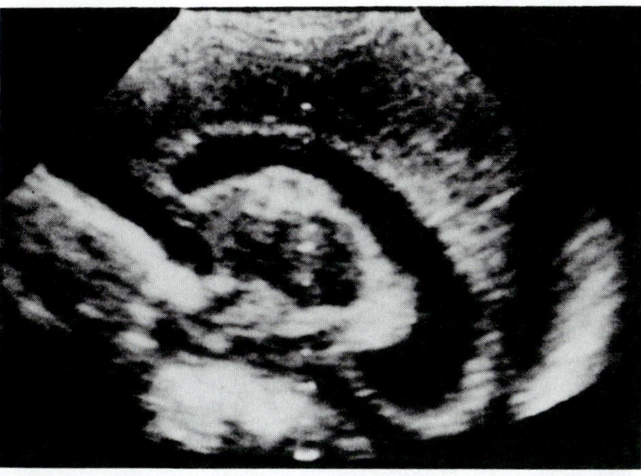

B

Figure 10–49. (**A**) A coronal sonogram; (**B**) a parasagittal sonogram.

376. Ventricular dilatation usually occurs how many days after the initial hemorrhage?

(A) 1 day
(B) 5–7 days
(C) 1 month
(D) 1 year

377. The cerebellum is separated from the occipital lobe of the cerebrum by the

(A) interhemispheric fissure
(B) tentorium
(C) cerebellar vermis
(D) parieto-occipital sulcus

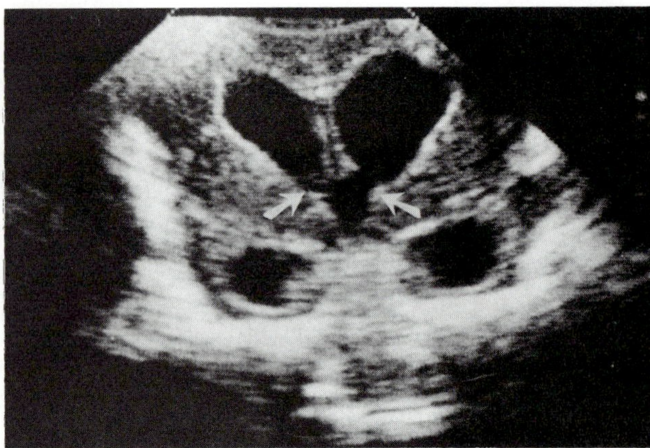

Figure 10–50. A coronal sonogram.

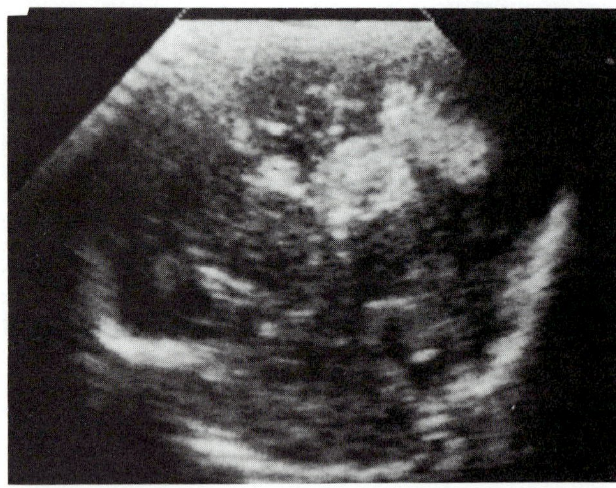

A

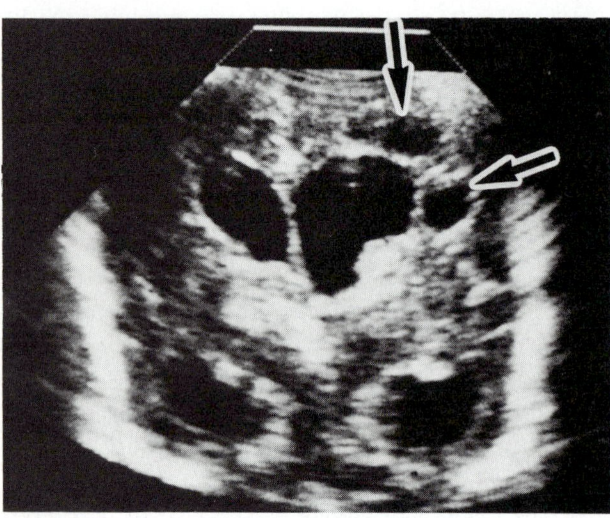

B

Figure 10–51. (A) A coronal sonogram taken of a 1-day-old neonate; (B) a coronal sonogram of the same infant taken at 30 days.

378. Which is *not* a true sonographic finding in complete agenesis of the corpus callosum?

(A) the lateral ventricles are widely separated
(B) the third ventricle is elongated and displaced
(C) the septum pellucidum is superior to the third ventricle
(D) the frontal horns of the lateral ventricles are sharply peaked

379. The sonogram in Fig. 10–50 shows

(A) marked ventricular dilatation of the lateral ventricles and third ventricle
(B) normal-sized lateral ventricles
(C) intraparenchymal hemorrhage
(D) none of the above

380. The arrows in Fig. 10–50 point to the

(A) interventricular foramina (foramina of Monro)
(B) vein of Galen
(C) fourth ventricle
(D) temporal horns

381. The findings in the sonogram in Fig. 10–51A are

(A) extensive intraventricular hemorrhage with an intraparenchymal hemorrhage
(B) intraparenchymal hemorrhage only
(C) intraventricular hemorrhage only
(D) subependymal hemorrhage only

382. The arrows in Fig. 10–51B point to

(A) cysts within the ventricle
(B) porencephalic changes associated with previous intraparenchymal hemorrhage
(C) subependymal hemorrhage
(D) subarachnoid hemorrhage

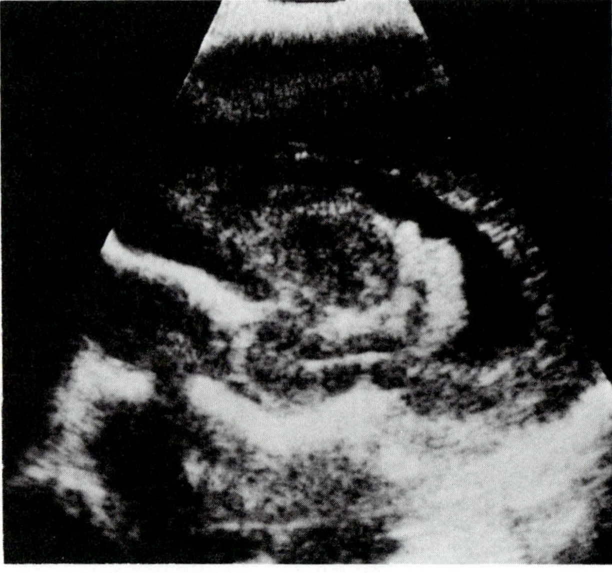

Figure 10–52. A parasagittal sonogram.

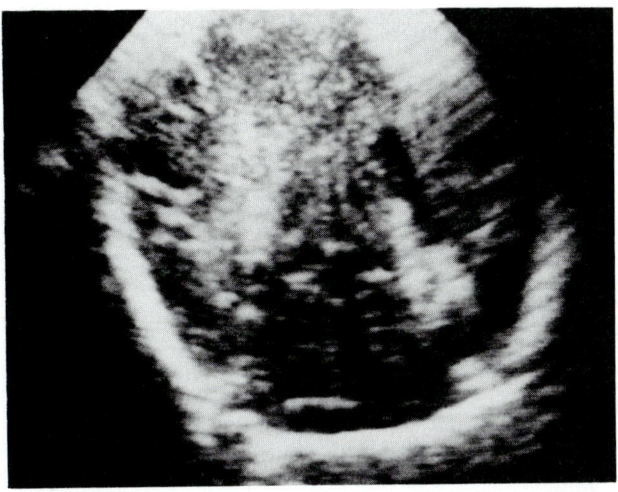

A

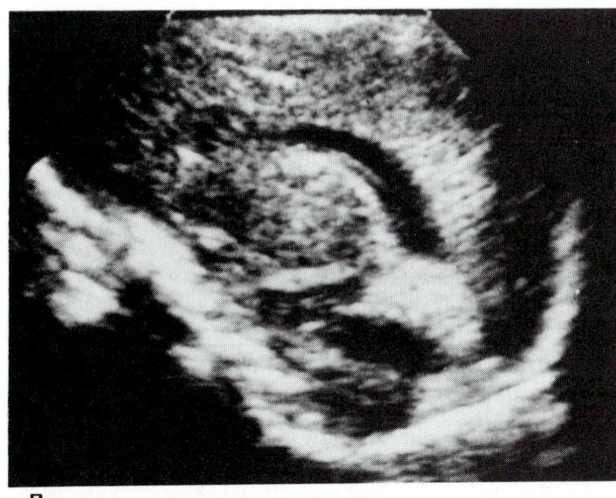

B

Figure 10–53. (**A**) A coronal sonogram; (**B**) a left parasagittal sonogram.

383. The image shown in Fig. 10–52 could be improved by

(A) increasing the near-field time gain compensation
(B) increasing the overall gain
(C) including all the important anatomy
(D) none of the above

384. The choroid plexus in Fig. 10–52 is

(A) normal
(B) abnormal
(C) not shown

385. The abnormal finding in Fig. 10–53A and B is

(A) intraventricular hemorrhage that is layering in the left occipital horn
(B) germinal matrix hemorrhage only
(C) intraparenchymal hemorrhage
(D) none of the above

386. The echogenic structure within the occipital horn in Fig. 10–53B is

(A) the choroid plexus
(B) intraventricular hemorrhage layering within the occipital horn
(C) an ependymal tumor
(D) none of the above

387. A sagittal cranial sonogram in a 2-day-old neonate shown in Fig. 10–54 demonstrates

(A) intraparenchymal hemorrhage
(B) intraventricular hemorrhage layering within the lateral ventricle
(C) normal sonogram
(D) subependymal hemorrhage only

388. An intraventricular hemorrhage

(A) occurs only with an intraparenchymal hemorrhage
(B) occurs only with a subependymal hemorrhage
(C) occurs only with a choroid plexus hemorrhage
(D) is life threatening

389. Which of the following does *not* occur as a result of a vein of Galen aneurysm?

(A) cardiac failure
(B) hydrocephalus
(C) enlarged aorta
(D) quadrigeminal cyst

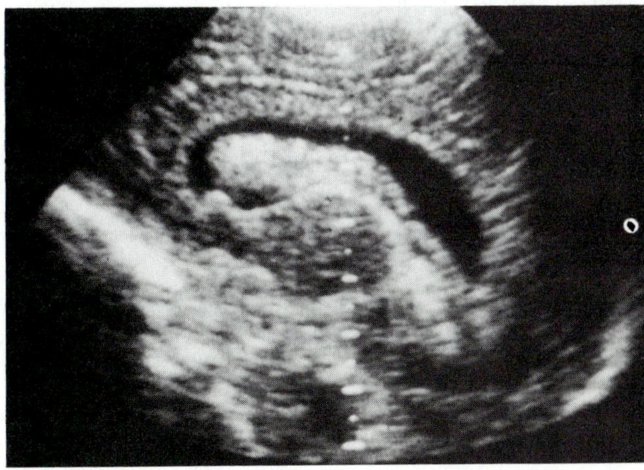

Figure 10–54. A parasagittal sonogram.

390. Which of the following does *not* apply to arachnoid cyst?

(A) arachnoid cysts lie between the pia mater and the subarachnoid space
(B) they do not communicate with the ventricles or the arachnoid space
(C) they contain cerebrospinal fluid
(D) they are usually found in the sylvian fissure, middle fossa, and interhemispheric fissure
(E) they are usually congenital and acquired

391. Which of the following statements is true about the arachnoid granulations?

(A) arachnoid granulations lie in the cingulate sulcus
(B) they lie in the pericallosal artery where cerebrospinal fluid is reabsorbed by the blood
(C) they lie in the sagittal sinus and reabsorb cerebrospinal fluid as it circulates
(D) they lie in the ventricular system and reabsorb cerebrospinal fluid as it circulates

392. Which of the following best describes the sylvian fissure?

(A) it separates the parietal lobe from the occipital lobe
(B) it separates the frontal lobe from the temporal lobe; the basilar artery pulsates there
(C) it separates the frontal lobe from the temporal lobe and forms a right angle with the central sulcus; the middle cerebral artery pulsates there
(D) it lies superior to the corpus callosum.

393. Figure 10–55 shows sagittal and coronal cranial sonograms of a 3-month-old infant who had an average gestational age of 36 weeks. The abnormal sonographic finding demonstrates

(A) intraventricular hemorrhage
(B) a cyst in the choroid plexus of the temporal horn of the lateral ventricle
(C) a simple cyst in the glomus part of the lateral ventricle
(D) an arachnoid cyst in the quadrigeminal cistern

394. The echogenic structure the arrow points to in the sagittal cranial sonogram shown in Fig. 10–56 is

(A) intraparenchymal hemorrhage
(B) sylvian fissure
(C) circular sulcus
(D) fissure of Rolando

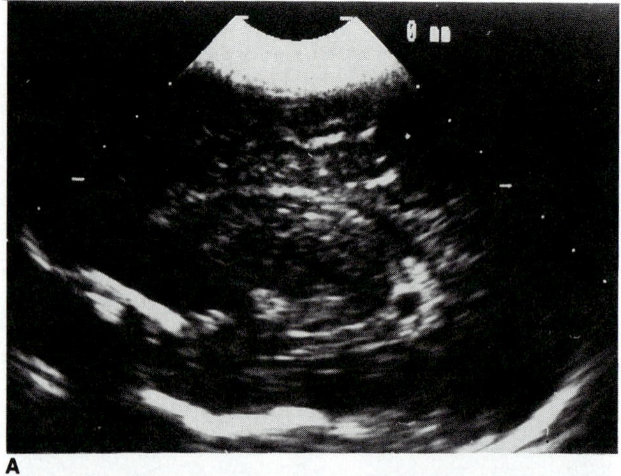
A

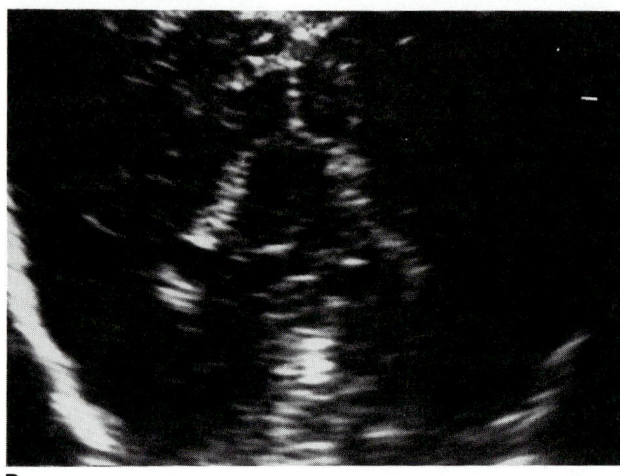
B

Figure 10–55. (**A**) A parasagittal sonogram; (**B**) a coronal sonogram

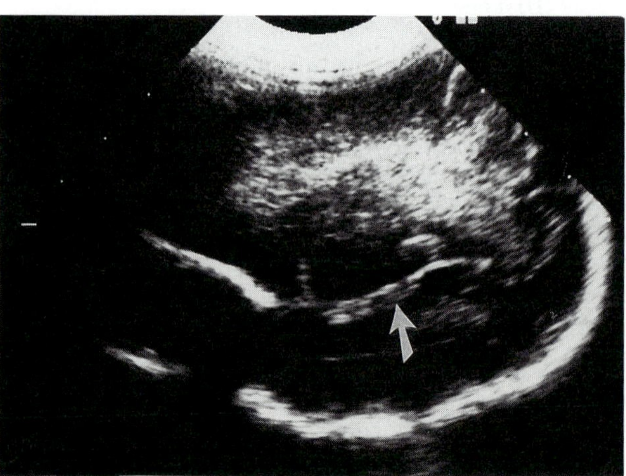

Figure 10–56. A parasagittal sonogram.

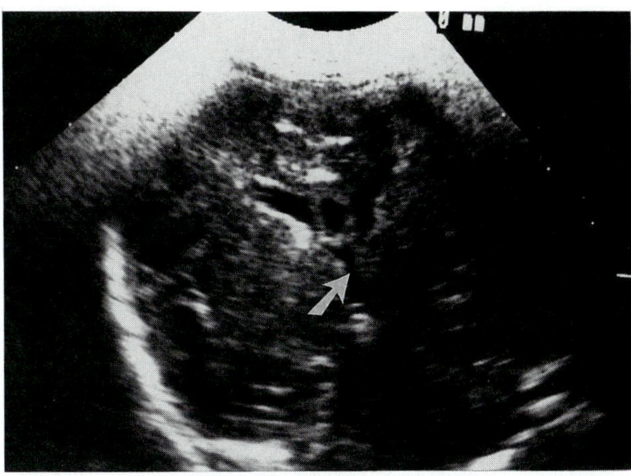

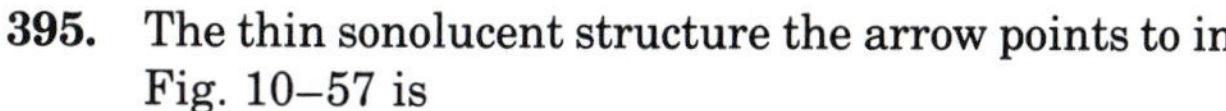

Figure 10–57. A coronal sonogram.

395. The thin sonolucent structure the arrow points to in Fig. 10–57 is

(A) porencephalic cyst
(B) cavum septum pellucidum
(C) fourth ventricle
(D) third ventricle

396. The echogenic structure the straight arrow points to in Fig. 10–58 is the

(A) interhemispheric fissure
(B) sylvian fissure
(C) corpus callosum
(D) cingulate sulcus

397. The bilateral sonolucent structures the open arrows point to in Fig. 10–58 represent

(A) trigone region of the lateral ventricles
(B) bodies of the lateral ventricle
(C) frontal horns of the lateral ventricle
(D) porencephalic cysts

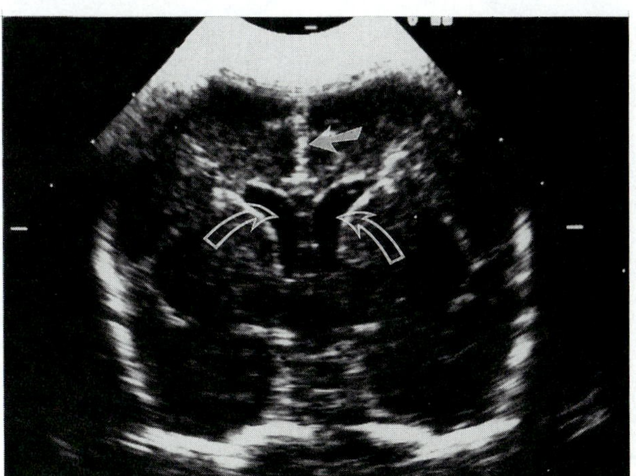

Figure 10–58. A coronal sonogram.

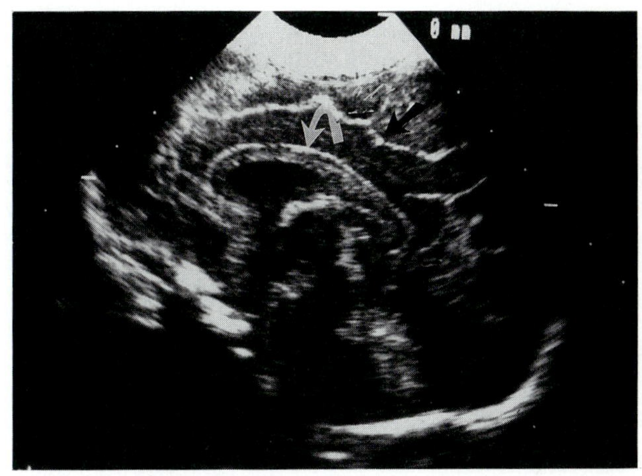

Figure 10–59. A midsagittal sonogram.

398. The straight black arrow in Fig. 10–59 points to

(A) calcarine sulcus
(B) circular sulcus
(C) tentorium
(D) cingulate sulcus

399. The curved arrow in Fig. 10–59 points to

(A) corpus callosum
(B) interhemispheric fissure
(C) choroid plexus
(D) none of the above

400. The central nervous system consists of the brain and spinal cord. The spinal cord is referred to as the distal continuation of the central nervous system. The terminal portion of the spinal cord is the

(A) filum terminale
(B) conus medullaris
(C) cauda equina
(D) pia mater

401. At what level of the vertebrae does the spinal cord terminate?

(A) fifth lumbar vertebra
(B) the lumbosacral joint
(C) the first lumbar vertebra
(D) the second lumbar vertebra

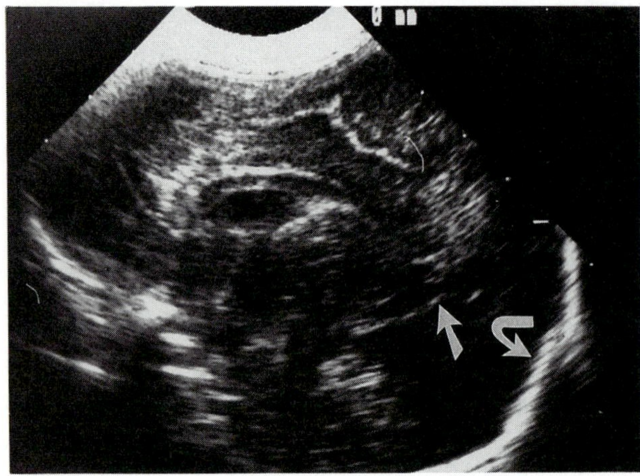

Figure 10–60. A sagittal sonogram.

402. The straight arrow in Fig. 10–60 points to an echogenic line called the

(A) callosal sulcus
(B) central sulcus
(C) parieto-occipital sulcus
(D) cerebellar vermis

403. The highly echogenic structure that the curved arrow points to in Fig. 10–60 is the

(A) frontal bone
(B) temporal bone
(C) occipital lobe of the cerebrum
(D) occipital bone

404. There are four grades of intracranial hemorrhage. What grade of hemorrhage is demonstrated on the coronal and sagittal sonograms in Fig. 10–61A and B?

(A) grade IV
(B) grade I
(C) grade III
(D) grade II

405. Which statement best explains the extent of the intracranial hemorrhage shown in Fig. 10–61 A and B?

(A) an intraparenchymal hemorrhage only is present
(B) parenchymal and germinal matrix hemorrhages are present
(C) parenchymal, germinal matrix, and intraventricular hemorrhages are present
(D) only intraventricular hemorrhage

406. The sonogram shown in Fig. 10–62 was taken from a premature neonate. The sonographic findings demonstrate a

(A) lipoma
(B) bilateral germinal matrix hemorrhage
(C) unilateral germinal matrix hemorrhage
(D) none of the above

407. The abnormal sonographic findings shown in Fig. 10–63 include

(A) a Dandy-Walker cyst
(B) dilatation of the fourth ventricle because of obstruction at the foramen of Magendie
(C) atresia of the foramen of Magendie
(D) none of the above

408. Dandy-Walker cysts are associated with

(A) absence of the inferior vermis
(B) dilatation of the fourth ventricle because of obstruction at the foramen of Magendie
(C) atresia of the foramen of Magendie
(D) none of the above

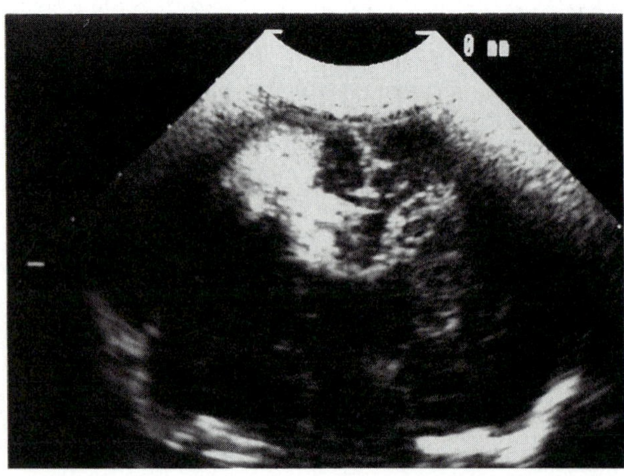

A

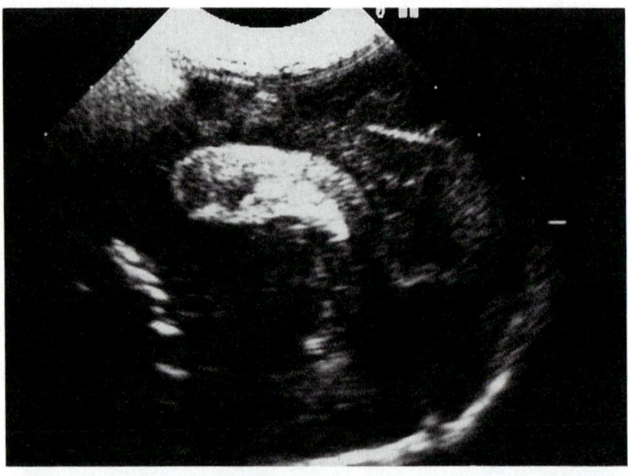

B

Figure 10–61. (**A**) A coronal sonogram; (**B**) a parasagittal sonogram.

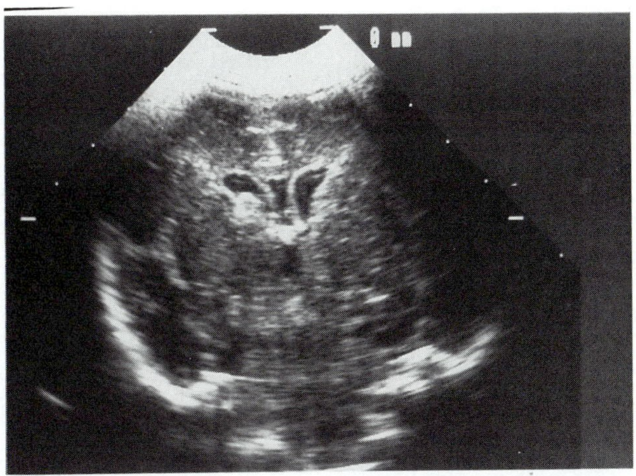
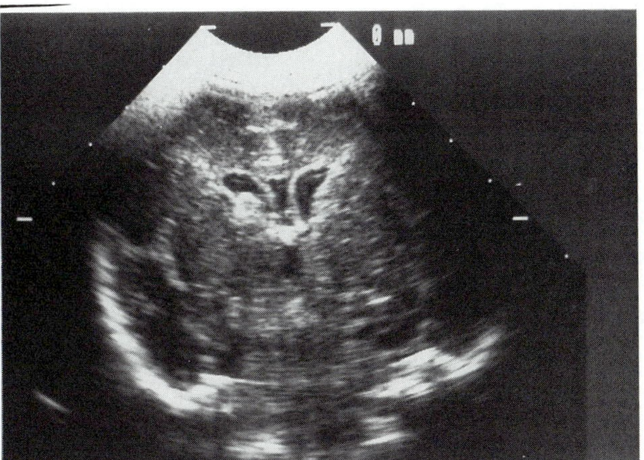

Figure 10–62. A coronal sonogram.

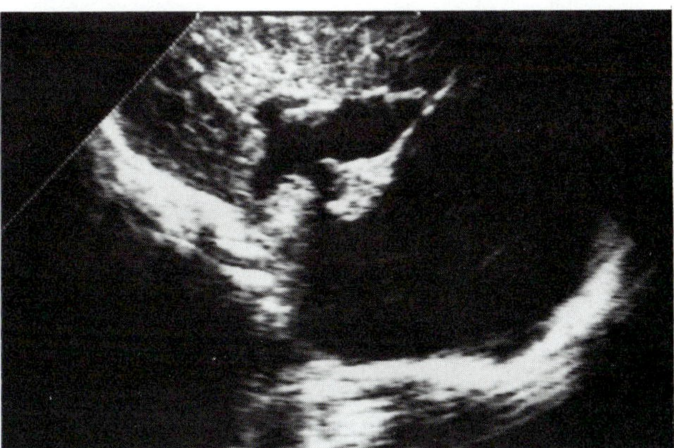

Figure 10–63. A midsagittal sonogram.

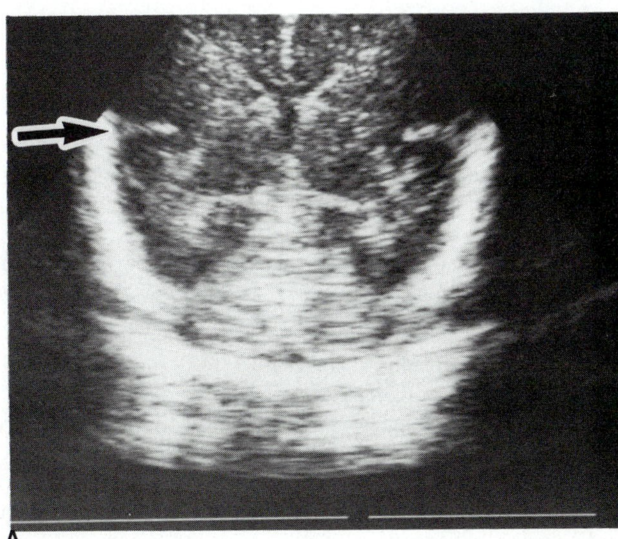

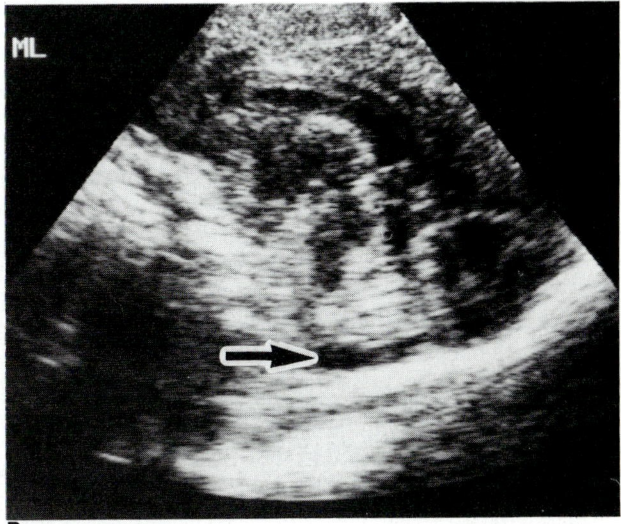

Figure 10–64. (**A**) A coronal sonogram; (**B**) a midparasagittal sonogram.

409. The arrow in Fig. 10–64A points to

(A) choroidal fissure
(B) sylvian fissure
(C) fissure of Rolando
(D) none of the above

410. The arrow in Fig. 10–64B points to

(A) cisterna magna
(B) vein of Galen
(C) vermi of the cerebellum
(D) none of the above

411. What region of the lateral ventricular system is the first to dilate in hydrocephalus?

(A) the third ventricle
(B) occipital horns
(C) frontal horns
(D) temporal horns

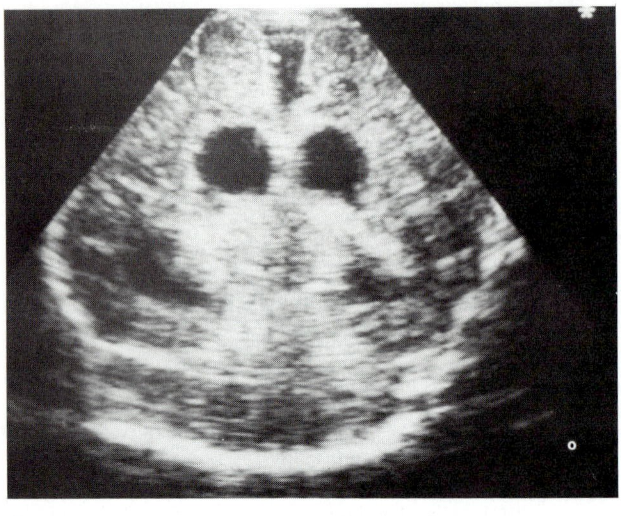
A

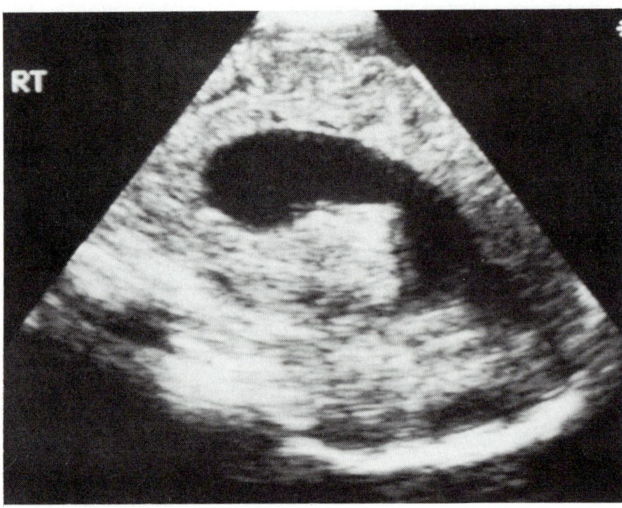

B

Figure 10–65. (**A**) A coronal sonogram; (**B**) a right parasagittal sonogram.

412. The abnormal sonographic findings shown in Fig. 10–65A and B include

(A) marked atrophy of the cerebrum
(B) increased subarachnoid fluid
(C) multiple intracerebral hemorrhages
(D) none of the above

413. The asphyxial pattern in Fig. 10–65A and B consists of

(A) multiple punctate echogenicities throughout the cerebrum
(B) atrophy on follow-up cranial sonograms
(C) intracerebral calcification
(D) A and B

414. The correct placement for a ventriculoperitoneal (V-P) shunt catheter is

(A) frontal horns anterior to the foramen of Monro
(B) frontal horns posterior to the foramen of Monro
(C) trigone of the lateral ventricle
(D) the roof of the third ventricle

415. Which of the following is associated least with complete agenesis of the corpus callosum?

(A) absence of the septum pellucidum
(B) enlarged septum pellucidum
(C) wide separation of the lateral ventricle
(D) displacement of the third ventricle

416. Which of the following is or are *not* seen in septo-optic dysplasia?

(A) septum pellucidum
(B) frontal horns
(C) thalamus
(D) occipital horns

417. Dilatation of the vein of Galen is most likely to cause obstruction

(A) at the level of the third ventricle and the aqueduct of Sylvius
(B) of the cavum septum pellucidum
(C) at the level of foramen of Magendie
(D) to the tentorium cerebelli

418. Which of following is *not* a characteristic of schizencephaly?

(A) the corpus callosum is absent
(B) the septum pellucidum is absent
(C) the ventricle has an unusual shape
(D) the septum pellucidum is dilated

419. Which of the following statements best describes rubella?

(A) it is a febrile viral disease characterized by eruptions closely resembling measles; it is also called German measles
(B) it is a parasitic infection of the fetus produced by an intracellular protozoan
(C) it is a communicable disease characterized by fever and rash and is more common among children
(D) it is a febrile viral disease characterized by swelling of the parotid gland

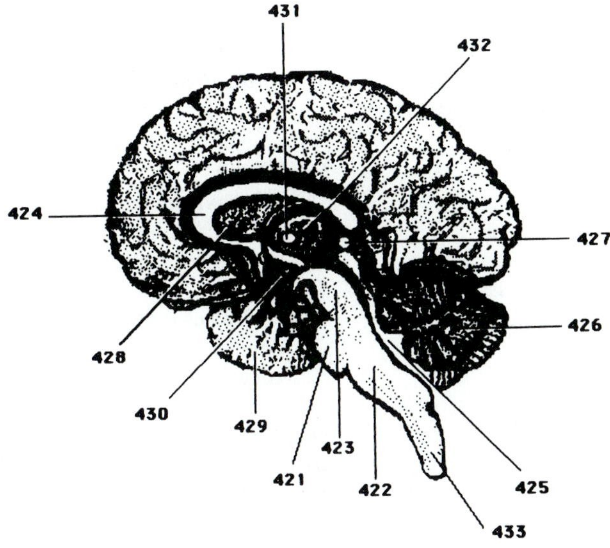

Figure 10–66. A diagram of a sagittal section of the brain.

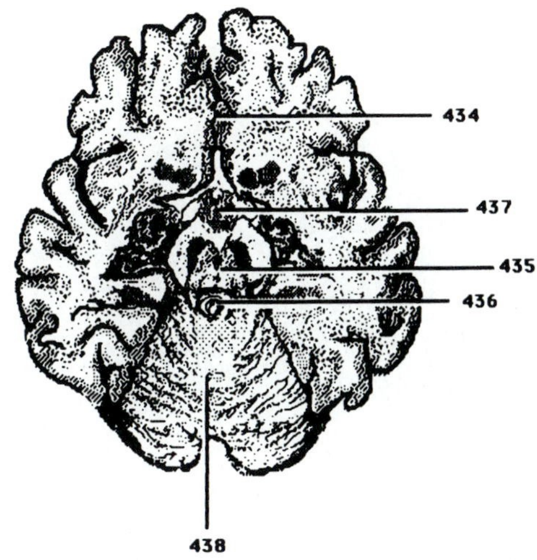

Figure 10–67. A diagram of a coronal section of the brain.

420. In the event of convulsions in a child requiring a cranial sonogram, the sonographer should (1) prevent the child from biting his or her tongue by placing the (sonographer's) fingers between the child's teeth, (2) prevent the child from biting his or her tongue by placing a wooden tongue blade wrapped with gauze between the child's teeth, (3) prevent injury, (4) try to force the child's mouth open if the child has already clamped his or her jaws down

(A) all of the above
(B) 2 and 4
(C) 1 and 4
(D) 2 and 3

Questions 421 through 433: Identify the structures to which the arrows point in Fig. 10–66, then place in Column A the letter corresponding to the appropriate item in Column B.

COLUMN A	COLUMN B
421. _____	(A) corpus callosum
422. _____	(B) thalamus
423. _____	(C) cerebellum
424. _____	(D) pineal body
425. _____	(E) pons
426. _____	(F) spinal cord
427. _____	(G) cerebral peduncle
428. _____	(H) septum pellucidum
429. _____	(I) medulla oblongata
430. _____	(J) interthalmic adhesion
431. _____	(K) fourth ventricle
432. _____	(L) third ventricle
433. _____	(M) temporal lobe

Questions 434 through 438: Identify the structures to which the arrows point in Fig. 10–67, then place in Column A the letter corresponding to the appropriate item in Column B.

COLUMN A	COLUMN B
434. _____	(A) cerebral aqueduct
435. _____	(B) cerebellum peduncle
436. _____	(C) cerebellum
437. _____	(D) hypothalamus
438. _____	(E) gyrus and sulcus

Questions 439 through 443: Match the structures to which the arrows point in Fig. 10–68, then place in Column A the letter corresponding to the appropriate item in Column B.

COLUMN A	COLUMN B
439. _____	(A) corpus callosum
440. _____	(B) septum pellucidum
441. _____	(C) third ventricle
442. _____	(D) caudate nucleus
443. _____	(E) pons

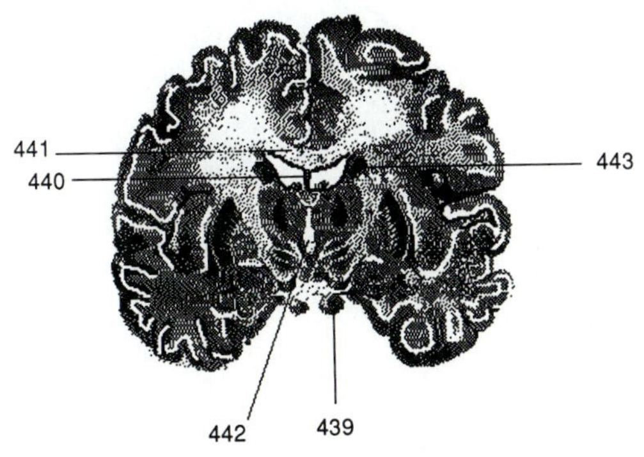

Figure 10–68. A diagram of a coronal section of the brain.

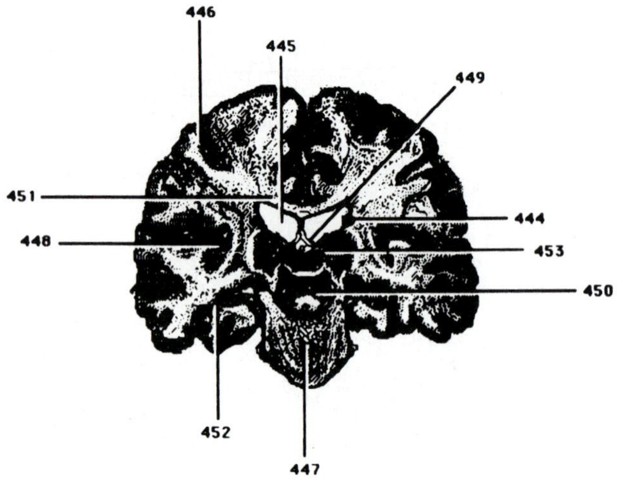

Figure 10–69. A diagram of a coronal section of the brain.

Questions 444 through 453: Match the structures to which the arrows point in Fig. 10–69, then place in Column A the letter corresponding to the appropriate item in Column B.

COLUMN A	COLUMN B
444. ______	(A) lateral ventricle
445. ______	(B) cerebellar peduncle
446. ______	(C) pons
447. ______	(D) corpus callosum
448. ______	(E) caudate nucleus
449. ______	(F) hippocampus
450. ______	(G) sylvian fissure
451. ______	(H) sulcus
452. ______	(I) column of fornix
453. ______	(J) thalamus

Questions 454 through 460: Identify the structures to which the arrows point in Fig. 10–70, then place in Column A the letter corresponding to the appropriate item in Column B.

COLUMN A	COLUMN B
454. ______	(A) internal capsule
455. ______	(B) temporal lobe
456. ______	(C) caudate nucleus
457. ______	(D) putamen
458. ______	(E) pericallosal artery
459. ______	(F) frontal lobe
460. ______	(G) corpus callosum

Questions 461 through 467: Identify the structures to which the arrows point in Fig. 10–71, then place in Column A the letter corresponding to the appropriate item in Column B.

COLUMN A	COLUMN B
461. ______	(A) dura mater
462. ______	(B) subdural space
463. ______	(C) pia mater
464. ______	(D) superior sagittal sinus
465. ______	(E) arachnoid villus
466. ______	(F) falx cerebri
467. ______	(G) subarachnoid space

Questions 468 through 471: Identify the structure to which the arrows point in Fig. 10–72, then place in Column A the letter corresponding to the appropriate item in Column B.

COLUMN A	COLUMN B
468. ______	(A) pericallosal artery
469. ______	(B) middle cerebral artery
470. ______	(C) callosomarginal artery
471. ______	(D) anterior cerebral artery

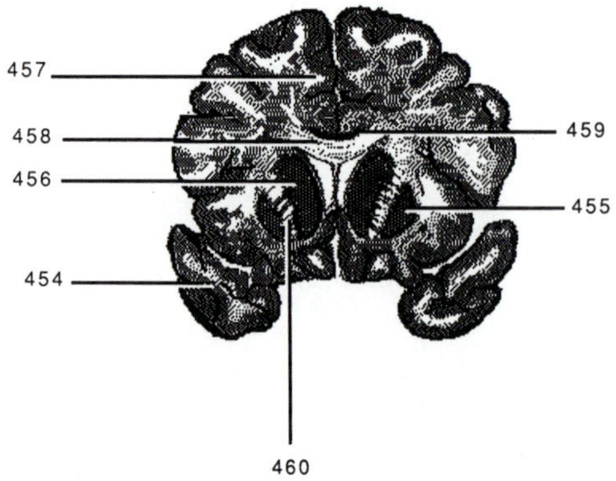

Figure 10–70. A diagram of a coronal section of the brain.

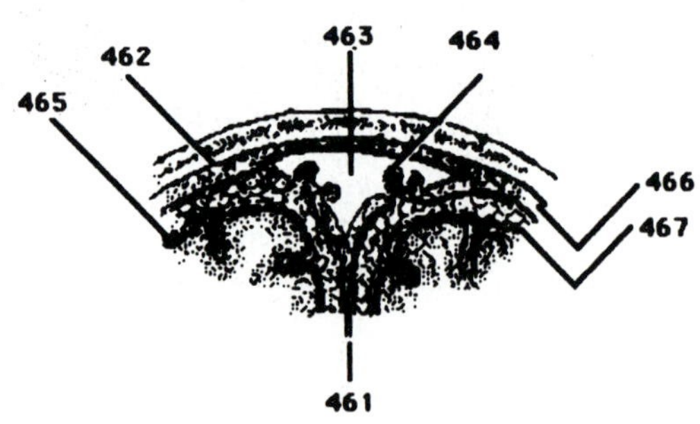

Figure 10–71. A diagram of a coronal section of the meninges and cortex.

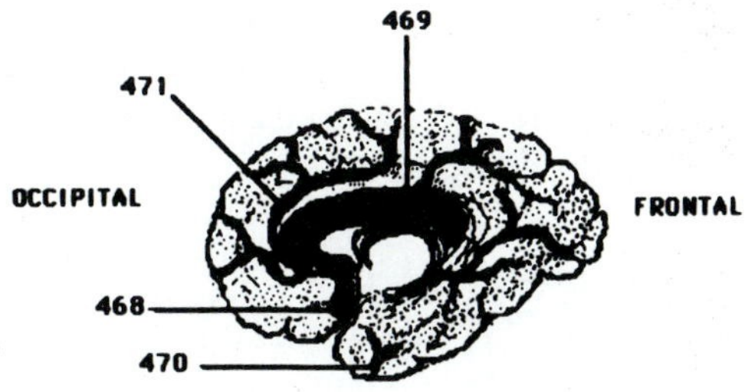

Figure 10–72. A diagram of the lateral aspect of the internal carotid artery and its divisions.

Questions 472 through 480: Identify the structures to which the arrows point in Fig. 10–73, then place in Column A the letter corresponding to the appropriate item in Column B.

COLUMN A	COLUMN B
472. _____	(A) anterior communicating artery
473. _____	(B) vertebral artery
474. _____	(C) basilar artery
475. _____	(D) posterior communicating artery
476. _____	(E) anterior inferior cerebellar artery
477. _____	(F) anterior spinal artery
478. _____	(G) posterior cerebral artery
479. _____	(H) internal carotid artery
480. _____	(I) anterior cerebral artery

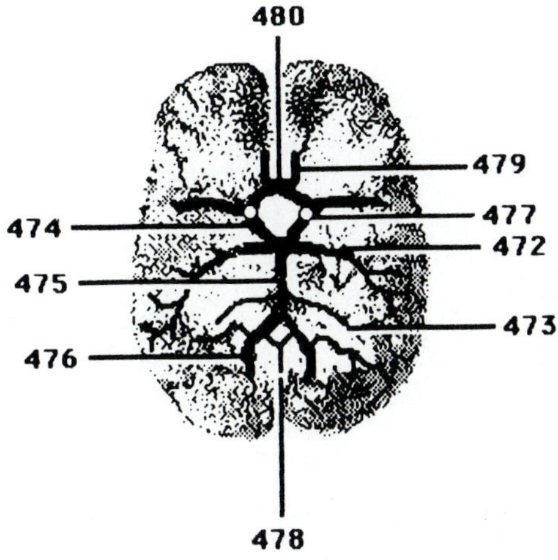

Figure 10–73. A diagram of the arteries at the base of the brain.

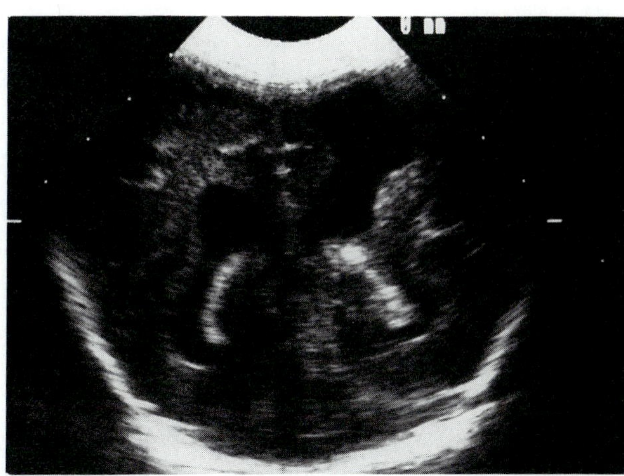

A

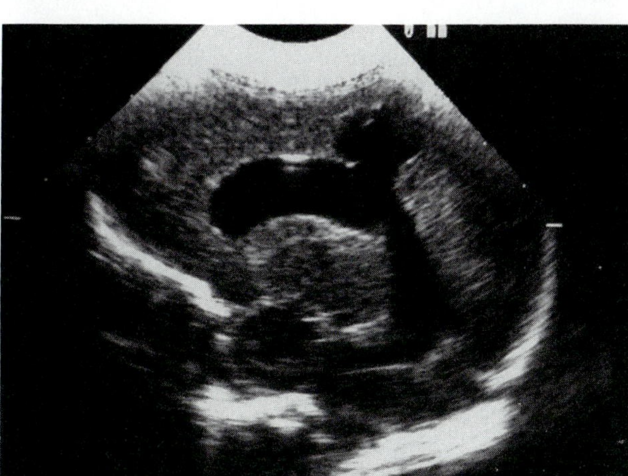

B

Figure 10–74. (A) A coronal sonogram; (B) a parasagittal sonogram.

481. The sonograms shown in Fig. 10–74 were taken from a 4-week-old premature neonate. The abnormal findings include

(A) arachnoid cyst
(B) enlarged ventricles and an area of porencephaly in the posterior horn of the right lateral ventricle
(C) enlarged ventricles with an area of porencephaly at the region of the body of the left lateral ventricle
(D) isolated porencephalic cyst

482. The abnormal findings in Fig. 10–74 are the result of

(A) isolated germinal matrix hemorrhage
(B) resolving intraparenchymal and intraventricular hemorrhages
(C) subarachnoid hemorrhage
(D) none of the above

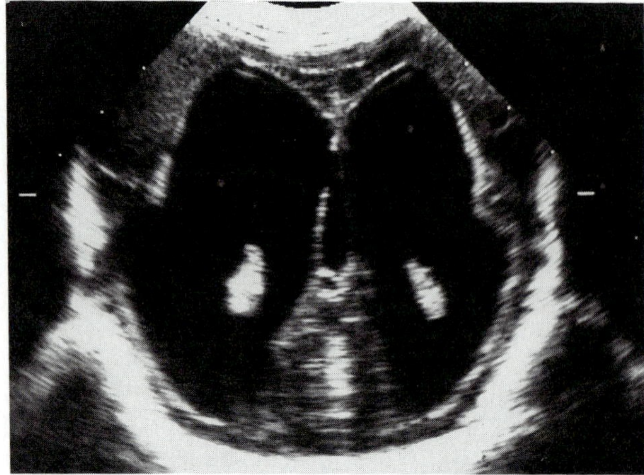

A

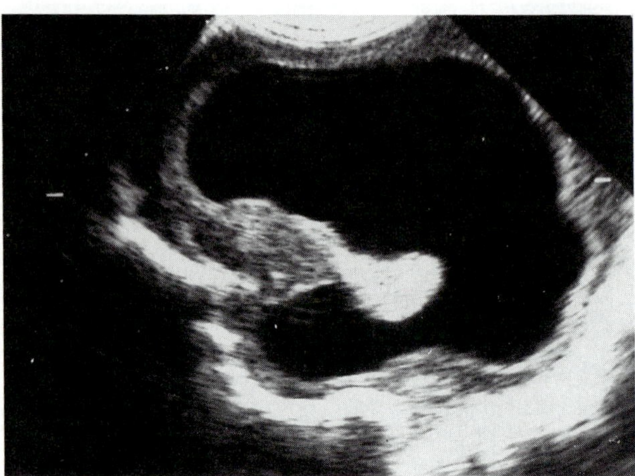

B

Figure 10–75. (**A**) A coronal sonogram; (**B**) a parasagittal sonogram.

483. These sonograms shown in Fig. 10–75 were taken from a 1-month-old premature infant. The abnormal findings include

(A) lobar holoprosencephaly
(B) alobar holoprosencephaly
(C) hydrocephalus
(D) Dandy-Walker cyst

484. The bilateral echogenic structures seen in the sonolucent cavities in the coronal view in Fig. 10–75 are

(A) clots
(B) choroid plexus
(C) the ethmoid and sphenoid bones
(D) bilateral lipomas

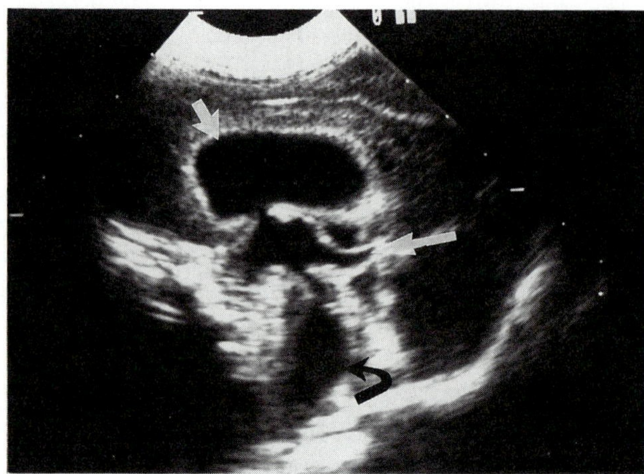

Figure 10–76. A midsagittal sonogram.

485. The sonogram shown in Fig. 10–76 is a midsagittal view of the head of a 1-month-old infant. Which statement best describes the abnormal findings?

(A) an enlarged cavum septum pellucidum, enlarged third and fourth ventricles, a dilated foramen of Monro, dilated aqueduct of Sylvius
(B) an enlarged lateral ventricle, an enlarged third ventricle, an enlarged fourth ventricle, a dilated foramen of Monro, and a dilated aqueduct of Sylvius
(C) all the abnormalities in A plus a posterior fossa cyst
(D) a dilated cavum septum pellucidum only is present

486. Identify the structure the long straight arrow points to in Fig. 10–76.

(A) foramen of Monro
(B) supraoptic recess
(C) infundibular recess
(D) pineal recess

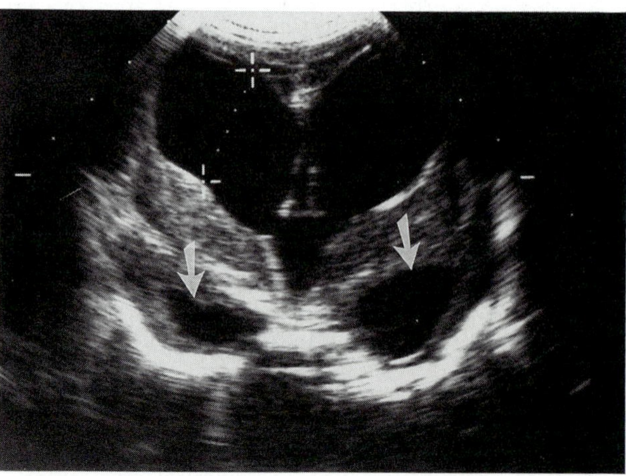

Figure 10–77. A coronal sonogram.

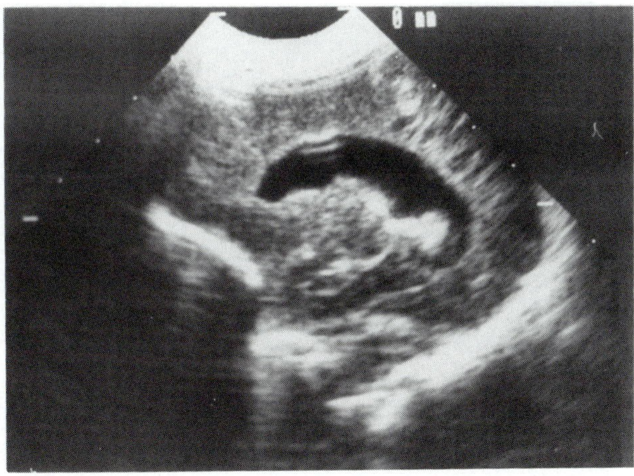

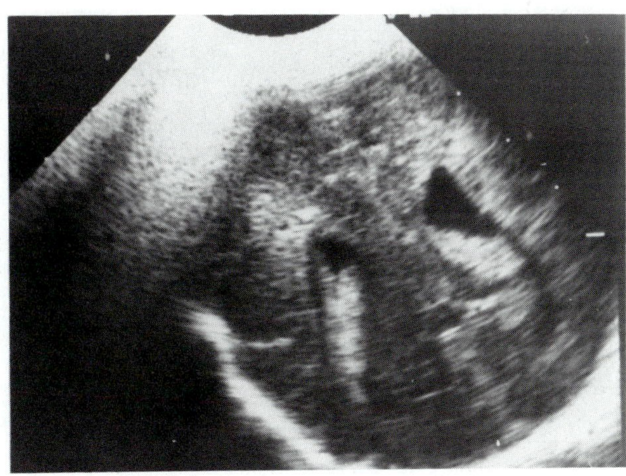

A B

Figure 10–78. (**A**) A parasagittal sonogram; (**B**) a coronal sonogram.

487. Identify the enlarged structure the curved black arrow points to in Fig. 10–76.

(A) third ventricle
(B) fourth ventricle
(C) cerebrum
(D) quadrigeminal cistern

488. Identify the structure the short arrow points to in Fig. 10–76.

(A) one of the lateral ventricles
(B) cavum septi pellucidi
(C) cisterna magna
(D) a cyst in the interhemispheric fissure

489. The two sonolucent areas the arrows point to in Fig. 10–77 are

(A) bilateral porencephalic cysts in the temporal lobes
(B) porencephalic cysts in the frontal lobe
(C) temporal horns of the lateral ventricles
(D) frontal horns of the lateral ventricles

490. The sonographic findings in Fig. 10–78A and B suggest

(A) subependymal hemorrhage
(B) resolving intraventricular hemorrhage and periventricular leukomalacia
(C) enlarged lateral ventricles
(D) B and C

491. The abnormal sonographic findings shown in Fig. 10–79A and B include

(A) intraparenchymal hemorrhage
(B) grade III type of intracranial hemorrhage
(C) germinal matrix hemorrhage with subependymal cysts
(D) none of the above

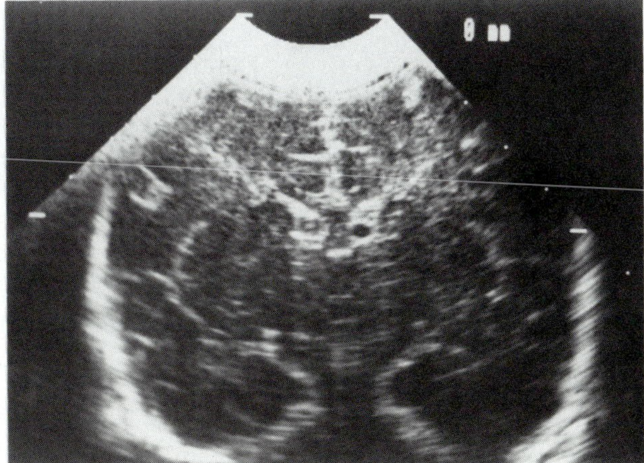

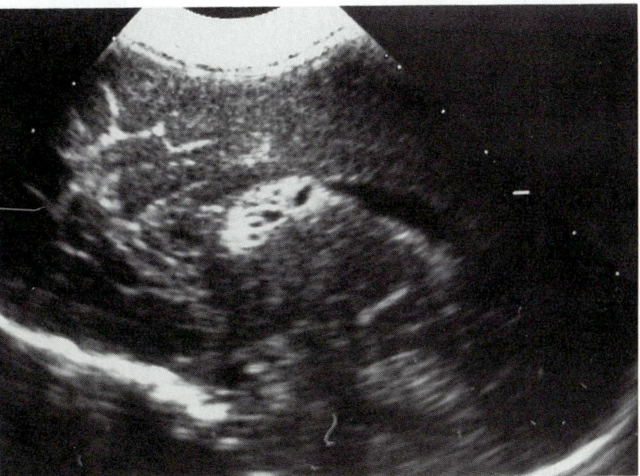

A B

Figure 10–79. (**A**) A coronal sonogram; (**B**) a parasagittal sonogram

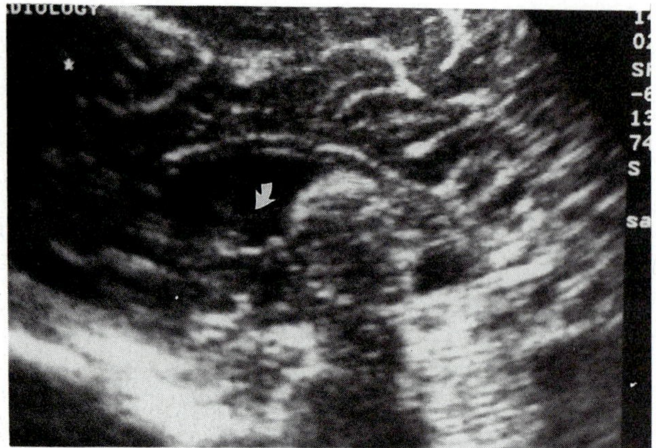

Figure 10–80. A midsagittal sonogram.

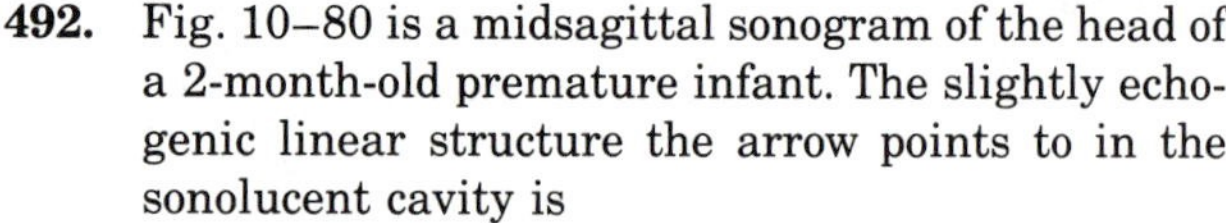

492. Fig. 10–80 is a midsagittal sonogram of the head of a 2-month-old premature infant. The slightly echogenic linear structure the arrow points to in the sonolucent cavity is

(A) septal vein
(B) anterior cerebral artery
(C) corpus callosum
(D) pericallosal artery

493. Fig. 10–81 is a sagittal sonogram taken from a 2-week-old premature neonate born at 31 weeks' gestational age. The structure the arrow points to is

(a) clot in the third ventricle
(B) massa intermedia
(C) interthalamic adhesion
(D) B and C

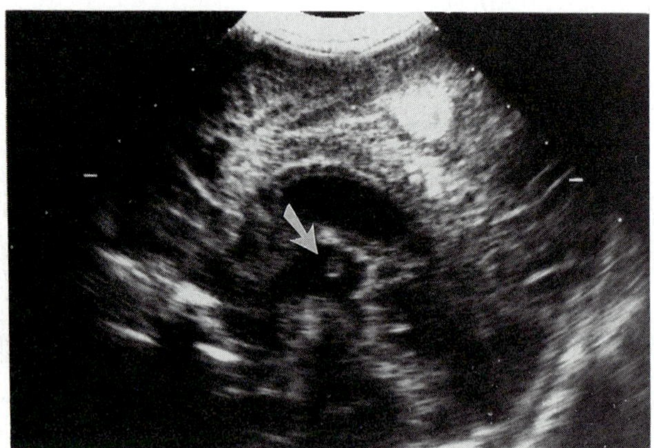

Figure 10–81. A sagittal sonogram.

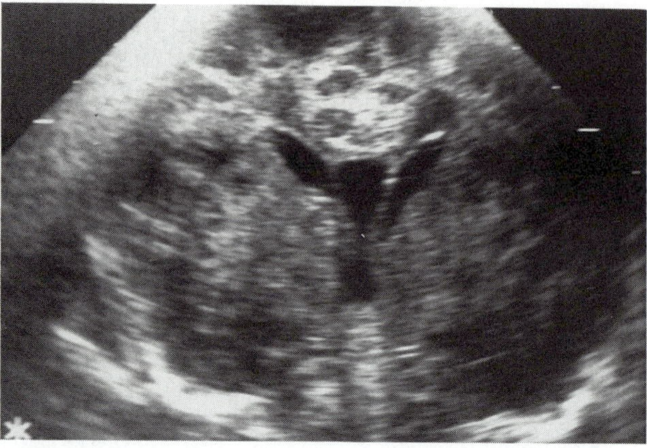

A

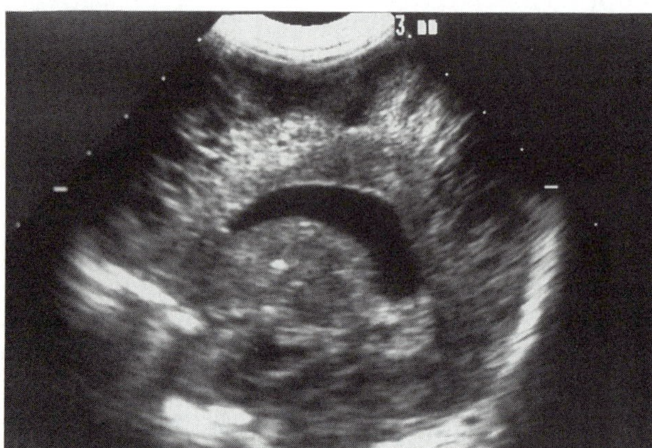

B

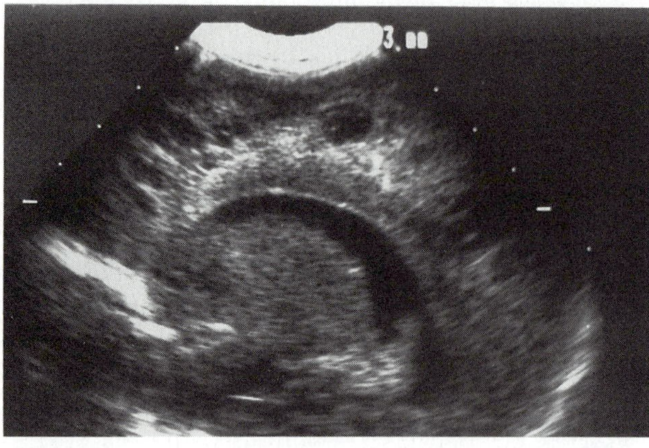

C

Figure 10–82. (**A**) A coronal sonogram; (**B**) a parasagittal sonogram; (**C**) a parasagittal sonogram.

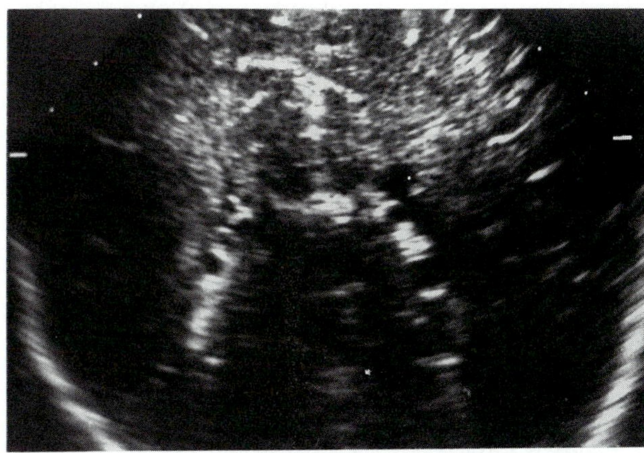

Figure 10–83. A coronal sonogram.

494. The abnormalities demonstrated in Fig. 10–81 also include

(A) intraparenchymal hemorrhage
(B) grade IV intracranial hemorrhage
(C) A and B
(D) subependymal hemorrhage

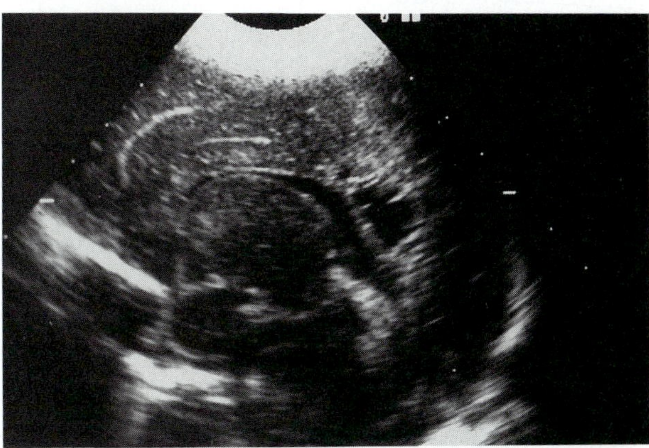

A

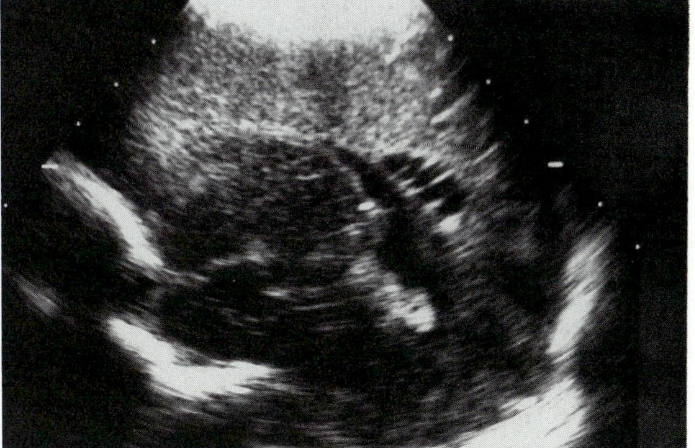

B

Figure 10–84. (**A**) A right parasagittal sonogram; (**B**) a left parasagittal sonogram.

495. The sonograms in Fig. 10–82 were taken from a 3-week-old neonate born at 31 weeks' gestational age. Which statements best describe the abnormal findings?

(A) encephalomalacia and enlarged ventricles
(B) diffuse hemorrhagic infarction
(C) periventricular leukomalacia
(D) A and B

496. Fig. 10–83 is a magnified coronal sonogram from a full-term neonate with a history of persistent pulmonary hypertension. The incidental finding is

(A) arachnoid cysts
(B) multiple irregular-shaped cysts in the glomus part of the choroid plexus
(C) intraventricular hemorrhage
(D) none of the above

497. The bilateral sagittal cranial sonograms in Fig. 10–84 demonstrate

(A) porencephalic cysts that communicate with the ventricles
(B) periventricular leukomalacia
(C) intraventricular hemorrhage
(D) B and C

498. At what level of the lateral ventricle is the coronal sonogram in Fig. 10–85 taken?

(A) occipital horns
(B) body
(C) frontal horns
(D) trigone region

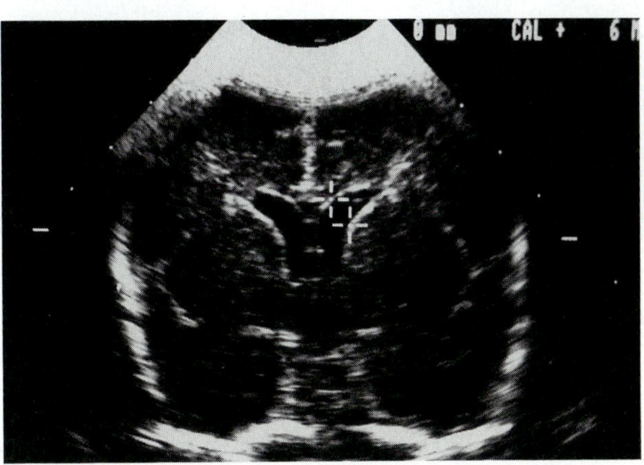

Figure 10–85. A coronal sonogram.

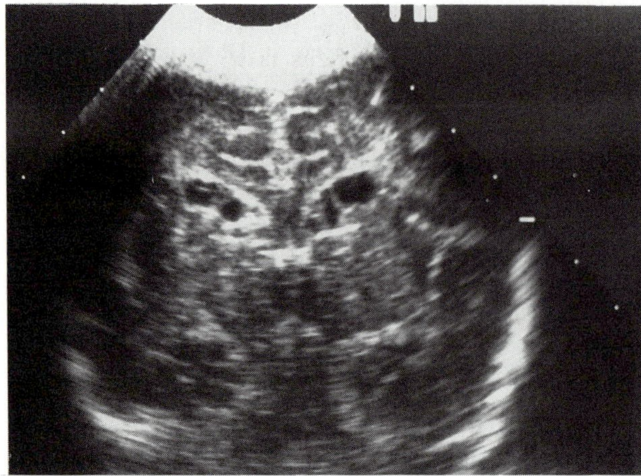

A

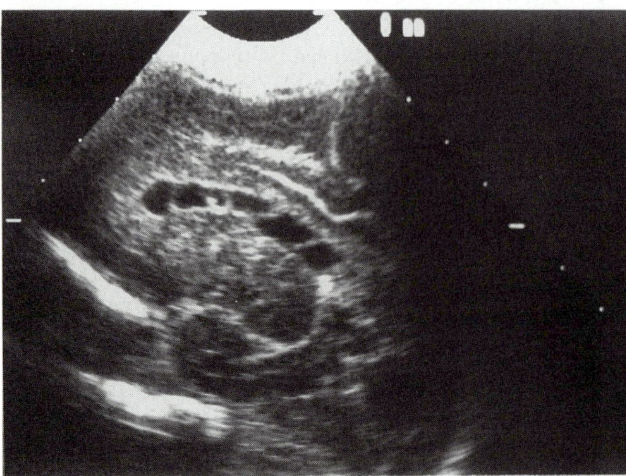

B

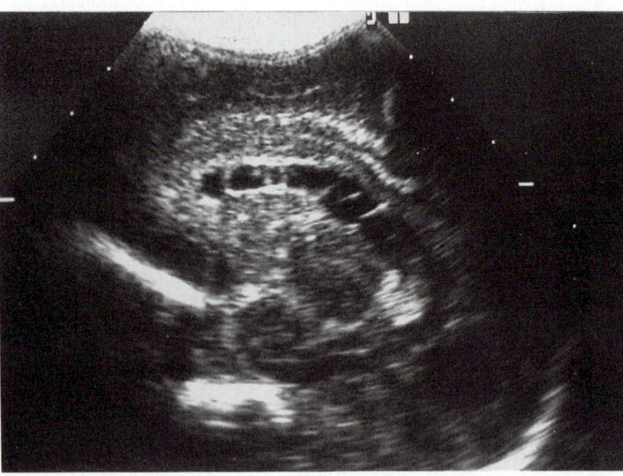

C

Figure 10–86. (**A**) A coronal sonogram; (**B**) a right parasagittal sonogram; (**C**) a left parasagittal sonogram.

499. With the development of hydrocephalus, which of the following portions of the lateral ventricle will dilate first?

(A) frontal horns
(B) temporal horns
(C) occipital horns
(D) body

500. The sonograms in Fig. 10–86 were taken from a 2-day-old full-term neonate with abnormal chromosomes, kidneys, and upper and lower extremities. The abnormal intracranial findings include

(A) cysts within the lateral ventricles
(B) septated lateral ventricles
(C) bilateral germinal matrix cysts
(D) bilateral porencephalic cysts in the frontal lobe of the cerebrum

501. Which of the following vessels supplies blood to the part of the brain lying in the anterior and middle cranial fossae?

(A) external carotid artery
(B) internal carotid artery
(C) vertebral artery
(D) basilar artery

502. Eight out of 12 neonates with meningitis usually develop

(A) ventriculitis
(B) intracranial hemorrhage
(C) abscess
(D) encephalomalacia

503. The most widely used frequency in cranial sonography of infants is

(A) 7.5 MHz
(B) 3.5 MHz
(C) 5.0 MHz
(D) 2.0 MHz

504. In cranial sonography, many neonates are examined in incubators and are attached to various types of equipment. Which of the following equipment can be removed?

(A) endotracheal tubes linked to a respirator
(B) scalp vein infusions
(C) an audible electrocardiographic monitor
(D) none of the above

505. When scanning neonates, excessive pressure should *not* be applied to the anterior fontanelle because it may

(A) cause increased heart rate
(B) cause slowing of the heart
(C) cause increased body temperature
(D) cause none of the above

506. An intraparenchymal hemorrhage is also known as

(A) intracerebral hemorrhage
(B) intraventricular hemorrhage
(C) intracranial hemorrhage
(D) choroid plexus hemorrhage

507. Which of the following best describes a subarachnoid hemorrhage?

(A) it may be seen as separation of the brain and skull or widening of the sylvian fissure or falx cerebri
(B) it occurs most commonly in temporal and frontal areas
(C) it is always echogenic
(D) it is usually the result of trauma and occurs in full-term infants

508. Which of the following statements best describes subarachnoid cisterns?

(A) subarachnoid cisterns are also known as lateral ventricles and contain cerebrospinal fluid
(B) they are a localized enlargement of the subarachnoid spaces where the dura mater and arachnoid do not follow the contour of the brain closely with the pia mater
(C) the subarachnoid cisterns serve as reservoirs for cerebrospinal fluid
(D) B and C

509. The quadrigeminal cistern is also known as

(A) ambient cistern
(B) vein of Galen cistern
(C) cistern veli interpositum
(D) cisterna magna

510. Optimal visualization of the subarachnoid cisterns in the fetus occurs in the

(A) second and late third trimesters
(B) second and early third trimesters
(C) late first and early second trimesters
(D) third trimester only

511. Enlargement of the subarachnoid spaces with ventriculomegaly in a fetus is an important clue in recognizing

(A) noncommunicating hydrocephalus
(B) communicating hydrocephalus
(C) nonobstructive hydrocephalus
(D) B and C

Match the definitions in Column B with the terms they define in Column A.

COLUMN A

512. periventricular leukomalacia
513. tentorium cerebelli
514. sulci
515. choroid plexus
516. cisterna magna
517. pia mater
518. corpus callosum
519. cavum septum pellucidum
520. insula
521. gyri
522. aqueduct stenosis

COLUMN B

(A) a enclosed space located caudad to the cerebellum, between the cerebellum and the occipital bone serving as a reservoir for cerebrospinal fluid
(B) folds on the surface of the brain
(C) special cells located in the ventricles that secrete cerebrospinal fluid
(D) softening of the white matter surrounding the ventricles
(E) congenital obstruction of the third and fourth ventricles resulting in ventricular dilation
(F) a group of nerve fibers above the third ventricle that connects the left and right sides of the brain
(G) a transverse division of dura mater forming a partition between the occipital lobe of the cerebral hemispheres and the cerebellum
(H) a triangular area of cerebral cortex, lying deeply in the lateral cerebral fissure
(I) grooves on the surface of the brain separating the gyri
(J) a cavity filled with cerebrospinal fluid that lies between the anterior horns of the lateral ventricle
(K) the inner membrane covering the brain and spinal cord.

Each of the following commonly used terms in Column B has an alternative name. Enter the alternative name for each term in Column A.

COLUMN A	COLUMN B
523. ______	massa intermedia
524. ______	temporal horn
525. ______	anterior horn
526. ______	occipital horn
527. ______	pineal gland
528. ______	germinal matrix hemorrhage
529. ______	trigone
530. ______	foramen of Monro

531. When doing a portable sonogram on a premature infant located in the neonatal intensive care unit, infection control is

(A) not necessary because the newborn has a lot of natural immunities
(B) not necessary because newborn isolates prevent all microorganism from entering
(C) a major concern because many infections originate from the hospital environment
(D) a nurse's responsibility

532. Term infants on extracorporeal membrane oxygenation (ECMO) who bleed intracranially can exhibit (1) hemorrhages in unusual locations, (2) hemorrhages originating in the germinal matrix, (3) a hemorrhage that sonographically is echogenic in appearance, (4) a hemorrhage that sonographically is hypoechoic or anechoic in appearance.

(A) 1 and 2
(B) 1 and 3
(C) 1 and 4
(D) all of the above

533. The major cerebral vascular feature of the brain at 24–28 weeks of gestation is well-developed circulation to the (1) basal ganglia, (2) cerebral cortex, (3) brain stem, (4) vermis of the cerebellum.

(A) 1 and 2
(B) 1 and 3
(C) 1 and 4
(D) 2 and 4

534. In periventricular leukomalacia, scans taken 3–6 weeks after the initial insult can demonstrate (1) markedly decreased vascular pulsations, (2) cysts in the echogenic areas previously described, (3) markedly increased vascular pulsations, (4) echo intensities at the external angle of the lateral ventricles and returning to a normal appearance.

(A) 1 and 2
(B) 2 and 4
(C) 1 and 4
(D) all of the above

535. On sonography, severe asphyxia of a term infant's brain at birth can sonographically demonstrate

(A) cerebral edema
(B) cortical necrosis
(C) diminished vascular pulsations
(D) all of the above

536. Early scans of a preterm infant brain that has periventricular leukomalacia can reveal

(A) increased echogenicity at the external angle of the lateral ventricles
(B) normal echogenicity surrounding the lateral ventricles
(C) cysts varying from a few small ones to multiple variably sized ones
(D) markedly decreased vascular pulsations

537. The main nutrient vessel of the subependymal germinal matrix tissue is the

(A) pericallosal artery
(B) callosal marginal artery
(C) posterior cerebral artery
(D) Heubner's artery

538. The period of maximum proliferation of neurons in the developing brain is

(A) 1–9 weeks of gestation
(B) 10–18 weeks of gestation
(C) 19–28 weeks of gestation
(D) 29–40 weeks of gestation

539. A well-defined hyperechoic mass observed contiguous sonographically with the corpus callosum is most likely to be

(A) a lipoma
(B) a glioma
(C) hemorrhage
(D) calcifications

540. The vessel that is insonated when a continuous-wave Doppler probe is placed on the anterior fontanelle and angled anteriorly is

(A) posterior cerebral artery
(B) middle cerebral artery
(C) pericallosal artery
(D) basilar artery

541. When a pulsed-wave Doppler transducer is placed on the anterior fontanelle, which cerebral vessel can be insonated with correct angulation of the probe?

(A) anterior cerebral artery
(B) pericallosal artery
(C) basilar artery
(D) internal carotid artery
(E) all of the above

542. When evaluating the intracerebral vessels of an infant's brain, the optimal frequency range for a continuous-wave Doppler transducer is

(A) 1–3 MHz
(B) 4–5 MHz
(C) 1–10 MHz
(D) 5–10 MHz

543. When using a transcranial approach with the transducer placed 0.5–1 cm anterior to the ear and superior to the zygomatic process, the vessel that can be evaluated most accurately in the newborn infant's brain is the

(A) middle cerebral artery
(B) anterior cerebral artery
(C) posterior cerebral artery
(D) posterior communicating artery

544. Which one of the following illustrations reveals the correct placement of a continuous-wave transducer through the anterior fontanelle for optimal waveform velocity of blood flow?

(A) A and B
(B) A
(C) B
(D) C

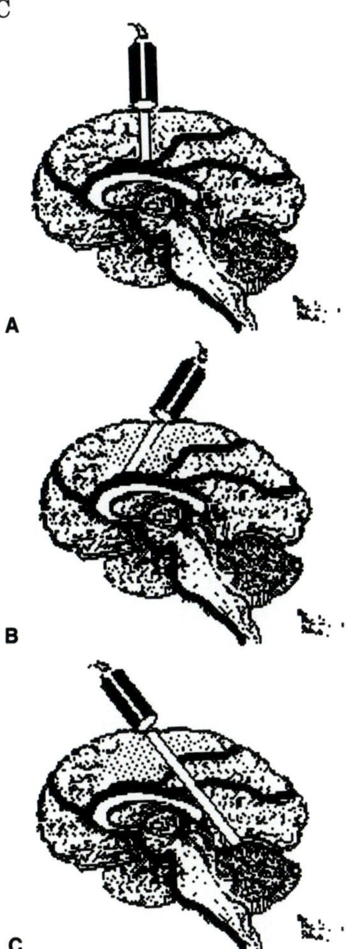

Questions 545–547: Identify the regions in the following diagram by placing the correct letters in the blanks.

545. end diastole _____

546. peak systole _____

547. cardiac cycle _____

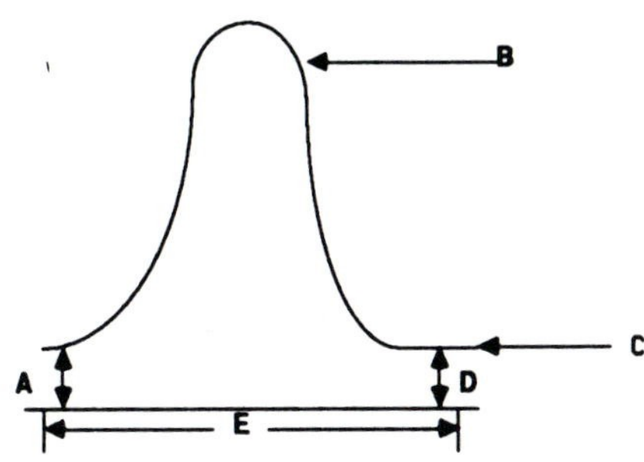

548. A normal pulsed-wave Doppler or continuous-wave tracing of an anterior cerebral artery demonstrates (1) forward flow throughout the cardiac cycle, (2) a triphasic pattern with reversal of flow in early diastole, (3) a vessel of high resistance, (4) a vessel of low resistance.

(A) 1 and 2
(B) 1 and 3
(C) 1 and 4
(D) 2 and 4

549. In a normal tracing of a cerebral vessel in an infant's brain, the maximum systolic amplitude is equivalent to the

(A) peak height
(B) area under the curve
(C) slope
(D) minimum height

550. With a real-time transducer, the vein of Galen normally is not a visible anatomic structure. To obtain a Doppler signal with a duplex scanner, the cursor would have to be placed (1) at the level of the vermis cerebellum, (2) in the appropriate area in the quadrigeminal plate cistern, (3) in the temporal lobe of the cerebral hemisphere, (4) beneath the splenium of the corpus callosum.

(A) 1 and 2
(B) 1 and 3
(C) 2 and 4
(D) 2 and 3

551. In a normal tracing of a cerebral vessel in an infant's brain, the end-diastolic amplitude is equivalent to the

(A) peak height
(B) area under the curve
(C) slope
(D) minimum height

552. The pressure and flow waveforms are influenced by

(A) cardiac contraction
(B) physical properties of the arterial walls
(C) the blood within the vessel
(D) the outflow impedance from the arterial tree
(E) all of the above

553. When using a Doppler probe (a continuous-wave or range-gated pulsed Doppler transducer), the scattering of the ultrasound by blood is attributed to the

(A) erythrocytes
(B) leukocytes
(C) platelets
(D) neutrophils

554. A Doppler tracing of an anterior cerebral artery in an infant with asphyxia can reveal (1) low pulsatility indexes, (2) high pulsatility indexes, (3) high diastolic forward flow, (4) low diastolic forward flow.

(A) 1 and 3
(B) 1 and 4
(C) 2 and 3
(D) 2 and 4

555. A Doppler tracing of an anterior cerebral artery in an infant with an intraventricular hemorrhage can reveal (1) low pulsatility indexes, (2) high pulsatility indexes, (3) high diastolic forward flow, (4) low diastolic forward flow.

(A) 1 and 3
(B) 1 and 4
(C) 2 and 3
(D) 2 and 4

Answers and Explanations

At the end of each explained answer there is a number combination in parentheses. The first number identifies the reference source; the second number or set of numbers indicates the page or pages on which the relevant information can be found.

1. **(A)** 1 and 2. Although all of the fontanelles and sutures can be used as an acoustic window to bypass the bone interface, the anterior and posterior fontanelles are used most frequently because of easy access to the paraventricular structures. *(1:24–25)*

2. **(A)** Periventricular calcifications. Infection of the fetal brain includes toxoplasmosis, rubella, cytomegalovirus, and herpes simplex (TORCH). These infections are acquired in utero; however, the diagnoses are usually made in the neonatal-infant period. All TORCH symptoms are characterized by periventricular calcifications. *(27:197)*

3. **(A)** Echoencephalography. A-mode echoencephalography was among the first sonographic techniques used to determine the position of midline structures of the brain. *(3:52)*

4. **(B)** The anterolateral fontanelle. The sphenoidal fontanelles are positioned anatomically anterior and lateral. *(5:345)*

5. **(D)** 12 months. Where several sutures meet, a triangular space is formed that encloses a membrane called a "soft spot" or fontanelle. The time that the fontanelles close varies with age. The mastoid fontanelles close completely by age 1 year. *(5:346)*

6. **(D)** 2–3 months. The posterior fontanelle closes at an early age; it is the first of all the fontanelles to close. *(5:346)*

7. **(D)** 18 months. The anterior fontanelle is the largest fontanelle and is the last to close. *(5:346)*

8. **(A)** Premature fusion of the cranial sutures. The prefix cranio relates to the cranium or skull. The suffix synostosis pertains to closure of the sutures. *(27:83)*

9. **(D)** Low temperature. Hypothermia (lowered body temperature) is defined as the reduction of body temperature below 35°C or 95°F. The clinically dramatic consequences of keeping a neonate in a cold environment, such as an air-conditioned ultrasound room, could result in shivering and lowered body temperature. *(22:716)*

10. **(D)** All of the above. There are multiple causes of hydrocephalus in utero. In addition to the causes listed, spina bifida and meningomyeloceles can cause hydrocephalus. *(27:70)*

11. **(D)** Posterolateral fontanelle. This is because the mastoidal fontanelles are positioned anatomically posterior and lateral. *(5:345)*

12. **(C)** 2–3 years. The parietal bones are relatively thin when compared with other cranial bones; therefore, measurements can be obtained up to 2 to 3 years after birth. *(2:180)*

13. **(A)** 40–60%. Studies indicate a higher incidence of intracranial hemorrhage in infants born at less than 32 weeks of gestation or in those whose birthweight is less than 1500 g. *(2:180; 8:209)*

14. **(E)** B, C, and D. The advantages of using a real-time linear array in neurosonography is to provide portable imaging of critically ill infants noninvasively and without ionization. In addition, it produces a dynamic portrayal of vascular pulsation. *(2:198–199)*

15. **(D)** 1, 2, 3, and 5. Linear-array real-time transducer produces a rectangular image. The type of transducer can be used to image the infant's brain. However, in visualizing the neonatal brain, it is

limited because of the small size of the fontanelle compared to the size of the transducer. In addition, the rectangular image produced by linear-array real-time fails on many occasions to visualize the inner walls of both sides of the calvarium simultaneously. *(2:180–199)*

16. **(A)** 1 only. The image must be sharp and clear. To avoid motion, the shutter speed on the multi-image camera must be faster than the frame rate of the videotape recorder. Experts have proved that the best method is exposure directly from the TV monitor through a multi-image camera. *(1:26, 2:181)*

17. **(D)** All of the above. The A-mode is a graphic presentation. This was used to evaluate hydrocephalus, mass lesions, and midline shift. *(2:179)*

18. **(A)** Axial. The sagittal and coronal CT views are useful but subject to artifacts: therefore, the axial plane is most compatible with sonography. *(1:24)*

19. **(B)** 2–3 months. The sphenoidals and posterior fontanelles close at about the same time. *(5:346)*

20. **(B)** 5 mm. The transducer should be placed on the parietal bone to obtain axial scans of the infant brain. Several sections should be obtained at intervals of 5 mm from above the external auditory meatus to the top of the infant cranium *(2:182)*

21. **(A)** They both diverge laterally as the project from the body of the lateral ventricles. The temporal horns (inferior horns) of the lateral ventricles are curved downward and extend laterally from the body of the ventricles. The tip of their inferior end extends around the posterior aspect of the thalamus. The occipital horns (posterior horns) of the lateral ventricles extend laterally from the body of the lateral ventricle and into the occipital lobe. *(2:183, 187; 8:29–31)*

Please see Study Guide for explanations for Questions 22–28.

22. **(C)** The posterior horn of the lateral ventricle. This is also called the occipital horn. *(1:29)*

23. **(B)** The choroid plexus and trigone of the lateral ventricle and the fourth ventricle. The trigone is also called the atrium. *(1:29)*

24. **(A)** The foramina of Monro and the third ventricle. *(1:29)*

25. **(D)** The frontal horn of the lateral ventricle. This is also called the anterior horn. *(1:29)*

26. **(A)** The third ventricle. *(1:29)*

27. **(B)** The temporal horn. This is also called the inferior horn. *(1:29)*

28. **(C)** The cavum septum pellucidum. *(1:29)*

29. **(D)** The lateral ventricular width/hemispheric width ratio is obtained by measuring the distance from the middle of the falx cerebri (midline echo) to the lateral wall of the lateral ventricle and dividing this by the distance from the falx cerebri (midline echo) to the inner table of the skull. Both measurements are taken from the same image. *(2:183; 27:64)*

30. **(C)** 35%. The percentage of the lateral ventricle width–hemispheric width ratio depends on when the sonogram was performed. The ratio is much higher in early pregnancy; however, as pregnancy advances there will be rapid growth of the cerebral hemispheres, which results in a decrease in the ratio. *(2:183; 27:64)*

31. **(D)** The external auditory meatus. The transducer is placed on the parietal bone above the ear. The tube-like passage in the ear is called the external auditory meatus. *(1:29)*

32. **(B)** 1 and 2. The axial scan gives the best anatomic levels for measurement in lateral ventricle width–hemispheric width ratio and for demonstrating a gravitational effect from blood cast. *(1:109; 2:183)*

33. **(D)** 2 and 4. The medial walls of the lateral ventricle may or may not be seen, depending on the angle of the sound beam. Because it is not usually seen with a normal gain setting, the actual width of the lateral ventricle is not measured. Therefore, the lateral ventricle height–hemispheric width ratio measures the ventricular size and appears to be the most useful index at this time. *(2:183)*

34. **(D)** 3 only. The caudate nucleus lies adjacent to the lateral wall of the lateral ventricle and extends posteriorly, tapering as it follows the curvature of the inferior lateral border of the body of the lateral ventricle. The tail extends into the roof of the temporal horn (inferior horn). *(2:183)*

35. **(D)** All of the above. The germinal matrix cannot be depicted as a distinct structure by computed tomography or sonography. The germinal matrix is a structure of the fetus that begins early in gestation and regresses as pregnancy advances. By 32 weeks to term, it may be completely absent. The location of the germinal matrix is above the caudate nucleus in the subependymal region of the lateral ventricle. *(2:183; 27:44)*

36. **(D)** The choroid is largest in the frontal horn and trigone region of the lateral ventricle. When the

head position of an infant changes, the choroid will fall to the gravity-dependent position. There is no choroid plexus in the frontal or occipital horn of the lateral ventricles. *(2:187; 8:235)*

37. **(A)** Anterior to the telea choroidea. The location is above the caudate nucleus; however, the most common site is anterior to the telea choroidea—the point at which the choroid attaches to the floor of the lateral ventricles. *(2:187; 27:121)*

38. **(A)** Above the caudate nucleus in the subependymal layer of the lateral ventricle. The germinal matrix forms the entire subependymal layer of the lateral ventricles in early gestation. After 24 weeks of gestation, the germinal matrix is present only over the head of the caudate nucleus. *(2:183; 27:45)*

39. **(D)** All of the above. The thalami are egg-shaped structures that sandwich the third ventricle. They lie inferior to the body of the lateral ventricle. The anterior margins are close to the columns of fornices and the foramen of Monro. The inferior margins are bound by the hypothalamus and the roof of the temporal horn. *(2:183; 27:42)*

40. **(D)** Echo-free space inferior to the cerebellum. The cisterna magna is anechoic (echo-free) and normally can be relatively large. It is located inferior to the cerebellum and should not be confused with a cyst. *(2:183; 27:186)*

41. **(D)** Middle cerebral arteries. On real-time sonography, a dense echo representing the Sylvian fissure can be seen near the lateral aspect of the brain on most coronal scans. The identification of symmetric pulsation in this fissure is the result of the middle cerebral arteries. *(1:95; 27:63)*

42. **(A)** The fissure and sulci both appear echogenic. The normal premature brain has numerous echogenic sulci. The echogenicity is caused by normal vascular structures. The fissures and cisterns also are echogenic. *(2:183; 27:209)*

43. **(A)** Telea choroidea. The point at which the choroid attach to the floor of the lateral ventricles is located behind the foramen of Monro. *(2:187; 27:121)*

44. **(B)** Between 32 and 40 weeks. The germinal matrix normally begins to regress around the 32nd week of gestation, first around the third ventricle, then around the temporal and occipital horns. The regression persists until birth, when it ceases to exist as a distinct structure. *(2:187; 27:45)*

45. **(A)** The cavum septum pellucidum. This structure is located between the frontal horns of the lateral ventricles. The third ventricle lies below the frontal horns and sandwiches between the thalami. *(2:187; 27:42)*

46. **(C)** 4 only. The caudate nucleus is divided into the head, body, and tail. It lies next to the lateral wall of the lateral ventricles. The head is the largest and is anterior in location. The caudate nucleus tapers as it extends posterior. The tail follows the curvature of the inferior horn of the lateral ventricle and the roof of the temporal horn. Both the caudate nucleus and the choroid plexus taper as they approach each other. *(2:190; 27:41)*

47. **(D)** 4 only. The cavum septum pellucidum is located between the frontal horns of the lateral ventricles. *(2:187; 27:42)*

48. **(B)** Bodies of the lateral ventricles. The fornix is the anatomic landmark dividing the cavum septum pellucidum anteriorly and the cavum vergae posteriorly. *(2:187; 27:42)*

49. **(C)** Thalami. *(2:187)*

50. **(A)** Increased echogenicity inferior and lateral to the frontal horn and body of the lateral ventricle. *(2:190; 27:121)*

51. **(D)** All of the above. The germinal matrix is a fetal structure consisting of loosely organized proliferating cells and connective tissue that give rise to neurons of the cerebral cortex and basal ganglia. It also contains many thin-walled veins. *(2:187; 27:45)*

52. **(D)** 67%. The incidence of germinal matrix hemorrhage varies with age. At 28 weeks, approximately two-thirds of fetuses have such hemorrhages. *(27:135)*

53. **(B)** 5%. The incidence of germinal matrix hemorrhage decreases as gestational age increases. *(2:187; 27:135)*

54. **(A)** A subependymal hemorrhage. The normal choroid tapers as it courses anterior to the foramen of the Monro. If a bulging density is seen after tapering, this finding may suggest subependymal hemorrhage. *(2:190)*

55. **(C)** A slightly oblique coronal view. An oblique coronal scan can result in a large choroid when compared to the other side. This pitfall can result in a false-positive diagnosis of subependymal hemorrhage. *(2:190)*

56. **(C)** An intraparenchymal hemorrhage. Most intraparenchymal hemorrhages appear as increased

echogenicity in the brain parenchyma and occur as a result of a subependymal hemorrhage. *(2:190; 27:126)*

57. **(A)** An intraventricular hemorrhage. These hemorrhages present as high-density echoes in the ventricles. They may present with clots or high-density cerebrospinal fluid blood levels. These findings are more evident with change of head position. *(27:123)*

58. **(C)** 7–14 days. The high-density echo within the brain parenchyma will present as an echogenic "rind" with a hypoechoic center at about this time (second stage). *(2:190; 27:128)*

59. **(D)** 2–4 weeks. At about this time, the clot settles in a dependent fashion and clot retraction can be depicted around the hemorrhage (third stage). *(2:190; 27:128)*

60. **(D)** Porencephaly. About 2 to 3 months after the hemorrhage, necrosis and phagocytosis are completed and an anechoic area termed porencephaly can be depicted (fourth stage) *(2:190; 27:128)*

61. **(C)** 1 and 2. The normal choroid plexus is echogenic and bulbous posteriorly. Therefore, an isolated choroid plexus hemorrhage may be difficult to diagnose. However, if a clot is attached to the choroid but is not in the subependymal area, an isolated choroid plexus hemorrhage is highly likely. *(2:191; 27:126)*

62. **(C)** A subdural hemorrhage. This type causes the sulci and gyri to appear prominent because they are outlined peripherally by the extracerebral blood. *(2:192)*

63. **(C)** Computed tomography. In neonates, a subarachnoid hemorrhage can be a difficult diagnostic problem both for computed tomography (CT) and sonography. However, CT is the preferred method of imaging to distinguish a subdural hemorrhage from a subarachnoid hemorrhage. *(27:147)*

64. **(C)** 90%–100%. Both computed tomography (CT) and sonography are reliable in the detection of intracranial hemorrhage. CT presents an image based on atomic number and density; as a result, a hemorrhage can become isodense and not be detectable at about 5 to 10 days. Ultrasound can detect intracranial hemorrhage for a much longer period than CT. The sensitivity of sonography in detecting an intracranial hemorrhage when compared to CT, is about 90–100% *(2:193; 27:117)*

65. **(D)** 5-10 days. On computed tomography, a hemorrhage can become isodense and may not be detectable after 5 to 10 days. *(2:197)*

66. **(A)** Same density. The term isodense denotes "same density" as soft tissue. This term is used in computed tomography (CT). A hemorrhage, for example, is presented as high density on CT and can become isodense after 5 to 10 days. *(22; 27:117–119)*

67. **(C)** 4 only. Pleural effusion is not among the many possible causes of intracranial hemorrhage. *(1:196; 7:100–107)*

68. **(D)** All of the above. There are many possible causes of intracranial hemorrhage: maternal ingestion of aspirin, infantile pneumothorax, hypoxia, extrauterine stress, hyaline membrane disease, acidosis, ischemia, hypertension, and hypercarbia. *(1:196; 7:100–107)*

69. **(C)** True. Intraoperative sonography can be used to identify the location of a cystic or solid spinal lesion and its extent. *(32:173)*

70. **(A)** A child during the first 28 days after birth. *(9:2)*

71. **(C)** All of the above. All of the given choices are associated with intracranial hemorrhage. (See the explanation for the answer to Question 68 for other possible causes.) *(7:100–107)*

72. **(A)** White matter surrounding the ventricles. This is the most common site for periventricular leukomalacia in premature infants. *(9:85–86)*

73. **(D)** Tuberous sclerosis. Developmental brain defects in organogenesis are classified in different groups such as neural tube closure, diverticulation, neuronal proliferation, and neuronal migration, organization, and myelination. Tuberous sclerosis is a disorder of histogenesis. *(27:91–93)*

74. **(A)** From 29 days after birth to 1 year. *(9:2)*

75. **(A)** Myelination. This occurs after birth, so defects of myelination are not called congenital. *(27:91, 93)*

76. **(B)** Papille et al. These authors developed the system in 1978 for grading of cerebroventricular hemorrhage (CVH) in that manner. *(41:56,59)*

77. **(E)** B and C. Scanning the infant in the isolette with the room temperature at about 75 to 78°F will prevent heat loss. *(27:5)*

78. **(A)** Alcohol. High-temperature sterilization, such as steam or heat, can damage the piezoelectric crys-

tals as well as the bonding cements. Oils also may damage bonding cements. Thus, sterilization with a glutaraldehyde-based solution or cleansing between examinations is recommended. *(27:9)*

79. **(E)** A, B, and D. Magnetic resonance, computed tomography, and static scanners were not designed for portable imaging of critically ill infants. *(27:5)*

80. **(A)** It can be done portably. Cranial sonography does not require transporting the critically ill infant. Scanning can be done in the isolette with portable real-time equipment. It allows identification of pulsating vascular structures. And it has no partial volume effect or isodense effect. *(2:198–199)*

81. **(D)** All of the above. Real-time images are normally obtained through the fontanelle; however, by the second year the bones of the vault interlock at the sutures and result in closure of the fontanelles. To obtain adequate studies in children older than 2, the images are obtained by scanning through openings in the bony cranium, such as craniotomy defects. *(1:23)*

82. **(C)** 1, 2, and 4. Because the fontanelles and sutures are normally open in infants younger than 18 months, this allows technically adequate studies. *(1:23)*

83. **(C)** 1, 2, and 3. Isolettes are equipped with heaters; thus, scanning in the isolette with portable real-time equipment prevents heat loss. If the infant has to be removed from the isolette, the room temperature should be controlled to maintain the infant's normal body temperature. *(1:24)*

84. **(D)** Intracranial hemorrhage. The term intraventricular hemorrhage was formerly used to refer to all types of cranial hemorrhage and caused some confusion in the terminology. The accepted term now is intracranial hemorrhage, which refers to any hemorrhage within the cranial vault. *(8:209;27:117)*

85. **(C)** Intraventricular hemorrhages. This type of hemorrhage is presented as echogenic material within the ventricles. An echogenic clot or elevated levels of blood in the cerebrospinal fluid may be present with a gravitational effect. *(27:123)*

86. **(B)** Subependymal hemorrhage. This type of hemorrhage originates in the germinal matrix and for this reason is also called a germinal matrix hemorrhage. These hemorrhages present as highly echogenic foci in the region of the caudate nucleus. However, the most common site is the telea choroidea. *(27:121)*

87. **(A)** Intraparenchymal hemorrhage. This type of hemorrhage is present at first as a homogeneous, highly echogenic focus. However, as hemorrhagic resolution proceeds through its stages, a variety of heterogeneous sonographic appearances can be identified. *(27:128)*

88. **(D)** Choroid plexus hemorrhages. This type of hemorrhage can be difficult to diagnose because both the normal choroid plexus and a choroid plexus hemorrhage appear echogenic. However, a choroid plexus that is heterogeneous in texture, irregular in contour, and bulbous in the anterior region, with echogenic foci extending from the choroid plexus into the ventricle would strongly suggest hemorrhage. *(8:209–211; 27:126)*

89. **(A)** 1, 2, and 3. This ımaginary line is called the orbitomeatal line, a radiographic baseline, or the canthomeatal line. The Reid's baseline is an imaginary line drawn from the infraorbital rim to the external auditory meatus. *(12:86)*

90. **(A)** Morphine sulfate. This medication has the fewest side effects. The use of chloral hydrate, Valium, and phenobarbital is not recommended in neonates because of their risks and side effects. *(27:3)*

91. **(C)** All of the above. A light dimmer is helpful not only for better viewing of the TV monitor on the real-time equipment but also for helping the infant stay quieter. Feeding the infant or providing a pacifier during the examination also may help. *(1:23)*

92. **(B)** 1, 2, and 3. Infants should be protected when restrained. Immobilization can be achieved by wrapping the infant's lower extremities together with an ace bandage or sheets. Five-pound sandbags also can be used to restrain the legs. Any device that might cause injury is not recommended. *(1:23)*

93. **(B)** 2 and 3. Studies indicate that intracranial hemorrhage is more common in infants born at less than 32 weeks' gestation and with birthweights less than 1500 g. *(27:117)*

94. **(B)** One parallel to a line 10° from the radiographic baseline. The transducer should be positioned over the parietal bones and 10° parallel from the canthomeatal line (radiographic baseline). *(8:184)*

95. **(A)** A subdural hemorrhage. Choroid plexus hemorrhages and subdural hemorrhages are more typical among full-term infants. *(27:118)*

96. **(B)** 90°. Coronal scans should be performed at 90° from the orbitomeatal line (canthomeatal line) and

the transducer should be angled to sweep from anterior to posterior. *(1:49)*

97. **(B)** 60°. All four ventricles and the posterior brain can be depicted when the transducer is angled 60°. *(1:50)*

98. **(A)** 150° from the orbitomeatal line and perpendicular to the clivus. The transducer should be positioned over the posterior fontanelle and should sweep anterior at 5 mm intervals. *(1:51)*

99. **(B)** 1 and 2. The fontanelles are used as an acoustic window by allowing an opening through which ultrasound can travel with little or no obstruction to bypass bony interfaces. *(10:15)*

100. **(B)** 3 only. The organisms associated most often with congenital infections of the nervous system are toxoplasmosis, rubella, cytomegalovirus, and herpes simplex (TORCH). Syphilis is associated but rare. Gonococcal infections are not among the organisms most often associated with congenital infections of the nervous system. *(1:186; 27:197)*

101. **(C)** 1, 2, and 4. The sonographic findings include periventricular calcifications, ventricular enlargement, and a small head (microcephalus). *(1:185; 27:197–199)*

102. **(D)** An isolated subependymal hemorrhage. There is no ultrasound grading system for intracranial hemorrhage. Therefore, the computed tomography classifications in current use are modified for sonography. The grades are from Grade I to Grade IV. Grade I is an isolated subependymal germinal matrix hemorrhage. *(8:210; 27:131)*

103. **(A)** The temporal and occipital horns. The lateral ventricle widens as it extends posteriorly from the body. This region of the lateral ventricle is called atrium or collateral trigone. It is formed by the junction with the temporal and occipital horns. *(8:216; 27:40)*

104. **(B)** Atrium. The trigone of the ventricle also is referred to as the atrium of the lateral ventricle. *(8:216–217)*

105. **(A)** Cerebral aqueduct. The foramen or passage between the third and fourth ventricles also is known as the aqueduct of Sylvius. *(8:217)*

106. **(A)** 1, 2, and 4. Hydranencephaly is a congenital deformity characterized by severe loss of cerebral tissue. The falx, midbrain, basal ganglia, and cerebellum are intact. *(8:191)*

107. **(B)** Dysgenesis of the vermis of the cerebellum. Dandy-Walker cysts are associated with dysgenesis (defective development) of the cerebellar vermis. *(8:191; 27:103)*

108. **(A)** 1 and 3. The purpose of a ventriculoperitoneal (V-P) shunt is to decrease the intraventricular pressure caused by hydrocephalus by shunting the fluid from the ventricle into the peritoneal cavity. *(8:246)*

109. **(B)** A ventriculoperitoneal (V-P) shunt. *(8:242)*

110. **(A)** 1 only. Clinical signs pertain to bedside observation. An x-ray and sonography are not clinical signs. *(9:221–222)*

111. **(A)** Aqueductal stenosis. This condition also can be associated with other abnormalities. *(8:224)*

112. **(A)** 2 and 3. Subarachnoid and intraventricular hemorrhages are the most common cause of obstructed flow resulting in ventricular enlargement. *(8:244)*

113. **(A)** Cephalohematomas. These are also called subperiosteal hematomas and refer to hemorrhages beneath the periosteum. *(1:194)*

114. **(D)** A traumatic delivery. *(1:194)*

115. **(A)** A mildly echogenic mass separating the scalp from the bony scalp. Sonographically, this type of hematoma is seen as a mildly echogenic mass separating the scalp from the bony calvarium (subdural region). *(1:194–198)*

116. **(A)** 40 weeks. Between the septum pellucidum is a fluid-filled cavity called the cavum septum pellucidum. The dorsal extension of the cavum septum pellucidum is called the cavum vergae. The fornix is the anatomic landmark dividing this single structure into two names. The cavum vergae is the first to start closure at about 24 weeks of gestation. The cavum septum pellucidum begins to close at term (40 weeks). *(8:218; 27:42)*

117. **(A)** The first ventricle. The lateral ventricles are the first and second largest of the four ventricles. *(8:216)*

118. **(B)** False. The lateral ventricles are divided anatomically into segments. The frontal horn extends anteriorly from the foramen of Monro to the body of the lateral ventricles posteriorly. *(8:216; 27:39)*

119. **(C)** The choroid plexus extends from the floor of the ventricle and medial aspects of the temporal

horn, the roof of the third ventricle, and the roof of the fourth ventricle. The choroid plexus is located in various positions of the ventricles. The choroid plexus can be found in each lateral ventricle and the third and fourth ventricles as well. There is no choroid plexus in the frontal and occipital horns. *(27:44, 166)*

120. **(B)** 5–7 days. An intracranial hemorrhage can occur during the first week of life. Because the incidence is higher in infants born before 32 weeks of gestation, sonographic screening is recommended soon after birth. *(8:214; 27:134)*

121. **(B)** False. A normal study on the first day following birth does not exclude further development. A hemorrhage can develop 3 to 5 days after birth. *(8:214; 27:134)*

122. **(C)** 3 and 4. Dandy-Walker syndrome is characterized by continuity of the fourth ventricle with a posterior fossa cyst and hydrocephalus. *(8:191)*

123. **(A)** Hydrocephalus. When a flashlight is positioned on the head of a newborn, the head may glow with light. This transillumination is associated with hydrocephalus. *(21:739, 801)*

124. **(C)** An intracranial hemorrhage because no choroid extends into this area. There is no choroid plexus in either the frontal or the occipital horn. *(27:44, 166)*

125. **(D)** The cause of hydranencephaly is unknown. However, the theoretical cause is thought to be intrauterine bilateral supraclinoid internal carotid arterial occlusion. *(8:191; 27:85)*

126. **(D)** The brainstem and a portion of the occipital lobe remain. Hydranencephaly is a congenital deformity characterized by a fluid-filled head with massive disruption of the cerebral hemispheres. The falx cerebri, cerebellum, and basal ganglia are usually intact. *(8:191; 27:84)*

127. **(A)** Severe hydrocephalus. The differential diagnoses for hydranencephaly are severe hydrocephalus, alobar holoprosencephaly, and massive subdural effusions. *(8:191; 27:86)*

128. **(A)** The corpus callosum. *(8:216–218)*

129. **(D)** The septum pellucidum. *(8:216–218)*

130. **(B)** The head of the caudate nucleus. *(8:216)*

131. **(A)** Posterior from the foramen of Monro to the collateral trigone. In other words, the ventricle extends from the intraventricular foramen (foramen of Monro) to the atrium (collateral trigone). *(8:216)*

132. **(A)** Above the corpus callosum. The pericallosal artery is the terminal branch of the anterior cerebral artery. It courses over the superior margin of the corpus callosum. *(8:218)*

133. **(B)** Region of the sylvian fissure and in the circle of Willis. The middle cerebral artery is the continuation of the internal carotid artery. *(7:87; 27:63)*

134. **(C)** 1 and 4. Frontal and occipital cortical mantle measurements are obtained in the axial scan. The frontal cortical measurements are taken from the lateral wall of the frontal horn extending anteriorly to the inner surface of the skull. The occipital is obtained by measuring the distance from the lateral wall of the occipital horn extending posteriorly to the inner surface of the skull. *(7:93; 27:158)*

135. **(D)** It is impossible in most cases to distinguish between an intracranial hemorrhage and a choroid plexus hemorrhage because both blood and the choroid are echogenic and both are homogeneous in texture. Although blood is echogenic and homogeneous in the first stage, it becomes heterogeneous in texture as it retracts. *(7:101)*

136. **(D)** Intraparenchymal hemorrhage. Extension of blood into the brain parenchyma is one of the most severe forms of hemorrhage. *(7:101)*

137. **(D)** 2 weeks. Hydrocephalus occurs first, followed by an increased head circumference approximately 14 days later. *(7:25)*

138. **(A)** Every 3 days until 2 weeks of age. *(7:117)*

139. **(B)** 18 days. The formation of the neural plate and its closure to form the neural tube is called neurulation. The time for this stage of development is approximately 18 or 19 days to begin and 26 days to close. *(13:270)*

140. **(A)** The prosencephalon. During embryologic development, the brain vesicles form the forebrain or prosencephalon, the midbrain or mesencephalon, and the hindbrain or rhombencephalon. *(13:370)*

141. **(D)** All of the above. Air bubbles can be eliminated by using liquid soap. *(13:277; 27:28)*

142. **(D)** Temporal and parietal bones. There are two squamous sutures, one on each side of the cranial bones. *(5:345)*

143. **(D)** All of the above. The circle of Willis is formed by eight arteries: two posterior cerebral arteries (ver-

tebral arteries), two anterior cerebral arteries (vertebral arteries), two internal carotid arteries, and one posterior and one anterior communicating arteries. *(15:12)*

144. **(C)** 12–16 weeks. *(27:74)*

145. **(C)** Normal septal veins. The presence of these veins represents normal intracranial anatomy in neonates. They extend vertically from the walls of the cavum septum pellucidum and should not be misinterpreted as pathology. *(38:623–624)*

146. **(A)** Linear-array real-time. The shape of the image depends on the equipment used: sector real-time (pie-shaped image), linear-array real-time (rectangular image), or automated scanner (panoramic image). *(1:20)*

147. **(B)** Frontal and parietal bones. *(5:344–347)*

148. **(C)** The two parietal bones and the occipital bone. *(5:344–347)*

149. **(D)** 20 weeks. The ventricular ratio is not constant, and it normally decreases in size as the gestational age increases. At 20 weeks gestation, the ventricles occupy more than 50% of the brain hemisphere. *(1:96)*

150. **(B)** The cerebrospinal fluid pathways within the brain are blocked. Hydrocephalus can be acquired or congenital. It is divided into noncommunicating or obstructive (blockage of cerebrospinal fluid within the brain) and communicating or nonobstructive (blockage of cerebrospinal fluid within the ventricular system). *(16:1539)*

151. **(C)** Cerebrospinal fluid is blocked within the ventricular system. *(16:1539)*

152. **(D)** A head that is largely filled with fluid and a severe loss of cerebral tissue. This congenital deformity of the head is characterized by complete or almost complete absence of the cerebral hemispheres. The head is largely filled with cerebrospinal fluid. *(1:152; 8:191)*

153. **(B)** Atresia of the foramen of Magendie and foramen of Luschka secondary to the failure of the vermis cerebellum to develop. The etiology of Dandy-Walker syndrome is believed to be failure of the vermis of the cerebellum to develop, which results in occlusion of the foramina of Magendie and Luschka. *(1:153; 27:80)*

154. **(A)** 1 and 2. Microcephaly is associated with Meckel-Gruber's syndrome, chromosomal abnormalities, rubella, and toxoplasmosis. *(27:85)*

155. **(A)** A congenital abnormality of the brain with elongation of the pons and fourth ventricle and downward displacement of the medulla into the cervical canal. The elongation of the pons is characterized by displacement of the fourth ventricle. *(27:95)*

156. **(B)** 1 only. Dandy-Walker syndrome is defined as cystic dilatation of the fourth ventricle with dysgenesis of the cerebellar vermis. *(8:191)*

157. **(D)** All of the above. Congenital hydrocephalus has multiple causes. Dandy-Walker malformation and chromosomal abnormalities can also be included. *(8:244)*

158. **(A)** Within the peritoneal cavity, in the right atrium, and in the gallbladder. The proximal end of the tube is normally placed within the ventricle, and the distal end is usually placed within the peritoneal cavity. However, other body cavities such as the right atrium or the gallbladder have been used. *(1:234; 8:246; 27:166)*

159. **(D)** All of the above. Holoprosencephaly is a developmental abnormality characterized by a single large midline ventricle and diverticulation of the forebrain. *(8:191–192)*

160. **(A)** One-way valve at the distal portion of the tube. This valve prevents back-flow of cerebrospinal fluid. The shunt has a distal and a proximal end and is used to remove excessive fluid from the ventricle to other body parts. *(8:246)*

161. **(D)** All of the above. Repeated infections also can be included in this list. *(1:235)*

162. **(D)** There are 12 pairs of cranial nerves and 31 pairs of spinal nerves. *(15:4)*

163. **(A)** L2. The spinal cord is shorter than the vertibral column and ends at about the second lumbar vertebra. *(15:4)*

164. **(D)** Two internal carotid and two vertebral arteries. These are the two main pairs of arteries that supply the brain with blood. *(15:8)*

165. **(B)** Basilar artery. The pons is the anatomic level at which the vertebral artery changes its name to the basilar artery. *(15:8)*

166. **(B)** Posterior cerebral artery. The cerebrum is the anatomic level at which the basilar artery changes its name to the posterior cerebral artery. *(15:8)*

167. **(A)** Loss of sensation on the left side of the body. Each side of the brain connects with the opposite

side of the body; therefore, obstruction of the right carotid artery causes loss of sensation on the left side. *(15:8)*

168. **(D)** All of the above. The central nervous system consists of the cerebellum, cerebrum, spinal cord, pons (brain stem), and medulla *(15:3)*

169. **(D)** Movement of extracellular fluid from blood. Only about 40% of cerebrospinal fluid is elaborated by the choroid plexus. The other 60% is produced by the movement of extracellular fluid from blood. *(27:155)*

170. **(D)** None of the above. The germinal matrix cannot be depicted by any of the three methods. *(27:44)*

171. **(A)** Basilar artery. The two vertebral arteries unite to form the basilar artery, which can be identified in the interpeduncular cistern in the notch of the heart-shaped cerebral peduncles. *(1:99; 27:63)*

172. **(B)** The trigone posteriorly. The occipital horn extends from the collateral trigone posteriorly into the occipital lobe. *(8:216)*

173. **(A)** It normally connects with the subarachnoid or ventricular fluid. Normally the cavum septum pellucidum does not connect with the subarachnoid or ventricular fluid. *(8:218)*

174. **(B)** Foramen of Monro. Each lateral ventricle is connected to the third ventricle via the foramen of Monro (the intraventricular foramen). *(27:40)*

175. **(F)** A, B, and D. Polymicrogyria (many small gyri) is associated with Chiari malformation, toxoplasmosis, cytomegalovirus, and abnormal thickening of the cortex. *(27:113)*

176. **(E)** A and B. A subependymal cyst is secondary to an intracranial hemorrhage, followed by porencephaly, then hydrocephalus. *(27:138)*

177. **(D)** The pericallosal artery. This artery is the terminal branch of the anterior cerebral artery. It courses above the superior margin of the corpus callosum. *(8:218–219)*

178. **(D)** The cerebral aqueduct. This is also called the aqueduct of Sylvius. *(27:40)*

179. **(C)** 1 and 3. The supraoptic recess also is called the preoptic recess. The infundibular recess is below the supraoptic recess. *(8:38)*

180. **(D)** 2 and 4. The two posterior recesses on the third ventricle are the pineal recess and the suprapineal recess. *(8:217)*

181. **(A)** An interthalamic adhesion. The place of fusion on the medial surfaces of the thalami on both sides of the third ventricle is called a massa intermedia or an interthalamic adhesion. *(18:38)*

182. **(C)** Grade O–IV. *(41:56, 59)*

183. **(C)** Normal-sized ventricles with no debris within them. The sonographic findings of ventriculitis include echogenic ventricular walls, septated ventricles, debris within the ventricles, and ventricular dilatation. *(40:83, 84, 91)*

184. **(C)** The palatine bone. The palatine is a facial bone. (See the explanation for the answer to Question 185.) *(39:190)*

185. **(C)** The skull is made up of one frontal bone, two parietal bones, two temporal bones, and one occipital, sphenoid, and ethmoid each. *(39:190)*

186. **(D)** The cerebellum. *(39:338)*

187. **(B)** 2. Periventricular leukomalacia can be found at the level of the white matter around the foramen of Monro and also between the middle cerebral artery and the posterior cerebral artery. However, it is most commonly found near the occipital horns and trigone (atrium) of the lateral ventricle. *(21:760)*

188. **(A)** A subarachnoid hematoma. Below the arachnoid is the subarachnoid space, which is located between the arachnoid and pia mater. *(18:3)*

189. **(B)** 1 and 3. The orbitomeatal line can be used as a reference point when scanning an infant's skull. It also is referred to as the radiographic baseline or the canthomeatal line. *(12:86)*

190. **(B)** The right and left lateral ventricles. *(20:301)*

191. **(A)** 40%. This percentage is produced by the choroid plexus. The remainder is produced by movement of the extracellular fluid. *(27:155)*

192. **(C)** 532–576 mL/day. In an adult the amount of cerebrospinal fluid produced daily is between 600 to 700 ml. In children it is less. *(18:9; 27:156)*

193. **(B)** An intraparenchymal hemorrhage. Any hemorrhage into the brain parenchyma is called an intraparenchymal hemorrhage. *(8:209–215)*

194. **(D)** A germinal matrix hemorrhage. *(1:194)*

195. **(C)** An epidural hematoma. The accumulation of blood between the dura mater and the inner table of the skull. *(1:194)*

196. **(B)** A subdural hematoma. *(1:194)*

197. **(C)** The infundibular horn. The lateral ventricles are comprised of five parts: the frontal horn, the body (corpus), the trigone (atrium), the posterior horn, and the inferior horn. *(18:28–31)*

198. **(C)** The inferior horn (cornu). *(18:29)*

199. **(B)** The posterior horn (cornu). *(18:29)*

200. **(A)** The temporal horn (cornu). *(18:29)*

201. **(A)** Intraventricular foramen. *(18:29)*

202. **(A)** The ophthalmic artery. Symmetric pulsatile arteries that are normally seen with real-time sonography are the middle cerebral, the anterior cerebral, the basilar, the pericallosal, and the carotid. *(1:94–98)*

203. **(B)** The cerebral hemispheres. They are paired brain matter separated from the midline by the falx cerebri. *(20:294)*

204. **(B)** Posterior to the foramen of Monro and superior to the third ventricle. *(27:192)*

205. **(A)** The spinal cord. The brain stem consists of the diencephalon, the midbrain, the pons, and the medulla oblongata. *(39:357)*

206. **(A)** 1, 2, and 3. The cavum septum pellucidum is not related to the Chiari II malformation. However, the massa intermedia is related, with enlargement in 82% to 90% of cases. Hydrocephalus and meningomyelocele also are associated. *(1:140)*

207. **(C)** 1 and 2. The differential diagnosis for hydrocephalus with a similar sonographic appearance is hydranencephaly. *(8:191)*

208. **(A)** Intracranial infections can be bacterial or viral

BACTERIAL	VIRAL
Diplococcus pneumoniae	toxoplasmosis
Haemophilus influenzae	mumps
bacterial meningitis	cytomegalovirus
	herpes simplex

(1:184)

209. **(A)** Epidural and subdural hemorrhages more typically occur in term infants. *(27:118)*

210. **(D)** The facial anomalies that can be associated with holoprosencephaly are cleft palate (fissure), cleft lip (fissure), cyclopia (single orbital fossa), cebrocephaly (characterized by a defective nose and closed eyes), and ethmocephaly (characterized by a defect of the ethmoid bone). *(1:174)*

211. **(C)** The incidence of intracranial infection is 20/10,000 premature births and 2/10,000 term births. *(1:184)*

212. **(D)** All of the listed answers are functions of the hypothalamus including the controlling of body temperature, sleep, heart rate, glandular secretions of the stomach, hunger, and water and electrolyte balance. *(20:304)*

213. **(B)** The brain is invested by three membranes termed PAD for pia, arachnoid, and dura mater. *(18:1–4)*

214. **(A)** The prefix *leuko* denotes white. The suffix *malacia* denotes morbid softening. Therefore, leukomalacia translates into morbid softening of the white matter. If this occurs around the ventricles, it is called periventricular leukomalacia. *(21:760; 22:868)*

215. **(C)** Neuropathic complications of periventricular leukomalacia include hemorrhage and cavitation within the cerebral white matter. *(19:127)*

216. **(D)** The thalamus is one of two ovoid structures that lie on either side of the third ventricle. It is *not* one of the cranial nerves. See Study Guide, p. 519. *(20:308–309)*

217. **(A)** A deep groove in the brain is called a fissure. *(20:294)*

218. **(B)** The central fissure is also called central sulcus or fissure of Rolando. *(20:295)*

219. **(D)** The place of fusion between the third ventricle and the medial surface of the thalami is called the massa intermedia or interthalamic adhesion. *(18:38)*

220. **(D)** The pineal nerve is *not* a cranial nerve. *(18:99–109)*

221. **(D)** All of the above. *(18:19–106)*

222. **(D)** The septum pellucidum. The dura mater is comprised of three structures: the falx cerebri, the falx cerebelli, and the tentorium cerebelli. *(20:287)*

223. **(D)** The etiology of a porencephalic cyst is a subependymal hemorrhage that extends into the brain parenchyma, an infection, an infarction, or trauma. *(1:153; 27:186)*

224. **(D)** All of the above. Holoprosencephaly may be associated with trisomy, toxoplasmosis, amino acid

abnormalities, rubella, diabetes, and endocrine dysgenesis. *(1:174)*

225. **(B)** 2 and 4. Computed tomography is the method of choice in screening subarachnoid and subdural hemorrhages. *(1:198)*

226. **(C)** 1 and 3. Sonography should be the imaging modality of choice for investigation of premature infants with a subependymal or intraparenchymal hemorrhage. Computed tomography is a better choice for term infants with subarachnoid and subdural hemorrhage. *(1:198)*

227. **(B)** A subdural hematoma. The gyri and sulci of the brain are more prominent in a subdural hematoma and are usually obscured in intracranial infections, infarctions, and intracranial hemorrhages, with the exception of subdural hematoma. *(27:209)*

228. **(B)** 24–32 weeks. The germinal matrix subsequently regresses in size and is absent at birth. *(1:196)*

229. **(D)** Cyclopia. This is a developmental anomaly, not a tumor. *(1:226)*

230. **(A)** 1 and 3. Brain tumors are rare in infants and children. The constitute only 12 to 15% of tumors in infants and children and are less frequent in infants younger than 2 years. *(1:226)*

231. **(A)** Ischemic lesions of the neonatal brain characterized by necrosis of periventricular white matter. *(21:760)*

232. **(B)** 1, 3, and 4. Dandy-Walker syndrome is characterized by cystic dilatation of the fourth ventricle. It is associated with cerebellar vermian dysgenesis, agenesis of the corpus callosum, and holoprosencephaly. *(1:153)*

233. **(A)** 1, 2, and 3. The causes of an arachnoid cyst are arachnoid lesions, entrapment of subarachnoid or cisternal space, and abnormal leptomeningeal formation. *(1:153)*

234. **(D)** All of the above. There are many explanations for periventricular leukomalacia, including infarction, ischemic injury, hypoxic injury, and failure of arterial perfusion. *(9:85–86; 19:127–128; 23:705–707)*

235. **(A)** Sylvian fissure. This fissure, also called the lateral sulcus is at a right angle to the longitudinal fissure. *(20:295)*

236. **(D)** Sulcus. A deep groove is called a fissure. *(20:295)*

237. **(F)** A, C, and D. The most common infections acquired in utero are toxoplasmosis, rubella, cytomegolovirus, and herpes simplex (TORCH). *(27:197)*

238. **(E)** A, B, and C. Macrocephalus, an enlarged head, is not associated with toxoplasmosis. *(27:199)*

239. **(D)** To increase the viscosity of the newborn's respiratory secretions. The reason for placing an infant in an isolette is to maintain an environment similar to that of the uterus, with heat, humidity and oxygen. The isolette also provides isolation and protection from infection. *(24:242)*

240. **(D)** All of the above. *(18:7–8)*

241. **(A)** It usually is not viable in utero. Generally, anencephalic fetuses are viable in utero but die soon after birth. *(27:77)*

242–244. See Fig. 10–23, p. 521 in the Study Guide.

245–259. See Fig. 10–19, p. 520 in the Study Guide.

260–262. See Fig. 10–23, p. 521 in the Study Guide.

263–270. See Fig. 10–3, p. 518 in the Study Guide.

271–272. See Fig. 10–24, p. 521 in the Study Guide.

273–276. See Fig. 10–25, p. 521 in the Study Guide.

277–284. See Fig. 10–16, p. 520 in the Study Guide.

285–296. See Fig. 10–26, p. 521 in the Study Guide.

297–311. See Fig. 10–5, p. 518 in the Study Guide.

312–320. See Fig. 10–4, p. 518 in the Study Guide.

321–324. See Fig. 10–10, p. 519 in the Study Guide.

325–326. See Fig. 10–11, p. 519 in the Study Guide.

327–332. See Fig. 10–12, p. 519 in the Study Guide.

333–335. See Fig. 10–8, p. 519 in the Study Guide.

336–340. See Fig. 10–9, p. 519 in the Study Guide.

341–342. See Fig. 10–7, p. 519 in the Study Guide.

343–348. See Fig. 10–6, p. 518 in the Study Guide.

349. **(A)** Hypoxia. Hypoxic and ischemic injuries account for the greatest number of fetal deaths. *(21:752)*

350. **(A)** A decrease in the size of the sylvian fissure as the neonatal brain matures. Lissencephaly is characterized sonographically by large sylvian fissures and ventricles. *(27:111)*

351. **(D)** Suffocation. *(22)*

352. **(F)** Death of tissue. *(22)*

353. **(J)** Deficiency of blood in a body part. *(22)*

354. **(G)** Diminished content of glucose in the blood. *(22)*

355. **(E)** Low oxygen content. *(22)*

356. **(B)** Accumulation of body acid. *(22)*

357. **(C)** Lack of oxygen. *(22)*

358. **(H)** Excess carbon dioxide in the blood. *(22)*

359. **(A)** Cessation of breathing. *(22)*

360. **(I)** Incomplete closure of the neural tube. *(22)*

361. **(A)** The cavum septi pellucidi. This fluid-filled median cavity in the septum pellucidum is also referred to as the fifth ventricle. The posterior extension of the cavum septi pellucidi is the cavum vergae (sixth ventricle). These structures are presented on cranial sonography in premature infants and lie between the frontal horns and body of the lateral ventricles. *(8:218; 38:623)*

362. **(A)** Spina bifida. Anencephaly denotes the absence of the cranial vault and brain tissue. It is associated with multiple congenital anomalies such as spina bifida and meningocele. *(27:77)*

363. **(D)** 2 and 4. *(27:199)*

364. **(D)** Remove all dressings and fracture weights carefully before scanning. Sonographers can reduce unnecessary accidents among infants by being conscious about safety measures. Do not remove any dressing or fracture weights without permission. Always wash your hands before and after scanning. Check for the patient's proper name and identification before scanning, and never leave an infant unattended. *(28:23, 216)*

365. **(D)** 1, 3, 4, and 5. The reasons for placing premature babies in incubators are to maintain environmental conditions similar to those in utero, protect the infant from infection, and to supply oxygen. *(28:88)*

366. **(A)** Prevent strain on the neck. *(28:88)*

367. **(C)** Semi-Fowler's position. This position assists in drainage and prevents pressure on the site. *(28:89)*

368. **(D)** Supine position. This is the usual position to assist in drainage. Too rapid reduction of fluid may lead to seizure. *(28:89)*

369. **(D)** Use bar soap in preference to liquid soap and be certain that the soap dish is of organisms causing disease. Liquid soap is preferred to bar soap because the soap dish and sink are considered contaminated. *(31:30)*

370. **(B)** 2, 3, and 5. The entries should be written only after the sonogram has been done and must include the time and date. Use a pen, *not* a pencil. Do not erase if you make an error; just draw a line through the mistake, write the word "error" over it, and continue the entry. *(30:75)*

371. **(E)** All of the above. The sonographer is responsible for the patient during a sonographic examination. Good observations and reports are the responsibility of all health care professions. *(30:652)*

372. **(A)** The first 2 years of life. *(30:428)*

373. **(B)** An "old" germinal matrix hemorrhage that has undergone fibrinolysis. *(31:280)*

374. **(B)** That the clot has undergone fibrinolysis and therefore has been present for at least 3 days. The hypoechoic appearance indicates that fribinolysis has occurred. *(31:280)*

375. **(B)** A bilateral germinal matrix hemorrhage with mild ventricular dilatation of the left lateral ventricle. *(31:281)*

376. **(B)** 5–7 days. Ventricular dilatation is usually observed 5 to 7 days after the initial cerebroventricular hemorrhage (CVH). It may spontaneously resolve up to 14 days after the initial CVH. *(31:262–264)*

377. **(B)** The tentorium. *(39:338)*

378. **(C)** The septum pellucidum is superior to the third ventricle. It is not present in complete agenesis of the corpus callosum. *(27:105)*

379. **(A)** Marked ventricular dilatation of the lateral ventricles and third ventricle. *(27:124)*

380. **(A)** Interventricular foramina (foramina of Monro). The arrows in the figure point to the dilated foramina of Monro. *(31:278)*

381. **(A)** An extensive intraventricular hemorrhage with

an intraparenchymal hemorrhage. The sonogram shows an extensive intraventricular hemorrhage bilaterally and a large intraparenchymal hemorrhage in the left parietal area. *(31:283)*

382. **(B)** The arrows in the figure point to hypoechoic areas representing porencephalic changes in the periventricular brain matter where the intraparenchymal hemorrhage was. *(31:283)*

383. **(A)** Increasing the near-field TGC. This would improve the depiction of the most proximal portion of the brain. *(31:37)*

384. **(A)** Normal. The normal choroid plexus can appear slightly bumpy, as is shown in the figure. Sometimes, intraventricular clots can layer upon the choroid plexus making it appear "bumpy." *(31:383)*

385. **(A)** An intraventricular hemorrhage that is layering in the left occipital horn. *(31:282)*

386. **(B)** An intraventricular hemorrhage layering within the occipital horn. The choroid plexus does not usually extend into the occipital horn; therefore, any echogenic interfaces within the occipital horn usually represent an intraventricular hemorrhage. *(31:282)*

387. **(B)** An intraventricular hemorrhage layering within the lateral ventricle. *(31:281)*

388. **(B)** Occurs only with a subependymal hemorrhage. An intraventricular hemorrhage usually occurs as a sequela of a germinal matrix hemorrhage (GMH). Note that a subependymal hemorrhage is the same as GMH. *(31:287)*

389. **(D)** A quadrigeminal cyst is not caused by a vein of Galen aneurysm. However, it may be a differential diagnosis because of its location and cystic components. Doppler evaluation should exclude a differential diagnosis. *(27:192)*

390. **(A)** Arachnoid cysts lie between the arachnoid membrane and the dura mater and not between the pia mater and the subarachnoid space. Acquired arachnoid cysts are found in cisterns adjacent to the third ventricle, sella, and posterior fossa. *(27:87, 188, 189)*

391. **(C)** They lie in the sagittal sinus and reabsorb cerebrospinal fluid as it circulates. *(27:155, 156)*

392. **(C)** It separates the frontal lobe from the temporal lobe and forms a right angle with the central sulcus: the middle cerebral artery pulsates there. The central sulcus also is known as the lateral sulcus. The anterior artery also pulsates there. *(39:347; 27:47)*

393. **(C)** A simple cyst in the glomus part of the lateral ventricle. A study done with fetuses that had simple choroid plexus cysts revealed a normal karyotype and no significant related abnormalities. Babies were delivered with no neurological abnormalities at the time of the neonatal examination. *(43:78)*

394. **(B)** The sylvian fissure. The structure is shown in the sagittal view. *(40:42)*

395. **(D)** The third ventricle. *(40:38, 39)*

396. **(A)** The interhemispheric fissure. The structure is shown in the coronal view. *(40:34, 36)*

397. **(C)** The frontal horns of the lateral ventricle. The horns are slightly dilated. *(40:39)*

398. **(D)** The cingulate sulcus. *(40:45)*

399. **(A)** Corpus callosum. *(40:45)*

400. **(B)** The conus medullaris. The spinal cord is the distal continuation of the central nervous system. It terminates as the conus medullaris at the end of the second lumbar vertebra. *(44:125)*

401. **(D)** The second lumbar vertebra. (See the explanation for the answer to Question 400.) *(44:125)*

402. **(C)** Parieto-occipital sulcus. *(40:45)*

403. **(D)** The occipital bone. *(41:14)*

404. **(A)** Grade IV hemorrhage. *(27:133)*

405. **(C)** Parenchymal, germinal matrix, and intraventricular hemorrhages are present. *(27:133)*

406. **(C)** A unilateral germinal matrix hemorrhage. *(27:125)*

407. **(A)** A Dandy-Walker cyst. The sonogram shows a typical Dandy-Walker cyst. *(34:73)*

408. **(D)** All of the above. Dandy-Walker cysts are associated with dilatation of the fourth ventricle because of atresia of the foramen of Magendie and absence of the inferior vermis. *(1:153; 34:73)*

409. **(B)** The sylvian fissure. *(36:821)*

410. **(A)** The cistern magna. *(36:821)*

411. **(B)** The occipital horns. A change in shape without a change in size occurs first in the frontal horns. However, the occipital horns enlarge first and the frontal horns enlarge last. *(27:158)*

412. **(A)** Marked atrophy of the cerebrum. This can be seen secondary to profound ischemia. *(37:417)*

413. **(D)** A and B. Initially, multiple punctate echogenicities can be seen throughout the brain parenchyma. On follow-up scans a few weeks after birth, brain atrophy can be identified. *(37:417)*

414. **(A)** Frontal horns anterior to the foramen of Monro. The reason for this position is to avoid obstruction of the shunt tip by choroid plexus. No choroid plexus extends into the frontal horns or the occipital horns of the lateral ventricle. *(27:166)*

415. **(B)** An enlarged septum pellucidum. In complete agenesis of the corpus callosum there is no septum pellucidum or corpus callosum. In addition, the third ventricle undergoes upward displacement. *(27:105)*

416. **(A)** The septum pellucidum. In septo-optic dysplasia, schizencephaly, and agenesis of the corpus callosum, the septum pellucidum is absent. *(27:108)*

417. **(A)** At the level of the third ventricle and the aqueduct of Sylvius. *(27:192)*

418. **(D)** The septum pellucidum is dilated. Schizencephaly is characterized by agenesis of the corpus callosum and septum pellucidum in addition to unusually shaped frontal horns of the lateral ventricles. *(27:112)*

419. **(A)** It is a febrile disease characterized by eruptions resembling measles; it is also called German measles. If German measles occurs during the first trimester of pregnancy, the child may have a congenital defect. *(9:136)*

420. **(D)** 2 and 3. *(30:428)*

421–433. See Figure 10–17, p. 520 in the Study Guide.

434–438. See Figure 10–13, p. 519 in the Study Guide.

439–443. See Figure 10–14, p. 519 in the Study Guide.

444–453. See Figure 10–15, p. 520 in the Study Guide.

454–460. See Figure 10–22, p. 521 in the Study Guide.

461–467. See Figure 10–27, p. 522 in the Study Guide.

468–471. See Figure 10–18, p. 520 in the Study Guide.

472–480. See Figure 10–28, p. 522 in the Study Guide.

481. **(C)** Enlarged ventricles with an area of porencephaly at the region of the body of the left lateral ventricle. *(27:128, 129)*

482. **(B)** Resolving intraparenchymal and intraventricular hemorrhages. The irregularity noted in the choroid plexus region is a sign of intraventricular hemorrhage. *(27:133)*

483. **(C)** Hydrocephalus. The abnormal finding is a severe form of post hemorrhagic hydrocephalus. *(40:111, 117)*

484. **(B)** The choroid plexus. *(40:37)*

485. **(B)** The abnormal findings in Figure 10–76 revealed enlarged lateral ventricle, an enlarged third ventricle, an enlarged fourth ventricle, a dilated foramen of Monro, and a dilated aqueduct of Sylvius. *(27:164)*

486. **(D)** The pineal recess. The recess is dilated. The recesses of the third ventricle are as follows: supraoptic, infundibular, pineal, and suprapineal. *(27:40, 41, 44)*

487. **(B)** The fourth ventricle. *(27:164)*

488. **(A)** One of the lateral ventricles. The ventricle is enlarged. *(41:129)*

489. **(C)** The temporal horns of the lateral ventricles. Both are enlarged. *(41:128)*

490. **(D)** A resolving intraventricular hemorrhage and periventricular leukomalacia. The lateral ventricles are enlarged, and small cystic areas are seen in the periventricular regions. *(40:120)*

491. **(C)** A germinal matrix hemorrhage with subependymal cysts. *(40:112, 113)*

492. **(A)** The septal vein. *(38:623)*

493. **(D)** The massa intermedia. The massa intermedia (or interthalamic adhesion) is visualized best in the presence of ventricular dilatation. *(27:41, 99; 40:89)*

494. **(C)** A and B. An intraparenchymal hemorrhage or a grade IV hemorrhage also is present. An isolated parenchymal hemorrhage is considered to be grade IV when any or all of the following are present: a subependymal hemorrhage, an intraventricular hemorrhage, and hydrocephalus. *(27:132; 45:312)*

495. **(D)** A and B. This neonate may have had a generalized cerebral edema that led to multiple areas of infarction termed encephalomalacia or porencephaly. *(27:213)*

496. **(B)** Multiple irregular-shaped cysts in the glomus part of the choroid plexus. (See also the explanation for the answer to Question 393.) In addition, a study involving complex choroid plexus cysts revealed trisomy 18 and 21. *(43:78, 81)*

497. **(D)** B and C. The abnormality demonstrated is bilateral periventricular leukomalacia and intraventricular hemorrhage. *(40:12)*

498. **(C)** The frontal horns. *(27:17)*

499. **(C)** The occipital horns. The frontal horns will dilate last because the occipital horns are larger and can provide more room for expansion before moving to the frontal horns. *(27:158)*

500. **(B)** Septated lateral ventricles. In these sonograms, multiple partitions are seen extending to the lateral walls of the ventricles. This particular case is congenital; however, septated ventricles usually occur in ventriculitis. *(40:83)*

501. **(B)** The internal carotid artery. This artery terminates by dividing into the anterior and middle cerebral arteries. *(39:692,693; 41:19, 20)*

502. **(A)** Ventriculitis. These neonates initially develop meningitis, edema, and cerebritis. Eight of 12 neonates with meningitis develop ventriculitis. Late complications include subdural effusion, enlarged ventricles, and ventricular septations. *(27:199)*

503. **(C)** 5.0 MHZ. As the head enlarges, a 3.5 MHZ focus transducer can be used; 7.5 MHZ transducers are best for use in extremely small infants (below 1500 g) because of their excellent near-field resolution. *(46:1)*

504. **(D)** None of the above. Special care must be taken not to dislodge the following when examining babies in incubators: endotracheal tubes linked to a respirator, scalp vein infusions, and audible electrocardiographic monitors. Removing them would endanger the neonate's life. *(46:4)*

505. **(B)** Cause slowing of the heart. *(46:5)*

506. **(A)** Intracerebral hemorrhage is the same as intraparenchymal hemorrhage. Intracranial hemorrhage includes all the different types of hemorrhage within the cranium. *(46:5,7)*

507. **(A)** A subarachnoid hemorrhage may be seen as separation of the brain and skull or widening of the sylvian fissure or falx cerebri and as densely echogenic or echolucent areas. *(46:7)*

508. **(D)** B and C. Subarachnoid cisterns are localized enlargements of the subarachnoid spaces that occur in areas where the dura mater and arachnoid do not follow the contour of the brain closely with its covering, the pia mater. Subarachnoid cisterns serve as reservoirs for cerebrospinal fluid. *(47:365)*

509. **(B)** The vein of Galen cistern. It lies in the angle between the superior surfaces of the cerebellum and the mesencephalon. *(47:365)*

510. **(B)** Second and early third trimesters. During these trimesters, the distance of the fetal head from the transducer allows the use of a 5 MHz probe, which gives clear resolution of prominent subarachnoid spaces in the majority of cases. *(47:370)*

511. **(D)** B and C. Important clue in recognizing communicating hydrocephalus. Communicating hydrocephalus is also known as nonobstructive hydrocephalus. *(47:369, 371)*

512. **(D)** Periventricular leukomalacia is softening of the white matter surrounding the ventricles. *(58:G8–G54)*

513. **(G)** The tentorium cerebelli is a transverse division of dura mater forming a partition between the occipital lobe of the cerebral hemispheres and the cerebellum. *(58:G8–G54)*

514. **(I)** Sulci are grooves on the surface of the brain separating the gyri. *(58:G8–G54)*

515. **(C)** The choroid plexus comprises special cells located in the ventricles that secrete cerebrospinal fluid. *(58:G8–G54)*

516. **(A)** The cisterna magna is an enclosed space located caudad to the cerebellum, between the cerebellum and the occipital bone, serving as a reservoir for cerebrospinal fluid. *(58:G8–G54)*

517. **(K)** The pia mater is the inner membrane covering the brain and spinal cord. *(58:G8–G54)*

518. **(F)** The corpus callosum is a group of nerve fibers above the third ventricle that connects the left and right sides of the brain. *(58:G8–G54)*

519. **(J)** The cavum septum pellucidum is a cavity filled with cerebrospinal fluid that lies between the anterior horns of the lateral ventricle. *(58:G8–G54)*

520. **(H)** The insula is a triangular area of cerebral cortex, lying deeply in the lateral cerebral fissure. *(58:G8–G54)*

521. **(B)** Gyri are folds on the surface of the brain. *(58:G8–G54)*

522. **(E)** Aqueduct stenosis is a congenital obstruction of the third and fourth ventricles resulting in ventricular dilation. *(58:G8–G54)*

523.	interthalamic adhesion	massa intermedia	*(18:38)*
524.	inferior horn	temporal horn	*(18:30)*
525.	frontal horn	anterior horn	*(18:30)*
526.	posterior horn	occipital horn	*(18:30)*
527.	epiphysis cerebri	pineal gland	*(58:G42)*
528.	subependymal hemorrhage	germinal matrix hemorrhage	*(1:198)*
529.	atrium	trigone	*(8:216)*
530.	interventricular foramen	foramen of Monro	*(18:30)*

531. **(C)** Neonates are particularly susceptible to infection because their immunologic system is immature. This is a major concern because many infections originate from the hospital environment. Infection control is the responsibility of all health care workers. *(59:1060)*

532. **(C)** 1 and 40. These are a direct result of systemic anticoagulation. A reduction of heparin concentrations to minimal therapeutic levels has resulted in subsequent clotting of these hemorrhages and progression to a "normal" echogenic appearance. When an "ECMO" baby is heparinized, the hemorrhages become anechoic in appearance, *not* echogenic. *(48:165)*

533. **(B)** Cerebral cortex. The major feature of the brain at 24–28 weeks of gestation is the well-developed circulation to the basal ganglia and the brain stem. *(49:184)*

534. **(B)** All of the above. Periventricular leukomalacia is a region of coagulation necrosis. The infarcts can range from small white areas of gliosis to varying degrees of cystic cavitation. Resultant thinning of white matter can lead to secondary enlargement of the lateral ventricles. *(50:60)*

535. **(D)** All of the above. The predominantly cortical flow of the full-term brain places the cortex at increased risk. *(49:194)*

536. **(A)** Increased echogenicity at the external angle of the lateral ventricles. Ischemic lesions may occur at the watershed boundary zones of the periventricular white matter and the centrum semiovale as periventricular leukomalacia. *(50:61)*

537. **(D)** Heubner's artery. This is the main nutrient vessel of the subependymal germinal tissue, which is destined to give rise to much of the glial cell population of the hemisphere. *(49:183)*

538. **(B)** 10–18 weeks of gestation. The important growth and development of the cerebral hemispheres is as follows: the maximum proliferative spurt of neuron is 10–18 weeks' gestation, the spurt in the proliferation of glial cells commences from about 20 weeks' gestation, and the elaboration of dendritic processes and dendritic spines occurs mainly from 26 weeks onward. *(49:182)*

539. **(A)** A lipoma. Lipomas of the corpus callosum are benign nonsurgical lesions. They do not grow out of proportion to cerebral growth and because of their vascularity and the involvement of the pericallosal arteries, surgery is dangerous. *(51:450)*

540. **(C)** Pericallosal artery. The anatomic course of the artery reflects around the corpus callosum so that an anterior angulation of a Doppler probe will illicit a signal from the vessel. *(52:184)*

541. **(E)** All of the above. The pulse-waved Doppler instrument offers the advantage of allowing determination of a flow-velocity profile from a specific area within a blood vessel and separation of flow components of individual vessels. *(53:34)*

542. **(D)** 5–10 MHz. The continuous-wave Doppler transducer can either be flat or be a pencil probe with an ultrasonic frequency of 5–10 MHz. *(52:180)*

543. **(A)** Middle cerebral artery. This artery can be evaluated best through the cranial vault because the newborn skull has a single pliable bony layer without the dipole. *(54:499)*

544. **(C)** B. Note that to obtain the optimal tracing of the cerebral blood-flow velocity, the beam of ultrasound is almost directly down the vessel. *(5:185)*

545. **(C)** End-diastole is the minimum value. *(54:501)*

546. **(B)** Peak-systole is the maximum value. *(54:501)*

547. **(E)** One cardiac cycle. *(54:501)*

548. **(C)** 1 and 4. This tracing has one systolic peak with continuous forward blood flow during diastole. *(55:678)*

549. **(A)** Peak height. *(55:678)*

550. **(C)** 2 and 4. To obtain a signal from the vein of Galen, the cursor must be placed in these areas. Flow in the vein of Galen is consistently easy to identify. Doppler signals from this vein are constant and always indicate a forward direction similar to that of venous flow in many other parts of the body. *(56:181)*

551. **(D)** Minimum height. The end-diastolic amplitude is equivalent to the minimum height of the blood velocity waveform. *(55:678)*

552. **(E)** All of the above. The pressure and flow waveforms are influenced by cardiac contractility, the density of blood, the elasticity of the vessel wall, and the cerebrovascular resistance. *(55:679)*

553. **(A)** Erythrocytes. The shifted frequencies of the waveform are produced by motion of the red blood cells. *(52:180)*

554. **(A)** 1 and 3. The fact that infants with asphyxia have low pulsatility and high diastolic flow probably represents a decrease in resistance of the cerebrovascular system in response to the asphyxia. *(57:599)*

555. **(D)** 2 and 4. The fact that infants with an intraventricular hemorrhage have high pulsatility indexes and extremely low forward diastolic flow may represent an increase in resistance in response to the hemorrhage. *(57:599)*

REFERENCES

1. Babcock DS, Han BK. *Cranial Ultrasonography of Infants.* Baltimore: Williams & Wilkins, 1981.
2. Winsberg F, Cooperberg PL. Real-time ultrasonography: clinics in diagnostic ultrasound. In Rumack CM, Johnson ML (eds): *Real-Time Ultrasound Evaluation of the Neonatal Brain,* Vol. 10. New York: Churchill Livingstone, 1982.
3. King DL, William McK. *Diagnostic Ultrasound.* St. Louis: CV Mosby, 1974.
4. Ora BA, Eddy L, Hatch G, Solida B, et al. The anterior fontanelle as an acoustic window to the neonatal ventricular system. *J Clin Ultrasound* **8**:65–67, February 1980.
5. Williams PL, Warwick R. *Gray's Anatomy,* 36th ed. Philadelphia: WB Saunders, 1980.
6. Bartrum RJ, Crow HC. *Real-time Ultrasound: A Manual for Physicians and Technical Personnel.* Philadelphia: WB Saunders, 1983.
7. Sanders RC, Thomas LS. *Ultrasound Annual.* New York: Raven Press, 1982.
8. Howard WR, William JZ, Babcock DS, et al. *Seminars in Ultrasound,* Vol. 3, No. 3. New York: Grune & Stratton, 1982.
9. Fenichel GM. *Neonatal Neurology,* Vol. 2. New York: Churchill Livingstone, 1980.
10. Haller JO, Shkolnik A, Slovis T. *Clinics in Diagnostic Ultrasound, Vol. 8: Ultrasound Pediatrics.* New York: Churchill Livingstone, 1981.
11. Helen LB, Sandra KM. *The Developing Person: A Life Span Approach.* San Francisco: Harper & Row, 1980.
12. Mallet M. *A Handbook of Anatomy and Physiology for Student X-ray Technicians,* 4th ed. Chicago: American Society of Radiologic Technologists, 1962.
13. Hagen-Ansert S. *Textbook of Diagnostic Ultrasound,* 2nd ed. St. Louis: CV Mosby, 1983.
14. William M. *The American Heritage Dictionary of the English Language.* New York: American Heritage, 1971.
15. Goldberg S. *Clinical Neuroanatomy Made Ridiculously Simple.* Miami: Med Master, 1979.
16. Robbins S, Cortran R. *Pathologic Basis of Disease,* 2 ed. Philadelphia: WB Saunders, 1979
17. Sutton D. *A Textbook of Radiology and Imaging,* Vol. 2, 3rd ed. New York: Churchill Livingstone, 1980.
18. Carpenter M. *Core Text of Neuroanatomy,* 2nd ed. Baltimore: Williams & Wilkins, 1978
19. Farmer T. *Pediatric Neurology,* 3rd ed. Philadelphia: Harper & Row, 1983.
20. Hole J Jr. *Human Anatomy and Physiology,* 3rd ed. Dubuque, IA: Wm C Brown, 1984.
21. Gordon BA. *Neonatology, Pathophysiology and Management of the Newborn.* Philadelphia: JB Lippincott, 1975.
22. *Dorland's Illustrated Medical Dictionary,* 24th ed. Philadelphia: WB Saunders, 1965.
23. Schaffer AJ, Avery ME. *Diseases of the Newborn,* 4th ed. Philadelphia: WB Saunders, 1977.
24. Waechter EH, Blake FG. *Nursing Care of Children,* 9th ed. Philadelphia: JB Lippincott, 1976.
25. Hellman LM, Pritchard J, Wynn RM. *Obstetrics,* 14th ed. New York: Appleton-Century-Crofts, 1971.
26. Danforth DN. *Textbook of Obstetrics and Gynecology,* 2nd ed. New York: Harper & Row, 1971.
27. Rumack CM, Johnson MI. *Perinatal and Infant Brain Imaging: Role of Ultrasound and Computed Tomography.* Chicago: Year Book, 1984.
28. Thompson DE. *Pediatric Nursing: An Introductory Text,* 4th ed. Philadelphia: WB Saunders, 1981.
29. Marlow RD. *Textbook of Pediatric Nursing,* 5th ed. Philadelphia: WB Saunders, 1977
30. Hafen QB, Karren JK. *Prehospital Emergency Care and Crisis Intervention,* 2nd ed. Englewood, CO: Morton, 1983.
31. Fleischer AC, James AE. *Real-time Sonography: Textbook with Accompanying Videotape.* Norwalk, CT: Appleton-Century-Crofts, 1985.

32. Rubin J. Intraoperative ultrasonography of the spine. **146:**173–176, *Am J Radiol* 1983.
33. Grant E, Kerner M, Schellinger D. Evaluation of porencephalic cyst from intraparenchymal hemorrhage in neonates: Sonographic correlation. *Am J Radiol* **138:**467, 1982.
34. Grant E, Schellinger D, Richardson J. Real-time ultrasonography of the posterior fossa. *J Ultrasound Med* **2:**73, 1983.
35. Taylor KWJ. Atlas of ultrasonography. In Mannes E, Sivo J (eds): *The Neonatal Head,* Vol. 1, 2nd ed. New York: Churchill Livingstone, 1984.
36. Shuman W, Rogers J, Mack L. Real-time sonographic sector scanning of the neonatal cranium: technique and normal anatomy. *AJNR* **2:**349–356, 1981.
37. Babcock D, Ball W Jr. Postasphyxial encephalopathy in full-term infants: Ultrasound diagnosis. *Am J Radiol* **148:**417–423, 1983.
38. Goldstein R, Filly R, et al: Septal veins: A normal finding on neonatal sonography. *Am J Radiol* **161:**623–624, 1986.
39. Hole JW Jr. *Human Anatomy and Physiology,* 3rd ed. Dubuque, IA: Wm C Brown, 1984.
40. Naidich TP, Quencer RM (Eds): *Clinical Neurosonography: Ultrasound of the Central Nervous System.* NY: Springer Verlag, 1986.
41. Levene M, Williams J, Fawer CL. *Ultrasound of the Infant Brain.* London: Spastics International Medical Publications, and Philadelphia: JB Lippincott, 1985.
42. *Dorland's Illustrated Medical Dictionary,* 26th ed. Philadelphia: WB Saunders, 1985.
43. Hertzberg S, Kay HH, Bowie JD. Fetal choroid plexus lesions. *J Ultrasound Med* **8,** 1989.
44. Kapit W, Elson LM. *The Anatomy Coloring Book.* NY: Harper & Row, 1977.
45. Sanders RC. *Clinical Sonography: A Practical Guide.* Boston: Little, Brown, 1984.
46. Martin J. *Ultrasound Technology Series. Cranial Sonography in Infants: Technicare Ultrasound.* New Brunswick, NJ: Johnson & Johnson, 1983.
47. Pilu P, Louis P, Roberto R, et al. The fetal subarachnoid cisterns: an ultrasound study with report of a case of congenital communicating hydrocephalus. *J. Ultrasound Med* **5,** 1986.
48. Bowerman RA, Zwischenberger JB, Andrews AF, et al. Cranial sonography of the infant treated with extracorporeal membrane oxygenation. *Am J Radiol* **145,** 1985.
49. Wigglesworth JS, Pape KE. An integrated model for haemorrhage and ischaemic lesions in the newborn brain: Early human development. *Early Human Dev* **2**(2):179–199, 1978.
50. Manger MN, Feldman RC, Brown WJ, et al. Intracranial ultrasound diagnosis of neonatal periventricular leukomalacia. *J. Ultrasound Med* **3:**59–63, 1984.
51. Christtenen RA, Pinckney LE, Higgins S, et al. Sonographic diagnosis of lipoma of the corpus callosum. *J Ultrasound Med* **6:**449–451, 1987.
52. Perlman JM. Neonatal cerebral blood flow velocity measurement. *Clin Perinatol* **12:**179–193, 1985.
53. Bada HS, Fitch CW. Uses of transcutaneous Doppler ultrasound technique in newborn infants. *Perinatol Neonatol* **7:**27–35, 1983.
54. Raju TNK, Zikos E. Regional cerebral blood velocity in infants: a real time transcranial and fontanellar pulsed Doppler study. *J Ultrasound Med* **6:**497–507, 1987.
55. Gray PH, et al. Continuous wave Doppler ultrasound in evaluation of cerebral blood flow in neonates. *Arch Dis Child* **58:**677–681, 1983.
56. Grant EG, White EM, Schellinger D, et al. Cranial Doppler sonography of the infant. *Radiology* **163:**177–185, 1987.
57. Miles RD, Menice JA, Bashiru M, et al. Relationships of five Doppler measures with flow in vitro model and clinical findings in newborn infants. *J Ultrasound Med* **6**(10):597–599, 1987.
58. Tortora GJ, Anagnostakos NP. Principles of anatomy and physiology, 6th ed. New York: Harper & Row, 1990.
59. Olds SB, London ML, Ladewig PA. Maternal-newborn nursing: A family-centered approach, 3th ed. California: Addison-Wesley, 1988.

mother lying on her left side. This will relieve pressure on the inferior vena cava (IVC). In addition, an anticoagulant medication such as heparin is administered. *(2:945; 3:140)*

199. **(F)** All of the above. Studies of children born with a previous history of intrauterine growth retardation (IUGR) confirms that it occurs more frequently in males than in females and results in speech defects, central nervous system (CNS) abnormalities, and diminished intelligence. *(3:139)*

200. **(C)** Trophoblastic disease is *not* associated with intrauterine growth retardation (IUGR). *(3:140)*

201. **(C)** The decidua of early intrauterine pregnancy is divided into decidua basalis, decidua parietalis (vera), and decidua capsularis. This marked hypertrophic change in the endometrium occurs no matter where the pregnancy is located. The uterine mucosa responds by a decidual reaction due to hormonal stimuli. However, when an ectopic pregnancy occurs, the uterine decidua responds by a cast off—decidual cast. This should *not* be confused with the normal decidua in an early pregnancy. *(3:57)*

202. **(D)** Pseudocyesis denotes false pregnancy. *(3:119)*

203. **(A)** The scanning plane in which spina bifida is best recognized is the transverse scan with real-time apparatus. Spina bifida is recognized sonographically as a U-shaped pedicle of the vertebral body. *(29:246)*

204. **(A)** The ideal time for detecting spina bifida is 17–18 weeks because the spinal echo is too small for reliable visualization before 16 weeks and the spinal curvature increases after 20 weeks. *(3:181)*

205. **(B)** Fluid-filled masses in the vagina could be Gartner's duct cyst, urine in the vagina, or hematocolpos. Vagina agenesis is absence of the vagina. *(41:48–61)*

206. **(D)** All of the above. The functions of the yolk sac are: nutrition—transfer of nutrients to the embryo; hemopoiesis—blood cell development; development of sex glands—gives rise to sex cells that later become spermatogonia or oogonia; and the formation of the embryonic digestive tube. *(21:751–752; 22:18)*

207. **(A)** Sonographically, the yolk sac may appear to be floating freely in the gestational sac and near the fetus. However, embryologically, the yolk sac is located in the chorionic cavity between the amnion and the chorion. *(22:128)*

208. **(A)** The yolk sac usually detaches from the midgut loop at the 6th week. *(22:129)*

209. **(B)** The yolk sac reduces in size as pregnancy advances. However, it may persist throughout pregnancy and continue to persist into adulthood. In about 2% of adults, the proximal intra-abdominal part of the yolk sac is presented as a diverticulum of the ilium, called Meckel's diverticulum. *(22:129)*

210. **(C)** On sonography, the yolk sac measures 2–5 mm in diameter. *(29:68)*

211. **(A)** A blighted ovum is a fertilized ovum that has been arrested (termination of development). Sonographically, the gestational sac is empty (anembryonic sac). *(39:48)*

212. **(B)** The ovarian follicle grows and accumulates fluid within it (follicular cyst). After ovulation, the fluid from the follicle spills into the cul-de-sac. Fluid also may be seen in pelvic inflammatory disease (PID), ectopic rupture, and endometriosis. Myoma is least likely to cause fluid in the cul-de-sac. *(3:302; 20:593)*

213. **(D)** The thin ringlike structure that surrounds the gestational sac is the amniotic membrane, which excludes the yolk sac. *(64:165)*

214. **(G)** A thickened "rind" of choriodecidual tissue is *not* a sonographic finding of a blighted ovum. *(3:15–16; 20:593)*

215. **(A)** The term *missed abortion* implies retention of a dead embryo or fetus. This is not to be confused with incomplete abortion, which refers to a portion of the products of conception passed, or a blighted ovum, which refers to an empty gestation sac. *(3:302)*

216. **(B)** The normal spine is seen as a closed circle, whereas spina bifida produces U-shaped echoes. *(3:180)*

217. **(E)** There is a geographic difference in the incidence of anencephaly. It occurs more frequently in the United Kingdom than in the United States. *(1:101)*

218. **(B)** Holoprosencephaly is an intracranial problem, whereas anencephaly is an abscence of the cranium. *(1:101–104)*

219. **(A)** The most common position for twin gestation is one cephalic and the other breech. *(10:59)*

220. **(A)** Malpresentation is any position other than vertex or cephalic. *(10:61)*

221. **(A)** This scan demonstrates an enlarged uterus with irregular uterine contour. The uterine texture is heterogeneous. These patterns are typical of subserosal fibroid. A tumor that grows outward toward the serosa is called subserosal leiomyoma. *(63:272)*

222. **(C)** This sonogram demonstrates an omphalocele primarily with herniated liver. *(63:134)*

223. **(E)** All of the above. Overdistension of the urinary bladder can result in serious diagnostic error. Inadequate filling of the bladder also can result in error. Overdistension of the urinary bladder may result in closure of an incompetent cervix due to bladder compression on the cervix; placenta previa due to bladder compression on the lower uterine segment; closure of the gestational sac due to bladder compression that causes both sides of the sac walls to meet resulting in a loss of the anechoic center or a change in sac shape (distortion); nonvisualization of the internal iliac vein due to displacement. *(1:199; 20:686)*

224. **(E)** A, C, and D. The solution of this problem is to distend the urinary bladder or to have a nurse help by gently applying pressure to elevate the fetal head as you scan. The elevation of the patient's feet (Trendelenburg's position) also helps. *(29:359)*

225. **(E)** The biparietal diameters (BPDs) of twins should be within 4 mm of each other. Because the BPD of twin gestation is normally less than a single pregnancy, it is recommended that 1–2 mm should be added to compensate for the difference. *(14:74)*

226. **(A)** Cardiac anomalies are sometimes present with omphalocele. Herniation of the fetal heart through abdominal wall defect can be depicted sonographically and referred to as ectopia cordis (ectopic heart). *(63:134)*

227. **(J)** A–G. The reasons for bladder distension prior to sonographic examination are sonic window—the urine-filled bladder provides a low attenuation pathway to which ultrasound can propagate; anatomical reference point—the anechoic space created by the urine-filled bladder permits rapid anatomical orientation; mass mobility—a mobile mass will be pushed by the distended bladder, whereas a nonmobile mass will remain fixed in the pelvis; decrease in the angle of incidence—the distended bladder pushes the uterus posteriorly and thus reduces the angle of incidence; demonstration of the cervix—the distended bladder helps to better visualize the cervix to help rule out placenta previa; fetal head elevation—the distended bladder elevates the fetal head out of the pelvis for obtaining a more accurate BPD; bowel displacement—the distended bladder pushes the bowel cephalad and out of the true pelvic cavity. The air contained within bowel loops will prevent adequate visualization of the pelvic viscera; uterine displacement—the bladder pushes the uterus cephalad and away from the symphysis pubis where the uterus can be best evaluated; mass comparison—the cystic characteristic of the fluid-filled bladder can be used as a comparison in evaluating the characteristic of a cystic mass. *(20:502; 25:98)*

228. **(B)** The urinary bladder can be distended with 250 mL of normal saline via a Foley catheter. *(26:2)*

229. **(C)** The fetus would be lying on its right side with the left side up toward the maternal anterior abdominal wall. *(1:41)*

230. **(B)** The fetus would be lying on its left side with the right side up toward the maternal anterior abdominal wall. *(1:41)*

231. **(A)** The horizontal position of the fetal heart is largely due to a large liver size. *(1:46)*

232. **(B)** When the umbilical cord is cut and the placenta circulation is ceased, the umbilical vein becomes thrombosed and converted into the ligamentum teres of the liver. *(1:49)*

233. **(A)** The ductus venosus also becomes obliterated. Its remnant is called ligamentum venosum of the liver. *(1:50)*

234. **(A)** The portal sinus remains open (patent) and becomes proximal to the left portal vein. *(1:50)*

235. **(D)** All of the above. A single umbilical artery (SUA) is associated with twins, the offspring of maternal diabetes mellitus, and congenital anomalies. *(29:371)*

236. **(B)** The normal umbilical cord contains a single umbilical vein and two arteries. *(29:371)*

237. **(B)** A large umbilical vein is associated with Rh isoimmunization. *(19:237)*

238. **(C)** Ovulation occurs approximately 14 days after the first day of the last menstrual period. *(1:1)*

239. **(A)** Esophageal atresia *is* a closure or absence of the esophagus. *(29:231)*

240. **(D)** When the stomach and duodenal bulb are distended, fluid gives it a double fluid appearance,

which is called the double-bubble sign, a term taken from radiography. *(29:232)*

241. **(F)** Bilateral renal abscence (agenesis) is associated with Potter's syndrome, pulmonary hypoplasia, and olighydramnios. *(1:72)*

242. **(D)** Normally, the fetal bladder empties every 60 minutes. *(1:73)*

243. **(C)** The most common cause of hydronephrosis of the fetus is obstruction at the ureteropelvic junction (UPJ). This can also occur at the uterovesical junction (UVJ). *(1:74)*

244. **(C)** Zygote.

245. **(B)** Cleavage.

246. **(A)** Morula.

247. **D)** Blastocyst. *(22:36)*

248. **(D)** Intrauterine growth retardation (IUGR) is *least* associated with the double-ring sign. *(3:297–309; 14:108–110)*

249. **(J)** The placenta is usually large in multiple gestation and Rh isoimmunization. *(1:141–156)*

250. **(H)** The placenta is thin in IUGR and placental insufficiency. *(1:141–156)*

251. **(D)** Multiple gestation is more often associated with hydramnios. *(3:139–146)*

252. **(P)** Intrauterine growth retardation and renal agenesis are more often associated with oligohydramnios. *(1:67–77; 20:598–605)*

253. **(A)** 3. Straight and well defined. Its texture is homogeneous with no densities. *(1:143)*

(B) 2. Subtle undulations with few scattered echogenic areas and no densities. *(1:143)*

(C) 4. Indentations extending into, but not to, the basal layer. Linear, commalike echogenic densities with basal stippling. *(1:143)*

(D) 1. Indentations communicating with the basal layer. Circular densities with echo-spared areas in the center and large irregular densities that cast acoustic shadowing. *(1:143)*

254. **(D)** Hemorrhage in the second or third trimester may be associated with placenta previa and placental abruption. However, placenta previa is the most common cause of painless vaginal bleeding in the second and third trimesters. The bleeding associated with placenta previa is usually bright red. Placental abruption's characteristic symptom is uterine pain with vaginal bleeding (the blood is usually dark). *(1:151; 7:503)*

255. **(D)** The most common benign tumor of the uterus is fibroid, also called myoma, leiomyoma, and fibromyoma. The most common malignant tumor of the uterus is leiomyosarcoma. *(27:427, 452)*

256. **(C)** There is a much higher incidence of fibroids in blacks than in whites. *(3:388; 27:427)*

257. **(C)** Fibroids are divided into three groups: (1) submucous, situated beneath the endometrium; (2) interstitial (intramural) situated in the muscular wall; and (3) subserous (subperitoneal) situated beneath the peritoneum. *(27:429)*

258. **(A)** Nägele's rule is a mathematical methodology for the estimation of duration of pregnancy. The expected date of confinement (EDC) is achieved by applying the Nägele's rule: add 7 days to the first day of the last menstrual period; subtract 3 calendar months, and add 1 year. *(2:304–305)*

259. **(A)** Leiomyosarcoma is a malignant fibroid. *(4:452)*

260. **(D)** The growth of fibroids is stimulated by estrogen. Therefore, birth control pills and pregnancy will also stimulate its growth. *(27:437)*

261. **(H)** The duration of pregnancy can be broken down into 280 days, 40 weeks, 9 calendar months, and 10 lunar months. A calendar month is 29 to 30 days; a lunar month is a period of four 7-day weeks (28 days). *(2:304–305)*

262. **(A)** This situation is most common in the anterior placenta. However, it also can occur in the posterior placenta. *(39:60)*

263. **(D)** All of the above. See the answer to question 227 for explanation.

264. **(E)** The chorionic plate is most easily depicted when the ultrasound beam is perpendicular to its surface. The chorionic plate is most difficult to depict when the ultrasound beam is parallel to its surface, such as fundal, lateral, and placenta previa. *(20:596)*

265. **(G)** All of the above. See the answer to question 224 for explanation.

266. **(B)** Endometriosis can be best described as ectopic locations of endometrial tissue such as on broad ligament, ovaries, or pelvic peritoneum. *(29:484)*

267. **(D)** The sonographic findings abruptio placentae are retroplacental clot and partial separation occurring at the margin of the placenta. *(39:60)*

268. **(B)** To calculate the EDC add 7 days, subtract 3 calendar months, and add 1 year to the first day of the last menstrual period (LMP). *(28:586)*

269–275. See Fig. 8–114.

276–279. See Fig. 8–115.

280. **(A)** 3. The head is larger than the abdomen at 12 to 24 weeks.

(B) 2. At 32 to 36 weeks, the head and body are about the same size.

(C) 1. After 36 weeks, the abdomen is larger than the head. *(10:79)*

281. **(A)** If an Rh^- mother and a Rh^+ father conceived a baby, there is a possibility that the baby may be Rh^+. Because the baby's Rh^+ red cells are foreign to the Rh^- mother, her body may respond by creating antibodies that cause damage to the Rh^+ cells (isoimmunization). Usually, Rh disease does not manifest itself until the second or third pregnancy. *(12:90)*

282. **(G)** The paramesonephric or müllerian ducts form both male and female reproductive systems. In the female, the müllerian ducts on each side grow toward each other. The lower portions of the ducts fuse to form a single uterovaginal cavity. The upper portions of the ducts that do not fuse remain as the paired fallopian tubes. The wolffian ducts also are called pronephric ducts or mesonephric ducts, which grow upward to form the ureters. *(22:279; 29:536)*

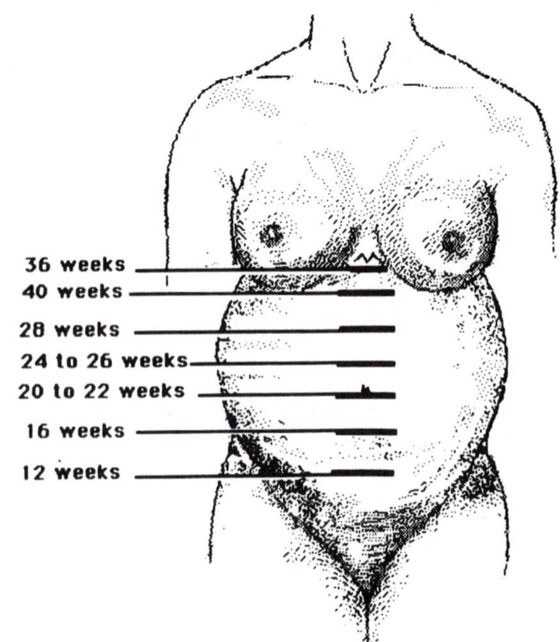

Figure 8–114. Diagram of the fundal height at various stages during pregnancy.

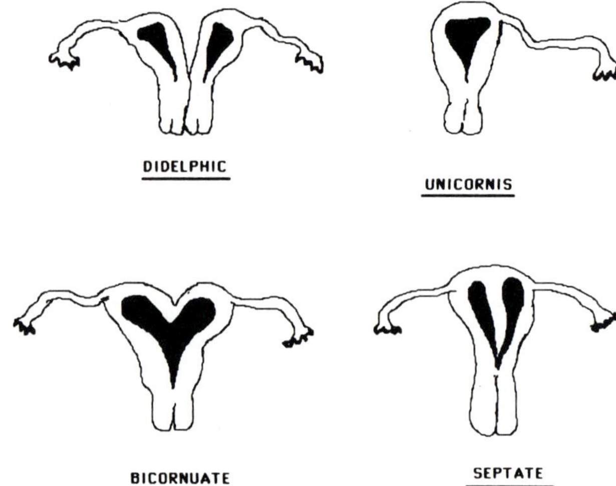

Figure 8–115. Diagram showing developmental anomalies of the uterus.

283. **(C)** Complete malfusion of the ductus paramesonephricus can result in a didelphic uterus. *(10:95; 29:536)*

284. **(A)** Partial malfusion of the ductus paramesonephricus can result in a bicornuate uterus. *(10:95; 29:536)*

285. **(B)** Minimal malfusion of the ductus paramesonephricus can result in a septate uterus. *(10:95; 29:536)*

286. **(B)** Arrested development of the paramesonephric duct results in uterine aplasia. *(29:536)*

287. **(C)** Unilateral arrested development of the paramesonephric duct results in uterus unicornis. *(29:536)*

288. **(A)** The kidneys should be scanned in patients suspected of any uterine anomaly. *(29:536)*

289. **(E)** Dysgerminoma is a malignant, *not* a benign, tumor. *(17:1289; 29:495)*

290. **(B)** Dermoid cysts are more common in younger women. *(27:561; 30:159)*

CHAPTER 1

ULTRASONIC PHYSICS AND INSTRUMENTATION

Trudy Dubinsky, Steven Horii, Charles S. Odwin, Ronald R. Price, Arthur C. Fleischer, and Milagros Garay

Study Guide

WHAT IS ULTRASOUND?

Ultrasound is a mechanical, longitudinal wave that carries variations of quantities referred to as *acoustic variables*. Ultrasound is above the range of human hearing (20,000 hertz [or cycles per second] or greater).

Ultrasound waves are produced by oscillatory motion of the particles in a medium, creating regions of compression and rarefaction. The continued movement of particles propagating through a medium is the result of collision between particles that make up the medium.

Ultrasound can be continuous or pulsed. In the *continuous* mode the vibratory motions are produced by the source in an uninterrupted stream, whereas in the *pulsed* mode the sound is delivered in a series of packets, or pulses. In almost all of the diagnostic applications of ultrasound, *pulsed ultrasound* is used.

The following terms are commonly used in diagnostic medical sonography:

Mechanical wave. A wave that requires a medium in which to travel and therefore cannot propagate in a vacuum.

Longitudinal wave. A wave in which the particle motion travels parallel to the energy source (as opposed to shear or transverse waves, which travel perpendicular).

Acoustic variable. Each of the following is considered an acoustic variable: *pressure, temperature, density, particle motion.* Note that all of these variables change as an acoustic wave passes through the medium.

Parameters of a wave (Fig. 1–1A).

The following terms are common to all waves:

Cycle. A cycle is composed of one compression and one rarefaction, or a complete positive and negative change in an acoustic variable.

Frequency (*f*). The number of cycles per second. Frequency describes how many times the acoustic variable (whether it be pressure, density, particle motion, or temperature) changes in one second. *Units:* hertz (Hz), megahertz (MHz).

$$\text{frequency } (f) = \frac{\text{propagation speed}}{\text{wavelength}}, \qquad f = \frac{c}{\lambda}$$

Period. The time it takes for 1 cycle to occur; the inverse of frequency. *Units:* seconds (s), microseconds (μs).

$$\text{period} = \frac{1}{\text{frequency}}, \qquad p = \frac{1}{f}$$

As the frequency increases, the period decreases. Conversely, as the frequency decreases, the period increases.

Wavelength (λ). The distance that the wave must travel in 1 cycle. Wavelength is determined by both the source of the wave and the medium in which it is propagating (Fig. 1–1B). *Units:* meters (m), millimeters (mm).

$$\text{wavelength } (\lambda) = \frac{\text{propagation speed } (c)}{\text{frequency } (f)}, \qquad \lambda = \frac{c}{f}$$

With a velocity or propagation speed (*c*) of 1540 m/s, the wavelength of 1 MHz is 1.54 mm, of 2 MHz is 0.77 mm, and of 3 MHz is 0.51 mm.

Propagation speed. The maximum speed with which an

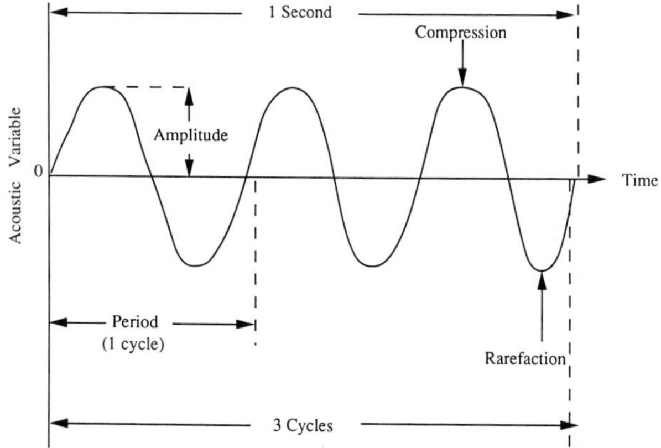

Figure 1–1A. The parameters of a wave. The frequency of this wave variable is 3 Hz (or cycles per second). A period is 1 complete cycle; therefore this wave consists of 3 periods. *Note:* The vertical direction is compression and downward direction is rarefaction and both represent pressure and density. Otherwise, it represents a positive (upward) or negative (downward) change in the acoustic variable.

acoustic wave can move through a medium, determined by the density and stiffness of the medium. Propagation speed increases proportionally with the stiffness (ie, the more stiff the medium the faster the variable will travel). Density is the concentration of mass per unit volume, and propagation speed is inversely proportional to density. *Units:* meters/second (m/s), millimeters/microsecond (mm/μs).

$$\text{propagation speed} \approx \sqrt{\frac{\text{elasticity (stiffness)}}{\text{density}}}, \qquad c \approx \frac{e}{p}$$

It should be emphasized that *compressibility* is the opposite of stiffness. If compressibility increases, then the propagation speed decreases.

Propagation speed is greater in solids > liquids > gases. Propagation speed (c) is equal to frequency (f) times wavelength (λ) $\{c = f \times \lambda\}$. Since the propagation speed is constant for a given medium, if the frequency increases the wavelength will decrease. Conversely, if the frequency decreases the wavelength will increase.

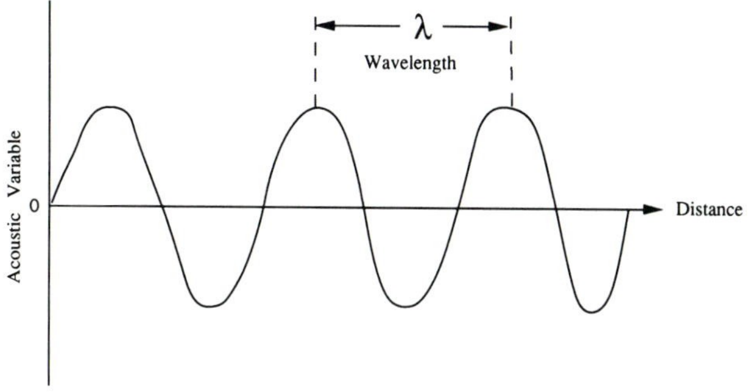

Figure 1–1B. A wavelength represents the distance between two adjacent wave peaks.

Example

If the frequency of an ultrasound wave traveling through soft tissue is increased from 5 to 10 MHz, what happens to the wavelength?
Steps to Solution:

$$\text{propagation speed} = 1540 \text{ m/s or } 1.54 \text{ mm/}\mu\text{s}$$

$$\text{frequency} = 5 \text{ MHz}$$

$$\frac{\text{propagation speed}}{\text{frequency}} = \text{wavelength}$$

$$1.54 \text{ mm/}\mu\text{s}/5 \text{ MHz} = 0.31 \text{ (mm)}$$

$$\text{frequency} = 10 \text{ MHz}$$

$$1.54 \text{ mm/}\mu\text{s}/10 \text{ MHz} = 0.154 \text{ (mm)}$$

Doubling the frequency halves the wavelength in a given medium. Note how the wavelength gets smaller.

PARAMETERS USED TO DESCRIBE PULSED WAVES

Pulse repetition frequency (PRF). The number of pulses per second. *Units:* hertz (Hz), kilohertz (kHz).

The PRF used depends on imaging depth: As the imaging depth increases, the PRF must decrease. This phenomenon is characteristic of the pulse–listening period–receiving cycle of the transducer. The longer it takes the returning signals (echoes) to come back to the transducer, the greater the interval between pulses. Therefore, the farther away a target, the longer the return trip, and the greater the interval between transmissions of the pulsed wave.

Pulse repetition period (PRP). The time from the beginning of one pulse to the beginning of the next (Fig. 1–2A). *Units:* seconds (s), milliseconds (ms).

$$\text{PRP} = \frac{1}{\text{PRF}}$$

The PRP increases as imaging depth increases. When depth decreases the PRP decreases.

Pulse duration (PD). The time it takes for a pulse to occur: the period of the ultrasound in the pulse multiplied by the number of cycles in the pulse (see Fig. 1–2A). *Units:* seconds (s), milliseconds (ms).

$$\text{pulse duration} = \text{number of cycles } (n) \times \text{period } (p)$$

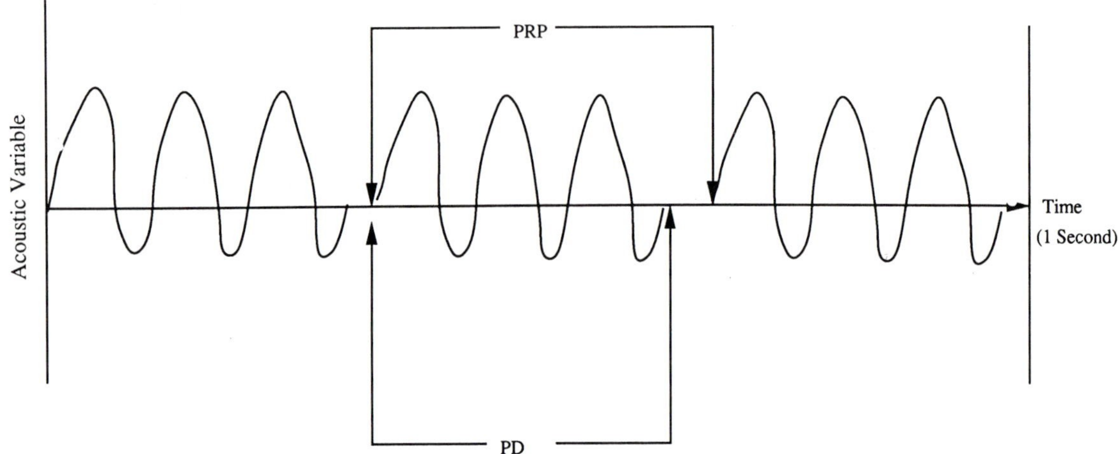

Figure 1–2A. Pulse repetition period (PRP).

Duty factor. The fraction of time that the transducer is generating a pulse. *Maximum value:* 1.0. In continuous wave the transducer is always generating a pulse. A second transducer acts as the listening device. *Minimum value:* 0.0. The transducer is *not* being excited (therefore no pulse will be generated). In clinical imaging, using pulse echo system the duty factor ranges from 0.001 to 0.01. *Units:* unitless.

$$\text{duty factor} = \frac{\text{PD } (\mu\text{s})}{\text{PRP (ms)} \times 1000}$$

Note: Since the duty factor is unitless and PD is usually in microseconds, it is necessary to divide by 1000 to cancel out the units in the formula. In using this formula, the units must match (PD and PRP both must be in seconds, milliseconds, or microseconds). If not, a correction factor, such as the 1000 in the denominator, must be used.

The duty factor can also be computed by the following formula:

$$\text{duty factor} = \frac{\text{PD} \times \text{PRF}}{1000}$$

Spatial pulse length (SPL). The distance over which a pulse occurs (Fig. 1–2B). *Unit:* millimeters (mm).

$$\text{spatial pulse length (SPL)} = \text{wavelength } (\lambda) \times \text{number of cycles in a pulse } (n)$$

Amplitude. The maximum variation that occurs in an acoustic variable. It indicates the strength of the sound wave. To arrive at this variation, the undisturbed value is subtracted from the maximum value and the unit for the acoustic variable is applied (Fig. 1–3). Peak-to-peak amplitude (P–P) is the maximum to minimum value.

Power. The rate of energy transferred. The power is proportional to the wave amplitude squared. *Unit:* watts (W).

$$\text{power} \approx \text{amplitude}^2$$

Intensity. The power in a wave divided by the area of the beam. *Unit:* Watts per centimeter squared (W/cm^2).

$$\text{intensity} = \frac{\text{power (W)}}{\text{area (cm}^2)}$$

Note: The intensity is proportional to the amplitude squared. If the amplitude doubles, then the intensity quadruples.

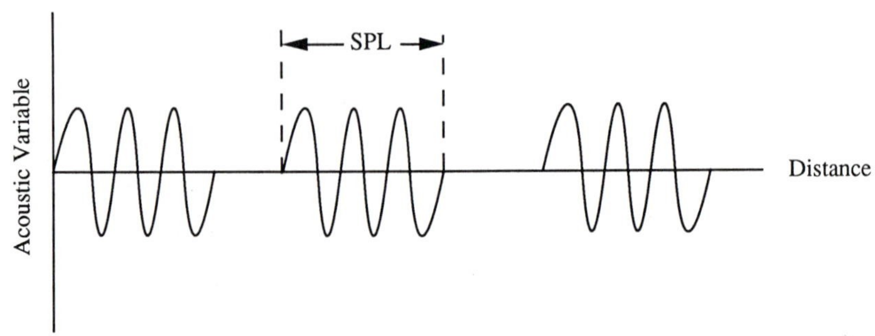

Figure 1–2B. Spatial pulse ıength (SPL).

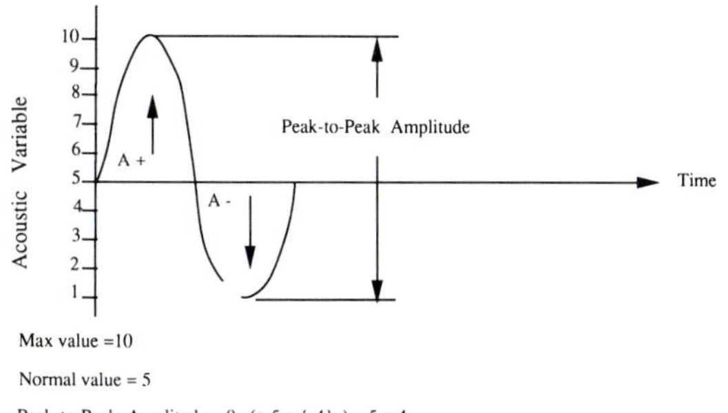

Figure 1–3. A wave amplitude. Amplitude is equal to the maximum value minus the normal value. Peak-to-peak amplitude (P–P) is equal to the maximum plus absolute value of the minimum.

POWER AND INTENSITY

The ultrasound power and the intensity of the ultrasound beam are not identical, although the two terms are sometimes used interchangeably. The *ultrasound power* is the rate at which work is done; it is equal to the work done divided by the time required to do the work. The intensity is the power per unit area and represents the strength of the ultrasound beam. The intensities used in diagnostic medical sonography applications range from 1 to 50 mW/cm^2. Understanding of the ultrasound intensity is important when studying the biologic effects of ultrasound in tissue (discussed later in this chapter).

Intensities have both a peak value and an average value. The intensity of the sound beam as it travels through a medium varies across the beam (*spatial intensity*) and with time (*temporal intensity*).

Spatial peak (SP). Intensity at the center of the beam.

Spatial average (SA). Intensity averaged throughout the beam.

Temporal peak (TP). Maximum intensity in the pulse, (measured when the pulse is on).

Temporal average (TA). Intensity averaged over one on–off beam cycle (takes into account the intensity from the beginning of one pulse to the beginning of next).

Pulse average (PA). Intensity averaged over the duration of the single pulse.

Six intensities result when spatial and temporal considerations are combined:

spatial peak–temporal peak	SPTP (highest)
spatial average–temporal peak	SATP
spatial peak–temporal average	SPTA
spatial average–temporal average	SATA (lowest)
spatial average–pulse average	SAPA
spatial peak–pulse average	SPPA

In pulsed ultrasound, the TP is greater than the PA, which is greater than the TA. When using continuous wave ultrasound, however, TP and TA intensities are the same.

Spatial peak intensity is related to SA by the beam uniformity ratio (BUR).

Beam uniformity ratio (BUR) is a unitless coefficient that describes the distribution of ultrasound beam intensity in space. The higher the SP, the more concentrated and the higher the SA, the less concentrated the intensity. *Units:* unitless.

$$\text{spatial average} = \frac{\text{spatial peak intensity (W/cm}^2)}{\text{beam uniformity ratio}},$$

$$\text{SA} = \frac{\text{SP}}{\text{BUR}}$$

$$\text{spatial peak} = \text{beam uniformity ratio} \times \text{spatial average}$$

$$\text{(SP)} = \text{BUR} \times \text{SA}$$

Temporal average intensity is related to TP by the duty factor (DF). *Units:* unitless.

$$\text{duty factor} = \frac{\text{temporal average}}{\text{temporal peak}},$$

$$\text{DF} = \frac{\text{TA}}{\text{TP}}$$

Attenuation

Attenuation is the reduction of the sound beam's amplitude and intensity as it travels through a medium. It is the reason why the echoes from deep structures are weaker than those from more superficial structures. The factors that contribute to attenuation are:

Absorption. The conversion of sound energy into heat. Absorption is the major source of attenuation in soft tissues.

Scattering. *Diffuse scattering* is the redirection of the sound beam after it strikes rough or small boundaries, when the wavelength is larger than the reflecting surface. Liver parenchyma and red blood cells represent diffuse scattering.

Reflection. The return of a portion of the ultrasound beam back toward the transducer (an echo). Of interest in diagnostic sonography is *specular reflection,* which occurs when the wavelength of the pulse is much smaller than the boundary it is striking and the surface is smooth. The best examples of specular reflectors are the diaphragm, liver capsule, and gallbladder walls. Reflection of the ultrasound beam depends on the *acoustic impedance mismatch* at the boundary between two media (discussed in detail later in this chapter).

The unit in which attenuation is given is the decibel (dB). *The decibel is the unit of intensity ratio, or power; it is the quantity obtained by taking 10 times the log of the ratio of two intensities.*

$$\text{decibels (dB)} = 10 \log \frac{\text{final intensity}}{\text{initial intensity}}$$

Attenuation coefficient is the attenuation per unit length of sound wave travel. For soft tissue, it is approximately half of the operating frequency of the transducer; that is, for every centimeter per megahertz (MHz) there is approximately 0.5 dB of attenuation. For example, if the operating frequency of a transducer is 5 MHz, then the attenuation coefficient is approximately 2.5 dB/cm.

$$\text{attenuation (dB)} = \text{attenuation coefficient (dB/cm)} \times \text{pathlength (cm)}$$

Note: Pathlength is the distance the sound beam travels in a medium. The actual calculation of decibel values is complex and need not be part of the sonographer's bank of common knowledge, but the sonographer should understand that since decibels are exponents, a small change in decibels can mean a large change in resulting values. The most useful way to handle these values is to memorize the commonly encountered ones (Table 1–1).

Example 1

The ultrasound beam produced by a 4-MHz transducer has an initial intensity of 20 mW/cm^2 after traveling through 3 cm of tissue. What is the intensity of the beam at the end of this path?

Given: Frequency is 4 MHz; original intensity is 20 mW/cm^2; pathlength is 3 cm; attenuation coefficient is ½ frequency, ie, ½(4 MHz) = 2 dB/cm.

Then: If attenuation is attenuation coefficient × pathlength, then attenuation is 2 dB/cm × 3 cm = 6 dB.
If attenuation is 0.25, then the decibel value is −6 dB.

(See Table 1–1.)

TABLE 1–1. DECIBEL VALUES OF ATTENUATION

Decibels (dB)	Value
−3 dB	(1/2) 0.5
−6 dB	(1/4) 0.25
−9 dB	(1/8) 0.13
−10 dB	(1/10) 0.10
−20 dB	(1/100) 0.01
−30 dB	(1/1000) 0.001

To obtain the final intensity, multiply the intensity ratio by the original intensity:

$$\text{mW/cm}^2 \times 0.25 = 5 \text{ mW/cm}^2$$

The intensity was therefore reduced to 25% of its original value. Another way to do this example is to note that a 3-dB reduction means halving a value. Since 6 dB = 3 dB + 3 dB, an attenuation of 6 dB reduces the power by one-half (20 W → 10 W), then by one-half again (10 W → 5 W).

Example 2

After passing through soft tissue media, an ultrasound beam with an initial intensity of 100 mW/cm^2 has a remaining intensity of 0.01 mW/cm^2. Calculate the amount of attenuation.

Given: Initial intensity is 100 mW/cm^2; final intensity is 0.01 mW/cm^2.

Then: If decibels $= 10 \log \frac{0.01}{100} = 10 \log \frac{1}{10{,}000}$

$$= 10\,(-4) = 40 \text{ dB}$$

Note: In strict mathematical terms the 40 dB should be negative, but for our purpose it can be simply stated as 40 dB of attenuation.
The attenuation, therefore, was 40 dB (−40 dB).

The *half-intensity depth* is the distance at which the intensity will be half that of the original; the distance the sound beam will travel through a medium before its intensity is reduced by 50%. It is calculated by the formula:

$$\text{half-intensity depth} = \frac{3}{\text{attenuation coefficient (dB/cm)}}$$

The half-intensity depth can also be calculated from the frequency:

$$\text{half-intensity depth} = \frac{6}{\text{frequency (MHz)}}$$

The half-intensity depth is a good indicator of the frequency that should be selected to view different structures in the body. For example, if 50% of the intensity is gone before one reaches a certain depth, then it is obvious that deeper structures will receive less of the sound beam and thus generate weaker echoes. To visualize deep structures it therefore is necessary to use a lower frequency.

Time gain compensation (TGC). An electronic compensation for tissue attenuation.

Echoes

Echoes are the reflections of the sound beam as it travels through the media. An echo is generated each time the beam encounters an acoustic impedance mismatch, but its strength depends on a number of factors. One very impor-

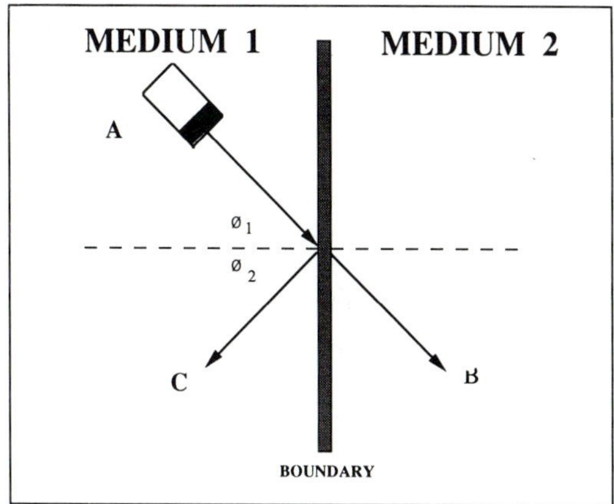

Figure 1–4A. (**A**) An oblique incidence striking a boundary; (**B**) refraction of the sound beam; (**C**) reflection of the sound beam. *Note:* An oblique incidence is *not* a normal incidence. A normal incidence is 90° (perpendicular). An incidence beam can be

1. Perpendicular (normal)
2. Oblique incidence (an incidence beam at an oblique angle) *not* perpendicular

The angle of incidence is the angle of any of the incidence beams.

tant factor, the *angle of incidence,* is the angle at which the incident beam strikes a boundary. The angle of incidence is equal to the angle of reflection (Fig. 1–4A).

Perpendicular Incidence. A beam traveling through a medium perpendicular to a boundary and encountering the boundary at a 90° angle (Fig. 1–4B). Perpendicular incidence is also known as *normal incidence.*[1] The portion of the beam that is not reflected continues in a straight line; this is called *transmission.*

Perpendicular incidence will produce a reflection when the acoustic impedance changes at the boundary. *Acoustic impedance is the product of the density of a medium and the velocity of sound in that medium.*

Acoustic impedance (rayls) = density (kg/m) × propagation speed (m/s)

$$Z = p \times c$$

At an acoustic impedance mismatch the sound beam will proceed (transmission), be reflected, or both.

The relationship between *perpendicular incidence* and the *intensity* of the echoes can be characterized by the following formulas:

$$\text{intensity reflection coefficient (IRC)} = \left(\frac{z_2 - z_1}{z_2 + z_1}\right)^2$$

$$\text{intensity reflection coefficient (IRC)} = \frac{\text{reflected intensity}}{\text{incident intensity}}$$

$$\text{intensity transmission coefficient (ITC)} = \frac{\text{transmitted intensity}}{\text{incident intensity}}$$

The ITC can also be calculated by the formula:

$$\text{ITC} = 1 - \text{IRC}$$

$$\text{Incident intensity} = \text{IRC} \times \text{incident intensity} + \text{ITC} \times \text{incident intensity}$$

Example

Given two media, one with an acoustic impedance of 20 rayls and the other with an acoustic impedance of 40 rayls, calculate the intensity reflection coefficient (IRC), the intensity transmission coefficient (ITC), the reflected intensity and the transmitted intensity. (Assume that the incident intensity is 10 mW/cm².)

$$Z_1 = 20 \text{ rayls}; Z_2 = 40 \text{ rayls}$$

$$\text{IRC} = \left(\frac{40 - 20}{40 + 20}\right)^2 = \left(\frac{20}{60}\right)^2 = \left(\frac{1}{3}\right)^2 = \frac{1}{9} = 0.11$$

Given: The IRC is 0.11.

Then: ITC = 1 − IRC

ITC = 1 − 0.11 = 0.89

If the reflected intensity is equal to the IRC times the original intensity, then reflected intensity = 0.11 × 10 mW/cm² = 1.1 mW/cm².

If the transmitted intensity is equal to the ITC times the original intensity, then transmitted intensity = 0.89 × 10 mW/cm² = *8.9 mW/cm².*

Oblique incidence. An angle of incidence that is not 90° perpendicular to a boundary. The angle of transmission will be equal to the angle of incidence as long as the propagation speeds of the media on each side of the boundary are equal. If the propagation speeds are

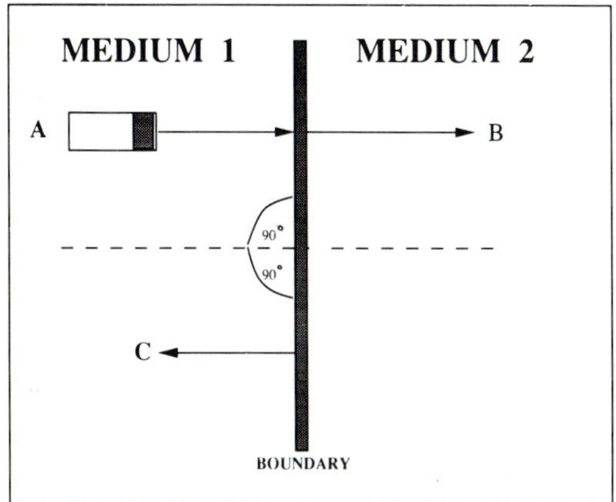

Figure 1–4B. The transmission of the perpendicular incidence sound beam, also called *normal incidence.* (**A**) Normal incidence striking a boundary perpendicularly; (**B**) the intensity transmitted; (**C**) reflection of energy at the boundary of medium 1 and medium 2. *Note:* Beam (**C**) actually travels back along the beam coming from (**A**), but it is depicted separately.

different, however, then the angle of incidence will not be equal to the angle of transmission. The change in direction, the difference in the angle of incidence and the angle of transmission (Fig. 1–5A, B, and C), is called *refraction* (Snell's law).

The angle of incidence is equal to the angle of reflection, but the angle transmission is variable and can be calculated as follows:

$$\text{angle of transmission} = \text{angle of incidence} \times \frac{\text{propagation speed (medium 2)}}{\text{propagation speed (medium 1)}}$$

ϕ_2 = angle of transmission

ϕ_1 = angle of incidence

$$\phi_2 = \phi_1 \times \frac{C_2}{C_1}$$

Note: The above equation is only an approximation; at larger angles it is subject to larger error. To obtain true accuracy use the full form of Snell's law.

$$\sin \phi_2 = \sin \phi_1 \times \frac{C_2}{C_1}$$

The *range equation* is the relationship between the round-trip travel time of the pulse and the distance to a reflector. This equation determines the position a reflector will have in depth on the display monitor.

$$\text{distance to the reflector (mm)} = \frac{1}{2} \times \text{propagation speed (mm/}\mu\text{s)} \times \text{pulse round-trip time (}\mu\text{s)}$$

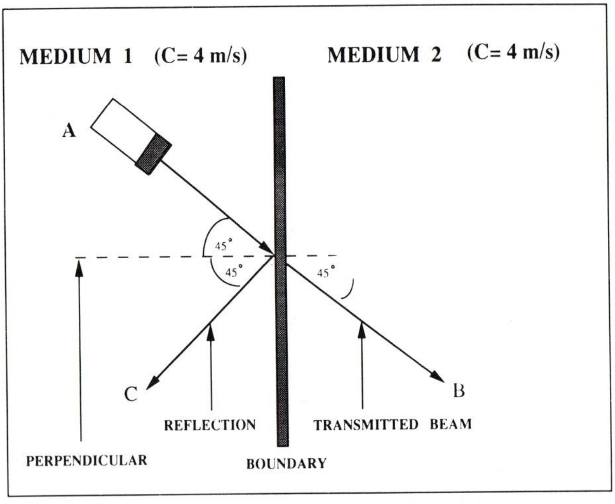

Figure 1–5B. In medium 1, the propagation speed is 4 m/s; in medium 2, the propagation speed is 4 m/s, therefore the angle incidence will be equal to the angle of transmission with *no* refraction. (**A**) Incidence striking a boundary; (**B**) transmitted beam; (**C**) reflected beam.

If we assume the propagation speed to be constant at 1540 m/s or 1.54 mm/μs, then one-half the propagation speed is equal to 0.77 mm/μs and the formula can be simplified:

$$\text{distance to the reflector } (d) = 0.77 \times \text{pulse round-trip time } (t)$$

If we assume that for every 13 μs the pulse travels 1 cm, then $d = t/13$. The value of (t) must be given in microseconds if the propagation speed is in millimeters per microseconds. The range equation defines the position a reflector will have in depth on the display monitor.

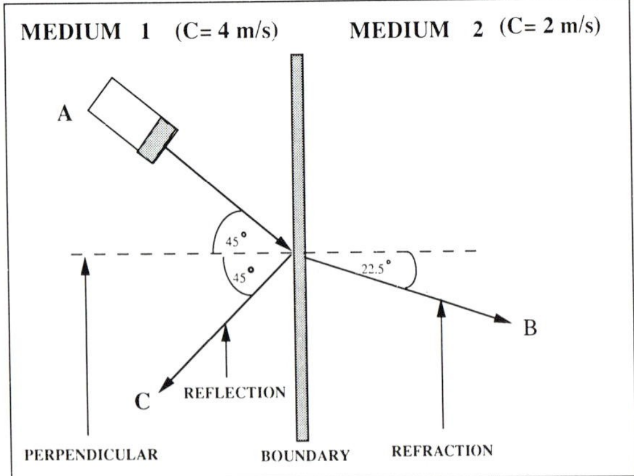

Figure 1–5A. In medium 1, the propagation speed is 4 m/s; in medium 2, the propagation speed is 2 m/s, therefore the beam bends towards the normal plane. (**A**) Incidence striking a boundary; (**B**) refraction of the sound beam; (**C**) reflected beam.

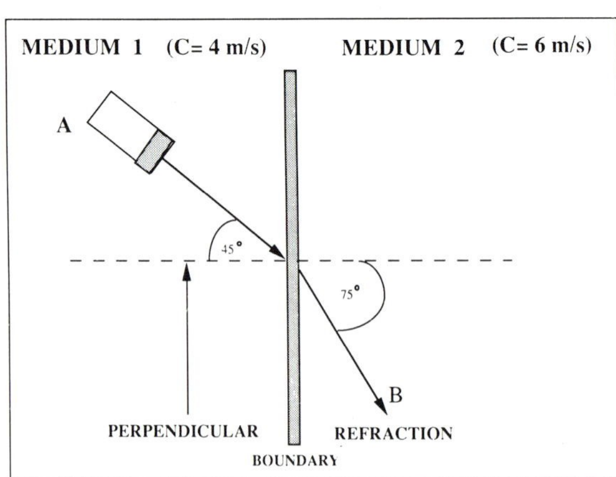

Figure 1–5C. In medium 1, the propagation speed is 4 m/s; in medium 2, the propagation speed is 6 m/s, therefore the beam bends away from the normal angle. (**A**) Incidence striking a boundary; (**B**) refraction of the sound beam; (**C**) reflected beam.

TRANSDUCERS

A *transducer* is a device that converts one form of energy to another. In diagnostic sonography the transducer converts electrical energy to pressure energy (acoustic energy) and vice versa.

1. *Active element*
   A. *Piezoelectric principle.* The conversion of electrical energy to pressure energy and vice versa. Ultrasound (pressure energy) is generated by electric stimulation of the piezoelectric element causing expansions and contractions of the element that in turn generate the ultrasound pulse. The resultant ultrasound pulse produces a similar distortion of the element and then converts back to an electric signal (Fig. 1–6).
   B. *Material.* The active element can be *natural* (eg, quartz, tourmaline, Rochelle salt) or *synthetic* (eg, lead zirconate titanate (PZT), barium titanate, lithium sulfate). Synthetic elements are most commonly used in today's diagnostic equipment because of their availability and low cost. To turn one of these manufactured substances into a piezoelectric element, it is heated to its Curie point, or the temperature at which a ferroelectric material, such as many piezoelectric materials, loses its magnetic properties. The dipoles within the material are then polarized with an electric current. When the element cools the dipoles are fixed (Fig. 1–7). The material is cut and shaped, then housed in the transducer.
   C. *Properties of elements (crystals).* The frequency of the acoustic wave produced by a standard pulsed-wave imaging system is determined by the *thickness* of the piezoelectric element and the *propagation speed* of the crystal. The propagation speed of the crystal is approximately three to five times greater than the speed of ultrasound in soft tissue, namely, 4 to 8 mm/μs. The thinner the crystal, the greater the frequency.

$$\text{frequency (MHz)} = \frac{\text{propagation speed of the crystal (mm/}\mu\text{s)}}{2 \times \text{thickness (mm)}}$$

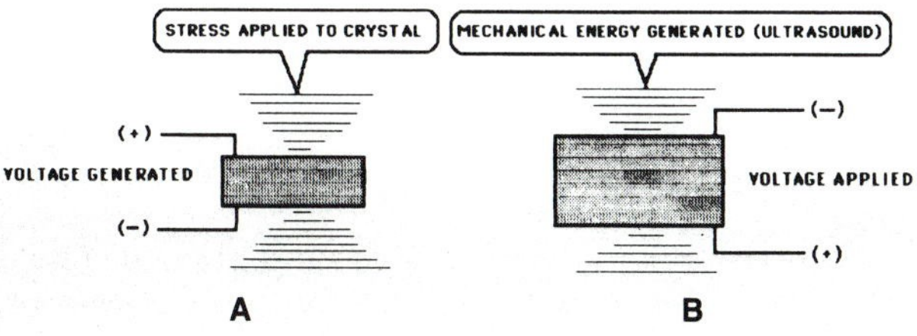

Figure 1–6. Applied electrical voltage. (**A**) Physical compression on the crystal will generate a potential difference across the faces of the crystal. The effect is called *piezoelectric effect.* (**B**) Voltage applied on the crystal will generate mechanical energy (ultrasound). The effect is called *reverse piezoelectric effect.*

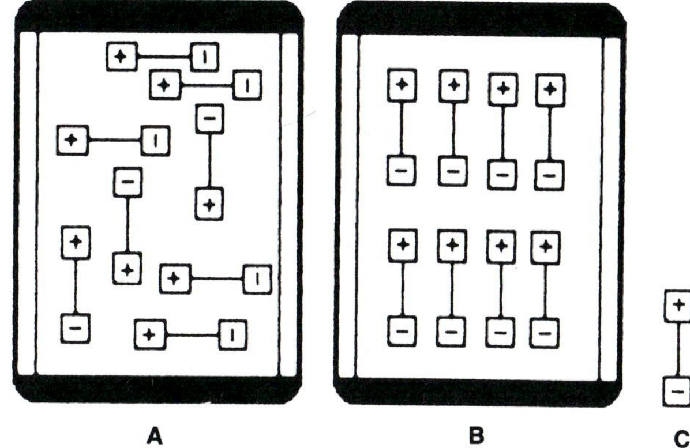

Figure 1–7. Synthetic material with dipoles. (**A**) nonpolarized; (**B**) polarized; (**C**) dipole.

The diameter of the crystal does not affect the pulse frequency; it does, however, determine the *lateral resolution.* Neither the impedance of the matching layer nor the thickness of the backing material is a primary determinant of ultrasound pulse frequency.

In contrast to pulse wave, *the frequency of continuous wave ultrasound is equal to the frequency of the electric voltage that drives the piezoelectric crystal.* In simpler terms, when the pulser of a continuous wave system produces an electric signal with a frequency of 6 MHz, the frequency of the emitted acoustic signal will also be 6 MHz.

2. *Damping material (backing material).* An epoxy resin attached to the back of the element that absorbs the vibrations and reduces the number of cycles in a pulse (Fig. 1–8). By reducing the number of cycles the following are accomplished:
   A. Pulse duration (PD) and spatial pulse length (SPL) are reduced.

$$\text{pulse duration (PD)} = \text{number of cycles } (n) \times \text{time } (t)$$

where t = period of ultrasound in pulse.

$$\text{spatial pulse length (SPL)} = \text{number of cycles } (n) \times \text{wavelength } (\lambda)$$

By reducing these two factors the axial resolution will be improved.

$$\text{axial resolution } (R_A) = \frac{\text{SPL}}{2}$$

   B. *Bandwidth* (the width of the frequency spectrum) is increased by increasing the damping. When the bandwidth increases, the quality factor (Q factor) of the transducer decreases.

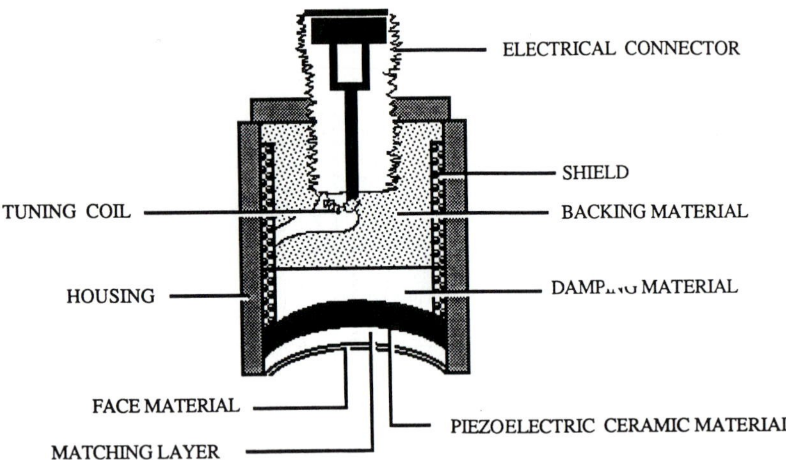

Figure 1–8. Components of a transducer.

$$\text{quality factor} = \frac{\text{operating frequency}}{\text{bandwidth}}$$

C. The duty factor is decreased.

3. *Matching layer.* A substance placed in front of the transducer element's face material to decrease the reflection at the transducer–tissue interface. The matching layer is necessary because the impedance difference between the transducer crystal and the soft tissue is so large that most of the energy will be reflected back at the skin surface. The matching layer provides an intermediate impedance, allowing transmission of the ultrasound beam into the body.

   The thickness of the matching layer is usually equal to one-quarter of the wavelength.[1] Multiple layers are often used to avoid reflections caused by the variety of frequencies and wavelengths present in short pulses. In addition to the matching layer of the transducer, a *coupling gel* is used to form a transducer surface–skin contact that will eliminate air and prevent reflection at this boundary.

Bandwidth and Quality Factor

The transducer produces more than one frequency. For example, the operating frequency may be 3.5 MHz, but a spectrum of other frequencies are also generated known as the bandwidth. The shorter the pulse the more of these other frequencies are generated. Therefore, the bandwidth and the pulse length are inversely proportional; as the pulse length decreases, the bandwidth increases (Fig. 1–9). Continuous-wave ultrasound has a very narrow bandwidth.

If the bandwidth increases, the Q factor decreases. If, however, the operating frequency increases, the Q factor increases. A low Q factor indicates:

1. broad bandwidth
2. low operating frequency
3. shortened pulse length
4. uniform near field (Many frequencies in a pulse result in a more uniform intensity distribution.)

Types of Transducers

There are several ways to classify transducers; one is the way the sound beam is swept (or steered). This process can be either mechanical or electrical.

A *mechanical transducer* (Fig. 1–10) has a scan head that contains a single disk-shaped active element. One type of mechanical transducer is the *oscillatory or rotary type,* which has an element that is physically attached to a mechanical device to move it through a pathway (see Fig. 1–10A). A second type has an *oscillatory mirror* that mechanically moves while the element remains stationary (see Fig. 1–10B).

Focusing the beam produced by a mechanical transducer is achieved by curvature of the crystal, a curved lens on the crystal, or the reflecting mirror. Focusing occurs at a *specific depth* on both the horizontal and vertical planes. To change the focal depth the operator must select another transducer with the desired focal zone. The mechanical transducer produces a sector-shaped image (see Fig. 1–10C). *Mechanical transducers are mechanically steered (MS) and mechanically focused (MF).*

The *annular array* is a mechanical transducer. The transducer element consists of 5 to 11 rings of transducer elements mounted on a mechanically moved (steered) arm (Fig. 1–11). The advantage of the annular array over the single element transducer is the presence of many elements, allowing for electronic focusing. By focusing trans-

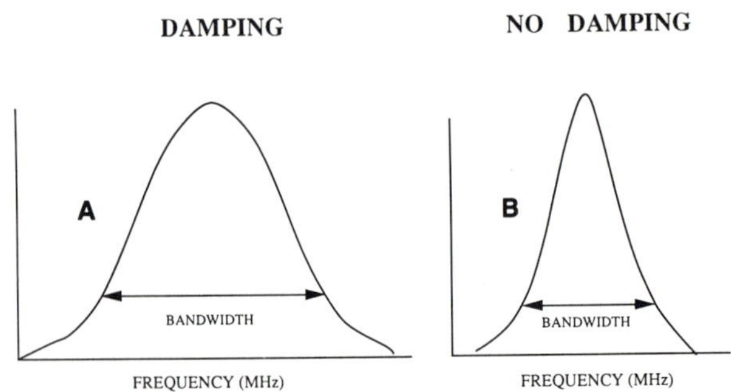

Figure 1–9. Bandwidth **(A)** with damping, **(B)** without damping. *Note:* Damping increases bandwidth.

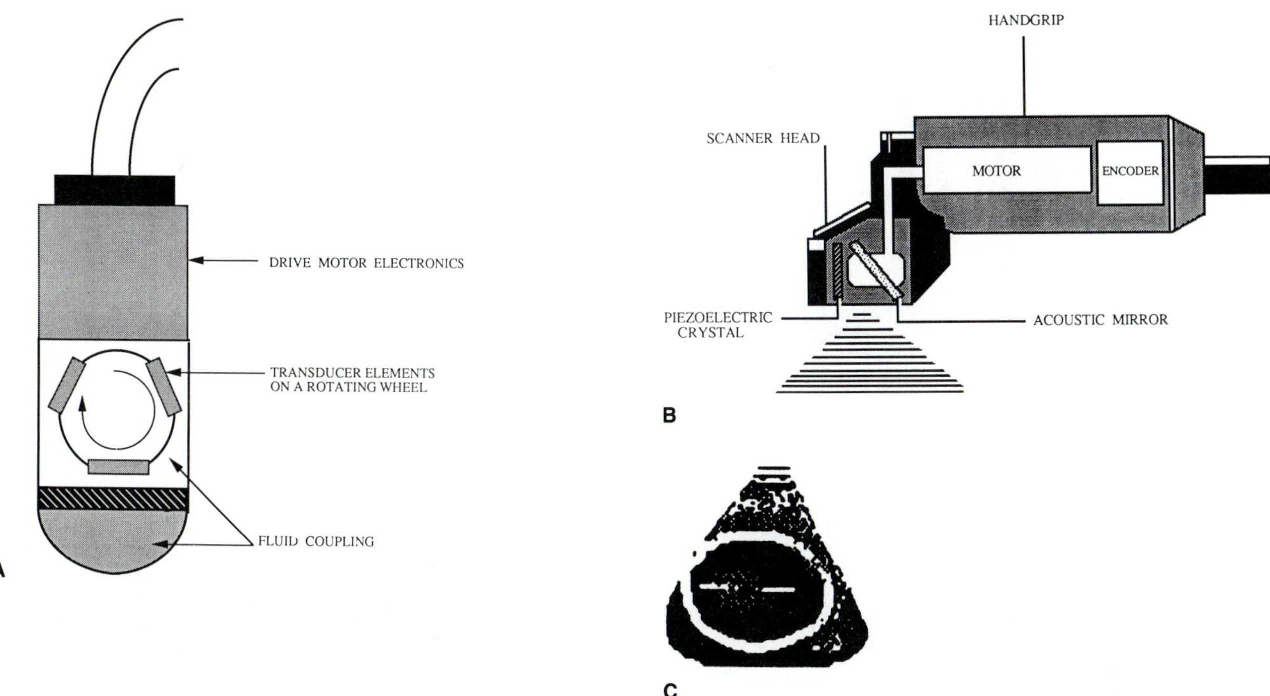

Figure 1–10 (**A**) mechanical sector real-time transducer that is mechanically steered and mechanically focused. (**B**) A mechanical sector real-time transducer that moves a mirror instead of the transducer. (**C**) Image presentation from a mechanical sector.

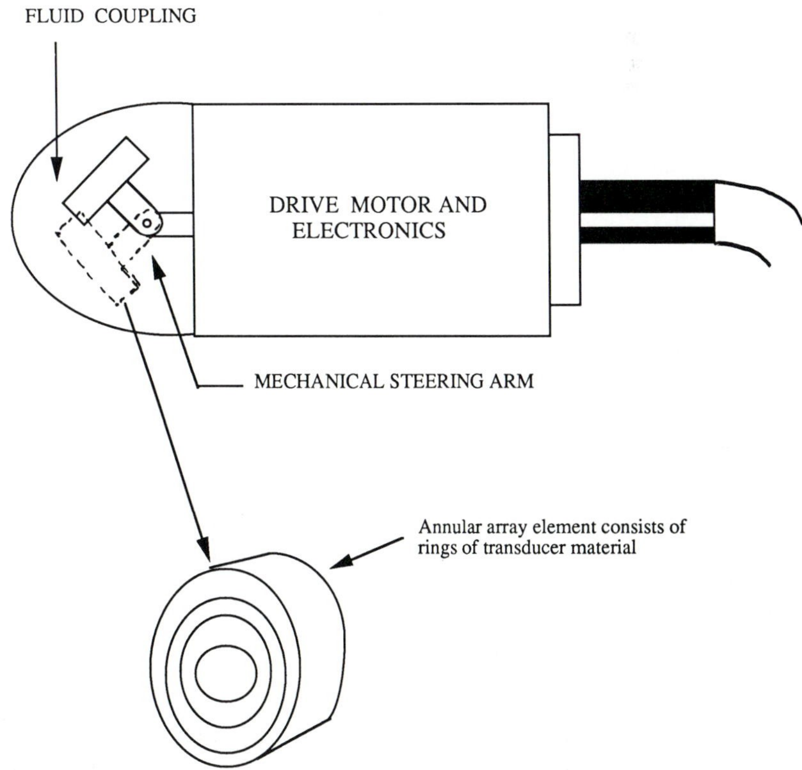

Figure 1–11. Annular array real-time transducer probe that contains four transducer rings (multi-element) on a mechanically steered shaft.

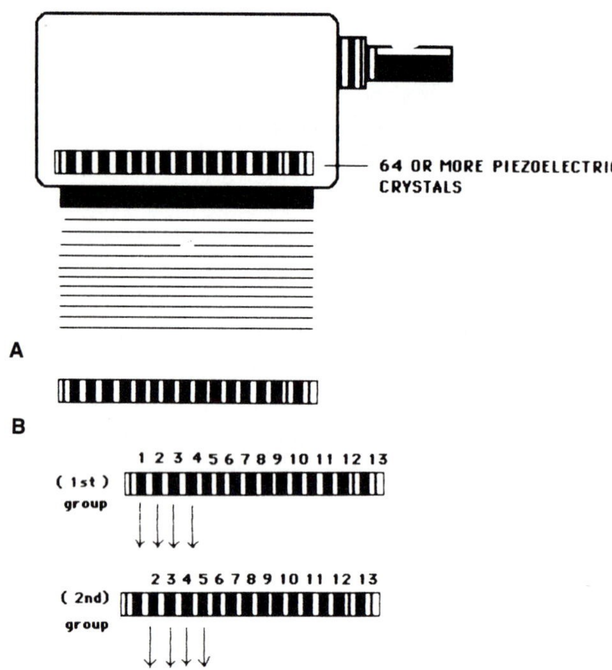

Figure 1–12. Linear sequential array. (**A**) A real-time linear-array transducer. (**B**) Design of a linear segmental phased-array transducer. These transducers consist of a long strip of piezoelectric crystals divided into elements, which are arranged next to each other; (**C**) Operation of a linear segmental phased-array transducer. The crystal elements are pulsed in groups of four in this example, with each group sending and receiving in succession.

mission and reception of the ultrasound energy, greater depth resolution is achieved. The image produced by an annular array is also a sector. *Annular arrays are mechanically steered (MS) and electronically focused (EF).*

An *electronic transducer* is an assembly of multiple elements called an *array.* There are many types of arrays, each with a particular set of characteristics:

Linear sequential array (linear array). Shown in Fig. 1–12. This type of transducer produces a rectangular image (Fig. 1–13B).

Curved array (radial array, convex array). The array of transducer elements are arranged with specific curvature (Fig. 1–14). Focusing the beam is achieved by internal and electronic focusing; there is no beam steering. The curved design of the transducer head creates a *sector or trapezoid image.*

Sector phased array (phased array). The voltage pulses are applied to the entire groups of elements with varying time delays. The beam can be electronically focused (EF) and steered (ES). The image format is sector (Fig. 1–15).

Focusing Techniques

Transducers can be either mechanically or electronically focused. *Mechanical focusing* is accomplished by using a curved crystal or an acoustic lens for each element. This type of focusing is usually applied to mechanical transducers and will improve lateral resolution by limiting the beam width.

There are two types of electronic focusing: transmit focusing and receive focusing.

Transmit focusing. Electronic focusing during transmission. It is accomplished by firing a group of elements with a small time delay (nanoseconds) between various elements in the group. The wavefront generated by each element in the group will arrive at a specific point in space, resulting in a focused beam. Using transmit focus will improve lateral resolutions and create several possible focal zones. Multizone transmit focusing will result in a slower frame rate. If, for example, there are three focal zones, then the frame rate will be reduced compared to a single focus zone. If the rate is very slow, then the image will flicker causing a "perceived" distortion of the image.

Receive focusing. Electronic focusing of the received echoes; by electronically delaying the return of the

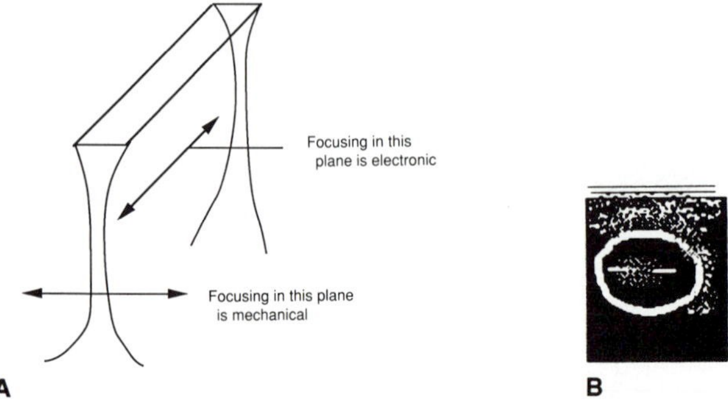

Figure 1–13. Linear sequential array. (**A**) Focusing in the plane of the long axis of the transducer is electronic; focusing in the plane perpendicular to the long axis is mechanical. (**B**) Image presentation from a linear phased array transducer. Note the rectangular image.

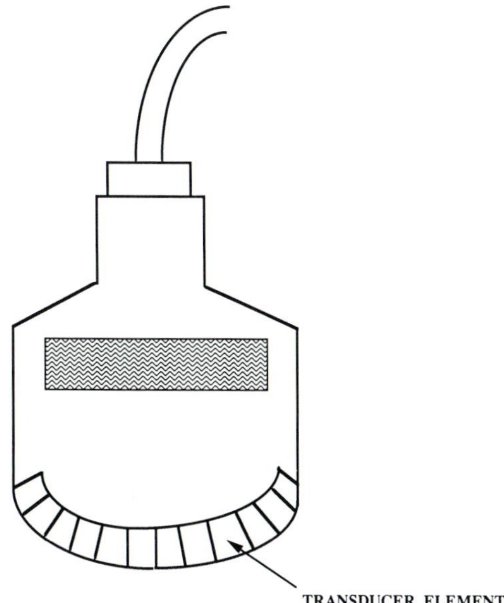

Figure 1–14. Curved linear array. The array of transducer elements are arranged with a specific curvature. There is no beam steering; focusing of the beam is achieved internally by mechanical and electronic means.

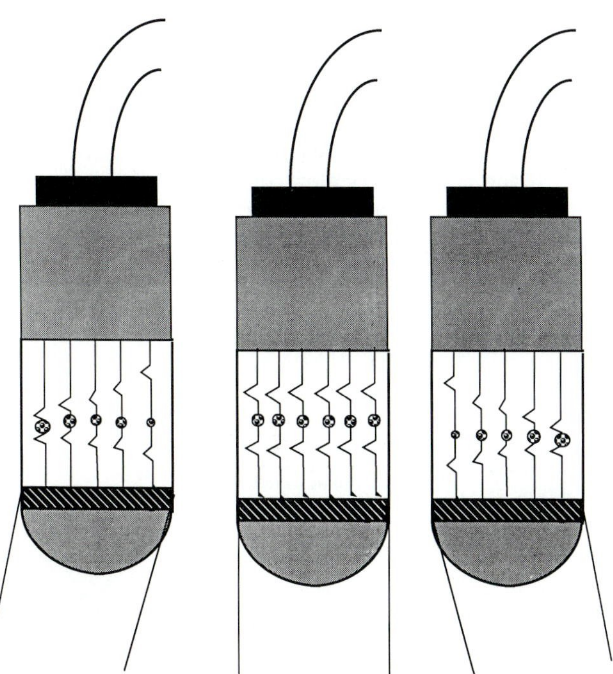

Figure 1–15. Sector phased array real-time transducer. This diagram illustrates how electronic pulses are used to steer the ultrasound beam.

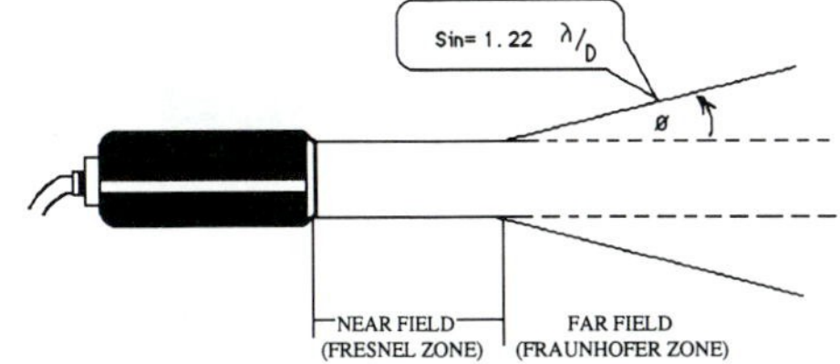

Figure 1–16. The ultrasound beam from an unfocused transducer.

signals to the processing system within the diagnostic unit, the optimum range of the focal zone can be extended. This process will enhance image clarity.

Note: Many phased arrays are capable of both transmit and receive focusing. Both transmit and receive electronic focusing are sometimes called *dynamic focusing* because focusing is done as the beam is being generated or received.

Sound Beam

A *sound beam* is the acoustic energy emitted by the transducer. The beam can be pulsed or continuous wave. *Pulsed waves follow Huygens' principle, which states that the resultant beam is a combination of all sound arising from different sources (wavelets) on the transducer crystal face. Focusing is the superimposition (algebraic summation) of all sound waves in the beam.*[1–3] As the various wavelets within a beam collide, interference (constructive and destructive) results in the formation of a sound beam (Fig. 1–16).

Constructive interference. The waves are in phase, producing an increase in amplitude.

Destructive interference. The waves are not in phase, producing a decrease in amplitude or even zero amplitude. Zero amplitude occurs if the out-of-phase waves completely cancel each other.

The beam is composed of a near zone, a focal point, and a far zone.

1. *Near zone (near field, fresnel zone).* The portion of the sound beam in which the beam diameter narrows as the distance from the transducer increases until it reaches its narrowest diameter. This distance is the *near zone length* (NZL). At the far end of the NZL the diameter of the beam is equal to

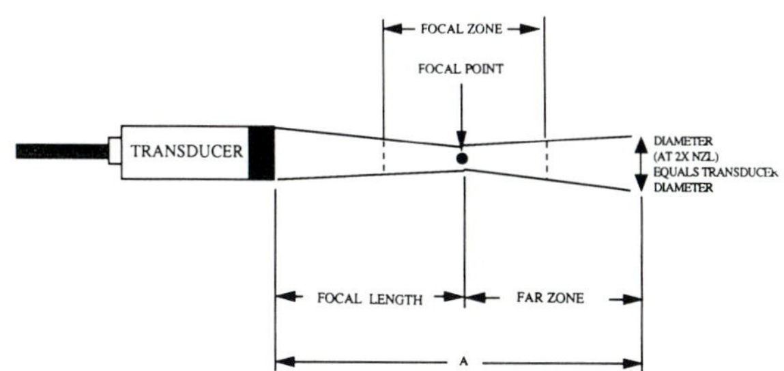

Figure 1–17. The components of the ultrasound beam in a focused transducer. (A) Note that the diameter of the beam is equal to the diameter of the transducer face.

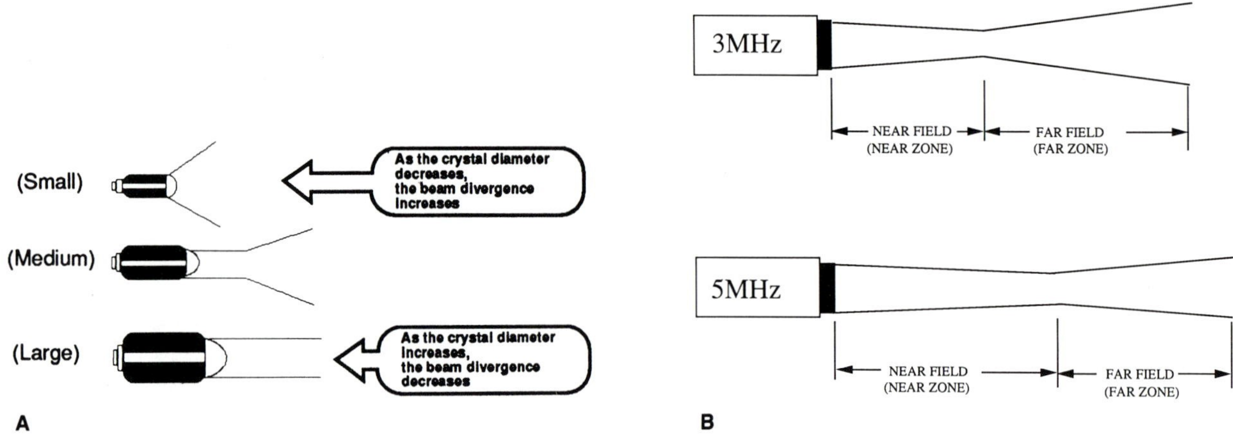

Figure 1–18 (A) Beam diversion with increasing crystal diameter. **(B)** Transducer crystal size shown in relationship to frequency. *Note:* The higher the frequency of the transducer, the smaller the beam diameter and the longer the near-zone. The angle of beam divergence in the far field is smaller with a higher frequency transducer.

one-half the diameter of the transducer. The NZL is also related to the frequency: Increasing the frequency increases the NZL, and vice versa. Components of the beam of a focused transducer are shown in Fig. 1–17.

2. *Focal point.* The point at which the beam reaches its narrowest diameter. As the diameter narrows the beam width resolution improves, becoming the best at the focal point. The *focal zone* is the distance between equal beam diameters that are some multiple of the diameter of the focal point (often two times the diameter of the focal point). The focal zone extends toward the transducer from the focal point, and toward the far zone. The *focal length* is the region of the beam from the transducer to the focal point.
3. *Far field (far zone, Fraunhofer zone).* The portion of the sound beam (after the NZL) in which the diameter of the beam increases as the distance from the transducer increases. At a distance of two times the NZL, the beam diameter once again equals the diameter of the transducer. The divergence of the beam in the far field is inversely proportional to the crystal diameter and frequency. The larger the transducer element and the higher the frequency, the smaller the angle of divergence in the far field (Fig. 1–18A and B).

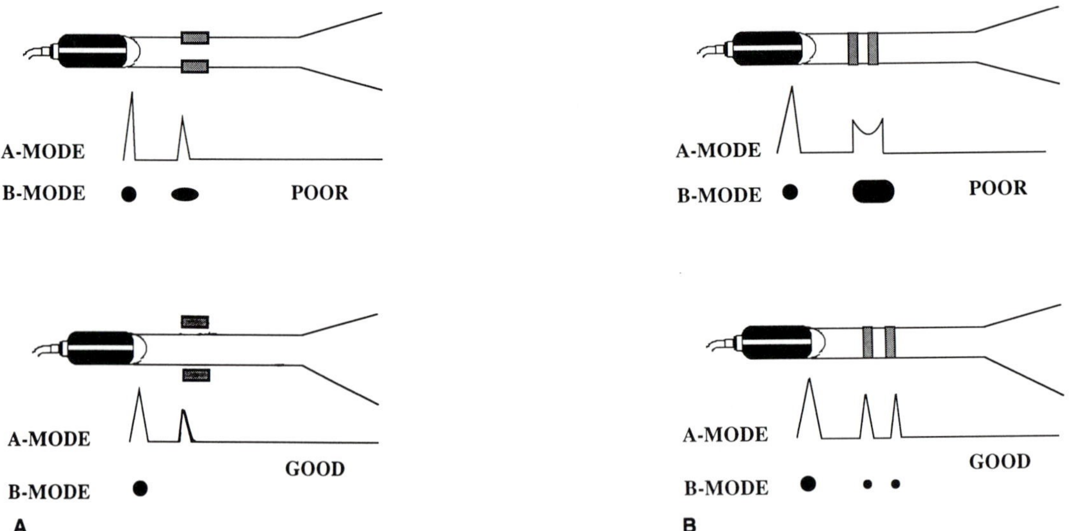

Figure 1–19 (A) *Lateral Resolution:* the ability of the ultrasound beam to separate two structures lying at a right angle (perpendicular) to the beam direction. Lateral resolution is also referred to as azimuthal, transverse, angular, or horizontal. **(B)** *Axial Resolution:* The ability of the ultrasound beam to separate two structures lying along the path of (parallel to) the beam direction. Axial resolution is also referred to as linear, longitudinal, depth, or range.

Resolution

There are two types of resolution, lateral and axial (Figs. 1–19A and B).

Lateral resolution (azimuthal, transverse, or angular resolution). Equal to the beam diameter (see Fig. 1–19A). The distance between two interfaces has to be greater than the beam diameter (width) for the two interfaces to be resolved as separate entities. Lateral resolution applies to interfaces perpendicular to the direction of the sound beam. With an unfocused transducer, lateral resolution is best in the near field; with a focused transducer, the lateral resolution is best at the focal point. A transducer with a smaller diameter will improve lateral resolution in the near zone, but will decrease the lateral resolution as the beam diverges in the far zone.

Axial resolution (linear, range longitudinal, or depth resolution). Related to the spatial pulse length (SPL). Two interfaces at different depths will be distinguished from each other only if the distance between them is equal to or greater than one-half the SPL (see Fig. 1–19B).

$$\text{axial resolution} = \frac{\text{spatial pulse length (SPL)}}{2}$$

To obtain maximum image quality, axial resolution (R_A) should be as small as possible. Axial resolution improves when wavelength or the number of cycles per second decreases (both of these factors are related to SPL). Frequency also affects the axial resolution. As the frequency increases the wavelength decreases, thus the axial resolution improves. However, as the frequency increases the depth of penetration decreases, creating a need to compromise resolution for adequate penetration into the tissues. This compromise is the reason why the frequency range for diagnostic procedures is usually between 2 and 10 MHz.

IMAGING PROCESS

The components of a pulsed-echo diagnostic ultrasound system are the pulser, receiver, scan converter, and display (Fig. 1–20).

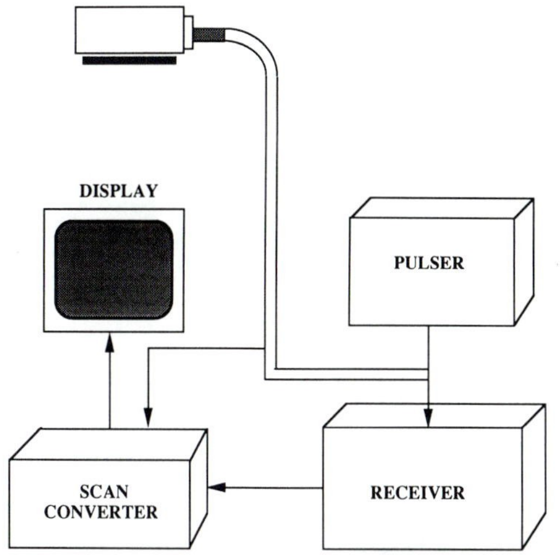

Figure 1–20. Components of a pulsed-echo diagnostic ultrasound system.

Pulser

The *pulser* produces an electric voltage that activates the piezoelectric element, causing it to contract and expand to produce the longitudinal compression wave (sound beam). A second function of the pulser is to signal the receiver and scan converter that the transducer has been activated. Each electric pulse generates an ultrasonic pulse. The number of ultrasonic pulses per second is defined as the *pulse repetition frequency* (PRF). With array transducers, the pulser is responsible for the delay and variations in pulse amplitude needed for electronic control of beam scanning, steering, and shaping. In improving the dynamic range of multi-element transducers the pulser suppresses grating lobes, a process termed *dynamic apodization.*[1]

Increasing the power output control of a system will raise the intensity by signaling the pulser to put out more voltage. To reduce the potential for harmful bioeffects, it is desirable to keep the power low. Therefore, to increase the number of echoes displayed it is recommended that the operator increase the gain control, not the power.

Receiver

The receiver processes electric signals returned from the transducer (ie, ultrasonic reflections converted into electric signals by the transducer). Processing involves amplification, compensation, compression, demodulation, and rejection (Fig. 1–21).

Amplification. The process that increases small electric voltages received from the transducer to a level suitable for further processing. This process is sometimes referred to as "over-all-gain" enhancement or increase. Gain is the ratio of output electric power to input electric power and is measured in decibels (dB). *Dynamic range* is the range of values between the minimum and maximum echo amplitudes. It is the ratio of the largest power to the smallest power in the working range of the diagnostic unit. Dynamic range is also expressed in decibels.

Compensation. Also referred to as gain compensation, swept gain, or time gain compensation. It is the mechanism that compensates for the loss of echo strength caused by the depth of the reflector. It allows reflectors with equal reflection coefficients to appear on the screen with equal brightness and to compensate, to a certain extent, for the effects of attenuation caused by greater depth. For the average soft tissues, the attenuation coefficient is equal to one-half the frequency (expressed in decibels per centimeter).

Compression. The internal process in which larger echoes are equalized with smaller echoes. Compression decreases dynamic range.

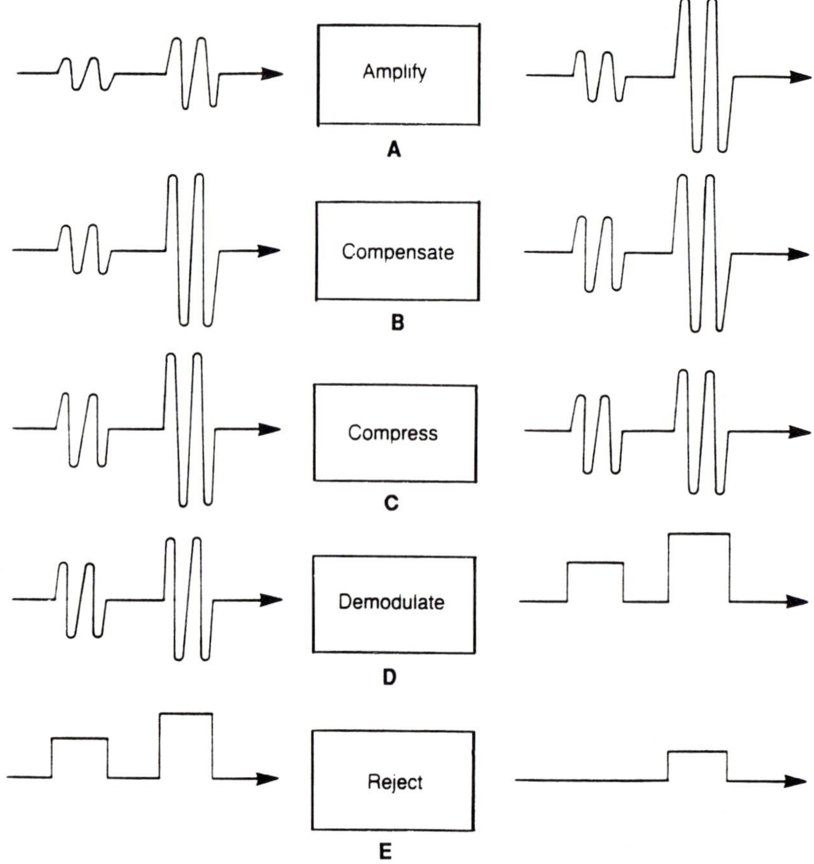

Figure 1–21. The five functions of the receiver. (**A**) Amplification of both pulses. (**B**) Amplification of the weaker pulses. (**C**) The difference between the pulse amplitudes is reduced. (**D**) The pulses are converted to another form. (**E**) The weaker pulse is rejected. *(Kremkaw FW. Diagnostic Ultrasound: Principles, Instruments, and Exercises, 3rd ed. Philadelphia: WB Saunders, 1989.)*

Demodulation. The process of converting voltages delivered to the receiver to a more useful form. Demodulation is done by rectification (removal of negative components, replacement with positive values) and smoothing (averaging of the new wave form).

Rejection. Also termed suppression or threshold. Rejection is the elimination of smaller amplitude voltage pulses produced by weaker reflections. This mechanism helps to reduce noise by removing low-level signals that do not contribute to meaningful information in the image.

Scan Converter (Memory)

The *scan converter, or memory,* transforms the incoming echo data into a suitable format for the display, storing all of the necessary information for the two-dimensional image. As the tissue is scanned, several images (frames) are acquired per second. Memory allows for a single scan consisting of one or more frames to be displayed. Most instruments have enough memory to store the last several frames scanned (cine loop). There are two types of scan converters (memories): analog and digital.

Analog scan converters. Found in older machines, these consist of semiconductors arranged in square matrices. As the ultrasound pulse transverses the tissues, an electronic beam scans the square matrix. It is swept in the same direction as the beam in the body. The current within the electronic beam corresponds to the intensity of the returning echoes. If the echoes are weak the current in the electronic beam is decreased, and vice versa. The strengths of the electrical charges are precisely what are stored in the individual insulators of the matrix. These electronic charges have values that correspond to brightness levels. To read the stored images, the electronic beam is scanned across the stored matrix. The stored charge in each element affects the current in the electronic beam, and together these charges are used to vary the brightness of display.

Digital scan converters. Store image brightness values as numbers instead as of electrical charges. A digital scan converter consists of three components: an analog-to-digital (A–D) converter, which changes the voltages of received signals into numeric values; a

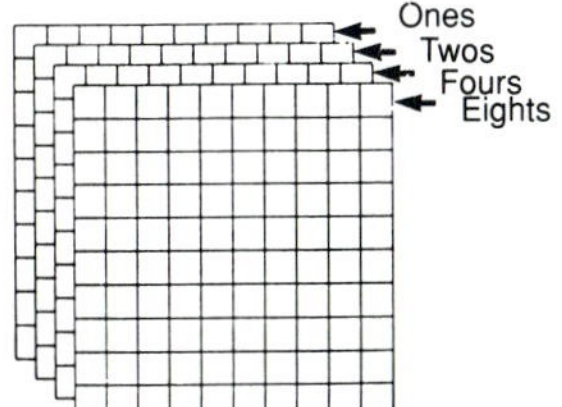

Figure 1–22. A 10 × 10 pixel, 4-bit-deep digital memory. *(Kremkau FW. Diagnostic Ultrasound: Principles, Instruments, and Exercises. 3rd ed. Philadelphia: WB Saunders, 1989.)*

digital memory, which stores these image echo values; and a circuit, which translates these stored numbers back into analog (voltage) values when needed (a digital-to-analog, or D–A, converter).

The digital memory component is the same as computer memory. Modern computers use circuits that have only two states: off and on. Within the computer, these states may be represented, for example, by the absence or presence of electrical current, the open or closed condition of switches, or the direction of magnetization on a magnetic disk or tape. Each of these examples has two states, which the computer considers zero (0) or one (1). At first, it seems that this system, called the *binary number system,* or binary,[4] is not very useful for computing, but it can represent any number that the more common decimal system can. Instead of using increasing powers of 10, as the decimal system does, the binary system uses increasing powers of 2. In the decimal system, the right-most digit represents units, the next to the left tens, the next hundreds, etc. In the binary system, the right-most binary digit or bit is ones, the next left twos, the next fours, the next eights, etc[1] (Fig. 1–22).

Display

How is this system used to represent ultrasound images? Imagine that the image is divided into many small squares similar to a checkerboard. Each square is assigned a number that represents the ultrasound echo amplitude. For example, for white-on-black displays, the highest echo value is white, and the lowest is black (the reverse is true for black-on-white displays).[2] A square located in a part of the image that has the highest echo values (eg, echoes in a gallstone) would be assigned a high number value, while a square in the surrounding bile would receive a small number value. In color flow imaging, each square would be assigned a number that represents the Doppler shift value. If the squares are made small enough, then the eye will not be able to see them as separate. Typically, ultrasound images are divided into 512 by 512 of these little squares.[1]

The squares are called picture elements, or pixels. The number 512 is a power of two (two to the ninth power) and also happens to fit well in a standard television frame. This number yields an image containing 262,144 pixels.

If each of these pixels could store only one binary value, then the results would be very much like an old bistable image, having only black and white values. Each pixel could be either black or white, with no gray values. To store gray scale images each pixel must have more than one binary digit (or bit). For example, with three bits per pixel each pixel could represent eight different shades of gray. To calculate how many different shades of gray can be represented by a pixel containing a set number (n) of data bits, the following formula can be applied:

$$\text{number of shades} = 2^n$$

The largest value that can be represented by a given number of bits is calculated by the formula:

$$\text{largest value for } n \text{ bits} = 2^n - 1$$

If, for example, we are considering 3 bits, we could represent eight different shades of gray with the largest gray value equal to seven.

Most ultrasound machines generate images with 4 to 8 bits of gray scale (16 to 256 shades of gray). Color-flow Doppler machines need more bits to represent the various colors. Since the machine makes no distinction of color (to the machine the image is only an array of numbers), the color values are stored as a number value for each of three primary colors. Combinations of these three primaries (usually red, green, and blue) can yield almost any color.

Fig. 1–22 is an example of a 10 × 10 pixel matrix with 4 bits/pixel. To calculate how many bits an ultrasound image contains, the following formula can be applied:

$$\begin{aligned}\text{number of bits/image} &= \text{number of image rows}\\ &\times \text{number of image columns}\\ &\times \text{number of bits/pixel}\end{aligned}$$

or

$$\begin{aligned}\text{number of bits/image} &= \text{total number of pixels}\\ &\times \text{number of bits/pixel}\end{aligned}$$

In computer terminology, 8 binary digits or 8 bits equals 1 *byte.* To determine the number of bytes of memory an image requires, divide the number of bits per image by eight:

$$\text{number of bytes/image} = \frac{\text{number of bits per image}}{8}$$

Examples

If an image has 10 pixel columns and rows with 2 bits/pixel, then:

$$\text{number of bits/image} = 10 \times 10 \times 2 = 200 \text{ bits}$$

TABLE 1–2. UNIT OF MEASUREMENT IN COMPUTER TERMINOLOGY

Unit	Prefix	Symbol	Quantity
byte[a]	kilo-	K	1000[a]
byte	mega-	M	1,000,000
byte	giga-	G	1,000,000,000

[a] 1 kilobyte equals 1024 characters, but can be rounded off to 1000.

$$\text{number of bytes/image} = \frac{200 \text{ bits/image}}{8} = 25 \text{ bytes}$$

If a 512 × 512 pixel image has 8 bits/pixel, then:

$$\text{number of bits/image} = 512 \times 512 \times 8 = 2{,}097{,}152 \text{ bits}$$

$$\text{number of bytes/image} = \frac{2{,}097{,}152}{8} = 262{,}144 \text{ bytes}$$

A single image can thus contain over 2 million bits or more than ¼ million bytes. To reduce the number of digits used to describe these values, multipliers are applied, such as kilo-, mega-, giga- (Table 1–2). These multipliers are not identical to their counterparts in the metric system, however. For example, 1 kilobit is not 1000 bits, but 1024 bits or 2 to the 10th power. For convenience, large numbers may be rounded (eg, 262,144 bytes may be rounded to 260 kilobytes).

The image can be stored in the digital memory as numbers, but it cannot be viewed unless the numbers are converted back to an image. Otherwise, a large list of numbers is all that would be displayed. The third part of the digital scan converter does this conversion: It takes the number values stored in the memory and changes them back into an analog voltage. The voltage varies the brightness of a spot on the cathode ray tube, generating an image that the human eye can interpret. The hardware that performs this function is the digital-to-analog (D–A) converter.

DYNAMIC IMAGING

Dynamic imaging is simply the process of viewing an image in motion. The dynamic image is displayed on a *cathode-ray tube* (CRT), the unit of visual display that receives electrical impulses and translates them into the picture on the screen by varying the brightness of the trace or lines displayed. The CRT in Fig. 1–23 is an electrostatic deflection CRT; another type, the magnetic deflection CRT, substitutes a magnetic coil to serve the same function as the deflection plates (ie, to move the electron beam). The front face of the CRT, the screen, is phosphor coated and displays the product of the aforementioned process in the form of a recognizable image.

A *frame* is a single image composed of multiple scan lines. To produce a dynamic or moving image, numerous

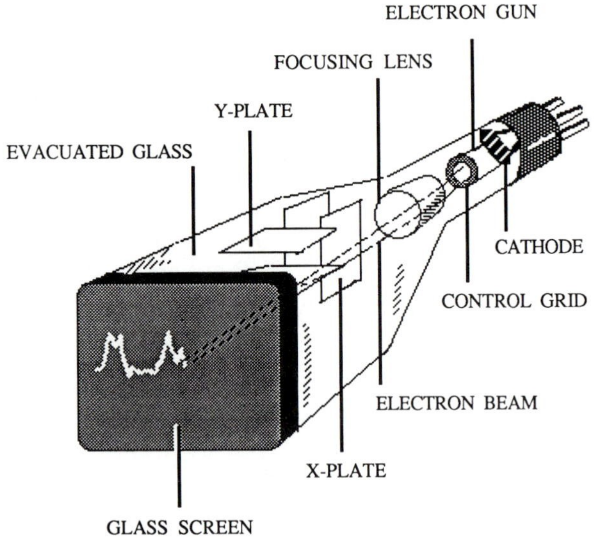

Figure 1–23. Basic structure of a cathode ray tube (CRT). *(Modified from McDicken W: Diagnostic Ultrasonics: Principles and Use of Instruments, 2nd ed. New York, Wiley, 1981, p 15).*

frames are required. To freeze a frame, or stop the image to record or view it, the memory of the system is activated. The *frame rate* (FR) is the number of frames displayed or scanned per second. In most diagnostic medical sonography or echocardiography systems, the frame rate is usually 10 to 60 frames/s. If the display frame rate is below 20/s, then the real-time image appears to flicker, preventing the eye from integrating the images.

The pulse repetition frequency (PRF) is the number of pulses produced by the transducer in a given time period. It is related to the number of lines per frame and the frame rate by the formula:

$$\text{pulse repetition frequency (PRF)} = \text{lines per frame (LPF)} \times \text{frame rate (FR)}$$

The PRF, LPF, and FR are directly related to the propagation speed. The maximum effective velocity is 77,000 cm/s, or one-half the propagation speed of ultrasound in soft tissues (1540 m/s or 154,000 cm/s). The one-half value results from the pulse having to make a round-trip to be received.

$$\text{depth} \times \text{LPF} \times \text{FR} = 77{,}000$$

Note: LPF × FR = PRF. Hence the equation can also be stated

$$\text{depth} \times \text{PRF} = 77{,}000$$

Improving image quality by increasing the lines per frame will reduce the frame rate if the depth remains constant. Increasing the depth of penetration while maintaining a constant number of lines per frame also reduces

the frame rate. The frame rate can be increased if the depth of penetration is decreased, assuming the LPF is constant.

The *display format* refers to how the image appears on the screen, as either a rectangular display or a sector display. A *rectangular display* image appears in the form of a rectangle. The width of the display is given in centimeters; the *line density* is expressed as the number of lines per centimeter. To determine the line density for a rectangular display the lines per frame are divided by the display width in centimeters:

$$\text{line density (lines/cm)} = \frac{\text{lines per frame (LPF)}}{\text{display width (cm)}}$$

A *sector display* yields a pie-shaped image. The scans form an angle so that the line density is expressed as lines per degree.

$$\text{line density (lines/degree)} = \frac{\text{lines per frame (LPF)}}{\text{sector angle (degrees)}}$$

The *scan converter,* electronic circuitry in the machine's display, transforms a rectangular or arc-shaped image into a rectangular video frame, and adds the text and graphics (such as depth markers).

Modes of Display

The *A-mode,* or amplitude mode, is a one-dimensional graphic display with vertical deflections of the baseline. The height of the deflection represents the amplitude, or strength, of the echo; the distance in time is a function of where on the baseline the deflection occurs.

The *B-mode,* or brightness mode, displays the echoes as variations in the brightness of a line of spots on the CRT. The position of the spot on the baseline is related to the depth of the reflecting structure; the brightness is proportional to the strength of the echo. Each row of spots represents information obtained from a single position of the transducer or scanning beam. When successive rows of these spots are integrated into an image, a B-scan is produced.

The *M-mode,* or motion mode, is a two-dimensional recording of the reflector's change in position, or motion, against time. Most M-modes display the brightness of the signal in proportion to the strength of the echo. This mode is most commonly used for the study of dynamic structures such as the heart.

ARTIFACTS

Unlike the Grecian urn, which is an *artifact* from a past culture, the term in diagnostic medical sonography has a very different implication. It refers to something seen on an image that does not, in reality, exist in the anatomy studied. An artifact can be beneficial to the interpretation of the image, or it can detract from this process. For example, certain artifacts are known to occur in cystic structures and are notably absent from a solid mass, and this information can therefore be used in a beneficial way when determining the nature of a mass. Conversely, there are artifacts that can appear similar to the placenta, making delineation of the limits of the placenta more difficult. Artifacts can be subdivided by the physical principles that produce them, namely: resolution artifacts, propagation artifacts, attenuation artifacts, or miscellaneous artifacts.

Resolution Artifacts

Axial resolution. The failure to resolve two separate reflectors parallel to the beam.

Lateral resolution. The failure to resolve two separate reflectors perpendicular to the beam.

Speckle. Scatter in tissues, causing interference effects referred to as noise.

Section thickness. The finite width of the beam producing extraneous echoes, or debris, in normally anechoic, or echo-free, structures.

Propagation Artifacts

Reverberation. Repetitive reflections between two highly reflective layers. The bouncing back and forth increases travel time, causing the signals to be displayed at different depths. The reverberations are seen on the image as equally spaced bands of diminishing amplitude.

Refraction. The change in direction of the sound beam as it passes from one medium to another. This phenomenon will cause a reflection to appear improperly positioned on the image.

Multipath. Because the returning signal does not necessarily follow the same path as the incident beam, the time required for some parts of the signal to return to the transducer will vary, causing reflections to appear at incorrect depths.

Mirror image. Generated when objects present on one side of a strong reflector are also shown on the other side of the reflector. Such artifacts are commonly seen around the diaphragm.

Attenuation Artifacts

Shadowing. The reduction in echo strength of signals arising from behind a strong reflector or attenuating structure. Structures such as gallstones, renal calculi, and bone will produce shadowing.

Enhancement. An increase in the amplitude of echoes located behind a weakly attenuating structure. The increase pertains to the relative strength of the signals as compared with neighboring signals passing through more highly attenuating media. For example, stronger reflections may be seen behind a fluid-

filled structure than behind a solid structure (eg, the urine-filled bladder versus a solid tumor of the uterus).

Refraction or edge shadowing. The beam may bend at a curved surface and lose intensity, producing a shadow. If the beam is traveling from a higher velocity medium (less dense) to a low-velocity medium, a narrower shadow will be generated. Conversely, a sound beam traveling from a low-velocity medium to a higher one will project a wider shadow.

Miscellaneous Artifacts

Comet tail. Produced by a strong reflector; similar in appearance to reverberation. The comet tail, however, is composed of thin lines of closely spaced discrete echoes.

Ring down. Thought to be caused by a resonance phenomenon and is associated with gas bubble. It also appears very similar to reverberation, producing numerous parallel echoes. Sometimes discrete echoes cannot be differentiated, giving the appearance of a continuous emission of sound.

Propagation speed error. Most diagnostic ultrasound equipment operates on the assumption that the speed of sound in the body is 1540 m/s. This is not always true, as different tissues do have different propagation speeds. If the beam passes from a medium of one speed into a medium of a greater speed, then the calculated distance will be less than the actual distance, causing the echo to be erroneously displayed too close to the transducer. If the propagation speed decreases, then the echo will appear farther from the transducer than it actually is.

Side lobes. The result of the transducer element being finite in size. The difference in vibration at the center and edge results in acoustic energy emitted by the transducer flowing along the main axis of the sound beam. The energy that diverts from the main path is the cause of the side lobes, which will generate reflections at improper, off-axis locations in the image.

Grating lobes. Seen with linear array transducers, which also produce off-axis acoustic waves as a result of the regular spacing of the active elements. All grating lobes will cause reflections to appear at improper, off-axis locations in the image.

QUALITY OF PERFORMANCE

To guarantee efficiency of performance, all ultrasound diagnostic equipment is tested under a quality assurance (QA) program. To ensure that the instrument is operating correctly and consistently, it is checked for

1. imaging performance
2. equipment performance and safety

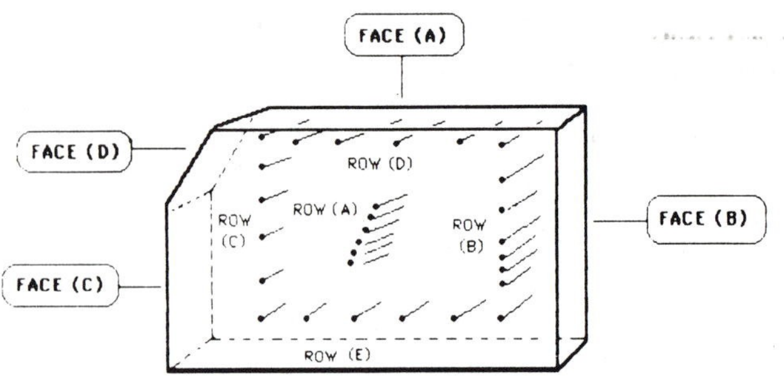

Figure 1–24. AIUM 100-mm test object.

3. beam measurements
4. acoustic output
5. preventative maintenance

AIUM Test Object

The American Institute of Ultrasound in Medicine (AIUM) has designed a test object specifically to measure imaging performance of an ultrasound system (Fig. 1–24). The AIUM test object is a "tank" consisting of a series of stainless steel rods, 0.75 mm in diameter, arranged in a specific pattern between two transparent plastic sides, with the other boundaries formed by thin, acrylic plastic sheets.[1,4] The tank is filled with a mixture of alcohol, an algae inhibitor, and water, which allows the propagation speed to approximate the speed of sound in soft tissues (1540 m/s). The results obtained are not affected by normal fluctuations in room temperature; the speed varies less than 1% for a temperature variation of 5° Celsius (5° C).

The following factors are measured by the AIUM test object (Table 1–3):

System sensitivity. Measured by determining the weakest signal that the system will display.

Axial resolution. Determined by placing the transducer on face A and scanning rod group (a). The six rods are separated by 4, 3, 2, and 1 mm, respectively. The system's axial resolution in millimeters is equal to the distance between the two closest yet distinguishable echoes.

Lateral resolution. Measured by placing the transducer on face B and scanning rod group (b). The lateral resolution is equal to the distance between the two closest rods in this group.

Dead zone. The region of the sound beam in which imaging cannot be performed; the area closest to the transducer. To determine the extent of the dead zone, the transducer is placed on face A and rod group (d) is scanned. The distance from the transducer to the first rod imaged is equal to the length of the dead zone.

Range accuracy (depth accuracy). Measured by placing the transducer on face A and scanning rod group (e). For the system to be operating properly, the echoes should appear at their actual depths and spacings within 1 mm (The rods in this group are 2 cm apart).

TABLE 1–3. PERFORMANCE MEASUREMENTS FOR THE AIUM TEST OBJECT

Measurement	Row	Test Object Face	Parameter Tested
Dead zone	D	Face (A)	The distance measured between the transducer face and the first rod depicted
Lateral resolution	B	Face (B)	Linear measurement of the echoes produced by Row D
Depth calibration	C or E	Face (A) or (B)	The distance measured between the first and the last line in Row E
Registration	E	Face (A), (B), (C), and (D)	Good Poor
Axial resolution	A	Face (A)	5 mm to 1 mm pins spaced at decreasing intervals of 1 mm in Row A
Digital calipers	E	Face (C)	A distance of 10 cm or 100 mm measured on the horizontal pins in Row E, indicating the digital calipers are functioning correctly
Liquid velocity	E	Face (C)	The cursors are positioned at the leading edge echo to the other end leading edge echo, on the horizontal pins in Row E. A 100 mm measurement indicates the liquid medium velocity is correct

Checking the range accuracy ensures the accuracy of the internal calipers of the system.

In addition to the AIUM test object, other devices have been designed to measure different parameters of imaging performance. The *beam profiler* is designed to record three-dimensional reflection amplitude information. It consists of a pulser, receiver, transducer, and tank equipped with rods placed at different distances from the transducer.[1]

The transducer is pulsed and scanned across the rods. The fluctuation in amplitude of each reflection returning to the transducer is recorded in an A-mode pattern. The *hydrophone* is one of several devices that measure acoustic output; it consists of a small transducer element mounted on a narrow tube.[1] When used with an oscilloscope, the voltages produced in response to variations in pressure can be displaced and evaluated. The output produced by the hydrophone permits calculation of the period, pulse repetition period, and pulse duration. The hydrophone can also be used as a beam profiler.

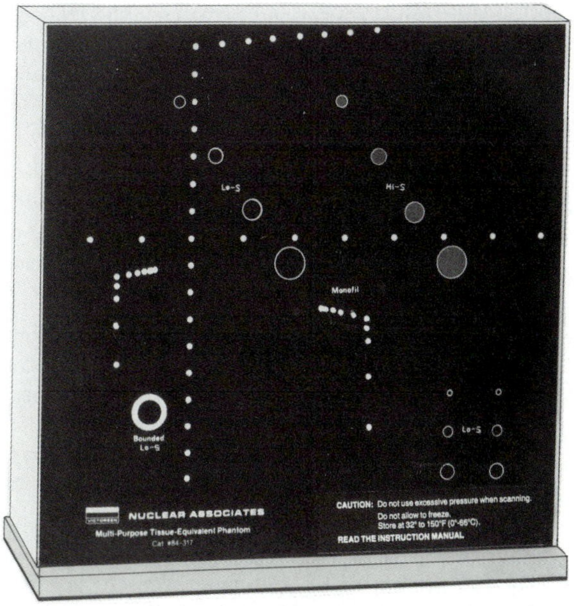

Figure 1–25. Multi-purpose tissue/cyst phantom. *(Courtesy of Nuclear Associates, Carle Place, NY. Printed with permission.)*

Tissue/Cyst Phantom

This test device contains a medium that simulates soft tissue (Fig. 1–25). Enclosed in the phantom are structures that mimic cysts and solid masses and a series of 0.375-mm targets, in two groups. Each group measures depth and angular resolution. The phantom is used to evaluate the ultrasound system and transducer performance. Sonographic equipment can be evaluated for depth and angular resolution, vertical and horizontal distance calibration, and ring down.[5]

Bioeffects

To date, there is no concrete evidence to support any truly detrimental bioeffects from the application of diagnostic ultrasound to human tissues.[1] The study of possible effects is ongoing, however, and the definitive answer has not been found. It is generally agreed that the potential value of the information obtained from the procedure far outweighs the possibility of deleterious effects. Greater study of the microscopic effects of sound on tissue will have to take place before additional conclusions can be reached. To clarify what is known to date, the potential bioeffects are categorized in three groups: mechanical effects, thermal effects, and cavitation.

Mechanical effects include all types of damage not categorized as thermal or cavitational. There is very little information on this type of effect.

Thermal effects are produced primarily by the mechanisms of attenuation. As a major component of attenuation, absorption by the tissue leads to a rise in tissue temperature. Increased temperatures can cause irreversible damage, depending on the extent of the exposure. It is generally agreed that *exposure producing a maximum temperature of 1° C can be used without any effects. A rise*

in temperature of the tissues to 41° C or above is considered dangerous to a fetus. The longer that this temperature is maintained, the greater the potential risk for damage.[1]

Cavitation is the result of pressure changes in the medium causing gas bubbles to form; it can produce severe tissue damage. The two types of cavitation are stable cavitation and transient cavitation. *Stable cavitation* involves microbubbles already present in tissue that respond by expanding and contracting when pressure is applied. These bubbles can intercept and absorb a large amount of the acoustic energy. Stable cavitation can result in shear stresses and microstreaming in the surrounding tissues.

Transient cavitation is dependent on the pressure of the ultrasound pulses. The tissue bubbles expand and collapse violently. This type of cavitation can cause highly localized, violent effects involving enormous pressures, markedly elevated temperatures, shock waves, and mechanical stress. Cavitation may occur with short pulses. It has been shown that pulses with peak intensities of greater than 3300 W/cm^2 can induce cavitation in mammals.[1] Precise determination of when cavitation will occur is not currently within our capabilities. For specific conditions of homogeneous media, it is possible to estimate an index for the cavitation threshold.

The following guidelines are adapted from an official statement by the American Institute of Ultrasound in Medicine (AIUM): *Bioeffects Considerations for the Safety of Diagnostic Ultrasound.* Bethesda, MD, American Institute of Ultrasound Medicine, 1988. The reader is urged to read the full AIUM text.

Intensity. No independently confirmed significant biological effects in mammalian tissues exposed in vivo with unfocused transducers with intensities below 100 mW/cm^2 and below 1 W/cm^2 for focused transducers.

Exposure. Exposure times can be > 1 s and < 500 s for an unfocused transducer; and < 50 s/pulse for a focused transducer. No significant bioeffects have been observed even at higher intensities than noted above (as long as the intensity × time product is < 50 J/cm^2).

Thermal. A maximum temperature rise of 1° C is acceptable, but an increase in the in situ temperature to 41° C or greater is hazardous to fetuses.

Cavitation. Can result if pressure peaks are greater than 3300 W/cm^2. However, it is not possible to specify a threshold at which cavitation will occur.

Randomized studies are the best method for assessing potential effects. *There are no independent confirmed biologic effects on patients or operators.*[1]

COMPUTERS AND ULTRASOUND

The majority of modern ultrasound equipment is computerized or has some computer capabilities. Today's ultrasound equipment can calculate gestational age, store nomograms, store patient data, and transfer sonographic images from one hospital to another via a modem (modulator/demodulator).

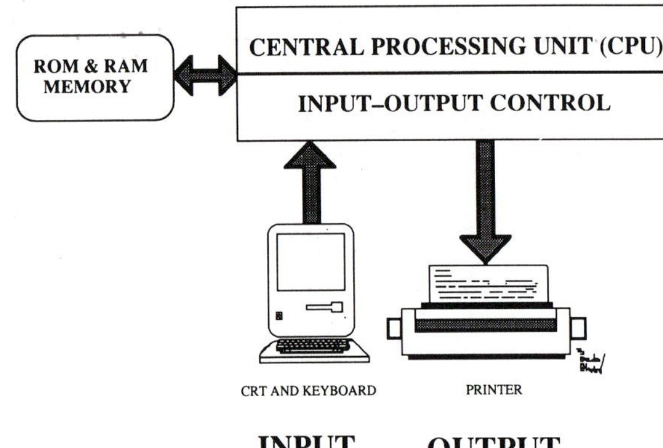

Figure 1–26. Computer organization.

What Is a Computer?

A computer is a device that contains a microprocessor and can perform high-speed mathematical calculations, assemble and store data, and perform logic operations. The graphics in this book, for example, were processed and stored by a computer.

The Computer Brain. The "brain" of the computer (Fig. 1–26) comprises three general parts:

1. the central processing unit (CPU)
2. the memory unit
3. the input–output unit

The *main computer storage* (MCS) is the memory of the computer. There are two kinds of computer memory[6]:

ROM (Read-only memory). ROM is permanent and unchangeable. It is installed by the computer manufacturer and contains instructions needed by the CPU when the computer is turned on.

RAM (Random-access memory, or read and write). RAM is temporary and changeable. It is usable memory for the operator to change depending on needs. This is temporary memory because when the computer is turned off, the RAM is lost. However, data can be extracted from the RAM before the computer is turned off to be stored permanently on a floppy disk or hard disk for use at a later time.

When the sonographer looks at the contents of the memory, he or she is *reading*. When the sonographer is entering or changing information, he or she is *writing* (read and write memory).

REFERENCES

1. Kremkau FW. *Diagnostic Ultrasound: Principles, Instruments and Exercises,* 3rd ed. Philadelphia: WB Saunders, 1989.

2. Edelman SK. *Understanding Ultrasound Physics: Fundamentals and Exam Review.* Houston: EPS Publishers, 1990.
3. Pinkney N. *A Review of the Concepts of Ultrasound Physics and Instrumentation,* 4th ed. Philadelphia: Sonior, 1983.
4. Bushong SC, Archer RB. *Diagnostic Ultrasound: Physics, Biology, and Instrumentation.* St. Louis: Mosby–Year Book, 1991.
5. *Diagnostic Ultrasound: Test Equipment and Accessories.* New York: Nuclear Associates, Catalog U-2, 1991, pp. 2–3.
6. Shelly G, Cashman T. *Computer Fundamentals for an Information Age.* Brea, CA: Anaheim Publishing, 1984.

Questions

GENERAL INSTRUCTIONS: For each question, select the best answer. Select only one answer for each question unless otherwise specified.

1. An example of a nonspecular reflector is

   (A) the liver surface
   (B) the diaphragm
   (C) red blood cells
   (D) any structure that does *not* produce a strong echo

2. The spatial pulse length

   (A) determines penetration depth
   (B) usually decreases with frequency
   (C) is improved with rectification
   (D) determines lateral resolution

3. Axial resolution

   (A) is improved in the focal zone
   (B) depends on the TGC slope
   (C) is improved by digital scan converters
   (D) depends on the wavelength

4. Lateral resolution

   (A) and ring-down are the same
   (B) depends on the beam diameter
   (C) improves with frequency
   (D) cannot be measured in the far zone

5. The beam of an unfocused transducer diverges

   (A) because of inadequate damping
   (B) in the Fresnel zone
   (C) in the Fraunhofer zone
   (D) when the pulse length is long

6. Reverberation artifacts are a result of

   (A) electronic noise
   (B) improper TGC settings
   (C) the presence of two or more strong reflecting surfaces
   (D) an angle of incidence that is too small

7. Grating lobes are essential for the proper operation of a linear phased array.

   (A) true
   (B) false

8. Electronically steered scanners always produce higher resolution images than do mechanically steered scanners.

   (A) true
   (B) false

9. An annular array scanner uses mechanical beam steering.

   (A) true
   (B) false

10. A linear sequenced array cannot be dynamically focused.

    (A) true
    (B) false

Questions 11 through 15: Match the following group of wires with its function for the AIUM test object (Fig. 1–27).

11. registration or B-mode alignment _____

12. axial resolution _____

13. lateral resolution _____

14. dead zone _____

15. depth calibration _____

16. Decreasing the spatial pulse length

    (A) reduces the field of view
    (B) reduces lateral resolution
    (C) improves axial resolution
    (D) improves lateral resolution

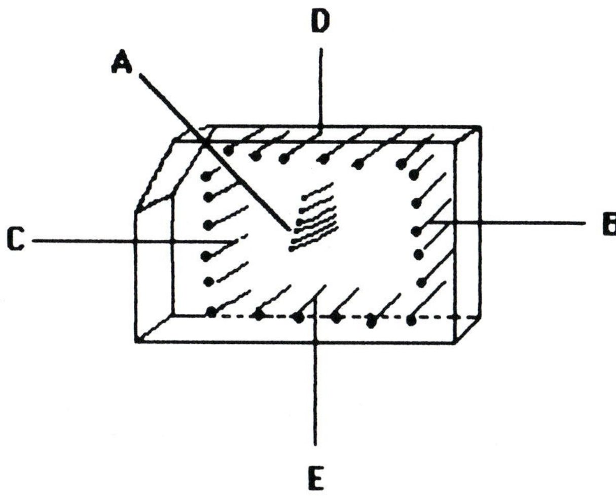

Figure 1–27. AIUM 100-mm test object.

17. How much will a 3.5-MHz pulse be attenuated after passing through 2 cm of soft tissue?

(A) 7 dB
(B) 3.5 dB
(C) 17 dB
(D) 1.75 dB

18. Propagation speed errors result in

(A) reverberation
(B) improper axial position
(C) shadowing
(D) a Doppler shift

19. Enhancement is caused by

(A) strongly reflecting structures
(B) propagation speed errors
(C) Snell's law
(D) weakly attenuating structures

20. The Doppler shift frequency is

(A) directly proportional to the velocity of the reflector
(B) greater in pulsed Doppler systems
(C) greater at high intensity levels
(D) dependent on the number of transducer elements being used

21. The number of frames per second necessary for a real-time image to be flicker free is

(A) more than 15
(B) less than 10
(C) between 6 and 10
(D) between 3 and 6

22. The SPTA intensity will always be larger than the SATA intensity.

(A) true
(B) false

23. The intensity of the ultrasound beam is usually greater at the focal zone because of

(A) decreased attenuation
(B) the smaller beam diameter
(C) diffraction effects
(D) a shorter duty factor

24. If the amplitude is doubled, the intensity is

(A) doubled
(B) cut in half
(C) increased by four times
(D) unchanged

25. The attenuation for soft tissue is

(A) increased with tissue thickness
(B) determined by the scope of the TGC curve
(C) increased with decreasing wavelength
(D) unimportant when using digital scan converters

26. The acoustic impedance of the matching layer

(A) can be chosen to improve transmission into the body
(B) must be much larger than the transducer material to reduce attenuation
(C) is not necessary with real-time scanners
(D) must be made with the same material as the damping material

27. In a pulse–echo system, the quality factor should be made as large as possible.

(A) true
(B) false

28. The beam diameter is constant in the near zone.

(A) true
(B) false

29. The operating frequency

(A) depends on the transducer's ring-down time
(B) depends on the thickness of the crystal
(C) is increased as the crystal diameter is decreased
(D) depends on the strength of the pulser

30. The period of an ultrasound wave is

(A) the time at which it is no longer detectable
(B) determined by the duty factor
(C) the time of one wavelength
(D) independent of the frequency

31. The dynamic range of a system

(A) is increased when specular reflectors are scanned
(B) is decreased when shadowing is present
(C) can be increased through the use of coupling gel
(D) is the ratio of smallest to largest power level that the system can handle

32. The intensity of an ultrasonic beam can be measured with radiation force balance.

(A) true
(B) false

33. Increasing the pulse repetition period

(A) improves resolution
(B) increases the maximum depth that can be imaged
(C) decreases the maximum depth that can be imaged
(D) increases refraction

34. Ultrasound bioeffects

(A) do not occur
(B) do not occur with diagnostic instruments
(C) are not confirmed below 100 mW/cm^2 SPTA
(D) are not confirmed below 1 W/cm^2 SPTA

35. No refraction can occur at an interface if the media impedances are equal.

(A) true
(B) false

36. Smaller transducers always produce smaller beam diameters.

(A) true
(B) false

37. The ultrasound beam profile can be measured with a hydrophone.

(A) true
(B) false

38. The pulsed-Doppler system yields better depth resolution than the continuous wave (CW) system.

(A) true
(B) false

39. The gray-scale display was made possible when digital scan converters replaced analog scan converters.

(A) true
(B) false

40. Videotape recorders operating at 30 frames per second cannot be used with mechanical real-time units because the frame rate is too slow.

(A) true
(B) false

41. Linear phased array scanners need no form of mechanical focusing since focusing is performed electronically.

(A) true
(B) false

42. The frame rate of real-time scanners depends on the number of lines used to form the image.

(A) true
(B) false

43. It is *not* possible to steer an annular phased array electronically.

(A) true
(B) false

44. The near zone length should be kept as short as possible.

(A) true
(B) false

45. What percentage of intensity of an ultrasound pulse incident on an interface of 0.25 and 0.75 rayls is reflected?

(A) 50%
(B) 100%
(C) 25%
(D) 75%

46. Axial resolution can be improved by using

(A) higher frequency transducers
(B) lower frequency transducers
(C) larger transducers
(D) poorly damped transducers

47. When particle motion of a medium is parallel to the direction of a wave propagation, the wave being transmitted is called a

(A) longitudinal wave
(B) shear wave
(C) surface wave
(D) lamb wave

48. The wavelength in a material having a wave velocity of 1500 m/s employing a transducer frequency of 5 MHz is

(A) 0.3 mm
(B) 0.3 cm
(C) 0.6 mm

49. The factor that determines the amount of reflection at the interface of two dissimilar materials is

(A) the index of refraction
(B) the frequency of the ultrasonic wave
(C) Young's modulus
(D) the specific acoustic impedance

50. The equation that describes the relationship among propagation, wavelength, and frequency is

(A) $V = f\lambda$
(B) wavelength = 2(frequency × velocity)
(C) $Z = pV$
(D) wavelength = frequency + velocity

51. Which of the following can occur when an ultrasonic beam reaches the interface of two dissimilar materials?

(A) reflection
(B) refraction
(C) mode conversion
(D) all of the above

52. The acoustic impedance of a material is

(A) directly proportional to density and inversely proportional to velocity
(B) directly proportional to velocity and inversely proportional to density
(C) inversely proportional to density and velocity
(D) equal to the product of density and velocity

53. The average velocity of ultrasonic waves in soft tissue is

(A) 1540 ft/s
(B) 3300 m/s
(C) 1540 m/s
(D) 300×10^6 m/s

54. Receiver-angle values in CW Doppler analysis do *not* influence the final Doppler shift.

(A) true
(B) false

55. Refraction occurs due to difference in _____ across an interface between two materials.

(A) acoustic impedance
(B) wave velocity
(C) density
(D) none of the above

56. Reflection factor at an interface between two materials depends primarily on the change in _____ across the interface.

(A) acoustic impedance
(B) wave velocity
(C) density
(D) none of the above

57. The velocity of sound waves is primarily dependent on

(A) angulation
(B) reflection
(C) the material through which the sound is being transmitted and the mode of vibration
(D) none of the above

58. Increasing the frequency of an ultrasonic longitudinal wave will result in _____ in the velocity of that wave.

(A) an increase
(B) a decrease
(C) no change
(D) a reversal

59. The change in direction of an ultrasonic beam, when it passes from one medium to another, in which elasticity and density differ from those of the first medium is called

(A) refraction
(B) rarefaction
(C) angulation
(D) reflection

60. A long near zone can be obtained by

(A) using a higher frequency transducer
(B) adding a convex lens to the transducer
(C) decreasing the diameter of the transducer
(D) increasing the damping

61. If a 2-MHz frequency is used in human soft tissue, the wavelength is approximately

(A) 0.75 mm
(B) 0.15 mm
(C) 0.21 mm
(D) 0.44 mm

62. The ratio of particle pressure to particle velocity at a given point within the ultrasonic field is

(A) interference
(B) impedance
(C) incidence
(D) noise

63. What is the following formula used to determine?

$$\frac{2 \times \text{velocity of reflector} \times \text{original frequency}}{\text{velocity of sound}}$$

(A) shift in frequency due to the Doppler effect
(B) degree of attenuation
(C) distance a wave front travels
(D) amount of amplification necessary to produce diagnostic ultrasound

64. The principle which states that all points on a wavefront can be considered as point sources for the production of spherical secondary wavelets was postulated by

(A) Doppler
(B) Young
(C) Huygens
(D) Langevin

65. A 10-dB difference in signal intensity is equivalent to a ______ difference.

(A) twofold
(B) tenfold
(C) hundredfold
(D) thousandfold

66. The level below which signals are *not* transmitted through an ultrasound receiver system is the

(A) sensitivity level
(B) threshold or negative level
(C) impedance level
(D) dynamic range level

67. Gray-scale systems typically use ______ as a means of signal dynamic range reduction.

(A) rejection
(B) compression
(C) relaxation
(D) elimination

68. The strength of the echo is related to the height of the deflection on the oscilloscope for the ______ display.

(A) A-mode
(B) B-mode
(C) B-scan
(D) M-mode

69. Which of the following is *not* a method for restricting the dynamic range of the signal?

(A) suppression
(B) rejection
(C) compression
(D) relaxation

70. Most of the scan converters currently in use are of the ______ type.

(A) analog
(B) digital
(C) bistable
(D) static

71. The fraction of time that pulsed ultrasound is actually on is the

(A) duty factor
(B) frame rate
(C) cavitation
(D) intensity transmission coefficient

72. The ability of an imaging system to detect weak reflections is called

(A) compression
(B) demodulation
(C) gain
(D) sensitivity

73. Which of the following image shapes is produced by a linear sequenced array real-time transducer?

A B C D

74. The major factor in determining the acoustic power output of the transducer is the

(A) size of the transducer
(B) magnitude of the voltage spike
(C) amount of amplification at the receiver
(D) amount of gain

75. Two primary mechanisms that produce sound changes in cells or tissues are

(A) oscillations and radiation
(B) absorption and reflection
(C) direct and indirect
(D) thermal and cavitational

76. The ______ relates bandwidth to operating frequency.

(A) near zone
(B) piezoelectric crystal
(C) quality factor
(D) far zone

77. The extraneous beams of ultrasound generated from the edges of individual transducer elements and not in the direction of the main ultrasonic beam are called

(A) a phased array
(B) impedance artifacts
(C) side lobes
(D) acoustic errors

78. The product of the period and the number of cycles in the pulse is the

(A) pulse repetition frequency
(B) continuous wave
(C) pulse repetition period
(D) pulse duration

79. The substance typically used as a matrix on the imaging surface of an analog scan converter tube is

(A) mercurous chloride
(B) silicon oxide
(C) manganese sulfide
(D) lithium fluoride

80. Specular reflection occurs when

(A) the frequency is small compared with the wavelength
(B) the object that causes the reflection is small
(C) the reflector surface is smooth as compared with the wavelength
(D) the angle of incidence and the angle of reflection differ by at least 45°

81. The refractive index of water is slightly altered when a sound beam passes through it, thus causing compression and rarefaction of the water molecules. The phenomenon is the basis for the ______ technique of beam measurement.

(A) isoamplitude
(B) Schlieren
(C) relative echo
(D) attenuator calibration

82. Artifacts appearing as parallel, equally spaced lines are characteristic of

(A) acoustic shadowing
(B) off-normal incidence
(C) specular reflection
(D) reverberation

83. An increase in reflection amplitude from reflectors that lie behind a weakly attenuating structure is called

(A) the incidence angle
(B) enhancement
(C) the intensity reflection coefficient
(D) the effective reflecting area

84. The amount of dispersion in the far field of an ultrasound beam can be decreased by

(A) using a transducer with a convex face
(B) using a larger diameter transducer
(C) decreasing the intensity of the beam in the near field
(D) using a lower frequency transducer

85. Longitudinal or axial resolution is directly dependent on

(A) depth of penetration
(B) spatial pulse length
(C) damping
(D) the angle of incidence

86. The transducer ______ is equal to the ratio of the operating frequency to the frequency bandwidth.

(A) frequency
(B) Q factor
(C) resolution
(D) polarity

87. The technique that uses an optical system to produce a visible image of an ultrasonic beam is the ______ technique.

(A) M-mode
(B) B-scan
(C) Schlieren
(D) kinetic scanning

88. Which of the following is the least obstacle to the transmission of ultrasound?

(A) muscle
(B) fat
(C) bone
(D) blood

89. The ratio of the largest power to the smallest power that the ultrasound system can handle is the

(A) dynamic range
(B) gain
(C) rejection
(D) amplification factor

90. Ultrasound waves in tissue are called ______ waves.

(A) shear
(B) lateral displacement
(C) rotational vibration
(D) longitudinal

Questions 91 through 99 refer to Fig. 1–28.

91. The row of wires in the middle are used to check

(A) lateral resolution
(B) axial resolution

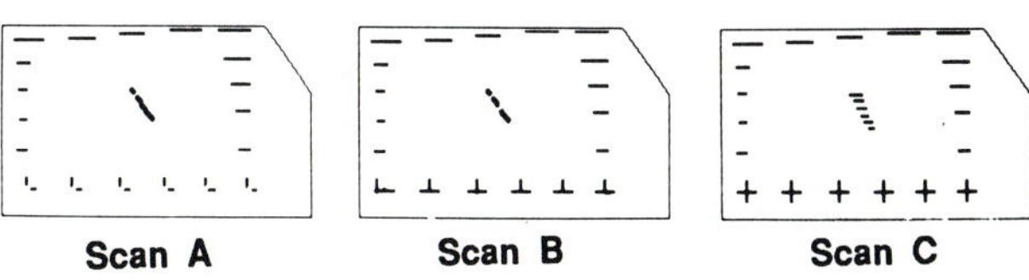

Figure 1–28. Diagram of the AIUM 100-mm test object.

(C) dead zone
(D) horizontal distance calibration
(E) all of the above

92. Which of the diagrams shows correct arm registration?

(A) scan A
(B) scan B
(C) scan C
(D) all the above
(E) none of the above

93. The row of wires on top is used to check

(A) dead zone
(B) vertical distance calibration
(C) horizontal distance calibration
(D) axial resolution
(E) none of the above

94. While using the AIUM test object to test an articulated-arm scanner you obtain an image similar to scan A. You should

(A) call for service
(B) increase the contrast setting
(C) switch to another type of transducer
(D) try another test object

95. The row of wires on the bottom is used to check for

(A) axial resolution
(B) lateral resolution
(C) horizontal caliper check
(D) vertical distance calibration
(E) dead zone

96. All except the following can be checked when the test object is scanned from the top only.

(A) axial resolution
(B) lateral resolution
(C) vertical distance calibration
(D) horizontal distance calibration

97. Which of the following parameters cannot be evaluated by the AIUM test object?

(A) gray scale
(B) dynamic range
(C) azimuthal resolution
(D) depth resolution
(E) both A and B
(F) all of the above

98. Scanning a test object from three sides without erasing would be used to check

(A) gray scale
(B) depth resolution
(C) horizontal distance calibration
(D) registration
(E) all of the above

99. When using the AIUM test object, which of the following should be kept constant for comparisons?

(A) output power
(B) TGC
(C) reject
(D) transducer, MHz, and focus
(E) all of the above

100. Which type of ultrasound machine can be used with the AIUM test object?

(A) linear array
(B) static scanner
(C) phased array
(D) annular array
(E) sector scanner
(F) all of the above
(G) A and C only

101. There are many types of natural and synthetic crystals that possess and exhibit piezoelectric properties. Which of the following are not natural?

(A) tourmaline
(B) quartz
(C) lead zirconate titanate (PZT-4 or PZT-5)
(D) barium titanate
(E) rochelle salt
(F) lithium sulfate
(G) lead metaniobate
(H) ammonium dihydrogen phosphate

102. Which of the following materials would not be suitable as acoustic insulators for transducer backing?

(A) cork
(B) rubber
(C) oil
(D) araldite loaded with tungsten powder
(E) epoxy resin
(F) B and E only
(G) all of the above

103. Ultrasound can be described as a(an)

(A) mechanical vibration that can be transmitted through matter
(B) mechanical vibration that can be transmitted through a vacuum
(C) electromagnetic wave that can be transmitted through tissues
(D) x-ray that can be transmitted through soft tissues

104. If the frequency of sound is below 16 Hz it is called

(A) infrasound (subsonic)
(B) audible sound
(C) ultrasound
(D) x-rays

105. If the frequency of sound is above 20 kHz it is called

(A) infrasound (subsonic)
(B) ultrasound
(C) audible sound
(D) x-rays

106. If the frequency of sound is between 16 Hz and 20 kHz it is called

(A) x-rays
(B) audible sound
(C) ultrasound
(D) infrasound (subsonic)

107. Which of the following is not among the spectrum of electromagnetic waves?

(A) x-rays
(B) ultrasound
(C) ultraviolet
(D) infrared
(E) visible light

108. The term Hertz denotes

(A) density
(B) milliwatts per centimeter square (mW/cm^2)
(C) kilogram
(D) cycle per second

109. An ultrasound transducer converts

(A) electrical energy into light and heat
(B) electrical energy into mechanical energy and vice versa
(C) mechanical energy into radiation
(D) sound into ultrasound

110. Which of the following is(are) an example(s) of a transducer?

(A) battery
(B) loudspeaker
(C) light bulb
(D) human being
(E) all of the above
(F) none of the above
(G) A and B only

111. When electric voltage is applied on both faces of a piezoelectric crystal, the crystal will

(A) increase in size
(B) decrease in size
(C) lose its polarization
(D) increase or decrease in size depending on the voltage polarity

112. The abbreviation 5 MHz denotes

(A) 5 hundred thousand cycles per second
(B) 5 hundred million cycles per second
(C) 5000 cycles per second
(D) 5 million cycles per second

113. The function of the damping material in the transducer housing is to

(A) reduce pulse duration
(B) improve axial resolution
(C) reduce spatial pulse length
(D) improve lateral resolution
(E) A and B only
(F) A and D only
(G) A, B, and C only

114. What is the velocity of ultrasound in human soft tissue at 37°C?

(A) 1540 meters per second
(B) 1540 miles per second
(C) 741 miles per hour
(D) 1087 meters per second

115. In physical science, the word period denotes

(A) the pressure or height of a wave
(B) the speed of a wave
(C) the time it takes to complete a single cycle
(D) propagation

116. Longitudinal waves are characterized by

(A) motion of particles parallel to the axis of wave propagation
(B) motion of particles perpendicular to the axis of wave propagation
(C) twisting action of the particles in motion
(D) surface vibrating particles

117. Transverse waves are characterized by

(A) motion of particles parallel to the axis of wave propagation
(B) surface vibrating particles
(C) motion of particles perpendicular to the axis of wave propagation
(D) twisting action of the particles in motion

118. Ultrasound wave propagation causes displacement of particles in a medium. The regions of greatest particle concentration are called

(A) acoustic impedance
(B) condensations
(C) rarefactions
(D) attenuation

119. Ultrasound wave propagation causes displacement of particles in a medium. The regions of lowest particle concentration are called

(A) acoustic impedance
(B) condensations
(C) rarefactions
(D) attenuation

120. The prefix piezo- is derived from a Greek word that denotes

(A) electric
(B) transducer
(C) crystal
(D) pressure

121. Axial resolution is

(A) the ability to distinguish two objects parallel to the ultrasound beam
(B) the ability to distinguish two objects perpendicular to the ultrasound beam
(C) the same as depth, longitudinal, and range resolution
(D) the same as azimuthal, angular, and transverse resolution
(E) both A and D
(F) both A and C

122. Lateral resolution is

(A) the same as depth, longitudinal, and range resolution
(B) the ability to distinguish two objects perpendicular to the ultrasound beam
(C) the ability to distinguish two objects parallel to the ultrasound beam
(D) the same as azimuthal, angular, and transverse resolution
(E) both A and B
(F) both B and D

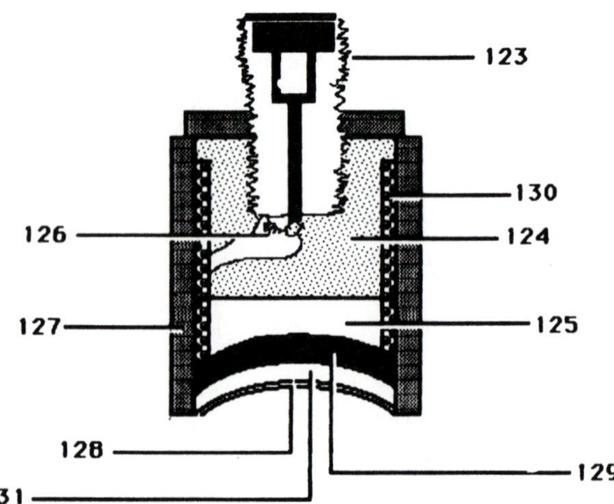

Figure 1–29. Components of a transducer.

Questions 123 through 131: Match the structures in Fig. 1–29 with the list of parts given.

123. _____	(A) tuning coil
124. _____	(B) damping material
125. _____	(C) electrical connector
126. _____	(D) piezoelectric ceramic material
127. _____	(E) housing
128. _____	(F) shield
129. _____	(G) matching layer
130. _____	(H) backing material
131. _____	(I) face material

Questions 132 through 140: Match the structures in Fig. 1–30 with the list of parts given.

132. _____	(A) cathode
133. _____	(B) Y-plate
134. _____	(C) glass screen
135. _____	(D) electron gun
136. _____	(E) evacuated glass
137. _____	(F) X-plate
138. _____	(G) control grid
139. _____	(H) electron beam
140. _____	(I) focusing lens

141. If frequency increases, the wavelength will

(A) decrease
(B) increase
(C) increase 10 times
(D) remain the same

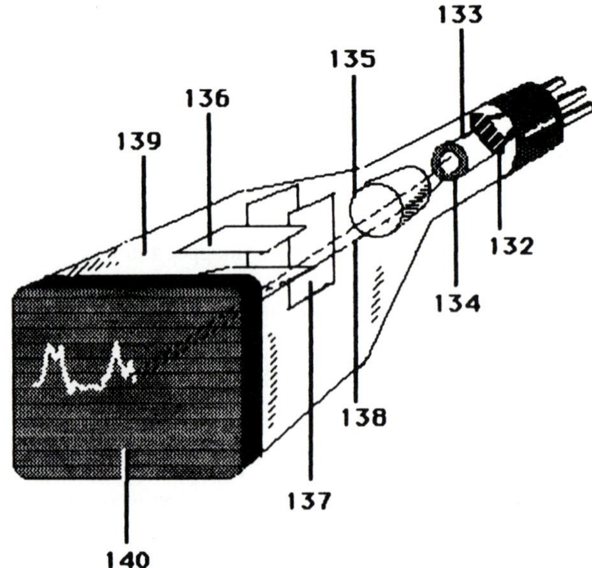

Figure 1–30. Basic structure of a cathode ray tube (CRT).

142. If frequency decreases, the wavelength will

(A) decrease
(B) increase
(C) increase 10 times
(D) remain the same

143. As frequency increases, the penetration will

(A) decrease
(B) increase
(C) increase 10 times
(D) remain the same

144. As frequency increases, the resolution will

(A) decrease
(B) increase
(C) increase 10 times
(D) remain the same

145. As frequency increases, the beam width will

(A) decrease
(B) increase
(C) increase 10 times
(D) remain the same

146. Ultrasound has difficulty in propagating through

(A) air
(B) bone
(C) $BaSO_4$
(D) IVP contrast
(E) all of the above
(F) A, B, and C only
(G) A and B only

147. Which of the following *cannot* be used as a coupling medium?

(A) water
(B) saline
(C) barium sulfate
(D) aqueous gels

148. Attenuation denotes

(A) progressive weakening of the sound beam as it travels
(B) density of tissue and the speed of sound in the tissues
(C) the redirection of the ultrasound back to the transducer
(D) bending of the transmitted wave after crossing an interface

149. The piezoelectric effect can be best described as

(A) density of tissue and the speed of sound in the tissues
(B) mechanical deformation that results from high voltage applied on faces of the crystal, and in turn generates ultrasound
(C) piezoelectric crystals subjected to pressure resulting in electrical charge appearing on their surfaces
(D) having a damaging effect on crystal due to high voltage

150. The reverse piezoelectric effect can be best described as

(A) density of tissue and the speed of sound in the tissues
(B) mechanical deformation that results from high voltage applied on faces of the crystal, and as a result generate ultrasound
(C) piezoelectric crystals subjected to pressures resulting in electrical charges appearing on their surfaces
(D) having a damaging effect on crystal due to high voltage

151. The parameter used to express attenuation is

(A) $\left(\frac{Z_2 - Z_1}{Z_2 + Z_1}\right)^2 \times 100$
(B) $\text{dB} = 10 \log_{10} \frac{I_2}{I_1}$
(C) $Z = pV$
(D) $\frac{\sin i}{\sin r} = \frac{V_1}{V_2}$

152. A waveform transfers ______ from one point in space to another point in space.

(A) particles
(B) matter
(C) energy
(D) mass

153. In a mechanical wave, there are material particles that

(A) oscillate around an equilibrium point
(B) move forward at a set rate
(C) move away from an equilibrium point
(D) move backward at a set rate

154. Wavelength is a measure of

(A) time
(B) voltage
(C) distance
(D) pulse duration

155. Ultrasonic waves are

(A) mechanical
(B) x-ray

(C) electromagnetic
(D) solar

156. Acoustic impedance is

(A) the amount of tissue × the speed of sound in tissue
(B) the density of tissue × the speed of sound in tissue
(C) the transducer frequency × the speed of sound in tissue
(D) the distance from one interface to the next

157. Amplitude is measured in

(A) W/cm^2
(B) $A = pV$
(C) $\frac{\sin i}{\sin r} = \frac{V_1}{V_2}$
(D) dB

158. The spectrum of ultrasonic frequency is

(A) less than 20 Hz
(B) above 20,000 Hz
(C) 20–20,000 Hz
(D) 1–3 million Hz

159. Period is inversely proportional to

(A) velocity
(B) watts
(C) hertz
(D) frequency

160. As the ultrasound beam becomes more perpendicular to the organ interface

(A) scattering becomes greater
(B) there are more refracted echoes
(C) there are fewer specular echoes
(D) there are more specular echoes

161. A decibel (dB) describes the

(A) ratio of two sound intensities
(B) sum of two sound intensities
(C) amount of scattering
(D) velocity of the sound wave

162. Axial resolution is also known as all of the following except

(A) depth
(B) range
(C) azimuthal
(D) longitudinal

163. Which of the following has the highest sound velocity?

(A) soft tissue
(B) bone
(C) air
(D) water

164. According to the AIUM, no significant biologic effects have been proven in mammals exposed to

(A) SPTA intensities above 100 mW/cm^2
(B) SPTA intensities below 100 mW/cm^2
(C) SPTP intensities below 10 mW/cm^2
(D) SATP intensities below 2 mW/cm^2

165. Temporal peak intensity is measured at

(A) the time the pulse is present
(B) the center of the beam
(C) the time cavitation occurs
(D) none of the above

166. Which of the following has the lowest intensity?

(A) SPTP
(B) SATP
(C) SPTA
(D) SATA

167. What is the definition of the beam uniformity ratio?

(A) the spatial average intensity divided by the spatial intensity
(B) the spatial peak intensity divided by the spatial average intensity
(C) the temporal average intensity divided by the spatial average intensity
(D) the temporal peak intensity divided by the spatial peak intensity

168. The duty factor of a pulsed echo system is normally less than

(A) 10%
(B) 100%
(C) 1%
(D) 25%

169. A shortened spatial pulse length results in

(A) better lateral resolution
(B) low frequency
(C) poor resolution
(D) better axial resolution

170. The equation for measuring the relationship among velocity, frequency, and wavelength is

(A) $\left(\frac{Z_2 - Z_1}{Z_2 + Z_1}\right)^2 \times 100$
(B) $V = f\lambda$
(C) $Z = pV$
(D) $\frac{\sin i}{\sin r} = \frac{V_1}{V_2}$

171. Attenuation of an ultrasound beam can occur by

(A) divergence of a beam
(B) scattering
(C) reflection
(D) all of the above

172. Attenuation coefficient of sound can be defined by which of the following units?

(A) dB/cm/MHz
(B) dB/cm^2/Hz
(C) cm/Hz/dB
(D) m/dB/cm^3

173. If the transducer Q factor is low, the bandwidth will be

(A) narrow
(B) high
(C) wide
(D) low

174. Axial resolution can be improved by

(A) reducing the spatial pulse length
(B) increasing the spatial pulse length
(C) lowering the transducer frequency
(D) all of the above

175. Axial resolution is primarily affected by

(A) beam width
(B) spatial pulse length
(C) strength of the echo
(D) velocity of the medium

176. Which of the following will improve both axial and lateral resolution?

(A) short pulse length
(B) narrow beam width
(C) increase beam diameter
(D) increase transducer frequency

177. All of the following are also known as lateral resolution except

(A) azimuthal
(B) transverse
(C) range
(D) angular

178. Continous wave Doppler has a duty factor of

(A) less than 1%
(B) 100%
(C) greater than 100%
(D) 50%

179. Acoustic impedance is defined as

(A) density × propagation speed
(B) frequency × propagation
(C) elasticity + propagation
(D) density × elasticity

180. Acoustic impedance is defined by which of the following?

(A) rayons
(B) meters/dB
(C) mW/cm^2
(D) rayls

181. Acoustic impedance is not dependent on which of the following?

(A) frequency
(B) density
(C) stiffness
(D) none of the above

182. The height of the vertical spike on the A-mode display corresponds to

(A) the strength of the echo
(B) the distance to the reflector
(C) round-trip time of the echo
(D) the pulse repetition frequency

183. B-mode ultrasound includes all of the following except

(A) static scans
(B) M-mode scans
(C) real-time scans
(D) all of the above are B-mode

184. The correct equation for calculating the percentage of reflection is

(A) $R = \left(\frac{Z_2 - Z_1}{Z_2 + Z_1}\right)^2 \times 100$

(B) $R = \frac{Z_1 \times Z_2}{2}$

(C) $R = \sqrt{Z_1 + Z_2 \times \pi}$

185. The reflection coefficient between water and air is

(A) 1%
(B) 50%
(C) 75%
(D) nearly 100%

186. What happens to the ultrasound beam beyond the critical angle?

(A) 100% is transmitted
(B) 100% is reflected
(C) 75% is transmitted, 25% is reflected
(D) 75% is reflected, 25% is transmitted

187. Rayleigh scattering occurs if the particle dimensions are

(A) less than the wavelength
(B) greater than 3 mm
(C) greater than the wavelength
(D) none of the above

188. One of the acoustic parameters that determines the intensity of an ultrasound wave is

(A) waveform
(B) particle displacement
(C) period
(D) power

189. Power is defined as energy per unit

(A) mass
(B) distance
(C) time
(D) force

190. The ability to resolve structures lying perpendicular to the axis of the ultrasound beam is called

(A) lateral resolution
(B) axial resolution
(C) depth resolution
(D) longitudinal resolution

191. In most soft tissue the attenuation coefficient varies approximately

(A) inversely with frequency
(B) with the square of the frequency
(C) logarithmically with frequency
(D) directly with frequency

192. Ultrasound absorption in a medium results in

(A) conversion of ultrasound into heat
(B) dissipation of ultrasound into x-rays
(C) conversion of ultrasound into visible light
(D) dissipation of ultrasound into gamma rays

193. The typical value of attenuation in soft tissue is

(A) 2 dB/cm²/Hz
(B) 1 dB/cm/Hz
(C) 2 dB/cm²/MHz
(D) 0.5 dB/cm/MHz

194. False echoes are produced by

(A) reflection
(B) rarefaction
(C) reverberation
(D) diffraction

195. Approximately what percentage of the ultrasound beam will be transmitted between fat and muscle?

(A) 1%
(B) 10%
(C) 50%
(D) 99%

196. Huygens' principle describes

(A) multiple point sources
(B) refraction
(C) velocity
(D) cathode ray tubes

197. Enhancement occurs posterior to

(A) strong attenuations
(B) weak attenuations
(C) strong diffractors
(D) weak diffractors

198. The role of sound attenuation in tissue is expressed in terms of

(A) half-value layer
(B) Huygens' principle
(C) duty cycle
(D) spatial peak

199. Improper location of an echo may be due to

(A) shadowing
(B) Huygens' principle
(C) density error
(D) propagation speed error

200. The range equation explains

(A) side lobes
(B) distance to reflector
(C) attenuation
(D) calibration

201. For a specular reflector

(A) the angle of incidence is equal to the angle of reflection
(B) the angle of incidence is greater than the angle of reflection
(C) there is no dependence on beam angle
(D) the angle of incidence is equal to the angle of transmission

202. Which of the following is determined by the medium?

(A) intensity
(B) period
(C) propagation speed
(D) amplitude

203. Which of the following is not an acoustic variable?

(A) density
(B) pressure
(C) temperature
(D) force

204. The acronym TGC denotes

(A) tissue gain characteristic
(B) time gain compensation
(C) transducer generator control
(D) temperature generator control

205. The propagation speed for fat is

(A) higher than 1540 m/s
(B) lower than 1540 m/s
(C) equal to 1540 m/s
(D) cannot be measured

206. Which of the following has a propagation speed closest to the average soft tissue?

(A) bone
(B) air
(C) fat
(D) muscle

207. Arrange the following media in terms of propagation velocity, from lowest to highest.

(A) air, fat, muscle, bone
(B) bone, fat, air, muscle
(C) bone, muscle, fat, air
(D) muscle, air, fat, bone

208. As frequency increases, backscatter

(A) decreases
(B) is not affected
(C) increases
(D) is reflected

209. The angle at which total reflection occurs is called

(A) critical angle
(B) warp angle
(C) reflectivity angle
(D) diffraction angle

210. The pulse repetition frequency is the number of pulses occurring per

(A) wave
(B) returning echo
(C) microsecond
(D) second

211. The unit(s) used for the duty factor is (are)

(A) rayls
(B) m/s/Hz
(C) m/μs/MHz
(D) unitless

212. The typical value for attenuation coefficient for 6 MHz ultrasound in soft tissue is

(A) 3 dB/cm
(B) 1 dB/cm/Hz
(C) 3 dB/cm^2
(D) 2 dB

213. Normal incidence occurs when the ultrasound beam travels ______ to the boundary between the two media

(A) parallel
(B) perpendicular
(C) obliquely
(D) at 1540 m/s

214. The amount of energy transmitted and/or reflected at the boundary between two media depends on

(A) acoustic impedance mismatch
(B) the frequency of the beam
(C) the propagation speed of the first medium
(D) the propagation speed of the second medium

215. Which of the following has a higher acoustic impedance coefficient?

(A) solid
(B) liquid
(C) gas
(D) all the above have an equal acoustic impedance coefficient

216. According to Snell's law, the transmission angle is greater than the incidence angle if the propagation speed

(A) of medium 2 is greater than that of medium 1
(B) of medium 1 is greater than that of medium 2
(C) of the two media are equal
(D) is calculated at 3 dB down

217. According to the range equation, which of the following are necessary to calculate the distance to the reflector?

(A) attenuation coefficient and type of reflector
(B) density and type of reflector
(C) propagation speed and pulse round-trip time
(D) density and pulse round-trip time

218. The mirror image artifact is commonly seen around which of the following structures?

(A) kidney
(B) pancreas

(C) spleen
(D) diaphragm

219. The comet tail artifact can be seen posterior to an object that has

(A) a much lower acoustic impedance than its surroundings
(B) a much higher acoustic impedance than its surroundings
(C) either a much lower or a much higher acoustic impedance than its surroundings
(D) the same acoustic impedance as its surroundings

220. Which of the following may produce the comet tail artifact?

(A) liver-kidney interface
(B) spleen-kidney interface
(C) tissue-gas interface
(D) gas-fluid interface

221. If the ultrasound beam passes through a mass in the liver that contains fat, how might the diaphragmatic echo posterior to it appear?

(A) closer than it really is
(B) farther than it really is
(C) will not be affected
(D) will not be visualized

222. Bandwidth can be increased by

(A) increasing the quality factor
(B) increasing frequency
(C) increasing pulse length
(D) increasing damping

223. Which of the following is not a control affecting the amplification of echoes?

(A) output
(B) compression
(C) time gain curve
(D) balance

224. On some sonographic equipment, adjusting the compression will affect which of the following processes?

(A) slope position
(B) dynamic range
(C) output
(D) balance

225. Generally, ultrasound transducers have

(A) better axial resolution than lateral resolution
(B) better lateral resolution than axial resolution
(C) better azimuthal resolution than radial resolution
(D) equal axial resolution and lateral resolution

226. The pulse repetition frequency of an ultrasound unit is typically

(A) 1 Hz
(B) 10 Hz
(C) 100 Hz
(D) 1000 Hz

227. B-mode display denotes

(A) basic modulator
(B) beam motion
(C) beam modulator
(D) brightness modulation

228. What percentage of the time is a typical pulsed ultrasound system capable of receiving echoes?

(A) 100%
(B) 99.9%
(C) 75%
(D) 50%

229. If the frequency doubles, what happens to the wavelength?

(A) increases fourfold
(B) increases twofold
(C) decreases by one-half
(D) no relationship to wavelength

230. Which of the following does not display a sector format?

(A) linear-sequenced array
(B) electronic-phased array
(C) mechanical rotating wheel
(D) mechanical wobbler

231. The equation for measuring acoustic impedance is

(A) $\left(\frac{Z_2 - Z_1}{Z_2 + Z_1}\right)^2 \times 100$
(B) $V = f\lambda$
(C) $Z = pV$
(D) $\frac{\sin i}{\sin r} = \frac{V_1}{V_2}$

232. Which of the following are most commonly used in ultrasound transducers?

(A) lead zirconate titanate (PZT)
(B) barium sulfate
(C) metaniobate
(D) quartz

233. Transmit–delay focusing in a linear array transducer will

(A) improve axial resolution
(B) improve lateral resolution
(C) improve the frequency
(D) decrease the depth of penetration

234. For real-time systems, which of the following is not related to the others?

(A) frame rate
(B) lines per frame
(C) pulse repetition frequency
(D) frequency

235. The pulse repetition frequency is

(A) pulses emitted per second
(B) time from the beginning of one pulse to the beginning of the next
(C) the time during which the pulse actually occurs
(D) cannot be defined

236. Which of the following is not a role of the pulser?

(A) driving the transducer
(B) telling the receiver when the ultrasound pulses are produced
(C) telling the memory when ultrasound pulses are produced
(D) beam steering

237. Demodulation is a process of

(A) converting the voltage delivered to the receiver from one form to another
(B) decreasing the differences between the smallest and largest amplitudes
(C) eliminating the smaller amplitude voltage produced by electronic noise
(D) rejecting weak echoes to reduce noise

238. Which of the following are not operator adjustable?

(A) compensation and rejection
(B) amplification and compensation
(C) demodulation and compression
(D) rejection and amplification

239. Which of the following varies with distance from the transducer?

(A) lateral resolution
(B) frequency
(C) axial resolution
(D) spatial pulse length

240. A period can be described by which number on the following diagram?

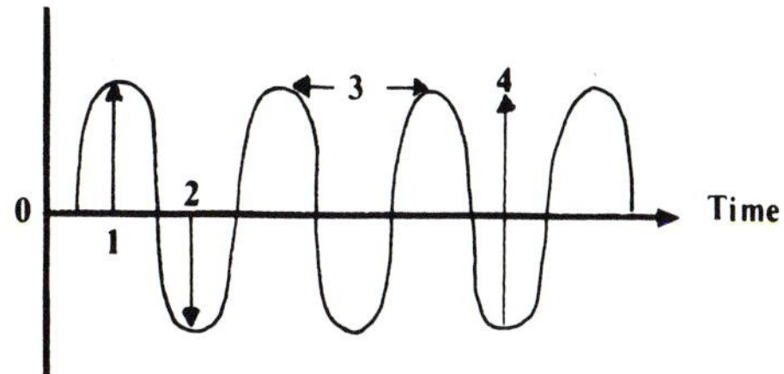

(A) #2
(B) #1
(C) #3
(D) #4

241. Increasing axial resolution by increasing frequency also results in

(A) increasing penetration
(B) decreasing half-intensity depth
(C) decreasing the pulse repetition frequency
(D) none of the above

242. Reflection refers to

(A) the bending of the ultrasound beam as it crosses a boundary
(B) conversion of ultrasound to heat
(C) redirection of a portion of the ultrasound beam from a boundary
(D) the scattering of the ultrasound beam in many directions

243. Digital computers use a special number system called

(A) digital number system
(B) alphanumeric system
(C) chronologic system
(D) binary number system

244. The term *bit* in computer science denotes

(A) binary digit
(B) buffer
(C) baud rate
(D) BASIC programming

245. An 8-bit binary number is referred to as

(A) byte
(B) baud rate
(C) buffer register
(D) BUS

246. Which of the following is not an example of computer hardware?

(A) monitor
(B) program
(C) disk drive
(D) printer

247. The acronym RAM denotes

(A) reset-auxiliary memory
(B) random-access memory
(C) retailing American microcomputers
(D) retailing American machines

248. The acronym ROM denotes

(A) read-only memory
(B) read-only modem

(C) retailing only microcomputers
(D) run-output machine

249. Which of the following is not an input device?

(A) keyboard
(B) printer
(C) disk drive
(D) magnetic disk

250. The type of permanent memory that is produced at the time of manufacture and cannot be changed by the computer user is called

(A) RAM
(B) ROM
(C) PROM
(D) EPROM

251. The type of programmable memory that allows the user to write, store, or erase data is called

(A) PLA
(B) ROM
(C) PROM
(D) EPROM

252. The acronym CPU denotes

(A) computer program update
(B) central processing unit
(C) capacitor power unit
(D) computer portable unit

253. The most common binary word length in microprocessors is

(A) 8, 16, or 32 bits
(B) 12 or 24 bits
(C) 128K bytes
(D) 64K bytes

254. An 8-bit word microcomputer with 128K words of memory can store how many bits of data?

(A) 1000
(B) 128,000
(C) 1,048,576
(D) 128

255. The contents of EPROM can be completely erased by which of the following applications?

(A) light waves
(B) infrared
(C) ultrasound
(D) ultraviolet light

256. A sonographic image can be transferred from one computer to another by way of

(A) fixed disk drive
(B) modem
(C) printer
(D) keyboard

257. The most commonly used programming language for personal computers is

(A) COBOL
(B) FORTRAN
(C) BASIC
(D) LOGO

258. The unit for measuring the speed of data communication is called

(A) buffer
(B) booting
(C) output unit
(D) baud rate

259. Which of the following disks has the highest storage capacity and fastest access time?

(A) 3½-in microfloppy double density
(B) Hard disk
(C) 5¼-in minifloppy
(D) 3½-in microfloppy high density

260. The acronym BASIC denotes

(A) basic American scientific instructional code
(B) basic American scientific information center
(C) beginner's all-purpose symbolic instruction code
(D) business application software information center

261. A modem is an electronic device that

(A) simulates human voice
(B) prints data
(C) translates signals from digital into analog and analog into digital
(D) senses data from a card inserted into it

262. Each binary digit in a binary number is represented in memory by a memory element, which at any time is in one of ______ states.

(A) many
(B) two
(C) none of the above

263. In binary numbers, how many values are used for each digit?

(A) 10
(B) multiples of 10
(C) 2
(D) 5

264. The number 30 in binary is

(A) 0110
(B) 1110
(C) 1001
(D) 1111
(E) none of the above

265. How many gray levels (echo amplitude levels) can a 4-bit deep digital scan converter store?

(A) 2
(B) 4
(C) 8
(D) 16
(E) 32

266. An ultrasound instrument that could represent 64 shades of gray would require a(n) ______ bit memory

(A) 8
(B) 6
(C) 4
(D) 16

267. Which of the following are effects seen in tissue at high ultrasound intensities?

(A) fusion, ionization
(B) heating, cavitation
(C) expansion, encrustation
(D) reabsorption, dehydration

268. Which of the following is the correct list of functions performed by the receiver system in the ultrasound machine (B-scanner)?

(A) inspection, detection, correction, rejection, depression
(B) randomization, amplification, modulation, rectification, limitation
(C) amplification, compensation, compression, rejection
(D) expansion, contraction, band limitation, sonification

269. A large amplitude pulse from the pulser results in

(A) a long duration pulse from the transducer
(B) a short duration pulse from the transducer
(C) shutdown of the receiver
(D) a large amplitude pulse from the transducer
(E) a large amplitude pulse from the display

270. Voltage pulses from the pulser go to the

(A) transducer and display
(B) transducer and receiver
(C) transducer and TGC control
(D) display and image memory
(E) amplifier and receiver

271. The five major components of a pulse–echo ultrasound system are

(A) flux capacitor, image memory, transducer, scan arm, amplifier
(B) interrossitor, pulser, receiver, display, power supply
(C) image memory, display, scan arm, TGC control, foot switch
(D) transducer, receiver, image memory, pulser, display

272. Transducers are focused by two major methods: internal focusing and external focusing. These methods can be accomplished by

(A) thickening the crystal and adding a water path
(B) cutting a curved transducer element and/or using an acoustic lens
(C) "doping" the crystal with metal ions and damping
(D) using a crystal pulse and a bandwidth limiter
(E) all of the above will focus a transducer element

273. The unit applied to the Q factor (quality factor) that describes the ratio of operating frequency to bandwidth is called

(A) megahertz (MHz)
(B) percent
(C) millimeter per microsecond
(D) Fresnel
(E) none of the above; Q factor is unitless

Questions 274 through 282: Match the terms in Column A with the correct definition in Column B.

COLUMN A

274. acoustic shadow ______
275. acoustic enhancement ______
276. anechoic ______
277. artifact ______
278. echogenic ______
279. hyperechoic ______
280. hypoechoic ______
281. interface ______
282. sonolucent ______

COLUMN B

(A) without echoes
(B) echoes of lower amplitude than the normal surrounding tissues
(C) the surface forming the boundary between two media having different acoustic impedances
(D) an echo that does not correspond to the real target
(E) reduction in echoes from a region distal to an attenuating structure
(F) a tissue or structure that does not have internal echoes (echo-free)

(G) an increase in echoes from a region distal to a weakly attenuating structure or tissue
(H) echoes of higher amplitude than the normal surrounding tissues
(I) a structure that possesses echoes

283. The backing material that is usually constructed in a continuous-wave Doppler transducer is

(A) epoxy resin
(B) cork
(C) air
(D) tungsten powder

284. Transducers with continuous-wave operation are commonly used in which of the following applications?

(A) diagnostic, surgical, therapeutic, and Doppler
(B) diagnostic and surgical
(C) diagnostic and Doppler
(D) surgical, therapeutic, and Doppler

285. Which of the following waves are visible under normal conditions?

(A) water waves
(B) x-ray waves
(C) radio waves
(D) sound waves

286. Ultrasound can travel in all of the following *except*

(A) IVP contrast
(B) solid tissue
(C) vacuum
(D) blood

287. The Greek letter lambda (λ) represents

(A) period
(B) wavelength
(C) frequency
(D) velocity

288. The time it takes to complete a single cycle is called

(A) period
(B) wavelength
(C) frequency
(D) velocity

289. A wave vibration at 20 cycles per second has a frequency of

(A) 20 MHz
(B) 20 Hz
(C) 20 kHz
(D) 120 kHz

290. A wave vibrating at 1 million cycles per second has a frequency of

(A) 1 GHz
(B) 1 kHz
(C) 1 MHz
(D) 100 MHz

291. The device that produces the ultrasound beam is commonly called a

(A) cathode-ray tube (CRT)
(B) scan converter
(C) transducer
(D) mechanical arm

Questions 292 through 294: Match the questions in Column A with the correct answer in Column B.

COLUMN A

292. Which statement best describes A-mode? ______
293. Which statement best describes B-mode? ______
294. Which statement best describes M-mode? ______

COLUMN B

(A) a graphical presentation with vertical spikes arising from a horizontal baseline; the height of the vertical spikes represents the amplitude of the deflected echo
(B) a two-dimensional image of internal body structures displayed as dots; the brightness of the dots is proportional to the amplitude of the echo; the image is applicable to both real-time and static scanners
(C) a graphical presentation of moving structures in a waveform; the display is presented as a group of lines representing the motion of moving interfaces versus time
(D) unidimensional presentation of moving structures displayed in a pie-shaped or rectangular image; the image is applicable only to real-time scanners

295. Which of the following is *not* an essential part of the cathode-ray tube (CRT)?

(A) electron gun
(B) fluorescent screen
(C) silicon
(D) deflection system (horizontal and vertical plates)

296. The CRT used in ultrasound usually encloses

(A) air
(B) vacuum
(C) oil
(D) gas

297. The positively (+) charged CRT terminal is called the

(A) anode
(B) cathode
(C) both anode and cathode

298. The negatively (−) charged CRT terminal is called the

(A) anode
(B) cathode
(C) both anode and cathode

299. The intensity of the ultrasound beam

(A) is measured in watts
(B) is always constant
(C) depends on the beam diameter
(D) is measured with the AIUM phantom

300. Whose principle states, "All points on an ultrasound waveform can be considered as point sources for the production of secondary spherical wavelets"?

(A) Doppler's
(B) Curie's
(C) Huygens'
(D) Young's

301. The fraction of time that a pulsed ultrasound system is actually producing ultrasound is called the

(A) duty factor
(B) curie factor
(C) frame rate
(D) transmission factor

302. Real-time ultrasound instrumentation can be classified as

(A) annular, sector, linear, and static scanners
(B) sector scanners only
(C) sector, linear, and annular scanners
(D) static scanners only

303. The speed at which ultrasound propagates within a medium depends primarily on

(A) its frequency
(B) the compressibility of the medium
(C) its intensity
(D) the thickness of the medium

304. An artifact that results from a pulse that has traveled two or more round-trip distances between the transducer and the interface is called

(A) a multipath
(B) a side lobe
(C) reverberation
(D) scattering

305. The ratio of output electric power to input electric power is termed

(A) power
(B) intensity
(C) gain
(D) voltage

306. Multipath artifacts result from

(A) echoes that return directly to the transducer
(B) shotgun pellets
(C) echoes that take an indirect path back to the transducer
(D) none of the above

307. A scan converter will accept echo signals from the receiver and store them in the "memory" of the instrument. Identify the types of memory used in scan converters.

(A) gray scale and bistable
(B) analog and digital
(C) static and real-time
(D) none of the above

308. To achieve the best possible digital representation of an analog system, the echo signals should undergo

(A) postprocessing
(B) preprocessing
(C) rectification
(D) amplification

309. Near zone length may be increased by increasing

(A) wavelength
(B) wavelength and bandwidth
(C) transducer diameter
(D) frequency and transducer diameter

Questions 310 through 319: Match the terms in Column A with the correct definition in Column B.

COLUMN A	COLUMN B
310. density ______	(A) rate at which work is done
311. propagation ______	(B) mass divided by volume
312. frequency ______	(C) conversion of sound to heat
313. power ______	(D) number of cycles per unit time
314. duty factor ______	(E) density multiplied by sound propagation speed
315. bandwidth ______	(F) range of frequencies contained in the ultrasound pulse
316. acoustic impedance ______	(G) the product of pulse duration and pulse repetition rate
317. absorption ______	(H) progression or travel
318. quality factor ______	(I) operating frequency divided by bandwidth
319. intensity ______	(J) power divided by area

320. Which of the following is a true definition for a highly damped transducer?

(A) increased efficiency, sensitivity, and spatial pulse length
(B) decreased efficiency, sensitivity, and spatial pulse length
(C) increased efficiency and sensitivity, but decreased spatial pulse length
(D) decreased efficiency, but increased sensitivity and spatial pulse length

321. Gain compensation is necessary due to

(A) reflector motion
(B) gray scale
(C) attenuation
(D) resolution

322. The frequency bandwidth may be determined by which of the following?

(A) spectral analysis
(B) Schlieren system
(C) hydrophone analysis
(D) cathode analysis

323. Analog scan converters

(A) function perfectly as peak deflectors
(B) have greater image sharpness than digital scan converters
(C) store any increment of signal amplitude
(D) have better image uniformity than digital scan converters

324. The gray-scale resolution for a 5-bit digital instrument that has a dynamic range of 42 dB is

(A) 1.9 dB
(B) 3 dB
(C) 1.3 dB
(D) 0.07 dB

325. If it takes 0.01 second for a pulse emitted by the transducer to reach an echo source of soft tissue, what distance must the pulse travel in order to be recorded?

(A) 1540 cm
(B) 30.8 m
(C) 15.4 m
(D) both A and C

326. An artifact that is produced from interaction of the incident beam with a curved surface and results in an acoustic shadow is referred to as

(A) a ghost artifact
(B) an edge artifact
(C) a comet tail artifact
(D) a ring down artifact

327. An artifact that results from refraction of the ultrasound beam at a muscle–fat interface and gives rise to double images is called

(A) a split image artifact
(B) an edge artifact
(C) a comet tail artifact
(D) a ring down artifact

328. An artifact that would *least* likely produce a pseudomass is

(A) a comet tail artifact
(B) a multipath artifact
(C) a mirror image artifact
(D) a slide lobe artifact

329. Split image artifact is more noticeable in

(A) athletic patients and mesomorphic habitus patients
(B) patients with underdeveloped rectus muscle
(C) mesomorphic habitus patients and patients with underdeveloped rectus muscle
(D) all of the above

330. Select the least likely cause or causes for a split image artifact:

(A) abdominal scar
(B) lateral margins of the rectus muscles
(C) gas bubble
(D) refraction of the sound beam at a muscle–fat interface

331. The most likely cause for a beam thickness artifact is

(A) metallic surgical clips
(B) gas bubble
(C) partial volume effect
(D) shotgun pellets

332. Beam thickness artifact is primarily dependent on

(A) position of the patient
(B) gas bubble
(C) beam angulation
(D) gravity

333. Which of the following is not true for side lobe artifact?

(A) caused by multiple side lobes of the transducer
(B) apparent in real-time image
(C) may be diffuse or specular in appearance
(D) not visible on real-time image

334. Which of the following is least likely to produce an acoustic shadow?

(A) bone interface
(B) metallic surgical clips
(C) gallstones
(D) gas interface

335. The most common type of artifact encountered in patients with shotgun wounds is

(A) comet tail artifact
(B) multipath artifact
(C) mirror image artifact
(D) side lobe artifact

336. The type of reverberation echo that usually results from a small gas bubble and appears as a high-amplitude echo occurring at regular intervals is called a

(A) multipath artifact
(B) mirror image artifact
(C) side lobe artifact
(D) ring-down artifact

337. The amount of splitting that occurs in a split image artifact for a given structure

(A) can be calculated using Snell's law
(B) cannot be calculated because it is an artifact
(C) can be calculated using the equation $Z = pV$
(D) can be calculated using a 5-MHz transducer with the equation: split (m/s) = $D\pi/T$

338. The first vertical deflection on the A-mode that corresponds to the transducer face is called

(A) bistable
(B) side lobe
(C) main bang
(D) gain

339. The type of real-time system that employs a combination of electronic and mechanical means is called

(A) wobbler sector real-time
(B) rotating wheel real-time
(C) annular-array real-time
(D) linear-sequenced array

340. If the amount of acoustic coupling medium is insufficient, what changes could result?

(A) decrease in amplitude of the returning echo
(B) increase in amplitude of the returning echo
(C) the transducer will slide on the skin easier
(D) no effect on the image

341. Which of the following is not a hard copy?

(A) x-ray film
(B) Polaroid film
(C) floppy disk
(D) videotape recorder

Questions 342 through 344: Each diagram represents modes of operation used in diagnostic ultrasound.

342. Identify the type of mode displayed in the following diagram.

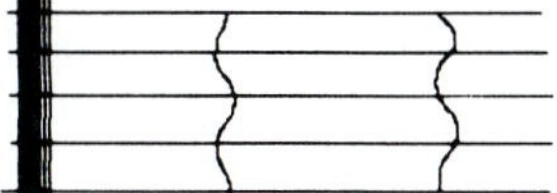

(A) B-mode
(B) A-mode
(C) M-mode
(D) R-mode

343. Identify the type of mode displayed in the following diagram.

(A) B-mode
(B) A-mode
(C) M-mode
(D) R-mode

344. Identify the type of mode displayed in the following diagram.

(A) B-mode
(B) A-mode
(C) M-mode
(D) R-mode

345. The effects of diagnostic ultrasound on human soft tissue are called

(A) sensitivity effects
(B) biologic effects
(C) neurologic effects
(D) pressure effect

346. The average propagation speed of ultrasound in soft tissue is

(A) 1.54 mm/μs
(B) 741 mph
(C) 1560 m/s
(D) 331 mm/s

Questions 347 through 350: Identify the regions on the diagram below by filling in the blanks to the right of each term given.

347. slope ______
348. delay ______
349. far gain ______
350. near gain ______

A B C D

DIAGRAM OF TGC CURVE

Questions 351 through 360: Match the terms in Column A with the correct definition in Column B.

COLUMN A

351. attenuation ______
352. bistable ______
353. bit ______
354. cavitation ______
355. coupling medium ______
356. damping ______
357. gray scale ______
358. matching layer ______
359. pixel ______
360. static imaging ______

COLUMN B

(A) picture element
(B) the production and behavior of bubbles in sound
(C) progressive weakening of the sound beam as it travels through a medium
(D) a liquid placed between the transducer and the skin
(E) the number of intensity levels between black and white
(F) having two stages
(G) binary digit
(H) a method of reducing pulse duration by electrical or mechanical means
(I) single-frame imaging
(J) plastic material placed in front of the transducer face to reduce the reflection at the transducer surface

361. The intensity of ultrasound is measured in

(A) kg/m^3
(B) N/m^2
(C) Hz
(D) W/cm^2

362. There is no known adverse biologic effect in tissue at intensities below

(A) 100 mW/cm^2 SPTA
(B) 1000 mW/cm^2 SAPA
(C) 10 W/cm^2 SPTP
(D) 500 m/Wcm^2 SATA

363. The acronym SPTA denotes

(A) static probe transmission amplitude
(B) static probe transmission absorption
(C) spatial peak temporal average
(D) sound propagation temperature artifact

Questions 364 through 370: Match the quantity in Column A with the correct unit in Column B.

COLUMN A

364. density ______
365. speed ______
366. frequency ______
367. work ______
368. intensity ______
369. wavelength ______
370. attenuation ______

COLUMN B

(A) W/cm^2
(B) kg/m^3
(C) m
(D) m/s
(E) J
(F) Hz
(G) dB

371. The general range of intensities in diagnostic ultrasound is

(A) 0.5 W/cm^2–2.0 W/cm^2 SPTA
(B) 0.002 W/cm^2–0.5 W/cm^2 SPTA
(C) 50 W/cm^2–100 W/cm^2 SPTA
(D) the general range of intensities in diagnostic ultrasound is unknown

372. The general range of intensities in therapeutic ultrasound is

(A) 0.5 W/cm^2–2.0 W/cm^2 SPTA
(B) 0.002 W/cm^2–0.5 W/cm^2 SPTA
(C) 50 W/cm^2–100 W/cm^2 SPTA
(D) the general range of intensities in therapeutic ultrasound is unknown

373. Which of the following characteristics does *not* apply to diagnostic ultrasound at normal diagnostic intensity levels?

(A) noninvasive
(B) atraumatic
(C) ionizing
(D) nontoxic

374. The most common result of high intensity ultrasound is

(A) cavitation
(B) brain damage
(C) fetal developmental anomalies
(D) heat

375. In the study of bioeffects, cavitation denotes

(A) production and behavior of gas bubbles
(B) necrosis
(C) cell membrane rupture
(D) chromosome breakage

376. The two types of cavitation are

(A) silent and noisy
(B) micro and macro
(C) membrane and nonmembrane
(D) stable and transient

377. An instrument used to detect frequency shift is called

(A) Doppler
(B) real-time
(C) A-mode
(D) static scanner

378. Specular reflections

(A) occur when the interface is larger than the wavelength
(B) occur when the interface is smaller than the wavelength
(C) arise from interfaces smaller than 3 mm
(D) are not dependent on the angle of incidence

379. Nonspecular reflections

(A) occur when the interface is larger than the wavelength
(B) occur when the interface is smaller than the wavelength
(C) arise from mirror-like surfaces
(D) are beam-angle dependent

380. The acronym SATA denotes

(A) static amplitude transmission average
(B) spatial average temporal average
(C) spatial average tissue absorption
(D) sound attenuation transmission average

381. The acronym SPPA denotes

(A) static probe power average
(B) static probe transmission absorption
(C) spatial peak pulse average
(D) sound propagation performance average

382. The mode not applicable to a Doppler instrument is

(A) static
(B) pulsed
(C) continuous
(D) audible

383. Which of the following transducers would be most useful for imaging superficial structures?

(A) 5-MHz, short-focus
(B) 3-MHz, long-focus
(C) 5-MHz, long-focus
(D) 2.5-MHz, short-focus

384. Which of the following transducers would be most useful for good penetration on an obese patient?

(A) 5-MHz, short-focus
(B) 3-MHz, long-focus
(C) 5-MHz, long-focus
(D) 2.5-MHz, short-focus

385. The digital memory represents a picture element called a

(A) pixel
(B) bistable
(C) real-time
(D) matrix

386. How many shades of gray can the human eye distinguish?

(A) about 16 shades
(B) between 16 and 32 shades
(C) more than 64 shades
(D) more than 124 shades

387. The most recent digital storage employs what size memory?

(A) 512 × 512 × 6-bit deep
(B) 64 × 64 × 2-bit deep
(C) 128 × 128 × 4-bit deep
(D) 16 × 16 × 2-bit deep

388. A disadvantage of pulsed-wave Doppler (PW) relative to continuous-wave Doppler (CW) is that

(A) it is unidirectional
(B) the Doppler shift depends on frequency
(C) it is subject to "aliasing"
(D) it does not provide in-depth information

389. Which of the following is (are) essential to a TGC display?

(A) static system
(B) real-time system
(C) bistable system
(D) all of the above

390. What is the effect of ultrasound absorption on tissues at normal intensity levels?

(A) dissipation of heat by conduction
(B) significant temperature elevations
(C) significantly lowered temperature
(D) necrosis

391. CRT monitors normally have how many horizontal lines?

(A) 16
(B) 64
(C) 100
(D) 525

392. How many frames per second are displayed by a CRT monitor?

(A) 525
(B) 30
(C) 16
(D) 60

393. How many times each second does the electron beam scan each field on a CRT monitor in order to produce a flicker-free display?

(A) 30
(B) 60
(C) 40
(D) 10

394. The dynamic range of the dots on the average oscilloscope or CRT monitor is

(A) 50–60 dB
(B) 20–25 dB
(C) 125 dB
(D) 525 dB

395. The term matrix, when referring to digital memory, denotes

(A) number of rows and columns
(B) analog
(C) pixel
(D) buffer

396. Digital memory resembles

(A) squares on a checkerboard
(B) a transducer
(C) an electron beam
(D) a hydrophone

397. A region that is anechoic is displayed as

(A) echo-free
(B) echogenic
(C) hyperechoic
(D) hypoechoic

398. A region that is hyperechoic is

(A) anechoic
(B) echogenic
(C) echo-free
(D) transsonic

399. Which of the following cannot be measured by a hydrophone?

(A) pressure amplitude
(B) spatial pulse length
(C) impedance
(D) intensity

400. The hydrophone is made up of

(A) x-rays
(B) transducer elements
(C) ultraviolet lights
(D) all of the above

401. Bioeffects at medium intensity levels on laboratory animals have resulted in

(A) cancer
(B) death
(C) growth retardation
(D) no effects

402. Which of the following is the least likely cause for attenuation?

(A) absorption
(B) reflection
(C) refraction
(D) scattering

403. Absorption refers to

(A) bending of the sound beam crossing a boundary
(B) conversion of sound to heat
(C) redirection of a portion of the sound from a boundary beam
(D) redirection of the sound beam in several directions

404. Diffraction refers to

(A) spreading-out of the ultrasound beam
(B) conversion of sound to heat
(C) redirection of a portion of the sound from a boundary beam
(D) bending of the sound beam crossing a boundary

405. Scattering refers to

(A) bending of the sound beam crossing a boundary
(B) conversion of sound to heat
(C) redirection of a portion of the sound from a boundary beam
(D) redirection of the sound beam in several directions

406. The method for sterilizing transducers is

(A) heat sterilization
(B) steam
(C) recommended by the transducer manufacturer
(D) autoclave

407. An example of an acoustic window is

(A) liver interface
(B) rib interface
(C) tissue/air interface
(D) tissue/bone interface

408. The binary number 1010 equals the decimal number

(A) 10
(B) 11
(C) 110
(D) 200

409. Real-time imaging is similar to

(A) static scanning
(B) fluoroscopy
(C) MRI
(D) all of the above

410. When attempting to identify fetal heart motion, the frame rate of the real-time system should be

(A) turned off to avoid confusion
(B) set at a slow rate
(C) set at a fast rate
(D) set at five frames per second

411. Select the recommended orientation for a transverse scan.

(A) all transverse scans should be viewed from the patient's feet
(B) all transverse scans should be viewed from the patient's head
(C) all transverse scans should be viewed lateral from the patient's right side
(D) all transverse scans should be viewed lateral from the patient's left side

412. The recommended orientation for longitudinal scans is

(A) the patient's head to the right of the image and feet to the left of the image
(B) the patient's head to the left of the image and feet to the right of the image
(C) the patient's head to the top (anterior) of the image and feet to the bottom (posterior) of the image
(D) none of the above

413. Demodulation is a function performed by the

(A) pulser
(B) amplifier
(C) receiver
(D) transmitter

414. Which of the following statements about ultrasound waves is not true?

(A) ultrasound waves are mechanical vibrating energy
(B) ultrasound waves can be polarized
(C) ultrasound waves are not part of the electromagnetic spectrum
(D) ultrasound waves cannot travel in a vacuum

415. The transducer crystal *most* likely to be employed in high-frequency work, above 18 MHz, is

(A) lithium sulfate
(B) PZT-5
(C) Rochelle salt
(D) quartz

416. The advantage that PZT-5 has over other ceramic material is that it is

(A) easy to shape
(B) effective at low voltage
(C) inexpensive
(D) all of the above

417. The trade name for lead zirconate titanate is

(A) $BaSO_4$
(B) quartz
(C) PZT-5
(D) synthetic-P

418. How many shades of gray can be displayed using a scan converter with 8 bits per memory element?

(A) 8
(B) 16
(C) 128
(D) 256

419. The transducer that would be best suited for intercostal scanning is

(A) linear-sequenced array real-time
(B) mechanical sector real-time transducer

(C) static with large diameter
(D) no type of transducer can scan between the intercostal space

420. The difference between real-time and fluoroscopy is

(A) ultrasound does not need contrast media
(B) fluoroscopy has potential biologic effects, whereas ultrasound has no known biologic effects at normal intensity level
(C) ultrasound is nonionizing
(D) a movie-like image is displayed, whereas real-time displays a single frame image
(E) all of the above
(F) A and D
(G) A, B, and C

421. Which of the following contrast media used in x-ray do *not* obscure the propagation of ultrasound?

(A) barium sulfate ($BaSO_4$) for upper GI examination
(B) hypaque for IVP examination
(C) air for lower GI examination
(D) telepaque for oral cholecystogram
(E) C and D
(F) B and D
(G) none of the above
(H) all of the above

Questions 422 through 430: Match each term in Column A with the correct definition in Column B.

COLUMN A	COLUMN B
422. acoustic lens ____	(A) unit of impedance
423. pixel ____	(B) the portion of the sound beam outside of the main beam
424. sector ____	(C) picture element
425. acousto-optical converter ____	(D) pie shaped
426. side lobe ____	(E) a change in frequency as a result of reflector motion between the transducer and the reflector
427. wavefront ____	(F) a device that changes sound waves into visible light patterns
428. rayl ____	(G) the ratio between the angle of incidence and the refraction
429. Snell's law ____	(H) imaginary surface passing through particles of the same vibration as an ultrasound wave
430. Doppler effect ____	(I) a device used to focus sound beams

431. Lateral resolution is equal to

(A) the wavelength
(B) the beam diameter
(C) the near-zone length
(D) the wave number

432. Which of the following materials are used to make acoustic lenses?

(A) aluminum
(B) Perspex (acrylic plastic)
(C) polystyrene
(D) ethylene oxide
(E) all of the above
(F) A, B, and C
(G) B and D

433. Ultrasound beams can be focused and defocused with the use of

(A) a concave or convex mirror
(B) acoustic lenses
(C) both A and B
(D) ultrasound beam cannot be focused, only light can

434. The normal range of wavelength in medical application is

(A) 0.1–1.5 mm
(B) 1.5–2 mm
(C) 2–5 mm
(D) 5.5–15 mm

435. Which of the following cannot be distinguished on diagnostic ultrasound?

(A) tissue
(B) solid mass
(C) individual cells
(D) male and female genitalia

436. Density is defined as

(A) unit of impedance
(B) force divided by area
(C) force multiplied by displacement
(D) mass per unit volume

437. Ultrasound absorption is directly proportional to

(A) viscosity
(B) frequency
(C) distance
(D) all of the above

438. The confirmed bioeffect(s) on pregnant women with the use of real-time diagnostic instruments is (are)

(A) brain damage
(B) fetal developmental anomalies
(C) growth retardation
(D) no known effect

439. The confirmed bioeffects on pregnant mice exposed to continuous wave ultrasound in a laboratory setting have resulted in

(A) cancer
(B) death
(C) neurocranial damage
(D) no known effect

440. Which of the following combinations of frequency and intensity would *most* likely result in cavitation?

(A) high frequency and low intensity
(B) low frequency and high intensity
(C) high frequency and high intensity
(D) intensity has no effect on cavitation

Questions 441 through 448: Match each term in Column A with the correct definition in Column B.

COLUMN A

441. in vivo ______
442. in vitro ______
443. spectral analysis ______
444. viscoelasticity ______
445. rejection ______
446. relaxation ______
447. red cell stasis ______
448. acoustic power ______

COLUMN B

(A) an in vivo phenomenon characterized by erythrocytes within small vessels stopping the flow and collecting in the low pressure regions of the standing wave field
(B) elimination of small amplitude echo
(C) a process of acoustic energy absorption
(D) energy transported per unit time
(E) tissue cultures in a test tube
(F) a method of analyzing a waveform
(G) the property of a medium characterized by energy distortion in the medium and irreversibly converted to heat
(H) living human tissue

449. Which of the following statements about bioeffects is (are) unconfirmed?

(A) ultrasound exposure in humans is accumulative
(B) most harmful bioeffects that occurred in experimental conditions have been confirmed in humans in a clinical setting
(C) intensity, frequency, and exposure time used on experimental animals were compatible to those used in a clinical setting
(D) continuous wave used in experimental studies gives the same tissue exposure as pulsed ultrasound used in a clinical setting
(E) the exposure of pregnant women to high intensity levels resulted in growth retardation of their offspring
(F) A and E
(G) all of the above are false or unconfirmed
(H) all of the above are true

450. The number of known human injuries resulting from diagnostic medical ultrasound exposure is

(A) 2500 in England
(B) 115 in the United States
(C) 1500 in Japan
(D) no exposure injuries in humans have been reported

451. What is the distinction between real-time scans and B-scans?

(A) no distinction; real-time scans are B-scans
(B) real-time scans display gray-scale images, whereas B-scans display bistable images
(C) real-time scans exhibit motion images, whereas B-scans exhibit static images
(D) B-scans are specific for static scanners; real-time scans are not

452. Transonic regions are always

(A) echo-free
(B) anechoic
(C) echogenic
(D) uninhibited to propagation

453. Which of the following is not related to real-time?

(A) A-mode
(B) static imaging
(C) dynamic imaging
(D) M-mode

454. Which of the following is *not* a component of the time-gain compensation (TGC) curve?

(A) gray scale
(B) far gain
(C) knee
(D) delay

455. The range of pulse repetition frequencies used in diagnostic ultrasound is

(A) 0.5–4 kHz
(B) 1–10 MHz
(C) 1–7 kHz
(D) 10–15 MHz

456. The spatial pulse length is defined as the product of the ______ multiplied by the number of ______ in a pulse.

(A) cycles, frequency
(B) frequency, velocity
(C) wavelength, cycles
(D) frequency, wavelength

457. Which of the following is (are) one-dimensional?

(A) B-mode and A-mode
(B) A-mode and M-mode
(C) B-mode
(D) static imaging

458. Continuous wave ultrasound is

(A) applicable to real-time instruments only
(B) used in all Doppler instruments
(C) used in some Doppler instruments
(D) applicable only to static scanners

459. Which imaging modality is audible?

(A) x-ray
(B) ultrasound
(C) Doppler
(D) computed tomography (CT)

460. Which mode requires two crystals: one for transmitting and one for receiving?

(A) A-mode
(B) M-mode
(C) continuous wave mode
(D) pulse-echo mode

Questions 461 through 464: Identify the components in Fig. 1–31 by correlating them with the list of terms given.

461. ______ (A) motor
462. ______ (B) acoustic mirror
463. ______ (C) scanner head
464. ______ (D) piezoelectric crystal

465. The normal range of intensities used in Doppler instruments is

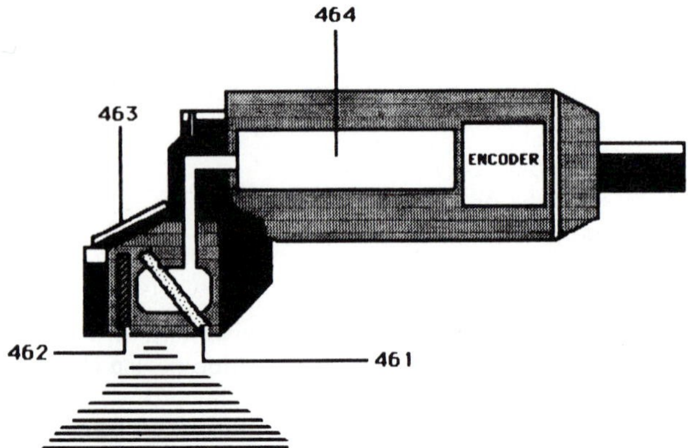

Figure 1–31. Diagram of a mechanical sector real-time transducer.

(A) 0.2–400 W/cm^2
(B) 0.2–400 mW/cm^2
(C) 400–800 mW/cm^2
(D) 800–900 mW/cm^2

466. If the media boundary is moving toward the source, the reflected sound wave will have

(A) a higher frequency than the incident frequency
(B) a lower frequency than the incident frequency
(C) no change in frequency
(D) be delayed

467. If the media boundary is moving away from the source, the result will be

(A) a higher frequency than the incident frequency
(B) a lower frequency than the incident frequency
(C) no change in frequency
(D) be delayed

468. A Doppler instrument that can distinguish between positive and negative shifts is called

(A) bistable
(B) a modulator–demodulator
(C) bidirectional
(D) a polarized shifter

469. Which statement about Doppler application is not true?

(A) color Doppler is not beneficial
(B) Doppler can produce audible sound
(C) Doppler instruments use both pulsed and continuous wave
(D) Doppler can display an image

Questions 470 through 474: Match the time gain compensation (TGC) controls in Column A with the control functions in Column B.

COLUMN A

470. near gain ______
471. far gain ______
472. slope ______
473. delay ______
474. knee ______

COLUMN B

(A) control used to suppress or increase echoes in the far field
(B) control used to suppress or increase echoes in the near field
(C) control used to delay the start of the slope
(D) control the upward incline of the TGC, used to display an even texture throughout an organ
(E) controls the point where the slope ends

475. The range of frequencies contained in an ultrasound pulse is called

(A) propagation
(B) bandwidth
(C) refraction
(D) rejection

476. Which quantity is unitless?

(A) Q-factor
(B) volume
(C) intensity
(D) force

477. Which of the following would *most* likely cause acoustic enhancement?

(A) a solid mass
(B) a fluid-filled mass
(C) a calcified mass
(D) a gallstone

478. Which of the following would *most* likely cause acoustic shadowing?

(A) gallbladder
(B) a fluid-filled mass
(C) a calcified mass
(D) urinary bladder

479. Continuous-wave Doppler uses how many piezoelectric element(s)?

(A) 1
(B) 2
(C) 64
(D) none

480. The greatest Doppler angle is achieved

(A) when the beam strikes a vessel at a sharp angle
(B) when the beam strikes a vessel perpendicular
(C) when the beam strikes a vessel at a 30° angle
(D) when the beam strikes a vessel at a 70° angle

481. If the power output of an amplifier is 100 times the power at the input, the gain is

(A) 10 dB
(B) 20 dB
(C) 30 dB
(D) 40 dB

482. Which control is used to minimize the effects of attenuation?

(A) reject
(B) field-of-view
(C) frame rate
(D) depth-gain compensation

483. When an ultrasound beam passes obliquely across the boundary between two materials, ______ will occur if there is a difference in ______ in the two materials.

(A) reflection, impedance
(B) reflection, density
(C) refraction, impedance
(D) refraction, propagation speed

484. A decreased pulse duration leads to

(A) better axial resolution
(B) decreased spatial resolution
(C) decreased longitudinal resolution
(D) better lateral resolution

485. What is the reflected intensity from a boundary between two materials if the incident intensity is 1 mW/cm^2 and the impedances are 25 and 75?

(A) 0.25 mW/cm^2
(B) 0.33 mW/cm^2
(C) 0.50 mW/cm^2
(D) 1.00 mW/cm^2

486. The near zone length of an unfocused transducer depends on

(A) frequency and thickness
(B) frequency and diameter
(C) resolution and field of view
(D) diameter and field of view

487. The frequency of a transducer depends primarily on

(A) overall gain
(B) the speed of ultrasound
(C) the element diameter
(D) the element thickness

488. An ultrasound beam that is normally incident on an interface will experience no

(A) attenuation
(B) refraction
(C) reflection
(D) absorption

489. The average speed of propagation of ultrasound in soft tissue is

(A) 1540 ft/s
(B) 1.54 dB/cm
(C) 1.54 mm/μs
(D) 1540 mW/cm^2

490. The duty factor for a system with a pulse duration (PD) of 5 μs and a pulse repetition period (PRP) of 500 μs is

(A) 0.1%
(B) 0.5%

(C) 1.0%
(D) 10.0%

491. Ultrasound is defined as sound with frequencies above

(A) 20 Hz
(B) 20 kHz
(C) 20 MHz
(D) 20 GHz

492. Frequency is a significant factor in

(A) propagation speed
(B) tissue compressibility
(C) tissue attenuation
(D) transducer diameter

493. In a pulse-echo system, a 3.5 MHz beam in 2 cm of tissue will be attenuated by

(A) 3.5 dB/cm
(B) 7.0 dB/cm
(C) 3.5 dB
(D) 7.0 dB

494. The characteristic acoustic impedance of a material is equal to the product of the material density and

(A) path length
(B) wavelength
(C) frequency
(D) propagation speed

495. For a focused transducer, the beam intensity will remain constant through the scan field.

(A) true
(B) false

496. For normal incidence, if the intensity reflection coefficient is 30%, the intensity transmission coefficient will be

(A) 30%
(B) 60%
(C) 70%
(D) 100%

497. A Fourier transform of a returning echo will result in a presentation of the ______ contained within the echo

(A) frequencies
(B) wavelength
(C) intensity
(D) power

498. The range equation relates

(A) frequency, velocity, and wavelength
(B) frequency, velocity, and time
(C) distance, velocity, and time
(D) distance, frequency, and time

499. The axial resolution of a system is determined by

(A) spatial pulse length
(B) beam intensity
(C) beam diameter
(D) spatial resolution

500. The Doppler shift frequency is zero when the angle between the receiving transducer and the flow direction is

(A) 0°
(B) 45°
(C) 90°
(D) 180°

501. The frame rate of real-time scanner that uses an electronic array will be limited only by the speed of the scan converter memory.

(A) true
(B) false

502. The dynamic range of a pulse-echo ultrasound system is defined as

(A) the ratio of the maximum to the minimum intensity that can be processed
(B) the range of propagation speeds
(C) the range of gain settings allowed
(D) none of the above

503. The digital scan converter will generally have a dynamic range that is ______ than other components of the system.

(A) larger
(B) smaller

504. The time-gain or depth-gain compensation control

(A) compensates for attenuation effects
(B) compensates for increased patient scan time
(C) compensates for machine malfunctions
(D) compensates for video-image drifts

505. A digital scan converter is essentially a

(A) radio receiver
(B) video monitor
(C) television set
(D) computer memory

506. A mechanical real-time scanner will always produce images at a slower frame rate than does an electronic realtime scanner.

(A) true
(B) false

507. Acoustic enhancement can be observed when scanning

(A) highly attenuating structures
(B) weakly attenuating structures
(C) highly reflective structures
(D) structures with large speed differences

508. Changes in the preprocessing controls will not affect the numbers stored in the scan converter.

(A) true
(B) false

509. The lateral resolution of a system

(A) is equal to the beam diameter
(B) is better at higher frequencies
(C) is constant throughout the image
(D) changes with gain settings

510. If the lines per degree in a mechanical sector scanner remain constant, a decreased sector angle can result in

(A) decreased resolution
(B) increased frame rate
(C) decreased frame rate
(D) increased resolution

511. The threshold control is equivalent to the

(A) TGC control
(B) DGC control
(C) modulation control
(D) reject control

512. If the actual propagation speed in soft tissue is 1700 m/s, current diagnostic scanners will display a reflector at a location ______ the transducer.

(A) too close to
(B) too far from
(C) displaced to the left of
(D) displaced to the right of

513. Continuous-wave (CW) ultrasound is used in

(A) static B-scanners
(B) bistable systems
(C) most modern B-scan systems
(D) some Doppler systems

514. If the gain of an amplifier is 18 dB, what will the new gain setting be if one reduces the gain setting by one-half?

(A) 9 dB
(B) 36 dB
(C) 15 dB
(D) 0.5 dB

515. Decreasing the pulse repetition period

(A) decreases spatial resolution
(B) decreases axial resolution
(C) decreases the maximum depth imaged
(D) increases the maximum depth imaged

516. The AIUM 100-mm test object

(A) measures power output
(B) measures beam intensity
(C) measures frequency
(D) measures spatial resolution

517. Real-time imaging is impossible without electronic arrays.

(A) true
(B) false

518. Grating lobes in electronic array systems

(A) increase with increased steering angle
(B) decrease with increased steering angle
(C) are eliminated at high frame rates
(D) are not likely to produce artifacts

519. The attenuation coefficient is expressed in units of

(A) mW/cm^2
(B) dB
(C) dB/cm
(D) mW

520. The wave equation relates

(A) time, mass, and distance
(B) time, velocity, and frequency
(C) wavelength, velocity, and frequency
(D) wavelength, distance, and frequency

521. The ability of a system to detect low-amplitude echoes accurately is referred to as

(A) resolution
(B) sensitivity
(C) accuracy
(D) dynamic range

522. The primary mechanisms whereby ultrasound can produce biologic effects are

(A) thermal and cavitation
(B) absorption and reflection
(C) reflection and transmission
(D) heat and cold

523. The near-zone length of a transducer depends on

(A) propagation speed and frequency
(B) frequency and transducer diameter
(C) field of view and transducer diameter
(D) path length

524. The AIUM Committee on Biological Effects (1982) stated that ______ biologic effects have been observed for ultrasound intensities below 100 mW/cm^2.

(A) no
(B) no confirmed
(C) few
(D) many

525. The intensity of a focused beam is generally

(A) constant
(B) highest at the transducer surface
(C) highest at the focal zone
(D) lowest at the transducer surface

526. The wavelength of a 5 MHz wave passing through soft tissue is approximately

(A) 0.1 mm
(B) 0.3 mm
(C) 0.5 mm
(D) 1.0 mm

527. An echo that has undergone an attenuation of 3 dB will have an intensity that is ______ than its initial intensity.

(A) three times smaller
(B) three times larger
(C) two times smaller
(D) two times larger

528. A pulse–echo system should have a high Q factor (quality-factor).

(A) true
(B) false

529. A 5 MHz transducer used in a pulse-echo system will generally produce

(A) a wide band of frequencies centered at 5 MHz
(B) frequencies only at 5 MHz
(C) frequencies only at 5 MHz or multiples of 5 MHz
(D) a wide band of frequencies above 5 MHz

530. The transducer ______ determines its ______.

(A) diameter, intensity
(B) damping, lateral resolution
(C) thickness, sensitivity
(D) thickness, resonance frequency

531. The axial resolution of a transducer can be improved with ______ but at the expense of ______.

(A) increased damping, sensitivity
(B) frequency, lateral resolution
(C) focusing, sensitivity
(D) focusing, lateral resolution

532. A material that changes its dimensions when an electric field is applied is called a ______ material.

(A) piezoelectric
(B) elastic
(C) inelastic
(D) compressible

533. The process of making the impedance values on either side of a boundary as close as possible to reduce reflections is called

(A) damping
(B) refracting
(C) matching
(D) compensating

534. When the pressure peaks of two waves coincide at a point to produce a new pressure that is larger than either of the two initial waves, the effect is called

(A) phase cancellation
(B) destructive interference
(C) enhancement
(D) constructive interference

535. Shadowing occurs with

(A) highly attenuating structures
(B) large changes in propagation speed
(C) low frequencies more often than with high frequencies
(D) weak reflectors

536. Reverberation artifacts

(A) occur most often at high frequencies
(B) occur with multiple strong reflecting structures
(C) occur only with real-time arrays
(D) cannot occur in color Doppler systems

537. A transducer with a large bandwidth is likely to have

(A) good axial resolution
(B) a large ring-down time
(C) poor resolution
(D) a high Q factor

538. The near zone is also referred to as the

(A) Fraunhofer zone
(B) Fresnel zone
(C) focal zone
(D) divergence zone

539. Refraction will not occur at an interface

(A) when high frequencies are used
(B) if the acoustic impedances are equal
(C) if the propagation speeds are significantly different
(D) with normal incidence of the ultrasound beam

540. Acoustic power output is determined primarily by

(A) the diameter of the transducer
(B) the thickness of the transducer
(C) the pulser voltage spike
(D) focusing

541. Specular reflections occur when

(A) the reflecting object is small with respect to the wavelength
(B) the reflecting surface is large and smooth with respect to the wavelength
(C) the reflecting objects are moving
(D) the angle of incidence and angle of reflection are unequal

542. The angle at which an ultrasound beam is bent as it passes through a boundary between two different materials is described mathematically by

(A) Huygen's principle
(B) Curie's principle
(C) Snell's law
(D) Doppler's law

543. An annular array real-time scanner

(A) is steered electronically
(B) is steered mechanically
(C) is not capable of electronic focusing
(D) is not used with digital-scan converters

544. The percentage of an ultrasound beam reflected at an interface between gas and soft tissue is approximately

(A) 90–100%
(B) 40–50%
(C) 1–10%
(D) < 1%

545. The percentage of an ultrasound beam reflected at an interface between fat and muscle is approximately

(A) 90–100%
(B) 40–50%
(C) 1–10%
(D) 0%

546. By using a waterpath offset,

(A) tissue attenuation can be reduced
(B) the focal zone can be moved to the skin surface
(C) lower frequencies can be used
(D) no reflections will occur at the skin surface

547. Ultrasound waves in tissue are referred to as

(A) shear waves
(B) transverse waves
(C) vibrational waves
(D) longitudinal compression waves

548. High-frequency transducers have

(A) shorter wavelengths and less penetration
(B) longer wavelengths and greater penetration
(C) shorter wavelengths and greater penetration
(D) longer wavelengths and less penetration

549. When the piezoelectric crystal continues to vibrate after the initial voltage pulse, this is referred to as

(A) ring-down time
(B) pulse delay
(C) pulse retardation
(D) overdamping

550. Annular phased arrays unlike linear phased arrays

(A) can be dynamically focused
(B) electronically focus in two dimensions rather than one
(C) can be used in Doppler systems
(D) can achieve high frame rates

551. Which group is arranged in the correct order of increasing propagation speed?

(A) gas, bone, muscle
(B) bone, muscle, gas
(C) gas, muscle, bone
(D) muscle, bone, gas

552. The lower useful range of diagnostic ultrasound is determined primarily by ______, whereas the upper useful range is determined by ______.

(A) resolution, penetration
(B) scattering, propagation speed
(C) cost, resolution
(D) scattering, resolution

553. Color Doppler systems are not subject to aliasing.

(A) true
(B) false

554. Which of the following is true?

(A) SPTA is always equal to or greater than SPTP

(B) SPTP is always equal to or greater than SPTA
(C) SATA is always equal to or greater than SATP
(D) SPTA is always equal to or greater than SATP

555. A beam-intensity profile is often mapped with

(A) a radiation force balance
(B) a SUAR phantom
(C) a hydrophone
(D) AIUM phantom

556. Real-time scanners are generally classified as either

(A) electronic or mechanical
(B) dynamic or fixed
(C) programmable or fixed
(D) static or electronic

557. The technique of passing an ultrasound beam through water so that compression and rarefaction of the water molecules allow the beam pattern to be measured is referred to as the

(A) Doppler method
(B) Schlieren method
(C) hydrostatic method
(D) water-density method

558. Pulse duration is the ______ for a pulse to occur.

(A) space
(B) range
(C) intensity
(D) time

559. The frame rate of a real-time scanner will not depend on

(A) the depth of view
(B) the line density
(C) the frequency
(D) the propagation speed

560. The unit of measure of SPTA is

(A) dB
(B) W/cm^2
(C) W
(D) Hz

561. The piezoelectric properties of a transducer will be lost if the crystal is heated above the

(A) dew point
(B) dynamic range
(C) Curie point
(D) linear range

562. If the amplitude of a wave is increased threefold, the intensity will

(A) decrease threefold
(B) increase threefold
(C) increase ninefold
(D) increase sixfold

563. A videotape recorder records at a rate of 30 frames/s and therefore cannot be used to record images from a mechanical scanner operating at lower frame rates.

(A) true
(B) false

564. If the frequency is increased, the ______ will be ______.

(A) velocity, increased
(B) attenuation, decreased
(C) velocity, decreased
(D) velocity, unchanged

565. Beam steering is achieved in a linear phased array by

(A) mechanical motion
(B) electronic time-delay pulsing
(C) an acoustic lens
(D) dynamic focusing

566. Dynamic focusing

(A) is made possible by array-based systems
(B) is made possible by acoustic lens
(C) is not possible in a linear-switched array
(D) is often used in single-element systems

567. Quality assurance measurements are not required with electronic scanners with digital scan converters.

(A) true
(B) false

568. Sound will travel ______ in 1 μs in soft tissue.

(A) 1540 m
(B) 1.54 cm
(C) 1.54 mm
(D) 0.75 mm

569. The arrow in Fig. 1–32 points to a

(A) ring-down artifact
(B) mirror image artifact
(C) side lobe artifact
(D) ghost artifact

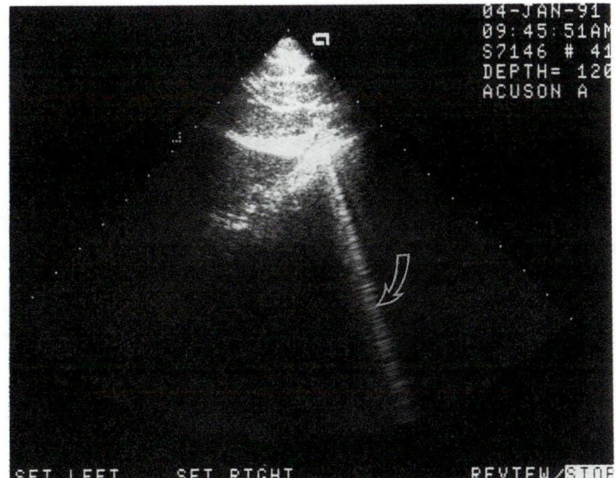

Figure 1–32. Sonogram of an artifact.

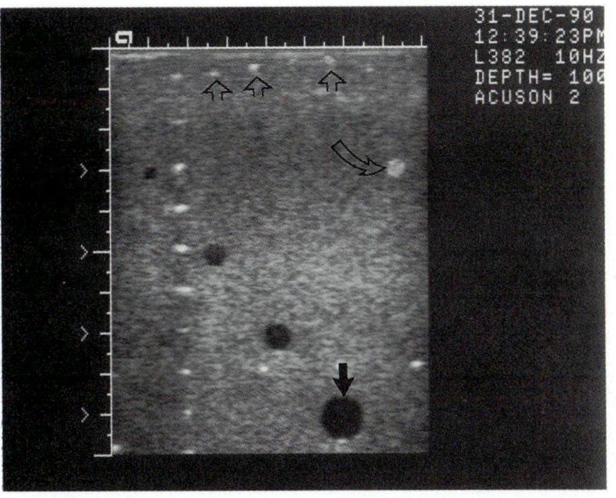

Figure 1–33. Image from a tissue-equivalent phantom.

570. In the image in Fig. 1–33, which represents a tissue-equivalent phantom, the small open arrows point to

(A) rods for measuring "ring down"
(B) parallel rods used for horizontal calibration
(C) rods used for axial resolution
(D) rods used for measure registration

571. In the image in Fig. 1–33, which represents a tissue-equivalent phantom, the curved open arrow points to

(A) a dead zone
(B) a simulated solid lesion
(C) a ghost artifact
(D) a side lobe artifact

572. In the image in Fig. 1–33, which represents a tissue-equivalent phantom, the solid black arrow points to

(A) a ghost artifact
(B) a dead zone
(C) a simulated cyst
(D) a side lobe artifact

Answers and Explanations

At the end of each explained answer there is a number combination in parentheses. The first number identifies the reference source; the second number or set of numbers indicates the page or pages on which the relevant information can be found.

1. **(C)** Red blood cells. Structures smaller than a wavelength will scatter sound in all directions and are sometimes called diffuse reflectors. *(2:42)*

2. **(B)** Spatial pulse length is defined as the product of the number of cycles in the pulse and its wavelength. This is generally shorter for higher frequencies since the wavelength is shorter. *(2:64)*

3. **(D)** Axial resolution, also called longitudinal, range, or depth resolution, is determined by the wavelength, damping, and frequency. Axial resolution improves with increased frequency. *(2:64)*

4. **(B)** Lateral resolution is defined as being equal to the beam diameter. *(2:65)*

5. **(C)** The beam of an unfocused transducer diverges in the Fraunhofer (far) zone. *(1:360)*

6. **(C)** Reverberation artifacts are present when two or more strong reflectors are located within the beam. One of these may be the transducer itself. *(2:142)*

7. **(B)** False. Grating lobes are an undesirable property of multi-element array transducers. *(4:31)*

8. **(B)** False. Resolution is a function of the focusing characteristics of any scanner and cannot be assumed to be better for any particular scanner configuration. *(1:390–399)*

9. **(A)** True. Annular arrays may be used for creating variable focusing in two dimensions but are not capable of electronic steering of the beam. *(5:233)*

10. **(B)** False. The focusing of a linear array is controlled by timing and is thus capable of dynamic focusing. *(4:29)*

11. **(A, B, C, D, E)** All rods must be used to check registration accuracy. *(2:158)*

12. **(A)** See Fig. 1–24 and Table 1–3, Study Guide. *(2:156)*

13. **(B)** See Fig. 1–24 and Table 1–3, Study Guide. *(2:156)*

14. **(D)** See Fig. 1–24 and Table 1–3, Study Guide. *(2:156)*

15. **(C or E)** See Fig. 1–24 and Table 1–3, Study Guide. *(2:156)*

16. **(C)** Decreasing the spatial pulse length improves axial resolution. Axial resolution is equal to one-half of the spatial pulse length. *(2:64)*

17. **(B)** A rule of thumb approximating the attenuation coefficient of a reflected echo in soft tissue is 0.5 dB/cm/MHz. Thus the attenuation coefficient will be one-half the operating frequency.

    attenuation (dB) = attenuation coefficient (dB/cm) $\times$ path length (cm)

    $$\text{dB} = 1.75\ \text{dB/cm} \times 2\ \text{cm} = 3.5\ \text{dB}$$

    (2:23)

18. **(B)** Improper axial (along-the-beam) position. *(2:139)*

19. **(D)** Weakly attenuating structures. *(2:139)*

20. **(A)** Directly proportional to the velocity of the reflector. *(1:386)*

21. **(A)** More than 15 frames per second. *Note:* The scan converter in most modern systems turns the scanning frame rate (which is the subject of this question) into a display frame rate (or video frame rate) which is usually faster (30 video frames/s). This is done by displaying the same scan frame more than once if the scan frame is less than the video rate. *(4:34)*

22. **(A)** True. Spatial peak (SP) values will always be greater than spatial average (SA) intensity values. *(2:21)*

23. **(B)** Smaller beam diameter. Intensity is defined as power per unit beam area; as the beam area decreases the intensity increases. *(2:18)*

24. **(C)** Increased by four times. Intensity equals the square of the amplitude. *(2:18)*

25. **(A)** Increased with tissue thickness. Attenuation is the product of the attenuation coefficient and path length. *(2:23)*

26. **(A)** Should be chosen to be at a value approximately equal to the mean of impedances of the material on either side of it. *(1:370)*

27. **(B)** False. The Q factor, or quality factor, of a transducer refers to the length of time that the sound persists. High-Q transducers tend to ring for a long time, whereas low-Q transducers ring for a shorter time. A low Q produces a short pulse length, which is necessary to provide good images. *(1:359)*

28. **(B)** False. The beam diameter reduces to one-half of the transducer diameter from the face of the transducer to the focal point. *(2:58)*

29. **(B)** Depends on crystal thickness. Thickness equals one-half the wavelength. *(2:50)*

30. **(C)** The time of one wavelength. *(2:6)*

31. **(D)** Ratio of smallest to largest power level. *(2:84)*

32. **(A)** True. Radiation pressure can be measured with a sensitive balance and converted to intensity. *(5:89)*

33. **(B)** Increases the maximum depth that can be imaged. *(4:36)*

34. **(C)** Are not confirmed below 100 mW/cm^2 SPTA. *(3:9)*

35. **(B)** False. Refraction comes as a result of changes in sound velocity across a boundary, not impedance. *(4:7)*

36. **(B)** False. Beam diameter depends on whether or not the transducer is focused, the distance from the transducer, and whether one is in the near field or far field. Small transducers produce greatly diverging beams in the far field. *(1:364)*

37. **(A)** True. A hydrophone is usually a very small piezoelectric crystal that can be moved in front of the transmitting crystal to map its beam characteristics. *(5:85)*

38. **(A)** True. Pulsed Doppler utilizes range gating to localize the signals to specific depths. *(5:385)*

39. **(B)** False. Gray-scale ultrasound images were also possible with analog storage devices. *(5:198)*

40. **(B)** False. If the imaging rate is slower than the video framing rate, frames are duplicated to fill in. *(4:44)*

41. **(B)** False. Linear arrays must also be focused in the direction perpendicular to the array axis to reduce the slice thickness. This is usually accomplished by mechanical focusing. *(1:394)*

42. **(A)** True. Real-time scanners display 15 to 60 images per second, called the frame rate. This rate must be greater than 15 frames per second to produce a flicker-free image. Each frame is made of scan lines, the number of lines per frame, and the number of frames per second are related to one another. *(4:35, 2:105)*

43. **(A)** True. Annular phased arrays must be steered mechanically, most frequently through the use of an oscillating acoustic mirror. *(3:4)*

44. **(B)** False. Images produced in the near zone have the best lateral resolution; therefore, the near zone length should be long enough to include all time regions-of-interest. *(1:362)*

45. **(C)** Twenty-five percent. The reflection coefficient (r) is equal to:

$$r = \left(\frac{Z_2 - Z_1}{Z_2 + Z_1}\right)^2 = \left(\frac{0.75 - 0.25}{0.75 + 0.25}\right)^2 = 0.25$$

where Z_1 and Z_2 are the acoustic impedances of each material. *(1:366)*

46. **(A)** Higher frequency transducers usually produce shorter spatial pulse lengths and thus improve axial resolution. *(2:64)*

47. **(A)** Longitudinal wave. *(4:2)*

48. **(A)** 0.3 mm.

$$\text{wavelength (mm)} = \frac{\text{velocity (mm/}\mu\text{s)}}{\text{frequency (MHz)}} = \frac{1.5}{5} = 0.3\ \text{mm}$$

(4:2)

49. **(D)** The specific acoustic impedance. The fraction of sound reflected at an interface (r) is given by:

$$r = \left(\frac{Z_2 - Z_1}{Z_2 + Z_1}\right)^2$$

where Z_1 and Z_2 are the acoustic impedance of the boundary material. *(1:366)*

50. **(A)** V or C = propagation velocity (cm/s)
f = frequency (cycles/s)
λ = wavelength (cm)
$V = f\lambda$ *(31:9; 12:2)*

51. **(D)** All of the above. Reflection refers to echoes; refraction refers to the bending of the beam; and mode conversion refers to a change in the propagation mode transverse, shear, surface, or longitudinal waves. *(5:15–19)*

52. **(D)** Equal to the product of density and velocity for longitudinal waves. *(1:365)*

53. **(C)** 1540 meters per second. *(1:353)*

54. **(B)** False. The magnitude of the Doppler shift frequency is directly related to the cosine of the angle between the direction of the blood flow and the receiver angle. The maximum shift frequency is therefore observed when the flow is along the receiver line-of-sight. *(1:386)*

55. **(B)** Wave velocity. Refraction is described by Snell's law, which relates the incident angle (θ_i) to the transmitted angle (θ_t) to the relative velocities of the two media making up the interface:

$$\frac{\sin \theta_i}{\sin \theta_t} = \frac{V_1}{V_2}$$

(1:367)

56. **(A)** Acoustic impedance. *(1:366)*

57. **(C)** The material through which the sound is being transmitted and the mode of vibration. *(1:353)*

58. **(C)** No change. The velocity of sound propagation depends on the material through which it is being transmitted and is independent of frequency. *(1:353)*

59. **(A)** Refraction. *(1:367)*

60. **(A)** Using a higher frequency transducer. The near zone length (x) is given by:

$$x = \frac{r^2}{\lambda}$$

where r is the radius of the transducer and λ is the wavelength. Thus, a longer near zone length is achieved by increasing the transducer diameter or increasing the frequency. *(1:367)*

61. **(A)** 0.75 mm. The wavelength can be determined by using the following equation:

$$\lambda = \frac{v}{f}$$

v = propagation velocity (m/s)
f = frequency (Hz)
λ = wavelength (m)

For example: $\lambda = \dfrac{1500 \text{ meters per second}}{2 \text{ MHz}}$

$$\lambda = \frac{1.5 \times 10^3 \text{ meters per second}}{2 \times 10^6 \text{ cycles per second}}$$

$$\lambda = 0.75 \times 10^{-3} \text{ meters}$$

$$\lambda = 0.75 \text{ mm}$$

(2:8; 12:2)

62. **(B)**

$$Z \text{ (impedance) for longitudinal waves} = \frac{\text{particle pressure}}{\text{particle velocity}}$$

(5:13)

63. **(A)** Doppler-shift formula. *(2:125)*

64. **(C)** Huygens. *(1:362; 5:26)*

65. **(B)** Tenfold difference in intensity or power. *(2:255)*

66. **(B)** Threshold, negative, or reject level. *(1:376)*

67. **(B)** Compression. *(2:84)*

68. **(A)** A-mode. *(1:370)*

69. **(D)** Relaxation processes are modes by which ultrasound may be attenuated in passing through a material. Suppression is another name for rejection. *(2:79–85)*

70. **(B)** Digital scan converter. *(3:31)*

71. **(A)** Duty factor. *(2:55)*

72. **(D)** Sensitivity. *(2:155)*

73. **(B)** Linear array transducers produce a rectangular image. (Sector scanners produce a pie-shaped image.) *(3:18–26)*

74. **(B)** Magnitude of the voltage spike applied to the transducer by the pulser. *(2:77)*

75. **(D)** Thermal and cavitational. *(2:171)*

76. **(C)** Quality factor, or Q factor, is equal to the operating frequency divided by the bandwidth. *(1:36)*

77. **(C)** Side lobes. *(5:29)*

78. **(D)** Pulse duration. *(2:15)*

79. **(B)** The silicon oxide matrix is charged by a scanning electron beam, producing an image pattern that can be displayed on a video monitor. *(5:198)*

80. **(C)** Reflectors whose boundaries are smooth relative to a wavelength behave as mirrors and are called specular reflectors. *(2:42)*

81. **(B)** Schlieren technique of measurement. *(1:362)*

82. **(D)** Reverberation. *(2:140)*

83. **(B)** Enhancement. *(2:146)*

84. **(B)** Using a larger diameter transducer. The dispersion angle in the far field (θ) is given as: $\sin \theta = 1.22\ \lambda/d$, where λ is the wavelength and d is the diameter of the transducer. The angle can be reduced by using either a larger transducer or a higher frequency (smaller wavelength). *(1:364)*

85. **(B)** Spatial pulse length.

$$\text{axial resolution (mm)} = \frac{\text{spatial pulse length (mm)}}{2}$$

(2:64)

86. **(B)** Quality factor (Q factor).

$$Q = \frac{f_0}{f_2 - f_1}$$

where f_0 is the central resonance frequency and $(f_2 - f_1)$ is the frequency bandwidth. *(2:53; 1:360)*

87. **(C)** Schlieren technique. *(1:362)*

88. **(D)** Blood. *(1:369)*

89. **(A)** Dynamic range. *(2:84)*

90. **(D)** Longitudinal waves. *(1:352)*

91. **(B)** Axial resolution. *(2:156)*

92. **(C)** Scan C. *(2:158)*

93. **(A)** Dead zone. *(2:156)*

94. **(A)** Call for service. *(6:23–24)*

95. **(C)** Horizontal caliper check. *(6:15)*

96. **(B)** Lateral resolution. *(6:19–26)*

97. **(E)** Gray scale and dynamic range. *(2:158; 6:19–24)*

98. **(D)** Registration. *(6:18)*

99. **(E)** All of the answers given are correct. *(6:10–24)*

100. **(F)** All of the answers given are correct. *(6:10–24)*

101. **(C, D, F, G, H)** Lead zirconate titanate, barium titanate, lithium sulfate, lead metaniobate, and ammonium dihydrogen phosphate are not natural. *(7:85–87; 8:28)*

102. **(C)** Cork, rubber, epoxy resin, and tungsten powder in araldite are good acoustic insulators. Water and oil are not. *(8:38–39)*

103. **(A)** Sound and ultrasound are mechanical vibrations that can propagate in matter, such as liquid and solid. However, sound or ultrasound cannot travel in a vacuum. *(10:1)*

104. **(A)** Infrasound (subsonic). *(10:1)*

105. **(B)** Ultrasound. *(10:1)*

106. **(B)** Audible sound. *(10:1)*

107. **(B)** The electromagnetic spectrum is a large family of electromagnetic waves. Light, x-rays, and infrared and ultraviolet rays are among its spectrum; ultrasound is not. (1:1–3)

108. **(D)** Cycle per second (cps). *(10:1)*

109. **(B)** Electrical energy into mechanical energy and vice versa. *(2:48)*

110. **(E)** All of the answers given are correct. *(2:48)*

111. **(D)** Increase or decrease depending on the polarity applied. *(2:49)*

112. **(D)** 1 mega = 1 million. Therefore, 5 MHz = 5 million cycles per second or 5 million Hz. *(10:1)*

113. **(G)** The damping material reduces pulse duration and spatial pulse length, and as a result it improves axial resolution. *(2:51)*

114. **(A)** Velocity of ultrasound transmitted through a medium depends on the properties of the medium: (1) temperature, (2) elasticity, and (3) density. The speed of ultrasound varies with temperature. However, temperature/velocity in human soft tissue can usually be ignored because body temperature is usually constant within a narrow range, for example: 94°F (low) to 106°F (high). The velocity of ultrasound in soft tissue at 37°C or 98.6°F (body temperature) is 1540 meters per second (1540 m/s). *(11:3; 9:55; 10:5)*

115. **(C)** A single cycle. *(11:2)*

116. **(A)** Particle motion parallel to (or in the same direction of) the axis of wave propagation. *(7:4)*

117. **(C)** Particle motion perpendicular to the axis of wave propagation. *(7:4)*

118. **(B)** Condensations. *(7:4)*

119. **(C)** Rarefactions. *(7:4)*

120. **(D)** Pressure. *(11:9)*

121. **(F)** *(2:64)*

122. **(F)** *(2:64)*

123–131. See Fig. 1–8 in the Study Guide. *(1:367; 2:98)*

132–140. See Fig. 1–23 in the Study Guide. *(12:2; 1:373)*

141. **(A)** If frequency increases, the wavelength decreases. *(2:140–141)*

142. **(B)** If frequency decreases, the wavelength increases. *(2:140–141)*

143. **(A)** As frequency increases, the penetration decreases. *(2:140–141)*

144. **(B)** As frequency increases, the resolution increases. *(2:140–141)*

145. **(A)** Higher frequency transmits shorter pulse and narrower beam width. *(9:31)*

146. **(F)** Air, bone, and barium sulfate ($BaSO_4$). The contrast material used for intravenous pyelogram (IVP) does not prevent the propagation of ultrasound. *(12:2; 13:413)*

147. **(C)** Barium sulfate ($BaSO_4$). A coupling medium is a liquid medium placed between the transducer and the skin to eliminate air gap. Air has a reflection coefficient approaching 100%, which results in almost zero transmission. Water or saline can also be used but they dry out faster than gel. *(13:10–11; 11:52)*

148. **(A)** The progressive weakening of the sound beam as it travels. Attenuation occurs because of (1) absorption, (2) reflection, and (3) scatter. Barium sulfate and air impair ultrasound transmissions. *(11:4)*

149. **(C)** When crystals are subjected to pressure resulting in electrical charge on their surfaces, it is called a piezoelectric effect. *(10:12)*

150. **(B)** When crystals are subjected to electrical impulse and generate ultrasound as a result, it is called reverse piezoelectric effect. *(10:12)*

151. **(B)** Attenuation is the amount of energy lost per unit of depth into the tissue. The parameter used to express the energy loss is the decibel (dB).

$$\text{dB} = 10 \log_{10} \frac{I_2}{I_1}$$

(12:5)

152. **(C)** Waves carry energy from one place to another through a medium. *(14:1)*

153. **(A)** A mechanical wave causes particles to oscillate around its equilibrium point. *(14:2)*

154. **(C)** Wavelength is the distance between two identical points on the waveform. *(14:4)*

155. **(A)** Ultrasonic waves are mechanical. A medium is required for propagation of sounds. *(14:1)*

156. **(B)** Acoustic impedance is defined as the density of tissue × the speed of sound in tissue ($Z = pc$). *(15:30)*

157. **(D)** Amplitude is defined as the height of the wave. For amplitude, dB = 20 log (amplitude ratio). *(15:3)*

158. **(B)** Ultrasound is above 20,000 cycles per second (Hz) and is above the audible range of sound. *(15:2)*

159. **(D)** The equation for period is:

$$\text{period} = \frac{1}{\text{frequency}}$$

(14:2)

160. **(D)** The direction of the returning echo is related to the beam angle. The more perpendicular the beam gets to an organ interface, the greater the specular reflection. *(15:5)*

161. **(A)** A decibel is the ratio of two sound intensities, highest to lowest (or vice versa). *(14:1)*

162. **(C)** Azimuthal is another name for *lateral* resolution. *(14:6)*

163. **(B)** Bone has the highest sound velocity due to its stiffness. *(14:8)*

164. **(B)** No significant biologic effects have been proven in mammals exposed below 100 mW/cm^2 spatial peak, temporal average (SPTA). *(2:175)*

165. **(A)** Temporal peak intensity is measured at the time the pulse is present. *(14:5)*

166. **(D)** SATA has the lowest intensity since the intensity is averaged over the whole beam profile (SA), and over the whole duration of exposure (TA). *(2:21)*

167. **(B)** The beam uniformity ratio is defined as the spatial peak intensity (measured at the beam center) divided by the spatial average intensity (the average intensity across the beam). *(2:19)*

168. **(C)** The duty factor is the fraction of time the transducer is emitting sound. In a pulsed echo system it is normally less than 1%. *(14:5)*

169. **(D)** Axial resolution is defined as one-half the spatial pulse length. Therefore, the shorter the spatial pulse length the better the axial resolution. *(14:6)*

170. **(B)** V = velocity of sound (cm/sec); f = frequency (cycle/sec); and λ = wavelength (cm). *(1:364)*

171. **(D)** Attenuation of an ultrasound beam can occur by divergence of a beam, scattering, and reflection. It can also occur by absorption. *(14:8)*

172. **(A)** Attenuation coefficient of sound is defined by dB/cm/MHz. *(14:12)*

173. **(C)** Transducer Q factor (quality factor) is equal to the operating frequency divided by the bandwidth. Therefore, if the transducer Q factor is low, the bandwidth is wide. *(14:6)*

174. **(A)** Axial resolution can be improved by shortening pulse length, increasing damping, and a higher-frequency transducer. *(14:6)*

175. **(B)** Axial resolution is primarily affected by spatial pulse length. Because the spatial pulse length is the product of wavelength, reducing the wavelength or increasing the frequency will affect axial resolution. *(2:64)*

176. **(D)** Increasing transducer frequency will improve both lateral and axial resolution but decrease depth of penetration. *(2:69)*

177. **(C)** Range resolution is another name for *axial* resolution. *(2:65)*

178. **(B)** The duty factor is the fraction of time that sound is being emitted from the transducer. In continuous wave the sound is being emitted 100% of the time. *(2:20)*

179. **(A)** Acoustic impedance (Z) is defined as density (p) × propagation speed (c). $Z = pc$. *(2:10)*

180. **(D)** Acoustic impedance is defined by the unit rayl. Density is defined by kg/m^3, and propagation speed by meters per second. *(2:10)*

181. **(A)** Acoustic impedance is dependent on density and stiffness. It does not depend on frequency. *(2:10)*

182. **(A)** The height of the vertical spike corresponds to the strength of the echo received by the transducer. *(6:60)*

183. **(B)** B-mode is an acronym for brightness modulation. Both real-time and static scanning are B-mode display. *(6:60)*

184. **(A)** The correct equation for calculating reflection percentage is:

$$R = \left(\frac{Z_2 - Z_1}{Z_2 + Z_1}\right)^2 \times 100$$

(31:14–15)

185. **(D)** The reflection coefficient between water and air interface is nearly 100%. Air prevents the sound from entering the body. It is for this reason that a coupling gel is necessary. *(13:8)*

186. **(B)** Beyond the critical angle, 100% of the sound beam is reflected and 0% is transmitted. *(13:9)*

187. **(A)** Rayleigh scattering occurs when the particle size is smaller than a wavelength (for ultrasound typically in the 1-mm range). *(13:9)*

188. **(B)** Particle displacement is an acoustic parameter which is related to the intensity of an ultrasound wave. Other intensity-related factors include sound velocity, pressure, amplitude, and density of the medium. *(13:4)*

189. **(C)** Power is defined as the rate at which work is done or energy is transferred (energy per unit time). *(2:269)*

190. **(A)** Lateral resolution is the minimum separation between two reflectors perpendicular to the sound path. *(2:65)*

191. **(D)** In most soft tissues the attenuation coefficient increases directly with frequency. As frequency is increased the attenuation coefficient increases, thereby limiting depth of perception. *(13:9)*

192. **(A)** Absorption is the conversion of sound into heat. Absorption, scattering, and reflection are all factors of attenuation. *(2:23)*

193. **(D)** The rule of thumb for attenuation in soft tissue is 0.5 dB per centimeter per megahertz. Therefore an ultrasound beam of 1-MHz frequency will lose 0.5 dB of amplitude for every centimeter traveled. *(11:4)*

194. **(C)** Reverberations produce false echoes. *(2:142)*

195. **(D)** The acoustic mismatch between fat and muscle is small; therefore, approximately 99% of the sound beam is transmitted. *(14:10)*

196. **(A)** Huygens' principle states that all points on a wavefront can be considered as a source for secondary spherical wavelets. *(14:3)*

197. **(B)** Enhancement is the "burst of sound" visualized posterior to weak attenuations. *(2:151)*

198. **(A)** Half-value layer (HVL—sometimes called half-intensity depth) is defined as the thickness of tissue that reduces the beam intensity by half. *(13:10)*

199. **(D)** Propagation speed error. The ultrasound machine assumes a speed of 1540 meters per second (1540 m/s). If the sound passes through a medium of a different velocity, the result is an error in the range equation. *(2:146)*

200. **(B)** Range equation explains the distance to the reflector, which is equal to one-half of the propagation speed × the pulse round-trip time. *(2:44)*

201. **(A)** For a specular reflector, the angle of incidence is equal to the angle of reflection. *(14:9)*

202. **(C)** Propagation speed is determined by the medium. Amplitude, period, and intensity are determined by the transducer. *(2:5)*

203. **(D)** Acoustic variables include density, pressure, temperature, and particle motion. *(2:5)*

204. **(B)** Time gain compensation. *(15:19)*

205. **(B)** The propagation speed for fat is 1440 meters per second (1440 m/s), which is lower than that of average soft tissue. *(2:10)*

206. **(D)** Muscle has a propagation speed of 1585 meters per second (1585 m/s), which is very close to average soft tissue at 1540 m/s. *(14:8)*

207. **(A)** A is correct, with the propagation velocity in this order respectively: 331 m/s, 1450 m/s, 1585 m/s, and 4080 m/s. *(2:9, 180)*

208. **(C)** Backscatter is increased by increasing frequency and increasing heterogeneous media. *(2:32)*

209. **(A)** Critical angle is the angle at which sound is totally reflected and none is transmitted. *(13:9)*

210. **(D)** The pulse repetition frequency (PRF) is the number of pulses occurring per second. The PRF is inversely proportional to the pulse repetition period. *(2:16)*

211. **(D)** The duty factor is the fraction of time that the transducer is emitting a pulse. It is unitless. *(2:15)*

212. **(A)** The attenuation coefficient is the attenuation per unit length of sound travel. Its typical value is 3 dB/cm, for 6 MHz sound in soft tissue (0.5 dB/cm/MHz × 6 MHz = 3 dB/cm). *(2:28)*

213. **(B)** Normal incidence is also known as perpendicular incidence. At normal incidence sound may be reflected or transmitted in various degrees. *(2:32)*

214. **(A)** The difference (mismatch) of acoustic impedance between two media is what determines how much energy will be transmitted and/or reflected. *(14:10)*

215. **(A)** Acoustic impedance is equal to the product of the density of a substance and the velocity of sound. The propagation speed in solids is higher than in liquids, and the propagation speed in gas is low. The increase in propagation speed is caused by increasing stiffness of the media, not by the density. *(2:180)*

216. **(A)** According to Snell's law,

$$\frac{\sin i}{\sin r} = \frac{V_1}{V_2}$$

the transmission angle is proportional to the incidence angle times the medium 2 propagation speed divided by the medium 1 propagation speed. *(2:30)*

217. **(C)** The propagation speed of the medium must be known in order to calculate the distance to the reflector. In addition, the round-trip must be measured. The distance to the reflector is equal to the product of the propagation speed and the pulse round-trip time divided by 2. *(2:45)*

218. **(D)** The mirror image artifact occurs around strong reflectors, for example the diaphragm. *(2:144–146)*

219. **(C)** The comet tail artifact is a type of reverberation artifact. The greater the acoustic impedance mismatch, the greater the possibility of this artifact to occur. *(16:7)*

220. **(C)** The acoustic impedance mismatch between tissue and gas is very great; therefore, it may produce the comet tail artifact. *(16:7)*

221. **(B)** Fat has a slower velocity than the liver. Therefore, the returning time of the echo to the transducer is delayed. Since the ultrasound machine assumes that everything in its path has a velocity of 1540 meters per second (1540 m/s), the diaphragm posterior to the fat is registered as farther than it actually is. *(19:58)*

222. **(D)** By increasing damping one also increases the bandwidth. Bandwidth is the range of frequency involved in a pulse. *(2:54)*

223. **(A)** Output affects the amount of energy leaving the transducer. It does not affect the amplification of echoes that are received. *(14:12)*

224. **(B)** The compression controls on some sonographic equipment, when adjusted, will reduce the dynamic range. Compression is the process of decreasing the difference between small and large amplitude echoes. *(14:13)*

225. **(A)** Ultrasound transducers generally can resolve reflectors along the sound path better than it can those perpendicular to it. *(2:69)*

226. **(D)** The number of electrical pulses produced per second is typically 1000 Hz. *(2:77)*

227. **(D)** Brightness modulation mode. This display is used in two-dimensional ultrasound images, real-time and static. *(6:60)*

228. **(B)** With a typical PRF of 1000 Hz, each pulse-receive interval is 1 millisecond (1000 microseconds) long. Since an average pulse is 1 microsecond long, this leaves 999 microseconds for receiving. 999/1000 is 99.9%. *(20:190)*

229. **(C)** Frequency equals velocity divided by wavelength. Since velocity is standard at 1540 m/s, doubling the frequency will result in decreasing the wavelength by one-half. *(2:8)*

230. **(A)** Real-time transducers display two formats: sector and rectangular. The linear-sequenced array transducer displays a rectangular format. *(2:120)*

231. **(C)** Z is the acoustic impedance; P is the material density; and V is the propagation velocity. *(12:2)*

232. **(A)** Lead zirconate titanate (PZT) is a ceramic material with piezoelectric properties. It is most commonly used in transducers because of its greater efficiency and sensitivity. *(6:50)*

233. **(B)** Transmit–delay focusing creates a narrow beam, which improves lateral resolution. *(14:19)*

234. **(D)** Pulse repetition frequency is equal to lines per frame and is related to time frame rate. Frequency has no relationship to this equation. *(2:77)*

235. **(A)** Pulse repetition frequency is the number of pulses emitted per second or pulse rate. *(2:140)*

236. **(D)** The pulser produces the electric voltage pulses; this in turn drives the transducer to emit ultrasound pulses. It also tells both the memory and receiver when the ultrasound pulses were produced. *(2:77)*

237. **(A)** Demodulation converts the voltage delivered to the receiver from one form to another by rectification and smoothing. *(2:82)*

238. **(C)** Demodulation and compression are not operator adjustable. Amplification, compensation, and rejection functions are operator adjustable. *(2:85)*

239. **(A)** Lateral resolution is dependent on beam diameter, which varies with distance from the transducer. *(2:65)*

240. **(C)** A period is the time it takes for one full cycle to occur. *(2:7)*

241. **(B)** Half-intensity depth decreases with increasing frequency. *(2:64)*

242. **(C)** Redirection of a portion of the sound beam from a boundary. *(11:5)*

243. **(D)** Computers use a special number system called binary numbers. The system uses two digits, 0 and 1. *(18:8.2)*

244. **(A)** Bit is an acronym for binary digit and represents the basic unit for storing data in the main computer memory. *(18:8.1)*

245. **(A)** Eight bits equal 1 byte. A bit is a unit of data in binary notation and assumes one of two states: "on" representing the number 1, or "off" representing the number 0. *(17:136)*

246. **(B)** A computer and its peripherals are categorized into hardware and software. Hardware is the term used to describe any of the physical embodiments of the computer, for example, the keyboard, disk drive, CRT, and printer. Computer programs are software. The software in turn runs the hardware. *(17:139)*

247. **(B)** Random-access memory. This type of memory is called random because it provides access to any storage location in the memory. *(18:8.13)*

248. **(A)** Read-only memory. This type of program memory provides access to read out only. *(18:8.13)*

249. **(B)** Any set of computer devices that transfers information or data from an external medium into the internal storage of the computer is called an input device. A printer is an output device. *(18:3.2)*

250. **(B)** ROM (read-only memory) is programmed into the computer at the time of manufacture. PROM (programmable read-only memory) can be written to by the programmer. *(18:8.13)*

251. **(D)** Erasable programmable read-only memory (EPROM) can be reprogrammed or erased. *(18:8.13)*

252. **(B)** Central processing unit (CPU). *(18:8.1)*

253. **(B)** Most microprocessors use 8-, 16- or 32-bit word length. The most common is a 16-bit. *(18:8.1–8.17)*

254. **(C)** While the symbol K represents kilo or 1000 in metric, in computer terminology K = 1024. The amount that can be stored in memory is then 128 × 1024 × 8 bits = 1,048,576 bits, referred to as 1 megabit. *(18:8.1–8.17)*

255. **(D)** Contents of EPROM are erased by exposing them to ultraviolet light. *(18:8.13)*

256. **(B)** Modem. *(18:11.5)*

257. **(C)** BASIC. *(18:13.8)*

258. **(D)** Baud rate. The measured speed is expressed in the number of bits per second (bps). *(18:11.9)*

259. **(B)** Hard disks have a larger storage capacity and faster access than do floppy disks. *(18:9.9)*

260. **(C)** Beginner's all-purpose symbolic instruction code (BASIC). *(18:13.8)*

261. **(C)** A modem is an acronym for modulator/demodulator. It is a device that translates digital data to analog signals and vice versa over standard telephone lines. *(18:11.5)*

262. **(B)** Two: off or on. "Off" represents the number 0. "On" represents the number 1. *(19:33; 17:137)*

263. **(C)** Two (0 or 1). *(19:31)*

264. **(E)** The number 30 is represented by 011110. To convert from decimal to binary, repeatedly divide by two and note the remainder.

30 ÷ 2 = 15 remainder 0	3 ÷ 2 = 1 remainder 1
15 ÷ 2 = 7 remainder 1	1 ÷ 2 = 0 remainder 1
7 ÷ 2 = 3 remainder 1	0 ÷ 2 = 0 remainder 0

(2:259)

265. **(D)** The binary system, which is used in digital scan converter memory, is based on the powers of two. For four bits, 2^4 (2 × 2 × 2 × 2) or 16 different gray levels can be represented. Another way of looking at this is to list all possible states:

0000	0100	1000	1100
0001	0101	1001	1101
0010	0110	1010	1110
0011	0111	1011	1111

There are 16 possible unique states. *(19:32)*

266. **(B)** Digital memory, where the electronic components are either on (1) or off (0), is based on the binary number system. We can say that the number of discrete levels possible, N, is equal to 2 raised to the power of that number of bits. $N = 2^n$. Therefore, to make 64 shades of gray would require 2^6 bit memory.

(2 × 2	4 × 2	8 × 2	16 × 2	32 × 2 = 64)
1 2	3	4	5	6

(19:32)

267. **(B)** At high ultrasound intensities, tissue damage has been observed to be caused by heat and cavitation. *(7:185)*

268. **(C)** The receiver processes echoes detected by the transducer. These echoes may be amplified (gain), compensated for depth (TGC), compressed (to fit into the dynamic range of the system), and rejected (eliminating low-level signals). *(19:27)*

269. **(D)** The greater the pulse amplitude (electronic voltage applied to the transducer), the greater the amplitude of the ultrasound pulse provided by the transducer. *(2:77)*

270. **(B)** The pulser produces electric voltage pulses which drive the transducer and at the same time tell the receiver that the transducer has been driven. *(2:77)*

271. **(D)** Components of a pulse–echo system include the *pulser* that produces the electrical pulse which drives the *transducer.* For each reflection received from the tissue by the transducer, an electrical voltage is produced that goes to the *receiver,* where it is processed for display. Information on transducer position and orientation is delivered to the *image memory.* Electric information from the memory drives the *display* (oscilloscope). *(2:75)*

272. **(B)** Transducers may be focused by using a curved piezoelectric transducer element (internal focusing) or by using an acoustic lens. *(19:20)*

273. **(E)** Quality factor (Q factor) is equal to the operating frequency divided by the bandwidth, and is unitless. *(2:54)*

274. **(E)** Reduction in echoes from a region distal to an attenuating structure. *(2:216)*

275. **(G)** An increase in echoes from a region distal to a weakly attenuating structure or tissue. *(2:212)*

276. **(A or F)** A structure that is echo-free. Not necessarily cystic unless there is good through transmission. A solid mass can be anechoic but will not have good through transmission. *(15:27)*

277. **(D)** An echo that does not correspond to the real target. *(21)*

278. **(I)** A structure that possesses echoes. *(15:27)*

279. **(H)** Echoes of higher amplitude than the normal surrounding tissues. *(21)*

280. **(B)** Echoes of lower amplitude than the normal surrounding tissues. *(21)*

281. **(C)** The surface forming the boundary between two media having different acoustic impedances. *(15:28)*

282. **(A or F)** A structure without echoes and with low absorption. Not necessarily cystic unless there is good through transmission. *Sonolucent* is a misnomer for *anechoic.* *(15:29; 21)*

283. **(C)** Air. There are numerable backing materials used for damping. Pulse–echo transducer backing materials are: (1) epoxy resin, (2) tungsten, (3) cork, and (4) rubber. Continuous-wave Doppler transducers have little or no backing materials. They are usually air backed. *(9:263; 22:33)*

284. **(D)** Surgical, therapeutic, and Doppler. Diagnostic application uses a pulse–echo transducer. *(9:311; 19:23; 22:33)*

285. **(A)** Not all waves are visible. Waves that appear on the surface of water (water waves) are visible. X-rays, radio waves, and sound waves are invisible waves. *(17:3)*

286. **(C)** In order for ultrasound to propagate a medium, the medium must be composed of particles of matter. A vacuum is a space empty of matter; therefore, ultrasound cannot travel in a vacuum. *(10:1; 25:19)*

287. **(B)** Wavelength. *(17:5)*

288. **(A)** Period. *(17:5)*

289. **(B)** Hertz (Hz) represents cycle per second (cps). Therefore, 20 cps = 20 Hz. *(17:5)*

290. **(C)** One MHz. *(17:5)*

291. **(C)** Ultrasound is produced by piezoelectric crystal. The crystal, damping material, and matching layer are enclosed in a device called a transducer. *(17:31)*

292. **(A)** A-mode is an acronym for amplitude mode. This mode is presented graphically with vertical spikes arising from a horizontal baseline. The height of the vertical spikes represents the amplitude of the deflected echo. *(22:2)*

293. **(B)** B-mode is an acronym for brightness modulation. This mode presents a two-dimensional image of internal body structures displayed as dots. The brightness of the dots is proportional to the amplitude of the echo. B-mode display is employed in all two-dimensional images, static or real-time. *(6:60; 22:2)*

294. **(C)** M-mode is an acronym for time–motion modulation. This mode is a graphical display of movement of reflecting structures related to time. M-mode is used almost exclusively in echocardiography. *(6:60; 22:2)*

295. **(C)** The cathode-ray tube (CRT) is formed by three essential elements: (1) the electron gun, (2) the fluorescent screen, and (3) the deflection system (vertical and horizontal plates). Silicon is a nonmetallic element found in the earth and used in computer semiconductors. *(24:234)*

296. **(B)** The cathode-ray tube (CRT) is enclosed by a glass tube containing a high vacuum. The manufacturer normally "degases" the tube (removes trapped air or gas) in order to provide a free passage for electrons. *(17:88; 9:13–15)*

297. **(A)** The anode is the counterpart of the cathode and is positively (+) charged. *(17:88)*

298. **(B)** The cathode consists of the electron gun and filament and is negatively (−) charged. *(17:88)*

299. **(C)** The intensity of the ultrasound beam depends on the beam diameter. Intensity is defined as the beam power divided by the beam cross-sectional area. *(2:18)*

300. **(C)** Huygens' principle *(1:362)*

301. **(A)** The fraction of time that a pulsed ultrasound is actually producing ultrasound is called the duty factor.

$$\text{duty factor (DF)} = \frac{\text{pulse duration (PD)}}{\text{pulse repetition period (PRP)}}$$

(2:55)

302. **(C)** Real-time ultrasound instrumentation is classified as

1. Sector — Linear-phased array (pie shaped); Wobbler or rotating wheel (pie shaped)
2. Linear-sequenced array——rectangular image
3. Annular——employs both mechanical and electronic (combination systems)

(3:15–30; 22:6–9)

303. **(B)** The speed at which ultrasound propagates within a medium depends primarily on the compressibility of the medium. *(34:1)*

304. **(C)** The reverberation artifact occurs when two or more reflections are present along the path of the beam. This gives rise to multiple reflections, which will appear behind one another at intervals equal to the separation of the real reflectors. *(11:40; 19:50)*

305. **(C)** Gain is the ratio of electric power. Gain governs the electric compensation for tissue attenuation and is expressed in decibels (dB). *(2:80; 9:89)*

306. **(C)** Multipath reverberation artifacts result from sound reflected from a highly curved specular surface when the echo takes an indirect path back to the transducer. *(6:28–29)*

307. **(B)** Both analog and digital scan converters are memory devices. An analog converter stores image information gathered during the scanning process and then retrieves and reads out the information to a vacuum tube similar to a CRT oscilloscope without the phosphor screen. A digital scan converter takes the incoming analog signals from the detector and converts them to binary numbers that are used to represent signal levels. These numbers are then stored in memory. *(19:31–32)*

308. **(B)** Echo signals that are in analog format as they emerge from the receiver are transferred to a digital format by an analog-to-digital (A–D) converter. Preprocessing then produces the best possible digital representation of the analog signal. *(19:32)*

309. **(D)** By increasing frequency (f) and/or transducer diameter, the near zone length is increased, as shown in the equation:

$$\text{near zone length} = \frac{(\text{transducer diameter})^2 f}{6}$$

(2:59)

310. **(B)** Mass divided by volume. *(2:209–217)*

311. **(H)** Progression or travel. *(2:209–217)*

312. **(D)** Number of cycles per unit time. *(2:209–217)*

313. **(A)** Rate at which work is done. *(2:209–217)*

314. **(G)** The product of pulse duration and pulse repetition rate. *(2:209–217)*

315. **(F)** Range of frequencies contained in the ultrasound pulse. *(2:209–217)*

316. **(E)** Density multiplied by sound propagation speed. *(2:209–217)*

317. **(C)** Conversion of sound to heat. *(2:209–217)*

318. **(I)** Operating frequency divided by bandwidth. *(2:209–217)*

319. **(J)** Power divided by area. *(2:209–217)*

320. **(B)** The damping material reduces spatial pulse length, efficiency, and sensitivity. *(2:15)*

321. **(C)** Gain is electric compensation for tissue attenuation. *(15:19)*

322. **(A)** Spectral analysis allows the determination of the frequency spectrum of a signal. *(17:16)*

323. **(C)** Analog scan converters store any increment of signal amplitude, whereas digital scan converters store the signal amplitude in discrete steps. *(17:30)*

324. **(C)** Gray-scale resolution is the ability of a gray-scale display to distinguish between echoes of slightly different amplitudes or intensities. The first step in this problem is to figure out how many shades of gray are contained in a 5-bit digital system. The total number of shades of gray is 32 ($2^5 = 32$). The next step is to divide the dynamic range (42 dB) by the number of levels. This will give the number of dB per level. 42 dB ÷ 32 gray levels = 1.3 dB/gray level. *(2:93)*

325. **(B)**

$$\begin{aligned}\text{Distance} &= \text{velocity} \times \text{time} \\ &= 1540 \text{ m/s} \times 0.01 \text{ s} \\ &= 15.4 \text{ m}\end{aligned}$$

However, 0.1 seconds is only the time to reach the echo source. The time of the round trip must be calculated by multiplying by 2. Round-trip distance = 15.4 m × 2 = 30.8 m. *(14:2)*

326. **(B)** An edge artifact. Edge shadowing results from refraction and reflection of the ultrasound beam on a rounded surface, for example, the fetal skull. *(28:42)*

327. **(A)** A split image artifact (ghost artifact) may produce duplication or triplication of an image, resulting in ultrasound beam refraction at a muscle–fat interface. *(26:29–34; 27:49–52)*

328. **(A)** Multipath, mirror image, and side lobe artifacts are most likely to produce a pseudomass. A comet tail artifact is least likely. *(28:27–43)*

329. **(A)** Split image artifact is more noticeable in athletic and mesomorphic habitus patients. *(27:49–52)*

330. **(C)** Split image artifact (ghost artifact) is *not* caused by a gas bubble. The most likely cause is refraction of the sound beam at a muscle–fat interface. The artifact is more evident at an interface between subcutaneous fat and abdominal muscle or between rectus muscle and fat in the pelvis. The artifact can also be produced by an abdominal scar. *(26:29–34; 27:49–52)*

331. **(C)** The most likely cause of beam thickness artifact is partial volume effect. This type of artifact occurs most often when the ultrasound beam interacts with a cyst or other fluid-filled structures. *(28:27–45)*

332. **(C)** Beam thickness artifacts depend on beam angulation, not gravity. Therefore, if an image of the gallbladder has what appears to be sludge, a change in the patient's position relative to the beam could differentiate pseudosludge caused by artifact from layering of biliary sludge. *(28:27–45)*

333. **(D)** Side lobe artifact is apparent in both static and real-time images. *(28:27–45)*

334. **(B)** Shotgun pellets and metallic surgical clips produce a trail of dense continuous echoes. Bone, gas, and gallstones produce distal acoustic shadow. *(28:27–45)*

335. **(A)** The most common type of artifact observed in patients with shotgun pellets or metallic surgical clips is the comet tail artifact. This type of reverberation artifact is characterized by a trail of dense continuous echoes distal to a strongly reflecting structure. *(16:1–17; 29:225–230)*

336. **(D)** A ring-down artifact is characterized sonographically as high-amplitude parallel lines occurring at regular intervals distal to a reflecting interface. This type of artifact is commonly associated with bowel gas. *(30:21–28)*

337. **(A)** It is possible to calculate the displacement in split images by using Snell's law. *(26:29–34)*

338. **(C)** The first vertical deflection at the start of the A-mode is called "main bang," or transducer artifact. *(11:26–27)*

339. **(C)** Annular-array real-time uses a combination of mechanical and electronic devices. The annular-array is used for dynamic focusing, the mechanical part for beam steering. *(22:9)*

340. **(A)** A decrease in the amplitude of the returning echo results in a fade-away picture. *(11:52; 22:21)*

341. **(D)** Hard copy is a term applied to any form of picture storage. A videotape recorder is hardware, whereas videotape is a hard copy (storage medium). *(11:35; 22:23)*

342. **(C)** M-mode stands for time-motion modulation. This mode displays a graphic representation of motion of reflecting surfaces. It is used primarily in echocardiography. *(10:44)*

343. **(A)** B-mode stands for brightness modulation. This mode displays a two-dimensional view of internal body structures in cross-section or sagittal section. The images, displayed as dots on the monitor, result from interaction between ultrasound and tissues. The brightness of the dots is proportional to the amplitude of the echo. Both static and real-time equipment use B-mode. *(10:44; 22:2)*

344. **(B)** A-mode stands for amplitude modulation. This mode displays a graphic representation of vertically deflected echoes arising from a horizontal baseline. The height of the vertical deflection is proportional to the amplitude of the echo, and the distance from one vertical deflection to the next represents the distance from one interface to another. A-mode is one-dimensional. *(10:44; 11:26; 22:2)*

345. **(B)** The effects of ultrasound on human soft tissue are called bioeffects or biologic effects. *(2:2)*

346. **(A)** 1.54 millimeters per microsecond (1.54 mm/μs) or 1540 meters per second (1540 m/s).

347. **(C)** Slope.

348. **(B)** Delay.

349. **(D)** Far gain.

350. **(A)** Near gain.

DIAGRAM OF TGC CURVE

(17:299–318; 19:26–27)

351. **(C)** Progressive weakening of the sound beam as it travels through a medium. *(2:209–217)*

352. **(F)** Having two stages (on or off), black-and-white image, no range of gray. *(2:209–217)*

353. **(G)** Binary digit. *(2:209–217)*

354. **(B)** The production and behavior of bubbles in sound at high intensities. *(2:209–217)*

355. **(D)** A liquid placed between the transducer and the skin. *(2:209–217)*

356. **(H)** A method of reducing pulse duration by mechanical or electrical means. *(2:209–217)*

357. **(E)** The number of intensity levels between black and white. *(2:209–217)*

358. **(J)** Plastic material placed in front of the transducer face to reduce the reflection at the transducer surface. *(2:209–217)*

359. **(A)** Picture element. *(2:209–217)*

360. **(I)** Single-frame imaging. *(2:209–217)*

361. **(D)** W/cm^2. *(17:242)*

362. **(A)** 100 mW/cm^2 SPTA. *(2:168)*

363. **(C)** Spatial peak temporal average. *(17:242)*

364. **(B)** kg/m^3. *(2:261)*

365. **(D)** m/s. *(2:261)*

366. **(F)** Hz. *(2:261)*

367. **(E)** J. *(2:261)*

368. **(A)** W/cm^2. *(2:261)*

369. **(C)** m. *(2:261)*

370. **(G)** dB. *(2:261)*

371. **(B)** 0.002 W/cm^2–0.5 W/cm^2 SPTA. *(17:250)*

372. **(A)** 0.5 W/cm^2–2.0 W/cm^2 SPTA. *(17:250)*

373. **(C)** Under normal intensity ranges, diagnostic ultrasound is atraumatic, nontoxic, noninvasive, and nonionizing. It is nonionizing because the intensity in diagnostic ultrasound range is not sufficient to eject an electron from an atom. *(10:26)*

374. **(D)** Heat. However, at the diagnostic intensity range, the heat produced has no known effect. *(10:26)*

375. **(A)** The production and behavior of gas bubbles (microbubbles) is called cavitation. Cavitation occurs when dissolved gases grow into microbubbles during the negative pressure phase of ultrasound wave propagation. There are two types of cavitation, stable and transient. Stable cavitation is a phenomenon in which microbubbles are formed and persist in a diameter with the passing pressure variations of the ultrasound wave. In transient cavitation, the microbubbles continue to grow in size until they collapse, producing shock waves. *(10:26–27; 35:156)*

376. **(D)** There are two types of cavitation, stable and transient. Stable cavitation is a phenomenon in

which bubbles are formed and persist. In transient cavitation the bubbles continue to grow in size until they collapse. *(10:26–27)*

377. **(A)** Doppler. *(10:61)*

378. **(A)** When an interface is smooth or "mirror-like," or larger than the wavelength, it is called a specular reflector. When the ultrasound beam strikes a specular reflector, the angle of reflection is equal to the angle of incidence. Therefore, reflection can be a critical factor when performing sonograms. The maximum amount of reflected echo occurs when the transducer is perpendicular to the interface. *(11:6; 12)*

379. **(B)** When an interface is smaller than the wavelength, usually less than 3 mm, it is called a nonspecular reflector. Nonspecular reflectors are not beam-angle dependent. *(11:6; 12)*

380. **(B)** Spatial average temporal average. *(17:242)*

381. **(C)** Spatial peak pulse average. *(17:242)*

382. **(A)** Since Doppler instruments are used for moving structures, static imaging does not apply. The Doppler instrument employs pulsed or continuous waves. The signal is amplified by a loudspeaker; thus the resulting sound is audible. *(22:10)*

383. **(A)** 5-MHz, short-focus. The choice of focal zone depends on what structure is to be imaged. The choice of transducer frequency depends on the amount of penetration and/or resolution needed. High-frequency transducers display good axial resolution but reduced tissue penetration. For superficial structures, a high-frequency transducer is most useful; for deep structures, low frequency is most useful. *(4:26–29)*

384. **(B)** 3-MHz, long-focus. See explanation for Question 383. *(4:26–29)*

385. **(A)** Pixel is short for picture element. *(11:32)*

386. **(A)** Under normal circumstances, the human eye can distinguish as many as 16 shades of gray. *(4:38)*

387. **(A)** 512 × 512 × 6-bit deep. *(11:32)*

388. **(C)** "Aliasing" results when the velocity exceeds the pulse repetition frequency (PRF). Aliasing is an artifact seen in Doppler ultrasound. *(34:1)*

389. **(D)** All of the above. *(4:43)*

390. **(A)** As ultrasound propagates through body tissue it undergoes attenuation, which is the progressive weakening of the sound wave as it travels. The causes of attenuation are:

1. absorption
2. reflection
3. scattering

When the sound wave is absorbed, it is then converted to heat. The heat generated from absorption is mostly removed by conduction. *(10:28; 11:5, 19:74)*

391. **(D)** Most commercial and standard CRT monitors use 525 horizontal lines. *(11:34)*

392. **(B)** CRT monitors display 30 frames per second. *(11:34)*

393. **(B)** Every one-sixtieth of a second reduces the flicker. *(11:34)*

394. **(B)** 20–25 dB. *(11:34)*

395. **(A)** Digital memory stores information divided into squares. The number of rows and columns of squares is called a matrix. *(11:32)*

396. **(A)** Digital memory is similar to squares on a checkerboard in which echoes are stored in a square corresponding to the location of the scanning plane. *(11:32)*

397. **(A)** Echo-free. *(21)*

398. **(B)** Echogenic. *(21)*

399. **(C)** Impedance cannot be measured by a hydrophone. *(2:163)*

400. **(B)** The hydrophone is made up of transducer elements. *(2:163)*

401. **(C)** When a beam is applied for 2–3 minutes on laboratory animals, the results are growth retardation and hemorrhage. These effects were observed in laboratory animals, not humans, and with continuous wave ultrasound. *(17:251)*

402. **(C)** Refraction and diffraction are least likely associated with attenuation. Refraction is the bending of the sound beam as it crosses an acoustic impedance mismatch. The spreading-out of an ultrasound beam is referred to as diffraction. *(9:48, 11:5)*

403. **(B)** Conversion of sound to heat. *(11:5)*

404. **(A)** The spreading-out of an ultrasound beam is referred to as diffraction. *(9:48, 11:5)*

405. **(D)** Redirection of the sound beam in several directions. *(2:215; 11:5; 9:60)*

406. **(C)** The transducer's piezoelectric ceramic is heat sensitive and should not be subjected to excessive heat sterilization, because the crystal in the transducer housing could become depolarized and lose its piezoelectric properties. Transducers are made up of a variety of materials, including plastic, crystals, bonding seals, steel or metal casing, but they are not all constructed alike. A disinfectant that is safe for some transducers may be destructive to others. The recommended method for sterilizing transducers is available from the manufacturer's user manual or from the manufacturer's technical support department. Any product used on transducers against the manufacturer instructions or precautionary measures could result in damage to the transducer and loss of the transducer warranty. *(33:130–131)*

407. **(A)** An acoustic window is a pathway through which the sound beam travels without interference. Examples are the liver and the urinary bladder. *(31:77)*

408. **(A)** The decimal number 10 may also be represented by the binary number 1010. *(2:96)*

409. **(B)** Real-time imaging is similar to x-ray fluoroscopy in that each displays motion of internal body parts. *(31:167)*

410. **(C)** The frame rate for real-time systems vary from 15 frames per second to 60 frames per second. A slow frame rate causes flickering. A frame rate higher than 15 frames per second is required to produce a flicker-free image. For fast-moving structures, a high frame rate is needed. *(4:34; 31:167)*

411. **(A)** All images of transverse scans should be viewed from the patient's feet, supine or prone. *(31:86)*

412. **(B)** In longitudinal (sagittal) scans the images are presented with the patient's head to the left of the image and feet to the right of the image in both supine and prone positions. *(31:86)*

413. **(C)** Within the receiver, a number of signal-processing functions take place: amplification, compensation, demodulation, compression, and rejection. *(2:84)*

414. **(B)** Because the particles in ultrasound waves oscillate in the same direction of wave propagation, no plane is defined. Therefore, ultrasound waves cannot be polarized. *(9:359; 10:1)*

415. **(D)** Quartz is the transducer crystal most likely to be employed. *(9:310)*

416. **(D)** All of the above. *(9:310)*

417. **(C)** PZT-5. *(9:310)*

418. **(D)** Two hundred fifty-six (256), or the number 2 raised to the power of 8 (the number of bits per memory element): $256 = 2^8$. *(34:32)*

419. **(B)** A real-time mechanical sector transducer allows greater maneuverability for small intercostal space scanning. *(3:173–174)*

420. **(G)** Both ultrasound and fluoroscopy evaluate moving structures in movie-like appearance. However, ultrasound is nonionizing because its intensity is insufficient to eject an electron from the atom. Fluoroscopy is ionizing and results in potential biologic effects. *(10:26)*

421. **(F)** The contrast media used for roentgenographic oral cholecystogram (x-ray of the GB) and intravenous pyelogram (x-rays of the kidneys) do not obscure the propagation of ultrasound. *(10:329)*

422. **(I)** A device used to focus sound beams. *(2:209–217)*

423. **(C)** Picture element. *(2:209–217)*

424. **(D)** Pie shaped. *(2:209–217)*

425. **(F)** A device that changes sound waves into visible light patterns. *(2:209–217)*

426. **(B)** The portion of the sound beam outside of the main beam. *(2:209–217)*

427. **(H)** Imaginary surface passing through particles of the same vibration as an ultrasound wave. *(2:209–217)*

428. **(A)** Unit of impedance. *(2:209–217)*

429. **(G)** The ratio between the angle of incidence and the refraction. *(2:209–217)*

430. **(E)** A change in frequency as a result of reflector motion between the transducer and the reflector. *(22:233–238)*

431. **(B)** The lateral resolution is defined as being equal to the beam diameter. *(32:32)*

432. **(F)** Perspex, aluminum, and polystyrene. Ethylene oxide is a gas, not a material used for lenses. *(9:317)*

433. **(C)** Both ultrasound and light can be focused and defocused by mirrors and lenses. *(9:317)*

434. **(A)** 0.1–1.5 mm. *(10:7)*

435. **(C)** Individual cells cannot be identified because they are smaller than the wavelength used in the medium. *(10:10)*

436. **(D)** Mass per unit volume. *(10:5)*

437. **(D)** The longer the distance traveled, the greater the absorption. Absorption increases with increased frequency, and the amount of frictional force encountered by the propagating sound wave (viscosity) determines the amount of absorption. *(10:18)*

438. **(D)** There are no confirmed biologic effects on human tissue exposed to intensities used in the diagnostic range below 100 m/Wcm^2. However, laboratory experiments on pregnant mice with intensities far greater than that used in the diagnostic range resulted in growth retardation in the offspring of the mice. *(17:251; 2:168)*

439. **(C)** Pregnant mice exposed to continuous wave ultrasound, applied for 2 to 3 minutes, experienced neurocranial damage, hemorrhage, and growth retardation. *(2:168)*

440. **(B)** A combination of low frequency and high intensity is most likely to cause cavitation resulting in tissue damage. *(17:250)*

441. **(H)** Living human tissue. *(21:1–12; 32:1–3)*

442. **(E)** Tissue cultures in a test tube. *(21:1–12; 32:1–3)*

443. **(F)** A method of analyzing a waveform. *(21:1–12; 32:1–3)*

444. **(G)** The property of a medium characterized by energy distortion in the medium and irreversibly converted to heat. *(21:1–12; 32:1–3)*

445. **(B)** Elimination of small amplitude echo. *(21:1–12; 32:1–3)*

446. **(C)** A process of acoustic energy absorption. *(21:1–12; 32:1–3)*

447. **(A)** An in vivo phenomenon, characterized by erythrocytes within small vessels stopping the flow and collecting in the low pressure regions of the standing wave field. *(21:1–12; 32:1–3)*

448. **(D)** Energy transported per unit time. *(21:1–12; 32:1–3)*

449. **(G)** All of the statements are false or unconfirmed at the present time. Experimental studies were conducted on pregnant mice, not pregnant women. The intensity, frequency, and exposure time were far greater than those used in a diagnostic setting. Continuous ultrasound was used in many of the experiments. *(17:251; 2:173–174)*

450. **(D)** At present, there are no known exposure injuries in humans in the clinical setting. Injuries have been reported only in laboratory animals. *(17:251; 2:173–174)*

451. **(A)** No distinction. All real-time scans are B-scans, and both static and real-time instruments employ B-mode. *(28:44–45)*

452. **(D)** The word transonic implies a region uninhibited to the propagation of ultrasound. An echo-free (anechoic) region does not guarantee the region to be transonic. For example, a homogenous solid mass can be echo-free but not transonic. Conversely, a region can exhibit echoes and be transonic. *(2:179)*

453. **(B)** Real-time is also referred to as dynamic imaging. A-mode and M-mode are also real-time modes. *(2:179)*

454. **(A)** The TGC is comprised of near gain, delay, slope, knee, and far gain. *(31:58–61)*

455. **(A)** The range of pulse repetition frequencies used in diagnostic ultrasound is 0.5 to 4 kHz. *(2:192)*

456. **(C)** Cycles, wavelength. The spatial pulse length (SPL) is defined as the product of the wavelength multiplied by the number of cycles in a pulse. *(35:61)*

457. **(B)** A-mode and M-mode. *(2:105–107)*

458. **(C)** Used in some Doppler instruments. Doppler instruments use both continuous or pulse waves. *(2:128)*

459. **(C)** Doppler. Doppler instruments employ an audio mode. *(10:62)*

460. **(C)** Continuous wave mode. Continuous wave mode requires two crystals, one for transmitting and the other for receiving. *(10:14)*

461. **(B)** Acoustic mirror. See Fig. 1–10B, p. 10, in the Study Guide.

462. **(D)** Piezoelectric crystal.

463. **(C)** Scanner head.

464. **(A)** Motor.

465. **(B)** 0.2–400 mW/cm^2. *(2:123)*

466. **(A)** Higher frequency than the incident frequency. *(2:123)*

467. **(B)** Lower frequency than the incident frequency. *(2:123)*

468. **(C)** Bidirectional. *(2:128)*

469. **(A)** Color Doppler is not beneficial. Color Doppler is very helpful in improving the ability to depict abnormal blood flow. *(2:129)*

470. **(B)** Control used to suppress or increase echoes in the near field. *(15:19–22)*

471. **(A)** Control used to suppress or increase echoes in the far field. *(15:19–22)*

472. **(D)** Control the upward incline of the TGC. Used to display an even texture throughout an organ. *(15:19–22)*

473. **(C)** Control used to delay the start of the slope. *(15:19–22)*

474. **(E)** Controls the point where the slope ends. *(15:19–22)*

475. **(B)** Bandwidth. Bandwidth is the range of frequencies contained in an ultrasound pulse. *(2:210)*

476. **(A)** Q factor. The Q factor is unitless. *(2:54)*

477. **(B)** A fluid-filled mass. Fluid-filled masses are characterized by sharp posterior walls and distal acoustic enhancement. The enhancement is associated with low attenuation. Solid and calcified masses demonstrate a different phenomenon, distal attenuation, the degree of which is determined by the attenuating properties of the mass. *(13:32)*

478. **(C)** A calcified mass. Calcified masses, gallstones or any high reflective or attenuating structure can produce an acoustic shadow. This results from failure of the sound beam to pass through the object. The urinary bladder, gallbladder, and any fluid-filled structure will demonstrate acoustic enhancement. In some circumstances both acoustic enhancement and acoustic shadowing can be seen, for example, a gallbladder with stones. *(2:216; 15:29)*

479. **(B)** 2. Continuous-wave Doppler uses two piezoelectric crystals, one for transmitting and the other for receiving the returning echoes. *(1:391)*

480. **(C)** When the beam strikes a vessel at a 30° angle. Doppler angle is the angle between the direction of propagation of the ultrasound beam and the direction of flow. Unlike real-time imaging of the abdominal organs in which the best images are obtained when the ultrasound beam has a perpendicular incidence, Doppler has a minimum shift at 90° (perpendicular) incidence, and a maximum shift when the transducer is oriented parallel to the direction of flow, even though parallel transducer orientation is not possible in most cases. Doppler application employs a Doppler angle of 30° to 60° with respect to the vessel. *(1:391)*

481. **(B)**

20 dB.

$$\text{dB} = 10 \log \left(\frac{\text{power out}}{\text{power in}} \right) = 10 \log (100) = 20 \text{ dB}$$

(34:3)

482. **(D)** Depth-gain compensation. *(1:376)*

483. **(D)** Refraction, propagation speed. Refraction occurs only if there is a change in propagation speed. *(1:367)*

484. **(A)** Better axial resolution. Axial resolution is related to the length of the pulse. The shorter the pulse, the better the axial resolution. *(1:378)*

485. **(A)** 0.25 mW/cm^2. The reflection fraction R:

$$R = \left(\frac{Z_2 - Z_1}{Z_2 + Z_1} \right)^2 = \left(\frac{75 - 25}{75 + 25} \right)^2 = 0.25$$

(1:366)

486. **(B)** Frequency and diameter. Near zone length (NZL) is the same as the Fresnel zone:

$$\text{NZL} = \frac{D^2}{4\lambda}$$

where D is diameter transducer (cm) and λ is wavelength (cm). *(1:362)*

487. **(D)** The element thickness.

thickness = ½ wavelength *(2:50)*

488. **(B)** Refraction. Refraction is described by Snell's Law which relates the incident angle (ϕ_i) and the transmitted angle (ϕ_t) to the relative velocities of the two media.

$$\frac{\sin \phi_i}{\sin \phi_t} = \frac{V_1}{V_2}$$

When there is normal incidence, $\phi_i = 0$, and the

sound will only change velocity and will not be bent. *(1:367)*

489. **(C)** 1.54 mm/μs or 1540 m/s. *(1:353)*

490. **(C)** 1.0%

$$DF = \frac{PD}{PRP} = \frac{5}{500} = \frac{1}{100} = 1\%$$

(2:155)

491. **(B)** 20 kHz (or 20,000 Hz). This is the upper limit of the audible range for human beings. *(34:1)*

492. **(C)** Tissue attenuation. Tissue attenuation increases with increased frequency. *(1:369)*

493. **(C)** 3.5 dB.

$$\text{total attenuation} = \text{attenuation coefficient} \times \text{path length}$$

$$dB = 1.75\ dB/cm \times 2\ cm = 3.5\ dB$$

The attenuation coefficient in dB/cm is by a rule-of-thumb equal to one half the frequency in MHz, ie, at 3.5 MHz, the attenuation coefficient is 1.75 dB/cm. *(2:23)*

494. **(D)** Propagation speed.

$$Z = \rho C,$$

where ρ is density and C is propagation speed. *(34:7)*

495. **(B)** False. Intensity depends upon beam diameter which is not constant.

$$\text{intensity} = \frac{\text{power}}{\text{beam area}}$$

(34:2)

496. **(C)** 70%.

100% = percent reflected + percent transmitted *(1:366)*

497. **(A)** Frequencies. *(1:360)*

498. **(C)** Distance, velocity, and time

distance = velocity × time *(34:1)*

499. **(A)** Spatial pulse length. (See answer for question 456.) *(2:64)*

500. **(C)** 90°

$$\text{Doppler shift frequency} = \frac{2fV}{C} \cos \theta$$

where V = velocity of blood flow; f, transducer frequency; c, velocity of sound. Since, cos 90 is 0, then the Doppler shift frequency is 0. *(1:386)*

501. **(B)** False. Frame rate depends upon the velocity of sound, the image depth, and the number of lines in an image. *(34:14)*

502. **(A)** The ratio of the maximum to the minimum intensity. *(2:6)*

503. **(B)** Smaller. The scan converter dynamic range is determined by its bit depth. *(34:30)*

504. **(A)** Compensates for attenuation effects. *(1:376)*

505. **(D)** Computer memory. *(34:32)*

506. **(B)** False. Frame rate is determined by the velocity of sound, the depth of the image, and the lines per frame and does not necessarily get reduced by the mechanical scanner. *(34:14)*

507. **(B)** Weakly attenuating structures. *(2:146)*

508. **(B)** False. Preprocessing alters the echo amplitudes before storage; thus, changes will cause the memory content to change. *(34:32)*

509. **(A)** Is equal to the beam diameter. *(2:65)*

510. **(B)** Increased frame rate. If the line density is kept constant, then the number of lines per image will decrease, making the time required per image smaller. *(34:14)*

511. **(D)** Reject control. *(1:376)*

512. **(A)** Too close to. The arrival time will be sooner than expected, causing the system to position the echoes too close. *(1:353)*

513. **(D)** Some Doppler systems. *(34:34)*

514. **(C)** 15 dB. For every change of 3 dB, the intensity will change by a factor of 2. *(2:255)*

515. **(C)** Decreases the maximum depth imaged. The pulse repetition period is the length of time allowed to collect echoes for each image line; a shorter PRP means less image depth. *(34:14)*

516. **(D)** Measures spatial resolution—using different rod-sets in the phantom, estimates of both axial and lateral resolution may be made. *(2:155)*

517. **(B)** False. Real-time scanning is achieved using a number of different designs of mechanically steered single-element transducers. *(34:26)*

518. **(A)** Increase with increased steering angle. In electronic array systems, minimum grating lobe artifacts are generated when the beam is projected normal to the plane of the array. Beams steered away from the normal will experience greater grating lobe artifacts. *(34:29)*

519. **(C)** dB/cm. Total attenuation is expressed in terms of dB, intensity in units of mW/cm^2 and power in units of mW. *(34:6)*

520. **(C)** Wavelength, velocity and frequency

$$C = \lambda f,$$

where C = velocity; λ, wavelength, f, frequency. *(34:1)*

521. **(B)** Sensitivity. *(2:155)*

522. **(A)** Thermal and cavitation. Thermal or heating effects are normally unmeasurable with diagnostic instruments. Further cavitation is also unlikely at current diagnostic levels. Cavitation refers to the growth and behavior of gas bubbles produced in tissue by ultrasound. *(34:17)*

523. **(B)** Frequency and transducer diameter. High frequencies and/or large diameter transducers produce long near-zones (Fresnel) lengths. *(1:362)*

524. **(B)** No confirmed. *(2:168)*

525. **(C)** Highest at the focal zone. This is true since the intensity is equal to the power/beam area, and the beam area is smallest at the focal zone. *(2:18)*

526. **(B)** 0.3 mm.

$$\lambda = \frac{V}{f} = \frac{1.54 \text{ mm}/\mu\text{s}}{5 \text{ MHz}}$$

$$\lambda = 0.3 \text{ mm}$$

(2:8)

527. **(C)** Two times smaller. A 3-dB attenuation change would correspond to a factor-of-two reduction, ie, one-half. For each decrease in intensity of 3 dB, the intensity is decreased by one-half. Thus, for 6 dB attenuation, the intensity is decreased by one-fourth. *(1:356)*

528. **(B)** False. A low Q factor implies a short spatial pulse length which means higher spatial resolution. *(1:359)*

529. **(A)** A wide band of frequencies centered at 5 MHz. *(1:360)*

530. **(D)** Thickness, resonance frequency. Specifically, thickness equals one-half wavelength, where wavelength is velocity divided by frequency. *(1:358)*

531. **(A)** Increased damping, sensitivity. Increased damping does improve axial resolution by making the spatial pulse length shorter; however, the result is to make the transducer less sensitive to small echoes. *(1:360)*

532. **(A)** Piezoelectric. *(34:4)*

533. **(C)** Matching. Usually a matching layer is added to the front surface of the transducer acoustic impedance intermediate between the impedance of the transducer and that of soft tissue. *(1:370)*

534. **(D)** Constructive interference. *(1:361)*

535. **(A)** Highly attenuating structures. *(2:139)*

536. **(B)** Occur with multiple strong reflectors. Reverberation artifacts are present when two or more strong reflectors are located in the beam. One of these may be the transducer itself. The sound in essence gets trapped between these reflectors. *(2:142)*

537. **(A)** Good axial resolution. A large bandwidth is equivalent to a short spatial pulse length. *(1:360)*

538. **(B)** Fresnel zone. The far zone is also known as the Fraunhofer zone. *(1:363)*

539. **(D)** With normal incidence of the ultrasound beam. At oblique incidence, a sound beam will be bent if there is a change in propagation speed across the boundary. With normal incidence, however, the beam will either slow down or speed up but not bend. *(34:7)*

540. **(C)** The pulser voltage spike. The larger the applied voltage, the greater the deformation of the crystal and consequently, the amplitude of the pressure wave produced. However, a larger crystal (same thickness) experiencing the same voltage will produce more acoustic energy. *(34:8)*

541. **(B)** The reflecting surface is large and smooth with respect to the wavelength. Reflectors whose boundaries are smooth relative to the wavelength behave as mirrors and reflect all frequencies equally. Small reflectors (diffuse or nonspecular) scatter the sound in all directions and show a frequency dependence. *(2:42)*

542. **(C)** Snell's law. *(34:6)*

543. **(B)** Is mechanically steered. An annular array is capable of focusing the beam electronically in both x and y directions, but is unable to electronically steer. It must be steered, therefore, by physically moving the transducer or alternatively an acoustic mirror. *(34:31)*

544. **(A)** 90–100%. Since the acoustic impedance of gas is so much smaller than that of soft tissue, there is almost 100% of the energy reflected. *(1:366)*

545. **(C)** 1–10%

$$Z_{\text{fat}} = 1.38$$

$$Z_{\text{muscle}} = 1.70$$

$$R = \left(\frac{1.70 - 1.38}{1.70 + 1.38}\right)^2 = 0.011\ (1.1\%)$$

where R is the percent of beam reflected. *(1:366)*

546. **(B)** Focal zone moved to skin surface. Often a detachable water path is used to allow the focal zone of a fixed focus transducer to be placed at a superficial location. *(34:28)*

547. **(D)** Longitudinal compression waves. Longitudinal implies that the variation in the pressure occurs in the direction of propagation. This is opposed to a transverse wave where variations occur perpendicular to the propagation. Transverse waves can occur in bone. *(34:1)*

548. **(A)** Short wavelength and less penetration. The wavelength is inversely related to the frequency and the attenuation is directly related to frequency.

$$\text{the half-intensity depth (cm)} = \frac{3\text{dB}}{f}$$

where f is the frequency in MHz. *(34:6)*

549. **(A)** Ring-down time. A long ring-down time is undesirable. It increases the spatial pulse length and thus decreases axial resolution. *(1:360)*

550. **(B)** Electronically focus in two dimensions rather than one. An annular phased array can be focused dynamically in two dimensions. A linear array can be focused dynamically only in the plane of the array. In the slice-thickness direction, perpendicular to the array plane, focusing is achieved by shaping the transducer elements or by acoustic lens. This is often referred to as double focusing. *(34:30)*

551. **(C)** Gas, muscle, bone. This ordering proceeds along increasing stiffness or lack of compressibility. *(34:2)*

552. **(A)** Resolution, penetration—At low frequencies, the axial resolution becomes unacceptable ($<$ 1 MHz), while at high frequencies the depth of penetration in the body becomes prohibitively small (10 MHz). *(34:6)*

553. **(B)** False. Color Doppler is basically a pulsed Doppler system with color encoding. As such, it suffers from aliasing at high flow velocities, ie, shift frequencies greater than one-half the pulse repetition frequency. *(34:37)*

554. **(B)** SPTP is always equal to or greater than SPTA. SPTP refers to spatial peak-temporal peak and SPTA refers to spatial peak-temporal average. In all cases, peak values will be at least as great as the average values by definition. For continuous wave ultrasound, there is no variation of the intensity in time, and peak values will be equal. *(2:21)*

555. **(C)** A hydrophone. A hydrophone is a small piezoelectric crystal that is moved in front of a transducer in a manner so that the beam pattern is mapped. A radiation force balance is used to quantify the total beam power. Other phantoms can be used to give qualitative estimates of beam profiles. *(2:163)*

556. **(A)** Electronic or mechanical. Electronic generally also refers to a transducer array, either linear or annular. Mechanical generally refers to a single element or physically moved annular arrays. *(34:26)*

557. **(B)** Schlieren method. Schlieren photography gives a two-dimensional photograph of the beam pressure profile. *(1:362)*

558. **(D)** Time. Pulse duration is equal to the period of a wave times the number of waves in a pulse, usually microseconds in length. *(2:14)*

559. **(C)** The frequency. The propagation speed does not significantly depend upon frequency, and thus the frame rate is not dependent. *(34:14)*

560. **(B)** W/cm^2. SPTA refers to intensity, which is power (watts) per unit beam area (cm^2). *(2:21)*

561. **(C)** Curie point. Crystals heated above the Curie

point lose their piezoelectric property. The Curie point for quartz is 573°C and for PET-4 is 328°C. *(1:358)*

562. **(C)** Increased ninefold. $I = A^2 = (3)^2 = 9$, where I is intensity and A is amplitude. *(1:388)*

563. **(B)** False. In many cases, electronic and mechanical scanners demonstrate a frame rate lower than 30 frames/s. *(34:32)*

564. **(D)** Velocity, unchanged. The velocity is essentially independent of frequency and is rather dependent upon the physical properties of the medium. *(34:1)*

565. **(B)** Electronic time-delay pulsing. The delay pulsing of the array elements can be used to form a wavefront which is directed at different angles. Pulsing can also be used to focus the beam at different depths. *(34:30)*

566. **(A)** Is made possible by array-based systems. Dynamic focusing is possible only with array-based systems since it is necessary to individually monitor echoes received from each location. *(34:30)*

567. **(B)** False. Quality assurance is essential for all systems in order to operate in a reproducible manner. *(34:37)*

568. **(C)** 1.54 mm. The velocity of ultrasound in tissues is 1.54 mm/μs. *(34:2)*

569. **(A)** Ring-down artifact. The arrow points to a ring-down artifact produced most probably by gas bubbles resulting in a tail of reverberation echoes. *(30:21–28)*

570. **(A)** Rods for measuring ring-down. The small open arrows point to a rod group used in measurement of the transducer dead-zone or ring-down distance. *(17:261–276)*

571. **(B)** A simulated solid lesion. *(17:261–276)*

572. **(C)** A simulated cyst. *(17:261–276)*

REFERENCES

1. Christensen EE, Curry T, Dowdey J. *Introduction to the Physics of Diagnostic Radiology,* 3rd ed. Philadelphia: Lea & Febiger, 1984
2. Kremkau FW. *Diagnostic Ultrasound: Principles, Instrumentation and Exercises,* 2nd ed. New York: Grune & Stratton, 1984.
3. Fleischer AC, James E. *Real-Time Sonography.* Norwalk, CT: Appleton-Century-Crofts, 1984.
4. Sanders R, James E. *The Principles and Practice of Ultrasonography in Obstetrics and Gynecology,* 3rd ed. Norwalk, CT: Appleton-Century-Crofts, 1984.
5. Wells PNT. *Biomedical Ultrasonics.* London: Academic Press, 1977.
6. Raymond H, Zwiebel W, et al. *Seminars in Ultrasound: Physics* 4(1), New York: Grune & Stratton, 1983.
7. Rose J, Goldberg B. *Basic Physics in Diagnostic Ultrasound.* New York: Wiley, 1979.
8. Wells PNT. *Physical Principles of Ultrasonic Diagnosis.* New York: Academic Press, 1969.
9. McDicken W. *Diagnostic Ultrasonics: Principles and Use of Instruments,* 2nd ed. New York: Wiley, 1981.
10. Goldberg B, Kotler M, Ziskin M, et al. *Diagnostic Uses of Ultrasound.* New York: Grune & Stratton, 1975.
11. Bartrum R, Crow H. *Real-Time Ultrasound: A Manual for Physicians and Technical Personnel.* Philadelphia: WB Saunders, 1983.
12. Powis R. *Ultrasound Physics: For the Fun of It.* Denver: Unirad, 1978.
13. Sarti D, Sample W. *Diagnostic Ultrasound Text and Cases.* Boston: GK Hall, 1980.
14. Pinkney N. *A Review of the Concept of Ultrasound Physics and Instrumentation.* Philadelphia: Sonior, 1983.
15. Saunders R. *Clinical Sonography: A Practical Guide.* Boston: Little, Brown, 1984.
16. Ziskin MC, Thickman DI, Goldberg NJ. The comet tail artifact. *J Ultrasound Med* **1**:1–7, 1982.
17. Powis R, Powis W. *A Thinker's Guide to Ultrasonic Imaging.* Baltimore: Urban & Schwarzenberg, 1984.
18. Shelly G, Cashman T. *Computer Fundamentals for an Information Age.* Brea, CA: Anaheim Publishing, 1984.
19. Hagen-Ansert S. *Textbook of Diagnostic Ultrasonography,* 2nd ed. St. Louis: CV Mosby, 1983.
20. Skelly A: Beyond 100 mW/cm^2. *A Bioeffects Primer: Part 1—Fundamentals,* vol 1, no 5. Philadelphia: JB Lippincott, Sept–Oct 1985.
21. Eggleton R. *American Institute of Ultrasound in Medicine: Recommended Nomenclature: Physics and Engineering.* Oklahoma City: AIUM, Aug 1979.
22. Wells P, Ziskin M. New Techniques and Instrumentation in Ultrasonography. In *Clinics in Diagnostic Ultrasound,* vol 5. New York: Churchill Livingstone, 1980.
23. Beiser A. *Modern Technical Physics,* 2nd ed. Menlo Park, CA: Cummings, 1973.
24. Rose J, Goldberg B. *Basic Physics in Diagnostic Ultrasound.* New York: Wiley, 1979.
25. Hussey M. *Diagnostic Ultrasound: An Introduction to the Interactions Between Ultrasound and Biological Tissues.* Glasgow: Blackie & Son, 1975.

26. Sauerbrei E. The split image artifact in pelvic ultrasonography: The anatomy and physics. *J Ultrasound Med* **4**:29–34, 1985.
27. Buttery B, Davison G. The ghost artifact. *J Ultrasound Med* **3**:49–52, 1984.
28. Laing F. Commonly encountered artifacts in clinical ultrasound. In Raymond H, Zwiebel W (eds). *Seminars in Ultrasound: Physics* 4(1), New York: Grune & Stratton, 1983.
29. Thickman D, Ziskin M, Goldenberg J, et al. Clinical manifestations of the comet tail artifact. *J Ultrasound Med* **2**:225–230, 1983.
30. Avruch L, Cooperberg P. The ring-down artifact. *J Ultrasound Med* **4**:21–28, 1985.
31. Wicks J, Howe K. *Fundamentals of Ultrasonographic Technique*. Chicago: Yearbook, 1983.
32. Edmonds P. *American Institute of Ultrasound in Medicine: Appendix relating to ultrasound tissue signatures*. Oklahoma City: AIUM-11375, April 1976.
33. Odwin C, Fleischer AC, Kepple D, et al. Probe covers and disinfectants for transvaginal transducers. *J Diagnostics Med Sonogr* 6(3):130–134.
34. Fleischer AC, Romero R, Manning FA, et al. *The Principles and Practice of Ultrasonography in Obstetrics and Gynecology,* 4th ed. Norwalk, CT: Appleton & Lange, 1991.
35. Bushong SC, Archer BR. Diagnostic Ultrasound: Physics, Biology, and Instrumentation. St. Louis: Mosby-Year Book, 1991.

CHAPTER 2

DOPPLER COLOR FLOW IMAGING INSTRUMENTATION

Raymond L. Powis

Study Guide

Color flow imaging arrived on the medical scene in answer to a basic medical need: to look at blood flow noninvasively. The technology emerged from the development of multigate Doppler systems, which first appeared in 1975.[1] Although these systems used color Doppler only inside an M-mode display, they established both the multigate approach and the use of color to encode motion. In 1983 the first real-time echocardiography color flow system became available commercially.[2] The first commercially available color flow vascular imaging device followed in 1986. Since then, nearly all ultrasound manufacturers have added color flow imaging capabilities to their product line.

The current applications of color flow imaging are extensive and increasing vigorously. Basic and clinical research is extending the usefulness of this imaging modality. And within the research engineering departments of many ultrasound companies, new technologies are shaping the speed and capabilities of color flow imaging. As in other parts of ultrasound, understanding the instrumentation can go a long way toward understanding how to conduct clinical examinations and read the images. This chapter briefly reviews color flow imaging instrumentation and how it fits into the major applications of imaging.

THE ESSENTIAL COLOR FLOW IMAGE

The primary feature of the color flow image is the coincident depiction of stationary soft tissues in gray scale and moving soft tissues in color. For the most part, the moving soft tissue is blood within the cardiovascular system. This relationship opens the use of color flow imaging to two major applications: cardiac imaging and vascular imaging. But, as you will discover, any moving echo source within and sometimes outside the scanning field can produce color in the image. Setting up the system correctly, however, will limit the color flow information to moving blood.

Color flow imaging is a direct extension of duplex imaging and Doppler multigate analysis. Duplex imaging is older than multigate analysis and has several different forms. It includes the combination of either a continuous-wave or a single-point (pulsed-Doppler) spectrum with an image.[4] The image can be an M-mode trace, a real-time B-mode image, or, almost paradoxically, a color flow image. (The paradox is not real, however. Color flow imaging and a single-point spectrum look at the same events, but they do so from different points of view. As a result, they can be profitably combined into a common presentation.)

Multigate analysis is a method of collecting Doppler data from several adjacent spatial locations. The system analyzes each sampling site for flow events using Doppler signal processing. The limitation of this form of signal treatment is time. Multigate systems look at each site serially; thus, as the number of sites increases, the time required to make an image also increases.[3] Conversely, as the image frame time increases, the image frame rate decreases.

Current machines use a number of modern signal-handling techniques to keep the image frame rates as high as possible. The essential color flow presentation provides the following pieces of information directly from the image: (1) the existence of flow, (2) its location in the image, (3) its location in the anatomy, (4) its direction relative to the transducer, (5) its direction relative to the anatomy, and (6) its pattern over space and time.

Because the color image shows flow over space and time, we can use the image to locate specific characteristics of the flow pattern. For example, the higher-velocity flow segments (major streamlines and poststenotic jets) are visible within the heart and larger vessels. In addition, the image clearly shows the difference between com-

plex flow patterns resulting from anatomy and poststenotic flow patterns (turbulence) associated with disease.[5]

The ability to clearly show the patterns of flow depends on advanced technologies focused on asking the right technologic questions. Everything comes together at the image, where we begin the discussion.

COLOR FLOW IMAGING TECHNOLOGY

Production of the Image

Color flow imaging begins by making a multigate image for both the gray-scale and the Doppler segments of the image. The system divides each beam location in the scanning plane into a series of small sampling sites, each of which translates into a specific location in the digital scan converter image.[6] Fig. 2–1 shows an example of this division using a linear array. The digital scan converter in the ultrasound machine determines the size and spacing of these sampling sites.

The sampling sizes depend on the type of image. For example, a gray-scale image requires sampling intervals no greater than one wavelength.[7] In this form of imaging, the system detects the echo signal amplitudes and converts them into gray-scale intensities. Sampling intervals that are greater than one wavelength simply do not display tissue texturing well enough to support good gray-scale imaging. To show the differences among tissues, a gray-scale image must be able to show the differences between the various tissue textures.

Sampling for Doppler information has a different set of requirements. Doppler signal processing requires more time than does amplitude detection. For example, a single pulse–listen cycle can provide the information for a single gray-scale image line of sight. Doppler, however, requires anywhere from 4 to 100 pulse–listen cycles to build a single Doppler image line of sight.[3] Practicalities will limit the dwelling time on each line of sight to a range of 4 to 32 cycles. As a result, the sampling intervals are usually larger and fewer than in gray-scale imaging. The smallest Doppler sampling sites are at one-wavelength intervals. Often, to shorten the time to form one frame of a real-time image, the Doppler sampling sites may be several wavelengths long. For vascular imaging, sampling sites larger than 1 mm provide a poor depiction of vascular flow patterns. Fig. 2–2 shows how the sampling intervals affect the depiction of flow patterns in a vessel.

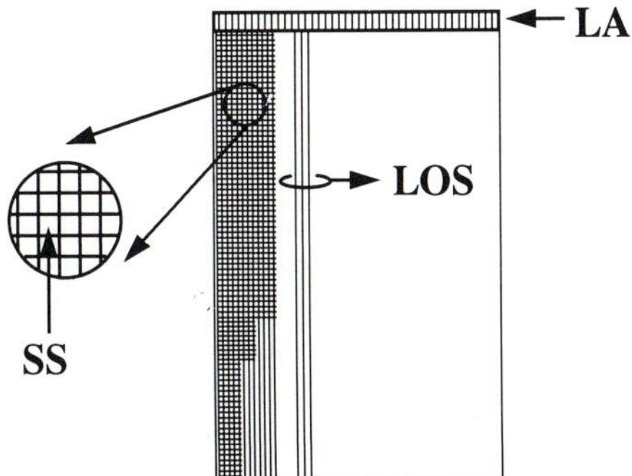

Figure 2–1. Sampling the scanning beams. LA is the linear array, SS is a sample site, and LOS represents the scanning lines of sight. Each sampling site represents a position in the digital scan converter.

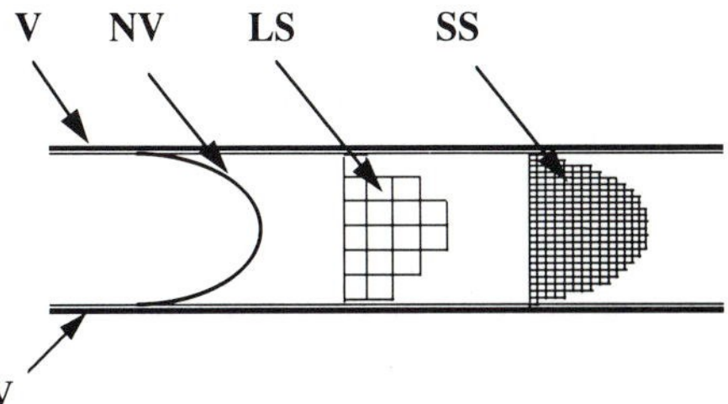

Figure 2–2. Flow image resolution and sampling intervals. W is the vessel wall, NV is the normal velocity profile, LS is the profile with large-interval sampling, and SS is the profile with small-interval sampling. The smaller the sampling, the better the depiction of flow.

The heart poses a different set of requirements. Because we do not need to see the same detailed flow patterns required in vascular imaging, color flow imaging in the heart can use larger sampling intervals.[2] By reducing the time required to make the colored portion of an image, frame rates can be speeded up enough to depict events in both adult and pediatric hearts. Even these techniques, however, may not be adequate. Higher frame rates may still require reducing the number of Doppler lines of sight in an image. Limiting Doppler signal processing to a specific region or window can help restore the frame rates to usable levels. Usually, the window can be moved to permit interrogating the entire image for flow. At each Doppler sampling site, the color flow imaging system looks at the returning echo signals for changes in phase and the Doppler shift frequencies.

Changes in Phase. The changes in echo signal phase or timing show that an echo source is moving and reveal the direction of its motion.[8] The reference for this motion is the transducer. As in duplex imaging, movement toward the transducer is called *forward* motion; movement away from the transducer is called *reverse*. The color flow system encodes this directional information into color, typically red and blue. Fig. 2–3 shows this color assignment geometry for a linear array. These same rules apply to every ultrasound beam in both sector and linear scanning fields. Because no universally accepted standard exists for assigning color to direction, most systems have a flow-reverse button that switches the color assignment. This often permits setting arterial flow in red and venous flow in blue.

Doppler Shift Frequencies. Each Doppler image sampling site is a range gate that represents the position of the Doppler sample volume. If the sample volume is within a pattern of flowing blood, a spectrum of Doppler

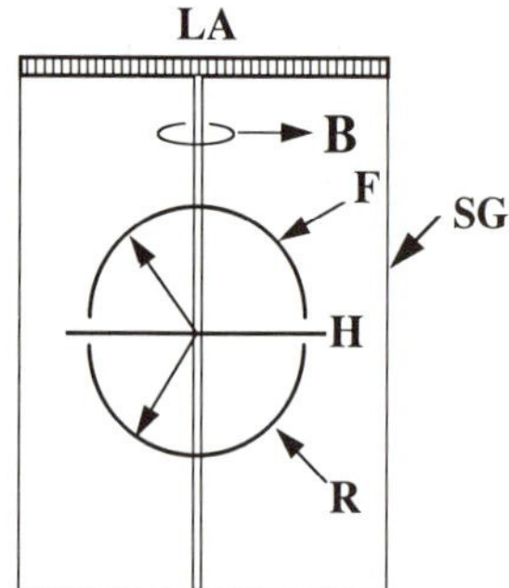

Figure 2–3. Color assignment to the direction of flow. LA is the linear array, B is the ultrasound beam, SG is the scanning field geometry, F is forward motion, R is reverse motion, and H is a horizontal line. Flow vectors pointing on the F arc are all one color. Flow vectors pointing on the R arc are the opposite color. Anatomy further restricts blood flow to the anatomy of the vessel.

shift frequencies appears. The system, however, cannot display a spectrum within each colored pixel that makes a color flow image. Instead, most color flow systems determine a representative frequency and encode this frequency into a color quality.[9]

All current color flow systems use some form of average frequency to represent the Doppler shift frequency within a sample site. The average frequency is a good choice because it is less sensitive to noise than are most alternatives. In some systems, the average frequency comes from an on-line spectral analysis.[9] In others, autocorrelation and signal-averaging techniques produce the average value.[2] Regardless of the type of system, the signal processing encodes the average frequency into one of several color qualities.

Color has three inherent qualities we can use to encode information: hue, brightness, and saturation. The hue of a color represents its basic frequency or wavelength. For example, red and blue are different hues; so are yellow and green. Some systems encode the Doppler shift frequency information into hue, presenting a variety of different colors, each representing a different Doppler shift frequency.[2]

The brightness of a color represents its energy content. For example, increasing or decreasing the illumination on a color patch changes the brightness of the color without changing its hue. In general, current designs avoid using color brightness to encode the average frequency, but may employ it to smooth the edges of the color boundaries.

Saturation is a measure of a color's purity. A color with 100% saturation is pure. For example, a pure or 100%-saturated red would appear on the screen as a deep red. Changing the saturation means adding some white light to the color; thus, a less saturated red appears whiter. Several systems use color saturation to encode the average frequency information.[10] In these images, jets and major streamlines appear whiter than the surrounding color.

Beam Contributions to Sampling

Forming the ultrasound beam and its subsequent motion have a strong role to play in making a color flow image. Most color flow imaging systems use a phased array, linear array, or curved linear array transducer. Only a few systems use a mechanical scan. This preference for electronic scanning is not merely a matter of chance.

The Doppler effect does not distinguish between a moving ultrasound beam and stationary echo sources or between a stable ultrasound beam with moving echo sources. A mechanical scanner has a steadily moving beam (Fig. 2–4). This continuous motion means that the Doppler signal processing always sees some movement between the tissue echo sources and the ultrasound beam. Common to the few color flow systems that use mechanical scanning is an inability to look at extremely slow blood velocities. This form of insensitivity appears as the system filters out the Doppler shift frequencies produced by the moving ultrasound beam. Along with the moving beam frequencies goes all the low-velocity information.

One clear advantage of the electronic systems is the formation of a stationary ultrasound beam (Fig. 2–4). In this scanning pattern, each beam appears at a fixed line-of-sight position in the scanning plane.[11] However, electronic beam forming and steering have a price as well. Every transducer, regardless of size, acts as if it were a hole or aperture in space.[12] In this model (Fig. 2–5), the ultrasound comes from a point source behind the aperture. As the waves travel through, the interaction of the aperture and the waves produces a diffraction pattern. Most of the energy comes through to form a large central lobe of energy. The remaining energy diffracts into a set of side lobes that broaden and smear the beam.

An array of transducers (linear and curved) produces a similar set of side lobes. Because these lobes come from the summation of side lobes from each transducer element, they are called grating lobes. When the electronic

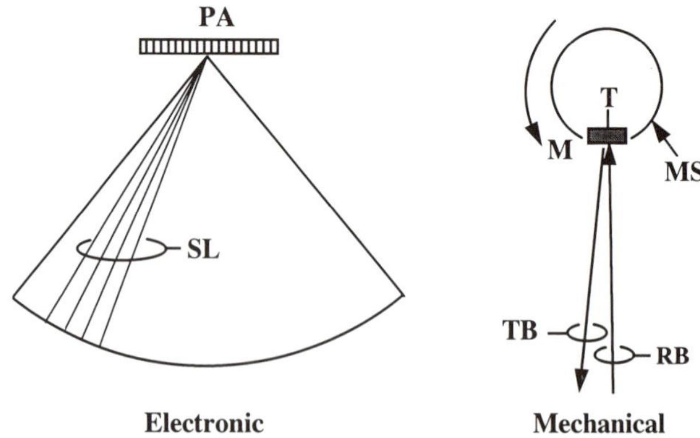

Figure 2–4. Electronic and mechanically steered beams. PA is a phased array, SL represents the scanning lines, MS is the mechanical scanning head, T is a transducer, M is the direction of motion, TB is the position of the transmit beam, and RB is the position of the receive beam. Electronic steering permits fixed positions for each scan line.

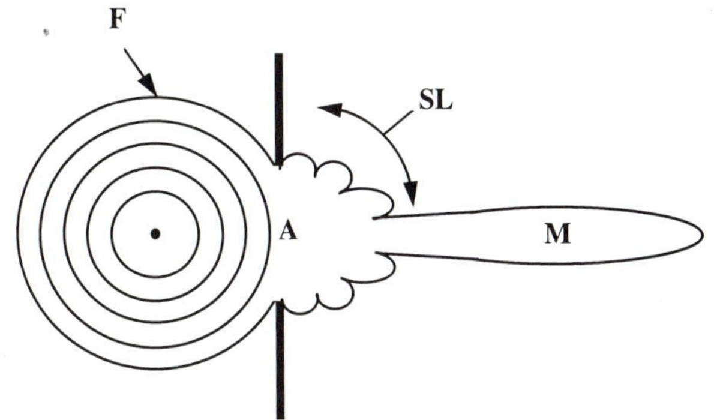

Figure 2–5. The transducer is a diffracting aperture. F is the virtual ultrasound field behind the aperture, A is the aperture, SL represents the diffraction side lobes, and M is the main beam. Each transducer acts like a diffracting hole in space.

control steers the beam perpendicular to the array, the grating lobes can be relatively small. By using several different cancellation techniques, engineers can suppress the grating lobes −60 dB (1/1000th) or more below the main lobe of energy. When the steered beam points off to the side, however, the number and size of the grating lobes increase (Fig. 2–6).[2] Again, the result is a smearing of the ultrasound beam and a loss of lateral resolution—a loss that can affect the accurate placement of color within an image.

Signal Processing

Once the echo signals are inside the machine, they face a diverse set of analyses. When and how these analyses occur will determine the character of the final color flow image.

Within the various machines, signal processing takes on two different forms. First, a system can use the same signal to make both the gray-scale and Doppler images. This is synchronous signal processing.[3] Second, the system can use different signals to form the gray-scale and Doppler images. This is asynchronous signal processing.[3] These two forms of signal processing are sufficiently different that they even have different names. High-resolution synchronous processing is currently called angiodynography,[6] whereas low-resolution synchronous imaging and both high- and low-resolution asynchronous imaging are termed color flow imaging. Angiodynography is, of course, a special form of color flow imaging.

Synchronous Signal Processing. Fig. 2–7 shows the basic organization of a synchronous signal-processing system. Replacing the linear array with a single transducer and replacing the B-mode image with an M-mode trace produced the earliest synchronous system: the M/Q system.[12] This system used the same signals to produce both an M-mode display and a point spectrum. All synchronous systems use the same transducer, coherent transmitter, and receiver because they extract different information from a common signal. After reception, the signals divide into two pathways: one for the gray-scale image, the other for the Doppler image.

Most cardiac color flow systems are synchronous.[2] Because they do not separate the signal processing events for gray scale and color, they permit higher frame rates. These systems focus on the phased array to form and steer the ultrasound beams (Fig. 2–8). At the same time, beam steering spreads the beam with grating lobes; the effects of these lobes appear in both the gray-scale and color images.

In synchronous vascular imaging, or angiodynography, the system shapes and focuses an ultrasound beam along a line of sight perpendicular to the linear array. Fig. 2–9 shows the organization of this system. The beam scans down the array to form a rectangular scanning field. Zone focusing on "transmit" and dynamic focusing on "receive" provide a narrow beam over the field of view.[13]

The system tests each sample site along each beam for flow. If flow exists, the corresponding image pixel becomes colored; if not, the pixel becomes gray scale. In this man-

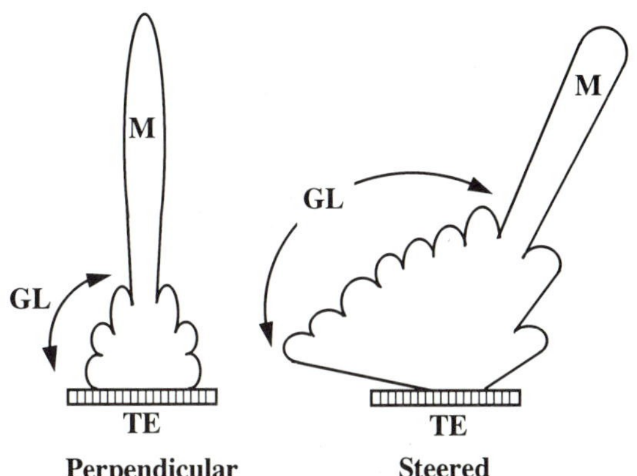

Figure 2–6. Grating lobe formation with beam steering. TE represents transducer elements, GL represents grating lobes, and M is the main lobe. Steering increases the formation of side lobes, smearing the ultrasound beam.

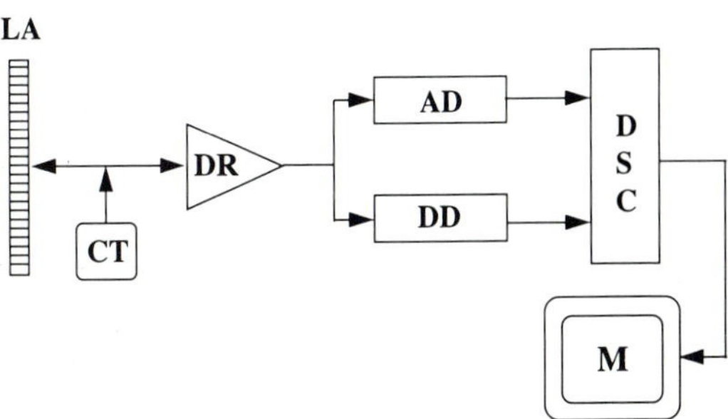

Figure 2–7. Synchronous signal processing. LA is the linear array, CT is a coherent transmitter, R is a receiver, AD represents amplitude detection, DD represents Doppler detection, DSC is the digital scan converter, and M is the color monitor. Synchronous signal processing uses the same signal to make the gray-scale and Doppler images.

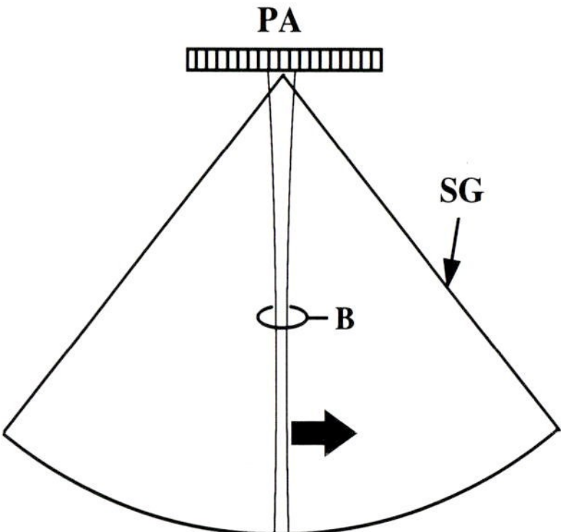

Figure 2–8. Formation of a phased array beam and steering. PA represents the phased array elements, B is the beam, SG is the scanning field geometry, and the arrow shows beam movement. The phased array has a limited aperture size that limits the focal spot size and focal range. Thus, focusing is poorest at the edges of the sector.

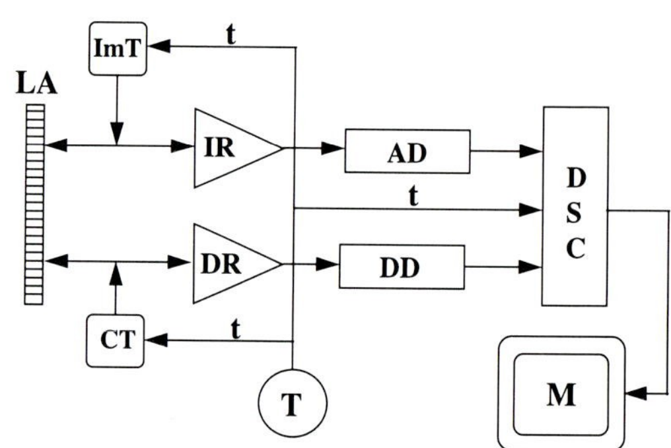

Figure 2–10. Asynchronous signal processing. LA is the linear array, ImT is the imaging transmitter, CT is the coherent transmitter, R is a receiver, AD represents amplitude detection, DD represents Doppler detection, DSC is the digital scan converter, M is the color monitor, T is a common timer with control signals (t), IR is the gray scale imaging receiver, and DR is the Doppler receiver. Asynchronous signal processing uses different signals for the gray-scale and color portions of the image.

ner, the processing builds the image on a sample-site by sample-site basis.

Gray-scale imaging depends on a mix of specular and scattering reflections. Doppler imaging, however, needs an angle of less than 90° between the beam and the flow streamlines. Synchronous vascular imaging systems use a mechanical wedge to establish the Doppler angle.[6] The wedge displaces one edge of the array about 18°, which in turn sets the ultrasound beams about 72° in relation to the vessels that are parallel or nearly parallel to the skin. In general, the wedge is a water-filled plastic device that slips on and off the array as needed. The choice of plastics and the internal architecture of the wedge reduces its attenuating effect on the echo signals to about 0.3 dB. The wedge does not affect focusing of the ultrasound beam, yet it suppresses reverberations within the wedge.

Asynchronous Signal Processing. Asynchronous signal-processing systems use different ultrasound beams and signals to create the gray-scale and Doppler images. Typically, they use separate transmitters for gray-scale and Doppler signals. Only the transducer array and a central coordinating timer are common throughout most of the signal pathway to the scan converter. In Fig. 2–10 the organization of this imaging system is illustrated.

Most asynchronous systems use beam steering to obtain the Doppler image, and they keep the beams perpendicular to form the gray-scale image. Fig. 2–11 shows how the two scanning fields interact. Because the system uses two different transmitters, the Doppler carrier frequency can be different from the imaging frequency. For example, imaging might be at 5.0 MHz and Doppler might be at 3.0 MHz.

The operating cycle interweaves the Doppler and gray-scale beams to produce two separate images. This interweaving reduces the potential frame rates for the system. Because the sample sites for the two fields of view do not coincide, they cannot accumulate into a common memory. Instead, they pass to separate memories and finally overlay one another in the digital scan converter.

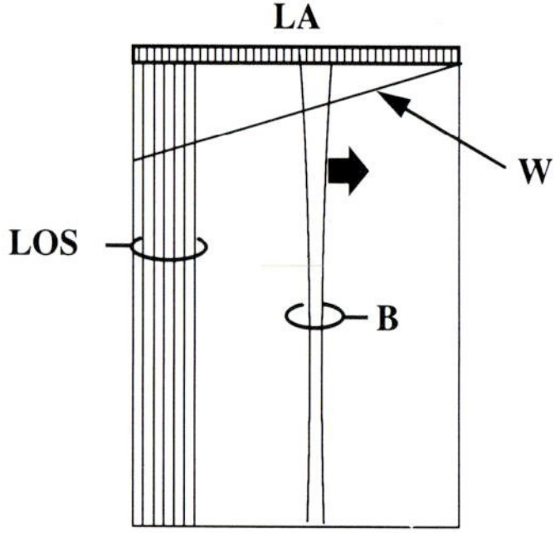

Figure 2–9. Scanning organization in angiodynography. LA is the linear array, LOS represents the scanning lines of sight, W is the wedge, B is the beam, and the arrow shows beam motion. The wedge provides a Doppler angle between the moving blood and the ultrasound beam.

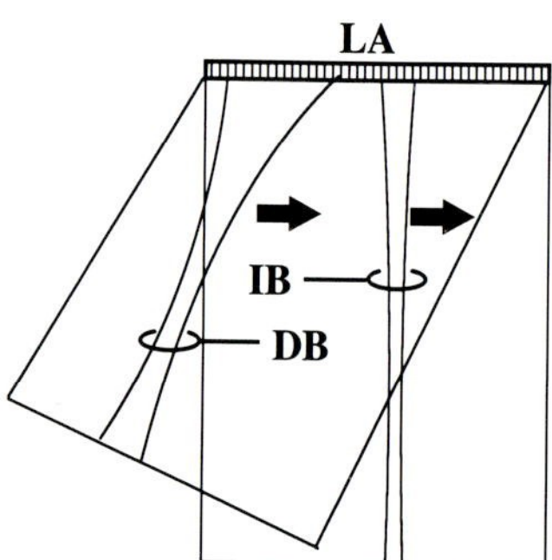

Figure 2–11. Scanning organization for asynchronous signal processing. LA is the linear array, DB is the Doppler beam, IB is the gray-scale beam, and the arrows show beam motion. Beam steering provides a Doppler angle for making the Doppler image. The Doppler and gray-scale frequencies can differ.

Because the two scanning fields have different orientations, the color imaging and the gray-scale images do not entirely correspond to one another (Fig. 2–11). Portions of the steered Doppler image are outside the gray-scale field, whereas portions of the gray-scale field are outside the Doppler field. To keep the overall image frame rate high, a system often confines the color to a small mobile window. This is a common practice for all color flow systems—both vascular and cardiac.

PRACTICAL ISSUES

Cardiac Imaging Requirements

In general, viewing the heart with ultrasound requires intercostal and subcostal imaging with low-frequency ultrasound.[2] For parasternal color flow imaging, the beam is placed at angles approximately 90° to the flow. As a result, apical and subcostal views of the heart are needed to place flow patterns parallel to the ultrasound beams. The phased array and the short-radius, curved linear arrays are the transducers of choice for viewing through these thoracic and abdominal windows. The sector angles range from 30° to 90°.

Because blood is a low attenuator (0.15 dB/cm per MHz), viewing the heart with ultrasound does not require the front-end design (delay lines and receivers) that vascular imaging requires. In addition, the high frame rates, combined with large fields of view, impose large sampling intervals on the cardiac image. And the scanning is on a sector format. All these factors combine to make the cardiac color flow device right for the heart and wrong for the vascular system.

Because the Doppler sampling intervals can be relatively large in echocardiography, detecting a regional turbulence is not always easy. To help find any disorganization of flow (spectral broadening) in a given location, most cardiac systems determine not only the mean frequency at a sample site but the signal variance as well.[2] In many cardiac devices, color coding for an increasing variance introduces green to the primary color.

Vascular Imaging Requirements

Vascular color flow imaging involves all available vessels, including the large, upper thoracic vessels and the deeper vessels in the abdomen. The linear array is used to view the peripheral vessels. This linear scanning field sets the stage for using changes in color to show changes in the direction of flow. In contrast, a sector scan of a linear vessel has a continuously changing Doppler angle (Fig. 2–12) and, thus, continuously changing color.

Sector scanning transducers such as the phased array and the curved linear array are used to view abdominal vessels. These transducers permit both subcostal and intercostal scanning to visualize the deeper abdominal vessels.

The sector fields, however, make reading the images more difficult. Identifying arteries and veins requires knowing both the direction of flow and the pulsatility of the flow. Large fields of view and longer processing times for the color flow image often make the frame rates too low to permit easy determination of pulsatility. The single-point spectrum and color flow image as well as reduced color regions can yield information about pulsatility.

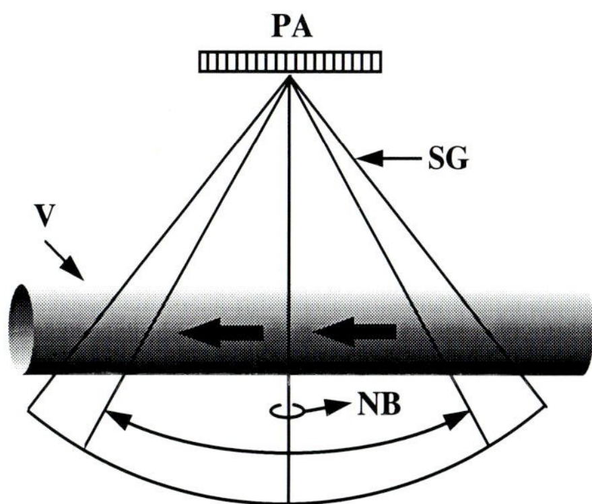

Figure 2–12. Vascular imaging with a sector scanning field. PA is a phased array, SG is the scanning field geometry, V is the vessel, and NB is the beam perpendicular to flow in the vessel (arrows). Because each beam position has a different Doppler angle, the colors in the image change rapidly.

Displays of Frequency and Velocity

All current color flow images using Doppler are two-dimensional maps of the Doppler shift frequencies. After all, color flow is Doppler, too.

Many systems show the color values in velocity (cm/s) rather than frequency. Such a color image display suggests a direct measurement of velocity. As in all color-flow Doppler determinations of velocity, the values represent a solution to the Doppler equation (Fig. 2–13). However, the velocity is not the absolute velocity of the red cells. Instead, it represents the closing velocity along the ultrasound beam. Absolute velocities would require continuous correction of angles for all flow patterns throughout the image. Fig. 2–14 shows the closing velocity relationship.

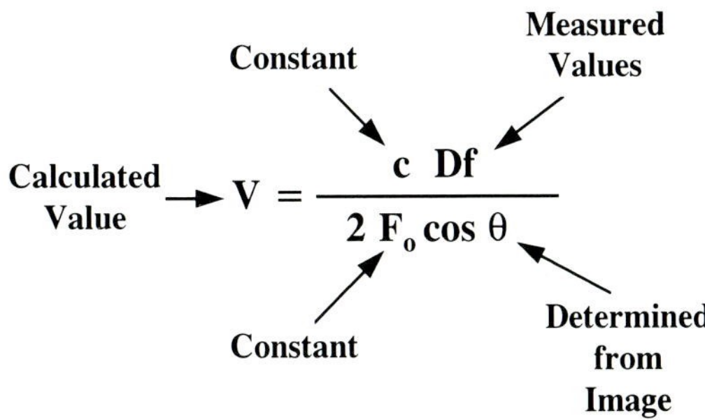

Figure 2–13. Calculation of velocity with the Doppler equation. *V* is the velocity, *c* is the ultrasound propagation velocity, *Df* is the Doppler shift frequency, F_0 is the carrier frequency, and θ is the Doppler angle. Doppler machines measure frequency and calculate velocity.

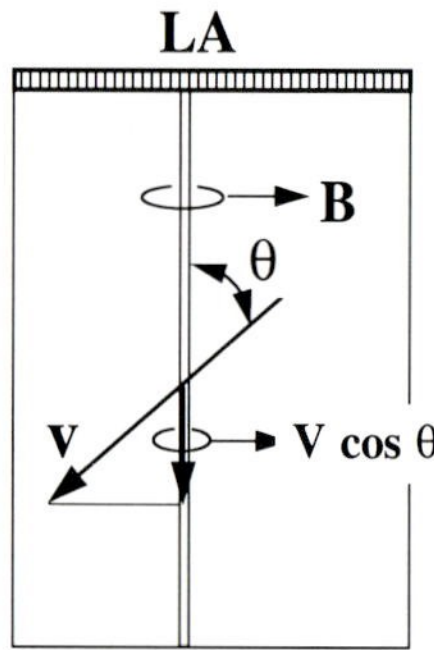

Figure 2–14. The closing velocity geometry. LA is the linear array, B is the ultrasound beam, SG is the scanning field geometry, *V* is the target velocity, and *V* cos θ is the closing velocity. Closing velocity is the component of motion along the ultrasound beam.

Color Flow Imaging Artifacts

Because color flow imaging incorporates both B-mode imaging and Doppler signal processing, it is subject to the same artifacts that affect ultrasound in general. Three primary sources of confusion in color flow imaging are (1) range ambiguity artifacts, (2) Doppler high-frequency aliasing, and (3) soft-tissue vibrations.

Fig. 2–15 shows the organization required to obtain a range ambiguity artifact. The high power and fast frame rates typical of color flow imaging offer ample opportunities for this artifact.[14] In color flow imaging, the artifact appears as diffuse nonpulsatile colors, suggesting flow that may not actually exist.

High-frequency aliasing occurs when the Doppler shift frequency exceeds the pulse repetition frequency (PRF) of the system.[8] As a result, the colors and spectra wrap around the display format and confuse the appearance of flow. To remove aliasing, a sonographer must either increase the PRF (shorten the field of view) or decrease the Doppler shift frequency.[12] The Doppler shift frequency can be decreased by either decreasing the Doppler carrier frequency or moving the Doppler angle closer to 90°.

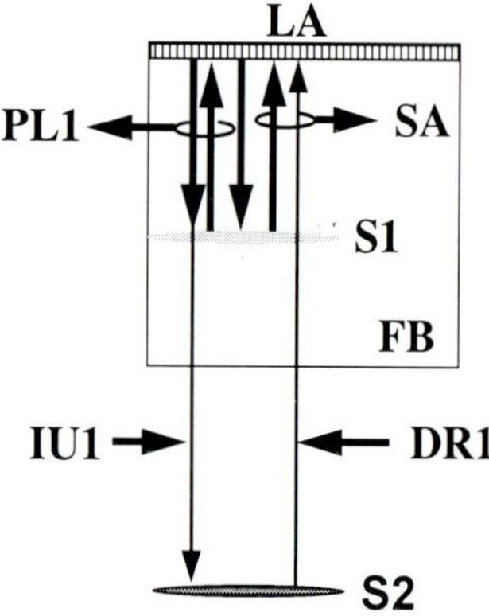

Figure 2–15. The range ambiguity artifact. LA is the linear array, PL1 is the initial pulse–listen cycle, IU1 is the incident ultrasound from PL1, S1 is an echo source inside the field boundary (FB), S2 is an echo source outside the scanning field, DR1 is the deeper returning echo, and SA represents the simultaneous arrival of the two echo signals. Range ambiguity occurs when echo sources outside the scanning field appear in the image.

A not uncommon problem is the mechanical vibration of soft tissues. For example, vibrations can occur if a patient talks. Such vibrations can fill an image of a carotid artery with diffuse colors. The low-frequency pulse from the heart also can fill an abdominal image with a burst of color. More often, the vibration comes from turbulent flow patterns within vessels that vibrate the surrounding soft tissues.[15]

Applying the Technology to Real Images

With some idea of how the various color flow systems work, we are now in a position to examine some examples of color flow imaging. They range from the depiction of flow within an M-mode recording to high-resolution imaging of the vascular system.

Fig. 2–16 shows the combination of an M-mode recording with color flow imaging. All motion in this image is referenced to the transducer as a closing velocity; that is, only as motion toward or away from the transducer. In this example, the Doppler frequencies have been calculated into closing velocities, which do not necessarily represent the true velocities of the cardiac blood flow. This system shows the increased Doppler shift frequencies (spectral broadening) by adding green to the primary di-

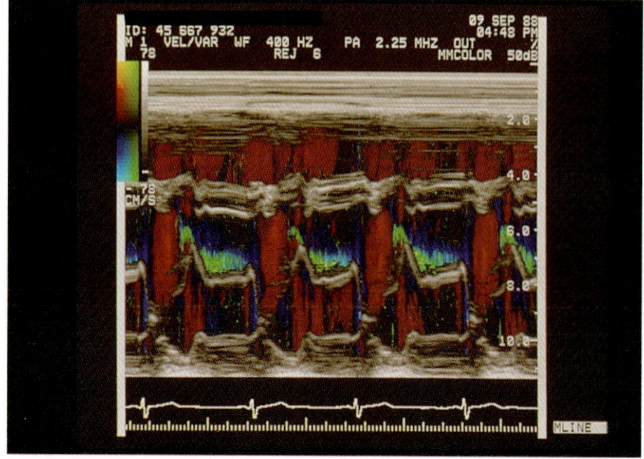

Figure 2–16. Color flow imaging of a mitral valve. This M-mode tracing views the mitral valve from the upper portion of the cardiac window, which is aimed down toward the mitral valve. Red is flow toward the transducer; blue is flow away. Closing velocity values (aliasing limits) appear on the color bar. The red flow between the interventricular septum and the closed mitral valve is ejection through the left ventricular outflow tract. During ventricular filling, the blue-green flow along the anterior mitral valve leaflet is reversed turbulent flow produced by an aortic regurgitation. Depth markers are at the right of the image, and an EKG trace provides timing at the bottom of the image. *(Reproduced with permission from Advanced Technology Labs, Bothell, WA.)*

rectional colors. As a result, the aortic regurgitation is quite evident in the color flow pattern.

Determining the true flow pattern is easier with a two-dimensional image of the heart. Fig. 2–17 provides a clear view of the heart in long axis, with the blood flow confined to the heart's chambers. Again, the Doppler frequency map is calculated into closing velocity values. True velocities would require a continuous angle correction throughout the image, which is not possible with current imaging technologies. This image shows a nonaxial regurgitating jet extending from the aortic root into the left ventricle. In this case, the color flow images show not only the existence of the jet but its nonaxial geometry.

Fig. 2–19 depicts a carotid artery with higher resolution, synchronous color flow imaging (angiodynography). The sampling rate in this image is at one-wavelength intervals (0.2 mm at 7.5 MHz) for both the gray scale image and the color portion of the image. The internal flow pattern of the vessel shows a normal flow separation and reversal in the carotid bulb. The flow direction is from image right to left, away from the transducer, causing the vessel to appear red. The higher Doppler shift frequencies are whiter, which clearly depicts the higher-velocity portions of the flow.

The beam steering that is typical of asynchronous signal processing changes the appearance of a similar carotid artery. This system also depicts different average Doppler shift frequencies with different color hues. As in Fig. 2–19, the image clearly shows the flow separation and reversal that is typical of a normal carotid bulb. This image also shows one of the hallmarks of normal blood flow, the nonaxial location of the higher-flow velocities.

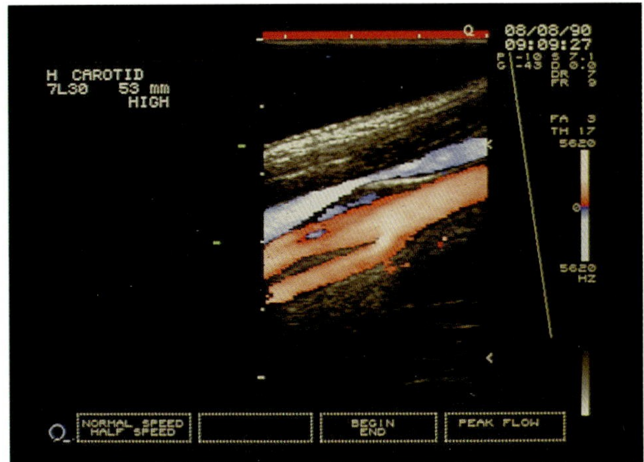

Figure 2–18. Color flow imaging of a carotid artery. This long-axis view of a normal carotid artery bifurcation shows the common carotid artery branching into internal (upper branch) and external (lower branch) carotid arteries. Flow is right to left, away from the transducer (red bar at the top of the image). The vessel above the carotid (blue) is the jugular vein. Within the carotid bulb is a normal flow separation and reversal (blue). Because higher Doppler shift frequencies are whiter, the major streamlines appear white in the image. The required Doppler angle comes from the wedge standoff (black triangular space at the top of the image). The peripheral dots are 1-cm markers, and the aliasing frequencies appear at the top and bottom of the color bar. *(Reproduced with permission from Quantum Medical Systems, Issaquah, WA.)*

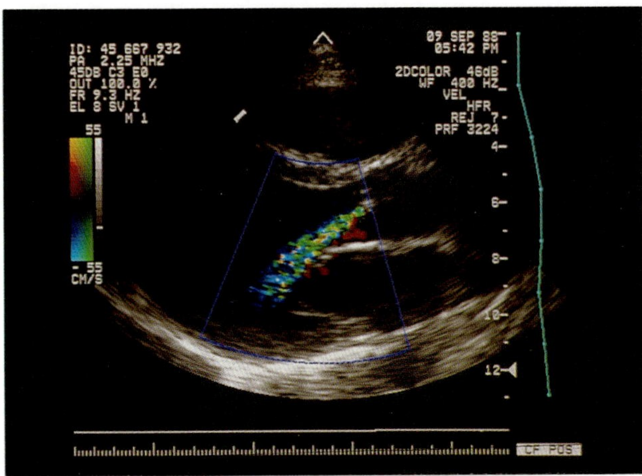

Figure 2–17. Cardiac color flow imaging. This parasternal long-axis view of the heart shows (from the top down) the right ventricle, the interventricular septum, and the left ventricle containing the mitral valve leaflets. Red is flow toward the transducer; blue is away. Closing velocity values (aliasing limits) appear on the color bar. The color-imaging window (blue boundary) shows a nonaxial blue-green turbulent jet (regurgitation) originating at the aortic root. Without color, the nonaxial quality of the jet could not be easily determined. *(Reproduced with permission from Advanced Technology Labs, Bothell, WA.)*

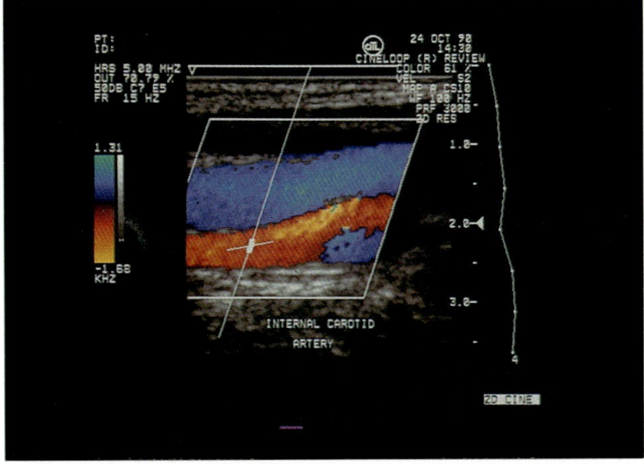

Figure 2–19. Color flow imaging of a carotid artery. The image shows the internal carotid artery and bulb. Flow in the artery (red) is from right to left, with a flow separation and reversal in blue. The major, nonaxial streamline (yellow) in the bulb is along the anterior wall. A small segment of aliasing (green) appears in the streamline. The more anterior blue vessel is the jugular vein. The Doppler angle for this image comes from beam steering. The white parallelogram shows the steering angle and the boundary for color signal processing in the image. The aliasing frequency limits appear on the color bar, with depth markers and a transmit focal point position on the right side of the image. *(Reproduced with permission from Advanced Technology Labs, Bothell, WA.)*

The beam steering in this image will not show flow throughout the image, but moving the color flow processing window and changing the scanning position permits a full interrogation of most vessels.

Any highly vascular tissue or structure is a good candidate for color flow imaging when trying to separate out ambiguous anatomy. Flow within major fetal vessels appears in Fig. 2–20. This image is formed with a convex linear array, producing a sector image pattern. Because of the complexity of the vascular anatomy and the changing angle between the vessels and the beams, color does not always indicate arteries and veins. Instead, the vessel pulsatility and its position relative to internal anatomical landmarks tell the story. If the system frame rate is too slow, then the single point, pulsed Doppler will be the most reliable means of determining the pulsatile flow patterns of arteries and the steady flow patterns of veins.

When wall disease in a vessel disturbs the flow pattern, a single point spectrum does not show the source or character of the disturbances. However, high-resolution color flow imaging, as in Fig. 2–21, clearly shows not only the irregularities of the vessel walls but the flow disturbances that result from these changes.

In the presence of stenosis, the flow within the narrowing increases velocity. The narrowing also often appears in the image as a physical narrowing of the color distribution, following the vessel. Fig. 2–22 shows these two results, the narrowing of the color distribution and the acceleration (whiter segments of the color) due to a carotid artery stenosis.

When frame rates are high enough and the Doppler sampling is fine enough, we begin to see some of the subtler flow physiology. Each pulse in the vascular system is a wave that travels down the vessels, only to reflect a por-

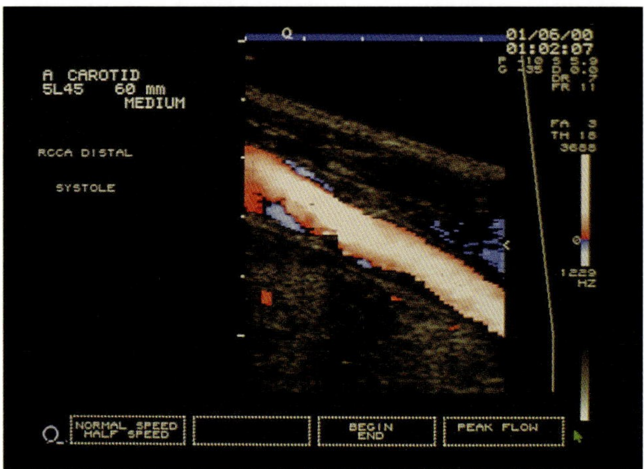

Figure 2–21. Color flow imaging of a carotid artery. This artery has irregular walls that cause flow disturbances (blue) at the walls. Flow is from right to left toward the transducer. The blue bar at the top represents flow away from the transducer. The color saturation shows a white major streamline that is crossing the vessel from the posterior to the anterior wall. The deviation of flow is more than 15° steeper than the vessel walls. The peripheral dots are 1-cm markers, and the aliasing frequencies appear at the top and bottom of the color bar. The black space at the top is a wedge standoff. *(Reproduced with permission from Quantum Medical Systems, Issaquah, WA.)*

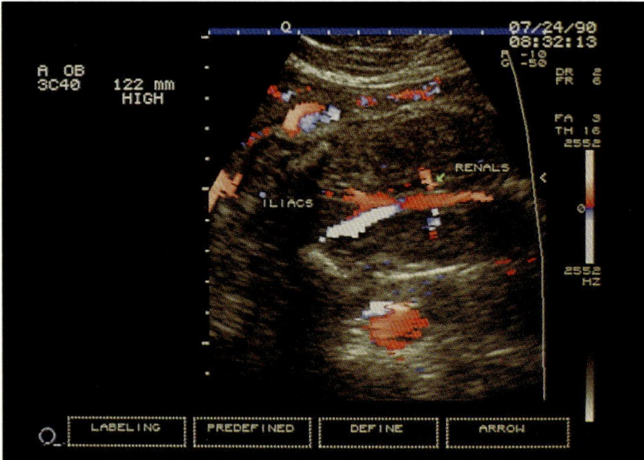

Figure 2–20. Color flow imaging of a fetal abdomen. This image shows the fetal aorta with renal and iliac branches. Flow away from the transducer is blue; flow toward the transducer is red. The peripheral dots are 1-cm markers, and the aliasing frequencies appear at the top and bottom of the color bar. A convex curved array forms the sector scanning field. *(Reproduced with permission from Quantum Medical Systems, Issaquah, WA.)*

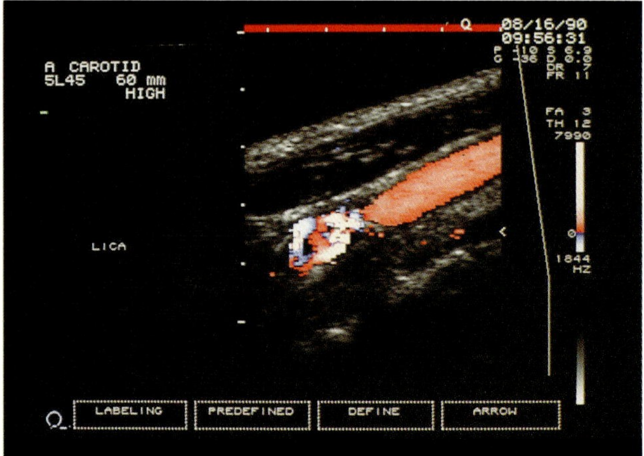

Figure 2–22. Color flow imaging of a carotid artery. This artery has a significant stenosis that is narrowing the flow channel (narrow color) and causing poststenotic turbulence (mixed colors). Flow is right to left, away from the transducer and is therefore colored red (red bar at the top represents flow away from the transducer). The peripheral dots are 1-cm markers, and the aliasing frequencies appear at the top and bottom of the color bar. The black space at the top of the image is a wedge standoff. *(Reproduced with permission from Quantum Medical Systems, Issaquah, WA.)*

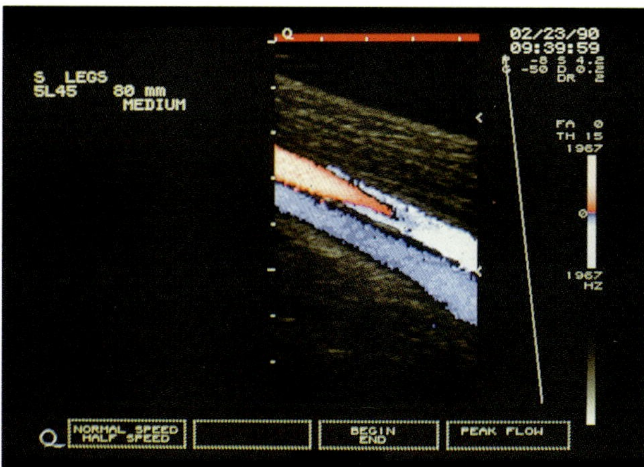

Figure 2–23. Color flow imaging of a superficial femoral artery and vein. These normal vessels show typical flow patterns during the cardiac and respiratory cycle. Arterial flow is from left to right, with a distally reflected pulse wave (blue) arriving to cross the incident pulse wave (red). The superficial femoral vein (blue posterior vessel) is flowing right to left as flow and color fill the vein's residual lumen. This color flow image clearly shows that the reversal of flow in a tri- or biphasic flow pattern comes from a traveling pulse wave. The peripheral dots are 1-cm markers, and the aliasing frequencies appear at the top and bottom of the color bar. The black space at the top of the image is a wedge standoff. *(Reproduced with permission from Quantum Medical Systems, Issaquah, WA.)*

tion of the energy at changes in hydraulic impedance. Fig. 2–23 shows the intersection of two traveling pulse waves: The red portion is the incident wave and the blue portion is the reflected wave. The color flow image and the Doppler spectrum show the connection between the triphasic flow pattern of this high-resistance vessel and the passing of forward and reversed pulse waves with the artery.

SUMMARY

Color flow imaging is a combination of gray-scale anatomical information and a colored depiction of flow events. It is an integrated image of form and function—anatomy and physiology. The color portion of the image is not an image of blood however; it is an image of motion.

Within each color flow system, the amplitudes of echo signals become gray-scale intensities, whereas the frequency content of the signals becomes color. The echo signals for both may be the same or be different even in carrier frequency. This imaging modality depends on the sophistication and speed of the signal processing. It also is an imaging modality that is changing, and will continue to change, the fields of ultrasound and medicine.

REFERENCES

See page 97.

Questions

GENERAL INSTRUCTIONS: For each question, select the best answer. Select only one answer for each question unless otherwise specified.

1. Duplex imaging combines gray scale with Doppler and can appear as

   (A) M-mode and spectrum
   (B) B-mode and spectrum
   (C) color flow imaging and spectrum
   (D) all of the above

2. Color flow imaging produces an image composed of

   (A) tissue echoes in gray scale and blood echoes in color
   (B) soft-tissue echoes in gray scale and blood motion in color
   (C) stationary tissues in gray scale and moving tissues in color
   (D) stationary tissues in gray scale and stationary blood in color

3. Angiodynography is a term used to describe

   (A) a form of high-resolution color flow imaging
   (B) a form of high-resolution magnetic resonance imaging
   (C) a new form of imaging relying on high-speed propagation velocities in soft tissues
   (D) the coloring of conventional angiograms

4. The Doppler effect occurs

   (A) only to waves traveling more than 1000 m/s
   (B) only to ultrasound waves with intensities greater than 500 mW/cm^2, SPTA
   (C) to all waves coming from a moving wave source
   (D) in ultrasound, but only when the targets are moving faster than 1.0 m/s

5. The Doppler effect depends on

   (A) the carrier frequency, the angle between echo source velocity and beam axis, and the reflectivity of blood
   (B) the closing velocity between transducer and tissue, carrier frequency, and ultrasound propagation velocity
   (C) the lowest Doppler-shift frequency detectable and the highest frequency without aliasing
   (D) the largest change in acoustical impedance within the moving blood

6. To calculate blood velocity using color flow imaging, a sonographer must

   (A) place a sample volume in the major streamline or jet within the vessel and set an angle correction parallel to the vessel wall
   (B) assume that all flow is parallel to the vessel wall
   (C) locate the major streamline and place the sampling angle at 60° to the vessel wall
   (D) place a sample volume in the major streamline or jet and set the angle correction parallel to the streamline

7. To preserve gray-scale texture, digital sampling for gray-scale images must be at intervals of

   (A) 0.6 mm
   (B) one wavelength or less
   (C) 1.0 mm
   (D) 3 dB

8. To preserve flow detail, digital Doppler sampling intervals for a vascular color flow image must be at intervals of

   (A) 1–2 mm
   (B) 1–2 cm
   (C) one wavelength or more but less than 1 mm
   (D) −6 dB

9. Gray-scale tissue texture in a color flow imaging system depends on

   (A) transmit focusing only
   (B) receive focusing only
   (C) the product of transmit and receive focusing
   (D) the speed at which the ultrasound beam is moved by the scanhead

10. The shape of the sample volume in pulsed Doppler has a major effect on the content of the Doppler signal

(A) true
(B) false

11. To form the color patterns in a color flow image, a color flow system samples down each Doppler image line of sight for

(A) the amplitude of the Doppler signal
(B) the velocities of red blood cells
(C) the average Doppler shift frequency
(D) the velocity spread within the sample site

12. The Doppler portion of a color flow image is a map of red-cell velocities

(A) true
(B) false

13. Separating moving soft tissue from moving blood in a color flow image tests for

(A) Doppler signal amplitudes only
(B) tissue signal amplitudes only
(C) Doppler signal frequencies only
(D) the relationship between the amplitudes and frequencies of the Doppler signals

14. A curving vessel within a color flow image shows color in the vessel when the beam and vessel are parallel and shows no color as the vessel turns. The loss of color means that

(A) the vessel is occluded
(B) the vessel is open, but the blood velocity is too low to complete the image
(C) the dark region is diseased
(D) the Doppler effect works only when the vessel is parallel to the ultrasound beam

15. The smallest vessels that appear in a color flow image are about 1 mm in diameter. The smaller vessels are absent because

(A) arterial blood velocities are too low in vessels that are less than 1 mm in diameter
(B) the smaller vessels are shadowed by the surrounding soft tissue
(C) soft tissue does not have many vessels that are less than 1 mm in diameter
(D) the smaller vessels do not reflect ultrasound as well as the larger vessels do

16. The color flow image provides information on (1) the existence of flow, (2) the location of flow in the image, (3) flow direction relative to transducer, (4) the maximum flow velocity.

(A) all of the above
(B) 1, 3, and 4
(C) 3 and 4
(D) 1, 2, and 3

17. Detecting flow in a color flow imaging system depends on the detection of

(A) changes in Doppler signal amplitude
(B) changes in Doppler signal frequency content
(C) changes in echo signal phase and frequency content
(D) changes in echo signal phase

18. One begins reading a color flow image by

(A) determining the maximum systolic frequency
(B) knowing the position of the scan plane on the patient's body
(C) knowing the direction of flow relative to the transducer
(D) determining the Doppler carrier frequency

19. Changes in the Doppler shift frequencies within a color flow image sample site appear in the image as

(A) nothing; the image only shows changes in phase
(B) different colors (hues)
(C) different levels of color saturation (purity)
(D) different colors (hues) *or* different levels of saturation (purity)

20. An angiodynogram shows changes in the frequency content of a Doppler sample site by

(A) changes in color
(B) changes in saturation
(C) changes in color texture
(D) the introduction of green markers

21. Cardiac color flow imaging shows changes in the frequency content of the Doppler sample site by

(A) changes in color
(B) changes in saturation
(C) changes in color texture
(D) the introduction of red markers

22. Color flow imaging systems determine the maximum Doppler shift frequency at each sample site.

(A) true
(B) false

23. A measurement of the peak systolic frequency in a carotid artery with a single point spectrum will be lower than a measurement of the color-encoded frequency at the same point.

(A) true
(B) false

24. The synchronous signal processing in angiodynography uses a Doppler carrier frequency that is the same as the imaging center operating frequency.

(A) true
(B) false

25. Asynchronous signal processing in color flow imaging requires the same frequency for both Doppler and gray-scale imaging.
(A) true
(B) false

26. Beam steering in asynchronous color flow imaging is used to provide
(A) a Doppler angle to typical blood flow
(B) a way of looking at the same soft-tissue targets at an angle different from the perpendicular beams
(C) an enlarged Doppler beam to improve Doppler sensitivity
(D) improved Doppler sensitivity to smaller vessels

27. The mechanical wedge in angiodynography is used to provide
(A) improved penetration through impedance matching
(B) improved beam focusing for the gray-scale image
(C) an attenuation system to remove side lobes
(D) a Doppler angle between the typical flow patterns in vessels

28. The ability to see flow in deep vessels is limited by the fact that
(A) blood has scattering units that are about the same size as soft tissue
(B) blood is moving faster than the surrounding tissues
(C) blood has an extremely low attenuation rate
(D) blood reflectivity is about 40 dB to 60 dB below that of soft tissue

29. Levels of output power and intensity for color flow imaging are generally higher than those for conventional gray-scale imaging.
(A) true
(B) false

30. Because Doppler signal processing requires more energy, synchronous signal processing always produces Doppler power levels that are higher than those for gray-scale imaging.
(A) true
(B) false

31. In general, tissue ultrasonic intensity levels are higher for single-point spectra than for color flow imaging with the same system.
(A) true
(B) false

32. Moving from gray scale only to full-screen color flow imaging in a system means that the image frame rate will probably
(A) decrease
(B) increase
(C) stay the same

33. Color flow imaging in the heart uses larger Doppler sampling intervals to increase the image frame rate than does vascular imaging.
(A) true
(B) false

34. Cardiac color flow imaging also works well in the vascular system because the design can handle the high attenuation rates in cardiac imaging.
(A) true
(B) false

35. Sampling intervals for cardiac color flow imaging and vascular color flow imaging are similar.
(A) true
(B) false

36. Cardiac color flow imaging is limited with a mechanical sector scanner because
(A) the cardiac attenuation rate is too high
(B) the ultrasound beams are always moving
(C) the beam has a fixed focal point
(D) the beam has too many side lobes

37. The phased array sector scanner and the linear array share common beam forming properties of (1) a stationary beam at each line of sight, (2) increased grating lobes with beam steering, (3) three dimensional dynamic focusing on receive, (4) the same aperture sizes for dynamic focusing.
(A) 1 and 2
(B) 1, 2, and 4
(C) 2, 3, and 4
(D) all of the above

38. Color flow imaging and angiodynography in the peripheral vascular system typically use
(A) the phased sector scan
(B) the linear array scan
(C) the curved linear scan
(D) a combination of A and B

39. Color flow imaging in the heart typically uses
(A) the phased sector scan
(B) the linear array scan
(C) the curved linear scan
(D) a combination of A and C

40. You are imaging a small vessel using 7.5 MHz color flow imaging with the lowest portrayable velocity of 6.0 cm/s. Changing only the carrier frequency to 5.0 MHz will change the lowest portrayable velocity to

(A) 1.5 cm/s
(B) 9 cm/s
(C) 6.0 cm/s; the vessel does not change
(D) 15 cm/s

41. Color flow imaging is unique because it does not have a major problem with high-frequency aliasing.

(A) true
(B) false

42. Both the color and a point spectrum in a stenosis show high-frequency aliasing. One strategy for removing the aliasing involves

(A) doing nothing. Aliasing cannot be removed from the system
(B) decreasing the system PRF
(C) decreasing the carrier frequency
(D) decreasing the Doppler angle toward zero

43. Increasing output power levels and PRFs to increase penetration and frame rates opens the system to the following artifact:

(A) high-frequency aliasing
(B) loss of low velocities
(C) tissue mirroring
(D) range ambiguity

44. The color coding of red arteries and blue veins and the slow high-resolution frame rates make the identity of arteries and veins in the abdomen direct and easy.

(A) true
(B) false

45. Turbulence in a vascular color flow image appears as

(A) a mottled pattern of colors
(B) a mottled pattern of red and blue with changing saturations
(C) a mottled green region
(D) A or B

46. Turbulence in a cardiac color flow image appears as

(A) a mottled pattern of colors
(B) a mottled pattern of red and blue with changing saturations
(C) a bright red region
(D) a mottled green region

Answers and Explanations

1. **(D)** All of the above. Color flow images can be used to locate a pulsed Doppler sample volume, as is the case with more conventional duplex imaging. *(5:1241)*

2. **(C)** Stationary tissue in gray scale and moving tissues in color. All moving tissues in a color flow imaging can produce color. Thus, stationary tissues are in gray scale, whereas moving tissues, including blood, are in color. *(3:236)*

3. **(A)** A form of high-resolution color flow imaging. Angiodynography is a form of high-resolution color flow imaging. It uses one-wavelength sampling intervals along each image line of sight. *(3:236, 5:1241, 9:27)*

4. **(C)** To all waves coming from a moving wave source. The Doppler effect happens to all waves coming from a moving source regardless of propagating velocity or power levels. *(12:172)*

5. **(B)** The closing velocity between transducer and tissue, carrier frequency, and ultrasound propagation velocity. The Doppler equation looks like the following,

$$Df = 2\ (f_o/c)\ V \cos \theta,$$

where f_o is the carrier frequency, c is the propagation velocity, and θ is the Doppler angle. $V \cos \theta$ is the closing velocity between the transducer and moving tissue. *(12:173)*

6. **(D)** Place a sample volume in the major streamline or jet and set the angle correction parallel to the streamline. Because the color pattern shows the location of the major streamline or jet, calculating velocity requires correction relative to the flow geometry, not the vessel. *(12:195)*

7. **(B)** One wavelength or less. This is necessary for textural information to reach the display in a digital scan converter. *(7:654)*

8. **(C)** One wavelength or more but less 1 mm. Digital sampling for vascular flow information requires such an interval because larger intervals cannot show the flow patterns within the vessel. *(3:236)*

9. **(C)** The product of transmit and receive focusing. The effective beam width results from the mathematical product of both functions. *(13:155, 11:620)*

10. **(A)** True. The sample volume and flow interact in a manner that depends on the geometry of the sample volume. *(8:9)*

11. **(C)** The average Doppler shift frequency. At each sample site, the color flow system determines the average Doppler shift frequency. *(3:236)*

12. **(B)** False. At each sample site, the system determines the average Doppler shift frequency. The display is then either these average frequencies or, in some cases, the calculated closing velocity. This velocity is the rate at which the flow is approaching or moving away from the transducer along the line of sight. *(3:236)*

13. **(D)** The relationship between the amplitudes and frequencies of the Doppler signals. The system will then avoid coloring strong slow-moving echo sources (tissue) but still color moderately fast weak echo sources (blood). *(15:647)*

14. **(B)** The vessel is open, but the blood velocity is too low to complete the image. As the vessel curves away from the beam, the Doppler frequencies become too low to be portrayed. The completeness of the image depends on the velocity of the blood flow, which is too slow for complete portrayal. *(2:19, 44)*

15. **(D)** The smaller vessels do not reflect ultrasound as well as the larger vessels do. Every living cell in the body is no more than two cell layers away from a red blood cell. The smaller vessels, however, are not sufficiently echogenic and vanish from the color display first because of their small echo signals. *(8:7)*

16. **(D)** 1, 2, and 3. Color provides information about the existence of flow, its location in the image, its location in the anatomy, the direction of the flow relative to the transducer, the direction of flow within the vessel, the flow pattern within the vessel, and the pulsatility of the flow. It does not indicate the velocity of the flow. *(5:1245)*

17. **(D)** Changes in echo signal phase. Like all directional Doppler systems, color flow systems detect the existence of motion with a change in echo signal phase. By measuring the direction of the phase change, the system shows whether the direction of motion is toward or away from the transducer. *(8:34)*

18. **(B)** Knowing the position of the scan plane on the patient's body. The expected flow pattern in any vessel comes from knowing how the scan plane is positioned on the patient. For example, the patient's head is always placed on the image left in long axis scans, and the patient's right side is on the image left in cross sectional scans. *(12:407)*

19. **(D)** Different colors (hues) *or* different levels of saturation (purity). The average frequency within each Doppler sample site is portrayed as a change in either color saturation (purity or whiteness) or hue (color). The object is to use the color to show flow patterns within the vessel lumen or heart chambers. *(2:44)*

20. **(B)** Changes in saturation. The angiodynogram uses only color saturation to show the average changes in Doppler shift frequency in each sampling site. *(3:236, 9:27)*

21. **(A)** Changes in color. Cardiac systems change color hues (frequencies) along red and blue lines to show changes in Doppler shift frequencies. Broadening frequencies in a sample site become shades of green. *(2:44)*

22. **(B)** False. Because only one frequency can come to the screen for each Doppler image pixel, all current systems use some estimate of the mean frequency. *(3:236)*

23. **(B)** False. Because color uses the average frequency at each location, the maximum systolic frequency will always be greater than the mean value. *(3:236, 9:27, 10:591)*

24. **(A)** True. Because synchronous signal processing uses the same echo signal for both Doppler and gray-scale signal processing, the frequency must be the same. *(3:236)*

25. **(B)** False. Asynchronous signal processing can, and often does, use different frequencies for the gray-scale image and the Doppler image. For example, it could image at 5.0 MHz and have a Doppler carrier of 3.0 MHz. *(3:236)*

26. **(A)** A Doppler angle to typical blood flow. All Doppler imaging requires a Doppler angle. In asynchronous systems that do not use a wedge, the angle comes from beam steering. *(12:173)*

27. **(D)** A Doppler angle between the typical flow patterns in vessels. Synchronous systems that keep the beams perpendicular to the transducer array (angiodynography) use a mechanical wedge to obtain the Doppler angle to the flow pattern of the vessel. *(9:27, 3:236)*

28. **(D)** Blood reflectivity is about 40 dB to 60 dB below that of soft tissue. The fact that blood reflectivity is about 1/100th to 1/1000th that of soft tissues translates into reflectivities that are much lower than those of soft tissues. *(8:18)*

29. **(A)** True. Because the reflectivity of blood is low, many color flow systems improve color penetration by greatly increasing the power of the transmitted Doppler output. *(3:236)*

30. **(B)** False. Synchronous signal processing systems are limited by the power levels of the common transmitter used for both gray-scale imaging and Doppler imaging. As a result, imaging with and without Doppler produces similar power levels. *(3:236, 9:27)*

31. **(A)** True. The single-point spectrum requires the ultrasound beam to linger over its position longer than is the case in either real-time gray-scale imaging or color flow imaging. *(3:236, 9:27)*

32. **(A)** Decrease. Color flow imaging requires dwelling on each line of sight for as few as 4 pulse–listen cycles to as many as 32 pulse–listen cycles. Various systems have different dwell times. The end result is a reduction in image frame rate for color flow imaging. *(3:236)*

33. **(A)** True. Real-time color flow imaging of the heart requires relatively high frame rates. In general, Doppler requires dwelling on each line of sight for some period of time. In addition, each Doppler sample site requires processing time to extract the average Doppler shift frequency. Restoring suitable cardiac frame rates requires decreasing the number of color flow lines of sight and the number of samples along each line. *(12:17, 9:27)*

34. **(B)** False. Cardiac color flow imaging does not work well for vascular imaging because the Doppler sampling intervals are too large. Imaging the heart also

involves a problem with reflectivities, not with tissue attenuation. *(3:236)*

35. **(B)** False. Doppler sampling for vascular imaging may be well below intervals of 1 mm. In contrast, sampling for echocardiography may be at 7 mm to 10 mm intervals or more. *(2:17)*

36. **(B)** The ultrasound beams are always moving. This is the case because mechanical systems lack a special motor that could move the beam in small steps. Because Doppler signal processing is keyed to relative movement and the beam is always moving, color does not work well in mechanical systems. *(2:17)*

37. **(A)** 1 and 2. The linear phased array and the phased linear array have stationary ultrasound beams at each line of sight in the scanning plane. Both arrays also have increased grating lobes with beam steering. They do not have three-dimensional dynamic focusing or apertures of the same size. *(9:27, 2:21)*

38. **(B)** The linear array scan. The linear array with a rectangular scanning field is the geometry used for vascular imaging. The sector-scanning geometry makes reading color ambiguous in the straighter segments of a vessel. *(2:44)*

39. **(D)** A combination of A and C. Color flow imaging of the heart uses the phased-array sector scan and the curved linear-array sector scan. These scanheads permit cardiac imaging from intercostal and subcostal windows. *(2:41)*

40. **(B)** Nine cm/s. Lowering the Doppler carrier frequency means that the same Doppler shift frequency requires a higher velocity. *(13:280)*

41. **(B)** False. Like all pulsed Doppler systems, color systems will alias when the Doppler frequencies exceed the PRF sampling limit. *(8:37)*

42. **(C)** Decreasing the carrier frequency. This moves all Doppler frequencies downward and may bring the high aliasing frequencies below the aliasing limit. *(12:192)*

43. **(D)** Range ambiguity. High frame rates (high PRFs) and high output power permit structures from outside the field of view to enter the image as a range ambiguity artifact. *(14:83)*

44. **(B)** False. The large fields of view for abdominal imaging slow the frame rate. In addition, vessel anatomy goes in all directions. Sorting out arteries and veins requires the spectrum to determine pulsatility. *(10:591)*

45. **(D)** A or B. In vascular color flow imaging, turbulence appears as broken streamlines. The image then takes on a mottled appearance either in color or in color saturation. *(10:591)*

46. **(D)** A mottled green region. In color flow echocardiography, the sampling intervals are too large to show turbulence. As a result, the system determines the spectral variance at each sampling site and expresses increased turbulence (increased variance) in green. *(2:12)*

REFERENCES

1. Fish PJ. Multichannel, direction resolving Doppler angiography. *Abstracts of 2nd European Congress of Ultrasonics in Medicine,* **72,** 1975.
2. Omoto R, ed. *Color Atlas of Real-Time Two-Dimensional Doppler Echocardiography.* Tokyo: Shindan-To-Chiryo, 1984.
3. Powis RL. Color flow imaging: understanding its science and technology. *JDMS* **4:**236–245, 1988.
4. Burns PN. *Instrumentation and clinical interpretation of the Doppler spectrum: carotid and deep Doppler.* In *Conventional & Color-Flow Duplex Ultrasound Course.* AIUM Spring Education Meeting, 29–38, 1989.
5. Persson AV, Powis RL. Recent advances in imaging and evaluation of blood flow using ultrasound. *Med Clin North Am* **70:**1241–1252, 1986.
6. Powis RL. Angiodynography: a new real-time look at the vascular system. *Applied Radiol* **January/February,** 1986.
7. Ophir J, Maklad NF. Digital scan converters in diagnostic ultrasound imaging. *Proc IEEE* **67:**654–664, 1979.
8. Atkinson P, Woodcock JP. *Doppler Ultrasound and Its Use in Clinical Measurement.* New York: Academic Press, 1982.
9. Powis RL. Color flow imaging technology. In *Basic Science of Flow Measurement.* Syllabus AIUM 1989 Spring Education Meeting, 27–33, 1989.
10. Merritt RBC. Doppler color flow imaging. *J Color Ultrasonography* **15:**591–597, 1987.
11. Havlice JF, Taenzer JC. Medical ultrasonic imaging: an overview of principles and instrumentation. *Proc IEEE* **67:**620–641, 1979.
12. Powis RL, Powis WJ. *A Thinker's Guide to Ultrasonic Imaging.* Baltimore: Urban & Schwarzenberg, 1984.
13. McDicken WN. *Diagnostic Ultrasonics: Principles and Use of Instruments,* 2nd ed. New York: John Wiley & Sons, 1981.
14. Goldstein A. Range Ambiguities in Real-Time Ultrasound. 9:83–90, 1981.
15. Middleton WD, Erickson S, Melson GL. Perivascular color artifact: pathologic significance and appearance on color Doppler US images. *Radiology* **171:**647–652, 1989.

CHAPTER 3

ADULT ECHOCARDIOGRAPHY

Henny Wasser Rudansky and Mark N. Allen

Study Guide

Echocardiography has evolved into a highly specialized field of ultrasound. It serves as an ideal noninvasive method to examine cardiac anatomy in the normal as well as the disease state. In addition, echocardiography provides valuable hemodynamic information regarding cardiac physiology. The combination of anatomical and functional information provided by echocardiography makes it the diagnostic technique of choice in a variety of clinical situations.

The heart is an extremely complex organ. Echocardiography provides a variety of techniques that can be applied to obtain moderately comprehensive information about a very dynamic organ. When performing an echocardiographic examination, it is important to consider not only the two-dimensional imaging information but also the Doppler findings. Both techniques should be performed as an integral part of an echocardiographic examination and should be used to complement one another.

Throughout this chapter M-mode, two-dimensional, and Doppler findings are discussed in each of the normal as well as abnormal conditions. The chapter begins by providing a description of Doppler echocardiography and its physical properties. The rest of the chapter combines these various techniques in a manner similar to that which should be done during an actual examination.

DOPPLER ECHOCARDIOGRAPHY

The Doppler effect was first described in 1842 by Christian Johann Doppler. Its basic principle states that as the source of sound moves toward one's ear, the frequency of that sound increases and the wavelength decreases. This is why a sound source moving toward you increases in loudness and decreases in loudness as it moves away from you. Doppler echocardiography allows quantification of blood flow velocities and direction of blood flow. It is the study of sound-wave reflections from blood cells as they course through the heart. To record these reflections, the sound beam must be parallel to blood flow. This is the opposite of imaging techniques in which the ideal position is perpendicular to the target. Three basic Doppler modalities are available: pulsed-wave, of which color flow mapping is one variation; continuous-wave; and high-pulsed repetition-frequency Doppler.

In pulsed-wave Doppler, a burst of sound waves is produced by electronically stimulating the piezoelectric crystal in the head of the transducer. Because short periods of time elapse between bursts of sound, reflected signals are allowed to return to the transducer. Thus, the time required to send the original signal and to receive can be determined. Given that the speed of sound in soft tissue also is known (1540 m/s), the depth of the target can then be calculated. The area under examination is called the sample volume. Therefore, the principal advantage of pulsed-wave Doppler is the ability to examine flow in one particular area at a given point in time while ignoring flow in other areas. Its major disadvantage is the inability to measure high velocities. Once flow reaches a particular velocity or frequency known as the Nyquist limit, a phenomenon called aliasing occurs. In this case, the Doppler signal appears to be ambiguous and the peak of the signal is not seen. The pulses are sent at a particular frequency, which is a physical characteristic of the machine known as the pulse repetition frequency or PRF. Sound frequencies received are measured if they fall within the PRF of the machine. Received sound frequencies outside the PRF are not well recorded and appear ambiguous.

When color encoding is used, blood flow is assigned colors according to the direction in which the blood is moving. Red indicates blood flowing toward the transducer, whereas blue indicates blood flowing away from the transducer.

Continuous-wave Doppler uses two separate crystals. One crystal transmits the signal; the other receives the incoming signals. The major advantage of continuous-wave Doppler is that peak velocities can be measured.

Aliasing is not a problem because a high pulse-repetition frequency is used. The major disadvantage is the inability to localize specific origins of the signals. Because they are continuously being sent and received, signals all along the path of the beam path are present.

The Doppler equation demonstrates the mathematical relationship between the velocity of the target (blood cells in the case of cardiac examinations) and the Doppler frequency.

$$f_d = f_r - f_t$$

$$f_d = \frac{2f_t V \cdot \cos\theta}{c}$$

where f_d = the Doppler frequency, f_t = the transmitted frequency, f_r = the received frequency, V = the velocity of blood cells, c = the speed of sound waves in a medium, and cos θ = cosine of the angle between the direction of the moving target and the path of the ultrasound beam.

The ideal angle is 0°. However, an angle of less than 20° will give a frequency shift. Angles greater than 20° will not yield good results.

Two basic types of blood-flow patterns exist within the heart. Laminar flow is the normal condition in which the blood cells are moving in a uniform direction and at a relatively uniform velocity. Cells traveling in the center of the vessel typically move slightly faster, whereas blood cells near the walls move slightly more slowly because of friction. The resulting Doppler signal is a well-defined spectral display.

The second type of flow pattern seen in the heart is turbulent flow. This is observed in narrowed or obstructed valves (stenosis), regurgitation, ventricular septal defect, and several other pathological conditions that are discussed in this chapter. In these conditions, blood cells no longer travel in a uniform direction; instead, they may travel in the opposite direction as they encounter an obstruction. The blood swirls much like water does when it encounters a dam. The modified or simplified Bernoulli equation can be used to calculate the pressure drop across the obstruction:

$$\Delta P = 4V^2,$$

where V is the velocity of blood flow distal to the obstruction and ΔP is the pressure drop across the obstruction.

The pressure half-time formula is useful for quantifying the degree of stenosis of the mitral valve. The theory behind this formula is that the time required for the peak velocity to be reduced by half is related to the degree of mitral stenosis. The formula is relatively simple and yields accurate results. The peak velocity is either divided by the square root of 1.4 or multiplied by 0.7. The time taken from the peak velocity to that value is the pressure half-time. The pressure half-time is then divided into the empirically derived number of 220. The resulting value is the area of the mitral valve.

ANATOMY AND PHYSIOLOGY OF THE HEART

In order to become proficient in the techniques of echocardiography, a thorough understanding of cardiac anatomy is essential. One must know the normal structures and be able to recognize normal variants from pathological states. There are numerous pathologies that affect the heart in the adult. These disease states can cause a variety of primary as well as secondary anatomical changes in the heart. Knowing what these changes are greatly enhances the echocardiographic examination. Once the student has an understanding of heart anatomy, the echocardiographic images are better understood. The basic two-dimensional echocardiographic views are illustrated in Figs. 3–1 through 3–8. These figures are from the American Society of Echocardiography and are the accepted nomenclature for two-dimensional imaging.

Left Ventricle

Anatomy. The left ventricle is the largest cardiac chamber, accounting for 75% of heart mass. It consists of two papillary muscles, has trabeculations in the apex, and a smooth-walled basal area. Its end-diastolic diameter is 3.6–5.2 cm, and its end-systolic diameter is 2.3–3.9 cm. The thickness of its wall in diastole measures 6–12 mm.

Hemodynamics. The ventricle receives oxygenated blood from the left atrium and pumps it through the aortic valve to the body by way of arteries, arterioles, and capillaries. Its systolic pressure is 100–120 mm Hg.

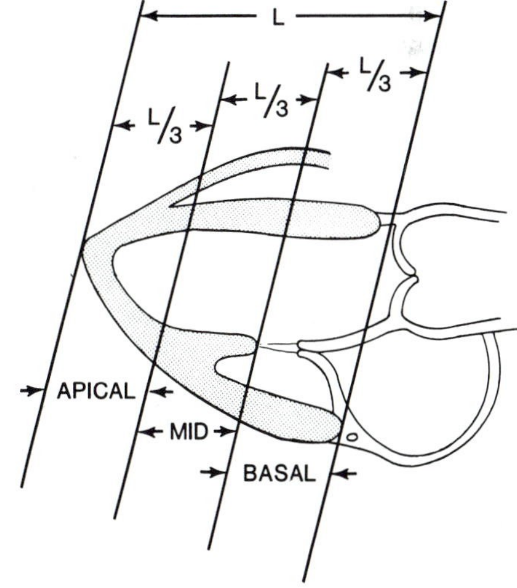

Figure 3–1. Parasternal long-axis view of the heart demonstrating the method of subdividing the myocardial walls along the long axis (L) into three regions of equal length using the left ventricular papillary muscles as landmarks. *(Reprinted with permission from the American Society of Echocardiography. Report of the ASE Committee on Nomenclature and Standards: Identification of Myocardial Wall Segments, November 1982.)*

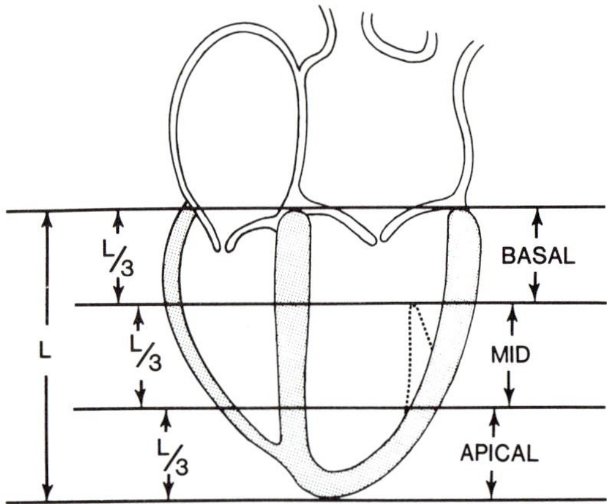

Figure 3–2. Apical four-chamber view of the heart demonstrating the method of subdividing the myocardial walls into three regions using the left ventricular papillary muscles as landmarks. (*Reprinted with permission from the American Society of Echocardiography. Report of the ASE Committee on Nomenclature and Standards: Identification of Myocardial Wall Segments, November 1982.*)

Echocardiographic Views. Almost all the standard views of the left ventricle allow visualization of at least part of the left ventricle. The apical views allow examination of the apex, which can be difficult to see in other views. The maximum internal dimensions are seen at end-diastole and should be measured at the onset of the QRS complex. The minimum internal dimensions are seen at end-systole and should be taken at the peak posterior motion of the interventricular septum.

Left Atrium

Anatomy. The left atrium is a smooth-walled sac, the walls of which are thicker than those of the right atrium.

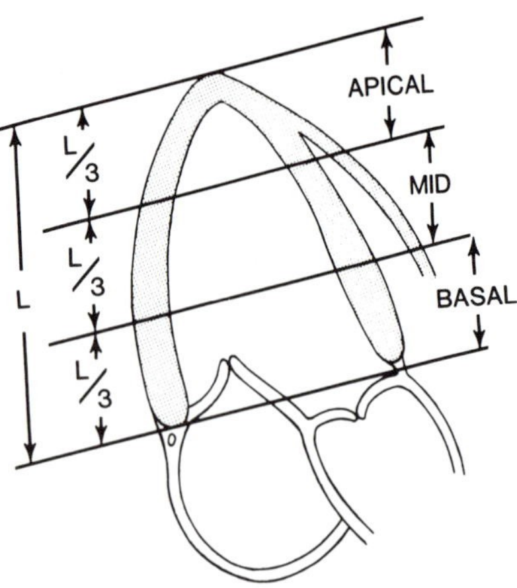

Figure 3–3. Apical long-axis view of the heart demonstrating the method of subdividing the myocardial walls into three regions of equal length. (*Reprinted with permission from the American Society of Echocardiography. Report of the ASE Committee on Nomenclature and Standards: Identification of Myocardial Wall Segments, November 1982.*)

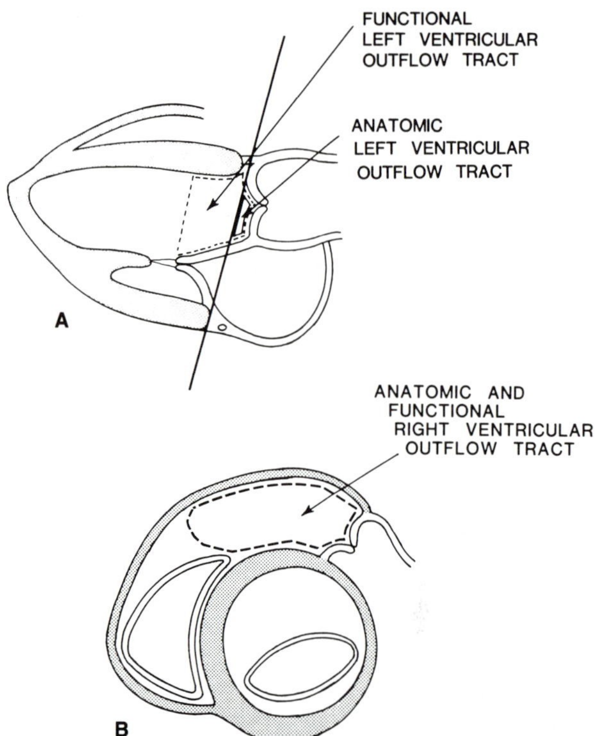

Figure 3–4. The functional and anatomic left ventricular outflow tracts of the heart are diagrammed in the upper panel (**A**), whereas the functional and anatomic right ventricular outflow tract is illustrated in the bottom panel (**B**). (*Reprinted with permission from the American Society of Echocardiography. Report of the ASE Committee on Nomenclature and Standards: Identification of Myocardial Wall Segments, November 1982.*)

The chamber receives four pulmonary veins: two (sometimes three) on the right and two (sometimes one) on the left. The interatrial septum is thin. The left auricle, or left atrial appendage, arises from the upper anterior part of the left atrium and contains small pectinate muscles. The average dimension of the chamber in the adult is 28–38 mm.

Hemodynamics. The mean pressure in the left atrium ranges from 1 mm Hg to 10 mm Hg. Oxygenated blood flows from the lungs and enters the atrium through the pulmonary veins. As left atrial pressure increases over that of the left ventricle, the mitral valve opens and blood then passes through the mitral valve and enters the left ventricle.

Echocardiographic Views. Maximal dimensions should be measured at end-systole. Measurements should be made from the leading edge of the posterior wall of the aorta to the leading edge of the posterior wall of the left atrium. This chamber is best seen from the parasternal long- and short-axis views; however, it also can be seen from the apical and subcostal views. In the left parasternal long-axis view, the descending aorta can be seen running posteriorly to the left atrium. Care must be given when

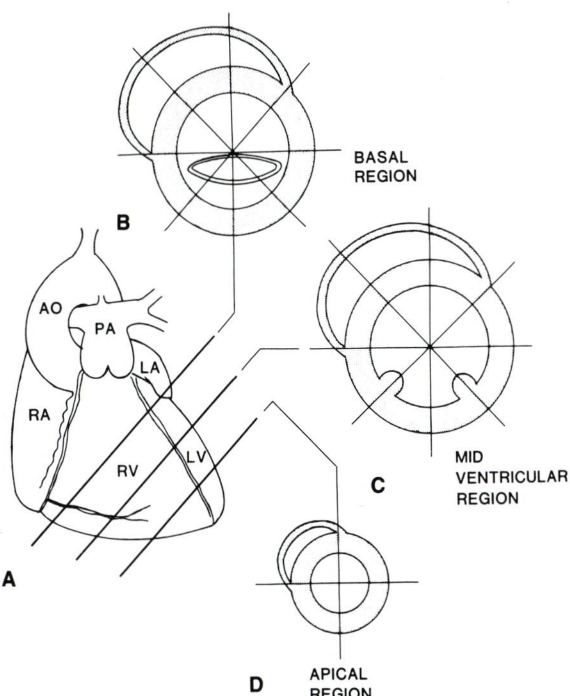

Figure 3–5. Diagram of the heart (**A**) and the short-axis views of the basal region (**B**), midventricular region (**C**), and apical region (**D**). (*Reprinted with permission from the American Society of Echocardiography. Report of the ASE Committee on Nomenclature and Standards: Identification of Myocardial Wall Segments, November 1982.*)

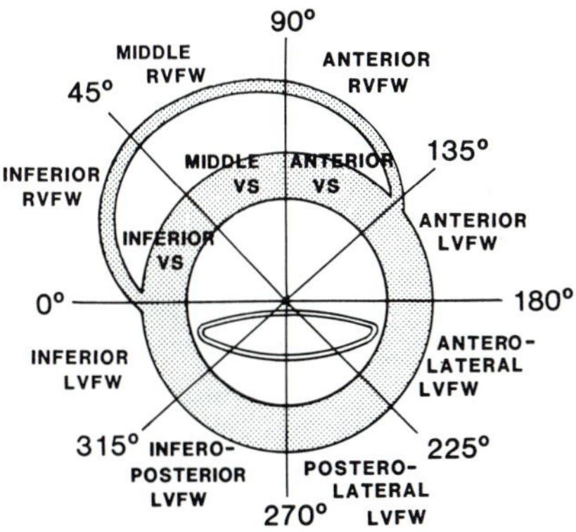

Figure 3–6. Short-axis view of the basal region of the heart demonstrating the method of subdividing the myocardial walls into segments using a coordinate system consisting of eight lines that are 45° apart. With this system, the left ventricular free wall (LVFW) is divided into five segments, whereas the ventricular septum (VS) and right ventricular free walls (RVFW) are subdivided into three segments each. (*Reprinted with permission from the American Society of Echocardiography. Report of the ASE Committee on Nomenclature and Standards: Identification of Myocardial Wall Segments, November 1982.*)

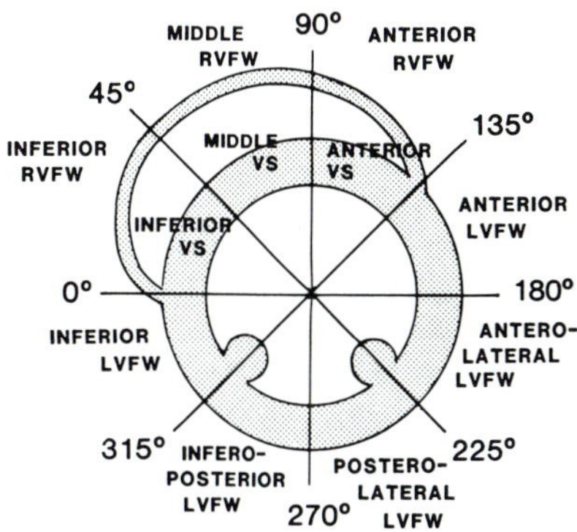

Figure 3–7. Short-axis view of the midventricular region of the heart demonstrating the method of subdividing the myocardial walls into segments using a coordinate system consisting of eight lines that are 45° apart. With this system, the left ventricular free wall (LVFW) is divided into five segments, whereas the ventricular septum (VS) and right ventricular free walls (RVFW) are subdivided into three segments each. (*Reprinted with permission from the American Society of Echocardiography. Report of the ASE Committee on Nomenclature and Standards: Identification of Myocardial Wall Segments, November 1982.*)

measuring the diameter of the left atrium so that the descending aorta is not included in the measurement because this will give an erroneous left atrial diameter.

Right Atrium

Anatomy. The right atrium has two parts: an anterior portion and a posterior portion. The two portions are separated by a ridge of muscle called the crista terminalis.

The smooth-walled posterior portion of the atrium is derived from the embryonic sinus venosus and receives the inferior and superior vena cavae. Guarding the opening (ostium) of the inferior vena cava is a thin fold of tissue called the eustachian valve, which is sometimes

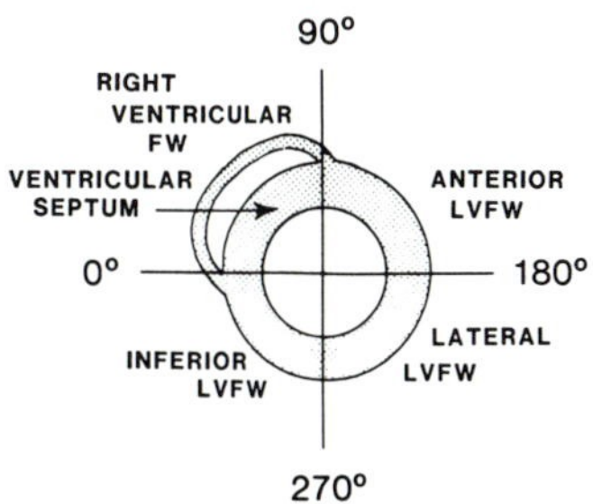

Figure 3–8. Short-axis view of the apical region of the heart demonstrating the method of subdividing the myocardial walls into segments using a coordinate system consisting of four lines that are 90° apart. With this system, the left ventricular free wall (LVFW) is subdivided into three segments, whereas the ventricular septum and right ventricular free wall (FW) are subdivided into one segment each. (*Reprinted with permission from the American Society of Echocardiography. Report of the ASE Committee on Nomenclature and Standards: Identification of Myocardial Wall Segments, November 1982.*)

large and complex and forms a network of tissues known as the network of Chiari. The coronary sinus also enters the right atrium anterior to the inferior vena cava. The coronary sinus also can be guarded by a thin fold of tissue called the thebesian valve.

The anterior portion, which represents the embryonic right atrium, is extremely thin and is trabeculated. The right atrial appendage, or right auricle, arises from the superior portion of the right atrium and contains pectinate muscle. The dimensions of the right atrium in adults range from 26–34 mm.

Hemodynamics. Deoxygenated blood from the body, head, and heart flows into the right atrium through the inferior vena cava, the superior vena cava, and the coronary sinus, respectively. When pressures in the right atrium increase above the pressures in the right ventricle, the tricuspid valve opens, allowing the blood to flow forward into the right ventricle. Mean pressures in this chamber range from 0–8 mm Hg.

Echocardiographic Views. Apical views are best for assessing the right atrium. Others include the subcostal and, to a lesser extent, the parasternal short-axis views.

Right Ventricle

Anatomy. The right ventricle is divided into a posterior inferior inflow portion and an anterior superior outflow portion. The inflow portion contains the tricuspid valve and is heavily trabeculated. The outflow portion, also called the infundibulum, gives rise to the pulmonary trunk. The subpulmonic area is smooth walled.

The right ventricle contains numerous papillary muscles that anchor the tricuspid valve. The ventricle contains numerous bands of muscle. One band, the moderator band, is readily seen in the apex of the ventricle by two-dimensional imaging. Internal diameters range from 7–26 mm.

Hemodynamics. Systolic pressures range from 15–30 mm Hg, and diastolic pressures range from 0–8 mm Hg.

Echocardiographic Views. The right ventricle is seen best from the apical and subcostal views. It also can be seen from the parasternal views.

Aorta

Anatomy. The aorta arises from the base of the heart and enters the superior mediastinum, where it almost reaches the sternum, then courses obliquely backward and to the left over the left bronchus. It then becomes the descending aorta and courses downward anterior to and slightly left of the vertebral column. The aorta is highly elastic and has three layers: (1) a thin inner layer called the tunica intima, (2) a thick middle layer called the tunica media, and (3) a thin outer layer called the tunica adventia. The diameter of the aortic root measures 2.5–3.3 cm.

Hemodynamics. Maximal velocities of blood flow in adults are 1.0–1.7 m/s.

Echocardiographic Views. The aortic root is seen from parasternal views. The ascending aorta, aortic arch, and descending aorta can be seen from the suprasternal view. As was mentioned earlier, part of the descending aorta also can be seen behind the left atrium in the long-axis view. The subcostal views allows visualization of the aortic root and valve.

Main Pulmonary Artery

Anatomy. The main pulmonary artery is located superior to and originates from the right ventricle. Immediately after leaving the pericardium, it bifurcates into a right pulmonary artery and a left pulmonary artery that enter the right and left lung, respectively.

Hemodynamics. This artery delivers deoxygenated blood from the right ventricle to the lungs. Flow velocities range from 0.6–0.9 m/s.

Echocardiographic Views. The artery is seen best from the parasternal short-axis view.

Mitral Valve

Anatomy. The mitral valve is an atrioventricular valve. It is located between the left atrium and left ventricle, is a thin yellowish-white membrane that originates at the annulus fibrous, a fibrous ring that surrounds the orifice of the valve. The valve has an anterior leaflet and a posterior leaflet, both of which have sawtoothlike edges. Both leaflets are attached to papillary muscles by cordae tendinae. The surface on the atrial side of the valve is smooth whereas the surface on the ventricular side is irregular.

Hemodynamics. Flow velocities across the valve range from 0.6–1.3 m/s. The valve's function is to prevent backflow of blood from the left ventricle into the left atrium.

Echocardiographic Views. The mitral valve is seen best from the long- and short-axis parasternal views and the apical view. Doppler measurements are obtained best from the apical four- and two-chamber views.

Aortic Valve

Anatomy. The aortic valve consists of three pocket-shaped thin smooth cusps named according to their location in relation to the coronary arteries. The cusp near the left coronary artery is the left coronary cusp, the cusp near the right coronary artery is the right coronary cusp, and the cusp that is not near a coronary artery is the noncoronary cusp. Because of its lunar or half-moon shape, the aortic valve is referred to as semilunar.

Hemodynamics. The function of the aortic valve is to prevent backflow of blood from the aorta into the left ventricle. The velocity of flow ranges from 1.0–1.7 m/s.

Echocardiographic Views. The valve is seen best from the parasternal views. It also can be seen from the apical four-chamber view with anterior angulation. The best Doppler measurements are obtained from the apical four-chamber view with anterior angulation, from the right parasternal window, and from the suprasternal view.

Tricuspid Valve

Anatomy. The tricuspid valve is an atrioventricular valve. It is located between the right atrium and ventricle. The atrial side is smooth; the ventricular side is irregular. Like the mitral valve, it is a thin yellowish-white membrane that originates at the annulus fibrous, a fibrous ring that surrounds the orifice of the valve. The valve has three leaflets—anterior, posterior, and medial—all of which are sawtoothlike in appearance. Each leaflet is attached to papillary muscles by cordae tendinae.

Hemodynamics. The function of this valve is to prevent backflow of blood from the right ventricle to the right atrium. The velocity of flow ranges from 0.3–0.7 m/s.

Echocardiographic Views. The valve is seen best from the parasternal short-axis and apical four-chamber views. The subcostal view also affords a good look. The best Doppler measurements are taken from the parasternal short-axis and apical four-chamber views.

Pulmonic Valve

Anatomy. The pulmonic valve consists of three thin smooth pocket-shaped cusps. Because of its shape, this valve, like the aortic valve, is called semilunar.

Hemodynamics. The function of this valve is to prevent backflow of blood from the main pulmonary artery to the right ventricle. The velocity of flow ranges from 0.6–0.9 m/s.

Echocardiographic Views. The pulmonic valve is seen best from the parasternal short-axis view. The best Doppler recordings are taken from the left parasternal short axis.

DISEASES AFFECTING THE VALVES

Mitral Valve Disease

Stenosis. Mitral valve stenosis results primarily from rheumatic disease. The valves may not become involved for many decades following rheumatic fever. Congenital mitral stenosis can occur but is extremely rare.

M-mode findings include (1) a flattened E-F slope (reduced diastolic filling), (2) anterior motion of the posterior leaflet, (3) thickened leaflets, and (4) an absent A wave in the absence of atrial fibrillation. Two-dimensional imaging also indicates thickening and shows doming of the leaflets in diastole.

Doppler measurements reveal a reduced rate of decrease in diastolic flow (reduced diastolic slope), a higher-than-normal peak velocity of flow, and spectral broadening on Doppler display. Secondary findings and complications include left atrial dilatation, pulmonary hypertension, a left atrial clot, and an exaggerated diastolic dip of the interventricular septum.

Regurgitation. Mitral regurgitation can occur as a result of mitral annular calcification, rheumatic mitral disease, flail mitral valve leaflet, conditions that may stretch the mitral annulus such as cardiomyopathies, myocardial infarction, mitral valve vegetations or other masses on the mitral valve or within the left atrium, papillary dysfunction, and mitral valve prolapse.

M-mode findings include (1) increased size of the left atrium, (2) exaggerated motion of the interventricular septum, (3) pulsations of the left atrial wall, and (4) preclosure of the aortic valve during systole. The first three findings are the result of volume overload.

Two-dimensional imaging reveals an increase in the size of the left atrium and exaggerated motion of the interventricular septum—all of which are the result of volume overload. In addition, pulsations of the left atrial wall and preclosure of the aortic valve during systole are observed.

Prolapse. The classic clinical findings in mitral valve prolapse are a systolic click (a sound that corresponds with the posterior displacement of the mitral valve leaflet into the left atrium) and a late systolic murmur (a sound that corresponds with the resulting mitral regurgitation that often occurs because of the prolapsing leaflets).

M-mode findings include late systolic posterior displacement of the anterior and posterior leaflets and anterior motion of the mitral valve in early systole. To achieve the best views for making the diagnosis, the ultrasound beam should be perpendicular to the valve from the parasternal windows. The two-dimensional findings reveal that the valve is bowing into the left atrium and, in many cases, thickened.

Flail Leaflet. The most common cause of flail leaflet is rupture of the chordae tendineae, which often occurs secondary to myocardial infarction. Rupture of papillary muscle is a less common etiology.

M-mode findings indicate coarse diastolic fluttering and systolic fluttering of the leaflet and visualization of part of the leaflet in the left atrium. Two-dimensional imaging indicates protrusion of the flail leaflet into the left atrium, noncoaptation of the two leaflets, and systolic and coarse diastolic motion of the flail leaflet. Doppler measurements indicate harsh, turbulent mitral regurgitation.

Annular Calcification. Mitral annular calcification results from the deposition of calcium in the annulus of the mitral valve. This is normally associated with aging. This condition can be caused by mitral regurgitation, conduction abnormalities, aging, or obstruction of the left ventricular outflow tract (LVOF).

M-mode findings reveal high-density echoes between the valve and the posterior wall of the left ventricle. Two-dimensional imaging reveals high-density bright echoes between the valve and the posterior wall of the left ventricle.

Aortic Valve Disease

Stenosis (versus Sclerosis). The cause of stenosis of the aortic valve can be congenital, the result of rheumatic heart disease, or degeneration. The effect is hypertrophy of the left ventricular walls.

M-mode findings indicate thickened cusps and restricted excursion of the cusps to less than 1.5 cm. Two-dimensional imaging not only reveals these M-mode findings but systolic doming of the cusps (the most important sign) as well. Doppler measurements reveal high-velocity jets greater than 1.7 m/s.

Regurgitation. The effects of regurgitation on atria, ventricles, and cardiac vessels result in dilation of the left ventricle. The condition can be caused by any one of the following: congenital (bicuspid cusp), rheumatic heart disease (the most common cause in adults), degeneration of the leaflet caused by infection, or aortic dilatation (Marfan syndrome).

M-mode findings reveal fluttering of the interventricular septum and diastolic fluttering of the mitral valve. Two-dimensional imaging indicates fine diastolic fluttering of the aortic valve, diastolic fluttering of the mitral valve, and fluttering of the interventricular septum. Spectral Doppler studies reveal diastolic flow, which appears above the baseline when in an apical position.

Tricuspid Valve Diseases

Stenosis. In stenotic disease of the tricuspid valve, the effects on atria, ventricles, and vessels cause dilatation of the right atrium.

M-mode findings indicate a reduced diastolic slope and thickening and decreased separation of the leaflets. Two-dimensional imaging reveals the most specific finding, systolic doming, as well as thickening of the leaflets. In Doppler measurements, the sample is placed in the right ventricle; the results indicate turbulent diastolic flow and slowed reduction in the velocity of flow during diastole.

Regurgitation. The primary cause of regurgitation is secondary to pulmonary hypertension. In rare cases, the condition can be caused by rheumatic heart disease, prolapse of the valve, or carcinoid heart disease. A secondary effect is dilatation of the right atrium and ventricle.

M-mode findings indicate a dilated right ventricle and anterior motion of the interventricular septum during isovolumetric contraction. Two-dimensional imaging reveals incomplete closure and diastolic fluttering of the leaflets, ruptured chordae, dilation of the right ventricle, and flattening of the interventricular septum. With Doppler measurements, turbulent flow can be detected in the right atrium during systole.

Pulmonic Valve Diseases

Stenosis. The causes of pulmonic valve disease are atherosclerosis, infectious endocarditis, and papillary fibroma. This disease is extremely rare in adults.

Regurgitation. M-mode findings reveal fluttering of the tricuspid leaflets, and Doppler measurements reveal early diastolic high-velocity, turbulent flow. The cause can be pulmonary hypertension or bacterial endocarditis or be secondary to pulmonary valvotomy.

Endocarditis

Types. Endocarditis can be caused by either bacteria or vegetation (funguslike growth) and, depending on the infecting organism, is classified as acute or subacute. Although the disease can occur in the endocardium of the heart, the infection usually affects the endocardium in specific valves and is more likely to affect the left heart than the right. Infection of the tricuspid and pulmonic valves is usually the result of intravenous (IV) drug abuse.

Bacterial Endocarditis. Predisposing factors for bacterial endocarditis include dental procedures, tonsilloadenoidectomy, cirrhosis, drug addiction, surgery, and burns.

Nonbacterial Endocarditis. Among the nonbacterial forms of the disease are systemic lupus erythematosus (SLE) and fungal (mycotic), nonbacterial thrombotic, Löffler's, marantic, and Libman-Sacks endocarditis. The most common manifestation of SLE is vegetation. Although this nonbacterial form of endocarditis primarily involves the mitral valve, it also can affect the mural endocardium. The mycotic form of the disease is usually subacute and can be caused by a variety of fungi—most commonly, *Candida, Aspergillus,* and *Histoplasma.* In the thrombotic form of nonbacterial endocarditis, the vegetation consists of fibrin and other blood elements.

Löffler's endocarditis is characterized by a marked increase of eosinophils. It primarily affects men in their forties who live in temperate climates. The disease affects both ventricles equally. Thickening of the inflow portions of the ventricles and the apices can be observed, as can formation of mural thrombi. Hemodynamically, diastolic filling is impaired because of increased stiffness of the heart. Atrioventricular valve regurgitation is a typical finding.

In the marantic form of the disease, the vegetation is nondestructive and sterile. It occurs in patients with malignant tumors and primarily affects the valves on the left

side of the heart. Embolus is the most serious complication.

Libman-Sacks endocarditis is characterized by vegetations or verrucae on the endocardium.

Hemodynamic Mechanisms. One common cause of subacute infectious endocarditis occurs when a high-velocity jet consistently hits a surface. Damage results when blood from a high-pressure area flows to a low-pressure area; this is called the Venturi effect. The site where vegetation has formed will usually be in the low-pressure area. When the mitral valve is involved and mitral regurgitation is present, the atrial side of the leaflets is the susceptible area. In this case, the high-pressure area is the ventricle and, because the mitral leaflets fail to coapt, the low-pressure area is the atrial side of the leaflets. The atrial wall that bears the brunt of the regurgitation also may become infected.

When the aortic valve is involved and aortic insufficiency is present, the aorta is the high-pressure area and the ventricle is the low-pressure area. Vegetations tend to form on the ventricular side of the aortic cusps because the cusps do not close completely in aortic regurgitation. The section of the ventricular wall hit by the regurgitant jet also may be damaged.

In ventricular septal defects (VSDs), the high-pressure area is the left ventricle in left-to-right shunting and the low-pressure area is the right ventricular side of the defect. The right ventricular wall directly across from the defect also can suffer damage and be prone to vegetation.

Echocardiographic Appearance. The presence of a mass on any valve leads to a diagnosis of infection caused by vegetation. However, echocardiography cannot differentiate between a new and old infection. M-mode patterns indicate shaggy echoes on the infected valve and detect 52% of vegetations. The technique of choice is two-dimensional imaging, which detects more than 80% of vegetations, reveals dense echoes on the valve, and often detects mobility of the mass.

Aortic Valve. Vegetation is seen best in diastole and is attached to the ventricular side of the cusps. This condition can cause reduced cardiac output and acute aortic regurgitation. The best views for two-dimensional imaging are the left parasternal long and short axes.

Mitral Valve. Predisposing factors to vegetational infection of the mitral valve include mitral valve prolapse, rheumatic valvulitis, and dysfunction of the papillary muscles with secondary mitral regurgitation and mitral annular calcification. Infection occurs most commonly on the atrial side of the leaflet.

The best views include the left parasternal short and long axes; the apical two- and four-chamber views also can be used. Vegetations as small as 2 mm in diameter are detectable or can be as large as 40 mm in diameter. Whereas M-mode imaging detects 14–65% of the vegetation, two-dimensional imaging detects 43–100%. Differential diagnoses include myomas, lipomas, and fibromas.

Tricuspid or Pulmonic Valve. Infections of the tricuspid or pulmonic valves are usually caused by IV drug abuse. Such infections are less common than left-sided infections; however, when they occur on the tricuspid valve, the infections can become larger than is typical of left-sided infections. They rarely occur on the pulmonic valve.

Prosthetic Valves

Types. Two types of prosthetic valves are available: mechanical and bioprosthetic. The mechanical types are ball-in-cage, disc-in-cage, and tilting-disc valves. The Starr-Edwards valve is the most common ball-in-cage type. The best view for observing excursion of the ball is the apical view when in the mitral and aortic positions. The disc-in-cage valve has less excursion than does the ball-in-cage type. The most common type of tilting-disc valve is the Bjork-Shiley, which consists of one disc that tilts. The less common St. Jude valve contains two tilting discs.

The most common bioprosthetic valve is the xenograft. A porcine heterograft is the most commonly used tissue; porcine pericardial tissue also can be used. Human homografts and facia lata tissue are sometimes used as valves.

Malfunctions. The following factors cause both types of prosthetic valves to malfunction: thrombi, regurgitation, stenosis, dehiscence, and vegetation.

Thrombi. Blood clots, the most common cause of valve malfunction, reduce the effective orifice and impair motion of the ball, disc, or leaflet tissue. Their major complication is the potential for an embolus. Two-dimensional imaging is the echocardiographic technique of choice for detecting the presence of a clot. The limitation of the technique is the masking effect produced by the highly reflective nature of the prosthetic material. Transesophageal echocardiography has proved to be useful for evaluating the formation of clots on prosthetic valves. In the Bjork-Shiley mitral prosthesis, there is a rounding to the E point on M-mode.

Regurgitation. Regurgitation can occur through the valve or around the sewing ring. Doppler echocardiography is the procedure of choice for detecting the problem. When masking is a problem from apical views, color Doppler is especially useful. Color flow Doppler not only allows spatial orientation but also demonstrates the direction of blood jets. Secondary echocardiographic findings for aortic prosthetic regurgitation include (1) fluttering of the mitral valve, (2) fluttering of the interventricular septum, and (3) evidence of volume overload in the left ventricle. Doppler echocardiography also is a procedure of choice for detecting paravalvular leaks with a high degree of sensitivity and specificity. In the Bjork-Shiley mitral valve, an early diastolic bump is noted by M-mode and two-dimensional imaging.

Stenosis. All prosthetic valves have some degree of obstruction. Doppler echocardiography can detect a valve with moderate to severe stenosis.

Dehiscence. In dehiscence, the valve becomes detached from its sewing bed. Disruption of suture lines securing the prosthesis to the sewing ring is usually the cause. The result is severe regurgitation, heart failure, or both, which can be detected by a Doppler examination. Two-dimensional imaging demonstrates an unusual rocking motion away from its normal excursion. Cinefluoroscopy can be helpful in assessing abnormal rocking motion.

Vegetation. As was mentioned earlier, vegetation is difficult to assess with echocardiographic techniques because it is often masked by the highly reflective properties of the prosthesis. These infections are usually found on bioprosthetic valves, are extremely mobile, and are more common in the aortic than the mitral position.

Degeneration. Degeneration is most common in bioprosthetic valves and usually occurs as a result of calcification of the area where the valve is joined to the surrounding tissue.

DISEASES AFFECTING THE PERICARDIUIM

The pericardium is composed of two layers. The inner layer is a serous membrane called the visceral pericardium, which is attached to the surface of the heart. This layer folds back upon itself to form an outer fibrous layer called the parietal pericardium. Between the two layers is the pericardial space, which is filled with a thin layer of fluid throughout. The functions of the pericardium are to (1) fix the heart anatomically, (2) prevent excessive motion during changes in body position, (3) reduce friction between the heart and other organs, (4) provide a barrier against infection, and (5) help maintain hydrostatic forces on the heart. Pericardial disease can be caused by any one of the following: malignant disease that spreads to the pericardium, pericarditis, acute infarction, cardiac perforation during diagnostic procedures, radiation therapy, SLE, or postcardiac surgery.

Effusion

In the normal pericardium, the pressure within the pericardial space is similar to the intrapleural pressure and lower than the right and left ventricular diastolic pressures. Increased intrapericardial pressure depends on three factors: the volume of the effusion, the rate at which fluid accumulates, and the characteristics of the pericardium. The normal intrapericardial space contains 15–50 mL of fluid, and it can tolerate the slow addition of as much as 1 to 2 L of fluid without increasing the intrapericardial pressure. However, if the fluid is added rapidly, the intrapericardial pressure increases dramatically.

Pericardial effusion can be diagnosed using M-mode and two-dimensional techniques. Three diagnostic criteria can be used: (1) posterior echo-free space, (2) obliteration of echo-free space at the left atrioventricular groove, and (3) decreased motion of the posterior pericardial motion.

Cardiac tamponade results when intrapericardial pressures increase. This problem is characterized by increased intracardiac pressures, impaired diastolic filling of the ventricles, and reduced stroke volume. The following echocardiographic findings are associated with cardiac tamponade:

- increased dimensions of the right ventricle during inspiration,
- decreased mitral diastolic slope (E-F),
- decreased end diastolic dimension of the right atrium or ventricle,
- posterior motion of the anterior wall of the right ventricle,
- collapse of the right ventricular free wall,
- diastolic collapse of the right atrial wall, and
- increased flow velocities across the tricuspid and pulmonic valve during inspiration.

Several findings can create a false positive diagnosis of pericardial effusion:

- Epicardial fat located on the anterior wall.
- Misinterpretation of normal cardiac structures such as the descending aorta or coronary sinus.
- Other abnormal cardiac or noncardiac structures.
- Confusion of pleural effusions with pericardial effusions.

Pericardial effusion can be differentiated from pleural effusion in several ways. First, in pericardial effusion, a large amount of fluid can collect posterior to the heart without any anterior collection. Second, a pericardial effusion tapers as it approaches the left atrium; a pleural effusion does not. Third, if both types of effusion occur simultaneously, a thin echogenic line should be noted between the two collections of fluid. And fourth, the descending aorta lies posterior to a pericardial effusion, whereas it lies anterior to a pleural effusion.

Pericarditis

Pericarditis comes in two forms: acute and constrictive. In acute pericarditis, the pericardium is inflamed. This form of the disease has a variety of etiologies: idiopathic causes, viruses, uremia, bacterial infections, acute myocardial infarction, tuberculosis, malignancies, and trauma. Echocardiography reveals thickening of the pericardium, with or without pericardial effusion.

In constrictive disease, the pericardium thickens and restricts diastolic filling of the heart chambers. Like the acute form, it has a variety of causes: tuberculosis, hemodialysis used to treat chronic renal failure, connective tissue disorders (eg, SLE, rheumatoid arthritis), metastatic infiltration, radiation therapy to the mediastinum, fungal or parasitic infections, and complications of surgery. Echocardiographic findings may include

- thickened pericardium,
- flattening of the left ventricular wall in mid and late systole,
- a rapid mitral valve E-F slope,
- exaggerated anterior motion of the interventricular septum,
- mid-diastolic premature opening of the pulmonic valve,
- inspiratory dilatation of hepatic veins and the inferior vena cava, and
- inspiratory leftward motion of the interatrial and interventricular septa.

DISEASES AFFECTING THE MYOCARDIUM

The term cardiomyopathy is used to describe a variety of cardiac diseases that affect the myocardium. Cardiomyopathies have been classified into three categories: (1) hypertrophic, which may or may not obstruct the left ventricular outflow tract, (2) dilated, and (3) restrictive. The classification depends on the anatomical characteristics of the left ventricular cavity as well as systolic-ejection and diastolic-filling properties of the left ventricle.

Hypertrophic Cardiomyopathy

Hypertrophic cardiomyopathy is characterized by concentric or asymmetric left ventricular hypertrophy, which results in an increase in left ventricular mass, with normal or reduced dimensions of the left ventricular cavity. Normal systolic function usually is preserved. Although asymmetric hypertrophy can occur anywhere within the left ventricle, the most common site is the proximal portion of the ventricular septum near the outflow tract. Asymmetric septal hypertrophy can be diagnosed when the ratio of septal thickness to posterior wall thickness is 1.3 to 1. When asymmetric hypertrophy is present obstruction most frequently occurs. Concentric hypertrophy may or may not lead to obstruction. A number of names are used to describe the obstructive forms of cardiomyopathy, including idiopathic hypertrophic subaortic stenosis, muscular subaortic stenosis, asymmetric septal hypertrophy, and hypertrophic obstructive cardiomyopathy.

Several echocardiographic findings, when found in conjunction, are highly specific for the diagnosis of obstructive cardiomyopathy. M-mode and two-dimensional findings include systolic anterior motion of the mitral valve, asymmetric septal hypertrophy, premature mid-systolic closure of the aortic valve, septal hypokinesis, and anterior displacement of the mitral valve. The size of the left ventricle is small to normal. Doppler examination reveals a decreased E wave in mitral flow with an exaggerated A wave. These findings suggest a decrease in diastolic compliance and an increase in left ventricular end diastolic pressures. In aortic flow, there is a midsystolic reduction of velocity. Fifty percent of patients demonstrate regurgitation in the mitral valve. Pulsed-wave Doppler is used to determine the obstructed area.

At rest, systolic anterior motion of the mitral valve may not be demonstrated. Because this motion is a diagnostic indication for this disease, provocative maneuvers are used to bring it out. Such techniques include the Valsalva's maneuver, amyl nitrate, and IV isoproterenol.

Dilated Cardiomyopathy

Dilated cardiomyopathy is characterized by globally reduced systolic function, with an ejection fraction of less than 40%, increased end-systolic and end-diastolic volumes, and, eventually, congestive heart failure. M-mode findings include increased end-diastolic and end-systolic dimensions of the left ventricle, reduced septal and posterior wall excursion, increased E point-to-septal separation, decreased aortic root movement, and a structurally normal aortic valve that opens slowly and drifts closed during systole because of reduced cardiac output. The principal two-dimensional echocardiographic findings include left ventricular dilatation and dysfunction, abnormal closure of the mitral valve, and dilatation of the left atrium. The abnormal closure of the aortic valve also is noted. Mitral regurgitation is a frequent Doppler finding in dilated cardiomyopathy. Hemodynamically, the left ventricle demonstrates signs of increased diastolic pressure in the left ventricle and decreased compliance. The walls of the left ventricle are normal in size. The right heart also may become enlarged as a result of the increased diastolic pressures in the left heart. The most common complication of dilated cardiomyopathy is the formation of thrombi and a potential cardiac source of emboli.

Dilated cardiomyopathies can be the result of a familial or x-linked cardiomyopathy, pregnancy, systemic hypertension, ingestion of toxic agents such as alcohol or other drugs, and a variety of viral infections. They also can be of unknown cause or idiopathic. This form of cardiomyopathy also can be found in severe coronary artery disease.

Restrictive Cardiomyopathy

Restrictive cardiomyopathy falls into two categories: endomyocardial fibrosis and infiltrative myocardial disease, which includes amyloidosis, sarcoidosis, hematochromatosis, Pompe's disease, and Fabry's disease. The characteristic feature of restrictive cardiomyopathy is increased resistance to left ventricular filling. The associated cardiac findings include elevated diastolic pressure in the left ventricle, hypertension and enlargement of the left atrium, and secondary pulmonary hypertension. The echocardiographic features include an increase in the thickness and mass of the left ventricular wall, a small-to-normal sized left ventricular cavity, normal systolic function, and a pericardial effusion. Restrictive cardiomyopathies are most common in East Africa; they account for only 5% of noncoronary cardiomyopathies in the western world.

Endomyocardial fibrosis involves formation of fibrotic sheets of tissue in the subendocardium. These sheets vary in thickness and result in increased stiffness of the

ventricles. The bright reflective characteristic of this tissue is easily seen with two-dimensional echocardiography. Other characteristic echocardiographic findings include a normal-sized left ventricle, increased thickness of the left ventricular wall, thrombus, and left atrial enlargement, which usually occurs because of elevated diastolic pressure of the left ventricle. The right heart is normal in size, with mildly reduced systolic function and increased wall dimensions. Tricuspid regurgitation is present because of the pulmonary hypertension that occurs because of elevated pressures in the left heart.

There are two basic varieties of endomyocardial fibrosis. One form, found primarily in temperate regions, results from hypereosinophilia and is therefore termed hypereosinophilic syndrome. This syndrome, also referred to as Löffler's endocarditis parietalis fibroplastica or Löffler's endocarditis, mainly affects men in their forties and is characterized by increased eosinophils of more than 1500/mm^3. The second form, obliterative endomyocardial fibrosis,[1] occurs primarily in subtropical climates and is especially common in Uganda and Nigeria. It accounts for 10–20% of all cardiac deaths in those countries. Large pericardial effusions are typical in this cardiomyopathy.

CARDIAC MASSES

Benign Tumors

Myxomas. Myxoma is the most common type of benign tumor, accounting for 30–50% of all benign tumors. Three times as many females as males are affected, and 90% of the tumors are found in the atria: 75–86% are found in the left atrium; 8–20% in the right atrium; and 5–11%, in the right atrium or left ventricle but rarely in both atria. Ninety percent of myxomas are pedunculated; the most common site of attachment is the interatrial septum near the fossa avalis. This tumor may be hereditary (autosomal dominant).

M-mode findings reveal echos behind the anterior leaflet of the mitral valve. Two-dimensional imaging reveals an echogenic mass in the affected chamber. The echo may be brightly echogenic to sonolucent because of hemorrhage or necrosis.

The clinical findings include the following: symptoms similar to those of mitral valve disease, embolic phenomena, no symptoms, symptoms similar to those of tricuspid valve disease, sudden death, pericarditis, myocardial infarction, symptoms similar to pulmonic valve disease, and a fever of unknown origin.

Rhabdomyomas. Rhabdomyoma, also called myocardial hamartoma, is the most common cardiac tumor found in infants and children and is associated with tuberous sclerosis. In 90% of the cases, multiple rhabdomyomas are involved. The tumor is yellow gray in appearance, ranges from 1 mm to several centimeters in diameter, and most commonly involves the ventricles. Large tumors may lead to intracavitary obstruction resulting in death.

Lipomas. Lipoma, the second most common benign tumor, affects people of all ages and is found equally often in males and females. Most of these tumors are sessile. Fifty percent are located in the subendocardium, 25% are found in the subepicardium, and 25% are intramuscular. The most common sites are the left ventricle, right atrium, and interatrial septum.

Fibromas. Fibromas occur in the connective tissue and are the second most common benign tumors found predominantly in children (most of whom are younger than 10 years). Almost all of these tumors occur in the ventricular myocardium.

Angiomas. Angiomas are extremely rare. They may occur in any part of the heart.[2]

Teratomas. Teratomas are extremely rare and occur more often in children. They are found most frequently in the right heart, but also can occur in the interatrial or interventricular septum.[2]

Cystic Tumors. Cystic tumors are usually small lesions found in the region of the A-V node.[2]

Malignant Tumors

Primary Cardiac Tumors. Angiosarcomas usually occur in adults and are twice as common in men as in women. They are usually found in the right atrium; the most common site is the interatrial septum. Other primary cardiac tumors are rhabdomyosarcomas, fibrosarcomas, lymphosarcomas, and sarcomas of the pulmonary artery.

Secondary Metastatic Tumors. Metastatic tumors usually invade the right heart. Usually they are clinically silent. However, they can cause superior vena cava syndrome because of obstruction, supraventricular arrhythmias, myocardial infarction, cardiomegaly, congestive heart failure, or nonbacterial endocarditis. Bronchogenic carcinomas, breast carcinomas, malignant melanomas, and leukemia's account for the vast majority of metastases to the heart. Bronchogenic carcinomas are the most common, followed by breast carcinomas, malignant melanomas, and leukemias. Spread of these tumors varies. Bronchogenic carcinomas spread via direct extension; breast carcinomas spread via the lymphatic channels; and metastases of malignant melanomas spread through the blood. Usually metastases involve the pericardium or the myocardium.[2]

Cardiac Thrombi

Left Ventricular Thrombi. Thrombi of the left ventricle occur in myocardial infarctions, left ventricular aneurysms, and cardiomyopathies. They usually form in the apex of the ventricle. Two-dimensional imaging can diagnose the clot with 90% sensitivity and specificity. Echocardiography reveals that the clot has distinct margins, is usually located near an akinetic or dyskinetic area, and may protrude within the ventricle or move with the adja-

cent wall. Protruding thrombi tend to be more echodense than mural thrombi, whereas mural thrombi have a layered appearance and are often echolucent along the endocardial border.

Thrombi form within the first 4 days after an infarction and occur in 30% of all anterior wall infarctions; they rarely occur in inferior wall infarctions. If they do not dissolve spontaneously, they may disappear with the use of anticoagulants.

Left Atrial Thrombi. Thrombi usually form in the left atrium in the presence of mitral valve disease (stenosis), an enlarged left atrium, and atrial fibrillation—conditions that predispose to blood stasis. The most common site is the atrial appendage. The echocardiographic appearance of these thrombi varies. In many cases, they are attached to the atrial wall and can be round or ovoid in shape. Their borders are often well defined, they demonstrate mobility, and their texture is uniform. Occasionally, they appear as a flat immobile mass or as a free-floating ball.

Thrombi of the Right Heart. Most thrombi form in the right heart in the presence of right ventricular infarction, cardiomyopathies, or cor pulmonale. They usually are immobile, heterogeneous sessile masses. In addition, secondary thrombi may occur. Their source is embolization from deep-vein thrombosis. Echocardiography typically reveals a long, serpentine, apparently free-floating mass with no obvious site of attachment. Patients are at a much higher risk for an embolus when the thrombus in any area of the heart is protruding or free floating.

Other Cardiac Masses. Because a number of foreign objects can mimic a thrombus, one must be aware of their presence and location. For example, right-heart catheters are often seen in both the right atrium and the right ventricle. These appear as highly reflective linear echoes.

Normal cardiac structures also can mimic intracardiac masses. The moderator band seen in the apex of the right ventricle appears as a thick muscular band extending from the free wall of the right ventricle to the interventricular septum. Occasionally, a prominent eustachian valve can be seen in the right atrium at the junction of the inferior vena cava. It appears as a thin, long, mobile structure in the right atrium, which also may contain thin filamentous structures known as the Chiari network that is a remnant of embryonic structures. The left ventricle also may contain long thin fibers known as false tendons or ectopic chordae tendineae. These filamentous structures traverse the left ventricle and typically are brightly reflective structures of no clinical significance.

DISEASES OF THE AORTA

Aortic Dilatation

The aorta is considered dilated when its diameter is greater than 37 mm. The average diameter of the adult aorta is 33–37 mm. M-mode measurements of the aorta should be taken at the level of the aortic annulus and the sinus of Valsalva. Aortic dilatation is seen most frequently in patients with annuloaortic ectasia or Marfan syndrome. In these patients, the medial layer of the aorta weakens and the aorta dilates. The dilatation occurs not only in the wall of the aorta but in the aortic annulus as well. This often leads to aortic insufficiency because the cusps of the aorta are unable to coapt during closure. Two-dimensional echocardiography can easily detect a dilated aorta.

Aortic Aneurysm

An aortic aneurysm can occur anywhere along the thoracic aorta. The most common sites are the arch and descending aorta, with most occurring just beyond the left subclavian artery. Aneurysms of the thoracic aorta often extend into the abdominal aorta.

A dissecting aortic aneurysm results from intimal tears of the aortic wall. The driving force of the blood destroys the media further and strips the intimal layer from the adventitial layer. Aortic dissections are classified according to the area and extent of the intimal tear. Type I tears extend from the ascending aorta and continue beyond the arch. Type II tears also begin a few centimeters from the aortic valve but are confined to the ascending aorta. Type III tears begin in the descending aorta, usually just distal to the origin of the left subclavian artery. More than 90% of patients with dissecting aneurysms experience severe pain. Dissections occur twice as often in men as in women and usually in the sixth and seventh decade of life. M-mode findings reveal extra linear echos within the aorta. Two-dimensional imaging is the echocardiographic tool of choice. Two-dimensional imaging allows visualization of the intimal flap, which divides the true lumen of the aorta from the false lumen. Color flow Doppler can be invaluable in localizing the site of intraluminal communication. Other echocardiographic evidence for dissection includes aortic regurgitation—the most commonly noted complication. Doppler is useful for detecting disturbed flow patterns in the left ventricular outflow tract. The left ventricle may become enlarged because of volume overload from the aortic regurgitation; pericardial effusion can be noted, and left pleural effusion also may be noted. The diagnosis of dissection should be made when an intima flap is seen in more than one view.

Aneurysms that occur in the sinus of Valsalva are seen best using two-dimensional imaging. They are observed most easily in the short-axis view during diastole. Rupture usually occurs into the right side of the heart, but it also can occur in the left heart and interventricular septum. Sinus of Valsalva aneurysms can be acquired or congenital in nature.

CONGENITAL HEART DISEASE

Aortic Stenosis

Abnormalities of the left ventricular outflow tract are the most common congenital heart disease found in the adult population. Obstruction can occur at the subvalvular, supravalvular, or valvular level. Congenital abnormalities

of the aortic valve occur in 1% of the population, with a higher prevalence among males. The most common malformation of the aortic valve is a bicuspid valve. Aortic coarctation, VSD, and isolated pulmonic stenosis are associated with the condition. As the valve ages, it becomes fibrotic and may calcify. By the fourth decade, 50% of all bicuspid aortic valves become stenotic.

Subvalvular stenosis also can occur. There are two types of subvalvular stenosis: discrete and subaortic. In discrete stenosis, a thin membrane obstructs the outflow tract or a more fibromuscular ridge obstructs the flow of blood. Subaortic stenosis, too, is more common in males. Aortic regurgitation is a frequent finding in subaortic stenosis. Discrete subvalvular stenosis is primarily an acquired rather than a congenital problem when it is present in adults.

Supravalvular stenosis also can be classified into two categories. The most frequent supravalvular narrowing is found in the ascending aorta just above the valve. Less frequently, the obstruction involves the ascending aorta, the aortic arch, and the descending aorta. Supravalvular obstruction can be a familial finding, but it also can be sporadic or as a result of rubella infection. When found in association with mental retardation, a diagnosis of Williams syndrome can be made.

Patients with congenital outflow obstruction usually present with left ventricular systolic hypertension and develop concentric left ventricular hypertrophy. The physical examination reveals a harsh systolic ejection murmur over the right parasternal border. Echocardiography has become the diagnostic tool of choice in making this diagnosis. M-mode echocardiography reveals a thickened valve with an eccentric closure line. Normally, the closure line of the aortic valve is centrally located. In a bicuspid aortic valve, however, the closure line is displaced toward either the anterior or the posterior wall of the aorta. Two-dimensional echocardiography reveals systolic doming of the cusps, which is seen in the left parasternal long-axis view. The left parasternal short-axis view reveals the presence of only two cusps. Pulsed-wave Doppler echocardiography can localize the area of obstruction and determine what type of obstruction is present. Continuous-wave Doppler examination allows quantification of peak and mean pressure gradients across the obstruction. Color flow Doppler examination allows assessment of blood flow direction.

Atrial Septal Defects

Atrial septal defects (ASD) is the second most common congenital abnormality found in adults. There are three classifications of ASDs, depending on their location: ostium secundum defects, ostium primum defects, and sinus venosus defects. Ostium secundum defects make up 70% of all ASDs found in adults. These are located near the fossa ovalis. Women are three times more likely than men to have this defect. Twenty percent of patients with this type of ASD have associated mitral valve prolapse. Other associated findings include mitral or pulmonic stenosis and atrial septal aneurysm. When an ASD and mitral stenosis exist simultaneously, the condition is called Lutembacher's syndrome. In isolated mitral stenosis, the left atrium is dilated because the valve area is reduced. In ASD the blood can escape across the atrial defect, thereby preserving the size of the left atrium.

Fifteen percent of all ASDs are the ostium primum type. These defects occur in the region of the ostium primum or the lower portion of the atrial septum. A common associated finding is a clefted anterior mitral valve leaflet.

Sinus venosus ASDs account for the other 15%. These defects occur in the upper portion of the atrial septum near the orifice of the inferior vena cava. The most common finding associated with this defect is partial anomalous pulmonary venous drainage.

Two-dimensional and M-mode echocardiography reveal a volume overload in the right heart. Findings indicative of right-sided volume overload include a dilated right ventricle and a flattening of the septum in diastole Two-dimensional imaging of the atrial septum allows direct visualization and localization of the defect. The views most commonly used to assess the atrial septum include the parasternal short-axis, the apical four-chamber, and the subcostal views. The latter view is the best one for visualizing the atrial septum. In addition to the secondary findings already described, two-dimensional imaging allows direct visualization of the defect. In septal defects, a dropout of echos is noted in the area of the defect. On echocardiography, the dropout of echos is characterized by a bright echo perpendicular to the atrial septum. This finding has been described as the "T" sign.

Doppler echocardiography also can help detect ASDs. In the absence of elevated pressures in the right heart, blood flows from the higher-pressure left ventricle to the lower-pressure right heart. In the subcostal view, a pulsed Doppler sample gate can be placed in the right heart near the atrial septum. The spectral display will reveal turbulent flow toward the transducer in late systole and throughout diastole. Color flow Doppler allows visualization of the interatrial shunt by superimposing a color coding on a two-dimensional image.

Contrast echocardiography can be used when imaging and when Doppler are unable to clearly identify the atrial defect. When used in conjunction with two-dimensional imaging, 92–100% of ASDs can be detected. Contrast agents injected into a vein enter the right heart, which is often highly opacified. In the presence of an ASD, small amounts of contrast material can be seen crossing the atrial septum into the left atrium and to the left ventricle. When the shunt is left to right, which is normally the case, a negative contrast effect can be noted. Contrast enhancement can be increased by having the patient perform the Valsalva maneuver or cough.

Patent Foramen Ovale

Patent (open) foramen ovale can be found in 27% of older patients. Left-to-right shunting does not normally occur when pressures are normal. A potential complication of the condition is paradoxical embolus.

Ventricular Septal Defects

VSDs are the most common defects found in infants and children. In the adult, ASDs are much more common. VSDs fall into two major classifications: muscular septal defects and membranous defects. Like ASDs, VSDs are classified according to the region involved.

Muscular Septal Defects. Muscular septal defects are entirely surrounded by muscle. Outlet defects occur in the most superior portion of the septum and make up part of the outflow region of the left ventricle. They are also referred to as outflow defects, subpulmonic or infundibular defects, or bulbar defects. These defects are bordered by the trabecula septomarginalis (right ventricular septal band) and the pulmonary valve annulus. Thus, they are the most difficult VSDs to image and are seen best from the subcostal and high parasternal positions.

A special form of outlet defect occurs above the crista supraventricularis. This defect is known as the supracristal ventricular defect; it also is referred to as the doubly committed subarterial defect because of its proximity to both semilunar valves. This defect also is seen best from the subcostal and high parasternal positions. Associated findings in this defect include (1) aortic valve prolapse because of lack of support, usually involving the right coronary cusp, (2) dilatation of the right coronary sinus of Valsalva, and (3) aortic insufficiency. The defect is usually small.

Inlet ventricular defects are bordered superiorly by the tricuspid valve annulus, apically by the tips of the papillary muscles, and anteriorly by the trabecula septomarginalis. They are also referred to as endocardial cushion defects, retrocristal defects, sinus defects, and inflow defects, which can be seen in several planes, including the parasternal, apical, and subcostal views. Because these defects are usually large, they can be confused with a double-inlet ventricle.

Trabecular defects are bordered by the chordal attachments of the papillary muscle to the apex. They extend from the smooth outlet septum to the inlet septum, are heavily trabeculated, and are usually large. They also can be multiple. These defects typically lead to hypertension of the right ventricle and may produce a right-to-left shunt if the pressures in the right heart exceed those in the left. A special type of muscular septal defect that occurs in the muscular septum is characterized by numerous small defects resembling Swiss cheese. This "Swiss cheese" defect occurs primarily in the apex.

Membranous Defects. Membranous septal defects occur in the region bordered by the inlet and outlet septums and the junctions between the right and noncoronary cusps of the aortic valve. This part of the septum is located at the base of the heart. Defects in this area are often referred to as perimembranous because they usually involve part of a surrounding muscular septum. Almost all planes can be used to image these defects, which occur more frequently than the muscular varieties.

Using two-dimensional imaging allows visualization of the septum. When the defect is large, a dropout of echoes is appreciated. In addition, a "T" artifact is observed. When imaging does not allow localization of the defect, color flow Doppler can be used. High-velocity turbulent flow usually can be seen as a mosaic color pattern in the area of the jet. Contrast echocardiography also can be used to localize the defect. Agitated solution can be injected into the right heart through a peripheral vein. Even a few bubbles seen entering the left ventricle are indicative of a right-to-left shunt when right-sided pressures are slightly elevated.

Tetralogy of Fallot

In adults, tetralogy of Fallot is the primary congenital disease producing cyanosis. In this condition, four specific findings are noted. The aorta overrides the perimembranous VSD. Infundibular or valvular pulmonic stenosis is present, resulting in right ventricular hypertrophy. M-mode criteria for diagnosing tetralogy of Fallot includes a break in the continuity of the anterior wall of the aorta from that of the interventricular septum as well as a narrowing of the right ventricular outflow tract. Two-dimensional imaging, however, allows direct visualization of the cardiac anatomy and is therefore the echocardiographic procedure of choice. Imaging often allows visualization of the VSD and gives valuable information about the amount of aortic override. Doppler echocardiography allows quantification of gradients across the obstruction of right ventricular outflow.

Pulmonic Stenosis

Eighty percent of all congenital obstructions of right ventricular outflow occur at the level of the pulmonic valve. The valve is often thickened with fusion of the cusps and can be seen doming in systole. Right ventricular hypertrophy occurs as a result of the increased resistance to flow. Two-dimensional imaging allows visualization of the valve, which usually appears thickened and with reduced excursion.

Persistent Ductus Arteriosis

Persistent ductus arteriosus (PDA) occurs when the ductus fails to close after birth. In utero, communication exists between the pulmonary circulation and the systemic circulation, the purpose of which in fetal circulation is to direct the flow of desaturated blood away from the coronary and cerebral circulation and toward the placenta. The ductus is located near the isthmus of the aorta near the origin of the left subclavian artery; it extends to the left pulmonary artery just beyond the bifurcation. In the absence of elevated pulmonary pressures, blood flows from the aorta to the pulmonary artery. In adults, the most common symptom of a PDA is dyspnea on exertion. In persistent ductus, the increased blood flow to the lungs results in dilatation of the pulmonary arteries, the left atrium and ventricle, and the aorta. If pulmonary pressure increases, the blood flow may reverse and travel from the pulmonary circulation toward the aorta. This condi-

tion is known as Eisenmenger's complex and is characterized by right-to-left shunting.

Coarctation of the Aorta

Twice as many men as women are likely to have coarctation of the aorta. Most patients with this condition are asymptomatic. The coarctation is manifested as left ventricular hypertension. On physical examination, a systolic murmur can be heard. The most common site of narrowing occurs in the thoracic aorta just distal to the left subclavian artery. This condition is often found in association with other congenital abnormalities such as VSD, PDA, a bicuspid aortic valve, and mitral valve abnormalities. It is the most common cardiac malformation found in Turner's syndrome.

The suprasternal notch offers the best view of the ascending aorta, the arch, and the descending aorta. Direct visualization of the coarctation is possible using two-dimensional imaging. Doppler echocardiography typically reveals increased velocities across the site of coarctation.

Ebstein's Anomaly

Ebstein's anomaly is characterized by downward displacement of the anterior or septal leaflet of the tricuspid valve into the right ventricle. As a result, the ventricle becomes "atrialized" and loses some of its pumping capacity. Associated findings include secundum-type ASDs, pulmonic stenosis or atresia, VSD, and mitral valve prolapse. Symptoms may not be evident until the patient is between 30 and 40 years old. The most common complication of this abnormality is failure of the right ventricle.

The M-mode criterion for this anomaly includes visualization of a large tricuspid valve leaflet, simultaneously seen with the anterior leaflet of the mitral leaflet. A delay time in closure of the tricuspid valve of 80 m/s or more to that of closure of the mitral valve is the second M-mode finding. Two-dimensional imaging allows direct visualization of the anatomy. Specific findings in imaging include an apically located tricuspid leaflet and a functionally small right ventricle. Ebstein's anomaly can be diagnosed if the leaflet is displaced 20 mm or more.

HYPERTENSIVE DISEASE

Systemic Hypertension

There are two basic types of systemic hypertension: essential or idiopathic and secondary hypertension. Both affect the diastolic and systolic pressure. The classification of blood pressure is shown in Table 3–1.

TABLE 3–1. CLASSIFICATION OF BLOOD PRESSURE

Range (mm Hg)	Category
Diastolic	
<85	Normal blood pressure
85–89	High normal blood pressure
90–104	Mild hypertension
105–114	Moderate hypertension
≥115	Severe hypertension
Systolic, when diastolic blood pressure is <90 mm Hg	
<140	Normal blood pressure
140–159	Borderline isolated systolic hypertension
≥160	Isolated systolic hypertension

Reprinted with permission from "The 1984 Report of the Joint National Committee on Detection, Evaluation, and Treatment of High Blood Pressure." Arch Intern Med 144, May 1984.

The cause of essential hypertension is unknown. Although several mechanisms may come into play, no specific cause has been well described. Secondary hypertension results in high blood pressure associated with any of the following: renal disease, endocrine disease, coarctation of the aorta, pregnancy, neurological disorders, acute stress, increased intravascular volume, alcohol and other drug abuse, increased cardiac output, and rigidity of the aorta.

The hemodynamic properties of systemic hypertension, whatever the cause, are similar. Initially, cardiac output increases, as does fluid volume. This increased fluid volume is transferred to the various organs and tissues. Once tissues receive more blood than they need, the blood vessels that deliver the blood constrict. This is known as vasoconstriction, which is an intrinsic property of systemic vessels such as arterioles and arteries. If this state continues, the vessels continue to exert resistance on the incoming blood (peripheral resistance). As a result, the heart beats against greater resistance and the vessels themselves become thicker.

As is the case with any muscle, hypertrophy occurs when stress is exerted. Just as the bicep increases in size when one does curls, so does the heart increase in size as it is forced to pump blood against increased peripheral resistance. Therefore, the main echocardiographic findings are increased muscle mass of the heart, especially the left ventricle. By M-mode criteria, the walls of the left ventricle are thick. The principal Doppler findings include (1) decreased transmitral E wave, (2) increased A wave, and (3) increased A-to-E-wave ratios.

Pulmonary Hypertension

In normal physiology, the pulmonary blood flow allows passage of blood to the lungs for three basic functions: oxygenation, filtration, and pH balance by excreting carbon dioxide. Blood coming in from the various tissues and organs of the body is directed to the right heart through the superior and inferior vena cavae. Once this deoxygenated blood enters the right atrium, it passes through the tricuspid valve into the right ventricle across the pulmonic valve and into the main pulmonary artery, which bifurcates into a left and right branch and directs blood to the left and right lobes of the lungs. Normally, the pulmonary circulation offers little resistance to blood flow: The normal peak systolic pressure ranges from 18–25 mm Hg, and the normal diastolic pressure ranges from 6–10 mm Hg. Pulmonary artery pressure in excess of 30 mm Hg systolic pressure and 20 mm Hg diastolic pressure represents elevated pulmonary pressures, or pulmonary hypertension.

Pulmonary Hypertension

Like systemic hypertension, pulmonary hypertension has two basic forms: primary and secondary. Primary pulmonary hypertension—also known as idiopathic, essential, or unexplained pulmonary hypertension—has no known discernible cause. Secondary pulmonary hypertension can be the result of any one of the following factors:

- increased resistance to pulmonary venous drainage,
- elevated left ventricular diastolic pressure,
- left atrial hypertension (mitral stenosis),
- pulmonary parenchymal disease, or
- pulmonary venous obstruction (cor triatriatum or pulmonary veno-occlusive disease).

Cor triatriatum is a congenital abnormality in which the common embryonic pulmonary vein is not incorporated into the left atrium. Instead, the pulmonary veins empty into an accessory chamber and communicate with the left atrium through a small opening. The result is obstruction of pulmonary venous flow that simulates mitral stenosis. In pulmonary veno-occlusive disease, the veins and venules of the lung become fibrotic.

M-mode findings reveal an absent or decreased A wave in the absence of right ventricular failure: a lack of respiratory variation in the A wave; an extended preejection period; midsystolic closure of the pulmonic valve, also known as midsystolic notch; and reduced ejection time of the right ventricle. Two-dimensional imaging indicates a dilated pulmonary artery and abnormalities in interventricular septal motion.

Doppler measurements reveal the following: a decreased acceleration time, a longer preejection period, a shorter ejection time, and tricuspid regurgitation. The acceleration time is the time interval between the onset of flow and the peak systolic flow. In pulmonary hypertension, the velocity of blood flow increases rapidly and peaks early in systole. This measurement is made by identifying the beginning of the Doppler signal and the peak velocity of the same signal. The time between the two is the acceleration time.

The preejection period is the time interval between the onset of the QRS complex to onset of flow in the pulmonary artery. In pulmonary hypertension, this time period increases.

Ejection time is the time from the onset of flow to the cessation of flow. In pulmonary hypertension, this time period becomes shorter. This measurement is made by taking the time between the beginning and end of the Doppler signal.

Tricuspid regurgitation occurs in the majority of patients with elevated pressures in the pulmonary artery. Continuous-wave Doppler can be used to localize the regurgitant jet and obtain the peak transtricuspid gradient using the modified Bernoulli equation. The peak gradient is the difference in systolic pressure between the right atrium and right ventricle. Estimation of the pulmonary pressures is accomplished by adding the right atrial pressures, which are determined by visual inspection of the jugular venous pulse. A more common way is to add the constant "10" to the peak systolic transtricuspid gradient. When stenosis of the pulmonic valve is present, however, one cannot determine pulmonary artery pressures using the peak transtricuspid regurgitant gradient.

CORONARY ARTERY DISEASE

The normal right and left coronary arteries supply the heart muscle with oxygenated blood (Table 3–2). The left coronary artery originates from the left coronary sinus of Valsalva, which bifurcates into two branches: the anterior interventricular or descending branch, also known as the left anterior descending branch, and the circumflex branch. The right coronary artery originates from the right coronary sinus of Valsalva.

The coronary anatomy can vary considerably in humans. In 67% of cases, the right coronary artery is the dominant artery. In these cases, this artery supplies the parts of the left ventricle and septum. In 15% of cases, the left coronary artery is the dominant one and supplies blood to all of the left ventricle and septum. In 18% of cases, the two arteries are equal; this situation is called the balanced coronary arterial pattern.

Abnormal Wall Motion

When the blood supply to the heart muscle is interrupted, the muscle is damaged and immediate changes in motion can be observed. The affected area can be identified using the various echocardiographic views. The wall segment

TABLE 3–2. NORMAL BRANCHES OF THE CORONARY ARTERIES

Coronary Artery	Major Branches	Area Supplied
Left coronary	Left anterior descending	Anterior left ventricular wall Anterior two-thirds of apical septum Anteroapical portions of left ventricle Anterior-lateral papillary muscle Midseptum Bundle of His Anterior right ventricular papillary muscle
	Circumflex*	Lateral left ventricular wall Left atrium
Right coronary	Numerous branches	Anterior right ventricular wall Posterior third (or more) of the interventricular septum Diaphragmatic wall of right ventricle Atrioventricular node

*If the circumflex terminates at the crux of the heart, it supplies the entire left ventricle and interventricular septum.

should be identified using the American Society of Echocardiography's recommendations (see the section of wall segment in the "Normal Anatomy" section).[3]

Complications of Ischemic Heart Disease

Ventricular Aneurysm. One complication of ischemic heart disease is ventricular aneurysm. Although aneurysms can form in any part of the left ventricle, more than 80% form in the apex and are the result of an anterior infarction. Of the 5–10% that form in the posterior wall, nearly half are false aneurysms.

The echocardiographic appearance of aneurysms includes thin walls that do not thicken in systole, a bulging wall, and dyskinetic motion to the affected area.

There are three types of ventricular aneurysms: anatomically true, functionally true, and anatomically false aneurysms. An anatomically true aneurysm is composed of fibrous tissue, may or may not contain a clot, and protrudes during both diastole and systole. Its mouth is wider or as wide as its maximum diameter, and its wall is the former left ventricular wall. An anatomically true aneurysm almost never ruptures once healed. A functionally true aneurysm also consists of fibrous tissue but protrudes only during ventricular systole.

An anatomically false aneurysm always contains a clot. Its mouth is considerably smaller than its maximum diameter, and it protrudes during both systole and diastole and may even expand. Its wall is composed of parietal pericardium. Because a false aneurysm often ruptures, immediate surgery is usually required.

Ventricular Septal Defect. A VSD occurs when a rupture occurs in the septum. Several echocardiographic techniques can be used to make the diagnosis. Two-dimensional imaging allows direct visualization of the defect. With contrast echocardiography with imaging, contrasting material can be seen filling the right ventricle and entering the left ventricle as blood moves back and forth through the defect. Negative contrast effect also can be noted. Doppler measurements can detect turbulent high-velocity signals on the right side of the ventricular septum. The best views include the left parasternal long- and short-axis views and the apical four-chamber view. Color Doppler can demonstrate communication between the left and right ventricles. The color jet appears as a mosaic pattern of high-velocity flow.

Thrombus. Thrombus, the most common complication of infarction, usually occurs in the apex in areas of dyskinesis. It can be laminar, lay close to the wall of the ventricle, or protrude into the cavity and be highly mobile. The diagnosis should be made when the thrombus is seen in several views.

Valve Dysfunction. An infarction is most likely to affect the mitral valve. Mitral regurgitation results if the papillary muscle is ruptured; if it becomes fibrosed; or if the mitral annulus is affected, resulting in incomplete closure of the leaflets.

Right Ventricular Involvement. Involvement of the right ventricle occurs primarily when the infarction is in the inferior wall or when the proximal right coronary artery is obstructed. Echocardiography reveals that the ventricle is dilated and its free wall moves abnormally.

REFERENCES

1. Feigenbaum H. *Endocardiopathy,* 4th ed. Philadelphia: Lea & Febiger, 1986.
2. Braunwald, E. *Heart Disease: A Textbook of Cardiac Medicine,* 3rd ed. Philadelphia: WB Saunders, 1988.
3. Report of the American Society of Echocardiography Committee on Nomenclature and Standards: Identification of Myocardial Wall Segments. 1982.

Questions

GENERAL INSTRUCTIONS: For each question, select the best answer. Select only one answer for each question, unless otherwise specified.

1. Which of the following views would best demonstrate all four cardiac chambers simultaneously?
   (A) left parasternal
   (B) right parasternal
   (C) subcostal
   (D) suprasternal

2. The three orthogonal planes for two-dimensional echocardiographic imaging are termed
   (A) long axis, short axis, and four chamber
   (B) apical, subcostal, and parasternal
   (C) suprasternal, right sternal border, and left sternal border
   (D) anterior, posterior, and coronal

3. Which of the following abnormalities are usually best demonstrated with the subcostal four-chamber view?
   (A) atrial septal defects and ventricular septal defects
   (B) mitral regurgitation and tricuspid regurgitation
   (C) mitral stenosis and tricuspid stenosis
   (D) aortic insufficiency and pulmonic insufficiency

4. The control that suppresses near-field echoes and enhances the intensity of the far-field echoes is called
   (A) attenuation
   (B) time-gain compensation
   (C) reject
   (D) compression

5. The tricuspid valve opens when
   (A) the right ventricular pressure drops below the right atrial pressure
   (B) the papillary muscle contracts
   (C) the velocity of blood flow in the right ventricle exceeds the velocity of flow in the right atrium
   (D) the pulmonic valve opens

6. Which of the following is *not* a remnant of the fetal circulation?
   (A) the eustachian valve
   (B) the coronary ligament
   (C) the foramen ovale
   (D) the ligamentum arteriosus

7. Blood normally flows from the right ventricle to the
   (A) pulmonary artery
   (B) aorta
   (C) right atrium
   (D) pulmonary vein

8. A pulmonary vein is normally attached to the
   (A) right ventricle
   (B) left ventricle
   (C) left atrium
   (D) right atrium

9. Which of the following statements regarding cardiac anatomy is false?
   (A) The heart tends to assume a more vertical position in tall thin people and a more horizontal position in short heavy people
   (B) The ligamentum arteriosum runs from the left pulmonary artery to the descending aorta
   (C) The coronary arteries arise from the sinuses within the pockets of the left and right coronary cusps of the aortic valve
   (D) The left ventricle constitutes most of the ventral surface of the heart

10. Left ventricular ejection time can be assessed from an M-mode echocardiogram by measuring the distance between the
   (A) aortic valve opening and closing points
   (B) mitral D and C points

(C) R wave and T wave
(D) mitral valve closure and aortic valve opening

11. Often, the best two-dimensional view for examining patients with chronic obstructive pulmonary disease is

(A) parasternal
(B) apical
(C) suprasternal
(D) subcostal

12. The two best transducer positions for Doppler investigation of systolic blood flow across the aortic valve are

(A) parasternal and suprasternal
(B) apical and right sternal border
(C) suprasternal and subcostal
(D) subcostal and apical

13. The size of the left atrium is measured on the M-mode

(A) at end-systole
(B) at the peak of the R wave
(C) with the onset of aortic valve opening
(D) at the beginning of the P wave

14. Doming of any cardiac valve on two-dimensional echocardiography is consistent with

(A) regurgitation
(B) decreased cardiac output
(C) stenosis
(D) congenital malformation

15. Two-dimensional images are best obtained when the ultrasound beam is directed ______ to the structure of interest. Doppler signals are best obtained when the ultrasound beam is directed ______ to the flow of blood.

(A) oblique, perpendicular
(B) parallel, perpendicular
(C) perpendicular, parallel
(D) perpendicular, oblique

16. Right ventricular systolic pressure overload can be caused by

(A) pulmonary insufficiency
(B) an atrial septal defect
(C) aortic stenosis
(D) pulmonary hypertension

17. Left ventricular measurements should be obtained from the parasternal long-axis view at the level of the

(A) mitral valve annulus
(B) tips of the mitral leaflets
(C) chordae tendineae
(D) papillary muscle

18. All of the following can cause paradoxical interventricular septal motion except

(A) left bundle branch block
(B) postpericardiotomy
(C) left ventricular volume overload
(D) severe tricuspid regurgitation

19. In a patient with volume overload of the right ventricle, the onset of ventricular systole is likely to show the interventricular septum moving

(A) toward the right ventricular free wall
(B) toward the left ventricular wall
(C) laterally
(D) not at all

20. A murmur that is associated with a thrill is likely to be

(A) organic in origin
(B) insignificant
(C) functional
(D) the result of an atrial septal defect

21. The Valsalva maneuver and the inhalation of amyl nitrite are techniques that are sometimes used during an echocardiographic examination when checking for

(A) mitral valve prolapse or systolic anterior motion of the mitral valve
(B) aortic stenosis or mitral stenosis
(C) aortic stenosis or aortic regurgitation
(D) a ventricular septal defect or pulmonic stenosis

22. Clubbing of the fingers and nail beds is a sign of

(A) cyanotic heart disease
(B) Marfan syndrome
(C) Barlow syndrome
(D) increased cardiac output

23. Even though two-dimensional echocardiography has largely replaced M-mode echocardiography for cardiac diagnosis, M-mode still has the advantage of

(A) defining spatial relationships of cardiac structures
(B) providing enhanced temporal resolution
(C) providing dynamic assessment of the velocity of blood flow
(D) providing superior lateral resolution

24. When attempting a parasternal short-axis view, if the left ventricle appears oval rather than circular, the echocardiographer should move the transducer

(A) medially
(B) laterally
(C) to a higher intercostal space
(D) to a lower intercostal space

25. A Doppler tracing of the mitral valve in which the A point is higher than the E point indicates

(A) high cardiac output
(B) low cardiac output
(C) decreased left ventricular compliance
(D) high left ventricular end-diastolic pressures

26. Which of the following is usually not a secondary finding in patients with mitral stenosis?

(A) a dilated left atrium
(B) a dilated right atrium
(C) a left ventricular thrombus
(D) a left atrial thrombus

27. The Doppler signal obtained from the apex in a patient with mitral stenosis is most likely to demonstrate all of the following except

(A) an increased diastolic peak velocity
(B) spectral broadening
(C) a decreased E-F slope
(D) a peak gradient occurring in late diastole

28. Torn chordae tendineae will cause

(A) aortic insufficiency
(B) myocardial infarction
(C) mitral insufficiency
(D) mitral stenosis

29. All of the following can produce false positive signs of mitral valve prolapse on an M-mode except

(A) pericardial effusion
(B) premature ventricular contractions
(C) improper placement of the transducer
(D) hypertrophic obstructive cardiomyopathy

30. Which of the following is a secondary echocardiographic finding in mitral regurgitation?

(A) a dilated left atrium
(B) left ventricular hypertrophy
(C) a hypokinetic left ventricle
(D) a dilated aortic root

31. The degree of mitral regurgitation is best estimated by measuring the

(A) width and length of the systolic jet by color Doppler
(B) peak velocity of the continuous-wave Doppler systolic mitral signal
(C) pressure half-time of the continuous-wave Doppler diastolic signal
(D) integral of the continuous-wave systolic curve

32. Which of the following is least likely to occur as a sequela of rheumatic fever?

(A) mitral stenosis
(B) mitral insufficiency
(C) aortic stenosis
(D) pulmonic stenosis

33. The two-dimensional echocardiogram of a patient with combined mitral and aortic stenosis is most likely to demonstrate

(A) a dilated left atrium and left ventricular hypertrophy
(B) a dilated left atrium and a dilated left ventricle
(C) a small left atrium and a small left ventricle
(D) systolic anterior motion of the mitral valve and left ventricular hypertrophy

34. The M-mode of the mitral valve in mitral stenosis is often missing an A wave. The reason is

(A) high initial diastolic pressures in the left ventricle
(B) concurrent atrial fibrillation
(C) decreased compliance of the left ventricle
(D) a dilated left atrium

35. A Doppler tracing that demonstrates a late diastolic mitral inflow velocity (A point) that is higher than the initial diastolic velocity (E point) can be seen with which of the following pathologies?

(A) aortic insufficiency
(B) hypertrophic cardiomyopathy
(C) mitral regurgitation
(D) a ventricular septal defect

36. If the two-dimensional examination demonstrates a markedly dilated and hyperkinetic left ventricle and a left atrium of normal size, one should suspect the presence of

(A) mitral regurgitation
(B) aortic regurgitation
(C) a ventricular septal defect
(D) aortic stenosis

37. Which group of echocardiographic findings would give a definitive diagnosis of mitral stenosis?

(A) a decreased E-F slope, a dilated left atrium, and a small left ventricle
(B) a thickened mitral valve, a dilated left atrium, and a small left ventricle
(C) a decreased E-F slope, a thickened mitral valve, and diastolic doming of the mitral valve
(D) a thickened mitral valve and a mitral diastolic velocity >1.5 m/s

38. A patient with mitral stenosis will usually have all of the following except

(A) a diastolic rumble on auscultation
(B) an increased E-F slope on M-mode
(C) a history of rheumatic fever
(D) a dilated left atrium

39. To obtain the true circumference of the mitral valve, one should obtain a short-axis view at the level of the

(A) papillary muscle
(B) chordae tendineae
(C) tips of the mitral leaflets
(D) mitral annulus

40. Secondary echocardiographic findings of mitral stenosis include all of the following except

(A) a dilated left atrium
(B) a dilated right atrium
(C) a dilated left ventricle
(D) a left atrial thrombus

41. A successful mitral valve commissurotomy would be *least* likely to demonstrate

(A) doming of the mitral valve
(B) mitral valve thickening
(C) an increase in pressure half-time
(D) a dilated left atrium

42. Left ventricular dilatation in a patient with mitral stenosis suggests

(A) severe mitral stenosis
(B) concomitant mitral regurgitation
(C) aortic stenosis
(D) hypertrophic cardiomyopathy

43. Early diastolic closure of the mitral valve is usually a sign of

(A) severe acute aortic regurgitation
(B) a left bundle branch block
(C) poor function of the left ventricle
(D) first-degree A-V block

44. Degenerative calcification of the mitral annulus can be accelerated by all of the following conditions except

(A) systemic hypertension
(B) aortic stenosis
(C) hypertrophic obstructive cardiomyopathy
(D) a ventricular septal defect

45. A mitral valve pressure half-time of 220 msec is consistent with a mitral valve area of

(A) 0.6 cm^2
(B) 1 cm^2
(C) 2.2 cm^2
(D) 5 cm^2

46. Echocardiographic findings of significant aortic stenosis include all of the following except

(A) reduced separation of the aortic valve cusp
(B) diastolic fluttering of the anterior mitral leaflet
(C) Doppler systolic velocities greater than 4 m/s
(D) thickened left ventricular walls

47. Which of the following causes the left ventricular walls to appear thick on an echocardiogram?

(A) mitral stenosis
(B) aortic insufficiency
(C) mitral regurgitation
(D) systemic hypertension

48. The presence of a systolic ejection murmur should alert one to look for

(A) a ventricular septal defect
(B) mitral regurgitation
(C) aortic stenosis
(D) patent ductus arteriosis

49. All of the following statements regarding a bicuspid aortic valve are true except

(A) the problem is a congenital one
(B) it may be associated with aortic stenosis
(C) it is often seen in conjunction with mitral stenosis
(D) it may be associated with coarctation of the aorta

50. The continuity equation is used to calculate the ______. It is most helpful in patients with ______.

(A) mitral valve area, mitral stenosis
(B) aortic valve area, poor left ventricular function
(C) aortic valve velocity, systemic hypertension
(D) degree of shunting, a ventricular septal defect

51. In patients with combined aortic stenosis and aortic insufficiency, which of the following parameters is best for assessing the severity of aortic stenosis?

(A) the maximum pressure gradient
(B) the mean pressure gradient
(C) the high pulse-repetition frequency
(D) the analog waveform

52. Which of the following two-dimensional views will best illustrate a color Doppler jet of aortic insufficiency?

(A) the apical long-axis view
(B) the suprasternal view
(C) the subcostal fine-chamber view
(D) the short axis view of the base

53. Which of the following is a secondary echocardiographic sign of aortic stenosis?

(A) a thickened aortic valve
(B) left ventricular hypertrophy
(C) a hyperdynamic left ventricle
(D) a dilated left ventricle

54. An M-mode finding of fine diastolic fluttering of the anterior mitral leaflet is consistent with

(A) aortic insufficiency
(B) mitral stenosis
(C) atrial fibrillation
(D) a prolonged heart rate

55. Diastolic velocity signals were detected in a patient's left ventricular outflow tract using pulsed Doppler. They could be detected between the tip of the anterior mitral leaflet and the aortic valve from the parasternal position. This is

(A) normal
(B) consistent with severe mitral regurgitation
(C) consistent with severe aortic regurgitation
(D) consistent with moderate aortic regurgitation
(E) consistent with moderate mitral regurgitation

56. The referring physician hears an Austin-Flint murmur. The M-mode echocardiogram of this patient is most likely to demonstrate

(A) a thickened mitral valve with a decreased E-F slope
(B) fine diastolic fluttering and possible flattening of the anterior mitral leaflet
(C) a thickened aortic valve with a decreased opening
(D) systolic posterior motion of the tricuspid valve

57. The best approach for obtaining the maximum aortic velocity in patients with aortic stenosis is from the

(A) left sternal border
(B) left supraclavicular region
(C) subcostal region
(D) right sternal border view

58. The best way to rule out an aortic dissection is with

(A) M-mode echocardiography
(B) transthoracic two-dimensional imaging
(C) color Doppler
(D) transesophageal echocardiography

59. Which echocardiographic finding is not associated with tricuspid insufficiency?

(A) a dilated right atrium
(B) tricuspid prolapse
(C) a dilated right ventricle
(D) a thickened anterior right ventricle wall

60. A tricuspid regurgitant velocity of 4 m/s indicates the presence of

(A) tricuspid stenosis
(B) severe tricuspid regurgitation
(C) a flail tricuspid leaflet
(D) pulmonary hypertension

61. Which of the following regarding tricuspid stenosis is *not* true?

(A) it occurs as a sequela to rheumatic fever
(B) Doppler echocardiography demonstrates a decreased pressure half-time
(C) two-dimensional echocardiography shows diastolic doming, and M-mode reveals a decreased E-F slope
(D) it is usually seen as part of the aging process

62. A peripheral contrast injection into the arm of a patient with severe tricuspid regurgitation is likely to demonstrate

(A) contrast in the pulmonary veins during diastole
(B) right-to-left shunting
(C) contrast in the inferior vena cava during ventricular systole
(D) left-to-right shunting

63. If the physician suspects carcinoid heart disease, the echocardiographer should pay special attention to the

(A) mitral valve
(B) tricuspid valve
(C) inferior vena cava
(D) interatrial septum

64. The velocity of a tricuspid regurgitant jet can be used to calculate

(A) the severity of tricuspid regurgitation
(B) right ventricular systolic pressure
(C) the severity of pulmonic regurgitation
(D) left atrial pressure

65. Coarse systolic fluttering of the pulmonic valve with an extremely high systolic velocity in the right ventricular outflow tract is most likely to be found in a patient with

(A) pulmonic regurgitation
(B) paradoxical interventricular septal motion
(C) infundibular pulmonic stenosis
(D) pulmonary hypertension

66. The most common window used to record peak pulmonic systolic velocity is

(A) suprasternal
(B) apical
(C) right parasternal
(D) left parasternal

67. The pulmonic valve is located where in relation to the aortic valve?

(A) cranial and lateral
(B) caudal and lateral
(C) cranial and medial
(D) caudal and medial

68. All of the following echocardiographic findings are associated with pulmonic stenosis except

(A) right ventricular hypertrophy
(B) M-mode demonstration of a steep pulmonic A wave
(C) midsystolic notching noted on M-mode
(D) systolic pulmonic Doppler velocities greater than 3 m/s

69. Valvular vegetations are best detected with

(A) M-mode echocardiography
(B) two-dimensional echocardiography
(C) Doppler echocardiography
(D) contrast injection

70. A 30-year-old intravenous drug abuser presents with an embolus to the right leg. The most likely cause of the embolic event is the presence of

(A) a left atrial myxoma
(B) mitral valve vegetation
(C) a right ventricular thrombus
(D) a myocardial abscess

71. Color Doppler assessment of prosthetic heart valves is especially helpful when checking for the

(A) presence of valve stenosis
(B) presence of paravalvular regurgitation
(C) presence of a clot
(D) valve area

72. A normally functioning Starr-Edwards valve

(A) may exhibit high Doppler velocities
(B) will echocardiographically resemble a bioprosthetic valve
(C) has a major and a minor orifice
(D) may exhibit mild-to-moderate regurgitation

73. A Bjork-Shiley is

(A) an example of a mechanical heart valve
(B) an example of a bioprosthetic heart valve
(C) not noticeable on the two-dimensional image
(D) a surgical procedure used to correct for transposition of the great vessels

74. Which of the following echocardiographic examinations is best used for evaluating the function of a prosthetic valve

(A) M-mode echocardiography
(B) high-pulse repetition-frequency Doppler echocardiography
(C) transesophageal echocardiography
(D) contrast echocardiography

75. All of the following are examples of mechanical prosthetic valves *except*

(A) St. Jude
(B) Bjork-Shiley
(C) Starr-Edwards
(D) Hancock

76. To check for prosthetic valve dehiscence, the echocardiographer should look for

(A) decreased valve excursion
(B) an abnormal mass of echoes on the valve
(C) abnormal rocking motion of the valve
(D) Doppler evidence of stenosis

77. A 26-year-old woman with significant mitral insufficiency is about to receive a mitral valve replacement. The surgeons are most likely to use a porcine valve because

(A) it tends to last longer
(B) it preserves myocardium better
(C) it often makes anticoagulation unnecessary
(D) it obstructs flow less

78. Prophylactic antibiotics are often recommended for individuals with mitral valve prolapse who are undergoing dental or surgical procedures

(A) because these patients are at a higher risk for endocarditis
(B) to prevent possible mitral regurgitation
(C) to prevent pneumonia
(D) because incisions on patients with mitral valve prolapse usually take longer to heal

79. One can be reasonably certain that a large amount of pericardial effusion is present by noting

(A) echocardiographic signs of cardiac tamponade
(B) a crescent-shaped pattern on the short-axis view
(C) a "swinging heart" on the two-dimensional examination
(D) a posterior echo-free space

80. Constrictive pericarditis

(A) impairs diastolic filling
(B) is sometimes referred to as "Dressler's syndrome"
(C) is detected by noting increased echogenicity of the pericardium
(D) is usually associated with a large pericardial effusion

81. Cardiac tamponade is most likely to occur when

(A) pressure in the pericardial cavity rises to equal or exceed the diastolic pressure in the heart
(B) there is a small pericardial effusion
(C) there is a large chronic pericardial effusion
(D) the pericardium becomes a sheath of fibrous tissue that interferes with diastolic filling

82. Which one of the following statements about pericardial effusion is false?

(A) pericardial effusion may be confused with epicardial fat
(B) an effusion may accumulate anteriorly without accumulating posteriorly
(C) a pericardial effusion can consist of blood or clear fluid
(D) In Dressler's syndrome, a pericardial effusion develops as a result of renal disease

83. A 38-year-old woman with a history of breast cancer is referred for an echocardiogram because she is experiencing shortness of breath. The echocardiogram is most likely to reveal

(A) metastasis to the left atrium
(B) metastasis to the right atrium
(C) a left atrial myxoma
(D) a pericardial effusion

84. All of the following can lead to a false-positive diagnosis of pericardial effusion on M-mode except

(A) the descending aorta
(B) a calcified mitral annulus
(C) ascites
(D) mitral valve prolapse

85. A false-negative sign of tamponade may occur in patients with

(A) pulmonic stenosis
(B) a pleural effusion
(C) mitral regurgitation
(D) loculated effusions

86. The pericardium appears as an extremely bright linear structure on the echocardiogram because

(A) it is a thick structure
(B) it is a fibrous band
(C) there is a large acoustic mismatch between lung tissue and pericardial tissue
(D) it contains calcium

87. Two echocardiographic techniques that are useful when evaluating for the presence of pericardial effusion are

(A) increasing reject and decreasing frame-rate
(B) decreasing time-gain control and increasing overall gain
(C) decreasing overall gain and increasing depth setting
(D) increasing reject and decreasing depth setting

88. The structure that often aids in differentiating a pericardial effusion from a pleural effusion on two-dimensional examination is the

(A) liver
(B) inferior vena cava
(C) pleural sac
(D) descending aorta

89. Flat mid-diastolic motion of the posterior wall on an M-mode echocardiogram suggests

(A) constrictive pericarditis
(B) left ventricular volume overload
(C) myocardial infarction
(D) dilated cardiomyopathy

90. The most striking echocardiographic feature of patients with an absent pericardium is

(A) excessive cardiac motion
(B) absence of bright linear pericardial echoes
(C) hypokinesis of the heart
(D) dyskinetic motion of the heart

91. The effect of systemic hypertension on the heart is

(A) thickening of the right ventricular free wall
(B) decreased systolic function of the left ventricle
(C) reduced compliance of the left ventricle
(D) right ventricular dilatation

92. Echocardiographic signs of outflow tract obstruction in hypertrophic cardiomyopathy include all of the following *except*

(A) midsystolic notching of the aortic valve
(B) left ventricular hypertrophy
(C) systolic anterior motion of the mitral valve
(D) high systolic velocity in the left ventricular outflow tract

93. A definitive diagnosis of amyloid heart disease is best made with

(A) M-mode echocardiography
(B) transthoracic echocardiography
(C) transesophageal echocardiography
(D) endomyocardial biopsy

94. All of the following can cause dilated (congestive) cardiomyopathy *except*

(A) coronary artery disease
(B) sarcoidosis
(C) viral myocarditis
(D) long-term alcohol abuse

95. All of the following are echocardiographic findings seen in dilated cardiomyopathy *except*

(A) increased systolic velocity in the left ventricular outflow tract
(B) dilated chambers
(C) global hypokinesis
(D) an increased E point-to-septal separation

96. Cardiac contusion

(A) is more likely to affect the right ventricle than the left ventricle
(B) is the same as a myocardial infarction
(C) occurs when there is underlying coronary artery disease
(D) leads to hypercontractility of the left ventricle

97. A 64-year-old man presents with an acute myocardial infarction of the anterior wall and an embolus to the right leg. Before beginning the examination, the echocardiographer should suspect the possibility of (choose the most likely diagnosis)

(A) an apical aneurysm with a mural thrombus
(B) mitral stenosis and a left atrial clot
(C) a right ventricular infarct with a clot
(D) vegetation on the mitral or aortic valve

98. All of the following echocardiographic findings are consistent with diastolic dysfunction of the left ventricle except

(A) M-mode demonstration of a mitral valve B notch
(B) M-mode demonstration of a high mitral A wave
(C) two-dimensional demonstration of an ejection fraction lower than 50%
(D) Doppler demonstration of a mitral valve E-to-A ratio >1.0

99. Akinesis of the anterior left ventricular wall is most likely to indicate obstruction of the

(A) right coronary artery
(B) left circumflex artery
(C) left anterior descending artery
(D) posterior descending artery

100. Pseudoaneurysms

(A) are usually hyperkinetic
(B) have a low risk of rupture
(C) have walls comprised of endocardium, myocardium, epicardium, and pericardium
(D) have a narrow neck

101. An increased E point-to-septal separation is usually a good indicator of

(A) high end-diastolic pressures in the left ventricle
(B) a reduced ejection fraction
(C) high initial diastolic pressures
(D) poor compliance of the left ventricle

102. A segment of the left ventricle that lacks systolic wall thickening and motion is best described as

(A) hypokinetic
(B) akinetic
(C) dyskinetic
(D) aneurysmal

103. Aneurysms in the inferior wall of the left ventricle may be associated with all of the following except

(A) an increased E point-to-septal separation
(B) thrombus formation
(C) mitral regurgitation
(D) occlusion of the left anterior descending coronary artery

104. The echocardiogram of a patient with a ruptured papillary muscle will exhibit

(A) mitral valve prolapse
(B) severe mitral regurgitation
(C) some degree of aortic insufficiency
(D) dyskinesis of the posterior left ventricular wall

105. Stress echocardiography

(A) is used instead of standard stress testing
(B) studies the acoustic properties of the myocardium
(C) allows for visualization of myocardial perfusion
(D) is used in diagnosing ischemic heart disease

106. Which of the following statements regarding left atrial myxomas is not true?

(A) they usually attach to the interatrial septum
(B) they may be pedunculated
(C) they do not recur once they are surgically removed
(D) clinically, they can mimic mitral stenosis

107. The QP/QS ratio is used to evaluate the severity of

(A) pulmonic stenosis
(B) ventricular septal defects
(C) aortic stenosis
(D) systemic hypertension

108. Which of the following would best describe the pulsed Doppler pattern of a patent ductus arteriosis if the sample volume were placed in the pulmonary artery from a short-axis view of the base of the heart?

(A) systolic flow below baseline
(B) continuous flow (systolic and diastolic) above baseline
(C) diastolic flow above baseline
(D) a biphasic systolic flow pattern below baseline

109. The best way to detect a small atrial septal defect is with

(A) two-dimensional echocardiography
(B) contrast injection echocardiography
(C) M-mode echocardiography
(D) pulsed-wave Doppler echocardiography

110. The most common type of atrial septal defect is

(A) primum
(B) secundum
(C) fenestrated
(D) sinus venosus

111. A ventricular septal defect with right-to-left shunting is consistent with

(A) Ebstein's anomaly
(B) tetralogy of Fallot
(C) Eisenmenger's syndrome
(D) a double-outlet right ventricle

112. Which of the following is not associated with Ebstein's anomaly?

(A) an abnormally large tricuspid valve
(B) infundibular pulmonic stenosis
(C) "atrialization" of the right ventricle
(D) an atrial septal defect

113. The echocardiogram of a patient with an endocardial cushion defect might exhibit

(A) a muscular ventricular septal defect and tricuspid valve vegetation
(B) a hypokinetic left ventricle and mitral valve vegetation
(C) overriding of the aorta and subpulmonic stenosis
(D) ostium primum atrial septal defect and an inlet ventricular septal defect

114. An echocardiographic diagnosis of coarctation of the aorta can be made by detecting a high-velocity Doppler jet in the

(A) left branch of the pulmonary artery
(B) aortic arch, proximal to the subclavian artery
(C) descending thoracic aorta
(D) abdominal aorta

115. The four principal components of tetralogy of Fallot include all of the following except

(A) a ventricular septal defect
(B) an override of the aorta
(C) an obstruction of pulmonary blood flow
(D) an atrial septal defect

116. Cor triatriatum

(A) is a fairly common congenital abnormality
(B) is a congenital malformation in which a fibrous membrane divides the left atrium into an upper and lower chamber
(C) results in mitral stenosis
(D) is a condition in which the pulmonary veins drain into the right atrium

117. The echocardiographic finding most commonly associated with left bundle branch block is

(A) left ventricular hypertrophy
(B) a hypercontractile interventricular septum
(C) paradoxical septal motion
(D) a dilated left ventricle

118. The echocardiographic pattern of the mitral valve in Fig. 3–9 is consistent with

(A) mitral stenosis
(B) mitral valve vegetation
(C) a mechanical prosthetic valve
(D) a calcified mitral valve annulus

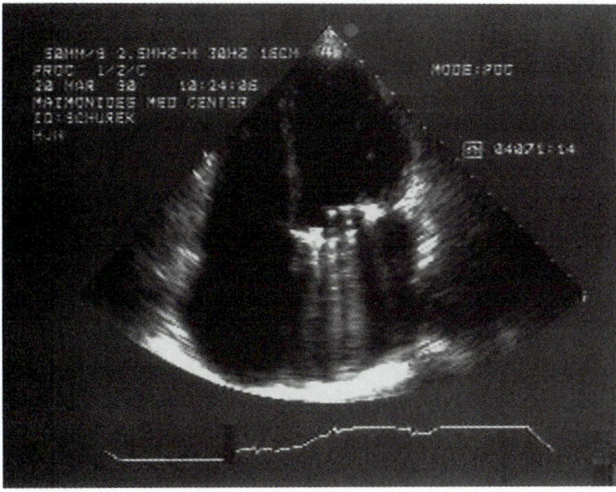

Figure 3–9. Apical four-chamber view.

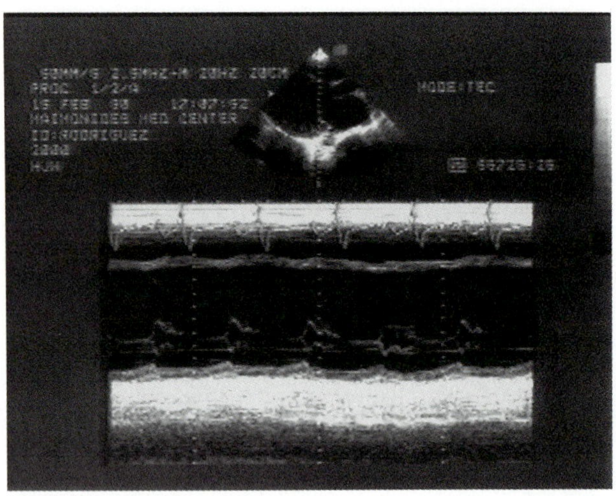

Figure 3–10. M-mode echocardiogram at the level of the mitral valve.

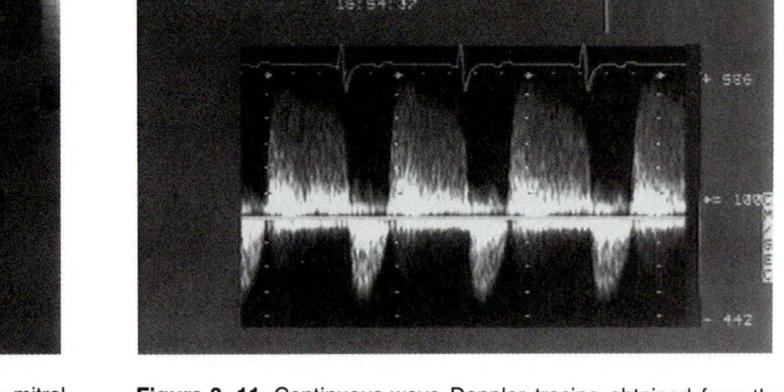

Figure 3–11. Continuous-wave Doppler tracing obtained from the apical position.

119. The M-mode pattern in Fig. 3–10 suggests that the ejection fraction of the left ventricle is

(A) normal
(B) mildly increased
(C) significantly increased
(D) significantly decreased

120. What other hemodynamic information could be derived from the M-mode (Fig. 3–10)?

(A) cardiac output is increased
(B) left ventricular end-diastolic pressure is increased
(C) the systolic ejection period is prolonged
(D) atrial flutter is present

121. The Doppler tracing in Fig. 3–11 demonstrates

(A) aortic stenosis and aortic insufficiency
(B) mitral stenosis and mitral regurgitation
(C) tricuspid stenosis and tricuspid regurgitation
(D) mitral stenosis and aortic stenosis

122. The echocardiographic findings in Fig. 3–12 indicate that the patient probably has a history of

(A) hypertension
(B) diabetes mellitus
(C) rheumatic fever
(D) coronary artery disease

123. The arrow in Fig. 3–12 is pointing to

(A) a side-lobe artifact
(B) papillary muscle
(C) chordae tendineae
(D) the anterior mitral leaflet

124. Fig. 3–13 demonstrates echoes within the left ventricular cavity. These echoes are

(A) artifactual
(B) caused by a mural thrombus
(C) caused by stagnant blood
(D) caused by a high near-gain setting

Questions 125 through 131: Match the numbered structures in Fig. 3–14 with the correct term given in Column B.

COLUMN A	COLUMN B
125. ______	(A) left ventricle
126. ______	(B) coronary sinus
127. ______	(C) left atrium
128. ______	(D) right ventricle
129. ______	(E) pericardial effusion
130. ______	(F) descending aorta
131. ______	(G) pleural effusion
	(H) aortic root
	(I) right atrium

132. Fig. 3–15 demonstrates

(A) a large pleural effusion
(B) pneumomediastinum
(C) ascites
(D) a large pericardial effusion

133. The echocardiographic examination of this patient should include analysis of the motion of the

(A) interventricular septum
(B) right ventricular wall
(C) left ventricular wall
(D) tricuspid valve

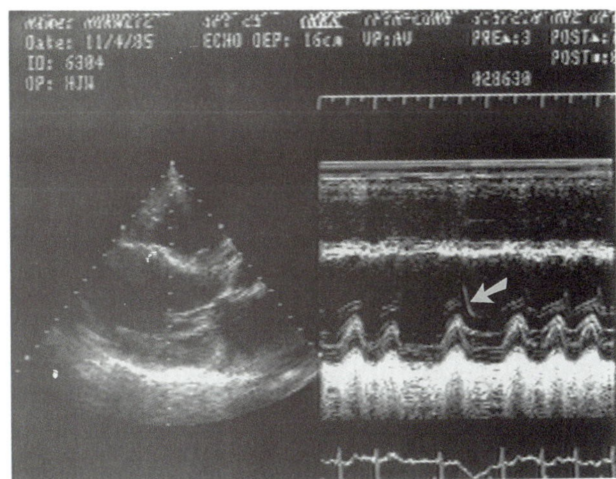

Figure 3–12. Split-screen display of a two-dimensional long-axis (left) and a correlating M-mode pattern (right). Note M-mode scan plane indicated by cursor (arrow).

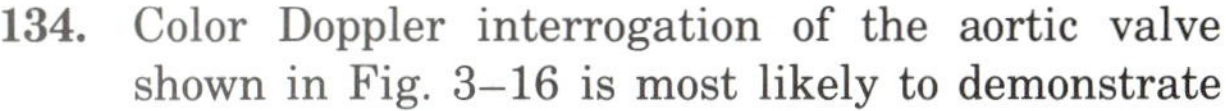

134. Color Doppler interrogation of the aortic valve shown in Fig. 3–16 is most likely to demonstrate
    (A) a narrow diastolic jet directed at the anterior mitral leaflet
    (B) a diastolic jet filling the left ventricular outflow tract and extending deep into the left ventricle
    (C) a normal pattern of blood flow
    (D) a narrow systolic jet directed at the anterior mitral leaflet

135. The arrow in Fig. 3–17 is pointing to
    (A) a fistula between the aorta and right ventricle
    (B) the coronary sinus
    (C) the left main coronary artery
    (D) the origin of the right coronary artery

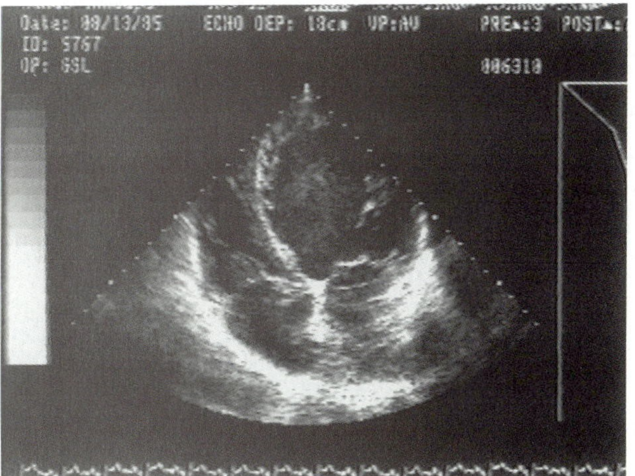

Figure 3–13. Apical four-chamber view showing a dilated left ventricle.

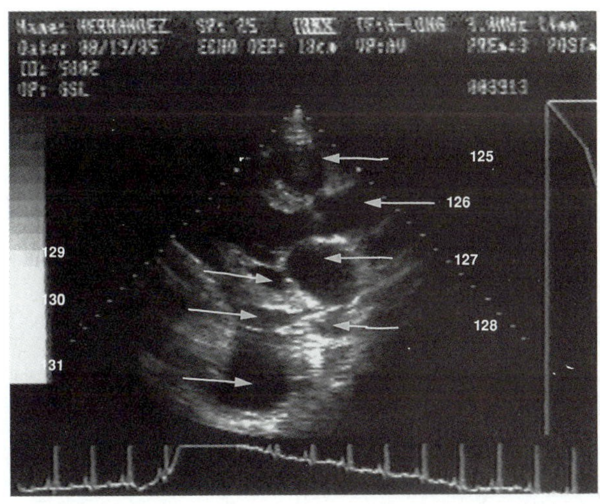

Figure 3–14. Parasternal long-axis view with an increased depth setting.

136. The right ventricular outflow tract is located medial to the arrow in Fig. 3–17.
    (A) true
    (B) false

137. The contrast study in Fig. 3–18 shows
    (A) left-to-right shunting at the atrial level
    (B) no shunting of blood
    (C) right-to-left shunting at the atrial level
    (D) right-to-left shunting at the ventricular level

138. A secondary finding noted on Fig. 3–18 is a moderate-sized pericardial effusion.
    (A) true
    (B) false

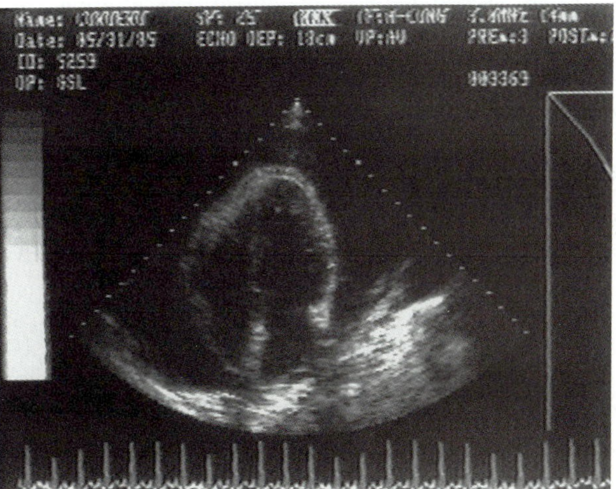

Figure 3–15. Apical four-chamber view.

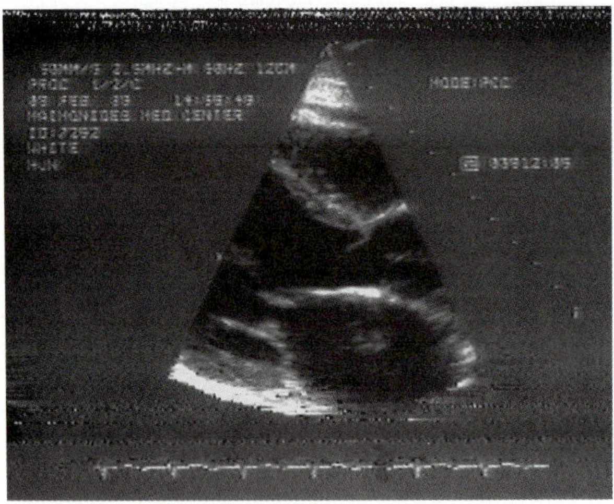

Figure 3–16. Narrow sector parasternal long-axis view.

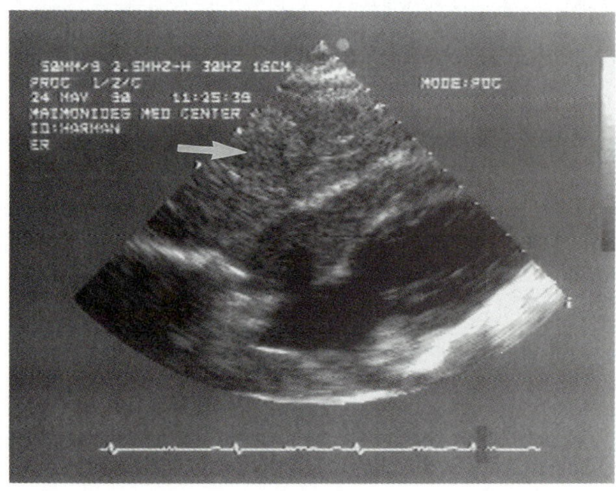

Figure 3–18. Subcostal four-chamber view with contrast injection.

139. The arrow in Fig. 3–18 is pointing to

(A) lung tissue
(B) liver parenchyma
(C) a mediastinal tumor
(D) the spleen

140. The absence of an A wave and midsystolic notching of the pulmonic valve on the M-Mode in Fig. 3–19 is consistent with

(A) pulmonic stenosis
(B) tricuspid stenosis
(C) mitral stenosis
(D) pulmonary hypertension

141. What other abnormality should be ruled out in the presence of the abnormality noted on the M-mode of the tricuspid valve in Fig. 3–20?

(A) tricuspid stenosis
(B) pulmonary hypertension
(C) mitral valve prolapse
(D) atrial septal defect

142. An 85-year-old woman with a long history of chest pain is sent for an echocardiogram. The M-mode of the mitral valve is shown in Fig. 3–21. The M-mode of the aortic valve would be likely to demonstrate

(A) diastolic fluttering
(B) delayed opening
(C) midsystolic notching
(D) systolic fluttering

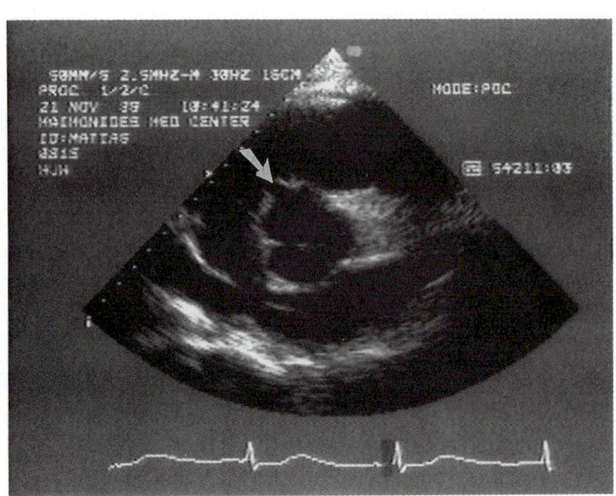

Figure 3–17. Short-axis view of the base of the heart.

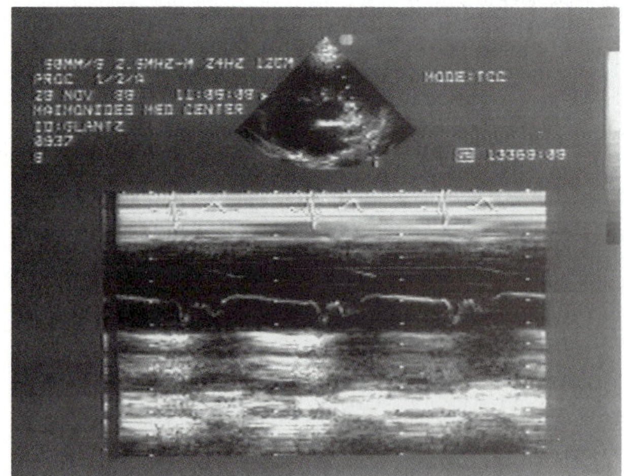

Figure 3–19. M-mode of the pulmonic valve.

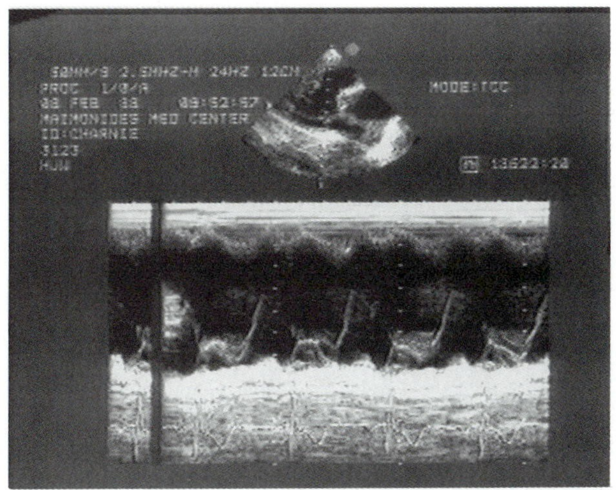

Figure 3–20. M-mode of the tricuspid valve.

143. An extremely tall slender young man was referred for an echocardiogram because he has a murmur. Echocardiographic findings in Fig. 3–22 include

(A) a biscupid aortic valve
(B) a cleft mitral valve
(C) a dilated aortic root
(D) left ventricular hypertrophy

144. Which echocardiographic view would be best for further evaluation of this abnormality?

(A) the long-axis suprasternal view
(B) the short-axis view of the base of the heart
(C) the apical four-chamber view
(D) the subcostal four-chamber view

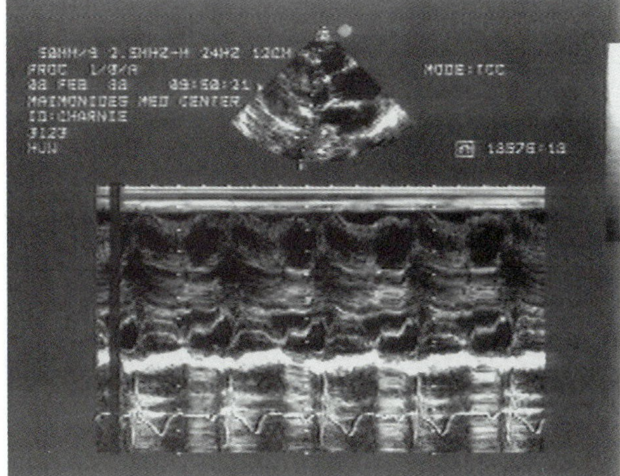

Figure 3–21. M-mode echocardiogram at the level of the mitral valve.

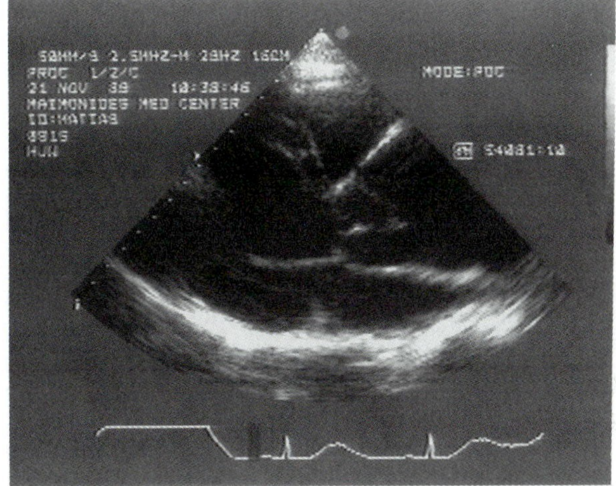

Figure 3–22. Parasternal long-axis view.

145. The left ventricle in Fig. 3–23 demonstrates

(A) hypertrophic cardiomyopathy
(B) an infiltrative tumor
(C) a large apical thrombus
(D) a myxoma

146. The mitral valve in Fig. 3–24 is

(A) normal
(B) flail
(C) stenotic
(D) prolapsing

147. The arrow in Fig. 3–25 is pointing to the

(A) left subclavian artery
(B) right pulmonary artery
(C) superior vena cava
(D) left pulmonary vein

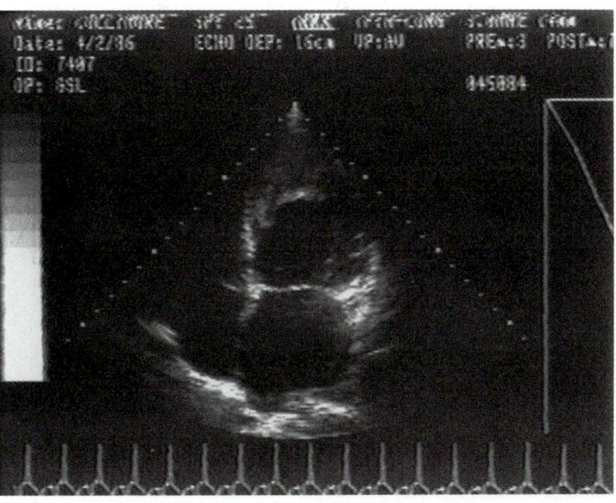

Figure 3–23. Apical four-chamber view.

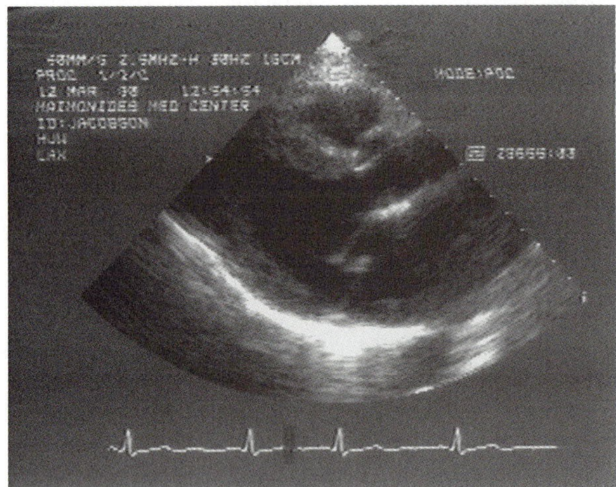

Figure 3–24. Parasternal long-axis view.

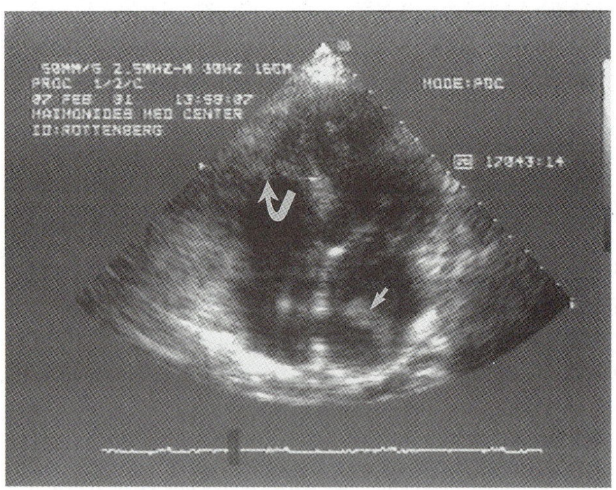

Figure 3–26. Apical four-chamber view.

148. Posterior to this structure is an echo-free space. This represents
   (A) the left atrium
   (B) a pleural effusion
   (C) pericardial effusion
   (D) the superior vena cava

149. The curved arrow in Fig. 3–26 is directed at
   (A) a pacemaker wire
   (B) the Chiari network
   (C) false chordae tendineae
   (D) the moderator band

150. The arrow in Fig. 3–26 is pointing to a structure that most likely represents
   (A) a right atrial myxoma
   (B) a left atrial thrombus
   (C) the left pulmonary vein
   (D) the eustachian valve

151. The echocardiographic findings in the long-axis view presented in Fig. 3–27 include
   (A) a dilated left atrium, mitral stenosis, and a pericardial effusion
   (B) aortic stenosis, a calcified mitral annulus, and basal septal hypertrophy
   (C) a dilated coronary sinus, left ventricular hypertrophy, and mitral valve vegetation
   (D) a dilated aortic root, a dilated left ventricle, and a thickened mitral valve

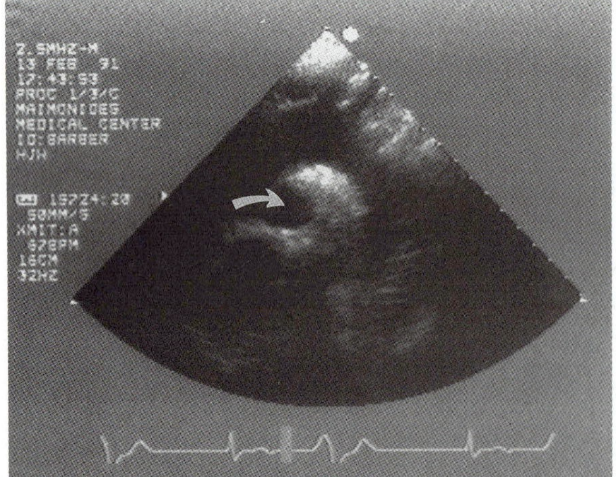

Figure 3–25. Suprasternal notch long-axis view of the aorta and transverse arch.

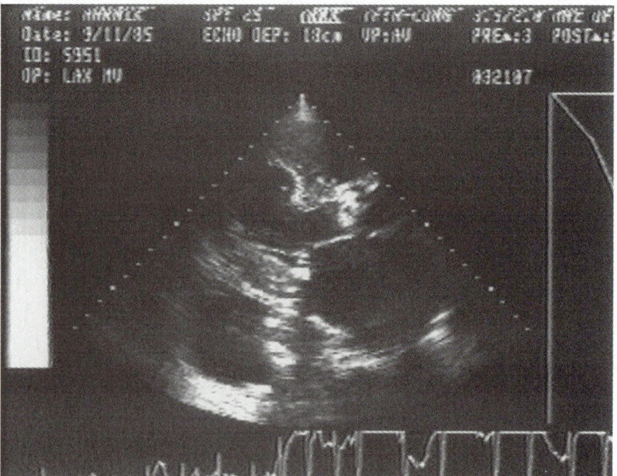

Figure 3–27. Parasternal long-axis view with slightly increased depth setting.

152. These findings are most consistent with

(A) rheumatic heart disease
(B) congenital heart disease
(C) subacute bacterial endocarditis
(D) an aged heart

153. The mitral valve diastolic waveforms in Fig. 3–28C are not uniform. This is caused by

(A) high end-diastolic pressure of the left ventricle
(B) faulty technique
(C) inspiration
(D) atrial fibrillation

The following study is of a 58-year-old woman who vaguely remembers a childhood illness that included pain in her joints. She was presented with a trans-ischemic attack and atrial fibrillation. For questions 154 through 156, refer to Fig. 3–28A, B, and C.

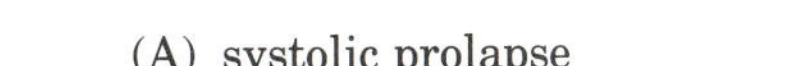

154. The mitral valve demonstrates

(A) systolic prolapse
(B) diastolic doming
(C) myxomatous degeneration
(D) hyperkinesis

155. Which chamber is significantly dilated?

(A) the left atrium
(B) the left ventricle
(C) the right atrium
(D) the right ventricle

156. Auscultation of this patient is most likely to reveal

(A) a midsystolic click
(B) a systolic ejection murmur
(C) a systolic rumble
(D) an opening snap

157. The arrow in Fig. 3–28B is pointing to the

(A) coronary sinus
(B) inferior vena cava

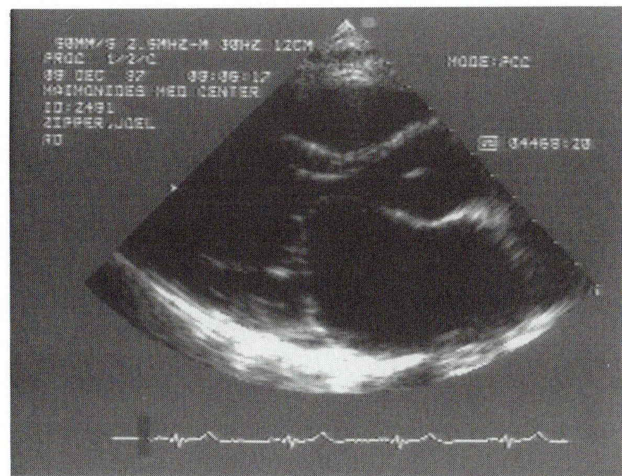

A

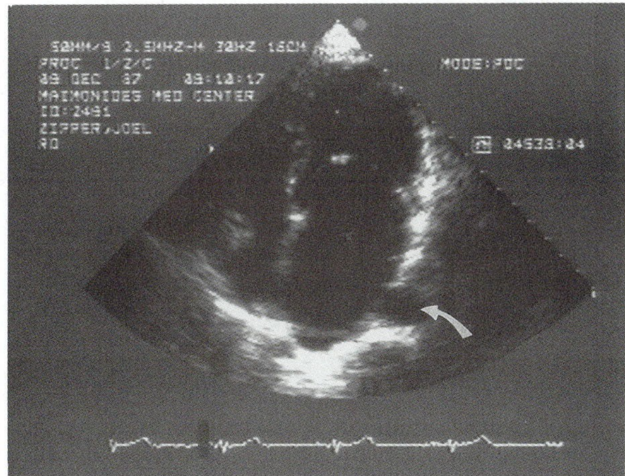

B

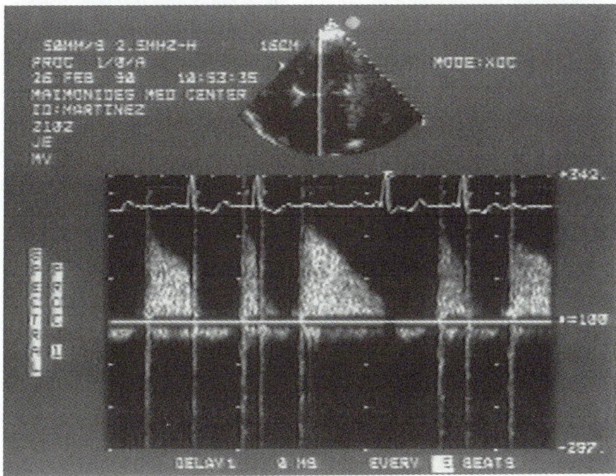

C

Figure 3–28. (**A**) Parasternal long-axis view; (**B**) apical four-chamber view; (**C**) continuous-wave Doppler tracing of mitral inflow from the apical position.

(C) descending aorta
(D) left pulmonary vein

158. The pressure half-time derived from the Doppler tracing of the mitral valve in Fig. 3–28C can be used to estimate

(A) the mitral valve area
(B) the mitral valve gradient
(C) the severity of aortic insufficiency
(D) the ejection fraction

A 52-year-old woman presents with chronic dyspnea. Chest x-ray reveals cardiomegaly. For questions 159 through 162, refer to Fig. 3–29A and B.

159. The most striking feature of this echocardiogram is

(A) left atrial compression
(B) mitral valve doming
(C) left ventricular hypertrophy
(D) right ventricular dilatation

160. Additional findings on this echocardiogram include

(A) a dilated aortic root, mitral valve prolapse, and a dilated coronary sinus
(B) a thickened mitral valve, a prominent interatrial septum, a small left ventricle, and a pericardial effusion
(C) a calcified mitral annulus, an extracardiac mass, and pleural effusion
(D) left atrial dilatation, systolic anterior motion of the mitral valve, and a thickened aortic valve

161. Given all the above information, the most likely diagnosis is

(A) hypertrophic obstructive cardiomyopathy
(B) Marfan syndrome
(C) endomyocardial fibrosis
(D) amyloid cardiomyopathy

162. The best way to substantiate this diagnosis is by obtaining

(A) a CT scan
(B) an endomyocardial biopsy
(C) a cardiac catheterization
(D) an electrocardiogram

A 64-year-old male sustained a myocardial infarction one week before this echocardiogram. He developed congestive heart failure and became hypotensive. A new murmur was detected on auscultation. For questions 163 through 167, refer to Fig. 3–30A and B.

163. The echocardiogram reveals a

(A) dilated cardiomyopathy
(B) ventricular septal defect
(C) cleft mitral valve
(D) pseudoaneurysm

164. Which of the following would be the most helpful in confirming the diagnosis

(A) color flow Doppler imaging
(B) M-mode echocardiography
(C) continuous-wave Doppler imaging
(D) pulsed-wave Doppler imaging

165. The arrow in Fig. 3–30B is pointing to a linear structure called the

(A) coronary sinus
(B) left anterior descending coronary artery
(C) left pulmonary vein
(D) left circumflex coronary artery

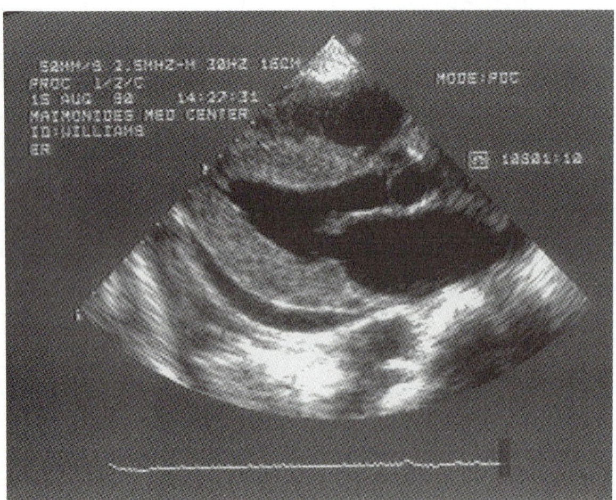

A

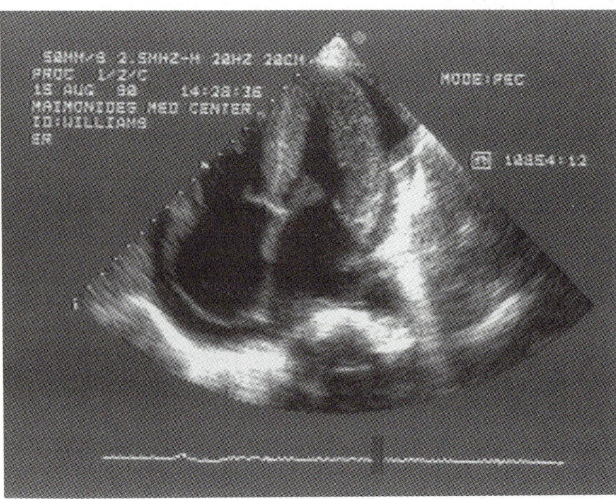

B

Figure 3–29. (**A**) Parasternal long-axis view; (**B**) apical four-chamber view.

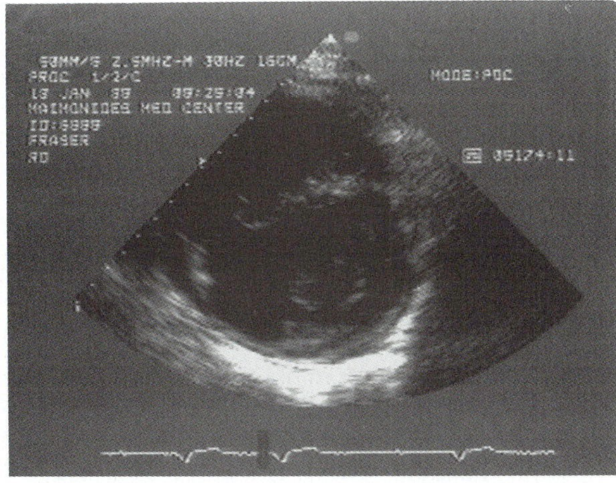

A

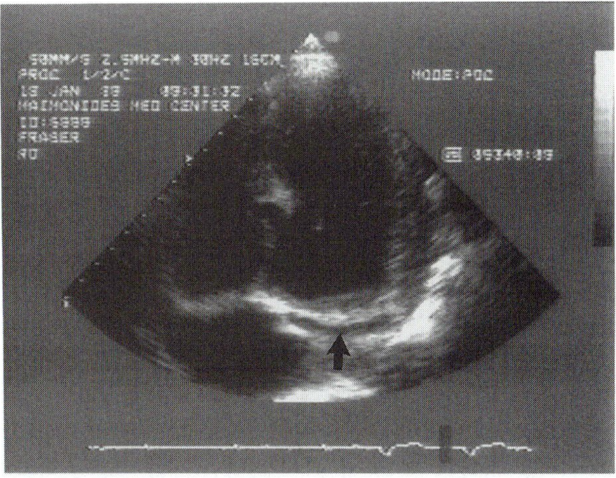

B

Figure 3–30. (**A**) Parasternal short-axis view at the level of the papillary muscles; (**B**) modified apical four-chamber view: The transducer is angled posteriorly and the depth setting is decreased.

166. This linear structure contains

(A) serous fluid
(B) deoxygenated blood
(C) oxygenated blood
(D) air

167. In Fig. 3–30B, in what direction would the transducer need to be directed to visualize the left ventricular outflow tract?

(A) anteriorly
(B) medially
(C) laterally
(D) inferiorly

A 34-year-old woman is extremely nervous at the time of the examination. She states that she often experiences chest pain and palpitations. Auscultation reveals a systolic murmur. For questions 168 through 171 refer to Fig. 3–31A and B.

168. The mitral valve demonstrates

(A) diastolic doming
(B) prolapse of the anterior leaflet
(C) prolapse of the posterior leaflet
(D) systolic anterior motion

169. Continuous-wave Doppler evaluation of the mitral valve from the apical position would most likely demonstrate a

(A) systolic curve below baseline greater than 3 m/s
(B) diastolic signal above baseline with a decreased pressure half-time
(C) systolic curve above baseline less than 3 m/s

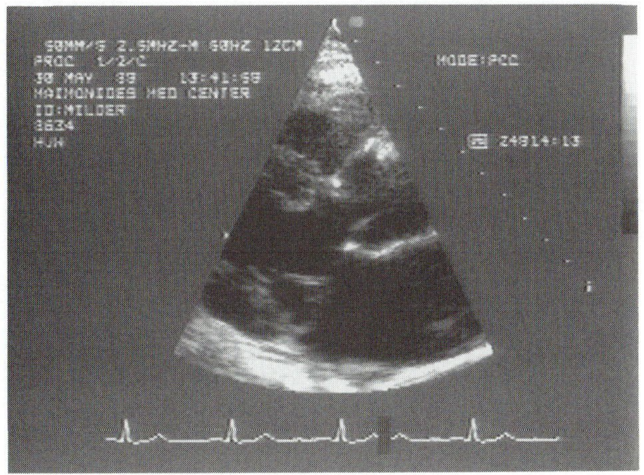

A

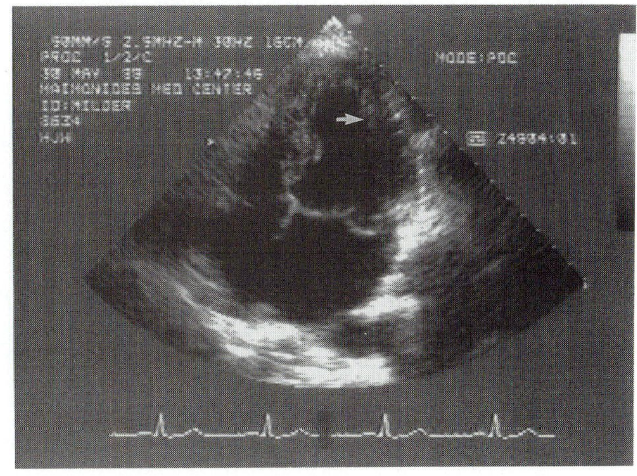

B

Figure 3–31. (**A**) Narrow sector parasternal long-axis view; (**B**) apical four-chamber view.

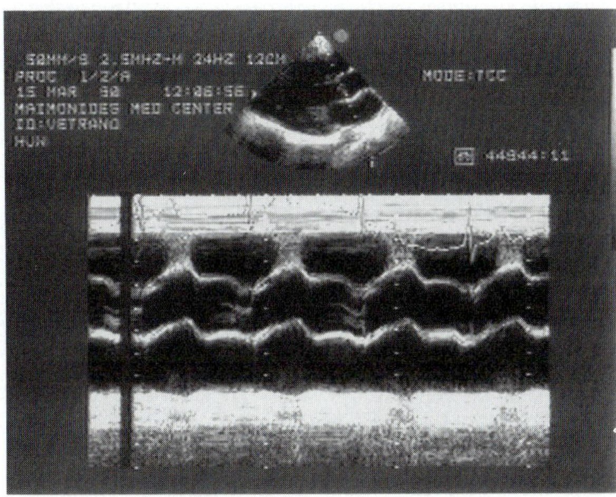

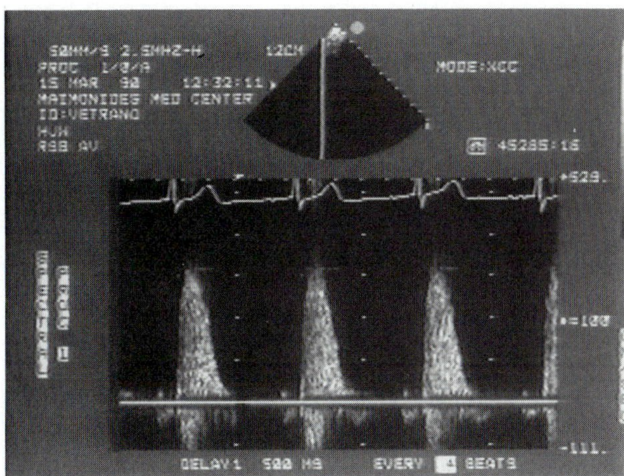

A

B

Figure 3–32. (**A**) M-mode tracing at the aortic valve level; (**B**) Continuous-wave Doppler tracing of aortic flow from the right sternal border (calibration marks are 1 m/s).

(D) diastolic curve below baseline greater than 3 m/s

170. The arrow in Fig. 3–31B is pointing to the posterior wall of the left ventricle.

(A) true
(B) false

171. The dropout of echoes in the interatrial septum in Fig. 3–31B is most likely

(A) a primum atrial septal defect
(B) a secundum atrial septal defect
(C) artifactual
(D) the result of interatrial septal prolapse

A 23-year-old male was referred for an echocardiogram because a systolic ejection murmur was heard on auscultation. For questions 172 through 175, refer to Fig. 3–32A and B.

172. The M-mode of the aortic valve in Fig. 3–32A demonstrates

(A) slight thickening of the valve with a normal opening
(B) the absence of aortic valve echoes
(C) systolic fluttering of the aortic valve
(D) a thickened aortic valve with a markedly decreased opening

173. According to the Doppler tracing in Fig. 3–32B, the peak aortic gradient using the simplified Bernoulli formula is approximately

(A) 4 mm Hg
(B) 16 mm Hg
(C) 36 mm Hg
(D) 100 mm Hg

174. The most likely diagnosis for this patient is

(A) aortic valve vegetation
(B) congenital aortic stenosis
(C) moderate aortic insufficiency
(D) rheumatic heart disease

175. Two-dimensional examination of the aortic valve is most likely to demonstrate

(A) systolic doming
(B) a mass of echoes in the left ventricular outflow tract
(C) diastolic doming
(D) four aortic cusps

A 38-year-old woman, who recently had extensive dental work performed, presented with fever, chills, and a transischemic attack. Auscultation revealed a grade 2/6 systolic murmur. For questions 176 through 181, refer to Fig. 3–33A, B, and C.

176. The mitral valve is

(A) normal
(B) doming
(C) exhibiting shaggy irregular echoes
(D) flail

177. The most likely diagnosis for this patient is

(A) rheumatic heart disease
(B) subacute bacterial endocarditis
(C) ruptured papillary muscle
(D) mitral valve prolapse

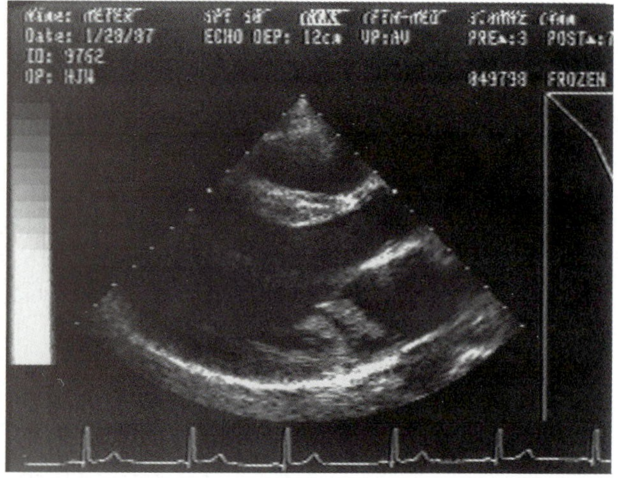

A

B

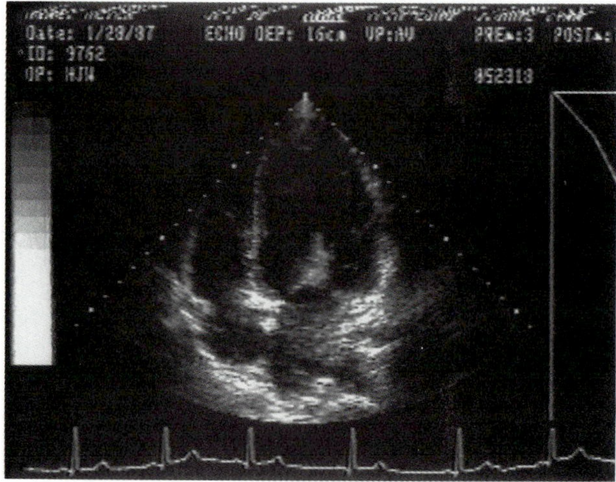

C

Figure 3–33. (**A**) Parasternal long-axis view; (**B**) parasternal short-axis view at the papillary muscle level; (**C**) apical four-chamber view.

178. The mitral valve excursion is most likely

(A) reduced
(B) increased
(C) normal
(D) absent

179. Apical continuous-wave Doppler examination of the mitral valve is most likely to demonstrate a

(A) systolic waveform below baseline
(B) diastolic waveform below baseline
(C) diastolic waveform above baseline greater than 3 m/s
(D) systolic waveform above baseline

180. By referring to all three echocardiographic views presented in this case, one could suggest that the mass of echoes on the mitral valve

(A) is stationary
(B) prolapses into the left atrium
(C) prolapses into the left ventricle
(D) prolapses into the left atrium and left ventricle

181. The arrow in Fig. 3–33B points to

(A) a mural thrombus
(B) the posteromedial papillary muscle
(C) vegetation
(D) a cleft mitral valve

Answers and Explanations

1. **(C)** Subcostal. Standard parasternal and suprasternal views do not demonstrate all four cardiac chambers. Only the apical and subcostal windows allow visualization of all cardiac chambers. *(1:80)*

2. **(A)** Long axis, short axis, and four chamber. The American Society of Echocardiography has standardized two-dimensional views of the heart into three basic orthogonal planes for which all views can basically be categorized. *(2:212)*

3. **(A)** Atrial septal defect and ventricular septal defect. If the ultrasound beam is not oriented perpendicular to the interatrial and interventricular septum, there may be false dropout of echoes. The subcostal approach allows the ultrasound beam to be perpendicular to the cardiac chambers, thereby allowing a better demonstration of atrial or ventricular septal defects. In addition, any gap noted in the interatrial or interventricular septum when the subcostal four-chamber view is used should be considered real. *(1:92)*

4. **(B)** Time-gain compensation. The time-gain compensation control allows the echocardiographer to selectively increase or decrease the gain at different depths of tissue. The objective is to achieve a uniform echocardiographic image without artifactually adding or eliminating information. *(3:52)*

5. **(A)** The right ventricular pressure drops below the right atrial pressure. The atrioventricular valves open when ventricular pressure drops below atrial pressure. *(3:38)*

6. **(B)** The coronary ligament. This ligament defines the bare area of the liver and is the only choice that does not represent a remnant of fetal circulation. *(4:30)*

7. **(A)** Pulmonary artery. The right side of the heart pumps deoxygenated blood through the pulmonary artery to the lungs for reoxygenation. (The pulmonary artery is the only artery in the body that carries deoxygenated blood.) *(3:9)*

8. **(C)** Left atrium. Four pulmonary veins transport oxygenated blood from the lungs to the left atrium. (The pulmonary veins are the only veins in the body that carry oxygenated blood.) *(3:9)*

9. **(D)** The left ventricle constitutes most of the ventral surface of the heart. The right ventricle, although less muscular than the left ventricle, dominates the ventral surface of the heart. *(3:25)*

10. **(A)** Aortic valve opening and closing points. Left ventricular ejection time—the time it takes for blood to be ejected from the left ventricle—can be obtained from an M-mode tracing of the aortic valve by measuring the time interval between opening and closing of the valve. *(3:156)*

11. **(D)** Subcostal. Lung expansion in patients with chronic obstructive pulmonary disease often obliterates the apical and parasternal position. This lung expansion also tends to shift the heart inferiorly, making the subcostal view the best approach for scanning the heart. *(5:79)*

12. **(B)** Apical and right sternal border. The most common windows used to record systolic blood flow across the aortic valve are the apical, right parasternal, and suprasternal. *(6:128)*

13. **(A)** At end-systole. M-mode measurements of the left atrium, left ventricle, and right ventricle are done at a point when the chambers are at their largest. The left atrium is largest at end-systole. *(3:82)*

14. **(C)** Stenosis. Doming is a main two-dimensional feature of any stenotic valve. The valve domes when it opens because the commissures are fused, causing the body of the valve to separate more widely than the tips. *(1:251)*

15. **(C)** Perpendicular, parallel. Because of the differences in transducer orientation for optimum two-dimensional and Doppler studies, one rarely obtains excellent-quality images and wave forms

simultaneously and may have to relinquish quality in one to obtain excellent-quality images in the others. *(1:104)*

16. **(D)** Pulmonary hypertension. The constant pressure overload of pulmonary hypertension causes right ventricular hypertrophy until the ventricle fails, at which point the right ventricle wall dilates. *(3:217)*

17. **(C)** Chordae tendineae. Left ventricular dimensions have been standardized to be obtained at the level of the chordae tendineae. *(7:1072)*

18. **(C)** Left ventricular volume overload. Right ventricular volume overload may cause paradoxical interventricular septal motion (anterior motion of the interventricular septum at the onset of systole). *(1:164)*

19. **(A)** Toward the right ventricular free wall. Right ventricular volume overload causes paradoxical septal motion, whereby the septum moves toward the right side of the heart in systole rather than toward the left side of the heart. *(1:164)*

20. **(A)** Organic in origin. A thrill is a murmur that produces a vibratory sensation when palpated. It is almost always organic in origin. *(8:51)*

21. **(A)** Mitral valve prolapse or systolic anterior motion of the mitral valve. The Valsalva maneuver and the inhalation of amyl nitrite decrease left ventricular volume and reduce the diameter of the left ventricular outflow tract, thereby stimulating mitral valve prolapse or systolic anterior motion of the mitral valve. *(3:222)*

22. **(A)** Cyanotic heart disease. Clubbing occurs when there is widening and cyanosis of the distal ends of the fingers and toes. *(9:18)*

23. **(B)** Providing enhanced temporal resolution. M-mode is still used in many laboratories to take measurements and to evaluate events that occur too rapidly for the eye to perceive, such as diastolic fluttering of the anterior mitral leaflet. This is the case because M-mode provides far better temporal (time) resolution than does two-dimensional echocardiography and allows for better analysis of intracardiac events. *(3:78)*

24. **(C)** To a higher intercostal space. If the transducer is placed too low relative to the position of the heart, the sector plane passes obliquely through the left ventricle, producing an ovoid image. *(3:110)*

25. **(C)** Decreased left ventricular compliance. This situation, referred to as reversed E-to-A ratio, indicates decreased left ventricular diastolic compliance. Conditions that cause this include left systemic hypertension, hypertrophic cardiomyopathy, and coronary artery disease. *(3:240)*

26. **(C)** A left ventricular thrombus. Left ventricular function is not impaired in mitral stenosis. Because thrombi tend to form in areas of poor blood flow, the likelihood of finding a left ventricular thrombus is low. *(1:489)*

27. **(D)** A peak gradient occurring in late diastole. The peak gradient in mitral stenosis usually occurs in early diastole. *(10:132)*

28. **(C)** Mitral insufficiency. Ruptured chordae tendineae always result in mitral regurgitation, the onset of which is often abrupt and acute. *(3:189)*

29. **(D)** Hypertrophic obstructive cardiomyopathy. This causes anterior motion of the mitral valve. It is not a source of confusion for mitral valve prolapse, in which the mitral valve moves posteriorly in systole. *(11:211)*

30. **(A)** A dilated left atrium. This is a secondary sign of mitral regurgitation. The left ventricle usually dilates as well and becomes hyperkinetic in response to the volume overload. *(1:266)*

31. **(A)** Width and length of the systolic jet by color Doppler. Color Doppler provides a spatial display of regurgitant flow. Quantification of the severity of mitral regurgitation is based roughly on the size and configuration of the regurgitant jet. *(12:87)*

32. **(D)** Pulmonic stenosis. The pulmonic valve is the valve that is least likely to be deformed by rheumatic fever. When pulmonic stenosis is noted on an echocardiogram, it is usually a congenital abnormality rather than a sequela of rheumatic fever. *(9:1711)*

33. **(A)** A dilated left atrium and left ventricular hypertrophy. Mitral stenosis causes the left atrium to dilate, and aortic stenosis leads to left ventricular hypertrophy. *(3:186, 206)*

34. **(B)** Concurrent atrial fibrillation. Mitral stenosis often leads to atrial fibrillation. The A wave of the mitral valve corresponds to the P wave on the electrocardiogram. Because the P wave is absent in atrial fibrillation, the A wave will be absent as well. *(11:333)*

35. **(B)** Hypertrophic cardiomyopathy. Under normal circumstances, the mitral E point, which represents rapid ventricular filling, is higher than the mitral A point, which corresponds to atrial contraction.

This relationship between the two points is altered when there is decreased left ventricular compliance (as is the case with hypertrophic cardiomyopathy). *(6:155)*

36. **(B)** Aortic regurgitation. Aortic regurgitation causes a left ventricular volume overload pattern on the echocardiogram (a dilated and hypercontractile left ventricle). Mitral regurgitation usually causes dilatation of both the left atrium and the left ventricle. *(5:231)*

37. **(C)** A decreased E-F slope, a thickened mitral valve, and a mitral distal velocity >1.5 m/s. Both thickening of the mitral valve and a reduced E-F slope must be noted to be sure the pathology is mitral stenosis. Diastolic doming of the mitral valve also is a specific sign of mitral stenosis. *(1:251)*

38. **(B)** An increased E-F slope on M-mode. One M-mode criterion for mitral stenosis is a decreased E-F slope. *(1:249)*

39. **(C)** Tips of the mitral leaflets. The mitral valve is funnel shaped, with the true orifice at the narrow end. Measurement of the size of the orifice should therefore be done at the tips of the leaflets at the point where the chordae tendineae merge with the body of the valve. *(3:161)*

40. **(C)** A dilated left ventricle. Unless there is concomitant mitral regurgitation, the size of the left ventricle will be normal or smaller than normal. *(13:64)*

41. **(C)** An increase in pressure half-time. A successful mitral valve commissurotomy should lead to a decrease in the pressure half-time. The other findings will usually remain, although the left atrium may decrease slightly in size. *(13:65)*

42. **(B)** Concomitant mitral regurgitation. Pure mitral stenosis leads to a dilated left atrium and a normal or smaller-than-normal left ventricle. Aortic stenosis and hypertrophic cardiomyopathy cause the left ventricular walls to appear thickened. Only concomitant mitral regurgitation will cause left ventricular dilatation as well. *(1:139)*

43. **(A)** Severe acute aortic regurgitation. Severe acute aortic insufficiency can cause an elevated left ventricular diastolic pressure, which in turn causes the mitral valve to close early. *(1:295)*

44. **(D)** A ventricular septal defect. Conditions such as systemic hypertension that stress the area of the mitral annulus can lead to premature calcification of the mitral annulus. *(9:1035)*

45. **(B)** 1 cm^2. Studies done by Hatle and co-workers found that a mitral valve with an area of 1 cm^2 exhibits a Doppler pressure half-time of 220 m/s. *(14:1096)*

46. **(B)** Diastolic fluttering of the anterior mitral leaflet. This is a finding of aortic insufficiency. *(3:210)*

47. **(D)** Systemic hypertension. This produces pressure overload of the left ventricle that, in turn, leads to left ventricular hypertrophy. Choices B and C cause a left ventricular volume overload pattern on the echocardiogram (dilated and hyperkinetic left ventricle). *(15:104)*

48. **(C)** Aortic stenosis. A systolic ejection murmur can be heard with this disorder. *(3:204)*

49. **(C)** It is often seen in conjunction with mitral stenosis. A bicuspid aortic valve is a congenital abnormality in which one of the aortic commissures is fused, leading to the formation of two aortic cusps instead of the usual three. Bicuspid valves tend to become stenotic in adulthood. Although they are sometimes seen in conjunction with coarctation of the aorta, a bicuspid valve and mitral stenosis have no direct association. *(3:202)*

50. **(B)** The aortic valve area, poor left ventricular function. When aortic stenosis is found in conjunction with a poorly moving left ventricle, standard estimations of the degree of aortic stenosis will be inaccurate. The continuity equation compensates for ventricular hypocontractility, allowing for a more accurate estimate of the aortic valve area. *(3:207, 16:105)*

51. **(B)** The mean pressure gradient. Aortic insufficiency may cause a high initial instantaneous gradient. When there is combined aortic stenosis and insufficiency, the mean pressure gradient is more specific for estimating the severity of aortic stenosis. *(6:137)*

52. **(A)** The apical long-axis view. All Doppler procedures are best performed with the ultrasound beam directed parallel to the flow of blood. Of the choices presented, the apical long-axis view provides the optimum angle to image acquisition. *(1:104)*

53. **(B)** Left ventricular hypertrophy. Aortic stenosis causes pressure overload of the left ventricle. This overload leads to left ventricular hypertrophy. *(11:203)*

54. **(A)** Aortic insufficiency. The anterior mitral leaflet flutters rapidly when hit by an aortic insufficiency

jet. These oscillations are best detected by M-mode. Atrial fibrillation causes coarse diastolic fluttering of the anterior mitral leaflet. *(1:294)*

55. **(D)** Consistent with moderate aortic regurgitation. The grading of aortic insufficiency with Doppler echocardiography is similar to the grading method used in cardiac catheterization laboratories. An aortic insufficiency jet that extends from the aortic valve to the tips of the anterior mitral leaflet is consistent with moderate aortic regurgitation. *(17:339)*

56. **(B)** Fine diastolic fluttering and possible flattening of the anterior mitral leaflet. An Austin-Flint murmur represents functional mitral stenosis caused by inhibition of anterior leaflet motion resulting from compression by a strong aortic insufficiency jet. This would appear on M-mode as fine diastolic fluttering of the anterior mitral leaflet with inhibition of opening. *(9:77)*

57. **(D)** The right sternal border. When obtainable, the right sternal border approach is usually best for acquiring maximum aortic valve velocities. The patient is turned onto his or her right side, and the Doppler probe is directed into the aortic root. *(18:89)*

58. **(D)** Transesophageal echocardiography. Because of the high-resolution images it provides of the thoracic aorta, transesophageal echocardiography has been highly successful in evaluating patients with suspected aortic dissection. *(19:216)*

59. **(D)** A thickened anterior right ventricle wall. Thickening of the right ventricular walls is usually caused by right ventricular pressure overload. Tricuspid insufficiency causes right ventricular volume overload. *(1:162)*

60. **(D)** Pulmonary hypertension. The right ventricular systolic pressure in this ventricle is approximately 74 mm Hg (using the formula $4\ V^2 + 10$). Because right ventricular pressures are basically equal to pulmonary artery pressures, the pulmonary artery pressure in this instance is roughly 74 mm Hg, thus indicating the presence of pulmonary hypertension. *(3:161)*

61. **(D)** It is usually seen as part of the aging process. Tricuspid stenosis is a rare condition that usually occurs as a sequela to rheumatic fever. Its echocardiographic findings are similar to those of mitral stenosis. *(3:198)*

62. **(C)** Contrast in the inferior vena cava during ventricular systole. With severe tricuspid regurgitation, the regurgitant volume extends all the way back into the right atrium and sometimes into the inferior vena cava as well. By injecting contrast, this regurgitant volume can be "seen" with M-mode or two-dimensional echocardiography. *(1:305)*

63. **(B)** Tricuspid valve. The echocardiographer should pay special attention to this valve because carcinoid heart disease presents as thickening and rigidity of the tricuspid valve leaflets. Severe tricuspid regurgitation is usually detected with Doppler. *(1:305)*

64. **(B)** Right ventricular systolic pressure. By using the modified Bernoulli equation and an estimate of jugular venous pressure, systolic pressure in the right ventricle can be determined. *(3:112)*

65. **(C)** Infundibular pulmonic stenosis. This is caused by hypertrophied muscle bands in the right ventricular outflow tract. Echocardiographically, it can be distinguished from valvular pulmonic stenosis by noting a step-up in Doppler velocities proximal to the pulmonic valve. In addition, the muscular ridge produces turbulence of blood, which hits the pulmonic valve and causes it to flutter. *(1:393)*

66. **(D)** Left parasternal. Pulmonary artery flow velocities are usually obtained from the left parasternal short-axis view at the level of the aortic root. *(10:80)*

67. **(A)** Cranial and lateral. This relationship is best appreciated from the short-axis view of the base of the heart. *(3:27)*

68. **(C)** Midsystolic notching noted on M-mode. Midsystolic notching is a sign of pulmonary hypertension. *(3:388)*

69. **(B)** Two-dimensional echocardiography. The spatial orientation of two-dimensional echocardiography provides for a better assessment of the size, location, and motion of valvular vegetations. *(3:277)*

70. **(B)** Mitral valve vegetation. Intravenous drug abusers have an increased incidence of endocarditis because of microorganisms that enter the bloodstream via unsterile needles. Vegetations usually form on the valves of the right side of the heart, but they may settle on left-sided valves as well. One complication of valvular vegetation is an embolic event. *(3:276)*

71. **(B)** Presence of paravalvular regurgitation. The spatial orientation of color Doppler allows for a quick assessment of blood flow in the region surrounding the prosthetic valve. *(12:141)*

72. **(A)** May exhibit high Doppler velocities. The normal Doppler velocities across any prosthetic valve will be slightly higher than those of a native valve.

A Starr-Edwards, or ball-in-cage valve, tends to exhibit the highest velocities. *(3:349)*

73. **(A)** An example of a mechanical heart valve. The Bjork-Shiley is a tilting-disc mechanical heart valve. *(3:314)*

74. **(C)** Transesophageal echocardiography. This is a major application in the evaluation of prosthetic heart valves, particularly in the mitral position. *(3:358)*

75. **(D)** Hancock. This valve is an example of a heterograft (bioprosthetic) valve. *(3:334)*

76. **(C)** Abnormal rocking motion of the valve. Valve dehiscence refers to a condition in which the prosthetic valve loosens or separates from the sewing ring and causes an abnormal rocking motion and a paravalvular leak. *(3:346)*

77. **(C)** It often makes anticoagulation unnecessary. Mechanical valves require constant anticoagulation. Women during childbearing years would therefore be more likely to receive a bioprosthetic valve, which would not require anticoagulation. *(20:1392)*

78. **(A)** Because these patients are at a higher risk for endocarditis. Because bacteremias occur during dental or surgical procedures, prophylactic antibiotics are often administered to susceptible patients (such as mitral valve prolapse patients) in an attempt to prevent bacterial endocarditis. *(20:1151)*

79. **(C)** A "swinging heart" on the two-dimensional examination. Excessive motion of the heart can sometimes be noted with massive pericardial effusion. *(1:558)*

80. **(A)** Impairs diastolic filling. The rigid and fibrotic pericardial sac impairs diastolic filling of the cardiac chambers. *(3:268)*

81. **(A)** Pressure in the pericardial cavity rises to equal or exceed the diastolic pressure in the heart. Tamponade occurs when intrapericardial pressures rise and impair cardiac filling. Although cardiac tamponade is usually seen in association with a large pericardial effusion, a small effusion may cause tamponade if the rate of accumulation of pericardial fluid exceeds the ability of the pericardium to accommodate the increased volume. *(15:213)*

82. **(D)** In Dressler's syndrome, a pericardial effusion develops as a result of renal disease. Dressler's syndrome, also known as postmyocardial infarction syndrome, is the development of pericardial effusion 2-to-10 weeks after infarction. *(9:1287)*

83. **(D)** A pericardial effusion. Neoplasms from the thoracic region often lead to pericardial effusion. *(20:1254)*

84. **(D)** Mitral valve prolapse. The descending aorta, a calcified mitral annulus, and ascites can cause echo-free spaces that may be misleading on an echocardiogram. Although a large effusion in which the heart exhibits excessive motion may lead to false mitral valve prolapse, prolapse will not lead to a false-positive diagnosis of pericardial effusion. *(1:552)*

85. **(A)** Pulmonic stenosis. Diastolic collapse of the right ventricular walls is a good indicator of tamponade. Pulmonic stenosis, or any other form of right ventricular pressure overload, leads to thickening of the right ventricular walls. A thickened wall is unlikely to collapse in diastole. *(1:565)*

86. **(C)** There is a large acoustic mismatch between lung tissue and pericardial tissue. A greater mismatch between two structures results in brighter reflected echoes from the interface between them. Because there is an extremely large acoustic mismatch between lung (air) and pericardium (tissue), the interface created by the two will cause a bright echo to appear on the echocardiogram. *(1:2)*

87. **(C)** Decreasing overall gain and increasing depth setting. Decreasing the gain allows for differentiation between the pericardium and epicardium, and increasing the depth setting helps define the borders of the effusion. *(11:249)*

88. **(D)** Descending aorta. Because the descending aorta lies posterior to the pericardial effusion and anterior to the pleural effusion, it often aids in differentiating between the two. *(1:554)*

89. **(A)** Constrictive pericarditis. The pericardium limits cardiac motion. When the pericardium is surgically removed (eg in constrictive pericarditis), the heart expands and exhibits excessive motion. *(1:575)*

90. **(A)** Excessive cardiac motion. Again, because the pericardium limits cardiac motion, the heart exhibits excessive motion when the pericardium is surgically removed. *(1:575)*

91. **(C)** Reduced compliance of the left ventricle. Systemic hypertension causes pressure overload of the left ventricle. As in all pressure-overload situations (eg aortic stenosis), the left ventricle hypertrophies and may become noncompliant, leading to diastolic dysfunction. *(11:273)*

92. **(B)** Left ventricular hypertrophy. This condition can be present in the absence of an obstruction. *(1:522)*

93. **(D)** Endomyocardial biopsy. Several echocardiographic signs are suggestive of amyloid heart disease, but a definitive diagnosis can be made only with an endomyocardial biopsy performed in the catheterization laboratory. *(20:1215)*

94. **(B)** Sarcoidosis. This is an infiltrative process that can lead to restrictive cardiomyopathy. *(11:317)*

95. **(A)** Increased systolic velocity of the left ventricular outflow tract. Velocities are low because of decreased cardiac output. *(3:230)*

96. **(A)** Is more likely to affect the right ventricle than the left ventricle. Cardiac contusion may be seen following a blunt trauma to the chest (such as a steering-wheel injury). Because the right ventricle is the most anterior structure of the heart, it is the one most susceptible to injury. *(3:301)*

97. **(A)** An apical aneurysm with a mural thrombus. Apical aneurysms sometimes develop following an anterior wall myocardial infarction. Because aneurysms are a likely site for thrombus, choice A is the most likely answer. *(1:489)*

98. **(C)** Two-dimensional demonstration of an ejection fraction lower than 50%. The ejection fraction is a measure of systolic left ventricular function. *(20:51)*

99. **(C)** Left anterior descending artery. This artery supplies the anterior wall of the left ventricle and the anterior portion of the interventricular septum. *(3:237)*

100. **(D)** Have a narrow neck. The best way to differentiate a true aneurysm from a pseudoaneurysm is to look at the width of its neck. Pseudoaneurysms tend to have a narrow neck because they result from a tear in the myocardium. *(1:486)*

101. **(B)** A reduced ejection fraction. An E point-to-septal separation of more than 10 mm correlates with a reduced ejection fraction. *(11:205)*

102. **(B)** Akinetic. Lack of systolic thickening and motion is referred to as akinesis. *(11:287)*

103. **(D)** Occlusion of the left anterior descending coronary artery. Blood to the inferior wall of the left ventricle is usually supplied by the right coronary artery. *(1:467, 21:93)*

104. **(B)** Severe mitral regurgitation. Doppler interrogation of a patient with ruptured papillary muscle will usually demonstrate this condition. *(3:249)*

105. **(D)** Is used in diagnosing ischemic heart disease. Stress echocardiography is used as an adjunct to standard stress testing in diagnosing patients with suspected coronary artery disease. Resting wall motion is compared to wall motion during and after stress. *(3:250)*

106. **(C)** They do not recur once they are surgically removed. Although characterized as a benign tumor, a myxoma may recur if some cells remain after excision of the tumor. *(20:1285)*

107. **(B)** Ventricular septal defects. The QP/QS ratio refers to the ratio of pulmonary-to-systemic blood flow. It can be calculated echocardiographically to determine the magnitude of left-to-right shunting of blood. *(6:161)*

108. **(B)** Continuous flow (systolic and diastolic) above baseline. Shunting of blood from the aorta to the pulmonary artery occurs in both systole and diastole. *(18:220)*

109. **(B)** Contrast injection echocardiography. Even a small atrial septal defect can be detected by noting the presence or absence of microbubbles. *(1:406)*

110. **(B)** Secundum. Atrial septal defects occur most commonly in the area of the foramen ovale, where they are termed ostium secundum defects. *(3:381)*

111. **(C)** Eisenmenger's syndrome. In this syndrome, the pulmonary vascular resistance is equal to or greater than the systemic vascular resistance, leading to right-to-left shunting. *(20:589)*

112. **(B)** Infundibular pulmonic stenosis. In Ebstein's anomaly, the tricuspid valve is large and partially adherent to the walls of the right ventricle so that the valve orifice is displaced apically. Therefore, most of the right ventricle functions as part of the right atrium. It is frequently associated with an atrial septal defect. Infundibular pulmonic stenosis is not part of the spectrum of this disorder. *(3:406)*

113. **(D)** Ostium primum atrial septal defect and an inlet ventricular septal defect. Endocardial cushion defects occur when the atrial and ventricular components of the cardiac septum fail to develop properly. *(3:381)*

114. **(C)** Descending thoracic aorta. Coarctation of the aorta is a constrictive malformation of the aortic

arch, usually located just distal to the origin of the left subclavian artery. The obstruction increases the velocity of blood flow beyond the point of constriction. *(3:396)*

115. **(D)** An atrial septal defect. The fourth component is right ventricular hypertrophy. *(3:421)*

116. **(B)** Is a congenital malformation in which a fibrous membrane divides the left atrium into an upper and lower chamber. Cor triatriatum is a rare abnormality in which an embryonic membrane in the left atrium fails to regress. It can be detected echocardiographically by noting a linear echo traversing the left atrium. Doppler echocardiography will detect high-velocity flow across a hole in the membrane. *(3:402)*

117. **(C)** Paradoxical septal motion. Left bundle branch block often causes this motion. *(1:231)*

118. **(C)** A mechanical prosthetic valve. This high echogenicity of the mitral valve is characteristic of a mechanical prosthetic valve. *(3:347)*

119. **(D)** Significantly decreased. The M-mode demonstrates a dilated and hypokinetic left ventricle. The markedly increased E point-to-septal separation is consistent with a decreased left ventricular ejection fraction. *(23:140)*

120. **(B)** Left ventricular end-diastolic pressure is increased. There is a mitral valve B notch, which is consistent with high end-diastolic pressure in the left ventricle. *(24:69)*

121. **(A)** Aortic stenosis and aortic insufficiency. The systolic waveform below baseline is consistent with moderate aortic stenosis. A mitral regurgitation waveform would be wider and is usually of higher velocity. The diastolic waveform above baseline is too high a velocity to be caused by mitral or tricuspid stenosis and is consistent with aortic insufficiency. *(6:78)*

122. **(D)** Coronary artery disease. The interventricular septum is hypokinetic and more echogenic than the posterior left ventricular wall. These findings are consistent with an old myocardial infarction. *(1:478)*

123. **(C)** Chordae tendineae. The M-mode cursor in this long-axis view is directed beyond the tips of the mitral leaflets at the level of the chordae tendineae—the level at which left ventricular measurements are obtained. *(11:12)*

124. **(C)** Caused by stagnant blood. The cloud of fuzzy smokelike echoes in the left ventricle is the result of blood stasis. It is usually seen when there is a severe decrease in left ventricular contractibility. *(1:492)*

125–131. If you are having a difficult time orienting yourself to an echocardiographic image, find a structure that is easy for you to recognize and work your way from there. For example, if you can identify the aortic root, you can then follow the anterior wall of the root as it continues into the interventricular septum. The posterior wall of the root will follow into the anterior mitral leaflet, and so on. 125. right ventricle, 126. aortic root, 127. left atrium, 128. descending aorta, 129. left ventricle, 130. pericardial effusion, 131. pleural effusion. *(1:558)*

132. **(D)** A large pericardial effusion. A massive circumferential pericardial effusion is demonstrated in this four-chamber view. *(11:253)*

133. **(B)** Right ventricular wall. The presence of tamponade should be ruled out in patients with pericardial effusion, especially a massive one. A fairly specific echocardiographic sign of tamponade is diastolic collapse of the right ventricle, the right atrium, or both. *(25:561)*

134. **(B)** A diastolic jet filling the left ventricular outflow tract and extending deep into the left ventricle. This long-axis view demonstrates a flail right coronary cusp of the aortic valve. The cusp is seen extending into the left ventricular outflow tract in diastole. Color Doppler would be likely to demonstrate severe aortic insufficiency, which choice B describes. *(12:100)*

135. **(D)** The origin of the right coronary artery. With slight superior angulation from a standard short-axis view of the aortic valve, the ostia and proximal segments of the right coronary artery can be visualized. *(11:23)*

136. **(B)** False. The right ventricular outflow tract is located lateral to the origin of the right coronary artery. *(1:102)*

137. **(A)** Left-to-right shunting at the atrial level. There is a washout effect in the right atrium as blood from the left side of the heart enters the contrast-filled right atrium. *(11:355)*

138. **(B)** False. A pericardial effusion would appear on a subcostal four-chamber view as an echo-free space anterior to the right ventricle. *(11:251)*

139. **(B)** Liver parenchyma. To obtain a subcostal four-chamber view, the transducer is placed on the abdo-

men and angled in a cephalic direction. Therefore, liver parenchyma will occupy the near field of the image. *(3:129)*

140. **(D)** Pulmonary hypertension. An absent A wave and midsystolic notching (flying W sign) are consistent with this condition. *(3:388)*

141. **(C)** Mitral valve prolapse. The M-mode in Fig. 3—20 demonstrates late-systolic tricuspid valve prolapse. Tricuspid valve prolapse almost always occurs in patients with concomitant mitral valve prolapse. *(1:305)*

142. **(C)** Midsystolic notching. Fig. 3–21 is an example of systolic anterior motion of the mitral valve. This is one classic echocardiographic sign of hypertrophic obstructive cardiomyopathy. The midsystolic obstruction of the left ventricular outflow tract will often be demonstrated on the M-mode of the aortic valve as well as by midsystolic notching. *(26:6)*

143. **(C)** A dilated aortic root. This patient exhibits characteristic findings of Marfan syndrome, a connective tissue disorder. There is a linear echo near the aortic valve suggesting aortic root dissection, another complication of Marfan syndrome. This syndrome often causes ascending aortic dilatation as well as myxomatous degeneration of the aortic and mitral valves. *(11:242)*

144. **(A)** The long-axis suprasternal view. Because the aortic root is dilated, echocardiographic evaluation should follow the length of the aorta to determine the extent of the aneurysm. The suprasternal long-axis view allows for visualization of the aortic arch and the proximal portion of the descending aorta. Further investigation should include a modified apical two-chamber view for evaluating the thoracic aorta and a subcostal approach for interrogating the abdominal aorta. *(3:121, 137)*

145. **(C)** A large apical thrombus. This thrombus is seen filling the apex, with a piece of the medial segment protruding into the left ventricle. Most thrombi are associated with anterior infarctions and are located in the apex in the majority of cases. *(1:489)*

146. **(B)** Flail. The tip of the posterior leaflet can be seen protruding into the left atrium, which is consistent with a flail mitral valve. *(27:1383)*

147. **(B)** Right pulmonary artery. The artery is seen in its short axis. *(11:36)*

148. **(A)** The left atrium. This atrium can sometimes be visualized posterior to the right pulmonary artery on the suprasternal long-axis view. *(11:36)*

149. **(D)** The moderator band. This is a muscular strip located in the apical third of the right ventricle. It is sometimes misdiagnosed as a right ventricular apical thrombus. *(3:117, 294)*

150. **(B)** A left atrial thrombus. This is seen protruding into the left atrium. (The bright linear echo in the right atrium originates from a pacemaker wire.) *(1:592)*

151. **(B)** Aortic stenosis, a calcified mitral annulus, and a pericardial effusion. The aortic valve is markedly calcified; there is a bright echo posterior to the mitral valve, representing a calcified mitral annulus; and the base of the interventricular septum is hypertrophied. The posterior echo-free space represents pleural effusion, as opposed to a pericardial effusion, because it does not taper at the descending aorta. *(1:345, 283)*

152. **(D)** An aged heart. When seen together, these findings usually indicate signs of aging. *(9:1658)*

153. **(D)** Atrial fibrillation. The electrocardiogram at the top of the Doppler tracing indicates this fibrillation. The variations from beat to beat reflect the altering lengths in diastolic filling periods that occur with atrial fibrillation. *(11:333)*

154. **(B)** Diastolic doming. The mitral valve is bulging into the left ventricle in diastole because the valve is stenotic and cannot accommodate all the blood available for delivery into the left ventricle. *(1:251)*

155. **(A)** The left atrium. Even without using the centimeter markers as a gauge, one can determine that the left atrium is dilated. On the long axis-view, the aortic root and left aorta should be approximately the same size. The apical four-chamber view is extremely useful for assessing relative chamber size. The right and left atria should be roughly the same size (although the left atrium is usually slightly larger), and they should be smaller than the ventricles. *(11:368)*

156. **(D)** An opening snap. The opening snap often affords the first clue to the diagnosis of mitral stenosis. *(20:185)*

157. **(C)** Descending aorta. A portion of the aorta can be seen lying behind the left atrium on the apical four-chamber view. *(1:98)*

158. **(A)** The mitral valve area. The pressure half-time, or the time it takes for the initial pressure drop of the mitral valve to be halved, can be used to measure mitral valve area. A pressure half-time of 220 msec has been shown to correlate with a valve area of 1.0 cm^2. *(18:117)*

159. **(C)** Left ventricular hypertrophy. The left ventricular walls are thickened and exhibit increased echogenicity. *(28:188)*

160. **(B)** A thickened mitral valve, a prominent interatrial septum, a small left ventricle, and pericardial effusion. The mitral valve and interatrial septum are slightly thickened, there is a small-to-moderate-sized pericardial effusion, and the left ventricle is small. *(1:535)*

161. **(D)** Amyloid cardiomyopathy. This patient exhibits classic features of this disease. The infiltrative process of the disease causes thickening of the ventricles, interatrial septum and valves. Pericardial effusion is another finding sometimes associated with this disease. *(3:232)*

162. **(B)** An endomyocardial biopsy. This has been shown to be helpful in identifying amyloid cardiomyopathy. *(3:232)*

163. **(B)** Ventricular septal defect. The short-axis and modified four-chamber views demonstrate a gap in the posterior aspect of the midsection of the interventricular septum. Given the patient's history and the irregular borders on the echocardiogram, one can assume that this defect is acquired rather than congenital. *(29:506)*

164. **(A)** Color-flow Doppler imaging. This is particularly useful for quickly determining the location and quantifying the extent of abnormal blood flow in patients with ventricular septal defects. *(3:243)*

165. **(A)** Coronary sinus. When imaged from the apical two-chamber view, the coronary sinus appears as a circular structure in the atrioventricular groove. By rotating to a four-chamber view and angling posteriorly, one can follow the coronary sinus as it courses along the length of the posterior atrioventricular groove. *(20:29)*

166. **(B)** Deoxygenated blood. The coronary sinus carries venous blood to the right atrium. *(30:211)*

167. **(A)** Anteriorly. By tilting the scan plane anteriorly from this posteriorly directed apical four-chamber view, the aorta and left ventricular outflow tract can be imaged. *(3:131)*

168. **(C)** Prolapse of the posterior leaflet. The posterior mitral leaflet bulges beyond the plane of the mitral annulus, which is consistent with prolapse. *(3:189)*

169. **(A)** A systolic curve below baseline greater than 3 m/s. Mitral valve prolapse, especially to the degree shown in this study, is most likely to be accompanied by some degree of mitral regurgitation, which is detected from the apical window with Doppler echocardiography by noting a systolic curve below baseline usually greater than 3 m/s. *(6:74)*

170. **(B)** False. The arrow is pointing to the lateral wall of the left ventricle. *(11:25)*

171. **(C)** Artifactual. A dropout of echoes in the interatrial septum is not an uncommon finding when visualized from the apical four-chamber view. If this were a true atrial septal defect, a "T sign" would likely be noted. *(1:404)*

172. **(A)** Slight thickening of the valve with a normal opening. This thickening is noted best in diastole. The leaflets appear to open widely in systole. (They open in close proximity to the walls of the aortic root.) *(1:279)*

173. **(C)** 36 mm Hg. Using the simplified Bernoulli equation, the peak aortic gradient can be obtained by squaring the peak velocity (in this case 3 m/s) and then multiplying by four. *(18:23)*

174. **(B)** Congenital aortic stenosis. In this disorder, the valve may be thin or minimally thickened, and M-mode may demonstrate a normal opening if the cursor was directed at the body of the leaflets rather than at the restricted tips. The best way to determine if congenital aortic stenosis is present is by noting Doppler evidence of increased velocities across the valve. *(1:384)*

175. **(A)** Systolic doming. This occurs in congenital aortic stenosis because the body of the leaflets expands to accommodate systolic flow while the tips of the leaflets restrict blood flow. (Normally, the tips of the aortic valve open wide and lie parallel to the aortic root in systole.) *(1:383)*

176. **(C)** Exhibiting shaggy irregular echoes. The mitral valve has a mass of shaggy echoes with irregular borders attached to it. *(3:277)*

177. **(B)** Subacute bacterial endocarditis. Because of the patient's history and the echocardiographic demonstration of an irregular mass attached to the mitral valve, this is the most likely diagnosis. *(20:1141)*

178. **(B)** Increased. Unlike calcium, which tends to inhibit valve opening, vegetations are likely to increase valve excursion. Because calcium and vegetations can look similar echocardiographically this difference can aid in the diagnosis. *(3:277)*

179. **(A)** Systolic waveform below baseline. A mitral valve vegetation will usually cause the mitral valve to be regurgitant. Mitral regurgitation can be de-

tected by continuous-wave Doppler from the apical four-chamber view by noting systolic flow below baseline. *(6:74)*

180. **(D)** Prolapses into the left atrium and left ventricle. In Fig. 3–33A, the mass is in the left atrium. In Fig. 3–33B and C, the mass appears in the left ventricle. Therefore, one could deduce that the mass is prolapsing into the left atrium in systole and into the left ventricle in diastole. *(1:312)*

181. **(B)** The posteromedial papillary muscle. On the opposite wall of the left ventricle, one can see the anterolateral papillary muscle. Between the two papillary muscles, the tip of the mitral valve vegetation can be seen protruding into the left ventricle. *(3:113)*

REFERENCES

1. Feigenbaum H. *Echocardiography,* 4th ed. Philadelphia: Lea & Febiger, 1986.
2. Henry WL, DeMaria A, Gramik R. *Nomenclature and Standardization in Two-Dimensional Echocardiography.* Raleigh, NC: American Society of Echocardiography, 1980.
3. Craig M. *Diagnostic Medical Sonography: A Guide to Clinical Practice. Vol 2. Echocardiography.* Philadelphia: JB Lippincott, 1991.
4. Cosgrove DO, McCready VR. *Ultrasound Imaging: Liver, Spleen, Pancreas.* New York: John Wiley & Sons, 1982.
5. Weyman AE. *Cross-sectional Echocardiography.* Philadelphia: Lea & Febiger, 1982.
6. Kisslo J, Adams D, Mark DB. *Basic Doppler Echocardiography.* New York: Churchill Livingstone, 1986.
7. Sahn DJ, DeMaria A, Kisso J, Weyman A. Recommendations regarding quantitation in M-mode echocardiography: results of a survey of echocardiographic measurements. *Circulation* **58:**1072–1083, 1978.
8. Sokolow M, McIlroy MB, Cheitlin MD. *Clinical Cardiology,* 5th ed. Norwalk, CT: Appleton & Lange, 1990.
9. Braunwald E. *Heart Disease: A Textbook of Cardiovascular Medicine,* 3rd ed. Philadelphia: WB Saunders, 1988.
10. Goldberg SJ, Allen HD, Marx GR, Flinn CJ. *Doppler Echocardiography.* Philadelphia: Lea & Febiger, 1985.
11. Harrigan P, Lee R. *Principles of Interpretation in Echocardiography.* New York: John Wiley & Sons, 1985.
12. Kisso J, Adams DB, Belkin RN. *Doppler Color Flow Imaging.* New York: Churchill Livingstone, 1988.
13. Salcedo E. *Atlas of Echocardiography,* 2nd ed. Philadelphia: WB Saunders, 1985.
14. Hatle L, Angelsen B, Tromsdal A. Noninvasive assessment of atrioventricular pressure half-time by Doppler ultrasound. *Circulation* **60:**1096–1104, 1979.
15. Gravanis MB. *Cardiovascular Pathophysiology.* New York: McGraw-Hill, 1987.
16. Popp RL. Echocardiography, *N Engl J Med* **323:**101–109, 1990.
17. Aobanu J, et al. Pulsed Doppler echocardiography in the diagnosis and estimation of severity of aortic insufficiency. *Am J Cardiol* **49:**339–343, 1982.
18. Hatle L, Angelsen B. *Doppler Ultrasound in Cardiology: Physical Principles and Clinical Applications.* Philadelphia: Lea & Febiger, 1985.
19. Currie PJ. Transesophageal echocardiography: new window to the heart. *Circulation* **80:**215–218, 1989.
20. Hurst JW. *The Heart,* 6th ed. New York: McGraw-Hill, 1986.
21. Wasser HJ, Greengart A, et al. Echocardiographic assessment of posterior left ventricular aneurysms. *J Diagn Med Sonography* **2:**93–95, 1986.
22. Driscoll DJ, Fuster V, McGoon DC. Congenital heart disease in adolescents and adults: atrioventricular canal defect. In Brandenburg RO, Fuster V, Giulani ER, et al. (eds): *Cardiology: Fundamentals and Practice.* Chicago: Year Book Medical Publishers, 1987.
23. D'Cruz IA, Lalmalani GG, et al. The superiority of mitral E point-ventricular septum separation to other echocardiographic indicators of left ventricular performance. *Clin Cardiol* **2:**140, 1979.
24. D'Cruz IA, Kleinman D, Aboulatta H, et al. A reappraisal of the mitral B-bump (B-inflection): its relationship to left ventricular dysfunction. *Echocardiography* **7:**69–75, 1990.
25. Williams GJ, Partidge JB, Right ventricular diastolic collapse: an echocardiographic sign of tamponade. *Br Heart J* **49:**292, 1983.
26. Doi YL, McKenna WJ, et al. M-mode echocardiography in hypertrophic cardiomyopathy: diagnostic criteria and prediction of obstruction. *Am J Cardiol* **45:**6–14, 1980.
27. Child JS, Skorton DJ, Taylor RD, et al. M-mode and cross-sectional echocardiographic features of flail posterior mitral leaflets. *Am J Cardiol* **44:**1383–1390, 1979.
28. Sigueira-Filho AG, Cunha CL, Tajik AJ, et al. M-mode and two-dimensional echocardiographic features in cardiac amyloidosis. *Circulation* **63:**188–196, 1981.
29. Chandraratna PAN, Balachandran PK, Shah PM, Hodges M. Echocardiographic observations on ventricular septal rupture complicating myocardial infarction. *Circulation* **51:**506–510, 1975.
30. Berne RM, Levy MN. *Cardiovascular Physiology,* 4th ed. St. Louis: CV Mosby, 1981.

CHAPTER 4

PEDIATRIC ECHOCARDIOGRAPHY

Diana Kawai Yankowitz

Study Guide

INTRODUCTION

Effective echocardiographic evaluation of congenital heart disease requires an appreciation of malformation severity and cardiovascular hemodynamics. A complete echocardiographic study involves the use of every modality available. Anatomy should be carefully delineated by two-dimensional (2-D) imaging because malformations frequently occur in combination rather than as isolated lesions. Doppler techniques provide information on shunt patterns, flow volumes, gradients through obstructions, and severity of regurgitation. Color flow Doppler facilitates rapid detection of flow abnormalities and qualitative assessment of such flow characteristics as direction, timing, and degree of turbulence. Pulsed-wave (PW) Doppler provides range (spatial) resolution of flow patterns. Quantification of high-velocity flows require the use of continuous-wave (CW) Doppler. M-mode is used primarily to evaluate subtle movements and to measure chamber, vessel, and wall size. Contrast echocardiography is useful in the demonstration of intracardiac and extracardiac shunts, particularly in cases in which 2-D and color flow imaging is suboptimal.

The study outline is intended as a guide for the entry-level pediatric echocardiographer and, as such, includes malformations that occur with relative frequency as well as those that occur rarely but are relatively straightforward. The outline includes a definition of the anatomic malformation, a list of variants, the hemodynamic effect of the lesion, characteristic clinical findings, key echocardiographic concepts, the natural history of the disease, commonly associated cardiac malformations, interventional catheterization techniques, and palliative as well as corrective surgical procedures. Complex malformations such as single ventricle, double-inlet ventricle and double-outlet ventricle are beyond the scope of this chapter. For information regarding these malformations, the reader is referred to more extensive texts.

Sample examination questions are provided following the text to give the reader an appreciation of the scope of knowledge required to perform routine diagnostic pediatric echocardiograms. The questions are *not* intended to be a comprehensive review but to assist the reader in determining what needs to be studied in greater detail.

For discussions of normal anatomy, general scanning technique, echocardiographic physics and instrumentation, and acquired heart disease that is not specific to the pediatric population, the reader is referred to other chapters within this book. Acquired pathologies that occur in the pediatric as well as adult population include mitral valve prolapse, rheumatic heart disease, cardiac masses, cardiomyopathies, pericardial effusions, and bacterial endocarditis. Evaluation of ventricular function in the pediatric population is identical to that of the adult population and, therefore, will not be repeated within this chapter.

SEGMENTAL ANATOMY

When evaluating congenital heart disease, the echocardiographer begins by determining whether the heart is located in the left chest (levocardia), right chest (dextrocardia), or directly posterior to the sternum (mesocardia). The direction in which the apex is pointing is also noted. The echocardiographer should demonstrate segmental anatomy by delineating situs, ventricular looping, and great vessel relationship. This may be done by documenting anatomic landmarks for each chamber and vessel, as follows:

1. Situs[2,49]
   - A. Types
     - (1) Solitus—normal
       - Descending aorta and left atrium to the left
       - Inferior vena cava to the right
     - (2) Inversus—mirror image visceral placement
       - Very rare
     - (3) Left atrial isomerism—double left sidedness

- Both atria have left atrial morphology
- 70% have interrupted inferior vena cava with dilated azygos vein located posterior to the aorta on the same side of the spine or direct hepatic vein drainage into atria bilaterally (2-D transverse subcostal views; confirm venous versus arterial structures by Doppler from sagittal views)
- Usually have polysplenia
- Frequently have complex cardiac anomalies

(4) Right atrial isomerism—double right sidedness
- Inferior vena cava located anterior to the aorta on the same side of the spine
- Usually have asplenia
- Frequently have other cardiac lesions

B. Determined by
(1) Positions of descending aorta and inferior venae cavae in the abdomen
(2) Positions of the atria as proven by anatomic landmarks
a. Right atrium
- Entrance of superior and inferior venae cavae (contrast echo)[69]
- Presence of eustachian valve
- Right atrial appendage (broad connection to atrium)
—parasternal or subcostal sagittal views

b. Left atrium
- Entrance of pulmonary veins (posterior subcostal coronal plane)
- Left atrial appendage (tubular, with narrow connection)
—parasternal long or short axis, subcostal, apical four-chamber views

2. Ventricular connection (looping)[12,64,66]
A. Types
(1) Dextro—right ventricle to the right
(2) Levo—right ventricle to the left
B. Determined by positions of the ventricles as proven by anatomical landmarks
(1) Right ventricle
- Trabeculated endocardial surface
- Tricuspid valve (three leaflets)
—annulus inserts more apically than the mitral valve
—chordal insertion into ventricular septum or free wall
- Moderator band

(2) Left ventricle
- Smooth endocardial surface
- Mitral valve (two leaflets)
- Two prominent papillary muscles

3. Great vessel relationship[2]
A. Types
(1) Dextro—aortic valve to the right of the pulmonic valve
(2) Levo—aortic valve to the left of the pulmonic valve
B. Determined by positions of the great arteries as proven by anatomical landmarks
(1) Pulmonary artery
- Bifurcates soon after exiting the heart
- Posterior course from base of the heart

(2) Aorta
- Superior course from base of the heart, to form aortic arch
- Coronary arteries

NORMAL HEMODYNAMICS[1]

chamber/ vessel	mean	diastolic	systolic
Right atrium		<9 mm Hg	<9 mm Hg
Right ventricle		<7 mm Hg	<30 mm Hg
Pulmonary artery	<20 mm Hg		<30 mm Hg
Left atrium	<12 mm Hg		<17 mm Hg
Left ventricle		<12 mm Hg	<140 mm Hg (within 5 mm Hg of arm pressure)
Aorta	determined by blood pressure cuff on arm		

IMPORTANT DOPPLER CALCULATIONS

1. Conversion of frequency shift into velocity by use of the Doppler equation[18]
2. Estimation of pressure gradient by application of the modified Bernoulli equation[18]
3. Determination of flow volume[43]
4. Determination of pulmonary to systemic flow ratio, referred to as Q_p: Q_s[10,58,59]
5. Estimation of valve area by use of the continuity equation[51]

ESTIMATION OF PULMONARY ARTERY PRESSURE

The development and progression of elevated pulmonary artery pressure is of concern in any patient with congenital heart disease. Pulmonary artery pressures rise in response to increased flow volume and/or pressure as pulmonary vascular resistance becomes elevated. Increased flow volume and/or high pressure cause the intimal and medial layers of the pulmonary arterioles to hypertrophy, thereby increasing pulmonary vascular resistance. With prolonged exposure to high-flow volume and/or pressure, the patient develops pulmonary hypertension and eventually pulmonary vascular obstructive disease, which is irreversible. When pulmonary artery pressures exceed

systemic pressures, blood flow through intra- and extracardiac shunts reverses, such that they become pulmonary to systemic or right to left shunts. Mixing of deoxygenated blood with oxygenated blood leads to cyanosis. The right ventricle eventually fails owing to the increased resistance against which it must work to eject blood. Pulmonary vascular disease that results from prolonged increased volume and pressure to the pulmonary vascular bed from a systemic to pulmonary (left to right) shunt is referred to as Eisenmenger's syndrome.[15]

Echocardiographic Signs of Elevated Pulmonary Artery Pressure (Pulmonary Hypertension)

- Dilated right ventricle with thickened right ventricular free wall
- Disappearance of the "a" wave on the pulmonic valve M-mode[22,27]
- Midsystolic closure of the pulmonic valve on M-mode, also known as the "flying W"[72]
- Tricuspid and/or pulmonic regurgitation in the absence of structural abnormalities of the valves[60]

Estimation of Systolic Pulmonary Artery Pressure

- Peak tricuspid regurgitation gradient plus 7 mm Hg (assumed central venous pressure)[60,73]
- Enhancement of tricuspid regurgitation Doppler tracing by use of echocardiographic contrast[5]

Estimation of Diastolic Pulmonary Artery Pressure

- End-diastolic pulmonary regurgitation gradient plus 7 mm Hg (assumed central venous pressure)[28]

Estimation of Mean Pulmonary Artery Pressure

- Acceleration time (AcT) divided by ejection time (ET) of flow through the right ventricular outflow tract as recorded by PW Doppler[21]

SIMPLE SHUNT LESIONS

Persistent Patent Ductus Arteriosus (PDA)

Anatomy. The ductus arteriosus is a vessel connecting the left pulmonary artery to the descending aorta (immediately distal to the level of the left subclavian artery) that allows blood to bypass the pulmonary circulation during fetal life. Shortly after birth, this vessel should close so blood may enter the pulmonary circulation to be oxygenated. When the vessel remains patent, it is referred to as a persistent patent ductus arteriosus.

Hemodynamics. During fetal life, pulmonary vascular resistance is higher than systemic vascular resistance; therefore, pulmonary pressure is higher than systemic pressure, so blood flows from the pulmonary artery to the descending aorta. After birth, pulmonary vascular resistance decreases and becomes much lower than systemic vascular resistance. The reversal in pressure differences between the pulmonary and systemic circulations causes a reversal of flow through a persistently patent ductus arteriosus, such that blood from the descending aorta enters the pulmonary circulation. The resulting increase in pulmonary flow continues into the left atrium as a volume overload causing the left atrium and ventricle to dilate. The magnitude of the systemic to pulmonary shunt is determined by the difference between the pulmonary and systemic vascular resistances, the difference in pulmonary artery and descending aortic pressures, and by the luminal diameter of the ductus arteriosus.[1]

Clinical Presentation.[1,11] Patients are usually asymptomatic; in cardiac failure if shunt is large.

- Physical exam: bounding pulses
- Auscultation: systolic murmur in infants, continuous murmer at older age
- ECG (electrocardiogram): variable
- Chest x-ray: enlarged pulmonary artery and aorta, increased vascular markings, ductus "bump" off the descending aorta

Key Echocardiographic Concepts

- 2-D visualization of the ductus entering the pulmonary artery (parasternal short axis or high parasternal view)[42,48]
- 2-D visualization of the ductus entering the descending aorta (suprasternal notch or high parasternal view)[55,56]
- Continuous flow in the pulmonary artery by PW or color flow Doppler[23,39]
- Diastolic flow reversal in the descending aorta distal to the left subclavian artery by PW or color flow Doppler[51,57]
- Demonstration of shunt by contrast echocardiography[3,42]
- Left atrial to aortic root ratio (LA/Ao ratio) greater than 1.2 in the absence of left ventricular failure[3]
- Estimation of pulmonary artery pressure by determining the pressure gradient through the duct by CW Doppler and subtracting this value from the systolic blood pressure[51]

Populations at Increased Risk[1]

- Preterm infant
- Infant born at altitudes greater than 4500 m above sea level
- Rubella syndrome
- Family history
- Complex congenital heart disease[15]

Natural History.[1] A large shunt may cause congestive heart failure, failure to thrive, and recurrent respiratory

infections. Pulmonary vascular obstructive disease will develop if left untreated.

Treatment[1]

- Indomethicin: to close ductus medically
- Prostaglandin E_1: to keep ductus patent in the presence of a "duct-dependent" lesion, in which the ductus is necessary to provide pulmonary circulation
- Umbrella closure (interventional catheterization)[36]
- Foam plastic plug closure (interventional catheterization)
- Surgical ligation

Postoperative Echocardiographic Evaluation. Left atrial and ventricular size should regress to normal. Color flow or PW Doppler should be used to check for residual shunting.

Other Systemic to Pulmonary Shunts

Echocardiographic Concepts

- PW Doppler documentation of diastolic descending aortic flow reversal to evaluate patency of the shunt
- Localization of shunt by PW Doppler (determine the level at which the diastolic reversal begins)
- Visualization of shunt on 2-D and color flow Doppler

Types

A. Aorticopulmonary Window: a defect in the walls of the ascending aorta and main pulmonary artery resulting in blood shunting between these structures; Doppler findings similar to persistant patent ductus arteriosus except reversal of flow may be detected in the ascending as well as descending aorta.[51]

B. Surgically Created Systemic to Pulmonary Shunts[1,34]

1. Blalock-Taussig: subclavian artery to pulmonary artery on side opposite the aortic arch; modified versions may be placed on either side; current shunt of choice
2. Central: anastamosis or conduit between the pulmonary artery and aorta
3. Glenn: superior vena cava to right main pulmonary artery; persistent left superior vena cava with innominate vein communication results in a steal phenomenon; occlusion may lead to various complications, including superior vena cava syndrome
4. Potts: descending aorta to pulmonary artery; difficult to control size; older technique
5. Waterston: ascending aorta to right pulmonary artery; difficult to control size; older technique

Atrial Septal Defects (ASDs)

Anatomy. Incomplete septation of the atrial septum results in a "hole" or communication through which blood may flow directly from one atrium into the other. Types of atrial septal defects, as determined by physical location, are listed below.[44,48]

- Secundum: area of the foramen ovale; most common
- Primum: posterior, near the atrioventricular valves; associated with cleft mitral valve and mitral regurgitation
- Sinus venosus: posterior and superior, near the entrance of the superior vena cava; associated with anomalous right pulmonary venous return into the right atrium
- Coronary sinus: area of the entrance of the coronary sinus; rare; associated with persistant left superior vena cava, absent coronary sinus, and complex congenital heart disease[47]

Hemodynamics. Blood is "shunted" from the higher pressure left atrium to the lower pressure right atrium causing a volume overload and, therefore, dilatation of the right atrium, right ventricle, and pulmonary arteries. Doppler interrogation reveals blood flow through the interatrial septum and increased flow velocities through the tricuspid and pulmonic valves.

Clinical Presentation.[1,11] Patients are usually asymptomatic.

- Physical exam: systolic impulse may be felt at the lower left sternal border
- Auscultation: fixed splitting of the second heart sound, systolic crescendo-decrescendo (ejection) murmur that is heard best at the upper left sternal border
- ECG: right ventricular hypertrophy
- Chest x-ray: enlarged heart and increased pulmonary vascular markings

Key Echocardiographic Concepts

- Visualization of defect on 2-D and with color flow Doppler (subcostal long and short, parasternal short axis, and apical four-chamber views)[39,48]
- PW Doppler tracing characteristic of left to right shunt through an atrial septal defect[24]
- Degree of right atrial and ventricular dilatation to estimate severity
- PW Doppler technique to calculate Q_p:Q_s (ie, magnitude of the shunt)
- Use of echocardiographic contrast to confirm the presence of a shunt[13,68]

Associated Disease[3,11]

- Mitral valve prolapse
- Left ventricular inflow obstruction (Lutenbacher's syndrome)
- Subaortic stenosis
- Atrial septal aneurysm

Natural History [1,11]

- May close spontaneously
- Pulmonary vascular obstructive disease may develop, usually in adulthood

Treatment

- Elective surgical suture closure
- Elective surgical patch closure with pericardial or Teflon patch

Postoperative Echocardiographic Evaluation

- Right atrial and ventricular size should regress to normal
- Color flow, PW Doppler, or contrast echo[69] should be used to check for residual shunting around the patch

Ventricular Septal Defects (VSDs)

Anatomy. A communication exits between the ventricles as a result of incomplete septation. Type is determined by location, as listed below.[45,48]

- Perimembranous: including the membranous septum and frequently portions of the muscular septum directly under the aortic valve
- Malalignment: the aorta or pulmonary artery overrides the interventricular septum
- Inflow (atrioventricular canal, endocardial cushion): posterior, at the level of the atrioventricular valves
- Doubly committed subarterial (subpulmonic, supracristal): immediately proximal to the pulmonic valve, in the right ventricular outflow tract
- Muscular: in the body of the ventricular septum
- Apical: in the apical septum
- Left ventricular to right atrial shunt: rare; mimics tricuspid regurgitation[17]

Hemodynamics. Blood from the higher-pressure left ventricle courses through the communication into the lower pressure right ventricle. The greatest volume of blood is shunted during systole when the pressure difference between the ventricles is most pronounced. Because the pulmonic valve is open during systole, the high-velocity jet from the left ventricle proceeds through the right ventricle directly into the pulmonary artery. The pulmonary vasculature, therefore, is affected more by the increased volume and pressure than the right ventricle. The increased blood volume proceeds into the left atrium and ventricle causing dilatation of these chambers.

Clinical Presentation. [11] Patients usually are asymptomatic; may present in cardiac failure if shunt is large

- Physical exam: palpable thrill over the chest
- Auscultation: harsh holosystolic murmur; variably split second heart sound
- ECG: dilated pulmonary artery, pulmonary vessels, left atrium, left ventricle
- Chest x-ray: left ventricular hypertrophy with or without right ventricular hypertrophy

Key Echocardiographic Concepts

- Visualization of defect on 2-D or of the shunt (jet) by color flow Doppler[38,39,48]
- Systolic flow into the right ventricle through the interventricular septum by PW or CW Doppler[58,61]
- Evidence of shunt by contrast echocardiography[45]
- Estimation of right ventricular pressure by determining the pressure gradient through the VSD by CW Doppler and subtracting this value from the systolic blood pressure[32]
- Restrictive versus nonrestrictive VSD[15]
- Estimation of the magnitude of the shunt by calculation of the Q_p:Q_s by Doppler technique

Associated Disease

- Multiple ventricular septal defects may occur
- Aortic insufficiency (particularly with doubly committed subarterial and perimembranous types)[46,48]
- Membranous subaortic stenosis[9]

Natural History [1,15]

- Small defects may close spontaneously
- Risk of developing endocarditis
- Aneurysms of tricuspid valve tissue may partially or completely occlude perimembranous VSDs[45]
- Doubly committed subarterial VSDs may develop aortic valve herniation (prolapse) and subsequent aortic insufficiency of increasing severity[46]
- Development of pulmonary vascular obstructive disease if a significant defect remains open
- Increased risk of progression of pulmonary vascular obstructive disease if closure is delayed beyond 2 years of life

Treatment

- Elective surgical stitch or patch closure
- Repair of aortic valve herniation

Postoperative Echocardiographic Evaluation

- Left atrial and ventricular size should regress to normal[3]
- Assess for peripatch residual shunts by PW Doppler, color flow, or contrast echo[15,23,69]
- Assess for patch dehiscence[3]

Atrioventricular Septal Defects (AVSDs)

Anatomy. A spectrum of malformations that occur at the crux of the heart where the atrioventricular valves, interatrial septum, and interventricular septum intersect. These malformations may also be referred to as endocar-

dial cushion defects or atrioventricular canals. Any combination of the following malformations may exist. When there is atrial, ventricular, and atrioventricular valve involvement, the patient is said to have a complete atrioventricular septal defect[52]:

- Ostium primum atrial septal defect
- Inlet ventricular septal defect
- Atrioventricular valve malformation: including cleft mitral valve, single atrioventricular valve, overriding atrioventricular valve, straddling atrioventricular valve
- Common atrium: interatrial septum is completely absent (associated with atrial isomerism)

Hemodynamics. The defects are generally large; therefore, equalization of pressures may occur between chambers resulting in bidirectional shunting through septal defects. The right heart is dilated due to volume and/or pressure increase. Atrioventricular valve regurgitation may cause atrial dilatation.

Clinical Presentation.[1,11] Patients are usually symptomatic during infancy.

- Physical exam: failure to thrive, fatigue, dyspnea, heart failure, recurrent respiratory infections
- Auscultation: variety of murmurs
- ECG: left axis deviation, biventricular hypertrophy
- Chest x-ray: gross cardiomegaly with increased vascular markings

Key Echocardiographic Concepts

- 2-D evaluation of size and positions of ventricular and atrial septal defects
- Relative right ventricular and left ventricular size by 2-D[52]
- Atrioventricular valve competency by PW or color flow Doppler[58]
- Structure of the atrioventricular valves, particularly chordal attachments[45]
- Assessment of pulmonary artery pressure by Doppler methods

Associated Disease[1,3,52]

- Left heart and aortic obstructive lesions
- Muscular ventricular septal defects
- Atrial isomerisms

Natural History

- Pulmonary vascular obstructive disease develops at an early age[11]

Treatment.[1] Surgery is usually done during the first year of life

- Elective surgical repair of atrioventricular valves and patch closure of septal defects
- Pulmonary artery band: surgical palliation in which supravalvular pulmonary stenosis is created to limit blood flow to the pulmonary vascular bed to retard progression of pulmonary vascular disease

Postoperative Echocardiographic Evaluation

- After definitive repair, evaluate ventricular function, check for residual shunts and assess competency of atrioventricular valves.
- After pulmonary artery banding, determine the anatomic position of the band and the pressure gradient across it by CW Doppler.

OBSTRUCTIVE LESIONS

Left Ventricular Outflow Obstructions

Anatomy. Various types of obstruction are listed below.[1,3,15,48]

- Bicuspid aortic valve: one of the commissures remains fused; the most common type of congenital heart disease; frequently hemodynamically insignificant until adulthood
- Unicuspid aortic valve: in place of a valve, there is a membrane with an orifice
- Discrete subaortic stenosis: membrane or ridge in the left ventricular outflow tract; may also affect the anterior leaflet of the mitral valve
- Dynamic subaortic stenosis (idiopathic hypertrophic subaortic stenosis, hypertrophic obstructive cardiomyopathy): thickened interventricular septum; genetically transmitted
- Tunnel aortic stenosis: diffuse narrowing of the left ventricular outflow tract; rare
- Supravalvular aortic stenosis: localized or diffuse narrowing of the ascending aorta, generally just distal to the sinuses of Valsalva; usually associated with the William syndrome

Hemodynamics. Obstruction increases resistance to flow out of the left ventricle. The left ventricle must therefore generate higher systolic pressures to force the blood past the obstruction. This pressure overload results in thickening of the left ventricular walls.

Clinical Presentation.[1,11] Patients are usually asymptomatic unless obstruction is severe.

- Physical exam: anacrotic notch and prolonged upstroke in peripheral arterial pulse; left ventricular lift and precordial systolic thrill may be palpable
- Auscultation: ejection click and systolic ejection murmur, narrowed splitting of the second heart sound; reversed splitting of the second heart sound if obstruction is severe
- ECG: left ventricular hypertrophy
- Chest x-ray: enlarged left ventricle, dilated ascending aorta

Key Echocardiographic Concepts

General Concepts

- High-velocity, turbulent jet distal to obstruction by PW or color flow Doppler[18,23]
- Increased thickness of left ventricular walls[3]
- Prolonged time to peak velocity (acceleration time to left ventricular ejection time ratio greater than 0.30 suggests pressure greater than 50 mm Hg, greater than 0.55 requires surgery)[18]
- Estimation of pressure gradient through the obstruction by CW Doppler-peak systolic pressure gradient greater than 75 mm Hg with a normal cardiac output is critical aortic stenosis and a surgical emergency[1,18,48]
- Estimation of valve area by continuity equation—area less than 0.5 cm^2/m^2 of body surface area is critical aortic stenosis and a surgical emergency[1]
- Calculation of left ventricular wall stress[3]
- Estimation of left ventricular pressure as posterior left ventricular wall thickness at end systole divided by end-systolic diameter multiplied by 225[6]

Bicuspid Aortic Valve

- Delineation of configuration of cusps by 2-D
- Doming of cusps on 2-D
- Aortic eccentricity index greater than 1.5 determined by M-mode[3]

Discrete Subaortic Stenosis[3,48]

- 2-D visualization of the membrane from the parasternal long axis or apical five-chamber view
- Premature closure or midsystolic notch on the aortic valve M-mode or PW Doppler tracing
- Coarse systolic fluttering of the aortic cusps on M-mode
- Increased velocity of flow proximal to the aortic valve by PW and color flow Doppler

Dynamic Subaortic Stenosis[37]

- 2-D demonstration of distribution of myocardial thickening
- Late systolic peak on CW Doppler tracing

Tunnel Aortic Stenosis

- 2-D visualization of diffusely narrow left ventricular outflow tract, hypoplastic aortic valve with thick cusps, and hypoplastic ascending aorta[48]

Associated Disease[1]

- Bicuspid aortic valve: aortic insufficiency, coarctation of the aorta
- Unicuspid aortic valve: aortic insufficiency
- Discrete subaortic stenosis: aortic insufficiency

Natural History[1]

- Obstruction usually progresses
- Development of aortic regurgitation

Treatment.[1,15] Patients are generally prophylaxed and restricted from participating in competitive sports

- Valvular aortic stenosis: intervention when peak systolic pressure gradient exceeds 75 mm Hg or orifice size decreases to 0.5 cm^2/m^2 of body surface area
  - —Percutaneous balloon valvuloplasty[30]
  - —Commissurotomy
  - —Aortic valve replacement
- Discrete subaortic stenosis: surgical resection of the membrane
- Supravalvular aortic stenosis: surgical resection of obstruction when pressure gradient exceeds 50 mm Hg
- Tunnel aortic stenosis: left ventricular to descending aorta valved conduit,[65] Konno procedure (widening of aortic root and left ventricular outflow tract)

Postoperative Echocardiographic Evaluation. Evaluate for residual or restenosis and aortic insufficiency.

Shone Syndrome

A constellation of left-sided obstructive lesions occur together: supravalvular mitral ring, parachute mitral valve, discrete membranous subaortic stenosis, and coarctation of the aorta.[48]

Coarctation of the Aorta

Anatomy. A discrete or diffuse narrowing of the aorta, most commonly located immediately distal to the left subclavian artery in the area of the ductus arteriosus. Infrequently, the coarctation will occur proximal to the ductus arteriosus or a portion of the aortic arch may be hypoplastic. In either of these cases, patency of the ductus arteriosus may be necessary to perfuse the descending aorta and maintain life.[1]

Hemodynamics. Obstruction to flow at the level of the coarctation results in a build-up of pressure proximal to the obstruction and decreased flow distal to it.[15] Left ventricular walls thicken in response to increased resistance. A high-velocity jet through the obstruction may weaken the aortic wall immediately distal to the obstruction causing poststenotic dilatation.

Clinical Presentation.[1,11] Patients are usually asymptomatic; if severe during infancy, will present in heart failure.

- Physical exam: systemic hypertension, with systolic blood pressure much higher in the upper extremi-

ties than in the lower extremities[15]; weak femoral pulses; upper body may be more well developed than the lower body
- Auscultation: systolic murmur along the left sternal border transmitting to back and neck; bruits from collateral vessels in older children
- ECG: right ventricular hypertrophy in symptomatic infants; left ventricular hypertrophy in older children
- Chest x-ray: inverted "3" sign at level of coarctation; prominant descending aorta; rib notching in children older than 8 years

Key Echocardiographic Concepts

- 2-D visualization of obstruction within the aortic lumen[19,35]
- Determination of gradient by CW Doppler tracing through the coarctation[16]
  —Velocity of flow proximal to the obstruction should be taken into consideration[58]
- Decreased pulsatility on the PW Doppler tracing of the descending aorta (blunted acceleration and slow deceleration of flow that does not return to baseline during diastole)[58]

Associated Disease[1,35]

- Bicuspid aortic valve (found in as many as 50% of patients with coarctation of the aorta)
- Additional levels of left heart obstruction
- Ventricular septal defects
- Transposition of the great arteries
- Double-outlet right ventricle

Natural History. If unrelieved, as many as 80% of patients die before reaching the age of 50 years[1]

Treatment.[1,15] Early repair appears to decrease probability of residual systemic hypertension

- Surgical resection of constricted area and primary anastamosis or graft placement
- Subclavian flap procedure: use of proximal portion of left subclavian artery to widen aortic lumen

Postoperative Echocardiographic Evaluation

- Assessment of the lumen size and pressure gradient in the area of the reanastamosis
- PW Doppler spectral tracing of the descending aortic flow may continue to appear somewhat blunted

Hypoplastic Left Heart Syndrome

A spectrum of left-sided hypoplasia in which the left atrium, mitral valve, left ventricle, aortic valve, and aorta may be hypoplastic, stenotic, or atretic. Frequently associated with an atrial septal defect through which pulmonary venous return flows into the right atrium and a patent ductus arteriosus, which in turn supplies the descending aorta.[48]

Treatment[4]

- Cardiac transplantation
- Norwood procedure

Pulmonary Stenosis

Anatomy. Obstruction may occur at various levels along the right ventricular outflow tract and the pulmonary arterial system. Types are listed below.[1,11]

- Valvular stenosis: fusion or dysplasia of cusps
- Infundibular stenosis: hypertrophy of muscle bands in the right ventricular outflow tract; usually associated with a ventricular septal defect or valvular pulmonary stenosis[48]
- Double chamber right ventricle: hypertrophied anomalous muscle bundles in the right ventricle, effectively dividing the right ventricle into two chambers with a communication between them; associated with valvular pulmonary stenosis, perimembranous ventricular septal defects, and subaortic stenosis[9,45]
- Peripheral pulmonary stenosis: may occur as a distinct shelf in the pulmonary artery, discrete narrowing of the pulmonary artery branches, or as diffuse tapered narrowing of the pulmonary artery branches[7]

Hemodynamics. Increased resistance to right ventricular outflow results in a pressure overload to this chamber. The right ventricular walls thicken and the chamber dilates. Blood flow into the pulmonary arterial system is at high velocity and turbulent. Eddy currents produced distal to the obstruction may cause poststenotic dilatation of the pulmonary artery.[48]

Clinical Presentation.[1] Patients are usually asymptomatic.

- Auscultation: systolic ejection murmur
- ECG: right ventricular hypertrophy
- Chest x-ray: prominant pulmonary artery trunk; large right atrium

Key Echocardiographic Concepts

- Thickened right ventricular free wall
- 2-D visualization and measurement of pulmonary valve annulus in candidate for balloon angioplasty of valvular stenosis[54]
- 2-D visualization of anomalous muscle bundle and orifice from parasternal and subcostal views[54]
- Accentuation of the "a wave" on M-mode[1]
- Doppler estimation of pressure gradient from all available positions[14]

Natural History[1]

- Increased risk of endocarditis
- Mild valvular and peripheral stenosis (right ventricular pressure less than 50 mm Hg and a pres-

sure gradient of less than 40 mm Hg) is considered benign and may or may not progress

- Severe stenosis (right ventricular pressure greater than 100 mm Hg and a pressure gradient greater than 80 mm Hg) requires relief
- Infundibular stenosis and anomalous muscle bundles tend to become progressively more obstructive

Treatment. When patient becomes symptomatic or pressure gradient exceeds 50 mm Hg[15]

- Balloon valvuloplasty: to relieve valvular and peripheral stenosis[30]
- Surgical valvotomy[1]
- Surgical resection of infundibular muscle or anomalous muscle bundles

Postoperative Echocardiographic Evaluation

- Assess patency of area of former obstruction
- Assess presence and severity of pulmonary insuffiency

Pulmonary Atresia

Anatomy. Imperforate membrane or thick fibrous band in place of a pulmonary valve or complete absence of the main pulmonary artery.[7]

Hemodynamics. Life is dependent upon a persistent patent ductus arteriosus or collateral vessels. A ventricular septal defect usually coexists and acts as an outlet to systemic venous return.[15]

Clinical Presentation.[1] Severe cyanosis and hypoxemia are seen in the neonate.

- Auscultation: possibly the murmur of a persistent ductus arteriosus
- ECG: right ventricular hypertrophy; right axis deviation
- Chest x-ray: boot-shaped heart; reticular or decreased pulmonary vascular markings

Key Echocardiographic Concepts[1,54]

- 2-D delineation of anatomy
  —right ventricular outflow tract, location and size of main pulmonary artery and branches (subcostal coronal and parasternal short axis)
  —associated malformations
- Contrast echocardiography to delineate anatomy
- Doppler and color flow delineation of flow patterns

Associated Disease[54]

- Persistent ductus arteriosus
- Atrial septal defect or patent foramen ovale
- Malformations of the tricuspid valve
- Coronary arterial sinusoids

Natural History

- Death when the persistent ductus arteriosus closes or systemic to pulmonary collateral flow becomes insufficient to sustain minimal blood oxygenation requirements[1]

Treatment[1,15]

- Prostaglandin E_2: to keep the ductus arteriosus patent
- Palliation with a surgically created systemic to pulmonary shunt
- Surgical reconstruction and/or placement of a prosthetic valve

Postoperative Echocardiographic Evaluation

- Evaluative patency of systemic to pulmonary shunt
- Evaluate patency of reconstructed area

Left Ventricular Inflow Obstruction

Anatomy. Left ventricular inflow is obstructed by a membrane in the left atrium or a decrease in the mitral orifice size. Various forms exist, as listed below.[45,48]

- Valvular mitral stenosis: rare; dysplastic valve leaflets, chordae and papillary muscles
- Parachute mitral valve: all chordae insert onto a single papillary muscle
- Arcade mitral valve: chordae insert onto multiple papillary muscles; may be regurgitant
- Double orifice mitral valve: rare; tissue bridge divides mitral valve into two halves with chordae from each half inserting onto a particular papillary muscle; may be regurgitant; associated with atrioventricular malformation[25]
- Cortriatriatum: rare; left atrial membrane immediately superior to the fossa ovalis and left atrial appendage
- Supravalvular ring: more common than cortriatriatum; left atrial membrane immediately superior to the mitral valve annulus; usually associated with other mitral valve anomalies[44,63]
- Mitral valve hypoplasia: small mitral valve annulus and leaflets
- Mitral atresia: imperforate mitral valve may be associated with a large ventricular septal defect, straddling tricuspid valve, or double-outlet right ventricle

Hemodynamics. Obstruction to left ventricular inflow results in a build-up of pressure in the left atrium causing it to dilate. Pulmonary veins become congested because they cannot empty easily into the left atrium.

Clinical Presentation[1]

- Physical exam: history of recurrent respiratory infections

- Auscultation: diastolic murmur heard best at the apex
- ECG: left atrial enlargement
- Chest x-ray: left atrial enlargement; increased pulmonary vascular markings; right heart enlargement

Key Echocardiographic Concepts

- Delineation of anatomy by 2-D
- Doppler estimation of pressure gradient
- Estimation of orifice size by application of the continuity equation

Associated Disease[1]

- Other levels of left heart obstruction
- Secundum and primum atrial septal defects
- Transposition of the great arteries
- Double-outlet right ventricle

Natural History. Eventually develop pulmonary vascular obstructive disease[1]

Treatment[1]

- Valvular: commissurotomy or valve replacement
- Cortriatriatum and supramitral ring: surgical excision of membrane[54]

Postoperative Echocardiographic Evaluation

- Evaluate residual stenosis and regurgitation

Tricuspid Atresia

Anatomy. A dense band of tissue replaces the tricuspid valve preventing direct communication between the right atrium and ventricle. A large atrial septal defect or patent foramen ovale must coexist to provide an outlet to the right atrium (obligatory shunt).[45] The right ventricle is usually small.[15]

Hemodynamics. Deoxygenated systemic venous blood returns to the right atrium and is shunted into the left atrium where it mixes with oxygenated pulmonary venous return. This mixing of deoxygenated blood with the pulmonary venous return results in desaturation of the oxygenated blood and, therefore, cyanosis. The right atrium and left heart are generally dilated owing to increased flow volume. Because the right ventricle receives blood only indirectly through a ventricular septal defect, it is generally small.[11]

Clinical Presentation.[1,11] Patients are cyanotic with a history of hypoxic spells.

- Physical exam: clubbing of the fingers; delayed growth; hyperactive cardiac impulse at the apex
- Auscultation: single first heart sound; no murmur
- ECG: left ventricular hypertrophy; left axis deviation
- Chest x-ray: decreased vascular markings

Key Echocardiographic Concepts

- 2-D visualization of dense fibrous band across tricuspid annulus and absence of tricuspid valve leaflets
- Dilated right atrium[45]
- Atrial septal defect or single atrium
- Small right ventricle or right ventricular outflow tract

Associated Disease[1,11]

- Atrial septal defect or patent foramen ovale
- Ventricular septal defect and pulmonary stenosis
- Pulmonary atresia
- Transposition of the great vessels

Natural History

- Early death without intervention[1]

Treatment[1]

- Pulmonary artery band (surgical palliation to restrict flow to the pulmonary bed)
- Systemic to pulmonary shunt (surgical palliation to increase flow to the pulmonary bed)
- Balloon atrial septostomy (interventional catheterization to increase interatrial shunting)
- Park blade septostomy (interventional catheterization to increase interatrial shunting)
- Fontan procedure: definitive physiologic correction; the right atrium is connected to the pulmonary artery by placement of a patch or conduit in the hope of increasing pulmonary flow[34]

Postoperative Echocardiographic Evaluation

- Assess for right atrial contractility and adequacy of flow through the pulmonary artery

Tricuspid Hypoplasia/Stenosis

Anatomy. Small tricuspid valve annulus, usually associated with critical pulmonary stenosis, pulmonary atresia with intact interventricular septum, or Ebstein anomaly.[45]

Imperforate Tricuspid Valve

Anatomy. Membrane exists in place of a tricuspid valve, which may be surgically opened.[45]

MALFORMATION OF THE TRICUSPID VALVE

Ebstein Anomaly of the Tricuspid Valve

Anatomy. The septal leaflet is tethered to the interventricular septum and attaches at least 8 mm distal to the tricuspid valve annulus.[3] Other tricuspid leaflets may also adhere to the ventricular wall and be dysplastic.[75]

This malformation results in a large "functional" right atrium and small "functional" right ventricle. The dysplastic nature of the leaflets and chordae prevents effective coaptation resulting in varying degrees of tricuspid insufficiency and stenosis.[45] Contractility of the right ventricle is affected by its size.

Hemodynamics. The right atrium is dilated owing to the volume overload that results from the tricuspid regurgitation. The size of the right ventricle varies with the severity of tricuspid valve leaflet displacement.

Clinical Presentation.[1,11,75] Cyanosis, dyspnea on exertion, and profound weakness or fatigue may be present.

- Physical exam: prominant left chest
- Auscultation: systolic and diastolic murmurs; loud, widely split first heart sound—"sail sound"; triple or quadruple rhythm
- ECG: right atrial hypertrophy; right bundle branch block; Wolff-Parkinson-White syndrome; paroxysmal supraventricular tachycardia
- Chest x-ray: enlarged heart: decreased pulmonary vascular markings; right atrial enlargement

Key Echocardiographic Concepts

- 2-D delineation of the anatomy of the tricuspid valve and degree of displacement and tethering of each leaflet from parasternal short axis, apical four-chamber and subcostal long- and short-axis views[50]
- Determination of the size of the functional right ventricle—if less than 35% of the size of the anatomic right ventricle, prognosis is poor[3]
- Severity of tricuspid regurgitation
- Tricuspid valve closure delayed greater than 90 m/s after mitral valve closure on M-mode[3]

Associated Disease[1,50,75]

- Persistent patent ductus arteriosus
- Atrial septal defect or patent foramen ovale with right to left shunting
- MVP
- Pulmonary stenosis
- Pulmonary atresia with intact ventricular septum
- Congenitally corrected transposition of the great vessels
- Ventricular septal defect

Natural History[1,50,75]

- Increased risk of endocarditis
- Prognosis is better with a larger functional right ventricle
- Prognosis is good if the child survives infancy but generally poor if there are associated lesions

Treatment[1,50,75]

- Annuloplasty: repair of the valve annulus to make it smaller
- Valve replacement
- Valve repair
- Plication of some of the atrialized portion of the right ventricle

Postoperative Echocardiographic Evaluation

- Assess right ventricular function and residual tricuspid insufficiency and/or stenosis

COMPLEX CONGENITAL HEART DISEASE

Tetralogy of Fallot

Anatomy. In this malformation, a large perimembranous ventricular septal defect is associated with a malalignment of the aorta, such that the aortic root overrides the septal defect. The malalignment of the aortic root contributes to the infundibular pulmonary stenosis that occurs as part of this malformation.[54]

Hemodynamics. The large size of the ventricular septal defect allows equalization of left and right ventricular pressures, such that the shunting through the defect is bidirectional. The overriding aorta receives blood from both ventricles, thereby mixing deoxygenated with oxygenated blood.

Clinical Presentation.[1,11] Cyanosis and a history of "tet spells" (transient cerebral ischemia resulting in limpness, paleness, and unconsciousness); history of squatting may present.

- Physical exam: prominant left chest, "clubbing" of fingers; right ventricular heave
- Auscultation: single second heart sound; systolic ejection murmur
- ECG: right ventricular hypertrophy; right axis deviation
- Chest x-ray: boot-shaped heart with decreased vascular markings

Key Echocardiographic Concepts[54]

- 2-D visualization of large perimembranous VSD and assessment of degree of aortic override
- 2-D assessment of degree and levels of right ventricular outflow obstruction
- Size of pulmonary artery and branches from high parasternal short axis and suprasternal notch views (aneurysmally dilated in cases of absent pulmonic valve)[29]
- Thickened RV free wall
- 2-D delineation of coronary artery and aortic arch anatomy to determine surgical approach[8]

Associated Disease[1,3,29,54]

- Valvular pulmonary stenosis or pulmonary atresia
- Congenitally absent pulmonic valve
- Right-sided aortic arch
- Atrial septal defect
- Atrioventricular malformation
- Mitral stenosis
- Coronary artery anomalies
- Persistent left superior vena cava

Natural History.[1] Severe infundibular stenosis may result in a fatal "tet spell," in which the infundibulum becomes totally occluded. Pulmonary vascular obstructive disease develops.

Treatment[1]

- Palliation by surgical creation of a systemic to pulmonary shunt
- Patch closure of ventricular septal defect and possible myomectomy of the right ventricular outflow tract, or pulmonary valvotomy

Postoperative Echocardiographic Evaluation

- Evaluation of patency of surgically created systemic to pulmonary shunt
- Evaluation of residual right ventricular outflow obstruction and residual shunting around ventricular septal defect

Transposition of the Great Arteries (TGA)

Anatomy. The aorta arises from the embryologic right ventricle and the pulmonary artery arises from the embryologic left ventricle. Terminology is listed below.

- C-transposition of the great arteries (congenitally corrected, L-transposition): ventricular inversion with the great vessels originating from the incorrect ventricle; blood flow sequence is normal; however, there is a high incidence of associated congenital heart disease
- D-transposition of the great arteries (frequently referred to simply as transposition of the great arteries or complete transposition): the ventricles are concordant with the atria; however the aorta originates from the right ventricle and the pulmonary artery originates from the embryologic left ventricle

Hemodynamics

- C-TGA: Blood flows in the normal sequence—from the systemic veins into the right atrium, through the mitral valve into the left ventricle, and out the pulmonary artery, returns to the left atrium via the pulmonary valves, courses through the tricuspid valve, into the right ventricle and out the aorta.
- D-TGA: Blood flows in two parallel circuits. It flows from the systemic veins into the right atrium, through the tricuspid valve, into the right ventricle and out the aorta, to return again through the systemic veins. Pulmonary venous return flows into the left atrium, through the mitral valve into the left ventricle, and out the pulmonary artery, to return again through the pulmonary veins. In short, deoxygenated blood flows in a continuous loop, and oxygenated blood flows in a separate continuous loop. Unless a communication exists between the systemic and pulmonary circulations (ie, an obligatory shunt), this situation is incompatible with life. In the newborn period, a left to right shunt occurs at the level of the foramen ovale and through a persistent ductus arteriosus, allowing mixing of oxygenated with deoxygenated blood.

Clinical Presentation for D-TGA.[1,11] Newborns become cyanotic, as the ductus arteriosus closes.

- Physical exam: normal weight, healthy-looking infant
- Auscultation: no murmurs; single second heart sound
- ECG: right ventricular hypertrophy
- Chest x-ray: cardiomegaly; narrow mediastinum; increased vascular markings

Key Echocardiographic Concepts[53]

- Identify situs by delineating anatomic atrial landmarks on 2-D
- Identify ventricular morphology (embryologic origins) by delineating anatomic landmarks on 2-D
- Identify great vessel morphology and relationship (will course in parallel fashion)
- Identity and evaluate magnitude of shunt through the obligatory shunt defect(s)
- Delineate coronary artery anatomy for consideration of surgical approach[8]
- Identify and evaluate associated congenital heart disease

Associated Disease for D-TGA[3,53]

- Patent ductus arteriosus: obligatory shunt; most common associated heart disease
- Aortic arch anomalies: coarctation, hypoplastic segment, interrupted aortic arch
- Atrial septal defect or patent foramen ovale: obligatory shunt
- Ventricular septal defect: obligatory shunt; with or without juxtaposed atrial appendages
- Outflow tract obstruction: fixed or dynamic
- Straddling atrioventricular valve: chordae from one atrioventricular valve attach into both ventricles
- Atrioventricular malformation: rare
- Pulmonary origin of coronary artery

Natural History. Patients with congenitally corrected transposition may never know they have congenital heart disease unless there is associated congenital heart dis-

ease, in which case the natural history is determined by the associated disease.

Patients with D-transposition of the great vessels must be palliated or repaired on an emergent basis because occlusion of the obligatory shunt would result in immediate death. The mortality rate in the absence of intervention is 95% at the end of 2 years of life.[27]

Treatment[1,3,34]

Prostaglandin E_1 Treatment: palliation; to keep ductus arteriosus patent until an atrial shunt or definitive surgical procedure can be performed

Balloon Atrial Septostomy (Rashkind Procedure): palliative interventional catheterization technique in which a distended balloon catheter is torn across a patent foramen ovale or small atrial septal defect creating a large atrial septal defect

Surgical Atrial Septectomy (Blalock-Hanlon Operation): palliation

Mustard Procedure (Atrial Switch): surgical excision of the interatrial septum and placement of a baffle made of pericardium or synthetic material to redirect right atrial flow through the mitral valve into the left ventricle and allow pulmonary venous return to flow around the baffle into the tricuspid valve

Senning Procedure (Atrial Switch): surgical reconstruction of the atrial wall and interatrial septum to create an intra-atrial baffle redirecting venous flow through the atria

Rastelli Procedure (Intraventricular Repair and Extracardiac Conduit): surgical procedure in which a tunnel is constructed through a large ventricular septal defect such that left ventricular outflow is directed to the aortic valve and a valved conduit is placed between the right ventricle and pulmonary artery

Jatene Procedure (Arterial Switch): surgical procedure in which the great arteries are taken off their trunks and moved such that each is reanastamosed to the trunk that will restore a normal blood flow sequence; coronary arteries also are removed and reimplanted into the neoaorta.

Postoperative Echocardiographic Evaluation. Evaluation of left ventricular function

- Balloon atrial septostomy: 2-D visualization of definitive tear in the interatrial septum and calculation of atrial septal defect size to interatrial septal length ratio[27]
- Mustard and Senning procedures: rule out superior vena cava or pulmonary venous obstruction and baffle leaks[1,51] by PW Doppler, color flow Doppler, or contrast echocardiography[69]
- Jatene procedure: evaluate anastomotic sites of great arteries for possible constriction[1]

Truncus Arteriosus

Anatomy.[1,11] A rare malformation in which a single large great artery (common trunk) arises from the heart and receives outflow from both ventricles. In most cases, the common trunk overrides the large ventricular septal defect which must be present. The valve of the common trunk frequently has more than three cusps. Pulmonary circulation occurs in one of the following ways:

- Type I: main pulmonary trunk arises from the common trunk (usually from the posterior aspect) and bifurcates into right and left branches
- Type II: right and left pulmonary arteries arise separately from the left posterolateral aspect of the common trunk
- Type III: right and left pulmonary arteries arise separately from lateral aspects of the common trunk
- Type IV: no pulmonary arteries exist; pulmonary circulation is through bronchiole arteries arising from the descending aorta

Hemodynamics.[1] The large ventricular septal defect causes equalization of pressures between the ventricles. Flow into the pulmonary circulation is at systemic pressures because the pulmonary arteries arise from the aorta and there is no pulmonary valve. There may be decreased flow to the pulmonary circulation if there is stenosis of the pulmonary branches or in type IV.

Clinical Presentation.[1,11] Patients are cyanotic.

- Physical exam: early congestive heart failure or hypoxic spells
- Auscultation: single second heart sound; systolic ejection click and murmur
- ECG: biventricular hypertrophy
- Chest x-ray: cardiomegaly; biventricular enlargement; wide mediastinum

Key Echocardiographic Concepts

- 2-D delineation of anatomy
- Color flow and PW Doppler evaluation of truncal valve (rule out stenosis or insufficiency)
- 2-D and color flow localization of pulmonary arteries (suprasternal notch views may be most helpful)
- Evaluation of size of pulmonary arteries

Associated Disease.[1] Usually, truncus arteriosus is an isolated lesion.

- Right aortic arch
- Truncal valve stenosis and/or insufficiency
- Aortic arch anomalies
- Persistent patent ductus arteriosus
- Coronary ostial anomalies

- Absence of a branch pulmonary artery on the side of the arch
- Atrial septal defect

Natural History.[1] If left untreated, death in infancy from heart failure or later from pulmonary vascular obstructive disease. Without intervention, survival beyond 1 year is unusual.

Treatment[1]

- Removal of the pulmonary arteries from the aorta and placement of a valved conduit between the right ventricle and pulmonary arteries
- Pulmonary artery banding palliation; may make definitive repair difficult or impossible

Postoperative Echocardiographic Evaluation

- Evaluate competency of the conduit valve and evaluate anastomatic areas for stenosis.
- Evaluate placement of pulmonary artery band and gradient across it

ANOMALIES OF THE CORONARY ARTERIES

Kawasaki Syndrome (Mucocutaneous Lymph Node Syndrome)

Anatomy. Acquired coronary artery disease may occur as a sequela to a childhood disease known as Kawasaki disease. Around 15% of patients develop cardiovascular involvement in the form of coronary artery aneurysm formation. The proximal branches appear to be most frequently involved. Distal aneurysms may occur in addition, although rarely without proximal involvement.[31]

Clinical Presentation.[33] Usually seen January to April; patients have fever of over 5 days' duration, lethargy, and irritability.

- Physical exam: bilateral conjunctivitis; dry, fissured lips; strawberry tongue; polymorphous truncal rash; erythema of palms and soles; desquamation of fingertips and toes; cervical lymphadenopathy
- Lab tests: elevated white count, platelet count, erythrocyte sedimentation rate, α_2-globulin, immunoglobulin E, transaminase, and lactic acid dehydrogenase
- ECG: infrequent, minimal changes

Key Echocardiographic Concepts

Acute Phase[8,31]

- Left ventricular dysfunction
- Valvular regurgitation
- Pericardial effusion

Convalescent Phase

- 2-D demonstration of saccular or fusiform coronary aneurysms (Table 4–1)
- Segmental wall motion abnormalities

TABLE 4–1. ECHOCARDIOGRAPHIC VIEWS USED TO EVALUATE CORONARY ARTERY ANATOMY

Coronary Artery	Echocardiographic View
Proximal right, left main, proximal left anterior descending, proximal left circumflex	Parasternal short axis High parasternal short axis (caudal angle) Subcostal 4 coronal
Distal right coronary	Subcostal coronal (acute margin of heart) Subcostal short axis (sagittal) Posterior apical 4 chamber (posterior atrioventricular groove)
Posterior descending	Parasternal short axis Subcostal coronal Apical 4 chamber
Left circumflex	Parasternal short Parasternal long Subcostal sagittal
Distal left anterior descending	Parasternal long Parasternal short Subcostal coronal

(Data from references 17 and 66.)

Natural History. The majority of aneurysms resolve; however, those with diameters larger than 8 mm are at increased risk for thrombosis, which may result in myocardial infarction.[31]

Treatment. Patients with aneurysms are usually treated with an aspirin per day to decrease the risk of thrombosis. Serial echocardiographic exams are generally performed, with coronary angiography at intervals to determine whether coronary artery bypass surgery is indicated.[1]

Anomalous Origin of the Left Coronary Artery

Anatomy. A rare malformation in which the left coronary artery originates from the main pulmonary artery rather than from the aortic root.[8]

Hemodynamics. The myocardium of the left ventricle is inadequately perfused with oxygen because the blood flowing into the left coronary artery is deoxygenated blood from the pulmonary artery.

Clinical Presentation.[8] Symptomatic in infancy.

- Physical exam: irritable, dyspneic, tachypneic
- Auscultation: mitral insufficiency murmur
- ECG: left ventricular hypertrophy with anterolateral myocardial infarction
- Chest x-ray: enlarged heart

Key Echocardiographic Concepts[8]

- 2-D visualization of left coronary artery originating from the pulmonary artery

- 2-D visualization of a dilated right coronary artery originating from the right sinus of Valsalva
- PW Doppler or color flow demonstration of diastolic flow entering the main pulmonary artery just distal to the pulmonary valve
- Decreased left ventricular contractility
- Mitral insufficiency

Natural History. In the absence of intervention, permanent myocardial damage occurs.

Treatment. Surgery to reimplant the left coronary artery into the aortic root.[8]

Coronary Arteriovenous Fistula

Anatomy. A variably tortuous coronary artery courses along the surface of the heart or within the myocardium to empty into a cardiac chamber or great vessel. Generally, it is the right coronary artery that is involved, and the site of drainage is usually a right heart structure.[8]

Hemodynamics. Rather than perfusing the myocardium, blood from the coronary artery flows into the cardiac chamber or vessel into which it empties.

Clinical Presentation. Generally, patients remain asymptomatic until the fourth decade of life.[26]

- Auscultation: atypical continuous murmur

Key Echocardiographic Concepts[71]

- 2-D demonstration of a dilated coronary artery
  —normal ratios of coronary artery diameter to aortic root diameter
  —left coronary artery = 0.17 ± 0.03
  —right coronary artery = 0.14 ± 0.03
- 2-D demonstration of origin, course, and site of drainage of the fistula
- Color flow Doppler visualization and PW Dopple confirmation of a continuous, turbulent jet entering a cardiac chamber or great vessel in a location in which shunt lesions do not enter
- PW Doppler demonstration of turbulent late systolic, early diastolic flow in a dilated coronary artery supplying the fistula

Natural History[71]

- Spontaneous closure may occur
- Bacterial endocarditis
- Congestive heart failure due to volume overload and myocardial ischemia

Treatment. Elective surgical ligation of the fistula.[71]

Postoperative Echocardiographic Evaluation. Check for residual flow through the fistula.

VENOUS MALFORMATIONS

Persistent Left Superior Vena Cava

Anatomy. In this relatively common malformation (0.5% of the general population and 3–5% of patients with congenital heart disease), a superior vena cava persists in the left chest. The left superior vena cava may empty into coronary sinus (62%), pulmonary venous atrium (21%), common atrium (17%), or rarely into a left-sided pulmonary vein. In most cases, there is also a right superior vena cava, and in 45–60% of cases, a communication exists between the two superior venae cavae.[74]

Hemodynamics. Systemic venous blood returns to the cardiac chamber to which the left superior vena cava connects. Deoxygenated blood mixes with oxygenated blood (right to left shunt) if the left superior vena cava drains into a left heart structure.

Key Echocardiographic Concepts[44]

- Dilated coronary sinus
- Contrast echocardiography[20]
- 2-D and color flow visualization of the left superior vena cava
- Absent or small innominate vein

Associated Disease[74]

- Atrial septal defect
- Complex congenital heart disease

Total Anomalous Pulmonary Venous Return

Anatomy. All of the pulmonary veins drain into something other than the left atrium. The types of anomalous drainage are listed below.[44,70]

- Supracardiac: pulmonary veins drain directly into the superior vena cava or form a vertical vein that empties into the innominate vein, superior vena cava, or persistent left superior vena cava
- Cardiac: pulmonary veins drain into the right atrium or coronary sinus
- Infracardiac: pulmonary veins form a common vein that descends below the diaphragm and empties into the portal vein

Hemodynamics. Increased flow into a systemic vein, right atrium, or coronary sinus[70] and ultimately, the right heart. There is an obligatory right to left shunt at the atrial level.[11]

Clinical Presentation Without Obstruction.[11] Mild cyanosis; asymptomatic.

- Physical exam: poor growth; prominant left chest; right ventricular heave
- Auscultation: fixed, widely split second sound
- ECG: right ventricular hypertrophy

- Chest x-ray: enlarged right heart; increased pulmonary vascular markings; snowman- or figure 8–shaped mediastinum

Clinical Presentation in the Presence of Obstruction.[11] Cyanosis; symptomatic during newborn period.

- Physical exam: tachypnea; dyspnea; right ventricular failure
- Auscultation: no murmurs
- ECG: right ventricular hypertrophy
- Chest x-ray: normal size heart; increased pulmonary vascular markings

Key Echocardiographic Concepts[44,70]

- Absence of normal pulmonary venous return into the left atrium by 2-D and color flow Doppler
- Dilated coronary sinus
- Turbulent flow noted in systemic vein or right atrium by color flow Doppler
- Localization of anomalous venous structures by use of 2-D and color flow Doppler from the subcostal and suprasternal positions
- Color flow Doppler interrogation of anomalous venous structures to rule out obstruction
- Contrast echocardiography

Associated Disease

- Atrial septal defect

Natural History.[11] Obstruction of the common vein or entry into a systemic venous structure will result in pulmonary edema and right heart failure, complete obstruction will cause death. Eventually, pulmonary vascular obstructive disease will develop.

Treatment. Surgical anastamosis of the common vein with the left atrium and closure of the atrial communication.

Postoperative Echocardiographic Evaluation

- Assessment of ventricular function
- Evaluate area of anastamosis to rule out obstruction

INTRAOPERATIVE ECHOCARDIOGRAPHY

Echocardiography is used increasingly in the operating room to enable surgeons to delineate anatomy and evaluate repair effectiveness. The most common method is epicardial echocardiography, in which the transducer and cable are encased in a sterile sheath and left in the sterile field. The surgeon scans "on heart" after the chest is opened and before the patient is put on cardiopulmonary bypass. This technique offers increased resolution when compared with "on chest" scanning because a higher-frequency transducer may be used owing to decreased depth penetration requirements. In some cases, the surgeon may decide to change the surgical approach based on anatomic and hemodynamic information obtained at this time. The role of the echocardiographer is to manipulate the echocardiographic equipment; setting gain and depth, image processing, manipulating Doppler and M-mode functions, and recording the scan. The most useful modalities are 2-D imaging and color flow Doppler. When the repair is completed, the surgeon may choose to image epicardially after the patient is taken off of bypass and before the chest is closed. Should the repair appear to be unsatisfactory, the surgeon may elect to put the patient back on bypass and revise the repair before closing the chest. Comparison of prebypass versus postbypass right and left ventricular function has proven helpful in perioperative medical management. When used routinely, intraoperative echocardiographic imaging and color flow Doppler impacts on as many as 50% of surgical cases.[67]

TRANSESOPHAGEAL ECHOCARDIOGRAPHY

Pediatric transesophageal echocardiography is an invasive technique that has been performed in the operating room, catheterization laboratory, and intensive care unit in patients who are anesthetized or sedated. Currently available transducers image in the transverse plane only and have color flow Doppler and pulsed Doppler capabilities. Uniplane transverse imaging is helpful in the evaluation of the following entities: ventricular function, atrioventricular connection, ventriculoarterial connection, interatrial septum, atrioventricular valve morphology, semilunar valve morphology, normal pulmonary venous connections, and identification of coronary artery origin. Color flow Doppler is useful in evaluating competency of valves and in searching for residual defects. Owing to limitations in peak velocity resolution and the angle of incidence, pulsed Doppler applications appear to be of limited usefulness.[41] A report of experience with a prototype uniplane longitudinal transesophageal probe confirms improved utility with the addition of this imaging plane. Longitudinal imaging allowed improved imaging of the interatrial septum, interventricular septum, and left ventricular inflow tract. The ventricular outflow tracts and superior vena cava, which were inadequately imaged in the transverse plane were well demonstrated in the longitudinal plane.[40] The utility of this technique will improve with the development of a pediatric-size biplane transducer, improved resolution, and the addition of steerable continuous-wave Doppler. Owing to current limitations, it may best be utilized in the operating room as a complementary technique with epicardial echocardiography.[62]

REFERENCES

1. Adams FH, Emmanouilides GC, Riemenschneider TA (eds): *Moss' Heart Disease in Infants, Children & Adolescents,* 4th ed. Baltimore: Williams & Wilkins, 1989.

2. Anderson R, Ho SY: Echocardiographic diagnosis and description of congenital heart disease: Anatomic principles and philosophy. In St John Sutton M, Oldershaw PJ (eds): *Textbook of Adult and Pediatric Echocardiography and Doppler.* Boston: Blackwell Scientific, 1989, pp 573–606.
3. Armstrong, WF: Congenital heart disease. In Feigenbaum H (ed): *Echocardiography,* 4th ed. Philadelphia: Lea & Febiger, 1986, pp 365–461.
4. Bash SE, Huhta JC, Vick GW, et al: Hypoplastic left heart syndrome: Is echocardiography accurate enough to guide surgical palliation? *J Am Coll Cardiol* **7**(3):610–616, 1986.
5. Beard JT, Byrd BF: Saline contrast enhancement of trivial Doppler tricuspid regurgitation signals for estimating pulmonary artery pressure. *Am J Cardiol* **62:**486–488, 1988.
6. Brenner JI, Baker KR, Berman MA: Prediction of left ventricular pressure in infants with aortic stenosis. *Br Heart J* **44:**406–410, 1980.
7. Burrows PE, Freedom RM, Rabinovitch M, et al: The investigation of abnormal pulmonary arteries in congenital heart disease. *Radiol Clin North Am* **23**(4):689–717, 1985.
8. Caldwell RL, Ensing GJ: Coronary artery abnormalities in children. *J Am Soc Echo* **2**(4):259–268, 1989.
9. Cassidy SC, Van Hare GF, Silverman NH: The probability of detecting a subaortic ridge in children with ventricular septal defect or coarctation of the aorta. *Am J Cardiol* **66:**505–508, 1990.
10. Cloez JL, Schmidt KG, Birk E, Silverman NS: Determination of pulmonary to systemic blood flow ratio in children by a simplified Doppler echocardiographic method. *J Am Coll Cardiol* **11**(4):825–830.
11. Fink, BW: Congenital Heart Disease: A Deductive Approach to Its Diagnosis, 2nd ed. Chicago: Year Book Medical, 1985.
12. Foale R, Stefanini L, Rickards A, et al: Left and right ventricular morphology in complex congenital heart disease defined by two-dimensional echocardiography. *Am J Cardiol* **49:**93, 1982.
13. Fraker TD, Harris PJ, Behar VS, et al: Detection and exclusion of interatrial shunts by two-dimensional echocardiography and peripheral venous injection. *Circulation* **59**(2):379–384, 1979.
14. Frantz, EG, Silverman NH: Doppler ultrasound evaluation of valvar pulmonary stenosis from multiple transducer positions in children requiring pulmonary valvuloplasty. *Am J Cardiol* **61:**844–849, 1988.
15. Fuster V, Driscoll DJ, McGoon DC: Congenital heart disease in adolescents and adults. In Brandenburg RO, Fuster V, Giulani ER, McGoon DC (eds): *Cardiology: Fundamentals and Practice.* Chicago: Year Book Medical, 1987, pp 1386–1458.
16. George B, DiSessa TG, Williams R, et al: Coarctation repair without cardiac catheterization in infants. *Am Heart J* **114**(6):1421–1425, 1987.
17. Goldfarb BL, Wanderman KL, Rovner M, et al: Ventricular septal defect with left ventricular to right atrial shunt: Documentation by color flow Doppler and avoidance of the pitfall of the diagnosis of tricuspid regurgitation and pulmonary hypertension. *Echocardiography* **6**(6):521–525, 1989.
18. Hatle L, Angelsen B: *Doppler Ultrasound in Cardiology: Physical Principles and Clinical Applications,* 2nd ed. Philadelphia: Lea & Febiger, 1985.
19. Huhta JC, Gutgesell HP, Latson LA, et al: Two-dimensional echocardiographic assessment of the aorta in infants and children with congenital heart disease. *Circulation* **70**(3):417–424, 1984.
20. Huhta JC, Smallhorn JF, Macartney FJ, et al: Cross-sectional echocardiographic diagnosis of systemic venous return. *Br Heart J* **44:**718–723, 1980.
21. Kitabatake A, Inoue M, Asao M, et al: Noninvasive evaluation of pulmonary hypertension by a pulsed Doppler technique. *Circulation* **68:**302–309, 1983.
22. Kosturakis D, Goldberg SJ, Allen HD, et al: Doppler echocardiographic prediction of pulmonary arterial hypertension in congenital heart disease. *Am J Cardiol* **53:**1110–1114, 1984.
23. Kyo S: Congenital heart disease. In Omoto R. (ed): *Color Atlas of Real-Time Two-Dimensional Doppler Echocardiography.* 2nd ed. Philadelphia: Lea & Febiger, 1987, pp 149–209.
24. Lin F, Fu M, Yeh S, et al: Doppler atrial shunt flow patterns in patients with secundum atrial septal defect: Determinants, limitations and pitfalls. *J Am Soc Echo* **1**(2):141–149, 1988.
25. Lipshultz SE, Sanders SP, Mayer JE, et al: Are routine preoperative cardiac catheterization and angiography necessary before repair of ostiuum primum atrial septal defect? *J Am Coll Cardiol* **11**(2):373–378, 1988.
26. Lloyd TR, Mahoney LT, Marvin WJ, et al: Identification of coronary artery to right ventricular fistulae by color flow mapping. *Echocardiography* **5**(2):115–120, 1988.
27. Marantz P, Capelli H, Ludomirsky A, et al: Echocardiographic assessment of balloon atrial septostomy in patients with transposition of the great arteries: Prediction of the need for early surgery. *Echocardiography* **5**(2):99–104, 1988.
28. Masuyama T, Kodama D, Kitabatake A, et al: Continuous wave Doppler echocardiographic detection of pulmonary regurgitation and its application to noninvasive estimation of pulmonary artery pressure. *Circulation* **74:**484–492, 1986.
29. McIrvin DM, Murphy DJ, Ludomirsky A: Tetralogy of Fallot with absent pulmonary valve. *Echocardiography* **6**(4):363–367, 1989.
30. McKay RG: Balloon valvuloplasty for treating pul-

monic, mitral and aortic valve stenosis. *Am J Cardiol* **61:**102G–108G, 1988.

31. Meyer RA: Echocardiography in Kawasaki disease. *J Am Soc Echo* **2**(4):269–275, 1989.
32. Murphy DJ, Ludomirsky A, Huhta JC: Continuous-wave Doppler in children with ventricular septal defect: noninvasive estimation of interventricular pressure gradient. *Am J Cardiol* **57:**428–432, 1986.
33. Neches WH: Kawasaki syndrome. In Anderson RH, Neches WH, Park SC, Zuberbuhler JR (eds): *Perspectives in Pediatric Cardiology.* Mt Kisco, NY: Futura Publishing, 1988, pp 411–424.
34. NeSmith J, Philips J: The sonographer's beginning guide to surgery for congenital heart disease. *J Am Soc Echo* **1**(5):384–387, 1988.
35. Nihoyannopoulos P, Karas S, Sapsford RN, et al: Accuracy of two-dimensional echocardiography in the diagnosis of aortic arch obstruction. *J Am Coll Cardiol* **10**(5):1072–1077, 1987.
36. Perry SB, Keane JF, Lock JE: Interventional catheterization in pediatric congenital and acquired heart disease. *Am J Cardiol* **61:**109G–117G, 1988.
37. Rakowski H, Sasson Z, Wigle ED. Echocardiographic and Doppler assessment of hypertrophic cardiomyopathy. *J Am Soc Echo* **1**(1):31–47, 1988.
38. Ritter S, Rothe W, Kawai, D, et al: Identification of ventricular septal defects by Doppler color flow mapping. *Clin Res* **36**(3):311A, 1988.
39. Ritter SB: Application of Doppler color flow mapping in the assessment and the evaluation of congenital heart disease. *Echocardiography* **4**(6):543–556, 1987.
40. Ritter SB: Pediatric transesophageal color flow imaging 1990: The long and short of it. *Echocardiography* **7**(6):713–725, 1990.
41. Roberson DA, Muhiudeen IA, Silverman NH: Transesophageal echocardiography in pediatrics: Technique and limitations. *Echocardiography* **7**(6):699–712, 1990.
42. Sahn DJ, Allen HD: Real-time cross-sectional echocardiographic imaging and measurement of the patent ductus arteriosus in infants and children. *Circulation* **58**(2):343–354, 1978.
43. Sahn DJ, Valdes-Cruz LM: Ultrasound Doppler methods for calculating cardiac volume flows, cardiac output, and cardiac shunts. In Kotler MN, Steiner RM (eds): *Cardiac Imaging: New Technologies and Clinical Applications.* Philadelphia: FA Davis, 1986, pp 19–31.
44. Sanders SP: Echocardiography and related techniques in the diagnosis of congenital heart defects Part I: Veins, atria and interatrial septum. *Echocardiography* **1**(2):185–217, 1984.
45. Sanders SP: Echocardiography and related techniques in the diagnosis of congenital heart defects Part II: Atrioventricular valves and ventricles. *Echocardiography* **1**(3):333–391, 1984.
46. Schmidt KG, Cassidy SC, Silverman NH: Doubly committed subarterial ventricular septal defects: Echocardiographic features and surgical implications. *J Am Coll Cardiol* **12**(6):1538–1546, 1988.
47. Schmidt KG, Silverman NH: Cross-sectional and contrast echocardiography in the diagnosis of interatrial communications through the coronary sinus. *Int J Cardiol* **16:**193–199, 1987.
48. Seward JB, Tajik AJ, Edwards WD, Hagler DJ: *Two Dimensional Echocardiographic Atlas.* Vol I: *Congenital Heart Disease.* New York: Springer-Verlag, 1987.
49. Silverman NS, Araujo LML: An echocardiographic method for the diagnosis of cardiac situs and malpositions. *Echocardiography* **4**(1):35–57, 1987.
50. Silverman NS, Birk E: Ebstein's malformation of the tricuspid valve: Cross-sectional echocardiography and Doppler. In Anderson RH, Neches WH, Park SC, Zuberbuhler JR (eds): *Perspectives in Pediatric Cardiology.* Mt Kisco, NY: Futura Publishing, 1988, pp 113–125.
51. Silverman NH, Schmidt KG: The current role of Doppler echocardiography in the diagnosis of heart disease in children. *Cardiol Clin* **7**(2):265–297, 1989.
52. Silverman NH, Zuberbuhler JR, Anderson RH: Atrioventricular septal defects: Cross-sectional echocardiographic and morphologic comparisons. *Int J Cardiol* **13:**309–331, 1986.
53. Smallhorn J: Complete transposition. In St John Sutton M, Oldershaw P (eds): *Textbook of Adult and Pediatric Echocardiography and Doppler.* Boston: Blackwell Scientific, 1989, pp 791–808.
54. Smallhorn J: Right ventricular outflow tract obstruction. In St John Sutton M, Oldershaw P (eds): *Textbook of Adult and Pediatric Echocardiography and Doppler.* Boston: Blackwell Scientific, 1989, pp 761–790.
55. Smallhorn JF: Patent ductus arteriosus—evaluation by echocardiography. *Echocardiography* **4**(2):101–118, 1987.
56. Smallhorn JF, Huhta JC, Anderson RH, et al: Suprasternal cross-sectional echocardiography in assessment of patent ductus arteriosus. *Br Heart J* **48:**321–330, 1982.
57. Snider AR: Doppler echocardiography in congenital heart disease. In Berger M (ed): *Doppler Echocardiography in Heart Disease.* New York: Marcel Dekker, 1987.
58. Stevenson JG: Doppler evaluation of atrial septal defect, ventricular septal defect, and complex malformations. *Acta Paediatr Scand* 329 (suppl):21–43, 1986.
59. Stevenson JG: The use of Doppler echocardiography for detection and estimation of severity of patent ductus arteriosus, ventricular septal defect and atrial septal defect. *Echocardiography* **4**(4):321–346, 1987.
60. Stevenson JG: Comparison of several noninvasive

methods for estimation of pulmonary artery pressure. *J Am Soc Echo* **2**(3):157–171, 1989.

61. Stevenson JG, Kawabori I, Dooley T, et al: Diagnosis of ventricular septal defects by pulsed Doppler echocardiography. *Circulation* **58**(2):322–326, 1978.
62. Stumper O, Kaulitz R, Sreeram N, et al.: Intraoperative transesophageal versus epicardial ultrasound in surgery for congenital heart disease. *J Am Soc Echo* **3**(5):392–401, 1990.
63. Sullivan ID, Robinson PJ, DeLeval M, et al: Membranous supravalvular mitral stenosis: A treatable form of congenital heart disease. *J Am Coll Cardiol* **8**(1):159–164, 1986.
64. Sutherland GR, Smallhorn JF, Anderson RH, et al: Atrioventricular discordance: Cross-sectional echocardiographic morphological correlative study. *Br Heart J* **50:**8, 1983.
65. Sweeney MS, Walker WE, Cooley DA, et al: Apicoaortic conduits for complex left ventricular outflow obstruction: 10-year experience. *Ann Thorac Surg* **42**(6): 609–611, 1986.
66. Tani L, Ludomirsky A, Murphy DJ, et al: Ventricular morphology: Echocardiographic evaluation of isolated ventricular inversion. *Echocardiography* **5**(1):39–42, 1988.
67. Ungerleider RM: The use of intraoperative echocardiography with Doppler color flow imaging in the repair of congenital heart defects. *Echocardiography* **7**(3):289–304, 1990.
68. Valdez-Cruz LM, Sahn DJ: Ultrasonic contrast studies for the detection of cardiac shunts. *J Am Coll Cardiol* **3**(4):978–985, 1984.
69. Van Hare GF, Silverman NH: Contrast two-dimensional echocardiography in congenital heart disease: Techniques, indications and clinical utility. *J Am Coll Cardiol* **13**(3):673–686, 1989.
70. Van Hare GF, Schmidt KG, Cassidy SC, et al: Color Doppler flow mapping in the ultrasound diagnosis of total anomalous pulmonary venous connection. *J Am Soc Echo* **1**(5):341–347, 1988.
71. Velvis H, Schmidt KG, Silverman NH, et al: Diagnosis of coronary artery fistula by two-dimensional echocardiography, pulsed Doppler ultrasound and color flow imaging. *J Am Coll Cardiol* **14**(4):968–976, 1989.
72. Weyman AE, Dillon JC, Feigenbaum H, et al: Echocardiographic patterns of pulmonic valve motion with pulmonary hypertension. *Circulation* **50:**905–910, 1974.
73. Yock PG, Popp RL: Noninvasive estimation of right ventricular systolic pressure by Doppler ultrasound in patients with tricuspid regurgitation. *Circulation* **70**(4):657–662, 1984.
74. Zellers TM, Hagler DJ, Julsrud PR: Accuracy of two-dimensional echocardiography in diagnosing left superior vena cava. *J Am Soc Echo* **2**(2):132–138, 1989.
75. Zuberbuhler JR, Anderson RH: Ebstein's malformation of the tricuspid valve: Morphology and natural history. In Anderson RH, Neches WH, Park SC, Zuberbuhler JR (eds): *Perspectives in Pediatric Cardiology.* Mt Kisco, NY: Futura Publishing, 1988, 99–112.

Questions

1. The most common type of atrial septal defect is

   (A) primum
   (B) secundum
   (C) sinus venosus
   (D) single atrium

2. Which transducer position is most helpful in the 2-D visualization of atrial septal defects?

   (A) left parasternal
   (B) apical
   (C) subxiphoid
   (D) right parasternal

3. Partial anomalous pulmonary venous return is most commonly associated with which type of atrial septal defect?

   (A) secundum
   (B) priumum
   (C) sinus venosus
   (D) coronary sinus

4. What is the most common congenital heart lesion in the pediatric population?

   (A) mitral stenosis
   (B) atrial septal defect
   (C) ventricular septal defect
   (D) pulmonary stenosis

5. A "T-sign" artifact demonstrated by ——— is useful in the detection of ventricular septal defects.

   (A) M-mode
   (B) 2-D
   (C) pulsed-wave Doppler
   (D) continuous-wave Doppler
   (E) color flow Doppler

6. A small muscular ventricular septal defect may be most easily localized by

   (A) M-mode
   (B) 2-D
   (C) pulsed-wave Doppler
   (D) continuous-wave Doppler
   (E) color flow Doppler

7. Which of the following will *not* cause a reversal of flow in the descending aorta during diastole?

   (A) large patent ductus arteriosus with severe pulmonary hypertension (suprasystemic pulmonary pressures)
   (B) severe aortic insufficiency
   (C) surgically created systemic to pulmonary shunt with normal pulmonary artery pressures
   (D) large patent ductus arteriosus with normal pulmonary artery pressures

8. Which of the following may be associated with valvar aortic stenosis?

   (A) patent ductus arteriosus
   (B) coarctation of the aorta
   (C) ventricular septal defect
   (D) pulmonary stenosis
   (E) all of the above

9. The most commonly associated lesion in patients with coarctation of the aorta is

   (A) ventricular septal defect
   (B) bicuspid aortic valve
   (C) patent ductus arteriosus
   (D) aortic stenosis
   (E) mitral stenosis

10. In the normally related heart, the aortic valve lies

    (A) anterior and to the left of the pulmonary valve
    (B) anterior and to the right of the pulmonary valve
    (C) posterior and to the right of the pulmonary valve
    (D) posterior and to the left of the pulmonary valve

11. Which of the following surgical procedures is *not* frequently used to treat transposition of the great arteries?

    (A) Senning procedure
    (B) Mustard procedure
    (C) Jatene procedure
    (D) Fontan procedure

12. Which of the following is also known as the arterial switch procedure?

(A) Rashkind procedure
(B) Mustard procedure
(C) Jatene procedure
(D) Senning procedure

13. When the aorta and pulmonary artery are transposed, they course ——— as they exit the heart.

(A) parallel to each other
(B) perpendicular to each other
(C) wound around each other
(D) in no particular relationship to each other

14. Balloon atrial septostomy is most commonly performed in infants who have

(A) Ebstein anomaly of the tricuspid valve
(B) transposition of the great arteries
(C) truncus arteriosus
(D) tetralogy of Fallot

15. Of all children who suffer from Kawasaki disease, ——— will develop coronary artery aneurysms.

(A) 2%
(B) 15%
(C) 50%
(D) 75%
(E) 100%

16. Which of the following groups is most likely to develop coronary artery aneurysms as a complication of Kawasaki disease?

(A) toddlers
(B) infants
(C) adolescents
(D) adults

17. Which of the following is *not* useful in the assessment of pulmonary artery pressure?

(A) peak Doppler gradient through a patent ductus arteriosus
(B) peak Doppler gradient of tricuspid regurgitation
(C) end-diastolic Doppler gradient of pulmonary insufficiency
(D) acceleration time to ejection time ratio calculated from a right ventricular outflow tract velocity curve
(E) all of the above are useful in estimating pulmonary artery pressure

18. A child with tetralogy of Fallot is upset and crying during the echocardiogram. The Doppler gradient through the right ventricular outflow tract will be ——— than if the child were sleeping peacefully.

(A) greater
(B) less
(C) outflow obstruction in tetralogy of Fallot is not affected by the patient's activity

19. A 3-year-old child with Kawasaki disease is referred to echocardiology. Which of the following views is not really necessary in the 2-D evaluation of the coronary arterial system?

(A) subcostal transverse
(B) parasternal short axis
(C) apical five chamber
(D) subcostal coronal
(E) all views are helpful

20. Which of the following Doppler findings is *not* characteristic of coarctation of the aorta?

(A) forward flow through the descending aorta extending throughout diastole
(B) normal or slightly increased velocity of flow in the aorta proximal to the left subclavian artery
(C) rapid acceleration and deceleration of the Doppler signal taken from the descending aorta
(D) Doppler signal from the descending aorta does not return to baseline during diastole
(E) high-velocity flow detected in the descending aorta distal to the left subclavian artery

21. Careful echocardiographic evaluation of a child with complex congenital heart disease reveals absence of the inferior vena cava above the level of the renal arteries. The aorta is to the left of the spine. What is this child's situs most likely to be?

(A) solitus
(B) inversus
(C) left atrial isomerism
(D) right atrial isomerism

22. The characteristic aortic valve M-mode tracing from a patient with discrete membranous subaortic stenosis demonstrates

(A) an asymmetric closure line
(B) early closure and partial reopening
(C) gradual closure (drifting closed)
(D) prolonged ejection time

23. Which of the following should *not* be included in the differential diagnosis when a Doppler tracing such as that in Fig. 4–1 is obtained from the descending aorta?

(A) patent ductus arteriosus
(B) severe aortic regurgitation
(C) arteriovenous malformation
(D) aortic to pulmonary window
(E) coarctation of the aorta

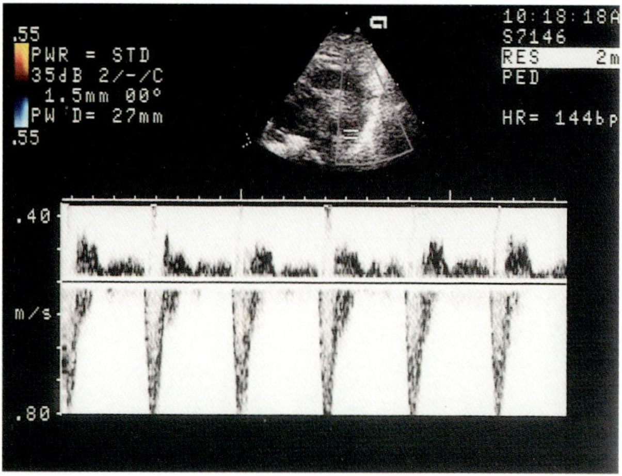

Figure 4–1. Pulsed Doppler spectral tracing of flow in the descending aorta as obtained from the suprasternal notch view.

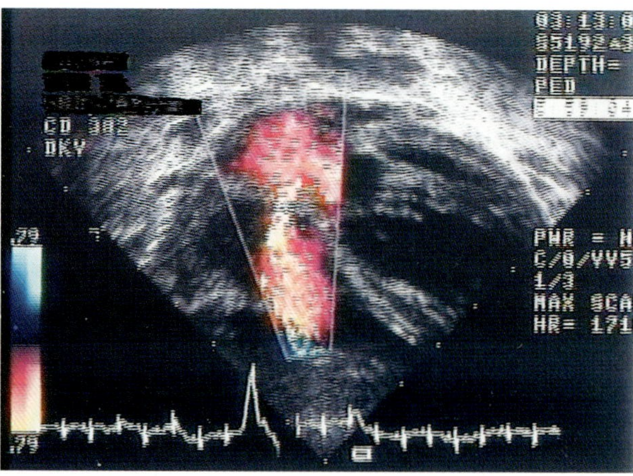

Figure 4–3. Color flow Doppler image of a subcostal four-chamber view presented with the apex down (anatomically correct) presentation. The patient is an 8-month-old female with trisomy 21.

24. An echocardiogram was requested for a premature infant in the neonatal intensive care unit who appeared clinically to be in congestive failure and in whom a murmur was heard. The color flow Doppler image in Fig. 4–2 was taken from the ductus view, which is a parasternal sagittal view. The closed aortic valve may be appreciated in the center of the image. This image demonstrates

(A) a small patent ductus arteriosus
(B) a moderate patent ductus arteriosus
(C) a large patent ductus arteriosus
(D) no ductus arteriosus

25. The image in Fig. 4–3 was taken from an 8-month-old female with trisomy 21. The color flow Doppler image was taken from the subcostal 4 chamber view. The image demonstrates

(A) a left to right shunt through a primum atrial septal defect
(B) a right to left shunt through a primum atrial septal defect
(C) a left to right shunt through a secundum atrial septal defect
(D) a right to left shunt through a secundum atrial septal defect
(E) a normal heart

26. The images presented in Fig. 4–4 were taken from the cardiac apex of a cyanotic infant. These images demonstrate

(A) a normal heart
(B) an isolated inflow ventricular septal defect
(C) single atrium
(D) tricuspid atresia with ventricular septal defect
(E) tricuspid atresia with intact ventricular septum

27. The color flow Doppler image presented in Fig. 4–5 was taken from an 8-year-old male with a systolic murmur. The image is of the parasternal short axis view during early systole and demonstrates a left to right shunt through a(n)

(A) inflow ventricular septal defect
(B) membranous ventricular septal defect
(C) muscular ventricular septal defect
(D) doubly committed subarterial ventricular septal defect

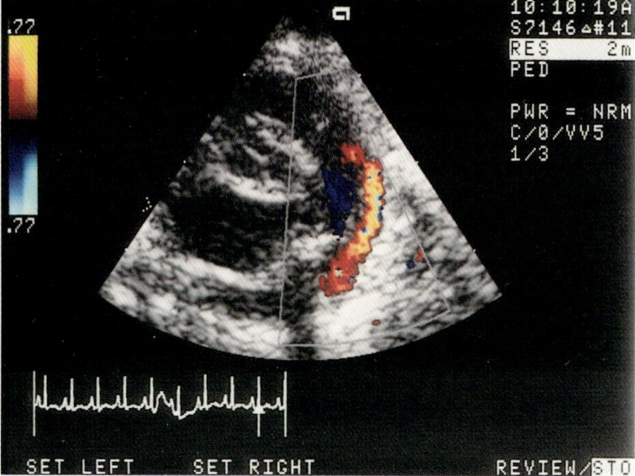

Figure 4–2. Color flow Doppler image of a modified short-axis parasternal view, known as the "ductus view." The patient is a premature infant in congestive heart failure in whom a murmur is heard.

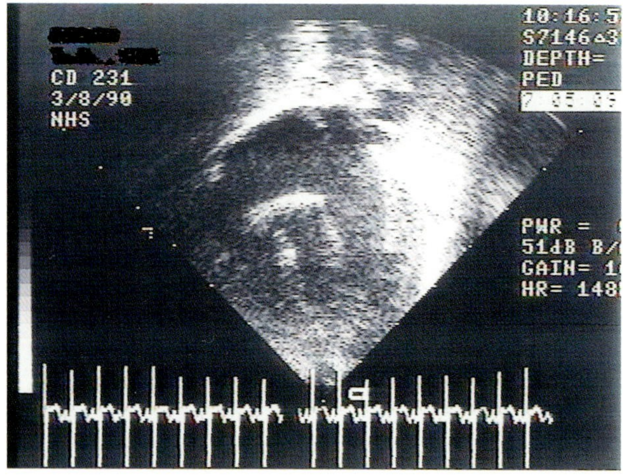

A

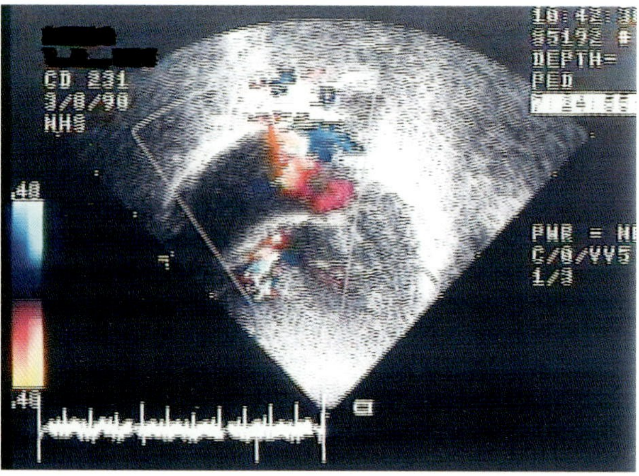

B

Figure 4–4. Apical four-chamber view presented with the apex down. (**A**) 2-D image. (**B**) Color flow Doppler image. The patient is a cyanotic infant.

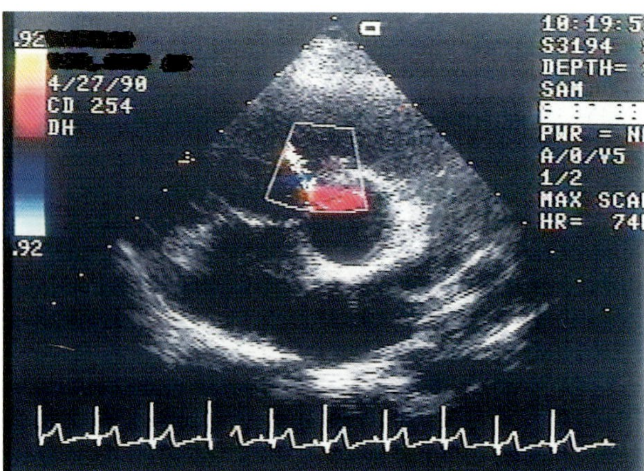

Figure 4–5. Color flow Doppler image of the parasternal short-axis view at the level of the semilunar valves taken in early systole. The patient is an 8-year-old male in whom a systolic murmur may be heard.

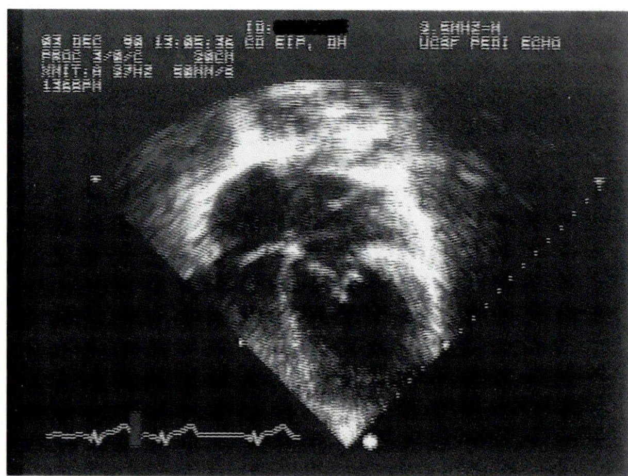

Figure 4–6. 2-D image of the apical four-chamber view presented with the apex down.

28. The 2-D image in Fig. 4–6 was taken from the cardiac apex and demonstrates

    (A) a normal apical four-chamber view
    (B) tricuspid atresia
    (C) Ebstein anomaly of the tricuspid valve
    (D) ventricular inversion

29. The 2-D image of the parasternal long-axis view presented in Fig. 4–7 was taken during diastole and demonstrates

    (A) a normal heart
    (B) valvular aortic stenosis
    (C) discrete membranous subaortic stenosis
    (D) ideopathic hypertrophic subaortic stenosis

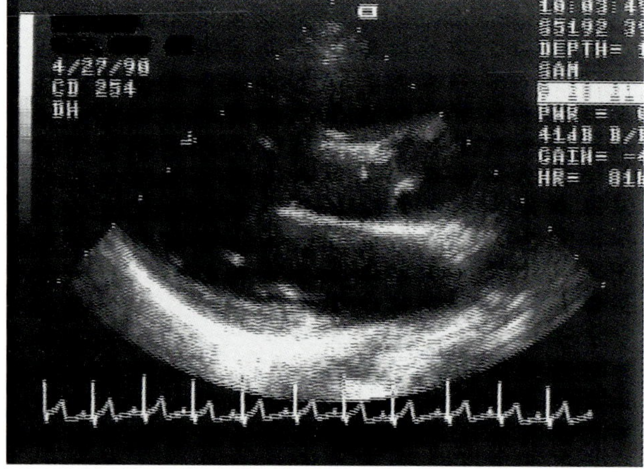

Figure 4–7. 2-D image of a parasternal long-axis view taken in diastole.

30. If the left ventricular outflow tract of the patient presented in Fig. 4–7 was interrogated by PW Doppler, what is the most proximal location at which an increase in velocity would be detected?

(A) just proximal to the aortic valve
(B) at the aortic valve
(C) just distal to the aortic valve
(D) in the aortic root
(E) distal to the left subclavian artery

31. The 2-D parasternal short-axis view image presented in Fig. 4–8 was taken from a young child who had recently had Kawasaki disease. This view demonstrates

(A) left coronary artery involvement
(B) right coronary artery involvement
(C) both left and right coronary arteries are involved
(D) normal coronary arteries

32. The 2-D parasternal short-axis view image presented in Fig. 4–9 was taken from an infant who was diagnosed as having tetralogy of Fallot. This image demonstrates

(A) a normal right ventricular outflow tract
(B) infundibular pulmonary stenosis only
(C) infundibular and valvular pulmonary stenosis
(D) infundibular pulmonary stenosis with hypoplasia of the pulmonary valve and main pulmonary artery

33. Which of the following views would *not* be helpful in delineating the size of left and right pulmonary arteries in the patient imaged for Fig. 4–9?

(A) suprasternal coronal view
(B) apical outflow view

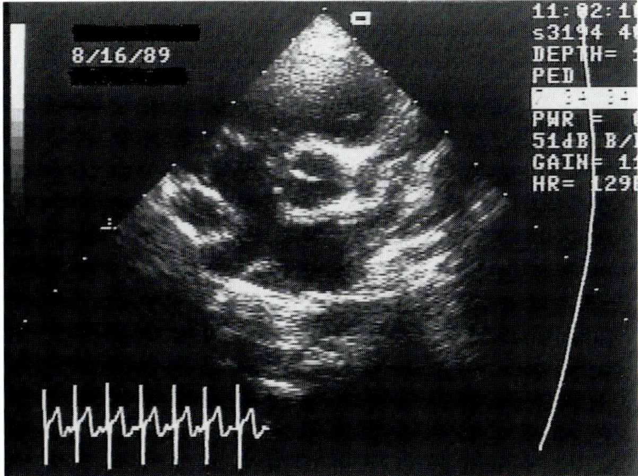

Figure 4–8. 2-D image of a parasternal short-axis view at the level of the semilunar valves. The patient is a young child who is in the convalescent phase of Kawasaki's disease.

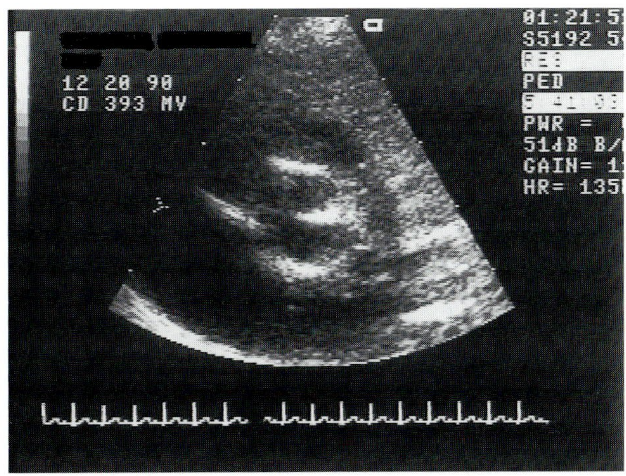

Figure 4–9. 2-D image of a parasternal short-axis view at the level of the semilunar valves. This infant has been diagnosed as having tetralogy of Fallot.

(C) subcostal short axis (sagittal) view
(D) high left parasternal view
(E) all of the above views would be useful

34. Which of the following methods is most reliable for estimating pulmonary artery pressures?

(A) thickness of the right ventricular free wall
(B) determination of the peak regurgitant gradient through the tricuspid valve
(C) determination of the peak regurgitant gradient through the pulmonic valve
(D) dividing the acceleration time by the ejection time of flow as obtained from the main pulmonary artery

35. In which of the following surgically created shunts is the subclavian artery used?

(A) Central
(B) Glenn
(C) Waterston
(D) Blalock-Taussig
(E) Potts

36. What is needed to estimate Q_p: Q_s in a patient with a ventricular septal defect?

(A) diameters and peak flow velocities through the pulmonary and aortic valves
(B) peak pressure gradient through a tricuspid regurgitation jet
(C) diameters and peak flow velocities through the tricuspid and aortic valves
(D) diameters and peak flow velocities through the pulmonary and mitral valves

37. The shunt through the atrial septal defect of a patient with tricuspid atresia is

(A) always left to right
(B) always right to left
(C) may be bidirectional
(D) nonexistant

38. The 2-D parasternal view presented in Fig. 4–10 was taken from an adolescent girl with Marfan syndrome. What abnormalities may be seen which are frequently associated with Marfan syndrome?

(A) dilated aortic root and mitral valve prolapse
(B) aortic aneurysm dissection
(C) ideopathic hypertrophic subaortic stenosis
(D) herniation of the sinus of Valsalva

39. The 2-D image presented in Fig. 4–11 was taken from the apex in a child who has had corrective surgery for transposition of the great arteries. The echogenic line in the left atrium represents

(A) cortriatriatum
(B) supramitral ring
(C) total anomalous pulmonary venous return
(D) an interatrial baffle

40. If a patient has total anomalous pulmonary venous return, the right atrium should be

(A) atretic
(B) small
(C) normal in size
(D) dilated

41. The most useful modality in the delineation of anatomy in total anomalous pulmonary venous return is

(A) 2-D
(B) M-mode
(C) PW Doppler
(D) CW Doppler
(E) color flow Doppler

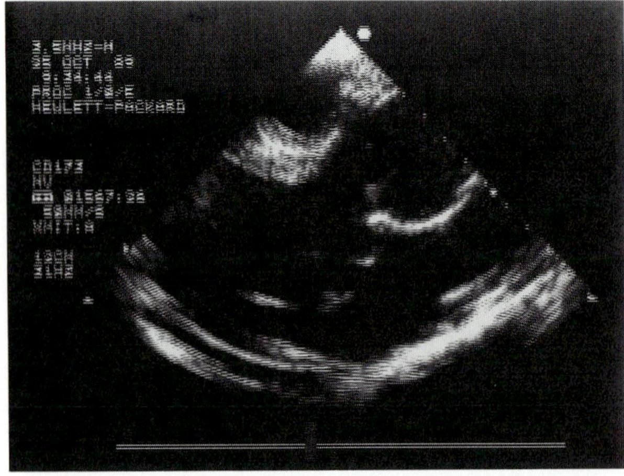

Figure 4–10. 2-D image of a parasternal long-axis view. The patient is an adolescent girl thought to have Marfan syndrome.

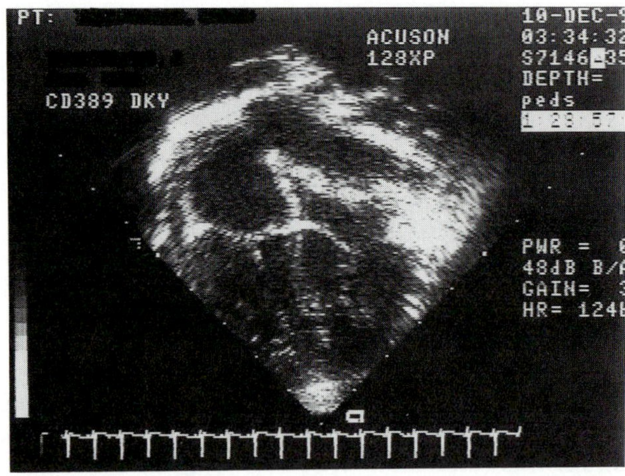

Figure 4–11. 2-D image of an apical four-chamber view presented with the apex down. This young child has had a previous repair for transposition of the great vessels.

TRUE OR FALSE: Indicate whether each of the following statements is true or false.

42. Patent ductus arteriosis is more commonly seen in low birth weight premature infants than in term infants.

43. Patency of the ductus arteriosus may be desirable in some cases.

44. In cortriatriatum, the left atrial appendage is continuous with the anatomic left atrium and not with the proximal chamber that receives flow directly from the pulmonary veins.

45. Children with trisomy 21 frequently have partial atrioventricular septal defects.

46. Patients with truncus arteriosus are usually quite cyanotic in infancy.

47. Individuals with Ebstein anomaly of the tricuspid valve are always symptomatic.

48. Distal coronary artery aneurysms are common in the absence of proximal aneurysm formation in patients who have had Kawasaki disease.

49. In patients with coarctation of the aorta, the gradient through the obstruction should approximate the difference in systolic blood pressures taken from the arm and leg of the patient.

50. Persistent left superior vena cava may exist in the absence of a dilated coronary sinus.

For each of the following transducer positions, indicate (true or false) whether the position could yield the highest pressure gradient estimate in a patient with valvular pulmonary stenosis.

51. parasternal

52. apical

53. subcostal

54. suprasternal

The 2-D image in Fig. 4–12 was obtained by placing the transducer at the cardiac apex of an infant. The infant was referred to echocardiology because of an enlarged heart on chest x-ray and cardiac failure. A systolic murmur may be heard at the apex. Indicate whether statements 55–60 are true or false for this image.

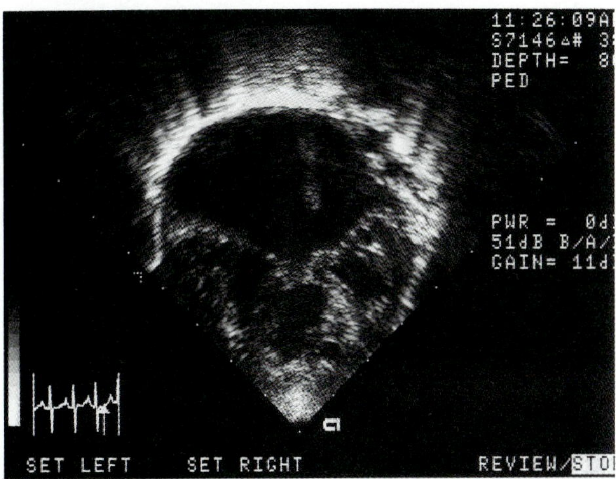

Figure 4–12. 2-D image of an apical four-chamber view presented with the apex down. This infant was in cardiac failure and reportedly had an enlarged heart on chest x-ray. A systolic murmur may be heard at the apex.

55. There is a secundum atrial septal defect.

56. There is a primum atrial septal defect.

57. The tricuspid valve appears normal.

58. The left ventricle is significantly smaller in size than the right ventricle.

59. The diagnosis for this patient is Ebstein anomaly of the tricuspid valve.

60. The systolic murmur is probably due to aortic stenosis.

Answers and Explanations

1. **(B)** Sinus venosus is the rarest form, and single atrium is not considered to be an atrial septal defect because there is complete absence of the atrial septum. *(15:1391)*

2. **(C)** In the subxiphoid position, the sound beam is perpendicular to the interatrial septum, thereby utilizing the axial resolution of the transducer. The atrial septum may also be visualized from the parasternal short axis view but it is more parallel to the sound beam and, therefore, may not be resolved optimally. In the apical position, the sound beam is parallel to the atrial septum, and the atrial septum is a great distance from the transducer, so echocardiographic dropout may be mistaken for an atrial communication. *(48:144–147)*

3. **(C)** Sinus venosus atrial septal defects are bordered posteriorly by the posterior atrial wall and superiorly by the entrance of the superior vena cava. Because of this, the upper right pulmonary vein may empty into the right atrium or superior vena cava. *(1:175)*

4. **(C)** Atrial septal defect and pulmonary stenosis are also common. Mitral stenosis is relatively uncommon in the pediatric population. *(1:190)*

5. **(B)** The "T" artifact is visualized on 2-D echocardiography as a prominence of echoes at the edges of the septal tissue. *(3:415)*

6. **(E)** Muscular VSDs may occur anywhere and be very small. Color flow Doppler allows relatively rapid evaluation of the entire interventricular septum. Visualization of a jet of turbulent flow identifies a VSD. PW or CW Doppler interrogation can be tedious and may miss a small muscular defect in an unusual position. *(39:544–548)*

7. **(A)** When pulmonary pressures exceed systemic pressures, the flow through the patent ductus arteriosus will be right to left; therefore, there would be no reversal in the descending aorta. All of the other choices should cause a reversal of flow in the descending aorta. *(51:285–287)*

8. **(E)** Although patent ductus arteriosus and coarctation of the aorta are more commonly associated with valvar aortic stenosis, ventricular septal defect and pulmonary stenosis may also be associated. *(1:224)*

9. **(B)** Although all of the listed malformations may be associated findings, bicuspid aortic valve has been reported to be an associated finding in as much as 85% of cases. *(1:244)*

10. **(C)** The aortic valve is posterior and to the right of the pulmonic valve in the normally related heart. The aortic valve is located centrally in the base of the heart, whereas the pulmonic valve is anterior and left. *(2:578–581)*

11. **(D)** The Fontan procedure was originally developed to treat patients with tricuspid atresia. Although it is now used in a modified form to treat other forms of complex congenital heart disease, it is not commonly used to treat patients with transposition of the great arteries. *(1:357–359,402–417)*

12. **(C)** The Rashkind procedure is an interventional catheterization technique that also is known as a balloon atrial septostomy. The Mustard and Senning procedures also are known as atrial switches. *(1:402–417)*

13. **(A)** Normally related great vessels course perpendicular to each other. Demonstration of this relationship rules out transposition of the great vessels. *(48:498)*

14. **(B)** The purpose of an atrial septostomy is to mix deoxygenated systemic venous return with oxygenated pulmonary venous return. In truncus arteriosus and tetralogy of Fallot, this mixing occurs through a large ventricular septal defect. In Ebstein

anomaly of the tricuspid valve, blood flow sequence is normal, therefore, mixing is not desirable. *(1:399–400)*

15. **(B)** There is about a 15% incidence of coronary artery aneurysm formation in children with Kawasaki disease. *(31:269)*

16. **(B)** Kawasaki disease is a childhood disease. Infants appear to be more likely to develop aneurysms than older children. *(31:273)*

17. **(E)** All of the above that are available should be used. *(18:223; 60:157–171)*

18. **(A)** The right ventricular outflow obstruction of tetralogy of Fallot is a dynamic obstruction; therefore, it may increase when the patient is distressed. *(1:278)*

19. **(E)** Although the proximal portions are the most frequently involved, the coronary system should be evaluated from every available view because aneurysms may occur anywhere. *(31:269–273)*

20. **(C)** In coarctation of the aorta, the descending aortic flow pulsatility is blunted such that the Doppler signal shows a slow acceleration and deceleration. *(18:217–221)*

21. **(D)** In situs solitus, the aorta descends anterior and to the left of the spine and the inferior vena cava ascends to the right of the spine. In situs inversus, the opposite is true. In left atrial isomerism, the inferior vena cava is frequently interrupted. *(49:35–56)*

22. **(B)** An asymmetric closure line is suggestive of a bicuspid aortic valve. Gradual closure is suggestive of depressed left ventricular contractility. Ejection time may be prolonged in severe valvular aortic stenosis. *(3:380–386)*

23. **(E)** Reversal of flow during diastole, as shown in Fig. 4–1, may be seen in any of the other conditions. The characteristic PW Doppler pattern in the descending aorta is very different for coarctation of the aorta. *(18:217–228; 51:279–295)*

24. **(B)** From the ECG, we can see that this is an end-diastolic frame. The 2-D image shows closed aortic and pulmonary valves, confirming that this is an end-diastolic frame. Red color representing flow toward the transducer may be appreciated coming into the main pulmonary artery from the patent ductus arteriosus. *(23:161–162,189–190)*

25. **(C)** The red jet seen traversing the interatrial septum represents flow coming toward the transducer, therefore, it is shunting from the left atrium to the right atrium. Portions of the superior and inferior interatrial septum may be seen on the 2-D image. *(39:548–550)*

26. **(D)** The mitral valve is open in Fig. 4–4A. A thick band of tissue appears in place of a normal tricuspid valve. A ventricular septal defect may be appreciated at the top of the ventricular septum in this image. In Fig. 4–4B, flow through the ventricular septal defect into the right ventricle is demonstrated by color flow Doppler during systole. *(3:374–375)*

27. **(B)** Flow through an inflow ventricular septal defect would be visualized at the level of the mitral annulus. Flow through a doubly committed subarterial ventricular septal defect would be visualized just proximal to the pulmonary valve in this view. Flow through a muscular ventricular septal defect would be visualized in the muscular portion of the ventricular septum. This portion of the ventricular septum is visible from the parasternal short axis at the level of the mitral valve and more apically. *(3:155–161, 183–188)*

28. **(D)** The mitral valve is always higher on the ventricular septum in the absence of an inflow ventricular septal defect. In this case, the atrioventricular valve of the right-sided ventricle inserts higher on the ventricular septum than the atrioventricular valve of the left-sided ventricle. *(48:324–325)*

29. **(C)** The aortic valve is closed and does not appear thickened. There is an echogenic line that extends posteriorly from the ventricular septum just proximal to the aortic valve. This represents a discrete subaortic membrane. In idiopathic hypertrophic subaortic stenosis, the interventricular septum would be significantly thickened. *(48:424–427)*

30. **(A)** Valvular aortic stenosis would cause the velocity of flow to increase just distal to the valve. Supravalvular aortic stenosis would cause the velocity of flow to increase in the aortic root. Coarctation of the aorta would cause the velocity of flow to increase past the level of the left subclavian artery. *(3:382)*

31. **(C)** The left coronary artery appears mildly dilated, and the large circle noted in the right atrium is the right coronary artery (with aneurysmal dilatation) as it courses within the right atrioventricular groove. *(31:268–273)*

32. **(D)** The entire right ventricular outflow tract is small in caliber. *(48:434)*

33. **(E)** The pulmonary artery branches may be imaged from all of these views. *(54:767–782)*

34. **(B)** The thickness of the right ventricular free wall may not be proportionate to the increase in pulmonary artery pressure. The end-diastolic and not peak gradient of pulmonary regurgitation may be used. Acceleration and ejection time should be measured from the right ventricular outflow tract. *(60:157–171)*

35. **(D)** The subclavian artery is used in the construction of the Blalock-Taussig shunt. In a central shunt, the pulmonary artery is connected to the aorta directly or via a conduit. In the Waterston shunt, the ascending aorta is connected to the right pulmonary artery, and in the Potts anastomosis, the descending aorta is connected to the pulmonary artery. *(34:384–385)*

36. **(A)** Q_p: Q_s is a comparison of pulmonary flow to systemic flow used to estimate the amount of blood flow through a systemic to pulmonary shunt. Flow is calculated by multiplying area by velocity of flow. This calculation must be done for the systemic circulation and for the pulmonary circulation. When the shunt is at the level of the ventricles, pulmonary flow may be calculated by using the pulmonary valve or the mitral valve (ie, pulmonary venous return). The systemic flow may be calculated by using the aortic valve or tricuspid valve (ie, systemic venous return). The calculation is done to determine how much more blood is going through the pulmonary vasculature than the systemic vasculature. *(10:825–827; 59:339–344)*

37. **(B)** Because the atrial septal defect is the only outlet for the blood in the right atrium, it is an obligatory right to left shunt. *(3:375)*

38. **(A)** Patients with Marfan syndrome are also at risk for aortic dissections, but only a limited amount of the aorta is visualized here. The other two abnormalities are not frequently associated with this syndrome. *(1:792–793)*

39. **(D)** The echogenic line visualized in the left atrium in Fig. 4–11 is an interatrial baffle constructed to redirect blood flow in what is known as an "atrial switch." *(48:552–557)*

40. **(E)** Because pulmonary venous flow returns directly to the right atrium, it will be dilated. *(3:368–371)*

41. **(E)** Color flow aids tremendously in demonstrating the anomalous channels and connections. *(70:341–347)*

42. **True.** Constriction of the ductus is physiologically delayed in this group. *(1:209–218)*

43. **True.** Prostaglandin E may be administered to keep the ductus arteriosus patent in infants with severe right ventricular outflow obstruction or atresia or great vessel malformations. *(1:221–222)*

44. **True.** The membrane inserts proximal to the left atrial appendage in cortriatriatum and distal to it in supravalvar mitral ring. *(1:599–602)*

45. **False.** These children more commonly have the complete form of atrioventricular defect. *(1:176)*

46. **False.** Significant cyanosis during infancy occurs only when there is associated pulmonary stenosis. *(1:507)*

47. **False.** There is a spectrum of severity in this malformation, and mild forms may remain asymptomatic. *(11:142)*

48. **False.** It is very rare to have distal involvement in the absence of proximal aneurysm formation. *(31:275)*

49. **True.** In severe cases, it may be difficult to obtain a reliable Doppler signal because of decreased flow through the area of obstruction. The Doppler derived gradient may be somewhat higher than the systolic pressure differences measured from the arm and thigh because peak systolic pressure occurs at slightly different times in these two areas; therefore the blood pressure method yields a peak to peak pressure difference, whereas the Doppler method yields an instantaneous pressure difference. *(18:217–219)*

50. **True.** Suprasternal coronal evaluation of the extracardiac vessels should be included in patients in whom this may be a concern for planning of surgical procedures. *(74:137)*

51. **True.** This has traditionally been the most common position for evaluation of pulmonary valve stenosis. *(54:765)*

52. **True.** The sound beam is angled anteriorly, and the transducer is moved to just below the left nipple. *(14:844–848)*

53. **True.** The sound beam is angled anteriorly and slightly to the left. *(54:765)*

54. **True.** In a few cases, this may be the only position from which a diagnostic Doppler signal can be obtained. *(14:844–848)*

55. **False.** The area of the fossa ovalis appears to be intact. *(1:173–174)*

56. True. The portion of atrial septum just above the level of the atrioventricular valves is absent. *(52:309–314)*

57. False. There is a common atrioventricular valve with chordal insertions onto the ventricular septum. *(52:315–319)*

58. True. The left ventricle is about one third the size of the right ventricle. The interventricular septum may be seen bowing into the left ventricle. *(52:319–330)*

59. False. The diagnosis is an unbalanced complete atrioventricular septal defect. In Ebstein anomaly of the tricuspid valve, the tricuspid valve leaflets are adherent to the right ventricular walls. *(48:293–305)*

60. False. The systolic murmur is probably due to atrioventricular valve insufficiency. *(1:181–187)*

REFERENCES

References appear on page 160.

CHAPTER 5

GENERAL ABDOMINAL SONOGRAPHY

Trudy Dubinsky, Arthur C. Fleischer, and Rena Dubinsky

Study Guide

LIVER

The liver is intraperitoneal. This means that it is surrounded by peritoneum except for a segment known as the bare area posterior to the dome of the liver.

Riedel's lobe is a normal variant of the right lobe of the liver whereby the right lobe projects inferiorly and may be mistaken for a pseudotumor.

Lobes, Ligaments, and Fissures (Figs. 5–1 and 5–2)

Lobes. The liver is divided into three lobes: the *right*—anterior and posterior segments; the *left*—medial (quadrate) and lateral segments; and the *caudate*—lies on the posterosuperior surface of the liver.

Guidelines. Hepatic veins are intersegmental (outlining the segments of the liver). They subdivide the liver as follows: (1) middle hepatic vein—divides the liver into right and left lobes; (2) left hepatic vein—divides the left lobe into medial and lateral segments; and (3) right hepatic vein—divides the right lobe into anterior and posterior segments. Both the right and left hepatic veins drain blood from the caudate lobe.

Since hepatic veins can only be recognized sonographically on superior sections of the liver, additional landmarks such as ligaments and fissures are needed. These landmarks may be used to define segmental anatomy on more caudad sections.

Table 5–1 is a guide to the anatomic structures useful in defining segmental anatomy.

Ligamentum Venosum. The ligamentum venosum is a remnant of the fetal ductus venosus. It divides the caudate lobe from the left lobe. It may be visualized sonographically on transverse and longitudinal scans as an echogenic line extending transversely from the porta hepatis.

Ligamentum Teres. The ligamentum teres is a remnant of the fetal umbilical vein, which lies in the left intersegmental fissure, dividing the left lobe of the liver into medial and lateral segments. Sonographically, it may be visualized on a transverse scan as a round hyperechoic density just to the right of the midline.

Falciform Ligament. The falciform ligament is the portion of the peritoneum reflected around the ligamentum teres, attaching the liver to the diaphragm and abdominal wall.

Main Lobar Fissure. Main lobar fissures separate the right and left lobes and may be visualized sonographically as an echogenic line extending from the porta hepatis to the neck of the gallbladder.

Parenchymal Architecture

The normal liver is homogeneous in texture, and its echogenicity may be compared to renal sinus > pancreas > liver > spleen > renal cortex.

Vasculature of the Liver—Hepatic Vein, Portal Vein, Hepatic Artery

Hepatic Vein. There are three hepatic veins: right, middle, and left. These veins drain into the inferior vena cava.

Portal Vein. The portal vein is formed by the confluence of the splenic vein and the superior mesenteric vein. It courses cephalad and rightward into the porta hepatis, bifurcating into right and left. The main *undivided* portal trunk lies immediately anterior to the inferior vena cava, just cephalad to the head of the pancreas and caudal to the caudate lobe.

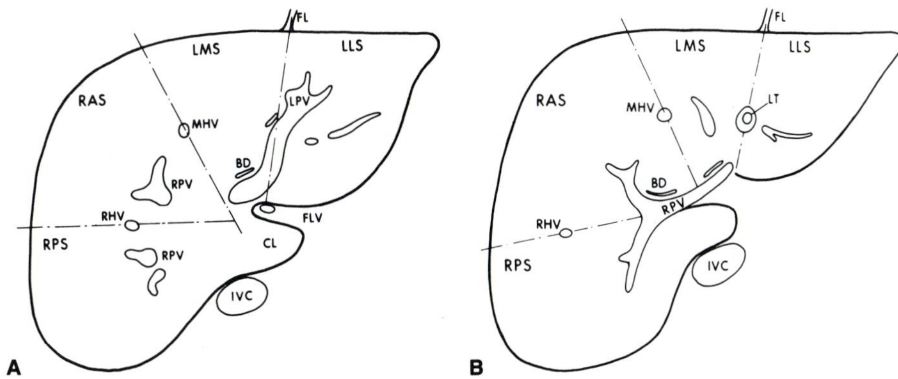

Figure 5–1. (**A**) Graphic representation. IVC = inferior vena cava; RPS, RAS = right lobe posterior and anterior segments; LMS, LLS = medial and lateral segments of left lobe; FLV = fissure of ligamentum venosum; RPV = right portal vein branch; RHV, MHV = right and middle hepatic veins; BD = bile duct. (**B**) Graphic representation. IVC = inferior vena cava; RPS, RAS = right lobe posterior and anterior segments; LMS, LLS = medial and lateral segments of left lobe; FL = falciform ligament; LT = ligamentum teres. *(Reprinted with permission from Sexton CC, Zeman RK. Correlation of computed tomography, sonography and gross anatomy of the liver. AJR 141:711–718, 1983.)*

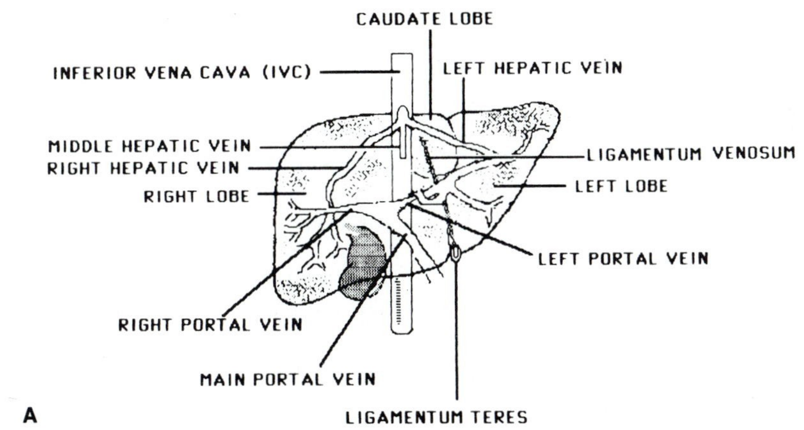

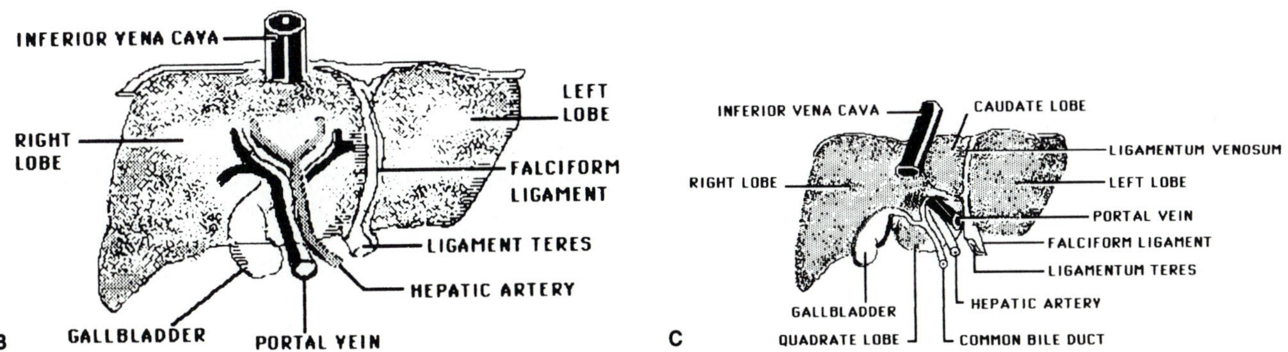

Figure 5–2. (**A**) Lobes, ligaments, and fissures. (**B**) Anterior projection of the liver. (**C**) Posterior projection of the liver.

TABLE 5–1. ANATOMIC STRUCTURES USEFUL FOR DIVIDING AND IDENTIFYING THE HEPATIC SEGMENTS

Structure	Location	Usefulness
RHV	Right intersegmental fissure	Divides cephalic aspect of anterior and posterior segments of right hepatic lobe and courses between anterior and posterior branches of RPV
MHV	Main lobar fissure	Separates right and left lobes
LHV	Left intersegmental fissure	Divides cephalic aspects of medial and lateral segments of left lobe
RPV (anterior)	Intrasegmental in anterior segment of right hepatic lobe	Courses centrally in anterior segment of right hepatic lobe
RPV (posterior)	Intrasegmental in posterior segment of right hepatic lobe	Courses centrally in posterior segment of right hepatic lobe
LPV (initial)	Courses anterior to caudate lobe	Separates caudate lobe posteriorly from medial segment of left lobe anteriorly
LPV (ascending)	Turns anteriorly in left intersegmental fissure	Divides medial and lateral segments of left lobe
IVC fossa	Posterior aspect of main lobar fissure	Separates right and left hepatic lobes
GB fossa	Main lobar fissure	Separates right and left hepatic lobes
Ligamentum teres	Left intersegmental fissure	Divides caudal aspect of left hepatic lobe into medial and lateral segments
Fissure of ligamentum venosum	Left anterior margin of caudate lobe	Separates caudate lobe from medial and lateral segments of left lobe

Reprinted with permission from Callen PW: J Clin Ultrasound 7(2):81, 1979, and John Wiley & Sons, Inc.

The left portal vein is also the umbilical portion of the portal vein, which is of variable size. Organs of the gastrointestinal tract, the gallbladder, the pancreas, and the spleen are drained by the tributaries of the portal vein that enter the liver via the main portal vein to bring nutrients to the liver cells.

How does one differentiate sonographically between portal veins and hepatic veins?

1. Portal veins have brighter walls owing to collagen within the wall
2. The branching angles have different orientation:
   a. Portal veins branch horizontally and are oriented toward the porta hepatis
   b. Hepatic veins branch longitudinally and are oriented toward the inferior vena cava
3. The caliber of a hepatic vein increases as it courses toward the diaphragm and inferior vena cava
4. The caliber of the portal vein increases as it nears the porta hepatis
5. Hepatic veins will vary in size during respiration

How does one differentiate sonographically between portal vein and bile duct? These are not to be confused in the normal liver because one does not see intrahepatic bile ducts unless there is dilatation due to disease or obstruction.

Hepatic Artery. The hepatic artery is visualized normally on transverse scans at the level of the hepatoduodenal ligament (just cephalad to the head of the pancreas and adjacent to the porta hepatis). Both the common bile duct and hepatic artery lie anterior to the portal vein at this level, with the common bile duct being more lateral.

PORTAL TRIAD

Portal vein Hepatic artery Bile duct	All travel together in a collagenous sheath (Glisson's capsule) extending throughout the liver.

Common Bile Duct. The common bile duct runs posterior to the head of the pancreas to enter the duodenum. This can be visualized on a sagittal or a right anterior oblique scan.

Several diseases of the liver with clinical findings, supporting laboratory data and sonographic anatomy are detailed in Tables 5–2 to 5–5.

Table 5–6 offers a simplified guide to laboratory tests for specific liver diseases.

GALLBLADDER

The gallbladder is a pear-shaped structure lying in a fossa on the visceral surface of the liver. It is attached to the lateral portion of the porta hepatis at the cystic duct. The cystic duct runs inferiorly and joins the common hepatic duct to form the common bile duct.

The gallbladder has a fundus, body, and neck. Hartmann's pouch is that portion of the neck that is closest to the cystic duct. Stones tend to accumulate at this point and cause obstruction. The cystic duct is markedly tortuous at its junction with the neck of the gallbladder. This is termed the spiral valve of Heister, which is a misnomer because it is not a true valve; bile flows freely in both

TABLE 5–2. FOCAL DISEASE OF THE LIVER

	Clinical Findings	Laboratory Data	Sonographic Anatomy
Cysts			
Congenital			
Simple liver cyst	Asymptomatic, may cause hepatomegaly	Normal liver function	Echo-free Smooth regular walls Posterior enhancement, usually solitary
Polycystic disease	More than 50% associated with renal polycystic disease; produces gross hepatomegaly and usually does not interfere with liver function	Normal liver function	Multiple cysts of various sizes found within the liver parenchyma
Acquired Lesions			
Traumatic (hematoma)	RUQ pain, hepatomegaly, hypotension	Drop in hematocrit Leukocytosis	Mixed echo pattern; may be predominantly cystic (fresh blood) to predominantly echogenic, chronic condition (old blood) Irregular walls Some through transmission—less than a cyst but more than a solid structure
Inflammatory lesions (abscess)	Fever, chills, RUQ pain, hepatomegaly	Leukocytosis	Predominantly fluid filled; with variable amounts of echos and irregular borders An abscess may contain gas or calcification—watch for shadowing
Hydatid cysts	Asymptomatic or RUQ pain and hepatomegaly—the tapeworm *Echinococcus* causes infection, with sheep, pigs, or cows being the intermediate host	Positive Casoni test Eosinophilia	Well-circumscribed cystic mass with smaller cysts surrounding or within it to give a multilocular appearance; the smaller cysts may contain echoes and/or calcification; when only one cyst is present, it cannot be differentiated from a simple cyst
Primary Solid Tumor			
Benign			
Liver cell adenoma	Most common in women who used oral contraceptive pills Patients present with palpable abdominal mass	Normal liver function	Well-defined solid mass of increased echogenicity
Focal nodular hyperplasia (FNH)	Similar to adenoma occurs in both sexes	Normal liver function	Variable sonographic pattern, usually echogenic
Cavernous hemangioma (most common benign tumor)	Generally asymptomatic; most lesions are small but may become quite large		Variable and nonspecific—cannot be distinguished, eg, from hepatomas, adenomas
Malignant			
Primary hepatic tumors Hepatomas (hepatocellular carcinoma) associated with longstanding cirrhosis Hepatoblastoma—found in children Angiocarcinoma Bile duct tumor Sarcoma	Primary findings (acute): jaundice, weight loss, hepatomegaly, palpable mass; (chronic): ascites, portal hypertension, splenomegaly	Abnormal hepatocellular function, increased alkaline phosphatase, increased levels of α-fetoprotein in serum	Variable and nonspecific, small or large, diffuse or circumscribed—cannot be distinguished from a benign or metastatic tumor Portal vein thrombosis, highly suggestive of hepatoma

(*continued*)

TABLE 5–2. (*Continued*)

	Clinical Findings	Laboratory Data	Sonographic Anatomy
Metastatic Solid Tumor			
Metastatic spread to the liver is common	Hepatomegaly, weight loss, RUQ pain, ascites, jaundice, splenomegaly	Abnormal hepatocellular function, increased serum bilirubin Increased alkaline phosphatase	Variable patterns Well-defined echogenic mass—search the intestines and urogenital tract for the primary Well-defined echo-poor mass—may come from any primary Defined calcific masses—may come from ovary, colon, or rectum Diffuse, miliary—may come from any primary Cystic mass—mucin secreting, especially ovary and pancreas
Lymphoma	Hepatomegaly, splenomegaly retroperitoneal nodes		Decreased echogenicity
Diffuse Liver Disease			
Fatty change—accumulation of fat within the hepatocytes	Causes: alcoholism, by-pass surgery for obesity, corticosteroid administration, malignancy, diabetes mellitus, obesity, protein malnutrition	Abnormal hepatocellular function	Liver enlarges especially the left and/or caudate lobe Regenerating nodules Liver is unduly bright and echogenic As the disease progresses, there is a loss of through transmission; decreased visibility of vessels
Cirrhosis—diffuse fibrotic process that involves the entire liver	Chronic injury to hepatocyte. May develop portal hypertension, ascites, splenomegaly, collateral circulation; jaundice may be seen Alcohol abuse is by far the most common cause	Abnormal hepatocellular function Slight increase in AST (SGOT) and ALT (SGPT) Alkaline phosphatase may or may not be elevated	Liver is shrunken and very echogenic; disproportionate enlargement of caudate lobe Through transmission is very poor Irregular shape; regenerating nodules Ascites Collateral vessels will be seen in the region Patent umbilical vein in severe portal hypertension; cannot trace the course of the major hepatic veins
Hepatitis			
Viral hepatitis is a diffuse inflammatory process of the liver; types: A, B, and non-A, non-B	Malaise, nausea, fever, and pain followed by jaundice. Liver is enlarged and tender	Elevation of SGOT and SGPT over 1000 units Serum bilirubin increased Alkaline phosphatase increased	Acute hepatitis—the echogenicity of the liver is reduced, the renal cortex being more echogenic than the liver Chronic hepatitis—the echogenicity is that of a bright liver as in early cirrhosis with increased echogenicity of portal veins Acute and/or chronic hepatitis—patchy liver, areas of increased and decreased echogenicity; hepatomegaly

(*continued*)

TABLE 5–2. (*Continued*)

	Clinical Findings	Laboratory Data	Sonographic Anatomy
Chronic Passive Congestion of the Liver			
	History of heart failure Hepatomegaly, dilatation of the inferior vena cava	Normal or slightly abnormal hepatocellular function	Texture changes are similar to those seen in fatty infiltrate of the liver; changes are accompanied by dilatation of the hepatic veins, inferior vena cava, mesenteric, and splenic veins, hepatomegaly
Glycogen Storage Disease			
Groups of hereditary disorders of carbohydrate metabolism resulting in glycogen accumulation in hepatocytes	Hypoglycemia Decreased glucose-6-phosphatase		Hepatomegaly Diffuse increased liver echogenicity Splenomegaly

TABLE 5–3. VASCULAR ABNORMALITIES WITHIN THE LIVER

	Etiology	Clinical Findings	Sonographic Findings
Portal hypertension	Owing to cirrhosis in >90% of cases. May be due to obstruction, tumors, or prolonged congestive heart failure	Ascites—46% Formation of collateral venous channels Splenomegaly GI bleeding as a consequence of abnormal venous channels	Portal vein enlargement, >1.3 cm Lack of distension of the splenic and superior mesenteric veins during respiration Patent umbilical vein >3 mm bull's-eye pattern in the ligamentum teres Splenorenal, gastrorenal, hemorrhoidal, intestinal varices
Portal vein obstruction	Related to thrombosis or direct invasion of the portal vein by tumors	Associated with hepatocellular carcinoma, pancreatic, GI cancer or lymphoma	Nonvisualization of the portal vein Echogenic material within the portal vein Dilatation of the splenic and superior mesenteric veins proximal to the point of obstruction
Budd-Chiari syndrome	Caused by obstruction of the hepatic veins	The liver becomes enlarged and tender with ascites. The most common finding is unexplained partial or complete fibrous obliteration of the major hepatic veins	An enlarged and hypoechoic caudate lobe Reduced or nonvisualization of hepatic veins Ascites

TABLE 5–4. CAUSES OF JAUNDICE

Medical Jaundice (Nonobstructive)		Surgical Jaundice (Obstructive)
Hepatocellular Disease—disturbance within the liver cells that interferes with the excretion of bilirubin Hepatitis Drug-induced cholestasis Fatty liver (most commonly caused by alcohol) Cirrhosis	Hemolytic Disease—an increase in red blood cell destruction; the hepatocytes cannot deal with the severe hemolysis efficiently with resulting increase in indirect bilirubin (nonobstructive jaundice) Sickle-cell anemia Cooley's anemia	Interference with flow of bile caused by obstruction of the biliary tract, typical course includes Choledocholithiasis Pancreatitis Pancreatic pseudocyst Mass in the head of pancreas Hepatoma Metastatic carcinoma Cholangiocarcinoma Mass in the portahepatis (enlarged lymph nodes)

TABLE 5–5. LIVER FUNCTION TESTS

1. Alkaline Phosphatase: Normally found in serum. Its level rises in liver and biliary tract disorders when excretion is impaired, as in obstructive jaundice, biliary cirrhosis, acute hepatitis, and granulomatous liver disease.
2. α-Fetoprotein (AFP): A protein produced by fetal liver, yolk sac, GI tract, and hepatocellular carcinoma (hepatoma) germ cell neoplasms and other cancers in adults. AFP level used to monitor chemotherapy treatment and prenatal diagnosis neural tube defects in fetus. Rarely positive in other cases.
3. Ammonia:
   Normally metabolized in the liver and excreted as urea
   Increased in hepatocellular disease
4. Bromsulfalein Retention (BSP):
   After IV rejection of the dye, BSP is bound to albumin and is removed from the blood by the liver
   If liver is not functioning properly, abnormal amounts of BSP remain in the blood
   Diseases with large retained amounts of BSP:
      Acute hepatitis (83%)
      Cirrhosis (87%)
      Extrahepatic obstruction (79%)
      Metastatic liver cancer (93–100%)
      Chronic congestion (88%)
5. Bilirubin:
   Derived from the breakdown of hemoglobin in red blood cells
   Excreted by the liver in the bile (main pigment)
   When destruction of red blood cells increases greatly or when the liver is unable to excrete normal amounts, the bilirubin concentration in the serum increases
   If increased too high, jaundice may occur
   Intrahepatic and extrahepatic obstruction may be determined by the levels of indirect and direct bilirubin
      Obstruction is indicated by the increase in direct bilirubin
      Increased red blood cell destruction/hemolysis is indicated by an increase in indirect bilirubin
6. Casoni Test: Blood test positive for eosinophilia, tapeworm echinococcal disease, hydatid cysts
7. Hematocrit: Volume percentage of erythrocytes in whole blood. A drop in hematocrit can indicate hematoma due to liver trauma.
8. Leukocytosis: A substantial increase in white blood cells above normal limits as in inflammatory lesions or abscess in liver.
9. Prothrombin Time:
   Prothrombin is converted to thrombin in the clotting process by action of vitamin K that is absorbed in the intestine and stored in the liver
   In obstructive liver disease, IV administration of vitamin K returns prothrombin time to normal
   In parenchymal tissue disease, vitamin K injection will not alter the prothrombin time
   Deficiency can cause uncontrolled hemorrhage
10. Aspartate Aminotransferase (AST), formerly Serum Glutamic Oxaloacetic Transaminase (SGOT):
    This enzyme is increased in liver cell necrosis due to:
       Viral hepatitis
       Toxic hepatitis
       Other acute forms of hepatitis
    Helpful in detecting acute hepatitis before jaundice occurs and in following the course of hepatitis
    No significant increase occurs in chronic liver disease such as cirrhosis or obstructive jaundice
11. Alanine Aminotransferase (ALT), formerly Serum Glutamic Pyruvic Transminase (SGPT):
    This enzyme is increased higher than SGOT in hepatitis
    It falls slowly and reaches normal levels in 2–3 months
    SGPT is especially valuable in assessing jaundice
       If jaundice is caused by liver cell disease
          >300 U
       If jaundice is due to a condition outside the liver
          <300 U
12. Urinary Bile and Bilirubin:
    There may be spillover into the blood in:
       Obstructive liver disease
       Excessive red blood cell destruction
    Bile pigments are found in urine when there is obstruction of the biliary tract
    Bilirubin is found alone when there is excessive breakdown of red blood cells
    Bile and bilirubin are not normally found in urine
13. Urinary Urobilinogen:
    This test differentiates between:
       Complete obstruction of the biliary tract
       Incomplete obstruction of the biliary tract
    Urobilinogen is a product of hemoglobin breakdown and may be elevated in:
       Hemolytic diseases
       Liver damage
       Severe infections
    Urobilinogen does not increase or there is no excess amount found in urine in cases of complete obstructive jaundice
14. Fecal Urobilinogen:
    Considerable amounts are found in the feces but an increase or decrease in normal amounts may indicate hepatic digestive abnormalities
       Decrease with complete obstruction of biliary tree
       Increase may suggest an increase in hemolysis

Nuclear Medicine Tests

Planar Liver Scan: Radioactive isotope is injected—an area that does not take up the radiopharmaceutical (cold spot) will signify abscess, tumor, necrotic/abnormal tissue, or a cirrhotic liver

SPECT Liver Scan: Used for ruling out hemangiomas and is more precise in locating and resolving space-occupying lesions

directions owing to pressure gradients. Physiologically, the gallbladder contracts in response to cholecystokinin, the release of which is stimulated by food in the gut.

Congenital anomalies of the gallbladder are rare, though a gallbladder may be intrahepatic or may have septations or folds. When the fundus of the gallbladder is sharply bent over itself, it is termed a phrygian cap, a fold or kink between the body and infundibulum of the gallbladder, also termed a junctional fold.

The gallbladder is a thin-walled structure having a maximum wall thickness of 3 mm. Table 5–7 outlines causes of gallbladder wall thickness.

TABLE 5–6. SUMMARY OF LABORATORY TESTS IN SPECIFIC LIVER DIAGNOSES

	Hematological Disease	Hepatitis	Cirrhosis	Obstructive Jaundice	Carcinoma
SGOT		++	+	+	+
SGPT		+++	+	+	+
Alkaline Phosphatase		+	+	+++	++
α-Fetoprotein					+++
Bilirubin					
Indirect	+++				
Direct		+++	+++	+++	
Ammonia		+++			

Symbols: + = increase; ++ = marked increase; +++ = very marked increase.

Causes of a Large Gallbladder

A large gallbladder can be caused by prolonged fasting; IV hyperalimentation; obstruction of the cystic duct (hydrops of the gallbladder); and obstruction of the distal common bile duct (the gallbladder will enlarge before the biliary tree because it has the greatest surface). Therefore, if one encounters a patient with an enlarged gallbladder and slightly dilated common bile duct with an increase in serum bilirubin, one should suspect a common duct obstruction.

Other causes of a large gallbladder include a Courvoisier gallbladder, which constitutes any enlarged gallbladder due to any malignancy affecting the distal common bile duct (pancreatic carcinoma, common duct carcinoma, or duodenal carcinoma; diabetes (long-standing insulin diabetes), and postvagotomy.

Causes of a Small Gallbladder

A small gallbladder usually presents after the patient has eaten. It can also be caused by congenital hypoplasia (extremely rare); chronic cholecystitis (the gallbladder becomes chronically scarred); biliary obstruction (at the level of the common hepatic duct, before the entry of the cystic duct—bile is not going to pass the obstruction and will not be able to fill the gallbladder); and hepatitis (bile production down).

Gallbladder Disease

Cholelithiasis—Intraluminal Echoes with Shadowing. Gallstones have 100% confidence if you demonstrate three criteria:

1. echogenic focus—echogenic due to the acoustic mismatch between stones and bile
2. acoustic shadow—most of the sound is absorbed with very little sound going through, producing a shadow
3. gravity dependent—put patient in decubitus position; the stones should be gravity dependent and fall to the gallbladder (GB) fundus

Beware. Causes of acoustic shadowing in the area of the GB are:

- spiral valves of Heister—folds in the neck of GB

TABLE 5–7. GALLBLADDER WALL THICKENING

Causes of Gallbladder Wall Thickening >3 mm	Sonographic Features
1. Contracted normal gallbladder 2. Inappropriate TGC and/or gain 3. Ascites (1–3: The gallbladder wall will appear thickened) 4. Hypoproteinemia (hypoalbuminemia): patient has inadequate amount of serum protein. Patients will have thickened bowel and gallbladder walls 5. Congestive heart failure (CHF): patient will have thickened bowel and gallbladder wall 6. Acute hepatitis—sympathetic infection: gallbladder responds to the infection in the liver	Diffuse thickening of the gallbladder wall
7. Carcinoma—primary or secondary: gallbladder wall irregularly thickened, associated with cholelithiasis	Irregular thickening of the gallbladder wall with cholelithiasis
8. Cholecystitis—acute or chronic: any inflammation will cause edema of the walls	Thickening of the gallbladder wall with associated cholelithiasis
9. Adenomyomatosis–noninflammatory gallbladder disease	An outpouching of the surface epithelium into the gallbladder wall and hypertrophy of the muscular layer of the wall; present in 25% of all patients, yet only 5% have symptoms; is associated with cholelithiasis
10. AIDS	Thickening of the gallbladder wall[44]

- edge effect—in any cystic structure, you might get refraction at the fluid, with the solid surface producing a shadow at the periphery due to refraction of sound. This will be seen especially on transverse sections of the GB
- junctional fold—normal fold between neck and body
- loop of duodenum

Intraluminal Echoes Without Shadowing/With Motility. The causes of intraluminal echoes with shadowing and with motility are viscous bile, sludge, blood, or pus. Sludge is made up of cholesterol crystals and bilirubin precipitate. Sludge is of no clinical significance, and not all sludge goes on to develop stones. Sludge will be present in:

- people who have been fasting for long periods of time will develop sludge owing to hypotonic gallbladder
- alcoholics have sludge for unknown reasons
- patients with biliary obstruction—the GB cannot empty well owing to the obstruction and stasis of bile ensues
- patients on IV hyperalimentation

Important Differential. If the patient is febrile, toxic, and hypotensive with extreme right upper quadrant pain and the GB is visualized filled with multiple intraluminal echoes, thickened wall, or with stones, this may represent hemorrhage or pus in a gangrenous or emphysematous GB.

Intraluminal Echoes Without Shadowing and Without Motility. The causes of intraluminal echoes without shadowing and without motility are:

- polyps
- GB carcinoma (CA)—the most common primary malignancy of the biliary tree. Pancreatic CA is the most common CA to *obstruct* the biliary tree
  Gallbladder carcinoma presents in many ways:
  - solid mass in the head of the GB fossa with no bile filling the lumen
  - diffusely irregular GB, with thickened wall and a small lumen
  - symmetrically thickened
  - soft tissue mass that casts shadow but is not gravity dependent
  - GB carcinoma associated with stones
  - chronic cholecystitis may lead to GB carcinoma
- artifacts, eg, partial volume
- mucosal folds, eg, junctional fold at the junction of the GB body and neck
- cholesterosis—strawberry GB (multiple fixed mural plaques)
- adenomyomatosis—Rokitansky-Aschoff sinuses

Sonographic Nonvisualization of the Gallbladder. The reasons for nonvisualization of the GB sonographically are: patient is not NPO and is physiologically contracted; duodenal gas or gas in the hepatic flexure; if the patient has had a cholecystectomy; ectopic GB; chronic cholecystitis with stones filling the lumen; and solid mass obliterating the GB. If you do not see the GB at all, but you see highly reflective shadows coming from where the GB should be, follow main lobar fissure from right portal vein to the GB fossa. It may be a completely contracted GB.

Beware. Causes of shadow simulators are:

- bowel, not a clear shadow
- high-level echoes within the liver
- air in the biliary tree from surgery. When you connect the common bile duct (CBD) to the jejunum (Whipple procedure), the sphincter of Oddi that normally blocks objects from going into biliary tree is now open
- sphincter of Oddi becomes fibrotic owing to the constant passage of stones and remains open
- fistula in GB or ducts allows air in
- porcelain GB—calcium in the wall of the GB; 20% of patients with porcelain GB will develop CA, and this is an indicator for cholecystectomy

Cholecystitis—Inflammation of the Gallbladder. Acute cholecystitis is inflammation of the GB wall, promoted by an obstruction of the cystic duct, usually by a stone. The problem with cholecystitis is that it sometimes presents as a calculus without stones or halo effect.

Chronic cholecystitis is the most common form of symptomatic GB disease and is associated with gallstones in 90% of the cases.

Table 5–8 outlines the sonographic and clinical findings for acute and chronic cholecystitis.

Complications of Cholecystitis. Emphysematous GB, porcelain GB, and carcinoma of the GB are complications of cholecystitis.

Emphysematous Gallbladder

- more common in males than in females
- occurs as a result of anaerobic infection (clostridia)
- signs and symptoms—right upper quadrant (RUQ) pain, fever and leukocytosis
- sonographic finding is the appearance of gas in the GB wall
- cholelithiasis in only 50%
- gangrene in 75%; perforation in 20%

Porcelain Gallbladder

- calcification of the GB wall
- associated cancer 10–20%
- frequently associated with cholelithiasis 95% of the time
- three sonographic patterns:
  1. echogenic line in GB fossa with posterior shadowing
  2. echogenic near and far walls with some shadowing
  3. irregular clumps of wall echoes with shadowing

TABLE 5–8. ACUTE VERSUS CHRONIC CHOLECYSTITIS

Etiology	Clinical Findings	Sonographic Findings
Acute Cholecystitis		
1. Obstruction of cystic duct by calculi 80–95% 2. Bacterial infection within biliary tract 3. Pancreatic reflux	1. RUQ pain, especially postprandial 2. Vomiting 3. Positive Murphy's sign 4. Leukocytosis	1. Enlarged gallbladder 2. Thickened gallbladder wall >3 mm (usually >5 mm) 3. Halo sign suggesting subserosal edema 4. Sludge or stone 5. Occasionally, one can see bizarre echoes in the gallbladder wall suggestive of necrosis, as in acute gangrene
Chronic Cholecystitis—Recurrent Inflammatory Changes		
1. Gallbladder mucosa scarred and inflamed due to previous infections 2. Long-standing intermittent presence of stones impacting cystic duct	1. Gallbladder usually is nontender	1. Stones 2. Generally small or normal gallbladder 3. Thickened gallbladder wall 4. Double arc and shadowing. The first arc is the gallbladder wall and the second is the stone followed by the shadow that represents contracted gallbladder with stone—WES sign: W = wall of gallbladder; E = echo of calculi; S = shadow of calculi

Carcinoma of the gallbladder

- more common in women than men
- etiology: gallbladder stones?
- signs and symptoms—RUQ pain, obstructive jaundice, cholangitis
- sonographically, thickened GB walls, poorly defined mass in the RUQ, and gallstones always exist

Benign Tumors of the Gallbladder. Polyps, hyperplastic cholecystoses, and adenomas are benign GB tumors.

Polyps. Most of polyps are not true neoplasms but rather cholesterol polyps. They do not shadow and do not move as the patient moves.

Hyperplastic Cholecystoses (Adenomyomatosis). This is characterized by:

- hyperplasia of epithelial and muscular elements of GB wall
- epithelial lined intramural diverticula (Rokitansky-Aschoff sinuses)
- localized, annular and diffuse varieties
- most common in fundus
- ultrasound demonstrates:
  1. nonspecific wall thickening; Rokitansky-Aschoff sinuses add specificity
  2. Rokitansky-Aschoff sinuses may be filled with bile, sludge, or calculi and thus vary from anechoic to echogenic with distal shadow or reverberation
  3. segmental disease may appear as focal wall thickening or bandlike constriction

Adenomas (pedunculated adenomatous polyps). These have been associated with CA in certain situations. They do not shadow and do not move.

Causes of pericholecystic fluid are acute cholecystitis, pericholecystic abscess, ascites, pancreatitis, peritonitis, and acquired immunodeficiency syndrome (AIDS).

Causes of gallstones in children are hemolysis, e.g., sickle cell disease, cystic fibrosis, malabsorption syndrome (Crohn's disease), hepatitis, and congenital biliary anomalies (choledochal cyst, biliary atresia).

BILE DUCTS

Intrahepatic radicles in the liver converge to form the main right and left hepatic ducts at the porta hepatis. The right and left hepatic ducts unite to form the common hepatic duct.

The common hepatic duct joins with the cystic duct to form the common bile duct (Fig. 5–3). The common bile duct travels along the hepatoduodenal ligament (ligament between the liver and duodenum), behind the duodenal bulb and posterior aspect of the pancreatic head to enter the second portion of the duodenum. The common bile duct joins with the pancreatic duct at the ampulla of Vater.

The extrahepatic biliary tree or common duct is always anterior to the portal vein.

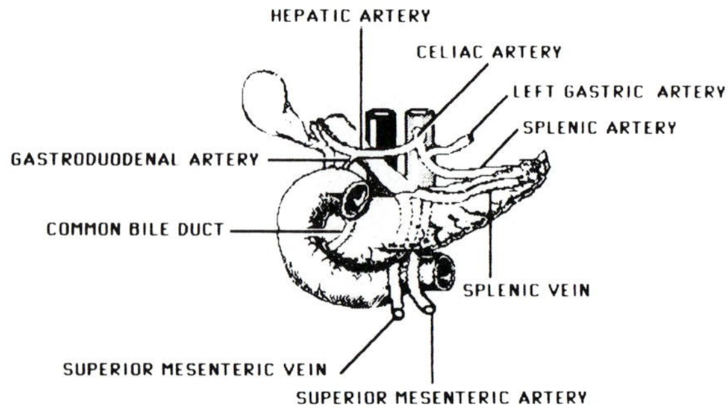

Figure 5–3. The common bile duct and surrounding vasculature.

The normal common bile duct measures ≤8 mm in luminal diameter, not including the wall. In older patients who are not jaundiced and have no pain, a common bile duct of 10–12 mm may be considered normal. This is due to the common bile duct becoming ectatic with age.

An enlarged common bile duct after a cholecystomy is normal, but one must rule out retained stones in the common bile duct or postoperative stricture.

The portion of the duct that is seen anterior to the right portal vein is the common hepatic duct. The common hepatic duct measures ≤4 or 5 mm.

The cystic duct is not seen sonographically, and intrahepatic biliary radicles are not visualized unless dilated.

Improper functioning of the bile duct and/or liver malfunction can cause jaundice (Table 5–4).

Sonographic Criteria for Biliary Tree Dilatation—Intrahepatic[31]

1. The bile duct runs anterior to the portal veins. When dilated, the sonographer will see the parallel channel sign (double-barrel shotgun sign)
2. Too many tubular structures are visible in the periphery of the liver
3. Stellate formation of the tubes near the porta hepatis
4. Enhancement of echoes distal to the ducts

Sonographic Criteria for Biliary Tree Dilatation—Extrahepatic[31]

1. Common bile duct lumen is larger than 6 mm
2. False-negative obstruction. If obstruction happens within 12 to 24 hours prior to sonography, the ducts may not yet be dilated
3. False-positive obstruction. The dilated common bile duct might be present, but no stone is present because the patient will have passed the stone

Table 5–9 outlines how to locate bile duct obstruction.

TABLE 5–9. LOCATING THE POINT OF COMMON BILE DUCT OBSTRUCTION

Remember—the ducts dilate proximal to the site of obstruction.

Intrahepatic biliary dilatation Common bile duct (normal) Gallbladder (normal)	1. Look for bile duct tumors, ie, cholangiocarcinoma, Klatskin tumor. Suspect stone in common hepatic duct. If biliary dilatation is confined to one lobe or another, suspect stone in right or left hepatic duct 2. Sclerosing cholangitis—inflammation and fibrosis of bile duct, with intrahepatic calculi a common complication. 3. Metastatic involvement and enlargement of porta hepatis lymph nodes 4. Biliary atresia is the most common and fatal liver disorder in children in the United States. Jaundice is the most common symptom. 5. Choledochal cyst—fusiform dilatation of the bile duct. Bile ducts are dilated above that point
Intrahepatic biliary dilatation Common bile duct dilatation Gallbladder enlarged	1. Stones in the common bile duct 2. Pseudocyst obstructing common bile duct 3. Acute pancreatitis—swollen pancreatic head will lead to obstructed bile flow 4. Chronic pancreatitis—fibrotic and shrunken pancreas will lead to obstructed bile flow 5. Carcinoma of the pancreatic head
Intrahepatic biliary dilatation Common bile duct dilatation Gallbladder small	Chronic cholecystitis

Congenital Anomalies of the Bile Ducts

The Jaundiced Infant

Biliary Atresia. This is the most common fatal liver disorder in children in the United States. In atresia of *intrahepatic radicles,* there is *no sonographic evidence of biliary* radicles. The condition is *untreatable.*

In atresia of *extrahepatic radicles,* there is an anastomosis of the biliary tree to the jejunum; in this case, you will see dilated intrahepatic radicles.

The Jaundiced Child

Choledochal Cyst. Cystic dilation and outpouching of the wall, involving *the common duct.* Classic triad is patient

with jaundice, RUQ pain, RUQ mass.[26] Diagnosed sonographically by demonstrating common duct or biliary radicles going into the cystic mass. This will help in the diagnosis of choledochal cyst. Also, the sonographer must see GB separate from the cyst.

Caroli's Disease. Caroli's disease is an inherited trait characterized by a segmental saccular dilatation of the *intrahepatic ducts.* It may be associated with cystic kidney disease, in particular renal tubular ectasia. Caroli's disease leads to bile stasis, stones, bacterial growth, abscesses, cholangitis, and decreased liver function due to compression of hepatocytes.

Sonographically, Caroli's disease presents as multiple liver cysts continuous with the biliary tree; stones and echoes may appear within the biliary ducts.

Cholangitis

Inflammation of the bile ducts caused by bacterial infection of the biliary tract is almost always associated with obstruction; eg, choledocholithiosis, biliary stricture, and neoplasms. The signs and symptoms are Charcot's triad (biliary colic), jaundice, and chills and fever. Laboratory tests show leukocytosis, increased serum bilirubin, increased alkaline phosphatase, and bacteremia.

Choledocholithiasis

Calculi in the common bile duct is usually caused by GB stones. The signs and symptoms are biliary colic, jaundice, episodes of cholangitis, and GB stones. Laboratory tests show increased serum bilirubin and increased serum alkaline phosphatase. Sonographically, stones can be seen in the duct.

Acquired Immunodeficiency Syndrome (AIDS)

In AIDS, dilated ducts may be seen in the context of right upper quadrant (RUQ) pain, increased liver function tests, and jaundice. These signs and symptoms are thought to be secondary to papillary inflammation and edema. The probable cause is cytomegalovirus, *Cryptospordium,* or *Mycobacterium avium intracellulare.* A sclerosing cholangitislike pattern may develop with irregular areas of dilatation and duct wall thickening.[44]

Malignant Tumors of the Biliary Tree

Adenocarcinoma and Squamous Cell Carcinoma. Signs and symptoms are anorexia, weight loss, right upper quadrant pain, and jaundice. Predisposing factors associated with carcinoma of the biliary tree are inflammation, cholelithiasis and chronic ulcerative colitis.[24] All branches of the biliary tree may be affected, from the common bile duct to the smallest biliary radicle. A *Klatskin tumor* is the name given to carcinoma arising at the confluence of the hepatic ducts. This location offers the worst prognosis for it allows considerable obstruction to occur before the tumor attains a significant size to be diagnosed.[24]

Sonographic Appearance of Klatskin Tumor. Dilatation of the intrahepatic ducts but not the extrahepatic ducts is seen. The tumor usually occurs at union of the right and left hepatic ducts. It presents as a small, solid mass of the hepatic hilum. Lymphadenopathy is commonly associated with Klatskin tumor.

Nuclear Medicine Test

Hepato Biliary Scan. To rule out cystic and/or common bile duct obstruction, fat-soluble radionuclide is injected. If both the cystic duct and common bile duct are patent, the radionuclide will appear in the GB and bowel within a half hour postinjection.

PANCREAS

The pancreas lies transversely in the body within the retroperitoneal cavity. The gland is divided into head, body, and tail (from right to left). The boundaries of the pancreas are arbitrary, relating to its surrounding anatomy. The size and shape of the pancreas can be variable, and it is relatively larger in children than in adults. Approximate normal measurements are, head—2.5 cm, body—2.0 cm, and tail—2.0 cm in anteroposterior dimension.

The head of the pancreas is anterior to the inferior vena cava and right renal vein and medial to the second portion of the duodenum. The common bile duct can be seen on the posterolateral margin of the pancreatic head. The gastroduodenal artery is located on the anterolateral surface. Both will appear as sonolucent circular structures within the head of the pancreas.

The pancreatic body is the largest part of the gland. It lies anterior to the superior mesenteric vein, superior mesenteric artery, splenic vein, and aorta. Posterior to the superior mesenteric artery and anterior to the aorta, one also can visualize the left renal vein.

The pancreatic tail lies anterior to the left kidney and medial to the splenic hilum. The splenic artery forms the superior border and the splenic vein the posterior border.

Extending the entire length of the gland is the pancreatic duct. The primary duct is called Wirsung's duct. It enters the second part of the duodenum at the ampulla of Vater along with the common bile duct. The secondary duct is called Santorini's duct. It enters the second part of the duodenum separately, approximately 2 cm proximal to the ampulla of Vater.

Fig. 5–4 demonstrates the pancreas and its related landmarks.

The echogenicity pattern of the pancreas consists of fine homogeneous echoes equal to, or more echogenic than, the normal liver. Since the pancreas has no true capsule, it tends to blend in with the surrounding retroperitoneal fat. The pancreatic duct can be commonly seen as a cystic tubular structure running from the head to the tail of the pancreas. Its normal caliber is 2–3 mm, being largest in the head, and decreasing in size to the tail where it is smallest.

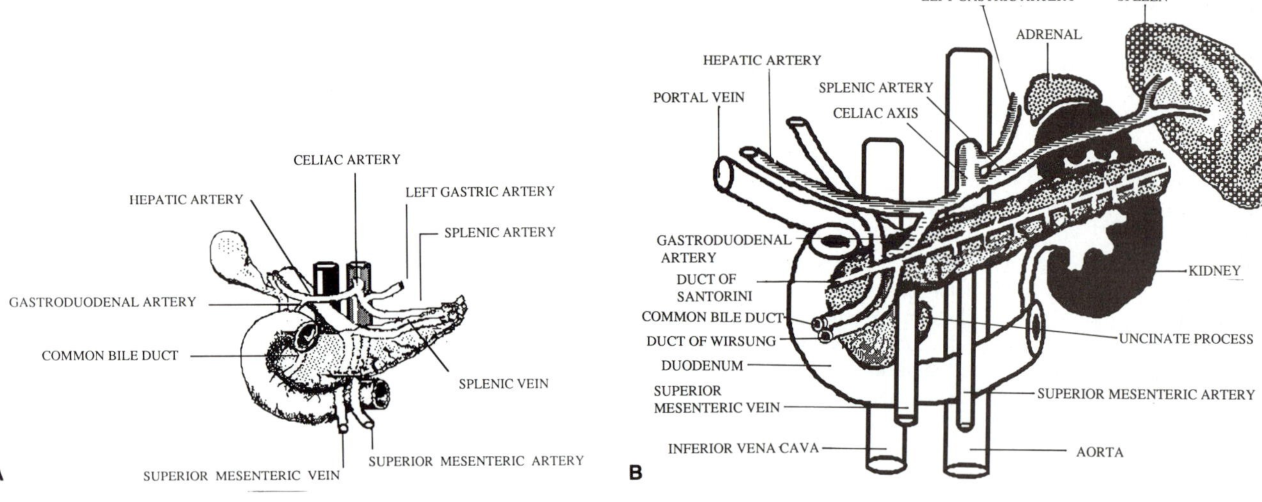

Figure 5–4. (**A**) Structures related to the pancreas; (**B**) Vascular anatomy related to the pancreas. *(Reprinted with permission from Fleischer AC, James AE. Diagnostic Sonography: Principles and Clinical Applications. Philadelphia: Saunders, 1989.)*

The endocrine function of the pancreas is to secrete insulin via the islets of Langerhans. The three exocrine enzymes are trypsin, lipase, and amylase.

Pancreatic Diseases (Table 5–10)

Pancreatitis: Inflammation of the Pancreas. Causes of pancreatitis in older patients include alcohol—most common in men, biliary tract disease—most common in women, trauma, surgery, perforated peptic ulcer disease, and drugs.

Causes in younger patients include infectious agents—mumps, mononucleosis; hereditary—cystic fibrosis; and congenital pancreatitis (rare).

Pancreatitis can be generalized into two discrete forms, acute (edematous and hemorrhagic), and chronic (recurrent and calcific).

Acute Pancreatitis

Edematous. The pancreas goes through inflammatory changes and interstitial edema. The gland enlarges and swells; consequently a less echogenic pancreas will be noted. Acute pancreatitis may also be associated with intraperitoneal or retroperitoneal fluid.

Hemorrhagic. There is rapid progression of the disease due to the autodigestion of pancreatic tissue. Frequently, areas of fresh blood (hence the name) and fat necrosis are seen. It is the least common form of pancreatitis but the more urgent. Sonographically, the pancreas will have a very varied appearance from heterogeneous to hypoechoic. The pancreatic duct may be enlarged larger than 2 mm, and peripancreatic fluid may be present.

Chronic Pancreatitis. There is continued destruction of pancreatic parenchyma, usually associated with chronic alcoholism and biliary tract disease. The pancreas will appear smaller and more echogenic.

Pancreatic Carcinoma. Pancreatic carcinoma can be subdivided generally into adenocarcinoma, cystadenocarcinoma, and endocrine-active tumors such as islet cell carcinoma. Adenocarcinoma is the most common and is usually located within the head. Sonographically, the pancreatic borders are irregular, the parenchymal pattern changes, and the gland enlarges. Dilatation of the pancreatic duct may be seen, and one should also look for dilatation of the common bile duct secondary to enlargement of the pancreatic head.

Cystadenocarcinoma is visualized sonographically as an irregular cystic lobulated tumor with thick walls. It is more commonly seen in the body or tail.

Islet cell carcinomas are usually small and well circumscribed. Seventy-five percent cause endocrine hypersecretion and are usually found in the pancreatic tail. They are visualized sonographically as solid masses with cystic degeneration.

With any type of pancreatic carcinoma, clinically one can see an increase in alkaline phosphatase and bilirubin secondary to obstruction leading to jaundice and liver metastasis. Lymphadenopathy may also be seen.

Benign Tumors. Benign pancreatic tumors that are sonographically visualized include islet cell tumors, cystadenoma, papilloma of the duct, and duct cell adenoma. It is also possible to visualize pancreatic cysts, abscesses, metastatic diseases (to the pancreas), and lymphomas, all of which have the same sonographic appearances as when seen in other areas of the body (Table 5–11).

TABLE 5–10. PANCREATIC DISEASE

	Acute Pancreatitis	Chronic Pancreatitis	Adenocarcinomas	Islet Cell Tumors
Etiology	In males—Alcoholism increases gastric secretions, causes constriction of ampulla of Vater causing back-up of pancreatic secretions		The risk of pancreatic CA is increased in smokers, diabetics, and coffee drinkers	Develops from B cells of islet of Langerhans; 30% of these tumors are malignant
Clinical Findings				
Presentation	1. Abdominal pain characteristically in epigastrum or periumbilical, usually radiating to the back 2. Nausea and vomiting 3. Abdominal distension due to a decrease in gastric and intestinal motility and chemical peritonitis	1. May present with symptoms identical to acute pancreatitis or may have no pain 2. Pain increases with consumption of alcohol and fatty foods 3. Weight loss 4. Abnormal stools	1. Pain is the most common sympton 2. Jaundice 3. Weight loss 4. Palpable gallbladder (Courvoisier's sign)	1. Hypoglycemia 2. Elevated plasma insulin levels
Size	Enlarged (swollen)	Normal to small	Irregular, nodular Focal enlargement	Focal enlargement Small 1–2 cm Well encapsulated Maybe multiple
Usual site in gland	Entire gland	Entire gland (but may be focal)	Usually in the head	Body and tail
Sonographic findings				
Texture (compared to normal pancreas)	Generalized decrease in echogenicity of the entire gland	Generalized increase in echogenicity (focal or diffuse) of gland	Generalized decrease in echogenicity	Homogeneous and solid, frequently hypoechoic, whereas some may be echogenic
Attenuation (compared to normal pancreas)	Decreased	Increased	Decreased	
Shape	Generalized enlargement of the gland with smooth contours	Normal to small in size with irregular contours	Borders of mass are irregular	Borders of mass are smooth
Calcification	None	Yes	No	No
Associated sonographic findings	1. Dilatation of the biliary tree and calculi 2. Pancreatic pseudocyst	1. Dilatation of the pancreatic duct, possibly with stones 2. Pancreatic pseudocyst 3. Calcification of the gland in 50% of patients with malabsorption syndromes 4. Dilated common bile duct	1. Dilatation of the pancreatic duct 2. Biliary dilatation–jaundice if mass is in pancreatic head 3. Lymph nodes 4. Portal venous system involvement 5. Ascites	
Laboratory values	Serum amylase increased in 24 h Serum lipase increased in 72–94 h	Serum amylase (the pancreas must be intact to synthesize amylase and release, so in chronic pancreatitis serum amylase may not be elevated) Serum lipase	Increased bilirubin, Increased alkaline phosphatase } Due to biliary obstruction Increased amylase Increased lipase	Decrease in the 2-hour postprandial (PP) blood sugar

TABLE 5–11. PANCREATIC MASSES

Pancreatic Growths	Sonographic Anatomy	Clinical Pathology
Cysts		
True Cyst	Sonographic features of a true cyst—smooth walls, echo free, good through transmission	True cysts have an epithelial lining and are usually found continuous with the pancreatic duct and/or arising from within the gland; most commonly found in the head
Pseudocyst	Pseudocysts generally take on the contour of the available space and may present as more than one "cyst." They are usually well defined with thick and echogenic borders. Internally they are anechoic, but debris may be seen on the dependent portion. Increased through transmission can also be seen posteriorly.	Pancreatic enzymes found outside of pancreatic duct. These enzymes can track anywhere. Sequelae in 2–60% of pancreatitis, usually appears 7 to 10 days after presenting symptoms; most commonly seen in alcoholic pancreatitis. If pseudocyst ruptures, can lead to pancreatic ascites
Benign Tumors		
Islet Cell Tumors	Well-circumscribed lesions of predominantly low-level echoes (may resemble an adenocarcinoma)	Most frequent benign tumor found within the pancreatic body and tail and presents as a small, solid mass with areas of cystic degeneration; 75% cause endocrine hypersecretion; 25% are nonfunctioning; 10% undergo malignant changes
Cystadenoma	The pancreas is lobulated with predominantly cystic areas, cannot be differentiated from malignant counterpart cystadenocarcinoma	Rare benign tumor arising from pancreatic duct, usually in tail
Malignant Tumor		
Adenocarcinoma	The pancreas demonstrates focal enlargement and is less echogenic than normal with ill-defined borders	Fourth or fifth most common cause of cancer death. Malignant solid tumor commonly found within the pancreatic head. Tumor becomes quite large. Patient presents with pain, weight loss, and jaundice
Associated Findings	Pancreatic duct dilatation Biliary tract dilatation Liver metastases Nodal metastases Portal venous system involvement Compression of inferior vena cava Large gallbladder (Courvoisier's sign) Laboratory values: Increased alkaline phosphatase (liver metastases), increased SGOT, increased serum amylase, increased bilirubin	Ascites; superior mesenteric vessel displacement posteriorly; a tumor of the uncinate process can cause anterior displacement of this vessel
Cystadenocarcinoma	The pancreas is lobulated with predominantly cystic areas. Can have similar appearance to pseudocyst	Rare malignant solid tumor commonly found within the tail and body. It presents as a cystic mass with solid components

SPLEEN

The spleen is the largest mass of reticuloendothelial tissue in the body. It normally measures about 12–14 cm in length, 7 cm in width, and 3 cm in anteroposterior dimension. It is situated in the left hypochondriac region, inferior to the diaphragm and posterolateral to the stomach. The left kidney, left adrenal gland, tail of the pancreas, and left colic flexure are all related to the visceral surface of the spleen.

Note that the spleen may be ectopic in location and/or accessory spleens may be present (usually in the area of the splenic hilum). Asplenia (congenital) is rare and often associated with congenital heart disease.

A fibroelastic capsule covers the spleen, the framework being composed of small fibrous bands that penetrate throughout the spleen. The capsule in turn is surrounded by peritoneum (thus the spleen is intraperitoneal).

The spleen is not essential to life, but it has important functions, particularly as the main component of the reticuloendothelial system. It is important because it functions in the breakdown of hemoglobin and formation of bile pigment; the filtration of organisms or other foreign material from the blood stream; the formation of anti-

bodies and immunity; as a reservoir for blood; and blood formation in the fetus or where there is severe anemia.

Tumors of the Spleen

In general, primary tumors of the spleen, either benign or malignant, are rare.

Malignant Tumors of the Spleen. These may be *primary* and arise from the capsule (sarcoma) or from the splenic tissue (lymphoma). *Secondary* malignant tumors of the spleen are metastatic from breast, malignant melanoma, or ovaries.

Benign Tumors of the Spleen. These include congenital cysts, cysts associated with polycystic disease, hemangioma (most common primary tumor of the spleen), and lymphangioma.

Rupture of the spleen is common with trauma. Spontaneous rupture can also occur in certain disease states when the spleen is enlarged and soft.

Sonographically, the spleen can be imaged by placing the patient supine, left lateral oblique, and prone. The spleen should appear as fine homogeneous low-level echoes as seen within the liver.

The pathological sonographic appearances of the spleen can be divided into two categories, focal and diffuse.

It is important to remember that the stage at which the sonographer sees the patient during the course of the illness will influence the echogenicity of the spleen (Table 5–12).

Splenic Enlargement (Splenomegaly)

Size and Mass. The size of the spleen varies with energy and nutritional state of the person. It also varies at different states in life—at birth, it has the same proportion to total body weight as in the adult. What is really important is the relationship of the spleen to body size and nutritional state of the individual.

TABLE 5–12. SONOGRAPHIC APPEARANCE OF THE SPLEEN

Focal		Diffuse	
Sonolucencies	***Echogenic***	***Decreased Echogenicity***	***Increased Echogenicity***
Splenic cysts		Congestion	Leukemia
Abscess		Multiple myeloma	Lymphoma
Lymphoma		Lymphopoiesis	
Metastases	Metastases	Granulocytopoiesis (eg, acute or chronic infection)	
		Erythropoiesis (as in sickle-cell disease, hemolytic anemia, thalassemia)	

The approximate "normal" mass of the spleen in the adult is length—12–14 cm; width—7 cm; anteroposterior—4 cm.

Rule of thumb for splenomegaly is that if the anterior margin of the spleen extends more anteriorly than the anterior wall of the abdominal aorta on a transverse section, and the patient is in the supine position, this represents splenomegaly. Note that this may be seen in a very thin patient without being pathologically enlarged (eyeball technique most commonly used) (Table 5–13).

KIDNEY

The paired kidneys and ureters are retroperitoneal, lying against the deep muscles of the back. The kidney is covered by a fibrous capsule that is closely applied but not adherent to the renal parenchyma.

The capsule is seen by sonography as a strong continuous specular reflector surrounding the cortex.

Surrounding the encapsulated kidney is a collection of fat in the perinephric space. Located superior, anterior, and medial to each kidney is the adrenal gland. Enclosing the kidney, perinephric fat, and adrenal is a fibrous sheath known as Gerota's fascia.

TABLE 5–13. CAUSES OF SPLENIC ENLARGEMENT AND SHRINKAGE

Minimal	Moderate	Massive
Enlargement		
1. Acute splenitis	1. Acute leukemia	1. Chronic leukemia
2. Acute splenic congestion	2. Infectious mononucleosis	2. Lymphoma
3. Acute febrile disorders	3. Cirrhosis with portal hypertension	3. Hodgkin's disease
Bacteremic states	4. Chronic splenitis	4. Parasitic infections
Systemic toxemias	5. Tuberculosis	5. Primary tumors of the spleen
Systemic lupus erythematosus	6. Sarcoid tumor	
Intra-abdominal infections	7. Chronic congestive splenomegaly	
	8. Cancer	
	9. Iron deficiency anemias	
	10. Hemolytic anemias	
Shrinkage		
1. Myelofibrosis 2. Sickle-cell disease	The spleen *shrinks* and becomes strongly reflective	

The kidney parenchyma has two distinct areas: the outer cortex and the inner medullary pyramids, which surround the renal sinus. The renal parenchyma is measured from the margin of the renal sinus to the surface of the kidney. Renal size varies with the body size, age, and sex of the individual. Average adult size is 11.5 cm in length, 6 cm in width, and 3.5 cm in thickness.

Sonographically, the parenchyma can be resolved into cortex and medullary pyramids. The cortex is usually composed of uniform, closely spaced, relatively low-level echoes of an intensity less than that of either the normal liver or spleen parenchyma. The medullary pyramids are displayed as round or blunted hypoechoic zones between the cortex and renal sinus. These are separated from each other by bands of cortical tissue called columns of Bertin that also extend inward to the renal sinus. Intense specular echoes may be seen at the boundary between cortex and medulla. These represent the arcuate vessels.

The inner echogenic portion of the kidney consists of the renal sinus. The renal sinus contains fat, calyces, infundibula, renal pelvis, connective tissue, renal vessels, and lymphatics. The entrance to this sinus is termed the hilum and through it passes various blood vessels, nerves, lymphatic vessels, and the ureter.

The superior end of the ureter is expanded to form a funnel-shaped sac called the renal pelvis, which is located inside the renal sinus. The pelvis is divided into two or three tubes called major calyces, and they in turn are divided into 8 to 18 minor calyces. Each minor calyx is indented by the apex of a medullary pyramid called the renal papilla.

In a fluid-restricted subject, the infundibula (the major and minor calyces) are collapsed and not distinguishable within the echo-dense renal sinus fat. During diuresis, these structures can often be identified as narrow channels traversing the sinus. When the renal pelvis is partially extrarenal in location, it may be seen as a fluid-filled structure medial to the kidney.

Maternal pyelocalietasis without mechanical obstruction is commonly observed during pregnancy and involves the right kidney more than the left. Fetal pyelectasis is also common in utero.

ANTERIOR TO THE RIGHT KIDNEY	ANTERIOR TO THE LEFT KIDNEY	POSTERIOR TO THE KIDNEYS
Right adrenal	Left adrenal	Diaphragm
Liver	Stomach	Quadratus lumborum muscles
Duodenum	Spleen	Psoas muscle
Right colic (hepatic) flexure	Pancreas	
Small intestine	Jejunum	

Functions of the Kidneys

The kidneys serve in the excretion of inorganic compounds, eg, Na^+, K^+, Ca^{++}; excretion of organic compounds, eg, creatinine; blood pressure regulation; erythrocyte volume regulation; and vitamin D and Ca^{++} metabolism.

The ultimate goals of kidney functions are to (1) maintain salt and water balance, (2) regulate the fluid volume in the body, (3) maintain acid base balance.

Renal Congenital Anomalies

Renal congenital anomalies include incorrect position, number, and shape.

Position. Embryologically, the kidneys form in the pelvis in an anteroposterior orientation. They then ascend and rotate to the adult position, so that the upper pole of each kidney is more medial than the lower pole. Their ascension is usually completed by the fifth to sixth year of life. Incomplete ascension leads to ectopic kidneys.

Number. Anomalies of kidney number would include a solitary kidney (single functioning kidney with the other atrophied), unilateral renal agenesis (absence of one kidney and ureter), and a supranumary kidney (duplication of the kidney, pelvis, and ureter).

Unilateral renal agenesis is frequently associated with other anomalies; eg, bicornuate uterus, unicornuate uterus, uterine and vaginal septations.

Bilateral renal agenesis (Potter's syndrome) is associated with oligohydramnies and pulmonary hypoplasia, and it is fatal soon after birth.

Shape. Anomalies of kidney shape include hypertrophied columns of Bertin, fetal lobulation, dromedary humps, renunculus and fusion of the kidneys (ie, horseshoe-shaped kidneys and lump kidneys). Also included in this category are the congenital cystic diseases that distort the shape of the kidney, infantile polycystic disease, adult polycystic disease, and multicystic disease.

Multicystic Dysplastic Kidney (Potter 2). This is the most common cause of an abdominal mass in the newborn. It is usually unilateral, with the kidney presenting with cysts of various shapes and sizes owing to atresia of the ureter, pelvis, or both.

Polycystic Diseases. Polycystic disease may be present at birth or may not manifest until adult life.

Infantile Polycystic Disease. This is the least common and most fatal of the three anomalies of kidney shape. It is inherited as an autosomal recessive trait and is more common in females (2:1). Sonographically, it presents as bilateral, echogenic, enlarged kidneys (the cysts classically are too small to be resolved). If survival past infancy occurs, hepatic fibrosis becomes a complication with death resulting from hepatic failure and/or bleeding from esophageal varices (Potter 1).

Adult Polycystic Disease. This is inherited as autosomal dominant and occurs relatively frequently. The disease may be latent for many years and then manifest itself for

unknown reasons. Sonographically, adult polycystic disease presents as bilateral, randomly distributed cortical cysts of various sizes. Associated findings include cysts in the liver, pancreas, and spleen. Destruction of the residual renal tissue in advanced stages leads to renal failure (Potter 3).

Medullary Cystic Disease. This is inherited with both dominant and recessive modes of transmission. Clinically, patients present with renal failure. Sonographically, there are small cysts confined to the medullary portion of both kidneys.

Renal Transplants

The transplanted kidney is placed within the ileopelvic region. A baseline sonogram should be obtained following the transplant to determine its exact location, size, and texture.

Acute failure of the transplanted kidney may be produced by acute rejection, acute tubular necrosis, or arterial obstruction. It is important to differentiate between these complications for correct treatment to be administered.

Acute rejection sonographically appears as enlarged kidney with increased cortical echogenicity (58%); decreased renal sinus echogenicity; irregular sonolucent areas in the cortex (47%); enlarged and decreased echogenicity of the pyramids; distortion of the renal outline; and indistinct corticomedullary junction.

Rejection due to **acute tubular necrosis** usually results in a normal sonogram. In rejection due to **acute renal arterial occlusion,** the sonographic anatomy remains grossly normal. However, duplex Doppler studies may reveal an absence of reduction of diastolic flow.

Perinephric fluid collections commonly associated with the transplanted kidneys are lymphocele, urinoma, abscess, and hematoma (Table 5–14).

TABLE 5–14. PERINEPHRIC FLUID COLLECTIONS[a]

Type	Sonographic Findings	Clinical Findings
Abscess (Renal carbuncle is a confluence of several small abscesses)	Usually echogenic with irregular thickened walls; gas may be encountered within an abscess and will be highly reflective resulting in shadowing	High white blood cell count and flank pain; patient is febrile
Hematoma	May resemble an abscess depending upon the degree of clot/liquification	Drop in hematocrit
Urinoma	Usually appears anechoic if not superimposed with infection	An encapsulated collection of extravasated urine
Lymphocele	Anechoic, but may contain echoes if superimposed by hemorrhage	Collection of lymphatic fluid

[a] Abscess, hematoma, urinoma, and lymphocele are commonly associated with renal transplantation, although it is not exclusive.

Hydronephrosis

There are two major classifications of hydronephrosis, intrinsic and extrinsic.

Intrinsic Hydronephrosis. This may occur as a result of:

- stricture
- renal calculi
- renal neoplasm
- bleeding and blood clot
- ureterocele
- pyelonephrosis
- tuberculosis

Extrinsic Hydronephrosis. This may be the result of:

- pregnancy (usually right-sided)
- pelvic masses
- bladder neck obstruction
- neurogenic bladder
- trauma
- retroperitoneal fibrosis
- prostatic hypertrophy
- urethritis
- inflammatory lesions—pelvic, gastrointestinal, retroperitoneal

Congenital Hydronephrosis. This is present at and existing from the time of birth. It may present as:

- UPJ obstruction
- ectopic ureterocele
- retrocaval ureter
- posterior urethral valves

False-Positive Hydronephrosis. This denotes a test result that wrongly *assigns* an individual to a diagnosis or category. In other words, the following list may mimic hydronephrosis.

- normal diuresis
- overdistended bladder
- parapelvic cyst
- renal sinus lipomatosis
- extra renal pelvis
- reflux—vesicoureteral
- diabetes insipidus

False-Negative Hydronephrosis. This denotes a test result that wrongly *excludes* an individual from a diagnosis or other category, in other words, patients suffering from severe dehydration or intermittent obstruction may indeed have hydronephrosis.

- severe dehydration
- nephrolithiasis with intermittent obstruction

Table 5–15 outlines clinical and sonographic findings associated with different renal masses.

Nephrolithiasis

Nephrolithiasis sonographically appears as a highly reflective echogenic foci with posterior shadowing. Nephrolithiasis may be composed of uric acid, cystine, or calcium, all of which sonographically appear the same. Staghorn calculi are large stones located in the center of the kidney.

Laboratory Values. In chronic obstruction, there is an increase in serum creatinine and BUN. In acute obstruction, there are no specific lab values. Urine may show hematuria and/or bacteria.

TABLE 5–15. RENAL MASSES

	Clinical Findings	Sonographic Findings
Cystic Masses		
Simple renal cyst	1. Seen in 50% of all patients over the age of 55 2. Usually originates in the renal cortex 3. Generally asymptomatic unless very large and obstructing the collecting system 4. Unilocular	1. Totally anechoic 2. Smooth, round border 3. Good through transmission
Atypical renal cyst	1. Septated or multilocular 2. The septation has no pathological significance	1. Fulfills all criteria for a cyst but, in addition, will have echogenic line or lines, ie, septations
Parapelvic cysts	Cysts located in the renal hilum developing from lymphatics or other nonparenchymal tissues in the renal hilar area	Similar to a simple cyst but located within the renal pelvis
Inflammatory cysts	1. Simple renal cysts that have become infected 2. An increase in leukocytosis	1. Complex pattern of internal echoes from inflammatory debris 2. Slightly thickened walls but not as thick as chronic abscess
Hemorrhagic cysts	6% of all renal cysts will hemorrhage	Complex echo pattern dependent upon state of hemorrhage (acute), hemorrhage (echogenic), chronic hemorrhage (more echogenic)
Calcified cysts	2% of all renal cysts will tend to have calcified walls	1. Anechoic 2. Smooth round borders that are highly echogenic or have echogenic foci 3. The calcified walls attenuate ultrasound, making it very hard to visualize
Renal abscess (carbuncle)[a]	1. May contain debris 2. Fever, chills, and flank pain 3. Elevated white blood cell count	1. Complex echo pattern due to debris 2. Walls are thickened and irregular 3. Gas may produce shadowing
Hydronephrosis	Obstruction a. *Intrinsic* within the collecting system either by a stone or stricture b. *Extrinsic,* a mass compresses the ureter or bladder outlet	The calices, infundibula, and pelvis dilate owing to the obstruction of urine flow. The sonographic picture may go from minor dilatation of the calices producing a cystic cauliflower effect to the gross dilatation of the pelvis and calices producing one large cystic area with little renal parenchyma
Pyonephrosis	Pus in the dilated collecting system complication of hydronephrosis that occurs secondary to urinary stasis and infection	Dilated pelvocaliceal system filled with internal echoes, shifting urine-debris level, may have shadowing due to gas-forming organisms
Renal Sinus Disease		
Renal sinus lipomatosis	More common in older patients; may be a sequelae to chronic calculous disease and inflammation. The renal sinus is replaced by fatty tissue	In replacement lipomatosis, the kidney is enlarged, the renal sinus appearing hypoechoic owing to the fat (one of the few times that fat will appear echo free rather than echogenic)

(*continued*)

TABLE 5–15. (*Continued*)

	Clinical Findings	Sonographic Findings
Benign Solid Tumor		
Angiomyolipoma, also called renal hamartoma (tumor composed of fat, muscle, and blood vessels)	More common in women than men (2 : 1). Symptoms are flank pain, hematuria, and hypertension	Discrete mass and highly echogenic
Adenomas (benign counterpart of renal cell carcinoma)	Asymptomatic, usually small and commonly found incidentally at autopsy	
Connective tissue tumors Hemangiomas Fibromas Myomas Lipomas	Gross hematuria	These tumors present as homogeneous echogenic lesions relating to their vascularity and fat content
Malignant Solid Tumor		
Hypernephroma (also known as adenocarcinoma, renal cell carcinoma, von Grawitz tumor)	1. Unilateral, solitary, and encapsulated 2. Affects males (2 : 1) more than females, most commonly after the age of 50 3. Hematuria 4. Metastases via the blood stream affecting the renal vein, inferior vena cava, contralateral kidney, ureter, peritoneum, liver, spleen, bone, heart, and brain 5. An arteriogram of the kidney demonstrates a mass with increased vascular supply and irregular branching	The tumor itself is well encapsulated and nonhomogeneous, ranging in echogenicity from hyperechoic to hypoechoic. Look for tumor thrombus infiltrating the inferior vena cava and renal vein
Transitional cell carcinoma (affects the urothelium and may be located anywhere within the urinary collecting system)	1. Occurs in the central portion of the kidney, the renal pelvis. Known to be invasive 2. Occasionally seen as a bulky discrete mass 3. Hematuria	Invasive tumor not well defined or encapsulated within the renal pelvis
Renal lymphoma	1. Relatively common in patients with widely disseminated lymphomatous malignancy 2. Overall kidney enlargement	Solid mass with very soft internal echoes. May appear similar to renal cysts but will demonstrate no through transmission
Wilms' tumor (nephroblastoma)	1. Most common malignancy of renal origin in children 2. Presenting symptoms are abdominal mass, hypertension, nausea, hematuria	1. Well encapsulated 2. The sonographic pattern varies according to the amount of necrosis and/or hemorrhage

[a] May appear as a solid mass early in their course.

Renal Failure

Renal failure occurs as a result of deterioration of renal function, which may be acute or chronic. Laboratory findings are increased serum BUN and serum creatinine levels.

Etiology

Prerenal Causes. Renal hypoperfusion secondary to a systemic cause can occur as a result of *vascular disorders* leading to renal failure and includes the following conditions.

Nephrosclerosis. Arteriosclerosis of the renal arteries, resulting in ischemia of the kidney. Nephrosclerosis develops rapidly in patients with severe hypertension.

Infarction. This may result from occlusion or stenosis of the renal artery.

Congestive Heart Failure. This may cause renal hypoperfusion secondary to the heart failure.

Sonography. Doppler is employed to detect arterial blood flow patterns.

Renal Parenchymal Disease—Infection and Inflammatory Disease

Acute Tubular Necrosis (ATN). Of the renal medical diseases, this is the most common cause of acute renal failure. The destruction of the tubular epithelial cells of the proximal and distal convoluted tubules may occur as a

result of ingestion or inhalation of toxic agents, ischemia due to trauma, hemorrhage, acute interstitial nephritis, cortical necrosis, and diseases of the glomeruli.

Pyelonephritis. Infection is the most *common* disease of the urinary tract, and the combination of parenchymal, caliceal, and pelvic inflammation constitutes pyelonephritis. Infection of the kidney is usually caused by bacteria ascending from the bladder or adjacent lymph nodes to the kidney.

Immunological Injuries. The nephrotic syndrome, glomerulonephritis, and lupus erythematosus are immunologic disorders involving the kidney.

Nephrotic syndrome is caused by deposition of antigen-antibody complexes on the glomerulus accompanied by proteinuria, hypoalbumenia, hyperlipidemia, and edema.

The etiology of *glomerulonephritis* is unknown, but it frequently follows other infections.

Systemic lupus erythematosus is an autoimmune disease. The echogenicity of the kidney will increase with increasing severity.

Metabolic Disorders. Diabetes mellitus, amyloidosis, gout, and nephrocalcinosis—deposition of calcium within the kidneys—are metabolic disorders associated with renal failure.

Chronic Nephrotoxicity. This is caused by exposure to radiation, heavy metals, industrial solvents, and drugs.

Sonography. In acute renal failure, the kidney may be normal sized or *enlarged.* In chronic renal failure, the kidney may be normal sized or *small.* As the case progresses from acute to chronic, the echogenicity of the kidney will increase. There is no definite correlation between the echogenicity of the kidney, kidney size, and degree of decreased renal function.

Postrenal Causes. These include urinary tract obstruction—hydronephrosis—which may be congenital or acquired intrinsically and extrinsically.

Sonography. There are varying degrees of dilatation of the renal sinus, calyces, infundibulum, and pelvis.

Renal Medical Disease (Table 5–16)

Type I. There are increased cortical echogenicity and an increase in corticomedullary differentiation. Type I diseases are those due to glomerular infiltrate such as acute and chronic glomerulonephritis, acute lupus nephritis, nephrosclerosis, any type of nephritis, and renal transplant rejection. All these disorders can increase the echo amplitude of the renal cortex to be more than that of liver and spleen. As the disease becomes more chronic, the kidney becomes smaller, the cortex has increased echogenicity, and eventually the medulla will become equally echogenic.

Type II. There is distortion of normal anatomy involving cortex and medullary pyramids, therefore, increased corticomedullary differentiation in either a focal or diffuse manner. The type II pattern is seen with focal lesions such as cysts, abscesses, hematomas, bacterial nephritis (lobar nephronia), infantile polycystic disease, adult polycystic disease, chronic pyelonephritis, and chronic glomerulonephritis.

BLADDER

The urinary bladder is located immediately behind the pubic bone. The apex of the bladder points anteriorly and is connected to the umbilicus by the median umbilical ligament, the remains of the fetal urachus. The ureters, enter at a superolateral angle, and the urethra extends from the bladder neck to the exterior of the body.

When distended with fluid, a normal bladder is seen as a symmetrical anechoic structure. It has a "sausage" shape on longitudinal scan, with a somewhat rounded appearance on a transverse scan. The bladder wall is seen as a thin, smooth, uniform echogenic line that usually measures from 3 to 6 mm in thickness. The normal bladder volume reaches 500 mL without major discomfort.

During an ultrasound examination of the bladder, wall thickness, irregularities of the wall, and bladder shape should be addressed. Table 5–17 reviews abnormalities that will distort the wall and shape of the bladder.

Ureters

Ureters lie on the anterior surface of the psoas near its medial edge. In the pelvis, they cross anterior to the common iliac vessels.

Congenital Anomalies of the Ureters. These include double or bifid ureters, narrowing, strictures, diverticuli, and hydroureter due to a congenital defect, as in polycystic kidney, or acquired as in a low ureteral obstruction.

Megaureter in Childhood

Primary—Nonobstructive, Nonrefluxing Megaureter. This includes *prune belly syndrome* (Eagle-Barrett syndrome), deficiency of the abdominal musculature, and urinary tract abnormalities; and *retroperitoneal fibrosis,* which fixes the ureters and prevents peristalsis leading to functional obstruction.

Secondary Megaureter. This is due to reflux of urine or obstruction.

Ureteral abnormalities are reviewed in Table 5–18.

ADRENAL GLANDS

The adrenal glands are triangular shaped structures situated superior and anteromedial to the upper pole of the kidneys. They measure 1 × 3 × 5 cm, but at birth are

TABLE 5–16. RENAL MEDICAL DISEASES

	Clinical Findings	Ultrasound Findings
Acute Pyelonephritis	Ninety percent of the patients are female; dysuria, frequency, fever, leukocytosis, bacteruria	Normal to enlarged kidney may have mild hydronephrosis. The corticomedullary area is enlarged and less echodense than usual. These low-level echoes may be produced by multiple small abscesses and areas of necrosis in the cortex and medulla
Chronic Pyelonephritis (urinary tract infection)	Affects males and females; occurs due to recurrent urinary tract infection or inadequately treated pyelonephritis proteinuria	Normal to small kidney parenchymal thinning; increased echogenicity due to fibrosis
Acute Lobar Nephronia (acute focal bacterial nephritis)	Inflammatory mass without drainable pus results from gram-negative bacteria that ascends from ureteral reflux, fever, chills, flank pain	Poorly defined cystic mass containing echoes that may disrupt the corticomedullary junction. Cannot be differentiated from an abscess
Xanthogranulomatous Pyelonephritis	Rare form of inflammatory disease found in patients with long-standing renal calculi	Renal enlargement with multiple anechoic to hypoechoic areas
Glomerulonephritis	Glomerular disease results from an immunological reaction in which antigen-antibody complexes in the circulation are trapped in the glomeruli. It is the most common cause of chronic renal failure. In the acute stage, will present with oliguria, edema, increased BUN, increased creatinine, increased serum K. In the chronic stage, the patient presents with polyuria and proteinuria to such a high extent that 50% of patients develop nephrotic syndrome	Increases the echo amplitude of the renal cortex with a decrease in kidney size as the disease progresses
Acute Tubular Necrosis (ATN)	The most common cause of acute renal failure may result from ischemia and the interruption or impairment of blood flow in and out of the kidney. This may be due to trauma/surgery. It is the most comon cause of renal failure in the postrenal transplant patient and toxin induced	Increase in kidney size, especially in the anteroposterior diameter; normal renal parenchyma; the medullary pyramids will appear more prominent and anechoic

proportionately much larger. Gerota's fascia encloses the kidneys, adrenals, and the perinephric fat.

The right gland lies posterior to the inferior vena cava and anterior to the right crus of the diaphragm.

The left gland lies between the spleen and the aorta, posterior to the tail of the pancreas. Sonographically, the normal adrenal glands in adults are difficult to visualize owing to their small size and their echo texture being similar to the surrounding retroperitoneal fat. The recommended modality for evaluation of the adrenals is computed tomography (CT). Occasionally, an adrenal tumor will be found on sonography. Therefore, to rule out adrenal pathology with sonography, one should observe displacement and/or compression of adjacent organs.

Right adrenal pathology will displace—

ANTERIORLY	POSTERIORLY
The retroperitoneal fat line	The right kidney
The inferior vena cava	
The right renal vein	

Left adrenal pathology will displace—

ANTERIORLY	POSTERIORLY AND INFERIORLY
Splenic vein	The left kidney

The adrenal gland consists of two distinct endocrine organs, the cortex and the medulla.

Adrenal Cortex

The adrenal cortex, which produces steroid hormones, is further subdivided into three zones: (1) zona glomerulosa, which produces mineralocorticoids (to regulate electrolyte metabolism); (2) zona fasiculata; and (3) the zona reticularis, which produces glucocorticoids (for regulation of carbohydrate metabolism) and androgens (for regulation of the secretion of androgens and estrogens, which are the sex hormones of an individual).

The adrenal cortical hormones are regulated by the adrenocorticotropic hormones (ACTH) of the anterior pituitary. A *decrease* in adrenal cortical function leads to an increased ACTH which then stimulates the adrenal cor-

TABLE 5–17. BLADDER ABNORMALITIES

Abnormality	Clinical Findings	Ultrasound Findings
Urachal Cyst: The urachus connects the apex of the bladder with the allantois (an embryological structure with no function in humans) through the umbilical cord. Normally, it fibroses at birth, but it may, in part or in whole, remain patent. The urachus lies in the space of Retzius.	A urachal cyst remains clinically silent until an infection develops, then there is vague abdominal pain and/or urinary complaints	A urachal cyst is seen as an echo-free tubular structure in the lower mid-abdominal anterior wall. The upper pole may extend from the umbilicus to the bladder
Diverticuli of the bladder: Pouchlike envaginations of the bladder wall	The diverticula constitute a site of urinary stasis that tends to become infected	Diverticula vary greatly in size and appear separate from the bladder. They are round, well-defined, thin-walled cystic masses. To help delineate it from an adnexal mass, have the patient void; it should disappear.
Reduplication: Complete reduplication of the bladder is rare	Unilateral reflex, obstruction or infection	One would visualize two separate bladders separated by a peritoneal fold
Reflux: Vesicoureteral reflex is a common urinary tract abnormality in children secondary to anomalies such as ectopia, posterior urethral valves, prune belly, neurogenic bladder, and primary congenital abnormalities of the bladder	Reflux may be a cause of chronic renal failure with scarring and atrophic changes in the kidney	Cysto-Conray (20%) is injected into the bladder. Each kidney is scanned while the contrast is injected. With each increasing grade of reflux, there is increasing kidney dilation
Bladder Neck Obstruction: The lower portion continuous with the urethra, is called the neck	In the male bladder, neck obstruction commonly is secondary to benign prostatic hypertrophy or carcinoma. With prolonged obstruction, the bladder will become thickened and trabeculate	Ultrasound demonstrates a thickened and irregular-walled bladder
Cystitis: Infection or inflammation of the bladder	Secondary to diverticula, urethral obstruction, fistulas, cystocele, bladder neoplasm, pyelonephritis, neurogenic dysfunction	When it is long standing, the bladder walls may show inflammatory changes and thickening. With a neurogenic bladder a pus-urine fluid level may be seen
Primary Benign Tumor: papilloma, epithelial	There may be papillary growths, nodular infiltrating	Small to massive solid tumors are seen projecting from the bladder wall, some may invaginate the bladder wall, and may be smooth or irregular in contour. May mimic benign prostatic hypertrophy or cystitis
Primary Malignant Tumor: 95% are transitional cell carcinoma; 5% are squamous cell carcinoma	Invasive growths, with 40% having metastases to lymph nodes and invasion of the prostate and seminal vesicles	

TABLE 5–18. URETERAL ABNORMALITIES

Abnormality	Clinical Findings	Ultrasound Findings
Posterior Urethral Valves	Posterior urethral valves are the most common cause of urinary obstruction in the male infant and are the second most common cause of hydronephrosis in the neonate. This obstruction is related to a flap of mucosa that has a slitlike opening in the area of the prostatic urethra.	Distended bladder with a thickened wall dilated; ureters medial and posterior to the bladder
Ureterocele	A ureterocele is a cystic dilatation of the submucosa of the intravesicular ureter (that portion of the ureter that enters the bladder)with narrowing of the ureteric orifice. This may cause obstruction of the ipsilateral ureter and can obstruct the bladder neck.	An anechoic thin-walled structure of variable size and shape projecting into the bladder
"Ureteral Jets" (not an abnormality but only appearing as one)	The term *ureteral jets* is used to describe the appearance of urine entering the bladder. These jets are seen during bladder filling and are not visible when the bladder is full. They are seen at regular intervals, each jet lasting from a fraction of 1–3 seconds.[36]	The urinary jet starts in the area of the ureter and flows toward the center of the bladder. Doppler may be used because the ureteral jet will cause a Doppler shift due to the continued changes in the turbulent flow of the urine

tex. An *increase* in concentration of adrenal hormones leads to a drop in ACTH secretion, which in turn leads to a drop in the activity of the adrenal cortex.

The adrenal cortex may be affected either by lesions that produce an excess of steroid hormones or by lesions that produce a deficiency. Be aware that adrenocortical hormones may be altered as a result of an overproduction or underproduction of ACTH that is a result of a pituitary tumor. Table 5–19 outlines possible adrenal gland malfunctions.

Adrenal Medulla

The adrenal medulla produces epinephrine (adrenalin) and norepinephrine. These hormones have a wide range of effect.

Epinephrine dilates the coronary vessels and constricts the skin and kidney vessels. It increases coronary output, raises oxygen consumption, and causes hyperglycemia.

Norepinephrine constricts all arterial vessels except the coronary arteries (which dilate). It is an essential regulator of blood pressure.

Epinephrine, in particular, is responsible for the fight-or-flight reaction. It stimulates the metabolic rate, allowing more available energy.

TABLE 5–19. ADRENAL GLAND MALFUNCTIONS

	Clinical Findings	Sonographic Findings
Adrenal Cortex		
Adrenocortical Hyperfunction		
Cushing's syndrome	Prolonged exposure to elevated plasma corticosteroids produces truncal obesity, rounded faces, mild hypertension, cardiac enlargement, and edema	May be solid, cystic, or complex appearing with focal zones of necrosis
Conn's syndrome	Hyperaldosteronism due to the increased secretion of aldosterone producing sodium retention, which leads to essential hypertension	
Adrenogenital syndrome	Exclusive oversecretion of androgens leading to virilism or masculinization in a female. Hypersecretion of estrogens (in the male) produces the feminizing syndrome	
Adrenocortical Hypofunction		
Addison's disease	Hypotension, small hearts, malaise, and weight loss, skin pigmentation, loss of body hair, and menstrual irregularity. 60% are due to idiopathic destruction, probably autoimmune in nature	
Adrenal Medulla		
Pheochromocytoma	Paroxysmal or sustained hypertension, angina, cardiac arrhythmias, and headaches. These features are due to the concentration of catecholamines released into the circulation	May grow to be quite large, may appear cystic, solid, or solid with calcific components
Neuroblastoma	Termed a nonfunctioning tumor (ie, tumors that do not produce epinephrine and norepinephrine) and arises from sympathetic nervous tissue. Most children are asymptomatic presenting with a palpable abdominal mass	The tumor appears echogenic and may be quite large
Adrenal Metastases	Most commonly from bronchogenic CA, lung adenocarcinoma, breast or stomach carcinoma	Metastases to the adrenals vary in size and echogenicity
Adrenal Cysts	None—patient may be asymptomatic	Strong back wall, no internal echoes, good through transmission. Adrenal cysts have the tendency to become calcified, which may appear as an echo-free structure, with an echogenic back wall but with poor through transmission.
Adrenal Hematomas	Especially encountered in infants	Varies from cystic to complex depending upon the age of the hematoma, ending in calcification

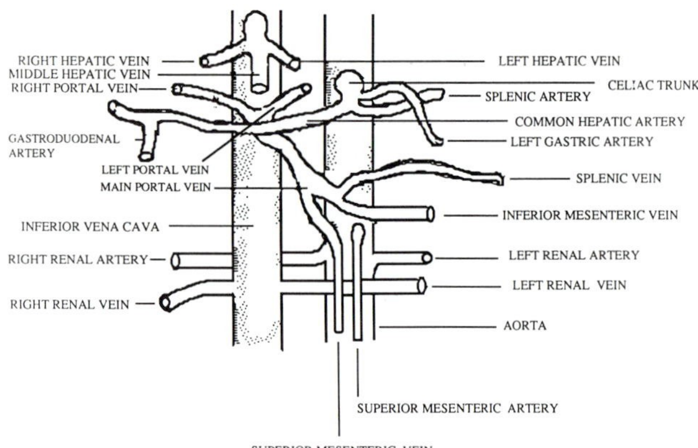

Figure 5–5. Prevertebral vessels. *(Reprinted with permission from Hagen-Ansert S. Textbook of Diagnostic Ultrasonography, 2nd ed. St. Louis: CV Mosby, 1983, p 113.)*

MAJOR LANDMARK VESSELS

Knowledge of the prevertebral vessels (Fig. 5–5) is extremely important, for they are the road maps and guideposts in helping to identify both normal anatomy and pathology.

Aorta

The aorta lies anterior to the spine and posterior to the pancreatic body. On sagittal scans, the superior aspect is most posterior.

Ventral Branches of the Aorta

Celiac. The celiac is only 2–3 cm long and has three branches:

1. Splenic artery—runs superior to the pancreas on its way to the spleen.
2. Left gastric artery
3. Hepatic artery—enters the porta hepatis with the portal vein. The gastroduodenal artery, a branch of the hepatic artery, delineates the anteriolateral aspect of the pancreatic head.

Superior Mesenteric Artery. The superior mesenteric artery (SMA) lies posterior to the body of the pancreas.

Inferior Mesenteric Artery. Originates from the abdominal aorta close to the umbilicus and is rarely seen on ultrasound.

Lateral Branches of the Aorta

Renal Arteries. There are two renal arteries, the left renal artery and the right renal artery. The right renal artery is the only vessel that runs posterior to the inferior vena cava.

Anatomy and Measurement. The aorta enters the abdomen at the first lumbar vertebra (L1) and follows the curvature of the spine to bifurcate at L4. If there is a separation between the aorta and the spine, adenopathy, fibrosis, or hematoma should be ruled out.

The normal AP dimension of the aortic lumen should be < 3 cm

- thoracic: 2.5 cm
- diaphragm: 2.5–3.0 cm
- mid-abdomen: 2.0–2.5 cm
- renals: 1.8–2.0 cm
- bifurcation: 1.5–1.7 cm
- iliac: 1.0–1.3 cm

Aortic aneurysms—increased aortic diameter greater than 3 cm.

- aneurysm: 3–6 cm
- signifant: > 5 cm
- surgical emergency: > 6 cm
- 50% survival of 1 year: > 6 cm
- 75% risk of fatal rupture: > 7 cm

Classification of Aneurysms. Aortic aneurysms may be true, dissecting, or false.

True Aneurysms. The three layers of the vessel (aorta) are dilated to form the aneurysm. They may be caused by: arteriosclerosis with hypertension; Marfan's syndrome is associated with aneurysm of the first portion of the aorta that usually extends to affect the aortic valve leading to aortic insufficiency; infections, especially as a result of bacterial endocarditis; trauma; congenital; and syphilis.

Clinical Findings: The clinical findings in true aortic aneurysms are pulsatile abdominal mass, back pain—most aneurysms start below renal arteries and extend down to common iliac arteries.

Types

- fusiform: gradual, spindle-shaped dilation of the vascular lumen, usually occurring below renal arteries to the bifurcation
- cylindrical: uniform dilation within the longitudinal diameter producing lengthening of the expanded vessel
- saccular: localized, spherical outpouching of the vessel wall, often containing thrombus; it is the least common type
- berry: small spherical aneurysm, 1–1.5 cm usually within cerebral circulation (middle cerebral artery)

Sonographic Findings. Generally, the vessel will show irregularities, tortuosities, and aortic wall calcification. An accurate measurement of the anteroposterior diameter should be performed.

Dissecting Aneurysm. Intima (inner wall) of aorta dissects and pulls away from other two walls; hemorrhage occurs between walls. Seventy percent begin in ascending aorta. They may be caused by cystic aneurysms, as in Marfan's syndrome, hemorrhage of vasa vasorum, and spontaneous rupture of the intima.[21]

Clinical Findings. Severe pain that mimicks myocardial infarction; the site of the pain may indicate the site of the aneurysm. Most severe type of aneurysm occurs most frequently in males and patients with hypertension.

Sonographic Findings. Demonstration of the intimal flap, which moves with aortic pulsation; differentiation between the true and false lumen is difficult.

False Aneurysm. An injury to the vessel wall and extravasation occurs; the extravasated blood is retained and walled off by the surrounding tissues, so the wall of the false aneurysm is not the vessel wall. False aneurysms mimic a true aneurysm. Trauma is the most common cause.

Sonographic Findings. A mass is adjacent to the vessel; usually has variable echogenicity.

Inferior Vena Cava

The inferior vena cava (IVC) lies to the right of the aorta and posterior to the pancreatic head. It extends from the union of the common iliac arteries to the right of L5 and travels cephalad. It then curves *anterior* to enter the right atrium.

The IVC normally contracts on exhalation and expands on inhalation or the Valsalva maneuver. The IVC remains dilated with hepatomegaly, pulmonary hypertension, congestive heart disease, constrictive pericarditis, right atrial myxoma, atherosclerotic heart disease, and right ventricular failure.

The most common tumor to involve the IVC is renal cell carcinoma and is usually on the right because of the close proximity to the IVC. Venous tumors may be seen as intraluminal echogenic nodules or thrombi and can cause generalized IVC dilation and innumerable diffuse low-amplitude echoes coming from the lumen. It may even extend to the renal artery. Wilm's tumor in children is similar to renal cell carcinoma.

Causes of IVC Displacement

- mass in posterior, caudate, or right hepatic lobe
- right renal artery aneurysm
- lymphadenopathy
- tortuous aorta
- right renal masses
- right adrenal masses; eg, pheochromocytoma
- retroperitoneal liposarcoma
- leiomyosarcoma
- osteosarcoma
- rhabdomyosarcoma

} retroperitonal tumors

Hepatic Veins. There are three hepatic veins, right, middle, and left, which drain into the inferior vena cava.

Renal Veins. There are two renal veins, the right renal vein and the left renal vein. The left renal vein runs anterior to the aorta but posterior to the SMA.

Portal System

Portal Vein. The portal vein is formed by the confluence of the superior mesenteric vein and the splenic vein in the region of the neck of the pancreas.

Splenic Vein. The splenic vein runs posterior to the pancreatic body and tail.

Superior Mesenteric Vein. The superior mesenteric vein lies posterior to the body of the pancreas but anterior to the uncinate process.

THYROID

The thyroid has two lobes connected anteriorly by a narrow band of tissue referred to as the isthmus.

The common carotid artery and the internal jugular vein lie posterior and lateral, defining the posterolateral margins of the thyroid. The "strap muscles" lie anterior to the lateral aspect of the pancreas defining the anterolateral margins of the pancreas.

Sonographically, the thyroid has a homogeneous echogenicity that is greater than the strap muscles.

Size

LOBES	ISTHMUS
Length: 4–6 cm	Length: 2 cm
Width: 1.5–2 cm	Width: 2 cm
Height: 2–3 cm	Height: 2–6 mm

Table 5–20 outlines pathologies of the thyroid that can be seen sonographically.

SCROTUM

The scrotum is a sac that is divided by a septum, the median raphe. Each space contains a testis, an epididymis, a portion of spermatic cord, and the ductus deferens (Fig. 5–6). The innermost wall of the scrotum is lined by a thin, double layer of peritoneum, the tunica vaginalis. This double layer of peritoneum normally contains a small amount of fluid.

The testicles are ovoid glands that measure about 4–5 cm in length. A dense white fibrous capsule, called the tunica albiguina, encases each testicle and then enters the gland, separating the testes into approximately 200 cone-shaped lobules. Within these lobules, two primary functions occur: spermatogenesis (the production of spermatozoa) and the secretion of testosterone by the interstitial cells (Leydig cells).

The secretions are carried through the lobules to the rete testis. A series of ducts, called efferent ductules, drain the rete testis, piercing the tunica albuginea and entering the head of the epididymis.

The epididymis consists of a single tightly coiled duct

TABLE 5–20. THYROID PATHOLOGY

Pathology Observable by Sonography	Sonographic Characteristics
Adenomas (benign). Most common nodule occurring in the thyroid. May be singular or multiple	Measures 5–30 mm. Varied sonographic appearance ranging from very echogenic to a solid homogeneous mass with few internal echoes, resembling a cyst. Most frequently it will present as a solid mass, often having an anechoic halo created by blood and edematous tissue compressing the surrounding parenchyma
Simple cyst. Usually developmental, such as thyroglosal duct and brachial cleft	No internal echoes, smooth walls, good sound transmission
Hemorrhagic cysts	Well-defined cysts, mass with irregular borders, and multiple septations
Acute thyroiditis	Diffuse enlargement and decreased echogenicity of lobes. One lobe, usually the right one, might be larger
Subacute thyroiditis	Diffuse enlargement with decreased echogenicity
Hashimoto's thyroiditis	Diffusely abnormal pattern, multiple small, low-level echoes with a decrease in the overall echogenicity of the gland
Goiter	Gland usually enlarged in its initial stages and may have normal echo pattern. In later stages, may have multiple discrete nodules (50%), diffusely nodular in homogeneous gland with no normal tissue (50%), nodules may display cystic degeneration and calcification
Graves' disease	Diffusely enlarged lobes and isthmus, homogeneous echo pattern as in normal gland or heterogeneous echo pattern. Only one lobe might be enlarged
Carcinoma—80% are papillary	May be as small as 2 mm or as large as 10 cm. Masses are usually singular and hypoechoic. Cystic degeneration and specks of calcification may be present

that drapes the posterior aspect of the testis. The most superior aspect of the epididymis is the head, followed by the body and tail. This duct continues as the ductus deferens (vas deferens), leaving the pelvis via the inguinal canal with the testicular artery, the draining veins of the scrotum, nerves, and lymphatics, to form the spermatic cord. Each spermatic cord now extends over the top and

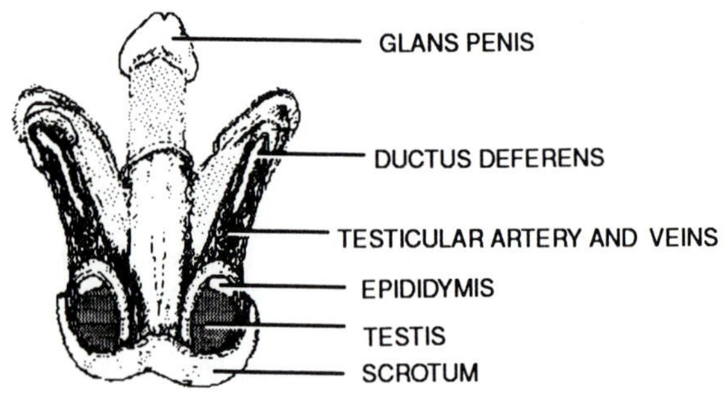

Figure 5–6. The male reproductive system.

down the posterior surface of the bladder, coming together to join with the duct from the seminal vesicle to form the ejaculatory ducts. The ejaculatory ducts pass through the prostate gland to terminate in the urethra.

Normal Sonographic Anatomy of the Scrotum

The normal testicle exhibits a homogeneous echo pattern of medium-level echogenicity. Posteriorly and superiorly capping the testis, the epididymial head is clearly distinguished owing to its coarser, more echogenic pattern. The body of the epididymis is harder to differentiate because of its posterior position and the tail is rarely seen. A brightly echogenic band, representing the mediastinum testis, is occasionally seen in the superior aspect.

On a transverse scan of the right side, the mediastinum testis is seen in the 9 o'clock position; on the left side, it is seen in the 3 o'clock position. Between the layer of the tunica vaginalis, a small amount of fluid is normally found.

The testicular artery and veins of the pampiniform plexus, which run along the posterior aspect of the testicle in the region of the epididymis, are not normally seen.

Scanning the testis transversely, comparing each testis and epididymis as to size and echogenicity, is the best guide for detecting lesions or enlargement.

Table 5–21 outlines scrotal pathology and associated sonographic and clinical findings.

DIAPHRAGM

The diaphragm is a dome-shaped muscle separating the thorax from the abdominal cavity. The diaphragm covers the superior border of the liver (and spleen) and sonographically can be identified as a curvilinear interface between the lungs and liver (spleen).

The *subphrenic space* is between the liver (or spleen) and the diaphragm and is a common site for abscess formation.

Crura of the Diaphragm

The diaphragmatic crura are right and left fibromuscular bundles that attach to the lumbar vertebra L3 on the right and L1 on the left and act as anchors to the diaphragm.

TABLE 5–21. SCROTAL PATHOLOGY

	Sonographic Anatomy	Clinical Pathology
Epididymis		
Acute epididymitis	The epididymis is enlarged and more hypoechoic	Specific epididymitis stemming from gonorrhea, syphilis, mumps, and/or tuberculosis
Chronic epididymitis	The epididymis is thickened, very echogenic, and may contain calcification	Nonspecific epididymitis is usually the result of a urinary tract infection Traumatic epididymitis due to strenuous exercise
Spermatocele	A cystic structure found superior to the testis, may be loculated and contain low-level echoes	A cystic mass of the epididymis containing spermatozoa
Testis		
Orchitis	The testis is enlarged and is less echogenic than the normal testis. An abscess of the testis appears as a localized area of inhomogeneity	Inflammation of a testis due to trauma, metastasis, mumps, or infection elsewhere in the body
Seminoma	Is usually hypoechoic compared to the rest of the testis but well circumscribed	Most common malignant tumor of patients between 30 and 40 years of age. Patients have elevated follicle-stimulating hormone levels
Teratoma	Areas of hemorrhage and necrosis are seen within this poorly circumscribed tumor	This tumor runs the spectrum from complete simple growth (benign) to the most malignant
Testicular torsion	An enlarged testicle is seen due to the edema. May have areas of infarcts and necrosis	Usually occurs in prepubertal boys. There is torsion of the spermatic cord, which causes strangulation of the blood supply to the testis, which in turn causes edema
Intratesticular hemorrhage	Appears as echogenic areas	
Pampiniform Plexus		
Varicocele	Numerous anechoic tortuous structures lying posterior to the testis and extending superiorly past the epididymis. May enlarge when patient is scanned in the upright position	Enlargement of the veins of the spermatic cord, commonly occurring on the left side
Scrotum		
Hydrocele	An accumulation of serous fluid between the parietal and visceral layers of the tunica vaginalis of the scrotum. Usually the result of inflammation of the epididymis or testis	The testis and the epididymis are surrounded by fluid
Inguinal hernia	Peristalsis of the mass will be visualized sonographically Echogenic foci that represent air within the loops of bowel will be noted	Herniation of the abdominal contents into the scrotal sac

The crura can be visualized anterior to the aorta above the level of the celiac artery. Below the celiac artery, the crura extend along the lateral aspects of the vertebral columns.

Sonography of Right Crus

Longitudinal Scans. The entire right crus can be seen as a solid hypoechoic longitudinally oriented structure immediately *posterior* and *parallel* to the inferior vena cava. It should not be confused with the right renal artery, which will appear as a circular structure crossing anterior to the crus and posterior to the IVC.

The right crus is also noted as a hypoechoic longitudinal structure *anterior and parallel to the aorta,* ending cephalically near the esophagogastric (EG) junction. This represents the anterior decussation of the crus.

Transverse Scans. The right crus is seen posterior to the IVC, extending between the IVC and aorta, until it reaches anterior to the aorta. The right adrenal and right kidney are posterolateral to the right crus.

Sonography of Left Crus

Longitudinal Scan. The left crus cannot be visualized longitudinally.

Transverse Scans. The left crus can be seen as a hypoechoic structure running anterior and lateral to the aorta.

It is closely associated with the left adrenal, splenic vasculature, and esophagogastric junction.

FLUID COLLECTIONS

Ascites

Ascites is an abnormal collection of serous fluid in the peritoneum. It may be:

- transudative—anechoic/freely mobile usually benign, free-floating bowel in the abdomen
- exudative—internal echos/loculated—associated with infection and malignancy
- bowel matted or fixed to posterior abdominal wall—associated with malignancy
- nonmobile fluid associated with coagulated hematoma (trauma)

Pathology Associated with Ascites

- Congestive heart failure
- Infection (inflammatory process)
- Kidney failure
- Liver failure/disease—end-stage fatty liver, cirrhosis
- Malignancy
- Ruptured aneurysm
- Pyogenic peritonitis
- Tuberculosis
- Portal venous system obstruction
- Obstruction of lymph nodes/vessels
- Acute cholecystitis
- Ectopic gestation
- Postoperative

Clinical Presentation. The clinical presentation of ascites is that of an enlarged abdomen.

Sonographic Findings. Accumulations occur (supine position) in the following order:

1. inferior tip—right lobe liver
2. superior portion—right flank
3. pelvic cul-de-sac
4. right paracolic gutter—lateral and anterior to liver
5. Morison's pouch

- ascites is found inferior to the diaphragm
- gross (massive) ascites—extrahepatic portion of falciform ligament seen attaching liver to anterior abdominal wall
- ascites may cause upward displacement of liver
- may cause gallbladder wall to appear thickened
- liver may appear more echogenic
- may see patent umbilical vein
- changing patient's position to observe fluid movement may be useful
- disproportional accumulations in lesser sac suggestive of adjacent organ pathology (ie, acute pancreatitis, pancreatic CA)

Abscess

An abscess is a circumscribed collection of pus (acute/chronic). A cavity formed by liquefactive necrosis within solid tissue.

Pathology Associated with Abscesses

- Penetrating trauma (wounds)
- Postsurgical procedures
- Retained products of conception
- Pelvic inflammatory disease (PID)
- Chronic bladder disease
- Sepsis—blood-borne bacterial infection
- Long-standing hematoma
- Postcholecystectomy—site of GB
- GI tract—peptic ulcer perforation; bowel spill during surgery (peritonitis)
- Urinary tract infection (UTI)
- Infected ascites with septa/debris
- Amebic abscess—may be densely echogenic

Clinical Presentation. Pain, spiking fever, chills, elevated white blood cell count, solitary or multiple sites, tenderness.

Hepatic Abscess

Intrahepatic. Abscess associated with sepsis; penetrating trauma to liver.

- location: within liver parenchyma
- differential diagnosis: solid tumor, usually round lesion with scattered internal echoes, variable through transmission

Subhepatic. Abscess associated with cholecystectomy.

- location: inferior to liver; fluid collection anterior to right kidney (Morrison's pouch); bed of GB (postcholecystectomy)

Subphrenic. Abscess associated with bacterial spill into peritoneum during surgical procedure; bowel rupture; peptic ulcer perforation; trauma.

- location: fluid collection above liver, inferior to diaphragm; transmission variable; gas (dirty shadowing)

General Sonographic Findings. A variable, complex, solid, cystic lesion with septa, debris, and scattered echoes; through transmission may be good; mass/cyst with shaggy/thick irregular walls; mass displacing surrounding structures; complex mass with dirty gas shadowing from within. *Presence of gas within a mass demonstrates an abscess.*

General Differential Diagnosis. Necrosing tumor with fluid center (these usually have thicker walls and *no gas*).

Ascites Versus Abscess

A localized area of ascites may be mistaken for an abscess. Place the patient in the erect or Trendelenburg position; ascites will shift but an abscess will not.

Pleural Effusion

Pleural effusions are a nonspecific reaction to an underlying pulmonary or systemic disease such as cirrhosis. Obtaining fluid for analysis may allow a more specific diagnosis.

Sonographic appearance shows a pleural effusion to be a usually echo-free, wedge-shaped area that lies posteromedial to the liver and posterior to the diaphragm. Occasionally, pleural effusions contain internal echoes, sometimes indicating the presence of a neoplasm. These echoes may be due to blood or pus (empyema), especially when the collection is loculated. Loculated effusions do not necessarily lie adjacent to the diaphragm and may be loculated anywhere on the chest wall. Sometimes effusions lie between the lung and the diaphragm and are known as subpulmonic. Right-sided pleural effusions can be easily assessed on a view looking through the diaphragm and the liver. Effusions on the left are more difficult to see in the supine position but sometimes can be seen with an oblique scan through the spleen.

RETROPERITONEUM

The retroperitoneum is the area between the posterior portion of the parietal peritoneum and the posterior abdominal wall, extending from the diaphragm to the pelvis.

Divisions

The retroperitoneum is divided into three areas by the renal fascia (Gerota's fascia): Fig. 5–7 demonstrates the division of the retroperitoneum into anterior pararenal and posterior pararenal spaces.[43]

1. The anterior pararenal space contains the retroperitoneal portion of the intestines and the pancreas

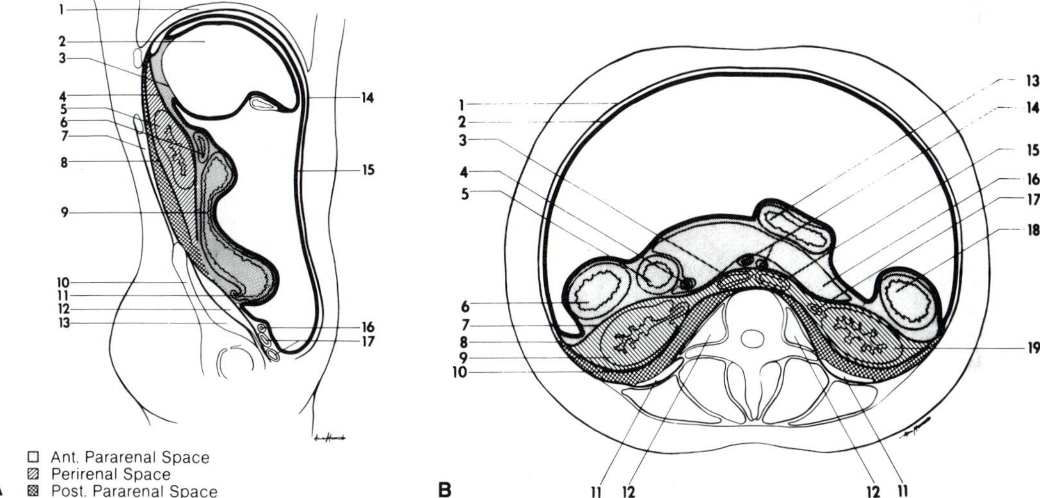

Figure 5–7. (**A**) Anatomy of the retroperitoneal compartments. Diagram of a right parasagittal view demonstrates the lumbar and iliac fossae. The lumbar fossa extends from the diaphragm (1) to the ilium (10). The anterior pararenal space is limited anteriorly by the peritoneum (15) and posteriorly by the anterior renal fascia (4). The perirenal space is contained between the anterior (4) and posterior (8) renal fascia. The posterior pararenal space lies between the posterior renal fascia (8) and the transversalis fascia (14) that continues about the entire abdomen. The retrofascial muscles (quadratus lumborum [7], psoas [12], and iliacus [13]) also are demonstrated. Note that the lumbar compartments are open inferiorly and merge as they enter the iliac fossa. 2 = liver, 3 = bare area of liver, 5 = kidney, 6 = duodenum, 9 = ascending colon, 11 = retrocecal appendix, 16 = ureter, 17 = iliac vessels. (**B**) Lumbar fossa of the retroperitoneum. Transverse sectional diagram viewed from below shows the relations between the retroperitoneal compartments on either side. The anterior pararenal space, bounded by the peritoneum (2) and anterior renal fascia (7), is continuous across the midline. The common bile duct (4), retroperitoneal portions of the duodenum (5, 13), ascending (6) and descending (18) colon, superior mesenteric vessels (14), and pancreas (16) are included in this space. The bilateral perirenal spaces are effectively separated from one another by the connective tissue sheaths surrounding the inferior vena cava (3) and aorta (15). The lateroconal fascia (8) is formed by the lateral fusion of the anterior (7) and posterior (10) renal fasciae. The transversalis fascia (1) lies behind the posterior pararenal space, forming the anterior boundary of the retrofascial spaces that include the quadratus lumborum (11) and psoas (12) muscles at this level. 9 = right kidney, 17 = right ureter, 19 = left kidney. *(Reprinted with permission from Koenigsberg M. Sonographic evaluation of the retroperitoneum. Semin Ultrasound 3:2, 1982.)*

2. The perirenal space contains the kidneys, ureters, adrenal glands, aorta, IVC, and retroperitoneal nodes
3. The posterior pararenal space contains the posterior abdominal wall, iliopsoas muscle, and quadratus lumborum muscle

Pathology
The retroperitoneal area is subject to infection, bleeding, inflammation, and tumors.

Anterior Pararenal Space. Pancreatic pathology, carcinoma of the duodenum, ascending and descending colon causing bowel thickening or infiltration resulting in a "bullseye" or inverted "bagel sign."

Perirenal Space. Kidney diseases, adrenal diseases, invasion or displacement of IVC, aortic aneurysms, ureteral abnormalities, sarcoma, liposarcoma, aortic, and retroperitoneal adenopathy.

Posterior Pararenal Space. Renal transplantation is usually performed in this extraperitoneal space within the iliac fossa, using the iliac vessels for anastomosis.

Primary Retroperitoneal Tumors
Primary retroperitoneal tumors are mostly malignant, rapidly growing, and the larger tumors are more likely to show evidence of necrosis and hemorrhage. Concurrence of mass with ascites indicates invasion of peritoneal surfaces.

Liposarcoma. Originates from fat. Liposarcoma has a complex echogenic pattern with thick walls.

Fibrosarcoma. Originates from connective tissue. Fibrosarcoma has a complex mostly sonolucent pattern, invading surrounding tissues.

Rhabdomyosarcoma. Originates from muscle. It occurs as a solid, complex or homogeneous echogenic mass, invading surrounding tissues.

Leiomyosarcoma. Originates from smooth muscle. It occurs as a complex echodense mass that may have areas of necrosis and cystic degeneration.

Teratoma. Originates from all three germ layers. Most teratomas occur in the vicinity of the upper pole of the left kidney. Ninety percent are benign. They are heterogeneously mixed echodense and cystic areas. Fifty percent occur in children.

Neurogenic Tumors. Originates from nerve tissue and occur mostly in the paravertebral region. They are heterogeneous and echodense.

Secondary Retroperitoneal Tumors
Secondary retroperitoneal tumors are primary recurrences from previously resected tumors or recurrent masses from previous renal carcinoma.

Ascitic fluid along with a retroperitoneal tumor usually indicates seeding or invasion of the peritoneal surface. Evaluation of the para-aortic region should be made for extension to the lymph nodes. The liver should also be evaluated for metastatic involvement.

Retroperitoneal Fibrosis
Retroperitoneal fibrosis is the formation of thick sheets of connective tissue extending from the perirenal space to the dome of the bladder. It encases, rather than displaces, the great vessels, ureters, and lymph channels, causing obstruction. Severe uropathy may ensue. The etiology of retroperitoneal fibrosis is usually idiopathic, but it may sometimes be associated with aortic aneurysm, the use of methysergide for vascular headaches, or retroperitoneal neoplasm.

Clinical Findings. The clinical findings in retroperitoneal fibrosis include hydronephrosis, hypertension, anuria, fever, leukocytosis, anemia, nausea and vomiting, weight loss, malaise, palpable abdominal or rectal mass, and abdominal, back, or flank pain. It is more frequent in males than females and is most common at ages 50 through the 60s.

Sonographic Findings. Retroperitoneal fibrosis appears as thick masses anterior and lateral to the aorta and IVC, extending from the renal vessels to the sacral promontory. The anechoic to hypoechoic sheets have smooth, well-defined anterior margins and irregular, poorly defined posterior margins. The differential diagnosis includes lymphoma, nodal metastases, and retroperitoneal sarcoma or hematoma.

Retroperitoneal Fluid Collections
Collections of fluids in the retroperitoneum include abscesses, hematomas, urinomas, lymphoceles, and cysts.

LYMPHATIC SYSTEM

The lymphatic system arises from veins in the developing embryo and is closely associated with veins throughout most parts of the body. Lymphatic vessels assist veins in their function by draining many of the body tissues and thus increasing the amount of fluid returning to the heart. The lymph vascular network does not form a closed-loop system like the blood vascular system. Lymph vessels begin as tiny, colorless, unconnected capillaries in the connective tissues. These merge to form progressively larger vessels that are interrupted at various sites by small filtering stations called lymph nodes. Lymph vessels ultimately drain into two principal lymph vessels: thoracic and right lymph ducts. These ducts, which have the appearance of small veins, pour about 2 L of lymph into the

brachiocephalic veins every 24 hours. The lymph vascular system has no pump of its own to push the lymph forward as the heart does blood. Therefore, lymph flow largely depends upon the kneading action of neighboring skeletal muscles alternately contracting and relaxing.

This lymphatic network has tremendous clinical significance. Interruption of lymph drainage in an area generally creates considerable swelling (edema) owing to the accumulation of fluids. In addition, the lymph vessels offer a variety of routes for cancer cells to move from one site to another (metastasis).

Lymph Nodes

Lymph nodes contain lymphocytes and reticulum cells, their function being one of filtration and production of lymphocytes and antibodies. All the lymph passes through nodes, which act as filters not only for bacteria but also for cancer cells. Enlargement of lymph nodes is a usual sign of an ongoing bacterial or carcinogenic process. Normal lymph nodes measure less than 1 cm in size. Sonographically, we can evaluate lymph nodes in the pelvis, retroperitoneum, portahepatis, perirenal, and prevertebral vasculature.

Function. The lymph nodes function in (1) the formation of lymphocytes, (2) the production of antibodies, and (3) the filtration of lymph.

Sonographic Appearance. In order to visualize lymph nodes they must be at least 2 cm in size. They are very homogeneous. Lymph nodes are typically hypoechoic but there is no through transmission. Lymphomas have a nonspecific appearance but in general:

- adenopathy secondary to lymphoma are usually sonolucent
- adenopathy secondary to metastatic disease is usually complex
- posttherapy enlarged nodes are usually very echogenic but may develop cystic areas secondary to necrosis

Periaortic nodes have specific characteristics: They may drape the great vessels anteriorly (obscuring sharp anterior vascular border); may have a lobular, smooth, or scalloped appearance; and with mesenteric involvement, they may fill most of the abdomen in an irregular complex pattern.

Sonographic Technique. Concentrate on prevertebral vessels, aorta, IVC; portahepatis (can produce *biliary* obstruction); spleen size; iliopsoas muscles; urinary bladder contour; perirenal; retroperitoneum; and pelvis.

Para-aortic lymph nodes are involved with lymphoma in 25% of cases and 40% with Hodgkin's disease. The sonographic appearance of these lymphomatous nodes varies from hypoechoic to anechoic with good thorough transmission. Occasionally, anechoic nodal masses may resemble cystic structures. Nodal enlargement secondary to other neoplasms or inflammatory processes, such as retroperitoneal fibrosis, may be indistinguishable from lymphomatous lymphadenopathy. Para-aortic or paracaval nodes frequently obscure the sharp anterior vascular border or compress the aorta or inferior vena cava. Decubitus viewing of the aorta and IVC facilitates sonographic imaging of the retroperitoneal area down to the aortic bifurcation.

Tumors of Lymphoid Tissue

Lymphomas (Tumors of Lymphoid Tissue). *Hodgkin's disease* (40%) is a malignant condition characterized by generalized lymphoid tissue enlargement (eg, enlarged lymph nodes and spleen). Twice as many males as females are affected. It usually occurs between the ages of 15 and 34 or after age 50. Histopathologic classification: Reed Sternberg cells and multinucleated cells are present.

Non-Hodgkin's (60%) *disease* is further subdivided into nodular and diffuse histopathologies. It is a heterogeneous group of diseases that consist of neoplastic proliferation of lymphoid cells that usually disseminate throughout the body. It occurs in all age groups with the incidence increasing with age.

Mesenteric nodal involvement is less than 4% in patients with Hodgkin's disease but more than 50% in non-Hodgkin's patients. Lymphomatous cellular infiltration of the greater omentum may be seen as a uniformly thick, hypoechoic band-shaped structure. The appearance of mesenteric nodes can resemble that of retroperitoneal nodes. Mesenteric masses may also appear as multiple cystic or separated masses that may resemble fluid-filled bowel loops. Perihepatic nodes, celiac axis nodes, splenic-hilar, and renal-hilar nodes may also be demonstrated sonographically. Although most are hypoechoic to anechoic, inhomogenous areas of increased echogenicity can be found in areas of focal necrosis within large nodes. Nodes can encase or invade adjacent organs and produce significant organ displacement, whereas portal nodes can produce biliary obstruction.

Extranodal Lymphoma. The liver, kidneys, GI tract, pancreas, and thyroid may show lymphomatous involvement.

Hepatic Lymphoma. Hepatic lymphomatous involvement presents as multiple hypoechoic or anechoic focal parenchymal defects. Although these anechoic lesions may resemble cystic structures, they rarely demonstrate enhanced posterior acoustic transmission or peripheral refractory shadowing. Hepatic abscesses, metastases from sarcomas or melanomas, focal areas of cholangitis, radiation fibrosis, and extensive hemosiderosis have presented with findings sonographically indistinguishable from hepatic lymphoma.

Renal Lymphoma. Less than 3% of all non-Hodgkin's lymphomas present with renal involvement, mainly Burkitt's lymphoma or diffuse histiocytic lymphomas.

Gastrointestinal Lymphoma. Fifteen percent of non-Hodgkin's lymphomas may present with gastrointestinal involvement. Sonographic features include a relatively hypoechoic mass with central sonodensity. Such findings are not specific for lymphomatous involvement, as gastric carcinoma or gastric wall edema may have a similar appearance.

Pancreatic Lymphoma. Ten percent of non-Hodgkin's patients present with pancreatic involvement—portions of tissue represented by focal hypoechoic or anechoic masses.

Thyroid Lymphoma. Lymphomatous thyroid masses also present in the same manner.

Inflammatory Conditions

There are three inflammatory conditions of the lymphatic system: acute and chronic lymphadentitis and infectious mononucleosis.

Common primary tumors with metastases to lymph are those of the breast, lung, melanoma, prostate, cervix, and uterus.

Sonographic Pitfalls

1. enlarged nodes can mimic an aortic aneurysm at lower gain settings on longitudinal scans; always scan in transverse to differentiate
2. aneurysms enlarge fairly symmetrically, whereas enlarged nodes tend to drape over prevertebral vessels
3. bowel can mimic enlarged nodes so check for peristalsis; nodes are reproducible, bowel is *not*

RETROPERITONEAL VERSUS INTRAPERITONEAL MASSES

The retroperitoneal location of a mass is confirmed when there is:

- anterior renal displacement
- anterior displacement of dilated ureters
- anterior displacement of the retroperitoneal fat pad—retroperitoneal lesions displace the fat pad ventrally and often cranially, whereas hepatic and subhepatic lesions produce inferior and posterior displacement. The vector of displacement may permit diagnosis of the anatomical origin of right upper quadrant masses.
- anterior vascular displacement—aorta, IVC, splenic vein, superior mesenteric vein

Questions

GENERAL INSTRUCTIONS: For each question, select the best answer. You are to select only one answer for each question unless otherwise instructed.

1. All of the following statements about the kidneys are true *except*

(A) the kidneys are intraperitoneal in location
(B) the average adult kidneys measure approximately 11–12 cm in length
(C) the kidneys may move with respiration
(D) the anteroposterior thickness of the normal adult kidneys are approximately 4–5 cm

2. The renal sinus echoes are produced by

(A) pelvis and calyces, renal vessels, fat, and areolar tissue
(B) perinephric fat
(C) renal parenchyma
(D) all of the above

3. The renal parenchyma is separated into cortex and medulla by the

(A) glomeruli
(B) renal fat
(C) arcuate vessels
(D) renal pelvis

4. The best approach for the evaluation of the left kidney is

(A) supine
(B) prone
(C) RAO
(D) coronal

5. All of the following statements about infantile hypertrophic pyloric stenosis are true *except*

(A) it causes projectile vomiting
(B) it is predominantly a disorder of male infants
(C) the hypertrophied pyloric muscle measures less than 3 mm
(D) it appears sonographically as a target-shaped lesion

6. To fulfill the criteria of a cyst, one must demonstrate sonographically

(A) an anechoic structure
(B) distal acoustic enhancement
(C) smooth walls
(D) all of the above

7. While performing an ultrasound examination, the sonographer finds that both kidneys measure 5 cm in length. They are very echogenic. One should consider the possibility of all of the following *except*

(A) chronic glomerulonephritis
(B) chronic pyelonephritis
(C) renal vascular disease
(D) renal vein thrombosis

8. Columns of Bertin may be confused with a pseudotumor. These may be found

(A) in the cortex surrounding and separating the renal pyramids and are unusually large
(B) in the major calyces as a rudimentary ureter
(C) in the minor calyces as a rudimentary calix
(D) outside the renal capsule

9. In the fasting patient, what is a common cause for sonographic nonvisualization of the gallbladder?

(A) contraction of the gallbladder due to chronic cholecystitis
(B) biliary sludge
(C) mobile stone
(D) the ingestion of oral contrast medium used in x-rays of the gallbladder prior to sonographic examination

10. In cases of renal trauma, sonography may be helpful in identifying a hematoma within the renal parenchyma. A hematoma typically presents as

(A) a sonolucent mass
(B) an echogenic mass
(C) a semicystic, semisolid mass
(D) all of the above

11. Extravasation of urine into the perinephric space (urinoma) may be found in cases of

(A) renal injuries
(B) renal transplants
(C) patients who have passed a renal stone
(D) all of the above

12. Hydronephrosis may be best demonstrated sonographically by which of the following patterns?

(A) distorted shape of the kidney outline
(B) multiple cystic masses throughout the renal parenchyma
(C) fluid-filled pelvocaliceal collecting system
(D) hyperechoic pelvocaliceal collecting system

13. Hydronephrosis may be caused by

(A) prostatic enlargement
(B) calculi
(C) congenital and/or inflammatory stricture
(D) pregnancy
(E) tumors
(F) all of the above

14. A 3-year-old boy presents with hematuria and a palpable left flank mass. Sonography depicts a solid renal mass. This finding would *most* likely represent

(A) hypernephroma
(B) Wilms' tumor
(C) neuroblastoma
(D) infantile polycystic kidney disease

15. A patient presents with right upper quadrant pain, fever, and elevated white blood cell count. The gallbladder appears enlarged with echogenic debris. This *most* probably represents

(A) porcelain gallbladder
(B) hydropic gallbladder
(C) empyema of the gallbladder
(D) carcinoma of the gallbladder

16. Acute cholecystitis is associated with

(A) right upper quadrant pain
(B) Murphy's sign
(C) stone impacted within the cystic duct
(D) fever and an elevated white blood cell count
(E) all of the above

17. A patient presents with ampulla of Vater obstruction, distension of the gallbladder, and painless jaundice. This is associated with

(A) hydrops of the gallbladder
(B) choledochal cyst
(C) Courvoisier's sign
(D) Hartmann's pouch

18. Gallbladder wall thickening may be due to

(A) ascites
(B) hypoproteinema
(C) right-sided congestive cardiac failure
(D) hepatitis
(E) acute cholecystitis
(F) chronic cholecystitis
(G) all of the above

19. Long-standing cystic duct obstruction will give rise to

(A) porcelain gallbladder
(B) hydropic gallbladder
(C) septated gallbladder
(D) gallbladder kink

20. The upper limits of the normal intraluminal diameter of the common duct should not exceed

(A) 4 mm
(B) 7 cm
(C) 7 mm
(D) 10 mm

21. In the normal adult, with gallbladder in place, the luminal diameter of the proximal common hepatic duct is less than or equal to

(A) 3–4 mm
(B) 5–6 mm
(C) 7–8 mm

22. Within the renal sinus, the following can be found *except*

(A) renal pyramids
(B) minor calyces
(C) major calyces
(D) the renal pelvis
(E) vessels
(F) lymphatics

23. The renal cortex contains one of the following

(A) Bowman's capsule and convoluted tubules
(B) renal pyramids
(C) major calyces
(D) minor calyces
(E) all of the above

24. Elevation of the following laboratory data may indicate renal failure *except* for

(A) blood urea nitrogen (BUN)
(B) alkaline phosphatase
(C) creatinine
(D) protein

25. A congenital abnormality in which both kidneys are united at their lower poles is termed a

(A) column of Bertin
(B) dromedary hump
(C) horseshoe kidney

26. Adult polycystic disease may be characterized by all of the following *except*

(A) it is a latent disease until the third or fourth decade
(B) it is an autosomal dominant disease
(C) it may have associated cysts in the liver, pancreas, and spleen
(D) the involved kidneys are small and extremely echogenic

27. Staghorn calculus refers to a large stone within the

(A) pancreas
(B) urinary bladder
(C) pelvis of the kidney
(D) common bile duct

28. Thickening of the gallbladder wall is a common feature in

(A) hypoalbuminemia
(B) cholecystitis—acute or chronic
(C) adenomyomatosis
(D) carcinoma of the gallbladder
(E) all of the above

29. Hypernephroma (renal adenocarcinoma) is characterized by

(A) the most common renal cell tumor representing three quarters of all adult renal malignancies
(B) irregular in shape but well-marginated solid mass
(C) tumor growth so large that it replaces the renal volume
(D) all of the above

30. Horseshoe kidneys may be confused sonographically with which of the following entities?

(A) carcinoma of the head of the pancreas
(B) lymphadenopathy
(C) hypernephroma

31. The pancreatic head lies

(A) caudad to the portal vein and medial to the superior mesenteric vein
(B) cephalad to the portal vein and medial to the superior mesenteric vein
(C) caudad to the portal vein and anterior to the inferior vena cava
(D) cephalad to the portal vein and anterior to the inferior vena cava

32. The liver is covered by a thick membrane of collagenous fibers intermixed with elastic elements. This membrane is called

(A) Glisson's capsule
(B) Gerota's fascia
(C) Bowman's capsule

33. The splenic vein is identified as

(A) anterior to the aorta
(B) anterior to the superior mesenteric artery
(C) caudad to the celiac axis
(D) all of the above

34. The proximal aorta is more posteriorly placed than the distal aorta with

(A) a gradual increase in size as it proceeds distally in the abdomen
(B) a generally horizontal course
(C) it decreases in size as it proceeds distally in the abdomen

35. Hepatic veins can be differentiated from portal veins because

(A) hepatic veins are not surrounded by bright acoustical reflections
(B) hepatic veins increase in caliber as the vessel approaches the diaphragm
(C) the angle formed by the branching of hepatic venous radicles will point superiorly to superomedially
(D) hepatic veins drain dorsomedially toward the inferior vena cava
(E) all of the above

36. The celiac trunk originates within the first 2 cm from the diaphragm and immediately branches into all of the following *except*

(A) common hepatic artery
(B) left gastric artery
(C) gastroduodenal artery
(D) splenic artery

37. The superior mesenteric artery arises 1 cm below the celiac trunk and runs

(A) anterior to the pancreas and posterior to the uncinate process
(B) cephalad to the pancreas and caudal to the uncinate process
(C) posterior to the pancreas and anterior to the uncinate process

38. The division into anatomic left and right lobes of the liver is along the line of attachment of the

(A) major hepatic fissure and middle hepatic vein
(B) ligamentum venosum

(C) falciform ligament
(D) middle hepatic duct

39. Which of the following is *not* true about pleural fluid?

(A) it can be anechoic
(B) it can be loculated
(C) it can be seen superior to the diaphragm
(D) it can be seen inferior to the diaphragm

40. In acute renal disease, the kidney size is

(A) generally enlarged
(B) generally small
(C) not affected

41. When the gallbladder fundus is folded over on itself, this is referred to as a

(A) junctional fold
(B) Hartmann's pouch
(C) phrygian cap

42. On a transverse sonogram, the common bile duct is located ______ to the head of the pancreas and lies ______ to the inferior vena cava

(A) anterior; medial
(B) posterior; posterior
(C) posterior; anterior

43. Which of the following statements regarding the spleen are *false?*

(A) a prominent bulge along the medial surface of the spleen can be seen in normal patients
(B) the normal-sized spleen should not extend caudal to the midportion of the left kidney
(C) the spleen is a retroperitoneal organ
(D) the sonographic texture of the normal spleen is homogeneous

44. Which statement about the kidneys is *false?*

(A) the kidneys are rigidly fixed on the abdominal wall
(B) the kidneys consist of an internal medullary and external cortical substance
(C) the kidneys rest on the psoas and quadratus lumborum muscles
(D) renal pyramids are found within the medullary region

45. Gallbladder carcinoma has a strong association with

(A) calculi and chronic mechanical irritation
(B) polypoid mass
(C) jaundice with weight loss
(D) bile duct obstruction
(E) chronic cholecystitis
(F) porcelain gallbladder
(G) all of the above

46. The inferior vena cava forms at the confluence of the

(A) right and left carotid veins
(B) right and left lumbar veins
(C) right and left common iliac veins

47. All of the following describe the inferior vena cava *except*

(A) Valsalva maneuver results in a change in the diameter of the inferior vena cava
(B) it lies immediately anterior to the surface of the spine, to the right of the aorta
(C) the caliber of the inferior vena cava increases as it courses cephalad
(D) it passes through the caval hiatus of the diaphragm to enter the left atrium

48. To distinguish dilated bile ducts from portal veins, all of these criteria can be used *except*

(A) distal acoustic enhancement
(B) echogenic walls
(C) parallel channel sign
(D) stellate pattern of the ducts near the porta hepatis
(E) numerous tubular structures within the periphery of the liver

49. A congenital dilation of the biliary tree is called

(A) sclerosing cholangitis
(B) Courvoisier gallbladder
(C) choledochal cyst

50. A fluid-filled mass anterior to the pancreas may be all of the following *except*

(A) pseudocyst
(B) loculated ascites
(C) aortic aneurysm
(D) fluid-filled stomach

51. The left renal vein runs

(A) between the aorta and the superior mesenteric artery
(B) posterior to the aorta
(C) posterior to the inferior vena cava
(D) parallel to the portal vein

52. The superior mesenteric vein

(A) enters the inferior vena cava at the level of the renal vein
(B) runs upward to the right of the superior mesenteric artery
(C) runs medially to enter the posterior and lateral aspect of the inferior vena cava
(D) none of the above

53. Throughout its course, the splenic vein relates to the

(A) anterior surface of the pancreatic body and tail
(B) anterior surface of the uncinate process
(C) posterior surface of the pancreatic body and tail

54. If on sonographic examination, one finds a patient with intrahepatic dilated ducts and a small gallbladder, this may indicate that the level of obstruction is

(A) at the common bile duct
(B) above the cystic duct
(C) below the cystic duct

55. The normal thickness of the gallbladder wall is

(A) 15 mm
(B) 7 mm
(C) 10 mm
(D) 3 mm
(E) 5 mm

56. Adenomyomatosis of the gallbladder is

(A) a disease of childbearing years
(B) an inflammation of the gallbladder
(C) associated with Murphy's sign
(D) a benign proliferation and thickening of the muscle and glandular layer

57. Strong specular reflections arising from the liver are the result of

(A) liver parenchyma
(B) Glisson's capsule
(C) portal veins
(D) hepatic arteries

58. An increase in parenchymal echogenicity within the liver may be due to

(A) alcohol abuse
(B) diabetes
(C) chemotherapy
(D) toxic substances
(E) all of the above

59. Hydronephrosis frequently occurs in

(A) renal hypoplasia
(B) duplication of ureters in a duplicated kidney collecting system
(C) horseshoe kidney

60. A patient presents with a dilated interhepatic duct, dilated gallbladder, and a dilated common bile duct. The level of obstruction should be at the

(A) proximal common bile duct
(B) distal common bile duct
(C) common hepatic duct

61. Sonographically, the gastroesophageal junction can be visualized

(A) anterior to the inferior vena cava
(B) anterior to the aorta and posterior to the left lobe of the liver
(C) it cannot be recognized sonographically

62. In cases of acute viral hepatitis, the liver parenchyma appears

(A) hyperechoic
(B) echogenic
(C) normal

63. The gallbladder contracts in response to gastrointestinal peptide hormones, chiefly

(A) gastrin
(B) peptine
(C) lipase
(D) cholecystokinin
(E) alkaline phosphatase

64. Diffuse thickening of the gallbladder wall an be seen with all of the following *except*

(A) acute cholecystitis
(B) hepatitis
(C) congestive heart failure
(D) elevated portal pressure

65. The best sonographic window to the left hemidiaphragm is the

(A) spleen
(B) kidney
(C) stomach
(D) left lung

66. The most frequent benign tumor of the pancreas is

(A) adenoma
(B) islet cell tumor
(C) cystadenoma

67. The most common primary neoplasm of the pancreas is adenocarcinoma. This

(A) is usually found in the head of the pancreas
(B) is accompanied by weight loss and painless jaundice
(C) is accompanied by a dilated gallbladder
(D) causes enlargement of the gland with irregular nodular border
(E) causes enlargement of the common duct
(F) all of the above

68. The portion of the pancreas that lies posterior to the superior mesenteric artery and vein is the

(A) head
(B) uncinate process
(C) body
(D) tail

69. High levels of serum amylase may be a result of all of the following *except*

(A) liver disease
(B) acute pancreatitis
(C) blockage of the pancreatic duct by a stone within the common bile duct

70. The pancreas produces all of the following *except*

(A) insulin
(B) glucagon
(C) bile
(D) lipase

71. On the medial border of each kidney is the renal hilum that contains

(A) the renal vein
(B) the renal artery
(C) the proximal ureter
(D) all of the above

72. The kidneys, the perinephric fat, and the adrenal glands are all covered by

(A) a true capsule
(B) Gerota's fascia
(C) peritoneum
(D) Glisson's capsule

73. The normal adult kidneys measure

(A) 6–9 cm in length and 4–5 cm in thickness
(B) 12–15 cm in length and 4–5 cm in thickness
(C) 10–12 cm in length and 4–5 cm in thickness

74. If a heavy deposition of fat (sinus lipomatosis) is found within the kidney on renal sonography, the renal sinus will appear

(A) enlarged
(B) mostly echo free
(C) mostly echogenic
(D) all of the above

75. If one does renal sonogram and finds a solid mass, one should

(A) end the examination and document what was found
(B) continue the examination and look at the pancreas for metastasis
(C) continue the examination and check the inferior vena cava and renal vein for tumor extension as well as the retroperitoneum for nodes
(D) continue the examination and check the aorta for tumor extension

76. Chronic pancreatitis may be associated with which of the following sonographic patterns?

(A) usually hyperechoic, with echogenicity greater than the liver
(B) a generalized decrease in the size of the pancreas
(C) occasionally one may see bright discrete echoes of calcification with a dilated pancreatic duct
(D) all of the above

77. Which of the following does *not* describe the pancreas?

(A) it lies within the peritoneal space
(B) it is a retroperitoneal structure
(C) it is nonencapsulated
(D) it is a multilobulated gland
(E) it is approximately 15 cm in length

78. One of the most frequent complications of pancreatitis is pseudocyst formation. Uncomplicated pseudocysts are usually

(A) echogenic with irregular walls and good ultrasound transmission distally
(B) echogenic with smooth walls and poor ultrasound transmission distally
(C) anechoic with smooth walls and good ultrasound transmission distally

79. Occasionally, a pseudocyst may have internal echoes and be confused with an abscess. To distinguish the two, one should look for

(A) calcification
(B) fluid in the pouch of Douglas
(C) gas

80. A pancreatic pseudocyst

(A) must be treated surgically
(B) may regress spontaneously
(C) must be treated with a diet of liquid lipase

81. Pancreatic pseudocysts are usually found in the area of the lesser sac. On occasion, a pancreatic pseudocyst may be found in the

(A) groin
(B) mediastinum
(C) the porta hepatis area
(D) pelvis
(E) all of the above

82. The pancreas is both an exocrine and endocrine gland. The endocrine function is to produce

(A) insulin
(B) lipase
(C) amylase
(D) carboxypeptide
(E) trypsin
(F) chymotrypsin

83. The exocrine products of the pancreas are carried within the

(A) blood stream
(B) acinar cells
(C) pancreatic duct

84. The maximum inner diameter of the pancreatic duct in young adults is

(A) 5 mm
(B) 2 mm
(C) 3 mm
(D) 4 mm

85. It is very important to image the duct within the substance of the pancreas. Structures that may be confused with the duct are

(A) collapsed stomach wall anteriorly
(B) portal vein posteriorly
(C) splenic vein posteriorly
(D) all of the above

86. The most common primary carcinoma of the pancreas is

(A) leiomyosarcoma
(B) adenocarcinoma
(C) lymphoma
(D) all of the above

87. All of the following statements pertaining to adenocarcinoma of the pancreas are *true except* that it is

(A) imaged as a solid, focally enlarged lobulated mass with low-level echoes
(B) usually found in the head of the pancreas
(C) associated with biliary obstruction
(D) not associated with biliary obstruction
(E) associated with pancreatic duct obstruction

88. If a mass in the area of the pancreatic head is found, special attention should be directed to which of the following areas?

(A) the portal vein
(B) the liver (for "fatty" changes)
(C) the common bile duct
(D) the spleen
(E) the kidney

89. When a pancreatic mass is imaged, raising the possibility of carcinoma, what other findings may lead to a diagnosis of malignancy?

(A) liver masses
(B) lymphadenopathic masses
(C) venous obstruction
(D) ascites
(E) inferior vena cava compression
(F) all of the above

90. The most common sonographic appearance of acute pancreatitis is

(A) usually hyperechoic, with echogenicity greater than the liver and irregular in shape
(B) the pancreas is enlarged with smooth contours, uniformly hypoechoic, demonstrating a decrease in ultrasound absorption, and an increase in through transmission
(C) the pancreas is enlarged with smooth contours, uniformly hypoechoic, demonstrating an increase in ultrasound absorption and a decrease in through transmission

91. What structure may be mistaken for a mass in the head of the pancreas?

(A) duodenum
(B) portal vein
(C) Riedel's lobe
(D) quadrate lobe

92. The liver's exocrine function includes producing

(A) glycogen
(B) urea
(C) heparin
(D) bile

93. The accessory duct of the pancreas is termed

(A) Wirsung's duct
(B) Santorini's duct
(C) Müllerian duct

94. The uncinate process of the pancreas extends

(A) lateral to the inferior vena cava and posterior to the superior mesenteric artery
(B) medial to the inferior vena cava and anterior to the portal vein

(C) medial to the inferior vena cava and posterior to the superior mesenteric vein

95. The extrahepatic portion of the falciform ligament

(A) runs between the inferior vena cava and the gallbladder
(B) is seen with ascites
(C) connects the liver to a lesser sac

96. The portion of the liver that is not covered by the peritoneum is termed

(A) quadrate lobe
(B) caudate lobe
(C) Riedel's lobe
(D) bare area

97. The right and left hepatic ducts unite to form the common hepatic duct most commonly

(A) in the porta hepatis
(B) within the hepatic parenchyma
(C) at the level of the pancreas

98. A patient with known carcinoma of the breast reveals unequivocal signs of biliary tree dilatation. However, the gallbladder is small and the common bile duct is normal. The sonographic findings that could be found include which of the following?

(A) stone in the cystic duct
(B) stone in the right hepatic duct
(C) enlarged lymph nodes in the porta hepatis

99. The main pancreatic duct is

(A) Santorini's duct
(B) Wirsung's duct
(C) Hirschsprung's duct

100. The ligamentum venosum is all of the following *except*

(A) a remnant of the umbilical vein
(B) a remnant of the ductus venosus
(C) a remnant of the fetal circulation, in which shunted oxygenated blood from the umbilical vein to the inferior vena cava bypasses the liver
(D) defines caudate lobe from left lobe of liver

101. Sonography is helpful in the evaluation of the transplanted kidney. Anechoic masses that occur around a renal transplant include

(A) urinoma
(B) lymphocele
(C) hematoma
(D) abscess
(E) all of the above

102. All of the following are causes of hydronephrosis *except*

(A) posterior urethral valves
(B) acute glomerulonephritis
(C) cancer of the ovary
(D) retroperitoneal tumor
(E) retroperitoneal fibrosis

103. A retroperitoneal abscess may *not* be found within

(A) the rectus abdominus muscle
(B) the psoas muscle
(C) the iliacus muscle
(D) the quadratus lumborum muscle
(E) none of the above

104. Which of the following is *not* retroperitoneal?

(A) kidney
(B) aorta
(C) psoas muscle
(D) spleen

105. Renal vein thrombosis is characterized sonographically by

(A) an enlarged kidney with decreased cortical echogenicity
(B) a normal-sized kidney with an increase in echogenicity
(C) decreased renal size with loss of corticomedullary definition
(D) all of the above may signify acute or chronic conditions

106. Dilatation of the intrahepatic biliary tree without dilatation of the extrahepatic duct includes all of the following *except*

(A) Klatskin tumor
(B) enlarged portal lymph nodes
(C) cholangiocarcinoma
(D) pancreatic carcinoma

107. The gastroduodenal artery

(A) is the first branch of the common hepatic artery
(B) proceeds caudally along the right anterolateral margin of the pancreatic head
(C) is seen in the transverse views directly anterior to the common bile duct
(D) all of the above

108. The liver may be divided segmentally with the right lobe, left lobe, and caudate lobe. The right lobe may be divided further into anterior and posterior segments and the left lobe into medial and lateral segments. The quadrate lobe is part of the

(A) lateral segment of the left lobe
(B) lateral segment of the right lobe
(C) medial segment of the left lobe
(D) posterior segment of the left lobe

109. The caudate lobe occupies much of the

(A) anteroinferior surface of the liver
(B) posteroinferior surface of the liver
(C) anterosuperior surface of the liver
(D) posterosuperior surface of the liver

110. The lobes of the liver are clearly defined by the hepatic veins that course between them to form the boundaries of the various hepatic segments and lobes. The hepatic veins are

(A) right and left
(B) right, left, and middle
(C) right, left, middle, and lateral

111. Within the liver there are three ligaments of primary importance to ultrasound. They are ligamentum teres, ligamentum venosum, and falciform ligaments. The ligamentum teres

(A) resides in the left intersegmental fissure
(B) is a remnant of the umbilical vein
(C) recannalizes in severe cirrhosis of the ligament
(D) is an echogenic spot on transverse scans
(E) is always seen above the portal vein
(F) all of the above

112. A dilated common bile duct without the presence of dilated intrahepatic biliary radicles suggests all of the following *except*

(A) acute obstruction of the common bile duct
(B) may appear in the presence of chronic infiltrative liver disease
(C) ascending cholangitis may be present
(D) a mass in the head of the pancreas

113. Cystic lesions within the liver include

(A) congenital cysts
(B) polycystic liver disease
(C) Caroli's disease
(D) all of the above

114. Shadowing from the area of the gallbladder fossa can be a source of confusion and error in ruling out cholithiasis. Sources of shadowing include

(A) spiral valve of Heister
(B) calcification within the liver
(C) air in the biliary tree
(D) all of the above

115. Complex lesions within the liver include

(A) biliary cystadenoma
(B) echinococcal cyst
(C) large cavernous hemangioma
(D) hematoma
(E) all of the above

116. The most common cause of pancreatitis in adults in the United States is

(A) biliary tract disease
(B) alcohol abuse
(C) trauma

117. Impaired fat digestion is an important indicator of pancreatic dysfunction. This is due to the reduction of

(A) insulin
(B) lipase
(C) amylase
(D) carboxypeptide
(E) trypsin

118. Which of the following is *least* likely to be associated with acute pancreatitis?

(A) ileus
(B) jaundice
(C) the pancreas becomes edematous
(D) the pancreas becomes diffusely enlarged
(E) anterior compression of the inferior vena cava

119. Which of the following is *least* likely to be associated with chronic pancreatitis?

(A) jaundice
(B) the pancreas becomes edematous
(C) the pancreatic duct may dilate and contain calculi
(D) the pancreas becomes fibrotic
(E) pseudocyst formation

120. Several techniques for imaging the pancreas are

(A) prone scan
(B) ingestion of fluid
(C) positioning the patient erect or sitting up
(D) positioning the patient right side up
(E) all of the above

121. The tail of the pancreas extends to the left and has all of the following relationships *except*

(A) the lesser sac lies anterior
(B) the left adrenal gland is anterior
(C) it lies in close relationship to the splenic hilum
(D) it lies anterior to the left kidney

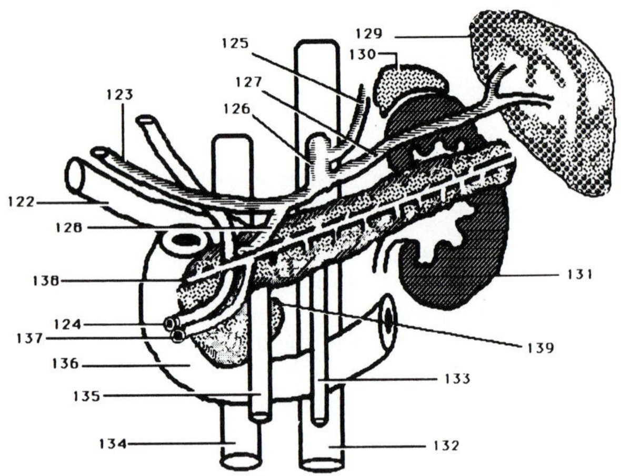

Figure 5–8. Diagram of the pancreas and other adjacent structures.

Questions 122 through 139: Identify the structures in Fig. 5–8 with the list of terms given in Column B.

COLUMN A	COLUMN B
122. ______	(A) spleen
123. ______	(B) gastroduodenal artery
124. ______	(C) kidney
125. ______	(D) inferior vena cava
126. ______	(E) splenic artery
127. ______	(F) left gastric artery
128. ______	(G) adrenal
129. ______	(H) superior mesenteric artery
130. ______	(I) superior mesenteric vein
131. ______	(J) celiac axis
132. ______	(K) common bile duct
133. ______	(L) portal vein
134. ______	(M) aorta
135. ______	(N) duodenum
136. ______	(O) Santorini's duct
137. ______	(P) Wirsung's duct
138. ______	(Q) uncinate process
139. ______	(R) hepatic artery

140. After cholecystectomy, the luminal diameter of proximal bile duct in normal individuals (ie, individuals with no current bile duct obstruction) is more than 5 mm in a significant (more than 10%) proportion of patients and may be up to 10 mm to be considered within normal limits.

(A) true
(B) false

141. Compare the echogenicities of the following structures and place them in decreasing echogenic order.

(A) pancreas > renal sinus > liver > spleen > renal parenchyma
(B) renal sinus > pancreas > liver > spleen > renal parenchyma
(C) renal sinus > renal parenchyma > pancreas > liver > spleen
(D) pancreas > renal sinus > renal parenchyma > liver > spleen

142. Splenomegaly may be the result of all of the following *except*

(A) an inflammatory process
(B) a left subphrenic abscess
(C) metastic disease to the spleen
(D) polycythemia vera
(E) chronic leukemia and lymphomas

143. With respect to thickening of the bowel wall

(A) the upper limit of normal is 5 mm when nondistended
(B) both inflammation and neoplasm can produce thickening
(C) the bowel wall itself is hypoechoic
(D) diminished or absent peristalsis on real-time is helpful in identifying a disease segment
(E) all of the above

144. A retroperitoneal sarcoma may displace

(A) the kidney posteriorly
(B) the spleen anteriorly
(C) the pancreas posteriorly
(D) the diaphragm inferiorly

145. An adrenal mass may displace the splenic vein

(A) anteriorly
(B) posteriorly
(C) medially

146. A fluid collection located between the diaphragm and the spleen may represent

(A) a pleural effusion
(B) a subcapsular hematoma
(C) a subphrenic abscess

147. At its maximum diameter, the normal adult adrenal rarely measures more than

(A) 2 cm
(B) 2 mm
(C) 3 cm
(D) 3 mm

148. The causes of a large gallbladder include all of the following *except*

(A) adenomyomatosis
(B) cystic duct obstruction
(C) pancreatic carcinoma
(D) diabetes mellitus
(E) a fasting patient
(F) common duct obstruction

149. Patients with right-sided heart failure and elevated systemic venous pressure may develop

(A) fatty liver
(B) portal-systemic anastomoses
(C) marked dilatation of the intrahepatic veins
(D) nonfocal liver disease

150. The body of the pancreas is bound on its anterior surface by

(A) the dorsum of the stomach
(B) the greater sac
(C) the splenic vein
(D) all of the above

151. Which of the following is associated with the pancreatic body?

(A) splenic vein lying posteriorly to the body
(B) splenic vein lying anteriorly to the body
(C) gastroduodenal artery
(D) common bile duct

152. The landmarks associated with the pancreatic head are

(A) the inferior vena cava lying posteriorly to the head
(B) the gastroduodenal artery outlining the anterolateral margin of the head of the pancreas
(C) the common bile duct marking the posterolateral margin of the head of the pancreas
(D) all of the above

153. Which landmark is most associated with the pancreatic neck?

(A) hepatic artery
(B) superior mesenteric vein
(C) porta hepatis
(D) superior mesenteric artery

154. Which of the following is *not* a true statement concerning the pancreas?

(A) the pancreas is a retroperitoneal organ
(B) the neck and body of the pancreas lies anterior to the superior mesenteric vein and superior mesenteric artery, respectively, and is usually found at the midline
(C) the pancreas has a true capsule
(D) the normal anteroposterior dimensions are 2.5 cm for the head, 2.0 cm for the body, and 2.0 cm for the tail
(E) the upper limits of the pancreatic duct are 3 mm
(F) the right renal vein lies posterior to the pancreatic head

155. Which of the following is *least* likely to be confused with hydronephrosis?

(A) an angiomyolipoma
(B) a multicystic kidney
(C) sinus lipomatosis
(D) a central renal cyst

156. The common bile duct is joined by the pancreatic duct as they enter the

(A) transverse portion of the duodenum
(B) first portion of the duodenum
(C) third portion of the duodenum
(D) second portion of the duodenum

157. On a sagittal scan, the portal vein is seen as a circular anechoic structure

(A) anterior to the inferior vena cava
(B) posterior to the aorta
(C) medial to the head of the pancreas
(D) inferior to the head of the pancreas

158. The prostate lies

(A) posterior to the symphysis pubis
(B) inferior to the urinary bladder
(C) inferior to the seminal vesicles
(D) all of the above

159. When performing transverse scans of the pelvis, to best visualize the prostate sonographically, one should

(A) angle the transducer 20° cephalad
(B) scan, angling the transducer 15° caudad
(C) scan, with 0° angulation
(D) scan, angling the transducer 15° cephalad

160. If the prostate is found to be enlarged, one should also check the

(A) spleen for enlargement
(B) scrotum for hydroceles
(C) kidneys for hydronephrosis
(D) liver for metastases

161. A 48-year-old female presents postcholecystectomy with right-upper quadrant pain, an elevated serum bilirubin (mainly conjugated), and bilirubin in her urine. It is true that

(A) she probably has hepatitis
(B) she probably has a stone, tumor, or stricture obstructing the bile duct
(C) the common duct will probably be less than 5 mm in internal diameter
(D) alkaline phosphatase will be normal

162. Acute prostatitis may be due to or complicated by all the following *except*

(A) hematogenous spread of infection to the prostate

(B) ascending or descending urinary infection
(C) acute cystitis and acute urinary retention
(D) trauma

163. The *most* common prostatic neoplasm is

(A) adenocarcinoma
(B) acute prostatitis
(C) benign cystic teratoma
(D) seminoma

164. A mirror-image artifact within the liver

(A) will appear as high-amplitude parallel lines occurring at regular periodic intervals
(B) will cause the gallbladder to fill in with echoes
(C) may result in a supradiaphragmatic projection of an infradiaphragmatic mass

165. The normal sonographic texture of the spleen is

(A) moderately echogenic but less echogenic than the liver
(B) hypoechoic
(C) strongly echogenic but more echogenic than the liver
(D) hyperechoic

166. The spleen is

(A) center for hematopoietic activity
(B) the largest organ of the reticuloendothelial system
(C) not a part of the reticuloendothelial system
(D) can contribute to the production of alkaline phosphatase

167. Which statement describes the correct anatomic location of structures adjacent to the spleen?

(A) the diaphragm is anterior, lateral, and inferior to the spleen
(B) the fundus of the stomach and lesser sac are medial and posterior to the splenic hilum
(C) the left kidney lies inferior and medial to the spleen

168. Benign ascites may be associated with

(A) peritoneal implants
(B) bowel that is matted posteriorly
(C) floating bowel loops

169. Malignant ascites may be associated with

(A) ascites that are anechoic and freely mobile
(B) bowels that are matted posteriorly
(C) floating bowel loops

170. The scrotum is an extraperitoneal sac that is divided by a septum into two compartments by the median raphe. Each compartment contains all of the following *except*

(A) a testis
(B) glomerulus
(C) an epididymis
(D) a portion of spermatic cord
(E) ductus deferens

171. Hematoceles are complicated hydroceles. The sonographic findings that accompany this abnormality include

(A) a cyst along the course of the vas deferens
(B) blood filling the sac that surrounds the testicle, secondary to trauma or surgery
(C) dilated veins caused by obstruction of the venous return
(D) a condition in which the testicles have not descended

172. Obstructive jaundice may be diagnosed sonographically by demonstrating

(A) a mass on the head of the pancreas with a dilated common bile duct
(B) an enlarged liver
(C) a fibrotic and shrunken liver
(D) cholangitis

173. In patients with uncomplicated acute epididymitis

(A) there is enlargement of the scrotum with focal or generalized thickening of the epididymis
(B) the epididymis is uniformly enlarged and more anechoic than usual
(C) a loculated fluid collection often containing low-level echoes appears cephalad to the testis

174. Acute hydroceles are *not* a result of

(A) trauma
(B) testicular torsion
(C) tumor
(D) infection of the testis or epididymis

175. The sonographic texture of the normal testis is

(A) heterogeneous with high-intensity echoes
(B) homogeneous with low-level echogenicity
(C) homogeneous with medium-level echogenicity
(D) variable echo pattern

176. Which of the following are benign lesions of the thyroid?

(A) adenomas
(B) diffuse nontoxic goiter
(C) adenomatous hyperplasia (multinodular goiter)
(D) thyroiditis
(E) thyroglossal duct cyst
(F) all of the above

177. When scanning a 22-year-old patient to rule out cholelithiasis, a single echogenic lesion is seen within the liver. This most probably represents

(A) a cavernous hemangioma
(B) a hematoma
(C) a hepatic cyst
(D) an abscess

178. Hyperthyroidism associated with a diffuse goiter is associated with

(A) papillary carcinoma
(B) Graves' disease
(C) Hashimoto's thyroiditis
(D) adenoma

179. Anatomic landmarks associated with the thyroid are the

(A) trachea medially, longus colli muscle laterally, carotid artery and strap muscles posteriorly
(B) trachea medially, longus colli muscles posteriorly, carotid artery and internal jugular vein laterally, strap muscles medially
(C) trachea medially, longus colli muscle posteriorly, carotid artery and internal jugular vein laterally, strap muscles anterolaterally
(D) trachea and strap muscles medially, longus colli muscle posteriorly, carotid artery inferiorly

180. If the sonogram suggests a mass in the head of the pancreas, the sonographer should

(A) examine the biliary radicles, common bile duct, and gallbladder to determine whether they are dilated
(B) outline the hepatic artery and splenic arteries to determine whether they are dilated
(C) scan the pancreas using the left kidney as a window, then end the examination
(D) examine both kidneys carefully to exclude a mass

181. The common carotid arteries can be differentiated from the internal jugular veins by all of the following *except*

(A) the jugular veins have a greater diameter than the carotids
(B) the jugular veins lie lateral to the carotids
(C) the trachea and esophagus lie medial to the common carotid arteries
(D) the jugular veins lie directly posterior to the thyroid lobes

182. The transducer of choice when scanning the thyroid gland should be

(A) a 5-MHz or higher short focus transducer if using the direct contact method
(B) a 5-MHz or higher medium focus transducer if using the direct contact method
(C) a 7.5-MHz short internal focus transducer if using a water bath technique
(D) none of the above

183. Which of the following is highly suspicious for prostatic carcinoma?

(A) a large cystic mass located within the prostate
(B) an enlarged prostate
(C) a well-encapsulated solid mass located within the prostate
(D) an uneven echo pattern and ill-defined borders
(E) none of the above; sonography cannot detect changes in the prostate due to prostatic carcinoma because the lesions are usually less than 1 mm.

184. Altered echogenicity within the prostate may indicate

(A) benign prostatic hypertrophy
(B) prostatic calculi
(C) prostatic neoplasm
(D) all of the above

185. The position of the parathyroid glands are variable. Most often they are located

(A) posterior to the thyroid lobes and medial to the common carotid arteries
(B) posterior to the thyroid lobes and anterior to the strap muscles
(C) anterior to the thyroid lobes and lateral to the anterior scalene muscles
(D) lateral to the thyroid lobes
(E) anterior to the trachea and within the isthmus of the thyroid

186. All of the following can mimic a parathyroid adenoma *except*

(A) minor neurovascular bundle
(B) longus colli muscle
(C) left lateral border of the esophagus
(D) intrathyroidal adenoma
(E) goiter

187. Normal measurements of the thyroid gland are

(A) there are no known normal measurements
(B) 3–4 cm in anteroposterior dimensions and in length
(C) 1–2 cm in anteroposterior dimensions and 4–6 cm in length
(D) 4–6 cm in anteroposterior dimensions and 1–2 cm in length

188. Thyroiditis will usually appear sonographically as

(A) multiple cysts within the thyroid
(B) diffusely enlarged thyroid lobes with decreased echogenicity
(C) diffusely enlarged thyroid lobes with no change in echogenicity
(D) small, echogenic thyroid

189. The halo sign as it pertains to thyroid masses is defined as a rim of sonolucency surrounding an intrathyroidal mass. It is most commonly encountered in

(A) cyst
(B) adenoma
(C) carcinoma
(D) thyroiditis

190. All of the following findings could suggest malignant neoplasm of the prostate *except*

(A) hypoechoic focal lesions
(B) uneven echo pattern, with irregular border
(C) an elevation of acid phosphatase
(D) overall enlargement of the gland with homogeneous echoes

191. The spermatic cord is composed of

(A) internal spermatic artery, vas deferens, testicular vessels, and nerves
(B) vas deferens, testicular vessels, nerves, and sperm
(C) vas deferens, testicular vessels, nerves, and efferent ductules
(D) vas deferens, testicular vessels, nerves, sperm, and efferent ductules
(E) vas deferens and its surrounding muscle

192. A varicocele is an

(A) abnormal dilatation of the draining veins of the scrotum seen in association with epididymitis
(B) abnormal dilatation of the draining veins of the scrotum seen in approximately 35–40% of infertile and subfertile men
(C) abnormal dilatation of the draining veins of the scrotum seen only with a malignant condition
(D) abnormal dilatation of the draining veins of the scrotum that cannot be sonographically differentiated from spermatoceles and epididymal cysts
(E) all of the above

193. Which of the following would sonographically appear as cystic fluid surrounding a testicle?

(A) tumor
(B) orchitis
(C) epididymitis
(D) hydrocele

194. All of the following disease states will cause upward displacement of the liver *except*

(A) excessive dilatation of the colon
(B) ascites
(C) abdominal tumor
(D) subphrenic abscess

195. Budd-Chiari syndrome is

(A) relative enlargement of the caudate lobe due to hepatic vein thrombosis
(B) relative shrinking of the caudate lobe due to hepatic vein thrombosis
(C) relative enlargement of the quadrate lobe due to hepatic vein thrombosis
(D) relative shrinking of all the lobes of the liver due to hepatic vein thrombosis
(E) metastatic disease of the liver from the gastrointestinal tract

196. The pyramidal lobe is a normal variant of the thyroid gland. Which of the following is its correct location?

(A) inferior extension of the right lobe
(B) superior extension of the isthmus
(C) inferior extension of the isthmus
(D) lateral extension of the isthmus

197. Ultrasonography of the urinary bladder is helpful in detecting

(A) bladder masses
(B) bladder calculi
(C) foreign bodies
(D) bladder diverticula
(E) all of the above

198. Epididymitis appears sonographically as a(n)

(A) enlarged prostate
(B) hypoechoic epididymis with diffuse enlargement of the gland
(C) hyperechoic epididymis with focal enlargement of the organ
(D) hydrocele that cannot be differentiated from it

199. On sonographic examination, a seminoma of the testicle may appear as a

(A) solid, homogeneous mass
(B) large, multilocular cystic mass
(C) small, simple cyst
(D) cannot be detected sonographically

200. Crytorchidism is a condition in which

(A) there is congenital agenesis of the testis
(B) the testicles have not descended and lie either in the abdomen or in the groin
(C) there is a benign enlargement of the testis
(D) the testicles do not produce the hormones that produce masculine features

201. The seminal vesicles

(A) produce sperm located within the prostate
(B) produce sperm located posterior to the bladder
(C) are the reservoir for sperm and are located posterior to the bladder
(D) are the reservoir for sperm and are located between the mediastinum testes and the pampiniform plexus

202. Infarcted testicle following testicular torsion will appear sonographically

(A) in the acute stage, indistinguishable from a hypoechoic tumor occupying the entire organ; in its chronic stage, small and echogenic
(B) in the acute stage, small and echogenic; in its chronic stage, indistinguishable from a hypoechoic tumor occupying the entire organ
(C) in its acute and chronic stages, indistinguishable from a hypoechoic tumor occupying the entire organ

203. The best way to distinguish hepatic veins from portal veins is by

(A) size, the hepatic veins are much smaller than the portal veins
(B) tracing them to their point of origin
(C) visualizing the pulsations of the hepatic veins
(D) visualizing the wall thickness of the vessels knowing that hepatic veins have thicker walls

204. The fundus of the stomach has the following anatomical relationship to the left lobe of the liver

(A) posteromedial
(B) anterolateral
(C) posterolateral
(D) anteromedial
(E) directly superior

205. Fatty infiltration of the liver may be due to all of the following *except*

(A) cardiac failure
(B) obesity
(C) alcoholic liver disease
(D) renal failure
(E) none of the above

206. Which of the following laboratory values may be elevated in the presence of liver metastases?

(A) blood urea nitrogen
(B) white blood count
(C) α-fetoprotein
(D) alkaline phosphatase
(E) none of the above

207. Metastatic lesions in the liver may appear sonographically as

(A) a target lesion ("bull's eye")
(B) echogenic
(C) anechoic
(D) complex
(E) none of the above

208. A cyst within a cyst (daughter cysts) is a classic example of which of the following liver masses?

(A) polycystic liver disease
(B) echinococcal (hydatid) cyst
(C) hepatoma
(D) hemangiomas
(E) pseudocysts

209. Riedel's lobe is a normal liver variant defined as a(n)

(A) elongated left lobe of the liver
(B) tonguelike extension of the caudate lobe
(C) tonguelike extension of the right lobe of the liver
(D) extra lobe of the liver visualized in some of the population

210. All of the following laboratory tests can be used for liver evaluation *except*

(A) bilirubin
(B) serum protein
(C) prothrombin time
(D) fetal antigen
(E) amylase
(F) SGOT

211. Given the clinical findings of a fever, right upper quadrant pain, and elevated white blood cell count, what should one expect to find in the patient's liver?

(A) abscess
(B) hepatoma
(C) hemangioma
(D) hematoma
(E) metastasis

212. Subphrenic abscess will

(A) push the liver up toward the diaphragm
(B) depress the liver away from the diaphragm
(C) enlarge the liver size
(D) never effect the liver; it is a separate entity
(E) none of the above

213. Portal vein size can be affected by

(A) Valsalva maneuver
(B) respiratory changes
(C) portal venous hypertension
(D) all of the above

214. Which of the following procedures would aid in distinguishing regenerating liver nodules from tumor masses?

(A) biopsy
(B) angiography
(C) isotope scan
(D) all of the above

215. Which of the following statements about the right crus of the diaphragm is *not* true?

(A) it is posterior to the right kidney
(B) it is anterior to the inferior vena cava
(C) it is posterior to the inferior vena cava
(D) it is posterior to the right adrenal gland

216. Structures that commonly alter the liver shape are

(A) diaphragm
(B) right kidney
(C) abdominal lymph nodes
(D) pancreas
(E) gallbladder
(F) all of the above except one

217. Lymphoma (Hodgkin's and non-Hodgkin's) can appear sonographically as

(A) echogenic
(B) anechoic
(C) focal lesion
(D) all of the above

218. Obstruction of lymph vessels can produce

(A) ascites
(B) effusion
(C) edema
(D) all of the above

219. Normal lymph nodes are no longer than

(A) 1 mm
(B) 1 cm
(C) 3 cm
(D) 4 cm
(E) dependent upon body habitus

220. When scanning a patient for lymphadenopathy, one should check the

(A) pelvis
(B) porta hepatis
(C) retroperitoneum
(D) perirenal area
(E) around the major blood vessels and their tributaries
(F) all of the above

221. In order to differentiate enlarged nodes from an aneurysm, one should

(A) have the patient perform the Valsalva maneuver
(B) scan the patient left anterior oblique
(C) know that aneurysms enlarge fairly symmetrically, whereas large nodes tend to drape over prevertebral vessels
(D) raise the overall gain
(E) decrease the overall gain

222. What is the approximate size at which lymph nodes can be depicted sonographically?

(A) 3 mm
(B) 10 mm
(C) 1.5 cm
(D) 3 cm

223. Sonographically, enlarged lymph nodes typically appear as

(A) solid masses
(B) complex masses
(C) anechoic masses with no demonstration of through transmission
(D) cystic masses with demonstration of through transmission

224. Which of the following will cause anterior displacement of the inferior vena cava?

(A) splenomegaly
(B) hydronephrosis
(C) enlarged lymph nodes
(D) pancreatitis

225. Which of the following can be potentially confused with the normal right adrenal gland?

(A) crus of the diaphragm
(B) bowel gas
(C) renal cyst
(D) aorta

226. To optimally scan the right adrenal, one should position the patient

(A) right anterior oblique
(B) left lateral decubitus
(C) right lateral decubitus
(D) erect

227. All of the following are functions of the spleen *except*

(A) production of plasma cells
(B) production of lymphocytes
(C) destruction of red blood cells
(D) destruction of white blood cells
(E) all of the above

228. Which of the following infectious diseases are associated with splenomegaly

(A) infective endocarditis
(B) tuberculosis
(C) syphilis
(D) schistosomiasis
(E) all the above

229. Which of the following vessels can be seen posterior to the inferior vena cava?

(A) right renal vein
(B) right renal artery
(C) left renal vein
(D) left renal artery
(E) no vessels course posterior to the inferior vena cava

230. A 35-year-old alcoholic male presented with epigastric pain. Sonography demonstrated a moderately enlarged gallbladder with a round, fluffy, nonshadowing mobile echo. This finding suggests

(A) a gallstone
(B) carcinoma of the gallbladder
(C) choledochal cysts
(D) a sludge ball

231. Cysts of the spleen are

(A) rare
(B) common
(C) of no clinical significance
(D) usually congenital

232. Metastases to the spleen occur more frequently with

(A) breast carcinoma
(B) colon carcinoma
(C) hepatitis
(D) leiomyoma

233. Metastases to the spleen

(A) are common
(B) only appear when the primary lesion has disseminated widely
(C) are usually the first sign of carcinoma
(D) are not known to occur

234. A spleen with overall decreased echogenicity is seen with all of the following *except*

(A) lymphopoiesis
(B) multiple myeloma
(C) congestion
(D) metastasis

235. The most common cause of splenomegaly in the United States is

(A) malaria
(B) portal hypertension
(C) syphilis
(D) mononucleosis

236. The retroperitoneal space is defined as the area between the

(A) posterior portion of the parietal peritoneum and the posterior abdominal wall muscles
(B) anterior portion of the parietal peritoneum and the posterior abdominal wall muscles
(C) anterior portion of the parietal peritoneum and the posterior portion of the visceral peritoneum
(D) posterior portion of the parietal peritoneum and the anterior portion of the visceral peritoneum
(E) none of the above

237. When assessing the upper retroperitoneum (ie, para-aortic lymph nodes) the best patient position for optimum visualization is

(A) prone
(B) supine
(C) RAO
(D) LAO

238. Primary retroperitoneal tumors are generally

(A) benign
(B) malignant
(C) very large
(D) none of the above

239. Urinomas are known to develop after

(A) urinary tract surgery
(B) subacute urinary obstruction
(C) chronic urinary obstruction
(D) trauma
(E) all of the above

240. The etiology of retroperitoneal fibrosis is

(A) iatrogenic
(B) unknown
(C) infectious
(D) blood borne

241. If retroperitoneal fibrosis is suspected, one should also check the

(A) kidneys for hydronephrosis
(B) liver for metastasis

(C) spleen for enlargement
(D) bladder for urinomas

242. The renal arteries are best seen on

(A) oblique sonogram
(B) transverse sonogram
(C) longitudinal sonogram
(D) they are not visualized

243. The largest major visceral branch of the inferior vena cava is the

(A) portal vein
(B) hepatic veins
(C) inferior mesenteric vein
(D) splenic vein

244. The spleen is variable in size, but it is considered to be which of the following?

(A) concave superiorly and inferiorly
(B) convex superiorly and concave inferiorly
(C) concave superiorly and convex inferiorly
(D) convex superiorly and inferiorly

245. When accessory spleens are present, they are usually located

(A) at the inferior margin of the spleen
(B) on the posterior aspect of the spleen
(C) near the hilum of the spleen
(D) near the kidney
(E) none of the above

246. Which of the following diseases would result in splenic atrophy?

(A) infectious mononucleosis
(B) typhoid fever
(C) splenitis
(D) sickle-cell anemia

247. The most common benign tumor of the spleen is

(A) fibroma
(B) osteoma
(C) chondroma
(D) cavernous hemangioma
(E) none of the above

248. When the spleen enlarges, it does so by extending

(A) inferomedially in an anterior position
(B) superomedially in an anterior position
(C) inferolaterally in a posterior position
(D) inferomedially in a posterior position

249. Which of the following vessels is *most* likely to appear round on a transverse sonogram?

(A) portal vein
(B) inferior vena cava
(C) right renal artery
(D) superior mesenteric artery

250. Alkaline phosphatase produced by cells lining the biliary tree is increased in all of the following *except*

(A) biliary obstruction
(B) pancreatic carcinoma
(C) hepatocellular disease
(D) presence of mass lesions in the liver

251. A hematoma in the posterior pararenal space will

(A) be located posteromedially and extend above and well below the level of the kidney
(B) be located posterior to the kidney and extend medially into the region of the pancreas
(C) be located posterior to the kidney, and extend laterally, to displace the kidney posteriorly
(D) extend up the lateral walls of the abdomen and displace the kidney anteriorly

252. A retroperitoneal sarcoma will displace which of the following organs anteriorly?

(A) kidney
(B) spleen
(C) pancreas
(D) all of the above

253. A hypertrophied column of Bertin is a

(A) benign tumor of the kidney
(B) malignant tumor of the kidney
(C) normal renal variant
(D) benign tumor of adrenal origin

254. If the patient has hydronephrosis, one may find all of the following *except*

(A) a renal calculus
(B) prostatic hypertrophy in a male or fibroid uterus in a female
(C) ureterocele
(D) renal vein thrombosis

255. An angiomyolipoma is

(A) rare
(B) benign tumor
(C) fatty tumor
(D) usually seen in middle-aged women
(E) all of the above

256. A hypernephroma is a solid renal mass. It is known as all of the following *except*

(A) renal cell carcinoma
(B) von Grawitz tumor
(C) adenocarcinoma of the kidney
(D) transitional cell carcinoma

257. All of the following will cause a false-positive abnormal intravenous pyleography *except*

(A) malrotated kidneys
(B) enlarged spleen or liver compressing the kidney
(C) dromedary hump
(D) renal vein thrombosis

258. With any renal tumor, one should also check for

(A) para-aortic nodes
(B) liver metastases
(C) tumor invasion of the inferior vena cava
(D) all of the above

259. The most common cause of nonvisualization of a kidney (unilateral) on intravenous pyelography is

(A) hydronephrosis
(B) renal calculus
(C) polycystic kidney disease
(D) pyelonephritis
(E) none of the above

260. All of the following will cause nonvisualization of the kidney on an intravenous pyelography *except*

(A) renal vein thrombosis
(B) renal artery occlusion
(C) pyonephrosis
(D) end-stage kidney disease
(E) all of the above

261. A pelvic kidney has a(n)

(A) abnormal appearance in a normal location
(B) normal appearance in an abnormal location
(C) normal appearance in a normal location
(D) all of the above

262. Ascites can be caused by all of the following *except*

(A) malignancy
(B) nephrotic syndrome
(C) congestive heart failure
(D) tuberculosis
(E) liver disease
(F) adenomyomatosis

263. Loculations within ascites are most commonly found in

(A) malignancy
(B) infection
(C) benign conditions
(D) A and B
(E) B and C

264. Internal echoes in ascitic fluid are suggestive of

(A) malignancy
(B) infection
(C) a benign condition
(D) A and B
(E) B and C

265. Acute pancreatitis may lead to all of the following *except*

(A) gallstones
(B) pancreatic pseudocyst
(C) pancreatic ascites
(D) common bile duct obstruction
(E) pancreatic abscess

266. Pancreatic pseudocyst may be found in the

(A) liver
(B) spleen
(C) mediastinum
(D) mesentary
(E) lesser sac
(F) all of the above

267. To best visualize the pancreatic tail, one should position the patient

(A) prone
(B) supine
(C) right anterior oblique
(D) left lateral decubitus

268. At times, what vessel can be confused with the pancreatic duct?

(A) superior mesenteric artery
(B) superior mesenteric vein
(C) splenic artery
(D) left renal artery

269. The splenic artery is located

(A) posterior to the body of the pancreas
(B) medial to the pancreas
(C) superior margin of the pancreas (body and tail)
(D) lateral to the uncinate process

270. Which of the following statements is true?

(A) the right kidney lies slightly higher than the left
(B) the right kidney lies slightly lower than the left
(C) both kidneys always lie at the same level
(D) none of the above

271. Signs of renal disease include all of the following *except*

(A) oliguria
(B) palpable flank mass
(C) generalized edema
(D) polyuria
(E) Murphy's sign

272. What percentage of the functioning renal parenchyma if lost will lead to the elevation of either blood urea nitrogen (BUN) or creatinine?

(A) 10%
(B) 20%
(C) 30%
(D) 40%
(E) 50%
(F) over 60%

273. The term *supernumerary kidney* refers to

(A) a pseudokidney in the renal fossa
(B) a double-collecting system
(C) the complete duplication of the renal system
(D) a pelvic kidney

274. To best evaluate the internal composition of a cyst, one should change

(A) the gain setting (TGC)
(B) the overall gain (power)
(C) the transducer to a higher frequency
(D) all of the above

275. Clinical symptoms associated with inflammatory renal masses include all of the following *except*

(A) fever
(B) chills
(C) flank pain
(D) hypoglycemia

276. The best way of delineating a dissecting aneurysm on sonography is to

(A) begin scanning in the transverse and record serial scans
(B) show an intimal flap vibration with the flow of blood
(C) have the patient lie left side down, so as to better visualize the lateral walls
(D) have the patient perform a Valsalva maneuver to dilate the aorta

277. Which of the following disorders may *not* produce a complex sonographic pattern?

(A) infected cyst
(B) hemorrhagic cyst
(C) hematomas
(D) congenital cyst
(E) abscesses

278. The abdominal aorta can be distinguished from the inferior vena cava by all of the following *except*

(A) change in gain setting
(B) anterior-posterior course
(C) left-right location
(D) Valsalva maneuver

279. With advanced chronological age, the pancreas

(A) becomes less echogenic and grossly enlarged
(B) decreases in size with increased echogenicity
(C) increases in size with no change in echogenicity
(D) increases in size with decrease in echogenicity

280. Which of the following are anatomically correct?

(A) the lesser sac is anterior and superior to the pancreas
(B) the greater sac is anterior and inferior to the pancreas
(C) the lesser sac is anterior and inferior to the pancreas
(D) A and B
(E) B and C

281. In comparison to the normal adult, the pancreas in children will be relatively

(A) more echogenic
(B) less echogenic
(C) the same echogenicity
(D) larger and less echogenic
(E) the same size and less echogenic

282. Compare the echogenicities of the following structures and place them in increasing echogenic order.

(A) renal sinus < pancreas < liver < spleen < renal parenchyma
(B) renal sinus < liver < spleen < pancreas < renal parenchyma
(C) pancreas < liver < spleen < renal sinus < renal parenchyma
(D) renal parenchyma < liver < spleen < pancreas < renal sinus

283. On a longitudinal scan, the pancreatic head can be seen

(A) anterior to the inferior vena cava
(B) caudad to the portal vein
(C) cephalad to the duodenum
(D) all of the above

284. The most common sonographic properties of a lymphoma are

(A) anechoic cystic mass with good through transmission and little ultrasound absorption
(B) relatively hypoechoic, solid mass with some decrease in through transmission and some increase in ultrasound absorption
(C) complex, predominantly cystic mass with internal debris; through transmission is increased and ultrasound absorption is decreased
(D) relatively hypoechoic solid mass with some increase in through transmission and some decrease in ultrasound absorption

285. Islet cell tumors of the pancreas are most likely to be located

(A) in the head, never in the body or tail
(B) frequently in the head, rarely in the body or tail
(C) never in the head, frequently in the body or tail
(D) rarely in the head, frequently in the body or tail

286. The normal right adrenal gland is located

(A) medial to the left kidney, inferior to the spleen
(B) superior to the right kidney, medial to the liver
(C) medial to the right kidney and liver
(D) anterior to the inferior vena cava

287. Addison's disease is a syndrome that results from

(A) chronic adrenal hypofunction
(B) thyroid hypofunction
(C) parathyroid hypofunction
(D) goiter

288. Anatomic landmarks helpful in locating the left adrenal gland are

(A) aorta, spleen, and left kidney
(B) gastric antrum, left kidney, and inferior vena cava
(C) left kidney, spleen, and inferior vena cava
(D) left kidney, left psoas muscle, and left hemidiaphragm

289. Adrenal hemorrhage sonographically appears

(A) echogenic
(B) anechoic
(C) complex
(D) all of the above

290. The spiral valves of Heister

(A) are located within the cystic duct
(B) may simulate a polypoid tumor
(C) may cause shadowing, therefore, simulating a stone
(D) all of the above

291. Landmarks for the right adrenal gland include

(A) liver, inferior vena cava, and right crus of diaphragm
(B) liver, right kidney, and aorta
(C) liver, right kidney, and right psoas muscle
(D) liver, inferior vena cava, and fourth part of duodenum

292. Which of the following masses are adrenal in origin and secrete hormones?

(A) adenoma
(B) teratoma
(C) pheochromocytoma
(D) neuroblastoma
(E) none of the above

293. Anterior displacement of the splenic vein can be caused by

(A) pancreatitis
(B) pseudocysts
(C) left adrenal hyperplasia
(D) aneurysm

294. Which of the following syndromes are associated with an adrenal mass?

(A) Frohlich's syndrome
(B) Cushing's syndrome
(C) Graves' syndrome

295. The vessel that originates from the celiac axis and is very tortuous is

(A) splenic artery
(B) proper hepatic artery
(C) right gastric artery
(D) none of the above

296. In reference to the gallbladder, a phrygian cap and Hartmann's pouch are

(A) two names for an enlarged gallbladder
(B) a fold at the gallbladder fundus and neck, respectively
(C) two names for the fold in the gallbladder neck
(D) two names for fold in the gallbladder fundus

297. Nonshadowing, nonmobile, echogenic foci seen within the gallbladder are most likely

(A) polyps
(B) calculi
(C) biliary gravel
(D) sludge balls

298. Echogenic bile within the gallbladder lumen may be caused by all of the following *except*

(A) hemobilia
(B) empyema
(C) long-standing cystic duct obstruction
(D) prolonged fasting
(E) all of the above can cause echogenic bile

299. The celiac axis is ______ to the origin of the superior mesenteric artery.

(A) caudal
(B) cephalad
(C) ventral
(D) medial

300. The inferior vena cava increases in diameter superior to the entrance of the

(A) renal vein
(B) portal vein
(C) superior mesenteric vein
(D) splenic vein

Question 301: Select the letter indicating the appropriate numbered choice(s).

301. Sonography is helpful in the evaluation of the dilated common bile duct. List the physiologic events given below in order of occurrence that lead to this phenomenon.

1. intrahepatic bile duct dilatation
2. common bile duct larger than 5 mm
3. stellate formation of the ducts near the porta hepatis
4. double-barrel shotgun sign

(A) 4, 2, 1, 3
(B) 2, 1, 4, 3
(C) 1, 3, 2, 4
(D) 1, 4, 3, 2

302. Jaundice in a pediatric patient is most probably due to

(A) hepatitis
(B) fatty infiltration
(C) biliary atresia
(D) cirrhosis

303. If a patient is in the right decubitus position, this means

(A) right side up and left side on the table
(B) left side up and right side on the table
(C) the patient is in a 45° angle
(D) the patient is being scanned coronally

304. Large gallbladders are detected in patients with

(A) diabetes
(B) hepatitis
(C) lymphoma
(D) cirrhosis

305. A patient presents with empyema of the gallbladder; the sonographer should expect to find

(A) pus within the gallbladder
(B) common bile duct obstruction
(C) stones within the gallbladder
(D) abscess surrounding the gallbladder

306. Which of the following laboratory values is higher with biliary obstruction than with liver disease?

(A) serum alkaline phosphatase
(B) serum glutamic oxaloacetic transaminase (SGOT)
(C) serum glutamic pyruvic transaminase (SGPT)
(D) lactic acid dehydrogenase (LDH)

307. The basic mechanisms in which jaundice occurs are all of the following *except*

(A) obstruction of intra- or extrahepatic ducts
(B) hepatocellular disease
(C) red blood cell destruction
(D) white blood cell destruction

308. Acute cholecystitis is associated with all of the following *except*

(A) gallbladder wall thickening greater than 3 mm
(B) obstruction of the cystic duct
(C) jaundice
(D) episode of right upper quadrant pain
(E) tender enlarged gallbladder (Murphy's sign)
(F) sonographic halo effect

309. Which of the following laboratory values is specific for a hepatoma of the liver?

(A) α-fetoprotein
(B) alkaline phosphatase
(C) bilirubin
(D) blood urea nitrogen (BUN)

310. Enlarged lymph nodes will usually appear sonographically as a

(A) heterogeneous mass with poor through transmission
(B) homogeneous mass with poor through transmission
(C) homogeneous mass with excellent through transmission

311. All of the following statements concerning the patterns periaortic nodes will follow are correct *except*

(A) they may drape or mantle the great vessels anteriorly
(B) they may displace the superior mesenteric artery posteriorly
(C) they may displace the great vessels anteriorly
(D) they may have lobular, smooth, or scalloped appearance
(E) as mesenteric involvement occurs, the adenopathy may fill most of the abdomen in an irregular complex pattern

312. A primary retroperitoneal tumor is one that originates independently within the retroperitoneal space. Most are malignant and may exhibit a variety of sonographic patterns. An example of a primary tumor that is retroperitoneal is

(A) hepatoma
(B) hypernephroma
(C) leiomyosarcoma
(D) adenocarcinoma

313. Retroperitoneal fluid collections may be

(A) urinoma
(B) hemorrhage
(C) abscess
(D) lymphocele
(E) all of the above

314. All of the following are characteristics for dilated intrahepatic bile ducts *except*

(A) the parallel channel sign
(B) irregular borders to dilated bile ducts
(C) echo enhancement behind dilated ducts
(D) decreasing size as they course toward the porta hepatis

315. The superior mesenteric artery is

(A) posterior to the body of the pancreas
(B) anterior to the splenic vein
(C) posterior to the renal vein
(D) usually larger in caliber than the superior mesenteric vein

316. Which of the following is *not* a remnant of the fetal circulation?

(A) ligamentum teres
(B) ligamentum venosum
(C) coronary ligament

317. A subhepatic abscess would be located

(A) superior to the liver
(B) inferior to the liver, anterior to the right kidney
(C) inferior to the liver, posterior to the right kidney

318. All of the following mass lesions are benign *except*

(A) hematoma
(B) hamartoma
(C) hepatic adenoma
(D) hepatoma
(E) hemangioma

319. If the ultrasound beam passes partially through bone where the speed of ultrasound is greater than in soft tissue, the transducer will register these echoes

(A) further away than they really are
(B) closer than they really are
(C) in their true position
(D) all of the above, depending upon which frequency transducer is used

320. If the ultrasound beam passes through a fatty tumor within the liver, and we know that the speed of sound in fat is lower than in soft tissue, where will this fatty tumor be placed?

(A) further away than it really is
(B) closer than it really is
(C) its true position
(D) all of the above, depending upon which frequency transducer is used

321. In which of the following ways does ascites sonographically affect the liver?

(A) there will be no effect
(B) the liver will appear more echogenic
(C) the ascites will attenuate the liver, resulting in decreased echoes

322. An obese patient has a known mass in the posterior aspect of the right lobe of the liver. Which transducer would help the most in visualizing it?

(A) 5-MHz short-focus transducer
(B) 3.5-MHz long-focus transducer
(C) 2.25-MHz long-focus transducer
(D) 2.25-MHz short-focus transducer

323. All of the following will cause jaundice *except*

(A) hemolytic disease
(B) obstructive disease
(C) hepatitis
(D) hepatocellular disease
(E) Reye's syndrome

324. The celiac artery arises from the ventral surface of the aorta. Its branches consist of the

(A) common hepatic, right gastric, splenic arteries
(B) common hepatic, left gastric, splenic arteries
(C) coronary, common hepatic, left gastric arteries
(D) splenic, right hepatic, right gastric arteries

325. A major branch of the common hepatic artery is the

(A) gastroduodenal artery
(B) coronary artery
(C) esophageal artery
(D) left gastric artery

326. The splenic artery

(A) originates from the anterior abdominal aorta
(B) lies posterior to the inferior aspect of the body of the pancreas
(C) is very tortuous and runs superior to the body and tail of the pancreas

327. Artifactual echoes may occur within cysts owing to each of the following *except*

(A) slice thickness artifacts
(B) side-lobe artifacts
(C) edge artifacts
(D) reverberation artifacts

328. Owing to the abrupt change in aortic caliber at the site of an aneurysm, laminar flow will be altered, thereby creating

(A) areas of increased echogenicity that will be seen as a result of calcification
(B) irregularities of flow that significantly increase the likelihood of clot formation and thrombus
(C) blood flow will not be altered

329. To detect irregularities of blood flow, the following may be used?

(A) A-mode
(B) B-mode
(C) Doppler sampling
(D) real-time study

330. Cavernous hemangiomas would be *least* likely to appear sonographically

(A) as an echogenic lesion
(B) distinguishable from a hepatoma
(C) as a smooth-walled, echo-free structure
(D) as a single or multiple lesions

331. An abscess may appear sonographically

(A) echo-free with smooth borders and good through transmission
(B) solid with smooth borders and no through transmission
(C) a variable echo texture with irregular borders and varied through transmission
(D) all of the above

332. Patients with portal hypertension may have

(A) dilated portal veins
(B) potential anastomoses between the portal and systemic circulation
(C) splenomegaly
(D) all of the above

333. In portal hypertension, potential anastomoses between the systemic circulation may open and bypass the liver. Those that can be seen sonographically include

(A) left umbilical vein
(B) lienorenal anastomoses
(C) anastomoses around the esophagus
(D) all of the above

334. During an ultrasound examination, a sonographer identifies a patent lumen within the umbilical vein. This finding may be associated with

(A) ascites
(B) an abscess
(C) portal hypertension
(D) an incidental finding

335. The major node-bearing areas in the retroperitoneum are

(A) the iliac nodes in the pelvis
(B) the hypogastric nodes within the pelvis
(C) para-aortic group in the upper retroperitoneum
(D) all of the above

336. Indications for scrotal sonography include all of the following *except*

(A) detection of testicular tumors
(B) evaluation of an enlarged, painful scrotum
(C) distinction between epididymitis and tumor involving the testicle
(D) a primary method for diagnosis of testicular torsion

337. Lymph nodes may be confused with all of the following *except*

(A) an abdominal aortic aneurysm
(B) chronic pancreatitis
(C) the crus of the diaphragm
(D) bowel

338. Sonography is used often in the evaluation of suspected palpable breast masses. In which situations is sonography of the breast *least* helpful?

(A) detection of microcalcifications associated with invasive ductal carcinoma
(B) evaluation of cystic breast masses
(C) in a patient concerned about irradiation exposure from radiographic mammographic examination
(D) detection of breast masses in the radiographically dense breast

339. The superior mesenteric vein can be differentiated from the superior mesenteric artery by all of the following *except*

(A) following the superior mesenteric vein into the portal vein
(B) respiratory variations are seen in the superior mesenteric vein
(C) on sagittal scan, the superior mesenteric artery angles away from the aorta and the superior mesenteric vein tends to parallel the aorta
(D) the superior mesenteric vein is smaller in caliber than the superior mesenteric artery

340. If the outer-to-outer dimension of an aortic aneurysm is found to be 7 cm, what percentage may rupture?

(A) 10–30%
(B) 30–50%
(C) 60–80%

341. Which vessel is not found posterior to the pancreas?
(A) splenic vein
(B) superior mesenteric artery
(C) superior mesenteric vein
(D) celiac trunk
(E) inferior vena cava

342. Which vessel is found anterior to the uncinate process?
(A) gastroduodenal artery
(B) superior mesenteric vein
(C) left gastric vein
(D) left renal vein

343. Which of the following statements are *true* if a patient has acute pancreatitis?
(A) amylase and BUN will both rise, but amylase remains higher for a longer period of time
(B) amylase and alkaline phosphatase will both rise, but amylase remains higher for a longer period of time
(C) amylase and lipase rise at the same rate, but lipase remains higher for a longer period of time

344. Acute hemorrhagic pancreatitis may occur from all of the following *except*
(A) alcoholism
(B) surgical trauma
(C) external trauma
(D) fibrocystic disease of the pancreas

345. One can determine if a lesion is cystic or solid within the liver by all of the following *except*
(A) posterior enhancement
(B) reverberation artifact
(C) through transmission
(D) amount of internal echoes
(E) well-defined borders

346. During a sonographic examination, a solid mass is found. The mass is seen superior to the left kidney, displacing the spleen anteriorly. The origin of this mass is most probably
(A) from the psoas muscle
(B) the stomach
(C) the tail of the pancreas

347. In the supine view, the spleen is considered enlarged if
(A) it crosses the medial aspect of the left kidney
(B) it displaces the stomach posteriorly
(C) its anterior border lies in front of the aorta and inferior vena cava
(D) it displaces the left kidney laterally

348. A pheochromocytoma is a benign hormone producing
(A) kidney tumor
(B) adrenal tumor
(C) splenic tumor
(D) pancreatic tumor

349. Enlarged lymph nodes are almost always anechoic and can be associated with fever of unknown origin. Lymphadenopathy can be found in
(A) the para-aortic area
(B) the celiac axis, displacing the pancreas anteriorly and involving the porta hepatis
(C) adjacent to the iliopsoas muscles in the pelvis
(D) all of the above

350. A 64-year-old male presents with renal failure with a BUN of 50 mg/dL and a creatinine of 1.5 mg/dL. The sonographer may expect to find
(A) hydronephrotic kidney
(B) small kidneys that are consistent with chronic glomerulonephritis
(C) normal kidneys that are consistent with acute pyelonephritis
(D) all of the above are consistent with renal failure

351. Optimal imaging of the left adrenal gland is achieved by the specific alignment of the
(A) left kidney to the aorta
(B) left kidney to the inferior vena cava
(C) superior mesenteric artery to the aorta
(D) tail of the pancreas to the aorta

352. The right adrenal is ______ to the kidney.
(A) lateral and superior
(B) anteromedial and inferior
(C) anteromedial and superior
(D) posterior and superior
(E) anterior and superior

353. The right adrenal gland tends to be located directly ______ to the inferior vena cava and ______ to the crus of the diaphragm.
(A) superior and posterior
(B) anterior and superior
(C) lateral and superior
(D) posterior and anterior

354. In children, a relatively common malignant tumor originating from the adrenal gland is called
(A) nephroblastoma
(B) hamartoma
(C) neuroblastoma
(D) cortical teratoma

355. The adrenal is an endocrine gland that can be divided into

(A) pelvis and sinus
(B) cortex and medulla
(C) major and minor calices

356. Above the level of the celiac axis the diaphragm can be visualized

(A) anterior to the inferior vena cava and posterior to the aorta
(B) posterior to the inferior vena cava and anterior to the aorta
(C) the crus of the diaphragm never crosses the aorta

357. The segments of the left lobe of the liver are

(A) medial and lateral
(B) anterior and posterior
(C) cephalad and caudad
(D) caudate and quadrate

358. A patent umbilical vein may be found in the

(A) ligamentum
(B) main lobar fissure
(C) ligamentum teres
(D) intersegmental fissure

359. A patient with ampullary carcinoma most likely will demonstrate all of the following *except*

(A) dilated pancreatic duct
(B) dilated common bile duct
(C) dilated hepatic veins
(D) dilated intrahepatic duct

360. The segments of the right lobe of the liver are

(A) medial and lateral
(B) anterior and posterior
(C) cephalad and caudad
(D) caudad and quadrate

361. In a dissecting aneurysm, the dissection is through

(A) the adventia
(B) the media
(C) the intima
(D) all three layers at once

362. Which of the following is *not* a type of aortic aneurysm?

(A) congenital
(B) mycotic
(C) atherosclerotic
(D) syphilitic
(E) phlebitis

363. The minimum anterior-posterior diameter for the diagnosis of aortic aneurysm is

(A) 1 cm
(B) 2 cm
(C) 3 cm
(D) above 3 cm

364. Abdominal aortic aneurysms are usually arteriosclerotic in origin. The most common type of aneurysm is

(A) dissecting
(B) saccular
(C) fusiform

365. What echo-poor linear structure may be visualized anterior to the aorta above the level of the celiac artery?

(A) superior mesenteric artery
(B) left renal vein
(C) crus of diaphragm
(D) none of the above

366. The inferior vena cava may be compressed and displaced anteriorly by

(A) mass lesion in the caudate lobe of the liver
(B) right renal artery aneurysm
(C) a tumor in the head of the pancreas
(D) right renal vein thrombosis

367. Dilatation of the inferior vena cava can be seen in which of the following pathologic conditions?

(A) hepatitis
(B) Valsalva maneuver
(C) right ventricular heart failure
(D) hydronephrosis

368. An 80-year-old male with dysuria and fatigue has an elevated serum acid phosphatase. Elevated acid phosphatases may be seen in

(A) acute pancreatitis
(B) acute cholecystitis
(C) hepatitis
(D) prostatic carcinoma
(E) hypernephroma

369. Artifactual echoes seen within the lumen of the aorta could be a result of all of the following *except*

(A) improper TGC (too high)
(B) poor lateral resolution
(C) thrombus
(D) improper overall gain (too high)

370. The gastroduodenal artery supplies the

(A) duodenum, parts of the stomach, and the head of the pancreas and arises from the common hepatic artery
(B) small bowel, the duodenum, the head of the pancreas and arises from the splenic artery
(C) duodenum, part of the stomach, the head of the pancreas and arises directly off the celiac axis
(D) stomach and the duodenum and arises from the superior mesenteric artery

371. Sonographically, one may recognize fatty infiltration of the liver by all of the following *except*

(A) hepatomegaly
(B) parenchymal echoes are brighter
(C) decreased vascular structures
(D) decreased through transmission
(E) a focal hyperechoic mass

372. End-stage fatty liver, like severe cirrhosis, may present with all of the following *except*

(A) ascites
(B) small shrunken liver
(C) biliary dilatation
(D) portal hypertension
(E) irregular liver borders due to liver nodules

373. The head of the pancreas is located anterior to the

(A) inferior vena cava
(B) aorta
(C) superior mesenteric artery
(D) splenic vein

374. The lesser sac is located between the

(A) pancreas and the inferior vena cava
(B) stomach and the pancreas
(C) abdominal wall and the stomach

375. Common bile duct obstruction is associated with

(A) a predominant increase in direct bilirubin
(B) a predominant increase in indirect bilirubin
(C) neither A nor B; the common bile duct is not in the liver

376. The renal pyramids are found in the

(A) cortex
(B) medulla
(C) renal sinus
(D) renal pelvis

377. Urine formation involves

(A) tubular reabsorption
(B) tubular secretion
(C) filtration
(D) all of the above

378. Urine passes, in the order given, through which of the following structures?

(A) glomerulus, urethra, bladder, ureter
(B) hilum, bladder, ureter
(C) renal pelvis, ureter, bladder, urethra
(D) hilum, urethra, bladder, ureter

379. Which of the following statements is true?

(A) Bowman's capsule is the fibrous capsule around the kidney
(B) a glomerulus, Bowman's capsule, and renal tubules together constitute a nephron
(C) nephrons are about the only structures, if not the only ones, in which active transport of substances through cell membranes does not occur
(D) the renal cortex secretes hormones called corticoids

380. A 34-year-old male presents with right-upper quadrant pain and recurrent attacks of pancreatitis. His laboratory values could indicate a(n)

(A) increase in blood urea nitrogen (BUN)
(B) decrease in serum amylase
(C) increase in lipase
(D) increase in indirect bilirubin

381. A jaundiced male child with a hemolytic disorder may be found to have

(A) a predominant increase in direct bilirubin
(B) a predominant increase in indirect bilirubin
(C) bilirubin generally does not increase in childhood

382. If a 68-year-old male is found to have choledocholithiasis on ultrasound, this may result in

(A) an increase in indirect bilirubin
(B) an increase in direct and a slight increase in indirect bilirubin
(C) bilirubin is not elevated in choledocholithiasis

383. A common anatomical variant is a bulge off the lateral border of the left kidney. This is termed a

(A) vascular pedicle
(B) Glisson's capsule
(C) dromedary hump

384. The most common intrascrotal inflammation is

(A) varicocele
(B) seminoma
(C) spermatocele
(D) epididymitis

385. On a longitudinal scan of the scrotum, a normal testicle is seen. Located superior to the testis is the

(A) ductus deferens
(B) rete testis
(C) head of the epididymis
(D) tunica albuginea

386. When measuring the diameter of the extrahepatic bile duct on ultrasound examination, which one(s) of the following statements is(are) true?

(A) one measures the luminal diameter (i.e., excludes the wall thickness)
(B) one measures the diameter from the outside of the wall (ie, includes wall thickness)
(C) one measures from the outside of one wall to the inside of the other

387. Which of the following is posterior to the spleen?

(A) right kidney
(B) left kidney
(C) stomach
(D) tail of pancreas

388. The stomach is located ______ to the spleen.

(A) anterior
(B) posterior
(C) lateral
(D) inferior

389. If a testicular tumor is found, one should also check

(A) the kidney for hydronephrosis
(B) the renal hilum for possible nodal metastases
(C) the abdominal cavity for ascites
(D) do nothing else; no further evaluation is necessary

390. The average dimensions of the testes are

(A) 6–7 cm long and 4–5 cm wide
(B) 4–5 cm long and 4–5 cm wide
(C) 4–5 cm long and 2.5–3 cm wide
(D) 3–4 cm long and 5–6 cm wide
(E) dependent on body habitus

391. The testes are considered to be

(A) endocrine glands
(B) exocrine glands
(C) both endocrine and exocrine glands
(D) neither an endocrine nor exocrine gland

392. Primary tumors found in childhood are

(A) hepatoblastoma found in the liver
(B) Wilms' tumor found in the pancreas
(C) neuroblastoma found in the kidneys

393. Hydroceles can be defined as serous fluid accumulated between the

(A) two layers of the tunica vaginalis
(B) tunica vaginalis and the tunica albuginea
(C) two layers of the tunica albuginea
(D) tunica albuginea and the testicle

394. Testicular malignancy is most often a disease affecting which of the following age groups?

(A) 80 years and above
(B) between 60 and 80 years
(C) between 40 and 60 years
(D) between 20 and 40 years
(E) between 10 and 20 years

395. Which one of the following statements is true?

(A) all neoplasms are benign
(B) all neoplasms are malignant
(C) a neoplasm is any new growth and therefore may be benign or malignant

Questions 396 through 403: Identify the structures in Fig. 5–9A with the list of terms in Column B.

COLUMN A	COLUMN B
396. ______	(A) gallbladder
397. ______	(B) left lobe
398. ______	(C) falciform ligament
399. ______	(D) right lobe
400. ______	(E) inferior vena cava
401. ______	(F) ligamentum teres
402. ______	(G) portal vein
403. ______	(H) hepatic artery

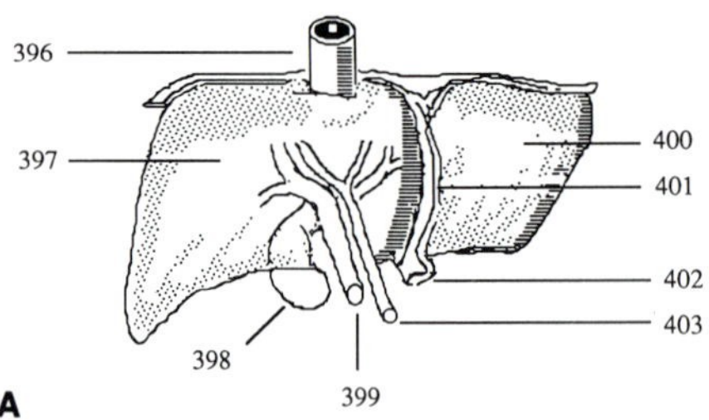

Figure 5–9A. Anterior projection of the liver.

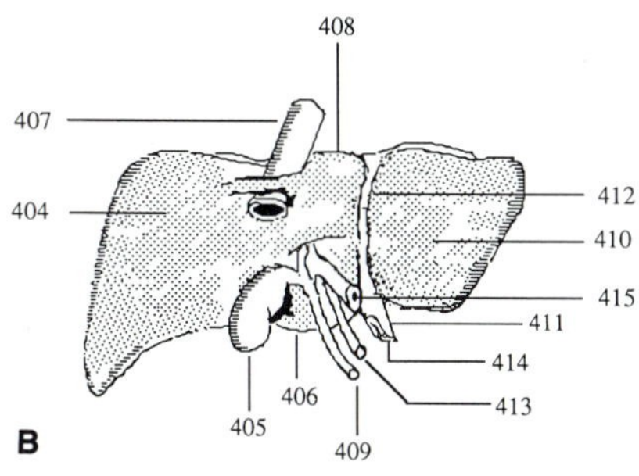

Figure 5–9B. Posterior projection of the liver.

Questions 404 through 415: Identify the structures in Fig. 5–9B with the list of terms in Column B.

COLUMN A	COLUMN B
404. ______	(A) gallbladder
405. ______	(B) left lobe
406. ______	(C) falciform ligament
407. ______	(D) right lobe
408. ______	(E) inferior vena cava
409. ______	(F) ligamentum teres
410. ______	(G) portal vein
411. ______	(H) hepatic artery
412. ______	(I) fissure for ligamentum venosum
413. ______	(J) common bile duct
414. ______	(K) caudate lobe
415. ______	(L) quadrate lobe (medial aspect of the left lobe)

Questions 416 through 426: Identify the structures in Fig. 5–10 with the list of terms in Column B.

COLUMN A	COLUMN B
416. ______	(A) cystic duct
417. ______	(B) ampulla of Vater
418. ______	(C) duodenum
419. ______	(D) fundus of the gallbladder
420. ______	(E) common hepatic duct
421. ______	(F) left hepatic duct
422. ______	(G) body of the gallbladder
423. ______	(H) right hepatic duct
424. ______	(I) neck of the gallbladder
425. ______	(J) infundibulum of the gallbladder (Hartmann's pouch)
426. ______	(K) common bile duct

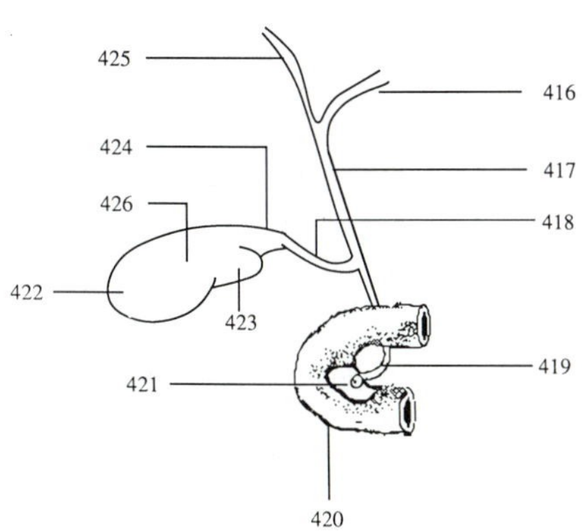

Figure 5–10. Extrahepatic biliary system.

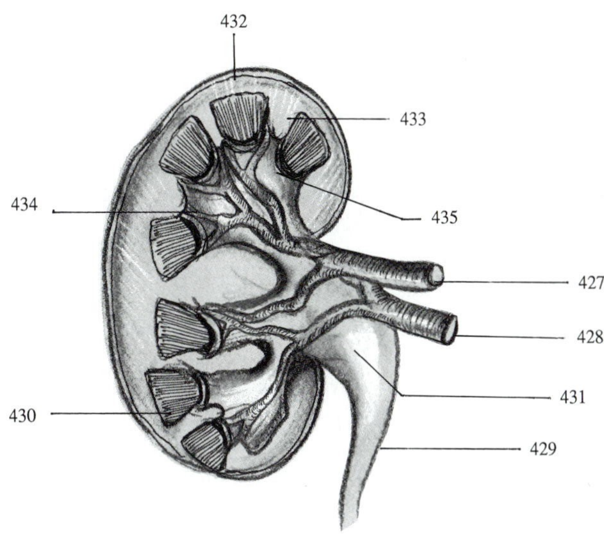

Figure 5–11. Kidney.

Questions 427 through 435: Identify the structures in Fig. 5–11 with the list of terms in Column B.

COLUMN A	COLUMN B
427. ______	(A) renal papilla
428. ______	(B) minor calyx
429. ______	(C) renal capsule
430. ______	(D) renal artery

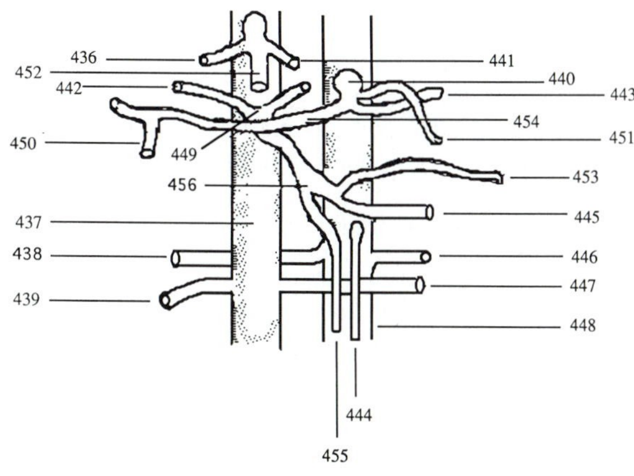

Figure 5–12. Prevertebral vessels.

431. ______ (E) ureter
432. ______ (F) renal pelvis
433. ______ (G) renal vein
434. ______ (H) pyramid
435. ______ (I) cortex

Questions 436 through 456: Match the numbered structures in Fig. 5–12 with the list of terms in Column B.

COLUMN A	COLUMN B
436. ______	(A) superior mesenteric artery
437. ______	(B) splenic vein
438. ______	(C) aorta
439. ______	(D) middle hepatic vein
440. ______	(E) celiac trunk
441. ______	(F) right hepatic vein
442. ______	(G) left hepatic vein
443. ______	(H) inferior vena cava
444. ______	(I) right renal vein
445. ______	(J) left renal artery
446. ______	(K) left renal vein
447. ______	(L) right renal artery
448. ______	(M) right portal vein
449. ______	(N) splenic artery
450. ______	(O) gastroduodenal artery
451. ______	(P) left portal vein
452. ______	(Q) inferior mesenteric vein
453. ______	(R) common hepatic artery
454. ______	(S) main portal vein
455. ______	(T) superior mesenteric vein
456. ______	(U) left gastric artery

Questions 457 through 466: Identify the structures in Fig. 5–13 with the list of terms in Column B.

COLUMN A	COLUMN B
457. ______	(A) vertebral body
458. ______	(B) trachea
459. ______	(C) common carotid artery
460. ______	(D) internal jugular vein
461. ______	(E) thyroid gland
462. ______	(F) strap muscles
463. ______	(G) esophagus
464. ______	(H) sternocleidomastoid muscle
465. ______	(I) parathyroid gland
466. ______	(J) longus colli muscle

Questions 467 through 473: Identify the structures in Fig. 5–14 with the list of terms in Column B.

COLUMN A	COLUMN B
467. ______	(A) testis
468. ______	(B) rete testis
469. ______	(C) epididymis body
470. ______	(D) septa
471. ______	(E) epididymis tail
472. ______	(F) epididymis head
473. ______	(G) seminiferous tubules

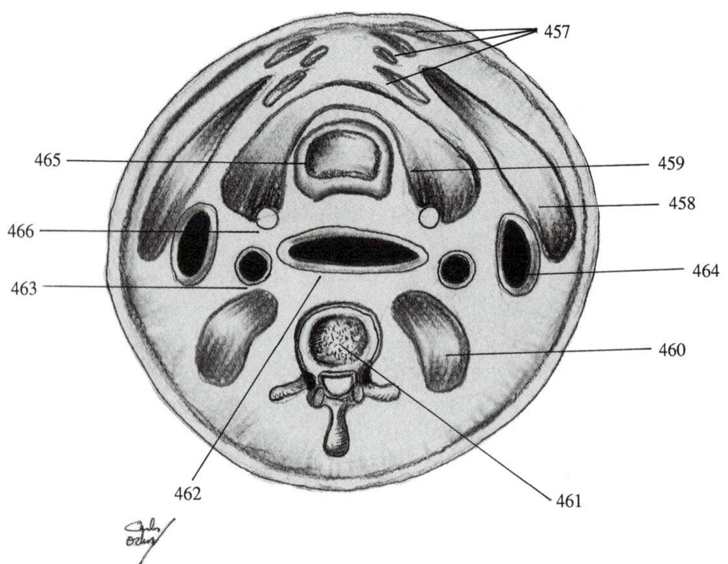

Figure 5–13. Cross-section of the thyroid.

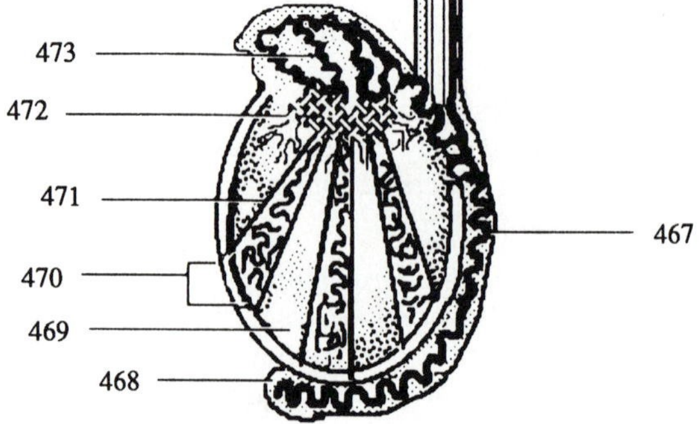

Figure 5–14. Longitudinal section of the testis.

474. In acute renal vein thrombosis, the kidney sonographically will *not* appear

(A) hydonephrotic
(B) enlarged
(C) more sonolucent

475. A 50-year-old female with a long history of alcoholism presents with increased abdominal girth. An ultrasound examination is performed and the most probable finding is

(A) liver metastases
(B) massive ascites with cirrhosis
(C) hepatoma

476. A known heroin addict presents with high fever and right flank pain. Ultrasound examination reveals expansion of the upper pole of the kidney by a mass with low-level echoes and a fluid level. This most probably represents

(A) a hypernephroma
(B) an abscess
(C) metastatic spread to the kidney
(D) hematoma

477. SGOT (serum glutamic oxalocetic transaminase) and SGPT (serum glutamic pyruvic transaminase) are highest in

(A) obstructive disease
(B) viral hepatitis and toxic hepatitis
(C) chronic cholecystitis

478. Which of the following laboratory values when elevated proportionally greater than the rest is an excellent indication of biliary obstruction?

(A) SGOT (serum glutamic oxalocetic transaminase)
(B) SGPT (serum glutamic pyruvic transaminase)
(C) prothrombin time
(D) alkaline phosphate
(E) serum amylase

479. A 1-week-old male infant presents with a left flank mass. An IVP demonstrates a normal right kidney but fails to demonstrate the left kidney. The ultrasound examination demonstrates many noncommunicating spherical cystic structures in the left renal fossa, the largest of which is located laterally. No true renal parenchyma is identified. The right kidney is normal sonographically. This most probably represents

(A) severe hydronephrosis
(B) polycystic kidneys
(C) a multicystic kidney
(D) nephroblastoma

480. A 6-year-old female child presents with recurrent fever, right upper quadrant pain, and jaundice. She has had similar episodes in the past. An oral cholecystogram fails to visualize the gallbladder. A sonogram is performed and the liver and gallbladder are normal. A 2-cm cyst is found medial and separate from the gallbladder but communicating with the common bile duct. This cystic structure most probably represents

(A) a choledochal cyst
(B) a pseudocyst
(C) an aortic aneurysm
(D) a mucocele

481. Ascites is usually due to

(A) obstruction of the portal venous system
(B) lymphoma
(C) severe colitis

482. A phlebolith is a

(A) venous calculus
(B) common bile duct calculus
(C) renal calculus
(D) arterial calculus

483. Chronic active hepatitis is a progressive destructive liver disease that eventually leads to

(A) liver cysts
(B) hepatoma
(C) cirrhosis
(D) pancreatitis

484. The term *fatty liver* is usually associated with which of the following conditions?

(A) diabetes
(B) chronic alcoholism
(C) obesity
(D) ulcerative colitis

485. Aneurysms of the popliteal arteries are

(A) usually arteriosclerotic
(B) found posterior to the knee joint
(C) associated with partially calcified walls
(D) all of the above

486. Chronic renal disease is associated with

(A) an enlarged kidney
(B) unilateral hydronephrosis
(C) dense, small echogenic kidneys
(D) a renal carbuncle

487. Gallstones may *not* produce symptoms; however, they can produce injury by

(A) the chronic irritation of calculi that may be a factor in the development of carcinoma of the gallbladder
(B) inducing inflammation (acute or chronic cholecystitis)
(C) causing obstruction at the neck of the gallbladder or in the bile ducts
(D) all of the above

Question 488: Select the letter indicating the appropriate numbered choice(s).

488. Sonography is helpful in evaluation of a solitary, hypofunctioning thyroid nodule (a cold nodule) that is initially encountered on a thyroid scintigram. List in order of greatest to least incidence the types of masses that can manifest as a solitary, hypofunctioning thyroid nodule.

1. cyst (such as a colloid cyst)
2. solid mass, malignant (such as follicular-papillary carcinoma)
3. solid mass, benign (such as an adenoma)

(A) 1, 2, 3
(B) 3, 2, 1
(C) 3, 1, 2

489. Obstruction of the common duct by pressure from outside the biliary tract is termed

(A) Courvoisier's law
(B) Raynaud's phenomenon
(C) Franconi's syndrome
(D) the Bernoulli effect

490. When performing a gallbladder examination, the patient is asked to be NPO (nothing by mouth) for approximately 12 hours before the examination because this will

(A) eliminate any gas that may collect in the bowel
(B) dehydrate the patient
(C) cause bile to collect within the gallbladder lumen

491. Sonography of a normally functioning transplanted kidney will appear

(A) more echogenic than usual
(B) with the renal cortex thinned, whereas the medullary pyramids increase in size
(C) not any different than a kidney found within the renal fossa
(D) with the renal sinus echoes occupying more space

492. Obstruction of the common bile duct by a mass in the head of the pancreas will lead to

(A) dilated gallbladder with dilated biliary radicles
(B) contracted gallbladder with dilated biliary radicles
(C) dilated biliary radicles with normal or shrunken gallbladder

493. A kidney can appear sonographically smaller than it actually is due to

(A) TGC (time gain compensation)
(B) gain
(C) scanning technique, imaging the kidney in an oblique rather than true long axis

494. Transplanted kidneys are usually placed

(A) within the kidney fossa
(B) in the pelvis along the iliopsoas margin
(C) in the pelvis posterior to the quadratus lumborum muscle

495. The membrane that lines the abdominal cavity is the

(A) visceral peritoneum
(B) parietal peritoneum
(C) pleura
(D) endometrial lining
(E) serosal lining

Questions 496 through 498: Refer to Fig. 5–15.

496. The echogenic line (*B*) represents the ligamentum venosum.

(A) true
(B) false

497. Echogenic foci (*A*) represents the ligamentum teres.

(A) true
(B) false

498. The portion of the liver between the inferior vena cava (IVC) and *B* is the caudate lobe.

(A) true
(B) false

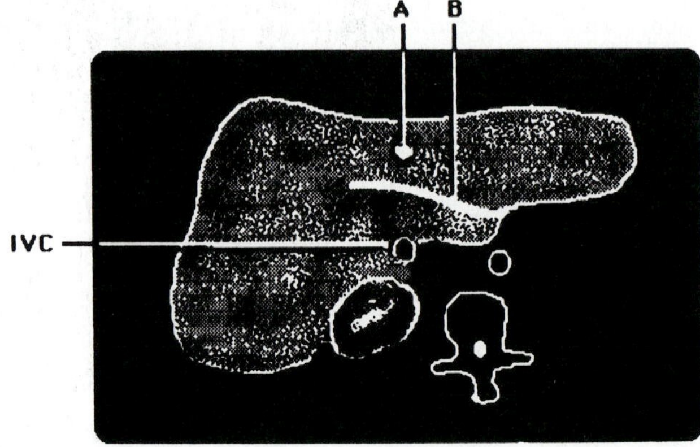

Figure 5–15. Schematic transverse scan of the liver.

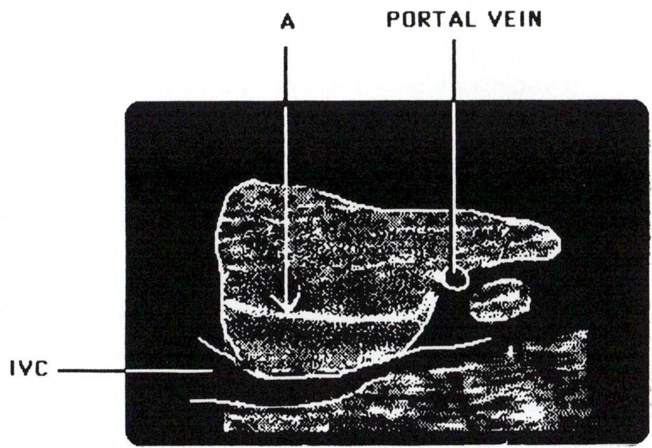

Figure 5–16. Schematic sagittal scan of the liver.

Questions 499 through 501: Refer to Fig. 5–16.

499. The arrow is pointing to the ligamentum teres.

(A) true
(B) false

500. The caudate lobe is cephalad to the portal vein.

(A) true
(B) false

501. The head of the pancreas is caudal to the portal vein.

(A) true
(B) false

502. When hypertrophic pyloric stenosis is delineated in short axis the abnormally hypertrophied muscle wall usually measures

(A) 5 mm or more
(B) more than 5 cm
(C) less than 2 mm
(D) about 5 mm

503. The sonographic findings of hydronephrosis may present with

(A) the calices and pelvis so grossly dilated that only a single large sac is seen
(B) multiple cystic areas within the kidney sinus
(C) very little renal parenchyma that can be visualized owing to the obstructing calices
(D) all of the above

504. To localize a dilated ureter, it is most helpful to

(A) place the patient in a supine position and scan the abdomen
(B) place the patient in a prone position and scan the abdomen
(C) scan the pelvis with a full bladder and evaluate the area posterior to the bladder
(D) all of the above

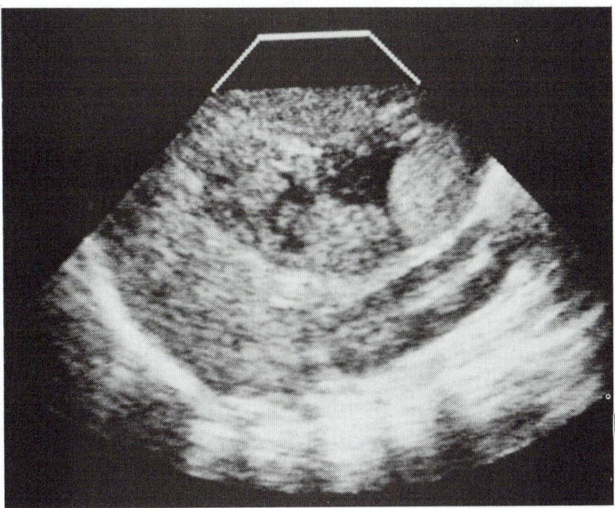

Figure 5–17. Sagittal sonogram taken through the right upper quadrant of a child.

505. The abnormal sonographic findings in Fig. 5–17 include

(A) a mass within the right kidney
(B) a large complex mass within the liver
(C) no abnormality
(D) pleural effusion

506. The most common liver mass found in children is

(A) hepatoblastoma
(B) metastatic disease
(C) polycystic liver and kidney disease
(D) hepatic fibrosis

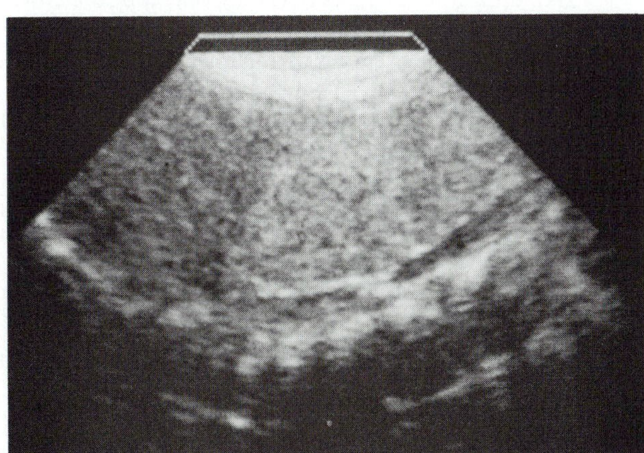

Figure 5–18. Sagittal sonogram through the right upper quadrant of a 9-hour-old neonate who failed to produce urine.

507. The abnormal sonographic findings in Fig. 5–18 include

(A) abnormal sonographic appearance of the right kidney suggestive of adult-type polycystic kidney disease
(B) abnormal sonographic appearance of the right kidney, highly suggestive of infantile polycystic disease
(C) abnormal sonographic appearance of the right kidney, most consistent with multicystic disease
(D) none of the above

508. In infantile polycystic disease

(A) cysts can be seen on sonography
(B) cysts are not seen because they are microscopic
(C) only a portion of the kidney is affected
(D) the other kidney appears normal because it is usually only unilateral

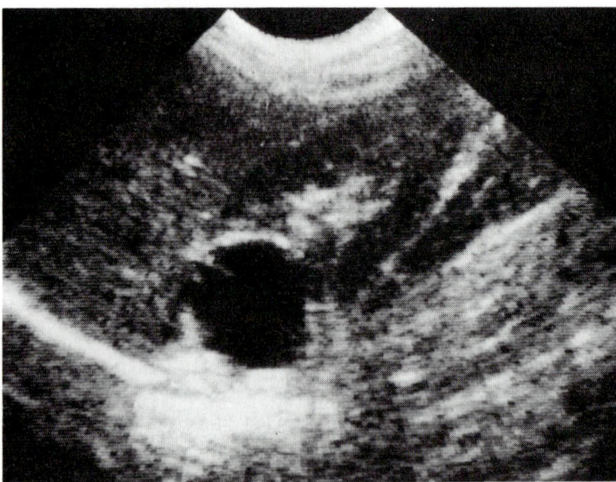

A

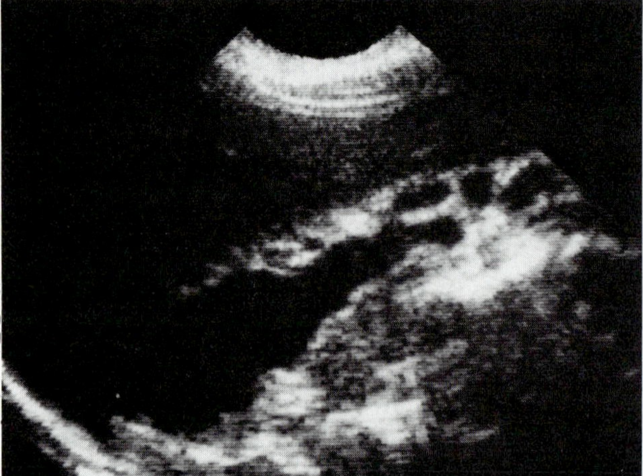

B

Figures 5–19. (A) and (B) Sagittal sonograms taken through the right upper abdomen. Figure 5–19A is lateral to Figure 5–19B.

509. The abnormal sonographic findings in Figs. 5–19A and B include a

(A) simple cortical cyst in the upper pole of the right kidney
(B) distended upper pole moiety of a duplex collecting system because the cystic mass seems to be contiguous with a distended ureter to the upper pole
(C) renal tumor
(D) large arteriovenous malformation

510. Typically, with a duplex collecting system, the upper pole moiety (Figs. 5–19A and B) is

(A) hydronephrotic due to reflux
(B) hydronephrotic due to obstruction from a ureterocele
(C) usually the least affected
(D) none of the above

511. The positive sonographic findings in Fig. 5–20 include

(A) cyst arising from the lateral aspect of the right kidney
(B) a 1-cm cyst seen lateral to an enlarged and flattened adrenal
(C) metastases in the liver
(D) none of the above

512. In renal agenesis, the adrenal

(A) has no abnormal shape and may mimic a kidney
(B) is also not present
(C) both A and B
(D) none of the above

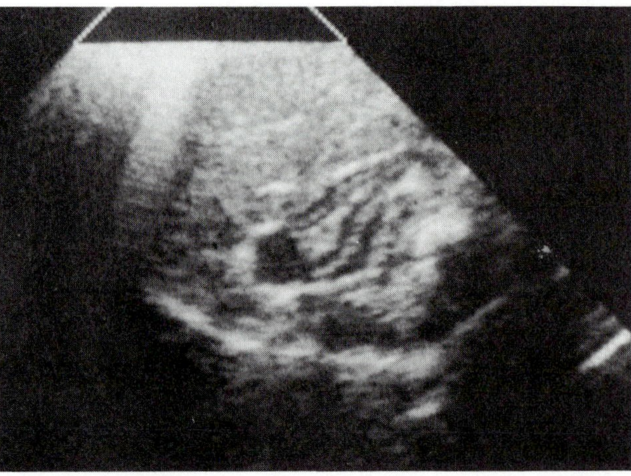

Figure 5–20. Transverse sonogram of the right upper abdomen in an anuric neonate.

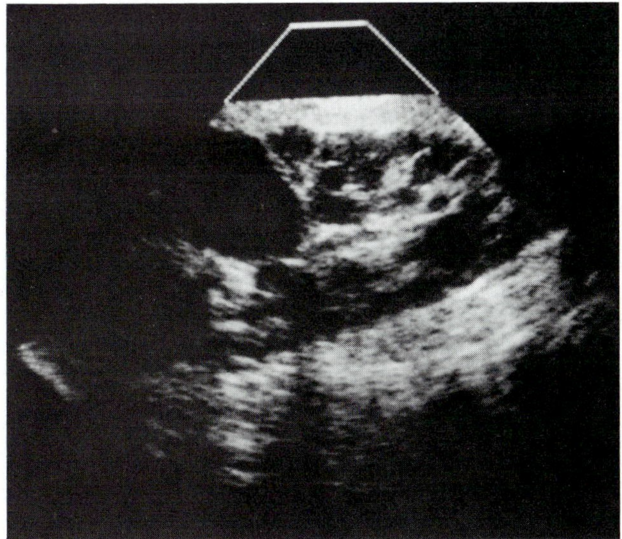

Figure 5–21. Coronal sonogram of the left kidney.

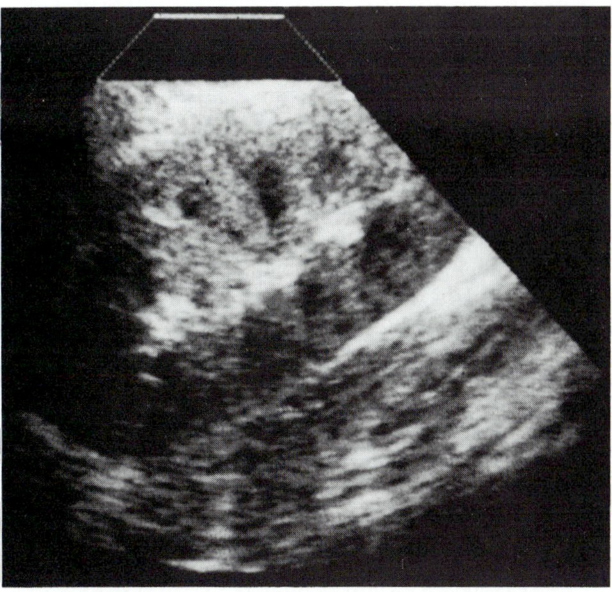

Figure 5–22. Long axis image of a renal transplant.

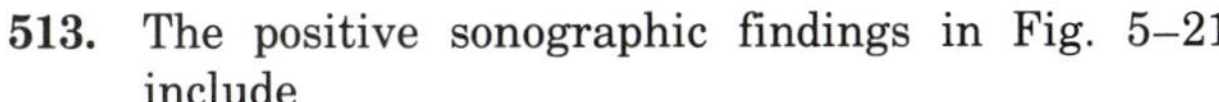

513. The positive sonographic findings in Fig. 5–21 include

(A) a solid tumor in the lower pole
(B) multiple cysts of various sizes, highly suggestive of adult-type polycystic disease
(C) marked hydronephrosis
(D) none of the above

514. In adult-type polycystic kidney disease, cysts may be found in

(A) the liver
(B) the pancreas
(C) the spleen
(D) any of the above

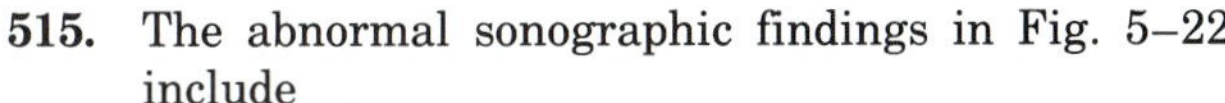

515. The abnormal sonographic findings in Fig. 5–22 include

(A) hydronephrosis
(B) the transplanted kidney appears normal
(C) very prominent medullary pyramids, consistent with acute rejection
(D) a large cyst in the upper pole of the transplanted kidney

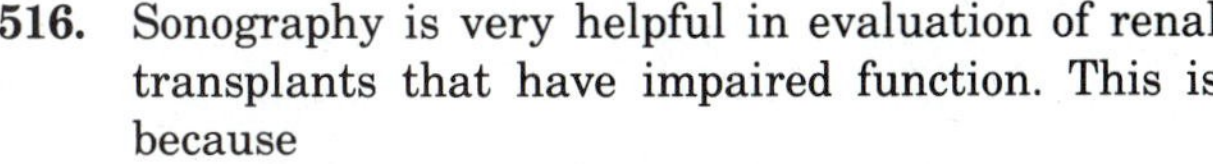

516. Sonography is very helpful in evaluation of renal transplants that have impaired function. This is because

(A) sonography can differentiate obstructive causes from rejection
(B) sonography is helpful because it can detect early rejection earlier and more reliably than the renal scintigram
(C) sonography is only helpful in detection of masses that can be treated surgically
(D) both A and C

517. The arrow in Fig. 5–23 points to

(A) a medullary pyramid
(B) the renal cortex
(C) a parapelvic cyst
(D) none of the above

518. The size of the kidney in normal adults is

(A) 10–12 cm in long axis, 5–6 cm in width, and 3–4 cm in anterior-posterior and transverse dimensions

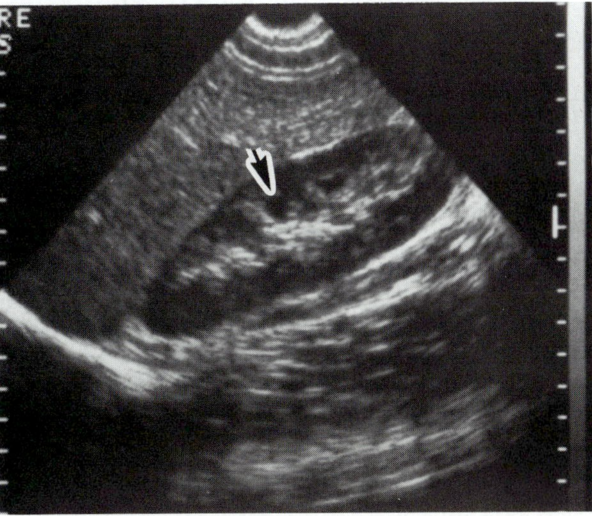

Figure 5–23. Sagittal sonogram through the right upper abdomen.

(B) there is too much variation and a normal range cannot be established
(C) the renal parenchyma (medulla and cortex) should measure at least 1 cm
(D) both A and B

519. The abnormal sonographic findings in Figs. 5–24A and B include

(A) gallbladder wall thickening
(B) viscid bile or sludge in the gallbladder
(C) a tumor within the gallbladder wall
(D) both A and B

520. Viscid bile within the gallbladder indicates

(A) the gallbladder has not been completely emptied, allowing viscid bile to build up within the lumen
(B) a normal finding that can be encountered in any patient
(C) that viscid bile typically is the precursor to small calculi and should be removed percutaneously
(D) both A and C

521. The abnormal sonographic findings in Fig. 5–25 include

(A) the pancreas as very echogenic; highly suggestive of chronic pancreatitis
(B) the pancreas is echogenic; but in older patients, it may normally be this echogenic
(C) both A and B
(D) none of the above

522. Sonography can be used intraoperatively in detecting pancreatic tumors. Most pancreatic tumors appear

(A) as hypoechoic focal lesions within the pancreas
(B) as echogenic lesions within the pancreas
(C) sonography is not useful in intraoperative pancreatic cases
(D) none of the above

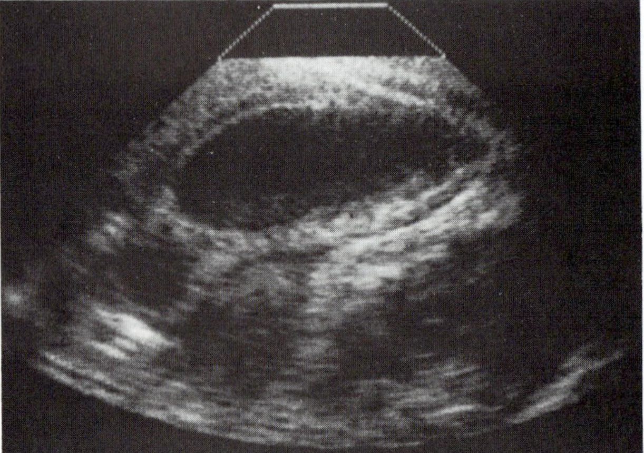

A

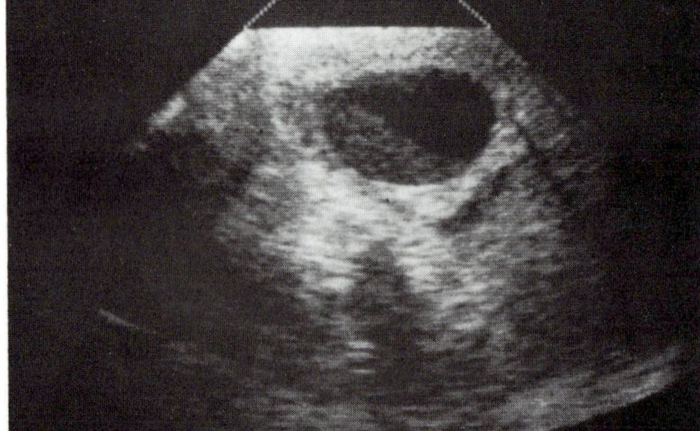

B

Figure 5–24. (**A**) Long axis view of the gallbladder. (**B**) Short axis view of the gallbladder.

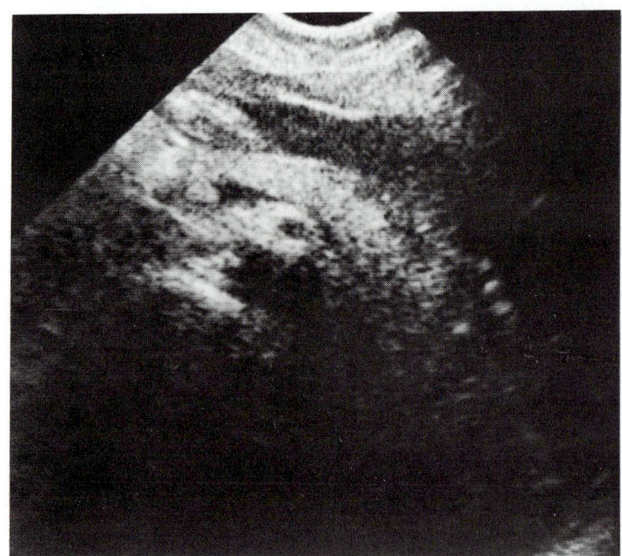

Figure 5–25. Transverse sonogram of the upper abdomen.

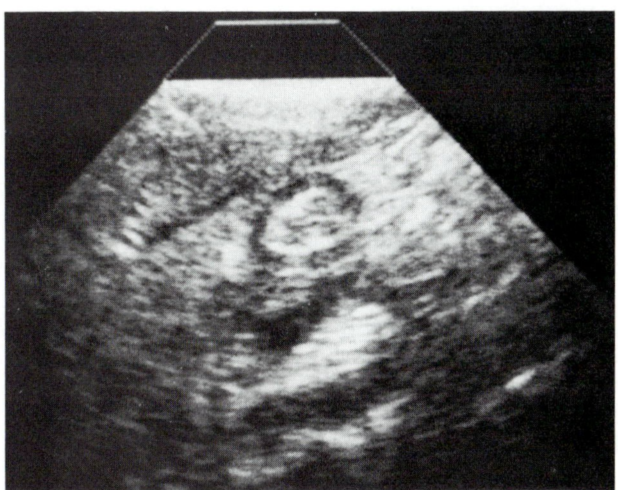

Figure 5–26. Sagittal sonogram taken through the midabdomen.

523. Sonographic findings in Fig. 5–26 include

(A) an abnormal mass in the upper abdomen most likely within the liver
(B) a structure that has a target configuration
(C) both A and B
(D) none of the above

524. The halo around the mass (Fig. 5–26) probably represents

(A) edema around a tumor
(B) the wall of the stomach
(C) both A and B
(D) none of the above

525. The anechoic structure immediately posterior to the gallbladder neck, as shown in Fig. 5–27, is probably

(A) a cystic tumor arising from the right adrenal
(B) a fluid-filled loop of bowel, probably transverse colon
(C) a fluid-filled loop of duodenum
(D) either B or C, but not A

526. Another maneuver to evaluate the gallbladder and the presence or absence of calculi within its lumen includes

(A) an upright view looking for stones to drop into the fundus
(B) a Trendelenburg view to see if the stone is impacted in the neck of the gallbladder
(C) both A and B
(D) none of the above

527. The structure depicted in Fig. 5–28 is the

(A) gallbladder
(B) stomach
(C) liver
(D) hydronephrotic right kidney

528. The malformation variant in the gallbladder that involves an acutely angulated pouch of the fundus is termed

(A) phrygian cap
(B) duplication of the gallbladder
(C) megagallbladder
(D) Smurf's cap

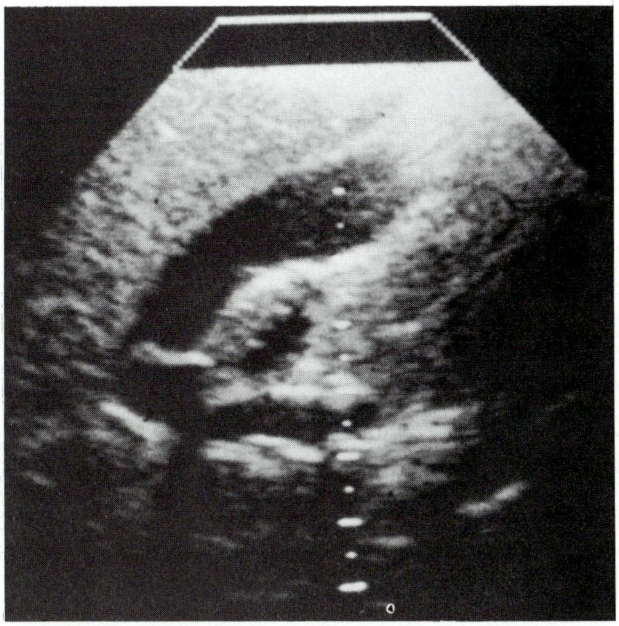

Figure 5–27. Sagittal sonogram of the right upper abdomen.

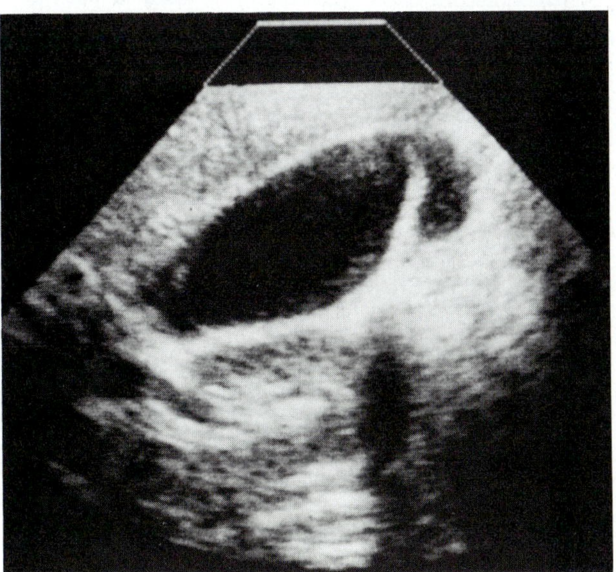

Figure 5–28. Sagittal sonogram of the right upper abdomen.

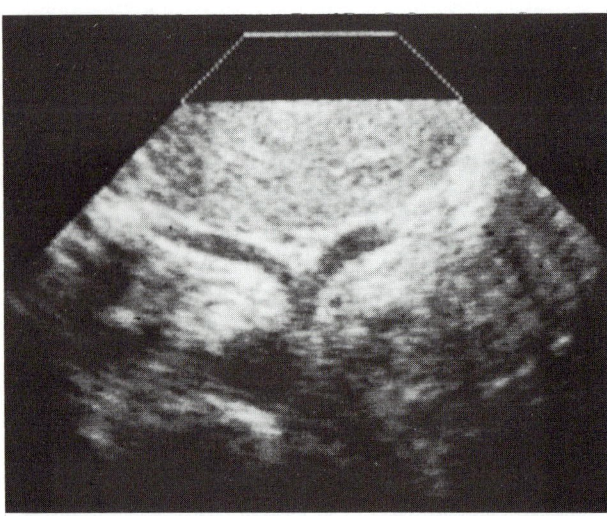

Figure 5–29. Transverse sonogram of the upper abdomen.

529. The vascular structures depicted in Fig. 5–29 include

(A) the aorta and superior mesenteric artery
(B) the aorta and celiac axis
(C) the aorta and splenic artery only
(D) none of the above

530. The normal celiac axis includes

(A) the common hepatic artery, splenic artery, and left gastric artery
(B) the superior mesenteric artery only
(C) A and B
(D) none of the above

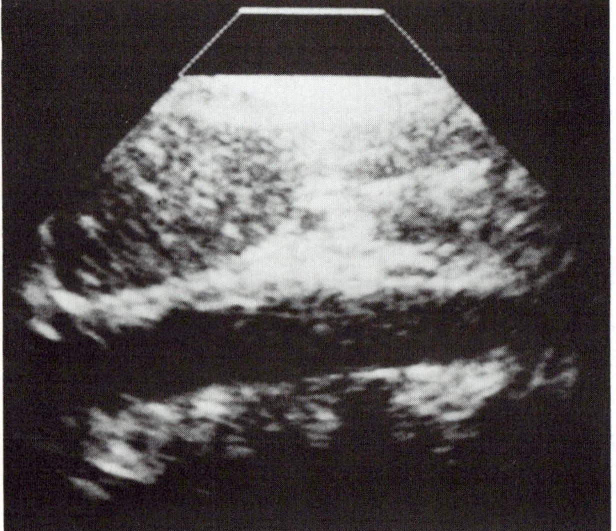

Figure 5–30. Sagittal image of the upper abdomen.

531. Structures identified in Fig. 5–30 include

(A) the abdominal aorta
(B) the left lobe of the liver
(C) the right kidney
(D) both A and B

532. The most frequent cause of abdominal aortic aneurysm is

(A) atherosclerosis
(B) mycosis
(C) trauma
(D) none of the above

533. The arrows in Fig. 5–31 delineate

(A) a hypertrophied pyloric muscle
(B) a normal pyloric muscle
(C) a lesion within the liver that obstructs the stomach
(D) none of the above

534. Hypertrophic pyloric stenosis can be diagnosed when

(A) the pyloric muscle is greater than 4 mm in thickness
(B) when the lumen of the pyloris remains totally open allowing reflux
(C) A and B
(D) none of the above

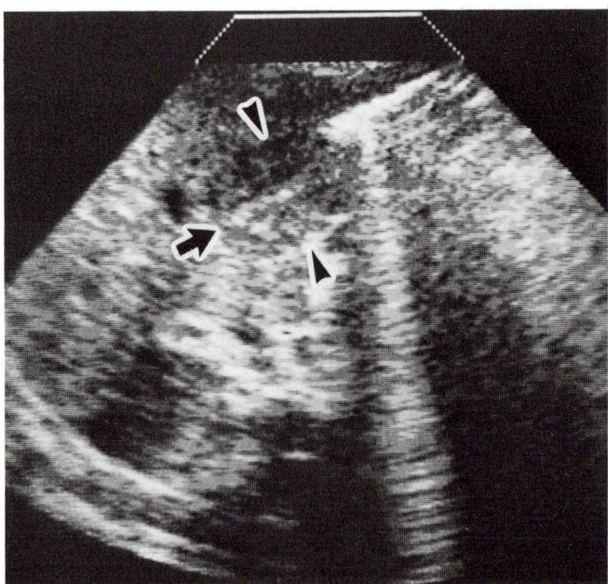

Figure 5–31. Transverse sonogram of a 2-week-old infant with excessive vomiting.

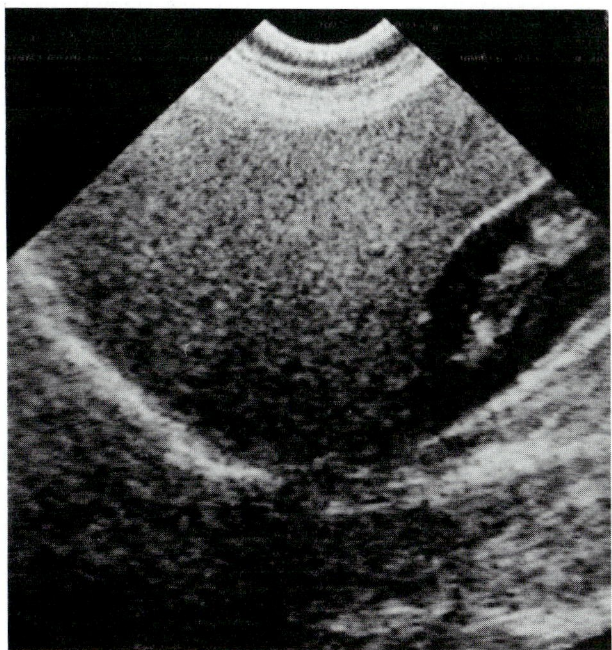

Figure 5–32. Sagittal sonogram obtained through the right upper abdomen.

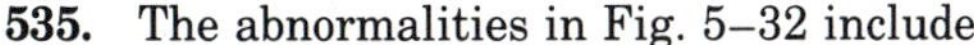

535. The abnormalities in Fig. 5–32 include

(A) the liver parenchyma is very echogenic when compared to the kidney
(B) there are no abnormalities
(C) there are metastases throughout the liver
(D) there are multiple masses in the kidney

536. Fatty metamorphosis of the liver can be assessed sonographically by noting

(A) increased echogenicity when compared with normal kidney
(B) normal vessels being identified throughout the liver
(C) A and B
(D) none of the above

537. The echogenic focus within the testicle (Fig. 5–33) represents

(A) a "burnt out" germ cell tumor
(B) the mediastinum of the testis
(C) an infarct
(D) none of the above

538. In testicular torsion

(A) the testes have a nonhomogeneous texture due to areas of hemorrhagic infarction
(B) the testes appear normal
(C) only after 2 weeks do the testes have an abnormal appearance
(D) none of the above

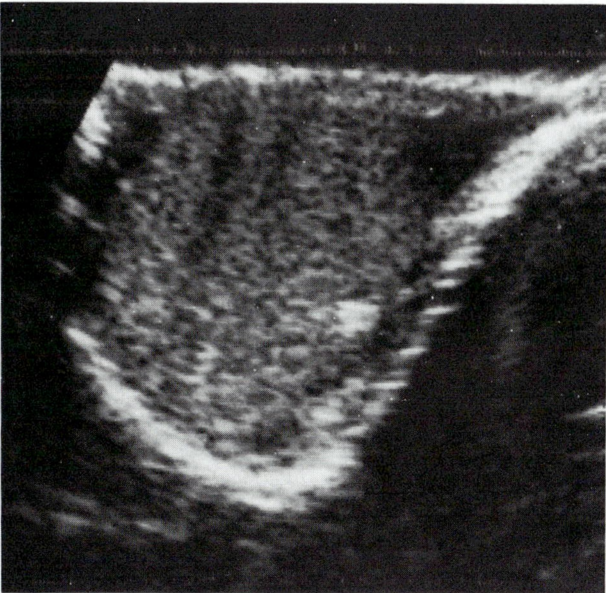

Figure 5–33. Transverse sonogram through the left hemiscrotum.

539. The abnormal sonographic features in Fig. 5–34 include

(A) marked hydronephrosis
(B) a calculus within the midpolar region
(C) a tumor in the upper pole
(D) all of the above

540. Sonography can occasionally detect renal calculi not seen on excretory urography or plain film radiography.

(A) true
(B) false

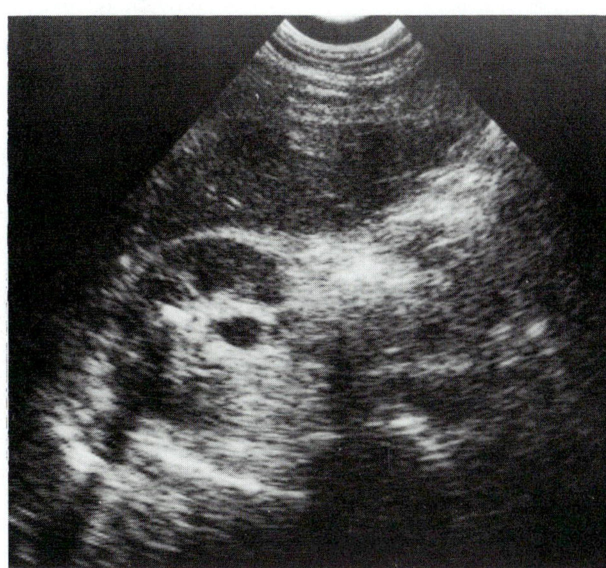

Figure 5–34. Transverse sonogram of the right kidney.

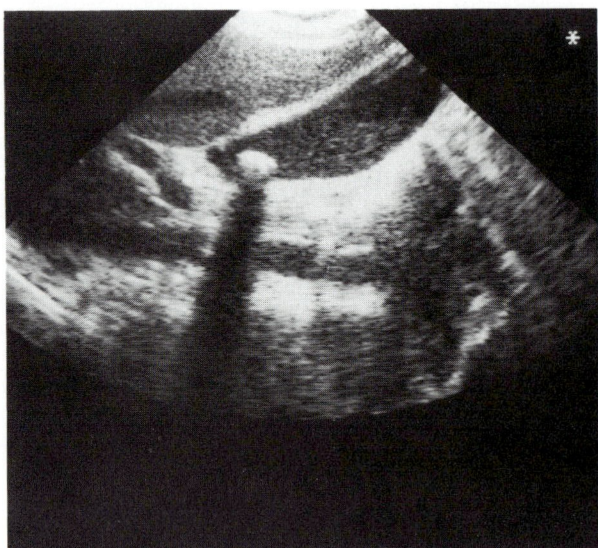

Figure 5–35. Long axis sonogram of the gallbladder.

541. The abnormal sonographic findings in Fig. 5–35 include

(A) a calculus within the gallbladder neck
(B) viscid bile within the gallbladder lumen
(C) A and B
(D) none of the above

542. The presence of intraluminal calculus indicates that there is cholecystitis.

(A) true
(B) false

543. The abnormal sonographic findings in Fig. 5–36 include

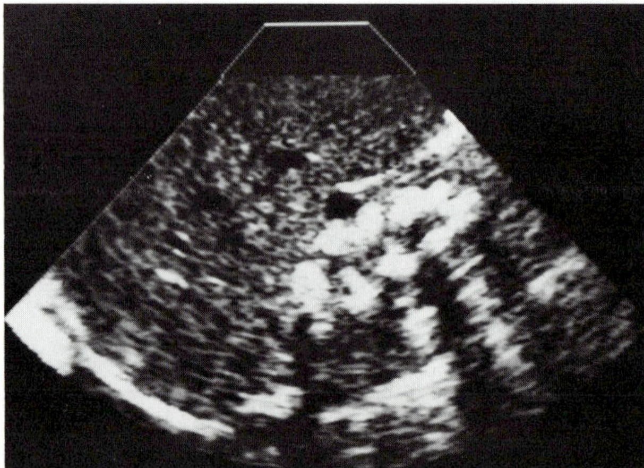

Figure 5–36. Sagittal sonogram through the liver and right kidney.

(A) a cortical cyst within the right kidney
(B) echogenic foci throughout the kidney probably representing a staghorn calculus
(C) focally echogenic medulla and cortex
(D) A and C

544. Disorders associated with this sonographic appearance (Fig. 5–36) include

(A) renal tubular acidosis
(B) medullary sponge kidney
(C) papillary necrosis
(D) all of the above

545. The abnormal sonographic findings in Fig. 5–37 include

(A) a renal tumor filling the renal pelvis
(B) a large renal calculus
(C) massive hydronephrosis
(D) all of the above

546. The type of renal calculi that may be nonopaque radiographically but appear as echogenic foci on sonography includes

(A) a calcium oxalate
(B) calcium bilirubinate
(C) cholesterol
(D) none of the above

547. The sonographic findings in Fig. 5–38 include

(A) massive splenomegaly
(B) a subphrenic abscess
(C) metastasis within the spleen
(D) normal-appearing spleen

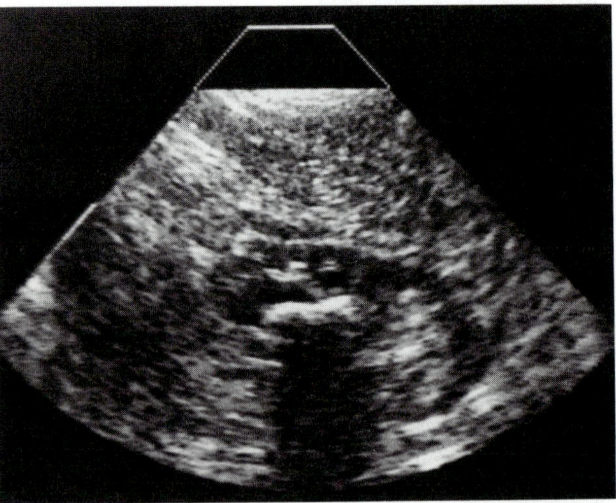

Figure 5–37. Transverse or short axis image of the left kidney. Plain film radiograph failed to reveal any abnormal calcifications.

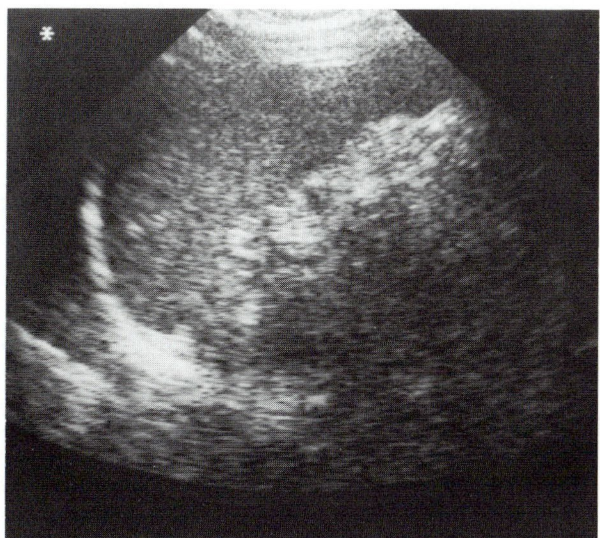

Figure 5–38. Coronal image through the left upper quadrant.

548. Splenomegaly can be encountered in

(A) chronic myelogenous leukemia
(B) portal hypertension
(C) sickle-cell crisis
(D) A and B

549. Fig. 5–39 depicts which of the following structures?

(A) the common hepatic duct
(B) a normal common bile duct
(C) the main portal vein
(D) all of the above

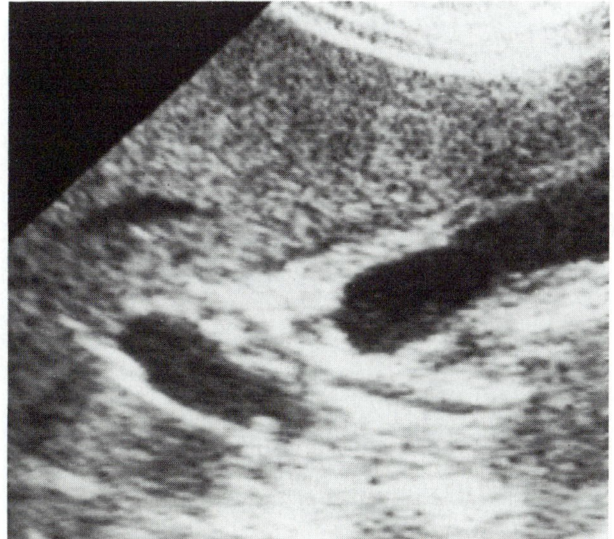

Figure 5–39. Magnified sagittal sonogram of the porta hepatis area.

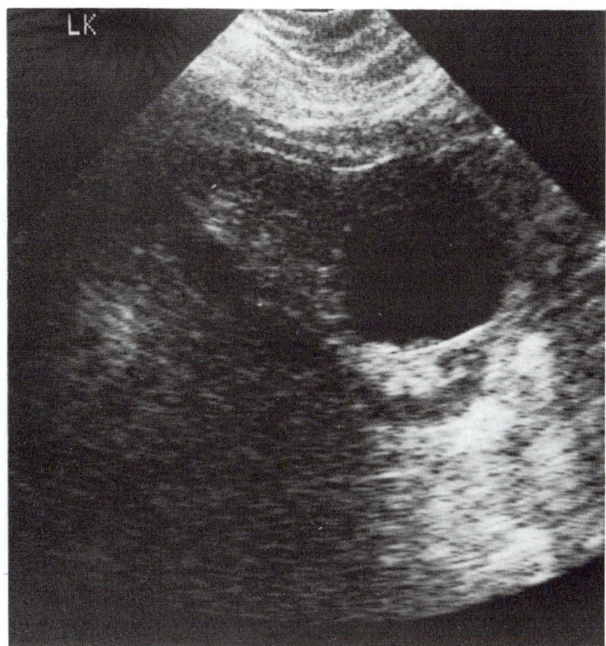

Figure 5–40. Coronal sonogram of the left kidney.

550. The common bile duct is formed by

(A) the right and left hepatic ducts joining the cystic duct
(B) the cystic duct joining the right hepatic duct
(C) the common hepatic duct joining the cystic duct
(D) none of the above

551. The abnormal sonographic findings in Fig. 5–40 include

(A) a solid mass in the lower pole
(B) a simple cyst in the lower pole
(C) hydronephrosis
(D) all of the above

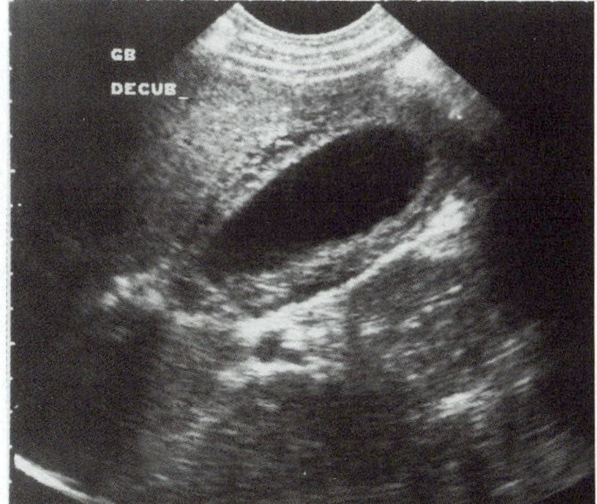

Figure 5–41. Sagittal image of the right upper quadrant.

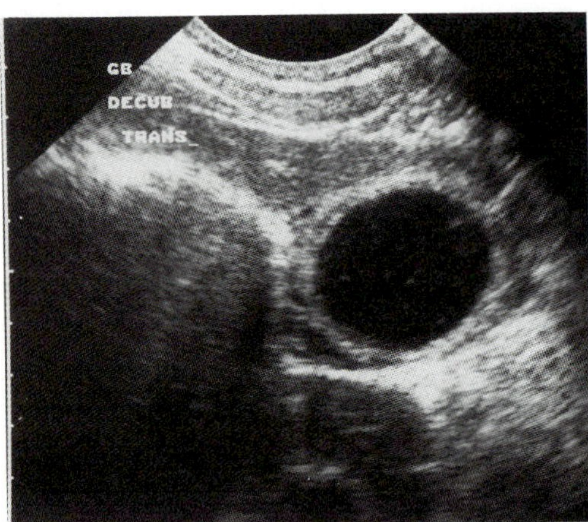

Figure 5–42. Transverse sonogram of the right upper quadrant.

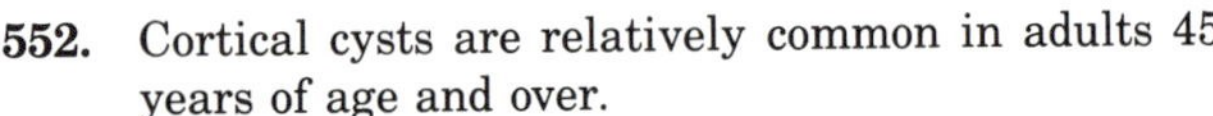

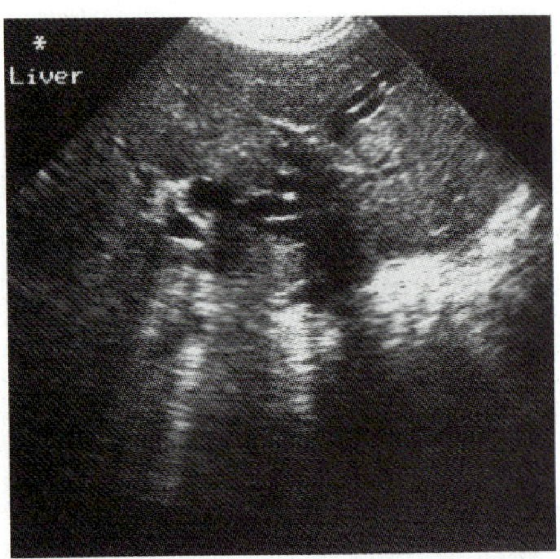

Figure 5–44. Transverse sonogram of the liver.

552. Cortical cysts are relatively common in adults 45 years of age and over.

(A) true
(B) false

553. Figs. 5–41 and 5–42 are long and short axes sonograms of the right upper quadrant of the abdomen, respectively. The abnormality is (are)

(A) marked thickening of the gallbladder wall
(B) gallstones
(C) sludge
(D) A and C

554. Causes of gallbladder wall thickening include

(A) cholecystitis
(B) nondistension
(C) hepatitis
(D) all of the above

555. Elicitation of pain while scanning over the gallbladder fundus is termed

(A) Chandelier's sign
(B) Murphy's sign
(C) Murphy's law
(D) Courvoisier gallbladder

556. Figs. 5–43, 5–44, and 5–45 were obtained during an abdominal sonogram performed on a 50-year-old man. The arrow in Fig. 5–43 points to

(A) the left portal vein
(B) a dilated intrahepatic duct in the left lobe
(C) an hepatic vein
(D) none of the above

557. The arrow in Fig. 5–45 points to

(A) a dilated common bile duct with a rat-tail deformity
(B) the main portal vein
(C) a hepatic vein
(D) hepatic artery

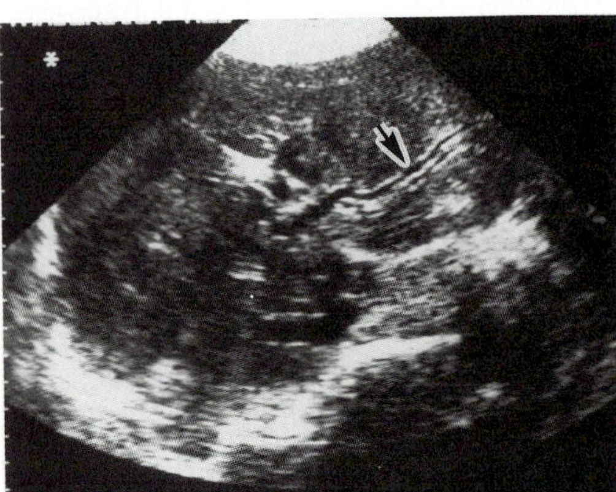

Figure 5–43. Sagittal image slightly left of midline.

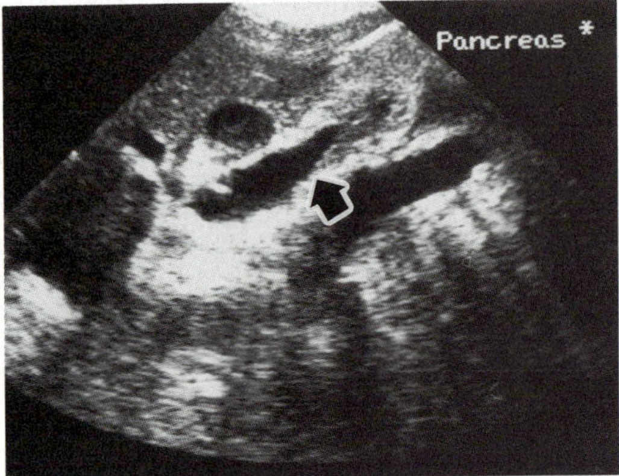

Figure 5–45. Sagittal image of the right upper quadrant.

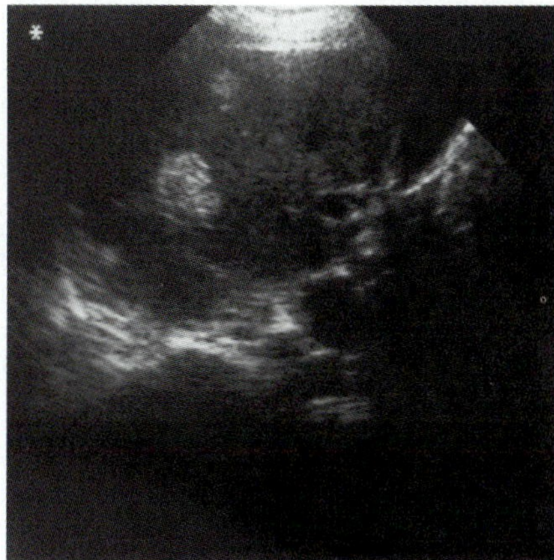

Figure 5–46. Transverse sonogram throughout the right hepatic lobe.

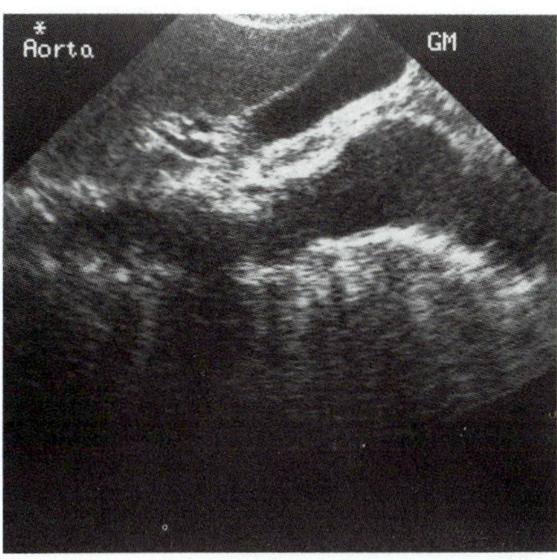

Figure 5–47. Midline longitudinal scan of the abdomen.

558. The most likely diagnosis is

(A) biliary obstruction due to cholelithiasis
(B) biliary obstruction due to pancreatitis
(C) distended portal vein due to portal hypertension
(D) distended hepatic vein due to chronic congestive heart failure
(E) obstruction of the distal common bile duct due to pancreatic tumor

559. Dilated intrahepatic ducts tend to be readily delineated in the left lobe because

(A) they are first affected by obstruction
(B) they course transversely in the left lobe
(C) they are bigger in the left lobe than in the right lobe
(D) none of the above

560. Fig. 5–46 is a transverse sonogram throughout the right hepatic lobe. The abnormality is

(A) an echogenic mass
(B) absence of portal vein
(C) a left-sided gallbladder
(D) none of the above

561. The most likely diagnosis is

(A) hemangioma
(B) metastases
(C) A or B
(D) neither

562. Hemangiomas can be diagnosed by

(A) needle biopsy
(B) a tagged red blood cell liver scan
(C) a computed tomographic (CT) scan
(D) an magnetic resonance imaging scan
(E) all of the above

563. Fig. 5–47 is a midline longitudinal scan of the abdomen. The abnormality is

(A) an ectopic gallbladder
(B) aneurysmal dilatation of the distal abdominal aorta
(C) total occlusion of the abdominal aorta by thrombus
(D) none of the above

564. An aneurysm is usually the result of

(A) degenerative joint disease
(B) atherosclerosis
(C) hypertension
(D) diabetes

565. Other arteries that may be affected by an aneurysm include

(A) the coronary arteries
(B) the carotids
(C) popliteal arteries
(D) all of the above

566. Fig. 5–48 is a midline sagittal transrectal sonogram of the prostate. The abnormality is

(A) dilatation of the prostatic urethra
(B) tumor within the transitional zone
(C) both A and B
(D) none of the above

567. The most likely diagnosis in the patient in Fig. 5–48 is

(A) carcinoma of the prostate stage A
(B) carcinoma of the prostate stage C
(C) idiopathic dilatation of the urethra
(D) iatrogenic dilatation of the urethra
(E) A and D

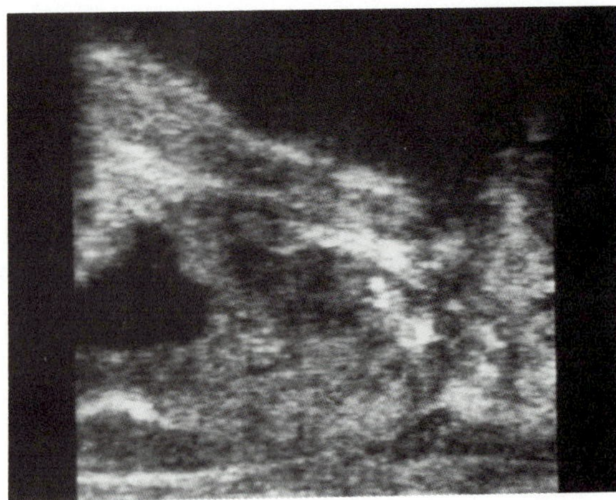

Figure 5–48. Midline sagittal transrectal sonogram of the prostate.

568. The prostatic-specific antigen (PSA) in the patient in Fig. 5–48 would most likely be

(A) normal
(B) elevated
(C) subnormal

569. Fig. 5–49 is an abdominal sonogram obtained through the right upper quadrant. The abnormality is

(A) an echogenic kidney
(B) hypoechogenic liver
(C) both A and B
(D) neither

570. The most likely diagnosis in the patient in Fig. 5–49 is

(A) a colonic tumor
(B) severe renal parenchymal disease
(C) a liver infarct
(D) none of the above

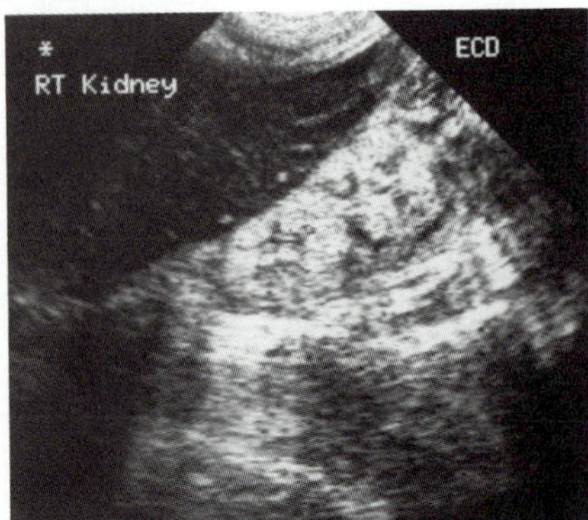

Figure 5–49. Sagittal sonogram obtained through the right upper quadrant.

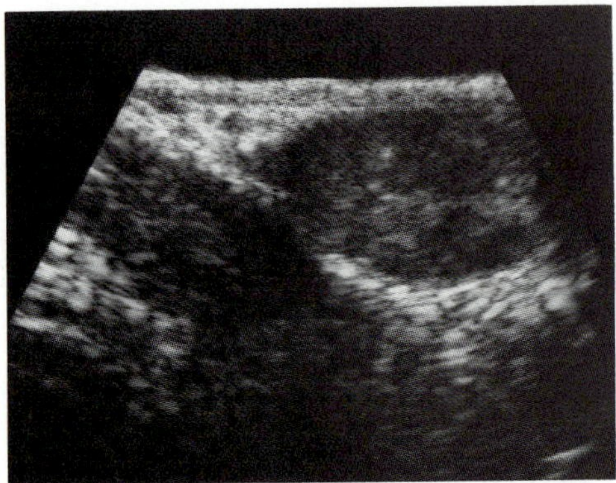

Figure 5–50. Long axis sonogram of the right hemiscrotum.

571. Normally, the liver is slightly more echogenic than the renal parenchyma because

(A) it has fibrous septa within the hepatic lobule
(B) the kidney has more water content
(C) the liver has more water content
(D) none of the above

572. Fig. 5–50 is a long axis sonogram of the right hemiscrotum. The abnormality is

(A) a diffusely abnormal testis
(B) enlarged and echogenic head of the epididymis
(C) a hydrocele
(D) none of the above

573. The most likely diagnosis in the patient in Fig. 5–50 is

(A) testicular tumor
(B) testicular torsion
(C) epididymitis
(D) A and C

574. The presenting symptom of a testicular tumor can be

(A) para-aortic lymphadenopathy
(B) mediastinum lymphadenopathy
(C) retroperitoneal lymphadenopathy
(D) all of the above

575. Fig. 5–51 is a parasagittal transrectal sonogram of the prostate rotated slightly from the midline. The abnormality is

(A) a small prostate
(B) absence of the seminal vesicle
(C) a hypoechoic lesion in the peripheral zone
(D) both B and C

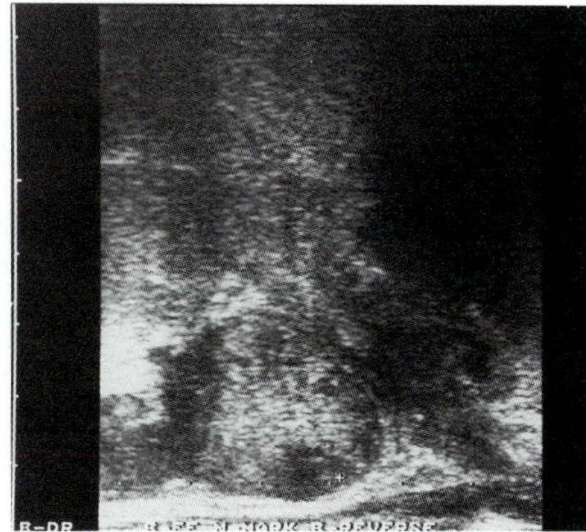

Figure 5–51. Parasagittal transrectal sonogram of the prostate rotated slightly from the midline.

576. The next procedure for definitive diagnosis after the sonogram would be

(A) useless—this finding is diagnostic
(B) transperineal biopsy
(C) transrectal biopsy
(D) either B or C

577. The approximate chance that a hypoechoic lesion in the peripheral zone is carcinoma is

(A) 2%
(B) 20%
(C) 50%
(D) 80%

578. The relative advantage of transrectal biopsy over transperineal biopsy includes

(A) an increased chance of infection in transperineal biopsy
(B) an increased chance of infection in transrectal biopsy
(C) increased incidence of hematospermia with transrectal biopsy
(D) none of the above

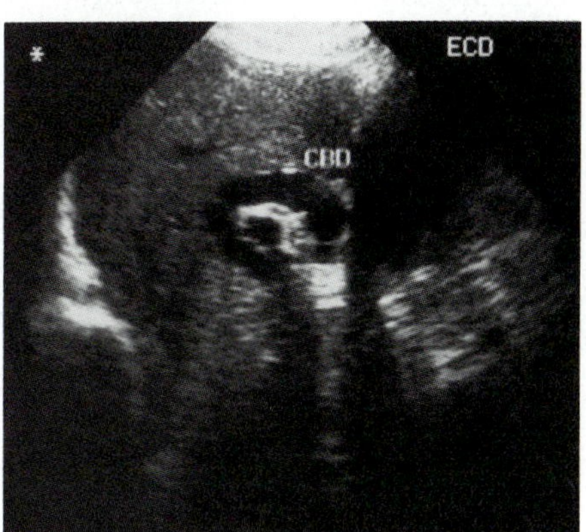

Figure 5–52. Long axis sonogram of the common bile duct.

579. Fig. 5–52 is a long axis sonogram of the common bile duct. The abnormality is

(A) thrombosed portal vein
(B) a dilated common bile duct
(C) aneurysm or dilatation of the hepatic artery
(D) A and B

580. The most likely cause of the abnormality shown in Fig. 5–52 is

(A) cholelithiasis
(B) tumor in the pancreatic head
(C) A or B
(D) neither

581. The common bile duct may distend with age and measure 7 mm or greater

(A) true
(B) false

582. Fig. 5–53 is a transverse sonogram of the left lobe of the liver. The arrow points to

(A) hepatic vessels
(B) hypoechoic lesions
(C) portal sinuses
(D) none of the above

583. Diagnostic possibilities in the findings in Fig. 5–53 include

(A) metastases
(B) hemangiomas
(C) infection foci
(D) A or C

584. The next step in the evaluation of the liver lesions seen in Fig. 5–53 would be

(A) a red blood cell liver scan
(B) liver-spleen scan

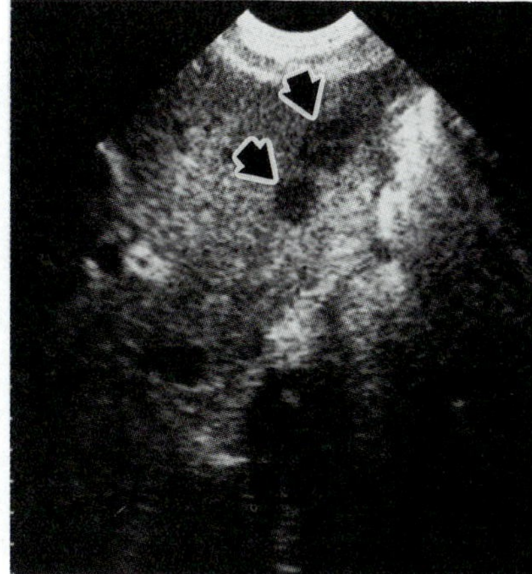

Figure 5–53. Transverse sonogram of the left lobe of the liver.

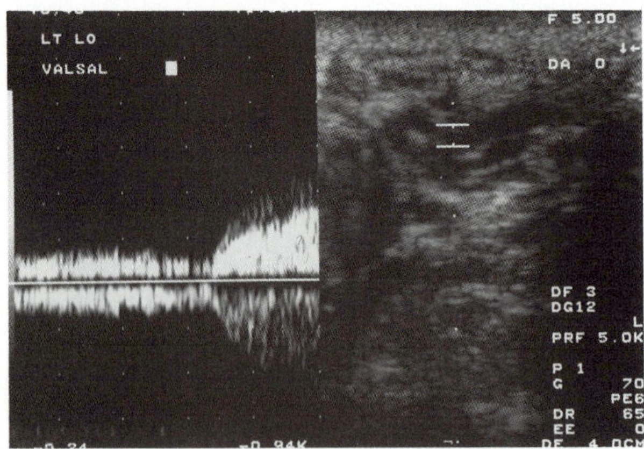

Figure 5–54. Duplex Doppler sonogram obtained in the upper hemiscrotum.

(C) computed tomography (CT) or magnetic resonance imaging (MRI) of the liver
(D) fine needle aspiration

585. Fig. 5–54 is a duplex Doppler sonogram obtained in the upper hemiscrotum. The abnormality is

(A) dilated spermatic duct
(B) dilated vessels near the head of the epididymis
(C) vascular tumor of the testes
(D) B or C

586. The waveform of a varicocele indicates

(A) increased flow within the varicocele
(B) decreased flow within the varicocele
(C) no change in flow after varicocele

587. The most likely diagnosis from the findings in Fig. 5–54 is

(A) varicocele
(B) testicular tumor
(C) testicular torsion
(D) A and C

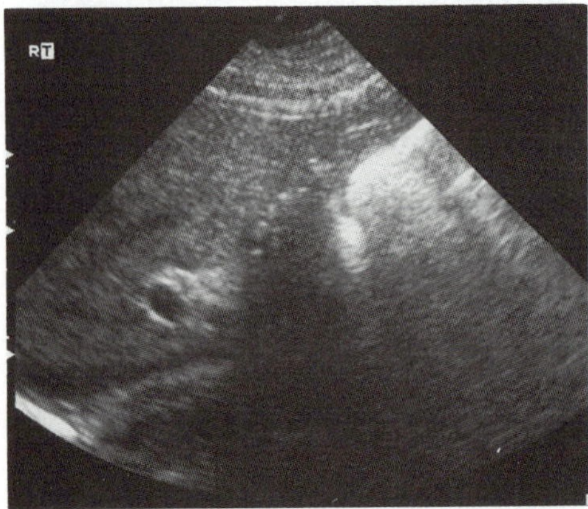

Figure 5–55. Long axis sonogram of the right upper quadrant.

588. Fig. 5–55 is a long axis sonogram of the right upper quadrant of the abdomen. The abnormality is (are):

(A) contracted gallbladder filled with stones
(B) contracted gallbladder without stones
(C) cyst in the liver
(D) nothing, the patient is status/postcholecystectomy

589. The most likely diagnosis in the patient in Fig. 5–55 is

(A) calculus cholecystitis
(B) hepatitis
(C) A and B
(D) neither

590. The patient in Fig. 5–55 is a good candidate for lithotripsy.

(A) true
(B) false

591. Fig. 5–56 is a longitudinal sonogram of the left kidney obtained in the prone position. The abnormality is

(A) a renal tumor affecting the upper pole
(B) distension of the renal pelvis and proximal ureter
(C) parapelvic cyst
(D) none of the above

592. The most likely diagnosis in the patient in Fig. 5–56 is

(A) vesicourethral reflex
(B) ureteropelvic junction obstruction
(C) pyelonephrosis
(D) ureterovesical junction obstruction
(E) A or D

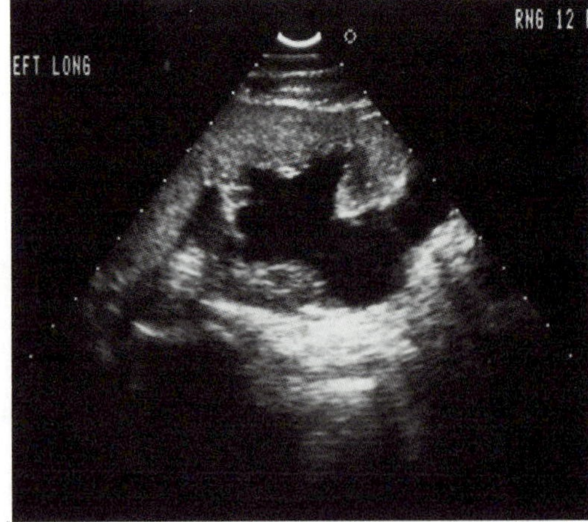

Figure 5–56. Longitudinal sonogram of the left kidney obtained in the prone position.

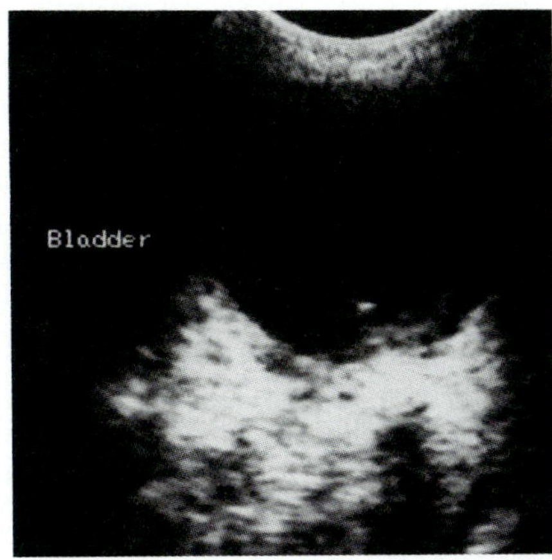

Figure 5–57. Transverse sonogram obtained through the urinary bladder.

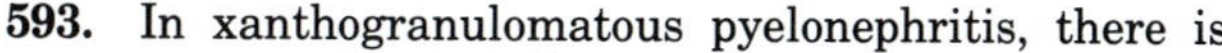

593. In xanthogranulomatous pyelonephritis, there is

(A) a calculus usually obstructing the renal collecting system
(B) parenchymal changes within the kidney secondary to infection
(C) multiple transitional cell tumors
(D) renal cell carcinomas
(E) A and B

594. Fig. 5–57 is a transverse sonogram obtained through the urinary bladder. The abnormality is

(A) a thickened bladder wall, particularly in the posterior portion of the wall
(B) bilateral ureteroceles
(C) A and B
(D) none of the above

595. The most likely diagnosis in the patient in Fig. 5–57 is

(A) bladder tumor (transitional carcioma)
(B) focal cystitis
(C) A or B
(D) none of the above

596. In a child, cystitis may be associated with

(A) chemotherapy
(B) frequent and painful urination
(C) renal infection
(D) all of the above

597. Fig. 5–58 is a longitudinal scan of the right upper quadrant. The abnormality is

(A) a hypoechoic texture to the renal parenchyma
(B) an echogenic texture to the liver
(C) no abnormality—this is a normal study
(D) none of the above

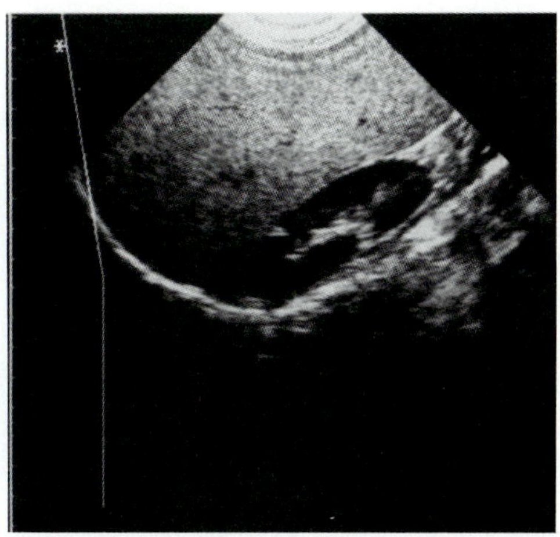

Figure 5–58. Longitudinal sonogram of the right upper quadrant.

598. Diagnostic possibilities in the patient in Fig. 5–58 include

(A) glycogen storage disease
(B) fatty metamorphosis
(C) hemochromatosis
(D) all of the above

599. A disorder associated with glycogen storage disease is

(A) multiple hepatic adenomata
(B) multiple hepatic tumors
(C) A and B
(D) none of the above

600. Fig. 5–59 is a transverse scan obtained through the right upper quadrant of a neonate. The abnormality is

(A) the absence of a right kidney
(B) an abnormal right adrenal

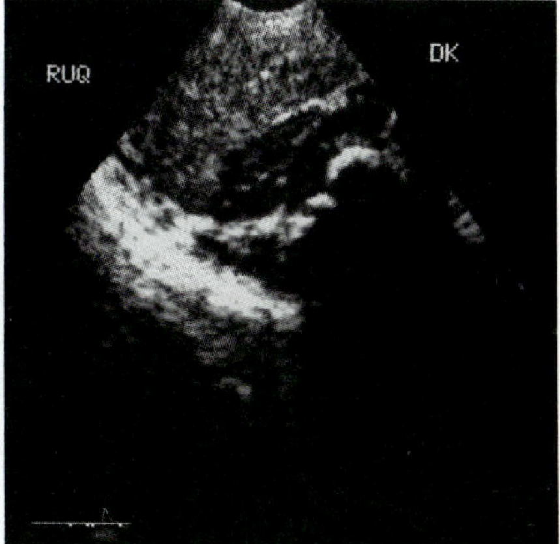

Figure 5–59. Transverse scan obtained through the right upper quadrant of a neonate.

(C) an abnormality of the right kidney with reduced parenchyma
(D) none of the above

601. Assuming that the findings are similar on the left side of the patient, the most likely diagnosis in the patient in Fig. 5–59 is

(A) chronic leiomyonephritis
(B) horseshoe kidney
(C) bilateral renal agenesis
(D) none of the above

602. In renal agenesis, the adrenal

(A) can appear elongated
(B) also is absent
(C) can contain multiple tumors
(D) none of the above

603. Fig. 5–60 is a long axis image of the gallbladder. The abnormality is

(A) a distended gallbladder with a markedly thickened wall
(B) multiple floating calculi
(C) an hydropic gallbladder
(D) none of the above

604. The most likely diagnosis in the patient in Fig. 5–60 is

(A) gallbladder hydrops probably secondary to obstruction
(B) cholelithiasis
(C) acalculus cholelithiasis
(D) none of the above

605. Hydrops of the gallbladder may be secondary to

(A) cholelithiasis
(B) obstruction of the distal common bile duct by pancreatic tumor
(C) obstruction of the distal common bile duct secondary to ampullary tumor
(D) obstruction of the cystic duct due to an anomalous portal vein
(E) all of the above

606. Fig. 5–61 is a long axis image of the gallbladder. The abnormality is

(A) diffuse thickening of the gallbladder wall
(B) difficult to determine because the gallbladder is not fully distended
(C) both A and B
(D) cholelithiasis

607. The most likely diagnosis in the patient in Fig. 5–61 is

(A) normal, nondistended gallbladder
(B) hyperplastic cholecystitis
(C) cholecystitis
(D) none of the above

608. Conditions that may be associated with gallbladder wall thickening include

(A) cholecystitis
(B) nondistension
(C) ascites
(D) right upper quadrant inflammatory bowel disease
(E) all of the above

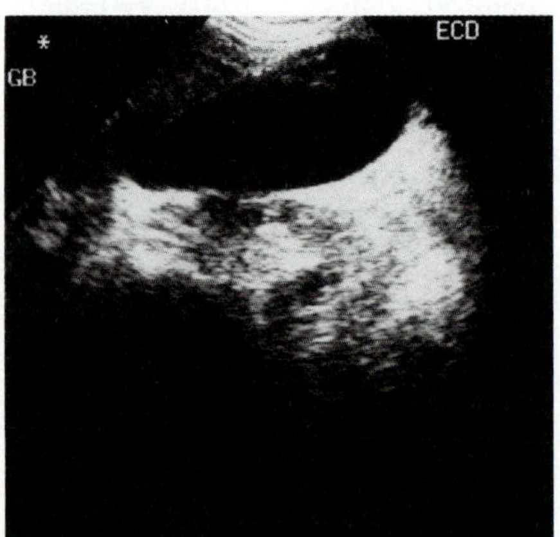

Figure 5–60. Long axis image of the gallbladder.

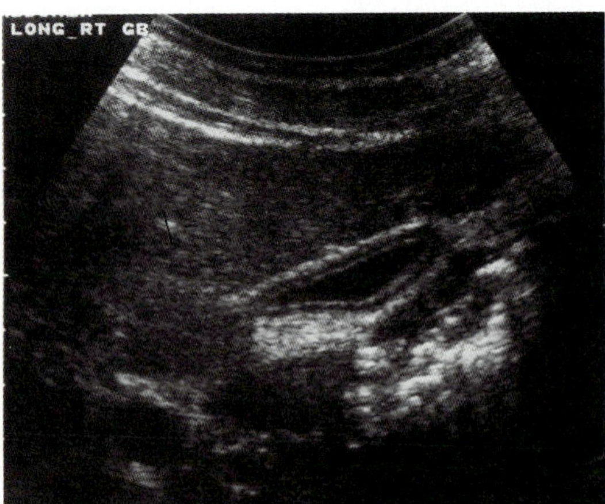

Figure 5–61. Long axis image of the gallbladder.

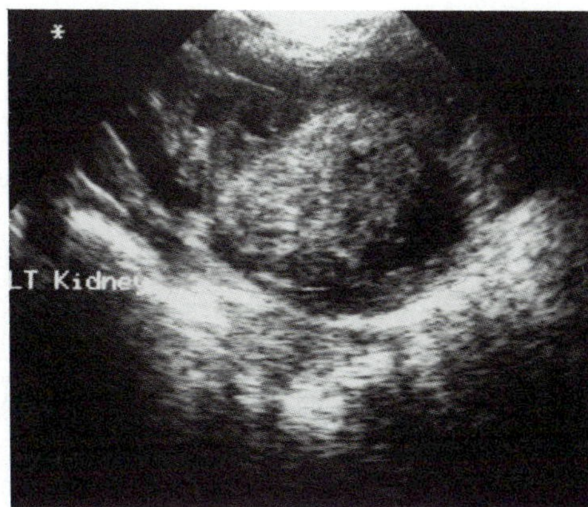

Figure 5–62. Long axis image of the left kidney obtained in the sagittal plane in the patient who is in a prone position.

609. Fig. 5–62 is a long axis image of the left kidney obtained in the sagittal plane in the patient in the prone position. The abnormality is

(A) large tumor involving the lower pole of the left kidney
(B) hydronephrosis
(C) adrenal tumor
(D) none of the above

610. Diagnostic possibilities in the patient in Fig. 5–62 include

(A) renal cell tumor
(B) angiomyolipoma
(C) transitional cell tumor
(D) A or B

611. Angiomyolipomas may be encountered in

(A) patients with tuberous sclerosis
(B) postmenopausal women
(C) prepubertal boys
(D) prepubertal girls
(E) A and B

612. Fig. 5–63 is a coronal image through the left upper quadrant of the abdomen. The arrow points to

(A) a small shrunken kidney
(B) the normal left adrenal
(C) a loop of bowel
(D) the splenic flexure

613. The most likely diagnosis in the patient in Fig. 5–63 is

(A) hepatic tumor
(B) splenic tumor
(C) normal left adrenal
(D) atrophic left kidney

614. A condition that may affect the adrenal is

(A) neonatal hypotension
(B) severe fulminant tuberculosis infection
(C) malignant lung carcinoma
(D) all of the above

615. Fig. 5–64 is a transverse image obtained in the upper abdomen. The cursors (+s) indicate

(A) an ectatic main pancreatic duct in an elderly patient
(B) a distended main pancreatic duct in a child
(C) the pancreatic duct appears to be in normal limits
(D) A or B

616. Given that this is a scan (Fig. 5–64) of a child the most likely diagnosis is

(A) hereditary pancreatitis
(B) chronic pancreatitis
(C) acute pancreatitis
(D) A or B

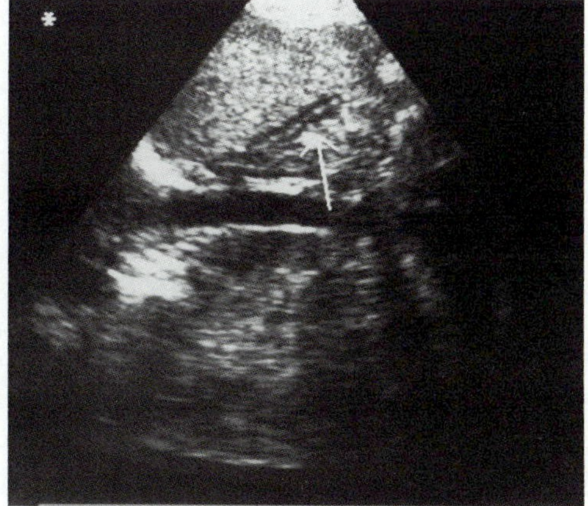
Figure 5–63. Coronal image through the left upper quadrant.

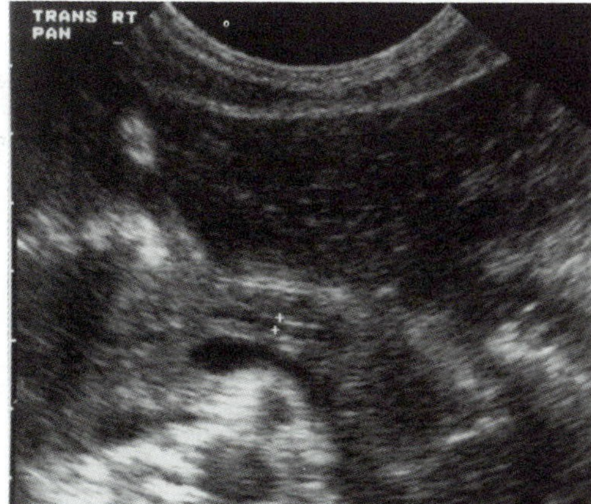

Figure 5–64. Transverse image obtained in the upper abdomen.

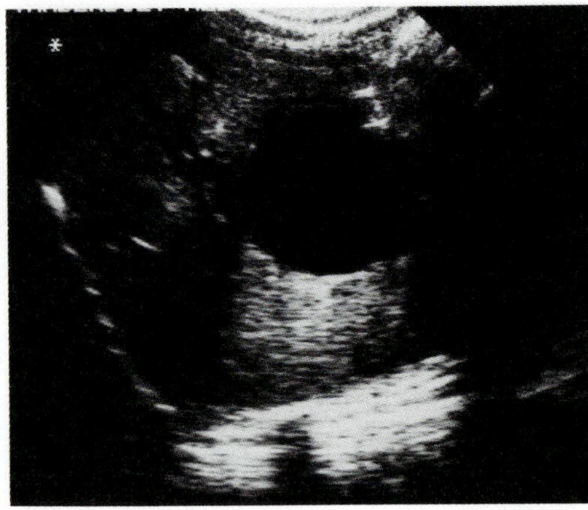

Figure 5–65. Parasagittal scan obtained through the liver.

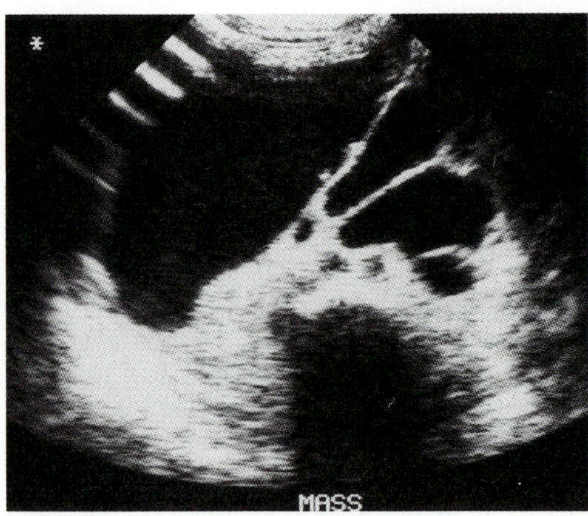

Figure 5–66. Transverse scan obtained through the abdomen of a child with a palpable mass.

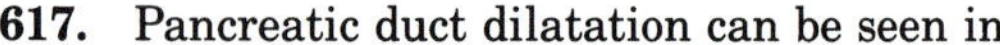

617. Pancreatic duct dilatation can be seen in

(A) pancreatic tumors
(B) chronic pancreatitis
(C) a normal ectatic duct in an elderly patient
(D) all of the above

618. Fig. 5–65 is a parasagittal scan obtained through the liver. The abnormality is

(A) a distended gallbladder
(B) a cystic mass related to the common bile duct
(C) a liver cyst
(D) none of the above

619. The most likely diagnosis in the patient in Fig. 5–65 is

(A) hydropic gallbladder
(B) choledochal cyst
(C) liver cyst
(D) none of the above

620. The types of choledochal cysts include

(A) type I—aneurysmal dilatation of the common bile duct
(B) type II—cystic diverticulum arising from common bile duct
(C) type III-choledochocele within the duodenum wall
(D) type IV—aneurysmal dilatation of the intrahepatic bile ducts
(E) all of the above

621. Factors that may contribute to development of a choledochal cyst include

(A) abnormal angulation of distal common bile duct and pancreatic duct
(B) abnormal fusion of the two tissues that fuse to form the pancreas
(C) retrograde secretion of pancreatic digestive juices in the wall of the pancreatic duct
(D) A and B
(E) none of the above

622. Fig. 5–66 is a transverse scan obtained through the abdomen of a child with a palpable mass. The abnormality is

(A) a cystic mass with several septations
(B) a cystic mass which appears to displace bowel and mesentery
(C) free fluid within the abdomen
(D) none of the above

623. The most likely diagnosis in the patient in Fig. 5–66 is

(A) mesenteric cyst
(B) complicated ascites
(C) ovarian carcinoma
(D) none of the above

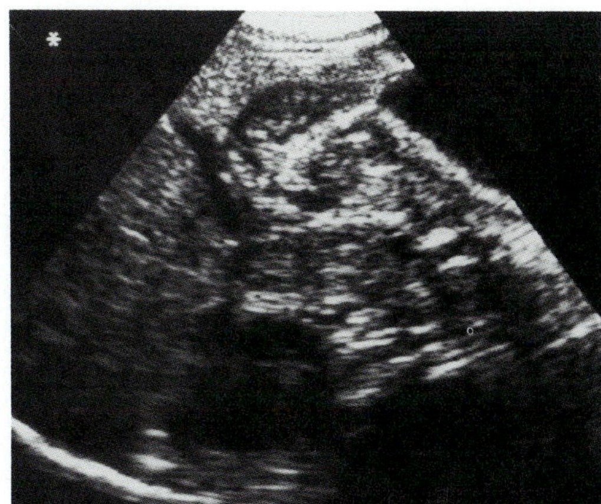

Figure 5–67. Longitudinal image through the gastric antrum of a child.

624. Figs. 5–67 and 5–68 are long and short axes sonograms through the gastric antrum of a child. The abnormality is

(A) thickened antrum wall
(B) shortened antrum
(C) lengthened pyloric canal
(D) A and C

625. The most likely diagnosis in the patient in Figs. 5–67 and 5–68 is

(A) normal stomach
(B) hypertrophic pyloric stenosis
(C) duodenal tumor
(D) none of the above

626. Criteria used for diagnosis of hypertrophic pyloric stenosis include

(A) a wall greater than 3 mm
(B) a wall less than 3 mm
(C) length greater than 14 mm
(D) length less than 14 mm
(E) A and C
(F) B and D

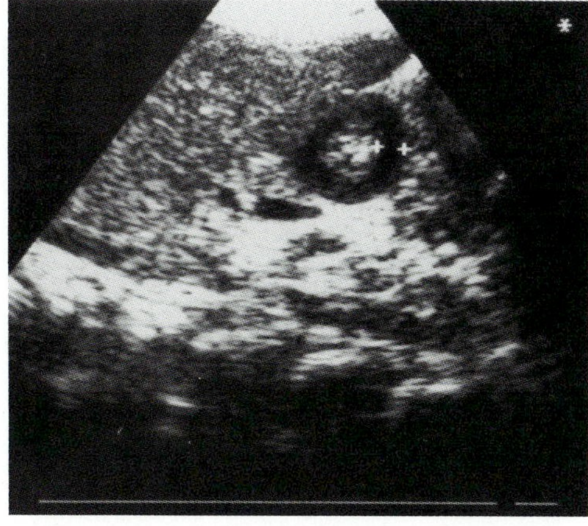

Figure 5–68. Transverse scan through the gastric antrum of a child.

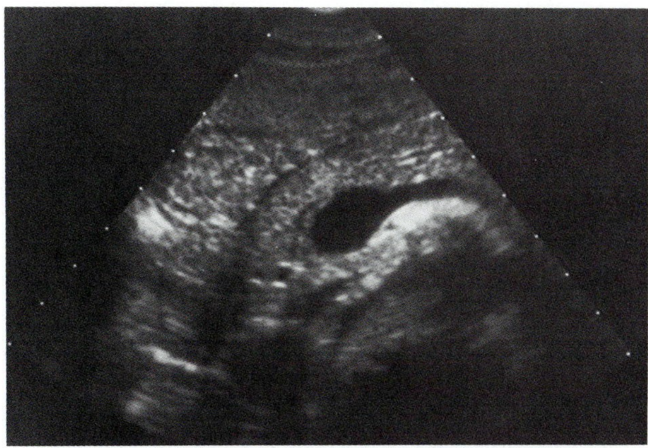

Figure 5–69. Transverse sonogram through the upper abdomen.

627. Fig. 5–69 is a transverse sonogram through the upper abdomen. The abnormality is

(A) enlarged and thickened pancreas
(B) dilatation of the main pancreatic duct
(C) dilatation of the duodenal bulb
(D) aneurysmal dilatation of the superior mesentery vein
(E) none of the above

628. The most likely diagnosis in the patient in Fig. 5–69 is

(A) pancreatitis
(B) normal
(C) gastric outlet obstruction
(D) portal hypertension

629. Fig. 5–70 is a long axis image in the upper outer quadrant of the right breast. The abnormality is

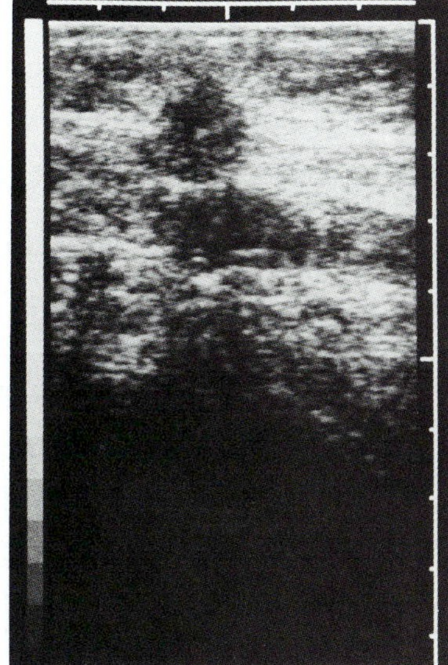

Figure 5–70. Long axis sonogram of the upper outer quadrant of the right breast.

(A) a cystic lesion within the breast
(B) a solid lesion with well-circumscribed borders
(C) a solid lesion with irregular borders
(D) none of the above

630. The most likely diagnosis in the patient in Fig. 5–70 is

(A) cyst
(B) fibroadenoma
(C) carcinoma
(D) mastitis

631. The sonographic findings in breast lesions are usually definitive and do not require future evaluation by biopsy or fine needle aspiration.

(A) true
(B) false

632. Fig. 5–71 is a transverse image in the right side of the neck at the level of the common carotid artery The abnormality is

(A) thrombosis of the common carotid artery
(B) a parathyroid mass
(C) a thyroid mass
(D) a mass within the strap muscles

633. The most likely diagnosis in the patient in Fig. 5–71 is

(A) parathyroid adenoma
(B) thyroid adenoma
(C) lymph node
(D) cannot tell

634. Parathyroid adenomas may be associated with

(A) hypercalcemia
(B) hypertension
(C) bloating
(D) headaches

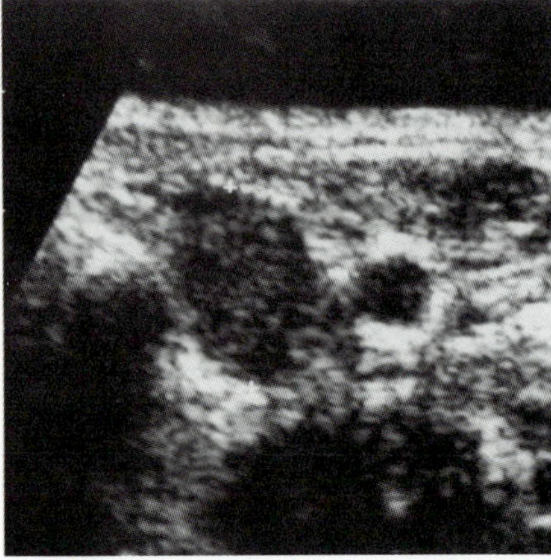

Figure 5–71. Transverse image of the right side of the neck at the level of the common carotid artery.

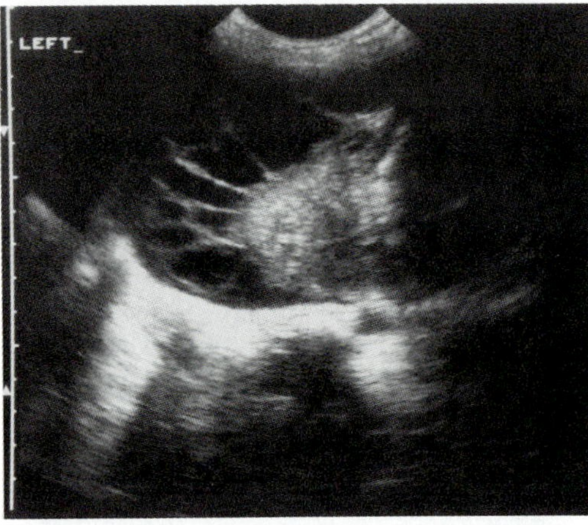

Figure 5–72. An upright coronal image of the lower left hemithorax of a 12-year-old child with fever and cough.

635. Fig. 5–72 is an upright coronal image of the lower left hemithorax of a 12-year-old child with fever and cough. The abnormality is

(A) loculated pleural effusion
(B) nonloculated pleural effusion
(C) hydronephrotic kidney
(D) none of the above

636. The most likely diagnosis in the patient in Fig. 5–72 is

(A) simple effusion
(B) cystic lung mass
(C) empyema
(D) none of the above

637. One of the findings useful in determining whether a fluid collection within the thorax will be successfully aspirated includes

(A) if there is deformation of shape with breathing
(B) how close it is to the chest
(C) if it has echogenic material within it
(D) all of the above

638. Regarding sonography of the appendix

(A) it is a clinically useful test for the diagnosis of acute appendicitis
(B) it is not a clinically useful test for the diagnosis of acute appendicitis
(C) it cannot be performed because the patient is usually too tender to tolerate adequate compression of the right lower quadrant
(D) bowel gas always obscures visualization in this region

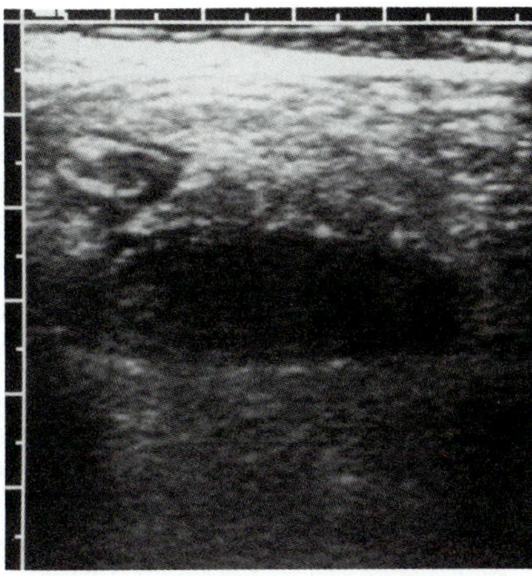

Figure 5–73. Sonogram of the right lower quadrant of the abdomen. *(Courtesy of John Worrell, M.D.)*

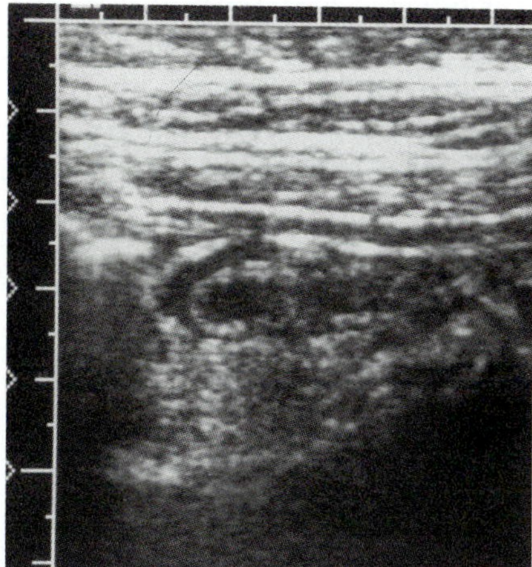

Figure 5–74. Sonogram of the right lower quadrant of the abdomen. *(Courtesy of John Worrell, M.D.)*

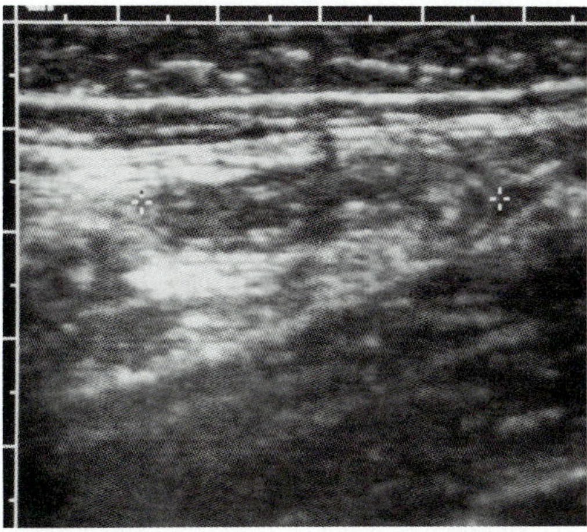

Figure 5–75. Sonogram of the right lower quadrant of the abdomen. *(Courtesy of John Worrell, M.D.)*

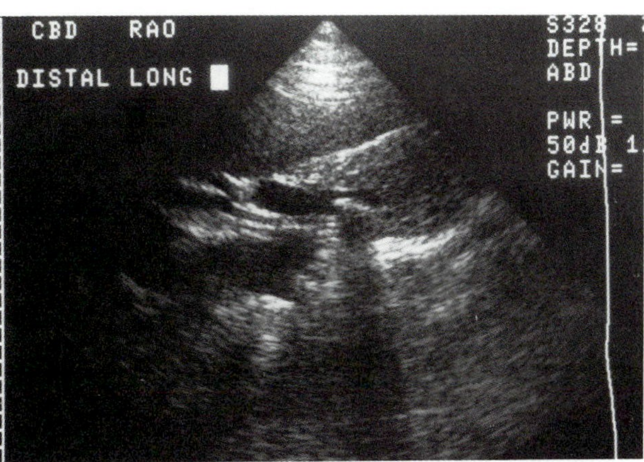

Figure 5–76. Longitudinal sonogram of the right upper quadrant.

639. Sonographic parameters used for diagnosis of an abnormal appendix include

(A) wall greater than 3 cm
(B) inability to compress completely with trans-abdominal pressure
(C) length of more than 1 cm
(D) presence of an appendicolith
(E) B and D

640. Figs. 5–73, 5–74, and 5–75 are sonograms of the right lower quadrant of the abdomen. The correct statements concerning these figures include

(A) Fig. 5–73 represents a normal appendix
(B) Fig. 5–74 represents a normal appendix
(C) Fig. 5–75 represents a normal appendix
(D) none of the above

641. The findings in Fig. 5–76 are consistent with

(A) pancreatic carcinoma
(B) cholelithiasis
(C) choledocholithiasis
(D) portal hypertension

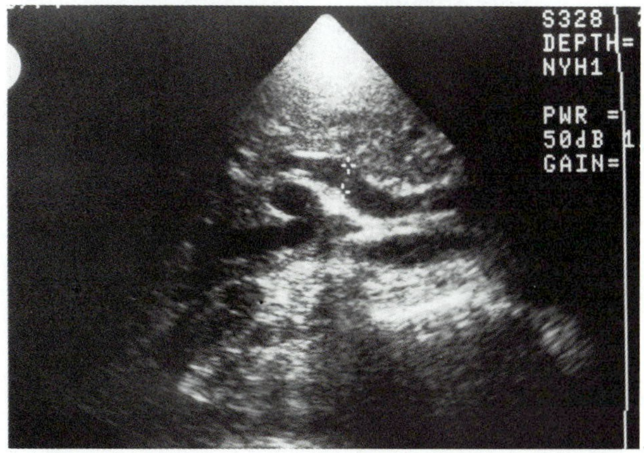

Figure 5–77. Sagittal sonogram of the right upper abdomen.

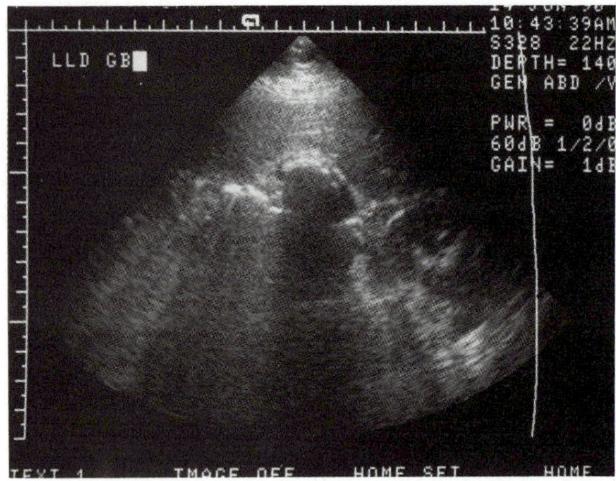

Figure 5–78. Longitudinal scan of the right upper quadrant.

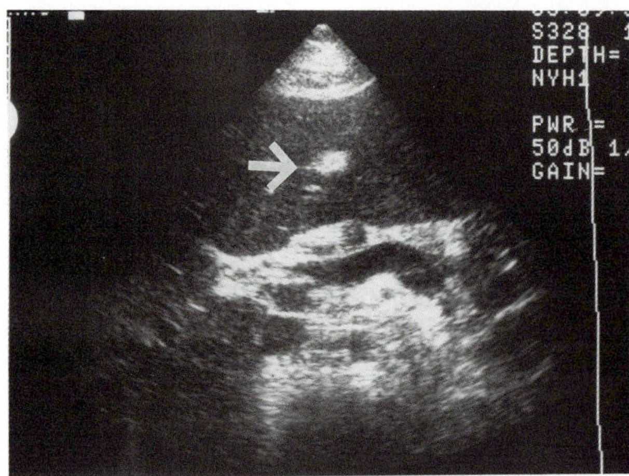

Figure 5–80. Transverse scan of the liver.

642. The findings in Fig. 5–77 are consistent with

(A) recanalized umbilical vein
(B) dilated common bile duct
(C) normal hepatic veins
(D) normal portal veins

643. The findings shown in Fig. 5–78 are consistent with

(A) chronic cholecystitis with cholelithiasis
(B) adenomyomatosis
(C) postprandial gallbladder contraction
(D) duodenal bulb

644. The arrow in Fig. 5–79 is pointing to

(A) main portal vein
(B) left portal vein
(C) hepatic duct
(D) hepatic artery

645. The arrow in Fig. 5–80 is pointing to

(A) dilated bile duct
(B) endothelioma
(C) mesenchymal hamartoma
(D) hepatocellular carcinoma
(E) ligamentum teres

646. The findings in Fig. 5–81 are associated with the following *except*

(A) alkaline phosphatase
(B) serum glutamic-oxaloacetic transaminase
(C) direct bilirubin
(D) α-fetoprotein
(E) jaundice

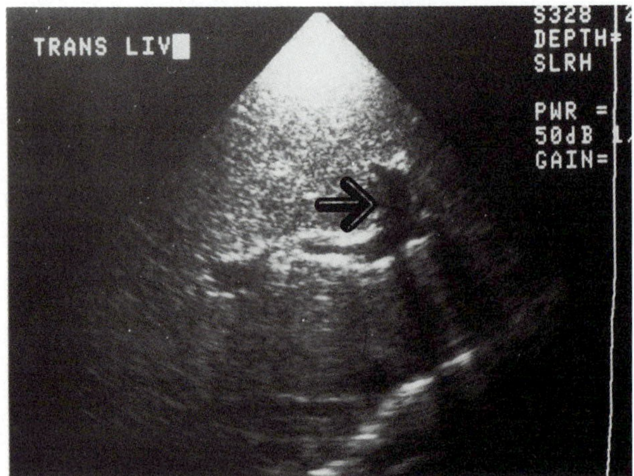

Figure 5–79. Transverse scan of the liver.

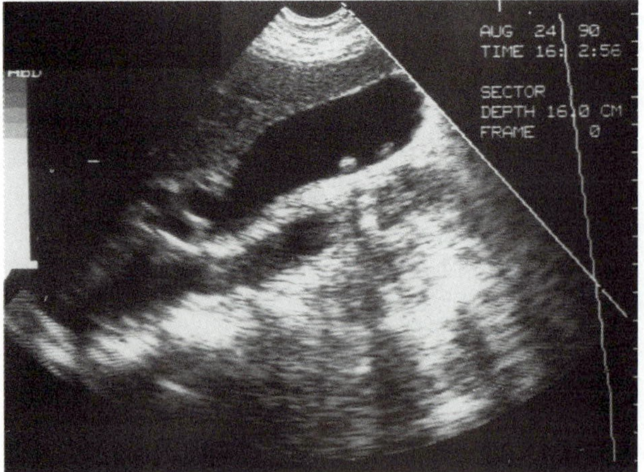

Figure 5–81. Longitudinal scan of the gallbladder.

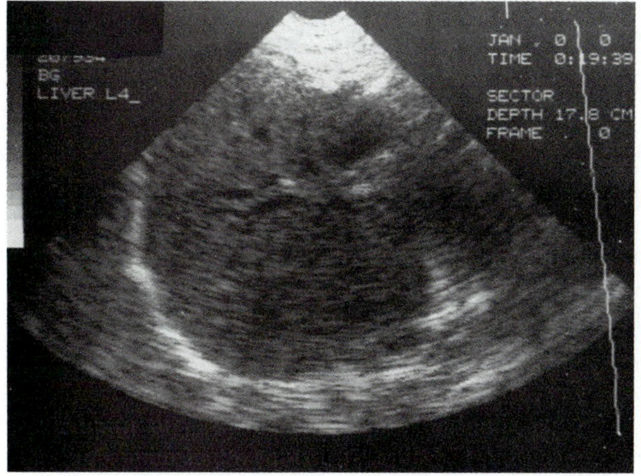

Figure 5–82. Longitudinal scan of the liver.

647. The findings in Fig. 5–82 are associated with a(n)

(A) decrease in direct bilirubin
(B) increase in indirect bilirubin
(C) increase in alkaline phosphatase
(D) increase in α-fetoprotein

648. The findings in Fig. 5–83 are associated with

(A) hypoproteinemia
(B) congestive heart failure
(C) acute hepatitis
(D) cholecystitis
(E) choledocholithiasis

649. The arrow in Fig. 5–84 is pointing to

(A) major lobar fissure
(B) ligamentum teres
(C) stone in the common bile duct
(D) stone within the cystic duct

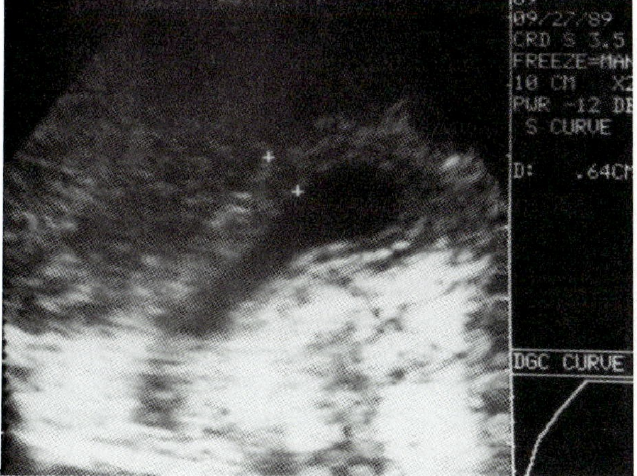

Figure 5–83. Magnified view of the gallbladder.

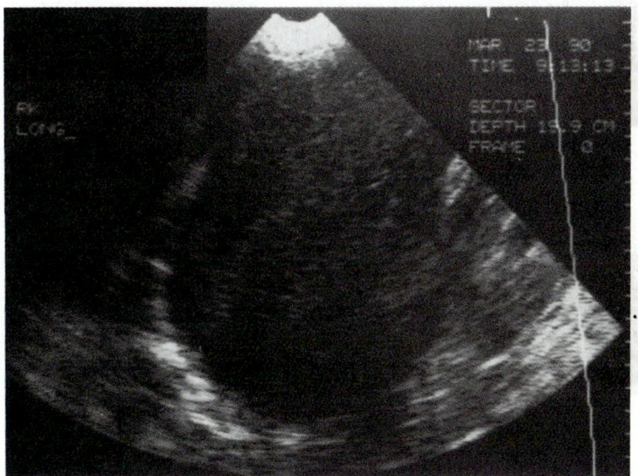

Figure 5–85. Longitudinal scan of the liver.

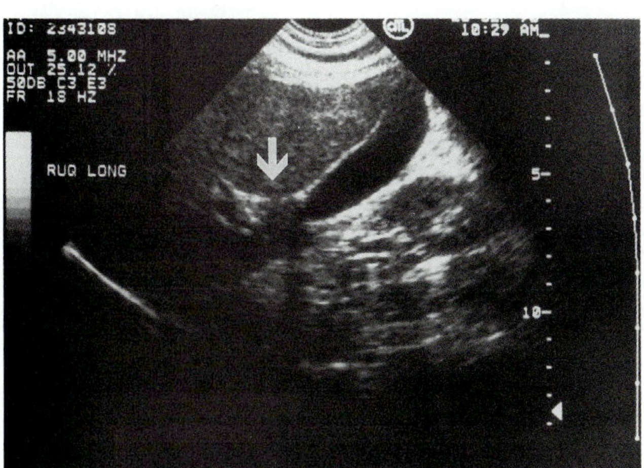

Figure 5–84. Longitudinal scan of the right upper quadrant.

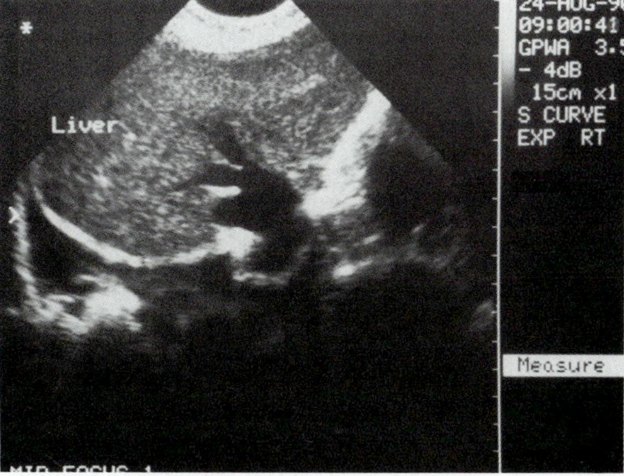

Figure 5–86. Transverse scan of the liver.

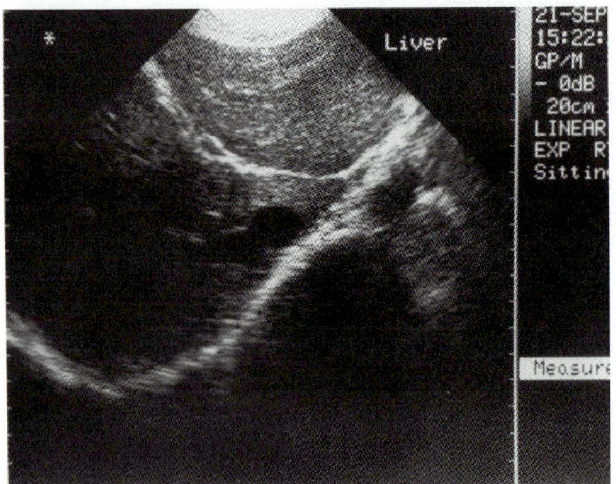

Figure 5–87. Transverse scan of the liver.

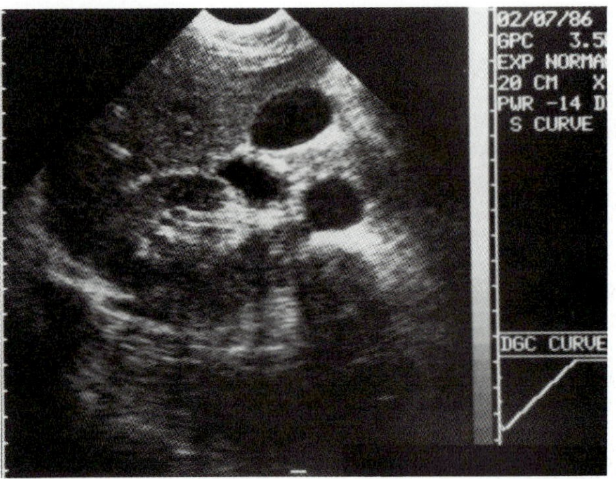

Figure 5–89. Longitudinal scan of the right upper quadrant.

650. The findings in Fig. 5–85 are suggestive of

(A) metastastic disease of the liver
(B) acute hepatitis
(C) fatty liver
(D) cirrhosis

651. The findings in Fig. 5–86 are representative of

(A) portal hypertension
(B) congestive heart failure
(C) cirrhosis
(D) normal scan

652. Which of the following ligaments are visualized in Fig. 5–87

(A) main lobar fissure
(B) ligamentum venosum
(C) coronary ligament
(D) ligamentum teres

653. The findings in Fig. 5–88 represent

(A) gallbladder carcinoma
(B) adenomyomatosis
(C) cholecystitis
(D) gallbladder papilloma

654. The findings in Fig. 5–89 are consistent with

(A) pancreatic carcinoma
(B) hydrops
(C) ascites
(D) normal duodenum

655. A patient presents with right upper quadrent pain, fever, nausea, and leukocytosis. The findings in Fig. 5–90 are most consistent with

(A) chronic cholecystitis
(B) gallbladder carcinoma
(C) adenomyomatosis
(D) acute cholecystitis

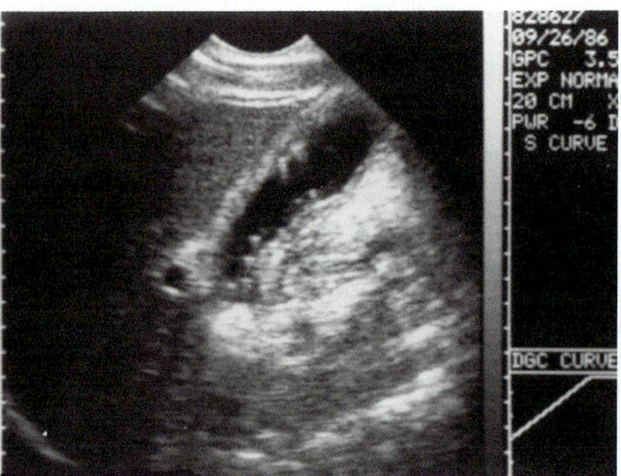

Figure 5–88. Longitudinal scan of the gallbladder.

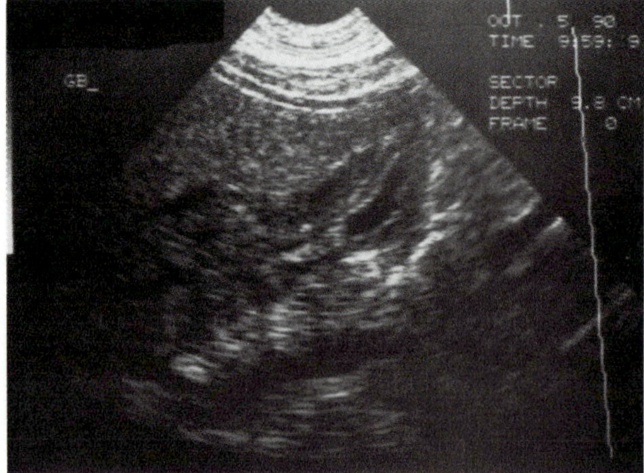

Figure 5–90. Longitudinal scan of the gallbladder.

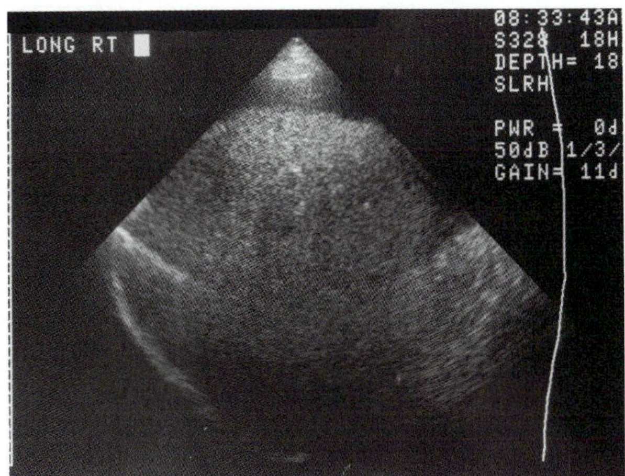

Figure 5–91. Longitudinal scan of the liver.

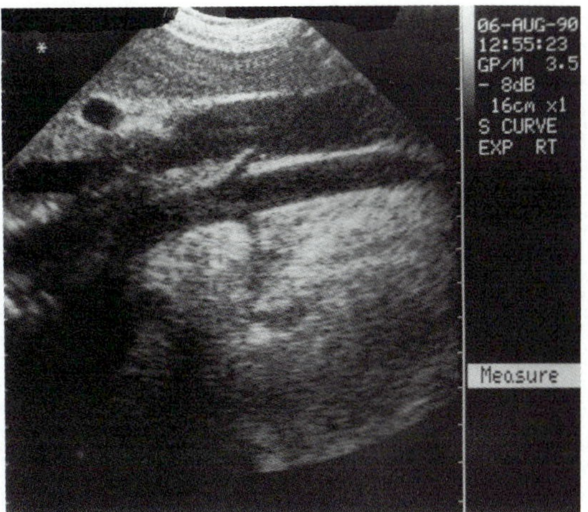

Figure 5–94. Coronal scan of the mid-abdomen.

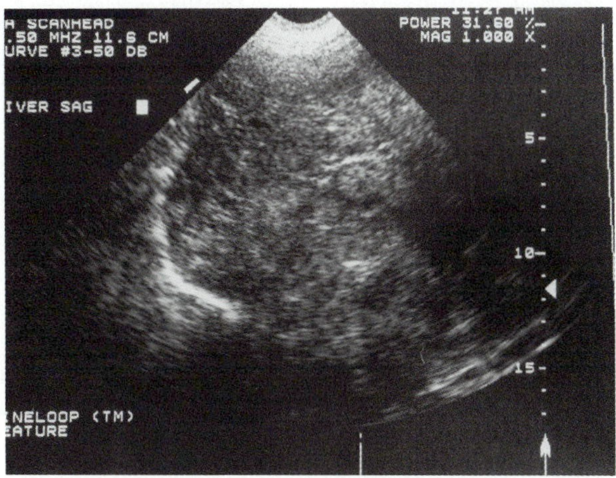

Figure 5–92. Longitudinal scan of the liver.

656. The findings in Fig. 5–91 are suggestive of

(A) liver metastases
(B) hepatoma
(C) cirrhosis
(D) fatty liver

657. A patient presents with an increase in direct bilirubin, SGOT, and alkaline phosphatase. The findings in Fig. 5–92 are suggestive of

(A) liver metastases
(B) hepatoma
(C) cirrhosis
(D) fatty liver

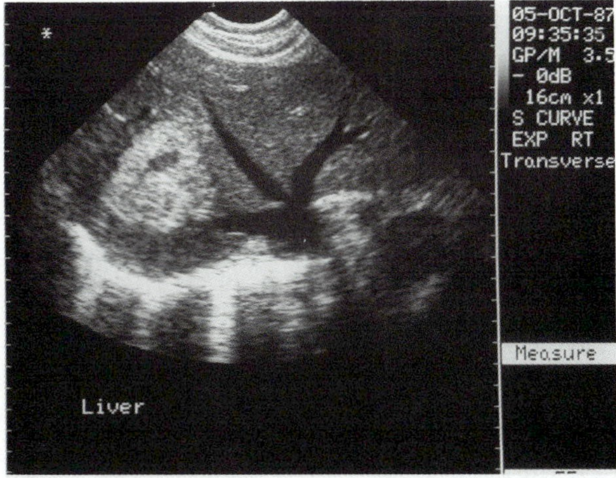

Figure 5–93. Transverse scan of the liver.

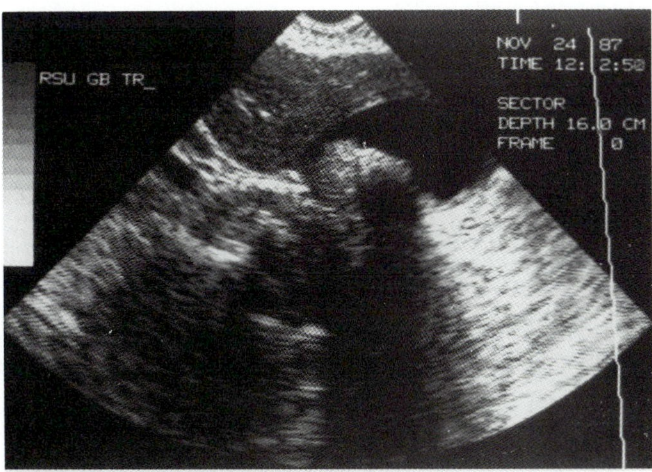

Figure 5–95. Longitudinal scan of the gallbladder.

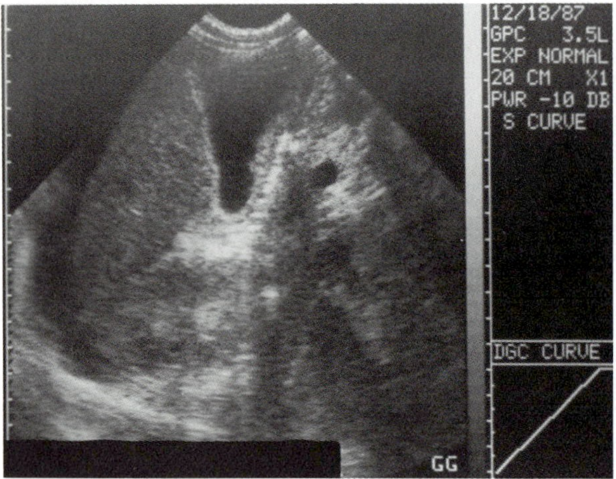

Figure 5–96. Longitudinal scan of the liver and gallbladder.

658. The hemangioma in Fig. 5–93 is located in

(A) posterior segment of the right lobe
(B) anterior segment of the right lobe
(C) anterior segment of the left lobe
(D) medial segment of the right lobe
(E) medial segment of the left lobe

659. Which vessels are visualized in Fig. 5–94?

(A) inferior vena cava, portal vein, left renal vein, right renal vein
(B) inferior vena cava, aorta, right hepatic artery, splenic vein
(C) inferior vena cava, aorta, left renal vein, right renal vein
(D) inferior vena cava, aorta, right renal artery, left renal artery

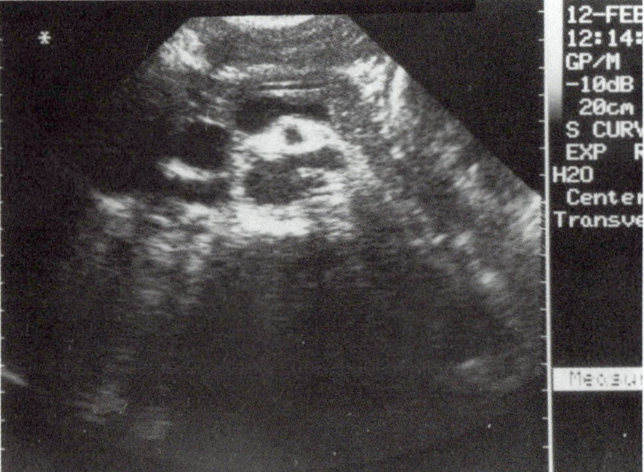

Figure 5–97. Transverse scan of the pancreas.

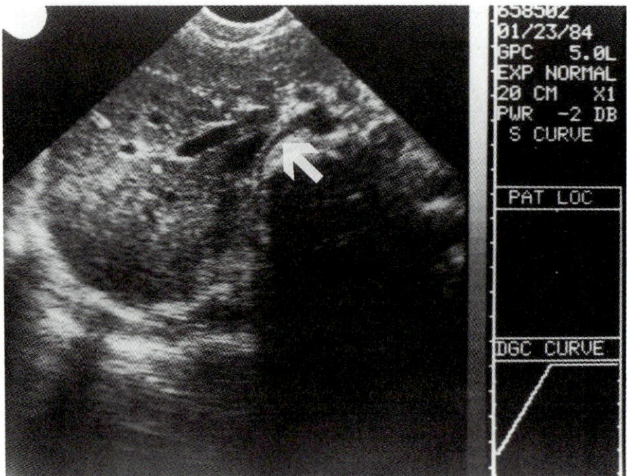

Figure 5–98. Transverse scan of the abdomen.

660. A patient with known pancreatic carcinoma presents with the findings in Fig. 5–95, which most likely represent

(A) cholilithiasis
(B) tumefactive biliary sludge
(C) carcinoma of the gallbladder
(D) cholidocholithiasis

661. A 53-year-old man with a history of liver cirrhosis presents with increased abdominal girth. Fig. 5–96 demonstrates a thickened gallbladder wall, which is most probably due to

(A) acalculus cholecystitis
(B) associated pancreatitis
(C) cirrhosis and the adjacent ascites
(D) cirrhosis
(E) the associated ascites

662. The findings in Fig. 5–97 are consistent with

(A) cholecystitis
(B) aortic aneurysm
(C) pancreatic carcinoma
(D) a normal pancreas

663. The arrow in Fig. 5–98 is pointing to

(A) the right crus of the diaphragm
(B) the right renal artery
(C) the right portal vein
(D) the right renal vein

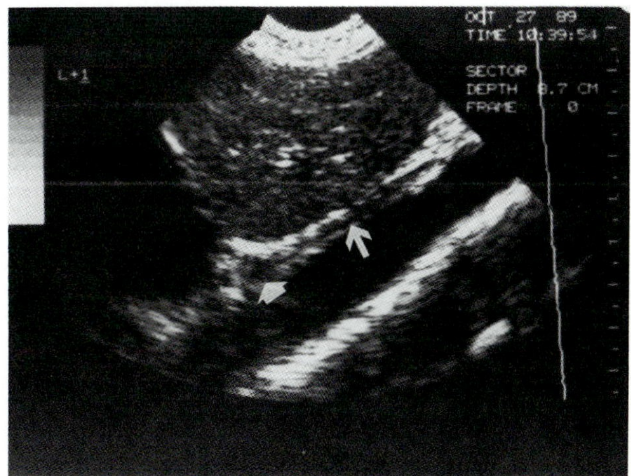

Figure 5–99. Longitudinal scan of the aorta.

664. The arrow in Fig. 5–99 is pointing to

(A) the inferior vena cava
(B) the superior mesenteric artery
(C) the celiac
(D) the right crus of the diaphragm

665. The arrowhead in Fig. 5–99 is pointing to

(A) esophagogastric junction
(B) hepatic artery
(C) portal vein
(D) superior mesenteric vein

666. The arrow in Fig. 5–100 is pointing to

(A) inferior vena cava
(B) superior mesenteric artery
(C) celiac artery
(D) right crus of the diaphragm

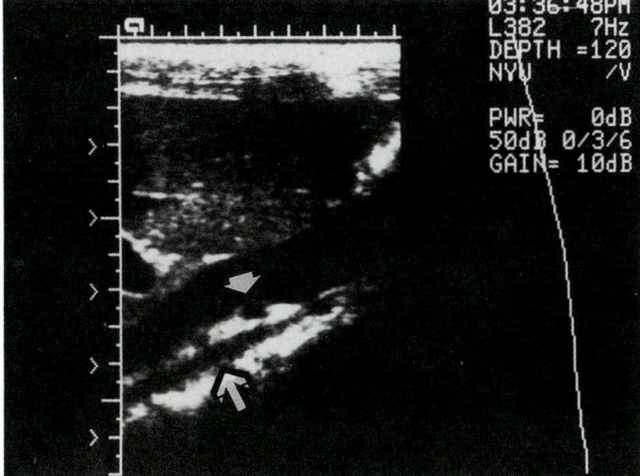

Figure 5–100. Longitudinal scan of the inferior vena cava.

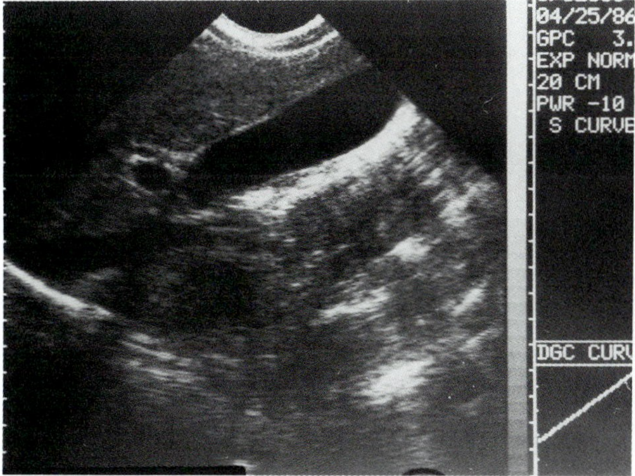

Figure 5–101. Longitudinal scan of the gallbladder.

667. The arrowhead in Fig. 5–100 is pointing to

(A) right renal artery
(B) right renal vein
(C) left renal artery
(D) left renal vein

668. The shadowing from the region of the gallbladder in Fig. 5–101 is most likely due to

(A) stones impacted in Hartmann's pouch
(B) cystic duct stone
(C) choledocholithiasis
(D) refraction artifact

669. There seem to be two hemangiomas in Fig. 5–102, one located superior and the other inferior to the diaphram, which are most probably due to

(A) slice-thickness artifact
(B) reflection
(C) mirror-image artifact
(D) refraction

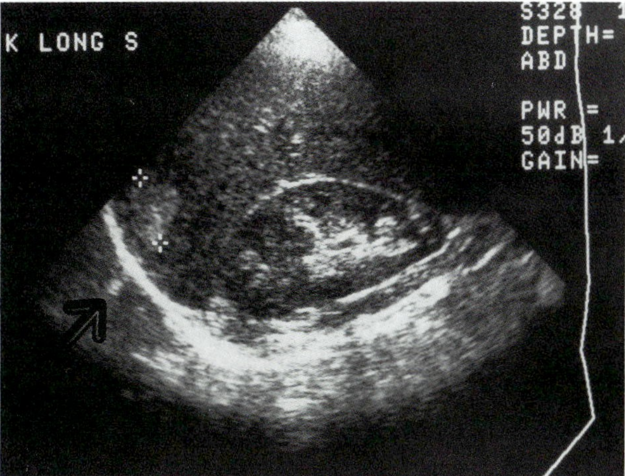

Figure 5–102. Longitudinal scan of the right upper quadrant.

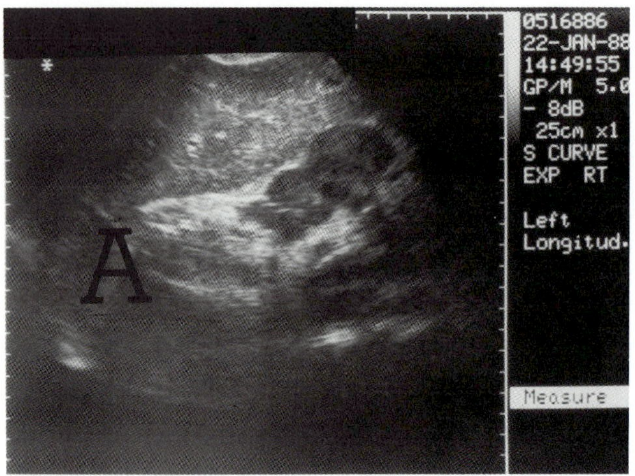

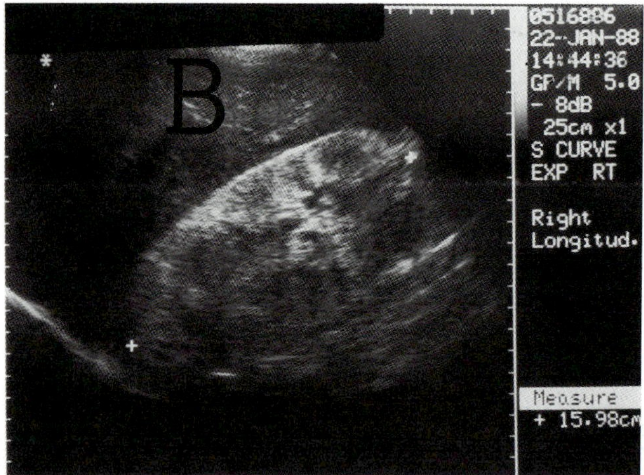

Figure 5–103. (**A**) Sagittal scan of the right upper quadrant. (**B**) Sagittal scan through the right kidney.

670. A 38-year-old man, who is an intravenous drug abuser, with a known mediastinal mass is seen in Fig. 5–103A and B. Fig. 5–103A demonstrates

(A) a mass near the head of the pancreas
(B) periportal lymphadenopathy
(C) chronic cholecystitis
(D) Klatzkin tumor

671. Fig. 5–103B demonstrates

(A) a normal kidney
(B) a kidney consistent with acute renal insufficiency
(C) a kidney consistent with chronic renal insufficiency
(D) renal cell carcinoma

672. The 32-year-old woman shown in Fig. 5–104 has a history of pancreatic carcinoma. The scan most likely represents

(A) celiac nodes
(B) an aortic aneurysm
(C) a horseshoe kidney
(D) a normal scan

673. Fig. 5–105 demonstrates

(A) a fusiform aneurysm
(B) a saccular aneurysm
(C) a cylindrical aneurysm
(D) a normal aneurysm

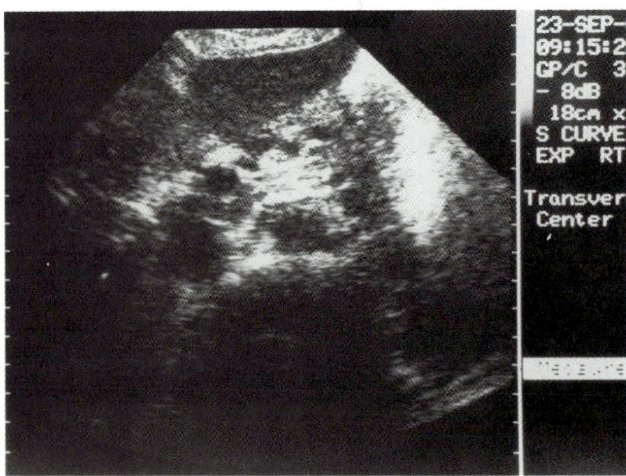

Figure 5–104. Transverse scan of the abdomen.

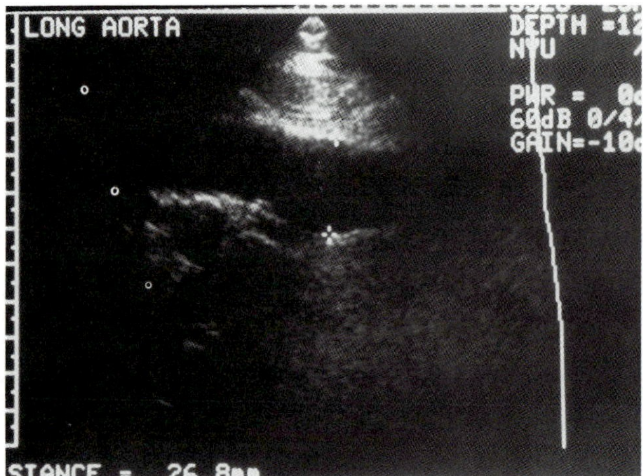

Figure 5–105. Longitudinal scan through the abdominal aorta.

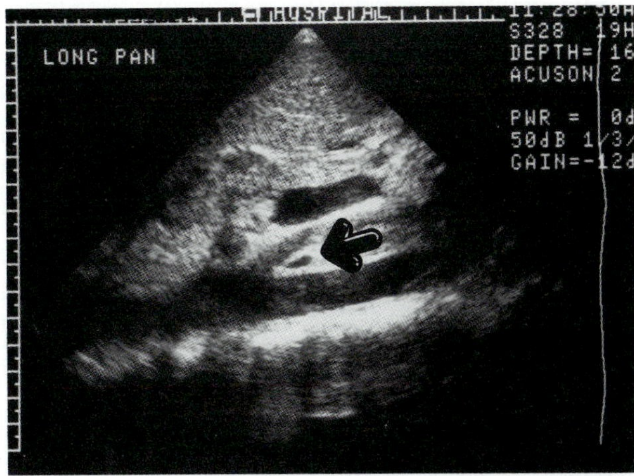

Figure 5–106. Longitudinal scan through the abdominal aorta.

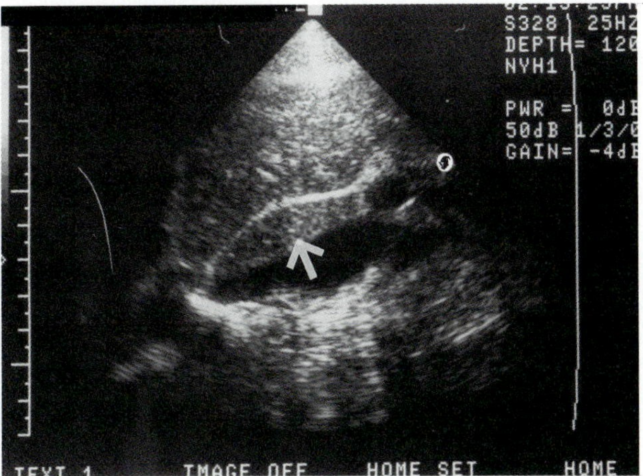

Figure 5–107. Sagittal scan through the right upper quadrant.

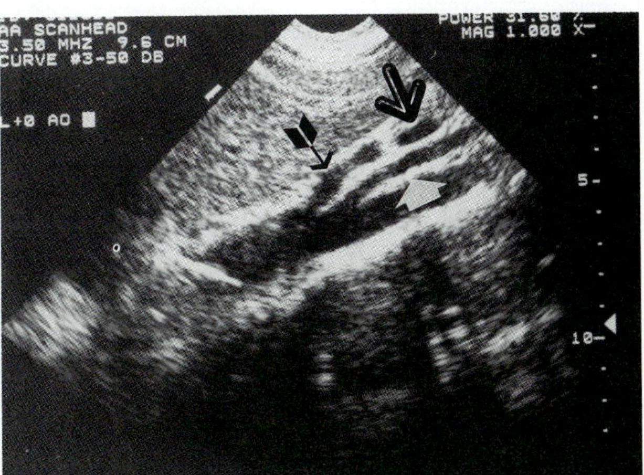

Figure 5–108. Sagittal scan through the right upper quadrant.

674. The arrow in Fig. 5–106 is pointing to

(A) right renal artery
(B) right renal vein
(C) left renal artery
(D) left renal vein

675. The arrow in Fig. 5–107 is pointing to

(A) head of the pancreas
(B) body of the pancreas
(C) caudate lobe of the liver
(D) quadrate lobe (medial aspect of the left lobe) of the liver

676. The thin black arrow in Fig. 5–108 is pointing to

(A) celiac artery
(B) superior mesenteric artery
(C) portal vein
(D) left gastric artery

677. The white arrowhead in Fig. 5–108 is pointing to

(A) celiac artery
(B) superior mesenteric artery
(C) portal vein
(D) left gastric artery

678. The larger black arrow in Fig. 5–108 is pointing to

(A) splenic vein
(B) portal vein
(C) inferior mesenteric vein
(D) left gastric artery

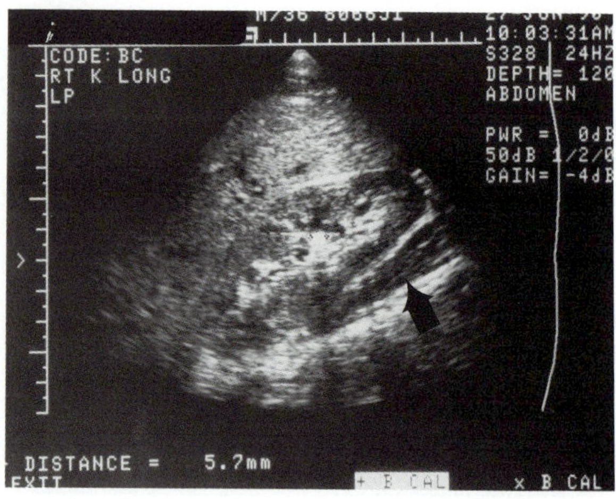

Figure 5–109. Longitudinal scan through the right kidney.

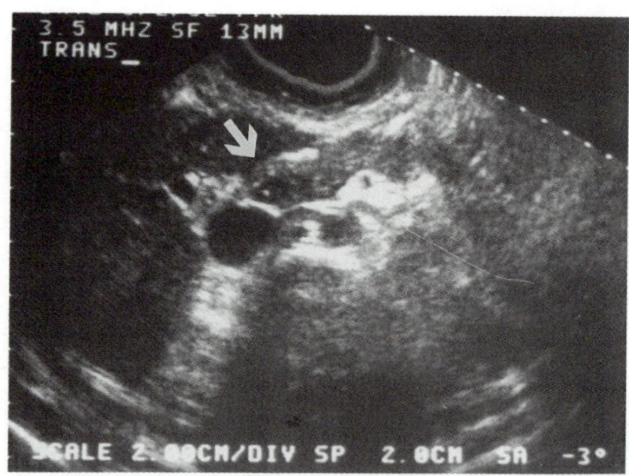

Figure 5–111. Transverse scan through the pancreas.

679. The arrow in Fig. 5–109 is pointing to

(A) levator ani muscle
(B) quadratus lumborum muscle
(C) psoas muscle
(D) internal oblique muscle

680. The patient in Fig. 5–110 presented with massive ascites. The arrow is pointing to

(A) ligamentum teres
(B) ligamentum venosum
(C) falciform ligament
(D) coronary ligament

681. The arrow in Fig. 5–111 is pointing to

(A) normal head
(B) normal body
(C) acute pancreatitis
(D) chronic pancreatitis
(E) adenocarcinoma

682. The arrow in Fig. 5–112 is pointing to

(A) normal body
(B) normal tail
(C) acute pancreatitis
(D) chronic pancreatitis
(E) adenocarcinoma

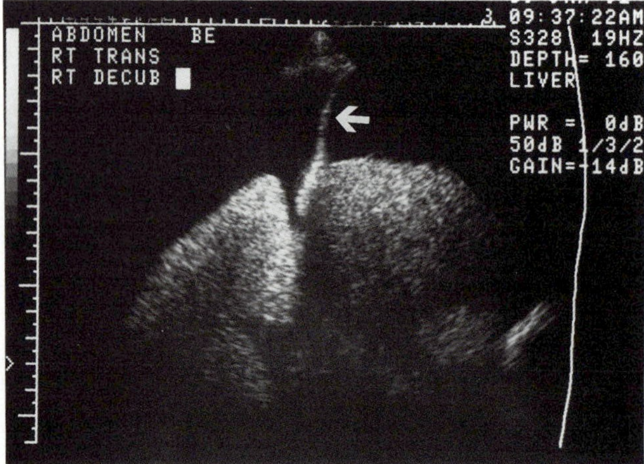

Figure 5–110. Transverse scan through the liver.

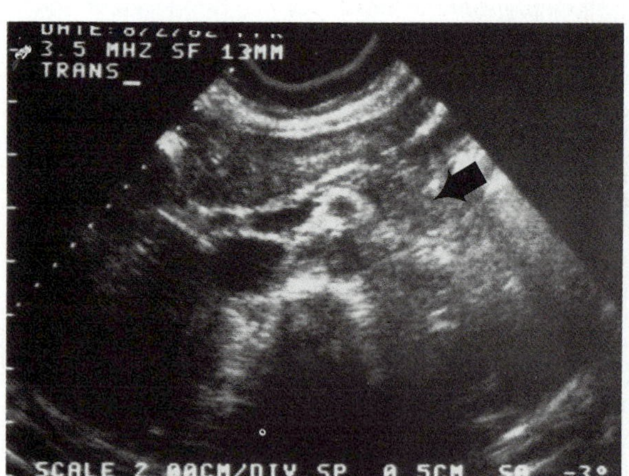

Figure 5–112. Transverse sonogram through the pancreas.

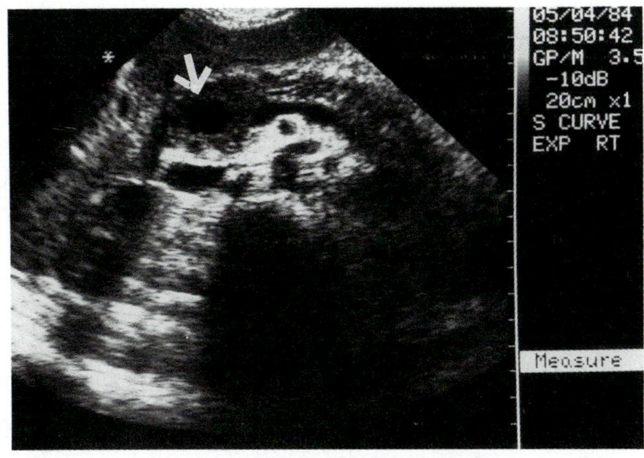

Figure 5–113. Transverse sonogram through the pancreas.

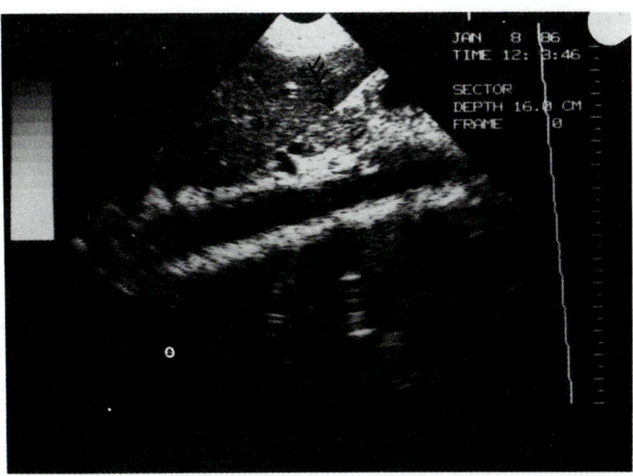

Figure 5–115. Longitudinal scan of the inferior vena cava.

683. The arrow in Fig. 5–113 is pointing to

(A) gastroduodenal artery
(B) common bile duct
(C) portal vein
(D) superior mesenteric vein
(E) hepatic artery

684. Fig. 5–114 is consistent with

(A) acute pancreatitis
(B) chronic pancreatitis
(C) adenocarcinoma
(D) islet cell tumor
(E) normal scan

685. The arrow in Fig. 5–115 is pointing to

(A) gastric antrum
(B) head of pancreas
(C) caudate lobe of liver
(D) body of pancreas
(E) adrenal gland

686. A 37-year-old man with a past history of repeated episodes of pancreatitis due to alcoholism presents with an epigastric mass. Fig. 5–116 suggests

(A) negative study
(B) pancreatic pseudocyst
(C) acute pancreatitis
(D) chronic pancreatitis
(E) adenocarcinoma

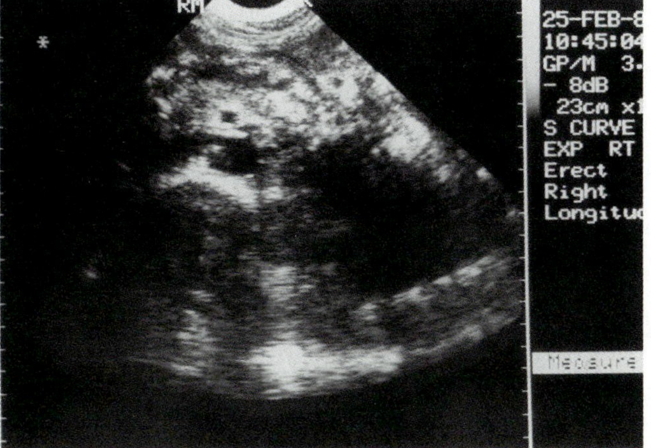

Figure 5–114. Transverse sonogram through the pancreas.

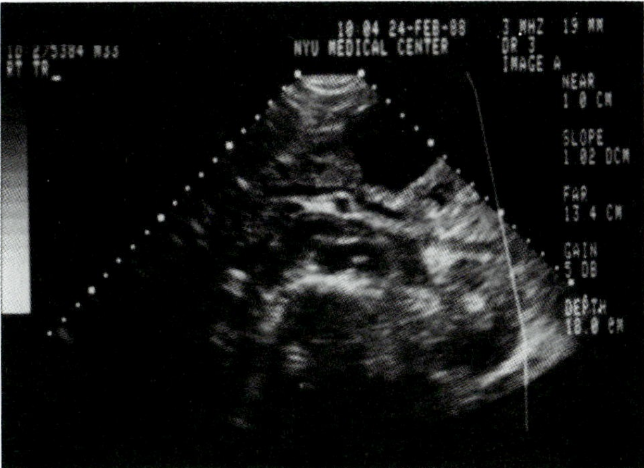

Figure 5–116. Transverse scan through the pancreas.

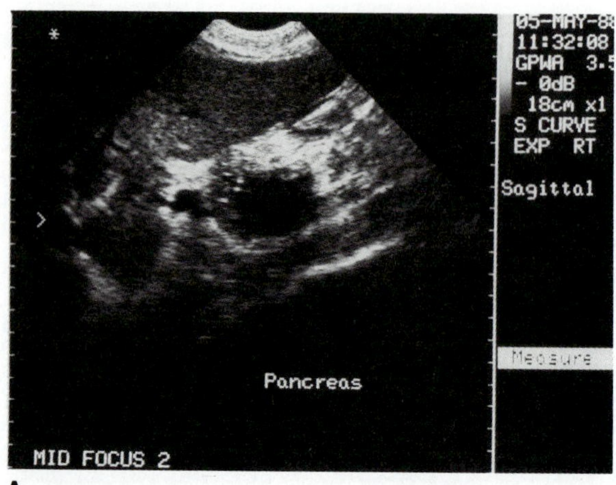

A

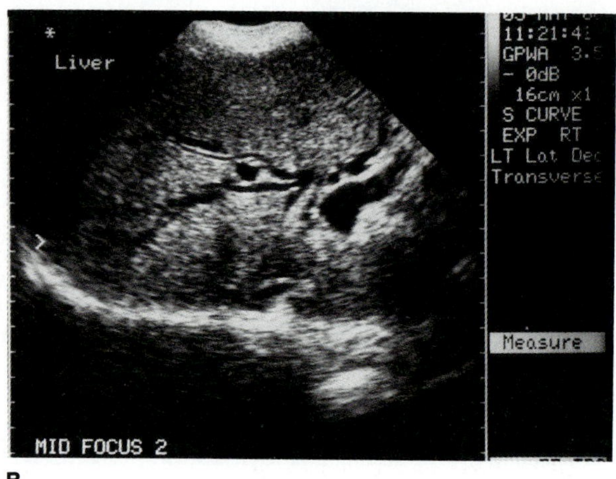

B

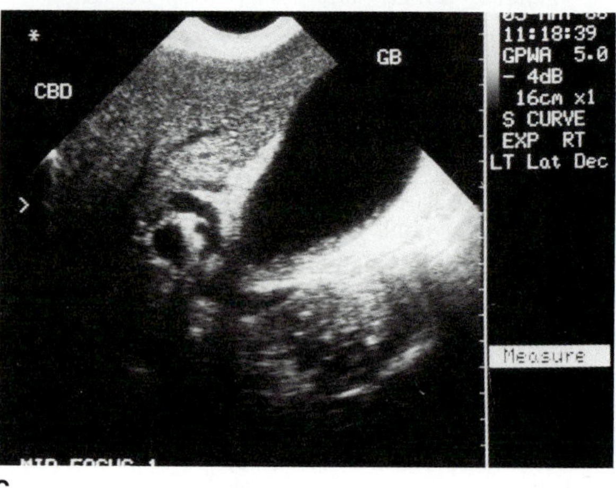

C

Figure 5–117. (**A**) Sagittal scan through the head of the pancreas. (**B**) Sagittal scan through the liver. (**C**) Sagittal scan through the gallbladder.

687. A 70-year-old man presents with a history of weight loss, abdominal pain, and anorexia. Figs. 5–117A–C suggest

(A) negative study
(B) pancreatic pseudocyst
(C) acute pancreatitis
(D) chronic pancreatitis
(E) pancreatic adenocarcinoma

688. In Fig. 5–118, the structures visualized within the liver are

(A) normal bile ducts
(B) dilated bile ducts
(C) hepatic arteries
(D) hepatic veins
(E) portal veins

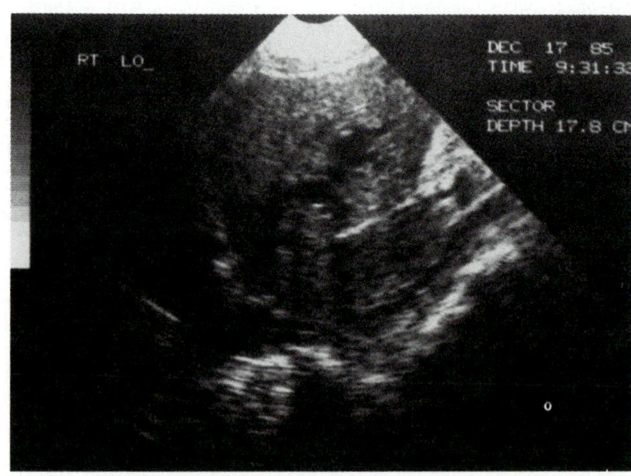

Figure 5–118. Sagittal scan through the liver.

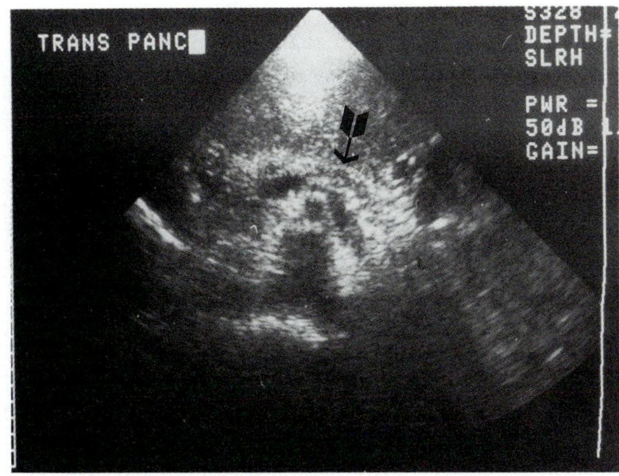

Figure 5–119. Transverse scan through the pancreas.

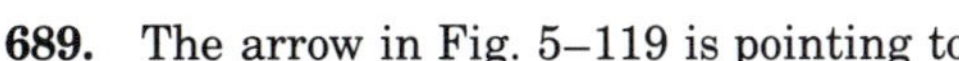

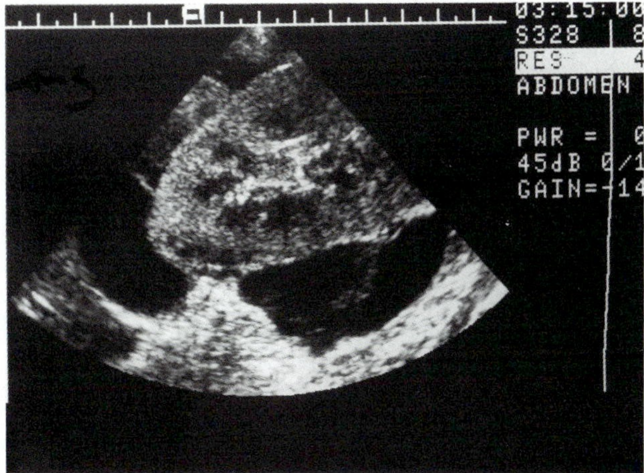

Figure 5–121. Longitudinal scan through the kidney.

689. The arrow in Fig. 5–119 is pointing to

(A) normal pancreas
(B) acute pancreatitis
(C) chronic pancreatitis
(D) adenocarcinoma
(E) islet cell tumor

690. As an incidental finding, this sagittal scan in Fig. 5–120 demonstrated two cystic structures within the liver. This is *most* likely

(A) liver metastases
(B) hydatid disease
(C) simple benign hepatic cysts
(D) lymphoma
(E) polycystic liver disease

691. The renal transplant patient in Fig. 5–121 was referred for a sonogram. The perirenal fluid collection may be associated with all of the following *except*

(A) abscess
(B) hematoma
(C) ascites
(D) urinoma
(E) lymphocele

692. Fig. 5–122 shows a 38-year-old man with a distended bladder and enuresis. The sonogram depicts

(A) an enlarged prostate
(B) a normal scan
(C) diffuse bladder wall thickening
(D) bladder neck obstruction
(E) endometriosis of the bladder

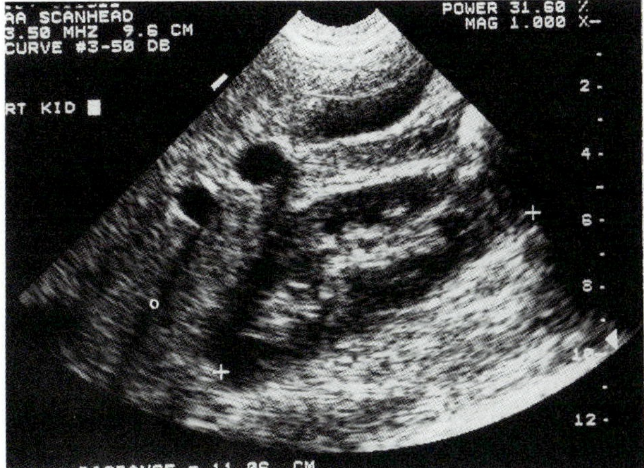

Figure 5–120. Longitudinal scan through the right upper quadrant.

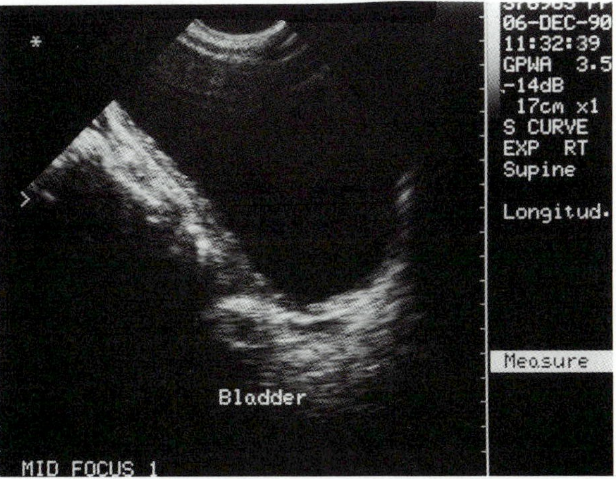

Figure 5–122. Longitudinal scan of a male pelvis.

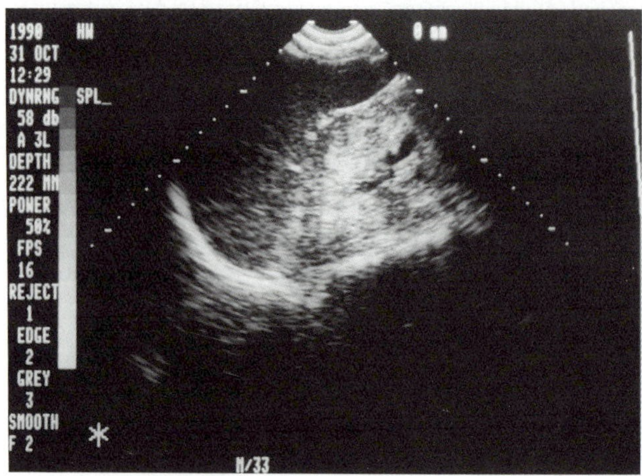

Figure 5–123. Longitudinal scan of the right kidney.

693. Which of the following laboratory values would you expect to be elevated in the patient in Fig. 5–123?

(A) serum glutamic oxaloacetic transaminase (SGOT) and serum glutamic pyruvic transaminase (SGPT)
(B) alkaline phosphatase and bilirubin
(C) amylase and lipase
(D) creatinine and blood urea nitrogen (BUN)
(E) acid phosphatase

694. Internal echoes inside the simple renal cyst shown in Fig. 5–124 may be due to all of the following *except*

(A) reverberation
(B) beam width artifact
(C) refraction
(D) attenuation
(E) side lobe artifact

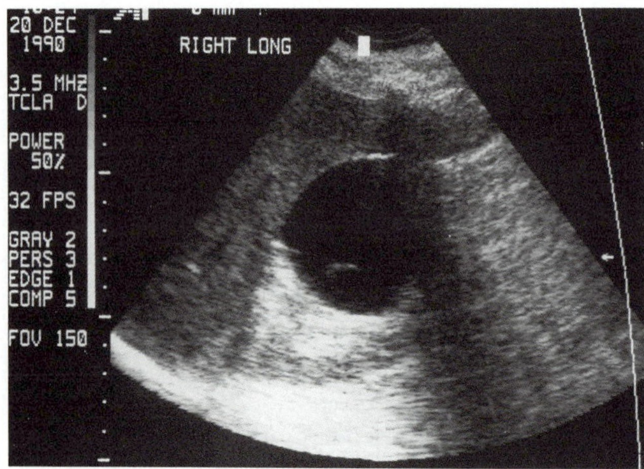

Figure 5–124. Longitudinal scan of the right kidney.

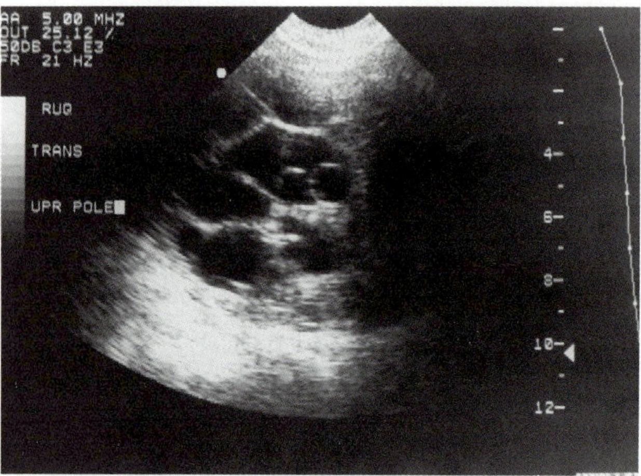

Figure 5–125. Transverse scan of the right kidney.

695. This transverse scan of the right kidney (Fig. 5–125) shows findings *most* consistent with

(A) parapelvic cysts
(B) chronic renal failure
(C) hydronephrosis
(D) adult polycystic kidney disease
(E) juvenile polycystic kidney disease

696. The newborn in Fig. 5–126 presented with a palpable abdominal mass. The sonogram suggests

(A) multicystic dysplastic kidney
(B) hydronephrosis
(C) infantile polycystic disease
(D) peripelvic cysts
(E) multiple renal cortical cysts

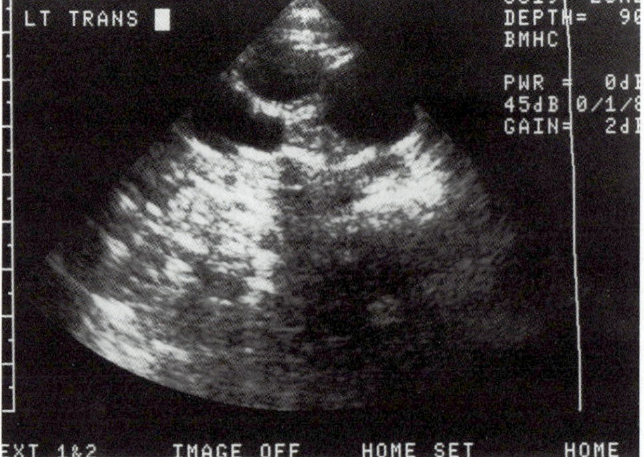

Figure 5–126. Transverse scan of the left kidney of a newborn baby.

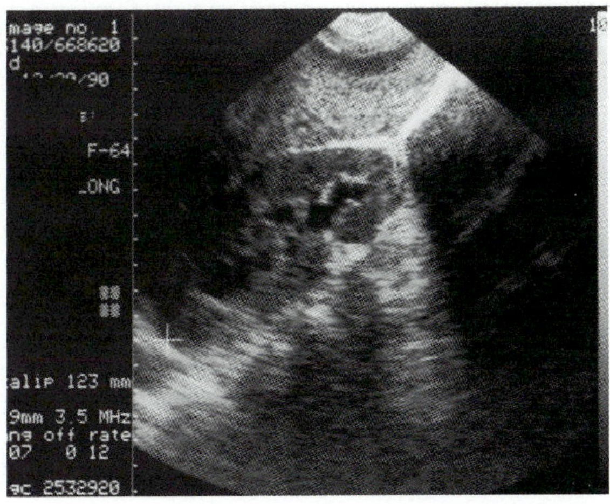

Figure 5–127. Longitudinal scan of the right kidney.

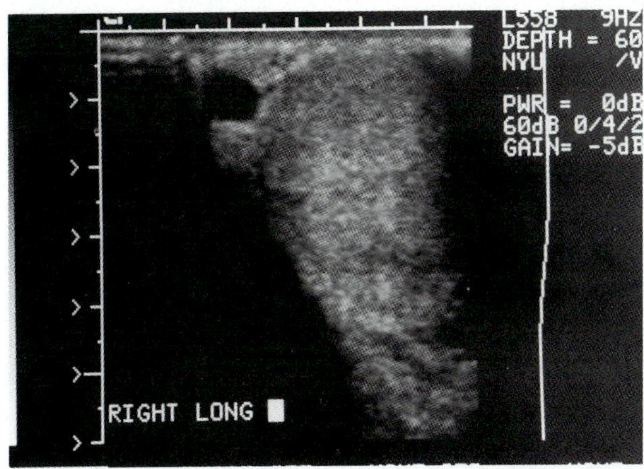

Figure 5–129. Longitudinal scan through the right testis.

697. Fig. 5–127 suggests that this patient may have all of the following *except*

(A) a normal scan
(B) benign prostatic enlargement
(C) prostatitis
(D) calculi
(E) retroperitoneal fibrosis
(F) pyelonephritis

698. The most obvious cause of hydronephrosis in the patient in Fig. 5–128 is

(A) angiomyolipoma
(B) vesicoureteral reflux
(C) tuberous sclerosis
(D) parapelvic cysts
(E) staghorn calculus

699. A scrotal ultrasound was performed on the 69-year-old man in Fig. 5–129. The findings are consistent with

(A) spermatocele
(B) epididymal cyst
(C) seminoma
(D) varicocele
(E) may be two of the above

700. A scrotal ultrasound was performed on the 78-year-old man in Fig. 5–130. The arrow is pointing to

(A) a fractured testicle
(B) normal head of epididymis
(C) the mediastinum
(D) seminoma
(E) testicular torsion

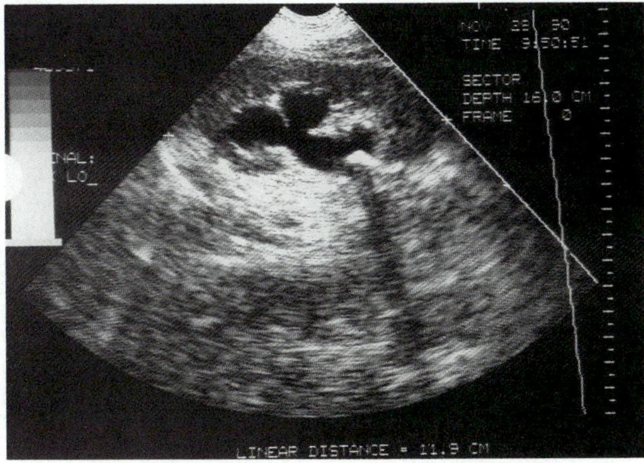

Figure 5–128. Coronal scan of the right kidney.

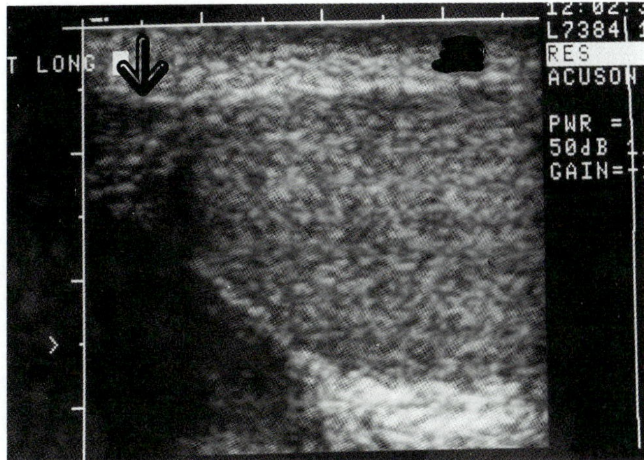

Figure 5–130. Magnified longitudinal scan of the right testis.

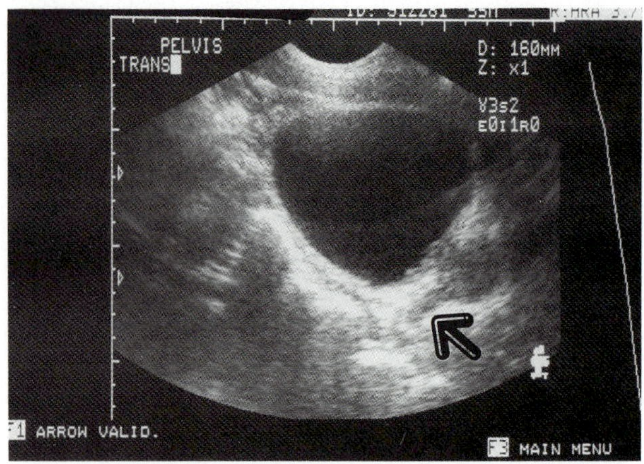

Figure 5–131. Longitudinal scan through a normal male pelvis.

701. Fig. 5–131 is a scan of a male pelvis. The arrow is pointing to

(A) prostate
(B) seminal vesicle
(C) prostatic urethra
(D) membranous urethra
(E) urethra

702. In Fig. 5–132, the arrow is pointing to

(A) spermatocele
(B) epididymal cyst
(C) cryptorchidism
(D) varicocele
(E) mediastinum testis

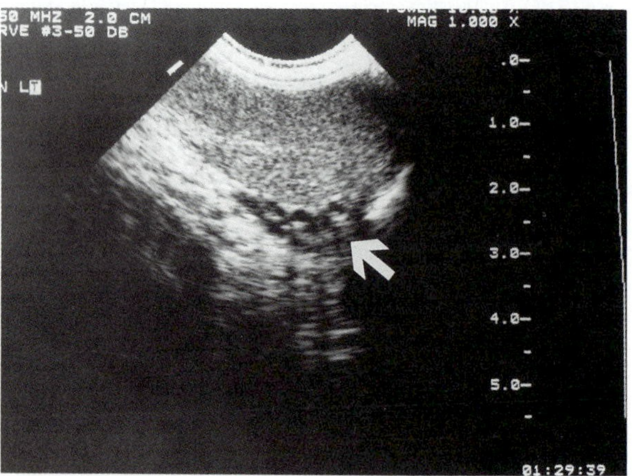

Figure 5–132. Longitudinal scan through the right testis.

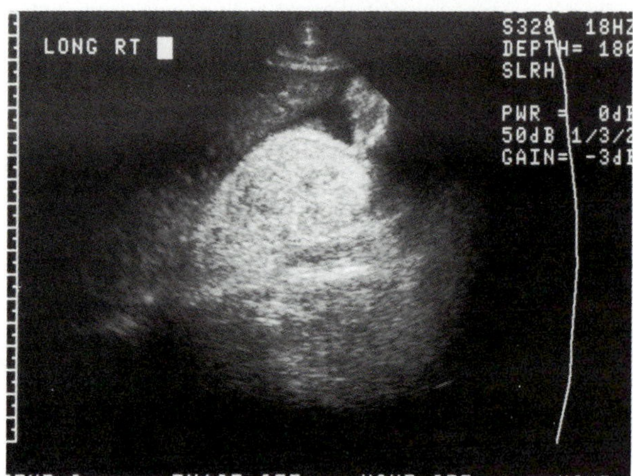

Figure 5–133. Longitudinal scan through the right kidney.

703. Fig. 5–133 is most consistent with

(A) acute pyelonephritis
(B) acute tubular necrosis
(C) tubular sclerosis
(D) chronic glomerulonephritis
(E) medullary nephrocalcinosis

704. Fig. 5–134 is consistent with

(A) acute pyelonephritis
(B) acute tubular necrosis
(C) tubular sclerosis
(D) acute focal bacterial nephritis
(E) an angiomyolipoma
(F) two of the above

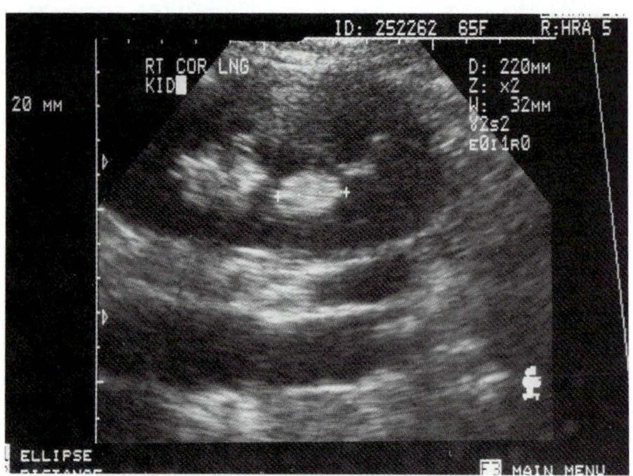

Figure 5–134. Coronal scan of the right kidney.

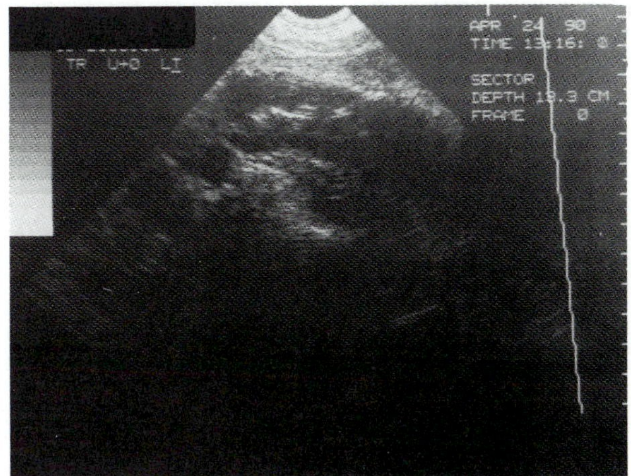

Figure 5–135. Transverse scan of the abdomen.

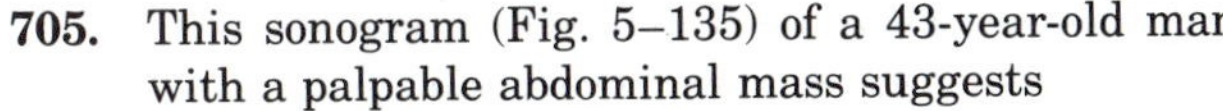

705. This sonogram (Fig. 5–135) of a 43-year-old man with a palpable abdominal mass suggests

(A) adenopathy
(B) aortic aneurysm
(C) horseshoe kidney
(D) dilated loop of bowel

706. The arrow in Fig. 5–136, showing a 14-day-old baby boy born 2 weeks prematurely, is pointing to

(A) normal adrenal
(B) perirenal hemorrhage
(C) retroperitoneal fat
(D) neuroblastoma
(E) pheochromocytoma

707. This is a scan (Fig. 5–137) of the left kidney. It suggests

(A) a parapelvic cyst
(B) hydronephrosis
(C) pyonephrosis
(D) urinoma
(E) renal infarction

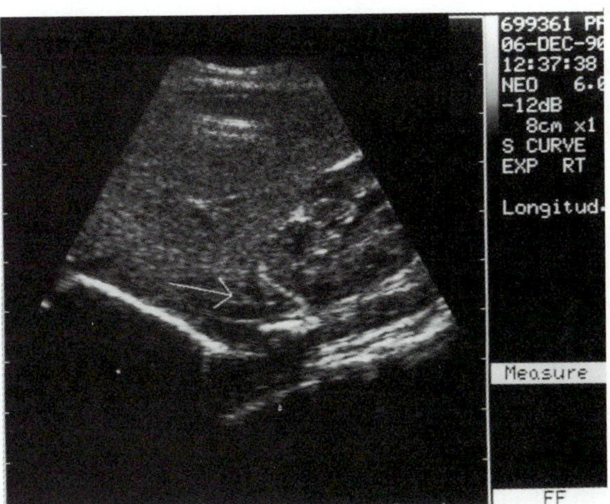

Figure 5–136. Longitudinal sonogram of a neonate through the area of the right kidney.

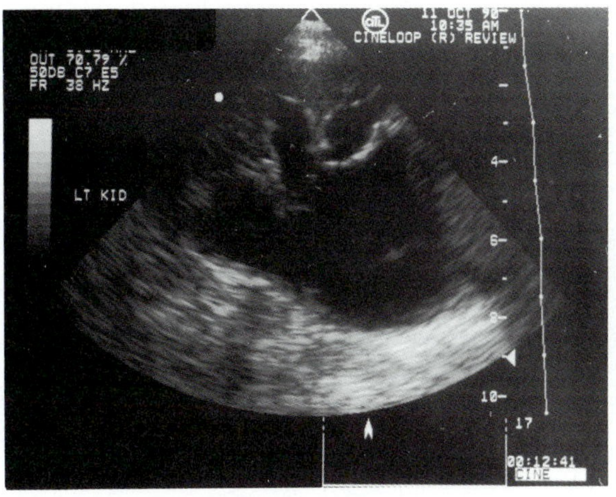

Figure 5–137. Coronal scan of the left kidney.

708. The thin black arrow in Fig. 5–138 is pointing to

(A) the renal sinus
(B) arcuate arteries
(C) pyramids
(D) simple renal cysts
(E) the major calyx

709. The open arrowhead in Fig. 5–138 is pointing to

(A) the renal sinus
(B) arcuate arteries
(C) pyramids
(D) simple renal cyst
(E) renal stones

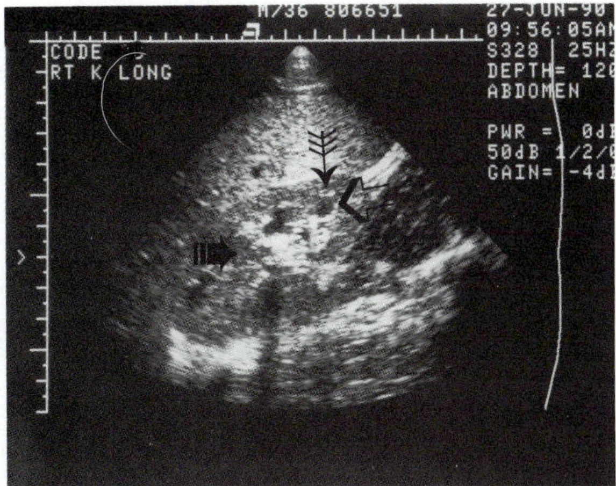

Figure 5–138. Longitudinal scan of the right kidney.

710. The larger black arrow in Fig. 5–138 is pointing to

(A) renal column of Bertin
(B) an angiomyolipoma
(C) dromedary hump
(D) bifid collecting system
(E) the renal pelvis

711. A patient presents with the sonogram reproduced in Fig. 5–139. The findings may be initiated by all of the following *except*

(A) stone in the common bile duct
(B) mass in the head of the pancreas
(C) ampullary carcinoma
(D) diffuse metastatic disease of the liver
(E) cirrhosis

712. A patient presents with the sonogram reproduced in Fig. 5–140. The findings may be initiated by all of the following *except*

(A) lymphoma
(B) portal hypertension
(C) infectious diseases
(D) myeloproliferative disorders
(E) neuroblastoma

713. The best position to place the patient to evaluate renal size and function is

(A) prone
(B) supine
(C) decubitus coronal
(D) transverse

Question 714: The following statements are either true or false.

714. Acute tubular necrosis is associated with

(A) increased renal size T _____ F _____

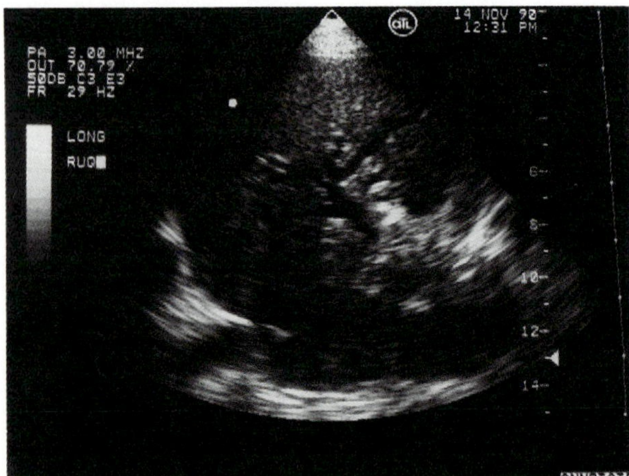

Figure 5–139. Longitudinal scan of the liver.

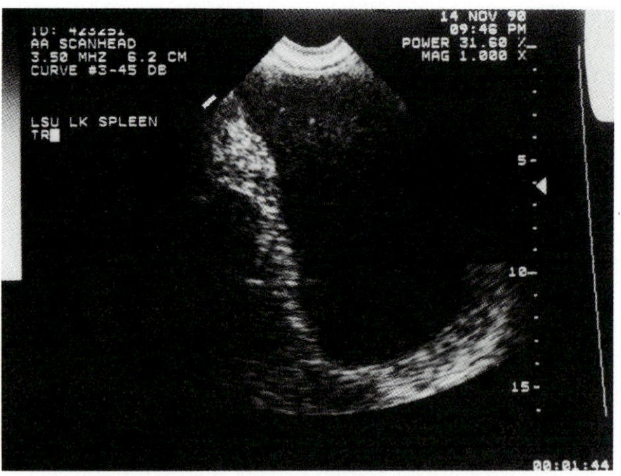

Figure 5–140. Longitudinal scan of the spleen.

(B) the medullary pyramids are prominent and anechoic T _____ F _____
(C) acute renal failure, of which acute tubular necrosis is the most common cause T _____ F _____
(D) a rise in serum creatinine of greater than 2.5 mg/dL T _____ F _____
(E) in renal transplantation, the most common cause of failure in the immediate post-transplant period is acute tubular necrosis T _____ F _____

715. The valves of Heister are located in

(A) common bile duct
(B) cystic duct
(C) gallbladder
(D) common hepatic duct

716. Chronic cholecystitis is associated with

(A) pancreatic pseudocyst
(B) gallbladder polyps
(C) gallbladder carcinoma
(D) increased α-fetoprotein levels

717. One may find associated with biliary dilatation all of the following *except*

(A) jaundice
(B) right upper quadrant pain
(C) increased alkaline phosphatase
(D) elevated amylase
(E) elevated acid phosphatase

718. People with diabetes may present with

(A) hypotonic and paralytic intestines
(B) renal insufficiency
(C) chronic distension of the gallbladder
(D) pancreatic phlegmon

719. If a patient presents with weight loss and jaundice, one would expect to find all of the below *except*

(A) liver metastasis
(B) dilated common bile duct
(C) hepatoma
(D) mass in the head of the pancreas
(E) hemangioma

720. Choledochal cyst is a

(A) cyst within the gallbladder
(B) focal dilatation of the biliary tree
(C) complication of a pseudocyst
(D) associated with adenomyomatosis

721. Carcinoma of the gallbladder would most likely appear as

(A) thin-walled enlarged gallbladder
(B) small gallbladder with thickened walls
(C) large gallbladder with a halo effect
(D) a diffusely thickened gallbladder with gallstones

Answers and Explanations

At the end of each explained answer there is a number combination in parentheses. The first number identifies the reference source; the second number or set of numbers indicates the page or pages on which the relevant information can be found.

1. **(A)** The kidneys are *not* intraperitoneal in location. They lie behind the parietal peritoneum; therefore, they are referred to as a retroperitoneal structure. *(2:308–309)*

2. **(A)** The renal sinus echoes are produced by the renal pelvis and calyces, renal vessels, fat, and areolar tissue. *(2:310)*

3. **(C)** Arcuate vessels separate the renal parenchyma into cortex and medulla. Sonographically, they may be visualized as bright echoes within this corticomedullary junction. *(2:310)*

4. **(D)** The best approach for evaluation of the left kidney is coronal. Satisfactory images of the left kidney are usually not obtainable in the supine and RAO positions due to overlying bowel gas. In patients with well-developed psoas muscles, the prone views may be of little value. *(2:318)*

5. **(C)** The normal pyloric muscle is 3 mm, and should measure less than 15 mm in total diameter. In the presence of pyloric stenosis, the muscle increases in size and measures more than 5 mm in thickness. *(34:1024)*

6. **(D)** All of the above. To fulfill the criteria of a cyst anywhere within the body, one must show an anechoic (echo-free) structure with good through transmission, distal acoustic enhancement, and well-defined smooth walls. *(1:109)*

7. **(D)** Renal vein thrombosis is associated with large kidneys. Small kidneys are associated with end-stage renal disease. (The normal adult kidneys range from 9 to 12 cm in length.) The renal parenchyma is normally less echogenic when compared to the liver parenchyma. However, in the presence of end-stage renal disease, the kidneys become more echogenic. End-stage renal disease may be due to chronic glomerulonephritis, chronic pylonephritis, and renal vascular disease. *(2:309; 10:60)*

8. **(A)** The columns of Bertin are the inward extensions of the cortex, surrounding and separating the renal pyramids of the medulla. At times, they may be confused with a pseudotumor. *(2:344; 10:52)*

9. **(A)** In the fasting patient, the most common cause for sonographic nonvisualization of the gallbladder is contraction of the gallbladder due to chronic cholecystitis. The contrast medium used to visualize the gallbladder in x-ray does not prevent ultrasound visualization. *(34:559)*

10. **(D)** All of the above. A hematoma may appear either sonolucent, echogenic, or as a semicystic, semisolid mass, depending on how soon after injury the patient is examined. A new hematoma will appear echo free, whereas old blood will appear quite echogenic. *(2:359)*

11. **(D)** All of the above. Urinomas often accompany renal injuries, renal transplants, and patients who have passed a renal stone. *(2:264, 362)*

12. **(C)** Fluid-filled pelvocaliceal collecting system. Sonographically, hydronephrosis presents with a spectrum of ultrasound appearances from a ring-shaped echo-free area in the region of the renal pelvis to a totally distended pelvocaliceal collecting system. Later, with progressive distention, large cystic areas are seen within the kidney with very little renal tissue identified. *(2:362)*

13. **(F)** All of the above. Hydronephrosis is a dilatation of the renal pelvis with associated atrophy of renal tissue resulting from an obstruction to the flow of urine. Possible causes may be prostatic enlargement, calculi, congenital and/or inflammatory strictures, pregnancy, and tumors, all of which can compress or block the outward flow of urine. *(4:363)*

14. **(B)** Wilms' tumor. This is a rapidly developing malignant tumor of the kidneys, usually affecting children before 5 years of age. *(4:372)*

15. **(C)** Empyema is a complication of acute cholecystitis with the development of purulent material within the gallbladder lumen. Since this is essentially an abscess, the patient is ill with fever and has local tenderness. Sonographically, the appearance is similar to acute cholecystitis with echogenic debris. *(1:252)*

16. **(E)** All of the above. Acute cholecystitis is associated with right upper quadrant pain, Murphy's sign, a stone impacted within the cystic duct, and in severe cases fever and an elevated blood count. *(2:124)*

17. **(C)** Courvoisier's sign. Courvoisier's law states that obstruction of the *common bile duct* by pressure from the *outside,* ie, by a carcinoma of the pancreas, produces a *distended* gallbladder. Obstruction by a stone from *within* produces *little* or *no distension* of the gallbladder. The gallbladder is thickened and contracted as a result of the inflammation, and the inflow of bile into the gallbladder is impeded. Classically, patients with a tumor in the head of the pancreas present with painless jaundice and a palpable Courvoisier gallbladder. *(2:127; 4:462)*

18. **(G)** All of the above. Causes of gallbladder wall thickening may include ascites, hypoproteinemia, right-sided congestive cardiac failure, hepatitis, and acute and chronic cholecystitis. In addition, carcinoma, primary or secondary adenomyomatosis, and a normal contracted gallbladder present with thickened walls. *(2:143)*

19. **(B)** Hydropic gallbladder. Complete obstruction of the neck of the gallbladder or the cystic duct leads to hydrops or mucocele of the gallbladder. In this condition, the bile within the gallbladder is absorbed and replaced by a mucoid secretion from the lining of the gallbladder. *(2:146)*

20. **(C)** The upper limits of the intraluminal diameter of the common duct should not exceed 7 mm. The term *common duct* was adopted in sonography to describe either the common hepatic or the common bile duct. The origin of the common duct, which is the anatomical point at which the cystic duct communicates with the common hepatic to form the common bile duct, cannot be visualized and/or differentiated sonographically; therefore one cannot recognize with surety if one sees the common hepatic or common bile, hence the term *common duct.* If one can visualize the duct at the level of the pancreas, at that point one can safely say it is the common bile duct. *(2:150)*

21. **(A)** In the adult, the luminal diameter of the proximal common hepatic duct should be less than or equal to 3–4 mm. *(3:157)*

22. **(A)** The renal pyramids are found within the medulla of the kidney not within the renal sinus. *(2:310; 3:194)*

23. **(A)** Bowman's capsule and the convoluted tubules are found within the renal cortex. *(3:194)*

24. **(B)** Alkaline phosphatase is elevated in hepatobiliary disease not in renal failure. Laboratory data that may indicate renal failure consists of an elevated blood urea nitrogen (BUN), creatinine, and increased protein in the urine. *(3:194)*

25. **(C)** Horseshoe kidney. This congenital abnormality occurs during fetal development with fusion of the upper or lower poles of the kidney. *(3:197)*

26. **(D)** The involved kidneys will be moderately to extremely enlarged resulting from an increase in the size of the individual cysts rather than an increase in their number. *(4:367)*

27. **(C)** A staghorn calculus is a large stone located within the pelvis of the kidney. *(3:207)*

28. **(E)** All of the above. Hypoalbuminemia, cholecystitis—acute or chronic, adenomyomatosis, and carcinoma of the gallbladder are all associated with thickening of the gallbladder wall. *(1:248)*

29. **(D)** All of the above. A hypernephroma, also known as a renal cell carcinoma, adenocarcinoma, or Grawitz's tumor, is the most common malignant renal tumor in adults. The tumor is an irregular in shape but well-marginated solid mass and may grow so large as to replace the renal volume. *(4:370)*

30. **(B)** Lymphadenopathy. Horseshoe kidneys occur during fetal development with fusion of the upper or lower poles of the kidney. The fused poles and the isthmus drape over the spine and may be confused with lymphadenopathy. *(3:197)*

31. **(C)** The pancreatic head lies caudad to the portal vein and anterior to the inferior vena cava. *(2:167)*

32. **(A)** Glisson's capsule is a dense fibrous membrane that surrounds the liver and encloses the portal vein, hepatic artery, and bile ducts within the liver. *(2:83)*

33. **(D)** All of the above. The splenic vein runs anterior to the aorta and superior mesenteric artery and caudad to the celiac axis to join with the superior mesenteric vein to become the portal vein. *(8:37)*

34. **(C)** In the normal individual, the abdominal aorta shows a gradual tapering of its luminal dimensions as it proceeds distally to its bifurcation. *(3:117–120)*

35. **(E)** All of the above. To distinguish hepatic veins from portal veins, all of the given anatomical considerations should be recognized. *(3:116)*

36. **(C)** The celiac trunk does *not* branch into the gastroduodenal artery. It does branch into the left gastric, splenic, and common hepatic arteries. *(3:118)*

37. **(C)** The superior mesenteric artery runs posterior to the neck of the pancreas, then emerges and crosses anterior to the uncinate process. *(3:120)*

38. **(A)** The division into anatomic right and left lobes of the liver is along the line of the major hepatic fissure and middle hepatic vein. *(3:130)*

39. **(D)** The pleural fluid may be anechoic to loculated and is found superior to the diaphragm. *(8:305)*

40. **(A)** In acute renal disease, the kidneys are enlarged and swollen. *(8:139)*

41. **(C)** When the gallbladder fundus is folded over on itself, this variation is termed a phrygian cap. *(1:228)*

42. **(C)** On transverse sonogram, the common bile duct is located anterior to the inferior vena cava and posterior to the head of the pancreas. The common bile duct will define the posterolateral aspect of the pancreatic head. *(1:260)*

43. **(C)** The spleen is *not* a retroperitoneal organ. It is an intraperitoneal organ, thus it is covered on both its anterior and posterior surfaces by the peritoneum. *(1:331)*

44. **(A)** The kidneys are *not* rigidly fixed on the abdominal wall. They may move downward during inspiration by as much as 2.5 cm. *(3:192)*

45. **(G)** Gallbladder carcinoma has a strong association with calculi and chronic mechanical irritation. It initially may begin as a polypoid mass eventually progressing to bile duct obstruction, jaundice, and weight loss. *(1:256)*

46. **(C)** The inferior vena cava forms at the confluence of the right and left common iliac veins. *(3:111)*

47. **(D)** The inferior vena cava passes through the caval hiatus of the diaphragm to enter the right, not the left, atrium. *(3:111)*

48. **(B)** Both bile ducts and portal veins have echogenic walls, therefore, this cannot be used as ultrasound criteria. *(1:260)*

49. **(C)** A choledochal cyst is not a true cyst but a congenital outpouching of the common duct that may cause obstructive jaundice in children. *(1:259)*

50. **(C)** A pancreatic pseudocyst, loculated ascites, and a fluid-filled stomach will all be found anterior to the pancreas. An aortic aneurysm is found posterior to the pancreas. *(5:175)*

51. **(A)** The left renal vein runs between the aorta and the superior mesenteric artery. *(3:116)*

52. **(B)** The superior mesenteric vein, a tributary of the portal vein, runs upward to the right of the superior mesenteric artery. *(3:114)*

53. **(C)** After leaving the spleen, the splenic vein courses along the posterior surface of the pancreatic body and tail. *(3:114)*

54. **(B)** If on sonographic examination one finds dilated intrahepatic ducts and a small gallbladder, the obstruction should be at the level of the common hepatic duct above the entry of the cystic duct. Bile is not going to pass the obstruction to fill the gallbladder. *(2:155)*

55. **(D)** The normal thickness of the gallbladder wall is 3 mm. Thicker walls suggest a pathological condition. *(1:248)*

56. **(D)** Adenomyomatosis is a benign proliferation and thickening of the muscle and glandular layer of the gallbladder with the formation of intramural diverticula. It is most common in the fundus where it appears as a focal mass. *(7:163)*

57. **(B)** Glisson's capsule is a strong specular reflector, having a large, smooth interface. The dimensions are much greater than the ultrasonic wavelength. *(2:83)*

58. **(E)** All of the above. An increase in the parenchymal echogenicity of the liver giving rise to a "fatty liver" may be due to alcohol abuse (most common), diabetes, chemotherapy, or toxic substances. *(2:102)*

59. **(B)** Hydronephrosis frequently occurs in a duplicated kidney collecting system. *(2:365)*

60. **(B)** If on sonographic examination, a patient is found to have dilated interhepatic ducts, a dilated common bile duct, and a dilated gallbladder (the

gallbladder enlarging before the biliary tree because it has the greatest surface area), one should expect obstruction at the distal common duct. *(2:155)*

61. **(B)** The gastroesophageal junction can sonographically be visualized anterior to the aorta and posterior to the left lobe of the liver. *(1:33)*

62. **(C)** In acute viral hepatitis, the liver parenchyma appears normal. *(2:103)*

63. **(D)** Cholecystokinin, a hormone released by the intestinal mucosa, stimulates the ejection of bile from the gallbladder. *(1:226)*

64. **(D)** Diffuse thickening of the gallbladder wall is a nonspecific finding and frequently is not a result of primary gallbladder disease. It can be seen with acute cholecystitis but may also be associated with hepatitis, congestive heart failure, and severe hypoalbumenic state. However, elevated portal pressure is *not* a recognized cause for diffuse gallbladder wall thickening. *(3:162)*

65. **(A)** The best sonographic window to the left hemidiaphragm is the spleen. *(8:302)*

66. **(B)** An islet cell tumor is the most common benign tumor of the pancreas. These tumors are usually small, well encapsulated, and most commonly found in the tail. Sonographically, they are very difficult to image owing to their small size. *(3:186)*

67. **(F)** All of the above. Adenocarcinoma is the most malignant tumor of the pancreas. These tumors may be quite large with irregular nodular borders and are commonly found within the pancreatic head. The enlarged gland causes obstruction of the common bile duct and possibly the pancreatic duct. Dilated bile ducts, an enlarged gallbladder (a Courvoisier gallbladder), weight loss, and painless jaundice are associated findings. *(3:186)*

68. **(B)** The uncinate process of the pancreas lies posterior to the superior mesenteric artery and vein. *(3:174)*

69. **(A)** High levels of serum amylase can be due to pancreatitis. One of the most common causes of pancreatitis is cholelithiasis. *(4:465)*

70. **(C)** Bile is produced within the liver *not* the pancreas. Lipase is an exocrine function and insulin and glucagon are endocrine functions of the pancreas. *(4:472)*

71. **(D)** All of the above. The renal hilum on the medial border of each kidney contains the renal vein, two branches of the renal artery, and the proximal ureter. *(3:192)*

72. **(B)** The kidneys, the perinephric fat, and the adrenal glands are covered by Gerota's fascia but not by a true capsule. *(3:192)*

73. **(C)** The normal adult kidneys measure 10–12 cm in length and 4–5 cm in thickness. *(2:309; 3:192)*

74. **(D)** Fat can sonographically present as either anechoic or echogenic depending upon its composition and location. In renal sinus lipomatosis, the renal sinus will be enlarged and its fat content runs the spectrum from echo-free to echogenic. *(5:318–319)*

75. **(C)** If one finds a solid renal mass, one should continue the examination and check the inferior vena cava and renal vein for tumor extension as well as the retroperitoneum for nodes. *(2:344)*

76. **(D)** All of the above. In the case of chronic pancreatitis, as the pancreas becomes more fibrotic, it will decrease in size and will appear more echogenic with an irregular outline. Dilatation of the pancreatic duct (over 2 mm) with calculi is a sequela of ductal obstruction. *(8:54)*

77. **(A)** The pancreas *does not* lie in the peritoneal space. It is a retroperitoneal organ. It is approximately 10–15 cm in length. The gland is multilobulated and nonencapsulated. Because there is no capsule, it is hard to visualize sonographically. *(3:174; 2:163)*

78. **(C)** Pseudocyst formation is a frequent complication of pancreatitis. Pseudocysts are usually located around the pancreas but may dissect through the retroperitoneum and be located anywhere in the body. An uncomplicated pseudocyst is one without any internal debris. Sonographically, it will appear anechoic, have smooth walls, and good ultrasound transmission distally. *(2:192)*

79. **(C)** The presence of gas within a mass confirms the diagnosis of an abscess. An abscess usually has a more irregular appearance than a pseudocyst and contains more internal echoes. *(2:192)*

80. **(B)** A pancreatic pseudocyst may regress spontaneously by draining into the communicating pancreatic duct and then into the bowel. *(2:192)*

81. **(E)** Pancreatic pseudocysts contain strong pancreatic enzymes. These enzymes can dissect into the porta hepatis area, or they can dissect through the esophageal or aortic hiatus to be found in the mediastinum. A pseudocyst may dissect into the retro-

peritoneal area and may extend into the pelvis and groin. *(2:197)*

82. **(A)** The endocrine function of the pancreas is to produce insulin. The exocrine function of the pancreas is to produce lipase, amylase, carboxypeptidase, trypsin, and chymotrypsin. *(3:175)*

83. **(C)** The acinar cells of the pancreas are the exocrine secretory cells. These cells secrete enzymes, which are carried by the pancreatic duct. *(3:175)*

84. **(B)** The maximum inner diameter of the pancreatic duct in young adults measures 2 mm. *(2:177)*

85. **(D)** All of the above. By visualizing pancreatic tissue on both sides of the pancreatic duct, one can avoid confusion between the pancreatic duct and the splenic or portal vein posteriorly. Confusion of the collapsed stomach wall anteriorly is best avoided by having the patient drink fluid. The splenic artery is located anteriorly and pulsations should be noted to avoid confusion. *(2:177)*

86. **(B)** Adenocarcinoma is the most common primary carcinoma of the pancreas. The clinical symptoms are weight loss, painless jaundice, nausea, vomiting, and changes in stool. *(3:186)*

87. **(D)** Adenocarcinoma of the pancreas is imaged as a solid focally enlarged lobulated mass with low-level echoes. It most commonly occurs in the pancreatic head, which in turn may lead to pancreatic duct obstruction or biliary duct obstruction. *(2:178)*

88. **(C)** When a mass is visualized in the area of the pancreatic head, one should check the liver for metastasis and dilation of the intrahepatic ducts. The common bile duct and the pancreatic duct should be checked for enlargement secondary to obstruction. *(2:177)*

89. **(F)** All of the above. Nodal masses, compression of the inferior vena cava, splenic vein, or portal vein posteriorly, and ascites are associated findings of pancreatic carcinoma. *(2:183)*

90. **(B)** In acute pancreatitis, the pancreas is enlarged and edematous demonstrating a decrease in ultrasound absorption. It is secondary to this that sonographically the pancreas becomes uniformly hypoechoic, with an increase in through transmission. *(2:183)*

91. **(A)** To delineate the duodenum from the pancreatic head, have the patient drink water and then scan a few minutes later. *(8:53)*

92. **(D)** Bile is an example of an exocrine function of the liver (the releasing of secretions via a duct). *(3:132)*

93. **(B)** Wirsung's duct is the main pancreatic duct and Santorini's duct is an accessory duct. *(1:275)*

94. **(C)** The head of the pancreas may extend medial to the inferior vena cava and posterior to the superior mesenteric vein. This extension is termed the uncinate process. *(3:174)*

95. **(B)** The extrahepatic portion of the falciform ligament can be visualized in ascites. It will appear as an echogenic band attaching the liver to the anterior abdominal wall. *(2:87)*

96. **(D)** The liver is considered to be an intraperitoneal structure. The portion of the liver that is devoid of peritoneum is termed the bare area. The bare area is located between the right and left triangular ligaments. *(2:85; 6:209)*

97. **(A)** The right and left hepatic ducts usually unite to form the common hepatic duct in the porta hepatis. Occasionally, they may unite within the hepatic parenchyma. *(1:228)*

98. **(C)** Lymphadenopathy is usually associated with carcinoma. A common site for enlarged nodes is in the porta hepatis. This in turn may cause dilatation of the intrahepatic ducts but will not affect the common bile duct or gallbladder because of the level of the obstruction. *(1:270)*

99. **(B)** The main pancreatic duct is Wirsung's duct. The duct starts at the tail of the pancreas, transverses the body, and courses to the head where it is largest in diameter. Normally, it should not exceed 2 mm in luminal diameter. *(2:176)*

100. **(A)** The ligamentum venosum is a remnant of the ductus venosus that shunts oxygenated blood from the umbilical vein to the inferior vena cava, bypassing the liver. In the adult, the ligamentum venosum is a landmark separating the caudate lobe from the left lobe of the liver. *(3:130; 6:211)*

101. **(E)** All of the above. All of the listed fluid collections are sonolucent masses that may occur around the renal transplant. To help differentiate between them, keep in mind the number of days or weeks at which they occur postoperatively. Abscesses usually occur immediately after surgery, hematomas appear early in the postoperative period, urinomas usually occur within the first 2 weeks, and lymphoceles occur between 2 weeks and 6 months. *(2:381)*

102. **(B)** Acute glomerulonephritis is *not* a cause of hydronephrosis. Posterior urethral valves obstruct the urethra directly and can lead to hydronephrosis. Ovarian cancer and retroperitoneal tumors may place extrinsic pressure on the ureters leading to hydronephrosis. Retroperitoneal fibrosis may encase and thereby obstruct the ureters also leading to hydronephrosis. *(2:415)*

103. **(A)** The rectus abdominus muscle is not considered to be retroperitoneal in location, therefore, a retroperitoneal abscess cannot be found there. *(3:231)*

104. **(D)** The spleen is an intraperitoneal organ. Retroperitoneal structures include the kidney, pancreas, aorta, vena cava, duodenum, and adrenal glands. *(3:231)*

105. **(D)** All of the above. Findings for renal vein thrombosis are determined by the stage of the disease. The order in which they appear (A, B, C) is from acute to chronic, respectively. *(2:373)*

106. **(D)** A Klatskin tumor is a ductal cancer at the bifurcation of the right and left hepatic ducts. *Cholangiocarcinoma* is a general term for ductal cancer. A Klatskin tumor, cholangiocarcinoma, and enlarged portal lymph nodes will only obstruct the intrahepatic biliary tree. Pancreatic carcinoma will first block the common duct before dilatation of the intrahepatic ducts can be seen. *(1:259; 2:144)*

107. **(D)** All of the above. The gastroduodenal artery is the first branch of the common hepatic artery. It proceeds caudally and is used as a landmark delineating the anterolateral aspect of the head of the pancreas. On transverse scans, it is seen as a round sonolucent structure anterior to the common bile duct. *(5:186)*

108. **(C)** The quadrate lobe is the medial segment of the left lobe. *(3:135)*

109. **(D)** The caudate lobe occupies much of the posterosuperior surface of the liver. It lies between the inferior vena cava and the ligamentum venosum. *(1:31)*

110. **(B)** There are three hepatic veins; right, left, and middle. They run intersegmentally and define the lobes of the liver. *(3:130)*

111. **(F)** The ligamentum teres is defined by all of the above and is an anatomic landmark which separates the caudal aspect of the left lobe of the liver into medial and lateral segments. *(3:130)*

112. **(D)** Acute obstruction of the common bile duct may not dilate the intrahepatic biliary radicles for a few days. In chronic infiltrative liver disease and cholangitis, the ducts cannot dilate easily due to secondary fibrotic narrowing. Given time, both of these circumstances will eventually lead to dilated intrahepatic biliary radicles to some degree. *(1:259)*

113. **(D)** Caroli's disease is cavernous ectasia of the biliary tree and may appear as focal cystic collections throughout the liver. Polycystic liver disease and congenital cysts are cystic lesions within the liver. *(2:108)*

114. **(D)** All of the terms given may lead to shadowing from the area of the gallbladder fossa. *(2:107)*

115. **(E)** All of terms given are complex lesions within the liver. Biliary cystadenoma is a rare benign tumor of the bile ducts. An echinococcal cyst is classically multiseptated with daughter cysts. A large cavernous hemangioma can be visualized but is best diagnosed by angiography or CT. The appearance of a hematoma depends on the stage of clot formation. *(2:111)*

116. **(A)** The most common cause of pancreatitis in adults in the United States is biliary tract disease. Alcohol abuse is the second most common cause followed by trauma. *(3:183)*

117. **(B)** Lipase secreted by the pancreas accounts for 80% of all fat digestion. The other 20% is secreted by the small intestine. *(3:176)*

118. **(B)** Jaundice is generally not seen in acute pancreatitis. Sonographically, the swollen pancreas is enlarged, becoming less echogenic and possibly pressing on the inferior vena cava anteriorly. *(3:184)*

119. **(B)** In chronic pancreatitis, the patient is usually jaundiced. The pancreas becomes small and fibrotic and echogenic calcifications are noted. Pseudocysts are commonly seen in association with chronic pancreatitis. *(3:184)*

120. **(E)** All of the techniques given may be useful in imaging the pancreas. The prone position is helpful in visualizing the tail. *(2:175)*

121. **(B)** The left adrenal is posterior, not anterior, to the tail of the pancreas. *(2:164)*

122. **(L)** Portal vein. *(8:49–51)*

123. **(R)** Hepatic artery. *(8:49–51)*

124. **(K)** Common bile duct. *(8:49–51)*

125. **(F)** Left gastric artery. *(8:49–51)*

126. **(J)** Celiac axis. *(8:49–51)*

127. **(E)** Splenic artery. *(8:49–51)*

128. **(B)** Gastroduodenal artery. *(8:49–51)*

129. **(A)** Spleen. *(8:49–51)*

130. **(G)** Adrenal. *(8:49–51)*

131. **(C)** Kidney. *(8:49–51)*

132. **(M)** Aorta. *(8:49–51)*

133. **(H)** Superior mesenteric artery. *(8:49–51)*

134. **(D)** Inferior vena cava. *(8:49–51)*

135. **(I)** Superior mesenteric vein. *(8:49–51)*

136. **(N)** Duodenum. *(8:49–51)*

137. **(P)** Duct of Wirsung. *(8:49–51)*

138. **(O)** Duct of Santorini. *(8:49–51)*

139. **(Q)** Uncinate process. *(8:49–51)*

140. **(A)** True. In a significant proportion of patients after cholecystectomy, the luminal diameter of the normal proximal bile duct is more than 5 mm and may be up to 10 mm. *(1:260)*

141. **(B)** In decreasing order of echogenicity is the renal sinus > pancreas > liver > spleen > renal parenchyma. *(2:165; 8:108)*

142. **(B)** A subphrenic abscess will displace the spleen inferiorly, not enlarge it. *(1:344)*

143. **(E)** All of the above. The thickening of the nondistended bowel wall greater than 5 mm whether due to inflammatory disease or a variety of neoplasm depends upon the amount of bowel wall infiltration. Absence of peristalsis on real-time and the bull's eye configuration will aid in the recognition of bowel abnormalities. *(2:299)*

144. **(B)** If a mass is solid, displacement of adjacent organs will aid in helping to evaluate the origin of the mass. In a retroperitoneal sarcoma, the kidney, spleen, and pancreas would be displaced anteriorly. *(8:110)*

145. **(A)** The splenic vein courses anteriorly to the left adrenal gland to join with the superior mesenteric vein to become the main portal vein. An adrenal mass may lead to anterior displacement of this vein. *(8:271)*

146. **(C)** A fluid collection located between the diaphragm and the spleen may represent a subphrenic abscess. *(8:110)*

147. **(C)** The normal adult adrenal rarely measures more than 3 cm at its maximum diameter. *(2:396)*

148. **(A)** Adenomyomatosis is a benign infiltrative disease that will *not* lead to a large gallbladder but rather to an irregular thickening of the gallbladder wall. *(3:152; 5:121)*

149. **(C)** Right-side heart failure will produce venous congestion of the liver, which in turn will lead to marked dilatation of the intrahepatic veins. *(2:104)*

150. **(A)** The body of the pancreas is bound on its anterior surface by the dorsum of the stomach. *(2:163)*

151. **(A)** The landmark associated with the pancreatic body is the splenic vein that lies posteriorly. The gastroduodenal artery defines the anterolateral and the common bile duct the posterolateral margins of the pancreatic head. *(1:274)*

152. **(D)** All of the above. The landmarks for visualizing the pancreatic head are the inferior vena cava lying posteriorly, the gastroduodenal artery defining the anterolateral margin, and the common bile duct defining the posterolateral margin. *(8:37)*

153. **(B)** The landmark most associated with the pancreatic neck is the superior mesenteric vein. *(1:274)*

154. **(C)** The pancreas *does not* have a true capsule; therefore when there is inflammation and/or obstruction, pancreatic enzymes are released, forming a pseudocyst. *(2:345–368)*

155. **(A)** Angiomyolipoma is least likely to be confused with hydronephrosis. It is a fatty tumor that is highly echogenic. *(2:345–368)*

156. **(D)** The common bile duct merges with the pancreatic duct just before entering the second portion of the duodenum. *(1:275)*

157. **(A)** On a sagittal scan the portal vein is seen as a circular structure anterior to the inferior vena cava and superior to the head of the pancreas. *(3:181)*

158. **(D)** All of the above. The prostate lies posterior to the symphysis pubis and inferior to the urinary bladder and seminal vesicles. *(8:159)*

159. **(B)** Owing to the prostate's posterior position, one must angle the transducer approximately 15° caudad to best visualize the gland. *(8:159)*

160. **(C)** If the prostate is found to be enlarged, one should check the kidneys for hydronephrosis. *(8:162)*

161. **(B)** The laboratory findings suggest obstructive jaundice; therefore, one must check for a stone or mass obstructing the bile duct. *(3:134)*

162. **(D)** Acute prostatitis is an infection and would not be caused by trauma. *(10:90)*

163. **(A)** Adenocarcinoma of the prostate is the most common prostatic neoplasm. *(10:91)*

164. **(C)** A mirror-image artifact occurs with highly reflective acoustic interfaces, such as the diaphragm and adjacent lung. This results in a supradiaphragmatic projection of an infradiaphragmatic mass. This artifact is noticed quite regularly when liver echoes are seen superior to the diaphragm. *(12:29)*

165. **(A)** The normal sonographic texture of the spleen is less echogenic than the liver but more echogenic than the cortex of the kidney. *(8:108)*

166. **(B)** The spleen is the largest organ of the reticuloendothelial system. *(10:76)*

167. **(C)** The left kidney lies inferior and medial to the spleen. The diaphragm is anterior, lateral, and superior to the spleen, and the stomach and lesser sac are anterior. *(5:245)*

168. **(C)** Benign ascites is generally anechoic and is freely mobile within the peritoneal cavity. The bowel is seen anteriorly floating. *(2:272; 5:425)*

169. **(B)** Malignant ascites may have echoes or septations. Matted bowel loops posteriorly and peritoneal implants may be seen. *(2:273; 5:437)*

170. **(B)** The glomerulus is part of the kidney *not* the scrotum. The scrotum contains the testes, epididymis, ductus deferens, and a portion of the spermatic cord. *(3:246)*

171. **(B)** Hematocele is a condition in which blood occupies the scrotal sac surrounding the testes as a result of trauma or surgery. *(8:295)*

172. **(A)** A mass in the head of the pancreas with a dilated common bile duct is most suggestive of obstructive jaundice. *(1:258)*

173. **(B)** The epididymis is uniformly enlarged and more anechoic than usual owing to the inflammatory process. On a sagittal sonogram, it will appear as a nonechogenic tubular structure along the underside of the testicle. *(5:388)*

174. **(B)** Acute hydroceles are a result of trauma, infection of the testicle or epididymis, and tumor. They are *not* caused by testicular torsion. *(3:247)*

175. **(C)** Sonographically, the testicles have a homogeneous texture of medium-level echogenicity. *(3:248)*

176. **(F)** All of the above. Adenomas (a true solitary thyroid nodule), diffuse nontoxic goiter (a compensatory enlargement of the thyroid due to thyroid hormone deficiency), adenomatous hyperplasia (multinodular goiter, most common), thyroiditis (as a result of infection or autoimmune disease), and thyroglossal duct cysts are all benign lesions of the thyroid. *(3:241)*

177. **(A)** A cavernous hemangioma is the most common benign hepatic lesion and presents as an echogenic, well-circumscribed tumor. *(3:241)*

178. **(B)** Hyperthyroidism associated with a diffuse goiter is known as Graves' disease. *(3:241)*

179. **(C)** The thyroid gland consists of two lobes, right and left, connected by a narrow isthmus. The trachea is medial to the lobes, the longus colli muscle lies posteriorly, the carotid artery and internal jugular vein laterally, and the strap muscles anterolaterally. *(11:38)*

180. **(A)** When there is extrinsic pressure and obstruction of the common bile duct (i.e., a mass in the head of the pancreas), the gallbladder, common bile duct, and biliary tree will be enlarged. *(1:260)*

181. **(D)** The jugular veins are lateral, not posterior, to the thyroid lobes. *(5:458)*

182. **(A)** Since the thyroid is a superficial structure, a 5-MHz or higher short focus transducer is appropriate (the higher the frequency, the better the resolution and the poorer the penetration). *(8:275)*

183. **(D)** Prostatic carcinoma presents sonographically as an enlarged prostate with ill-defined borders of uneven echogenicity. *(5:588)*

184. **(D)** All of the above. Prostatic neoplasm and prostatic calculi present with an uneven echo texture. Benign prostatic hypertrophy is an overall enlargement of the gland and may present with a heterogeneous echo pattern. *(8:162)*

185. **(A)** The four parathyroid glands, two on each side, lie posterior to the thyroid lobes and medial to the common carotid arteries. *(8:275)*

186. **(E)** A parathyroid adenoma is a discrete mass. A goiter is a diffuse enlargement of the thyroid. *(8:280)*

187. **(C)** The normal thyroid gland measures 1–2 cm in anteroposterior dimension and 4 to 6 cm in length. *(5:454)*

188. **(B)** Thyroiditis will present sonographically as diffusely enlarged thyroid lobes with decreased echogenicity, similar to other organs involved with diffuse inflammatory changes. *(5:476)*

189. **(B)** Most thyroid masses demonstrating a halo are adenomas. *(8:279)*

190. **(D)** Invasive prostatic carcinoma enlarges in an uneven fashion, with irregular and nondiscrete borders. An elevation of acid phosphatase is highly suggestive of prostate cancer. *(5:588)*

191. **(A)** The spermatic cord is composed of the internal spermatic artery, veins that drain the testis, nerves, and the vas deferens. All of these are enclosed by the cremaster muscle and layers of fascia. *(3:246)*

192. **(B)** Varicocele is a varicose dilatation of the veins of the pampiniform plexus, the draining veins of the scrotum, and is associated with infertility. *(2:469)*

193. **(D)** In a hydrocele, the testicle and the appendix epididymis are surrounded by serous fluid, which will appear cystic on ultrasound. *(8:299)*

194. **(D)** A subphrenic abscess will displace the liver inferiorly *not* upward. *(3:127)*

195. **(A)** Budd-Chiari syndrome is caused by hepatic venous congestion. There is relative enlargement of the caudate lobe due to hepatic vein thrombosis. *(1:44)*

196. **(B)** The pyramidal lobe is a superior extension of thyroid tissue arising from the isthmus. *(8:274)*

197. **(E)** All of the above. Sonography of the urinary bladder is extremely valuable in the diagnosis of foreign bodies, masses, calculi, and diverticula. *(3:297)*

198. **(B)** Epididymitis will appear sonographically as a diffuse enlargement of the gland with decreased echogenicity (hypoechoic). *(5:276; 10:42)*

199. **(A)** A seminoma is a solid malignant mass of the testicles that will appear sonographically homogeneous and well circumscribed. *(10:43)*

200. **(B)** Crytorchidism is a condition in which the testicles have not descended and lie either in the abdomen or in the groin. *(8:295)*

201. **(C)** The seminal vesicles are the reservoir for sperm and are located posterior to the bladder. *(8:295)*

202. **(A)** Owing to the interrupted blood supply, the acute infarcted testicle will appear sonographically indistinguishable from a hypoechoic tumor and in its *chronic* stage it will appear small and echogenic. *(8:300)*

203. **(B)** The best way to distinguish hepatic veins from portal veins is by tracing them from their point of origin. Hepatic veins may be traced into the inferior vena cava, whereas the portal system arises from the main portal vein. *(3:129)*

204. **(C)** The fundus of the stomach lies posterolateral to the left lobe of the liver. The remainder of the stomach is located inferior to the liver. *(3:130)*

205. **(D)** Fatty infiltration may be due to cardiac failure, obesity, and more commonly alcoholic liver disease. It is the damage to the hepatocytes that cause accumulation of fat within the liver cells. Renal failure does *not* cause fatty infiltration. *(3:139)*

206. **(C)** α-Fetoprotein and carcinoembryonic antigen are biochemical markers that indicate liver metastases. *(8:57)*

207. **(E)** None of the above. Metastatic lesions in the liver have no specific sonographic appearance. Liver metastases are usually suspected clinically by a palpable liver mass, an enlarged liver, and/or a sudden onset of ascites. *(1:146)*

208. **(B)** A daughter cyst is a classic example of an echinococcal (hydatid) cyst. Hydatid disease is caused by a parasite that enters through the digestive tract and is carried to the liver by the portal system. *(8:66)*

209. **(C)** Reidel's lobe is a normal liver variant. This tonguelike extension of the right lobe of the liver lies anterior to the right kidney. It may clinically lead to a palpable liver descending below the costal margin. *(8:71)*

210. **(E)** Bilirubin, serum protein, prothrombin time, fetal antigen, and SGOT are lab tests that may be used for evaluation of the liver. Serum amylase is elevated in acute pancreatitis. *(10:15)*

211. **(A)** There is no sonographic diagnostic appearance for a liver abscess due to the spectrum of appearances it may have. An abscess is suspected when sonographically one finds a liver mass, and clinically when the patient has an elevated white blood

cell count, right-upper quadrant pain, and is febrile. *(5:65)*

212. **(B)** A subphrenic abscess lies between the diaphragm and liver therefore depressing the liver away from the diaphragm. *(5:66)*

213. **(D)** All of the above. The normal portal vein measures up to 1.5 cm in luminal diameter. Its size can be affected by Valsalva maneuver, respiratory changes, and portal venous hypertension. *(5:78)*

214. **(D)** All of the above. Regenerative nodules can be distinguished from tumor masses by biopsy, angiography, and isotope scan. Enlarged portal vein, ascites, recanalized umbilical vein, and esophageal and splenic varices are associated findings. *(5:66)*

215. **(B)** The right crus of the diaphragm extends posterior to the inferior vena cava and posterior to the right kidney and adrenal gland. *(8:33)*

216. **(F)** All but the pancreas. Structures that commonly alter the liver shape are the diaphragm, right kidney, abdominal lymph nodes, and the gallbladder. *(1:54)*

217. **(D)** Lymphoma (Hodgkin's and non-Hodgkin's) can appear sonographically as focal lesions, both anechoic and echogenic. *(2:103)*

218. **(D)** All of the above. The function of lymph vessels is to absorb lymph that has filtered out of the blood capillaries. If the lymph vessel is obstructed, it may lead to edema, ascites, or an effusion of the affected location. *(2:208)*

219. **(B)** Normal lymph nodes are no larger than 1 cm. Sonographically, to be visualized they must be larger than 3 cm. *(10:84)*

220. **(F)** All of the above. The lymph nodes are closely related to the aorta and form a preaortic and a right and left lateral aortic (para-aortic) chain. Therefore, when scanning a patient for lymphadenopathy, one should check the pelvis, porta hepatis, retroperitoneum, perirenal area, and around the major blood vessels and their tributaries. *(10:84)*

221. **(C)** Para-aortic nodes have characteristic sonographic appearances. They can be differentiated from an aortic aneurysm by shape. Aneurysms enlarge fairly symmetrically, whereas large nodes tend to drape over prevertebral vessels in lobular fashion. *(10:86)*

222. **(D)** Sonographically, for lymph nodes to be visualized they must be enlarged up to at least 3 cm. *(10:86)*

223. **(C)** Sonographically, enlarged nodes appear as anechoic masses with no demonstration of through transmission on account of its composition. *(5:368)*

224. **(C)** Enlarged lymph nodes being closely related to the aorta and forming preaortic and para-aortic nodes may displace the inferior vena cava anteriorly. The spleen, pancreas, and kidneys are situated anterior to lymph nodes, therefore these organs could not be displaced anteriorly. *(5:368)*

225. **(A)** The right adrenal gland lies directly anterior to the crus of the diaphragm. Both are posterior to the inferior vena cava and may be confused with one another. *(5:336)*

226. **(B)** To optimally scan the right adrenal gland, one should position the patient in the left lateral decubitus position (right side up) because of the adrenal gland's location between the right lobe of the liver and the crus of the diaphragm. *(3:216)*

227. **(D)** The functions of the spleen include the production of plasma cells, lymphocytes and antibodies, storage of iron, and breakdown of red blood cells. *(10:75)*

228. **(E)** All of the above. Splenomegaly occurs in a vast range of infectious diseases. Infective endocarditis, tuberculosis, syphilis, and schistomiasis are only a few infectious diseases that cause splenomegaly. *(10:76)*

229. **(B)** The right renal artery can be seen as a pulsatile circular structure posterior to the inferior vena cava on a longitudinal scan. *(3:120)*

230. **(D)** Virtually all gallstones demonstrate an acoustic shadow. Biliary sludge and sludge balls are mobile and do not demonstrate an acoustic shadow. *(2:136)*

231. **(A)** Splenic cysts are rare. Care must be taken not to confuse them with a pseudocyst or renal cyst. *(10:79)*

232. **(A)** Metastases to the spleen occur more frequently with breast carcinoma. *(10:79)*

233. **(B)** Metastases of the spleen is a late sign of a carcinoma. It only appears once the primary lesion has disseminated widely. *(10:79)*

234. **(D)** A spleen with overall decreased echogenicity is seen with lymphopoiesis, multiple myeloma, and congestion. Metastasis to the spleen will not effect its overall appearance, but will appear as a mass of lesions. *(10:81)*

235. **(B)** The most common cause of splenomegaly in the United States is portal hypertension. The spleen will appear to have an overall decrease in echogenicity owing to congestion. *(2:234)*

236. **(A)** The retroperitoneal space is the area between the posterior portion of the parietal peritoneum and the posterior abdominal wall muscles. *(3:231)*

237. **(B)** When assessing the upper retroperitoneum, ie, para-aortic lymph nodes, it is best visualized with the patient in the supine position. This is because of the location of such nodes along the lateral and anterior margins of the aorta. *(3:231)*

238. **(B)** Primary tumors of the retroperitoneum are generally malignant. They can be cystic, solid, or complex depending upon their physical composition. *(3:237)*

239. **(E)** All of the above. A urinoma is a collection of urine located outside the genitourinary tract. Urinomas are known to develop after urinary tract surgery, trauma, or subacute or chronic urinary obstruction. *(3:237)*

240. **(B)** The etiology of retroperitoneal fibrosis is unknown. It is not an invasion of the body by pathogenic organisms (infections) or carried by the blood or physician induced (iatrogenic). *(3:238)*

241. **(A)** If retroperitoneal fibrosis is suspected, one should also check the kidneys for hydronephrosis because it may encase the ureters and thereby obstruct them. *(3:120)*

242. **(B)** The renal arteries are best seen on a transverse sonogram. *(3:120)*

243. **(B)** The right, middle, and left hepatic veins originate in the liver and drain into the inferior vena cava at the level of the diaphragm. They are the largest major visceral branch of the inferior vena cava. *(3:116)*

244. **(B)** The spleen is variable in size but is considered to be convex superiorly and concave inferiorly. When the spleen enlarges, it extends inferiorly and medially in an anterior position. *(3:221)*

245. **(C)** Accessory spleens are a common congenital anomaly and are usually located near the splenic hilum. *(3:221)*

246. **(D)** Sickle-cell anemia results in splenic atrophy. In its advanced stages, the spleen becomes small because of "autosplenectomy" from repeated infarcts. *(3:222)*

247. **(D)** The most common benign tumor of the spleen is a cavernous hemangioma. *(3:224)*

248. **(A)** Splenic size is variable with 14 cm in length being upper-normal. When the spleen enlarges, it does so inferomedially in an anterior position. *(1:331)*

249. **(D)** The superior mesenteric artery will appear as a round sonolucent dot surrounded by an echogenic ring. *(8:51)*

250. **(C)** Alkaline phosphatase is synthesized and excreted by hepatocytes. With obstruction, metastatic involvement and infiltrative disease, one sees a sharp rise in the production and synthesis of this enzyme. SGOT and SGPT are specific as indicators of hepatic function (hepatocellular disease). *(3:133)*

251. **(D)** If it is located in the posterior pararenal space, a hematoma will extend up the lateral walls of the abdomen and displace the kidney anteriorly. *(8:172)*

252. **(D)** All of the above. Solid masses tend to displace surrounding organs therefore indicating its place of origin. A retroperitoneal sarcoma will displace the kidney, pancreas, and spleen anteriorly. *(8:110)*

253. **(C)** A hypertrophied column of Bertin is a normal renal variant in which there is hypertrophy (enlargement) of the cortex between two pyramids. It will appear sonographically as normal renal tissue. *(8:133)*

254. **(D)** If a patient presents with hydronephrosis, one should look for the cause of the obstruction. This may include renal calculus, pelvic masses, prostatic hypertrophy, fibroid uterus, and ureteroceles. Renal vein thrombosis is *not* associated with hydronephrosis. *(8:143)*

255. **(E)** All of the above. An angiomyolipoma is a rare benign renal tumor usually seen in middle-aged women. It is composed of mostly fat and can be associated with tuberous sclerosis. *(8:145)*

256. **(D)** Hypernephroma is a malignant solid renal tumor also known as renal cell carcinoma, von Grawitz tumor, and adenocarcinoma of the kidney but *not* transitional cell carcinoma. *(8:145)*

257. **(D)** Malrotated kidneys, enlarged spleen or liver compressing the kidneys, and the presence of a dromedary hump will cause a false-positive abnormal intravenous pyelogram. Renal vein thrombosis will lead to nonvisualization of the affected kidney and is a true abnormality. *(8:150)*

258. **(D)** All of the above. Solid renal masses are considered malignant until proven otherwise. Therefore, one should also check for para-aortic nodes, liver metastases, and tumor invasion of the inferior vena cava. *(8:153)*

259. **(A)** The most common cause of unilateral nonvisualization of a kidney on intravenous pyelography is hydronephrosis. *(8:155)*

260. **(E)** All of the above. Renal vein thrombosis, renal artery occlusion, pyonephrosis, and end-stage renal disease will all lead to nonvisualization of the kidneys on intravenous pyelography. Other causes include hydronephrosis, a tumor large enough to involve the entire kidney, tumor obstructing the renal vein, multicystic kidney, and xanthogranulomatous pyelonephritis. *(8:155)*

261. **(B)** A pelvic kidney is a normal kidney in size and shape but is located in an abnormal position. *(8:151)*

262. **(F)** Ascites is free fluid located within the peritoneal cavity. It can be caused by malignancy, nephrotic syndrome, congestive heart failure, tuberculosis, and/or liver disease but not adenomyomatosis. *(8:120)*

263. **(D)** Loculations within ascites are more commonly found in malignancies and infections. Benign ascites tend to have no internal echoes or loculations. *(8:130)*

264. **(D)** Internal echoes within ascites are most commonly found in malignancies and infections. Benign ascites tend to be anechoic with no internal debris. *(8:130)*

265. **(A)** Acute pancreatitis may lead to pancreatic pseudocyst, pancreatic ascites, common bile duct obstruction, and/or chronic pancreatitis but *not* gallstones. *(8:48)*

266. **(F)** All of the above. Pancreatic pseudocysts may be found in the liver, spleen, mediastinum, mesentary, and lesser sac. Owing to its composition of enzymes, pseudocysts are capable of tracking anywhere in the body. *(8:48)*

267. **(A)** To best visualize the pancreatic tail, one should position the patient in prone position, using the left kidney as an acoustic window. *(2:175)*

268. **(C)** The splenic artery may be confused with the pancreatic duct. In order to differentiate between the two, remember that the splenic artery pulsates and the pancreatic duct does not. *(8:56)*

269. **(C)** The splenic artery courses along the superior margin of the pancreatic body and tail. *(8:50)*

270. **(B)** The right kidney lies slightly lower than the left because the right lobe of the liver occupies more of the right upper quadrant. *(3:192)*

271. **(E)** Signs of renal disease include oliguria, polyuria, palpable flank mass, generalized edema, pain, fever, and urgency but *not* Murphy's sign. *(3:194)*

272. **(F)** Over 60% of functioning renal parenchyma must be lost in order to elevate either the blood urea nitrogen (BUN) or creatinine. Since the kidneys have a significant reserve, an elevation of these laboratory values shows an already severely impaired kidney. *(3:194)*

273. **(C)** A supernumerary kidney is a complete duplication of the renal system. It is rare and generally found in the pelvis. *(3:197)*

274. **(D)** All of the above. To best evaluate the internal composition of a cyst, one should change the gain setting, overall power, and/or transducer to a higher frequency. All of these will lead to better resolution of the cyst. *(3:199)*

275. **(D)** Clinical symptoms associated with inflammatory renal masses include fever, chills, and flank pain but *not* hypoglycemia. *(3:204)*

276. **(B)** Sonographically, the best way of delineating a dissecting aneurysm is by showing the intimal flap waving along with the pulsations of blood through the aorta. *(2:55)*

277. **(D)** Lesions that produce complex echo patterns include infected cysts, hemorrhagic cysts, hematomas, and abscesses but *not* congenital cysts. Correlating the sonographic appearance with the clinical history may help to differentiate the pathology. *(2:327)*

278. **(A)** The abdominal aorta courses anteriorly, whereas the inferior vena cava has a horizontal course. The aorta is to the left of the inferior vena cava and is not affected by Valsalva maneuvers. *(8:35)*

279. **(B)** With advanced chronological age, the pancreas decreases in size with increased echogenicity. *(1:278)*

280. **(D)** The lesser sac is located anterior and superior to the pancreas and the greater sac is located anterior and inferior to the pancreas. The origin of the transverse mesocolon is the dividing line. *(1:275)*

281. **(B)** The pancreas in children will be relatively less echogenic. With increasing age and body fat deposition, there are increased amounts of fat within the parenchyma of the pancreas, accounting for an increase in its echogenicity. *(1:278)*

282. **(D)** A series of relative echogenicity has been established. It is from least echogenic to most, renal parenchyma < liver < spleen < pancreas < renal sinus. *(2:165)*

283. **(D)** All of the above. Several landmarks can be helpful in identifying the pancreatic head on a longitudinal scan. The pancreatic head is visualized directly anterior to the inferior vena cava, caudad to the portal vein, and cephalad to the duodenum. *(2:167)*

284. **(B)** The sonographic appearance of lymphoma has been known to vary but it is most commonly seen as a solid mass that is relatively hypoechoic and has some decrease of through transmission with an increase in ultrasound absorption. *(2:179)*

285. **(D)** Islet cell tumors of the pancreas are well-circumscribed solid masses with low-level echoes and are frequently found in the body and tail and rarely in the head of the gland. *(2:179)*

286. **(B)** The normal right adrenal gland is located superior to the right kidney and medial to the liver, posterior to the inferior vena cava, and anterior to the crus of the diaphragm. *(5:338)*

287. **(A)** Addison's disease is a syndrome that results from chronic adrenal hypofunction. The decrease in function may be due to a primary adrenal tumor or secondary to metastases. *(3:218)*

288. **(A)** Anatomical landmarks helpful in locating the left adrenal gland are the aorta, spleen, left kidney, and left crus of the diaphragm. *(5:340)*

289. **(D)** All of the above. Adrenal hemorrhage sonographically may appear either echogenic, anechoic, or complex depending upon the stage of clot organization. *(5:272)*

290. **(D)** All of the above. The spiral valves of Heister are located within the cystic duct. They are very tortuous and may simulate a polypoid tumor or cause shadowing simulating a stone. Note that there is no valvular action by the spiral valves of Heister. Bile flow is dependent upon the pressure gradient between the gallbladder and cystic duct. *(1:226)*

291. **(A)** The right adrenal gland is located superior and anteromedial to the upper pole of the right kidney. Anatomic landmarks include the liver, inferior vena cava, and right crus of diaphragm. *(5:271)*

292. **(C)** A pheochromocytoma is an adrenal tumor that secretes hormones that in turn elevate blood pressure. *(8:265)*

293. **(C)** Left adrenal hyperplasia, for whatever reason, may cause anterior displacement of the splenic vein and posterolateral displacement of the left kidney. *(8:271)*

294. **(B)** Cushing's syndrome may be associated with an adrenal mass or be caused by a mass in the anterior pituitary. The syndrome is characterized by an increase in androgen production, hypertension, truncal obesity, and a moon-shaped face. *(3:218)*

295. **(A)** The celiac axis has three branches, the common hepatic artery, left gastric artery, and splenic artery. Sonographically, only a short section of the splenic artery can be seen owing to its tortuous course. *(1:66)*

296. **(B)** A phrygian cap is a fold near the fundus of the gallbladder. If a fold is visualized near the neck of the gallbladder, it is termed Hartmann's pouch. *(2:132)*

297. **(A)** Gallbladder polyps can be distinguished from stones by the absence of shadowing or movement. *(1:255)*

298. **(E)** Long-standing cystic duct obstruction and prolonged fasting will cause the gallbladder to retain sludge. Other examples of echogenic bile within the gallbladder may be due to hemobilia and empyema of the gallbladder. *(2:146)*

299. **(B)** The celiac axis is cephalad to the superior mesenteric artery. *(3:120)*

300. **(A)** Blood that is returning from the kidneys via the renal veins to the inferior vena cava accounts for this enlargement. *(3:116)*

301. **(B)** 2, 1, 4, 3. The biliary tree generally dilates in a routine fashion when obstructed. First the common bile duct will dilate (larger than 5 mm in luminal dimension). This is followed by dilatation of intrahepatic ducts. Next, one can see the double-barrel shotgun sign and with increased obstruction, the biliary tree continues to dilate in a stellate formation. *(1:260)*

302. **(C)** The most common cause of jaundice in the pediatric patient is biliary atresia, a narrowing and obstruction of the intrahepatic bile duct. *(8:87)*

303. **(B)** Right decubitus, left coronal, or left side up view indicates that the right side of the patient is on the table and the left side is up. *(8:31)*

304. **(A)** Large gallbladders are detected in patients with diabetes, prolonged fasting, status-postvagotomy,

or the use of anticholinergic drugs and other causes. *(3:152)*

305. **(A)** Empyema of the gallbladder is a complication of acute cholecystitis, whereby purulent exudate fills the cavity. Since the gallbladder contains gas due to the bacteria in the exudate, posterior shadowing will be noted, but it will not be a "clean" shadow. *(1:252)*

306. **(A)** SGOT, SGPT, LDH, and alkaline phosphatase are all liver enzymes released from damaged hepatic cells. SGOT, SGPT, and LDH tend to be higher with intrinsic liver disease, whereas alkaline phosphatase levels tend to be higher with biliary obstruction. *(8:87)*

307. **(D)** Three mechanisms of jaundice are red blood cell destruction, hepatocellular disease, and obstruction of intra- or extrahepatic ducts. Red blood cell destruction occurs with hemolytic anemias. Hepatocellular disease is most commonly due to alcoholic liver disease. Obstruction of intra- or extrahepatic ducts is most commonly caused by cholelithiasis, choledocholithiasis, pancreatic tumors, and/or ductal tumors. *(8:88)*

308. **(C)** Acute cholecystitis is characterized by an edematous wall (the halo sign) greater than 3 mm, acute pain over the gallbladder (Murphy's sign), and/or a stone impacted within the cystic duct. *(1:248)*

309. **(A)** α-Fetoprotein and carcinoembryonic antigen (CEA) are laboratory values that are elevated in hepatoma of the liver. *(2:116)*

310. **(B)** Enlarged lymph nodes will usually appear sonographically as a homogeneous anechoic mass with poor through transmission. *(3:232)*

311. **(B)** Periaortic nodes will displace the superior mesenteric artery anteriorly *not* posteriorly. *(3:237)*

312. **(C)** Examples of primary retroperitoneal tumors seen on sonography are leiomyosarcomas, neurogenic tumors, fibrosarcomas, rhabdomyosarcomas, and teratomatous tumors. *(3:237)*

313. **(E)** All of the above. Retroperitoneal fluid collections include urinoma, lymphocele, abscess, and hemorrhage. To help to distinguish among them, their sonographic appearance and clinical correlation are necessary. *(3:238)*

314. **(D)** The parallel channel sign, irregular borders to dilated ducts, and echo enhancement behind dilated ducts are all characteristic of dilated intrahepatic bile ducts. It is the common bile duct near the porta hepatis that is the first to dilate and is greatest in size. *(1:260)*

315. **(A)** The superior mesenteric artery can be seen on transverse scans as an anechoic circle with an echogenic wall posterior to the body of the pancreas. *(3:120)*

316. **(C)** The ligamentum venosum is a remnant of the fetal ductus venosus and the ligamentum teres is a remnant of the fetal umbilical vein. The coronary ligaments define the bare area of the liver. *(1:30)*

317. **(B)** A subhepatic abscess would be located inferior to the liver and anterior to the right kidney. Other common sites for abscesses are subphrenic, perinephric, intrarenal, intrahepatic, pelvic, and around incisions. *(3:141)*

318. **(D)** The primary malignant tumor of the liver is a hepatoma. Another name for a hepatoma is hepatocellular carcinoma. Eighty percent of hepatomas occur in livers with preexisting cirrhosis. *(1:146)*

319. **(B)** The ultrasound instrument assumes that the speed of sound in all tissues in its path is 1540 m/s. The speed of sound through bone is greater than that in the average soft tissue. This is what causes the registration error of the reflector to appear closer to the transducer than its actual distance. *(3:58)*

320. **(A)** All ultrasound equipment is calibrated at 1540 m/s, the speed of sound in soft tissue. When the ultrasound beam goes through a fatty tumor with a lower propagation speed, the tumor will appear *further* than its actual distance. *(3:58)*

321. **(B)** When ascites is present it acts as an acoustic window. Therefore, the liver will appear more echogenic. *(2:83)*

322. **(C)** As one *decreases* the frequency of the transducer, one *decreases* the resolution but *increases* the depth of penetration. With an obese patient, depth of penetration is important, especially if a mass is suspected deep in the posterior aspect of the right lobe of the liver; therefore one should use a 2.25-MHz long-focused transducer. *(8:6)*

323. **(E)** Reye's syndrome typically occurs in childhood and is associated with fatty changes in the liver and encephalopathy. Jaundice is *not* associated with this disease. *(4:438)*

324. **(B)** The three branches of the celiac artery are the common hepatic, left gastric, and splenic arteries. *(2:38)*

325. **(A)** The gastroduodenal artery is a major branch of the common hepatic artery. *(2:38)*

326. **(C)** The splenic artery originates from the celiac axis and runs superior to the body and tail of the pancreas throughout most of its course. *(8:35)*

327. **(C)** Artifacts that cause spurious echoes result from a variety of sources including beam thickness and side-lobe artifacts, reverberation artifacts, electronic noise, and range ambiguity effects. Edge effects cause acoustic shadowing owing to reflection and refraction of sound. *(14:31–37)*

328. **(B)** Irregularities of flow within a vessel greatly increase the likelihood of clot formation and thrombus. *(2:48)*

329. **(C)** Doppler sampling across a vessel is utilized to detect irregularity of blood flow. *(2:48)*

330. **(C)** Hepatic hemangiomas are least likely to be echo-free structures with smooth walls. They generally appear echogenic and may present as solitary or multiple lesions. Sonographically, they cannot be distinguished from a hepatoma. *(10:17)*

331. **(C)** The sonographic appearance of an abscess has a variable echo texture from echo free to echogenic, with irregular borders, and varied through transmission. The sonographic appearance of an abscess is dependent upon the stage and age of the abscess. *(2:250)*

332. **(D)** All of the above. Patients with portal hypertension may have a portal vein greater than 11 ± 2 mm in luminal dimension, splenomegaly, portal venous collaterals, and a patent umbilical vein. *(2:66)*

333. **(D)** All of the above. Three main sites of potential anastomoses within the systemic circulation seen with ultrasound include the left umbilical vein, lienorenal anastomoses, and anastomoses around the esophagus. The most clinically significant anastomosis is esophageal varices. *(1:218)*

334. **(C)** In response to the pressure changes associated with portal hypertension, the umbilical vein located within the ligamentum teres recanalizes. *(1:221)*

335. **(C)** The para-aortic group is the major node-bearing region in the upper retroperitoneum. The major node-bearing regions in the pelvis are the iliac and hypogastric nodes. *(3:231)*

336. **(D)** Acute torsion of the spermatic cord, whereby the arterial blood supply to the testis is disrupted, has no specific sonographic characteristics. Therefore, ultrasound is not used as the primary method of diagnosis. *(2:474; 3:247)*

337. **(B)** Lymphocytes may be confused with an aortic aneurysm, the crus of the diaphragm, and bowel, because they are generally echo free, whereas chronic pancreatitis is echogenic. *(3:232)*

338. **(A)** Sonographic evaluation of the breast is certainly helpful in those patients who are concerned about being exposed to irradiation. More specifically, sonography is helpful in evaluating those masses thought to be cystic in patients who have radiographically dense breasts. The radiographic appearance of these breasts occasionally impairs detection of surrounding breast masses. Cysts represent 25% of palpable and/or mammographically detected masses. Ultrasound can detect cysts as small as 2 mm. The detection of microcalcifications associated with invasive ductal carcinoma cannot be ruled out by ultrasound. One must remember that the detection of an exact "type" of tumor can only be determined by a histologic diagnosis. *(3:268–269)*

339. **(D)** The superior mesenteric vein is larger, not smaller, in caliber than the superior mesenteric artery. *(8:50)*

340. **(C)** An aortic aneurysm of 6 cm or greater is considered a surgical emergency. At 7 cm, 60–80% are said to rupture. *(2:52)*

341. **(D)** The celiac trunk originates within the first 2 cm of the abdominal aorta; therefore, it is not found posterior to the pancreas. *(2:38; 3:118)*

342. **(B)** Landmarks for the uncinate process are the superior mesenteric vein anteriorly and the inferior vena cava posteriorly. *(2:163)*

343. **(C)** Amylase and lipase levels rise at the same rate, but lipase levels remain higher for a longer period of time. Amylase becomes elevated for many other reasons than acute pancreatitis; therefore, lipase is more consistent with, but not specific for, acute pancreatitis. *(10:45)*

344. **(D)** Alcoholism and surgical and external trauma can all lead to acute hemorrhagic pancreatitis. Cystic fibrosis is the most common childhood congenital disease causing the pancreatic tissue to fibrose with ductal enlargement. *(10:47)*

345. **(B)** A reverberation artifact results from a strong echo returning from a large acoustic interface to the transducer. This artifact appears in both cystic and solid masses and is not specific for delineating cystic structures. *(8:29)*

346. **(C)** Pancreatic tail masses lie superior to the kidney and displace the spleen anteriorly. *(8:110)*

347. **(C)** If the spleen is as thick as the normal kidney or thicker, and its anterior border crosses the aorta and inferior vena cava, it is considered to be enlarged. *(8:109)*

348. **(B)** A pheochromocytoma is a benign adrenal tumor that secretes epinephrine and norepinephrine. These two hormones are responsible for the clinical symptom of intermittent hypertension associated with a pheochromocytoma. *(3:218; 8:265)*

349. **(D)** All of the above. Common sites of lymphadenopathy include all of the listed possible answers. Other common sites include the left renal hilum and the porta hepatis. *(8:104)*

350. **(D)** All of the above are consistent with renal failure. Sonographic appearance of the kidneys depends upon the stage of renal failure (acute or chronic) the patient is in. Acutely, the kidneys are normal-sized or enlarged. Chronically, they are small. Hydronephrosis may be the sole cause of the renal failure. *(2:351; 8:133)*

351. **(A)** Optimal imaging of the left adrenal gland is achieved by the specific alignment of the left kidney to the aorta. *(2:376)*

352. **(C)** Both adrenal glands are located superior and anteromedial to the upper pole of their respective kidney. *(2:397; 8:267)*

353. **(D)** The right adrenal gland is located directly posterior to the inferior vena cava and anterior to the right crus of the diaphragm. *(2:397; 8:267)*

354. **(C)** A neuroblastoma is a relatively common malignant adrenal tumor seen in children. Sonographically, it appears as an echogenic mass. *(2:399)*

355. **(B)** The adrenal gland can be divided into cortex and medulla. The cortex secretes mineralocorticoids. The medulla secretes epinephrine and norepinephrine. *(3:215)*

356. **(B)** Above the level of the celiac axis the diaphragm can be visualized posterior to the inferior vena cava and anterior to the aorta. *(8:43)*

357. **(A)** The left hepatic vein separates the medial and lateral aspects of the left lobe of the liver. *(8:42)*

358. **(C)** A patent umbilical vein may be found in the ligamentum teres and is associated with portal hypertension. *(8:43)*

359. **(C)** Ampullary carcinoma is found within the ampulla of Vater, which is where the pancreatic duct and common bile duct enter the duodenum. The carcinoma will obstruct the pancreatic duct, leading to its dilatation, and obstruct the common bile duct, leading to its dilatation and progressive dilatation of the intrahepatic ducts. *(5:222)*

360. **(B)** The right hepatic vein separates the anterior and posterior segments of the right lobe. *(3:130)*

361. **(B)** A dissecting aneurysm is a hemorrhage into the aorta itself. The dissection is generally through the media of the aorta. *(4:290)*

362. **(E)** Phlebitis is an inflammation of the veins and therefore, is not a type of aortic aneurysm. *(4:290–293)*

363. **(D)** The minimum anterior-posterior diameter for the diagnosis of aortic aneurysm is above 3 cm. *(2:47)*

364. **(C)** The most common type of arteriosclerotic, aortic aneurysm is fusiform. Generally, it arises below the origin of the renal arteries and may continue down into the iliac vessels. *(2:47)*

365. **(C)** The crus of the diaphragm is visualized sonographically as an echo-poor linear structure. It runs anterior above the level of the celiac axis. Below that level, it extends along the lateral aspect of the vertebral column. *(1:65)*

366. **(B)** A mass in the caudate lobe of the liver and head of the pancreas would displace the inferior vena cava posteriorly. The right renal vein lies lateral to the inferior vena cava. The right renal artery lies posteriorly and can cause anterior displacement with pathology. *(3:120)*

367. **(C)** Dilatation of the inferior vena cava can be seen with right ventricular heart failure. The Valsalva maneuver will increase the size of the inferior vena cava but is not a pathologic condition. *(7:112)*

368. **(D)** Acid phosphatase is usually increased in patients with carcinoma of the prostate gland, particularly when metastases are present. *(4:385)*

369. **(C)** Thrombus will be visualized as echoes within the aorta but they are not artifactual. *(3:118)*

370. **(A)** The gastroduodenal artery arises from the common hepatic artery and supplies the duodenum, parts of the stomach, and the head of the pancreas. Sonographically, it can be visualized as a circular anechoic structure located in the anterior portion of the head of the pancreas. *(3:120)*

371. **(E)** Fatty infiltration of the liver usually causes a diffuse hyperechoic pattern not a focal mass. *(3:139)*

372. **(C)** Ascites, small liver portal hypertension, and irregular liver borders due to liver nodules may all be present with end-stage fatty liver as well as severe cirrhosis. The bile ducts do not dilate because of the fibrosis. *(3:139)*

373. **(A)** The head of the pancreas is located anterior to the inferior vena cava. *(3:181)*

374. **(B)** The lesser sac is located between the stomach and pancreas. *(3:78)*

375. **(A)** In biliary obstruction, the increase in direct bilirubin predominates, although the indirect bilirubin may also rise slightly. *(3:192)*

376. **(B)** The pyramids are located in the medulla of the kidney. *(3:192)*

377. **(D)** All of the above. The function of the kidneys is to excrete urine. Urine formation includes filtration in the glomeruli, tubular reabsorption, and tubular secretion, respectively. *(3:194)*

378. **(C)** Major calices of the kidney converge to form the renal pelvis located in the hilum of the kidney. The ureter emerges from the hilum and travels down to the urinary bladder entering it in its trigone. Urine is then stored in the bladder until it passes out of the body via the urethra. *(3:192)*

379. **(B)** Bowman's capsule and glomerulus together are termed the renal corpuscle or malpighian body. Extending from Bowman's capsule is a renal tubule. Each tubule has three sections: a proximal tubule, a descending limb, and an ascending limb. Together the Bowman's capsule, glomerulus, and renal tubules constitute a nephron. *(3:194)*

380. **(C)** A rise in lipase levels indicates acute pancreatitis or pancreatic carcinoma. Amylase levels will also rise with acute pancreatitis but are not as specific for this as the rise in lipase levels. *(3:176)*

381. **(B)** In hemolytic disease associated with abrupt breakdown of large amounts of red blood cells, the reticuloendothelial cells receive more bilirubin than it can detoxify. Therefore, one would present with an elevated indirect or unconjugated bilirubin. *(3:134)*

382. **(B)** With biliary obstruction at any level in the biliary tree, the direct bilirubin levels rise predominantly and the indirect bilirubin levels rise only slightly. *(3:134)*

383. **(C)** A dromedary hump is a common anatomical variant. It is visualized as a bulge off the lateral border of the left kidney consisting of normal renal tissue. *(3:134)*

384. **(D)** The most common intrascrotal inflammation is epididymitis. Acutely, the epididymis becomes enlarged and less echogenic. Chronically, the epididymis becomes very echogenic and may contain calcium. *(3:248)*

385. **(C)** The head of the epididymis is located superior to the testes. The rest of the epididymis courses along the posterior margin of the testicle inferiorly. *(2:461)*

386. **(A)** The sonographic diagnosis of ductal obstruction should be dependent upon the luminal diameter of the common bile duct at or below the porta hepatis. *(1:260)*

387. **(B)** The left kidney is located posterior to the spleen. *(10:74)*

388. **(A)** The stomach is located anterior to the spleen. *(10:74)*

389. **(B)** If a testicular tumor is found, one should also check the renal hilum for possible nodal metastases. Testicular tumors will not cause hydronephrosis or ascites. *(8:300)*

390. **(C)** The average dimensions of the testes are 4–5 cm long and 2.5–3 cm wide. Enlargement or atrophy is a sign of a pathological process. *(3:247)*

391. **(C)** The testes produce spermatozoa that travel via the spermatic cord; therefore, the testes are considered exocrine glands. They also are considered endocrine glands because they produce testosterone, a male sex hormone. *(3:246)*

392. **(A)** A hepatoblastoma is a primary malignant liver tumor found in childhood. Wilms' tumor is a childhood tumor found in the kidney. Neuroblastoma is the most common tumor of infancy and is adrenal in origin. *(3:143, 220, 320)*

393. **(A)** Hydroceles can be defined as serous fluid accumulated between the two layers of the tunica vaginalis. Sonographically, the testicle and epididymis are visualized surrounded by anechoic fluid. *(3:247)*

394. **(D)** Testicular malignancy usually affects men between 20 and 40 years of age. The most common type of testicular malignancy is a seminoma. Other types include embryonal carcinoma, choriocarcinoma, and teratomas. *(3:247)*

395. **(C)** A neoplasm is any new growth or development of abnormal tissue. The best way to know if a neoplasm is benign or malignant is to biopsy it. *(3:143)*

396. **(E)** Inferior vena cava.

397. **(D)** Right lobe.

398. **(A)** Gallbladder.

399. **(G)** Portal vein.

400. **(B)** Left lobe.

401. **(C)** Falciform ligament.

402. **(F)** Ligamentum teres.

403. **(H)** Hepatic artery.

404. **(D)** Right lobe.

405. **(A)** Gallbladder.

406. **(L)** Quadrate lobe (medial aspect of the left lobe).

407. **(E)** Inferior vena cava.

408. **(K)** Caudate lobe.

409. **(J)** Common bile duct.

410. **(B)** Left lobe.

411. **(C)** Falciform ligament.

412. **(I)** Fissure for ligamentum venosum.

413. **(H)** Hepatic artery.

414. **(F)** Ligamentum teres.

415. **(G)** Portal vein.

416. **(F)** Left hepatic duct.

417. **(E)** Common hepatic duct.

418. **(A)** Cystic duct.

419. **(K)** Common bile duct.

420. **(C)** Duodenum.

421. **(B)** Ampulla of Vater.

422. **(D)** Fundus of the gallbladder.

423. **(J)** Infundibulum of the gallbladder (Hartmann's pouch).

424. **(I)** Neck of the gallbladder.

425. **(H)** Right hepatic duct.

426. **(G)** Body of the gallbladder.

427. **(D)** Renal artery.

428. **(G)** Renal vein.

429. **(E)** Ureter.

430. **(H)** Pyramid.

431. **(F)** Renal pelvis.

432. **(C)** Renal capsule.

433. **(I)** Cortex.

434. **(B)** Minor calyx.

435. **(A)** Renal papilla.
(3:149,150,175,193,for answers 396–435)

436. **(F)** Right hepatic vein.

437. **(H)** Inferior vena cava.

438. **(L)** Right renal artery.

439. **(I)** Right renal vein.

440. **(E)** Celiac trunk.

441. **(G)** Left hepatic vein.

442. **(M)** Right portal vein.

443. **(N)** Splenic artery.

444. **(A)** Superior mesenteric artery.

445. **(Q)** Inferior mesenteric vein.

446. **(J)** Left renal artery.

447. **(K)** Left renal vein.

448. **(C)** Aorta.

449. **(P)** Left portal vein.

450. **(O)** Gastroduodenal artery.

451. **(U)** Left gastric artery.

452. **(D)** Middle hepatic vein.

453. **(B)** Splenic vein.

454. **(R)** Common hepatic artery.

455. **(T)** Superior mesenteric vein.

456. **(S)** Main portal vein. *(3:113,177, for answers 436–456)*

457. **(F)** Strap muscle.

458. **(H)** Sternocleidomastoid muscle.

459. **(E)** Thyroid gland.

460. **(J)** Longus colli muscle.

461. **(A)** Vertebral body.

462. **(G)** Esophagus.

463. **(C)** Common carotid artery.

464. **(D)** Internal jugular vein.

465. **(B)** Trachea.

466. **(I)** Parathyroid gland. *(3:240, for answers 457–466)*

467. **(C)** Epididymis body.

468. **(E)** Epididymis tail.

469. **(A)** Testis.

470. **(G)** Seminiferous tubules.

471. **(D)** Septula.

472. **(B)** Rete testis.

473. **(F)** Epididymis head. *(3:246, for answers 467–473)*

474. **(A)** Renal vein thrombosis may be a cause of renal failure. In *acute* renal vein thrombosis, the kidney becomes edematous *not* hydronephrotic. Sonographically, there is decreased cortical echogenicity and an increase in renal size. Later, there is increased echogenicity due to cellular infiltration. *(2:373; 11:38)*

475. **(B)** A long history of alcoholism implies cirrhosis with accompanying massive ascites. *(8:120)*

476. **(B)** High fever is an indication of an abscess. An abscess will sonographically appear as a complex mass. *(2:327)*

477. **(B)** SGOT and SGPT are enzymes that are released from damaged liver cells. High levels can be seen in an obstructive process but more commonly indicate intrinsic liver disease. Viral and toxic hepatitis are diseases intrinsic to the liver and will therefore lead to elevated levels of SGOT and SGPT. *(8:87)*

478. **(D)** Marked elevation of alkaline phosphatase is typically associated with biliary obstruction. Other liver enzymes will also rise but not in the same proportion. *(8:87)*

479. **(C)** A multicystic (dysplastic) kidney is a common cause of a neonatal mass. It is always a unilateral phenomenon. *(3:200)*

480. **(A)** A choledochal cyst is a focal cystic dilatation of the common duct. It will cause relative obstruction secondary to the segment of the biliary tree affected. This entity is usually congenital and treated by surgery. *(10:25)*

481. **(A)** Ascites is commonly associated with obstruction of the portal venous system, as in cirrhosis. *(4:484,572)*

482. **(A)** A phlebolith is a small stone or calcification that may occur in an organized thrombus within a vein; ie, a venous calculus. *(4:111)*

483. **(C)** Chronic active hepatitis may eventually lead to postnecrotic cirrhosis. The etiology of chronic active hepatitis is usually ideopathic but may be immunological or viral. *(4:445)*

484. **(B)** In the early stages of alcoholic cirrhosis, the liver enlarges and undergoes severe fatty changes. This is followed by a fibrofatty change. Ultimately, the liver undergoes fibrosis and shrinks. *(4:447)*

485. **(D)** All of the above. The popliteal artery is located posterior to the knee joint. Focal dilatation of this artery is usually due to atherosclerosis and is associated with partially calcified walls. *(4:290; 8:293)*

486. **(C)** In chronic renal disease, both kidneys are dense, small, and echogenic. *(5:314; 8:139)*

487. **(D)** Gallstones can produce injury by all of the listed alternative answers. Other possible complications include empyema of the gallbladder, ascending cholangitis, biliary cirrhosis of the liver, acute pancreatitis, and gallstone ileus. *(4:462)*

488. **(B and C)** Sixty percent of all masses that appear as a hypofunctioning thyroid nodule (cold nodule) on a nuclear medicine thyroid scintigram are adenomas and/or benign thyroid nodules. The remaining 40% are cysts and malignant nodules. *(3:242)*

489. **(A)** Courvoisier's law states that obstruction of the common bile duct by pressure from the outside (ie, mass in the pancreatic head) will produce a distended gallbladder. Obstruction by a stone (intrinsic pressure) will produce an inflamed contracted gallbladder. *(2:132; 4:462)*

490. **(C)** When food containing fat enters the small intestines, cholecystokinin is released and activates the gallbladder to empty its bile. A contracted gallbladder is very difficult to visualize. *(35:358–362)*

491. **(C)** A normally functioning transplanted kidney should not appear different from a normal kidney located within the renal fossa. *(3:211)*

492. **(A)** As stated in Courvoisier's law, obstruction of the common bile duct due to pressure from the outside will lead to dilated gallbladder and biliary radicles. *(4:462)*

493. **(C)** Time gain compensation (TGC) and gain cannot make an organ look larger or smaller. Imaging the kidney in an oblique view will shorten the kidney. *(8:143)*

494. **(B)** Transplanted kidneys are usually placed in the pelvis along the iliopsoas margin. The ureter of the donor kidney is anastomosed to the bladder. *(10:59)*

495. **(B)** The parietal peritoneum lines the abdominal cavity. Organs are said to be intraperitoneal if they are surrounded by peritoneum or retroperitoneal if they are only covered on their anterior surface. *(2:244)*

496. **(A)** True. *(1:45)*

497. **(A)** True. *(1:45)*

498. **(A)** True. *(1:45)*

499. **(B)** False. *(1:45)*

500. **(A)** True. *(1:45)*

501. **(A)** True. *(1:45)*

502. **(A)** Wall thickness of an abnormal bowel has been reported to be from 5 to 30 mm, averaging 23 mm. *(2:299)*

503. **(D)** All of the alternative answers are possible. The appearance of a hydronephrotic kidney is dependent on the severity of the hydronephrosis. *(8:140)*

504. **(C)** To localize a dilated ureter, scanning the pelvis with a full bladder and evaluating the area posterior to it may be helpful. Localization of the ureter is usually very difficult owing to overlying bowel gas. *(5:308)*

505. **(B)** There is a large complex mass within the liver. This mass is a hepatoblastoma. *(13:313)*

506. **(A)** The most common liver tumor in children is hepatoblastoma. *(13:313)*

507. **(B)** The renal architecture is disorganized and the kidney is enlarged indicating infantile polycystic kidney disease. In this disorder, the renal parenchyma appears echogenic and macroscopic cysts are not identified. *(13:307)*

508. **(B)** Microscopic cysts are not identified in infantile polycystic kidney disease because the disorder involves ectasis of the distal collecting ducts. *(13:307)*

509. **(B)** This cyst represents a dilated upper pole moiety in the duplex collecting system. *(13:304–305)*

510. **(B)** The hydronephrotic upper moiety implants ectopically and is associated with a ureterocele. *(13:304–305)*

511. **(B)** This structure is not a kidney because it does not have the typical configuration in transverse action. It represents the right adrenal that has an echogenic medulla in hypoechoic cortex. There is a cystic structure along its lateral aspect, which represents a remnant of dysplastic renal tissue. *(13:307)*

512. **(A)** In renal agenesis, the adrenal has an abnormal shape because the kidneys are not present. The abnormally shaped adrenal may mimic, to some degree, the sonographic appearance of a kidney. *(13:307)*

513. **(B)** This is a kidney in a patient affected by adult-onset polycystic kidney disease. *(13:228)*

514. **(D)** Cysts can be found in any of the given structures. *(13:214)*

515. **(B)** This is a normal renal transplant. *(13:238)*

516. **(D)** Since sonography can detect masses that may be surgically treated, it has an important role in

distinguishing surgically amenable causes of post-transplant poor renal function from those that occur as a result of rejection. *(13:216)*

517. **(A)** The arrow points to a medullary pyramid. *(13:26)*

518. **(D)** The size of the kidney in normal patients can be correlated with the patient's overall body height. Normal adult kidneys range from 10–12 cm in long axis, 5–6 cm in width, and 3–4 cm in anteroposterior dimension. The renal parenchyma (the medulla and cortex) ranges from 1.5–2.0 cm. *(13:210)*

519. **(A)** There is gallbladder wall thickening. *(13:184)*

520. **(D)** Viscid bile results from incomplete gallbladder emptying and represents the precursor to formation of calculi. *(13:184)*

521. **(B)** The pancreas may be echogenic in older adults owing to deposition of fat within the pancreatic lobules. *(13:194)*

522. **(A)** Most pancreatic lesions are hypoechoic. *(2:179)*

523. **(B)** This is the appearance of a normal stomach with an echogenic center and a hypoechoic halo representing the wall; ie, it has a target configuration. *(13:206)*

524. **(B)** The hypoechoic portion represents the wall of the stomach. *(13:206)*

525. **(D)** Either a fluid-filled loop of bowel, probably transverse colon, or a fluid-filled loop of duodenum may have the appearance shown in Fig. 5–27. *(13:178)*

526. **(A)** The upright view is helpful to detect any mobile calculi that move into the fundus when the patient stands upright. *(13:160–162)*

527. **(A)** This structure is an unusually shaped gallbladder. *(13:180)*

528. **(A)** The sonogram represents a phrygian cap, an anatomical variant. *(13:180)*

529. **(B)** The sonogram represents the aorta and celiac axis. *(13:202)*

530. **(A)** The common hepatic artery, splenic artery, and left gastric artery arise from the celiac axis. *(13:202)*

531. **(D)** The abdominal aorta and the left lobe of the liver are shown. *(13:202)*

532. **(A)** Atherosclerosis is the most common cause of abdominal aortic aneurysms. *(13:169)*

533. **(A)** The arrows delineate a hypertrophied pyloric muscle. *(13:323)*

534. **(A)** A muscle thickness of greater than 4 mm is diagnostic of hypertrophic pyloric stenosis. *(13:172)*

535. **(A)** The liver parenchyma is very echogenic compared to the kidney. *(13:199)*

536. **(C)** The hepatic parenchyma is more echogenic when compared with the kidney. *(13:199)*

537. **(B)** The echogenic focus represents the mediastinum of the testes through which many of these central vessels and tubules arise. *(18:112)*

538. **(A)** The testes appear as nonhomogeneous structures because interstitial hemorrhage associated with hemorrhagic infarction and testicular torsion is indicated. *(19:527)*

539. **(B)** The abnormal sonographic findings indicate a calculus in the midpolar region of the kidney. *(20:191)*

540. **(A)** True. Oxalate and uric acid stones are radiopaque but are echogenic on sonography. *(20:191)*

541. **(C)** There is evidence of viscid bile and a large calculus within the gallbladder lumen. *(22:499)*

542. **(B)** False. The presence of calculus within the gallbladder does not always indicate that there is active cholecystitis. However, there is a possible complication of perforation when cholelithiasis is associated with cholecystitis. *(23:798)*

543. **(D)** There is focal echogenicity within the cortex and medulla and an incidental finding of a small cortical cyst. *(13:199)*

544. **(D)** All of the suggested answers can be associated with echogenic medulla and cortex. *(27:830)*

545. **(B)** Abnormal sonographic findings indicate a large renal calculus with an associated shadow in the medial portion of the kidney. *(20:191)*

546. **(A)** Calcium oxalate stones may be radiopaque but are echogenic on sonography. *(20:191)*

547. **(D)** The spleen appears normal. *(28:537)*

548. **(D)** Splenomegaly is typically encountered in chronic myelogenous leukemia and portal hyper-

tension. In sickle-cell crisis, there is typically auto-infarction of the spleen producing a very small spleen. *(29:697)*

549. **(B)** The sonogram shows a normal common bile duct. *(30:703)*

550. **(C)** The common bile duct is formed from the confluence of the common hepatic duct and cystic duct. *(30:703)*

551. **(B)** Abnormal sonographic findings show that the mass has all the characteristics of a simple cyst in the lower pole of the kidney. *(32a:87)*

552. **(A)** Approximately one-third of normal adults over the age of 45 have cysts in their kidney. *(33:671)*

553. **(D)** The sonograms demonstrate marked gallbladder thickening with a small amount of intraluminal sludge. *(35:361)*

554. **(D)** All of the above. Gallbladder wall thickening (> 3.5) is associated with cholecystitis, hepatitis, ascites, alcoholic liver disease, hypoproteinemia, hypoalbuminemia, and a nondistended gallbladder. The patient has AIDS, and this pattern is consistent with cholecystitis associated with this disorder. *(35:361)*

555. **(B)** Murphy's sign *(35:361)*

556. **(B)** The sonogram demonstrates a dilated intrahepatic duct in the left lobe. *(35:363)*

557. **(A)** The abnormal sonographic findings indicate a dilated common bile duct with a rat-tail deformity of the distal common bile duct usually associated with tumors in the head of the pancreas. *(35:363)*

558. **(E)** This is an example of biliary duct obstruction both intra- and extrahepatic due to a pancreatic tumor. *(35:363)*

559. **(B)** The intrahepatic bile ducts course in a transverse plane in the left lobe, therefore, they are more readily detected on a transverse scan of the left lobe than bile ducts occurring within the right lobe. *(35:363)*

560. **(A)** An echogenic mass is noted. *(35:383)*

561. **(A)** This is an echogenic focus within the liver most consistent with a hemangioma. *(35:383)*

562. **(B)** A tagged red blood cell liver/spleen scan is most definitive in the diagnosis of hemangioma. *(35:383)*

563. **(B)** This is a typical fusiform dilated aneurysm of the distal abdominal aorta. *(35:402)*

564. **(B)** Atherosclerosis is the most common cause of an aneurysm. *(35:402)*

565. **(D)** All of the above. Aneurysmal dilation of an artery may occur in any area of the body. *(35:402)*

566. **(B)** There is a hypoechoic tumor that was found during a transrectal sonogram. The hypoechoic tumor appears to extend into the transitional zone. *(35:486)*

567. **(A)** Carcinoma of the prostate stage A. *(35:486)*

568. **(B)** Elevated. *(35:486)*

569. **(A)** An echogenic kidney. *(35:445)*

570. **(B)** Normally, the liver parenchyma should be more echogenic than the renal cortex in chronic renal disease. The kidney is found to be small and echogenic. This kidney had severe parenchymal disease and is markedly more echogenic that the liver. *(35:445)*

571. **(A)** The liver appears more echogenic because of the fibrous septa within the hepatic lobules. *(35:445)*

572. **(A)** This testis has a diffusely abnormal pattern consistent with a testicular tumor or possible testicular torsion. *(35:501)*

573. **(A)** This scan is diagnostic of a testicular tumor. In testicular torsion, one usually observes enlargement of the head of the epididymis, which in this case is normal. *(35:501)*

574. **(D)** Lymphadenopathy may be a presenting symptom associated with a testicular tumor. *(35:512)*

575. **(C)** The transrectal sonogram demonstrates a hypoechoic lesion in the peripheral zone. *(35:499)*

576. **(C)** Biopsy of this lesion through the transrectal approach would be preferred owing to its proximity to the rectum. *(35:499)*

577. **(B)** This has approximately a 20% chance of being carcinoma. *(35:499)*

578. **(D)** Transperineal and transrectal biopsy are the most common routes of obtaining prostate tissue using ultrasound guidance. Transrectal biopsy is preferred because of its closer proximity to the prostate. *(35:499)*

579. **(B)** This sonogram demonstrates a dilated common bile duct. *(35:363)*

580. **(C)** The most likely cause of this includes pancreatic tumor or gallstone in the distal common bile duct. *(35:363)*

581. **(A)** With age, the common bile duct may distend and measure 7 mm or greater. *(35:363)*

582. **(B)** The arrow points to hypoechoic lesions within the left lobe of the liver. *(35:397)*

583. **(C)** These hypoechoic lesions are the results of infectious foci. It is very unusual to have metastases with hypoechoic texture. Occasionally, lymphoma may produce hypoechoic liver metastases. Hemangiomas are echogenic. *(35:397)*

584. **(D)** A fine needle aspiration would be the next step to evaluate the nature of these liver lesions. *(35:397)*

585. **(B)** This sonogram is diagnostic of a varicocele, dilated vessels, near the head of the epididymis. *(35:513)*

586. **(A)** Increase flow within the dilated vessels can be seen with a Valsalva maneuver. *(35:513)*

587. **(A)** A varicocele appears as tortuous vessels near the head of the epididymis, mostly occurring on the left. *(35:513)*

588. **(A)** This patient has a contracted gallbladder filled with stones. *(35:360)*

589. **(A)** The sonogram demonstrates calculus cholecystitis. *(35:360)*

590. **(False)** With this many stones, the patient would not be a candidate for biliary lithotripsy. *(35:434)*

591. **(B)** This sonogram shows distension of the renal pelvis and proximal ureter. *(35:444)*

592. **(E)** This may be secondary to reflux or ureterovesicle junction (UVJ) obstruction. Since the proximal ureter is dilated, ureteropelvic junction (UPJ) obstruction is unlikely. *(35:444)*

593. **(E)** Xanthogranulomatous pyelonephritis is an inflammatory process accompanied by calculi. Sonographically, the kidney appears as an enlarged hydronephrotic kidney with stones obstructing within the renal collecting system. *(35:454)*

594. **(A)** This sonogram shows thickening of the posterior bladder wall. *(35:562)*

595. **(C)** This may be secondary to cystitis or tumor. *(35:562)*

596. **(D)** Chemotherapy, renal infection, frequent and painful urination is associated with cystitis in a child. *(35:562)*

597. **(B)** This sonogram shows marked increased echogenicity of the liver compared with the kidney. *(35:581)*

598. **(D)** All of the above. In the adult, glycogen storage disease, fatty metamorphosis, cirrhosis, and hemochromatosis all present with an echogenic liver. In the child, this is frequently a complication of glycogen storage disease. *(35:581)*

599. **(A)** These children have a greater incidence of multiple hepatic adenomata and tumors. Portions of normal liver may appear hypoechoic relative to the abnormal echogenic liver. *(35:581)*

600. **(A)** The absence of a right kidney. *(35:577)*

601. **(C)** This sonogram shows a flattened and relatively large adrenal in a patient with bilateral renal agenesis. *(35:577)*

602. **(A)** In neonates affected by this disease, the adrenals may be relatively long and misshapen. *(35:577)*

603. **(C)** This sonogram shows a markedly hydropic gallbladder. *(35:587)*

604. **(A)** Hydrops of the gallbladder may be related to obstruction at the level of a cystic or distal common bile duct. *(35:587)*

605. **(E)** All of the above will lead to an hydropic gallbladder. In addition, in mucocutaneous lymph node syndrome (Kawasaki's disease), there may be gallbladder hydrops related to obstruction of the neck by lymph nodes. *(35:587)*

606. **(B)** Difficult to determine because the gallbladder is not fully distended, and as one can see from the centimeter marker on the side of the image, this gallbladder is perhaps only 3 cm in length and is nondistended. *(35:358)*

607. **(A)** When the gallbladder is nondistended, the wall may look thickened just because the gallbladder wall is not fully stretched as in the distended state. *(35:358)*

608. **(E)** All of the above. There are a variety of nonphysiological conditions that can be associated with gallbladder wall thickening. These include cardiac

dysfunction, lymphadenophathy, right upper quadrant inflammatory process, and hyperplastic cholecystitis. *(35:358)*

609. **(A)** This sonogram shows a large mass in the lower pole of the left kidney. *(35:574)*

610. **(D)** In an adult, this would most likely represent a renal cell tumor; in a child, Wilms' tumor. Angiomyoneuromas may also have this appearance but typically have a more echogenic texture related to their fat content. *(35:574)*

611. **(E)** Angiomyolipomas are seen in patients with tuberous sclerosis and in postmenopausal women. *(35:574)*

612. **(B)** This sonogram shows the normal left adrenal. *(35:578)*

613. **(C)** Normal left adrenal. *(35:578)*

614. **(D)** All of the above are conditions that may affect the adrenal. *(35:578)*

615. **(D)** This sonogram demonstrates an ectatic or dilated main pancreatic duct. *(35:594)*

616. **(D)** Cystic fibrosis is a genetic disease affecting 1 in 2000 persons. The complications of cystic fibrosis are related to the increase in secretions of the exocrine glands. This leads to chronic pancreatitis and a small echogenic pancreas with a dilated duct. Hereditary pancreatitis is an autosomal dominant disease producing recurrent inflammation of the pancreas. Hereditary pancreatitis is not as common as cystic fibrosis. *(35:594)*

617. **(D)** Pancreatic tumors and chronic pancreatitis will lead to a dilated pancreatic duct. In elderly patients, the duct has lost its elasticity and will be ectatic and dilated. *(35:594)*

618. **(B)** This sonogram demonstrates a cystic mass contiguous with the common bile duct. *(35:591)*

619. **(B)** This is a choledochal cyst, of which there are at least three varieties. *(35:591)*

620. **(E)** All of the above are variations of choledochal cysts. *(35:591)*

621. **(E)** None of the above. A choledochal cyst occurs as a result of an anomalous insertion of the common bile duct into the pancreatic duct, permitting reflux of pancreatic juices into the bile duct leading to cholangitis, weakening, and dilatation. *(35:591)*

622. **(B)** A cystic mass that appears to displace the bowel and mesentery. *(35:600)*

623. **(A)** This is a mesenteric cyst. Bowel loops are displaced by the cyst and their mesentery is seen. Note how the cyst conforms closely to the contour of the anterior wall, pushing the bowel and mesentery posteriorly. An ovarian cyst and free fluid do not displace bowel posteriorly. *(35:600)*

624. **(D)** These sonograms demonstrate marked thickening and lengthening of the antral muscle (pyloric canal and muscle). *(35:604)*

625. **(B)** This is consistent with hypertrophic pyloric stenosis. *(35:604)*

626. **(E)** The criteria for this diagnosis include wall thickness greater than 3 mm and antral length greater than 14 mm. *(35:604)*

627. **(E)** None of the above. This transverse sonogram of the upper abdomen demonstrates a normal pancreas and duodenum. *(35:371)*

628. **(B)** Normal. *(35:371)*

629. **(C)** This real-time sonogram demonstrates a solid mass within irregular borders. *(35:737)*

630. **(C)** At biopsy, this was carcinoma. Fibroadenomas usually are well circumscribed, whereas carcinomas are not. *(35:737)*

631. **(B)** False. One cannot tell with an adequate degree of confidence whether a solid lesion is benign or malignant by its sonographic appearance. *(35:737)*

632. **(B)** A parathyroid mass. This is a large mass adjacent to the thyroid and right common carotid artery. *(35:737)*

633. **(A)** This represents a parathyroid adenoma or carcinoma. *(35:715)*

634. **(A)** Parathyroid adenoma may present with hypercalcemia. *(35:715)*

635. **(E)** None of the above. The chest radiograph demonstrates a large amount of fluid density in the left hemidiaphragm. *(35:744)*

636. **(C)** The sonogram demonstrates that this fluid density contains multiple loculations consistent with an empyema. *(35:744)*

637. **(A)** If the fluid seems to move with each breath, one can assume that it is nonloculated, simple effusion. *(35:744)*

638. **(A)** Sonography is useful in confirming the clinical impression of acute appendicitis. *(35:409)*

639. **(E)** The primary criteria for diagnosis of acute appendicitis is visualization of a noncompressible appendix. Other diagnostic criteria are muscular wall thickness greater than 3 mm, and the presence of an appendicolith. *(35:409)*

640. **(C)** 5–75 represents a normal appendix. *(35:409)*

641. **(C)** Choledocholithiasis. Ductal stones are identified by the presence of echogenic material within the duct. *(36:132)*

642. **(B)** The dilated common bile duct has an internal dimension if greater than 6 mm. Also note the "parallel channel" sign ("shotgun" sign), which represents the dilated hepatic duct and the portal vein. *(36:129)*

643. **(A)** In *chronic* cholecystitis, the gallbladder generally is contracted, with the walls being thickened, but rarely more than five times its size with associated cholelithiasis. Remember in *acute* cholecystitis, the gallbladder is *enlarged* with *thickened* walls and leukocytosis. *(36:107)*

644. **(B)** Main portal vein. It branches into left portal and right portal. The left portal vein proceeds cranially *vertically* along the anterior surface of the caudate lobe, whereas the right portal has a horizontal course. *(36:7, 9)*

645. **(E)** The ligamentum teres courses in the caudal aspect of the left intersegmental fissure and may be used as a landmark in dividing the left lobe into medial (quadrate) and lateral segments. Sonographically on a transverse scan, it appears as a round echogenic area. *(36:4)*

646. **(D)** In obstructive jaundice, alkaline phosphatase, and direct bilirubin will be markedly increased with SGOT also being increased. Keep in mind that SGOT also is markedly increased in hepatitis. *(38:172)*

647. **(C)** The sonogram demonstrates dilated biliary radicles. A serum alkaline phosphatase level greater than five times the upper limit of normal is characteristic of cholestatic hepatobiliary disease. *(40:369)*

648. **(D)** The sonogram suggests a *thickened* gallbladder wall (cholecystitis). A gallbladder wall greater than 3 mm is seen with hepatitis, ascites, alcoholic liver disease, hypoproteinemia, hypoalbuminemia, heart failure, systemic venous hypertension, and renal disease. *(36:107)*

649. **(A)** The major lobar fissure is seen on longitudinal scans as a linear echo coursing from the gallbladder to the porta hepatis. It divides the liver into left and right lobes. *(36:5)*

650. **(A)** Metastases are neoplastic involvement in the liver, causing liver enlargement with multiple nodules of varying sonographic patterns. Metastases have been described as hypoechoic, echogenic, bulls-eye, anechoic, and diffusly inhomogeneous. *(36:61)*

651. **(B)** The sonogram shows dilated hepatic veins and a dilated inferior vena cava. This is consistent with congestive heart failure. *(37:223)*

652. **(B)** The ligamentum venosum is noted here. The fissure for the ligamentum venosum contains the hepatogastric ligament, which is located between the caudate lobe and the left lobe of the liver. *(36:5)*

653. **(B)** This sonogram is suggestive of adenomyomatosis of the gallbladder. Sonographically, one should look for diffuse or segmental thickening of the gallbladder wall with intramural diverticula protruding into the lumen. *(36:19)*

654. **(D)** At the level of the gallbladder, one may see the fluid-filled second or descending portion of the duodenum, which runs along the right side of the inferior vena cava. *(36:611)*

655. **(D)** The clinical features of acute cholecystitis are *leukocytosis,* fever, nausea, vomiting, and referred shoulder pain if the inflammation irritates the diaphragm. Sonographically, the gallbladder is enlarged with a thickened wall greater than 5 mm. *(36:107)*

656. **(C)** The ultrasound findings in cirrhosis include increased echogenicity of the anterior portion of the liver, with decreasing echogenicity as one proceeds posteriorly owing to the difficulty of the beam to penetrate the cirrhotic liver. The echogenicity that is noted is much higher than that of the kidney. There may be associated ascites, splenomegaly, and portal hypertension. It is difficult to pinpoint when a liver changes from being a fatty to a cirrhotic but generally a fatty liver is homogeneously enlarged and echogenic. *(36:17)*

657. **(A)** This liver is enlarged and extremely heterogeneous consistent with metastatic disease. Metastatic patterns within the liver may vary from hypoechoic to echogenic. *(36:61)*

658. **(B)** The hemangioma is located between the right and middle hepatic veins; therefore it is in the anterior segment of the right lobe. The right hepatic

vein separates the right lobe into anterior and posterior segments; the middle hepatic vein divides the liver into right and left lobes. *(36:5)*

659. **(D)** When scanning coronally left side down and placing the transducer longitudinally on the patient's right side, the aorta will be seen posterior to the inferior vena cava. Sometimes one may also be able to see the renal arteries arising off the aorta. This scan is very beneficial to rule out lymphadenopathy. *(36:444)*

660. **(B)** Owing to long-standing obstruction, tumefactive biliary sludge has been described as a Courvoisier gallbladder. Because of the stasis, the sludge eventually will become so thick as to attenuate enough sound to cause distal shadowing. Metastatic tumor to the gallbladder should be suspected in the presence of focal gallbladder wall thickening in association with nonshadowing intraluminal soft tissue masses. *(36:104, 125)*

661. **(C)** Cirrhosis is a chronic and progressive disease leading to liver cell failure, portal hypertension, and ascites. The thickened gallbladder wall is most likely related to hypoproteinemia and to the adjacent ascites that will make the gallbladder appear thickened. *(36:17)*

662. **(D)** This is a sonogram of a normal pancreas. With high-resolution ultrasound, the pancreatic duct is routinely visualized. The normal pancreatic duct should not measure more than 2 mm in its internal diameter. *(36:174)*

663. **(B)** The arrow is pointing to the right renal artery, which lies posterior to the inferior vena cava. *(36:443)*

664. **(D)** The crura of the diaphragm are extensions (tendinous fibers) of the diaphragm that attach to the vertebral process of L3 on the right and L1 on the left. The right crus appears as a hypoechoic linear structure and can be visualized as it runs from posterior to the inferior vena cava to anterior to the aorta. *(36:387)*

665. **(A)** The esophagogastric junction can be seen anterior to the aorta and posterior to the left lobe of the liver. *(36:387)*

666. **(D)** Here we see the right crus of the diaphragm posterior to the inferior vena cava. *(36:387)*

667. **(A)** The right renal artery runs posterior to the inferior vena cava and anterior to the right crus of the diaphragm. *(36:387)*

668. **(D)** When an ultrasound beam having an oblique incidence (not on a perpendicular angle) is directed at an interface and travels between two media (liver and gallbladder) of different propagation speeds, refraction of the ultrasound beam will occur (Snell's law). Here we can see the beam refracting off the curved surface of the gallbladder wall. *(41:161)*

669. **(C)** The echogenic foci sitting superior to the diaphragm (arrow) is a mirror-image artifact. A mirror-image artifact is a duplication artifact secondary to the sound beam bouncing off (reflecting off) a strong reflector in its path; ie, the diaphragm. This strong reflector acts as a mirror and the image will present as two reflected objects rather than one. *(41:151)*

670. **(B)** The sonogram demonstrates periportal lymphadenopathy, which is characterized by enlarged lymph nodes that are secondarily involved in almost all infections and neoplastic disorders. Lymph nodes consist of lymphocytes and reticulum cells, their function being filtration and production of lymphocytes. All the lymph passes through these nodes that act as filters, not only for bacteria but also for cancer cells. Sonographically, we can evaluate lymph nodes in the pelvis, retroperitoneum, porta hepatis, and perirenal and prevertebral vasculature. The ultrasound appearance of lymphomatous nodes varies from hypoechoic to anechoic with very good sound transmission. *(36:419)*

671. **(C)** There is no definite correlation between kidney size and echogenicity with the degree of renal failure. Generally, if the kidney parenchyma (cortex) is more echogenic than the liver, chronic renal insufficiency should be considered. *(36:290)*

672. **(C)** The sonogram demonstrates celiac nodes surrounding the celiac artery and its winglike configuration. Note the increased distance between the celiac artery and the aorta due to these masses. *(36:426)*

673. **(A)** This sonogram depicts a fusiform aneurysm. The fusiform type is a gradual dilatation of the vascular lumen. The saccular type is a discrete round structure and the cylindrial aneurysm is a dilatation longitudinally producing lengthening of the expanded vessel in a uniform diameter. The aorta is considered aneurysmal if it exceeds 3 cm; greater than 6 cm requires surgery. *(36:451)*

674. **(D)** The left renal vein courses between the aorta and the superior mesenteric artery. *(36:448)*

675. **(C)** The caudate lobe of the liver is seen posterior to the ligamentum venosum. *(36:4)*

676. **(A)** The celiac artery is the first anterior branch of the abdominal aorta. *(36:445)*

677. **(B)** The superior mesenteric artery is the second branch of the abdominal aorta. *(36:445)*

678. **(A)** The splenic vein is noted posterior to the body of the pancreas, and on a longitudinal scan can be seen between the celiac artery and the superior mesenteric artery. *(36:445)*

679. **(B)** The kidney rests on the quadratus lumborum muscle that runs laterally to the psoas muscle. *(36:396)*

680. **(C)** The falciform ligament extends from the umbilicus to the diaphragm and can only be seen sonographically in patients with ascites. *(36:5)*

681. **(A)** Normal head, which lies anterior to the inferior vena cava. *(35:372)*

682. **(B)** Normal tail, which lies anterior to the splenic vein. *(35:371)*

683. **(B)** Common bile duct, which defines the posterolateral margin of the pancreas. In the head of the pancreas, the internal diameter should not be more than 4 cm. *(36:168)*

684. **(B)** Chronic pancreatitis is associated with a normal to small pancreas, increased echogenicity due to fibrotic changes, calcification, and ductal dilatation. *(35:375)*

685. **(B)** The head of the pancreas lies anterior to the inferior vena cava. *(36:167)*

686. **(B)** A pancreatic pseudocyst is a fluid collection that arises as a result of obstruction associated with pancreatitis. The pancreatic duct being obstructed increases in size until it can no longer dilate; it ruptures and allows pancreatic juices to escape. Blunt trauma is the most common cause of pseudocysts in children. Pseudocysts may track anywhere from the mediastinum to the pelvis. *(36:184)*

687. **(E)** Adenocarcinoma is found most often in elderly males, in whom the pancreatic head is affected 70% of the time. As a rule the mass is hypoechoic, with irregular borders. (Fig. 5–117A). Associated findings include dilation of the pancreatic duct, biliary dilation (Fig. 5–117B), and an enlarged gallbladder (Courvoisier gallbladder) (Fig. 5–117C). *(36:206)*

688. **(B)** There have been several ultrasound signs described for biliary dilatation. In this sonogram, we can recognize (1) tubular lucencies within the liver demonstrating acoustic enhancement—bile opposed to blood increases through transmission; (2) the tubules have a stellate (starlike with little points extending into the periphery) appearance as opposed to veins or arteries that are straight; (3) dilated ducts are generally seen running in pairs—as two tubular lucencies—normal bile ducts are not visualized within the liver. *(36:129)*

689. **(C)** The arrow is pointing to an example of chronic pancreatitis. With chronic pancreatitis, the pancreas generally is diffusely smaller and more fibrotic than usual with areas of calcification and ductal dilatation. In acute pancreatitis, the pancreas is generally diffusely larger and *less* echogenic than normal. In adenocarcinoma and islet cell tumors, the pancreas is generally focally enlarged in the pancreatic head with the former and the tail in the latter. *(36:196)*

690. **(C)** Because the patient was asymptomatic, this is most likely a simple benign hepatic cyst. *(36:36)*

691. **(C)** The perirenal fluid collection may be associated with lymphocele, a collection lymph fluid caused by injury to lymphatic channels during transplantation; hematoma, a collection of blood; and abscess, which are all associated with renal transplantation. Unfortunately it is difficult to differentiate one from the other. Urinoma is a collection of urine due to a urinary leak of a uretero pelvic or ureteroureter anastomosis. Abscess is a collection of pus due to an inflammatory response. Ascites is not associated with a renal transplant. *(36:335)*

692. **(C)** There is an irregular diffuse thickening of the bladder wall of unknown origin. The prostate is not enlarged, and there is no suggestion of a bladder neck obstruction that most commonly is secondary to benign prostatic hypertrophy or carcinoma. Endometrial tissue may be found penetrating the bladder wall and extending into the lumen in severe cases of endometriosis in premenopausal women. *(36:349)*

693. **(D)** Serum creatinine and BUN (blood urea nitrogen) are elevated in kidney disease. *(38:126)*

694. **(D)** Attenuation is the *decrease* in amplitude and intensity as a wave travels through a medium. On the contrary, one of the criteria for a cyst is the acoustic enhancement posterior to the cyst due to the nonattenuating characteristics of a cyst. *(41:173)*

695. **(D)** Adult polycystic kidney disease is an inherited autosomal dominant disease that most often manifests in the fourth decade. It manifests by cystic dilatation of the proximal convoluted tubules, Bowman's capsule, and the collecting tubules. It is mostly a bilateral process, with associated cysts

found in the liver (25–50%), pancreas, lungs, spleen, ovaries, and testes. Juvenile polycystic disease is part of the spectrum of infantile polycystic kidney diseases, whereby the kidney presents as enlarged and echogenic owing to the many *small* cystic interfaces found within the kidney *(36:236)*

696. **(A)** Multicystic dysplastic kidney disease is the most common cause of an abdominal mass in the newborn. It is usually unilateral, although the other kidney may be associated with abnormalities, and the left kidney is affected more than the right. Sonographic criteria of this disease are cysts of varying size with the largest in the periphery, absence of connections between the cysts, absence of an identifiable renal sinus, and absence of renal parenchyma surrounding cysts. *(36:232)*

697. **(A)** The sonogram is not normal. It depicts hydronephrosis. There are numerous causes for hydronephrosis: congenital anomolies, as in posterior urethral valves; bladder neck obstruction; acquired causes such as calculi; benign prostatic hypertrophy; tumors; inflammation; intrinsic causes such as calculi; pyelonephritis; and extrinsic causes such as neoplasm and retroperitoneal adenopathy. *(36:252)*

698. **(E)** Staghorn calculus is a large calculi within the renal collecting system that leads to hyronephrosis. An angiomyolipoma (renal hamartoma) is a benign renal tumor that is highly echogenic because of its fat content. Vesicoureteral reflux is a common urinary tract abnormality in children and stems from several congenital anomalies such as ectopia, posterior urethral valves, and prune belly syndrome. The reflux will eventually reach the kidney and may progress to hydronephrosis, but the ureteral reflux is not due to obstruction in the kidney but rather is ureteral in origin. Tuberous sclerosis is an inherited neurocutaneous disorder and is associated with angiomyolipomas in 40–80% of cases. Parapelvic cysts do not communicate with the collecting system and are lymphatic in nature. *(36:297, 298, 306)*

699. **(E)** The sonogram depicts an extratesticular mass. This may be a spermatocele (which is a cyst in the epididymis) containing spermatozoa or an epididymal cyst. A varicocele (enlargement of the veins of the spermatic cord) is also extratesticular but is found on the posterior surface, commonly occurring on the left, and sonographically appears tubular in shape. A seminoma is a malignant tumor within the testes. *(35:512)*

700. **(B)** A normal head of the epididymis is noted. *(35:506)*

701. **(B)** The arrow is pointing to the seminal vesicle, which is posterior to the bladder and superior to the prostate. *(35:489)*

702. **(D)** Varicoceles are enlargements of the veins of the pampiniform plexus, which runs along the posterior aspect of testicle and is more prominent on the left. Spermatocele and epididymal cyst are found in the epididymis. The mediastinum testis is found within the testis and connects the rete testis with the epididymis. Cryptorchidism is another name for undescended testes. *(35:503)*

703. **(D)** The sonogram depicts a small echogenic kidney with a loss of distinction between cortex medulla and renal sinus. This patient has chronic glomerulonephritis, which is the most common cause for chronic renal failure. *(36:291)*

704. **(F)** An angiomyolipoma (renal hamartoma) is a benign fatty renal tumor that presents as a discrete hyperechoic lesion. Of patients with tuberous sclerosis, 40–80% have angiomyolipomas. *(36:298, 306)*

705. **(C)** This is a sonogram of malrotated kidneys fused at the upper pole (horseshoe kidney) draped anterior to the vertebral vessels. *(35:460)*

706. **(A)** The sonogram shows normal adrenals. At birth, the normal neonatal adrenal is relatively thick and prominent, being one-third the size of the kidney. *(36:391)*

707. **(B)** This decubitus coronal sonogram depicts severe hydronephrosis, extending into the renal pelvis, with marked thinning of the renal parenchyma. Pyonephrosis is a collection of pus within the dilated collecting system due to the stasis of urine and would have internal echoes. The few echoes that are present within this hydronephrotic kidney are due to artifact. *(35:252)*

708. **(C)** The arrow is pointing to the renal pyramids, which are in the medulla. *(36:222)*

709. **(B)** The arcuate arteries, which are depicted as the small echogenic line above the pyramids are used as a landmark to differentiate the cortex from the medulla. *(36:224)*

710. **(A)** The renal column of Bertin is composed of cortical tissue (cortex) that extends into the medullary area between the pyramids. *(36:227)*

711. **(E)** The sonogram depicts dilated biliary radicles that are caused by obstructed bile ducts. This may be due to a stone, mass lesions in the area of the head of the pancreas, or tumor or metastatic lesions within the liver. Cirrhosis is related to "medical" jaundice and there will be no evidence of biliary dilatation. *(8:99)*

712. **(E)** A neuroblastoma is an adrenal tumor found in children. It will not cause splenomegaly. *(8:108)*

713. **(C)** The decubitus coronal position will provide the longest dimension to evaluate the kidney and will allow visualization of the renal pelvis extending into the renal hilum. *(36:222)*

714. **(T)** All of the answers are true. Acute tubular necrosis (ATN) is the most common cause of acute renal failure resulting in the accumulation of creatinine and nitrogenous wastes (BUN) in the body. ATN may be due to renal ischemia (the impairment of blood flow in and out of the body), trauma, toxin exposure, or a complication of surgery. Owing to the inflammatory changes, the kidney becomes edematous and congested; it therefore increases in size and the medullary pyramids appear more prominent and anechoic. *(36:287)*

715. **(B)** The valves of Heister are located within the cystic duct, at its junction with the neck of the gallbladder. *(37:228)*

716. **(C)** Gallbladder carcinoma is frequently associated with cholelithiasis, chronic cholecystitis, and/or calcification of the gallbladder wall. *(35:362;39:318)*

717. **(E)** Jaundice and right upper quandrant pain are associated with biliary obstruction. An increase in alkaline phosphatase is indicative of biliary obstruction, and one may see an increase in amylase if a tumor in the pancreatic head or pancreatitis is noted obstructing the common bile duct. Elevated acid phosphatase is associated with prostate carcinoma. *(38:185)*

718. **(D)** A large gallbladder, hypotonic intestines, and renal insufficiency are commonly seen in patients with diabetes. *(42:231)*

719. **(E)** Excessive weight loss is associated with carcinoma; therefore, liver metastases, dilated common bile duct (as may be present with adenocarcinoma within the pancreatic head), hepatoma, and pancreatic mass are correct. A hemangioma is the most common benign tumor of the liver. *(36:49)*

720. **(B)** Most commonly choledochal cyst is a cystic dilation of the common bile duct with the common hepatic duct being normal. Sonographically, one finds a large cystic mass in the porta hepatis with a dilated common hepatic or common bile duct entering the cyst. The gallbladder must be visualized as a separate structure. *(36:147)*

721. **(D)** A diffusely thickened gallbladder with localized infiltrating or fungating tumors protruding into the lumen. In 65–90% of cases, cholelithiasis is noted. *(36:119)*

REFERENCES

1. Cosgrove DO, McCready VR.: *Ultrasound Imaging: Liver, Spleen, Pancreas.* New York: Wiley, 1982.
2. Goldberg BB. *Abdominal Ultrasonography,* 2nd ed. New York: Wiley, 1984.
3. Hagen-Ansert SL. *Textbook of Diagnostic Ultrasonography.* 2nd ed. St. Louis: CV Mosby, 1983.
4. Anderson WAD, Scotti TM. *Synopsis of Pathology,* 10th ed. St. Louis: CV Mosby, 1980.
5. Sarti DA, Sample WF. *Diagnostic Ultrasound Text and Cases.* Boston: GK Hall, 1980.
6. Snell RS. *Clinical Anatomy for Medical Students.* Boston: Little, Brown, 1973.
7. Durrell C. Gallbladder ultrasonography in clinical context. Semin Ultrasound CT MR **5**(4):315, 1984.
8. Saunders RC, Campbell J, Guidi SM, et al. *Clinical Sonography: A Practical Guide.* Boston: Little, Brown, 1984.
9. Beeson PB, McDermott W, Wyngaarden JB. *Cecil's Textbook of Medicine,* 15th ed. Philadelphia: WB Saunders, 1979.
10. *SMDS Educational Outline Abdomen, Small Parts.* Vol. 2. Dallas: Society of Diagnostic Medical Sonographers, 1983.
11. *SMDS Educational Outline Abdomen, Small Parts.* Vol. 5. Dallas: Society of Diagnostic Medical Sonographers, 1983.
12. Lang FC. Commonly encountered artifacts in clinical Ultrasound. *Semin Ultrasound* **4**(1):22, 1983.
13. Fleischer AC, James AE: Real-Time Sonography. *Textbook with Accompanying Videotape.* Norwalk, CT: Appleton-Century-Crofts, 1984.
14. Hirsch J, Rogers J, Mack L. Real-time sonography of pleural opacities. *AJR* **136**:297, 1981.
15. Fleischer A, Winfield A, Page D. Synergistic use of sonomammography and x-ray mammography. *Postgrad Radiol* **5**:163, 1985.
16. Cole-Beuglet C, Sorino R, Kurtz A, et al. Fibroadenoma of the breast: Sonography correlate with pathology in 122 patients. *AJR* **140**:369, 1983.
17. Reading C, Carboneau J, James EM. *High resolution parathyroid sonography. AJR* **139**:539, 1982.
18. Hricak H, Filly R. Sonography of the scrotum. *Invest Radiol* **18**:112, 1983.
19. Bird K, Rosenfield A, Taylor K. Ultrasonography in testicular torsion. *Radiology* **147**:527, 1983.
20. King W, Kimme-Smith C, Winter J. Renal stone shadowing: An investigation of contributing factors. *Radiology* **154**:191, 1985.
21. Bernstein E, Chan E. Abdominal aortic aneurysm in high-risk patients. *Ann Surg* **200**:255, 1984.
22. Laing F, Federle M, Jeffrey R, et al. Ultrasonic eval-

uation of patients with acute right upper quadrant pain. *Radiology* **140**:499, 1981.

23. Gracie W, Randonoff D. The natural history of silent gallstones: The innocent gallstone is not a myth. *N Engl Med* **307**:798, 1982.
24. Jones T, Dubuisson R, Hughes J, et al. Abrupt termination of the common bile duct: A sign of malignancy identified by high-resolution real-time sonography. *J Ultrasound Med* **2**:345, 1983.
25. Simeone J, Muueller P, Ferrucci J, Jr et al. Sonography of the bile ducts after a fatty meal: An aid in detection of obstruction. *Radiology* **143**:211, 1982.
26. Kangarloo H, Sarti D, Sample W, Amundson G. Ultrasonographic spectrum of choledochal cysts in children. *Pediatr Radiol* **9**:15, 1980.
27. Shuman W, Mack L, Rogers J. Diffuse nephrocalcinosis: Hyperechoic sonographic appearance. *AJR* **136**:830, 1981.
28. Niederau C, Sonnenberg A, Muller J, et al. Sonographic measurements of the normal liver, spleen, pancreas, and portal vein. *Radiology* **149**:537, 1983.
29. Mittelstaedt C, Partain C. Ultrasonic-pathologic classification of splenic abnormalities: Gray-scale patterns. *Radiology* **134**:697, 1980.
30. Parulekar S. Ultrasound evaluation of common bile duct size. *Radiology* **129**:703, 1979.
31. Graif M, Manor A, Itzchak Y. Sonographic differentiation of extra- and intrahepatic masses. *AJR* **141**:553, 1983.

32a. Charboneau J, Hattery R, Ernst E, et al. Spectrum of sonographic findings in 125 renal masses other than benign simple cyst. *AJR* **140**:87, 1983.

32b. McClennan B, Stanley R, Melson G, et al. CT of the renal cyst: Is cyst aspiration necessary? *AJR* **133**:671, 1979.

33. Hole JW Jr. *Human Anatomy and Physiology,* 3rd ed. Dubuque, IO: William C. Brown, 1984.
34. Taylor KJW. *Atlas of Ultrasonography,* 2nd ed. New York: Churchill Livingstone, 1985.
35. Fleischer AC, James AE. *Diagnostic Sonography Principles and Clinical Applications.* Philadelphia, WB Saunders, 1989.
36. Mittelstaedt CA. *Abdominal Ultrasound.* New York: Churchill Livingstone, 1987.
37. Hagan-Ansert SL. *Textbook of Diagnostic Ultrasonography.* 3rd ed. St. Louis, CV Mosby, 1989.
38. Byrne JC, Saxton DF, Pelikan PK, Nungent PM. *Laboratory Tests, Implications for Nurses and Allied Health Professionals.* Reading, MA: Addison-Wesley, 1981.
39. Durrell CA. Gallbladder ultrasonography in clinical content. *Semin Ultrasound CT MRI* **5**(4):315, 1984.
40. Richter JM. *Evaluation of the jaundiced patient:* An internist's perspective. Semin *Ultrasound CT MRI* **5**(4):369–376, 1984.
41. Kremkau FW. *Diagnostic Ultrasound Principles, Instruments and Exercises.* 3rd ed. WB Saunders, 1989.
42. Fishman MC, Hoffman AR, Klausner AR, et al. *Medicine.* Philadelphia: JB Lippincott, 1981.
43. Koenigsberg M: Sonographic evaluation of the retroperitoneum. *Semin Ultrasound CT MRI* **3**:2, 1982.
44. Romano AJ, Sonnenberg VE, Casola GB, et al: Gallbladder and bile duct abnormalities in AIDS: Sonographic findings in eight patients. *AJR* **15**:123–129, 1988.

CHAPTER 6

ENDORECTAL PROSTATE SONOGRAPHY

Dunstan Abraham

Study Guide

The prostate is a heterogeneous oval-shaped organ that surrounds the proximal urethra. In the adult, the normal gland measures approximately 3.8 cm (cephalocaudal) by 3 cm (anteroposterior) by 4 cm (transverse).[1] It normally weighs about 20 g, but it can be slightly larger in men older than 40. The prostate is composed of glandular and fibromuscular tissue and is located in the retroperitoneum between the floor of the urinary bladder and the urogenital diaphragm. The base of the prostate, its superior margin, abuts the inferior aspect of the urinary bladder. The gland is bounded anteriorly by prostatic fat and fascia, laterally by the obturator internus and levator ani muscles, and posteriorly by areolar tissue and Denonvilliers' fascia, which separates it from the rectum.

The seminal vesicles are two saclike lateral structures that out pouch from the vas deferens and are situated on the posterior-superior aspect of the prostate between the bladder and the rectum. The seminal vesicles join the vas deferens to form the ejaculatory ducts, which then enter the base of the prostate to join the urethra at the verumontanum. The verumontanum is a midpoint region between the prostatic base and apex and surrounds the urethra. The size and fluid content of the seminal vesicles are variable.

The prostatic urethra courses through the substance of the gland and is divided into a proximal and a distal segment. The proximal segment extends from the neck of the bladder to the base of the verumontanum; the distal segment begins at this point and extends to the apex of the gland.

NORMAL SECTIONAL ANATOMY

The earlier anatomic descriptions of the prostate divided the gland into five major lobes (anterior, posterior, middle, and two lateral) or two zones (outer and inner). More recent histological studies, however, have divided the prostate into three glandular zones: the transitional, central, and peripheral zones. There is also a nonglandular region called the anterior fibromuscular stroma[2] (Fig. 6–1A and B).

Transitional zone. The transitional zone represents about 5% of the glandular prostate and is located in the central region on both sides of the proximal urethra.[2] The ducts of the transitional zone run parallel to the urethra and end in the proximal urethra at the level of the verumontanum.

Central zone. The central zone constitutes approximately 25% of the prostatic glandular tissue and is located at the base of the gland.[2] It is wedgelike in shape, is oriented horizontally, and surrounds the ejaculatory ducts throughout their course. The zone narrows to an apex at the verumontanum. Ducts of the vas deferens and seminal vesicles come together to form the ejaculatory ducts, which pass through the central zone and join the urethra at the verumontanum.

Peripheral zone. The peripheral zone constitutes about 70% of the glandular tissue.[2] This zone consists of the posterior, lateral, and apical parts of the prostate and also extends anteriorly. The ducts of the peripheral zone enter the urethra at, and distal to, the verumontanum.

Anterior fibromuscular stroma. The anterior fibromuscular stroma is a thick nonglandular sheath of tissue that covers the entire anterior surface of the prostate. This tissue is composed of smooth muscle and fibrous tissue.

NORMAL SONOGRAPHIC ANATOMY

Sonographically, the prostate is a homogeneous gland with low-level echoes. The periurethral glandular tissue that surrounds the proximal urethra is homogeneous and isoechoic. The central zone is normally more echogenic than the peripheral zone because it has a greater amount

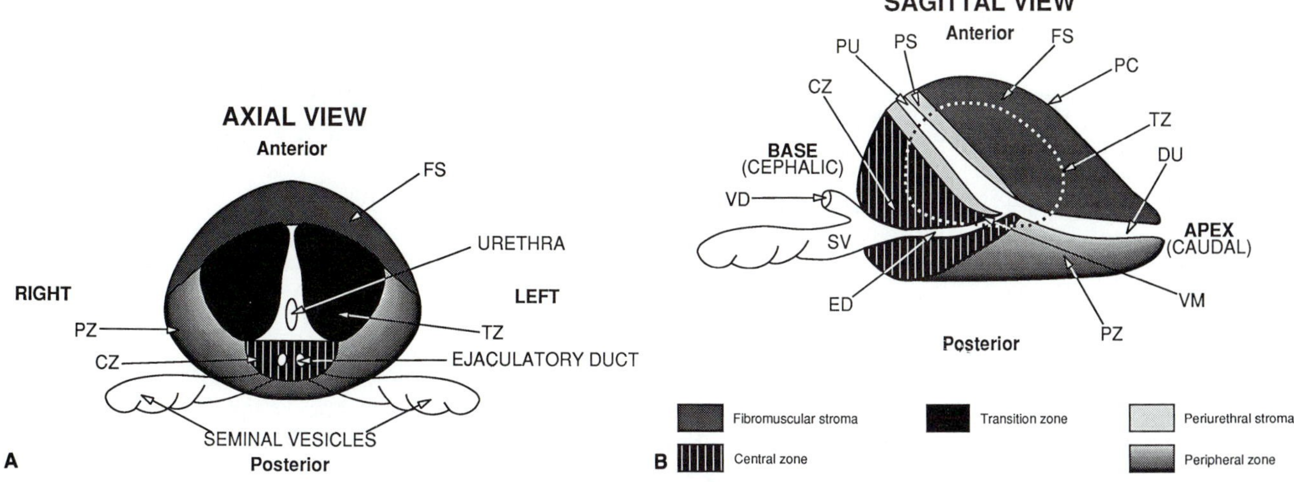

Figure 6–1. (**A**) An axial view of normal prostate anatomy: CZ is the central zone, FS is the fibromuscular stroma, TZ is the transition zone, and PZ is the peripheral zone. (**B**) Sagittal view of the normal prostate anatomy: SV is the seminal vesicle, ED is the ejaculatory duct, DU is the distal urethra, PC is the prostatic capsule, VD is the vas deferens, VM is the verumontanum, PU is the proximal urethra, CZ is the central zone, FS is the fibromuscular stroma, TZ is the transition zone, PS is the periurethral stroma, and PZ is the peripheral zone. *(Modified with permission from McNeal J E. Regional morphology and pathology of the prostate. Am J Clin Pathol 49:347–357, 1968 and Dakin R, et al. Transrectal ultrasound of the prostate: Technique and sonographic findings. JDMS 5(1):2, 1989.)*

of corpora amylacea (calcified deposits) in the central zone. The fibromuscular capsule, located anteriorly, is smooth, hyperechoic, and sharply defined.

The seminal vesicles are visualized as symmetrically paired structures that are slightly less echoic than the prostate. The vas deferens can be depicted as tubular hypoechoic structures joining the seminal vesicles medially. On transverse imaging, they are round or oval and are located between the seminal vesicles. The ejaculatory duct, when empty, can be seen as a hyperechoic line joining the urethra. The empty urethra is identified by its echogenic walls coursing through the prostate. When filled with fluid, the urethra is recognized more easily.

On longitudinal sections, the anterior space between the prostate and the seminal vesicles (prostate-seminal vesicle angle) is variable but is the same bilaterally. Similarly, the posterior space between the prostate and the seminal vesicle (or nipple) is symmetrical on both sides.[1]

INDICATIONS FOR SONOGRAPHY

Patients can be referred for endorectal prostate sonography for various reasons such as the following[3]:

- An abnormal digital rectal examination, as indicated by a palpable prostatic mass or a prostate with an asymmetrical size or shape.
- Biopsy guidance of sonographically detected abnormal areas.
- Clinical evidence of prostate cancer such as an elevated level of prostatic-specific antigen, an elevated level of prostatic acid phosphatase, or radiographically detected bone metastasis.
- Monitoring of a patient's response to therapy.
- Inflammation leading to the formation of a prostatic abscess.
- Infertility caused by the absence of the seminal vesicles or a bilateral obstruction of the ejaculatory ducts.
- Difficulties in voiding caused by an obstruction of the prostatic urethra.

EQUIPMENT AND EXAMINATION TECHNIQUES

Technical innovations have led to the availability of several types of endorectal imaging systems. The original systems were radial (axial) scanners that produced transverse-oriented slices of the prostate. Later, linear array scanners that imaged the gland in longitudinal sections were introduced. Today, biplanar endorectal probes that can produce both longitudinal and transverse sections of the gland are available, thus eliminating the need for two separate probes. The frequency of endorectal probes ranges from 5.0 to 7.5 MHz. A guide that is attached directly to the probe allows one to biopsy suspicious prostatic lesions safely and accurately.

Preparation of the patient for endorectal sonography begins with a self-administered enema 1 hour before the examination.[1] This enema not only eliminates fecal material from the rectum that might adversely affect the quality of the image but also reduces the risk of contamination of the prostate. The probe is sterilized and covered with a condom, and nonaerated water is placed in the system through an extension tube and an orifice on the probe.

The water and all residual air are then removed. The tip of the probe is lubricated, then inserted into the rectum. The nonaerated water can then be placed back into the system through the orifice on the probe. Because the distended cover on the probe increases the distance between the prostate and the transducer, the result is better imaging of the gland.

The patient can be examined in the lateral decubitus, lithotomy, or knee-chest position. Before the probe is inserted, a digital rectal examination is performed to exclude any obstructing lesions or rectal fissures. Axial scanning begins at the level of the seminal vesicles. The probe is then gradually withdrawn to image the gland sequentially down to the level of the apex. Sagittal imaging begins in the midline and shows the gland from base to apex with portions of the seminal vesicles. The probe is then rotated clockwise and counterclockwise to demonstrate the right and left sides of the gland.

PATHOLOGY

Prostatic Carcinoma

Prostatic carcinoma is the second leading cause of death among American men. In 1987 96,000 new cases were diagnosed and 27,000 lives were lost to this disease.[1] Although the etiology of prostatic cancer remains unclear, the factors implicated in its causation include age, genetic or racial makeup, hormonal influences, effects of benign prostatic hyperplasia, carcinogens in the environment and infectious agents. Anatomic studies have determined that 70% of prostate cancers originate de novo in the peripheral zone, 20% originate in the transitional zone, and 10% originate in the central zone.[1] Clinical symptoms include back pain and an obstruction of urinary outflow that may mimic benign prostatic hypertrophy.

The sonographic characteristics of prostatic carcinoma are variable. However, small cancers originating in the peripheral zone are anechoic to hypoechoic. As the tumor enlarges and extends into the central glandular region, it becomes more isoechoic to hyperechoic. The tumor also may spread outward beyond the prostatic capsule and disrupt this normally well-defined echogenic structure.[4] Several entities, however, may have ultrasound characteristics that are similar to those of intraprostatic malignancy. These include hyperplastic nodules, infarcts, focal inflammation, cystic atrophy, blood vessels, and muscle tissue.[5] Invasion of the tumor into the seminal vesicles can be seen as solid material within this normally fluid-filled structure. Invasion may make the size, shape, and echogenicity of the seminal vesicles asymmetrical in appearance.

Obliteration of the nipple or the prostate- seminal vesicle angle is another diagnostic criteria for invasion by the tumor.[1] However, because the nipple is not imaged consistently, this criterion is of limited usefulness. Staging of prostatic cancer with ultrasound also is feasible.

Benign Prostatic Hyperplasia and Hypertrophy

Benign prostatic hyperplasia affects 80–90% of adult men.[1] Its etiology is believed to be related to hormonal factors. The clinical symptoms of the disease may include decreased flow of urine, difficulty in initiating and terminating urination, nocturia, and urinary retention. Benign prostatic hyperplasia originates in the transitional zone and in periurethral glandular tissue.

The sonographic characteristics of hyperplasia nodules are variable. They can be hypoechoic, hyperechoic, or of mixed echogenicity. Enlargement of the central gland by benign prostatic hyperplasia causes lateral displacement of the peripheral zone. The prostatic calculi that are often encountered with benign prostatic hyperplasia are believed to be the result of stasis of prostatic secretions.

Benign prostatic hyperplasia causes the number of cells in the prostate to increase, whereas benign prostatic hypertrophy refers to an increase in the size of existing cells. Hyperplasia and hypertrophy often develop concurrently and result in the enlargement of the prostate gland.

Prostatitis

Inflammation of the prostate can be the result of acute or chronic bacterial infections or of unknown nonbacterial factors. Clinical symptoms of prostatitis may include fever, pelvic and low back pain, urinary frequency and urgency, and dysuria. Although prostatitis usually involves the peripheral zone in its initial stages, it can originate in any area of the gland.

In acute prostatitis, the main sonographic characteristics are (1) a hypoechoic rim surrounding the gland, (2) an echo-free halo surrounding the periurethral zone, and (3) diffuse low-level echogenic areas within the gland. In chronic prostatitis, diffuse inhomogeneous echogenicity and fluid-filled areas within the prostate is demonstrated, although this is a nonspecific finding.[1] Calculi also may be present.

A prostatic abscess may develop secondary to prostatitis. Endorectal sonography may show hypoechoic areas corresponding to liquefaction within the abscess.

Prostatic Cysts

Prostatic cysts are frequently congenital.[1] Sonographically, these cysts are anechoic, have sharp walls, and demonstrate good sound transmission.

REFERENCES

1. Rifkin M. *Ultrasound of the Prostate*. New York: Raven Press, 1988.
2. Lee F, Torp-Pedersen, ST, Siders DB, et al. Transrectal ultrasound in the diagnosis and staging of prostatic carcinoma. *Radiology* **170**:609, 1989.

3. Rifkin M. Prostate cancer ultrasound: Screening tool or hype? *Diagn Imaging*: 302–305, November 1988.
4. Lee F, Littrup PJ, Kumasaka GH, et al. The use of transrectal ultrasound in diagnosis, guided biopsy, staging and screening of prostate cancer. *Radiographics* **7**:627, 1987.
5. Waterhouse RL, Resnick MI. The use of transrectal prostatic ultrasonography in the evaluation of patients with prostatic carcinoma. *J Urol* **141**:233, 1989.

Questions

GENERAL INSTRUCTIONS: For each question, select the best answer. Select only one answer for each question, unless otherwise specified.

1. The fibromuscular stroma
   (A) covers the anterior surface of the prostate
   (B) is the major site of benign prostatic hypertrophy
   (C) is a nonglandular region
   (D) A and C

2. Which is *not* an indication for endorectal prostate sonography?
   (A) a palpable prostate mass
   (B) biopsy guidance of a palpable prostate nodule
   (C) an elevated prostatic-specific antigen
   (D) differentiation of a benign from a malignant nodule

3. Patients having endorectal prostate sonography are commonly examined in which of the following positions?
   (A) the lithotomy position
   (B) the erect position
   (C) the Trendelenburg position
   (D) Fowler's position

4. The transitional zone
   (A) is located centrally around the proximal urethra
   (B) represents about 5% of the gland
   (C) is the primary site of benign prostatic hyperplasia
   (D) is all of the above

5. Which one of the following statements is false?
   (A) the central zone constitutes approximately 25% of the glandular tissue
   (B) the central zone is located at the apex of the prostate
   (C) the vas deferens join the seminal vesicles in the central zone
   (D) none of the above

6. The peripheral zone accounts for which percentage of the prostatic glandular tissue?
   (A) 50%
   (B) 10%
   (C) 70%
   (D) 1%

7. Which of the following statements about the prostate is false?
   (A) its apex is located superiorly
   (B) its base abuts the urinary bladder
   (C) it has three zones
   (D) the urethra runs through the gland

8. Which of the following is a function of the prostate?
   (A) hormonal secretions
   (B) testosterone production
   (C) secretion of alkaline fluid
   (D) all of the above

9. The prostate is bounded anteriorly by
   (A) the obturator muscle
   (B) the levator ani muscle
   (C) fat and fascia
   (D) the obturator and levator ani muscles

10. The seminal vesicles join which of the following to form the ejaculatory duct?
   (A) the Denonvilliers' duct
   (B) the vas deferens
   (C) the verumontanum
   (D) the urethra

11. The ejaculatory duct joins the ______ at the verumontanum.
   (A) vas deferens
   (B) efferent ducts
   (C) epididymis
   (D) urethra

12. The seminal vesicles are located on which surface of the prostate?

(A) the anterior-inferior surface
(B) the posterior-inferior surface
(C) the posterior-superior surface
(D) none of the above

13. Which of the following statements about prostatic cancer is *not* true?

(A) it originates mainly in the central zone
(B) it is anechoic to hypoechoic in the early stage
(C) its associated factors include benign prostatic hyperplasia and hormonal influence
(D) all of the above are true

14. Benign prostatic hyperplasia

(A) involves the periurethral tissue
(B) affects 80–90% of adult men
(C) is sonographically variable
(D) involves all of the above

15. Sonographic features of acute prostatitis may include

(A) a hypoechoic "rim" around the prostate
(B) calcification in the peripheral zone
(C) diffuse low-level echoes within the gland
(D) A and C only

16. Benign prostatic hyperplasia appears to be caused by which of the following factors?

(A) nutritional factors
(B) hormonal factors
(C) unknown factors
(D) none of the above

17. Approximately what percentage of men are affected by benign prostatic hyperplasia?

(A) 20%
(B) 40%
(C) 50%
(D) 90%

18. Benign prostatic hyperplasia originates in which of the following areas of the prostate?

(A) the fibromuscular stroma
(B) the peripheral zone
(C) the ejaculatory ducts
(D) the transitional zone

19. Corpora amylacea are

(A) part of the anterior fibromuscular capsule
(B) calcified deposits in the prostate
(C) hypoechoic on endorectal ultrasound
(D) never seen on endorectal ultrasound

20. Tumor invasion may affect which of the following characteristics of the seminal vesicles?

(A) their size
(B) their shape
(C) their echogenicity
(D) all of the above

21. Obliteration of the nipple and the prostate-seminal vesicle angle may indicate

(A) prostatitis
(B) scarring of tissues
(C) tumor infiltration
(D) the need for a higher-frequency probe

22. Prostatic cysts

(A) occur secondary to obstruction
(B) can be congenital
(C) are anechoic with good enhancement
(D) all of the above

23. Clinical symptoms of prostatitis may include

(A) fever
(B) dysuria
(C) perineal pain
(D) all of the above

24. In its initial stages, prostatitis generally involves the

(A) peripheral zone of the prostate
(B) anterior capsule of the prostate
(C) ejaculatory duct
(D) none of the above

25. Which of the following can mimic intraprostatic cancer?

(A) focal inflammation
(B) blood vessels
(C) muscle tissue
(D) all of the above

26. Sonographic characteristics of prostatic cancer include

(A) a hypoechoic nodule in the peripheral zone
(B) distortion of the capsule
(C) obliteration of the "nipple"
(D) all of the above

27. The earliest prostate probes were

(A) biplanar
(B) radial scanners
(C) linear array scanners
(D) none of the above

28. An endorectal examination of the prostate should begin with

(A) transverse scanning
(B) longitudinal scanning
(C) views of the seminal vesicles
(D) a digital rectal examination

29. Prostate cancer is

(A) echogenic
(B) anechoic
(C) hypoechoic
(D) sonographically variable

30. The verumontanum is

(A) a midpoint region between the base and apex of the prostate
(B) a congenital abnormality of the prostate
(C) part of the peripheral zone
(D) none of the above

31. An echo-free "halo" around the periurethral zone may indicate

(A) tumor invasion
(B) benign prostatic hyperplasia
(C) prostatitis
(D) none of the above

32. An elevated prostatic-specific antigen may indicate

(A) prostatic inflammation
(B) prostatic cancer
(C) benign prostatic hyperplasia
(D) obstruction of the prostatic ducts

33. Which of the following narrows to an apex at the verumontanum?

(A) the central zone
(B) the peripheral zone
(C) the transitional zone
(D) the fibromuscular stroma

34. The normal adult prostate weighs approximately

(A) 10 g
(B) 20 g
(C) 30 g
(D) 40 g

35. Denonvilliers' fascia

(A) is located posterior to the prostate
(B) separates the prostate from the rectum
(C) covers the entire prostate
(D) is located posterior to and separates the prostate from the rectum

36. The normal adult prostate measures approximately

(A) 5 × 8 × 4 cm
(B) 8.3 × 3 × 6 cm
(C) 3.8 × 3 × 4 cm
(D) 5.8 × 4 × 5 cm

37. In 1987 the approximate number of new cases of prostate cancer diagnosed was

(A) 1000
(B) 10,000
(C) 100,000
(D) 200,000

38. Which statement about the seminal vesicles is incorrect?

(A) their absence does not usually affect fertility
(B) they are joined by the vas deferens
(C) they are normally less echoic than the prostate
(D) their size varies

39. Which of the following describes the normal prostate capsule?

(A) smooth and unbroken
(B) highly echogenic
(C) sharply defined
(D) all of the above

Questions 40 through 46: Identify the structures in Fig. 6–2A by matching them with the list of terms given in column B.

COLUMN A	COLUMN B
40. ______	(A) peripheral zone
41. ______	(B) central zone
42. ______	(C) seminal vesicles
43. ______	(D) transitional zone
44. ______	(E) ejaculatory duct
45. ______	(F) urethra
46. ______	(G) fibromuscular stroma

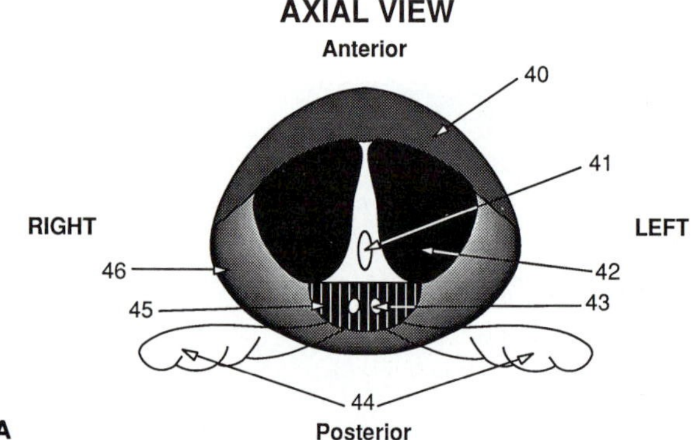

Figure 6–2A. An axial view of normal prostate anatomy. The numbers correspond to questions 40–46. *(Modified with permission from McNeal JE. Regional morphology and pathology of the prostate. Am J Clin Pathol 49:347–357, 1968 and Dakin R, et al. Transrectal ultrasound of the prostate: Technique and sonographic findings. JDMS 5(1):2, 1989.)*

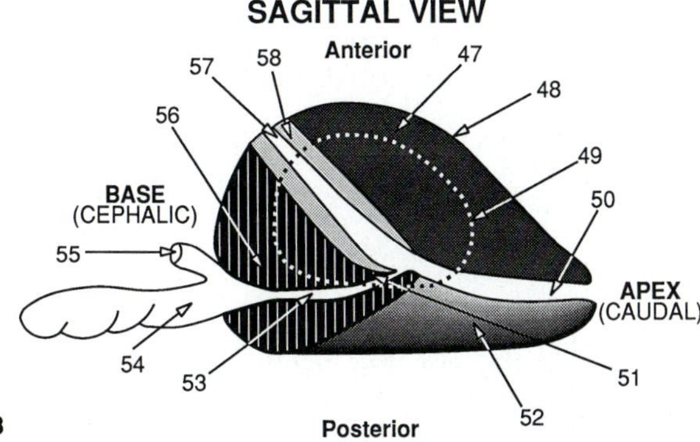

Figure 6–2B. A sagittal view of normal prostate anatomy. The numbers correspond to questions 47–58. *(Modified with permission from McNeal JE. Regional morphology and pathology of the prostate. Am J Clin Pathol 49:347–357, 1968 and Dakin R, et al. Transrectal ultrasound of the prostate: Technique and sonographic findings. JDMS 5(1):2, 1989.)*

Questions 47 through 58: Identify the structures in Fig. 6–2B by matching them with the list of terms given in column B.

COLUMN A	COLUMN B
47. _____	(A) proximal urethra
48. _____	(B) central zone
49. _____	(C) vas deferens
50. _____	(D) seminal vesicle
51. _____	(E) ejaculatory duct
52. _____	(F) peripheral zone
53. _____	(G) verumontanum
54. _____	(H) distal urethra
55. _____	(I) transitional zone
56. _____	(J) prostatic capsule
57. _____	(K) fibromuscular stroma
58. _____	(L) periurethral stroma

59. Fig. 6–3 represents a longitudinal scan taken to the right of midline. The structure indicated by the arrow is

(A) the proximal urethra
(B) a seminal vesicle
(C) the verumontanum
(D) none of the above

60. Fig. 6–4 represents a transverse scan. The structure indicated by the arrows is

(A) a tumor in the peripheral zone
(B) prostatitis involving the periurethral areas
(C) central gland calcification
(D) distortion of the prostatic capsule

61. Fig. 6–5 represents a longitudinal scan of a 60-year-old patient presenting with urinary frequency. He was referred for an endorectal prostate sonography examination. The area outlined by the markers indicates

(A) obliteration of the "prostate-seminal vesicle angle"
(B) a hypoechoic mass in the central zone
(C) a tumor in the peripheral zone
(D) bulging of the prostatic capsule

62. Fig. 6–6 represents a longitudinal scan. The region indicated by the white arrow is

(A) the fibromuscular stroma
(B) the seminal vesicle
(C) the peripheral zone
(D) the central zone

63. Fig. 6–6 represents a longitudinal scan. The region indicated by the black arrow is

(A) the peripheral zone
(B) the central zone
(C) the prostatic capsule
(D) none of the above

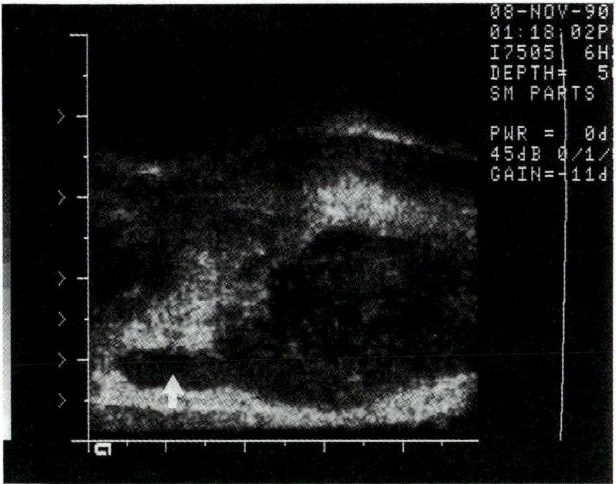

Figure 6–3. Longitudinal scan to the right of midline.

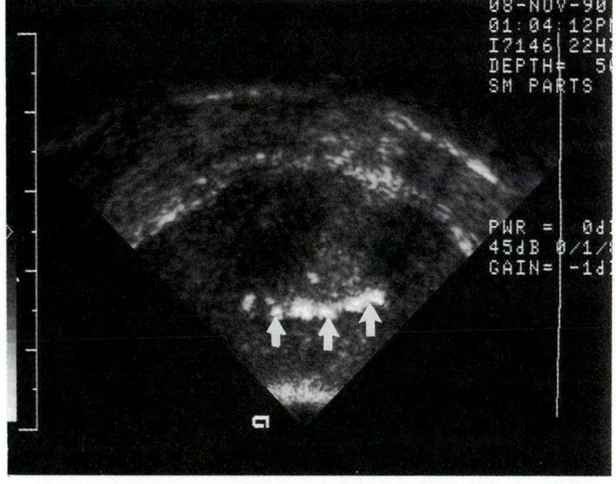

Figure 6–4. Transverse scan of the prostate.

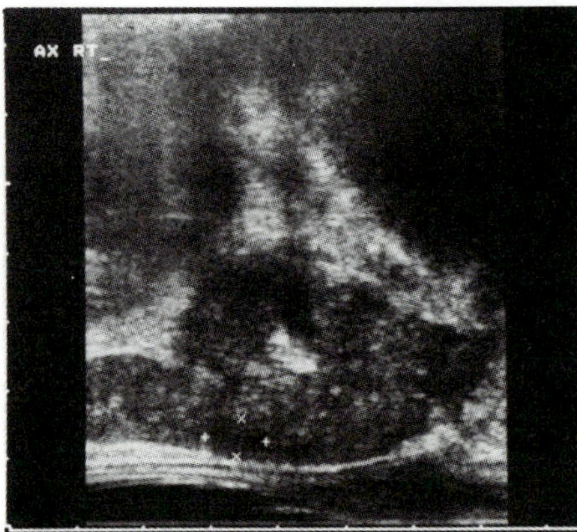

Figure 6–5. Longitudinal scan of the prostate.

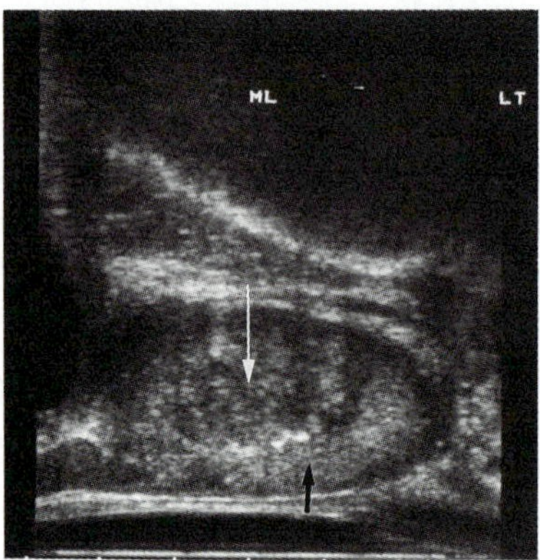

Figure 6–6. Longitudinal scan of the prostate.

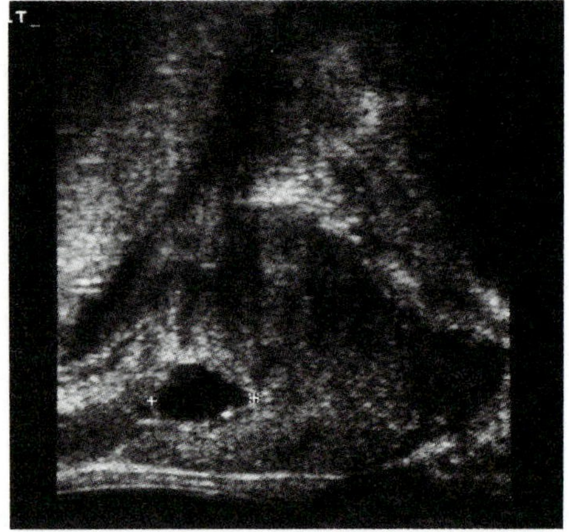
Figure 6–7. Longitudinal scan of the prostate.

64. Fig. 6–7 represents a longitudinal scan taken from a patient presenting with a history of infertility. The findings indicated by the markers probably represent

(A) benign prostatic hypertrophy
(B) a cyst in the ejaculatory duct
(C) extension of a tumor into the nipple region
(D) central gland disease

65. Fig. 6–8 represents a longitudinal scan of a 75-year-old man presenting with voiding difficulties and weight loss. This sonographic finding most likely represents

(A) diffuse cancer
(B) cancer confined to the peripheral zone
(C) benign prostatic hypertrophy
(D) none of the above

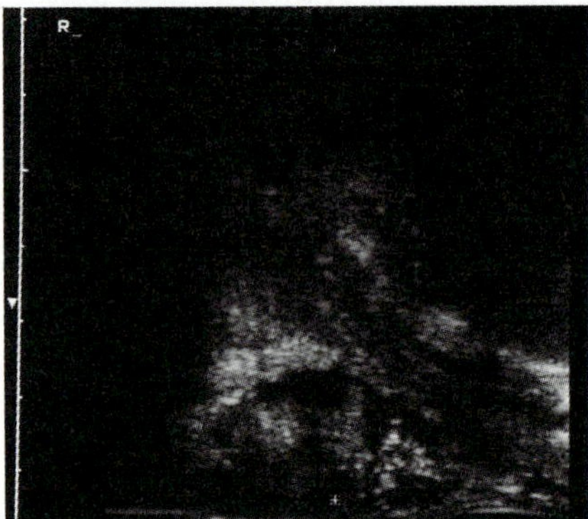

Figure 6–8. Longitudinal scan of the prostate.

Answers and Explanations

1. **(D)** Both A and C. The fibromuscular stroma is a nonglandular region that covers the anterior surface of the prostate. Therefore, both A and C are correct. *(2:612)*

2. **(D)** Differentiation of a benign from a malignant nodule. Ultrasound cannot make a specific diagnosis of prostatic diseases. Biopsy is required to establish the diagnosis. *(3:303)*

3. **(A)** The lithotomy position. Patients who are having endorectal prostate sonography can be examined in the left lateral decubitus, knee-chest, or lithotomy position. *(1:44)*

4. **(D)** Is all of the above. The transitional zone is located on both sides of the proximal urethra and represents 5% of the gland. It also is the primary site of benign prostatic hyperplasia. *(2:610)*

5. **(B)** The central zone is located at the apex of the prostate. The central zone is a triangular structure located at the base of the prostate with its apex at the verumontanum. *(7:89)*

6. **(C)** 70%. The peripheral zone constitutes more than two-thirds of prostatic glandular tissue. *(2:612)*

7. **(A)** Its apex is located superiorly. The apex of the prostate is located inferiorly. (see Fig. 6–1B in the study guide.)

8. **(C)** Secretion of alkaline fluid. The prostate discharges this fluid into the urethra to enhance the motility of sperm. *(6:2)*

9. **(C)** Fat and fascia. The prostate is bounded anteriorly by vessels, fat, lymphatics, nerves, and fascial tissues, collectively termed the anterior prostatic fat and fascia *(1:5)*

10. **(B)** The vas deferens. The seminal vesicles join the vas deferens to form the ejaculatory duct, which passes through the central zone. *(2:612)*

11. **(D)** Urethra. The ejaculatory duct empties into the urethra at the verumontanum *(2:612)*

12. **(C)** The posterior-superior surface. *(1:74)*

13. **(A)** It originates mainly in the central zone. Seventy percent of prostatic cancers originate de novo in the peripheral zone. *(1:146)*

14. **(D)** Involves all of the above. Benign prostatic hyperplasia occurs mostly in the transitional zone, and nodules occasionally develop in the periurethral glandular tissue. It affects 80–90% of men and is sonographically variable. *(1:191, 196)*

15. **(D)** A and C only. In acute prostatitis, the gland may be surrounded by a hypoechoic rim, have an echo-free halo around the periurethral zone, or have scattered low-level echoes within the gland. *(1:222, 7:218)*

16. **(B)** Hormonal factors. A variety of reasons are attributed to the formation of benign prostatic hyperplasia. A hormonal factor is one possible explanation. *(1:191)*

17. **(D)** 90%. It is estimated that 80–90% of adult men will be affected by benign prostatic hyperplasia. *(1:192)*

18. **(D)** The transitional zone. (See the explanation for the answer to Question 14).

19. **(B)** Calcified deposits in the prostate. Degenerated epithelial cells of the prostate are shed and become suspended in albuminous fluid. This mass of cells is called corpora amylacea. Calculi are formed by the consolidation of corpora amylacea. *(7:137)*

20. **(D)** All of the above. The diagnostic criteria for neoplasms invading the seminal vesicles include asymmetry in the size, shape, and echogenicity of the vesicles. *(1:239)*

21. **(C)** Tumor infiltration. The tumor will obliterate the "nipple" and "prostate-seminal vesicle angle." *(1:179)*

22. **(D)** All of the above. Prostatic cysts are frequently congenital and secondary to obstruction of the seminal vesicle and ejaculatory duct. The differential diagnosis includes a cyst in the wolffian duct or the vestigial müllerian duct and diverticula of the ejaculatory duct. *(1:235)*

23. **(D)** All of the above. The major symptoms of acute bacterial prostatitis include a high fever, chills, dysuria, perineal pain, and urinary frequency and urgency. *(6:5)*

24. **(A)** Peripheral zone of the prostate. Although prostatitis can originate in any area of the prostate, it initially presents in the peripheral zone. *(1:14)*

25. **(D)** All of the above. Hyperplastic nodules, cysts, infarcts, inflammation, blood vessels, and muscle tissue can simulate intraprostatic cancer. *(4:236)*

26. **(D)** All of the above. Early prostatic cancers can present an anechoic or hypoechoic lesions in the peripheral zone. They can break through the prostatic capsule causing distortion, or they can invade the seminal vesicles. *(1:161, 179)*

27. **(B)** Radial scanners. The earliest endorectal probes were radial scanners that required a specially designed chair. *(1:35)*

28. **(D)** A digital rectal examination. This examination should be done before the probe is inserted to exclude obstructing lesions, rectal fissures, or other pathology. *(1:43)*

29. **(D)** Sonographically variable. Prostate cancer first appears as anechoic-hypoechoic. It becomes isoechoic-hyperechoic as it spreads to the central gland. *(5:629)*

30. **(A)** A midpoint region between the base and apex of the prostate. (See Fig. 6–1B in the Study Guide.)

31. **(C)** Prostatitis. (See the explanation for the answer to Question 15.)

32. **(B)** Prostatic cancer. An elevated prostatic-specific antigen or an elevated level of prostatic acid phosphatase may indicate prostate cancer. *(3:304)*

33. **(A)** The central zone. (See Fig. 6–1B in the Study Guide.)

34. **(B)** 20 g. The normal postpubescent prostate weighs approximately that amount. *(1:5)*

35. **(D)** Is located posterior to and separates the prostate from the rectum. Denonvilliers' fascia separates the prostate from the rectum posteriorly. *(1:5)*

36. **(C)** 3.8 × 3 × 4 cm. This is the average normal size of the prostate. *(1:5)*

37. **(C)** 100,000. In 1987 96,000 new cases of prostate cancer were diagnosed and 27,000 deaths resulted from this disease. *(1:141)*

38. **(A)** Their absence does not usually affect fertility. In rare cases, infertility can be caused by absence of the seminal vesicles or by an obstruction in the bilateral ejaculatory duct. *(3:304)*

39. **(D)** All of the above. The normal prostatic capsule is smooth, well defined, and highly echogenic. *(4:234)*

40. **(G)** Fibromuscular stroma
41. **(F)** Urethra
42. **(D)** Transitional zone
43. **(E)** Ejaculatory duct
44. **(C)** Seminal vesicles
45. **(B)** Central zone
46. **(A)** Peripheral zone
47. **(K)** Fibromuscular stroma
48. **(J)** Prostatic capsule
49. **(I)** Transitional zone
50. **(H)** Distal urethra
51. **(G)** Verumontanum
52. **(F)** Peripheral zone
53. **(E)** Ejaculatory duct
54. **(D)** Seminal vesicles
55. **(C)** Vas deferens
56. **(B)** Central zone
57. **(A)** Proximal urethra
58. **(L)** Periurethral stroma

59. **(B)** A seminal vesicle. The structure demonstrated in Fig. 6–3 is the right seminal vesicle, which joins the vas deferens (not shown) to form the ejaculatory duct. (See Fig. 6–1B in the Study Guide.)

60. **(C)** Central gland calcification. Figure 6–4 shows bright echoes representing prostatic calcification, which can be solitary or can occur in clusters. *(7:139)*

61. **(C)** A tumor in the peripheral zone. The hypoechoic mass seen on the peripheral zone in Fig. 6–5 is characteristic of prostatic cancer. *(1:63)*

62. **(D)** The central zone. This zone (white arrow) in Fig. 6–6 is clearly demarcated from the peripheral zone (black arrow) by a curved band of echoes. *(7:42)*

63. **(A)** The peripheral zone. (See the explanation for the answer to Question 62.) *(7:42)*

64. **(B)** A cyst in the ejaculatory duct. The cystic structure shown in Fig. 6–7 is clearly located within the ejaculatory duct. *(1:231)*

65. **(A)** Diffuse cancer. Fig. 6–8 demonstrates diffuse hypoechoic masses throughout the prostate. This inhomogeneous pattern is consistent with diffuse malignancy. *(1:167)*

REFERENCES

1. Rifkin M. *Ultrasound of the prostate.* New York: Raven Press, 1988.
2. Lee F, Torp-Pedersen ST, Siders DB, et al. Transrectal ultrasound in the diagnosis and staging of prostatic carcinoma. *Radiology* **170**:609, 1989.
3. Rifkin M. Prostate cancer ultrasound: Screening Tool or hype? *Diagn Imaging* 302–305, November 1988.
4. Waterhouse RL, Resnick MI. The use of transrectal prostatic ultrasonography in the evaluation of patients with prostatic carcinoma. *J Urol* **141**:233, 1989.
5. Lee F, Littrup PJ, Kumasaka GH, et al. The use of transrectal ultrasound in diagnosis, guided biopsy, staging and screening of prostate cancer. *Radiographics* **7**:627, 1987.
6. Paulson D. Diseases of the prostate. *Clin Symposia* **41**(2):1989.
7. Resnick, M. *Prostatic Ultrasonography.* Philadelphia: BC Decker, 1990.

CHAPTER 7

TRANSVAGINAL SONOGRAPHY

Charles S. Odwin and Arthur C. Fleischer

Study Guide

INTRODUCTION

Transvaginal sonography involves the insertion of a specifically designed transducer into the vagina for imaging pelvic structures. Numerous names have been applied to this type of scanning, which can be confusing to students. Therefore, we will attempt to clarify these nomenclatures in the hope that students will easily understand the proper usage of terms used in transvaginal sonography and apply them appropriately.

The term *transvaginal* is a combination of Latin terms (L. *trans* through + *vagina* sheath), whereas the term *endovaginal* combines a Greek and a Latin term (Gr. *endon* within + L. *vagina* sheath). The terms *transvaginal* and *endovaginal* are both descriptive of the technical approach to scanning and are not specific for imaging of the vagina. In fact, only a small area of the vagina is imaged; the images are predominantly of the uterus and its adnexa.

The terms *endosonography* and *endocavity sonography* are general terms used to describe any introduction of the transducer into the body cavity: the vagina, rectum, or esophagus. Any introduction of a medical instrument into a body cavity is classified as an invasive procedure, unlike the term *transabdominal sonography,* in which the transducer is placed on the skin surface.

PHYSICAL CONCEPTS

The use of high-frequency transducers within the vaginal canal to image the uterus and its adnexa (ovaries, fallopian tubes, and ligaments) is founded on the basic concept of ultrasound physics. Placing the transducer in close proximity to the pelvic organs or structures allows the use of higher frequencies, which in turn provides better resolution, both axial and lateral. The resolution is not lost even in the presence of magnification resulting from a short focal zone.[1] The close proximity of the transducer also results in reduced attenuation and better focusing. Thus, transvaginal sonography allows earlier and more definitive diagnoses than are possible with conventional transabdominal techniques.[4]

Applications. The applications of transvaginal sonography include

- diagnosing ectopic pregnancies
- monitoring the follicles of an infertile patient who is undergoing ovulation induction
- guiding the placement of the needle during follicular aspiration or aspiration of fluid from the cul-de-sac
- evaluating the fallopian tubes
- evaluating blood flow to the gestational sac and uterine arteries with Doppler imaging
- achieving additional diagnostic information in conjunction with transabdominal sonography
- evaluating the fetal intracranial anatomy and prolapse of the umbilical cord during the second and third trimester[2]
- detecting the presence of placenta previa[2]

Advantages. Transvaginal sonography has a variety of advantages. For example, because it offers high resolution (improved images), it allows earlier and more definitive diagnoses.[4] Unlike transabdominal sonography, the transvaginal procedure does not require a full bladder; thus, it eliminates patient discomfort. Because emergency patients can be evaluated quickly, the procedure allows faster medical management. Transvaginal sonography also has a high degree of acceptance—most patients prefer it to the transabdominal procedure. Finally, as was mentioned earlier, transvaginal sonography often provides valuable additional information when used in conjunction with transabdominal sonography.

Disadvantages. Transvaginal sonography also has several disadvantages. The limited field of view means that large masses may not be seen because they are beyond the focal

zone of the transducer. For the same reason, the sonographer may be unable to document the uterine size. Because of the magnification in the near field, the sonographer may be unable to see both ovaries on the same image. The confined space of the vagina limits the mobility of the transducer.[1] Therefore, complete sequential and segmental images obtained with transabdominal sonography cannot be achieved with transvaginal sonography. In addition, only the presenting parts of the fetus and cervix can be seen in the second and third trimester pregnancy with the transvaginal approach.

Transducers. Transducers for transvaginal scanning have a specific size, shape, and frequency. Their diameter ranges from 12 mm to 16 mm; this smaller-than-usual diameter allows easy penetration within the vaginal lumen without causing the patient any discomfort. In addition, these transducers are twice as long as most transabdominal transducers. Because the normal length of the vaginal lumen is approximately 7.5 cm to 9.5 cm, the transvaginal transducer must be longer than usual so that part of it can be inserted and the other part can serve as a handle for the operator. The normal range of frequencies used in transvaginal sonography is 5–7.5 MHz, with a sector field of view of 90° to 115°. The larger the sector field of view, the larger the portion of the organ or structure that can be visualized.

Color Doppler. Transvaginal color Doppler is a combination of B-mode image, pulsed-wave Doppler, and a color flow display (triplex imaging).[5] The direction of blood flow is indicated by assigning color to the Doppler-shifted echoes superimposed on the gray-scale image. As was discussed in an earlier chapter, the direction of flow toward and away from the transducer is presented in different colors on the image. For example, red represents flow toward the transducer, blue represents flow away from the transducer, and a mixture of colors represents turbulent flow.

Color Doppler has two advantages. First, because a network of blood vessels occasionally can mimic follicles, color Doppler allows rapid differentiation between vascular structures and follicles. Second, it allows precise placement of the sample volume for Doppler waveform analysis.

PRECAUTIONARY MEASURES

The microorganisms that cause sexually transmitted disease, including the human immunodeficiency virus (HIV), are sometimes present in vaginal secretions. Although these microorganisms are usually transmitted through sexual contact with an infected partner, they can be transmitted by contaminated invasive medical instruments.[6,7]

Two methods are currently used to prevent transmission of infection with transvaginal transducers: (1) disinfection or sterilization of the transducer after each examination and (2) the use of disposable probe covers (condoms, rubber gloves, and sheaths). Both are required to prevent cross-infection from the transducer because, although the probe is covered, even a microscopic tear in the cover will expose the transducer to the vaginal membrane and the external cervical os. For the same reason, all vaginal transducers should be disinfected before they are returned to the manufacturer or technical support staff for maintenance or repair.

Disinfection or Sterilization

The first step in preparing the transvaginal transducer for an examination is disinfection or sterilization. Disinfecting agents destroy all disease-causing organisms except spores, whereas sterilizing agents, the most complete type of disinfectants, destroy all forms of microbial life—bacteria, viruses, fungi, and spores.[8]

Several methods of sterilization are available: autoclaves (steam or gas), ethylene oxide (cold gas), and chemical glutaraldehydes. The piezoelectric ceramic material of the transducer is heat sensitive. Therefore, steam autoclaves should not be used because excessive heat may depolarize the crystal in the transducer housing, thus eliminating its piezoelectric properties.

The cold-gas ethylene oxide method of sterilization, formerly used with ultrasound transducers, also is undesirable because it can take as long as 12 hours and is toxic to tissues.[9] Furthermore, a technique used to detoxify the transducer after sterilization typically requires an additional 8 hours.[9] The fact that the entire process of sterilization and detoxification with ethylene oxide takes at least 20 hours makes it an impractical procedure in a busy ultrasound department.

The use of chemical sterilizing solutions (eg, Cidex™, MetriCide™, Wavicide™, Cybact™) is the most practical method of sterilization. These high-level bactericidal, fungicidal, and virucidal agents are now used routinely to clean medical and surgical instruments (Table 7–1).[10] Some of them have gained significant acceptance for sterilizing transvaginal transducers because they can inactivate HIV-1 in just 60 seconds. These agents are available in the form of sprays, towelettes, and soak solutions. Some transducer manufacturers caution against immersing the transvaginal transducer in sterilizing solutions because these solutions could break the seal; the sprays and towelettes have gained considerable acceptance. The fact that transducers can now be disinfected in 10 minutes has resulted in increased productivity because they can be used more often.

Various less expensive chemicals also can inactivate HIV. For example, diluted household bleach (sodium hypochlorite) can inactivate HIV-1 in 1 minute and is recommended by the Centers for Disease Control. However, although all transvaginal transducers are composed of plastic, crystals, bonding material, and steel or some other metal, they are not necessarily constructed alike. Thus, a disinfecting or sterilizing agent may be safe for some transducers and be destructive to others (Table 7–2). For instance, bleach can destroy the bonding material and plastic of some transducer housings. Because this can

TABLE 7–1. HIGH-LEVEL DISINFECTANTS

Manufacturer	Brand Name	Microorganisms Affected
Wave Energy Systems	Wavicide™-01*	Herpes 1 and 2, HIV-1, cytomegalovirus, hepatitis B, *Candida albicans, Escherichia coli, Staphylococcus aureus, Streptococcus salivarius, Salmonella typhosa.*
Central Solutions	Pheno-Cen™ disinfectant spray*	*Salmonella choleraesuis, Trichophyton mentagrophytes, Staphylococcus aureus, Pseudomonas aeruginosa* HIV-1
Surgikos	Cidex Plus™ disinfectant solution* Cidex™ disinfectant solution*	Herpes 1 and 2, HIV-1, cytomegalovirus, adenovirus type 2, poliovirus type 1, rhinovirus, coxsackievirus B1, *B. subtilis, C. sporogenes*
Metrex Research Corp.	MetriCide™ 28 disinfectant solution* MetriCide™ disinfectant solution*	Herpes 1 and 2, HIV-1, cytomegalovirus, rhinovirus vaccinia, adenovirus, *T. mentagrophytes, Mycobacterium bovis, S. aureus, S. Choleraesuis*

*Registered with the Environmental Protection Agency as an inactivator of HIV-1 (AIDS virus).

Reprinted with permission, Odwin C, Fleischer A, Kepple DM, et al. Probe covers and disinfectants for transvaginal transducers. J. Diagn Med Sonogr 6:130–135, 1990.

cause the transducer to fail, bleach is not recommended by most transducer manufacturers. In other words, sonographers should not attempt to sterilize a transducer until they have carefully reviewed the manufacturer's instruction manual and have consulted with technical support staff regarding any changes that may have occurred since the manual was published.

While the transducer is being sterilized, the system should be turned off and the transducer should be disconnected from it to avoid an electric shock. The transducer scanning head (excluding the handle and cable connector) should then be placed in the sterilizing solution for 10 to 20 minutes, depending on the temperature of the solution and the product used. Immediately after sterilization, the transducer should be dried with a soft sterile cloth. Fig. 7–1 shows the method of immersing the ATL (Advanced Technology Laboratories, Bothell, Washington) transvaginal transducer for sterilization. This method of immersion is specific for the ATL; other manufacturers may use different methods and sterilizing agents.

Transvaginal Probe Covers

Probe covers are specially designed sheaths for covering the transducers; they are available in different sizes in order to fit all types of transducers. These covers are made up of a variety of material; latex, polyethylene, and polyurethane and are approved by the U.S. Food and Drug Administration (FDA). Probe covers are also available in sterile or nonsterile packs and are accessible from vendors (Table 7–3). Condoms are Class II medical devices approved for sexual use to prevent pregnancy and sexually transmitted diseases, including HIV. Although obviously

TABLE 7–2. MANUFACTURERS' RECOMMENDATIONS FOR DISINFECTION OR STERILIZATION OF TRANSVAGINAL TRANSDUCERS

Manufacturer	Products	Precautionary Measures
Acuson	Cidex™, MetriCide™, ProClide™	Do not sterilize with ultraviolet light. Do not sterilize with gas or dry heat. Do not autoclave. Do not use chlorine bleach. Do not use iodine compounds to clean or wipe
Diasonics	Cidex™	Use bleach only in an emergency situation as bleach could damage the steel jacket.
Advanced Technology Laboratories (ATL)	Cidex™, Wavicide™	Immerse transducer tip only; do not immerse handle. Do not gas or heat sterilize. Do not allow solution to enter strain relief joint or tracking adjustment slot.
Siemens	Chlorhexidinegluconat (Hibitance™) Cidex™, Gigasept™	Follow the manufacturer's directions. Never use phenol or other organic-based solvents. Never use heat (steam) or cold gas (ethylene oxide).
Toshiba	(Hibitance™), 0.5%, hypochlorous sodium 0.1%, glutaraldehyde 2% (Cidex™)	Dilute bleach (1 part bleach per 10 parts water). After disinfecting, rinse with sterile water.

*Using any of the products against the manufacturer's instructions or precautionary measures could void the transducer warranty.

From Odwin C, Fleischer A, Kepple DM, et al. Probe covers and disinfectants for transvaginal transducers. J Diagn Med Sonogr 6:130–135, 1990.

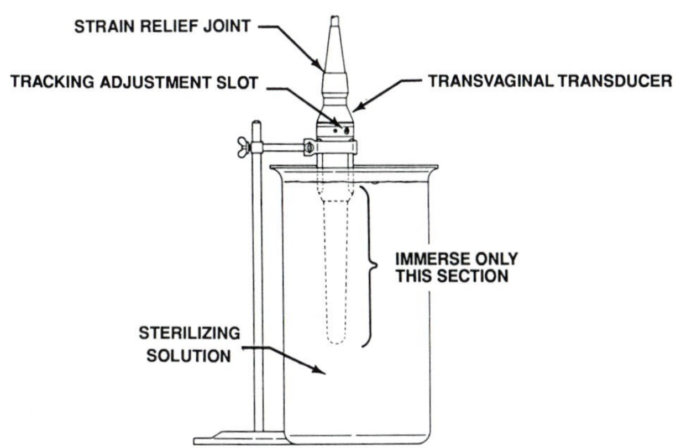

Figure 7–1. The ATL transvaginal transducer immersed in a solution. This method of sterilization is specific for the ATL; other manufacturers may use different methods and solutions. *(Reprinted with permission from Advanced Technology Laboratories (ATL).)*

not designed for use as a probe cover, they are sometimes used for this purpose because they are immediately available and moderately priced.

Three types of over-the-counter condoms are available: latex (rubber), natural lamb (made from the cecum of the lamb intestine), and artificial (synthetic) skin. The latex dry condom with a plain end is the most suitable and frequently used condom for transducer probes. Under an electron microscope, the surface of latex condoms demonstrate no pores. This intact barrier prevents the transmission of all bacteria and viruses.[11] (Only latex condoms have been approved by the FDA for the prevention of HIV).

Electron microscopy reveals that natural lamb condoms have occasional pores that are small enough to prevent transmission of sperm and some bacteria but are more than 10 times the size of HIV and more than 25 times the size of the hepatitis B virus.[11] Therefore, although natural lamb condoms are much stronger than latex condoms, the FDA does not recommend them for the prevention of HIV or hepatitis B infections.[11,12]

Because a loose-fitting condom on a transducer increases the chances that it will slip off during scanning, the sonographer must be familiar with the size of the transvaginal probe. Although all condoms have a rim on their proximal end, most will need additional support, such as a small rubber band or an orthodontal band, to secure them to the transducer shaft.

Over-the-counter condoms have a shelf life of 5 years and a 4% failure rate caused by tearing. The failure rate may be higher when they are used as probe covers in transvaginal sonography and even higher if an inappropriate lubricant is used. Oil-based lubricants such as petroleum jelly, cold cream, baby oil, and mineral oil should be avoided because they tend to cause latex condoms to deteriorate. Water-soluble products such as K-Y jelly,™, Surgilube™, and aqueous gels are appropriate lubricants. (Because some aqueous gels can affect the mobility or mortality of sperm, they should not be used when examining a patient who is undergoing artificial insemination.) The lubricant is applied to the outside of the probe cover after the cover has been secured over the transducer probe.

A white powder (talc) that manufacturers apply to latex condoms during production to keep them from sticking together may contain an embryotoxic compound that will conflict with transvaginal egg retrieval or embryo transfer. (In addition, latex may cause vaginal irritation if a patient is allergic to it.) Talc-coated latex condoms or transducer sheaths can be used for nontraumatic transvaginal scanning during pregnancy because the cervical os is normally closed and direct contact with the ovaries and the embryo does not occur. If talc must be avoided, the sonographer should not attempt to rinse it off with saline, which causes stickiness. The best method is to use a talc-free nonembryotoxic polyurethane probe cover (eg CIV-Flex™) (see Table 7–3).

All health care workers involved in invasive procedures that expose them to vaginal secretions or excretions

TABLE 7–3. DISPOSABLE PROBE COVERS FOR TRANSVAGINAL TRANSDUCERS

Manufacturer	Brand	Talc	Precautions
CIVCO Medical Instruments 418 B Avenue, Drawer Q Kalona, IA 52247	Latex*	Yes†	Can be damaged by heat or light; store in dark, cool, dry place. Do not lubricate with petroleum-based products.
	Polyethylene*	No	
	CIV-Flex (polyurethane)*	No	Nonembryotoxic.
	Enviro-Flex (polyethylene)*	No	
Schmid Laboratories Little Falls, NJ 07424	Latex condom (Ramses™)	Yes†	Avoid prolonged storage at temperatures above 100°F; do not lubricate with oil-based lubricants. Can be damaged by heat or light.
Carter-Wallace New York, NY 10153	Latex condom (Trojans™)	Yes†	Avoid prolonged storage at temperatures above 100°F; do not lubricate with oil-based lubricants. Can be damaged by heat or light.

*Approved by the Food and Drug Administration for transducers.
†Minimal amount.

should wear latex gloves when doing a procedure or cleaning instruments. The probe cover and gloves should be treated as potentially infectious waste and be disposed of accordingly immediately after the transvaginal examination.

POSITION OF THE PATIENT AND THE EXAMINATION TABLE

During the transvaginal examination, the patient is placed in the lithotomy position for insertion of the transducer and for scanning. The probe can be inserted by the patient, the physician, or the sonographer. When the insertion is done by the patient, the physician or sonographer holds the transducer cable so that the patient cannot accidentally drop the device.

The ideal table is a gynecologic examination table that allows numerous pelvic tilt positions and has stirrups for the patient's heels. The table is placed in a slight Fowler's position (also called the reversed Trendelenburg position) (Fig. 7–2). Elevation of the thighs allows the transducer to be moved freely from side to side (the horizontal plane).[7] The gynecologic examination table allows free upward and downward movement of the transducer (the vertical plane) and the slight Fowler's position of the table allows pooling of the small amount of peritoneal fluid normally found to pool in the region of the cul-de-sac which allows better delineation of pelvic structures. (The Trendelenburg position should not be used because it drains away this fluid.) If a gynecologic examination table is unavailable, a flat examination table can be prepared by placing a cushion that is 15–20 cm thick under the patient's pelvis.[7]

SCANNING TECHNIQUES

Three transducer maneuvers are commonly used in transvaginal sonography: (1) in and out, (2) rotating, and (3) angling, or up and down and side to side (Fig. 7–3). All of these maneuvers are limited by the size of the vaginal lumen. Fig. 7–3A illustrates the in-and-out motion of the transducer used to achieve variation in the depth of the imaging from cervix to fundus. Imaging of the cervix is optimized by gradually withdrawing the probe into the midvagina.[13] Fig. 7–3B illustrates the rotating motion of the transducer for obtaining various degrees of semiaxial to semicoronal planes. And Fig. 7–3C illustrates the angling motion of the transducer within the vaginal canal. With this angulation, one can obtain images of the anterior and posterior cul-de-sac, and with side to side movements can obtain images of the adnexa.

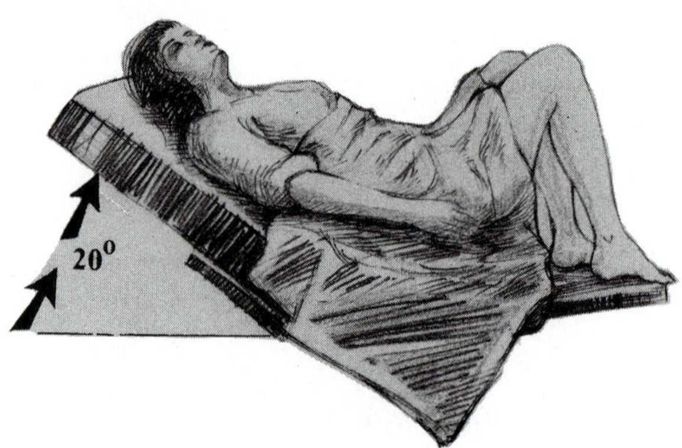

Figure 7–2. Examination table in a slight Fowler's position with a 20° elevation. The patient is in the lithotomy position.

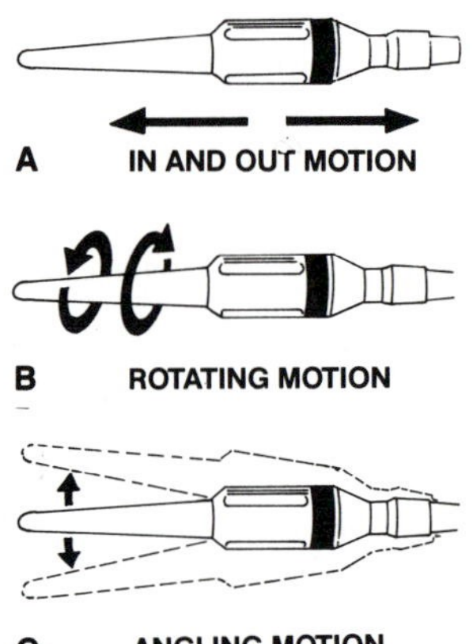

Figure 7–3. Scanning techniques: (**A**) in and out; (**B**) rotating motion; (**C**) angling motion. (*With permission from Advanced Technology Laboratories, Bothell, Washington.*)

Ovaries. The ovaries are normally situated anterior and medial to the internal iliac (hypogastric) vessels and can be recognized by their ovoid shape, their texture (Fig. 7–4), and the presence of graafian follicles. They are recognized more often in patients in the reproductive age group than in the postmenopausal age group.

Unlike transabdominal sonography, which allows the

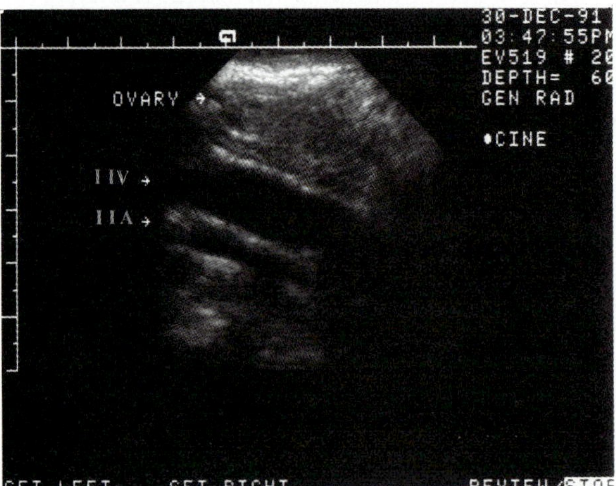

Figure 7–4. A demonstration of the ovary in close proximity to the internal iliac vein (IIV) and the internal iliac artery (IIA).

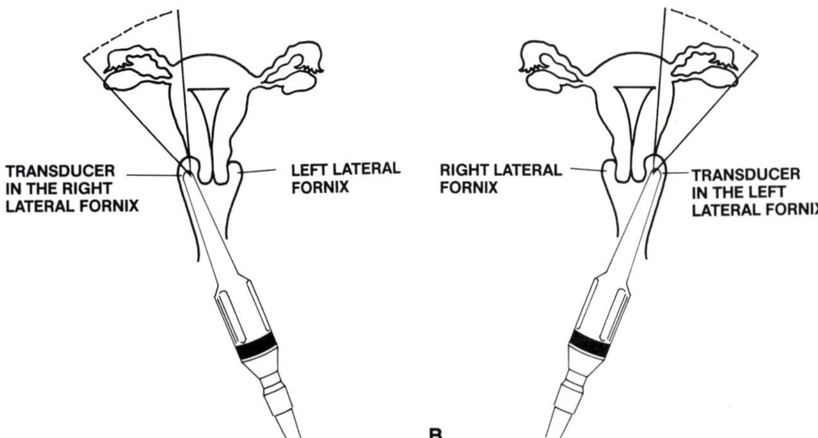

Figure 7–5 (**A**). A transvaginal transducer in the right lateral fornix; (B) a transvaginal transducer in the left lateral fornix. (*With permission from Advanced Technology Laboratories, Bothell, Washington.*)

simultaneous imaging of both ovaries relatively often, transvaginal sonography can best image only one ovary at a time. To image the right ovary, the sonographer moves the transducer handle toward the patient's left thigh so that the tip of the transducer probe is in the right lateral fornix (Fig. 7–5A). To image the left ovary, the sonographer moves the handle toward the patient's right thigh so that the tip of the probe is in the left lateral fornix (Fig. 7–5B). Although the ovaries can be depicted from almost any parauterine position, they are usually depicted either lateral to the uterus or in the cul-de-sac.

Uterus. Visualization of the texture and thickness of the uterine endometrium is greatly improved with transvaginal sonography. The appearance and thickness of the endometrium will vary, depending on the phase of the patient's menstrual cycle (Table 7–4).

Blood is supplied to the uterus from the uterine and ovarian arteries. The uterine artery gives rise to the arcuate arteries, which course within the outer myometrium (Fig. 7–6). Imaging of these vessels can be enhanced with triplex color vaginal sonography.

Because of the magnification and the relatively small field of view provided by transvaginal sonography, measurements that indicate the size of the uterus are obtained best with transabdominal sonography.

TABLE 7–4. ENDOMETRIAL THICKNESS

Menstrual Cycle	Measurements (mm)
Proliferative phase	4–8 mm in anteroposterior (including two layers)
Secretory phase	7–14 mm in anteroposterior (including two layers)
Postmenopausal	4–8 mm in anteroposterior (including two layers)
Postmenopausal hormone replacement therapy	6–10 mm in anteroposterior (including two layers)

Reprinted with permission from Fleischer A, Kepple D. Transvaginal Sonography: A Clinical Atlas. Philadelphia: JB Lippincott, 1992.

PREGNANCY

Pregnancy Test

A pregnancy test is a biochemical test of a woman's urine or serum to detect the presence of human chorionic gonadotropin (hCG). Although numerous tests are available, the radioimmune assay is specific for the beta subunit of hCG. Because of its specificity, reliability, and quantitative ability, this assay is the most acceptable one for ultrasonographic correlation. The values are reported in milli-international units per milliliter (mIU/mL), which can be reported in two different hCG levels[1]: International Reference Preparation (IRP) and Second International Standard (2nd IS). The level of hCG above which virtually all normal intrauterine pregnancy can be visualized with ultrasound is called a discriminatory zone. This zone will vary, depending on the type of transducer frequency and equipment used.[1] The level of serum beta hCG at which a 4 weeks' gestational sac can be depicted range from 420–800 mIU/mL (2nd IS) and 1,025–1,600 mIU/mL (IRP).[1,3]

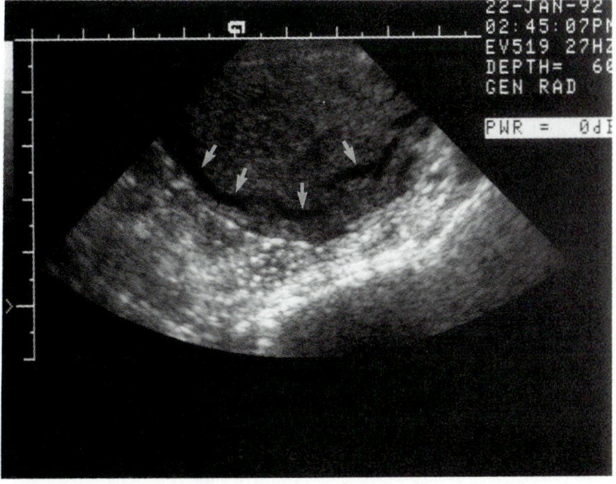

Figure 7–6. The small arrows point to the arcuate arteries in the outer myometrium.

Embryonic Period

The embryonic period extends from about the second week of gestation to the end of the 8th week, at which point the fetal period begins. Table 7–5 is a chronology of embryonic and fetal development from the 4th to the 14th week of gestation.

Gestation Sac. Documentation of intrauterine pregnancy can be made as early as 4 weeks with transvaginal sonography by the identification of a gestational sac within the uterus. The gestational sac has an anechoic center with a highly echogenic ring that represents the decidual reaction. The anechoic center of the gestational sac represents fluid within the sac. The sac size is about 5 mm when first depicted.[3] The gestational sac increases in size as pregnancy advances. By 5 weeks of gestation, the secondary yolk sac can be depicted within the gestational sac measuring about 3 mm in size.

Yolk Sac. The yolk sac lies in the chorionic cavity (the extraembryonic coelom) between the amnion and chorion. Its functions are to (1) form blood cells (hemopoiesis), (2) give rise to sex cells (sperm or egg), (3) supply nutrients from the trophoblast to the embryo during the second and third week while the uteroplacental circulation is being established, and (4) become incorporated into the embryo as the primitive gut.

Sonographically, the yolk sac can be depicted from the 5th to the 10th week of gestation. The sac is connected to the midgut by a narrow stalk called the yolk stalk, the vitelline duct, or the omphalomesenteric duct. This stalk (or pedicle) detaches from the midgut by the end of the 6th week, and the dorsal part of the yolk sac is incorporated into the embryo as the primitive gut.

As pregnancy advances, the yolk sac shrinks and becomes solid and its pedicle becomes relatively longer. The pedicle may prevail throughout the pregnancy and be recognized on the fetal surface of the placenta near the attachment of the umbilical cord; this situation is extremely rare and has no significance. In about 2% of adults, the proximal portion of the yolk stalk persists as a diverticulum of the ileum called Meckel's diverticulum.[9]

Lacunae. The lacunae appear at about 5 weeks on one side of the gestational sac in the choriodecidua and represent the beginning of uteroplacental circulation (intervillous spaces). They do not completely circle the sac; they appear at one end of it in a semicircle.[3] Sonographically, they appear as small round hypoechoic structures that measure about 2–3 mm. Transvaginal color Doppler can demonstrate blood flow in these spaces.

Yolk Sac–Embryo Complex. At approximately 6 weeks of gestation, the crown-rump length of the embryo measures 3–4 mm and abuts the yolk sac. The upper limb buds appear first, followed by the lower limb buds at 7 weeks.[3] The heart beat also can be seen at this time.[3] Also at about 6 weeks, a portion of the embryonic midgut temporarily protrudes into the umbilical cord. This physiologic herniation of the midgut (or gut migration) occurs because the liver and kidneys occupy most of the abdominal space. When the midgut is in the umbilical cord, it rotates 90° counterclockwise around the axis of the superior mesenteric artery. At the 8th week of gestation, the sonographic appearance of the physiologic herniation of the midgut is a hyperechoic bulging of the cord near the point where it enters the fetal abdomen.

Brain. The brain develops from three primary vesicles: the prosencephalon (forebrain), from which the cerebral hemispheres are derived; the mesencephalon (midbrain), which becomes the brain stem; and the rhombencephalon (hindbrain), which becomes the cerebellum, the medulla oblongata, and the pons. During the 5th week of embryonic development the prosencephalon divides into the telencephalon (the paired cerebral vesicles) and the diencephalon (which connects the cerebral vesicles to the brain stem), and the rhombencephalon divides into the metencephalon (the cerebellum and the pons) and the myelencephalon (medulla oblongata). Although these brain vesicles seem to be cystic (see Fig. 7–7), their sonographic appearance is normal for the developing brain at 8 weeks of gestation and should not be confused with hydro-

TABLE 7–5. CHRONOLOGICAL CHART: TRANSVAGINAL OBSTETRICAL SONOGRAPHY

Length of Gestation	Observations
4 weeks	The gestational sac is first seen at this time. It measures 4–5 mm and is surrounded by decidua with an anechoic center. No embryo or yolk sac is depicted at this time.
5 weeks	The yolk sac is first seen and measures 3–4 mm. The lacunar structures can be seen on one side of the gestational sac, and blood flow from its spaces can be depicted with color Doppler.
6 weeks	The fetal pole can be seen measuring 2–4 mm and abutting the yolk sac (yolk sac/embryo complex). The heartbeats can be seen, and the crown-rump length can be measured.
7 weeks	The limb buds first appear, and the amnion membrane and chorionic cavity can be seen.[3]
8 weeks	Sonolucent brain vesicles and midgut herniation are seen.
9 weeks	The placenta and choroid plexus are seen.
10 weeks	The intraventricular heart septum is seen.
11 weeks	The umbilical cord is visible.
12 weeks	The extraembryonic coelom is obliterated, and the midgut herniation disappears.
13 weeks	The orbital structures are seen.
14 weeks	The four-chamber heart becomes visible.[3]

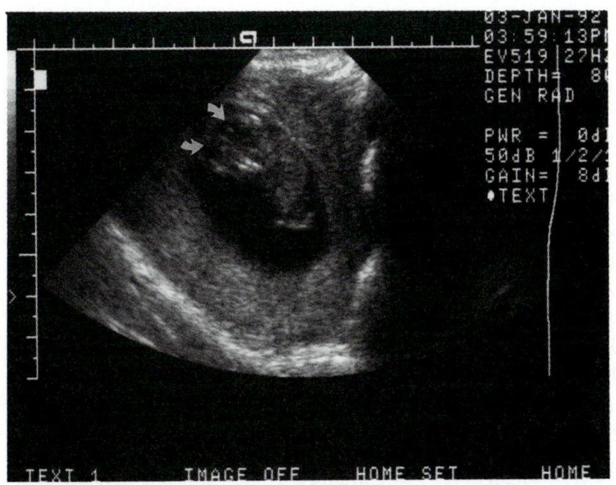

Figure 7–7. A transvaginal sonogram. The small arrows point to brain vesicles.

cephalus. The falx cerebri and choroid plexus are not sonographically evident at this time.

Fetal Period

The heart appears as a one-chambered structure until the 10th week; at 14 weeks, a view of the four-chambered heart can be obtained (Table 7–5). The midgut returns to the abdomen, where it undergoes a second rotation, which is 180° counterclockwise. Thus, the midgut undergoes a total rotation of 270°.[14] If the bowel fails to return to the abdomen during this second stage of rotation, an omphalocele may be the result. If development is normal, the herniation disappears completely after the 12th week and should not be confused with a defect of the abdominal wall.

REFERENCES

1. Goldstein SR. *Endovaginal Ultrasonography.* New York: Alan R Liss, 1988.
2. Rottem S. Scanning after the first trimester: Endovaginal ultrasound course. Syllabus. Spring Educational Meeting, Phoenix, AZ, by AIUM, April 9–10, 1989, pp. 33–35.
3. Timor-Tritsch IE, Rottem S. *Transvaginal Sonography,* 2nd ed. New York: Elsevier, 1991.
4. Sacks GA, Fleischer AC, Kepple DM, et al. Toshiba Medical Review: Clinical Applications of Transvaginal Sonography in Obstetrics and Gynecology. Toshiba Corp, Tokyo, No. 23, Feb 1988.
5. Kurjak A. *Transvaginal Color Doppler: A Comprehensive Guide to Transvaginal Color Doppler Sonography in OB/GYN.* Park Ridge, NJ: Parthenon, 1991.
6. Odwin C, Fleischer AC, Kepple DM, et al. Probe covers and disinfectants for transvaginal transducers. *J Diagn Med Sonography* **6**(3):130–135, 1990.
7. Axelrod D. *A Physician's Guide to Aids: Issue in the Medical Office.* Albany: New York State Department of Health, 1988.
8. Leach E. A new synergized glutaraldehyde-phenate sterilizing solution and concentrated disinfectant. *Infect Control* **2**:3–6, 1981.
9. Sigel B. *Operative Ultrasonography,* 2nd ed. New York: Raven Press, 1988.
10. Kennedy M. Evaluation of a glutaraldehyde-phenate solution used to disinfect endoscopes and instruments in a free-standing surgical facility. *JORRI* **111**(8), 1983.
11. Can you rely on condoms? *Consumer Rep* **45**:135–140, 1989.
12. Willis J. Precautions for Health Care Professionals. FDA Drug Bill **17**:16–17, 1987.
13. Fleischer AC, Kepple DM. *Transvaginal Sonography.* Philadelphia: JB Lippincott, 1992.
14. Moore KL. *The Developing Human: Clinically Oriented Embryology,* 3rd ed. Philadelphia: WB Saunders, 1982.

Questions

GENERAL INSTRUCTIONS: For each question, select the best answer. Select only one answer for each question unless otherwise indicated.

1. Fig. 7–8 is a transvaginal sonogram of a 23 year old woman with a uterus the size of a 10-week pregnancy and vaginal bleeding. The most likely diagnosis is

   (A) gestational trophoblastic disease
   (B) an incomplete abortion
   (C) a completed abortion
   (D) A or B

2. The level of β-hCG at which the gestational sac can first be depicted with transvaginal or transabdominal sonography is referred to as

   (A) the discriminatory zone
   (B) qualitative assay levels
   (C) a radioimmunoassay
   (D) β level

3. The abnormal findings in the transvaginal sonogram of a 10-week pregnancy shown in Fig. 7–9 include

   (A) an ancephalic fetus
   (B) a two-headed fetus
   (C) a massive sacrococcygeal teratoma
   (D) none of the above

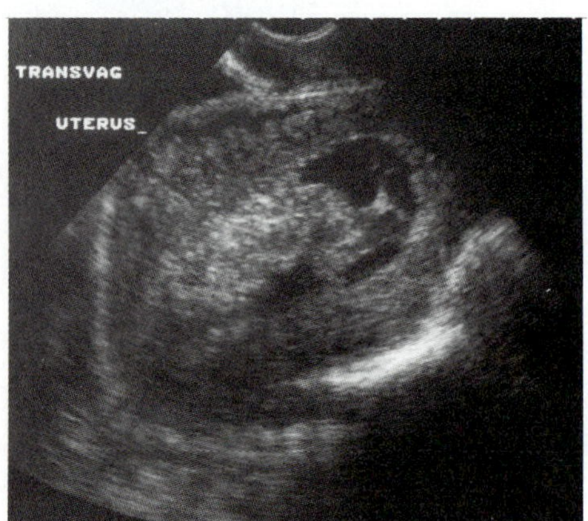

Figure 7–8. A transvaginal sonogram of the uterus.

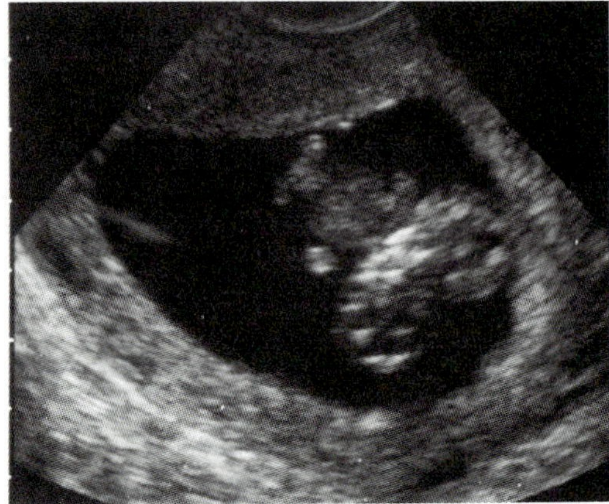

Figure 7–9. A transvaginal sonogram of a 10-week pregnancy.

4. Alpha-fetoprotein is elevated in

   (A) all types of neural tube defects
   (B) closed neural tube defects
   (C) neural tube defects occasionally associated with fetal regurgitation
   (D) none of the above

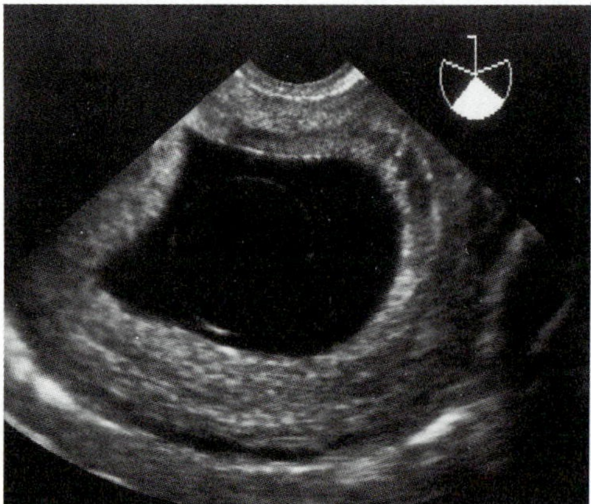

Figure 7–10. A transvaginal sonogram of an 8-week pregnancy.

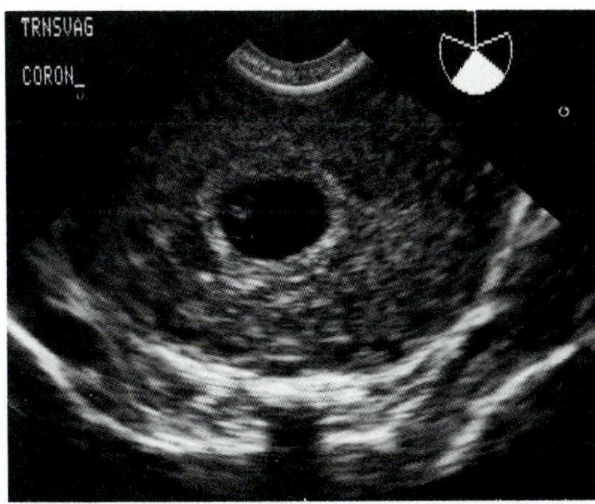

Figure 7–11. A transvaginal sonogram of an early pregnancy.

5. The thin rounded structure in the middle of the uterine lumen shown in the transvaginal sonogram in Fig. 7–10 is

   (A) the hydropic yolk sac
   (B) the amnion
   (C) the chorion
   (D) the placenta

6. Fusion of the amnion and chorion normally occurs between

   (A) 3 and 5 weeks
   (B) 5 and 8 weeks
   (C) 8 and 10 weeks
   (D) 14 and 16 weeks

7. The best estimate of gestational age in the transvaginal sonogram shown in Fig. 7–11 is

   (A) 3 weeks
   (B) 4 weeks
   (C) 5 weeks
   (D) 6 weeks

8. The "double bleb sign" refers to

   (A) the amnion, embryo, and yolk sac
   (B) hypoechoic areas behind the placenta
   (C) the rhombencephalon and spinal cord of the developing embryo
   (D) none of the above

9. Which of the following are true statements concerning the magnified transvaginal sonogram of an 8-week fetus shown in Fig. 7–12?

   (A) physiologic herniation of the bowel is seen
   (B) a yolk sac is seen
   (C) the amnion is seen
   (D) the rhombencephalon is seen
   (E) all of the above are seen

10. The area outside of the amnion is called

    (A) the chorionic cavity
    (B) the amniotic cavity
    (C) the extrafetal space
    (D) none of the above

11. Fig. 7–13 is a combined real-time image and M-mode of a patient presenting with first trimester bleeding. This sonogram demonstrates that

    (A) the embryo is living and has heart motion
    (B) the embryo is dead
    (C) only a clot is seen within the gestational sac
    (D) none of the above

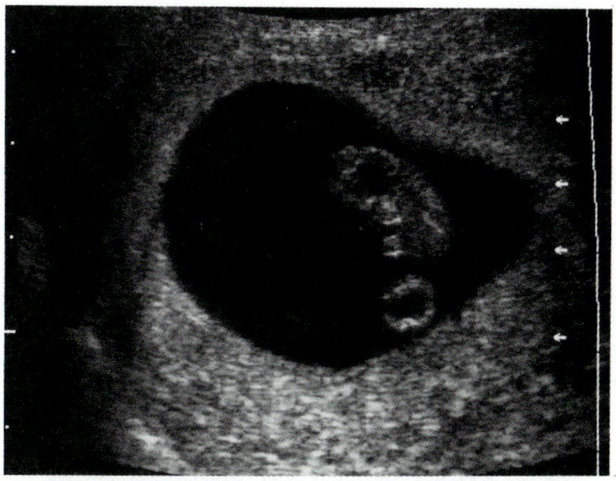

Figure 7–12. A magnified transvaginal sonogram of an 8-week pregnancy.

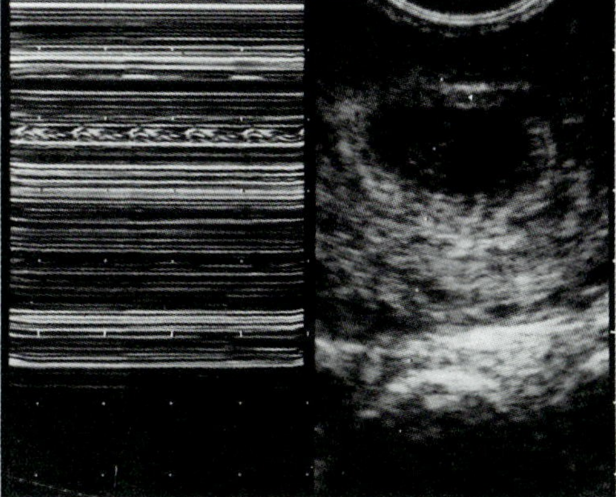

Figure 7–13. A combined real-time and M-mode image of a patient presenting with bleeding in the first trimester.

12. At what gestational age should fetal heart motion be detected on a transvaginal sonogram?

(A) 4 weeks
(B) 5 weeks
(C) 6 weeks
(D) 8 weeks

13. The following structures are depicted in the transvaginal sonogram of an 8-week embryo shown in Fig. 7–14.

(A) the chorion, yolk sac, and amnion
(B) the amnion, embryo, chorionic cavity, and lacunae
(C) the embryo, yolk sac, and amnion
(D) the yolk sac, embryo, and chorion

14. The embryonic period ends and fetal development begins at

(A) 4–10 weeks
(B) 7–8 weeks
(C) 8–20 weeks
(D) none of the above

15. Fig. 7–15 is a transvaginal sonogram of a 26-year-old woman who is 6-to-7 weeks pregnant. The yolk sac

(A) has an important function in hematopoiesis
(B) has an important function in the induction of neural tissue
(C) has no known function
(D) has the important function of producing yolk

16. The secondary yolk sac is located

(A) outside of the amniotic cavity
(B) within the amniotic cavity
(C) within the embryo
(D) none of the above

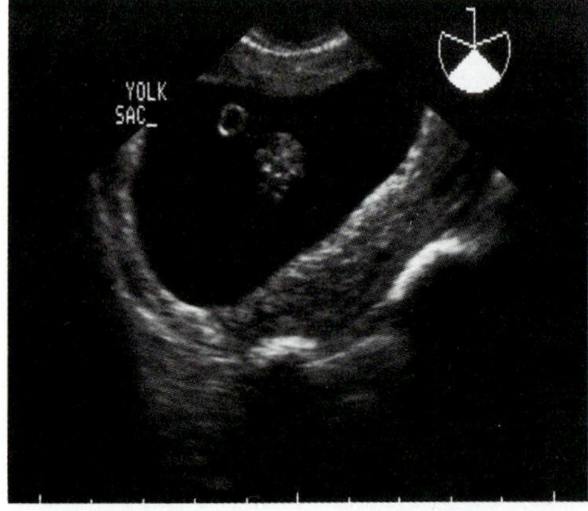

Figure 7–15. A transvaginal sonogram of a 6-to-7 week pregnancy.

17. Fig. 7–16 is a transvaginal sonogram of the left ovary in a patient undergoing ovulation induction with Pergonal®. The sonographic findings indicate that

(A) multiple follicles have developed
(B) there is hemorrhage within some of these follicles
(C) there is ovarian torsion
(D) A and B are present

18. Ovarian hyperstimulation syndrome typically occurs after

(A) the patient is pregnant and has received human chorionic gonadotropin (hCG)
(B) before the patient has received hCG
(C) failed induction of ovulation
(D) the patient has received intrauterine artificial insemination

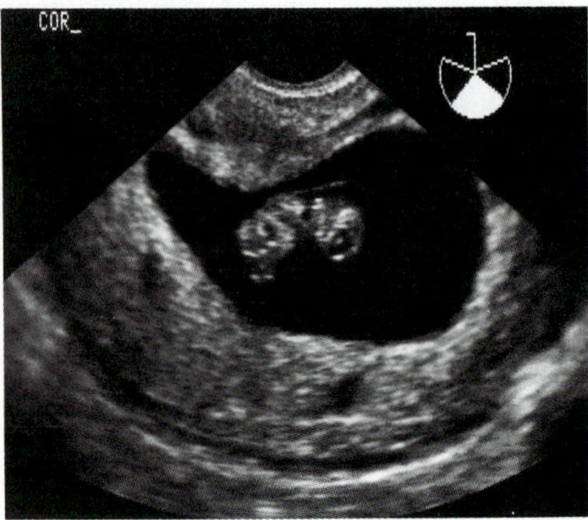

Figure 7–14. A transvaginal sonogram of an embryo at 8 weeks.

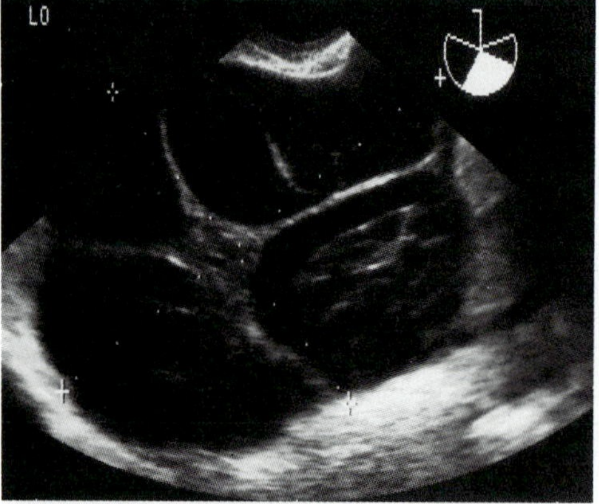

Figure 7–16. A transvaginal sonogram of the left ovary.

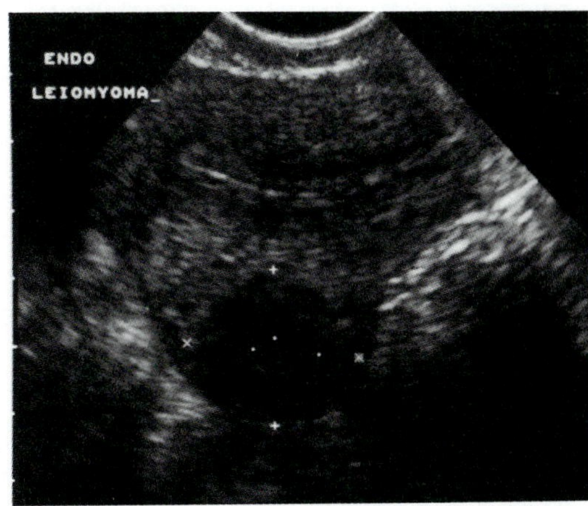

Figure 7–17. A transvaginal sonogram of an infertile patient.

19. Fig. 7–17 is a transvaginal sonogram of an infertility patient. The abnormal sonographic findings include

(A) an intramural leiomyoma
(B) an endometrial carcinoma
(C) a bicornuate uterus
(D) none of the above

20. A submucous leiomyoma can be diagnosed by transvaginal sonography.

(A) true
(B) false

21. Fig. 7–18 is a transvaginal sonogram of the left adnexa. This patient's adnexa has

(A) a cystic mass within the confines of the left ovary
(B) a cystic mass that is separate from the left ovary
(C) an ovary containing multiple immature follicles
(D) fluid in the cul-de-sac

22. A paraovarian cyst arises

(A) from the vestigial Gartner's duct
(B) from the vestigial wolffian duct
(C) within the mesovarium
(D) A and C

23. The following abnormalities are detected in Fig. 7–19, a transvaginal sonogram in the coronal plane of the right adnexa.

(A) a fusiform cystic structure
(B) an ovarian cyst
(C) a hydrosalpinx
(D) A and C

24. A hydrosalpinx can be identified on transvaginal sonography by showing

(A) its origin near the uterine cornua, as demonstrated by the endometrium
(B) relatively thick folds
(C) lack of ovarian tissue or stroma surrounding it
(D) all of the above

25. Fig. 7–20 is a transvaginal sonogram in the uterus in a coronal plane. The following observations can be made.

(A) the uterus is enlarged
(B) the uterus apparently has two endometria, which indicate a bicornuate uterus
(C) A and B
(D) none of the above

26. Bicornuate uteri are the result of

(A) abnormal fusion of the müllerian duct system
(B) multiparity
(C) A and B
(D) none of the above

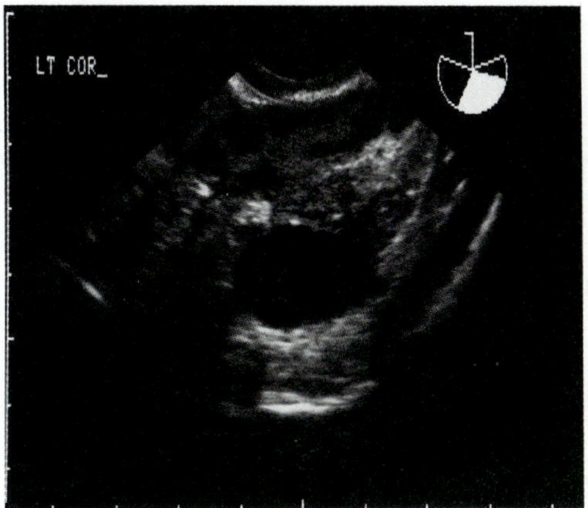

Figure 7–18. A transvaginal sonogram of the left adnexa.

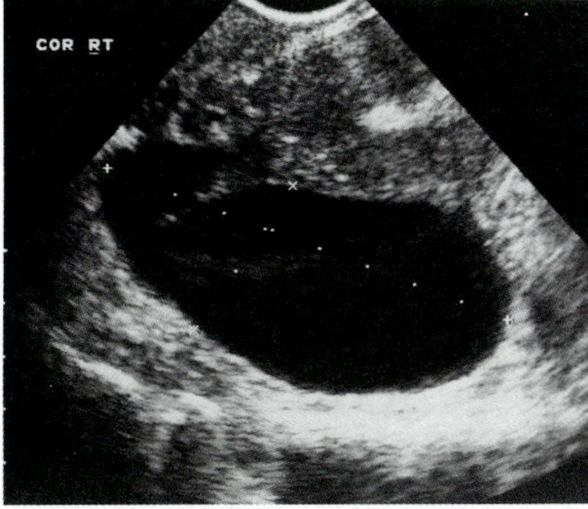

Figure 7–19. A transvaginal sonogram of the right adnexa.

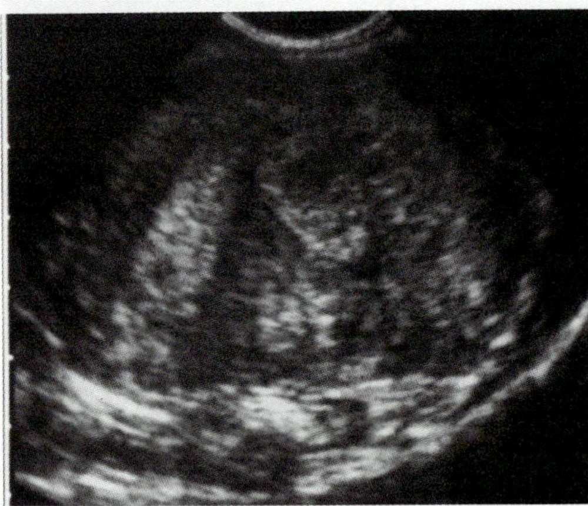

Figure 7–20. A transvaginal sonogram of the uterus.

27. The following findings are apparent in the transvaginal sonogram of the right ovary shown in Fig. 7–21.

    (A) the mass contained solid material that may be related to hemorrhage
    (B) the mass was either a tubo-ovarian abscess or an ovarian tumor such as mucinous cystadenoma
    (C) A and B
    (D) none of the above

28. In the differential diagnosis of corpora lutea, one also must consider

    (A) cystic tumors of the ovary
    (B) a hematosalpinx
    (C) endometriomas
    (D) all of the above

29. The position of the patient that enables free movement of the probe in the horizontal plane while performing transvaginal scanning is the

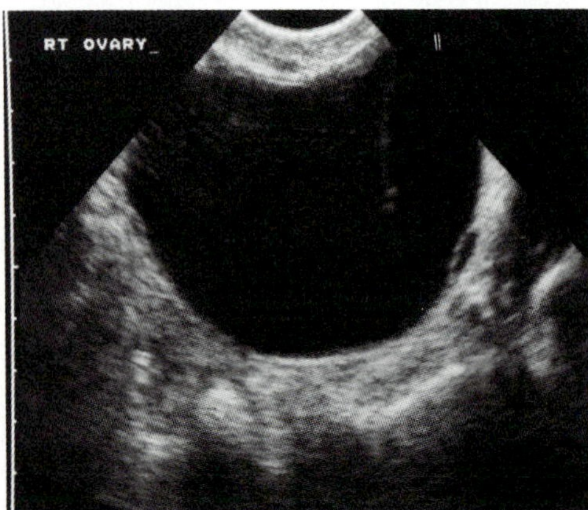

Figure 7–21. A transvaginal sonogram of the right ovary.

    (A) Trendelenburg position
    (B) lithotomy position
    (C) Sims' position
    (D) prone position

30. The position of the examination table for transvaginal sonography is

    (A) the Trendelenburg position
    (B) the lithotomy position
    (C) the Sims' position
    (D) the Fowler's position

31. When a gynecological examination table is *not* available for performing a transvaginal study, a regular flat examination table can be used if a foam cushion that is 15–20 cm thick is used to elevate the

    (A) pelvis
    (B) head
    (C) legs
    (D) knees

32. The range of transducer frequencies used in transvaginal sonography is

    (A) 3.5 to 5.0 MHz
    (B) 5.0 to 7.5 MHz
    (C) 2.5 to 3.5 MHz
    (D) none of the above

33. The most important prerequisite for transvaginal sonography is

    (A) emptying of the urinary bladder
    (B) adequate filling of the urinary bladder
    (C) putting the patient in the Trendelenburg position
    (D) selecting a low-frequency probe

34. Which of the following is *not* true for transvaginal sonography?

    (A) both ovaries are always seen simultaneously
    (B) an empty bladder is required before scanning
    (C) the ovaries are identified by the presence of follicles
    (D) a large mass can be missed

35. The most appropriate method of disinfecting the transvaginal probes from organisms, including the AIDS virus, is

    (A) diluted household bleach
    (B) ethylene oxide
    (C) an autoclave
    (D) a glutaraldehyde-based agent

36. Transvaginal sonography detects the embryological structures about

(A) 5 weeks earlier than does transabdominal sonography
(B) 1 week earlier than does transabdominal sonography
(C) 2 weeks earlier than does transabdominal sonography
(D) the same time as does transabdominal sonography

37. The diameter of a mature graafian follicle ranges from

(A) 3–5 mm
(B) 10–12 mm
(C) 18–24 mm
(D) 24–30 mm

38. On transvaginal sonography, the embryo is seen within the amniotic cavity and the secondary yolk sac is normally depicted within

(A) the amniotic cavity
(B) the extraembryonic coelom
(C) the trophoblast
(D) the umbilical cord

39. The level of β-human chorionic gonadotropin required to depict the gestational sac with transvaginal sonography is approximately

(A) 3600 mIU/mL 2nd IS
(B) 6500 mIU/mL IRP
(C) 1800 mIU/mL 2nd IS
(D) 1000 mIU/mL IRP

40. Preparation for a transvaginal study does *not* require

(A) application of a probe cover
(B) disinfecting of the probe
(C) emptying of the bladder
(D) a vaginal douche, antibiotic therapy, or both before the probe is inserted.

41. A fully distended bladder in a patient undergoing transvaginal sonography will

(A) occupy most of the image and displace organs of interest out of the focal range
(B) increase the focal range, allowing better image enhancement
(C) allow better visualization of pelvic organs
(D) produce low attenuation, resulting in reduced magnification

42. The transvaginal probe should be covered with a protective sheath before vaginal insertion. All of the following are recommended for this purpose except

(A) latex condoms
(B) lamb condoms
(C) latex gloves
(D) CIV-Flex™ probe covers

43. Which one of the following lubricants should *not* be used on latex probe covers?

(A) K-Y jelly™
(B) a coupling gel
(C) a water-based gel
(D) petroleum jelly

44. The examination table is tilted for transvaginal sonography to

(A) drain fluid out of and away from the cul-de-sac
(B) push the bowel cephalad out of the true pelvic cavity
(C) increase filling of the bladder to delineate the pelvic structures better
(D) pool intraperitoneal fluid into the cul-de-sac to outline pelvic organs better

45. What position should the patient be placed in for transvaginal sonography?

(A) the Sims' position
(B) the knee-chest position
(C) the lithotomy position with a slight Trendelenburg tilt
(D) the lithotomy position with a slight Fowler's tilt

46. The major limitation of transvaginal sonography is that

(A) it can be used only in the first trimester
(B) its field of view is limited
(C) it can be used only to evaluate an ectopic pregnancy
(D) it can be used only to evaluate follicles

47. The ideal examination table for transvaginal sonography is a

(A) gynecologic examination table with a variable pelvic tilt and stirrups
(B) x-ray table with Trendelenburg tilt and safety straps
(C) a stretcher with side rails
(D) flat immobile examination table

48. The use of a high-frequency transvaginal transducer results in

(A) less penetration, more magnification, and better resolution
(B) more penetration, less resolution, and less magnification
(C) greater penetration, more magnification, and better resolution
(D) no change

49. Transvaginal sonography is useful for evaluating all of the following except

(A) an ectopic pregnancy
(B) intrauterine growth retardation
(C) a third-trimester pregnancy
(D) a placenta previa

50. The acceptance rate among patients for transvaginal verses transabdominal sonography is

(A) 5%
(B) 20–35%
(C) 50–60%
(D) 82–93%

51. The small cystic space in the posterior cranium seen on transvaginal sonography during the 8th-to-10th week of gestation is most likely

(A) the rhombencephalon
(B) mild hydrocephalus
(C) a Dandy Walker cyst
(D) the choroid plexus

52. The echogenic bulging of the umbilical cord seen with transvaginal sonography near the abdominal insertion at about the 8th-to-10th week of gestation is most likely to represent

(A) a gastroschisis
(B) physiologic herniation of the midgut
(C) the yolk sac
(D) omphalocele

53. Transvaginal sonography can depict the fetal heart before a clear sonographic depiction of the embryo can be obtained

(A) by putting the M-mode cursor on the gestational sac
(B) by putting the M-mode cursor at the periphery of the yolk sac
(C) by putting the M-mode cursor on the trophoblast
(D) only if the embryo is at least sonographically evident

54. Which one of the following is *not* true of the urinary bladder with transvaginal sonography?

(A) the wall of the bladder cannot be identified when the bladder is nearly empty
(B) the nearly empty bladder can be on the right of the screen
(C) the nearly empty bladder can be on the left of the screen
(D) the nearly empty bladder may be in the true anatomic position

55. The hypoechoic parallel linear lines in the outer myometrium seen on transvaginal sonography represent

(A) arcuate vessels
(B) the external iliac vein
(C) the external iliac artery
(D) the internal iliac vein

56. The vascular web seen on transvaginal sonography near the lateral border of the cervix represents

(A) arcuate vessels
(B) uterine veins and arteries
(C) the external iliac artery
(D) the internal iliac vein

57. The round hypoechoic structures seen surrounding one region of the choriodecidua represent

(A) arcuate vessels
(B) lacunae
(C) the yolk sac
(D) the internal iliac vein

58. Which of the following is *not* true of transvaginal sonography (TVS) in the second and third trimesters?

(A) TVS is more precise in locating the placenta than is transabdominal sonography
(B) TVS can be helpful in evaluating prolapse of the umbilical cord and the intracranial anatomy
(C) transvaginal color Doppler can be used to detect abnormal patterns of blood flow
(D) TVS is useful in the first trimester
(E) all of the above are true

59. Identify the structure the arrow points to in Fig. 7–22.

(A) the yolk sac
(B) the embryo
(C) the umbilical cord
(D) the yolk stalk

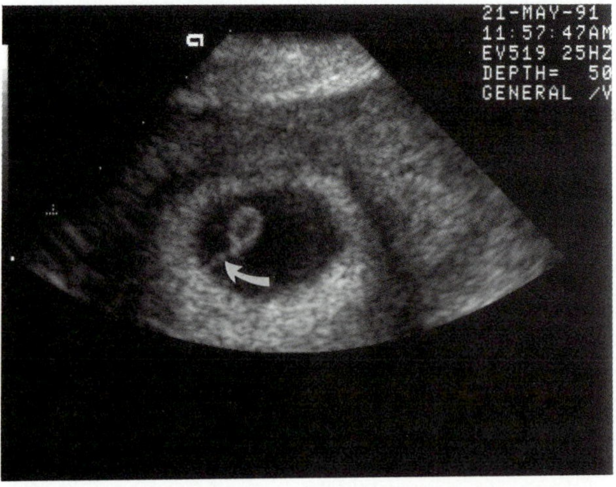

Figure 7–22. A transvaginal sonogram of an early pregnancy.

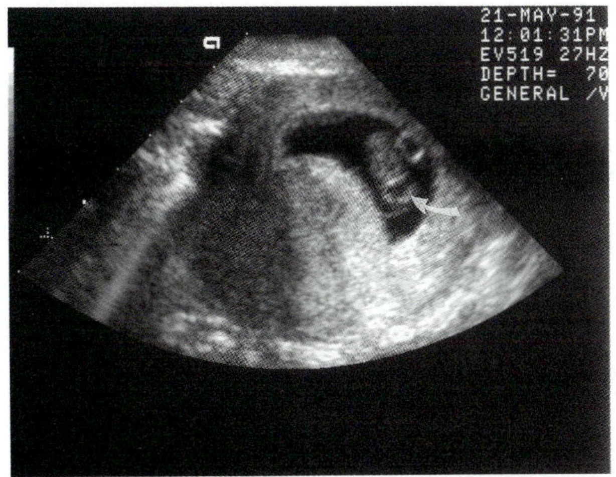

Figure 7–23. A transvaginal sonogram of an early pregnancy.

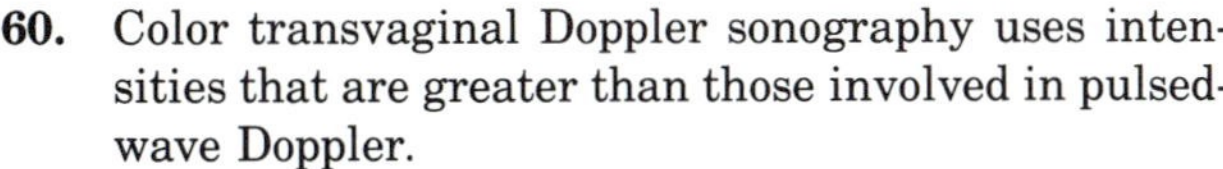

60. Color transvaginal Doppler sonography uses intensities that are greater than those involved in pulsed-wave Doppler.

(A) true
(B) false

61. Identify the structure the arrow points to in Fig. 7–23.

(A) the rhombencephalon
(B) the hydrocephalon
(C) the yolk sac
(D) the chorion

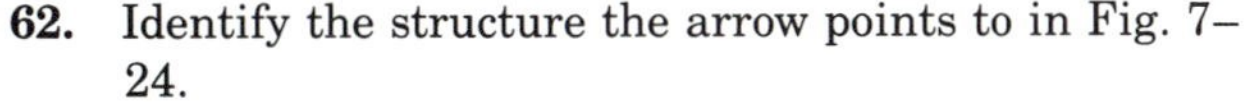

62. Identify the structure the arrow points to in Fig. 7–24.

(A) the ovarian vein
(B) a dermoid cyst
(C) a follicular cyst
(D) an ectopic pregnancy

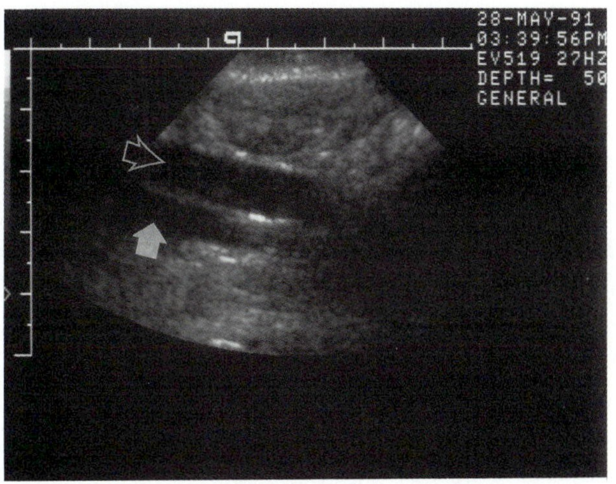

Figure 7–25. A transvaginal sonogram of the adnexa.

63. Identify the structure the closed arrow head points to in Fig. 7–25.

(A) the internal iliac vein
(B) the internal iliac artery
(C) the ovarian artery
(D) the ovarian vein

64. Identify the structure the open arrow head points to in Fig. 7–25.

(A) the internal iliac vein
(B) the internal iliac artery
(C) the ovarian artery
(D) the ovarian vein

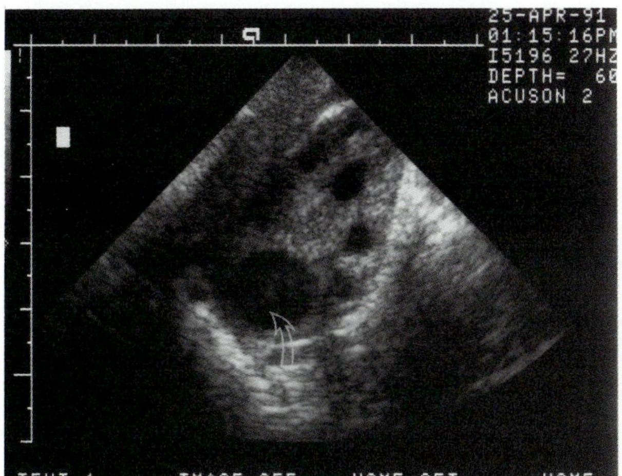

Figure 7–24. A transvaginal sonogram of the adnexa.

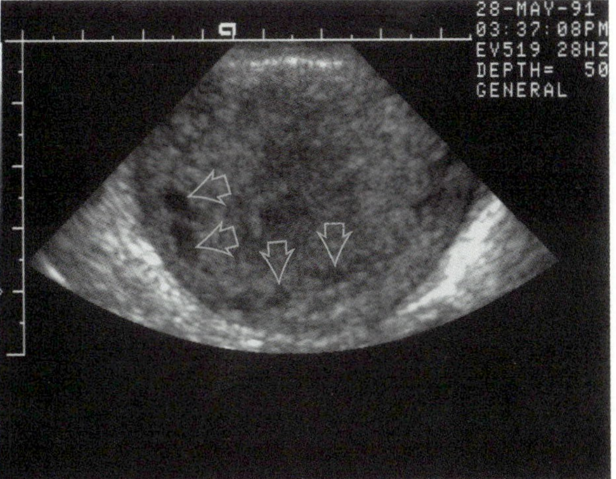

Figure 7–26. A transverse scan of the uterus.

65. Identify the structure the arrow heads point to in Fig. 7–26, a transverse scan of the uterus.

(A) the internal iliac vein
(B) the internal iliac artery
(C) the arcuate artery
(D) the azygos vein

66. Identify the structure the arrow heads point to in the transverse scan of the uterus depicted in Fig. 7–27.

(A) a double decuida
(B) the internal iliac artery
(C) lacunae
(D) the yolk sac

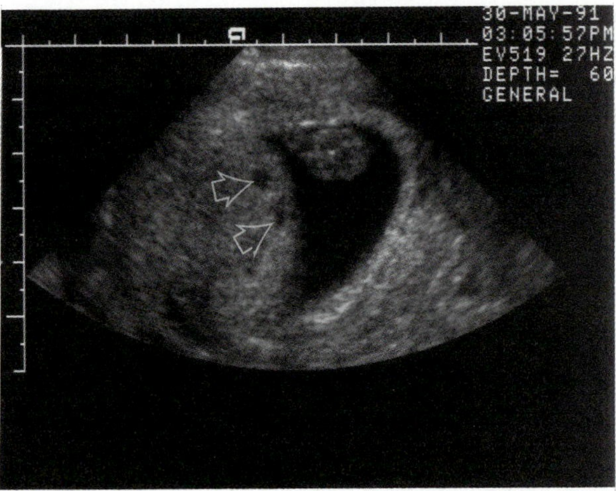

Figure 7–27. A transverse scan of the uterus.

Answers and Explanations

1. **(D)** A or B. Echogenic tissue within the uterine lumen can be the result of either an incomplete abortion or early trophoblastic disease. Vesicles do not form until approximately 12 weeks. Therefore, in the early stages of trophoblastic disease, the tissue appears as echogenic intraluminal material. *(8:95)*

2. **(A)** The discriminatory zone. The level of β-hCG at which the gestational sac can first be depicted with transvaginal or transabdominal sonography is referred to as the "discriminatory" zone of human chorionic gonadotropin. *(5:39–41)*

3. **(B)** A two-headed fetus. This sonogram shows a two-headed fetus that has a single pair of arms and legs. *(8:65)*

4. **(C)** Neural tube defects occasionally associated with fetal regurgitation. α-fetoprotein is elevated when there is a break in the skin, blood in the amniotic fluid or with a variety of disorders associated with neural tube defects, cystic hygroma, placental abnormalities, and fetal regurgitation. Closed neural tube defects such as closed spina bifida usually do not elevate α-fetoprotein. *(8:130)*

5. **(B)** The amnion. *(8:63)*

6. **(D)** 14 and 16 weeks. The amnion and chorion usually fuse during this period. *(8:125)*

7. **(D)** 6 weeks. This is the best estimate because there is an embryo, a yolk sac, and an amnion "double bleb sign." *(10:75)*

8. **(A)** The amnion, embryo, and yolk sac. The "double bleb sign" refers to seeing these three indicators and is best seen at approximately 6 weeks of gestation. *(10:75)*

9. **(E)** All of the above are seen. *(10:75)*

10. **(A)** The chorionic cavity. This area has developed from the extraembryonic coelom. *(10:75)*

11. **(A)** The embryo is living and has heart motion. Transvaginal sonography can reliably detect heart motion in living embryos at 6 weeks. *(10:25)*

12. **(B)** 6 weeks. *(8:40; 9:79)*

13. **(B)** The chorion, yolk sac, and amnion. The hypoechoic areas around outside of the developing amnion is called the chorionic cavity, which has developed from the extraembryonic coelom. The developing placenta represents blood lakes or lacunae. *(8:40)*

14. **(B)** 7–8 weeks. The embryonic period extends from the 4th to the 8th week. All major organs and systems are formed (organogenesis) during this period. After this embryonic period, the embryo is called a fetus. *(11:71–72)*

15. **(A)** Has an important function in hematopoiesis. This transvaginal sonogram demonstrates a 6–7 week embryo with a secondary yolk sac that is located outside of the amniotic cavity. The yolk sac produces blood elements for the embryo. *(8:67)*

16. **(A)** Outside of the amniotic cavity. The secondary sac lies between the amnion and chorion. *(10:75)*

17. **(D)** A and B are present. This transvaginal sonogram demonstrates an enlarged ovary that contains multiple follicles, some of which contain hemorrhage. The ovaries in these patients typically include numerous follicles. *(8:144)*

18. **(A)** The patient is pregnant and has received human chorionic gonadotropin. Ovarian hyperstimulation syndrome usually occurs after hCG is given. *(8:329)*

19. **(A)** An intramural leiomyoma. This transvaginal sonogram demonstrates an intramural leiomyoma that apparently does not involve the endometrial surface. In some infertile patients, a leiomyoma may distort the endometrial lining, therefore contributing to infertility. *(8:40)*

20. **(A)** True. A submucous leiomyoma is difficult to delineate with transabdominal sonography. It is diagnosed best with transvaginal sonography. *(8:272, 306)*

21. **(B)** A cystic mass that is separate from the left ovary. The differential diagnosis includes a paraovarian or peritoneal cyst. *(8:40)*

22. **(D)** From A and C. A variety of masses do not arise directly from the uterus or ovaries. For example, paraovarian cysts arise from the vestigial Gartner's duct in the mesovarium. *(8:263)*

23. **(D)** A and C. This sonogram demonstrates the typical appearance of a hydrosalpinx, which appears as a fusiform cystic structure arising from the area of the uterine cornua and has a rounded shape in its distal aspect. *(8:40)*

24. **(D)** All of the above. Hydrosalpinx usually appears as a fusiform structure that is separate from the ovary. It can be identified by the lack of ovarian tissue surrounding it. *(1:322, 328)*

25. **(C)** A and B. This transvaginal sonogram demonstrates two endometrial lumina in bicornuate or septate uteri. *(8:40)*

26. **(A)** Abnormal fusion of the müllerian duct system. Bicornuate uteri are the result of fusion abnormalities of the two tissue elements that form the uterus from the müllerian duct system. *(8:40)*

27. **(C)** A and B. This sonogram demonstrates an area of increased echogenicity within a predominantly cystic ovarian mass. This pattern is most likely to be seen in hemorrhagic corpora lutea, but it can also be seen in mucinous cystadenomas, tubo-ovarian abscesses, endometriomas, and dermoid cysts. *(8:264)*

28. **(D)** All of the above. (See the explanation of the answer to question 27.) *(8:264)*

29. **(B)** The lithotomy position. The elevated thighs in the lithotomy position allows free movements of the probe from side to side (horizontal plane). *(8:15)*

30. **(D)** The Fowler's position. The patient should be lying in the lithotomy position with the examination table in the Fowler's position (reverse Trendelenburg). The patient should *not* be placed in the Trendelenburg's position because it will drain the normal amount of fluid from the cul-de-sac that is used to outline structures. *(8:15)*

31. **(A)** Pelvis. A thick foam cushion under the pelvis allows free up-and-down movements of the probe (vertical plane). *(8:15)*

32. **(B)** 5 to 7.5 MHz. Transvaginal transducers range in frequency from 5 to 7.5 MHz. *(4:22)*

33. **(A)** Emptying of the urinary bladder. This is important because a filled bladder takes up most of the image, displacing adnexal structures out of the image. In addition, it contributes to unnecessary patient discomfort. *(2:15)*

34. **(A)** Both ovaries are always seen simultaneously. Transvaginal sonography can best demonstrate only one ovary at a time because of image magnification and the small focal area. *(1:59–65)*

35. **(D)** A glutaraldehyde-based agent. The most recent and practical method of sterilization is a glutaraldehyde-based chemical disinfectant. Diluted household bleach is effective in inactivating HIV-1 on environmental surfaces, but it could be destructive to the bonding material and plastic of some transducers. Glutaraldehyde-based chemical disinfectants are bactericidal, fungicidal, and virucidal and are effective in inactivating HIV-1 on environmental surfaces. *(3:131)*

36. **(B)** 1 week earlier than does transabdominal sonography. Transvaginal sonography detects the embryologic structures about a week earlier on the average. *(1:107)*

37. **(C)** 18–24 mm. *(1:143)*

38. **(B)** The extraembryonic coelom. The secondary yolk sac (the definitive yolk sac) lies in the chorionic cavity between the amnion and chorion. The chorionic cavity also is called the extraembryonic coelom. The extraembryonic coelom forms the primary yolk sac, which decreases in size and the secondary yolk sac develops. *(1:93; 4:22–27)*

39. **(D)** 1000 mIU/mL IRP. There are two different methods of reporting hCG. The International Reference Preparation (IRP) and the 2nd International Standards (2nd IS). The 2nd IS is approximately 50% of the IRP. The gestational sac can be depicted when the serum β hCG is 1,000 mIU/mL (IRP) or 500 mIU/mL (2nd IS). *(4:17)*

40. **(D)** A vaginal douche, antibiotic therapy, or both before the probe is inserted. This is not required because the transducer is normally disinfected and covered before the insertion. *(3:130–135)*

41. **(A)** Occupy most of the image and displace organs of interest out of the focal range. *(1:16)*

42. **(B)** Lamb condoms. Natural lamb condoms, when viewed under the electron microscope, show tiny pores

that are larger than the HIV or hepatitis B virus and may permit its transmission. *(3:130–135)*

43. **(D)** Petroleum jelly. The type of lubricants recommended for latex condoms are water-based products such as K-Y jelly™ and ultrasound coupling gel. Petroleum jelly or oil-based products can cause deterioration of the latex that results in fracture. *(3:130–135)*

44. **(D)** Pool intraperitoneal fluid into the cul-de-sac to outline pelvic organs better. *(1:15)*

45. **(D)** The lithotomy position with a slight Fowler's tilt. A slight Fowler's tilt is also called the reverse Trendelenburg position. *(2:15)*

46. **(B)** Its field of view is limited. Transvaginal sonography can also be used in the second and third trimesters as well as the first trimester. *(2:16; 4:59)*

47. **(A)** Gynecologic examination table with a variable pelvic tilt and stirrups. *(2:15)*

48. **(A)** Less penetration, more magnification, and better resolution. *(5:5)*

49. **(B)** Intrauterine growth retardation. Transvaginal sonography is unable to do the multiparameter measurements needed to assess either intrauterine growth retardation or a complete obstetrical survey because the focal zone is small. Furthermore, because the transducer also is limited to the confinement of the vagina, a sectional survey cannot be obtained. *(5:5–22)*

50. **(D)** 82–93%. *(4:4)*

51. **(A)** The rhombencephalon. The small cystic space in the posterior cranium seen on transvaginal sonography during the 8th-to-10th week of gestation is the hindbrain (rhombencephalon) *(4:16)*

52. **(B)** Physiologic herniation of the midgut. The normal migration of the midgut into the umbilical cord occurs during the 6th-to-10th week. The normal physiologic midgut herniation is seen on transvaginal sonography as an echogenic bulging of the cord and should not be confused with an omphalocele. *(5:70)*

53. **(B)** By putting the M-mode cursor at the periphery of the yolk sac. The yolk sac is normally seen before the embryo at about 5 week's gestation. The yolk sac is larger than the embryo at this time; later it becomes smaller than the embryo. Abutting the yolk sac is the embryological disk, which is too small to be depicted. If the M-mode is placed at the edge of the yolk sac at approximately 5½-to-6 weeks, the heartbeats can be depicted, not from the yolk sac, but from the adjacent but not-yet-apparent embryo. The heartbeats occur at 35 to 36 days menstrual age. *(4:14, 30)*

54. **(A)** The wall of the urinary bladder can be identified even though the bladder is nearly empty. The position of the bladder can be to the right or left of its normal anatomic position or be in its normal position. *(6:5)*

55. **(A)** Arcuate vessels. *(1:37)*

56. **(B)** Uterine veins and arteries. *(1:32)*

57. **(B)** Lacunae. These are seen surrounding one region of the choriodecidua in early pregnancy. *(1:90)*

58. **(E)** All of the above. Transvaginal sonography is used in the second and third trimesters for a more precise location of the placenta in relation to the internal os, presentation of the cord, and blood flow. *(6:35)*

59. **(D)** The yolk stalk. *(1:93)*

60. **(A)** True. The intensities used in color Doppler are much lower than those in duplex Doppler. *(7:52)*

61. **(A)** The rhombencephalon. *(10:75)*

62. **(C)** A follicular cyst. *(8:40)*

63. **(B)** The internal iliac artery. *(1:22)*

64. **(A)** The internal iliac vein. *(1:22)*

65. **(C)** The arcuate artery. The arrow is pointing to the arcuate artery in the myometrium. *(1:37)*

66. **(C)** Lacunae. *(1:37)*

REFERENCES

1. Timor-Tritsch IE, Rottem S. *Transvaginal Sonography,* and ed. New York: Elsevier, 1991.
2. Sacks GA, Fleischer AC, Kepple DM. Toshiba Medical Review: Clinical Applications of Transvaginal Sonography in Obstetrics and Gynecology. Toshiba Corp, Tokyo, No. 23:15–24, Feb 1988.
3. Odwin C, Fleischer A, Kepple DM, et al. Probe covers and disinfectants for transvaginal transducers. *J Diagn Med Sonography* **6**(3): 130–135, 1990.
4. Transvaginal Sonography. *Semin Ultrasound CT MR,* Philadelphia: WB Saunders, **11**(1): 1990.
5. Goldstein SR. *Endovaginal Ultrasound.* New York: Alan R Liss, 1988.
6. Rottem S. Scanning after the first trimester: Endo-

vaginal ultrasound course. Syllabus. Spring Educational Meeting. Phoenix, AZ, by AIUM, April 9–19, 1989, pp 33–35.

7. Fleischer AC, Rao B, Kepple DM. Transvaginal color Doppler sonography: preliminary experience. *Dyn Cardiovas Imaging* **3:** 52–58, 1990.
8. Fleischer A, James AE Jr. *Diagnostic Sonography: Principles and Clinical Applications.* Philadelphia: WB Saunders, 1988.
9. Pennell RG, Baltarowich OH, Kurtz AB, et al. Complicated first-trimester pregnancy: evaluation with endovaginal US versus transvaginal technique. *Radiology* **165:**79–83, 1987.
10. Bree RL, Edwards M, Bohn-Velez M, et al. Transvaginal sonography in the evaluation of normal early pregnancy: correlation with hCG level. *AJR* **153:** 75–79, 1989.
11. Langman J. *Medical Embryology,* 4th ed. Baltimore, MD: Williams & Wilkins, 1981.

CHAPTER 8

OB/GYN SONOGRAPHY

Charles S. Odwin, Arthur C. Fleischer, Dale R. Cyr, and Pamela M. Foy

Study Guide

ANATOMY OF THE FEMALE REPRODUCTIVE SYSTEM

Uterus

The uterus is a pear-shaped muscular organ located in a median position in the pelvic cavity between the urinary bladder and the rectum. Its functions are (1) menstruation, (2) pregnancy, and (3) labor.

The uterus consists of three anatomic subdivisions: (1) fundus, (2) corpus (body), and (3) cervix. The isthmus uteri is the slightly constricted region of the uterus between the body and the cervix (Fig. 8–1), and it is of special significance in sonography as it helps to identify the region of the internal os of the cervix. The walls of the uterus are made up of three layers: (1) endometrium (mucosal), (2) myometrium, and (3) serosa (peritoneum). The echotexture of the uterine myometrium is normally homogeneous, whereas the echotexture of the endometrium varies with the phase of the menstrual cycle.

Cul-de-Sac

The peritoneum covering the posterior wall of the uterus and cervix reflecting on the rectum forms a deep pouch called the posterior cul-de-sac (retrouterine pouch) or the pouch of Douglas. Anteriorly, the peritoneum reflected at the level of the isthmus uteri over the urinary bladder form a shallow pouch called the anterior cul-de-sac, or vesicouterine pouch. Sonographically, the posterior cul-de-sac may become distended with fluid because of a ruptured ovarian cyst, a ruptured ectopic pregnancy, ascites, or an abscess.

Fallopian Tubes

The fallopian tubes (oviducts) extend laterally from the superior lateral angle of the uterus to the ovaries and have four anatomic subdivisions: (1) interstitial, (2) isthmus, (3) ampulla, and (4) infundibulum (Fig. 8–1). The functions of the fallopian tubes are in fertilization and aiding in the transport of the ova from the ovaries.

Ovaries and Adnexa

The ovaries are solid ovoid structures measuring 3 cm by 2 cm by 1 cm. They are located, one on each side of the uterus, in a shallow depression called Waldeyer's fossa. Their functions are in (1) ovulation and (2) secretion of hormones.

Sonographically, the ovaries are adjacent to the internal iliac vessels. In the reproductive years, the presence of follicles helps to identify the ovaries. After menopause, the ovaries are more difficult to identify because of their reduced size and the absence of follicles. The adnexa are any accessory parts or structures that are lateral to the uterus. The ovaries, fallopian tubes, and broad ligaments are adnexal structures. A cystic mass or tumor also can be adnexal if it is within the region described.

Blood Supply

The uterus receives its blood supply from the uterine and ovarian arteries, which are branches of the internal iliac (hypogastric) arteries. The branches of the uterine arteries that penetrate the myometrium and travel parallel to the outer surface are called arcuate arteries.[8] These arcuate vessels are demonstrated sonographically as parallel anechoic linear structures in the outer myometrium (Fig. 8–2).

Size

The size and shape of the uterus vary according to the patient's age and parity. Before puberty and after menopause, the uterus is normally small in size, whereas an increase in the number of children born usually results in an increase in size.[1,2] The normal size of the adult uterus in women who have never been pregnant is approximately 7.5 cm long, 3 cm thick, and 5 cm wide. The size of the uterus in women who have had multiple pregnancies varies from 8 to 10 cm in length.

In an elderly woman, the uterus atrophies. Therefore, a uterus that is 9 cm or more long would be abnormal for a

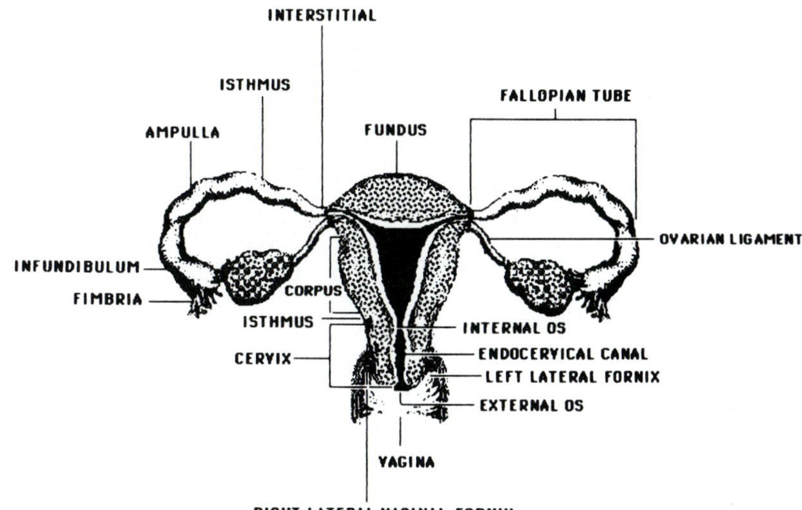

Figure 8–1. Diagram of the female reproductive organs (frontal view).

woman who is 65 years old. Sonographic measurements of the uterus should be correlated with the patient's age and parity to predict uterine enlargement. The two most common causes for uterine enlargement are pregnancy and fibroids.

Uterine Positions

The position of the uterus changes depending on the degree of bladder distention. The uterus is normally located in a anteverted position in 90% of women, forming an angle of 90° between the long axis of the vagina and the long axis of the uterine cavity.[3] The uterus can be in any one of the following positions:

- anteverted: the uterus tilts forward without a sharp angle between the corpus and cervix
- retroverted: the uterus tilts backward without a sharp angle between the corpus and cervix
- anteflexion: the uterine corpus is bent forward on the cervix, resulting in a sharp angle at the point of bending
- retroflexion: the uterine corpus is bent backward on the cervix, resulting in a sharp angle at the point of bending
- medianus: midline position
- dextroversion: right lateral deviation
- levoversion: left lateral deviation

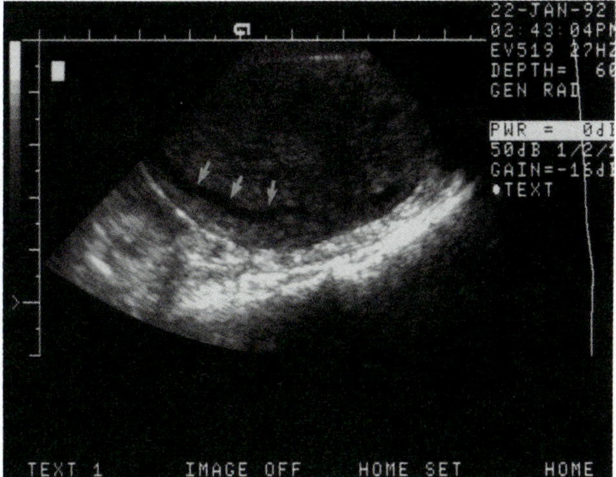

Figure 8–2. Transvaginal sonogram of the uterus. Arrows point to arcuate vessels.

The difference between the retroverted and retroflexion positions is the degree of bending. In the retroflexed uterus, the corpus bends backward on the cervix at the level of the isthmus uteri and causes a sharp angle at the point of bending; in the retroverted position, the uterus bends backward without changing the relationship of the corpus to cervix.[3]

Congenital abnormalities of the uterus such as uterine duplication and malformation result from improper fusion or incomplete development of the paramesonephric ducts (müllerian ducts). These various types of congenital uterine abnormalities, which are demonstrated in (Fig. 8–3), occur often in association with renal anomalies.[5] Although it is difficult to distinguish between a bicornuate and a septate uterus on sonograms, identification of two endometrial cavities is helpful in identifying the bicornuate uterus. These cavities are demonstrated best on transverse scans.

Urinary Bladder

The urinary bladder is a hollow muscular organ that is located behind the symphysis pubis. The floor of the bladder consists of a triangular area called the trigone. There are three openings in each angle: two orifices for the ureters, which convey urine to the bladder from the kidneys, and one urethral orifice, through which urine is expelled from the body. The bladder serves as a reservoir for urine and helps the urethra expel urine.

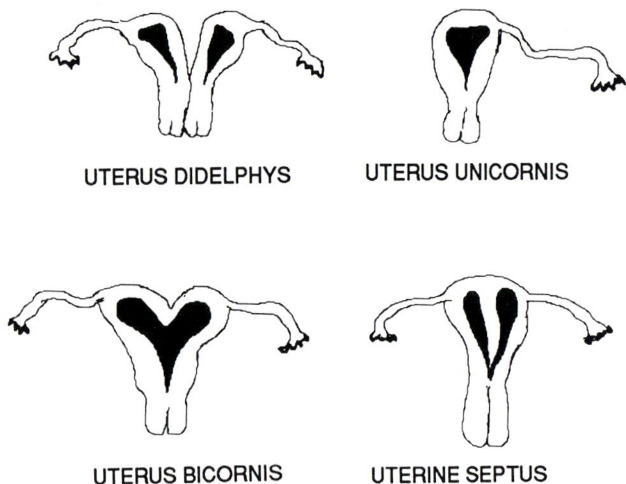

Figure 8–3. Diagram showing developmental anomalies of the uterus.

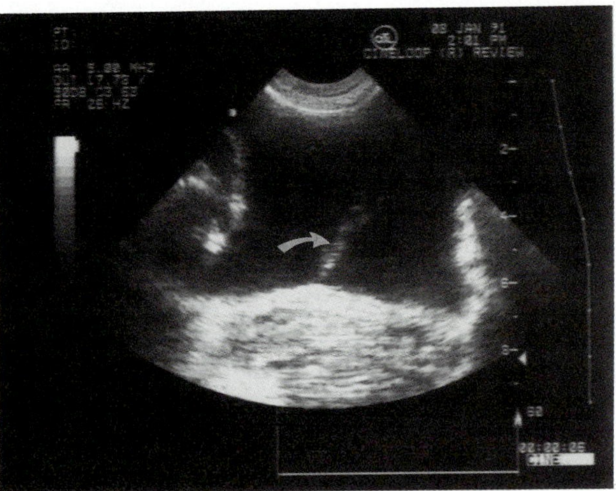

Figure 8–4. Sonogram of the urinary bladder with ureteral jet (arrow).

Bladder Distention. During a transabdominal sonographic examination of the pelvis, the urinary bladder must be distended for a variety of reasons. The reasons are the urine-filled bladder pushes the bowel cephalad out of the true pelvic cavity, it pushes the uterus cephalad away from the symphysis pubis, it permits rapid anatomic orientation, it provides a low-attenuation pathway to which ultrasound can propagate, and it helps to elevate the head of the fetus for easy measurements. Whereas a distended bladder is an extremely important prerequisite for a transabdominal study, an empty bladder is the most important prerequisite for a transvaginal study. The failure to fill the bladder adequately for transabdominal studies can result in serious diagnostic errors. On the other hand, an overdistended bladder can also result in errors.

When the bladder is being filled, urine can be observed entering the bladder on real-time and has been referred to as the "ureteral jets."[4] The jets begin at the ureteral orifices and flow toward the center of the bladder (Fig. 8–4).

Bladder Contour. Sonographically, the position and shape of the uterus have an effect on the urinary bladder. If the uterus is anteverted, the normally distended bladder has a mild indentation on its posterocephalad region. If the uterus is surgically removed or absent, the bladder has a different contour. Therefore, bladder contour depends on the shape and position of its surrounding structures.

PELVIC MASSES

A variety of pelvic masses can be depicted sonographically: solid, complex, and cystic. Tables 8–1, 8–2, and 8–3 describe the clinical and sonographic findings for the three types of masses.

OBSTETRIC HISTORY

Recording

Recording of the patient's obstetric history often provides the key to an accurate sonographic diagnosis. The sonographer has an opportunity to listen to the patient's complaints of illness during scanning and, on some occasions, may obtain information that the patient has not shared with her referring physician or radiologist. Because the sonographer-patient relationship can be of value in gathering information, the sonographer's basic knowledge of the patient's clinical history is essential.

Terminology

The term *gravidity* refers to the total number of pregnancies. A woman who has never been pregnant is called a nulligravida. A gravida is a pregnant woman, a primigravida is a woman who is pregnant for the first time, and a multigravida is a woman who has been pregnant several times.

The term *gravida* followed by an Arabic or roman numeral refers to the total number of previous pregnancies. For example, gravida 4 (IV) represents four pregnancies. The patient's past obstetric history also can be displayed in a series of four digits. For example, in the number 5235, the first digit refers to the number of full-term births, the second digit refers to the number of premature births, the third digit refers to the number of abortions, and the fourth digit refers to the number of children currently alive.[1]

TABLE 8–1. SOLID PELVIC MASSES

Mass	Type	Clinical Findings	Sonographic Findings
Leiomyoma, myoma, fibromyoma, fibroid	Solid	A benign tumor of the smooth muscle of the uterus. Growth is stimulated by estrogen. *submucous*—beneath the endometrium *interstitial*—in the muscular wall *subserous*—beneath the serosa May undergo softening and degeneration during pregnancy. Symptoms: pain and bleeding	Enlarged uterus (small in postmenopausal women) Irregular in contour (lobular or nodular) Inhomogeneous texture Calcifications Displacement of the uterus Degeneration (cystic changes) Poor ultrasonic penetration (attenuation)
Leiomyosarcoma	Solid	A malignant fibroid tumor with accelerated growth. Symptoms: pain and bleeding	Simular sonographic features as leiomyoma Indistinguishable from benign myoma
Dysgerminoma	Solid	A malignant germ cell tumor of the ovary that usually occurs in the second and third decades	Predominately solid with hypoechoic internal echoes
Adenomyosis	Solid	Benign invasion of the uterine musculature by the endometrium. Symptoms: dysfunctional uterine bleeding and dysmenorrhea	Endometrial echo complex Symmetrical uterine enlargement
Endometrial carcinoma	Solid	Malignant tumor most common after menopause; abnormal uterine bleeding	Thickening endometrial echo greater than 10 mm in width.[5] Irregular and inhomogeneous endometrial texture

Used with permission from Fleischer A, James E. Diagnostic Sonography: Principles and Clinical Applications. Philadelphia: WB Saunders, 1989.

PREGNANCY

Pregnancy Test

As was mentioned in an earlier chapter, levels of human chorionic gonadotropin (hCG) are reported in terms of two common standards: the International Reference Preparation (IRP) and the Second International Standard (2nd IS). The 2nd IS is approximately half the value of the IRP. Human chorionic gonadotropin is first detectable about 10 days after conception and is considered to be positive at levels of 30 mIU/mL IRP.[7]

The level of hCG above which virtually all normal intrauterine pregnancies can be visualized with ultrasound is called the discriminatory zone. A normal rise of hCG (an average of 66% every 48 hours, or double every

TABLE 8–2. COMPLEX PELVIC MASSES

Mass	Type	Clinical Findings	Sonographic Findings
Endometrosis	Complex	Ectopic endometrial tissue, the tissue bleeds during menses, producing hemorrhagic masses called endometriomas or chocolate cysts because of the dark-brown blood inside the cysts. Pain and infertility.	Multiple cystic adnexal masses with thick wall and low-level internal echoes. Small echogenic lesions posterior to the uterus
Benign cystic teratoma (dermoid cyst)	Complex	Most common benign germ cell tumor filled with material: bone, fat, hair, skin, teeth. More common among young women in the reproductive age group	Fluid-fluid levels Distal acoustic shadow Calcifications Tip of the iceberg sign[6]
Serous cystadenoma	Complex	Benign ovarian neoplasm, usually unilateral	Large cystic mass Usually unilocular The presence of ascites is indicative of serous cystadenocarcinoma
Mucinous cystadenoma	Complex	Multilocular, most common among postmenopausal women. Rupture may cause pseudomyxoma peritonei	Large multiseptated mass The presence of ascites is indicative of mucinous cystadenocarcinoma
Tubo-ovarian abscess	Complex	Masses containing inflammatory fluid or pus within the tube and ovaries	Fluid-fluid levels Hydrosalpinges Cystic mass with low level echoes

Used with permission from Fleischer A, James E. Diagnostic Sonography: Principles and Clinical Applications. Philadelphia: WB Saunders, 1989.

TABLE 8–3. CYSTIC PELVIC MASSES

Mass	Type	Clinical Findings	Sonographic Findings
Corpus luteum cyst	Cyst	Associated with pregnancy	Unilocular May contain low-level internal echoes Normally regress before the 16th week of pregnancy
Theca lutein cyst	Cyst	Associated with hydatidiform mole. Multilocular and bilateral	Multiseptated cystic mass
Polycystic ovaries (Stein-Leventhal syndrome)	Cyst	A build-up of follicles, with bilateral enlargement and a thick outer covering of the ovaries preventing overlation. Symptoms: oligomenorrhea, hirsutism obesity.[3]	Bilateral enlarge ovaries Multiple small cysts
Nabothian cyst	Cyst	Retention cyst formed in the cervix due to occlusion of the cervical gland	Small cystic mass in the cervix; can be multiple
Gartner's duct cyst	Cyst	Cyst formed at the lower ends of the primitive mesonephric tubules, generally located on the anterolateral vaginal walls.[7]	Small cystic mass in the vagina
Follicular cyst	Cyst	Functional cyst, regresses spontaneously. Development and growth due to hormones	Change in size during the menstrual cycle Small thin-wall unilocular cyst Fluid in the cul-de-sac (follicular spill) Focal internal echo (cumulus oophorus)

Used with permission from Fleischer A, James E. Diagnostic Sonography: Principles and Clinical Applications. Philadelphia: WB Saunders, 1989.

72 hours) is indicative of an intrauterine pregnancy; a falling hCG level is indicative of a nonviable intrauterine pregnancy or an ectopic pregnancy.[7]

The qualitative level of the serum β subunit of hCG should be correlated with the sonographic findings for a more accurate diagnosis.

Duration

The duration of a pregnancy can be calculated from the first day of the last normal menstrual period and is referred to as menstrual age. The average duration of a pregnancy is about 280 days, 40 weeks, 9 calendar months, or 10 lunar months. The expected date of delivery can be estimated by Nägele's rule, which is based on a 28-day menstrual cycle:

- identify the date when the last menstrual period began
- add 7 days
- subtract 3 months
- add 1 year

Development of the Embryo and Fetus

As a pregnancy progresses, the progressive enlargement of the uterus can be followed by examining the fundal height (Fig. 8–5). At 16 weeks' gestation, the fundus is palpable midway between the symphysis and the umbilicus and reaches the umbilicus at 20–22 weeks. Transabdominal sonography can depict the gestational sac at a menstrual age of approximately 5 weeks. The chronologic development of the embryo and fetus during a pregnancy is described in Table 8–4. At 5 weeks of gestation, the yolk sac and embryo are not visible sonographically with the transabdominal approach and appear to be completely so-

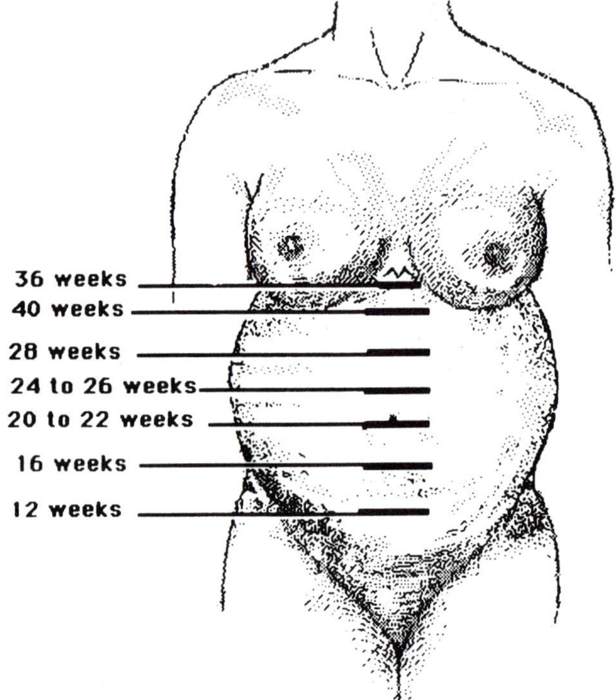

Figure 8–5. Diagram of the fundal height at various stages during pregnancy.

TABLE 8–4. CHRONOLOGICAL DEVELOPMENT OF THE EMBRYO AND FETUS

Gestational Age	Description	Developments
5 weeks	Average sac dimension = 1 cm	The sac is anechoic and surrounded by a thick "rind" of echoes. The sac is completely anechoic as echoes from the embryo are not yet visible. Sac size for gestational age can be performed.
6 weeks	Average sac dimension = 2 cm	Embryo appears, movements can be seen. Heart motion may be seen. CRL can be performed.
7 weeks	Average sac dimension = 4 cm	The embryo is about 10 mm. The heart motion can be seen. The yolk sac and umbilical stalk can be depicted.
8 weeks	Average sac dimension = 5 cm	Organogenesis is completed and the embryo is now called a fetus, which measures about 2 cm in length.
9 weeks	Average sac dimension = 6 cm	The fetus now measures about 3 cm in length. The placenta becomes recognizable.
10 weeks	Average sac dimension = 7 cm	The fetus now measures about 4 cm.
11 weeks		The fetus now measures about 5 cm. The yolk sac and umbilical stalk begin to disappear.
12 weeks		The fetus now measures about 6 cm. BPD can be obtained. End of first trimester. The decidua capsularis adheres to the decidua parietalis.
13–19 weeks	The fetus is extremely active and may change position several times during the ultrasound examination	The femur length, abdominal circumference, and BPD can be measured. The circumference of the head is greater than the abdominal circumference.
20–30 weeks	The fetus is extremely active and may change position several times during the ultrasound examination	Fetal abdominal wall defects and adrenal gland can be seen.
30–40 weeks	The fetus is less active and may not change its position during the examination.	Fetal head and body are equal in ratio from 32 to 36 weeks. Epiphyseal ossification is visible in the distal femur at 33 weeks.

Abbreviations: CRL, crown rump length; BPD, biparietal diameter.
The gestation sac grows about 1 cm a week, from the 5th week to the 10th week. The BPD can be done from 12 to 40 weeks, most accurate from 14 to 20 weeks. The CRL can be done from 6 to 12 weeks, most accurate from 8 to 12 weeks.
A rule of thumb for calculating the CRL is: CRL (cm) + 6.5 = gestational age in weeks

nolucent at this time. However, the gestational sac can be distinguished from blood in the uterine cavity by identifying the two decidua (the endometrium of pregnancy). The double decidua comprise the decidua capsularis (inner ring), which is the decidua overlying the gestational sac, and the decidua parietalis (outer ring), which is the decidua along the remainder of the uterine cavity. As the gestational sac enlarges, the unoccupied space between the two layers of decidua disappears and the double decidua are no longer apparent. The decidua basalis is the thick decidua beneath the implantation site (Fig. 8–6A).

The yolk sac–embryo appears at a menstrual age of

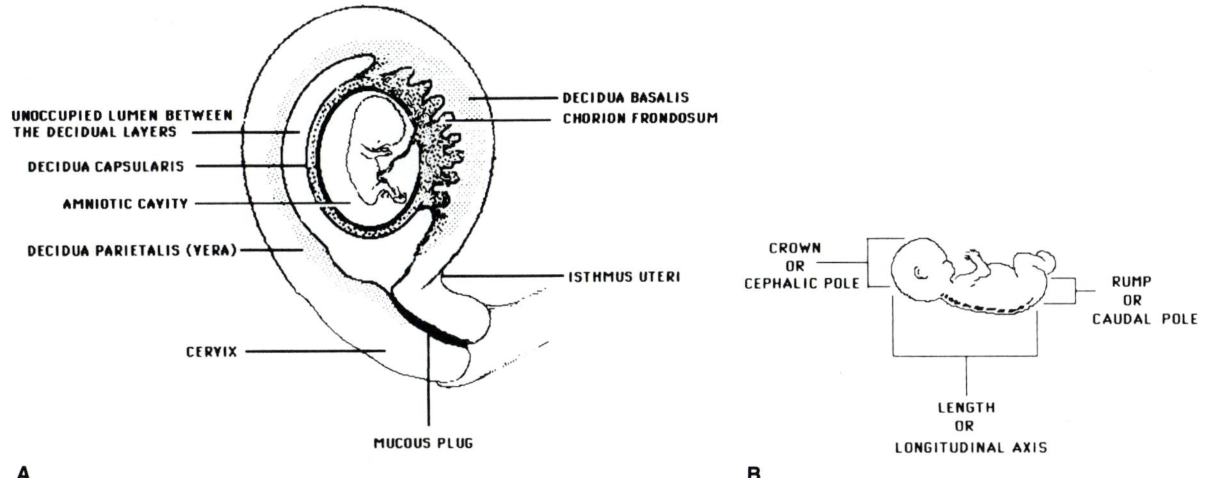

Figure 8–6. (**A**) Diagram of early pregnancy; (**B**) diagram of the fetal crown-rump length (the crown is the topmost part of an organ or structure, the rump is the buttocks, and the length is the long axis).

about 6 weeks, at which time the yolk sac is larger than the embryo. As the pregnancy advances, however, the embryo becomes larger than the yolk sac. The yolk sac lies in the chorionic cavity between the amnion and chorion. At about 10 to 12 weeks of menstrual age, the yolk sac shrinks, the amnion and chorion fuse, and the yolk sac is no longer visible.

OBSTETRIC ANOMALIES

A variety of obstetric anomalies can be depicted sonographically. The sonographic characteristics and features of these anomalies are described in Table 8–5.

Ectopic Pregnancy

Ectopic pregnancy denotes any pregnancy located outside the endometrial lumen. The term *ectopic* is a broad term used to describe any organ, structure, or pregnancy that is located away from its normal position; for example, an ectopic kidney or spleen. Ectopic pregnancy includes pregnancy located in the fallopian tubes, ovaries, or cervical canal. A pregnancy may be ectopic and yet be situated within the uterus.

The sonographic appearances of an ectopic pregnancy are multiple and depend on location, position, and whether it is ruptured or not. Some of these findings include (1) an enlarged empty uterus, (2) a ringlike adnexal mass, and (3) fluid in the cul-de-sac or subhepatic space. The possibility of coexistent intrauterine and ectopic pregnancy can occur but is a rare finding (reported to be between 1 in 2,000 to 1 in 30,000 deliveries).[31]

Blighted Ovum and Missed Abortion

A blighted ovum is a fertilized ovum that has become arrested. The gestational sac is without an embryo. The sonographic findings are: (1) failure of the gestational sac to grow normally, (2) a large gestational sac (3 cm) without an embryo, (3) a fluid-fluid level within the gestational sac, and (4) absent or irregular choriodecidual reaction.

A missed, or incomplete, abortion is defined as a dead embryo retained in the uterus before the 20th week of gestation. The sonographic findings are (1) no fetal heart

TABLE 8–5. OBSTETRICAL ANOMALIES

Anomalies	Characteristics	Sonographic Features
Anencephaly	Absence of the cranial vault and cerebral hemispheres. Predominantly occurs in female fetuses and is associated with spinal defects.	Hydramnios (polyhydramnios) Visible face with protruding eyes, giving a froglike appearance Absence of the cranial vault and inability to identify normal brain structures.
Acephalus	Fetus without a head	Complete absence of the head. Hydramnios (polyhydramnios)
Spina bifida	Midline bony defect of the vertebrae. Most common location is the posterior arches in the lumbosacral region. Characterized by elevated α-fetoprotein	A "horseshoe" or U-shaped spine on transverse scan, which provides a more reliable depiction than does a longitudinal scan Associated with hydrocephalus "banana sign" and "lemon sign"[30]
Meningomyelocele	Herniation of part of the spinal cord and meninges through a defect in the vertebral column. Most common in the lumbosacral region. Levels of alpha-fetoprotein are elevated.[9]	Hydramnios (polyhydramnios). Associated with hydrocephalus
Cephalocele	Protrusion of the meninges and brain through a bony defect of the skull. Elevated level of α-fetoprotein	Hydramnios (polyhydramnios). Associated with hydrocephalus, microcephaly
Ectopia cordis[9]	Ectopic fetal heart	Ectopic position of the fetal heart with real-time cardiac activity. Thoracic wall defect
Pentalogy of Cantrell[30]	1. Supraumbilical abdominal defect 2. Defect of the lower sternum 3. Deficiency of the diaphragmatic pericardium 4. Deficiency of the anterior diaphragm 5. Intracardiac abnormality	Hydramnios (polyhydramnios). Anterior wall defect. Fetal cardiac abnormality.
Omphalocele	Anterior wall defect with herniation of the abdominal contents; liver, spleen and bowel at the base of the umbilical cord. Covered with a membrane[7]	Hydramnios (polyhydramnios). Anterior wall defect. Unable to identify cord insertion Mass in amniotic fluid
Gastroschisis	Anterior wall defect with herniation of the abdominal contents; bowel to the right of midline with normal insertion of the umbilical cord. No membrane covering	Hydramnios (polyhydramnios) Anterior wall defect Bowel in amniotic fluid

Derived from Fleischer AC, Romero R, Manning FA, et al. The Principles and Practice of Ultrasonography in Obstetrics and Gynecology, 4th ed. Norwalk, Connecticut: Appleton & Lange, 1991.

motion on real-time, (2) reduced amniotic fluid, and (3) disorganized echoes in the uterine cavity.

Fetal Demise

Fetal demise is defined as death of the developing fetus after 20 weeks of gestation. The clinical and sonographic signs for fetal demise are numerous. The sonographic signs can be divided into specific and nonspecific.[29] The specific signs are (1) the failure to find the fetal heart tones on Doppler examination, (2) no fetal cardiac pulsation on M-mode, and (3) no movements or fetal heart pulsation seen on real-time sonography. The nonspecific signs are

- overlapping of the fetal sutures (Spalding's sign)
- hydramnios or oligohydramnios
- flattened (oblong) fetal head
- absence of the falx cerebri
- distorted fetal anatomy
- decrease in the biparietal diameter when measurements are repeated from one week to the next
- decrease in the size of the uterus
- edematous soft tissue around the head (the "halo" sign or Druel's sign)
- fragmentation of the fetal skin
- diffuse edema of the entire fetus (anasarca)
- separation of the amnion from the chorion after 20 weeks
- gas in the fetal circulatory system (Robert's sign)
- hydropic swelling of the placenta

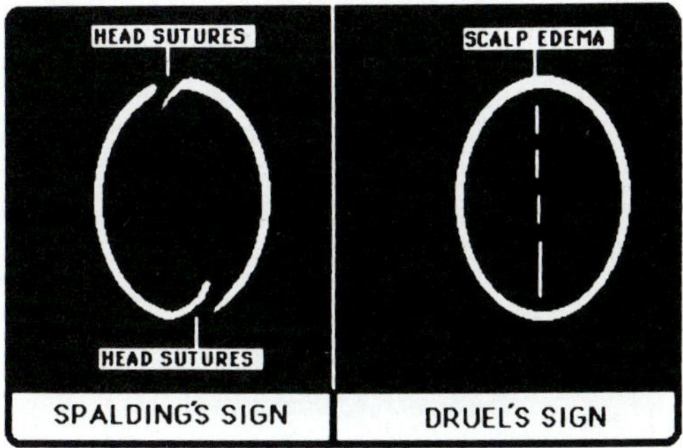

The clinical and laboratory findings of fetal demise are the failure of the uterus to grow, two negative pregnancy tests (serum beta hCG), no fetal movement, no heart sounds on auscultation, and red or brown amniotic fluid.

Amniotic Fluid Anomalies

The volume of amniotic fluid normally increases until the 34th week of gestation, then decreases as the pregnancy approaches term. The function of this fluid is to protect the fetus against possible injury and to regulate the fetal body temperature.[30] The fluid is produced by the kidneys, skin, and umbilical cord.[30]

The fetus normally swallows the amniotic fluid during pregnancy; therefore, if fetal swallowing is impaired, the amount of amniotic fluid can change.[1] An excessive amount of amniotic fluid is called hydramnios or polyhydramnios; a reduction in the normal amount of fluid is called oligohydramnios.

Hydramnios. A wide variety of maternal and fetal conditions are associated with hydramnios. The mnemonic MOTHER'S HOUSE serves as a memory key for 12 conditions associated with hydramnios.

- M meningomyelocele
- O omphalocele
- T twin–twin transfusion
- H hydrocephaly
- E erythroblastosis fetalis
- R retroperitoneal fibrosis
- S sacrococcygeal teratoma
- H hydrops fetalis
- O obstructive gastrointestinal anomalies
- U urethral stenosis
- S spina bifida
- E esophageal atresia

Oligohydramnios. The conditions associated with oligohydramnios are (1) fetal demise, (2) renal agenesis, (3) intrauterine growth retardation, (4) premature rupture of membranes, and (5) postmaturity. The mnemonic DRIPP serves as a key for memorizing the five conditions associated with oligohydramnios:

- D demise
- R renal agenesis
- I intrauterine growth retardation
- P premature rupture of membranes
- P postmaturity

Abnormal Presentation and Lie

The term *presentation* refers to the part of the fetus lying in closest proximity to the birth canal. The fetus can present in one of three presentations: cephalic, breech, and shoulder. Cephalic presentations are classified according to the degree of flexion or extension of the fetal head and represent about 96% of term deliveries.[1]

Cephalic presentations are (1) vertex, (2) face, and (3) brow. The terms *cephalic* and *vertex* are sometimes used incorrectly. The word *cephalic* is descriptive of the fetal head as the presenting part without being specific to what region of the head, whereas *vertex* is specifically descriptive of the region of the fetal head between the anterior and posterior fontanelles as the presenting part.

There are three types of breech presentations: (1) complete, (2) frank, and (3) footling (single or double footling) and represent only about 4% of term deliveries.[1]

The term *lie* refers to the relation of the long axis of the fetus to the long axis of the mother. There are three types of lie: (1) longitudinal, (2) transverse, and (3) oblique.

FETAL ECHOCARDIOGRAPHY

Fetal echocardiography has become an integral part of obstetric sonography. Sonographic examination of the in utero human heart can diagnose congenital heart disease, which may alter clinical care. The sonographer is obligated to perform a basic fetal heart survey on every fetal sonogram. The following sections outline the basics of fetal echocardiography, not only the American Registry of Diagnostic Medical Sonographers Examinations but for the sonographer who is performing obstetric sonography.

Fetal Anatomy and Cardiac Circulation

The complex development and transformation of the fetal heart is completed by the sixth week of gestation, and fetal cardiac circulation remains anatomically constant until birth. It is important to recognize that the fetal heart acts in unison as far as cardiac outputs are concerned, but left and right heart circulations differ in the parts of the fetus they perfuse. This section outlines crucial knowledge about the intracardiac anatomy and hemodynamics of the normal fetus. The fetal heart receives blood from the hepatic veins and ductus venosus of the fetal liver that ascend within the inferior vena cava and enter the right atrium. Once the blood approaches and actually enters the right atrium, the eustachian valve directs the flow of blood across the right atrium and toward the interatrial septum. The eustachian valve arises at the inferior vena cava or right atrial border of the inferior vena cava and is in direct communication with the lower edge of the septum secundum of the interatrial septum (the crista dividens). The eustachian valve–crista dividens complex directs approximately 60% of the highly oxygenated blood from the interior vena cava toward the atrial septum. The eustachian valve also reduces regurgitant flow during ventricular systole. Once the highly oxygenated blood from the inferior vena cava is channeled to the interatrial septum, the blood then continues through the septum via the hole in the atrial septum called the foramen ovale.

The foramen ovale allows highly oxygenated blood to enter the left atrium; consequently, the left heart circulation. No other normal in utero intracardiac pathways allow highly oxygenated blood to enter the left heart. The remaining volume of the blood pool in the inferior vena cava remains in the right atrium and mixes with blood entering the right atrium from the superior vena cava.

The blood in the right atrium that is not as oxygenated as the blood in the inferior vena cava traverses the tricuspid valve during diastole and enters the right ventricle. During systole, the tricuspid valve closes, and the ventricular blood volume is ejected through the outflow tract of the right ventricle and main pulmonary artery. Once the blood is in the main pulmonary artery, it can travel in two different pathways. Ninety percent of the blood continues in the artery and enters the ductus arteriosus, which acts as a shunt directing blood away from the traditional pulmonary circulation into the descending aorta for systemic circulation of the highly oxygenated blood. The remaining 10% of the blood in the main pulmonary artery enters the right and left pulmonary arteries that perfuse the nonfunctioning lungs of the fetus and returns to the left atrium through the pulmonary veins.

The left atrium is filled by pulmonary venous return and the highly oxygenated blood from the inferior vena cava. During diastole, the left atrial volume is emptied into the left ventricle through the mitral valve. The left ventricular volume passes through the left ventricular outflow tract during systole and continues through the aortic valve. At this point, the blood volume is distributed through the aortic arch and its cranial vessels, essentially supplying the cephalic aspect of the fetus (Fig. 8–7).[10,11]

The situation just described depicts the individualism of the circulation in the left and right hearts. The right heart largely perfuses the fetal body, whereas the left heart provides oxygenated blood to the fetal brain. Once the fetus is born, the thoracic pressures decrease and cardiac blood flows to the lungs, dramatically increasing the volume of the now-functioning lungs. These changes occur secondarily to the closing of the foramen ovale because of increased left heart pressures and closure of the ductus arteriosus, which becomes the ligamentum arteriosus and forces more pulmonary blood flow. At this point, the unique fetal cardiopulmonary circulation assumes the traditional circulatory pattern of the human.

Sonographic Anatomy and Techniques

The ability of the fetal echocardiogram to visualize normal or abnormal cardiac structures depends on the sonographer's knowledge and skill. The sonographer must have some understanding of traditional echocardiographic techniques because many of the multiple views potentially used in fetal echocardiography are identical to those used in adult and pediatric echocardiography.

The first step when observing the fetal heart is to orient oneself to the fetal anatomy. Determining the fetal lie and the location of the spine is essential because it

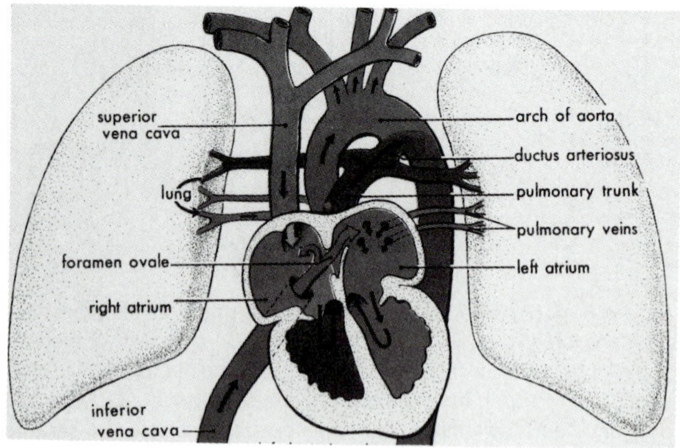

Figure 8–7. Schematic drawing demonstrating fetal cardiac circulatory system. *(Reproduced with permission from Moore KL, The Developing Human: Clinically Oriented Embryology, 4th ed, Philadelphia: WB Saunders, 1988, p. 326.)*

allows the sonographer to identify the left, right, cranial, caudal, dorsal, and ventral aspects of the fetus and the fetal heart.

Sonographic Views

Four-Chamber View. The fetal heart lies within the thorax in a horizontal plane that is perpendicular to the spine. Thus, the most important echocardiographic view, the four-chamber view, can be obtained with relative ease. The four-chamber view is obtained by imaging the fetal thorax in a transverse plane. Both atria, both ventricles, the atrioventricular valves (mitral and tricuspid), the atrial and ventricular septa, the moderator band, and the foramen ovale can be visualized in this view (Fig. 8–8).

Once the four-chamber view is imaged, orienting oneself to the anatomy of the fetal heart is crucially important. This is accomplished by visualizing the foramen ovale, which appears as a flap arising from the atrial septum and moving in and out of the left atrium. Because blood flows right to left through the foramen ovale, the flap of the foramen can only be within the left atrium. Occasionally, the foramen ovale cannot be visualized; in such cases, the sonographer relies on identification of the right ventricular moderator band. This band runs from the interventricular septum to the lower free wall of the right ventricle and can be seen within the apex of the right ventricle. These two parts of the intracardiac anatomy allow the sonographer to have a left-right cardiac orientation, which is essential for proper identification of normal or possibly abnormal structure. Valvular atresias, hypoplastic chambers, and septal defects can be identified from the four-chamber view.

Five-Chamber View. Additional cardiac anatomy can be visualized from the four-chamber view using subtle anterior angulation in relation to the fetal heart; this produces the five-chamber view (Fig. 8–9). The five-chamber view not only demonstrates the four chambers previously seen but also adds the left ventricular outflow tract and the proximal aortic root in relation to the ventricular septum. Further anterior angulation demonstrates the main pulmonary artery and the pulmonary valve arising from the right ventricle (Fig. 8–10). Thus, the five-chamber view orients the sonographer to the position of the great vessels in relation to the left and right ventricles.

Short-Axis View. Another important view that sonographers should be aware of is the short-axis view. To obtain this fetal echocardiographic view, the fetus must be imaged in a sagittal plane; consequently, the fetal heart is imaged in its transverse axis. The sonographer can sweep the entire heart, from its apexes to the aortic pulmonary window (Fig. 8–11), potentially demonstrating septal defects, hypoplastic chambers, and anomalies in the orientation of the great vessels.[12–16]

Fortunately, the sonographer does not need to be an expert in fetal echocardiography to see abnormalities on

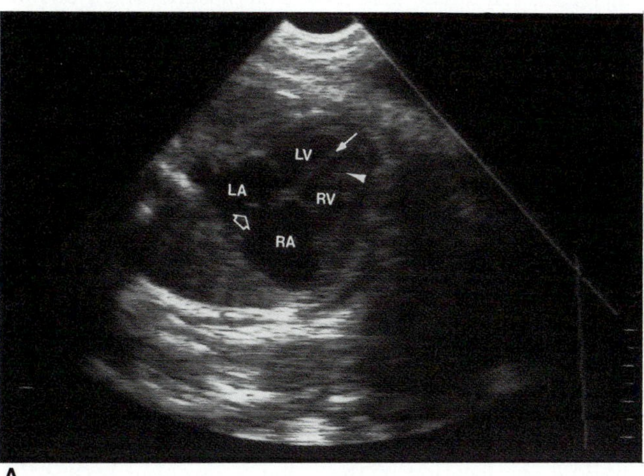

A

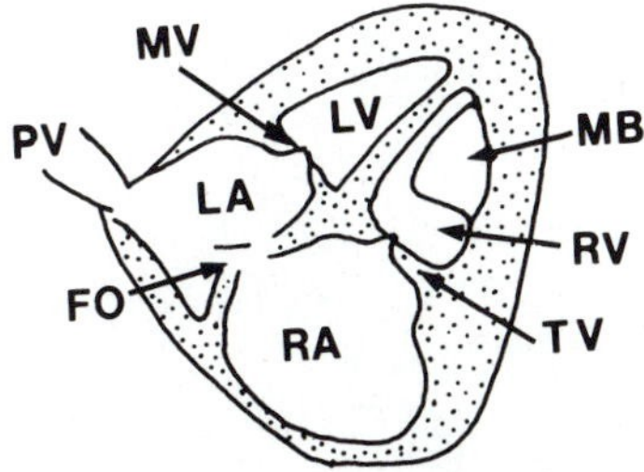

B

Figure 8–8. (**A**) Sonogram demonstrating the four chamber view: LA is the left atrium, RA is the right atrium, LV is the left ventricle, RV is the right ventricle (arrow), the arrowhead points to the moderator band, and the open foramen ovale (open arrowhead); (**B**) schematic diagram demonstrating a four-chamber view: FO is the foramen ovale, MB is the moderator band, TV is the tricuspid valve, and MV is the mitral valve. (*Reproduced with permission from Cyr DR, et al, A systematic approach to fetal echocardiography using real time/ two dimensional sonography. J Ultrasound Med 5:343–350, 1986.*)

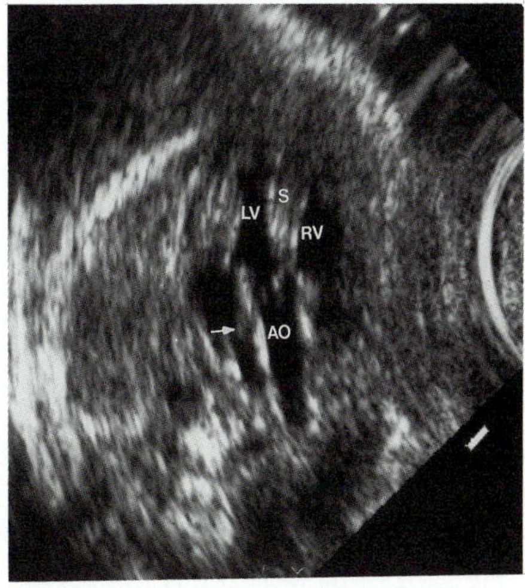

Figure 8–9. Sonogram demonstrating five-chamber view: AO is the aorta, LV is the left ventricle, S is the ventricular septum, RV is the right ventricle, and the arrow points to the left atrium.

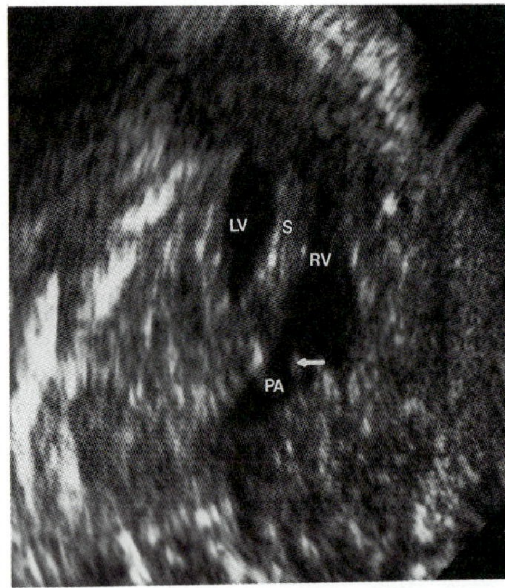

Figure 8–10. Sonogram demonstrating pulmonary artery from the five-chamber view: PA is the pulmonary artery (the arrow points to pulmonary valve), RV is the right ventricle, S is the ventricular septum, and LV is the left ventricle.

any given obstetrical sonogram. Recent studies have shown that 96% of fetal cardiac malformations, proved neonatally or pathologically, have been seen on the four-chamber view.[17,18] Therefore, the sonographer only needs to be proficient at obtaining the four- and five-chamber views to rule out the overwhelming majority of cardiac defects.

Other Views. Although they are beyond the scope of this chapter and will not be described in detail, several other fetal echocardiographic planes can be used to evaluate the fetal heart. These are the long-axis, aortic arch (suprasternal), right ventricular inflow, and right atrial inflow views. Table 8–6 demonstrates congenital abnormalities that can be identified sonographically, given the echocardiographic plane.[13]

M-MODE

Using M-mode in conjunction with two-dimensional imaging is essential in performing fetal echocardiograms. M-mode should be used to calculate heart rate (atrial or ventricular), measure the size of the atria and ventricles, or determine the type of cardiac arrythmia that is present.[22] Typical arrythmias that are diagnosed prenatally are premature atrial contractions, premature ventricular contractions, supraventricular tachycardias, and heart block. It is extremely important to evaluate both the atria and the ventricles with M-mode if this modality is to be used properly within the fetus.[19–21,23,24]

DOPPLER

Doppler plays a limited role in routine fetal echocardiography. The use of duplex sonography and color flow imaging is indicated only if congenital heart disease is suspected. Once a heart lesion is suspected, Doppler imaging helps distinguish abnormal flow patterns from dysplastic valves, abnormal great vessels, and septal defects. If Doppler is used in fetal echocardiography to aid in a diagnosis, it must be performed by experienced personnel.[12,24–28]

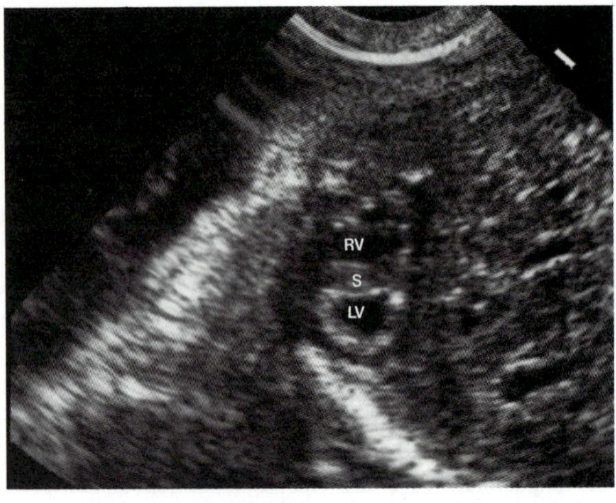

A

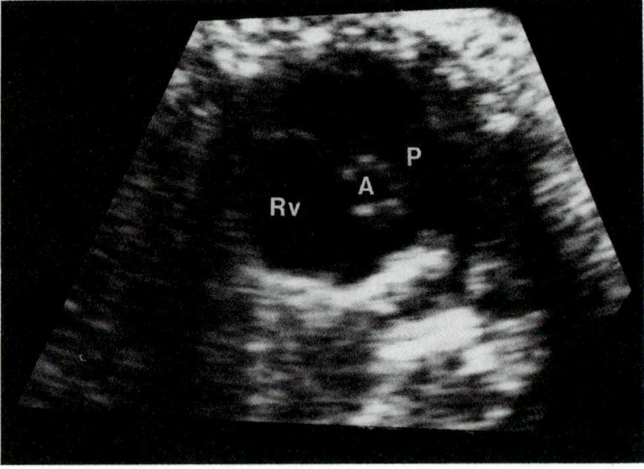

B

Figure 8–11. (**A**) Transverse sonogram in the short-axis view at the apical level: RV is the right ventricle, S is the ventricular septum, and LV is the left ventricle; (**B**) short axis view at the aortic-pulmonic window: A is the aorta (in transverse axis) and P is the main pulmonary artery.

TABLE 8–6. CONGENITAL CARDIOVASCULAR ANOMALIES DETECTABLE IN STANDARD ECHOCARDIOGRAPHIC VIEWS

Four-chamber anomalies
A hypoplastic ventricle (consider dilatation of the other ventricle)
Atresia of the mitral or tricuspid valve
A large atrial septal defect
A large ventricular septal defect
A-V canal (endocardial cushion defect)
Ebstein's anomaly
Pericardial and pleural effusions (hydrops)
Five-chamber anomalies (with aortic root)
Transposition of the great arteries
Aortic atresia
Long-axis left ventricle
Mitral stenosis or atresia
Aortic stenosis or atresia
Hypoplastic left ventricle
Cardiomyopathies (particularly endocardial fibroelastosis)
Pericardial effusion
Right ventricle inflow
Tricuspid atresia
Hypoplastic right ventricle
Ebstein's anomaly
Short-axis aortic level
Aortic stenosis or atresia
Pulmonic stenosis or atresia
Tricuspid atresia
Ebstein's anomaly
Large atrial septal defect
Large membranous ventricular septal defect
Ductus arteriosus (normal in fetus)
Truncus arteriosus
Transposition great arteries
Short-axis ventricles
Hypoplasia or dilatation either ventricle
Cardiomyopathy
Large muscular septal defect (including single ventricle)
Right atrial inflow
Tricuspid atresia
Ebstein's anomaly
Absent inferior vena cava (azygos continuation)
Suprasternal (aortic arch)
Coarctation
Interrupted arch
Underdeveloped pulmonary arteries (eg tetralogy of Fallot)

*Reproduced with permission from Cyr DR, et al. J Ultrasound Med **5**:343–350, 1986.*

REFERENCES

1. Cunningham FG, MacDonald PC, Gant NF. *Williams Obstetrics,* 18th ed. New York: Appleton & Lange, 1989.
2. Danforth DN, Dignam WJ, Hendricks CH, et al. *Obstetrics and Gynecology,* 3rd ed. New York: Harper & Row, 1977.
3. Netter FH, Oppenheimer E, Rock J. *The Ciba Collection of Medical Illustrations: Reproductive Systems,* vol. 2, 4th ed, Summit, NJ: Ciba Pharmaceutical, 1965.
4. Mittelstaedt C, Lawrence V. *Abdominal Ultrasound.* New York: Churchill Livingstone, 1987.
5. Fleischer A, James E. *Diagnostic Sonography: Principles and Clinical Applications.* Philadelphia: WB Saunders, 1989.
6. Sabbagha R. *Diagnostic Ultrasound: Application to OB/GYN,* 2nd ed. Philadelphia: JB Lippincott, 1987.
7. Goldstein S. *Endovaginal Ultrasound.* New York: Alan R Liss, 1988.
8. Callen PW. *Ultrasonography in OB/GYN,* 2nd ed. Philadelphia: WB Saunders, 1983.
9. Romero R, Pilu G, Jenty P, et al. *Prenatal Diagnosis of Congenital Anomalies.* Norwalk, CT: Appleton & Lange, 1988.
10. Kleinman CS, Copel JA, Weinstein EM, et al. Treatment of fetal supraventricular tachyarrhythmias. *J Clin Ultrasound* **13**:265–273, 1985.
11. Reed KL, Sahn DJ, Scagnelli S, et al. Doppler echocardiographic studies of diastolic function in the human fetal heart: changes during gestation. *J Am Coll Cardiol* **8**:391–395, 1986.
12. Allan LD, Chita SK, Al-Ghazali, et al. Doppler echocardiographic evaluation of the normal human fetal heart. *Br Heart J* **57**:528–533, 1987.
13. Cyr DR, Guntheroth WG, Mack LA, et al. A systematic approach to fetal echocardiography using realtime two-dimensional sonography. *J Ultrasound Med* **5**:343–350, 1986.
14. Cyr DR, Komarniski CA, Guntheroth WG, Mack LA. The prevalence of imaging fetal cardiac anatomy. *J. Diagn Med Sonography* **6**:299–304, 1988.
15. DeVore GR. Fetal echocardiography—a new frontier. *Clin Obstet Gynecol* **27**:359–377, 1984.
16. Rudolph AM. Distribution and regulation of blood flow in the fetal and neonatal lamb. *Circulation Res* **57**:811–821, 1985.
17. Benacerraf BR, Pober BR, Sanders SP. Accuracy of fetal echocardiography. *Radiology* **165**:847–849, 1987.
18. Copel JA, Pilu G, Green J, et al. Fetal echocardiographic screening for congenital heart disease: the importance of the four-chamber view. *Am J Obstet Gynecol* **157**:648–655, 1987.

19. Allan LD, Joseph MC, Boyd EGCA, et al. M-mode echocardiography in the developing human fetus. *Br Heart J* **47:**573–583, 1982.

20. DeVore GR, Donnerstein RL, Kleinman CS, et al. Fetal echocardiography. I. normal anatomy as determined by real-time–directed M-mode ultrasound. *Am J Obstet Gynecol* **144:**249, 1982.

21. DeVore GR, Siassi B, Platt LD. Fetal echocardiography. IV. M-mode assessment of ventricular size and contractility during the second and third trimesters of pregnancy in the normal fetus. *Am J Obstet Gynecol* **150:**981–988, 1984.

22. DeVore GR, Siassi B, Platt L. Fetal echocardiography. III. The diagnosis of cardiac arrhythmias using real-time-directed M-mode ultrasound. *Am J Obstet Gynecol* **146:**792, 1983.

23. Kenny JF, Plappert T, Doubilet P. Changes in intracardiac blood flow velocities and right and left ventricular stroke volumes with gestational age in the normal human fetus: a prospective Doppler echocardiographic study. *Circulation* **74:**1208–1216, 1986.

24. Moore KL. *The Developing Human: Clinically Oriented Embryology,* 3rd ed. Philadelphia: WB Saunders, 1982.

25. DeVore GR, Horenstein J, Siassi B, Platt LD. Fetal echocardiography. VII. Doppler color flow mapping: a new technique for the diagnosis of congenital heart disease. *Am J Obstet Gynecol* **156:**1054–1064, 1987.

26. Huhta JC, Strasburger JF, Carpenter RJ, et al. Pulsed Doppler fetal echocardiography. *J Clin Ultrasound* **13:**247–254, 1985.

27. Jeanty P, Romero R, Hobbins JC. Fetal pericardial fluid: a normal finding of the second half of gestation. *Am J Obstet Gynecol* **149:**529–532, 1984.

28. Reed KL, Meijboom EJ, Sahn DJ, et al. Cardiac Doppler flow velocities in human fetuses. *Circulation* **73:**41–46, 1986.

29. Sanders RC, James AE. *The Principles and Practice of Ultrasonography in Obstetrics and Gynecology,* 3rd ed. Norwalk, CT: Appleton-Century-Crofts, 1985.

30. Nyberg DA, Mahony BS, Pretorius DH. *Diagnostic Ultrasound of Fetal Anomalies: Text and Atlas.* St. Louis: Mosby-Yearbook, 1990.

31. Hann LE, Bachmann DL, Ardle CR. Coexistent intrauterine and ectopic pregnancy: A reevaluation. *Radiology* **152:**151, 1984

Questions

GENERAL INSTRUCTIONS: For each question select the best answer. Select only one answer for each question, unless otherwise indicated.

1. Which of the following is not among the general categories of gestational trophoblastic disease?
   (A) hydatidiform mole
   (B) chorioadenoma destruens
   (C) chondrosarcoma
   (D) choriocarcinoma

2. An invasive mole is also referred to as
   (A) hydatidiform mole
   (B) an endometrioma
   (C) a blighted ovum
   (D) chorioadenoma destruens

3. The variables that make up a fetal biophysical profile are
   (A) breathing movements
   (B) qualitative amniotic fluid volume
   (C) fetal tone
   (D) reactive fetal heart rate
   (E) all of the above
   (F) B and D only

4. The cephalic index is defined as the ratio of the biparietal diameter to
   (A) femur length
   (B) occipito-frontal diameter
   (C) abdominal circumference
   (D) binocular distances

5. Identify the signs and symptoms that are associated with hydatidiform moles from the following list: (1) thyrotoxicosis, (2) hyperemesis gravidarium, (3) uterus too large for dates, (4) elevated serum β-hCG, (5) hemorrhage, (6) passage of grape-like vesicles through the vagina, (7) preeclampsia, (8) pulmonary embolism.
   (A) 2, 4, and 5
   (B) 3, 4, 5, and 7
   (C) 2, 3, 4, and 5
   (D) all of the above

6. Hydatidiform mole is characterized by
   (A) benign proliferation of the trophoblast
   (B) malignant proliferation of the trophoblast
   (C) invasive proliferation of the trophoblast
   (D) all of the above

7. Figure 8–12 is a transverse sonogram of the uterus. The most likely diagnosis is
   (A) an unruptured ectopic pregnancy within the right fallopian tube
   (B) an incomplete abortion
   (C) an early embryonic demise of a twin intrauterine pregnancy
   (D) an intrauterine pregnancy in one horn of a bicornuate uterus

8. A solid mass may exhibit all of the following *except*
   (A) distal acoustic shadows
   (B) distal acoustic enhancement
   (C) irregular, poorly defined walls
   (D) an echo-free interior

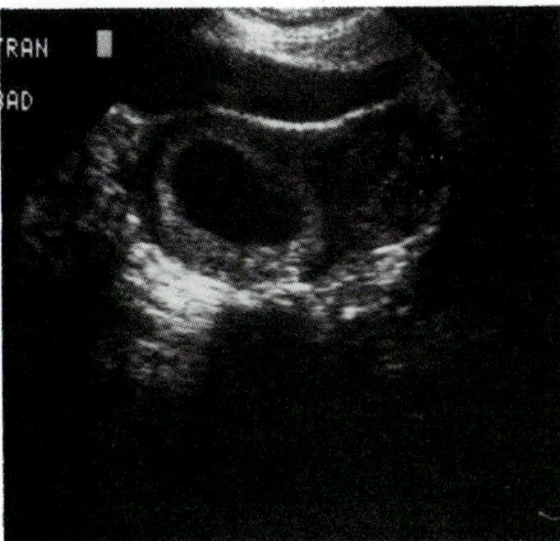

Figure 8–12. Transverse sonogram of the uterus.

9. The incidence of hydatidiform mole in the United States is approximately
   (A) 1 in 5000 patients
   (B) 1 in 500 patients
   (C) 1 in 250 patients
   (D) 1 in 1200–2000 patients

10. What percentage of hydatidiform mole has a coexistent fetus?
   (A) 20%
   (B) 30%
   (C) 5%
   (D) 2%

11. What type of cyst is commonly associated with hydatidiform mole?
   (A) a theca lutein cyst
   (B) a paraovarian cyst
   (C) a corpus luteum cyst
   (D) a follicular cyst

12. With the advent of gray-scale sonography, there has been a variety of sonographic appearances of hydatidiform mole. Which of the following are characteristic of its gray-scale appearance?
   (A) a snowstorm
   (B) a vesicular sonographic texture
   (C) a speckled appearance
   (D) a calcified appearance

13. Trophoblastic disease, which extends outside the uterus and spreads to the lungs or brain, is called
   (A) choriocarcinoma
   (B) hydatidiform mole
   (C) endometrioma
   (D) lung-gestational molar

14. How many weeks after suction evacuation of molar gestation does the serum β-human gonadotropin (β-hCG) return to the normal range?
   (A) 36 weeks
   (B) 20–30 weeks
   (C) 2–4 weeks
   (D) 10–12 weeks

15. What percentage of molar pregnancy results in choriocarcinoma?
   (A) 90%
   (B) 65%
   (C) 3–20%
   (D) 40–50%

16. Choriocarcinoma can metastasize to which of the following areas: (1) lungs and brain, (2) liver, (3) bone, (4) gastrointestinal tract?
   (A) 3 and 4
   (B) 2 and 3
   (C) 1 only
   (D) all of the above

17. Select the most effective form of contraceptive.
   (A) intrauterine contraceptive device (IUCD)
   (B) oral contraceptive
   (C) condom
   (D) vaginal contraceptive sponge

18. Which of the following countries has the greatest incidence of hydatidiform mole?
   (A) United States
   (B) Japan
   (C) France
   (D) Jamaica

19. Which of the following statements is a hypothetical explanation for the geographic variability in the incidence of hydatidiform mole?
   (A) hydatidiform mole is secondary to nutritional factors
   (B) it is the result of genetic predisposition
   (C) it is the result of increased parity in these areas
   (D) all of the above

20. The etiology of hydatidiform mole is
   (A) trophoblastic changes in a blighted ovum
   (B) hydatid swelling of the retained placenta in a missed abortion
   (C) fertilization of an ovum without any active chromosomal material
   (D) A and B only

21. How long does it usually take for theca lutein cysts to regress after molar evacuation?
   (A) 1–2 weeks
   (B) 4–5 weeks
   (C) 6 months
   (D) 2–4 months

22. A pregnancy within a bicornuate uterus
   (A) sometimes aborts
   (B) may go to term without complications
   (C) may result in decidual proliferation in the nongravid horn
   (D) all of the above

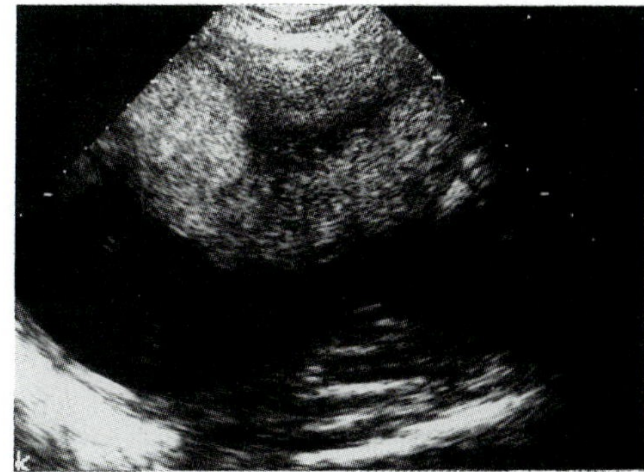

Figure 8–13. Transverse sonogram through the uterine fundus.

23. Figure 8–13 is a transverse sonogram through the uterine fundus in a 28-week pregnancy. The most likely diagnosis is

(A) a placental choriongioma
(B) abruptio placentae
(C) a large venous lake
(D) an overmature placenta

24. Which of the following is *not* among the characteristic echo patterns of an intrauterine contraceptive device?

(A) a distal acoustic shadow
(B) entrance–exit reflections
(C) a line of interrupted echo
(D) distal acoustic enhancement

25. The maximum number of interrupted echoes seen on a sonogram with a Lippes Loop in situ is

(A) two
(B) four
(C) five
(D) eight

26. The date of the last menstrual period indicates

(A) the date when fertilization occurred
(B) the date when menstrual bleeding ended
(C) the date when ovulation occurred
(D) the date when menstrual bleeding began

27. What percentage of intrauterine contraceptive devices demonstrate an entrance–exit reflection?

(A) 95%
(B) 65%
(C) 30%
(D) 20%

28. Concerning placental grading,

(A) there is a significant overlap of placental patterns in normal and abnormal pregnancies
(B) all grade III placentas will have a mature fetal pulmonary test
(C) it is a useful parameter in the diagnosis of intrauterine growth retardation
(D) continuous-wave Doppler will always be abnormal in grade III placentas
(E) A and C

29. Abruptio placentae

(A) may be life threatening to the fetus
(B) may be life threatening to the mother
(C) can be mistaken for a sustained uterine contraction
(D) all of the above

30. The accuracy of sonography in the diagnosis of molar gestation has been estimated to be more than

(A) 90%
(B) 50%
(C) 60%
(D) 20%

31. Which of the following diagnoses does *not* mimic the sonographic characteristic of hydatidiform mole?

(A) endometriosis
(B) hematoma
(C) uterine leiomyoma
(D) missed abortion

32. After hydatidiform mole is treated, a chest radiograph is recommended. The reasons for this are which of the following: (1) evidence of metastatic disease, (2) pleural effusion, (3) cardiomegaly, (4) a pulmonary embolism?

(A) 1 and 2
(B) 1 and 4
(C) all of the above
(D) none of the above

33. What percentage of patients diagnosed with hydatidiform mole will usually follow a benign course?

(A) 20%
(B) 10%
(C) 50%
(D) 80%

34. If the nylon thread attached to the IUCD cannot be visualized or palpated by a physician, the possibilities are which of the following: (1) detachment of the nylon thread, (2) expulsion of the device, (3) uterine perforation by the IUCD, (4) migration of the nylon thread?

(A) 1 and 2
(B) 2 and 4

(C) 4 only
(D) all of the above

35. Figure 8–14 is a transverse sonogram of the left upper quadrant in a gravid patient. The most likely diagnosis is

(A) an obstructed left kidney
(B) a fluid-filled, distended small bowel
(C) a fluid-filled, distended large bowel
(D) a ruptured spleen

36. In what anatomic site does fertilization of the ovum usually occur?

(A) the vagina
(B) the uterine cavity
(C) the ovary
(D) the fallopian tube

37. A Krukenberg's tumor is a

(A) benign ovarian tumor
(B) bilateral tumor of the ovary that has metastasized from primary tumor in the gastrointestinal tract.
(C) cystic tumor
(D) uterine tumor.

38. Which of the following is *not* a clinical symptom of a hydatidiform mole?

(A) preeclampsia
(B) hyperemesis gravidarum
(C) embolization
(D) hydrometrocolpos

39. The small bowel can be distinguished from the large bowel by

(A) a barium enema
(B) the presence of valvulae conniventes

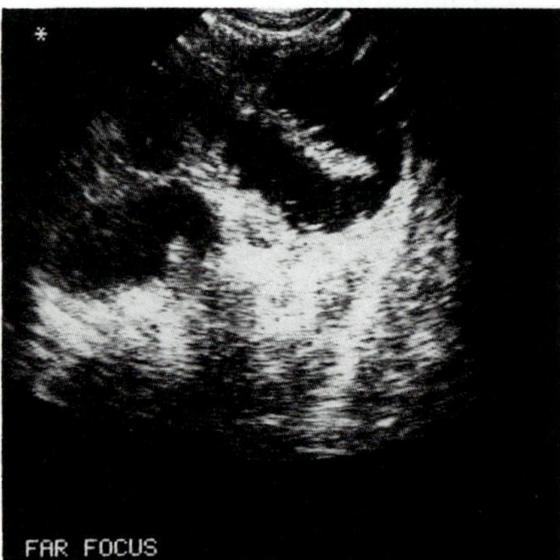

Figure 8–14. Transverse sonogram of the left upper quadrant in a gravid patient.

(C) the presence of haustra
(D) different peristaltic patterns

40. The term trophoblast denotes

(A) the extraembryonic peripheral cells of the blastocyst
(B) a rigid state of the flagellate microorganism
(C) the gestation sac
(D) the characteristics of a disease

41. The term pathognomonic denotes

(A) development of a morbid condition
(B) insanity
(C) the study of pathologic lesions
(D) the characteristics of a disease

42. What are most likely to produce numerous anechoic structures of about 3–5 mm in diameter in a classical sonographic appearance of hydatidiform mole?

(A) numerous hydropic villi
(B) calcifications
(C) theca lutein cysts
(D) fetal parts

43. The term proliferation denotes

(A) the characteristics of a disease
(B) the multiplication of similar forms
(C) the peripheral cells of the blastocyst
(D) the creation of holes

44. Perforation of the uterus by an intrauterine contraceptive device occurs most often during

(A) menstruation
(B) exercise
(C) intercourse
(D) insertion

45. During pregnancy, the maternal bowel is usually

(A) displaced superiorly by the gravid uterus
(B) displaced inferiorly by the gravid uterus
(C) not displaced
(D) filled with amniotic fluid

46. Although many imaging modalities are used today, the most reliable method of evaluating intrauterine contraceptive devices is

(A) a pelvic x-ray
(B) sonography
(C) computed tomography
(D) a hysterogram

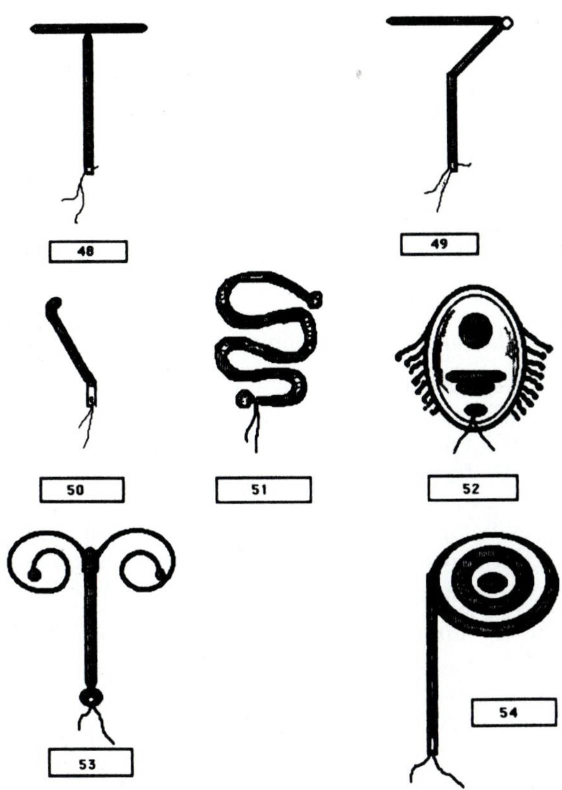

Figure 8–15. Diagram of intrauterine contraceptive devices.

47. How accurate is sonography in assessing the localization of an intrauterine contraceptive device in utero?

(A) 100%
(B) 50%
(C) 90%
(D) 99%

Questions 48 through 54: Match the devices in Fig. 8–15 with the list of terms in Column B.

COLUMN A	COLUMN B
48. ____	(A) Saf-T-Coil
49. ____	(B) Copper-T (Cu-T)
50. ____	(C) Copper-7 (Cu-7)
51. ____	(D) Gynekoil
52. ____	(E) Lippes Loop
53. ____	(F) Dalkon shield
54. ____	(G) Antigon device

55. Fetal death is defined as death of a fetus (1) at 20 weeks or more of gestation, (2) at any stage of gestation, (3) weighing 500 g or more, (4) after 36 weeks of gestation.

(A) 1 and 3
(B) 2 and 3
(C) 4 only
(D) all of the above

56. Which of the following conditions is most likely to require scanning of the right upper quadrant?

(A) intrauterine gestation 6 weeks size
(B) gonococcal pelvic inflammatory disease
(C) a 2 cm right ovarian cyst
(D) a 2 cm left ovarian cyst

57. Metastatic ovarian carcinoma can be associated with

(A) ascites
(B) peritoneal metastases
(C) omental metastases
(D) liver metastases
(E) all of the above

58. The endometrium can appear echogenic (1) particularly in the secretory phase, (2) in patients with pelvic inflammatory disease, (3) after dilatation and curettage, (4) in patients with endometritis, (5) after removal of an intrauterine contraceptive device.

(A) 1 and 3 only
(B) 4 only
(C) 1, 2, 3, and 5
(D) all of the above

59. Which of the following masses would be *least* likely to be encountered during pregnancy?

(A) leiomyoma uteri
(B) dysgerminoma
(C) dermoid cyst
(D) corpus luteum cyst

60. A 22-year-old gravid patient presents with oligohydramnios. Which of the following would be *least* likely?

(A) anencephaly
(B) postterm pregnancy
(C) renal agenesis
(D) premature rupture of the membranes

61. If spontaneous labor were allowed after fetal death, what percentage of mothers would deliver the fetus by the end of the third week?

(A) 50%
(B) 65%
(C) 80%
(D) 93%

62. What are the potential dangers if a demised fetus is allowed to remain in utero for more than 5 weeks?

(A) hypofibrinogenemia
(B) cytomegalovirus

(C) erythroblastosis
(D) rubella

63. The term liquefaction denotes

(A) echoes in the amniotic fluid
(B) the conversion of a solid material into a liquid form
(C) a fatty tumor
(D) a demised fetus

64. How accurate is real-time sonography at diagnosing fetal death?

(A) 50%
(B) 70%
(C) 80%
(D) 99%

65. The nonspecific signs of fetal death are which of the following: (1) polyhydramnios, (2) nonvisualization of the heartbeat on real-time, (3) sonographic spalding signs, (4) scalp edema, (5) loss of the falx cerebri, (6) echoes in the amniotic fluid?

(A) 2 only
(B) 1, 3, and 4
(C) 1, 3, 4, 5, and 6
(D) all of the above

66. The biparietal diameter can be determined as early as

(A) 14 weeks
(B) 12 weeks
(C) 8 weeks
(D) 6 weeks

67. What is the first structure seen in the early diagnosis of pregnancy by sonography?

(A) the gestation sac
(B) the fetal head
(C) the zygote
(D) the morula

68. The measurement(s) used to assess gestational age in the first trimester is

(A) the uterine size
(B) the biparietal diameter
(C) the gestation sac and crown-rump length
(D) the fetal abdominal circumference

69. A gestational sac generally refers to a pregnancy

(A) of less than 2 weeks
(B) between 4 and 10 weeks
(C) between 10 and 15 weeks
(D) between 4 and 36 weeks

70. When scanning a patient who is near term and complains of feeling faint, the sonographer should

(A) offer her fluid by mouth
(B) stop the examination and turn her on her side
(C) put her in Fowler's position
(D) fan her or turn on the air conditioner

71. Given a 24-year-old gravid patient whose last menstrual period began on 8/10/92, what date would her expected date of confinement be?

(A) 5/14/94
(B) 5/17/93
(C) 5/10/93
(D) 8/10/93

72. The patient is a 20-year-old multigravid patient, whose last menstrual period is uncertain. On the TV monitor a completely anechoic gestation sac with an average dimension of 1 cm is seen. The approximate gestational age is

(A) 8 weeks
(B) 4–5 weeks
(C) 9 weeks
(D) 10–12 weeks

73. Organogenesis is completed at

(A) 4 weeks
(B) 8 weeks
(C) 36 weeks
(D) 40 weeks

74. How early can the placenta be identified on sonography?

(A) 8 weeks
(B) 14 weeks
(C) 16 weeks
(D) 20 weeks

75. What is the uterine isthmus called during pregnancy?

(A) the gestation sac
(B) an ectopic pregnancy
(C) the placenta previa
(D) the lower uterine segment

76. A patient's parity is P4174. How many abortions has she had?

(A) four
(B) seven
(C) one
(D) six

77. What is the *most* common type of cyst seen in the first trimester of pregnancy?

(A) a corpus luteum cyst
(B) a follicular cyst
(C) a theca lutein cyst
(D) a paraovarian cyst

78. The patient is a 22-year-old multigravida, last menstrual period uncertain. A gestation sac is seen with an embryo. The crown-rump length is 2 cm. What is the approximate age of the embryo?

(A) 6 weeks
(B) 8.5 weeks
(C) 10.5 weeks
(D) 4–5 weeks

79. A gestational sac fills one-quarter of the uterine cavity and measures 1 cm in length, 1 cm in anteroposterior diameter, and 2 cm in transverse diameter. What is the average sac dimension of the gestation?

(A) 1.3 cm
(B) 2.5 cm
(C) 2.5 mm
(D) 1.1 mm

80. A near-term gravid patient lying face up for more than 15 minutes will sometimes become ill with fainting and nausea. She is probably experiencing

(A) supine hypotensive syndrome
(B) supine hypertensive syndrome
(C) morning sickness
(D) hyperemesis gravidarum
(E) none of the above

81. Fig. 8–16 is a longitudinal midline sonogram through the cervix. The most likely diagnosis is

(A) a fibroid
(B) feces in the rectum
(C) placenta previa
(D) a cystic ovarian tumor

82. The double-ring sign of the fetal skull is sometimes seen in which of the following conditions?

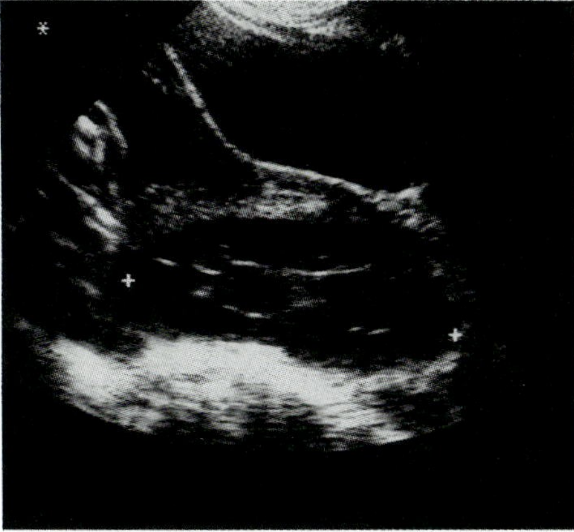

Figure 8–16. Sagittal midline sonogram through the cervix.

(A) maternal diabetes
(B) fetal demise
(C) sickle-cell anemia
(D) Rh isoimmunization
(E) fetal distress
(F) fetal anasarca
(G) hydrops fetalis
(H) all of the above
(I) A, B, and D only

83. The separation of the chorionic and amniotic membranes is normal

(A) after 24 weeks of gestation
(B) before 24 weeks of gestation
(C) after 16 weeks of gestation
(D) before 16 weeks of gestation

84. Amniotic band syndrome is a term for

(A) adhesions of torn amniotic membranes wrapped around fetal parts and producing congenital amputations
(B) complications of placental abruption
(C) a syndrome that occurs after the fetus swallows too much amniotic fluid
(D) A and C

85. Eighty percent of cystic hygromas occur in what region?

(A) the axilla
(B) the mediastinum
(C) the cervical region
(D) all of the above
(E) none of the above

86. Which of the following is the appropriate description of gastroschisis?

(A) normal insertion of the umbilical cord, with herniation of the bowel occurring most often on the right side of the umbilicus
(B) herniation of the abdominal contents, including the bowel and liver or spleen, with herniation at the base of the umbilical cord
(C) herniation of the umbilical cord
(D) herniation of bowel to the left of the umbilicus containing spleen covered by peritoneum

87. Cystic hygromas are

(A) malignant cysts of the thyroid
(B) benign developmental abnormalities of lymphatic origin
(C) another name for meningomyelocele
(D) benign cysts of the ovaries

88. A 30-year-old gravid patient, 8 months by dates, now presents with painless vaginal bleeding that has lasted for 5 days. The first condition to rule out by sonography is

(A) an ectopic pregnancy
(B) placenta previa
(C) an ovarian cyst
(D) hydatidiform mole

89. The clinical signs and symptoms for intrauterine pregnancy are which of the following: (1) Chadwick's sign, (2) Hegar's sign, (3) Goodell's sign, (4) quickening?

(A) 3 and 4
(B) 1 and 3
(C) 1, 3, and 4 only
(D) all of the above

90. How long does a postpartum uterus remain enlarged?

(A) 4–8 weeks after delivery
(B) 2–4 weeks after delivery
(C) 8–12 weeks after delivery
(D) 12–14 weeks after delivery

91. The abdominal circumference of the fetal abdomen should be taken at what level?

(A) the site of the cord insertion
(B) the portal sinus of the umbilical vein and the stomach
(C) the kidneys
(D) the heart

92. The thick "rind" of echoes surrounding the gestational sac are the (1) decidua capsularis, (2) syncytiotrophoblast, (3) decidua basalis, (4) yolk sac.

(A) 1 only
(B) 1 and 2
(C) 1, 2, and 3
(D) all of the above

93. Which of the following conditions or complications is *least* likely to occur?

(A) an ectopic pregnancy situated in the uterus
(B) menstruation following a hysterectomy
(C) a pregnancy following a hysterectomy
(D) a hysterectomy without a surgical scar on the skin
(E) a pregnancy in the uterus and outside the uterus at the same time

94. Parity P8257 indicates that

(A) the number of abortions is ______
(B) the number of term infants is ______
(C) the number of premature infants is ______
(D) the number of children currently alive ______

95. A sonographic characteristic of cystic hygroma is a

(A) multiseptated cystic mass
(B) solid mass on the anterior neck
(C) complex mass of the spine
(D) bilateral hyperechoic mass of the neck only

96. A large placenta is most likely to be seen in which of the following?

(A) multiple gestation
(B) Rh isoimmunization
(C) diabetics
(D) preeclampsia
(E) all of the above
(F) A, B, and C only

97. The most accurate biparietal diameter measurements are made at what week of gestation?

(A) 36 weeks
(B) 14–20 weeks
(C) 20–30 weeks
(D) 40 weeks

98. If a pregnant patient becomes faint (syncope) and nauseous during sonographic examination, this may be due to pressure of the

(A) uterus on the intestine
(B) uterus on the aorta
(C) uterus on the inferior vena cava
(D) transducer on the skin

99. Placental abruption is diagnosed by which of the following sonographic findings?

(A) retroplacental clot
(B) extramembranous clot
(C) both A and B
(D) neither A nor B

100. How accurate is placental localization with sonography?

(A) 95%
(B) 75%
(C) 80%
(D) 99%

101. If a localized thickening of the placenta and myometrium is seen, which changes within 20 minutes, this would most likely represent

(A) fibroid
(B) placenta previa
(C) placental abruption
(D) Braxton Hicks contractions

102. Placental abruption is defined as premature separation of the placenta from the uterine wall *after* the 20th week of gestation.

(A) true
(B) false

103. A 10-cm gestational sac is seen with a 25-mm embryo in it. Which one of the following measurements is *most* appropriate?

(A) crown-rump length (CRL)
(B) biparietal diameter (BPD)
(C) femur length (FL)
(D) gestational sac measurement

104. The term *ectopic pregnancy* denotes

(A) pregnancy in the fallopian tube
(B) pregnancy in the abdomen
(C) any abnormal pregnancy
(D) any pregnancy located outside of the endometrial lumen

105. The reason for shoulder pain in ectopic pregnancy is

(A) intraperitoneal bleeding with diaphragmatic irritation
(B) vomiting
(C) syncope
(D) fluid in the posterior cul-de-sac

106. If a multigravida uterus is 8.5 cm in length, the uterus is

(A) enlarged
(B) small
(C) normal size
(D) abnormal

107. Which of the following statements is *not* true concerning the yolk sac?

(A) the yolk sac should be included in measurements of crown-rump length (CRL)
(B) the yolk sac shrinks as pregnancy advances
(C) the yolk sac plays a role in blood development and transfer of nutrients
(D) the yolk sac is attached to the body stalk and is located between the amnion and chorion

108. Which of the following statements concerning intrauterine growth retardation (IUGR) is *not* true?

(A) chromosomal abberations are more common in asymmetrical IUGR than in symmetrical IUGR
(B) amniotic fluid volume is always abnormally low in IUGR
(C) abdominal circumference measurements are helpful in the diagnosis of IUGR
(D) IUGR is associated with hydramnios

Questions 109 through 126: Match the structures in Fig. 8–17 with the list of terms in Column B.

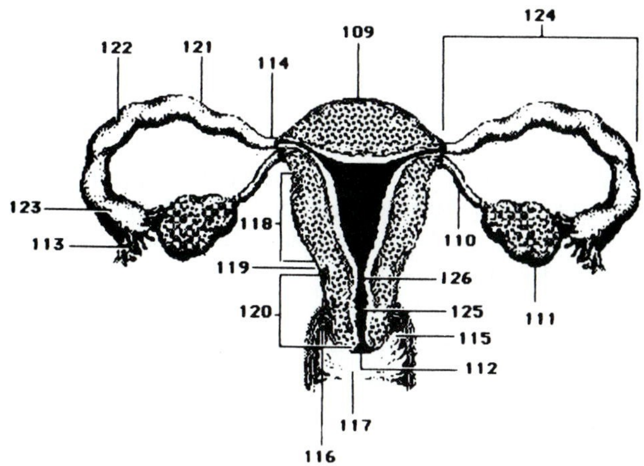

Figure 8–17. Diagram of the female reproductive organs (frontal view).

COLUMN A	COLUMN B
109. _____	(A) uterine cervix
110. _____	(B) fimbria
111. _____	(C) uterine fundus
112. _____	(D) right lateral vaginal fornix
113. _____	(E) left lateral vaginal fornix
114. _____	(F) interstitial portion of tube
115. _____	(G) vagina
116. _____	(H) isthmus uteri
117. _____	(I) external os of cervix
118. _____	(J) ovary
119. _____	(K) ovarian ligament
120. _____	(L) uterine corpus
121. _____	(M) fallopian tube
122. _____	(N) infundibulum
123. _____	(O) internal os of cervix
124. _____	(P) isthmus tubae
125. _____	(Q) ampulla
126. _____	(R) endocervical canal

127. Ectopic pregnancy is responsible for what percentage of maternal deaths?

(A) 26%
(B) 60%
(C) 70%
(D) 80%

128. What percentage of ectopic pregnancies occur in the fallopian tube?

(A) 50%
(B) 95%
(C) 20%
(D) 9%

129. Approximately how many days during the first 6 weeks after conception does the amount of human chorionic gonadotropin (hCG) double?

(A) 7 days
(B) 20 days
(C) 12 days
(D) 2 days

130. Fig. 8–18 is a transvaginal sonogram of a 24-year-old woman presented with 3 weeks of irregular vaginal bleeding and left pelvic pain. The most likely diagnosis is

(A) corpus luteum cyst
(B) unruptured ectopic pregnancy
(C) ruptured ectopic pregnancy
(D) A and B

131. Human chorionic gonadotropin (hCG) titers in ectopic pregnancy are frequently

(A) lower than patient with normal intrauterine pregnancy (IUP)
(B) higher than patient with normal intrauterine pregnancy (IUP)
(C) same as patient with normal intrauterine pregnancy (IUP)
(D) 50% higher than patient with normal intrauterine pregnancy (IUP)

132. The sonographic appearance of ectopic gestation include(s)

(A) enlarged nongravid uterus
(B) irregular adnexal mass or adnexal ring
(C) fluid in the cul-de-sac
(D) all of the above

133. An intrauterine pregnancy (IUP) with a coexistent extrauterine gestation occurs in what percentage of pregnancies?

(A) 2 in 10,000 pregnancies
(B) 1 in 6,000 to 30,000 pregnancies
(C) 5 in 10,000 pregnancies
(D) 1 in 5 to 1 in 50,000 pregnancies

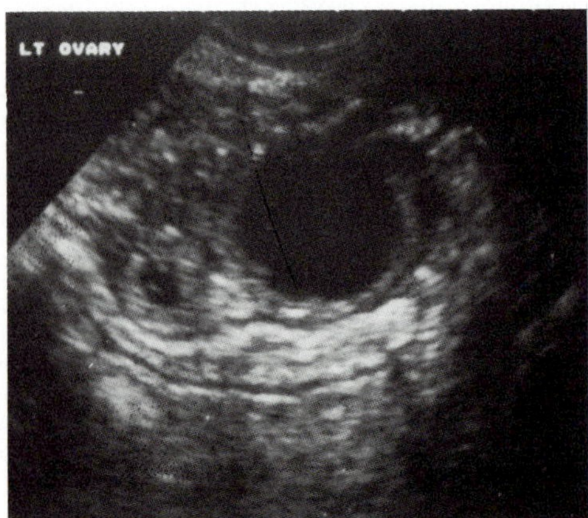

Figure 8–18. Transvaginal sonogram of the left adnexa.

134. What percentage of ectopic gestations demonstrate a pseudogestational sac?

(A) 60%
(B) 50%
(C) 40%
(D) 20%

135. A pseudogestational sac is *most* likely produced by

(A) yolk sac
(B) decidual cast
(C) ovarian tumor
(D) PID

136. Cystic hygromas are associated with

(A) Potter's syndrome
(B) Beckwith Wiedemann syndrome
(C) elevated levels of α-fetoprotein
(D) Turner's syndrome
(E) C and D only

137. The sonographic characteristics of cystic hygromas are which of the following: (1) thin-walled cyst, (2) hyperechoic mass on the neck, (3) multiseptated cystic mass, (4) echogenic mass in the cervical region?

(A) 2 and 3
(B) 1 and 3
(C) 4 only
(D) 1 only

138. On transvaginal and transabdominal sonography, the most common appearance of an unruptured ectopic pregnancy is

(A) "tubal ring"
(B) nonspecific adnexal mass
(C) a cystic adnexal mass
(D) complex adnexal mass

139. Which of the following is the appropriate description of omphalocele?

(A) normal insertion of the umbilical cord, with herniation of bowel occurring most often on the right side of the umbilicus
(B) protrusion of abdominal contents that may contain bowel, liver, or spleen with herniation at the base of the umbilical cord
(C) herniation of bowel only
(D) herniation of bowel to the left of the umbilicus containing spleen covered by peritoneum

140. Important facts to consider in the differential diagnosis of omphalocele versus gastroschisis are

(A) omphalocele has a normal insertion of the umbilical cord and is covered by parietal peritoneum or amniotic membrane
(B) gastroschisis has a normal insertion of the umbilical cord and is covered by parietal peritoneum or amniotic membrane
(C) gastroschisis has a normal insertion of the umbilical cord and is not covered by membrane
(D) both gastroschisis and omphalocele have a normal insertion of the umbilical cord; however, gastroschisis is covered by a membrane

141. The uterine findings on ectopic pregnancy typically include

(A) a pseudogestational sac
(B) thickened endometrium
(C) irregular decidualized endometrium
(D) all of the above

142. Twenty percent of cystic hygromas can occur in which of the following regions: (1) cervical region, (2) groin, (3) axilla, (4) mediastinum?

(A) all of the above
(B) 1 and 4 only
(C) 1 only
(D) 2, 3, and 4 only

143. Turner's syndrome is defined as

(A) retarded growth and sexual development with abnormal sex chromosomes
(B) bilateral renal agenesis with pulmonary hypoplasia
(C) blepharochalasis occurring in association with goiter
(D) paralysis of the soft palate, larynx, and tongue

144. The nonspecific signs of fetal death are which of the following: (1) echoes in the amniotic fluid, (2) the absence of the falx cerebri, (3) a decrease in biparietal diameter (BPD) measurements, (4) a double contour of the fetal head (sonographic halo sign)?

(A) 3 and 4
(B) 4 only
(C) all of the above
(D) none of the above

145. The proposed reasons for the development of an ectopic pregnancy include

(A) fallopian tube malfunction
(B) fallopian tube adhesions
(C) PID (pelvic inflammatory disease)
(D) fallopian tube diverticula
(E) all of the above

146. Once a patient has had an ectopic pregnancy, what are the chances of recurrence?

(A) 1 in 15
(B) 1 in 8
(C) 1 in 10
(D) 1 in 4

147. In what portion of the fallopian tube does ectopic pregnancy pose serious potential complications?

(A) isthmus
(B) ampullary
(C) infundibulum
(D) interstitial portion

148. How long after fetal death can scalp edema be seen?

(A) 2–3 days
(B) 5–10 days
(C) 10–20 days
(D) 8–10 days

149. Sonographic Spalding's sign is

(A) double contour of the fetal head
(B) "halo" sign
(C) overlapping of the fetal cranium
(D) all of the above

150. The most common location for an ectopic implantation is

(A) isthmus
(B) infundibulum
(C) interstitial portion
(D) ampullary portion

151. Sonographic masses that can mimic an ectopic pregnancy are

(A) hemorrhagic corpus luteum cyst
(B) tubo-ovarian abscess
(C) dermoid cyst
(D) B and C only
(E) all of the above

152. The sonographic demonstration of a double decidual sac, with or without a fetal pole, strongly suggests

(A) ectopic pregnancy
(B) intrauterine pregnancy (IUP)
(C) yolk sac
(D) fetal demise

153. The regions to scan for localizing fluid collection in an ectopic pregnancy are (1) anterior and posterior cul-de-sac, (2) paracolic recesses, (3) subhepatic space (Morrison's pouch), (4) adnexa.

(A) 1 and 2 only
(B) 1, 3, and 4 only
(C) all of the above

154. Which of the following statements is (are) *not* true for abdominal pregnancy: (1) the fetus may be alive at birth, (2) the placenta should be removed to prevent hemorrhage, (3) the uterus is separated from the fetus, (4) it can be missed on sonogram?

(A) 3 and 4 only
(B) 1, 3, and 4
(C) 2 only
(D) all of the above

155. Which neonates are considered growth retarded: (1) those born after 36 weeks, (2) those whose birth weight is on or above the 10th percentile, (3) those whose birth weight is on or below the 10th percentile?

(A) 2 and 3
(B) 1 and 2
(C) 1, 2, and 3
(D) 3 only

156. Conditions that are frequently associated with fetal hydrocephalus include

(A) meningomyelocele
(B) in utero exposure to TORCH (toxoplasmosis, rubella, cytomegalovirus, herpes)
(C) aqueductal stenosis
(D) Dandy-Walker syndrome
(E) all of the above

157. Fig. 8–19 is a longitudinal midline pelvic sonogram. The arrow points to

(A) bladder tumor
(B) pelvic kidney
(C) cystic mass
(D) normal uterus

158. After 34 weeks of gestation, approximately what percentage of fetuses are in the cephalic presentation?

(A) 80%
(B) 90%
(C) 60%
(D) 25%

159. The causes of cul-de-sac fluid are which of the following: (1) ruptured corpus luteum cyst, (2) ruptured hemorrhagic cyst, (3) ruptured ectopic gestation, (4) culdocentesis?

(A) 1 and 3
(B) 3 only
(C) 1, 2, and 3
(D) all of the above

Questions 160 through 168: Match the structures in Fig. 8–20 with the list of terms in Column B.

COLUMN A	COLUMN B
160. ______	(A) isthmus uteri
161. ______	(B) chorion frondosum
162. ______	(C) decidua parietalis (vera)
163. ______	(D) decidua capsularis
164. ______	(E) cervix
165. ______	(F) amniotic cavity
166. ______	(G) decidua basalis
167. ______	(H) unoccupied lumen between the decidual layers
168. ______	(I) mucous plug

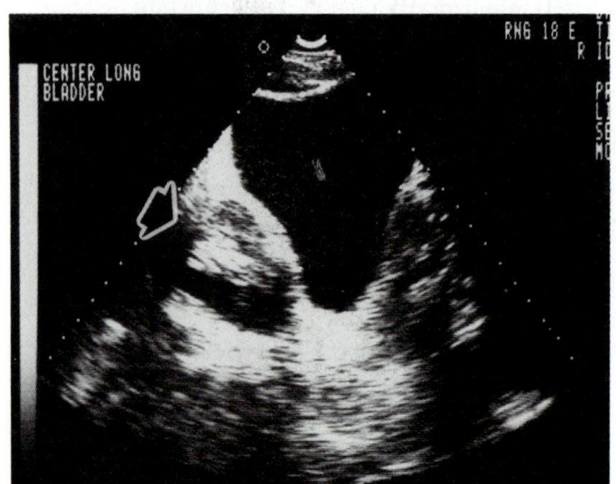

Figure 8–19. Sagittal midline pelvic sonogram.

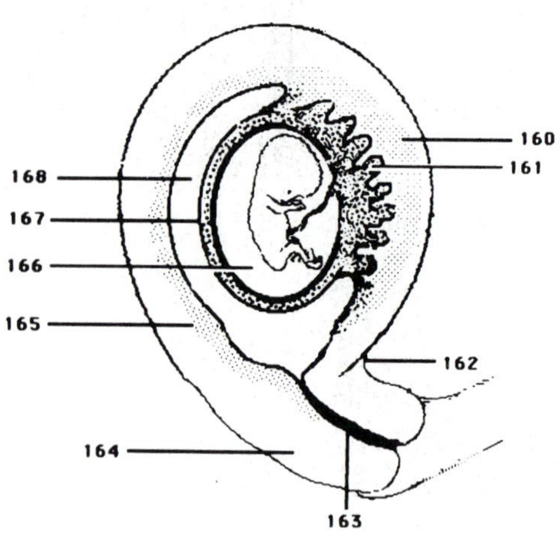

Figure 8–20. Diagram of early pregnancy.

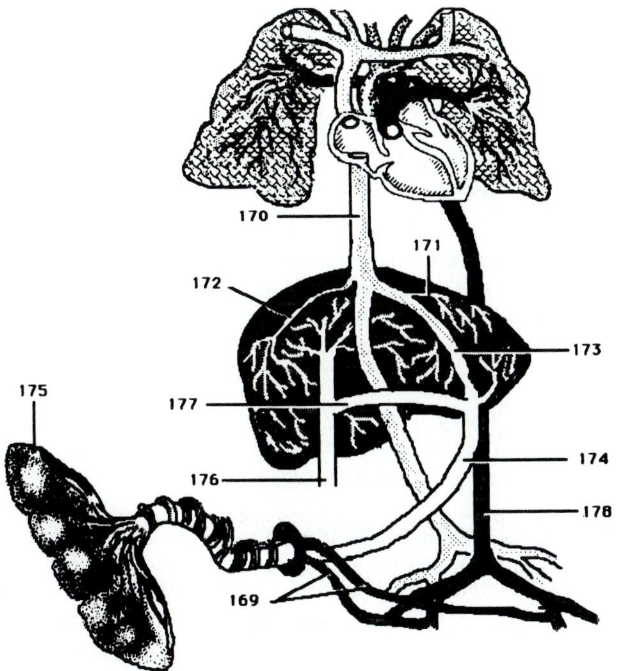

Figure 8–21. Diagram of the fetal circulatory system.

Questions 169 through 178: Match the structures in Fig. 8–21 with the list of terms in Column B.

COLUMN A	COLUMN B
169. _____	(A) placenta
170. _____	(B) inferior vena cava (IVC)
171. _____	(C) portal sinus
172. _____	(D) umbilical vein
173. _____	(E) aorta
174. _____	(F) left hepatic vein
175. _____	(G) right hepatic vein
176. _____	(H) ductus venosus
177. _____	(I) portal vein
178. _____	(J) umbilical arteries

179. Fetal ocular biometry has proven to be useful in evaluating

(A) hypotelorism
(B) hypertelorism
(C) anophthalmos
(D) gestational age
(E) microphthalmos
(F) all of the above

180. The interocular distance is measured from

(A) frontal process of the maxillary bone to the opposite maxillary process
(B) medial border of the orbit to the opposite medial border
(C) from inner canthus to outer canthus
(D) frontal process of the zygomatic bone to the opposite zygomatic bone
(E) all of the above

181. The biocular distance is measured from

(A) frontal process of the maxillary bone to the opposite maxillary process
(B) lateral border of the orbit to the opposite lateral border
(C) outer canthus to the inner canthus
(D) frontal process of the zygomatic bone to the opposite zygomatic bone
(E) all of the above

182. A cephalic index of 80% is

(A) suggestive of brachycephaly
(B) suggestive of dolichocephaly
(C) suggestive of hypertelorism
(D) normal

183. The crown-rump length (CRL) measurement is the longest length of the embryo

(A) excluding the limbs
(B) including the limbs
(C) including the yolk sac
(D) including the femur

184. Femoral length is measured from which of the following: (1) proximal femoral neck to the distal femoral condyles, (2) greater trochanter to the distal femoral condyles, (3) femoral head to the medial epicondyle, (4) femoral head to the intercondyle notch?

(A) 1 and 2 only
(B) 4 only
(C) 3 and 4 only
(D) none of the above

185. Hypertelorism denotes

(A) abnormally wide-spaced orbits
(B) abnormally closely spaced orbits
(C) smallness of the eyes
(D) absence of eyes

186. Hypotelorism denotes

(A) abnormally wide-spaced orbits
(B) abnormally closely spaced orbits
(C) smallness of the eyes
(D) absence of eyes

187. The accuracy of crown-rump length (CRL) measurement as a means of estimating gestational age has been statistically evaluated. The study showed

(A) 95% confidence limit of ± 4.7 days
(B) 85% confidence limit of ± 3 days

(C) 100% confidence limit of ± 3 days
(D) 99% confidence limit of ± 4.7 days

188. The structures that should *not* be included when measuring the embryo for a crown-rump length (CRL) are which of the following: (1) yolk sac, (2) femur, (3) spine, (4) humerus, (5) ulna and radius, (6) tibia and fibula, (7) placenta?

(A) 1 and 7 only
(B) 7 only
(C) 1, 3, and 6
(D) 1, 2, 4, 5, 6, and 7
(E) all of the above

189. The CRL should be performed between which weeks of gestation?

(A) 4 and 5 weeks
(B) 6 and 12 weeks
(C) 12 and 14 weeks
(D) 14 and 20 weeks

190. The most accurate methodology for the assessment of gestational age in the first trimester is

(A) femur length (FL)
(B) biparietal diameter (BPD)
(C) crown-rump length (CRL)
(D) orbital distance (OD)

191. The cardiac circulation of the fetus is different from that of adults. Some of these differences that are present in the fetus and *not* in the adult include

(A) shunting of blood across the foramen ovale
(B) presence of a ductus arteriosus
(C) presence of a ductus venosus within the heart
(D) all of the above.

192. The gestational sac can be seen on transabdominal sonography as early as

(A) 5 weeks' gestational age
(B) 2 weeks' gestational age
(C) 6 weeks' gestational age
(D) 7 weeks' gestational age

193. Ovarian carcinomas usually metastasize to

(A) bone
(B) lungs
(C) brain
(D) bowel

194. Sonographers should be familiar with the medication Clomid (clomiphene citrate) because of which of the following: (1) it is used to treat infertility, (2) it can be associated with multiple gestation, (3) the urinary bladder will not fill, (4) it will cause heart failure?

(A) 1 and 2
(B) 1 and 3
(C) 1 and 4
(D) all of the above

195. During the first 10 weeks of gestation, the gestational sac grows approximately

(A) 25 mm per week
(B) 1 mm per day
(C) 1 cm per week
(D) 3 cm per week or 30 mm per week

196. The accuracy of gestational sac volume measurement as a means of estimating gestational age has been reported as

(A) 95% confidence limit of ± 4.7 days
(B) confidence limit of ± 9 days
(C) confidence limit of ± 5 days
(D) confidence limit of ± 15 days

197. Which of the following are associated with intrauterine growth retardation (IUGR): (1) preeclamptic toxemia, (2) chronic renal disease, (3) maternal heart disease, (4) heavy smoking, (5) maternal malnutrition, (6) alcoholism?

(A) 1, 2, 5, and 6 only
(B) 2 and 6 only
(C) 1, 2, 3, 5, and 6 only
(D) all of the above

198. The treatment for intrauterine growth retardation (IUGR) includes which of the following: (1) bed rest, (2) having the mother lie on the left side, (3) administration of anticoagulant drugs, (4) the medication heparin?

(A) 1 only
(B) 4 only
(C) all of the above
(D) none of the above

199. Long-term follow-up studies of children born with previous intrauterine growth retardation (IUGR) confirm

(A) speech defects
(B) central nervous system (CNS) abnormalities
(C) diminished intelligence
(D) more frequent occurrence in males than in females
(E) B and C
(F) all of the above

200. In about 10% of intrauterine growth retardation (IUGR) cases there are fetal anomalies. These disorders include all of the following *except*

(A) trisomy 21
(B) trisomy 18
(C) trophoblastic disease
(D) Potter's syndrome
(E) neural tube defects

201. The term *decidua* denotes the transformed endometrium of pregnancy. The different regions of the decidua are divided into

(A) two regions called decidua basalis and chorionic villi
(B) one region called decidual reaction
(C) three regions called decidua basalis, decidua parietalis, and decidua capsularis
(D) three regions called endoderm, mesoderm, and ectoderm

202. Pseudocyesis denotes false

(A) cyst
(B) tumor
(C) decidua basalis
(D) pregnancy

203. In which of the scanning planes is spina bifida best recognized?

(A) transverse
(B) longitudinal
(C) oblique
(D) coronal

204. The ideal time for detecting spina bifida is

(A) 17–18 weeks
(B) 20–30 weeks
(C) 12–16 weeks
(D) 30–36 weeks

205. Fluid-filled masses in the vagina could include all of the following *except*

(A) Gartner's duct cyst
(B) vaginal agenesis
(C) urine in the vagina
(D) hematocolpos

206. The functions of the yolk sac are which of the following: (1) hemopoiesis, (2) development of sex glands, (3) formation of the embryonic digestive tube, (4) transfer of nutrients?

(A) 1 and 4
(B) 2 and 3
(C) 4 only
(D) all of the above

207. At 10 weeks of gestation, the location of the yolk sac is

(A) in the chorionic cavity between the amnion and the chorionic sac
(B) outside the chorionic cavity alongside the fetus
(C) inside the umbilical cord
(D) between the umbilical arteries

208. The yolk stalk usually detaches from the midgut loop at which week?

(A) 6th week
(B) 11th week
(C) 8th week
(D) 5th week

209. In about 2% of adults, the yolk stalk persists as a diverticulum of the ileum. This is known as

(A) Adams and Stokes' diverticulum
(B) Meckel's diverticulum
(C) Raymond's diverticulum
(D) Turner's diverticulum

210. On sonography, the yolk sac measures between

(A) 15 and 19 mm
(B) 1 and 2 cm
(C) 2 and 5 mm
(D) 15 and 25 mm

211. A blighted ovum is which of the following: (1) an empty gestational sac, (2) retention of a dead embryo, (3) arrested development of a fertilized ovum, (4) arrested development of a fetus after the first trimester?

(A) 1 and 3
(B) 2 only
(C) 2 and 3
(D) all of the above

212. Fluid in the cul-de-sac is least likely to be associated with

(A) ectopic pregnancy
(B) myoma uteri
(C) pelvic inflammatory disease (PID)
(D) ovulation
(E) follicular cyst

213. The thin ring-like structure that surrounds the gestational sac and excludes the yolk sac is most likely

(A) twin gestation sacs
(B) impending abortion or implantation bleeding
(C) blighted ovum
(D) not yet fused amnion
(E) all of the above

214. Which of the following is *not* among the sonographic findings of a blighted ovum?

(A) "tennis racquet" configuration of the sac
(B) disproportion between the gestational sac and uterine size
(C) failure of the gestation sac to increase in size by 75% in 1 week
(D) fragmentation of the sac
(E) weak surrounding echoes
(F) anembryonic sac after 8 weeks
(G) thickening of the decidua

215. A missed abortion is

(A) retention of a dead embryo or fetus
(B) anembryonic sac
(C) a blighted ovum
(D) an empty gestation sac

216. Which of the following statements is *not* true about spina bifida?

(A) spina bifida produces a U-shaped echo
(B) the spinal canal is seen as a closed circle in the presence of spina bifida
(C) over 80% of the cases of spina bifida are detectable sonographically
(D) the optimal time for sonographic examination is 17–18 weeks

217. Which of the following statements is *not* true about anencephaly?

(A) anencephaly has an incidence of 1 in 1000 births
(B) anencephaly has a female to male ratio of 4 to 1
(C) anencephaly is the most common anomaly effecting the central nervous system (CNS)
(D) anencephaly results from a failure of the neural tube to close completely
(E) anencephaly occurs more frequently in the United States than in the United Kingdom

218. Anomalies associated with anencephaly include all *except* which of the following: (1) spina bifida, (2) meningocele, (3) myelomeningocele, (4) cleft palate, (5) holoprosencephaly, (6) umbilical hernia, (7) polyhydramnios?

(A) 4 and 5 only
(B) 5 only
(C) 6 only
(D) 4, 5, and 6

219. The *most* common position for twin gestation is

(A) one in the cephalic and the other in breech presentation
(B) both in breech presentation
(C) both in cephalic presentation

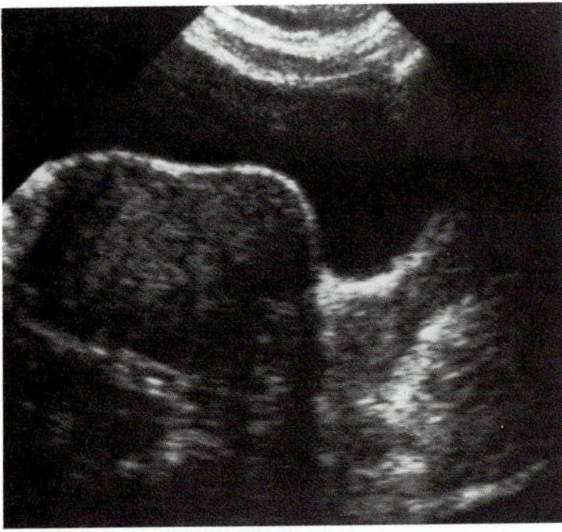

Figure 8–22. Sagittal midline sonogram.

(D) one in the cephalic and the other in transverse presentation

220. The following is a list of different presentations. Identify which is *not* a malpresentation.

(A) cephalic
(B) breech
(C) transverse
(D) oblique

221. Fig. 8–22 is of a 32-year-old woman in whom the uterus was found to be enlarged and firm on physical examination. The most likely diagnosis is

(A) subserosal fibroid
(B) submucosal fibroid
(C) hydatidform mole
(D) early pregnancy

222. Fig. 8–23 is a sonogram obtained through the abdomen of a 24-week fetus. The most likely diagnosis is

(A) herniated cord
(B) herniated bowel
(C) herniated liver
(D) normal bulging of the abdominal wall related to fetal breathing

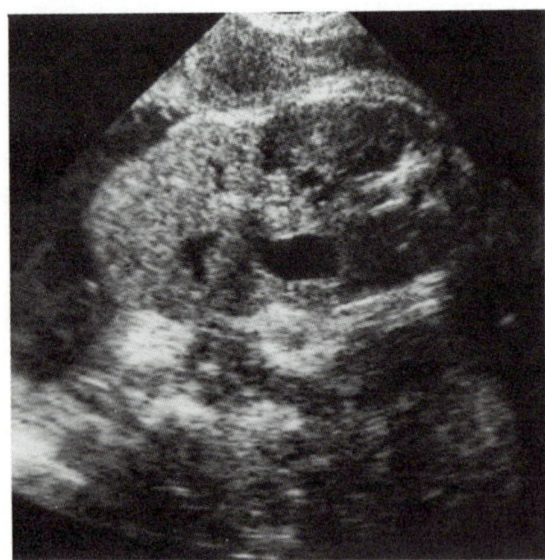

Figure 8–23. Transverse sonogram of the fetal abdomen.

223. Overdistension of the urinary bladder may cause

(A) anterior placenta to appear previa
(B) closure of an incompetent cervix
(C) distortion or closure of the gestational sac
(D) obscured visualization of the internal iliac vein
(E) all of the above
(F) A and B only

224. If the fetal skull is low in the pelvis, what maneuvers or techniques can the sonographer use to obtain an accurate biparietal diameter (BPD)?

(A) place the patient in Trendelenburg's position
(B) place the patient in Fowler's position
(C) apply gentle manual pressure to elevate the fetal head
(D) distend the urinary bladder
(E) A, C, and D

225. Which of the following statements is *not* true about biparietal diameter (BPD) measurement in twin gestation?

(A) the biparietal diameter (BPDs) of the twins should be within 4 mm of each other
(B) 1–2 mm should be added to the biparietal diameter (BPD) if the standard BPD chart for a singleton fetus is used
(C) if the biparietal diameter (BPD) of twin A is 6 mm less than twin B, growth retardation of twin A should be considered
(D) the biparietal diameters (BPDs) of twins are slightly smaller than those of a single fetus
(E) the biparietal diameters (BPDs) of twins should be within 1 to 2 cm of each other

226. Abnormalities usually associated with an omphalocele include

(A) ectopic heart
(B) cysts in the liver
(C) cysts in the kidney
(D) none of the above

227. All patients for transabdominal sonographic examination of the pelvis require the urinary bladder be physiologically distended prior to the sonographic examination. The reason(s) for this is (are)

(A) it produces a sonic window
(B) it establishes an anatomical reference point
(C) it helps evaluate the mobility of a mass
(D) it decreases the angle of incidence
(E) it helps demonstrate the cervix
(F) it helps elevate the head of the fetus for a more accurate measurement of the biparietal diameter (BPD)
(G) it pushes the bowel cephalad
(H) A and G
(I) F and G
(J) A–G

228. For patients who are unable to ingest fluid, or in the event of an emergency, the urinary bladder can be distended via a Foley catheter and

(A) 1 qt barium sulfate
(B) 250 mL saline
(C) 300 mL tap water
(D) 32 oz mineral oil

229. If the fetus is in a vertex presentation and the spine of the fetus is to the maternal right, the fetus is lying on its

(A) back and face up with the fetal head toward the fundus
(B) left side and the right side is toward the maternal anterior abdominal wall
(C) right side and the left side is toward the maternal anterior abdominal wall
(D) abdomen and face down with the fetal head toward the fundus

230. If the fetus is in a breech presentation and the spine of the fetus is to the maternal right, the fetus is lying on its

(A) back and face up with the fetal head toward the fundus
(B) left side and the right side is toward the maternal anterior abdominal wall
(C) right side and the left side is toward the maternal anterior abdominal wall
(D) abdomen and face down with the fetal head toward the fundus

231. In the fetus, the heart is in a relatively horizontal position. This is largely due to

(A) large liver size
(B) large kidneys
(C) fetal stomach
(D) umbilical vein

232. When the cessation of blood flow from the placenta occurs, the umbilical vein collapses to become

(A) ligamentum venosum
(B) ligamentum teres
(C) portal vein
(D) hepatic vein

233. When the cessation of blood flow from the placenta occurs, the ductus venosus collapses to become the

(A) ligamentum venosum
(B) ligamentum teres
(C) portal vein
(D) hepatic vein

234. When the cessation of blood flow from the placenta occurs, the portal sinus

(A) remains patent and becomes the proximal left portal vein
(B) remains patent and becomes the proximal right portal vein
(C) remains occluded and becomes the proximal right portal vein
(D) remains occluded and becomes the proximal left portal vein

235. A single umbilical artery (SUA) may be associated with

(A) twins
(B) diabetes mellitus
(C) congenital anomalies
(D) all of the above

236. The three vessels normally found in the umbilical cord are

(A) one artery and two veins
(B) two arteries and one vein
(C) one artery, one vein, and one portal sinus
(D) hepatic vein, portal vein, and umbilical vein

237. Measurement of the umbilical vein diameter is a useful indicator of

(A) intrauterine growth retardation (IUGR)
(B) Rh isoimmunization
(C) gestation age
(D) weight estimation

238. Ovulation occurs approximately

(A) always after intercourse
(B) on the 7th day of the menstrual cycle
(C) on the 14th day of the menstrual cycle
(D) on the 2nd day of the menstrual cycle

239. Which of the following statements is(are) *not* true about esophageal atresia?

(A) esophageal atresia is a narrowing of the esophagus
(B) esophageal atresia is a closure or absence of the esophagus
(C) 90% of fetuses have tracheoesophageal fistula
(D) repeated failure to identify the fetal stomach by sonogram in the presence of hydramnios is indicative of esophageal atresia

240. The characteristic ultrasound pattern of duodenal atresia is

(A) failure to identify the fetal stomach by sonography
(B) Chadwick's sign
(C) "triple-bubble" sign
(D) "double-bubble" sign

241. Fetal renal agenesis is associated with the following condition(s)

(A) pulmonary hypoplasia
(B) Turner's syndrome
(C) oligohydramnios
(D) Potter's syndrome
(E) A and B only
(F) A, C, and D only

242. Normally, the fetal bladder will empty every

(A) 10 minutes
(B) 15 minutes
(C) 3 hours
(D) 1 hour

243. The most common cause of hydronephrosis of the fetus is

(A) staghorn calculi
(B) ovarian tumor
(C) obstruction occurring at the ureteropelvic junction (UPJ)
(D) all of the above

Questions 244 through 247: Arrange in sequence in Column A the embryologic stages following fertilization listed in Column B.

COLUMN A	COLUMN B
244. _____	(A) morula
245. _____	(B) cleavage
246. _____	(C) zygote
247. _____	(D) blastocyst

248. The double-ring sign ("halo" sign) of the fetal head is seen in the presence of diseases or conditions affecting the fetus. From the following list, identify the condition *least* associated with this sign.

(A) fetal demise
(B) fetal distress
(C) sickle-cell anemia
(D) intrauterine growth retardation (IUGR)
(E) diabetes mellitus
(F) Rh isoimmunization
(G) fetal anasarca
(H) hydrops fetalis

249. Thinning of the placenta is seen in most of the following. Identify the condition(s) *least* associated with this.

(A) intrauterine growth retardation (IUGR)
(B) chronic hydramnios
(C) placental insufficiency
(D) preeclampsia
(E) polyhydramnios
(F) Rh isoimmunization
(G) multiple gestation
(H) A and C only
(I) D, A, and C only
(J) F and G only

250. Thickening of the placenta is seen in most of the following. Identify the condition(s) *least* associated with this.

(A) intrauterine growth retardation (IUGR)
(B) maternal and fetal heart disease
(C) placental insufficiency
(D) diabetes mellitus
(E) Rh isoimmunization
(F) multiple gestation
(G) transplacental syphilis
(H) A and C only
(I) A, B, C, and D only
(J) F and G only

251. Oligohydramnios is seen in the presence of diseases or conditions affecting the fetus. Identify the condition *least* associated with this.

(A) intrauterine growth retardation (IUGR)
(B) renal agenesis
(C) fetal demise
(D) multiple gestation

252. Hydramnios is seen in the presence of diseases or conditions affecting the fetus. Identify those *least* associated with this.

(A) anencephaly
(B) hydrocephaly
(C) spina bifida
(D) meningomyelocele
(E) multiple gestation
(F) fetal demise
(G) intrauterine growth retardation (IUGR)
(H) diabetes mellitus
(I) twin-twin transfusion
(J) renal agenesis
(K) esophageal and duodenal atresia
(L) erythroblastosis
(M) omphalocele
(N) porencephaly
(O) J and L
(P) G and J
(Q) all of the above

253. There are four classifications of the maturational process of the placenta, which are graded from 0 through III. Arrange the descriptive appearances in Column B to correlate with the grades in Column A.

COLUMN A	COLUMN B
A. 0 ____	(1) indentations communicating with the basal layer. Circular densities with echo-spared areas in the center and large irregular densities that cast acoustic shadowing
B. I ____	(2) subtle undulations with few scattered echogenic areas and no densities
C. II ____	(3) straight and well defined. Its texture is homogeneous with no densities
D. III ____	(4) indentations extending into, but not to, the basal layer. Linear, commalike echogenic densities with basal stippling

254. The *most* common cause of painless vaginal bleeding in the second and third trimesters of pregnancy is

(A) trauma
(B) ectopic pregnancy
(C) placental abruption
(D) placenta previa

255. The *most* common benign tumor of the uterus is fibroid. However, it has been known to have many other names. Identify the name that does *not* correlate.

(A) myoma
(B) leiomyomas
(C) fibromyomas
(D) leiomyosarcoma

256. Which of the following is *not* true about fibroids?

(A) higher incidence in blacks than in whites
(B) occur in 20% of females over 35 years of age
(C) higher incidence in whites than in blacks
(D) are the cause of at least 10% of all infertility problems

257. Fibroids can be classified into three groups; their names, which are based on their position in the various layers in the uterine wall, include which of the

following: (1) submucous, (2) pedunculated, (3) interstitial, (4) endometriosis, (5) endometritis, (6) adenomyosis, (7) subserous?

(A) 1, 2, and 4
(B) 2, 3, and 6
(C) 1, 3, and 7
(D) 1, 4, and 7

258. What is Nägele's rule?

(A) mathematical methodology to estimate expected date of confinement (EDC)
(B) methodology to estimate age based on fundal height
(C) sonographic methodology to estimate gestational age
(D) mathematical methodology for measurement of fibroid

259. A malignant fibroid is known as

(A) leiomyosarcoma
(B) cystadenofibroma
(C) lymphoma
(D) endometrioma

260. The growth of fibroids is stimulated by

(A) estrogen
(B) pregnancy
(C) infection
(D) A and B

261. What is the average duration of pregnancy

(A) 280 days
(B) 40 weeks
(C) 36 weeks
(D) 9 calendar months
(E) 10 lunar months
(F) all of the above
(G) C and D only
(H) A, B, D, and E only

262. Overdistension of the urinary bladder may compress the placenta and create a sonographic appearance similar to placenta previa. This situation is *most* common

(A) in the anterior placenta
(B) in the posterior placenta
(C) in the fundal placenta
(D) overdistension of the urinary bladder *cannot* create a sonographic appearance similar to placenta previa

263. The reason(s) for distending the urinary bladder prior to sonographic examination is which of the following: (1) it displaces gas-containing bowel from the pelvis, (2) it establishes an anatomic reference point, (3) it pushes the uterus cephalad and away from the symphysis pubis, (4) it acts as an acoustic window, (5) it is used as a comparison when the internal characteristics of a mass is evaluated?

(A) 1 and 2
(B) 1, 2, 3, and 4
(C) 1 and 4
(D) all of the above

264. The chorionic plate of the placenta is displayed as a strong linear echo on the inner surface. Where is the chorionic plate most difficult to depict if the fetus is *not* in the path of the ultrasonic beam?

(A) fundal placenta
(B) lateral placenta
(C) anterior placenta
(D) posterior placenta
(E) A and B
(F) all of the above

265. Difficulty can arise when the placenta is situated posteriorly and the fetus is in a cephalic position. In this situation, the sonographer should

(A) place the patient in Trendelenburg's position
(B) have a nurse gently elevate the fetal head by manual maneuver
(C) overdistend the maternal bladder
(D) measure the distance between the fetal calvarium and the anterior margin of the maternal sacrum
(E) B and D only
(F) A and B only
(G) all of the above

266. Endometriosis can be best described as

(A) malignant endometrial stroma
(B) ectopic endometrial tissue
(C) hematoma of the endometrium
(D) inflammation of the endometrium

267. The sonographic finding(s) in abruptio placentae is

(A) retroplacental clot
(B) separation occurring at the margin of the placenta
(C) large uterine veins and sinuses
(D) A and B
(E) all of the above

268. To calculate the expected date of confinement (EDC) you should

(A) measure the fundal height, multiply by 4 then divide by 7
(B) to the last menstrual period (LMP) add 7 days, subtract 3 calendar months, and add 1 year
(C) to the last menstrual period (LMP) subtract 7 days, add 3 calendar months, and add 1 year
(D) to the last menstrual period (LMP) add 5 days, subtract 9 calendar months, and add 1 year

Questions 269 through 275: Match the fundal height in Fig. 8–24 with the weeks of gestation in Column B.

COLUMN A	COLUMN B
269. ______	(A) 40 weeks
270. ______	(B) 36 weeks
271. ______	(C) 12 weeks
272. ______	(D) 16 weeks
273. ______	(E) 20–22 weeks
274. ______	(F) 28 weeks
275. ______	(G) 24–26 weeks

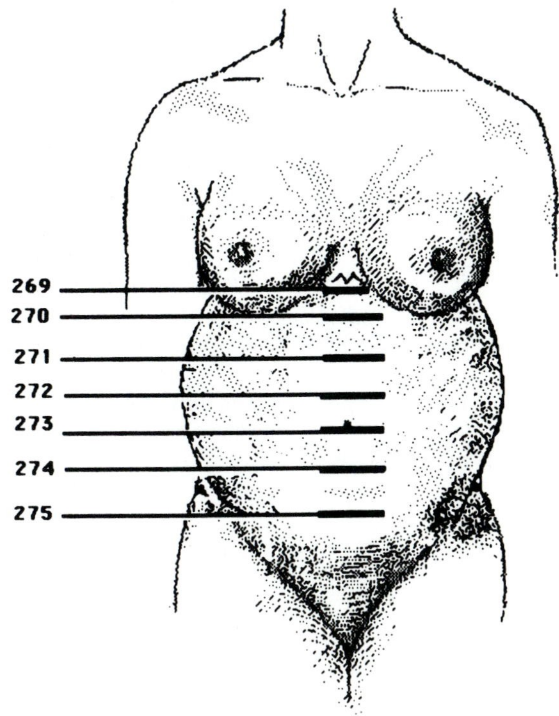

Figure 8–24. Diagram of the fundal height at various stages during pregnancy.

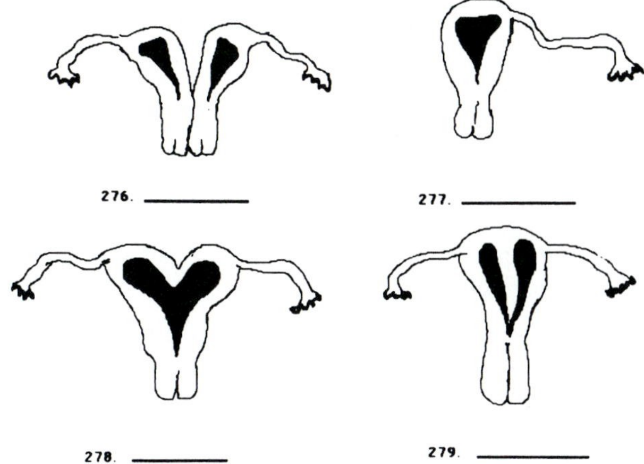

Figure 8–25. Diagram showing developmental anomalies of the uterus.

Questions 276 through 279: Match the type of developmental anomalies of the uterus shown in Fig. 8–25 with the terms in Column B.

COLUMN A	COLUMN B
276. ______	(A) bicornuate
277. ______	(B) septate
278. ______	(C) unicornis
279. ______	(D) didelphic

280. The ratio of head circumference to body circumference normally changes as pregnancy progresses. Match the weeks of gestation in Column A with the head and body ratio in Column B.

COLUMN A	COLUMN B
A. 12–24 ______	(1) abdomen larger than head
B. 32–36 ______	(2) head and body are equal
C. 36–40 ______	(3) head larger than abdomen

281. Rh isoimmunization results from which of the following combinations?

(A) mother Rh^- and father Rh^+
(B) mother Rh^+ and father Rh^-
(C) mother Rh^+ and father Rh^+
(D) mother Rh^- and father Rh^-

282. The name(s) of the ductal systems in the early development of the female fetus that form the internal genitalia is

(A) wolffian duct
(B) müllerian ducts
(C) ductus arterious
(D) ductus deferens
(E) A and D
(F) B and D
(G) A and B

283. Total malfusion of the ductus paramesonephricus could result in

(A) bicornuate uterus
(B) septate uterus
(C) didelphic uterus
(D) unicornuate uterus

284. Partial malfusion of the ductus paramesonephricus could result in

(A) bicornuate uterus
(B) septate uterus
(C) didelphic uterus
(D) unicornuate uterus

285. Minimal malfusion of the paramesonephricus could result in

(A) bicornuate uterus
(B) septate uterus
(C) didelphic uterus
(D) unicornuate uterus

286. Arrested development of the paramesonephric duct results in

(A) bicornuate uterus
(B) uterine aplasia
(C) septate uterus
(D) didelphic uterus

287. Unilateral arrested development of the paramesonephric duct results in

(A) bicornuate uterus
(B) uterine aplasia
(C) uterus unicornis
(D) didelphic uterus

288. If uterine malformations are seen, the sonographer should scan which organ?

(A) kidneys
(B) gallbladder
(C) spleen
(D) liver

289. Which of the following is *not* true of dysgerminoma?

(A) it is a solid malignant germ cell tumor of the ovary
(B) it is a counterpart of seminoma of the testis
(C) it is a relatively uncommon tumor accounting for about 2% of all ovarian cancers
(D) 90% are unilateral
(E) it is a solid benign tumor

290. Which of the following is *not* true of dermoid cysts?

(A) it may cast an acoustic shadow
(B) it is encountered more in women over 40 years
(C) it is also called benign cystic teratoma (BCT)
(D) most common benign germ cell tumor in the female
(E) it is unilateral in about 80% of cases
(F) the tumor has elements such as hair, tooth, bone, endoderm, ectoderm, mesoderm, and thyroid glandular tissue
(G) fat floats on top of fluid, therefore, one may see a fat-fluid level
(H) fat can be echogenic or anechoic
(I) sonographically, can produce a "tip of the iceberg" effect

291. The trophoblast in ectopic pregnancy secretes *more* human chorionic gonadotropin (hCG) than does the placenta of a normal pregnancy.

(A) true
(B) false

Questions 292 through 300: Match the terms in Column A to the correct description in Column B.

COLUMN A

292. Gravida ______
293. Multipara ______
294. Nullipara (Po) ______
295. Primipara (Pi) ______
296. Nulligravida (Go) ______
297. Primigravida (Gi) ______
298. Multigravida ______
299. Para ______
300. Trimester ______

COLUMN B

(A) a woman who has given birth two or more times
(B) one who has never been pregnant
(C) a woman who is pregnant
(D) a woman who has never given birth to a viable infant
(E) pregnant for the first time
(F) one who has been pregnant several times
(G) the number of pregnancies that have continued to viability
(H) a woman who has given birth one time to a viable infant, regardless of whether the child was living at birth and regardless of whether the birth was single or multiple
(I) a 3-month period during gestation

Questions 301 through 308: Match the terms in Column A to the correct description in Column B.

COLUMN A	COLUMN B
301. Adnexa ______	(A) dark green substance in the intestines of a full-term fetus
302. Eclampsia ______	(B) toxemia of late pregnancy characterized by convulsion and coma
303. Meconium ______	(C) any accessory parts, structures, or masses lateral to the uterus
304. Postpartum ______	(D) small amount of amniotic fluid, below 300 cc at term
305. Hydramnios ______	(E) excessive amount of amniotic fluid, above 2,000 cc at term
306. Oxytocin ______	(F) after birth
307. Oligohydramnios ______	(G) a hormone that stimulates uterine contractions
308. Preeclampsia ______	(H) toxemia of late pregnancy characterized by hypertension, albuminuria, and edema

Questions 309 through 314: Match the terms in Column A to the correct description in Column B.

COLUMN A	COLUMN B
309. Lightening ______	(A) painless uterine contraction
310. Chadwick's sign ______	(B) softening of the lower uterine segment
311. Hegar's sign ______	(C) the fetal head engages into the pelvis
312. Goodell's sign ______	(D) softening of the cervix
313. Braxton Hicks sign ______	(E) the mother's first perception of the movements of the fetus felt in utero from 16 to 18 weeks of pregnancy
314. Quickening ______	(F) bluish purple color of the vagina

Questions 315 through 318: Diabetes is one of the more common medical complications of pregnancy. Match the diabetic classification in Column A to the correct description in Column B.

COLUMN A	COLUMN B
315. Class A diabetes ______	(A) chemical diabetes before pregnancy
316. Class B diabetes ______	(B) onset before age 10, duration over 20 years, vascular lesions of benign retinopathy
317. Class C diabetes ______	(C) onset between ages 10 and 19, duration of 10–19 years, no evidence of vascular disease
318. Class D diabetes ______	(D) onset of clinical diabetes mellitus after age 20, duration less than 10 years, no evidence of vascular disease

319. The start of the first menstrual cycle is called

(A) amenorrhea
(B) dysmenorrhea
(C) menarche
(D) polymenorrhea

320. How long after fertilization does implantation of the blastocyst occur?

(A) 4 weeks
(B) 14 days
(C) 24 hours
(D) 7 days

321. A benign invasion of endometrial tissue into the myometrium is known as

(A) endometriosis
(B) pelvic inflammatory disease (PID)
(C) adenomyosis
(D) endomyosarcoma

322. Bacterial organisms that result in pelvic inflammatory disease (PID) are

(A) *Neisseria gonorrhoeae*
(B) *Escherichia coli*
(C) enterococci
(D) *Chlamydia trachomatis*
(E) *Streptococcus veridans*
(F) A and D only
(G) all of the above

323. The signs and symptoms of pelvic inflammatory disease (PID) are

(A) severe pelvic pain
(B) high fever
(C) leukocytosis
(D) rapid pulse rate
(E) vaginal discharge
(F) rebound tenderness
(G) A, B, and C
(H) B, C, and E
(I) all of the above

324. Endometriosis is a condition that mostly affects

(A) women who are infertile
(B) women who are in their thirties
(C) women who are multipara
(D) white women more than black women
(E) B and D only
(F) A, B, and D only
(G) all of the above

325. Women with endometriosis may have

(A) dyspareunia
(B) metromennorhagia
(C) dysmenorrhea
(D) all of the above

326. Endometriosis is

(A) ectopic endometrial tissue
(B) benign invasion of endometrial tissue into the myometrium
(C) endomyosarcoma with chocolate tissue
(D) inflammation of the endometrium

327. The sonographic features of endometriosis are

(A) chocolate cyst
(B) fluid-fluid levels
(C) cyst with irregular wall
(D) echo-free with relative smooth border
(E) cysts containing clumps of high-level echoes
(F) A, D, and C
(G) all of the above

328. Pelvic inflammatory disease (PID) of intrauterine contraceptive device (IUCD) users is more often associated with

(A) *Staphylococcus* infection
(B) gonorrhea
(C) actinomycosis
(D) *Escheria coli* infection

329. Prominent endometrial echo within the uterus can be seen in cases of

(A) ectopic gestation
(B) endometritis
(C) pelvic inflammatory disease (PID)
(D) menstruation (secretory phase)
(E) A, C, and D only
(F) all of the above

330. Which of the following can mimic pelvic inflammatory disease (PID)?

(A) endometriosis
(B) ectopic pregnancy
(C) multiple hemorrhagic cysts
(D) multicystic ovarian cancer
(E) all of the above

Questions 331 through 334: Match the terms in Column A to the correct description in Column B.

COLUMN A	COLUMN B
331. Aerobe ______	(A) pus in the fallopian tubes
332. Anaerobe ______	(B) organism that requires oxygen for life
333. Pyocolpos ______	(C) organism that does not require oxygen for life
334. Pyosalpinx ______	(D) pus in the vagina

335. The *most* common sonographic appearance(s) of a dermoid cyst(s) are which of the following: (1) totally anechoic, (2) completely solid, (3) predominantly solid, (4) complex mass with internal echoes and acoustic shadow?

(A) 1 and 4
(B) 2 and 3
(C) 2 only
(D) 4 only

336. The *most* common location for dermoid cyst(s) is (are)

(A) posterior cul-de-sac
(B) right adnexa
(C) left adnexa
(D) superior to the uterine fundus

337. Krukenberg's tumor is

(A) a secondary carcinoma of the ovaries with primary in the gastrointestinal tract
(B) a primary carcinoma of the ovaries with secondary in the gastrointestinal tract
(C) a benign ovarian tumor
(D) the most common ovarian tumor in children

338. The cause(s) of ectopic pregnancy is

(A) delayed transit of the fertilized zygote secondary to tube malfunction
(B) obstruction of the tube due to adhesions from pelvic inflammatory disease (PID)
(C) chronic salpingitis
(D) all of the above

339. When is the recommended time to perform genetic amniocentesis?

(A) 40 weeks' menstrual age
(B) 36 weeks' gestational age
(C) 20–24 weeks' menstrual age
(D) 16–19 weeks' gestational age

340. During which weeks of gestation is femur length measurement most accurate?

(A) 20–30
(B) 10–20
(C) 30–36
(D) 14–20

341. For safe amniocentesis, the needle should be placed

(A) through the thickest portion of the placenta but away from the fetus
(B) through the umbilical cord but away from the fetus and placenta
(C) avoiding the placenta, umbilical cord, and fetus
(D) through the fetal spine

342. The reasons(s) for amniocentesis are which of the following: (1) sex determination, (2) genetic disorders, (3) fetal maturity, (4) hemolytic disease?

(A) 2 and 3
(B) 2, 3, and 4 only
(C) 2 and 4
(D) all of the above

343. If the serum β human chorionic gonadotropin (β-hCG) is negative, the recommended procedure is

(A) sonogram may not be warranted
(B) laparoscopy
(C) dilation and curettage (D&C)
(D) suction curettage

344. How early can the fetal iliac crests be depicted on sonogram?

(A) 8 weeks
(B) 10 weeks
(C) 12 weeks
(D) 18 weeks

345. How long after fertilization does a corpus luteum cyst first begin to regress?

(A) 5 days
(B) 14 days
(C) 12–15 weeks
(D) 16–20 weeks

346. What types of fibroids are *most* likely to become pedunculated?

(A) interstitial
(B) subserous
(C) submucous
(D) leiomyosarcoma
(E) B and C
(F) A and D

347. Which of the following is *not* true of the fetal lungs on sonography?

(A) the fetal lungs are relatively homogeneous on sonogram
(B) the echogenicity of the lungs is similar to that of the liver
(C) in the third trimester, the lungs become more echogenic than the liver
(D) the fetal lungs expand only after birth. The fetal lungs contain air and are at rest in utero; thus the reason for nonvisualization by ultrasound

348. What is the normal rate of fetal chest wall movements in utero?

(A) 12–60 breaths per minute
(B) 60–80 breaths per minute
(C) 80–120 breaths per minute
(D) all of the above are untrue; thoracic movement occurs only after birth

349. Which of the following can be seen in the fetal lungs on sonography?

(A) type I cystic adenomatoid malformation
(B) type II cystic adenomatoid malformation
(C) pleural effusions
(D) pulmonary sequestration
(E) all of the above
(F) none of the above can be seen; the fetal lungs expand only after birth and also contain air; thus pulmonary lesions cannot be visualized by sonography

350. Which of the following statements is *not* true of ectopic pregnancy?

(A) once a patient has had an ectopic pregnancy, there is a 1 in 4 chance of recurrence
(B) the most common presenting symptoms of an ectopic pregnancy is pelvic pain
(C) ectopic pregnancy in the interstitial portion of the fallopian tube is more serious than in the ampullary portion
(D) ectopic pregnancy in the ampullary portion of the fallopian tube is more serious than in the interstitial portion

351. How long after conception in a normal intrauterine pregnancy (IUP) can the β human chorionic gonadotropin (β-hCG) be detected?

(A) 10 days
(B) 4 weeks
(C) 8 weeks
(D) 28 days

352. Immediately prior to ovulation, follicular cysts can be identified within the ovary. They range in size from

(A) 3 to 5 cm
(B) 25 to 30 mm
(C) 10 to 20 mm
(D) 5 to 10 cm

353. The normal adult ovaries measure

(A) 3 × 2 × 2 cm
(B) 2 × 2 × 4 cm
(C) 3 × 3 × 2 cm
(D) 3 × 2 × 1 mm

354. Which of the following medications could stimulate the growth of multiple follicles?

(A) Clomid (clomiphene citrate)
(B) Perganol (menotropins)
(C) Valmid (ethinamate)
(D) A and B only
(E) all of the above

355. Uterine size may vary according to the patient's age and parity. What is the approximate measurement for a 22-year-old nulligravida?

(A) 8 × 6 × 5 cm
(B) 6 × 3 × 3 cm
(C) 90 × 60 × 30 mm
(D) 100 × 60 × 30 mm

356. In order to identify and measure the ovaries, the recommended technique(s) is

(A) identify the internal iliac vessels running along the posterolateral aspect of the ovary
(B) measure length × thickness × width
(C) identify the internal iliac vessels running along the anteriolateral aspect of the ovary
(D) measure length × width × thickness and divide by 6
(E) A and B
(F) A and D

357. The postmenopausal ovaries are usually enlarged.

(A) true
(B) false

358. The human pelvis is formed by two innominate bones (ossa coxae), the sacrum, and coccyx. The term *innominate* is derived from the Latin word for nameless (*innominatus*). However, these bones do have names. Identify them.

(A) ischium
(B) ileum
(C) pubic
(D) ilium
(E) condyle
(F) A, B, and C
(G) A, C, and D

359. The method of terminating pregnancy is dependent upon the gestational age. Which method is used for up to 12 weeks' menstrual age?

(A) vacuum aspiration (suction curettage)
(B) hypertonic saline
(C) hysterectomy
(D) oxytocin

360. The method of terminating pregnancy is dependent upon the gestational age. Which of the following methods are *not* used after 14 weeks' menstrual age?

(A) vacuum aspiration (suction curettage)
(B) hypertonic saline
(C) hysterectomy
(D) oxytocin

361. Possible masses arising from the posterior aspect of the uterus can be confirmed further by

(A) barium enema with real-time sonography
(B) water enema with real-time sonography
(C) further distending the urinary bladder via a Foley catheter
(D) a radiograph
(E) all of the above

362. The normal variation(s) in the position of the uterus is

(A) anteflexed
(B) retroflexed
(C) anteverted
(D) retroverted
(E) midposition
(F) right lateral deviation
(G) left lateral deviation
(H) C and D
(I) A, B, C, and D
(J) all of the above

363. A T-shaped uterus is associated with

(A) a mother who ingested diethylstilbestrol (DES) when she was pregnant
(B) trauma to the supporting structure of the uterus
(C) relative deficiency of vitamins
(D) none of the above

Questions 364 through 367: Match the terms in Column A to the correct description in Column B.

COLUMN A	COLUMN B
364. Hydrometrocolpos	(A) watery fluid in the uterus and vagina
365. Hematometrocolpos	(B) pus in the uterus
366. Pyometrium	(C) blood in the uterus and vagina
367. Pseudopolyp	(D) tag of mucous membrane resembling a tumor with a pedicle

368. The sonographic appearance(s) of leiomyoma is

(A) nodular distortion of the uterine contour
(B) distortion of the endometrial echoes
(C) abnormal indentation on the bladder or rectum
(D) high-level echoes with distal shadow
(E) calcific degeneration
(F) the uterus cannot be separated from the mass
(G) uterine enlargement
(H) A, B, E, and G
(I) all of the above

369. The sonographic criterion or criteria for a cystic mass are

(A) anechoic even at high-gain settings
(B) smooth, well-defined wall
(C) distal acoustic enhancement
(D) distal acoustic shadow
(E) low-amplitude echoes posterior to the mass
(F) A, B, and E
(G) A, B, and C
(H) A, B, and D
(I) all of the above

370. The sonographic criterion or criteria for a solid mass are

(A) anechoic, without distal acoustic enhancement
(B) smooth, well-defined walls
(C) distal acoustic enhancement
(D) distal acoustic shadow
(E) low-amplitude echoes posterior to the mass
(F) internal echoes that increase with an increase in gain settings
(G) irregular and poorly defined walls and margins
(H) A, D, E, F, and G
(I) A, B, and C
(J) A, B, and E
(K) all of the above

371. Which of the following is *not* true of serous cystadenomas?

(A) thin-walled cyst without septations
(B) occasionally large with measurement of 15–20 cm
(C) more frequently seen in postmenopausal women
(D) more frequently seen with numerous internal septations

372. Which of the following is *not* true of mucinous cystadenomas?

(A) more frequently seen without internal septations
(B) occasionally large with measurement of 15–20 cm
(C) more frequently seen in postmenopausal women
(D) more frequently seen with numerous internal septations

373. In the event of malignant tumors, the sonographer should look for

(A) other tumors
(B) pleural effusions
(C) ascites in the pouch of Douglas
(D) ascites in both paracolic gutters
(E) A and D
(F) all of the above

374. If the peritoneal cavity becomes filled with a mucinous material from a ruptured ovarian cyst or cystadenocarcinoma, it is called

(A) ascites
(B) abscess
(C) pseudomyxoma peritonei
(D) hematoma

Questions 375 through 380: Squamous cell carcinoma of the cervix is the most common malignancy among women in the United States. Match the stages in Column A to the correct description in Column B.

COLUMN A	COLUMN B
375. Stage IVB	(A) carcinoma confined to the cervix
376. Stage 0	(B) lateral parametrial involvement
377. Stage IA	(C) microinvasive
378. Stage II	(D) carcinoma extending beyond the cervix
379. Stage IB	(E) carcinoma in situ
380. Stage IIB	(F) distant metastases

381. Stein-Leventhal syndrome is characterized by

(A) bilateral large cystic ovaries (polycystic ovaries)
(B) obesity
(C) hirsuitism
(D) infertility
(E) menstrual dysfunction

(F) A, D, and E
(G) all of the above

382. A large cyst of about 15–18 cm is situated in the broad ligament between the fallopian tube and ovaries with remnants of the wolffian body. This is *most* likely

(A) theca lutein cyst
(B) serous cystadenoma
(C) serous cystadenocarcinoma
(D) paraovarian cyst

383. Postpartum period refers to

(A) after childbirth
(B) after death
(C) after 20 weeks of gestation
(D) all of the above

384. Puerperium refers to the period

(A) after death
(B) 8–10 weeks after delivery
(C) 6–8 weeks before delivery
(D) 3–6 weeks after delivery

385. Which of the following structures is most likely *not* seen in a postpartum pelvic sonogram?

(A) uterus
(B) endometrial echo
(C) vagina
(D) ovaries

386. If sonograms were taken approximately 1 day after delivery, the fundal height and measurement of the uterus should be

(A) fundus at the level of the umbilicus and measuring 19–22 cm
(B) fundus midway between the symphysis pubis and umbilicus and measuring 10–12 cm
(C) fundus midway between the symphysis pubis and umbilicus and measuring 8–10 cm
(D) involuted back to its normal size, measuring about 7–8.5 cm

387. The *most* common complication(s) during the postpartum period is

(A) hemorrhage
(B) thromboembolism
(C) infection
(D) placenta previa
(E) A, B, and C
(F) all of the above

388. The normal volume of amniotic fluid

(A) increases with gestational age throughout pregnancy
(B) decreases with gestational age and increases near term
(C) increases with gestational age and decreases near term
(D) remains the same volume throughout pregnancy

389. The *most* common and accepted method for measuring the biparietal diameter (BPD) is from

(A) outer to outer edge
(B) outer to inner edge
(C) inner to inner edge
(D) mid-echo to mid-echo edge

390. The degree to which the head shapes may affect biparietal diameter (BPD) can be estimated by which of the following formulas?

(A) $HC = BPD_2 + OFD\pi$

(B) $V = 7 \frac{\pi}{6\,(BPD \div OFD)}$

(C) $CI = \frac{BPD}{OFD} \times 100$

(D) $BPD = \frac{BPD \times OFD}{1.256}$

391. Head circumference can be obtained with which of the following methodologies?

(A) real-time electronic caliper

(B) light pen with commercial computer measurement system

(C) map measurer

(D) formula head circumference $(HC) = \frac{BPD + OFD}{2}\pi$

(E) A and C only

(F) all of the above

392. The *least* reliable method for measuring femoral length is

(A) sector real-time
(B) static scanner
(C) linear-array real-time
(D) Doppler measurement

393. To reduce the chance of error when measuring the biparietal diameter (BPD), the sonographer should

(A) make sure the fetal head appears ovoid
(B) make sure the fetal head appears round
(C) obtain a sonogram at the level of the cavum septum pellucidum, thalamus, and anterior horns of the lateral ventricle
(D) obtain a sonogram at the level of the falx cerebri and lateral ventricles
(E) A and D
(F) B and C
(G) A and C
(H) all of the above

394. The kidneys of the fetus develop in which anatomic region?

(A) pelvis
(B) paraspinal position
(C) thorax
(D) flanks

395. The urinary bladder of the fetus is completely developed by

(A) 12 weeks
(B) 20 weeks
(C) 36 weeks
(D) 8 weeks

396. Fetal gender can be determined as early as

(A) 24 weeks
(B) 8 weeks
(C) 34 weeks
(D) 16 weeks

397. Definite evidence of a male fetus is obtained by visualization of the

(A) penis
(B) scrotum
(C) testicles
(D) prostate gland
(E) A, B, and C
(F) all of the above

398. What is the pathologic significance of isolated hydrocele in utero?

(A) renal agenesis
(B) multicystic kidneys
(C) no significance
(D) trauma to testicles

399. Definite evidence of a female fetus can be confirmed by

(A) nonvisualization of the scrotum
(B) nonvisualization of the penis
(C) depiction of the labia
(D) depiction of the urinary bladder

400. The accuracy in gender prediction in the second and third trimesters is

(A) 80–90%
(B) 50–60%
(C) always 100%
(D) 95–99.9%

401. The vessel in the umbilical cord that carries oxygenated blood and nourishment from the placenta to the fetus is

(A) one artery
(B) two veins
(C) one vein

402. The vessel in the umbilical cord that carries deoxygenated blood from the fetus to the placenta is

(A) two arteries
(B) two veins
(C) one vein

Questions 403 though 408: Match the terms in Column A to the correct description in Column B.

COLUMN A	COLUMN B
403. Placenta previa ______	(A) abnormal adherence of part or all of the placenta to the uterine wall
404. Placenta accreta ______	(B) premature separation of the placenta after 20 weeks of gestation
405. Placenta succenturiata ______	(C) accessory lobe of placenta
406. Abruptio placentae ______	(D) implantation of the placenta in the lower uterine segment
407. Placenta increta ______	(E) abnormal adherence of part or all of the placenta in which the chorionic villi invade the myometrium
408. Placenta percreta ______	(F) abnormal adherence of part or all of the placenta in which chorionic villi invade the uterine wall

409. The treatment for incompetent cervix is

(A) the McDonald procedure
(B) the Shirodkar procedure
(C) dilation and curettage (D&C)
(D) hysterectomy
(E) A and B

410. Which of the following has the largest percentage incidence of a single umbilical artery?

(A) singleton births
(B) twins
(C) abortuses
(D) fetuses with trisomy D

411. The causes of an incompetent cervix are

(A) several dilation and curettage procedures (D&Cs)
(B) exposure to diethylstilbestrol in utero
(C) hormonal influences
(D) all of the above

412. Incompetent cervix is treated at how many weeks of gestation?

(A) 24
(B) 28–36
(C) 14–18
(D) 8–10

413. Sonographers should pay attention to the technical aspects of the study when ruling out placenta previa or incompetent cervix. Which of the following is *least* likely?

(A) overdistended maternal urinary bladder can cause false-negative diagnosis of incompetent cervix
(B) an erect position should *not* be used because gravitational pressure from uterine contents can cause an abortion
(C) overdistended maternal urinary bladder can cause false-positive diagnosis of placenta previa
(D) fetal head can prevent visualization of a posterior placenta previa
(E) A, C, and D
(F) B and C only
(G) all of the above

414. Twins that result from union of one sperm and one ovum are called

(A) monozygotic
(B) dizygotic
(C) fraternal
(D) identical
(E) B and C
(F) A and D

415. Twins that result from union of two sperm and two ova are called

(A) monozygotic
(B) dizygotic
(C) fraternal
(D) identical
(E) B and C
(F) A and D

416. When is a neonate considered growth retarded?

(A) when the neonate's mean weight for gestational age is below the 10th percentile
(B) when the biparietal diameter (BPD) is less than 9.7 cm at term
(C) neonates born between 36 and 40 weeks
(D) when hydramnios is present at term

417. Which of the following methods is *least* reliable for diagnosing intrauterine growth retardation (IUGR)?

(A) total intrauterine volume (TIUV)
(B) head circumference
(C) abdominal circumference
(D) femur length

418. The formula for head circumference (HC) is

(A) $HC = \frac{\pi}{6\ c(AB + C^1)}$

(B) $HC = 0.523 \times ABC$

(C) $HC = \frac{BPD + OFD}{2}\pi$

419. Abdominal circumference measurement reflects primarily which organ size?

(A) stomach
(B) umbilical vein
(C) kidney
(D) liver

420. The formula for abdominal circumference is

(A) $AC = (D_1 + D_2) \times 1.57$

(B) $AC = \frac{\pi}{6\ (A + B^1)}$

(C) $AC = 0.523 \times ABC$

(D) $AC = \frac{BPD + OFD}{2}\pi$

421. Which of the following organs are responsible for amniotic fluid production?

(A) stomach
(B) umbilical vein
(C) kidney
(D) liver

422. Which of the following is *not* true of renal agenesis?

(A) associated with oligohydramnios
(B) associated with hydramnios
(C) associated with Potter's syndrome
(D) absence of the kidneys

423. The most common fetal renal anomaly is

(A) hydronephrosis
(B) polycystic kidney
(C) Wilms' tumor
(D) neuroblastoma

424. Most unilateral hydronephrosis is due to

(A) neuroblastoma
(B) polycystic kidney
(C) Wilms' tumor
(D) ureteropelvic junction obstruction

425. Bilateral hydronephrosis of a fetus in utero is associated with

(A) "prune belly" syndrome
(B) ureteropelvic junction obstruction
(C) oligohydramnios
(D) dilated urinary bladder
(E) Eagle-Barrett syndrome
(F) B, C, and D
(G) all of the above

426. Which of the following statements is *not* true of "prune belly" syndrome?

(A) predominantly a male disorder
(B) also known as Eagle-Barrett syndrome
(C) it is associated with cryptorchidism
(D) predominantly a female disorder

427. Which of the following is *not* true of infantile polycystic disease?

(A) it has an autosomal recessive type of inheritance
(B) it occurs bilaterally
(C) it is bilateral renal enlargement
(D) it can be diagnosed before birth
(E) it cannot be diagnosed before birth
(F) it occurs in Meckel's syndrome
(G) it is incompatible with life

428. Which of the following is *not* true of multicystic disease?

(A) it has an autosomal dominant type of inheritance
(B) it is usually unilateral
(C) it is bilateral renal enlargement
(D) it can be diagnosed before birth
(E) it cannot be diagnosed before birth
(F) it occurs in Meckel's syndrome

429. Sonography can depict all of the following *except*

(A) diaphragmatic hernia
(B) choledochal cyst
(C) meconium pseudocysts
(D) fetal alopecia

430. Hydramnios denotes

(A) excessive amount of amniotic fluid over 200 mL at term
(B) excessive amount of amniotic fluid over 2,000 mL at term
(C) reduced amount of amniotic fluid below 300 mL at term
(D) reduced amount of amniotic fluid below 200 mL at term

431. Oligohydramnios denotes

(A) excessive amount of amniotic fluid over 200 mL at term
(B) excessive amount of amniotic fluid over 2,000 mL at term
(C) reduced amount of amniotic fluid below 300 mL at term
(D) reduced amount of amniotic fluid below 2,000 mL at term

432. The formation of the umbilical cord in the early weeks of embryogenesis results from fusion of which structures?

(A) decidual basalis
(B) decidual capsularis
(C) body stalk
(D) yolk stalk
(E) A and B
(F) B and C
(G) C and D
(H) A and D

433. The blood vessels inside the umbilical cord are protected by a mucoid substance called

(A) chorionic fluid
(B) amniotic fluid
(C) Wharton's jelly
(D) estrogen

434. The *most* accurate time to obtain femur length is

(A) 14–20 weeks
(B) 20–30 weeks
(C) 6–12 weeks
(D) 30–40 weeks

435. Which of the following statements is true about twins?

(A) monozygotic twins also are known as fraternal twins
(B) dizygotic twins also are known as identical twins
(C) approximately 75% of twins are of the same sex
(D) twins produced from a single ova are called fraternal twins

436. The *most* common anomaly affecting the central nervous system (CNS) is

(A) spina bifida
(B) anencephaly
(C) encephalocele
(D) hydrocephalus

437. If fetal ascites are seen in a mother with an elevated Rh titer, it is most likely an indication of

(A) hepatosplenomegaly
(B) duodenal atresia
(C) umbilical cord anomalies
(D) heart failure

438. Artifactual ascites (pseudoascites) which can be produced by a linear array real-time, may be confused with true ascites. To avoid this confusion, the sonographer should use which of the following important techniques: (1) record the falciform ligament and its surrounding fluid, (2) record the pattern of intraperitoneal fluid, (3) change the patient's position and observe whether the fluid moves to a dependent position, (4) record the pattern of the retroperitoneal fluid as it surrounds the abdominal viscera?

(A) 3 and 4
(B) 1, 2, and 3
(C) 1 and 4
(D) all of the above

439. Which of the following anomalies are associated with erythroblastosis?

(A) ascites
(B) hepatosplenomegaly
(C) hydramnios
(D) increased umbilical vein diameter
(E) hydrops
(F) all of the above

440. Cleft palate is associated with

(A) hypotelorism
(B) alobar holoprosencephaly
(C) trisomy 13
(D) A and B only
(E) all of the above

441. A complex mass is seen near the buttocks of a fetus in utero. The mass has some calcific areas with distal acoustic shadows. This is most likely

(A) sacrococcygeal teratoma
(B) meconium
(C) encephalocele
(D) uteropelvic junction obstruction

442. The sonographic appearance of cleft palate is

(A) a coronal view through the maxilla showing absence of this bone below the nose
(B) a coronal view through the maxilla showing absence of this bone above the nose
(C) cystic mass protruding from the lip
(D) split in the zygoma
(E) A, C, and D
(F) all of the above

443. What blood vessel usually can be depicted posteromedial to the ovary?

(A) ovarian vein
(B) ovarian artery
(C) external iliac artery
(D) internal iliac artery

444. If a patient's blood pressure is 140/90 mm Hg or more with edema and proteinuria, these signs and symptoms are consistent with

(A) rubella
(B) Rh isoimmunization
(C) syphilis
(D) preeclampsia

445. A patient's blood pressure is 140/90 mm Hg or more with edema, proteinuria, and convulsions. These signs and symptoms are consistent with

(A) rubella
(B) Rh isoimmunization
(C) eclampsia
(D) syphilis

446. A hemolytic disease of newborns, characterized by anemia, jaundice, and hepatosplenomegaly is

(A) lymphangioma
(B) erythroblastosis fetalis
(C) Eagle-Barrett syndrome
(D) omphalocele

447. A patient who contracts German measles in the first 12 weeks of gestation may give birth to an infant with

(A) auditory defects
(B) patent ductus arteriosus of the heart
(C) macrocephaly
(D) microcephaly
(E) A and C
(F) A, B, and D
(G) C and D

448. The three stages of labor are which of the following: (1) dilatation of the cervix, (2) abdominal pain, (3) delivery of the baby, (4) expulsion of the placenta, (5) Braxton Hicks contractions?

(A) 2, 3, and 4
(B) 1, 3, and 4
(C) 5, 3, and 4

449. The external os of the cervix is said to be completely dilated at

(A) 10 cm
(B) 10 mm
(C) 25 cm
(D) 100 mm
(E) A and D
(F) all of the above

450. With current real-time equipment, how early can the fetal kidneys be depicted?

(A) 11 weeks
(B) 14 weeks
(C) 20 weeks
(D) 35 weeks

451. How much does the fetal head grow per week at 16 weeks of gestation?

(A) 5 mm per week
(B) 15 mm per week
(C) 2 cm per week
(D) 3 cm per week

452. If performing a BPD measurement and the midline echo is continuous and unbroken, this would indicate that the scanning plane is

(A) normal
(B) too high
(C) through the fetal neck
(D) correct

453. How much does the fetal head grow per week at 20 weeks of gestation?

(A) 5 mm per week
(B) 15 mm per week
(C) 2 cm per week
(D) 3.6 mm per week

454. How much does the fetal head grow per week at 32 weeks of gestation?

(A) 5 mm per week
(B) 15 mm per week
(C) 2.3 mm per week
(D) 3.5 cm per week

455. How much does the fetal head grow per week at 40 weeks of gestation?

(A) 5 mm per week
(B) 1.4 mm per week
(C) 2.3 mm per week
(D) 3.5 cm per week

456. Which of the following pelvic masses is *least* likely to enlarge during pregnancy?

(A) ovarian cystadenoma
(B) fibroid
(C) corpus luteum cyst
(D) dermoid cyst

457. The *most* common solid mass(es) associated with pregnancy is (are)

(A) dermoid
(B) leiomyomas
(C) leiomyosarcoma
(D) cystadenoma

458. The causes for a uterus too large for dates include

(A) multiple gestation
(B) oligohydramnios
(C) hydramnios
(D) wrong menstrual dates
(E) hydatidiform mole
(F) myoma
(G) A, C, and D
(H) A, C, D, E, and F
(I) A and D only
(J) all of the above

459. The causes for a uterus too small for dates include

(A) fetal death
(B) oligohydramnios
(C) hydramnios
(D) wrong menstrual dates
(E) hydatidiform mole
(F) intrauterine growth retardation (IUGR)
(G) A, B, D, and F
(H) A, C, D, E, and F
(I) A and F
(J) all of the above

460. The position of the uterus may be variable with parity. What percentage of women may have an anteverted uterus?

(A) 50%
(B) 10%
(C) 80%
(D) 90%

461. What degree of angle does the uterus normally have with the long axis of the vagina?

(A) 50°
(B) 10°

(C) 45°
(D) 80°
(E) 90°

462. If the peritoneum is reflected at the level of the isthmus on the anterior surface of the uterus to the upper aspect of the bladder, it is called

(A) anterior cul-de-sac
(B) pouch of Douglas
(C) vesicouterine pouch
(D) space of Retzius
(E) posterior cul-de-sac
(F) A and C
(G) B and E

463. If the peritoneum is reflected at the level of the posterior fornix of the vagina on the posterior surface of the uterus to the anterior aspect of the rectum, it is called

(A) posterior cul-de-sac
(B) pouch of Douglas
(C) vesicouterine pouch
(D) space of Retzius
(E) retrouterine pouch
(F) A, B, and E

464. The space between the bladder and pubis that is filled with extraperitoneal adipose tissue is called

(A) posterior cul-de-sac
(B) pouch of Douglas
(C) vesicouterine pouch
(D) space of Retzius
(E) retrouterine pouch

465. The three major pelvic side wall muscles seen on sonography are

(A) iliopsoas
(B) pubococcygeus
(C) obturator internus
(D) rectus
(E) gluteal
(F) A, B, and D
(G) C, E, and D
(H) A, B, and C

466. What is mittelschmerz?

(A) a disease of the iliopsoas muscles
(B) intermenstrual pain
(C) a name for infants of diabetic mothers
(D) a malignant blood disease

467. What was removed during surgery may be important clinical information for the sonographer to know. If a 27-year-old patient with a recent abdominal pregnancy of 37 weeks presents with a surgical Hx of status/post (S/P) C-section, which of the following organs or structures would almost never be removed in this case?

(A) placenta
(B) uterus
(C) cord
(D) fetus

468. An acardius anencephalic twin occurs in

(A) monozygotic twin pregnancy
(B) dizygotic twin pregnancy
(C) amniotic band syndrome
(D) B and C
(E) all of the above

469. If the heart is absent (acardius) on real-time in one of the fetuses of an anencephalic twin, it is correct to assume that

(A) one of the fetuses is dead and therefore only the other will move around on real-time
(B) both fetuses may move around and demonstrate flexion and extension of the limbs
(C) if there is no visible head or heart, there will be no movement

470. Anencephaly results from failure of the

(A) müllerian duct to close completely
(B) neural tube to close completely at its cephalic end
(C) neural tube to close completely at its caudad end

471. The standard range of error for biparietal diameter (BPD) measurements in the third trimester is

(A) 10 mm
(B) 5 mm
(C) 2 mm
(D) 4 mm

472. A method that an individual user can employ to test the range of error for biparietal diameter (BPD) is

(A) a series of measurements made on the same patient in 24 hours
(B) error = $(BPD + 2) \times \pi$
(C) neither A nor B

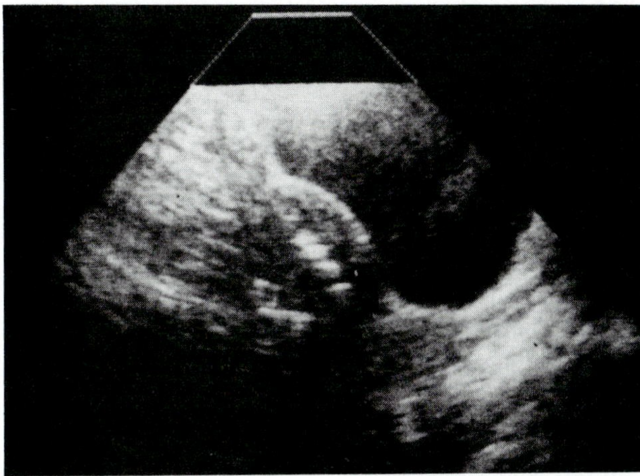

Figure 8–26. Sagittal midline sonogram through the uterus.

473. The sonographic findings in Fig. 8–26 include

(A) multiple echogenic interfaces probably arising from a Lippes loop IUCD
(B) echogenic material within the uterus probably secondary to sloughed endometrium
(C) A and B
(D) neither A nor B

474. The optimal placement of an intrauterine contraceptive device (IUCD) is

(A) in the cervix
(B) in the fundus only
(C) in the lumen of the uterus
(D) within the wall of the uterus

475. The sonographic findings in Fig. 8–27 include

(A) multiple immature follicles
(B) a mature follicle and two immature follicles
(C) polycystic ovary
(D) none of the above

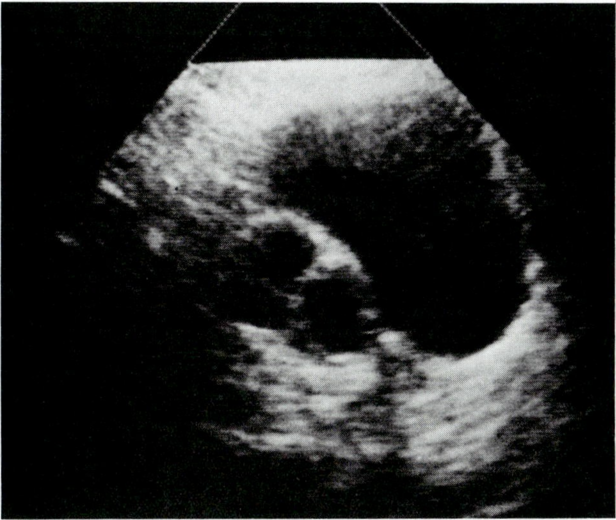

Figure 8–27. Sagittal sonogram obtained through the right adnexa of a patient undergoing ovulation induction.

476. Mature follicles measure approximately

(A) 2 cm
(B) 1 cm
(C) 3 cm
(D) 4 cm

477. Sonographic findings in Fig. 8–28 include

(A) ovarian cyst
(B) loculated predominantly cystic adnexal mass
(C) normal uterus
(D) loculated fluid collections

478. The most probable diagnosis of this mass (Fig. 8–28) includes

(A) endometrioma
(B) ovarian cyst
(C) cystic ovarian tumor
(D) A or C

479. Fig. 8–29 is a transverse sonogram through the mid-abdomen of a postmenopausal woman. The abnormal finding on this sonogram includes

(A) large ovarian tumor
(B) matted bowel
(C) simple ascites
(D) bowel obstruction

480. The condition in question 479 usually results from

(A) ovarian carcinoma
(B) renal failure
(C) liver failure
(D) congestive heart failure

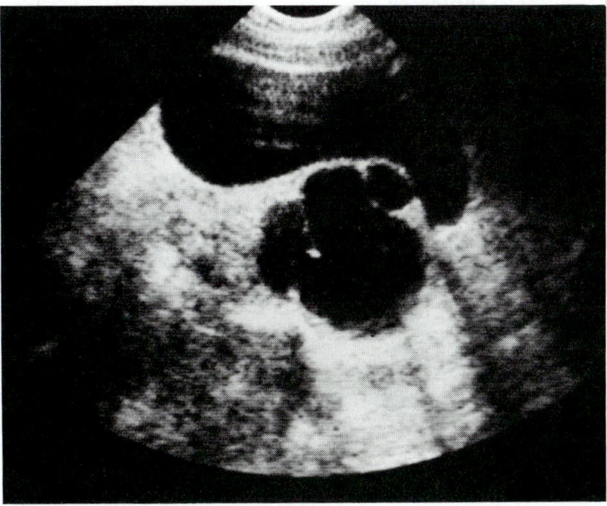

Figure 8–28. Sagittal sonogram obtained through the left adnexa.

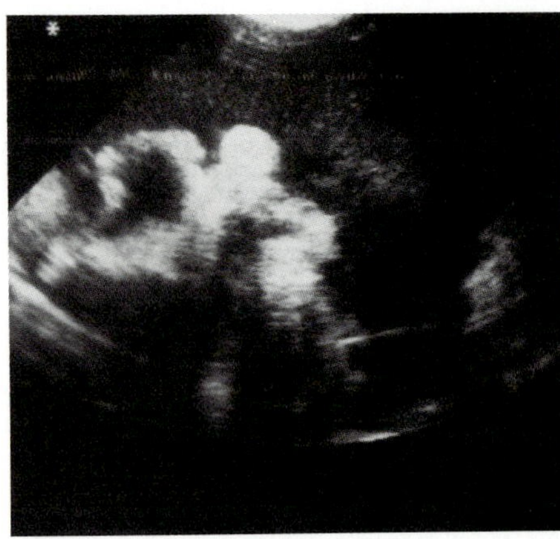

Figure 8–29. Transverse sonogram through the mid-abdomen.

481. Given the findings in Fig. 8–29, the most likely diagnosis is

(A) pseudomyxoma peritonei
(B) bowel obstruction
(C) bowel perforation
(D) appendicitis

482. The incidence of ovarian carcinoma in women in th United States over 50 years of age is

(A) 33 per 100,000
(B) 3 per 100,000
(C) 333 per 100,000
(D) cannot be estimated

483. Fig. 8–30 is a sonogram obtained through the lower face of a 29-week fetus. Sonographic findings include

(A) cleft palate
(B) cleft lip
(C) cleft lip and palate
(D) normal nose and lips

484. Cleft lip and palate is associated with

(A) chromosomal disorders
(B) Stein-Leventhal syndrome
(C) A and B
(D) none of the above

485. Fig. 8–31 is an image obtained through the arm and hand of a third-trimester fetus. The most likely diagnosis is

(A) one digit missing
(B) "hitchhiker thumb"
(C) A and B
(D) none of the above

486. Hydrops fetalis can be secondary to

(A) tumors obstructing venous return to the heart
(B) Rh isoimmunization
(C) diabetes mellitis
(D) A or B

487. The chorion and the amnion fuse at approximately

(A) 8–10 weeks
(B) 10–14 weeks
(C) 18–20 weeks
(D) they never fuse

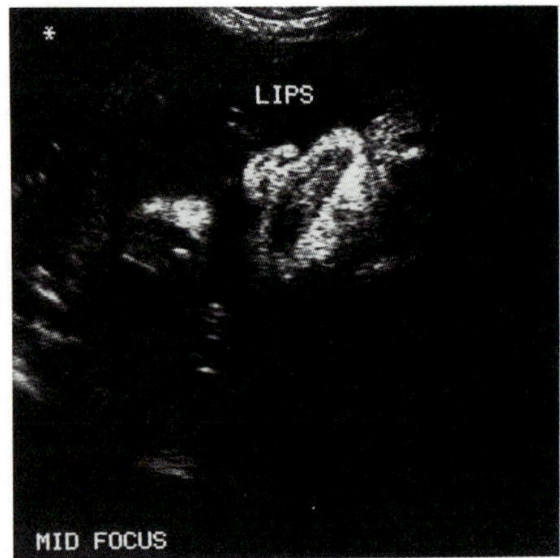

Figure 8–30. Sonogram obtained through the lower face of a fetus.

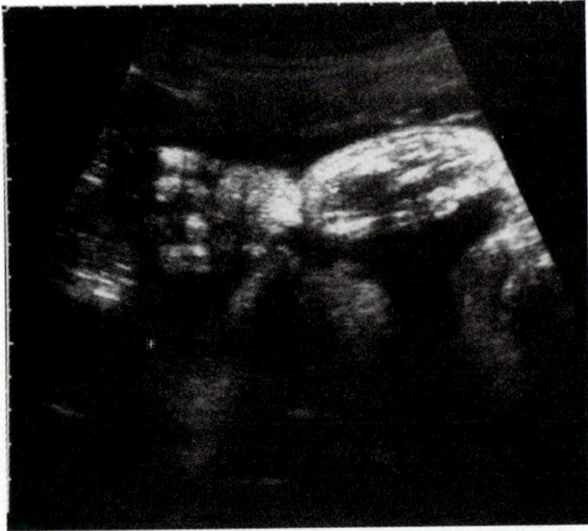

Figure 8–31. Sonogram obtained through the arm and hand of a third trimester fetus.

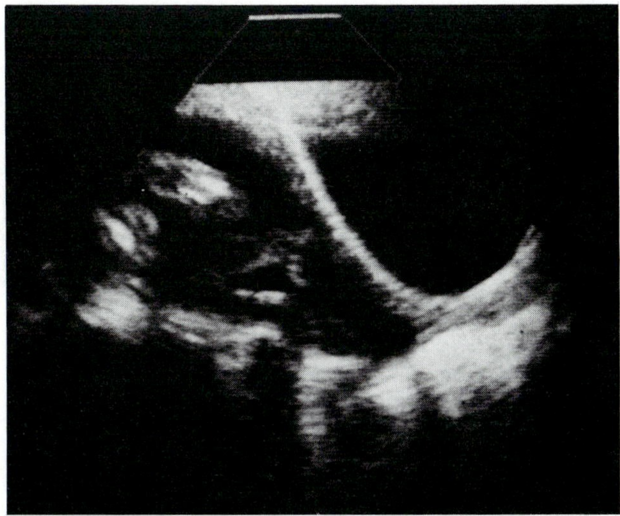

Figure 8–32. Sagittal sonogram of a second trimester pregnancy.

488. The linear interference related to the chorionic plate in Fig. 8–32 represents

(A) elevated chorion with subchorionic venous lakes
(B) a placental chorioangioma
(C) a placental tumor
(D) chorioamniotic separation

489. The term *limb reduction abnormalities* includes

(A) acheiria
(B) acheiropodia
(C) A and B
(D) none of the above

490. Mild pyelocaliectasis of the fetal renal collecting system may be related to

(A) maternal ingestion of fluid prior to sonographic study
(B) diuresis of the fetal kidney
(C) maternal diabetes
(D) A and B

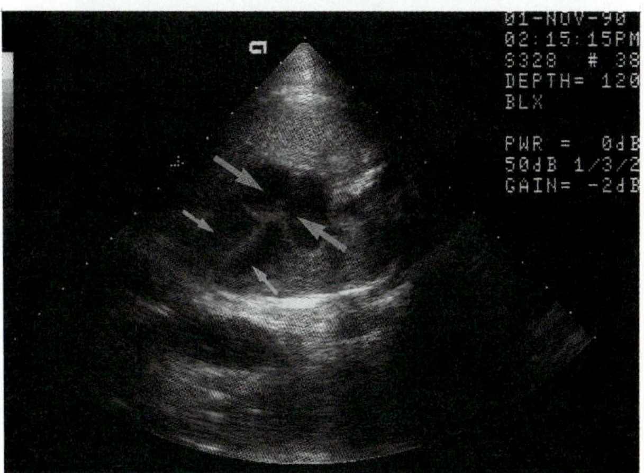

Figure 8–33. Sonogram obtained through the fetal thorax.

491. Fig. 8–33 is taken through the chest of a 30-week fetus. The large arrows point to

(A) the atria
(B) the ventricles
(C) the valves
(D) the papillary muscles

492. The short arrows point to

(A) the atria
(B) the ventricles
(C) the valves
(D) the papillary muscles

493. Maternal condition(s) that are associated with increased incidence of fetal heart malformations is

(A) diabetes mellitus
(B) certain medications such as lithium
(C) both A and B
(D) neither A nor B

494. In order to obtain the best femur length, the sonographer should

(A) obtain the entire length of the femur, including the femoral neck and head
(B) the diaphysis or shaft of the femur is the only portion that should be measured
(C) the femur is not a good measurement of gestational age because it has a wide variance
(D) none of the above

495. The uterus should involute to normal size

(A) 1 week after delivery
(B) approximately 4 weeks after delivery
(C) 1 year after delivery
(D) it never returns to normal size

496. Placenta previa most frequently occurs in

(A) multigravida patients
(B) patients with history of previous C-section
(C) patients with history of previous therapeutic abortion
(D) all of the above

497. Fig. 8–34 is an M-mode echocardiogram (vertical line/sec) of the same fetus shown in Fig. 8–33. The M-mode echocardiogram shows

(A) arrhythmia
(B) bradycardia
(C) tachycardia
(D) normal rhythm

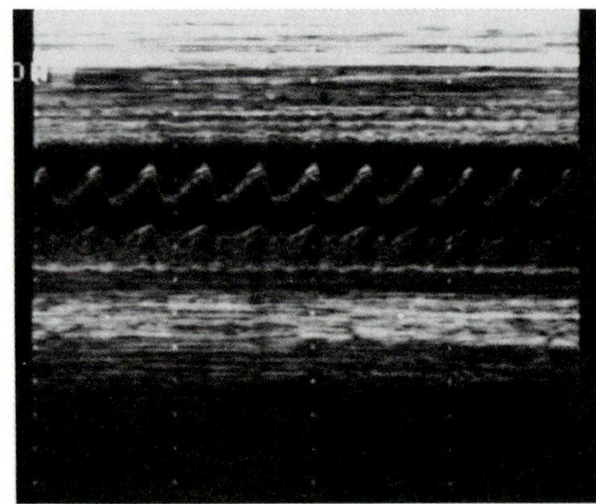
Figure 8–34. M-mode echocardiogram of the fetus.

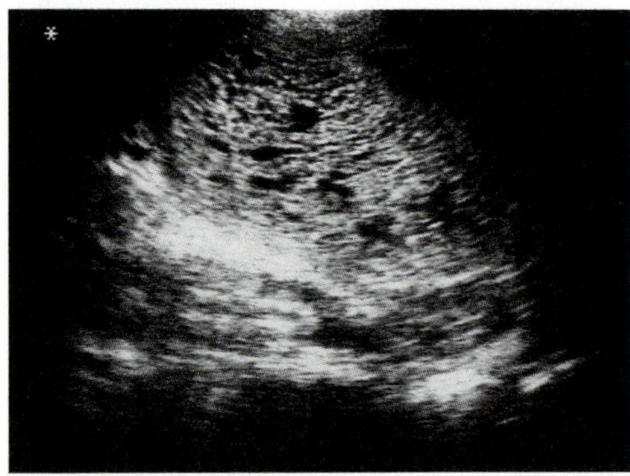
Figure 8–35. Transverse sonogram through the mid-abdomen.

498. Retrochorionic hemorrhage can be associated with

(A) a very poor prognosis for completion of pregnancy
(B) first and second trimester bleeding
(C) A and B
(D) neither A nor B

499. Arrhythmias may be associated with

(A) malformed hearts
(B) maternal lupus erythematosus
(C) maternal rheumatoid arthritis
(D) all of the above

500. The cervix normally measures

(A) no greater than 3 cm in length
(B) no less than 3 cm in length
(C) no less than 3 cm in anteroposterior dimension
(D) none of the above

501. The normal heart rate and rhythm of a second-trimester fetus is

(A) between 120 and 160 beats/minute
(B) can vary with the fetal state, breathing, and activities
(C) can demonstrate periodic premature ventricular contractions
(D) all of the above

502. The adrenal in the third-trimester fetus can be as much as ______ % the size of the kidneys.

(A) 70 (C) 30
(B) 50 (D) 10

503. Fig. 8–35 is a transverse sonogram through the mid-abdomen. The most likely diagnosis is

(A) molar tissue within the uterus
(B) a uterine fibroid
(C) normal pregnancy
(D) complicated ascites

504. The *most* common site for an ectopic pregnancy is

(A) ampullary portion of the fallopian tube
(B) isthmic portion of the fallopian tube
(C) interstitial portion of the fallopian tube
(D) within the ovary

505. Based on the sonogram in Fig. 8–35, one would expect that the pregnancy

(A) is less than 8 weeks
(B) is more than 14 weeks but less than 20
(C) cannot be predicted based on this sonogram
(D) is over 30 weeks

506. Sonography can be used in assessing the amount of retained tissue following a miscarriage. In the diagnosis of complete abortions, one must also consider the possibility of

(A) ectopic pregnancy
(B) concomitant intrauterine pregnancy
(C) A and B
(D) none of the above

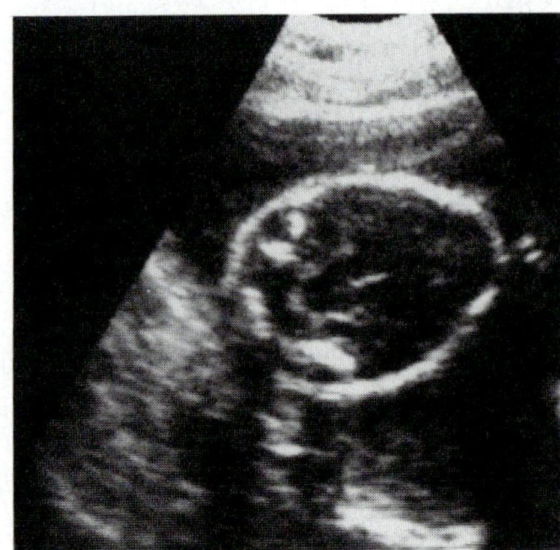
Figure 8–36. Transverse sonogram through the fetal head.

507. Fig. 8–36 is a transverse sonogram of a fetal head at 16 weeks' gestation. This sonogram most likely represents

(A) normally shaped fetal head
(B) "lemon head," or abnormally convex frontal bones
(C) "banana sign," or abnormally fusiform shape of the cerebellar hemispheres
(D) hydrocephalus
(E) B and C

508. The abnormality in the fetus in Fig. 8–36 is associated with

(A) meningomyelocele
(B) omphalocele
(C) gastroschisis
(D) fetal hydronephrosis

509. The maternal serum α-fetoprotein in the mother of the fetus in Fig. 8–36 would be most likely

(A) elevated
(B) decreased
(C) normal

510. The yolk sac has an important role in early hematopoiesis. It typically is largest

(A) between 5 and 9 weeks
(B) after 16 weeks
(C) only before the fifth week
(D) none of the above

511. The positive sonographic findings in Fig. 8–37 include

(A) herniation of brain and meninges through defect in posterior cranial fossa
(B) a large meningomyelocele arising from the neck
(C) a large cystic hygroma arising from the neck
(D) none of the above

512. Cystic hygromas

(A) result from a malfusion of lymphatic channels behind the neck
(B) can be associated with Turner's syndrome
(C) A and B
(D) neither A nor B

513. What is the most common nontrophoblastic primary tumor of the placenta?

(A) teratoma
(B) chorioangioma
(C) hydatidiform mole
(D) melanoma

514. Fig. 8–38 is a magnified longitudinal sonogram of a postpartum uterus. The most likely diagnosis is

(A) retained products of conception
(B) molar pregnancy
(C) uterine fibroid
(D) none of the above

515. Fig. 8–39 is a longitudinal sonogram of a third-trimester fetus. The arrow points to

(A) ascites
(B) polyhydramnios
(C) pericardial effusion
(D) fetal hydrops

516. The cause for immune hydrops is

(A) obstruction to venous return
(B) Rh isoimmunization
(C) congestive heart failure of the fetus
(D) all of the above

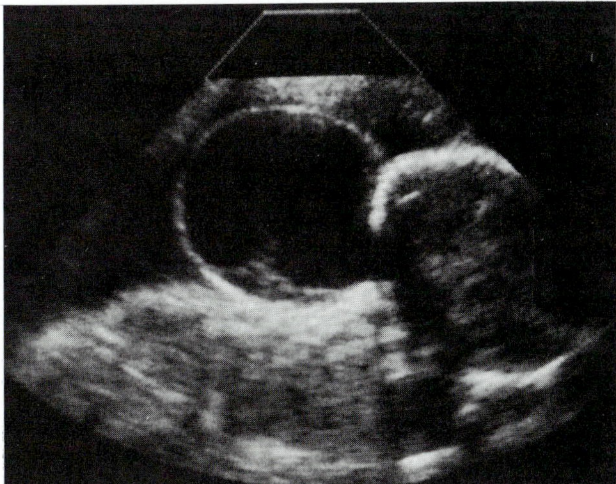

Figure 8–37. Transverse sonogram through the fetal head.

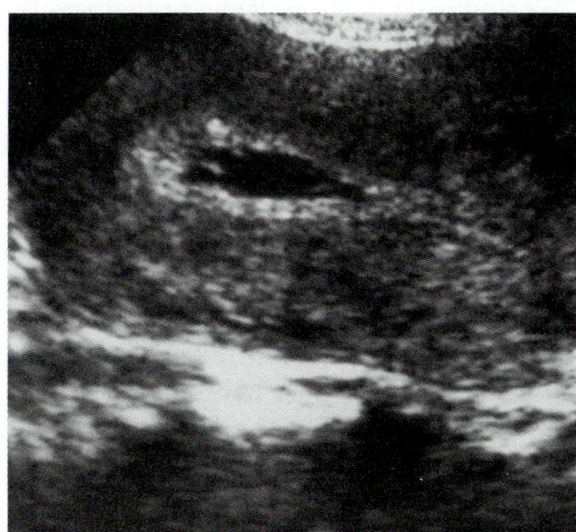

Figure 8–38. Magnified longitudinal sonogram of a postpartum uterus.

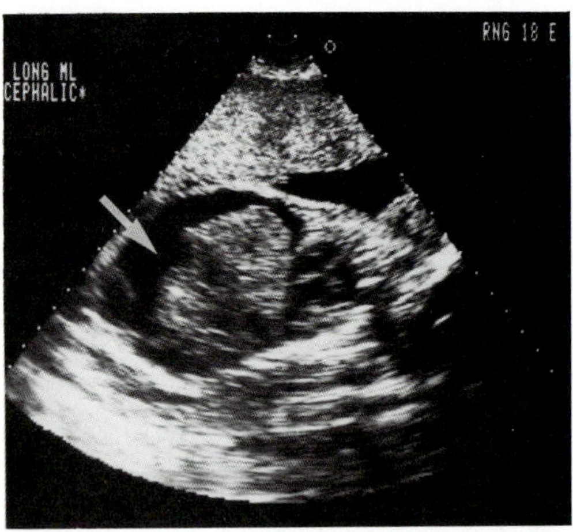

Figure 8–39. Sagittal sonogram of a third trimester uterus.

517. Fig. 8–40 is a midline longitudinal sonogram of the lower uterine segment in a 30-week intrauterine pregnancy. The most likely diagnosis is

(A) placenta previa
(B) amniotic sheet or band
(C) uterine septation
(D) none of the above

518. Genetic amniocenteses are performed between 16 and 18 weeks because

(A) the α-fetoprotein is highest at that time
(B) the aminocytes have the highest likelihood for successful harvesting of chromosomes
(C) it is easiest to do amniocentesis at this stage
(D) a first-trimester termination can be performed if there is abnormal chromosomes

519. Amniotic band syndrome can be associated with

(A) gastroschisis
(B) omphalocele
(C) anencephaly
(D) amputated fingers, toes, and extremities
(E) all of the above

520. One would expect that the α-fetoprotein in an anencephalic fetus to be

(A) usually normal because this is a closed neural tube defect
(B) usually abnormal because this is an open neural tube defect
(C) may be abnormal if associated with a menigomyelocele
(D) none of the above

521. Bowel may be seen herniated at the base of the umbilical cord between ______ and ______ weeks of gestation.

(A) 5 and 6 weeks
(B) 8 and 12 weeks
(C) 12 and 18 weeks
(D) 18 and 20 weeks

522. If a sonographer encounters a patient with a bicornuate uterus, what other structures should be imaged?

(A) brain
(B) liver
(C) kidneys
(D) nothing needs to be done because this is almost always an isolated anomaly

523. Figs. 8–41 and 8–42 are transverse scans of the fetal abdomen of different third-trimester fetuses. Fig. 8–41 demonstrates

(A) polycystic kidneys
(B) meconium-filled large bowels
(C) hydronephrosis
(D) none of the above

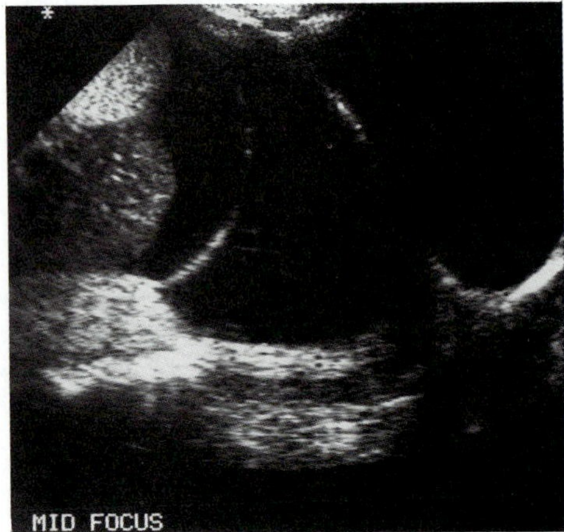

Figure 8–40. Midline sagittal sonogram of the lower uterine segment.

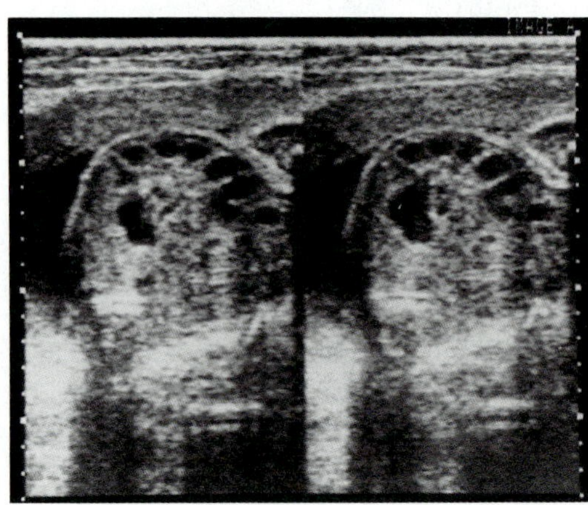

Figure 8–41. Transverse sonogram through the fetal abdomen.

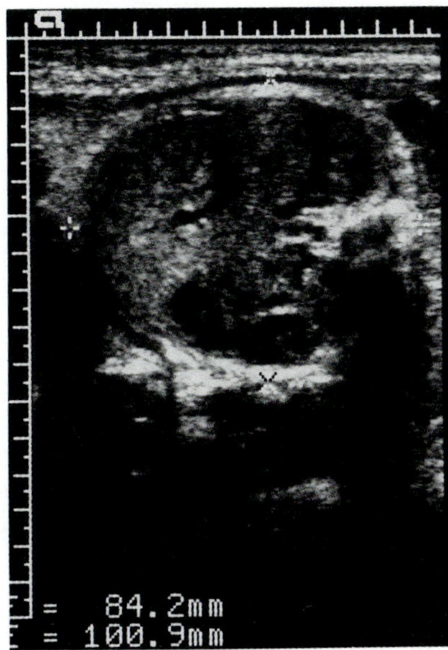

Figure 8–42. Transverse sonogram through the fetal abdomen.

524. Fig. 8–42 demonstrates

(A) fetal gallbladder
(B) portal sinus
(C) fetal stomach
(D) left adrenal
(E) all except for A

525. The type of intrauterine contraceptive device (IUCD) shown in Fig. 8–43 is

(A) Copper-7 (Cu-7)
(B) Lippes loop

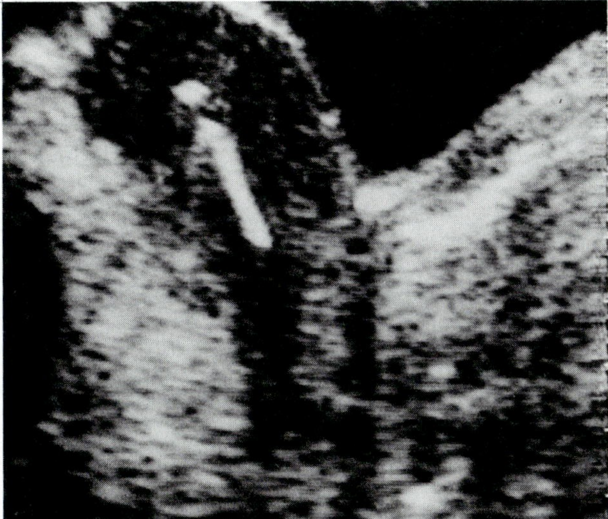

Figure 8–43. A magnified longitudinal pelvic sonogram in a patient with lost string.

(C) Dalkon shield
(D) none of the above

526. Complications of intrauterine contraceptive devices (IUCDs) include

(A) ectopic pregnancy
(B) ovarian abscess
(C) endometriosis
(D) A and B

527. A blighted ovum implies that

(A) a fetus has formed but has undergone disintegration
(B) an embryo has probably not been formed

528. Figs. 8–44 and 8–45 are obtained from a 28-week fetus. Fig. 8–44 represents

(A) hydrocephalus
(B) incorrect level for obtaining a biparietal diameter
(C) absence of the cavum septi pellucidi
(D) none of the above

529. Fig. 8–45 represents

(A) the proper level for obtaining an abdominal circumference
(B) omphalocele
(C) two dilated bowel loops
(D) double bubble

530. An overly distended urinary bladder may result in

(A) an anterior, low-lying placenta appearing as a placenta previa
(B) a posterior, low-lying placenta appearing as a placenta previa
(C) A or B
(D) none of the above

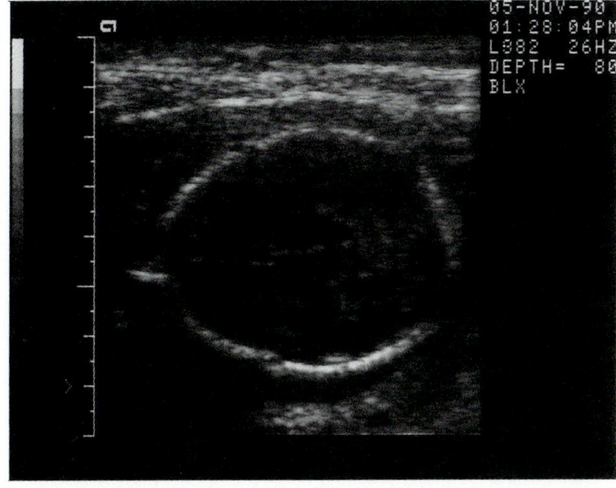

Figure 8–44. Transverse sonogram through the fetal head.

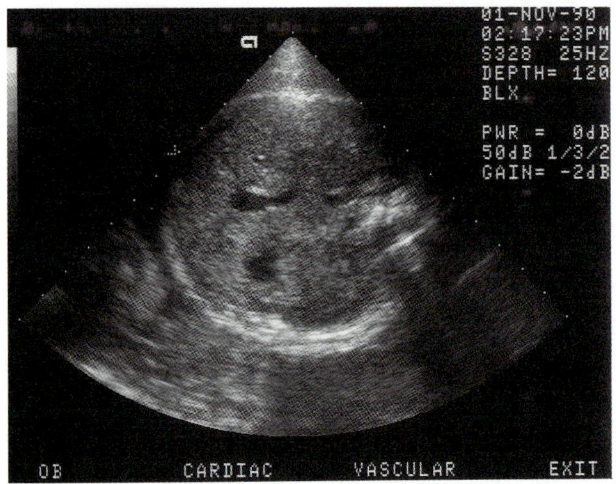

Figure 8–45. Transverse sonogram through the fetal abdomen.

531. A fetus with situs inversus would demonstrate what on the sonogram?

(A) inflammation of the renal sinus
(B) pelvic kidney
(C) transposition of the abdominal and thoracic viscera
(D) enlargement of the fetal viscera

532. With anencephaly, there is an approximately 30% incidence of spinal dysraphism.

(A) true
(B) false

533. Fig. 8–46 is a transvaginal sonogram of a 27-year-old woman with amenorrhea. A physical examination suggested a slightly enlarged uterus. An ultrasound examination was requested to rule out ectopic pregnancy. This sonogram shows

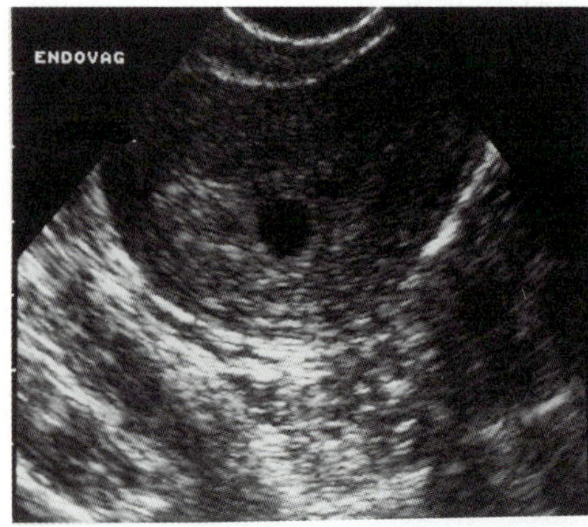

Figure 8–46. Transvaginal sonogram of the uterus.

(A) hydatidiform mole
(B) a chorionic sac within the decidualized endometrium
(C) a pseudogestational sac
(D) a nabothian cyst

534. Disorders that are frequently associated with a meningomyelocele include

(A) Chiari malformation
(B) polycystic kidneys
(C) omphalocele
(D) A and C

535. The abnormal sonographic findings in Fig. 8–47 include

(A) herniation of the liver outside of the abdomen
(B) large meningomyelocele
(C) extrophy of the heart
(D) none of the above

536. Omphalocele is usually associated with

(A) herniation of the bowel from an eccentric vent in the anterior abdominal wall at the umbilical cord insertion
(B) herniation of the bowel with normal umbilical cord insertion
(C) a solid mass extending from the coccyx
(D) cranial anomalies

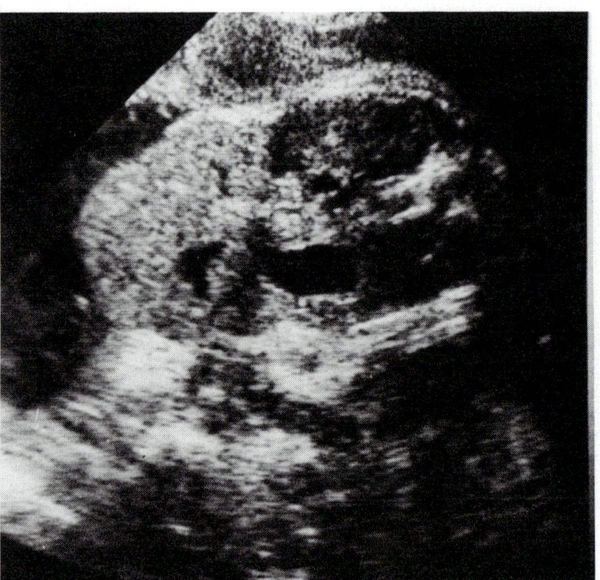

Figure 8–47. Transverse sonogram through the fetal abdomen at 30 weeks.

537. At what level of serum β human chorionic gonadrotropin (β-hCG) is the normal intrauterine gestational sac seen on transvaginal sonography with the Second International Standard?

(A) 65,000 mIU/mL
(B) 35,000 mIU/mL
(C) 1000 mIU/mL
(D) 500 mIU/mL

538. The cumulus oophorus consists of

(A) the oocyte
(B) clusters of granulosa cells that surround the oocyte
(C) A and B
(D) neither A nor B

539. The most likely diagnosis that can be made from Fig. 8–48 is

(A) a physiologic (follicular or luteal) ovarian cyst
(B) cystadenocarcinoma
(C) ruptured ectopic pregnancy
(D) A and B

540. A physiologic ovarian cyst may have internal echoes due to

(A) hemorrhage within the cyst
(B) fat within the cyst
(C) A or B
(D) neither A nor B

541. Fig. 8–49 is a transvaginal sonogram of an early intrauterine pregnancy. The most likely diagnosis is

(A) uterine contraction
(B) intramural uterine fibroid

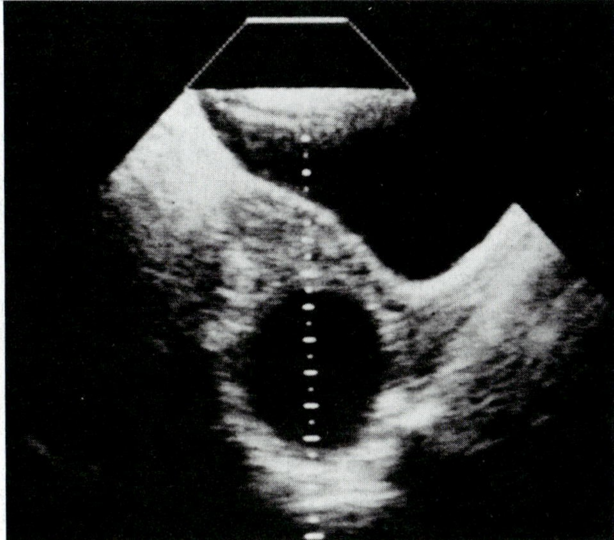

Figure 8–48. Sagittal midline pelvic sonogram of a 20-year-old patient with pelvic pain.

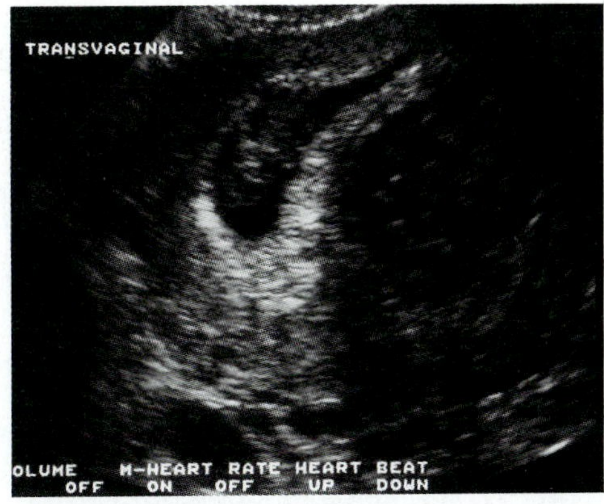

Figure 8–49. Transvaginal sonogram of a gravid uterus.

(C) dermoid cyst
(D) none of the above

542. The types of uterine fibroids include

(A) submucosal
(B) subserosal
(C) intramural
(D) all of the above

543. At what size should the gestation sac be in order to visualize the yolk sac in a normal intrauterine pregnancy with transvaginal sonography

(A) 1–2 mm
(B) 2–4 mm
(C) 4–6 mm
(D) 8–10 mm

544. Fig. 8–50 is a sagittal sonogram of a 28-year-old woman, gravida 3, para 2, who underwent ultrasound examination because of uncertain dates of her pregnancy. This image was taken at the level of the umbilical cord. The arrow points to

(A) allantoid cyst
(B) hemangioma of the umbilical cord
(C) thrombosis of the umbilical vessels
(D) three-vessel cord

545. Fig. 8–51 is a sagittal sonogram of a 30-year-old woman with uncertain menstrual date, who was re-

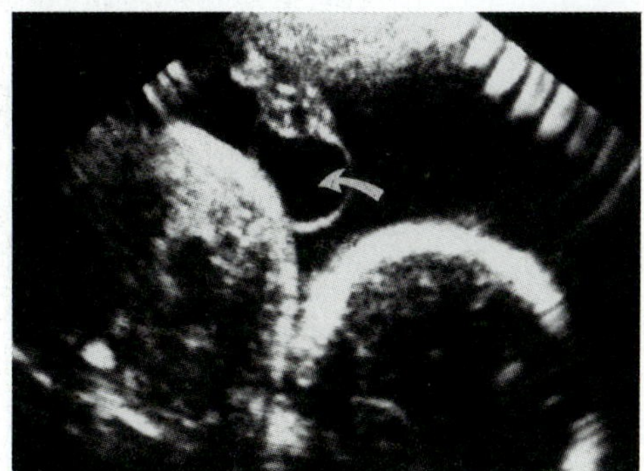

Figure 8–50. Sagittal sonogram of a gravid uterus.

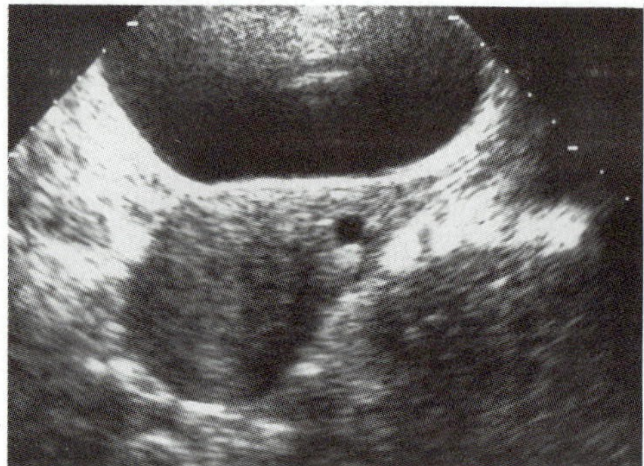

Figure 8–51. Sagittal midline pelvic sonogram.

ferred for a pelvic sonogram. This sonographic finding demonstrates

(A) blood in the uterine cavity
(B) retroverted uterus with a Bartholin cyst
(C) retroverted uterus with a gestation sac
(D) retroverted uterus with a nabothian cyst

546. Retrochorionic hemorrhage that occurs in the first trimester is usually associated with

(A) poor prognosis for completing the pregnancy
(B) ectopic pregnancy
(C) A or B
(D) neither A nor B

547. Fig. 8–52 is a transverse scan taken at the level of the uterine fundus of a 25-year-old woman who was referred for obstetrical sonogram with onset of vaginal bleeding and pelvic pain. This sonogram demonstrates

(A) mature placenta
(B) placental cyst
(C) total placenta previa
(D) abruptio placentae

548. The difference between a gestational sac and a pseudogestational sac is

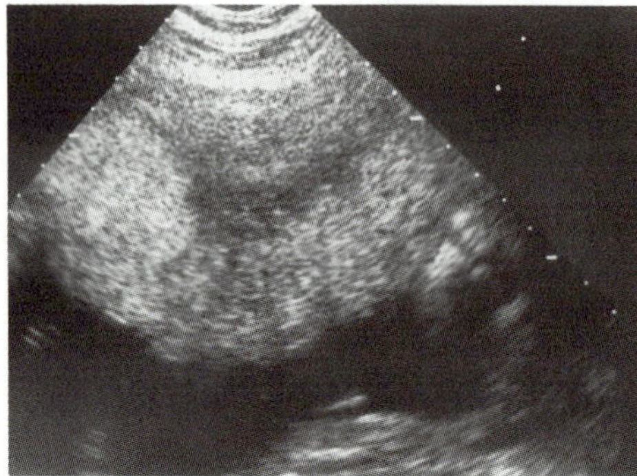

Figure 8–52. Transverse sonogram through the uterine fundus.

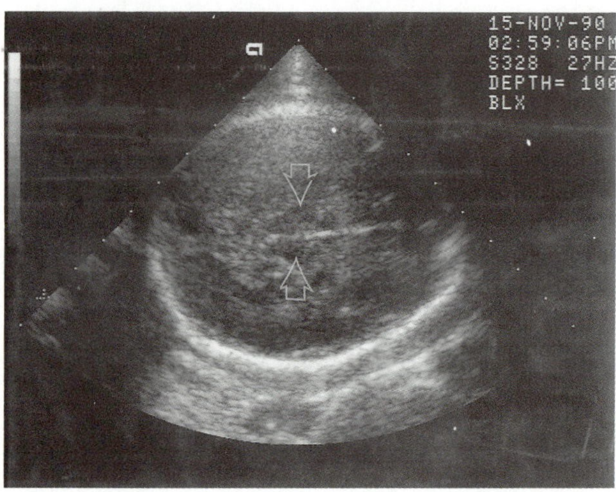

Figure 8–53. Transverse sonogram of the fetal head.

(A) a gestational sac usually has two layers of decidua
(B) a pseudogestational sac usually has two layers of decidua
(C) a pseudogestational sac is larger than most gestation sacs
(D) none of the above

549. Identify the structure the two arrowheads point to in Fig. 8–53

(A) cavum septum pellucidum
(B) thalamus
(C) cerebral peduncle
(D) choroid plexus

550. Identify the structure the arrow points to in Fig. 8–54

(A) cavum septum pellucidum
(B) thalamus
(C) cerebral peduncle
(D) third ventricle

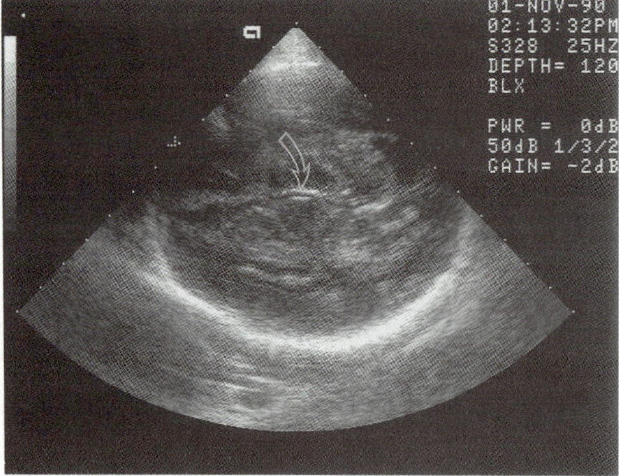

Figure 8–54. Transverse sonogram of the fetal head.

551. Identify the structure the open arrow points to in Fig. 8–55

(A) cavum septum pellucidum
(B) thalamus
(C) cerebral peduncle
(D) third ventricle

552. Identify the structure the solid arrow points to in Fig. 8–55

(A) cavum septum pellucidum
(B) thalamus
(C) cerebral peduncle
(D) third ventricle

553. Pregnancies that occur with an intrauterine contraceptive device (IUCD) in place are

(A) most likely to produce endometriosis
(B) associated with approximately 50% of completion
(C) usually associated with excessive vaginal bleeding
(D) B and C

554. Identify the structure the arrow points to in Fig. 8–56

(A) falx cerebri
(B) sylvian fissure/insula
(C) hydrocephalus
(D) choroid plexus

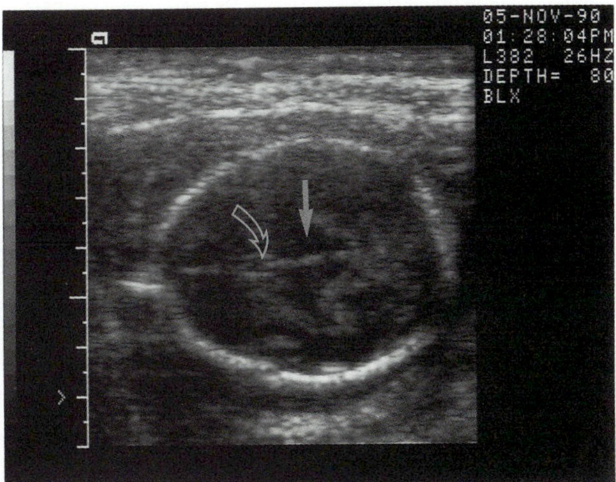

Figure 8–55. Transverse sonogram of the fetal head.

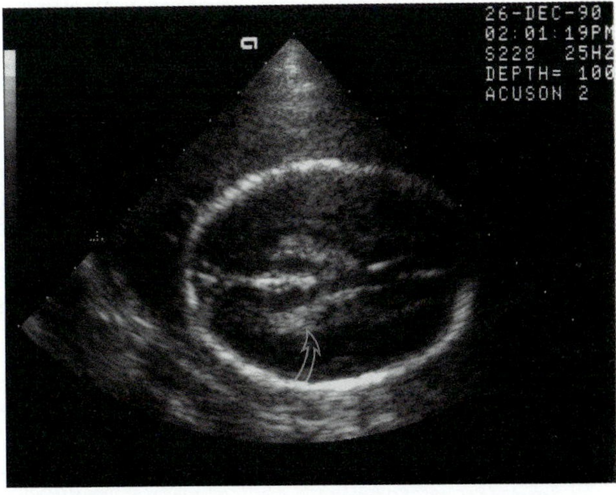

Figure 8–56. Transverse sonogram of the fetal head.

555. Fig. 8–57 shows a 28-year-old patient admitted because of severe preeclampsia and hyperemesis gravidarum. Give an impression of the sonogram in correlation with the clinical findings shown in these figures.

(A) fibroid
(B) large dermoid
(C) hydatidiform mole
(D) multiloculated papillary serous cystadenoma
(E) pseudocyesis

556. The differential diagnoses indicated in Fig. 8–57 are (1) leiomyoma, (2) missed abortion, (3) pseudocyesis, (4) multiloculated papillary serous cystadenoma, (5) hematoma.

(A) 1 and 5
(B) 1, 2, 4, and 5
(C) 1, 2, and 3
(D) all of the above

557. This study (Fig. 8–58) is of a 19-year-old gravida 2, para 0, with a sudden onset of vaginal bleeding and pelvic pain. The urinary chorionic gonadotropin (UCG) was negative. What is the impression of the sonograms in correlation with the clinical findings?

(A) pelvic inflammatory disease (PID)
(B) pedunculated fibroid
(C) dermoid
(D) ectopic pregnancy
(E) all of the above

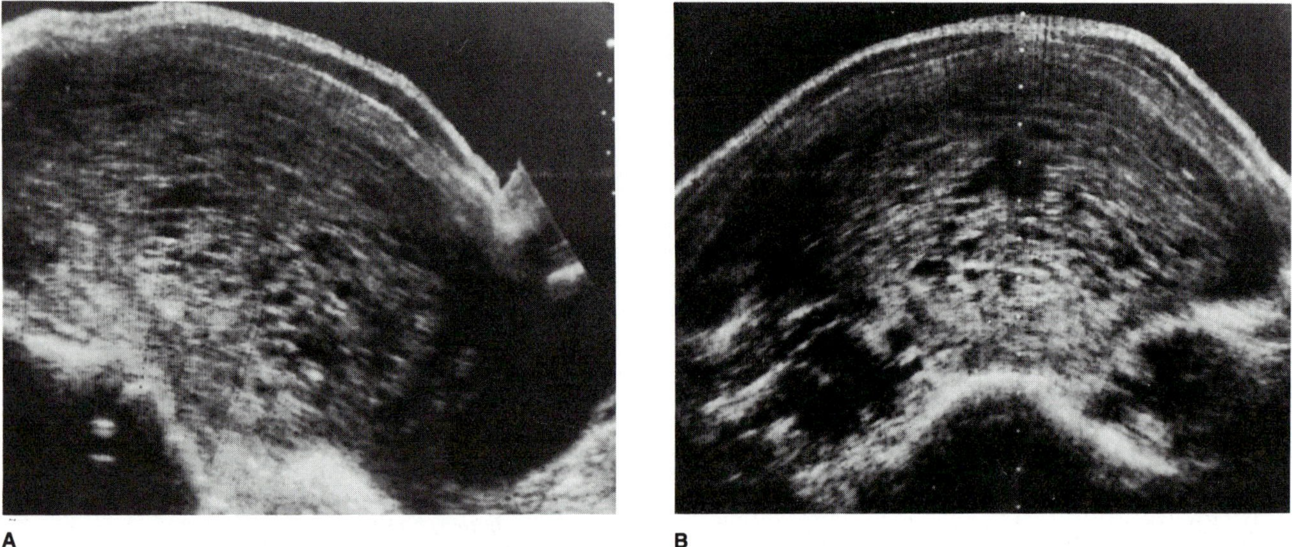

A B

Figure 8–57. (**A**) Static sagittal sonogram of the pelvis; (**B**) transverse sonogram of the pelvis.

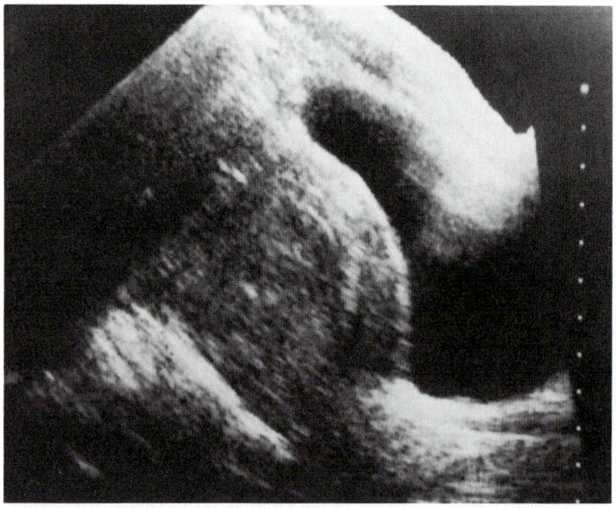

A 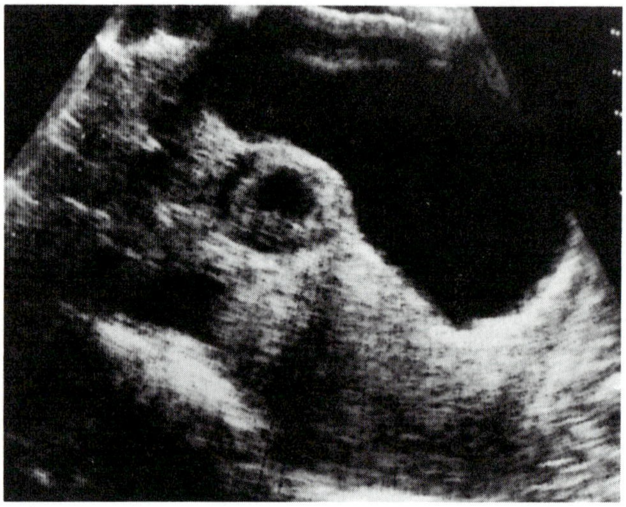 B

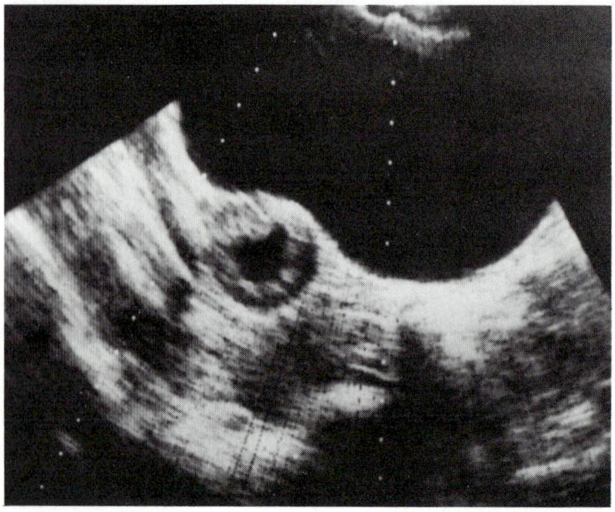

C

Figure 8–58. (**A**) Static sagittal midline sonogram of the uterus; (**B**) static sagittal sonogram obtained to the right of midline; (**C**) static transverse sonogram of the pelvis.

558. The differential diagnosis(es) indicated in Fig. 8–58 include

(A) pelvic inflammatory disease (infection in the right tube)
(B) pedunculated fibroid
(C) dermoid
(D) hermorrhagic cyst
(E) A and D only
(F) all of the above

559. The uterus shown in Fig. 8–58 appears

(A) small
(B) normal
(C) large
(D) atropic

560. Fig. 8–59 show an asymptomatic 35-year-old gravida 5, para 3. The patient's menstrual periods were uncertain. What is the impression of the sonograms in correlation with the clinical findings shown in this figure?

(A) calcified fibroid
(B) gestation sac
(C) dermoid
(D) Zipper ring
(E) the fetal head

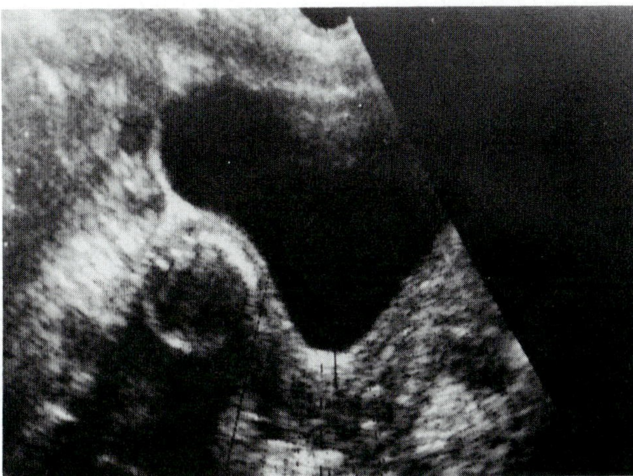

A

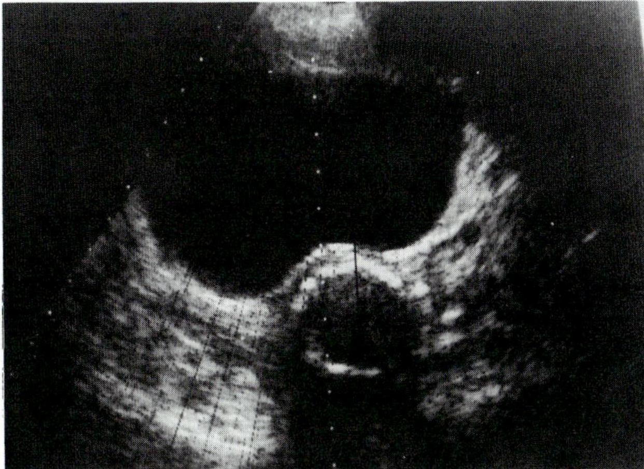

B

Figure 8–59. (**A**) Static sagittal midline sonogram of the uterus; (**B**) static transverse sonogram of the uterus.

561. The differential diagnosis(es) indicated in Fig. 8–59 include

(A) Zipper ring
(B) gestation sac
(C) dermoid
(D) hemorrhagic cyst
(E) B and C
(F) all of the above

562. The distal acoustic shadow seen in Fig. 8–59 is *most* likely due to

(A) calcification in a fibroid
(B) air in pessary ring
(C) artifact from the fetal skull
(D) calcified dermoid

563. The mass in Fig. 8–59 is

(A) cystic
(B) solid
(C) complex
(D) calcified
(E) B and D
(F) A and D

564. Fig. 8–60A shows a patient who underwent an ultrasound examination because of uncertain dating. The sonogram confirmed the presence of a singleton fetus in cephalic presentation. The real-time fails to demonstrate any heart motion. Scans of the fetal skull were taken with a static scanner. What is the impression of the sonogram in correlation with the findings shown in this figure: (1) fetal demise, (2) scalp edema, (3) Spalding's sign, (4) hydrocephalus?

(A) all of the above
(B) 1 and 2
(C) 1 and 4
(D) 1 and 3

565. Fig. 8–60B shows a 27-year-old gravida 3, para 2. This patient underwent an ultrasound because of Rh^- blood type and uncertain dating. The sonogram confirmed the presence of a singleton fetus in cephalic presentation with hydramnios. The real-time demonstrates fetal heart motion. Scans of the fetal skull were taken with a static scanner. What is the impression of the sonogram in correlation with the findings: (1) fetal demise, (2) scalp edema,

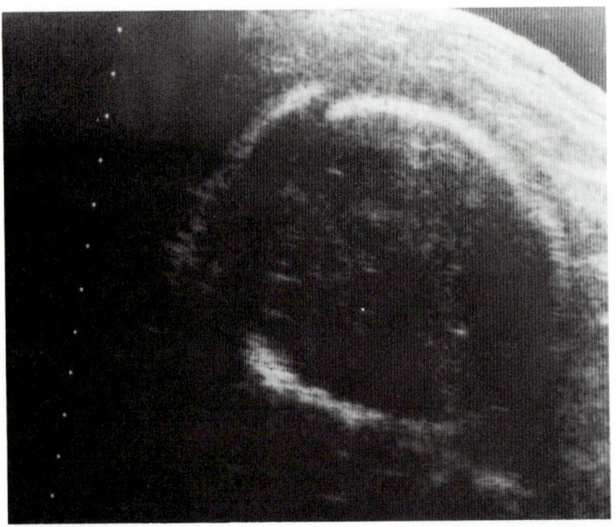

A

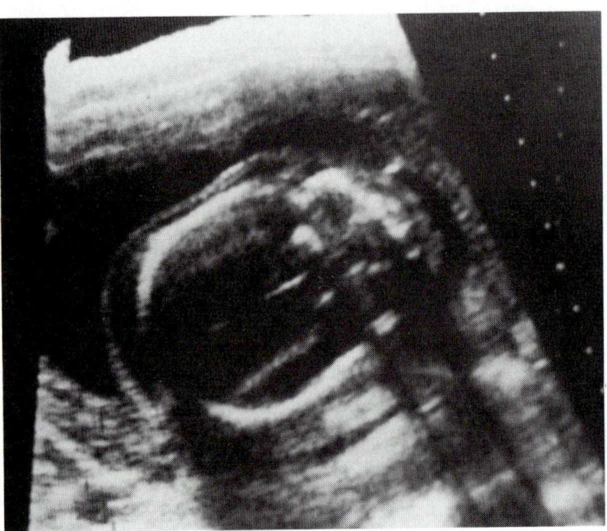

B

Figure 8–60. (**A**) Static transverse sonogram of a fetal head at 37 weeks; (**B**) static transverse sonogram of the fetal head at 27 weeks.

(3) Spalding's sign, (4) hydrocephalus, (5) erythroblastosis fetalis?

(A) all of the above
(B) 1 and 2
(C) 2 and 5
(D) 3 and 4

566. The differential diagnosis(es) for Fig. 8–60 without a given history is which of the following: (1) encephalocele, (2) cystic hygroma, (3) Spalding's sign, (4) microcephaly, (5) scalp edema?

(A) all of the above
(B) 2 and 4
(C) 5 only
(D) 3 only

567. Fig. 8–61 shows a 22-year-old nulligravida with pelvic pain. This patient underwent a sonographic examination because of pelvic pain and because her physician palpated a mass. The urinary chorionic gonadotropin was negative on two separate occasions. What is the impression of this sonogram in correlation with the clinical history given?

(A) an intrauterine pregnancy (IUP)
(B) ectopic pregnancy
(C) dermoid right adnexa
(D) polycystic ovaries

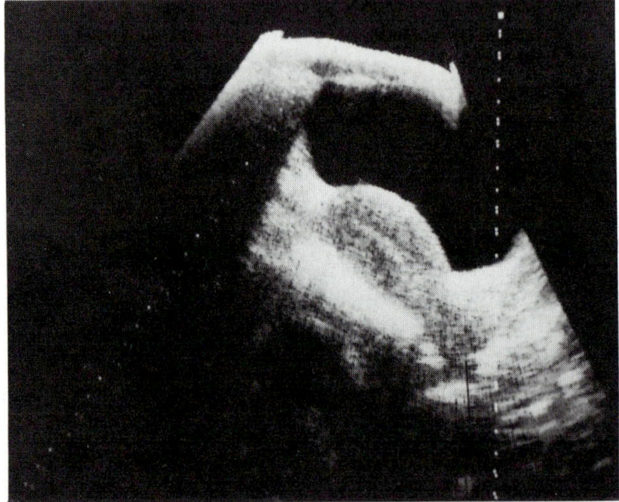

A

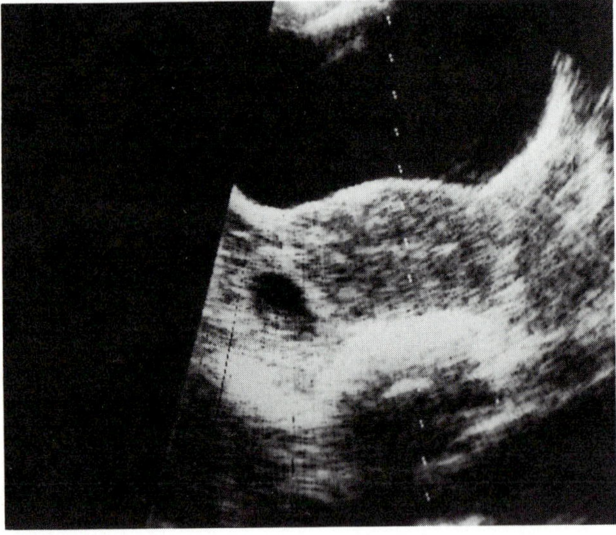

B

Figure 8–61. (**A**) Static sagittal midline sonogram of the uterus; (**B**) static transverse sonogram of the uterus.

568. The differential diagnosis(es) indicated in Fig. 8–61 includes which of the following? (1) dermoid cyst, (2) hemorrhagic cyst, (3) pelvic inflammatory disease (PID) (infection of the right tube), (4) pelvic inflammatory disease (PID) (infection of the left tube)?

(A) all of the above
(B) 1 and 2
(C) 2 and 3
(D) 2 and 4

569. A sonographer is employed in a private ultrasound clinic. The patient is a 27-year-old primigravida who is excited about her baby and asks for a Polaroid picture of the fetus. The sonographer's action should be

(A) give her the Polaroid picture and charge her $3.00 for film cost
(B) do *not* give her any picture; the pictures belong to the ultrasound clinic
(C) the patient pays for the sonogram and thereby it becomes her property. She has a legal right to have the picture

570. A sonographer is employed in a private ultrasound clinic. The patient is a 30-year-old multigravida who is excited about her baby. She asks you for the video home system (VHS) tape or a copy of it because she wants to show her family her baby. The sonographer's action should be

(A) give her the VHS tape and charge her $5.00 for tape cost
(B) do *not* give her any tape; the VHS tape belongs to the ultrasound clinic
(C) the patient pays for the sonogram and thereby it becomes her property. She has a legal right to have the picture

571. A sonographer is employed in a hospital ultrasound department. The patient is a 22-year-old primigravida who is excited about her baby. She asks you for a Polaroid picture of the fetus. The sonographer's action should be

(A) give her the Polaroid picture and charge her $3.00 for film cost
(B) do *not* give her any picture; the pictures are hospital property
(C) the patient pays for the sonogram and thereby it becomes her property. She has a legal right to have the picture

572. A sonographer is employed in a hospital ultrasound department. The patient is a 22-year-old being scanned to rule out ectopic pregnancy. The patient demands to see her medical chart. The sonographer's action should be

(A) do *not* give her the chart; the patient's medical chart is hospital property
(B) the patient's medical chart is hospital property; however, she has a legal right to make copies of it only upon proper request
(C) the patient pays for the sonogram and thereby all medical records become her property. She has a legal right to have the medical record and all information in it
(D) if the patient pays for the sonogram and other hospital services, she then has a legal right to have the medical record and all information it contains: She may copy it, take it home, or even destroy it if she wishes

573. If an inexperienced physician prescribed a wrong medication to a patient and an experienced nurse knew of the error but did *not* inform the physician, both the physician and the nurse could be charged with negligence. Conversely, in sonography, if an inexperienced physician issued an incorrect diagnosis but the experienced sonographer knew the correct diagnosis but did *not* inform the physician and as a result death occurs, who would be legally responsible?

(A) the sonographer is responsible because even though it was known that the physician was inexperienced, important information was deliberately withheld
(B) both could be charged with negligence
(C) the sonographer is an agent of the physician, and thus the sonographer may be guilty of withholding helpful information but not of negligence for the diagnosis because only the physician is ultimately responsible for the diagnosis

574. A sonographer is in a physician's office performing obstetric ultrasound but the physician is not there. The patient being scanned is 40 weeks' pregnant and begins to deliver on the ultrasound table. The ambulance is called and will arrive in 20 minutes. When the sonographer returns to the room, the baby's head is out with the umbilical cord around its neck. Attempts to remove the umbilical cord fail. What should be done?

(A) wait 20 minutes until the ambulance arrives
(B) use a thread to tie the cord at the end closest to the baby and cut the cord above the thread
(C) place two clamps on the cord about 2 inches apart and cut between them
(D) do not use any clamps on the cord, just cut it

575. A winglike double fold of peritoneum that extends from the lateral margins of the uterus to the pelvic walls and divides the pelvic cavity into anterior and posterior compartments is called

(A) fallopian tubes
(B) round ligaments
(C) broad ligaments
(D) iliopsoas muscle

576. Many obstetric real-time ultrasound examinations are performed by sonographers who may be asked by the referring physician to render a preliminary report at the time the study is performed. If the sonographer issues an incorrect preliminary report, who would be legally responsible?

(A) the sonographer who wrote the report
(B) the sonographer who did the sonogram
(C) the chief sonographer
(D) the physician

577. If a female sonographer is accused of sexually molesting a male patient in the ultrasound room, who would be legally responsible?

(A) a female sonographer *cannot* be liable for any sexual attack
(B) the female sonographer would be responsible
(C) the chief sonographer
(D) the physician is always responsible for the sonographer's behavior
(E) the male patient

578. If an obstetric real-time ultrasound examination was performed by a sonographer who missed a twin gestation and as a result the physician issued an incorrect diagnosis, who would be legally responsible?

(A) the director of the ultrasound department
(B) the patient is responsible if she fails to inform the sonographer she is having twins
(C) the sonographer and physician are both legally liable
(D) the physician who read the report
(E) the manufacturer of the ultrasound equipment is liable

579. The presence of a Y chromosome in the fertilized ovum means that the resulting infant will be

(A) a girl
(B) a boy
(C) have Down's syndrome
(D) have Patau's syndrome

580. Which one of the following does *not* take place in the uterus?

(A) pregnancy
(B) menstruation
(C) fertilization
(D) implantation

581. What is frank breech?

(A) when both feet are prolapsed into the lower uterine segment
(B) when one foot is prolapsed into the vagina
(C) when the fetal head is to the maternal right and the buttocks are to the maternal left
(D) when the buttocks descend first, the thighs and legs are extended upward along the anterior fetal trunk

582. What is complete breech?

(A) when both feet are prolapsed into the lower uterine segment
(B) when one foot is prolapsed into the vagina
(C) when the buttocks descend first, the knees are flexed, baby sitting cross-legged
(D) when the thighs and legs are extended upward along the anterior fetal trunk

583. What is footling breech?

(A) when one or both feet are prolapsed into the lower uterine segment
(B) when one foot is prolapsed into the fundus
(C) when the buttocks descend first, the knees are flexed, baby sitting cross-legged
(D) when the thighs and legs are extended upward along the anterior fetal trunk

584. What is the difference between vertex and cephalic?

(A) vertex is when the face is the presenting part and cephalic is when the fontanelles and the sagittal suture are the presenting part
(B) vertex and cephalic have the same meaning
(C) vertex is when the region between the anterior and posterior fontanelles and the sagittal suture are the presenting parts. Cephalic is a general term for head first

Questions 585 through 590: Match the acronym in Column A to the correct description in Column B.

COLUMN A	COLUMN B
585. PROM ______	(A) dust and clean
586. CPD ______	(B) fast urine output
587. FUO ______	(C) nothing by mouth
588. NPO ______	(D) fever of unknown origin
589. D&C ______	(E) cephalopelvic disproportion
590. TAH ______	(F) total abdominal hysterectomy
	(G) tubal abdominal hemorrhage
	(H) premature rupture of membranes
	(I) posterior right abdominal mass
	(J) dilation and curettage

591. The earliest the fetal kidneys can be depicted sonographically is

(A) 20 weeks
(B) 9 weeks
(C) 30 weeks
(D) 14 weeks

592. During pregnancy, the endocervical canal secretes a thick mucous that helps to seal the canal and protect it from bacteria. What is the name of this seal?

(A) seal of serosa
(B) seal of os
(C) corpus seal
(D) mucous plug

593. What is the normal circumference of the fetal kidneys in relationship to the fetal abdominal circumference?

(A) 27–30%
(B) 15–20%
(C) 50–60%
(D) 40–50%

Questions 594 through 597: Match the structures in Fig. 8–62 with the list of terms in Column B.

COLUMN A	COLUMN B
594. ______	(A) ovary
595. ______	(B) uterus
596. ______	(C) piriformis muscle
597. ______	(D) iliopsoas muscle

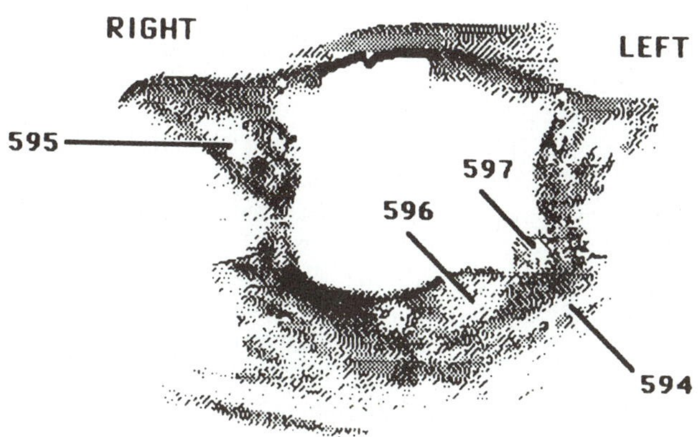

Figure 8–62. Diagram of a transverse scan of the pelvis.

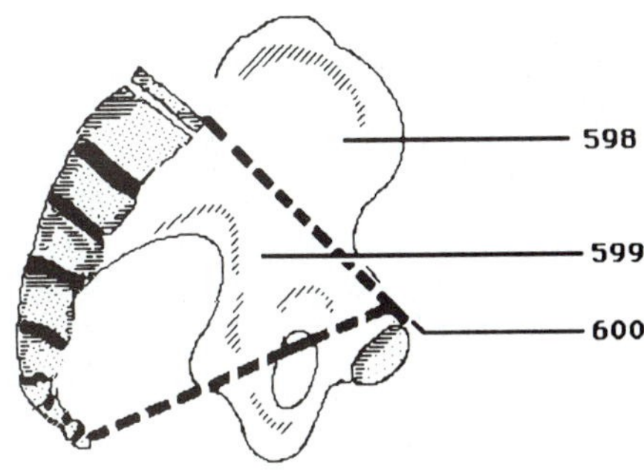

Figure 8–63. Diagram of the pelvic bones in the lateral view.

Questions 598 through 600: Match the structures in Fig. 8–63 with the list of terms in Column B.

COLUMN A	COLUMN B
598. ______	(A) false pelvis and pelvic major
599. ______	(B) true pelvis and pelvic minor
600. ______	(C) true pelvis and pelvic major
	(D) false pelvis and pelvic minor
	(E) linea terminalis

601. Identify the structure the solid arrow points to in Fig. 8–64

(A) cavum septum pellucidum
(B) falx cerebri
(C) cerebral peduncle
(D) sylvian fissure/insula

602. Identify the structure the open arrow points to in Fig. 8–64

(A) falx cerebri
(B) sylvian fissure/insula
(C) cerebral peduncle
(D) third ventricle

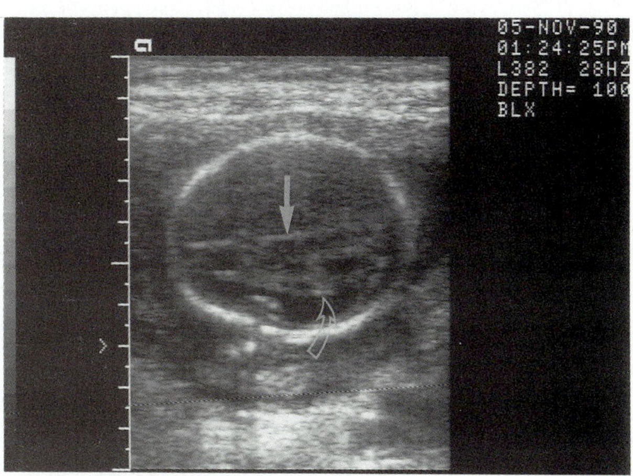

Figure 8–64. Transverse sonogram of the fetal head.

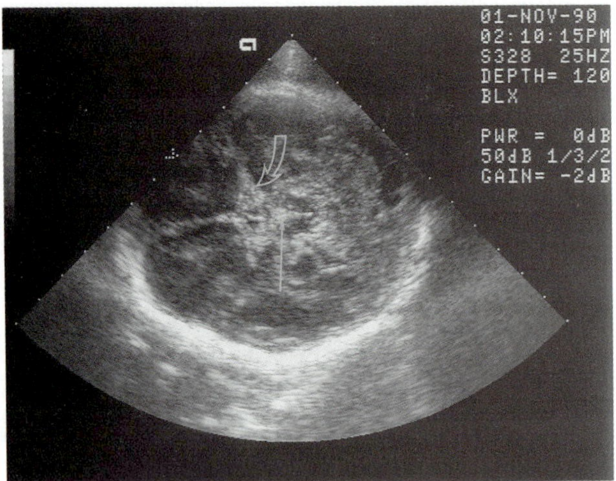

Figure 8–65. Transverse sonogram of the fetal head.

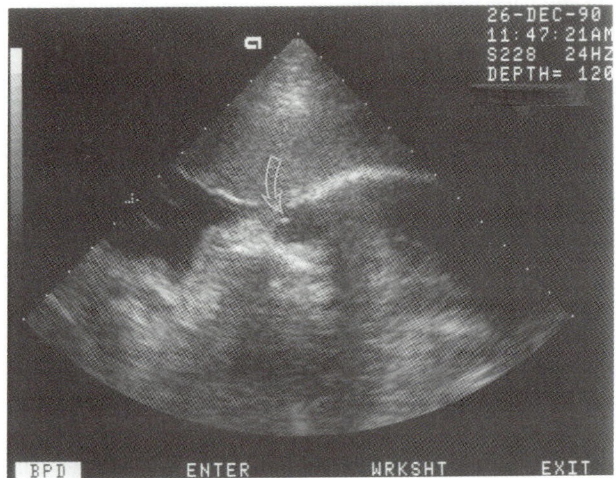

Figure 8–67. Sagittal sonogram of a gravid uterus.

603. Identify the structure the open arrow points to in Fig. 8–65

(A) falx cerebri
(B) cistern
(C) cerebral peduncle
(D) third ventricle

604. Identify the structure the solid arrow points to in Fig. 8–65

(A) falx cerebri
(B) basilar artery
(C) cerebral peduncle
(D) third ventricle

605. Identify the two structures the arrows point to in Fig. 8–66

(A) follicular cyst
(B) fetal limbs
(C) umbilical veins
(D) umbilical arteries

606. Identify the structure the arrow points to in Fig. 8–67

(A) lens
(B) eyebrow
(C) tooth buds
(D) nasal bone

607. Identify the structure the open arrow points to in Fig. 8–68 (sagittal sonogram)

(A) fetal bladder
(B) fetal stomach
(C) fetal heart
(D) ovarian cyst

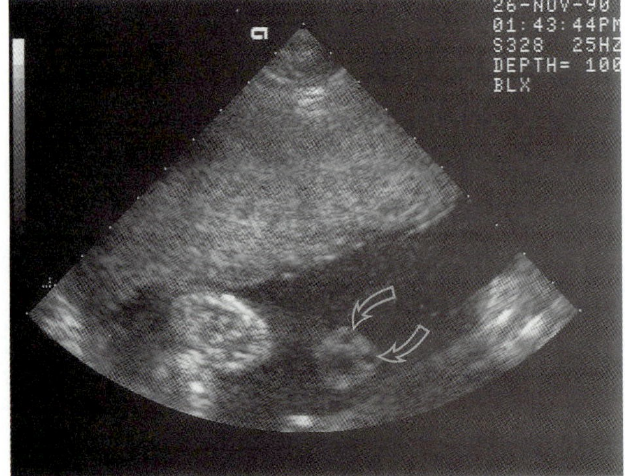

Figure 8–66. Transverse sonogram of a gravid uterus.

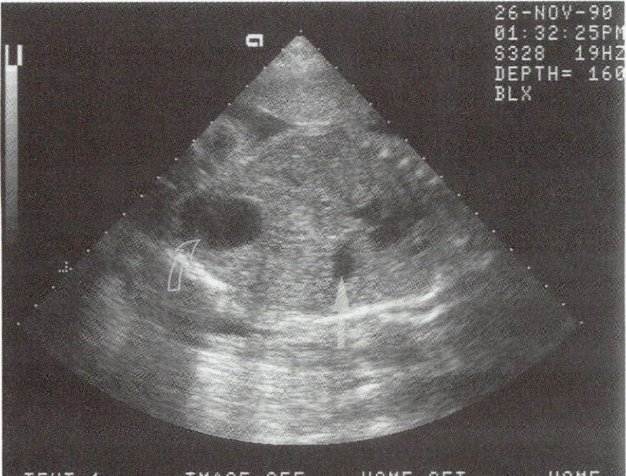

Figure 8–68. Sagittal sonogram of a gravid uterus.

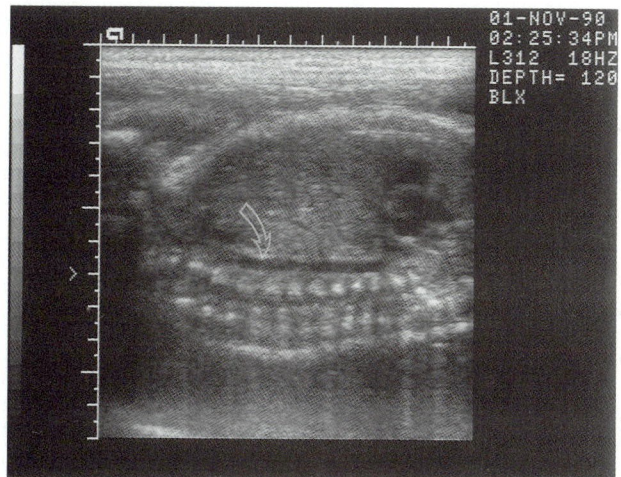

Figure 8–69. Sagittal sonogram of a gravid uterus.

608. Identify the structure the solid arrow points to in Fig. 8–68 (sagittal sonogram)

(A) fetal bladder
(B) fetal stomach
(C) fetal heart
(D) ovarian cyst

609. Identify the structure the arrow points to in Fig. 8–69 (sagittal sonogram)

(A) umbilical cord
(B) umbilical vein
(C) aorta
(D) spine

610. Identify the structure the arrow points to in Fig. 8–70 (transverse sonogram)

(A) umbilical cord
(B) female genitalia

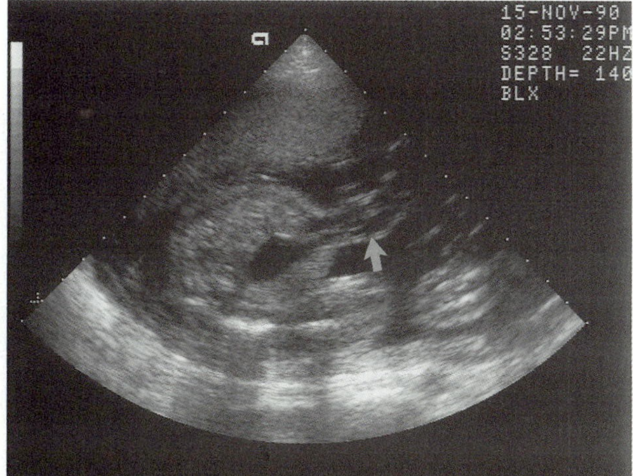

Figure 8–70. Transverse sonogram of a gravid uterus.

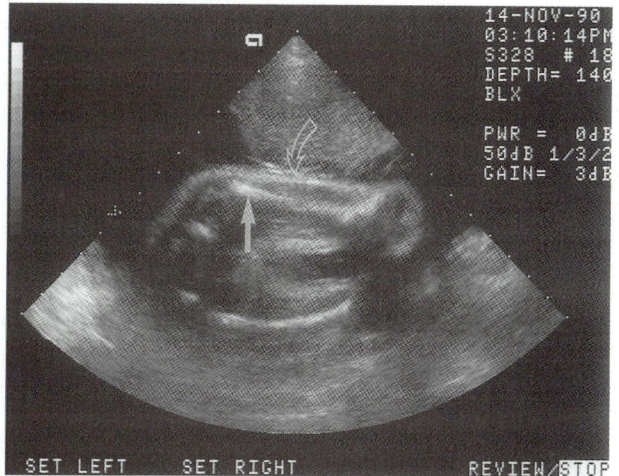

Figure 8–71. Transverse sonogram of a gravid uterus.

(C) male genitalia
(D) bladder

611. Identify the structure the open arrow points to in Fig. 8–71 (transverse sonogram)

(A) femur
(B) tibia
(C) fibula
(D) subcutaneous tissue/skin

612. Identify the structure the solid arrow points to in Fig. 8–71 (transverse sonogram)

(A) femur
(B) tibia
(C) fibula
(D) subcutaneous tissue/skin

613. Identify the hypoechoic line the arrow points to in Fig. 8–72 (sagittal sonogram)

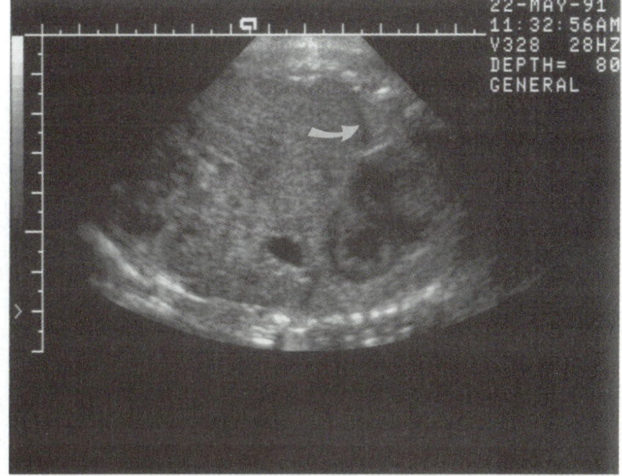

Figure 8–72. Sagittal sonogram of a gravid uterus.

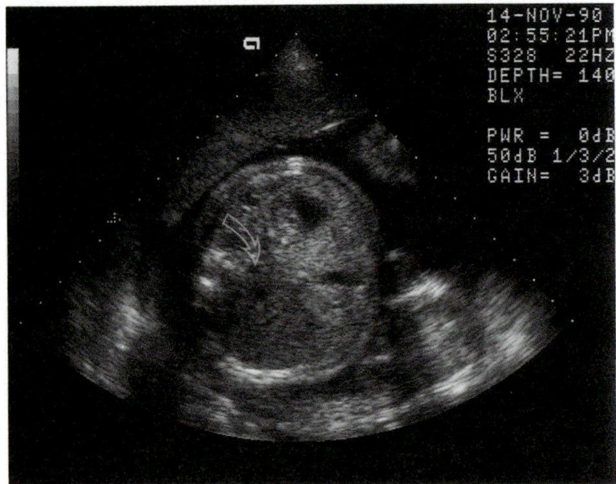

Figure 8–73. Transverse sonogram of a gravid uterus.

(A) heart
(B) stomach
(C) diaphragm
(D) kidney

614. Identify the structure the arrow points to in Fig. 8–73 (transverse sonogram)

(A) spine
(B) inferior vena cava
(C) gallbladder
(D) aorta

615. Identify the structure the arrow points to in Fig. 8–74 (transverse sonogram)

(A) ascites
(B) pleural effusion
(C) pseudoascites
(D) scalp edema

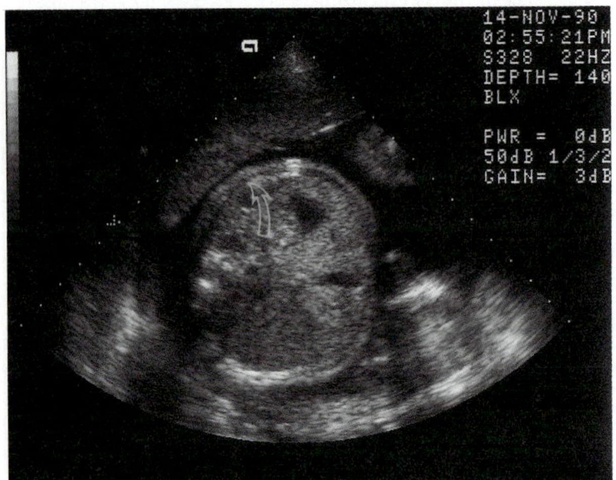

Figure 8–74. Transverse sonogram of a gravid uterus.

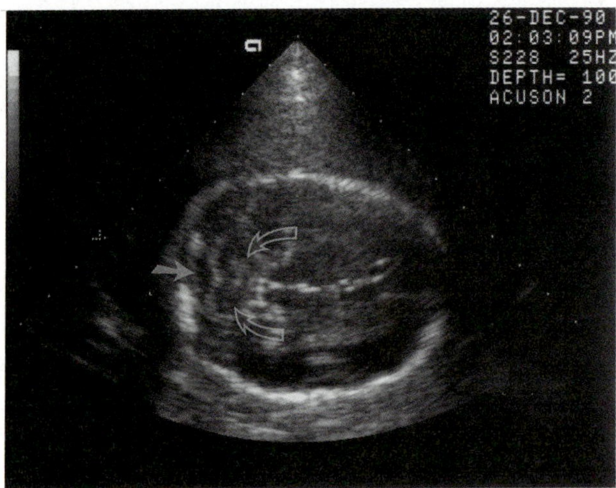

Figure 8–75. Transverse sonogram of the fetal head.

616. Identify the two structures the open arrows point to in Fig. 8–75 (fetal brain)

(A) cerebellar hemispheres
(B) thalami
(C) cerebral peduncles
(D) cisterna magna

617. Identify the anechoic structure the solid arrow points to in Fig. 8–75 (fetal brain)

(A) cerebellar hemispheres
(B) cavum septum pellucidum
(C) third ventricle
(D) cisterna magna

618. Identify the structures the arrows point to in Fig. 8–76 (transverse scan)

(A) kidneys
(B) adrenal glands
(C) bowel
(D) pectoralis muscles

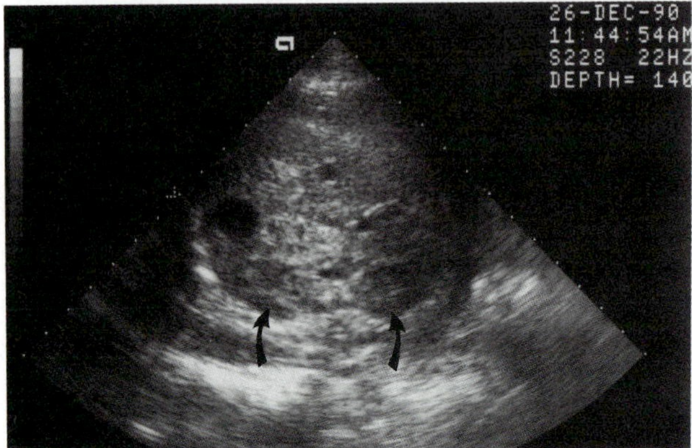

Figure 8–76. Transverse sonogram of a gravid uterus.

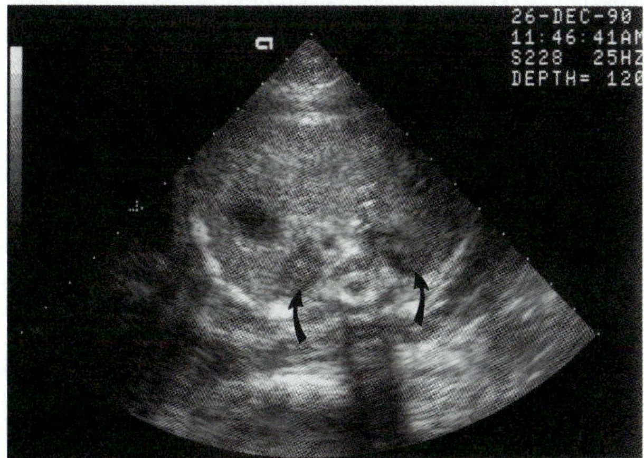

Figure 8–77. Transverse sonogram of a gravid uterus.

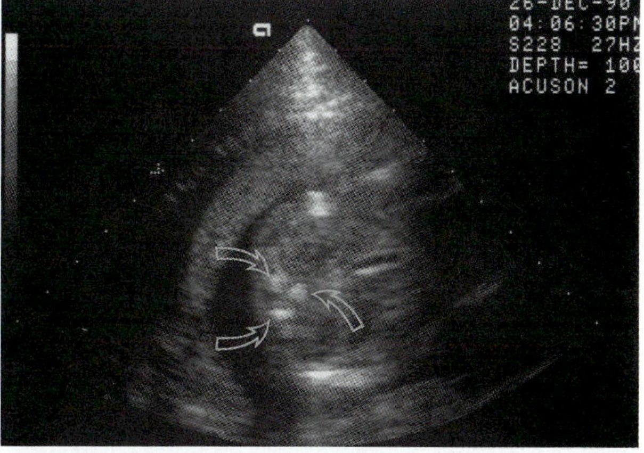

Figure 8–79. Transverse sonogram of a gravid uterus.

619. Identify the structures the arrows point to in Fig. 8–77 (transverse sonogram)

(A) kidneys
(B) adrenal glands
(C) bowel
(D) pectoralis muscles

620. Identify the structure the arrow points to in Fig. 8–78 (transverse sonogram)

(A) umbilical cord
(B) female genitalia
(C) male genitalia
(D) membrane separating the chorionic cavities

621. Identify the structures the arrows point to in Fig. 8–79 (transverse sonogram)

(A) one vein and two arteries
(B) spinal ossification centers
(C) kidney stones
(D) aorta, inferior vena cava, and portal vein

622. Identify the structure the arrow points to in Fig. 8–80 (sagittal sonogram)

(A) cervical spine
(B) thoracic spine
(C) lumbar spine
(D) sacral spine

623. Identify the structure the "0" arrow points to in Fig. 8–81 (sagittal sonogram)

(A) uterine fundus
(B) vagina
(C) intrauterine contraceptive device (IUCD)
(D) cervix

624. Identify the structure the "1" arrow points to in Fig. 8–81 (sagittal sonogram)

(A) uterine fundus
(B) vagina
(C) an intrauterine contraceptive device (IUCD)
(D) cervix

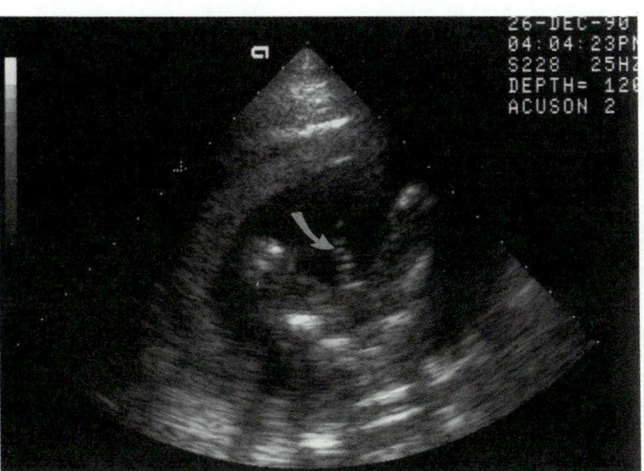

Figure 8–78. Transverse sonogram of a gravid uterus.

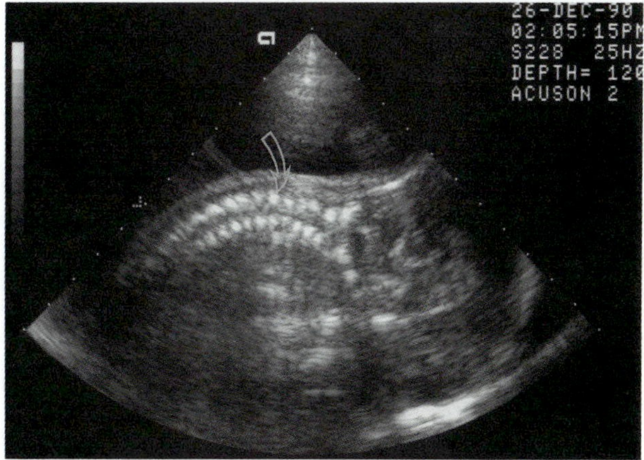

Figure 8–80. Sagittal sonogram of a gravid uterus.

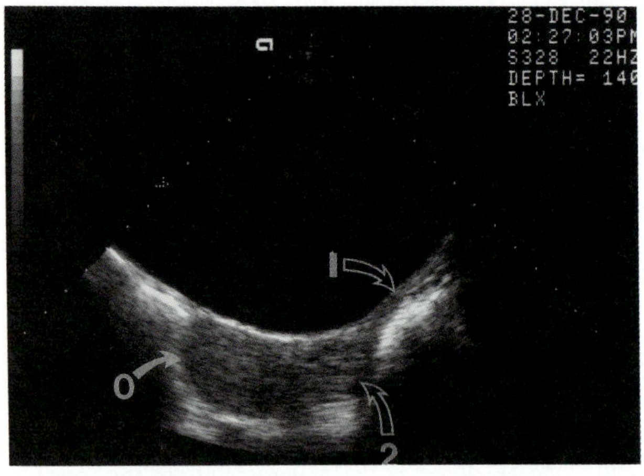

Figure 8–81. Sagittal sonogram of the uterus.

625. Identify the structure the "2" arrow points to in Fig. 8–81 (sagittal sonogram)

(A) uterine fundus
(B) vagina
(C) intrauterine contraceptive device (IUCD)
(D) cervix

626. Identify the structure the arrow points to in Fig. 8–82 (transverse pelvic sonogram)

(A) ovarian cyst
(B) follicular cyst
(C) left ovary
(D) right ovary

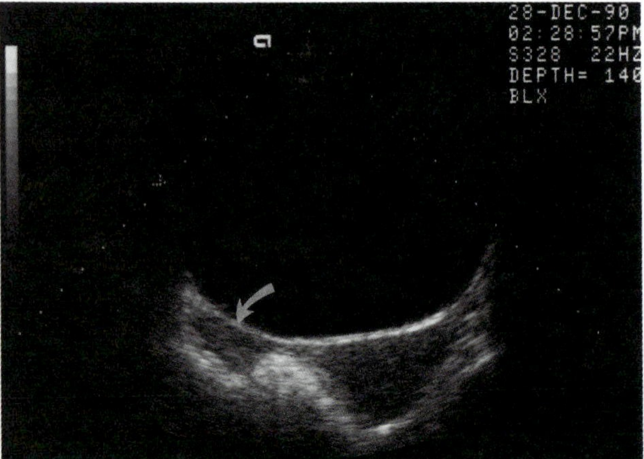

Figure 8–82. Transverse sonogram of the uterus.

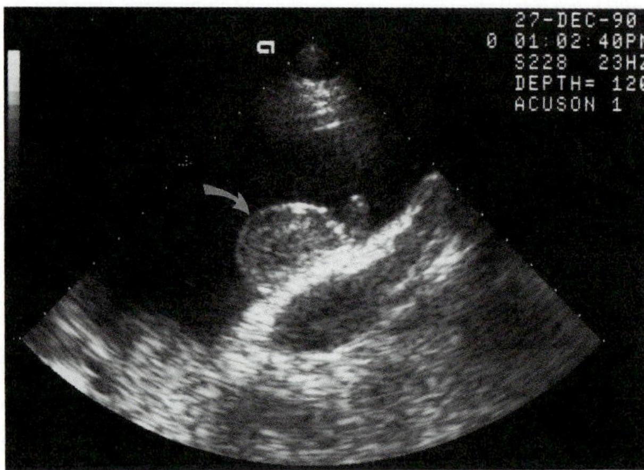

Figure 8–83. Sagittal sonogram of a gravid uterus.

627. Identify the structure the arrow points to in Fig. 8–83 (sagittal sonogram)

(A) omphalocele
(B) limb
(C) hydrocele
(D) gender

628. Identify the structure the arrow points to in Fig. 8–84 (transverse sonogram)

(A) umbilical vein
(B) stomach
(C) portal vein
(D) gallbladder

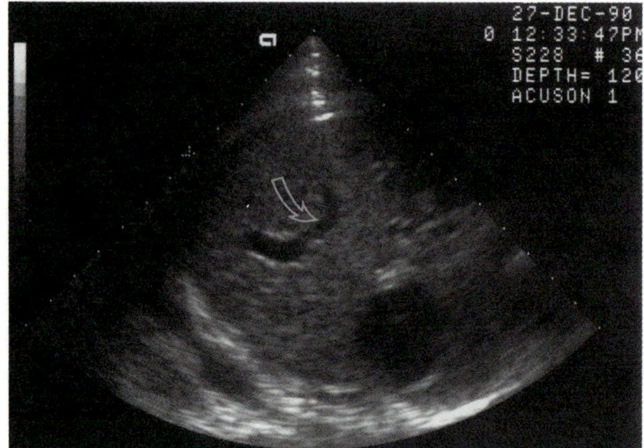

Figure 8–84. Transverse sonogram of a gravid uterus.

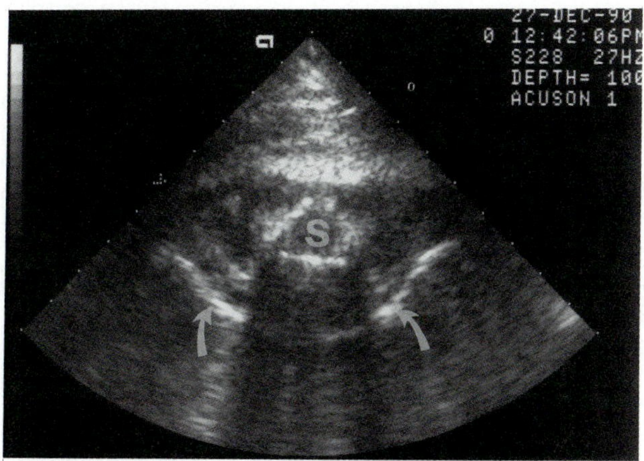

Figure 8–85. Transverse sonogram of a gravid uterus.

629. Identify the structures the arrows point to in Fig. 8–85 (transverse sonogram)

(A) iliac crests
(B) ribs
(C) scapulas
(D) clavicles

630. The anatomic location(s) of the ovaries is

(A) inferior to the uterus
(B) anterior to the uterus
(C) posterior to the uterus
(D) variable in position

631. A brief evaluation of the kidneys should be done following pelvic sonogram with sonographic evidence of pregnancy or a pelvic mass. The primary reason is to evaluate

(A) any degree of hydronephrosis
(B) renal stone
(C) hypernephroma
(D) renal agenesis

632. Sonographically, the broad ligaments are best demonstrated

(A) when surrounded by ascites
(B) with transvaginal sonography
(C) with over distention of the urinary bladder
(D) with a large myoma

633. The most common cause for enlargement of the uterus is

(A) ovarian carcinoma
(B) endometriosis
(C) myoma
(D) cystadenoma

634. Focal hypoechoic areas within the uterine myometrium are suggestive of

(A) gestational sac
(B) intrauterine contraceptive device (IUCD)
(C) myomas
(D) nabothian cyst

635. The thickness of the endometrium in the proliferative phase is approximately

(A) 2–4 mm
(B) 5–6 mm
(C) 6–10 mm
(D) 12–14 mm

636. The thickness of the endometrium in the secretory phase is approximately

(A) 2–4 mm
(B) 5–6 mm
(C) 6–10 mm
(D) 12–14 mm

637. In the postmenopausal patient in the absence of hormonal replacement therapy, the thickness of the endometrium is approximately

(A) 1–3 mm
(B) 2–4 mm
(C) 5–6 mm
(D) 6–8 mm

638. The eccentric position of the endometrial echo from the midline of the uterus suggests

(A) proliferative phase
(B) menstrual phase
(C) secretory phase
(D) leiomyomas

639. The muscle(s) that can be identified forming the boundaries of the true pelvis is

(A) piriform
(B) iliopsoas
(C) obturator
(D) all of the above

640. In the normal ovaries, follicular cysts first may be identified when they approach the size of

(A) 4–5 mm
(B) 5–10 mm
(C) 10–15 mm
(D) 18–24 mm

641. At what gestational age is the proximal tibial epiphyseal ossification center seen?

(A) 20 weeks
(B) 33 weeks
(C) 35 weeks

(D) the proximal tibial epiphyseal ossification center can only be seen by x-rays

642. At what gestational age is the distal tibial epiphyseal ossification center seen?

(A) 20 weeks
(B) 33 weeks
(C) 35 weeks
(D) the distal tibial epiphyseal ossification center can only be seen by x-rays

643. The cisterna magna appears sonographically as

(A) echogenic space superior to the cerebellum
(B) echogenic space inferior to the cerebellum
(C) echo-free space superior to the cerebellum
(D) echo-free space inferior to the cerebellum

644. Cranial bone defect resulting in herniation of the brain and meninges is referred to as

(A) spina bifida
(B) anencephaly
(C) hydrocephalus
(D) encephalocele

645. Incompetent cervix denotes

(A) absence of the cervix
(B) dilation of the cervix during the onset of labor
(C) premature dilation of the endocervix before the onset of labor
(D) inability of the cervix to dilate completely during the onset of labor

646. The distinguishing feature(s) of myoma uteri from focal myometrial contraction (FMC) is

(A) FMC attenuates the ultrasound beam and myoma does not
(B) FMC is always heterogeneous, whereas myoma are always homogeneous
(C) myomas are hypoechoic in relation to the adjacent myometrium, but an FMC tends to be isoechoic in relation to the myometrium
(D) FMC tends to distort both the serosal and endometrial contour, whereas myomas distort only the endometrial surface

647. Identify the structures the arrows point to in Fig. 8–86 of this transverse sonogram

(A) right and left ribs
(B) right and left clavicles
(C) right and left iliac crests
(D) right and left humerus

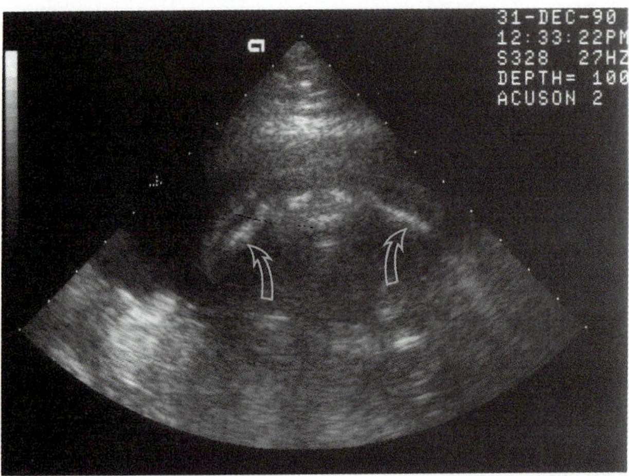

Figure 8–86. Transverse sonogram of a gravid uterus.

648. Identify the structures in Fig. 8–87 (sagittal sonogram)

(A) femur and subcutaneous thigh tissues
(B) tibia and fibula
(C) ulna and femur
(D) radius and subcutancous tissucs

649. Identify the structures the arrows point to in Fig. 8–88 (transverse sonogram)

(A) cross-section of the leg
(B) cross-section of the thigh
(C) the scrotum with calcification of the testicles
(D) the umbilical cord demonstrating the two arteries

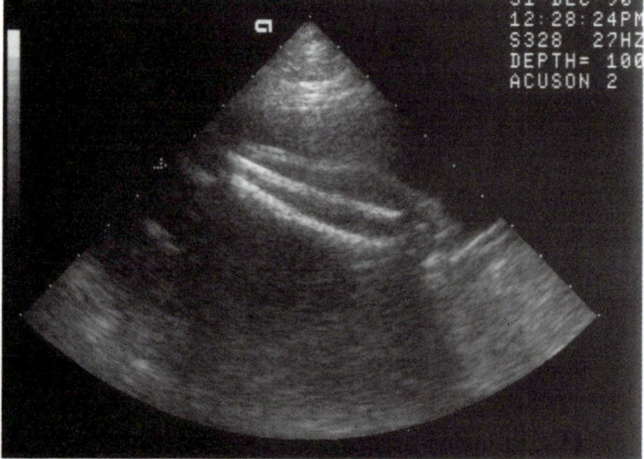

Figure 8–87. Sagittal sonogram of a gravid uterus.

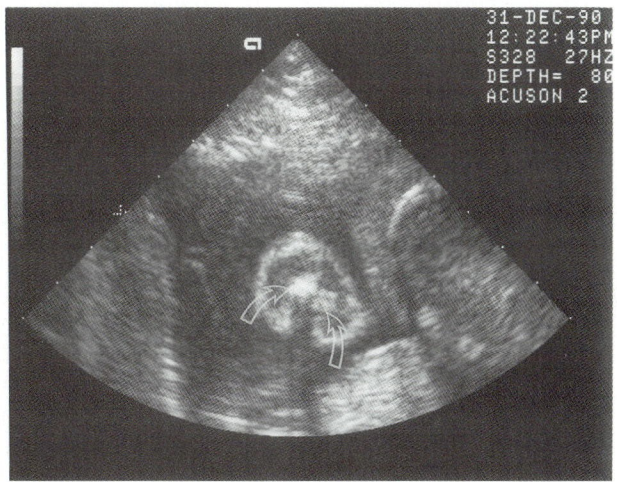

Figure 8–88. Transverse sonogram of a gravid uterus.

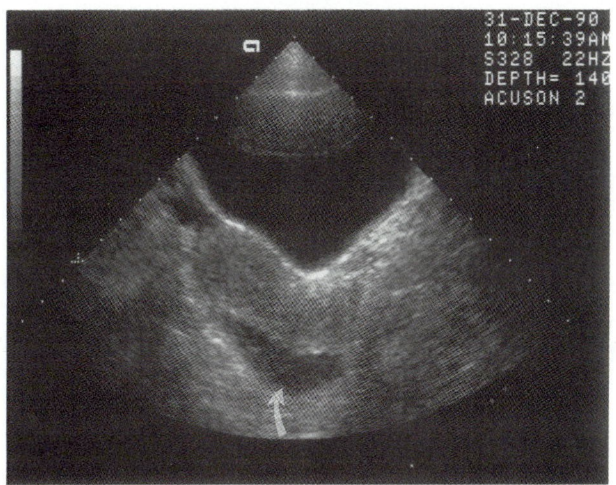

Figure 8–90. Sagittal sonogram of the uterus.

650. Identify the structures the solid arrow points to in Fig. 8–89 (transverse sonogram)

(A) foramen ovale
(B) intraventricular septum
(C) mitral valve
(D) tricuspid valves

651. Identify the structures the open arrow points to in Fig. 8–89 (transverse sonogram)

(A) foramen ovale
(B) intraventricular septum
(C) mitral valve
(D) tricuspid valves

652. Identify the structures the arrow points to in Fig. 8–90 (sagittal sonogram)

(A) fluid in Morison's pouch
(B) fluid in the vagina
(C) fluid in the anterior cul-de-sac
(D) fluid in pouch of Douglas

653. Identify the structures the arrows point to in Fig. 8–91 (transverse sonogram)

(A) broad ligaments
(B) ovaries
(C) hydrosalpinx
(D) fimbriae of the fallopian tube

654. Identify the structure the arrow points to in Fig. 8–92 (transverse sonogram)

(A) posterior placenta
(B) myoma
(C) retroplacental hematoma
(D) focal myometrial contraction

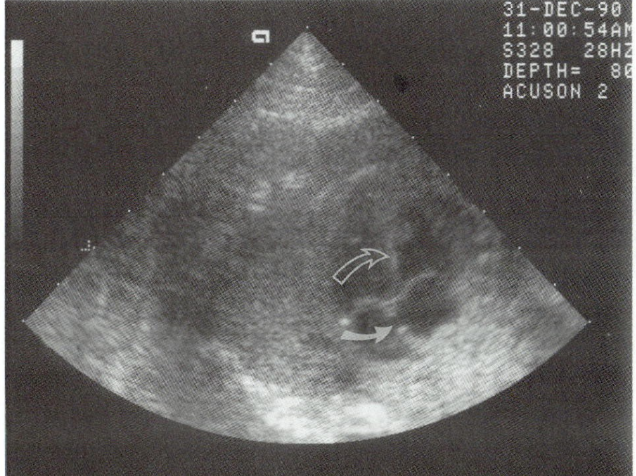

Figure 8–89. Transverse sonogram of a gravid uterus.

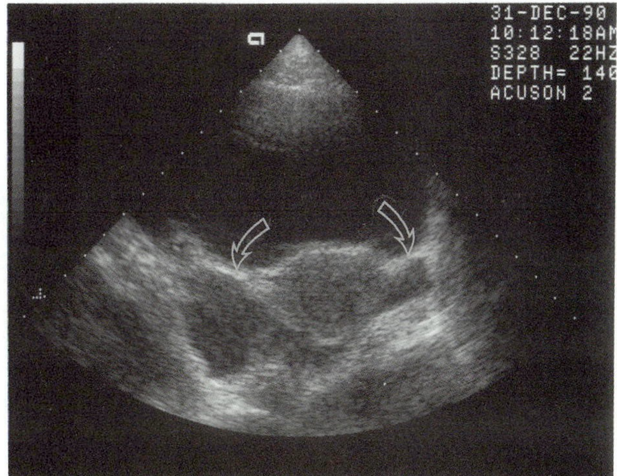

Figure 8–91. Transverse sonogram of the uterus.

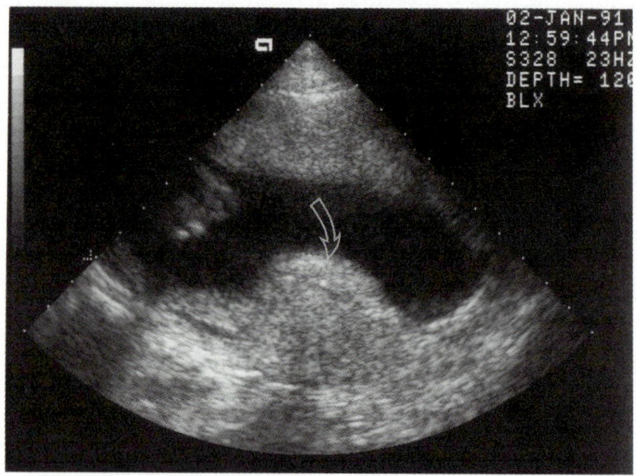

Figure 8–92. Transverse sonogram of a gravid uterus.

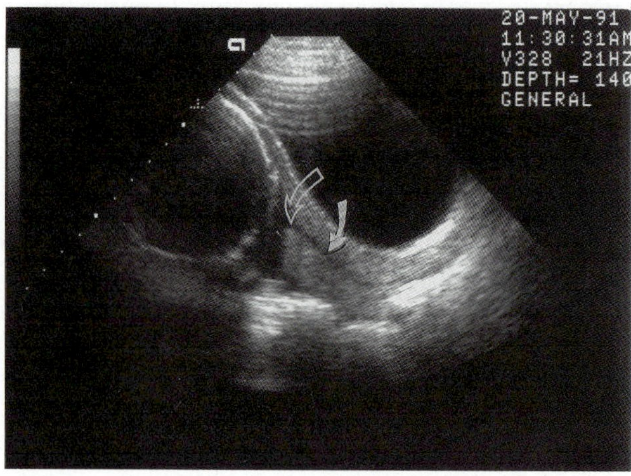

Figure 8–94. Sagittal midline sonogram of the cervical region.

655. Identify the structure the arrow points to in Fig. 8–93 of this transverse sonogram

(A) calcified patella
(B) distal femoral epiphyseal ossification center
(C) fracture of the femoral head
(D) fetal thumb

656. Identify the structure the open arrow points to in Fig. 8–94 (sagittal sonogram)

(A) internal os
(B) external os
(C) endocervical canal
(D) vagina

657. Identify the structure the solid arrow points to in Fig. 8–94 (sagittal sonogram)

(A) internal os
(B) external os
(C) endocervical canal
(D) vagina

658. Identify the structure the arrow points to in Fig. 8–95 (sagittal sonogram)

(A) aorta
(B) inferior vena cava
(C) spinal cord
(D) spinal canal

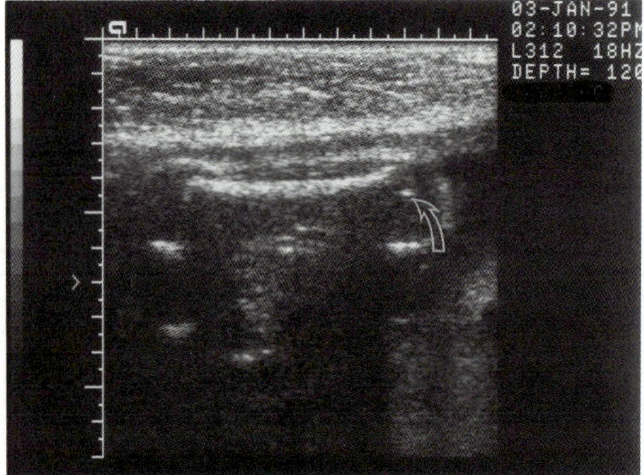

Figure 8–93. Transverse sonogram of a gravid uterus.

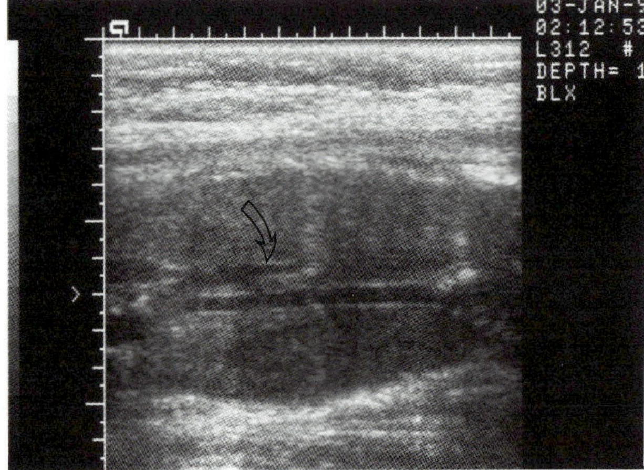

Figure 8–95. Sagittal sonogram of a gravid uterus.

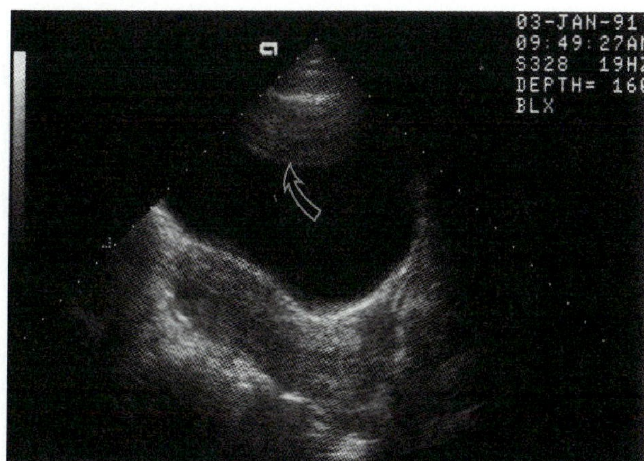

Figure 8–96. Sagittal sonogram of the uterus.

659. Identify the structure the arrow points to in Fig. 8–96 (sagittal sonogram)

(A) sludge in the bladder
(B) bladder wall defect
(C) bladder flap hematoma
(D) reverberation artifact

660. The chorion frondosum progressively develops to become

(A) fetal component of the placenta
(B) maternal component of the placenta
(C) the amnionic cavity
(D) the yolk sac and stalk

661. The decidua basalis progressively develops to become

(A) fetal component of the placenta
(B) maternal component of the placenta
(C) the amnionic cavity
(D) the yolk sac and stalk

662. The type of intrauterine growth retardation (IUGR) that demonstrates nonuniformity of fetal organ size due to uteroplacental insufficiency is referred to as

(A) macrosomia
(B) small for gestational age (SGA)
(C) symmetrical
(D) asymmetrical

663. Identify the structure the arrow points to in Fig. 8–97 (transverse sonogram)

(A) Foley catheter
(B) bladder septation
(C) ureterocele
(D) ureteral jet

664. Identify the structure the arrows point to in Fig. 8–98 (sagittal sonogram)

(A) sacral spine
(B) distal femoral epiphyseal ossification center
(C) iliac bones
(D) femurs

665. The cisterna magna is best demonstrated at what week of gestation?

(A) 12–16 weeks
(B) 15–28 weeks
(C) 28–30 weeks
(D) 30–35 weeks

666. Identify the structure the arrows point to in Fig. 8–99 (sagittal sonogram)

(A) labia majora
(B) limbs
(C) hydrocele
(D) scrotum

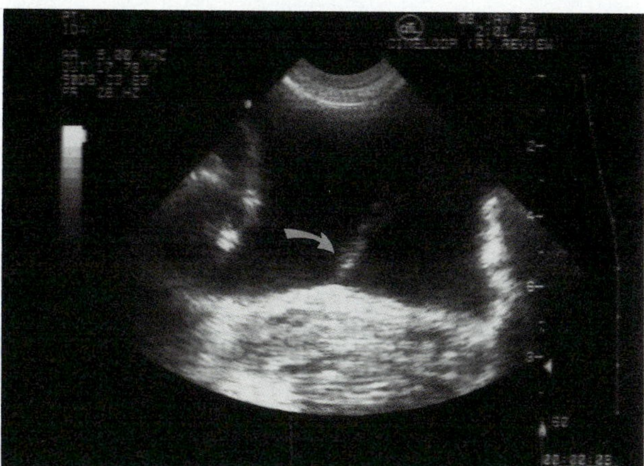

Figure 8–97. Transverse sonogram of the bladder.

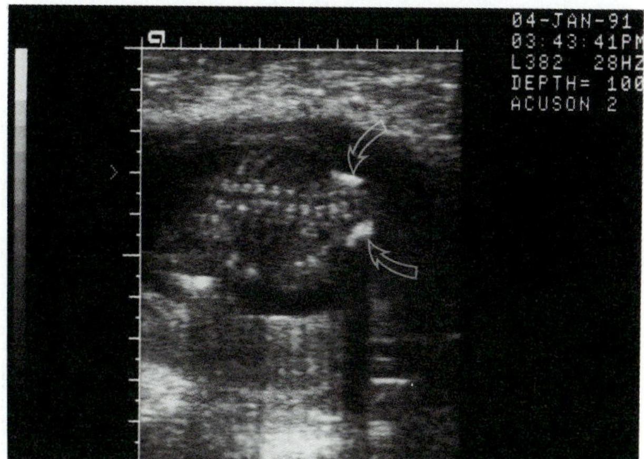

Figure 8–98. Sagittal sonogram of a gravid uterus.

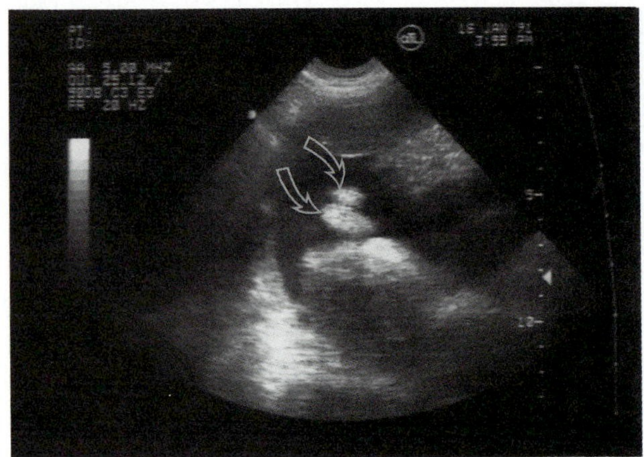

Figure 8–99. Sagittal sonogram of a gravid uterus.

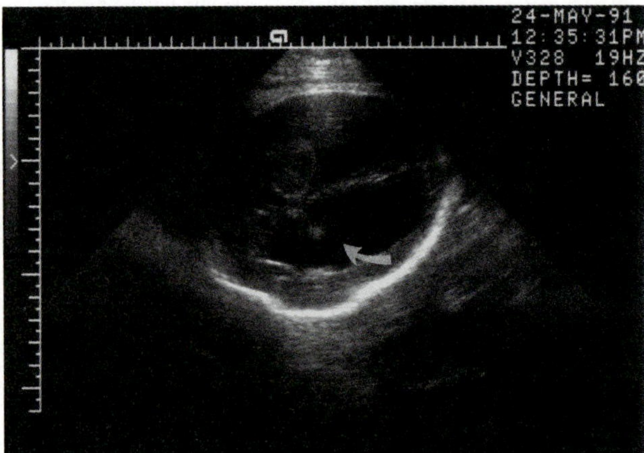

Figure 8–101. Transverse sonogram of the fetal head.

667. Identify the structure the solid arrow points to in Fig. 8–100 (sagittal sonogram)

(A) ectopic pregnancy
(B) hematometra
(C) nabothian cyst
(D) Gartner's duct cyst versus urine or blood in the vagina

668. Identify the structure the open arrow points to in Fig. 8–100 (sagittal sonogram)

(A) cul-de-sac fluid
(B) ovary
(C) fibroid
(D) nabothian cyst

669. Identify the structure the arrow points to in Fig. 8–101 (transverse sonogram)

(A) hydrocephalus
(B) falx cerebri
(C) thalami
(D) third ventricle

670. Identify the structure the open arrowhead points to in Fig. 8–102 (transverse sonogram)

(A) hydrocephalus
(B) falx cerebri
(C) thalami
(D) lateral ventricle

671. Identify the structure the solid arrowhead points to in Fig. 8–102 (transverse sonogram)

(A) hydrocephalus
(B) falx cerebri
(C) thalami
(D) lateral ventricle

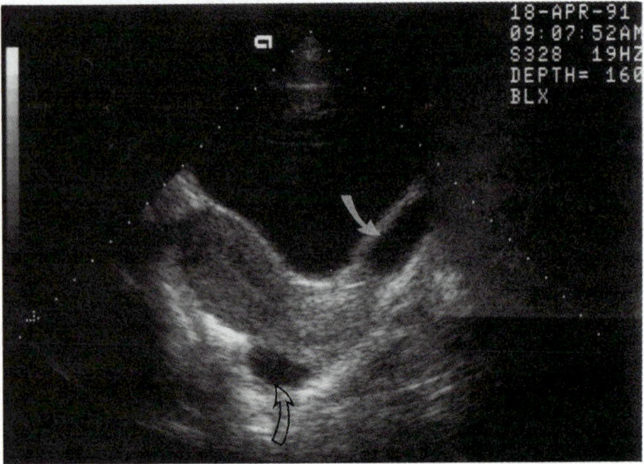

Figure 8–100. Sagittal sonogram of the uterus.

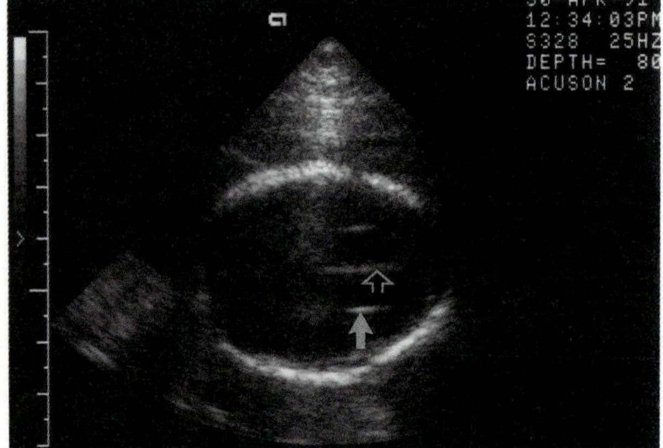

Figure 8–102. Transverse sonogram of the fetal head.

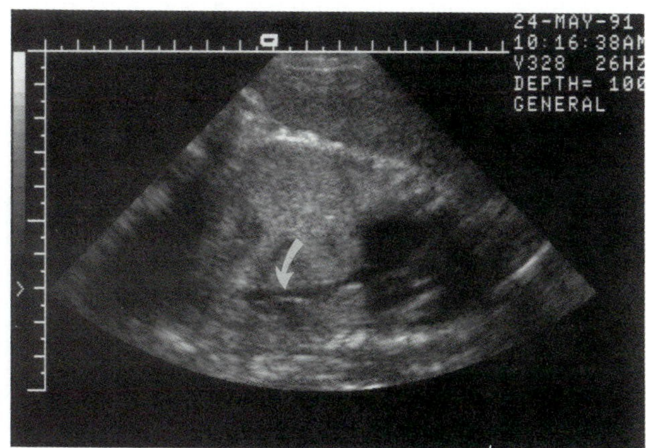

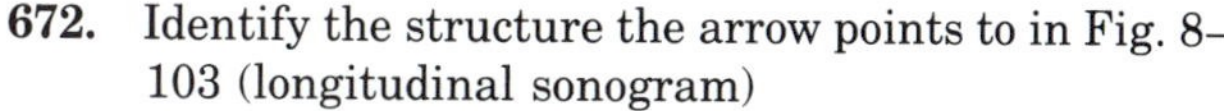

Figure 8–103. Sagittal sonogram of a gravid uterus.

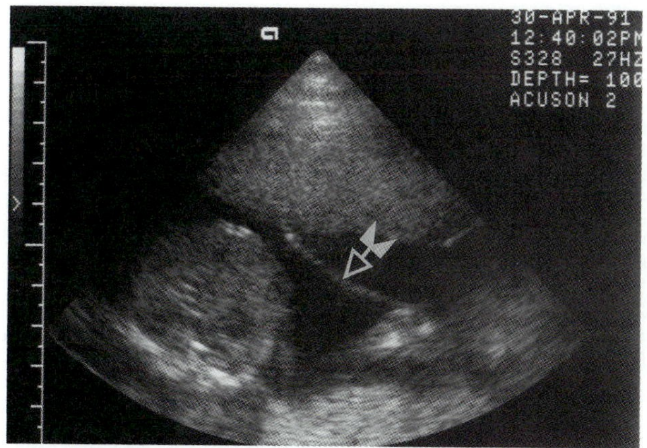

Figure 8–105. Transverse sonogram of a gravid uterus.

672. Identify the structure the arrow points to in Fig. 8–103 (longitudinal sonogram)

(A) inferior vena cava
(B) aorta
(C) umbilical vein
(D) spine

673. Identify the structure the solid white arrowhead points to in Fig. 8–104 (longitudinal sonogram)

(A) dividing membrane
(B) umbilical cord
(C) umbilical artery
(D) portal vein

674. Identify the structure the white arrowhead points to in Fig. 8–104 (longitudinal sonogram)

(A) umbilical vein
(B) umbilical cord
(C) umbilical artery
(D) portal vein

675. Identify the structure the black open arrow points to in Fig. 8–104 (longitudinal sonogram)

(A) umbilical vein
(B) umbilical cord
(C) umbilical artery
(D) portal vein

676. Identify the structure the arrow points to in Fig. 8–105 (transverse sonogram)

(A) umbilical vein
(B) umbilical cord
(C) chorionic plate
(D) dividing membrane

677. Identify the structure the closed curve white arrow points to in Fig. 8–106 (longitudinal sonogram)

(A) ascites
(B) liver
(C) lungs
(D) pleural effusion

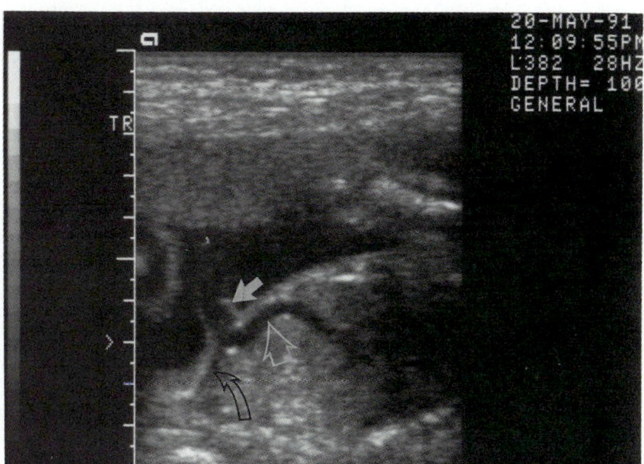

Figure 8–104. Sagittal sonogram of a gravid uterus.

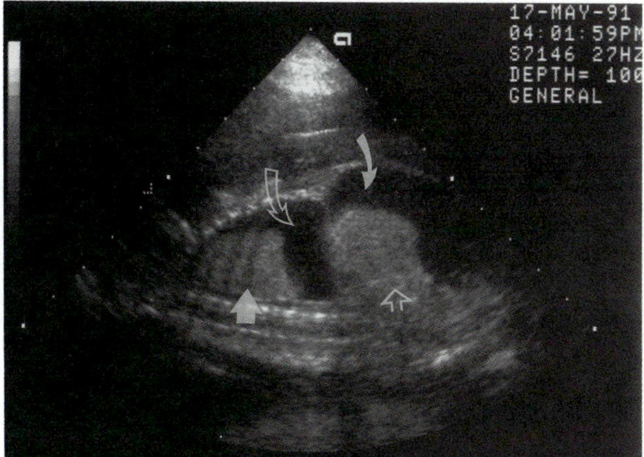

Figure 8–106. Sagittal sonogram of a gravid uterus.

678. Identify the structure the open white arrow points to in Fig. 8–106 (longitudinal sonogram)

(A) ascites
(B) liver
(C) lungs
(D) pleural effusion

679. Identify the structure the closed arrowhead points to in Fig. 8–106 (longitudinal sonogram)

(A) ascites
(B) liver
(C) lung
(D) pleural effusion

680. Identify the structure the open arrowhead points to in Fig. 8–106 (longitudinal sonogram)

(A) ascites
(B) liver
(C) lungs
(D) pleural effusion

681. Identify the structure the arrow points to in Fig. 8–107 (transverse sonogram)

(A) gastroschisis
(B) omphalocele
(C) conjoined fetal heads
(D) normal gut migration

682. In orienting to the fetal heart, the two most important pieces of cardiac anatomy to recognize are

(A) aorta and pulmonary vessels
(B) aorta and foramen of Monro
(C) foramen ovale and moderator band
(D) left ventricle and right atrium

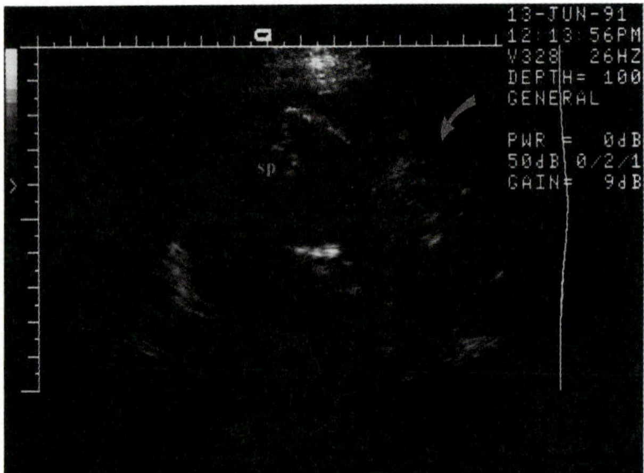

Figure 8–107. Transverse sonogram of a gravid uterus.

683. The transatrial flow pattern is

(A) left to right
(B) right to left
(C) atrial to ventricular
(D) none of the above

684. The eustachian valve's function is

(A) to allow blood to flow from the right ventricular to the main pulmonary artery
(B) to direct blood flow from the superior vena cava to the foramen ovale
(C) to direct blood flow from the inferior vena cava across the right atrium toward the foramen ovale
(D) to direct blood flow from the main pulmonary artery to the ductus arteriosus

685. When performing M-mode of the fetal heart to diagnose an arrhythmia, one should

(A) perform M-mode of the ventricles
(B) perform M-mode of the atria
(C) perform M-mode of both atria and ventricles
(D) isolate arrhythmic chamber and perform M-mode of that chamber

686. The most important cardiac view one can obtain from any fetal echocardiogram is

(A) five-chamber view
(B) four-chamber view
(C) long-axis view
(D) short-axis view

687. Of the right atrial blood volume, what percentage crosses the foramen ovale?

(A) 10%
(B) 100%
(C) 30%
(D) 60%

688. Of the blood flowing through the main pulmonary artery, what percentage of the volume continues through the ductus arteriosus?

(A) 90%
(B) 10%
(C) 100%
(D) none of the above

689. Of the total left atrial blood volume, what percentage fills the left atrium by pulmonary venous return?

(A) 90%
(B) 10%
(C) 50%
(D) 25%

690. 96% of all fetal cardiac malformations can be identified from what fetal echocardiographic plane?

(A) five-chamber view
(B) long-axis view
(C) short-axis view
(D) four-chamber view

691. If a sonographer is concerned about a coarctation of the aorta in the fetus, what would be the ideal view to obtain for visualization of the area of concern?

(A) four-chamber view
(B) long-axis view
(C) aortic arch (suprasternal) view
(D) right ventricular in-flow view

692. If the sonographer is concerned about transposition of the great vessels in the fetus, what basic fetal echocardiographic plane should one try to initially obtain?

(A) five-chamber view
(B) four-chamber view
(C) aortic arch (suprasternal) view
(D) none of the above

693. The left side of the fetal heart generally perfuses

(A) cranial aspects of the fetus
(B) systemic aspects of the fetus
(C) placenta
(D) none of the above

694. The right side of the fetal heart generally perfuses

(A) cranial aspects of the fetus
(B) systemic aspects of the fetus
(C) heart
(D) placenta

695. The crista dividens complex is associated with what cardiac anatomy?

(A) eustachian valve and foramen ovale
(B) right ventricular out-flow tract
(C) moderator band
(D) ductus arteriosus

696. The highest oxygenated blood is found in what fetal heart chamber?

(A) left ventricle
(B) left atrium
(C) right atrium
(D) right ventricle

697. What fetal cardiac vessel becomes a ligament after birth?

(A) main pulmonary artery
(B) ductus arteriosus
(C) distal aortic arch
(D) none of the above

698. If the foramen ovale cannot be visualized, what other portion of fetal cardiac anatomy should a sonographer strive for in determining cardiac situs?

(A) aorta
(B) pulmonary artery
(C) moderator band
(D) pulmonary veins

699. In theory, if a fetus has severe hypoplastic right heart syndrome, what part of the fetus would be spared?

(A) the systemic aspects of the fetus
(B) the cranial aspects of the fetus
(C) the placenta
(D) none of the above

700. The use of Doppler in fetal echocardiography is helpful in the following areas *except*

(A) dysplastic valves
(B) septal defects
(C) great vessel abnormality
(D) arrhythmia diagnosis

701. In the four-chamber view, the lie of the fetal heart is

(A) parallel to the fetal spine
(B) perpendicular to the fetal spine
(C) 45° to the fetal spine
(D) B and C

702. The image plane in the short-axis view will image the fetus in what anatomic plane?

(A) transverse
(B) sagittal
(C) coronal
(D) none of the above

703. The right atrium primarily receives blood from what vessels?

(A) pulmonary veins and inferior vena cava
(B) superior vena cava and pulmonary veins
(C) ductus arteriosus and inferior vena cava
(D) inferior vena cava and superior vena cava

704. Which of the following describes the systolic/diastolic ratio (S/D) in the umbilical artery during gestation

(A) progressive decline in S/D ratio from early pregnancy until term
(B) progressive increase in S/D ratio from early pregnancy until term

(C) S/D ratio is unchanged throughout pregnancy
(D) S/D ratio remains stable until term when it increases
(E) S/D ratio remains stable until term when it falls

705. The pulsatility index (PI) is

(A) (A − B)/A
(B) A/B
(C) (B · 100%)/A
(D) (A − B)/mean

706. All of the following may affect the flow velocity waveform of the umbilical artery *except*

(A) fetal breathing movements
(B) the angle of insonation
(C) fetal tachycardia
(D) epidural anesthesia
(E) uterine contractions

707. This continuous-wave Doppler image (Fig. 8–108) of a maternal vessel reveals absence of flow in systole and diastole. This is related to

(A) severe preeclampsia
(B) diabetes mellitus
(C) wall filter set too high
(D) twins

708. The normal typical configuration of an umbilical artery waveform

(A) has a triangular shape
(B) has a rapid acceleration during systole
(C) shows reversal of flow in diastole
(D) has a small amount of forward flow in diastole with a marked notch at the end of systole

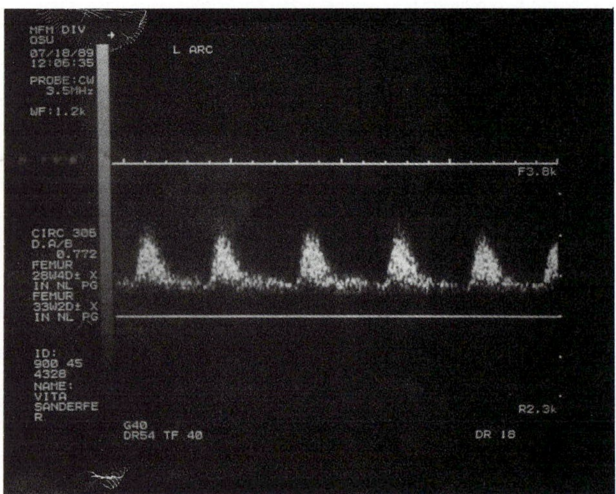

Figure 8–108. Continuous-wave Doppler image of a maternal vessel.

709. The A/B ratio of the umbilical artery in the third trimester is less than

(A) 0
(B) 1.0
(C) 2.0
(D) 3.0

710. The Pourcelot (or resistance) index is

(A) (A − B)/mean
(B) (A − B)/A
(C) A/B
(D) (B · 100%)/A

711. Blood flow in the uterine and fetoplacental circulation can be evaluated with a continuous wave or a duplexed Doppler machine and pregnancies complicated by _____ may be evaluated noninvasively

(A) intrauterine growth retardation (IUGR)
(B) diabetes
(C) maternal hypertension
(D) all of the above
(E) none of the above

712. Which type(s) of Duplex scanner(s) is available for obstetric Doppler applications

(A) mechanical sector
(B) electronically steered sector
(C) electronically steered linear
(D) offset linear
(E) all of the above

713. Pulsed Doppler examination of which fetal vessel offers an alternative method of studying fetal cardiac dysrhythmias

(A) fetal descending aorta
(B) fetal IVC
(C) fetal hepatic arteries
(D) fetal umbilical vein

714. Umbilical artery A/B ratios of the fetal end of the cord when compared to A/B ratios at the placental cord insertion are

(A) significantly lower
(B) significantly higher
(C) the same
(D) none of the above

715. With a transducer directed medially from the iliac vessels, the lateral uterine wall vessel may be insonated. The Doppler signals obtained from these uterine vessels in a normal pregnancy will exhibit a typical pattern of

(A) high pulsatility with low end-diastolic frequencies
(B) high pulsatility with low end-diastolic frequencies and diastolic notch
(C) low pulsatility with high end-diastolic frequencies
(D) high pulsatility with reversal flow in late systole and early diastole

716. The A/B ratio of the uterine or arcuate artery is less than ______ after 26 weeks of gestation

(A) 4.0
(B) 2.6
(C) 6.6
(D) 3.0

717. This pulsed Doppler tracing (Fig. 8–109) of the umbilical cord of a 24-week fetus reveals

(A) normal umbilical artery
(B) ectopic beats
(C) tachyarrhythmias
(D) fetal breathing

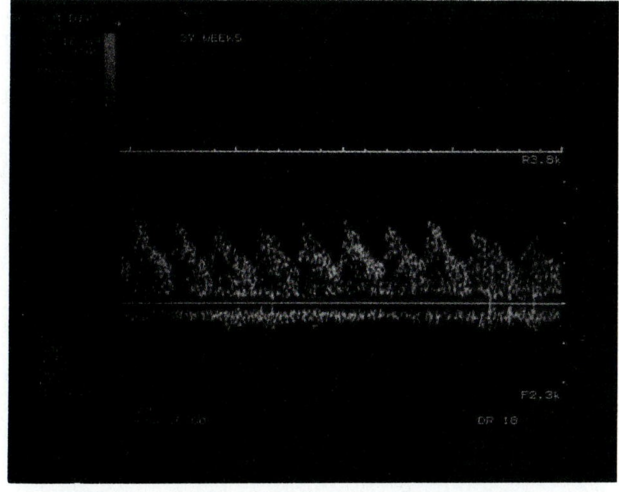

Figure 8–109. Doppler image of the umbilical cord.

Answers and Explanations

At the end of each explained answer there is a number combination in parentheses. The first number identifies the reference source. The second number or set of numbers indicates the page or pages on which the relevant information can be found.

1. **(C)** Gestational trophoblastic disease is categorized into three general types: (1) hydatidiform mole (benign), (2) chorioadenoma destruens (malignant nonmetastatic), and (3) choriocarcinoma (malignant and metastatic). Chrondrosarcoma is *not* among these types. *(2:558; 29:387–388)*

2. **(D)** Chorioadenoma destruens. *(2:558)*

3. **(E)** All of the above. Fetal biophysical profile is comprised of five variables: (1) qualitative amniotic fluid volume, (2) breathing movements, (3) reactive fetal heart rate, (4) fetal tone, and (5) body movements. *(29:184–185)*

4. **(B)** Occipito-frontal diameters. *(29:150)*

5. **(D)** All of the above. *(1:259, 270; 2:558–571; 3:255)*

6. **(A)** Benign proliferation of the trophoblast. The vesicles are filled with viscid material. *(1:259; 2:558)*

7. **(D)** An intrauterine pregnancy in one horn of a bicornuate uterus. The gestational sac is seen in the right horn; the nongravid left horn contains a decidual reaction. Although there is a slight chance of abortion in a bicornuate uterus, a more common anomaly associated with this complication of pregnancy is a septated uterus. *(63:296)*

8. **(B)** A solid mass exhibits the following sonographic patterns: internal echoes, irregular walls, and distal acoustic shadows or reduced echoes distal to the mass caused by increased attenuation. However, some solid masses can attenuate the ultrasound beam to such an extent that the mass will exhibit an echo-free interior, mimicking the interior of a cyst. A solid mass will *not* exhibit a distal acoustic enhancement—a finding that is typical of a cyst. *(56:343; 14:40)*

9. **(D)** 1 in 1200–2000 patients. The incidence of hydatidiform mole varies geographically. In the United States, the incidence is less than in the Far East, where 1 in 400 pregnancies experience hydatidiform mole. *(1:259; 3:256)*

10. **(D)** 2%. *(3:257)*

11. **(A)** A theca lutein cyst. These cysts are usually multiloculated and bilateral. *(29:394)*

12. **(B)** A vesicular sonographic texture. With the use of bistable equipment, the sonographic appearance of hydatidiform mole was formerly called "snowstorm." However, with the introduction of gray scale, a variety of sonographic appearances can be seen, depending on the duration of the mole. First trimester mole may mimic a blighted ovum, a threatened abortion, or a missed abortion, giving it an atypical appearance. In second trimester mole, the vesicles have a maximum diameter of 1 cm, giving it a typical vesicular sonographic texture. *(3:255; 29:390)*

13. **(A)** Choriocarcinoma. *(3:261; 29:388)*

14. **(D)** 10–12 weeks. *(1:264)*

15. **(C)** 3–20%. *(1:266; 29:387)*

16. **(D)** All of the above. Choriocarcinoma can metastasize in the kidney and pelvis as well as the liver, bowel, lungs, and brain. *(1:269; 29:388)*

17. **(B)** An oral contraceptive. *(3:335)*

18. **(B)** Japan. The incidence also is high in Hong Kong. *(1:259)*

19. **(D)** All of the above. *(1:261; 3:257)*

20. **(C)** The etiology of hydatidiform mole is fertilization of an ovum without any active chromosomal material. *(64:503)*

21. **(D)** 2–4 months. *(1:263)*

22. **(D)** All of the above. The chance of abortion in a bicornuate uterus is slight and, because of the decidual proliferation that occurs in the nongravid horn, the endometrial surfaces will be echogenic. Pregnancy in a bicornuate uterus can go to term without complications. *(63:296)*

23. **(B)** Abruptio placentae. This sonogram demonstrates a large hypoechoic area involving at least 50% of the basal plate surface of the placenta. This is secondary to a large abruption. *(63:176)*

24. **(D)** Distal acoustic enhancement. The sonographic characteristics of intrauterine contraceptive devices are multiple-double parallel interrupted echo (entrance-exit reflections) and/or multiple-high amplitude interrupted echoes with distal acoustic shadow. *(1:254)*

25. **(C)** Five. These echoes represent the transected ring of the loop. The anechoic space between the interrupted echoes represents the gaps between the loop. *(1:250)*

26. **(D)** The date when menstrual bleeding began. *(29:61)*

27. **(B)** 65% of IUDs demonstrate an entrance-exit reflection. *(1:251).*

28. **(E)** A and C. There is a significant overlap in morphologic aging of the placenta and its actual function; therefore, placental grading is of only limited use. *(63:119)*

29. **(D)** All of the above. Management of patients with placental abruption is critically important because acute abruptions may lead to disseminated intravascular coagulation in the mother and result in fetal death. Placental abruption can be mistaken for a sustained uterine contraction. *(63:176)*

30. **(A)** 90%. The accuracy of sonography in the diagnosis of molar pregnancy depends on the time duration. However, correlation of serum β-human gonadotropin and real-time sonography has been estimated at at least 90%. *(13:257)*

31. **(A)** The differential diagnoses that may mimic hydatidiform moles are missed abortions and leiomyoma uteri, hematomas, and multiloculated papillary serous cystadenomas but *not* endometriosis. *(3:259)*

32. **(B)** 1 and 4. A chest x-ray is recommended after treatment to look for evidence of metastatic disease and pulmonary embolism. *(1:264; 2:562)*

33. **(D)** 80%. *(1:264)*

34. **(D)** All of the above. There are four possibilities for the missing thread: the nylon thread may have been disconnected from the device, the device may have been expelled, unnoticed, during menstruation, the device may have perforated the uterine wall, or the thread may have been pulled up from the vagina into the uterus (thread migration). *(3:339)*

35. **(B)** A fluid-filled, distended small bowel. The sonogram demonstrates thin internal projections from valvulae conniventes. Obstruction of the small bowel during pregnancy may necessitate emergency surgery. *(63:420)*

36. **(D)** Fertilization of the ovum usually occurs in the ampullary portion of the fallopian tube. *(29:61)*

37. **(B)** Bilateral tumor of the ovary that has metastasized from a primary tumor in the gastrointestinal tract. Microscopically, the tumor has coarse and abundant stroma. The epithelial cells are large and laden with mucin. The tumor must display all of these characteristics to be called a Krukenberg tumor. If it lacks all of them, it may be a metastatic ovarian tumor. *(28:323; 40:1293)*

38. **(D)** Hydrometrocolpos is characterized by fluid in the uterus and vagina and is *not* a clinical symptom of hydatidiform mole. *(3:257)*

39. **(B)** The presence of valvulae conniventes. *(63:420)*

40. **(A)** The extraembryonic peripheral cells of the blastocyst. The trophoblast forms these cells, which form the wall of the blastocyst. *(22:33)*

41. **(D)** The characteristics of a disease. *(4:710)*

42. **(A)** The classic sonographic appearance of hydatidiform mole consists of echogenic intrauterine tissue that is separated by numerous anechoic areas of varying size (3–5 mm) that are randomly distributed throughout the uterine cavity. These areas are most likely to be represented by numerous hydropic villi. *(3:258–261)*

43. **(B)** The multiplication of similar forms. *(4:785)*

44. **(D)** Insertion. *(3:340)*

45. **(A)** Displaced superiorly by the gravid uterus. *(63:206–207)*

46. **(B)** Sonography. Before the use of sonograms, x-rays of the pelvis were the imaging modality of choice to locate lost intrauterine contraceptive devices (IUCDs). The hysterogram was a more accurate method than a plain x-ray; however, it was invasive and painful. Real-time sonography is nontoxic and atraumatic and is the most reliable method used today. Unfortunately, if the device is in an extrauterine position, it may not be depicted because of bowel echoes. Today, x-ray is the secondary method used to find an IUCD. *(3:339–340)*

47. **(D)** 99%. Although sonography is extremely accurate in locating an intrauterine contraceptive device (IUCD) in utero, it is less reliable in an extrauterine position. The accuracy in locating the device in utero can on some occasions be difficult. An interrupted blood clot, gas bubbles, and calcification within the uterine cavity can produce a strong echo with a distal acoustic shadow that mimics an IUCD. Therefore, the accuracy is not 100% but 99%. *(10:93; 29:598)*

48 to 54. See Fig. 8–110.

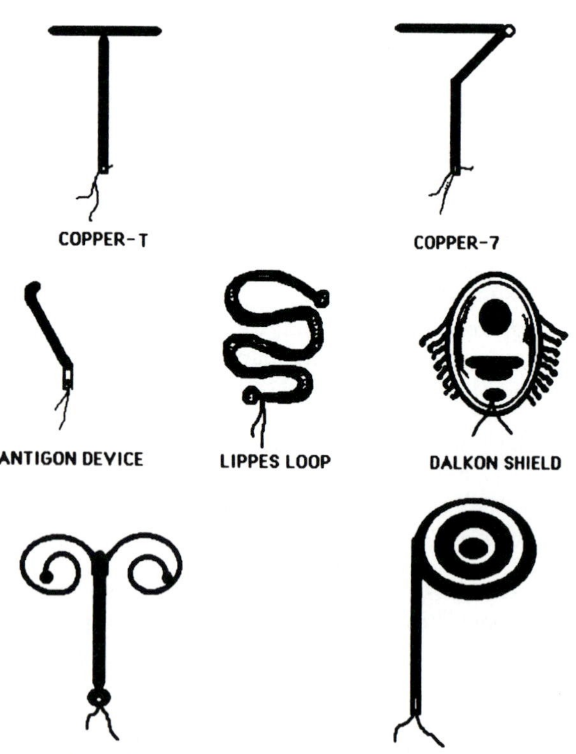

Figure 8–110. Diagram of intrauterine contraceptive devices.

55. **(A)** 1 and 3. Fetal death is defined as the death of a fetus at a gestational age of 20 weeks or more or a fetus weighing 500 g or more. Death of a fetus before 20 weeks is termed an abortion. *(5:75)*

56. **(B)** Gonococcal pelvic inflammatory disease. The spread of gonococci from the pelvis to the upper abdomen is a complication called Fitz-Hugh–Curtis syndrome. Sonographically, it presents as fluid in the subhepatic space (Morrison's pouch). All patients suspected of having pelvic inflammatory disease or an ectopic pregnancy should also have the upper abdomen scanned. *(1:217, 271; 2:405)*

57. **(E)** All of the above. There is a strong association with ovarian carcinoma and ascites. The tumor can implant on the peritoneum, omentum, and bowel. Metastatic spread to the liver also is associated. *(39:126)*

58. **(D)** All of the above. Decidual proliferation in ectopic pregnancy and endometrial carcinoma also can cause the endometrium to become echogenic. *(39:123)*

59. **(B)** The most common cystic mass encountered in pregnancy is a corpus luteum cyst, which usually regresses after the 12th to 14th week. The most common solid mass encountered in pregnancy is myoma uteri. Dermoid cyst is a common complex mass. Because dysgerminoma is a rare malignant germ cell tumor, it is least likely to be encountered. *(39:53–54, 129)*

60. **(A)** Anencephaly. Oligohydramnios is associated with premature rupture of membranes, intrauterine growth retardation, renal agenesis (Potter's syndrome), pulmonary hypoplasia, a post-term pregnancy, and fetal demise. *(29:197; 39:56)*

61. **(D)** 93%. *(5:75)*

62. **(A)** One in four mothers will develop hypofibrinogenemia, which is manifested by intravascular coagulation. *(5:75)*

63. **(B)** The conversion of a solid material into a liquid form. *(8:844)*

64. **(D)** 99%. Real-time sonography is the preferred method of diagnosing fetal death. The absence of fetal heart motion is a better indication of fetal death than is fetal movement because a fetus can be immobile and be alive or can be mobile and yet lack a heart (acardiac twin pregnancy). There have been cases of false-positive diagnosis with real-time; therefore, the accuracy is not 100% but 99%. *(29:431; 33:108–109)*

65. **(C)** 1, 3, 4, 5, and 6. The signs of fetal demise can be divided into specific and nonspecific. Real-time of the fetal heart is a specific sign. *(3:297–309)*

66. **(B)** 12 weeks. *(39:48)*

67. **(A)** The gestation sac is the first structure to be seen in the early diagnosis of pregnancy with today's sonographic equipment. The zygote and morula are early phases of embryologic development and are too small to be visualized sonographically. *(29:61–68)*

68. **(C)** The gestational sac and crown-rump length. These are the two measurements used in the first trimester of pregnancy to assess gestational age. The most accurate measurement is the crown-rump length; the sac size or volume is less reliable. *(29:70–71, 141)*

69. **(B)** Between 4 and 10 weeks. A gestation sac generally refers to pregnancy from 4 weeks gestational age (6 weeks menstrual age) to 10 weeks gestational age (12 weeks menstrual age). *(3:111–128)*

70. **(B)** Stop the examination and turn her on her side. *(2:239–240)*

71. **(B)** 5/17/93. The expected date of confinement or delivery can be estimated from the first day of the last menstrual period by Nägele's rule: Add 7 days to the first day of the last menstrual period, subtract 3 months, and add 1 year. *(2:305)*

72. **(B)** 4–5 weeks. At this stage of gestation (6 to 8 weeks menstrual age), the sac may be completely anechoic even though an embryo may be present embryologically. This is the result of the limited resolution of sonographic equipment. *(3:111–116; 29:66)*

73. **(B)** 8 weeks. *(3:115)*

74. **(A)** 8 weeks. At this stage of gestation, the placenta is recognized as an area of localized thickening of the gestation sac. This thickened area represents the chorion fondosum and decidua basalis, which will arborize and proliferate to form the placenta. *(57:214)*

75. **(D)** The lower uterine segment. *(2:22)*

76. **(B)** Seven. The patient's obstetric history is summarized in a series of digits called parity code. The first digit refers to the number of full-term births, the second digit is the number of premature births, the third digit is the number of abortions, and the fourth digit is the number of living children. *(2:304)*

77. **(A)** A corpus luteum cyst. This type of cyst usually regresses between 12 to 16 weeks. *(29:439)*

78. **(B)** 8.5 weeks. Once an embryo can be seen in the gestation sac, the crown-rump length should be measured and correlated to the nomogram for assessment of age. However, this is appropriate in a clinical setting. If you are in a classroom or an examination center and a nomogram is not readily available, an approximate age can be achieved by the rule-of-thumb method. Add 6.5 to the crown-rump length in centimeters to get an approximate age.

$$\text{CRL (cm)} + 6.5\ \text{cm} = \text{weeks}$$

For example, in the problem given: first convert 20 mm to centimeters by moving the decimal point one space to the left (2.0 cm). Now add 6.5, which will equal 8.5 weeks. *(5:4; 32:256)*

79. **(A)** 1.3 cm. The measurements of the gestational sac are taken in three dimensions. The first two measurements are taken in the longitudinal scan. The third is taken in the transverse scan. The first is the cephalocaudad measurement. The second is the anteroposterior diameter. The third is the transverse diameter taken in transverse scan. All the measurements are added and divided by 3 for the average sac dimension. *(1:25)*

80. **(A)** Supine hypotensive syndrome. *(2:239–340)*

81. **(D)** A cystic ovarian tumor. The figure demonstrates a cystic ovarian mass with thick irregular septations arising from a theca luteum cyst. *(63:125)*

82. **(H)** All of the above. The double-ring sign is most often associated with edema of the soft tissues but is seen in many other abnormalities as well. The double-ring sign in a fetus of a diabetic mother most often represents fat deposition within the subcutaneous tissue rather than scalp edema. *(1:63; 3:304–309; 14:108–109)*

83. **(D)** Before 16 weeks of gestation. The chorionic and amniotic membranes fuse at about 16 weeks. In a small percentage of cases, the amniotic and chorionic membrane fail to fuse. *(1:10; 6:1–8)*

84. **(A)** Adhesions of torn amniotic membranes wrapped around fetal parts and producing amputations. *(6:1–8)*

85. **(C)** The cervical region. *(1:63)*

86. **(A)** Normal insertion of the umbilical cord, with herniation of the bowel occurring most often on the

right side of the umbilicus. The umbilical cord is not involved in gastroschisis. There is no covering membrane and the opening in the abdominal wall is usually to the right of the umbilicus. *(1:71–72)*

87. **(B)** Benign developmental abnormalities of lymphatic origin. *(1:63)*

88. **(B)** Placenta previa. *(3:217; 11:222)*

89. **(D)** All of the above. The clinical signs and symptoms of early pregnancy are Hegar's sign, softening of the isthmus uteri; Chadwick's sign, bluish purple color of the vagina caused by the increased blood supply; Goodell's sign, softening of the cervix; and quickening, the first perception of fetal movement, which occurs at about 18 to 20 weeks of gestation. *(7:29–35; 12:54)*

90. **(A)** 4–8 weeks after delivery. A postpartum uterus remains enlarged 4 to 8 weeks after delivery. *(3:311)*

91. **(B)** The kidneys. Abdominal circumference of the fetal abdomen should be taken at the level where the umbilical vein joins the left portal vein and the fetal stomach. *(29:151)*

92. **(C)** 1, 2, and 3. The "rind" (choriodecidua) represents a combination of embryologic structures including decidual reaction, cytotrophoblast, and syncytotrophoblast. *(1:4; 29:66)*

93. **(B)** Menstruation following a hysterectomy. Pregnancy can be ectopic and yet situated in the uterus: for example, a cervical pregnancy. Hysterectomy without a skin scar is called a vaginal hysterectomy. Intrauterine with an extrauterine pregnancy occurs in about 1 of 6000 to 1 of 30,000 patients. Ectopic pregnancy following hysterectomy rarely occurs. In most cases an implanted fertilized ovum in the tube occurred a few days before hysterectomy. *(2:528; 27:636,155)*

94. **(A) 5, (B) 8, (C) 2, (D) 7.** The patient's obstetric history is summarized in a series of digits called a parity code. The first digit refers to the number of full-term births, the second digit is the number of premature births, the third digit is the number of abortions, and the fourth digit is the number of living children. The letter P before the digits represents parity. *(2:304)*

95. **(A)** A multiseptated cystic mass that is usually located posterior to the neck. *(1:63)*

96. **(F)** A, B, and C only. Preeclampsia is associated with small, not large, placenta. *(3:238)*

97. **(B)** The most accurate biparietal diameter measurements are made at 14–20 weeks of gestation. *(29:142)*

98. **(C)** Syncope and nausea may result from pressure of the gravid uterus on the inferior vena cava. *(2:239; 7:623)*

99. **(C)** Placental abruption is diagnosed by retroplacental clot and extramembranous clot. *(1:152–153; 39:60)*

100. **(D)** Placenta localization is 99% accurate from 8 weeks to term. *(3:216)*

101. **(D)** Contractions of the uterus (Braxton Hicks). *(29:336)*

102. **(A)** True. Premature separation of the placenta before the 20th week is called abortion. After 20 weeks, it is called an abruption. *(7:582)*

103. **(A)** The crown-rump length measurement is most accurate in the first trimester of pregnancy. The measurement should be done between 6 and 12 weeks. The embryo size is approximately 10–70 mm, respectively. *(29:72)*

104. **(D)** Ectopic pregnancy denotes any pregnancy located outside the endometrial lumen. The term *ectopic* is a broad term used to describe any organ or structure that is located away from its normal position, for example, ectopic kidney. Ectopic pregnancy includes pregnancy located in the fallopian tubes, abdomen, or cervical canal. A pregnancy may be ectopic and yet be situated within the uterus. *(7:311; 27:636)*

105. **(A)** Intraperitoneal bleeding usually results in diaphragmatic irritation. The diaphragm develops embryologically in the neck and shoulder region and descends downward. The nerves that supply the neck also supply the diaphragm and as a result, irritation results in referred shoulder pain. *(7:313)*

106. **(C)** The size and shape of the uterus varies with parity and age. The average multigravida uterus measures 8 to 9 cm in length × 5 cm in thickness × 6 cm in width. *(39:123)*

107. **(A)** The yolk sac lies in the chorionic cavity between the amnion and chorionic sac. It measures 5 mm to 1 cm. The yolk sac shrinks as pregnancy advances. It should *not* be measured in the CRL. *(29:68,428)*

108. **(D)** Hydramnios is *not* associated with intrauterine growth retardation (IUGR). *(29:160–171)*

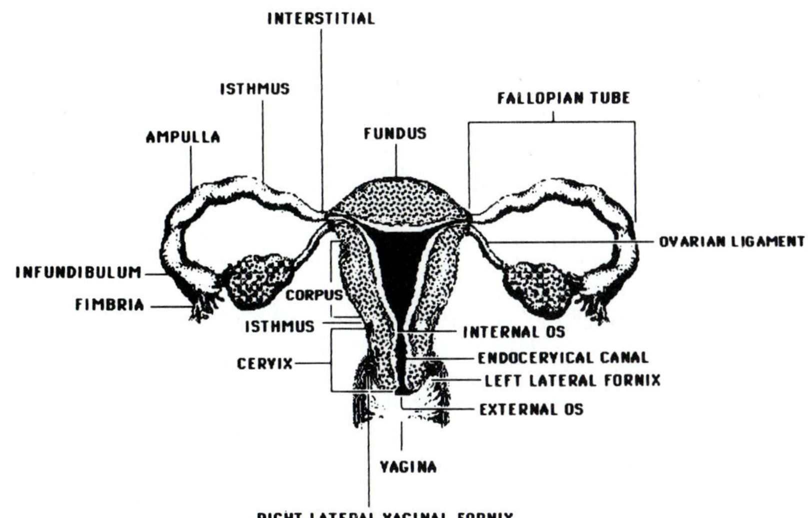

Figure 8–111. Diagram of the female reproductive organs (frontal view).

109 to 126. See Fig. 8–111.

127. **(A)** 26%. *(1:291)*

128. **(B)** 95%; the other 5% occur in the cervix, ovaries, and abdomen. *(1:292)*

129. **(D)** Every 2 days. *(1:293)*

130. **(D)** A and B. Transvaginal sonography greatly enhances the ability to diagnose ectopic pregnancy. An unruptured ectopic pregnancy appears as a "tubal ring" consisting of a concentric echogenic rim with a hypoechoic center. A corpus luteum cyst is identified on the left ovary. *(63:91–92)*

131. **(A)** Human chorionic gonadotropin titers in ectopic pregnancy are lower than patients with normal intrauterine pregnancy (IUP). This may be due to the defective function of the trophoblast or separation from the tubal wall that occurs in ectopic pregnancy. *(1:294)*

132. **(D)** All of the above; as well as fluid in the paracolic gutters and subhepatic space (Morison's pouch) are correct. *(1:294)*

133. **(B)** An intrauterine pregnancy (IUP) with a coexistent extrauterine gestation occurs in 1 in 6,000 to 1 in 30,000 pregnancies. *(58:41)*

134. **(D)** 20%. *(1:296)*

135. **(B)** A cast of the uterine decidua is the most likely cause of a pseudogestational sac. *(1:296)*

136. **(E)** C and D. Cystic hygromas are associated with elevated α-fetoprotein and Turner's syndrome. *(1:64)*

137. **(B)** 1 and 3. Sonographic characteristics of cystic hygromas are multiseptated cystic masses with thin walls. *(1:63)*

138. **(A)** On transvaginal and transabdominal sonography, a unruptured ectopic pregnancy typically appears as a "tubal ring" consisting of a concentric echogenic rim with a hypoechoic center. *(63:91–92)*

139. **(B)** Omphalocele is covered by a peritoneal sac covered with amnion that may be filled with bowel, liver, or spleen. The protrusion is at the base of the umbilical cord. *(1:71)*

140. **(C)** The important facts to consider are gastroschisis has a normal insertion of the umbilical cord and is *not* covered by membrane. In addition, gastroschisis herniates, often to the right side of the umbilicus. *(1:71–72)*

141. **(D)** All of the above. There are a variety of sonographic appearances of the uterine endometrium in ectopic pregnancy. In ectopic pregnancy, blood or secretions can accumulate within the uterine cavity, simulating the appearance of a gestation sac (pseudogestational sac). Decidual changes produce a slightly thickened endometrium similar to that encountered in the secretory phase of the cycle. *(63:89)*

142. **(D)** 20% can occur in the axilla, groin, and mediastinum; 80% occur in the cervical region. *(1:63)*

143. **(A)** Abnormal sex chromosomes and retarded growth and sexual development. *(8:1492)*

144. **(C)** All of the above. Nonspecific signs of fetal death are double contour of the fetal head due to scalp edema, absence of the falx cerebri due to liq-

uefaction of the brain, echoes in the amniotic fluid due to fragmentation of the fetal skin, and a decrease in biparietal diameter (BPD) measurements due to collapse of the cranial sutures after death. *(3:305–309; 29:430)*

145. **(E)** All of the above. The main reasons for development of an ectopic pregnancy include fallopian tube malfunction, adhesions, diverticula, and PID. Any mechanical obstruction of the fallopian tube that prevents the passage of the fertilization egg into the uterine cavity contributes to the development of ectopic pregnancy. Salpingitis, menstrual reflux, and tumors in the fallopian tube also have been implicated in the cause. *(1:291–292; 2:527)*

146. **(D)** The chances of ectopic pregnancy recurrence are 1 in 4. *(3:278)*

147. **(D)** Ectopic pregnancy in the interstitial portion of the fallopian tube poses potential serious complications because of forcible expulsion and rupture with hemorrhage. *(1:301)*

148. **(A)** Scalp edema can be seen 2–3 days, or 24–72 hours, after fetal death. *(3:309)*

149. **(C)** Sonographic Spalding's sign is the overlapping of the fetal cranium. *(3:309)*

150. **(D)** The ampullary portion of the fallopian is the most common and the isthmus is the next most common location for an ectopic implantation. *(2:528)*

151. **(E)** All of the above. The conditions that can mimic an ectopic pregnancy are hematoma, hemorrhagic corpus luteum cyst, dermoid cyst, hydrosalpinx, tubo-ovarian abscess. However, when the sonograms are correlated with the β-hCG, the differential diagnosis can be reduced considerably. *(29:412)*

152. **(B)** In 50% of intrauterine pregnancies (IUP), a double-line decidua can be seen. This finding can be used to differentiate between a pseudogestation sac (decidual cast) and an IUP. The double-line decidua represents the space between the decidua capsularis and the decidua parietalis (decidua vera). *(1:297)*

153. **(C)** All of the above. The areas to scan when screening for fluid collection in an ectopic pregnancy are the anterior and posterior cul-de-sac, paracolic recesses, adnexa, and the subhepatic space. *(1:300)*

154. **(C)** The placenta should be left in the abdominal cavity because removal will result in massive hemorrhage. *(2:545)*

155. **(D)** A neonate is considered growth retarded when the birth weight falls below the 10th percentile for gestational age. Birth weight by itself is not valid for intrauterine growth retardation (IUGR). *(18:99)*

156. **(E)** All of the above. In addition, spina bifida also is associated with fetal hydrocephalus. About 80% of fetuses having hydrocephaly may also have spina bifida. *(29:248)*

157. **(B)** Pelvic kidney. Vaginal delivery may be contraindicated in patients with a pelvic kidney. *(63:454)*

158. **(B)** 90%. *(10:56)*

159. **(D)** All of the causes given are correct. Free-fluid in the cul-de-sac can also be due to ascites or abscesses. Small amounts of fluid may be due to follicular spill from a ruptured follicular cyst. *(1:33; 39:126)*

160–168. See Fig. 8–112.

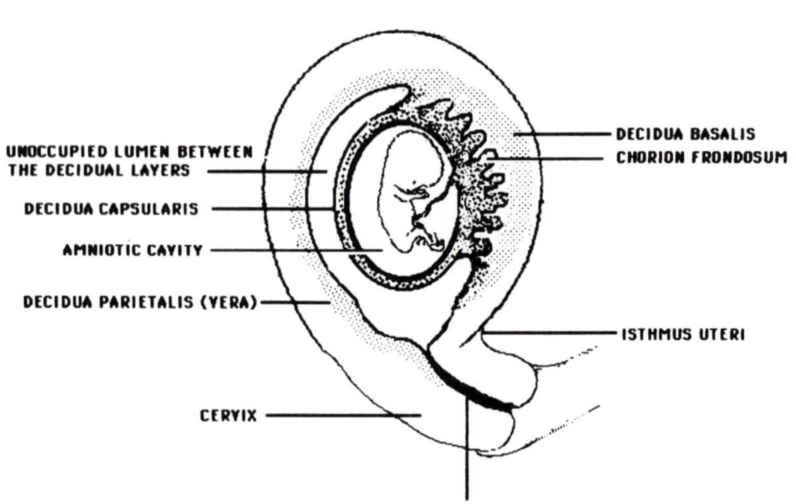

Figure 8–112. Diagram of an early pregnancy.

169–178. See Fig. 8–113.

179. **(F)** All of the above. Fetal ocular biometry has proven to be useful in evaluating hypertelorism, anophthalmos, microphthalmos, and gestational age. *(59:92)*

180. **(B)** From the medial border of the orbit to the opposite medial border. *(58:94)*

181. **(B)** From lateral border of the orbit to the opposite lateral border. *(58:94)*

182. **(D)** A cephalic index of 80% is normal. An index above 85% is suggestive of brachycephaly, whereas less than 75% is suggestive of dolichocephaly. *(59:92)*

183. **(A)** The crown-rump length (CRL) measurement is from the crown to the rump of the embryo excluding the limbs. *(19:223)*

184. **(A)** The two measurements (proximal femoral neck to distal femoral condyles and greater trochanter to the distal femoral condyles) differ by 1–2 mm. However, the measurement taken from the femoral neck to the distal end of the femoral condyles is easily obtainable and most recommended. *(19:233)*

185. **(A)** Hypertelorism denotes abnormally wide-spaced orbits. It does *not* denote smallness of the eyes (microphthalmos) or absence of the eyes (anophthalmos). *(59:93–98)*

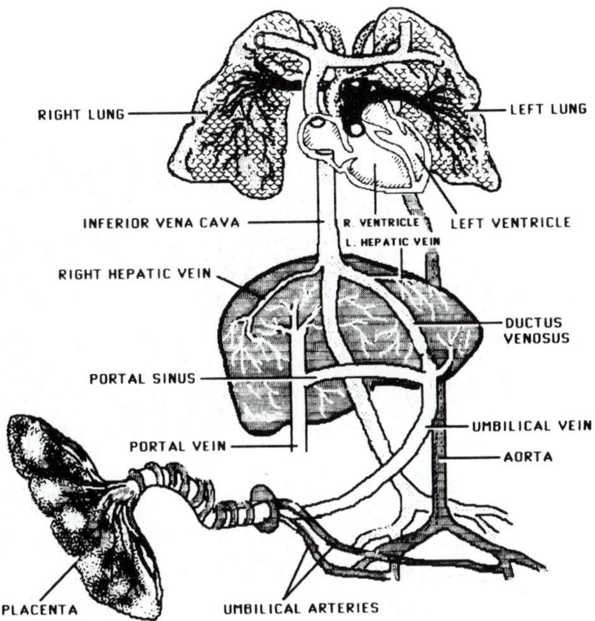

Figure 8–113. Diagram of the fetal circulatory system.

186. **(B)** Hypotelorism denotes abnormally closely spaced orbits. *(15:117)*

187. **(A)** Accuracy of crown-rump length (CRL) measurement shows a 95% confidence limit of ± 4.7 days. *(3:129)*

188. **(D)** Measure only the embryo from top of the head to buttocks (rump), excluding the limbs. *(3:127–129)*

189. **(B)** Crown-rump length measurement is most accurate between 6 and 12 weeks of gestation. After the 12th week, biparietal diameter (BP) should be done. *(41:184)*

190. **(C)** The most accurate methodology for assessment of gestational age in the first trimester is crown-rump length (CRL). *(18:337)*

191. **(D)** All of the above. The cardiac circulation of the fetus is different from that of the adult. The differences that are present in the fetus and not in the adult include an opening in the heart left by the septum secundum called the foramen ovale. It allows shunting of blood from the right atrium to the left atrium. After birth, the foramen ovale normally closes. The presence of ductus arteriosus and venosus are present in the fetus and not in the adult. *(22:308)*

192. **(A)** The gestational sac can be seen as early as 5 weeks with transabdominal sonography. Transvaginal sonography can depict the gestational sac one week earlier than the transabdominal method. *(64:39–46)*

193. **(D)** Metastases from ovarian carcinoma usually can implant on the serosa of bowel, the peritoneum, and the omentum. *(63:249)*

194. **(A)** Clomid (clomiphene citrate) is used for treating infertility and can result in multiple gestation. *(10:62)*

195. **(B)** The gestational sac grows approximately 1 mm per day. *(20:610; 29:427)*

196. **(B)** The accuracy of gestational sac volume measurement as a means of estimating gestational age has a confidence limit of ± 9 days. *(3:127)*

197. **(D)** All of the above. The conditions associated with intrauterine growth retardation (IUGR) are smoking and alcoholism, chronic renal disease, maternal heart disease, preeclamptic toxemia, maternal malnutrition, and anemia. *(3:140)*

198. **(C)** All of the above. The treatment for intrauterine growth retardation (IUGR) is bed rest with the

Contributors

Dunstan Abraham, MPH, RDMS
Adjunct Instructor, Diagnostic Medical Imaging Program, College of Health Related Professions
SUNY/Health Sciences Center at Brooklyn
Clinical and Adjunct Instructor
Diagnostic Ultrasound Technology Program
New York University Medical Center
Supervisor of Ultrasound
Bronx-Municipal Hospital Center
Bronx, New York

Mark N. Allen, BS, RDCS
Administrator and Chief Cardiac Sonographer
University of Rochester Medical Center
Rochester, New York

Dale R. Cyr, BS, RDMS
Chief Sonographer
University of Washington Medical Center
Seattle, Washington

Rena Dubinsky, BS, RDMS
Adjunct Instructor
Diagnostic Ultrasound Technology Program
New York University Medical Center
New York, New York

Trudy Dubinsky, MA, RDMS
Program Director
Diagnostic Ultrasound Technology Program
New York University Medical Center
New York, New York

Arthur C. Fleischer, MD
Professor of Radiology and Radiological Sciences
Professor of Obstetrics and Gynecology
Chief of Diagnostic Sonography
Vanderbilt University Medical Center
Nashville, Tennessee

Pamela M. Foy, BS, RDMS
Clinical Coordinator of Ultrasound Services
Department of Obstetrics and Gynecology
The Ohio State University
Columbus, Ohio

Milagros Garay, RDMS
Adjunct Instructor
Diagnostic Ultrasound Technology Program
New York University Medical Center
New York, New York

Thomas G. Hoffman, BS, RDMS, RVT
Adjunct Instructor, Diagnostic Medical Imaging Program, College of Health Related Professions
SUNY/Health Sciences Center at Brooklyn
Clinical and Adjunct Instructor
Diagnostic Ultrasound Technology Program
New York University Medical Center
Supervisor of Ultrasound
Weiler Hospital of the Albert Einstein College of Medicine
Bronx, New York

Steven Horii, MD
Associate Professor of Georgetown University Hospital
Georgetown University Hospital
Washington, D.C.

Sandra Katanick, RN, RVT
Former Field Applications Specialist–Peripheral Vascular
Acuson Computed Sonography
Mountain View, California
Executive Director of ICAVL
Rockville, Maryland

Charles S. Odwin, RT, RDMS
Clinical Instructor, Diagnostic Medical Imaging Program, College of Health Related Professions
SUNY/Health Sciences Center at Brooklyn
Clinical and Adjunct Instructor
Diagnostic Ultrasound Technology Program
New York University Medical Center
Supervisor of Ultrasound
Department of Radiology
Bronx-Lebanon Hospital Center
Bronx, New York

Chandrowti Devi Persaud, RT, RDMS
Clinical Instructor
New York University Medical Center
Diagnostic Ultrasound Technology Program
Sonographer
Bronx-Lebanon Hospital Center
Bronx, New York

Raymond L. Powis, PhD
Clinical Science and Communications Manager
Quantum Medical Systems
Issaguah, Washington

Ronald R. Price, PhD
Director, Division of Radiological Sciences
Professor of Radiology and Radiological Sciences
Vanderbilt University Hospital
Professor of Physics and Astronomy
Vanderbilt University
Nashville, Tennessee

David L. Rollins, MD
Director of Surgery
St. Vincent's Charity Hospital
Cleveland, Ohio

Henny Wasser Rudansky, BS, RDCS
Adjunct and Clinical Instructor, Diagnostic Medical Imaging Program, College of Health Related Professions
SUNY/Health Sciences Center at Brooklyn
Supervisor of Echocardiography
Department of Cardiology
Maimonides Hospital
Brooklyn, New York

Carolyn M. Semrow, BS, EE
Director of Vascular Research
St. Vincent's Charity Hospital
Cleveland, Ohio

Diana Kawai Yankowitz, BS, RDCS
Pediatric Echocardiographer
University of California San Francisco Medical Center
San Francisco, California

Contents

Preface

The clinical application of Diagnostic Medical Ultrasound has expanded considerably since the first edition was published. Accordingly, we have developed a comprehensive up-to-date self-examination and study guide which incorporates these new applications. This single multispecialty, comprehensive examination review has long been anticipated.

This edition is comprised of ten examination specialties with each specialty containing a study guide followed by numerous questions and explanations.

Over 3000 questions with accompanying answers and explanations and over 600 sonograms and illustrations are organized into a single textbook. Color images have also been added in order to cover the most current applications of diagnostic ultrasound. Candidates seeking RDMS, RDCS, and RVT certifications will find this edition informative and invaluable. In addition, this review guide was carefully revised for sonography students as a supplement to classroom lectures.

It is our desire that you will find this new edition not only a means to study for the Registry but a useful tool to enhance your professional growth and clinical effectiveness.

We applaud you in your search for knowledge and we thank you for the opportunity of sharing our experience with you.

Charles S. Odwin
Trudy Dubinsky
Arthur C. Fleischer

Acknowledgments

The creation of this textbook has been hard work, and without support it would not have been achieved. We wish to extend our thanks to all the Radiologists at the Bronx-Lebanon Hospital Center. I am deeply grateful to Richard A. Rosen, MD, Director of the Department of Radiology, Harvey Stern, MD, Associate Director of the Department of Radiology, and Walter McKoy, Administrator of the Department of Radiology, who were kind enough to allow me the time and flexibility to complete this text, and special thanks to David P. Neumann, MD, Chief Resident, for his constructive criticism of the first edition. I would especially like to thank Mrs. La Rosa Pinder for her secretarial assistance. To conclude, I wish to thank my ultrasound colleagues and students for their support and encouragement.

How to Use This Book

This book has been written as a study guide for review and self-examination and serves as a useful tool for preparation for the American Registry of Diagnostic Medical Sonography Examination and the ultrasound portions of the American Board of Radiology Examination.

To get the most from this book, first read the Study Guide then go through the Questions answering them all regardless of difficulty, just as you would take the actual test. The Questions are either multiple choice or matching, and many are accompanied by a sonogram or illustration.

At the end of each set of Questions, there is an Answer and Explanation section. In this section the answer is explained, and a reference is given for each answer. The first number of the reference indicates a book or journal, as numbered in the References section. The second number or numbers indicate the page or pages on which the relevant material can be found. If only one number is given, the reference is to the entire book.

Do not be discouraged if you are unable to answer all of the questions on the first try. We encourage you to try again.

Best wishes for success in your study of ultrasound.

This book is dedicated to the memory of Trudy Dubinsky, MA, RDMS, the founder and Program Director of the New York University Medical Center School of Diagnostic Medical Sonography. Trudy was a well-known, superb teacher whose dedication and contribution to her profession will always be remembered. She will be sadly missed.

McGraw-Hill

A Division of The ***McGraw-Hill*** *Companies*

Appleton & Lange's Review for the Ultrasonography Examination, Second Edition

11 12 13 14 15 CCI/CCI 0 9 8 7 6 5 4 3 2

ISBN: 0-8385-9073-X

Notice

Medicine is an ever-changing science. As new research and clinical experience broaden our knowledge, changes in treatment and drug therapy are required. The authors and the publisher of this work have checked with sources believed to be reliable in their efforts to provide information that is complete and generally in accord with the standards accepted at the time of publication. However, in view of the possibility of human error or changes in medical sciences, neither the authors nor the publisher nor any other party who has been involved in the preparation or publication of this work warrants that the information contained herein is in every respect accurate or complete, and they disclaim all responsibility for any errors or omissions or for the results obtained from use of the information contained in this work. Readers are encouraged to confirm the information contained herein with other sources. For example and in particular, readers are advised to check the product information sheet included in the package of each drug they plan to administer to be certain that the information contained in this work is accurate and that changes have not been made in the recommended dose or in the contraindications for administration. This recommendation is of particular importance in connection with new or infrequently used drugs.

Library of Congress Cataloging-in-Publication Data

Odwin, Charles S.
Appleton & Lange's Review for the ultrasonography examination / Charles S. Odwin, Trudy Dubinsky, Arthur C. Fleischer. — 2nd ed.
p. cm.
ISBN 0-8385-9073-X
1. Diagnosis, Ultrasonic—Examinations, questions, etc.
I. Dubinsky, Trudy. II. Fleischer, Arthur C. III. Odwin, Charles S. Ultrasonography examination and review. IV. Title: Appleton & Lange's review for the ultrasonography examination.
[DNLM: 1. Ultrasonography—examination questions. WB 18 027u]
RC78.7.U4038 1993
616.07'543'076—dc20
DNLM/DLC 92-49035
for Library of Congress CIP

Acquisitions Editor: Jane Licht
Production Editor: Karen W. Davis
Designer: Penny Kindzierski

Second Edition

Appleton & Lange's Review for the ULTRASONOGRAPHY EXAMINATION

Charles S. Odwin, RT, RDMS
Supervisor of Ultrasound
Department of Radiology
Bronx-Lebanon Hospital Center
Bronx, New York

Trudy Dubinsky,† MA, RDMS
Program Director
Diagnostic Ultrasound Technology Program
New York University Medical Center
New York, New York

Arthur C. Fleischer, MD
Professor of Radiology and Radiological Sciences
Professor of Obstetrics and Gynecology
Chief of Diagnostic Sonography
Vanderbilt University Medical Center
Nashville, Tennessee

†*Deceased.*

Appleton & Lange Reviews/McGraw-Hill
Medical Publishing Division

New York St. Louis San Francisco Auckland Bogotá Caracas Lisbon London
Madrid Mexico City Milan Montreal New Delhi San Juan
Singapore Sydney Tokyo Toronto